To
Lewis L. Gould, mentor above all
and
Simon Cordery, partner in all

ABOUT THE AUTHOR

Stacy A. Cordery is a professor of history at Monmouth College. She is the author of two books on Theodore Roosevelt and is the bibliographer for the National First Ladies' Library. She lives in Monmouth, Illinois, with her husband and son.

Alice

Alice Roosevelt Longworth,

from

White House Princess

to Washington Power Broker

Stacy A. Cordery

PENGUIN BOOKS

PENGUIN BOOKS

Published by the Penguin Group

Penguin Group (USA) Inc., 375 Hudson Street, New York, New York 10014, U.S.A.
Penguin Group (Canada), 90 Eglinton Avenue East, Suite 700, Toronto,
Ontario, Canada M4P 2Y3 (a division of Pearson Penguin Canada Inc.)
Penguin Books Ltd, 80 Strand, London WC2R 0RL, England
Penguin Ireland, 25 St Stephen's Green, Dublin 2, Ireland (a division of Penguin Books Ltd)
Penguin Group (Australia), 250 Camberwell Road, Camberwell,
Victoria 3124, Australia (a division of Pearson Australia Group Pty Ltd)
Penguin Books India Pvt Ltd, 11 Community Centre, Panchsheel Park, New Delhi – 110 017, India
Penguin Group (NZ), 67 Apollo Drive, Rosedale, North Shore 0632,
New Zealand (a division of Pearson New Zealand Ltd)
Penguin Books (South Africa) (Pty) Ltd, 24 Sturdee Avenue,
Rosebank, Johannesburg 2196, South Africa

Penguin Books Ltd, Registered Offices: 80 Strand, London WC2R 0RL, England

First published in the United States of America by Viking Penguin,
a member of Penguin Group (USA) Inc. 2007
Published in Penguin Books 2008

3 5 7 9 10 8 6 4 2

Grateful acknowledgment is made to the following for permission to use copyrighted works:
"The Return" from *Personae* by Ezra Pound. Copyright © 1926 by Ezra Pound. Reprinted by
permission of New Directions Publishing Corp.
Joanna Sturm for the use of selections from the Joanna Sturm Papers.

Photographic sources: Page numbers refer to the photo inserts between pages 110 and 111 and 430 and 431.
Joanna Sturm: 1 (top), 6 (top), 7, 8 (top), 11, 12, 13 (bottom), 15 (bottom), 17, 19, 20 (top),
21 (top), 24 (both), 25 (top), 26 (top), 27, 28 (both), 29 (both), 30 (both), 31 (both)
Library of Congress: 2 (both), 3 (both), 4, 5 (top), 9, 10 (bottom), 13 (top), 14 (both),
15 (top), 16, 18 (bottom), 22, 23 (bottom), 26 (bottom)
Theodore Roosevelt Collection, by permission of the Houghton Library,
Harvard University (bMS Am 1541.9 [142]): 1 (bottom)
Georgetown University Art Collection and Deborah Vollmer: 32
All other photographs are from the author's collection.

THE LIBRARY OF CONGRESS HAS CATALOGED THE HARDCOVER EDITION AS FOLLOWS:
Cordery, Stacy A.
Alice : Alice Roosevelt Longworth, from White House princess to Washington power broker / Stacy A. Cordery.
p.   cm.
Includes bibliographical references and index.
ISBN 978-0-670-01833-8 (hc.)
ISBN 978-0-14-311427-7 (pbk.)
1. Longworth, Alice Roosevelt, 1884–1980.   2. Children of presidents—United States—Biography.
3. Roosevelt, Theodore, 1858–1919—Family.   I. Title.
E757.3.C67 2007
973.91'1092—dc22
[B]   2006103087

Printed in the United States of America
Set in Fournier
Designed by Francesca Belanger
Family tree by Jeffrey L. Ward

Preface

FOR NEARLY ALL of her ninety-six years Alice Roosevelt Longworth occupied a unique place in the nation's culture. Part Old Guard, part New Woman, Theodore Roosevelt's eldest daughter embraced her celebrity status and understood the constraints of fame but still did precisely what she wanted. At the turn of the twentieth century she became America's Princess Alice, the intrepid First Daughter who flouted social rules and thereby invited other women to challenge convention. She married Representative Nicholas Longworth in the White House as "the nation's bride," showered with fairy tale presents from governments and citizens around the globe. Torn between her Republican husband and her Progressive father in the 1912 election, she personified the agony of the divided GOP. Meetings in her drawing room helped to change the course of history, as she fought successfully to keep the United States from joining the League of Nations in the early 1920s. Her syndicated newspaper columns criticizing the New Deal programs of her cousins Franklin and Eleanor Roosevelt found a receptive audience and cemented her reputation as a wit. When war erupted again in Europe, Alice Longworth became a founding member of America First to keep the United States neutral in that overseas conflagration. In her sixties during the early cold war years, she campaigned for Robert Taft, boosted Richard Nixon, and became a passionate anti-Communist. Through the Kennedy and Johnson years, she was an institution in the nation's capital and her salon continued to bring together the powerful and the amusing. She embraced her most comfortable role: the other Washington monument.[1]

This book is the first full biography of Alice Roosevelt Longworth based on her personal papers. Access to these untapped sources, not previously available to other biographers and scholars, has opened the way to a more nuanced view than formerly possible of the career of this remarkable American woman. Her tart witticisms were important and influential, but Alice Longworth's sway over governmental policy makers and Washington society was due to her incisive intelligence, eclectic interests, and personal magnetism. Alice's emotional connections with family members and friends, among them leading politicians and journalists, are also revealed in her letters and diaries.

Alice Roosevelt Longworth was the social doyenne in a town where socializing was state business. She had a habit of "taking up" promising public servants. Her approval meant instant access to insiders' Washington. Every president and countless foreign dignitaries requested audiences with her. Politicians, writers, scientists, journalists, and social climbers coveted invitations to her teas. It was worse to be ignored by "Mrs. L" than to be skewered by her, and her rapier-sharp dismissals were reserved for the pompous and the obsequious. She could help dispatch an ineffectual politician to an early professional death—who remembers Thomas Dewey today as anything but "the groom on the wedding cake"? The hundreds of gatherings she hosted played their part in the smooth workings of the American government. Alice collected Republicans and Democrats, hawks and doves, people with and people lacking society's approbation. Talk flowed freely around her, connections were made, deals struck. For five decades, the Longworth home was ground zero for serious socializing among politicians and those who sought to influence them; her salon bridged the two worlds of Washington—society and politics. Alice Longworth ignored the Junior League and women's clubs. She had no need of them: leaders of the free world came to her dinner table.

They came because she was a politician; never elected, always involved. The *Oxford English Dictionary* defines *politician* as "one versed in the theory or science of government and the art of governing." Alice Longworth read political philosophy and avidly followed the course of legislation and foreign affairs. Her patriotism and her partisanship burned like twin flames at the center of her philosophy. She cared deeply about the preservation of the United States and never took its continuation for granted. She grew up knowing Civil War veterans, lived through two epic world wars, and faced the cold war with trepidation and resolve. Alice Longworth expected to be disappointed by elected officials, but she never lost her love for the political game.

She had a cheerful countenance, and that sometimes disguised her habit of looking on the world with what she called "detached malevolence."[2] She laughed easily and often, finding humanity wryly funny in its capricious and frequently self-destructive march. She was personally shy—just one reason she never sought elected office. Alice brooked weakness from no one, least of all herself. She was a mother, a grandmother, an important aunt for younger Roosevelts. And, in the same way that Eleanor Roosevelt had a platform because of her husband's position, Alice was the eldest daughter of a charismatic president, the wife of the Speaker of the House of Representatives, the sister of the assistant secretary of the navy, and the lover of the chair of the Senate Foreign Relations Committee during the heady interwar years when foreign policy was debated fiercely across the nation. But it wasn't simply her name or her connections that made Alice a celebrity and a power broker. Pulitzer Prize–winning author Paul Horgan believed "her spirited character, her civilized gaiety, and her all-out convictions" made "her a figure of political consequence—one of the first American women to achieve this position." It also took her intellect. She was widely considered the most brilliant of her siblings; even Eleanor—who had no reason to love her cousin—admitted that Alice had "an extraordinary mind."[3]

Like all Roosevelts, Alice had wide-ranging interests. An autodidact with a lifelong passion for knowledge, she taught herself Greek at age eighty. Filling her bookshelves were tomes historical, philosophical, literary, and scientific—theories of evolution were a particular interest. She retained a fascination for subjects that had grabbed her as a girl: Romany culture, fairies, poetry. In common with all her clan, Alice could and did quote quite liberally great passages from Alexander Pope, William Shakespeare, Rudyard Kipling, Charles Lamb, Niccolò Machiavelli, Sir Thomas

Browne, and others. And the amount and type of poetry she cherished and recited from memory was staggering—from Ogden Nash's limericks to G. K. Chesterton's "Lepanto." Alice Longworth's extensive library contained battered and marked copies of anthologies such as *The Oxford Book of English Verse*, Burton Stevenson's *Home Book of Verse*, the Modern Library edition of *Anthology of Famous European and American Poetry*, and volumes from poets like E. A. Robinson, Ezra Pound, and Alfred Austin, usually inscribed to her by the authors. Alice and her brother Ted coedited a volume of poetry. She loved words and word games; dog-eared and annotated in her angular handwriting were *Brewer's Dictionary of Phrase and Fable*, *The Oxford Book of Green Verse in Translation*, and *Aesop's Book of Fables*.

Essentially, though, she was always, always Theodore Roosevelt's daughter—the first-born and the longest-lived of his children. Theodore Roosevelt is the key to understanding Alice. Her formative years were shaped by abandonment. The three pivotal adults in her young life—her mother (involuntarily), her father, her aunt—abrogated their principal duties as parents: they failed to love her unconditionally and they all left her prematurely. Alice grew up with no reason to trust anyone. "To thine own self be true" became the motto of a girl who was motherless; rejected by her father; forsaken by her surrogate mother, Auntie Bye; and widowed young by her unfaithful husband. The acting out that Alice did as a teenager in the White House was only partly to gain the attention of the father she so desperately needed to notice her. It was also the logical modeling of a child after her elders, in this case Theodore Roosevelt and his elder sister, Bye. Denied the example of her mother, Alice Hathaway Lee Roosevelt, who died in childbirth, and disinclined to follow any lead provided by her withdrawn and puritanical stepmother, Edith Kermit Carow Roosevelt, Alice looked instead to her distant father and her beloved aunt. They bequeathed to Alice tremendous cerebral and political gifts in lieu of reliable emotional sustenance. TR and Bye were lighthearted intellectuals who thrived on new ideas, interesting people, and challenging situations. Both loved life. Both had what a relative called "tremendous vitality" that they could impart to others like "a shot in the arm."[4] Both appreciated their social positions but fought injustice when they saw it. Bye's happy home, where Alice lived from birth to age three, had a revolving door. Through it came and went good friends and fascinating achievers of all sorts. Conversation at the dinner table danced along a wide collection of topics, setting an example Alice would emulate. After marriage, Bye relocated to Washington, D.C., and became the center of a constellation of brilliant people, especially politicians. When Roosevelt was president, her home was the "other White House."

Theodore Roosevelt was much like his elder sister, Bye: iconoclastic, boisterous, energetic, and larger than life, yet thoughtful, well read, disciplined, and charming. He was the unmistakable sire of Princess Alice. The fact that she did not wholly share his sense of noblesse oblige was perhaps a sign of the lack of nurturing she received when young. The ideas of duty and service that Edith and Theodore imparted to their own children Alice understood. But rejecting them was part of her fractured birthright. When she wanted to, she could be as proper as her perfect half sister, Ethel. But she had to want to. Independence was the substitute for parental love that Alice generated out of self-defense. Thus independence could be a mask— but more often it was a prop.

Alice Roosevelt Longworth decried sentimentalism and neediness. Her father's famous strenuous life was transmuted in her to a hyper-self-reliance. The torrent of books and articles he published was echoed in her newspaper columns, but even more in her famous wordplay. Weathering one of her gibes was the best letter of recommendation to her salon. She was a survivor; she was tough; she was impenetrable. Morbid grief about a dead mother won no points in a nursery fast filling with half siblings. Her own father never mentioned her mother to her; it was a clear sign to Alice that the unhappy past was gone—literally dead and buried. Alice lived in the present. Her friend journalist Bill Walton said she seldom indulged in reminiscing.[5] She sought to please herself, having learned early that adults could not be trusted. IF YOU CAN'T SAY SOMETHING GOOD ABOUT SOMEONE, SIT RIGHT HERE BY ME read the legendary needlepoint pillow in her sanctuary. Though she did not originate the phrase, she adored the pillow. Stepmother Edith would not have approved. But then the sanction of others never meant much to Alice.

Mrs. L of the barbed tongue, the heterodoxy, the one who, as she said, left the good deeds to Eleanor, is only the tip of the complex woman who was Alice Lee Roosevelt Longworth. "Her interest in politics is nothing less than joyous," a reporter wrote in 1929.[6] Politics was about power, about an agenda for the nation, about morals, about civic duty, but it was also about politicians. The human condition intrigued her. As a friend put it, tapping her temple, "She liked to be amused, but she would muse—deeply—about everything."[7] Alice Longworth immersed herself in books and took seriously the obligation to be an informed citizen in the democracy she loved. She commands our attention not only because of her many achievements, her position and use of power at the epicenter of the nation's capital, her inherently interesting and often sorrow-filled life, but because she was an early-model bad girl who snarled instead of smiling, who spoke up rather than shut up, and who surrounded herself with men and women of ideas rather than a house full of children.

In 1966, at age eighty-two, Alice Longworth had tea with two old friends. As the water boiled, the subject turned to historical memory and the tendency to Bowdlerize to protect heroes. "Mrs. L remarked that 'I can assure you *nothing happened*' was the most insidious phrase possible. She poked her hands, clenched, into the wine-colored velvet cushions of her sofa, darted a glance from one to the other, and said, 'If anyone ever brings forth my name into such a conversation, I want them to say, "Believe me, *plenty happened.*"' "[8]

Contents

Alice

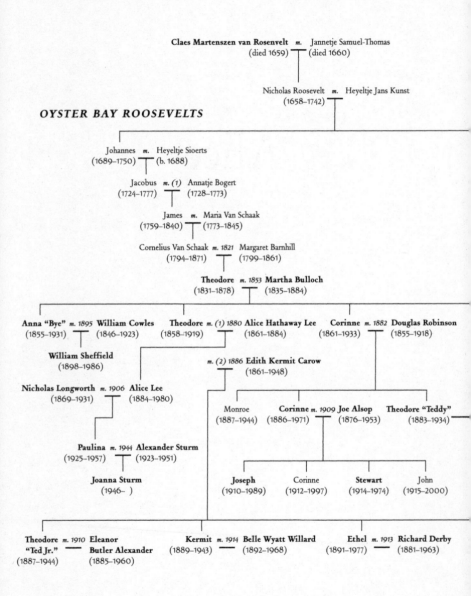

Claes Martenszen van Rosenvelt *m.* Jannetje Samuel-Thomas
(died 1659) ⊤ (died 1660)

Nicholas Roosevelt *m.* Heyeltje Jans Kunst
(1658–1742) ⊤

OYSTER BAY ROOSEVELTS

Johannes *m.* Heyeltje Sioerts
(1689–1750) ⊤ (b. 1688)

Jacobus *m. (1)* Annatje Bogert
(1724–1777) ⊤ (1728–1773)

James *m.* Maria Van Schaak
(1759–1840) ⊤ (1773–1845)

Cornelius Van Schaak *m. 1821* Margaret Barnhill
(1794–1871) ⊤ (1799–1861)

Theodore *m. 1853* **Martha Bulloch**
(1831–1878) ⊤ (1835–1884)

Anna "Bye" *m. 1895* **William Cowles**   **Theodore** *m. (1) 1880* **Alice Hathaway Lee**   **Corinne** *m. 1882* **Douglas Robinson**
(1855–1931) ⊤ (1846–1923)   (1858–1919)   (1861–1884)   (1861–1933) ⊤ (1855–1918)

William Sheffield
(1898–1986)

m. (2) 1886 **Edith Kermit Carow**
(1861–1948)

Nicholas Longworth *m. 1906* **Alice Lee**
(1869–1931) ⊤ (1884–1980)

Monroe   **Corinne** *m. 1909* **Joe Alsop**   **Theodore "Teddy"**
(1887–1944)   (1886–1971) ⊤ (1876–1953)   (1883–1934)

Paulina *m. 1944* **Alexander Sturm**
(1925–1957) ⊤ (1923–1951)

Joanna Sturm
(1946–)

Joseph   Corinne   **Stewart**   John
(1910–1989)   (1912–1997)   (1914–1974)   (1915–2000)

Theodore *m. 1910* **Eleanor**   **Kermit** *m. 1914* **Belle Wyatt Willard**   **Ethel** *m. 1913* **Richard Derby**
"Ted Jr." ⸺ **Butler Alexander**   (1889–1943) ⸺ (1892–1968)   (1891–1977) ⸺ (1881–1963)
(1887–1944)   (1885–1960)

HYDE PARK ROOSEVELTS

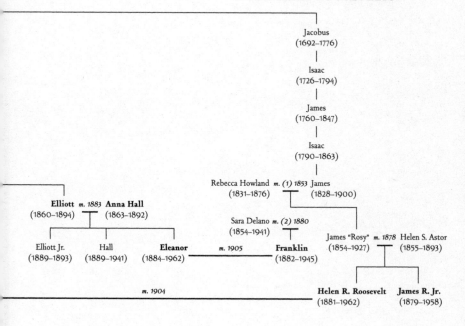

Jacobus
(1692–1776)

Isaac
(1726–1794)

James
(1760–1847)

Isaac
(1790–1863)

Rebecca Howland *m. (1)* 1853 James
(1831–1876)   (1828–1900)

Elliott *m.* 1883 **Anna Hall**
(1860–1894)   (1863–1892)

Sara Delano *m. (2)* 1880
(1854–1941)

James "Rosy" *m.* 1878 Helen S. Astor
(1854–1927)   (1855–1893)

Elliott Jr.   Hall   **Eleanor**   *m.* 1905   **Franklin**
(1889–1893)   (1889–1941)   (1884–1962)   (1882–1945)

m. 1904

Helen R. Roosevelt   **James R. Jr.**
(1881–1962)   (1879–1958)

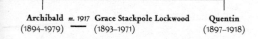

Archibald *m.* 1917 **Grace Stackpole Lockwood**   **Quentin**
(1894–1979)   (1893–1971)   (1897–1918)

Names in boldface are mentioned in *Alice.*

Chapter 1

"It Was Awfully Bad Psychologically"

A$_N$ APPALLING double tragedy overshadowed the joy that should have welcomed Alice Lee Roosevelt's entrance to the world on February 12, 1884. The popular, young New York assemblyman Theodore Roosevelt lost both his beautiful wife, Alice Hathaway Lee, and his beloved mother, Martha Bulloch Roosevelt, on Valentine's Day 1884. He gave the infant her mother's name, a wet nurse, a temporary home, and then relegated her to an afterthought. The family turned in upon itself, lost in grief at the sudden and unexpected deaths, too heartbroken to celebrate Alice's birth. It was the last time anything would eclipse Alice Roosevelt.

The grieving family into which Alice was born boasted a long pedigree with fascinating forebears and a comfortable wealth. Dutchman Claes Martenszen van Rosenvelt arrived in colonial America in the 1640s, well over a century before the thirteen colonies declared independence from Great Britain. Claes and Jannetje Samuel-Thomas van Rosenvelt's son Johannes became the paterfamilias of the Theodore Roosevelt side of the family (the Oyster Bay, Long Island, Roosevelts). Another son, Jacobus, sired what would become the Franklin D. Roosevelt side (the Hyde Park Roosevelts). Five generations of Roosevelt merchants and businessmen, trading in hardware, glass, and other goods, culminated in Cornelius van Schaak Roosevelt. In 1840, he was one of the founders of Chemical National Bank and the father of Theodore Roosevelt Sr., the future president's father. The Roosevelt family grew in size and wealth. By the time Theodore Roosevelt Jr. was born, the family was one of New York's oldest and most socially prominent.

Alice Roosevelt was descended on her mother's side from a Boston Brahmin banking family, the Lees, and through them the Cabots and the Lowells, the families immortalized in John Bossidy's poem about Boston, "Where the Lowells talk only to the Cabots / And the Cabots talk only to God." On Alice's father's side, New England Dutch merchants and patrician Bourbons met. Her paternal grandmother was Martha Bulloch Roosevelt, descendent of an established Southern family whose ancestor James Bulloch had come to America in 1729. Thus Alice enjoyed impeccable membership in the American aristocracy.[1]

Consciousness of their tenure in North America—a fundamental part of what made patricians patricians—suffused the Roosevelt clan. Alice would later jest that the Roosevelts had managed to stay "one step ahead of the bailiff from an island in the Zuider Zee."[2] Still, the family was one of New York's oldest and most socially prominent and such a long line of antecedents gave the Roosevelts an unshakeable social stature and the certainty of belonging. Even encroachment by nouveau riche industrial capitalists could not threaten their standing. The Roosevelts might be outspent but not outclassed, and no amount of money earned by an upstart Scottish immigrant such as Andrew Carnegie would ever erase the fact that the Roosevelts beat him to America. The Vanderbilts could not buy, after the fact, a generalship in the American Revolution, or a seat at the Philadelphia convention. Alice's ancestors had both.

Around Alice's unchanging and insular world, the rest of the United States was rapidly transforming under the combined forces of industrialization and urbanization, fueled by immigrants from all over the world. Industrialization brought new inventions such as the telephone, indoor plumbing, electric lights, and central heating. Urbanization crowded people into cities, and tenements piled family on top of family. Horse cars, electric trolleys, and suburban trains ferried the middle classes to work. Seventeen million immigrants came to the United States between 1900 and 1917. They powered America's second industrial revolution, but their different languages, religions, and expectations gave rise to labor unrest and cultural upheaval. The Republican Party controlled the presidency in eight out of ten elections between the end of the Civil War and Theodore Roosevelt's ascension to that office in 1901. The Grand Old Party was the pro-business advocate of national expansion and high tariffs. The GOP considered itself the moral arbiter for the nation, having successfully guided the country through the 1898 Spanish-American War and begun America's rise to world prominence. Although they could not vote, women entered college and the workforce in small but increasing numbers. Family size decreased as mothers chose to bear fewer offspring. The average life expectancy at the turn of the century was forty years for men and forty-eight years for women. African Americans, struggling under legal segregation after 1896, confronted increasing hostilities. Resistance took organized form in the 1890s, as the Afro-American Council and later the National Association for the Advancement of Colored People fought the uphill battle against institutionalized racism.

Roosevelt wealth and status protected Alice from such changes. In 1896, 5.5 million of America's 12.5 million families were working class, earning less than $500 annually. The Roosevelts were among the 1.5 million families bringing in more than $5,000 per year and owning 86 percent of the nation's wealth.[3] They ran the banks and the railroads, the law firms and the politicians. They also governed the social code. Victorian morality was synonymous with honorable men, demure women, and docile children. Etiquette prescribed a precise system of behavior appropriate to baptisms, funerals, and every life situation in between. Good breeding entailed hewing closely to the moral code, instilling class values in children, and never causing a public scandal. Women's names were to appear in newspapers only at marriage and death.

The Roosevelt family belonged to a social circle of New Yorkers called Knickerbockers. Like their Massachusetts counterparts, the Boston Brahmins, they constituted a closed society. Knickerbockers and Brahmins conducted business among themselves and spent their leisure time together. Parents pressured children to marry within their stratum, a frequent occurrence as the Old Money elites did not consistently mingle with the nouveaux riches until the late 1880s. In that decade, the arrivistes, such as the

Vanderbilts, the Harrimans, and the Goulds, amassed so much money that it became possible for them to "buy" their way into society—or so fretted conservative Knickerbockers.

Theodore Roosevelt was born just as the upstart Robber Barons were starting their fortunes. The elder son of Theodore Roosevelt Sr. and Martha "Mittie" Bulloch Roosevelt, Teedie, as he was called as a young boy, grew up in a loving and sheltered environment, blemished only by his physical condition. Asthma and his undersized body contributed to making him an advocate of "the strenuous life." As a young man, he was closest to his father and to his elder sister, Anna, called Bamie or Bye. Their father gave his time and money to charities like Mrs. Slattery's Night School for Little Italians and cofounded cultural institutions such as the Metropolitan Museum of Art. Inheriting his father's altruistic nature and sense of duty, Theodore would see beyond his class.

Mittie was a transplanted Southerner. She filled her children's heads with the escapades of their swashbuckling Confederate uncles. Her appreciation for their heroics took root especially in her eldest son, who avidly read sagas and legends of many cultures. Mittie and her children shared a close bond. She was their first teacher and a model of the ideal wife who provided support for her husband's activities and managed the family's networks. While Mittie had her quirks—she was consumed with a passion for cleanliness and depended greatly on her eldest daughter for assistance with household tasks—her husband and children adored her and her impish sense of humor.

Teedie's relationship with his brother, Elliott (who would be Eleanor Roosevelt's father), was affectionate but competitive. Elliott seemed to have all the good looks, the charisma, the physical prowess, and the sense of fun. Young Theodore was bookish. He immersed himself in heroic literature and nature studies, and these came to supplement a later love of hunting, taxidermy, and histories of warfare. However, Elliott lacked Theodore's tenacity and his moral core. Elliott died at the age of thirty-four, an alcoholic, drug addict, and adulterer, possibly also suffering from undiagnosed epilepsy.[4]

When TR was twenty years old and halfway through his degree at

Harvard College, his father succumbed to stomach cancer. The inheritance TR gained could not make up for the loss of "the best man [he] ever knew," the father of whom he did not feel worthy. His grief was profound. Less than five months after his father died, he mused to his diary, "Had a very good sermon. I was much struck with one remark, that Christianity gave us, on this earth, rest in trouble, not from trouble."[5]

After his father's death, Roosevelt could live lavishly. His $8,000 annual trust income was $3,000 a year more than the salary of the president of Harvard. The Brahmins were happy to claim him as one of their own, giving him an immediate circle of like-minded gentlemen friends. All of the best Harvard clubs, including the Porcellian and the Hasty Pudding, inducted Theodore into their ranks. He joined the Rifle Club, the Art Club, the Glee Club; served as president of the Natural History Society; and helped found the Finance Club. His habits were not those of a raucous student. Roosevelt did not smoke, detested "low humor," and taught Sunday School classes. He studied biology but found his love of the outdoors thwarted by Harvard's theoretical scientists, who preferred the classroom. Roosevelt turned to history and government. His undergraduate thesis, "The Practicability of Equalizing Men and Women Before the Law," considered the topic of women's rights, including property ownership, and argued that women ought to keep their birth names upon marrying. Roosevelt was an excellent student in the era of the "gentleman's C," but something about him always stood out. He lacked the undergraduate savoir faire that marked his sophisticated classmates, and was known for single-minded intensity in almost every task he approached. This was not a compliment.

Theodore Roosevelt never concentrated quite so hard as during his courtship of the striking and athletic Alice Hathaway Lee. Theodore met Alice when he was nineteen and she was seventeen. His diary rarely ran on a one-woman track, and very few days passed without mention of other females who caught his fancy, but when Roosevelt began a serious pursuit of Alice, he could confide to his diary, "Thank Heaven I am absolutely pure."[6]

Alice Hathaway Lee was born in Chestnut Hill, Massachusetts, on July

29, 1861. She was the daughter of George Cabot Lee and Caroline Watts (Haskell) Lee. Alice Lee was called Sunshine by family and friends, who all agreed it perfectly described her cheerful disposition. She was young, charming, independent minded, and beautiful. Photographs prove her to have been slim and delicate of feature. As a young woman, Alice was tall for the era, almost Theodore's height of five feet, eight inches. Her daughter would inherit her nose, mouth, and slender build. George Lee was a wealthy Boston banker whose affluence allowed Alice and her sisters to live well but not ostentatiously. The Lees prepared their daughters for marriage—a woman's career then—by making them practice ramrod-straight posture and probably by learning other "finishing" skills, such as embroidery, music, and a little French. Alice excelled at archery and tennis, and during walks could cover ground as rapidly as her swain.

Alice attended many balls and parties that featured Harvard's best young men. Her next-door neighbor and cousin, Dick Saltonstall, introduced her, in October 1878, to third-year student Theodore Roosevelt. Roosevelt's father had died nine months earlier, and TR's grief was still raw. He confided to his diary in April, "I have lost the only human being to whom I told *everything*, never failing to get loving advice and sweet sympathy in return; no one, but my wife, if ever I marry, will ever be able to take his place. I so wonder who my wife will be! 'A rare and radiant maiden' I hope; one who will be as sweet, pure and innocent as she is wise."[7]

While "absolutely pure," Roosevelt was clearly not immune to the charms of women. On New Year's Day 1878, TR chronicled his "twenty calls," including one on Edith Carow.[8] He and Edith had grown up together. One of her earliest memories was a visit from the Roosevelts. Four-year-old Edith immediately bonded with Teedie, age seven. But the Knickerbocker Carows were starting to feel the effects of the patriarch's alcoholism. Charles Carow's drinking interfered with his transatlantic shipping business, and the family fortunes suffered. Between her father's mounting troubles and her deepening friendship with the Roosevelt children, Edith became a sort of charity case in the Roosevelt household. Tutored alongside the Roosevelt children, active in their childhood games and able to match them at intellectual pursuits, Edith grew closest to Theodore's sister Corinne, but never lost her initial response to Theodore.

Edith was sweet on him then and until they were teenagers. During two weeks together in the summer of 1878, TR and Edith rowed, swam, and took companionable walks in the way of longtime friends. He drove her out to pick water lilies and spent, as he recounted to his diary, "a lovely morning with her."[9] But Edith and TR quarreled frequently, and one of their rows, Edith always maintained, resulted in the breaking off of what she called their engagement. Edith remembered later that TR proposed several times in 1877 and 1878, but got nowhere because of objections, based either on her youth or on some unsuitable characteristics of the Roosevelts, made by Edith's maternal grandfather. Corinne later suggested that it was *her* father who forbade marriage because of Charles Carow's alcoholism.[10] TR never spoke to his daughter about her mother so Alice Roosevelt Longworth would only have heard her stepmother's side of the story—the side that hurt the most. In this version Alice's mother was TR's second choice: her father picked Alice Lee only after Edith, his first love, had spurned him.

No hint of an engagement appears in TR's diary—but he was never candid there on the most intimate matters until after the fact. There is the intriguing notation from Thursday, August 22, 1878, that "Edith and I went up to the summer house," presumably to have the talk that resulted in their estrangement. This was followed immediately by, "My ride today was so long and hard that I am afraid it may have injured my horse." The next entry is dated two days later: "The other day a dog annoyed me very much while on horseback, and I told the owner I should shoot it; which threat I fulfilled while out riding with [cousin] West today, rolling it over with my revolver very neatly as it ran alongside the horse."[11] A horse lamed and a dog dead because of Roosevelt's fury at Edith's rejection? He had known Edith longer than any other woman. To tender a marriage offer to one like kin not long after his family circle was broken is not farfetched, and of the women he knew, he would have expected Edith to be the most sympathetic. For her to reject his attempt at patching the circle back together must have seemed both incredible and cruel to the grieving young man.

After Edith and TR's argument, fifty-six days passed without female companionship.[12] Instead, Roosevelt took twenty-mile horseback rides and rowing excursions, a five-day "yachting cruise," and a three-week hunting trip through the Maine woods. It wasn't until his eventful junior year at Harvard that he met the scintillating Alice Lee. On the eighteenth of October, TR confided that Saltonstall drove him over to the family manse at Chestnut Hill in Boston, where "all his family are just too sweet to me for anything," and where he met Alice Lee. It was truly love at first sight for TR. "I fell in love with her then," he recounted to a cousin, "...and only the third time I had seen her, I registered a vow in my journal that win her I would...."[13]

He became a regular presence at Chestnut Hill. "I really feel almost as if I were at home when I am over there," he wrote during one palliative stay. In the wake of his father's absence, he found patriarch Leverett Saltonstall "one of the best examples of a true, simple hearted 'gentleman of the old school' I have ever met." But Alice was the real enticement. The more he saw of "pretty Alice," the more he was certain in his objective toward her. And he saw quite a lot of her. By the end of April, TR and Alice sought time alone. At a theater party they "sat just behind the others," and during a walk, "Alice and I soon separated from the others and we did not return till nearly six."[14] They had their photographs taken together—that is, Alice and Theodore and the ubiquitous Rose, with some other friends. Dick's sister Rose Saltonstall was the socially dictated third person, since suitors of that class were not often allowed to be alone together.

Theodore's pursuit of Alice became ever more fervent, but she turned down his proposal. Roosevelt was distraught. He rode his horse back to Harvard in the "pitch dark" and "fell, while galloping down hill." It was, he chided himself, "a misadventure which I thoroughly deserve for being a fool."[15] It cost him another horse lamed.

Why Alice Lee declined Theodore's offer is not wholly apparent. George and Caroline Lee considered their daughter too young to know her mind. She hadn't even come out to society yet. It may be that the Lees wanted proof that Theodore would settle into a career that could provide for their daughter. What he would do to increase the Roosevelt fortune was not obvious when he asked for Alice's hand in marriage. Perhaps they objected to the peculiar mannerisms of the prospective son-in-law. His busy mind was occupied always with a plurality of thoughts, and they tumbled out of his mouth at such a rate that others sometimes had trouble understanding him. In TR's case, one avocation led to another. His childhood interest in the natural world grew into a serious study of the surrounding fauna. To learn better the science behind nature, Roosevelt studied Latin. To examine the animals he shot, he took up taxidermy, making his expensive clothes smell oddly of chemicals. His commitment to charitable work was also a bit strange to the other young men in Harvard Yard. The zealous way in which he lived his life applied to sports as well: he boxed, rowed, hunted, rode, walked (strenuously), and enjoyed every sport but baseball.

Yet Alice didn't reject him absolutely. In the miserable way of young love, TR was happy—and undeterred. Bubbling with optimism at the end of his junior year, he marveled, "I doubt if I ever shall enjoy myself so much again. I have done well in my studies and I have had a most royally good time with the Club, my horse, and above all, the sweet, pretty girls at Chestnut Hill, etc." After a summer spent at Oyster Bay—during which time he remembered to send Edith Carow a book for her eighteenth birthday—Roosevelt reappeared in Boston for his senior year. Of course it wasn't long before he and Dick Saltonstall presented themselves at Chestnut Hill, but Roosevelt's diary continues to provide evidence that while Alice Lee held his heart, his oldest friend still impressed him: "Had a most delightful call on Edith Carow; she is the most cultivated, best read girl I know."[16] Adjectives such as these he reserved for Edith alone.

He continued to see both women. In November 1878, he hosted a luncheon at the Porcellian in honor of his visiting sisters, who were charmed by Alice Lee. He whirled Alice across the floor at her coming-out party on December 2. At home over the Christmas holidays, TR saw Edith more than once. He lunched with her on Boxing Day, but spent the afternoon preparing for the arrival of Alice Lee, Rose and Dick Saltonstall, and three other friends. They "danced the old year out and drank the new year in," and a great party of them went out for a spree and supper.[17]

Finally—finally—on January 25, 1880, his exultant diary entry reads,

"I am so happy that I dare not trust in my own happiness. I drove over to the Lees determined to make an end of things at last; it was nearly eight months since I had first proposed to her, and I had been nearly crazy during the past year; and after much pleading my own sweet, pretty darling consented to be my wife. Oh, how bewitchingly pretty she looked! If loving her with my whole heart and soul can make her happy, she shall be happy." The success of his conquest freed Roosevelt's pen, and he confessed that "it was a real case of love at first sight—and my first love, too."[18] So much for Edith.

The weeks passed deliciously. Alice received a gratifying number of congratulations and basked in engagement parties in her honor. The women of the family tightened their circle around her. One week after the engagement, Bye sermonized, "Theodore is the one most truly like Father and the one from whom Father expected so much and on whom we all greatly lean; and now I feel sure you will help him lead a true and noble life worthy of his Father's name."[19] Alice understood. She never offered a challenge to the Roosevelt women, but seems to have blended into the family with ease; while her relatives provided Theodore with a true second home.

Theodore managed to tear himself away from the happy socializing to take one last hunting trip as a bachelor. "I do not know what I will do when you go out West for six weeks," Alice lamented. "What a good time we did have at Oyster Bay, I loved so much our pleasant little evenings in the summer house and all our lovely drives together. Teddy I love you with my whole heart and am never happier than I am when I am with you," she wrote. Their letters attest to their twin worries: his health and their fitness for marriage. On the eve of his departure, he confided, "I hope we have good sport, or, at any rate, that I get into good health. I am feeling pretty well now; and the Doctor said the very best thing for me was to go."[20]

In the fall of 1880, TR reluctantly left her side again and returned to New York to see about wedding plans. He also enrolled in law school at Columbia University—but without much enthusiasm and with no plans to practice law.[21] He called on his mother, for the two had much to discuss. Mittie and Caroline Lee assisted with the wedding preparations, and the latter had her hands full with a deluge of more than 250 wedding presents.

Early in the process, Alice crowed to TR, "Just think Teddy we have got 79 presents, I had them all out this afternoon for different people to see." In addition to her wedding gift, the groom gave the bride a "beautiful ring." "What an extravagant boy you are, Teddy," Alice purred.[22]

The wedding took place at noon on Wednesday, October 27, 1880, Theodore's twenty-second birthday. Elliott was his brother's best man, and Corinne was one of the four bridesmaids. The crowd overflowed Brookline's Unitarian church. Edith Carow was there and danced the soles off her shoes, subduing her lingering feelings for Theodore.[23] If the bridegroom noticed, he did not leave a record. The newlyweds spent a fortnight at the family home in Oyster Bay, New York, which Bye had prepared for them. "Teddy and I take lovely drives every morning and in the afternoon we either play tennis or walk," Alice wrote to thank her sister-in-law. "I never saw time go faster," she gushed to Bye. "I am so happy."[24] Alice and TR took a proper five-month European honeymoon in the spring of 1881, characterized apparently by the sweet harmony between them. The only trouble came from a physician who warned Theodore that his heart was so weak he should never undertake strenuous exercise. Characteristically, TR ignored him and climbed the 14,693-foot Matterhorn.

When they returned, glowing with good health and contentment, Theodore and Alice moved in with the Roosevelt family at 6 West Fifty-seventh Street. They had their own suite on the third floor. It was an idyllic time. The two began to entertain, going out most nights to join other society leaders. Alice attended meetings of her sewing circle.[25] Occasionally, she visited her family in Boston. She was busy there, with twenty callers in one day, she marveled once, and "everyone is so kind to me." But she worried about her husband stuck at home "making your little boats, up to all hours in the night; with no one to call you to bed." The nighttimes were hardest for them both. "I miss you so much more at night," the new bride confessed.[26] TR was researching and writing *The Naval War of 1812*—his "little boats." He found the project much more engrossing than law school, from which he eventually withdrew, degreeless.

In search of a useful career, Theodore Roosevelt won election to the New York State assembly from the Twenty-first District in 1881, one year after he had formally joined the Republican Party. He spent that fall at the state capital in Albany immersed in his political education. Bye conscientiously cut out newspaper clippings featuring TR and pasted them into her scrapbook. Roosevelt, at twenty-three, was the youngest assemblyman, and he had powerful backers among conservative Knickerbocker elites who tried to gauge his potential. His beautiful wife was by his side for that first winter of 1882. They lived in a boardinghouse that rang with tales of the days' business as Alice absorbed the Byzantine world of New York politics.

On weekends they returned to New York City and the family, where Bye hosted gatherings of politicians, writers, journalists, intellectuals, and reformers to help advance her brother's career. Bringing together influential people from many walks of life was a gift of Bye's, one she used quite freely on her brother's behalf throughout the rest of his life. Educated briefly at Les Ruches in Fontainebleau under the eagle eye of Marie Souvestre, Bye had been given an excellent grounding both in political philosophy and the social graces.

Older Roosevelts provided two different paths to politics. Theodore Sr. had been a Republican delegate to the GOP convention that kept two corrupt nominees—James G. Blaine and Roscoe Conkling—away from the presidency; later Roosevelt paid the price by being denied the position of collector of the Port of New York by Conkling. Still, he had no regrets. In the last letter he ever wrote to TR, Theodore Sr. told his impressionable son that he was proud of the fight he had made against "machine politicians" who "think of nothing higher than their own interests. I fear for your future," he worried. "We cannot stand so corrupt a government for any great length of time."[27]

A second path came from the example of TR's uncle Robert B. Roosevelt, who fought from the other side of the aisle. A lifelong Democrat, Uncle Robert was already well known for his commitment to the conservation of wildlife—he may have been TR's inspiration for his college plan of becoming a scientist—and his service in the U.S. Congress from 1871 to 1873. He was the author of such works as *Is Democracy Dishonesty?*, *The Washington City Ring*, and *Progressive Petticoats*. For the young assemblyman, Theodore Sr. and Robert set two examples of Roosevelts with a reform bent.

TR's background predisposed him to voting on behalf of his class. Nevertheless, he surprised many people, including his working-class constituents, when, during the Westbrook scandal, he made a name for himself as a reformer dedicated to clean government. After conducting his own research, Roosevelt concluded that Judge Theodore R. Westbrook was the pawn of Robber Baron Jay Gould and had profited illegally because of their business dealings. Roosevelt stood before the Albany assembly shaking with passionate indignation and called for the judge's impeachment. He lost, outmaneuvered by his senior colleagues, some of whom were themselves in Gould's pocket. But as a result, TR became a leader of the reform faction—cheered by some and hissed by others, whose class interests they accused Roosevelt of betraying.

Roosevelt turned a deaf ear to the "old family friend" who warned him to give up "the reform play" because he had "gone far enough, and that now was the time to leave politics and identify myself with the right kind of people, the people who would always in the long run control others...."[28] Roosevelt had intended to vote against a bill that would outlaw cigar making in homes, but he changed his mind after labor activist Samuel Gompers took him on a tour of the hovels where cigar makers, mostly Jewish immigrants, lived and worked. Aghast at the squalor, Roosevelt, taking a page from his father's book, decided the sweatshop system was immoral. People could not live healthily enough to participate in the democracy in such conditions. Between Westbrook and Gompers, Roosevelt found the gumption to step outside of himself and view life through the eyes of others. Thus began his career in public service, one in which he generally put the needs of the many above the greed of a few. The fork in TR's political road bent pragmatically leftward until very late in his life.

In October 1882, Assemblyman Roosevelt and his wife left Mittie and moved into their own home, a rented house at 55 West Forty-fifth Street. Alice's charm and beauty made them leaders of, in the jargon of the day, "the young married swells." Quiet evenings at home were the exception, but both husband and wife continued to delight in each other. In the summer of 1883, after undergoing an undefined gynecological surgery, Alice became pregnant. She couldn't find the words to tell Bye "how happy" the knowledge had made her.[29] Theodore's asthma resurfaced at the news. He threw himself into his second term in the legislature. When the session was over, Roosevelt returned to the Dakotas to hunt buffalo and regain his equilibrium. Having fallen in love with the wildness and the open skies around Medora, he invested ten thousand dollars in a ranch and began to animate it with cattle. He expected both a large return on his investment and to enjoy, once a year or so, the life of a cattle rancher.

The couple had also purchased more than fifty acres of land at rural Oyster Bay on which to build a home for their family. They joined other Roosevelts who had chosen the northern shore of Long Island for its proximity to Manhattan. The house was to be called Leeholm in Alice's honor, and would boast ten bedrooms and a large wraparound porch. They dreamed of a home filled with children—many of their own, and their nephews, nieces, and eventually grandchildren, too. Leeholm was a tangible commitment to their future, as tangible as the baby Alice carried. "My own tender true love," Roosevelt wrote Alice, "I never cease to think fondly of you; and oh how doubly tender I feel towards you now! You have been the truest and tenderest of wives, and you will be the sweetest and happiest of all little mothers."[30]

The Roosevelt family correspondence recorded nothing unusual during Alice Lee Roosevelt's pregnancy. Her mother-in-law remarked once about "how very large" Alice looked. She may have been commenting on the way Alice looked in a particular dress on a particular day, or she might have been viewing one of the symptoms of chronic nephritis. Theodore was not overly concerned about his wife. She had moved back into Mittie's house, and had Mittie's sister Anna Bulloch Gracie, Anna Hall Roosevelt (Elliott's wife), Mittie, Bye, and Corinne close by. Her own mother was a short train ride away in Boston. Theodore spent his weeks in Albany, rushing home for the weekend, except for the times an important bill kept him in the capital.

On February 6, 1884, Roosevelt wrote to his wife, "I look forward so much to seeing you tomorrow; I wish I could be with you to rub you when you get 'crampy.'" Theodore apparently understood the cramps as a normal part of pregnancy, not a warning sign of illness. He spent the weekend of February 9 to 11 with Alice in New York City. Corinne and her new husband, Douglas Robinson, had left their infant son in Bye's care while they were away in Baltimore. Mittie took to bed with what everyone thought was a severe cold. On Monday, the eleventh, Caroline Lee arrived to help her daughter through childbirth. Roosevelt attended hearings downtown that day and then left for the legislature, confident that the women were being well tended.

As he raced away toward Albany, Alice penciled what would be her last letter to her husband: "Darling Thee—I hated so to leave you this afternoon, I dont think you need feel worried about my being sick as the Dr told me this afternoon that I would not need my nurse before Thursday—I am feeling well tonight but am very much worried over the ~~baby~~ your little mother, her fever is still very high and the Dr is rather afraid of typhoid, it is not in the least catching. I will write again to-morrow and let you know just how she is—dont say anything about it till then. I do love my dear Thee so much, I wish I could have my little new baby soon.—ever Your loving wife, Alice."[31]

That evening at 8:30 p.m. Alice gave birth to a healthy, eight-and-three-quarter-pound girl. Anna Gracie bustled about taking care of the infant, while the doctor tended to Alice. Aunt Gracie wrote down an account of the birth. She described Alice crying "I <u>love</u> a little girl," and begging the doctor to tend to the infant as it was sneezing. As Aunt Gracie swaddled the newborn in flannel and set her down in an armchair the infant sneezed again. Alice begged, "Oh, don't let my baby take cold." Gracie remembered Alice remonstrating with the doctor to see to the infant. But he was concerned about the mother. While Aunt Gracie "made up the little Basinet with all the dainty, pretty little things her sweet little mother had laid aside," the family sent a telegram to Albany bearing the good news to the father, but advising him that Alice was "only fairly well." According to Aunt Gracie, "at eleven o'clock the baby's grandmother Lee told me 'Alice has had her child in her arms and kissed it.'"[32] The telegram reached Theodore on the thirteenth during the morning session of the legislature. This great news was stolen from him by the arrival of a second, dire telegram in midafternoon saying Alice had taken a turn for the worse.

Roosevelt left Albany in a fury to make the five-hour train trip home in ghastly weather. Dense fog and rain slowed all traffic in and out of New York. Roosevelt managed to arrive at 11:30 p.m. One hour earlier, Corinne and Douglas had returned home from Baltimore. Elliott threw open the doors of the house and warned them to go see their baby—who had been moved to another relative's home—before entering: "There is a curse on this house," Elliott cried to his sister. "Mother is dying, and Alice is dying too."[33] Inside, the women kept the vigil; Corinne at Alice's bedside and Bye at their mother's. Alice was a victim of an undiagnosed kidney ailment called Bright's disease. Mittie suffered from typhoid, an illness that annually killed several hundreds of city dwellers in the days before sanitation became a civic virtue.

Theodore gazed helplessly at his unconscious wife until called away for the last moments of his mother's life. All four of her children were present when Mittie died at 3:00 a.m. Theodore barely had time to register her death before he scaled the stairs to Alice's room. Eleven hours later, held tenderly by her devastated husband, Alice died. Their infant daughter remained—a living reminder that their joyous life together had not been a dream.

Two thousand people crowded the nave for the double funeral at the Fifth Avenue Presbyterian Church. Theodore suffered impassively through the eulogies and the burials. Four days later, he was back at the legislature. One grueling March day, TR reported twenty-one bills out of committee, and then stayed up all that night redrafting another bill. He couldn't think of his daughter—What did he know of infants? He couldn't face the horrible task of tending to the worldly affairs of his mother. The child and the legal responsibilities reminded him paralyzingly of his double loss. The routine of the statehouse, its masculine culture, and the endless work provided him with the stability to continue. "I think I should go mad if I were not employed," Theodore swore. "The more we work the better I like it," he wrote to Bye.[34]

As he poured himself into his career, he left much to his twenty-nine-year-old sister. Bye responded to the hundreds of condolence letters. It fell to her to organize and distribute their parents' possessions, including the house. Less than a fortnight after Mittie's death, it was done. Bye monitored the building of Leeholm. The agonizing chores were hers because Bye was the least encumbered—no family of her own, no remunerative employment—and because she was the responsible one, the eldest child, who had been more like an adult to her three siblings than one of them when they were younger. As she divided up the property of two lifetimes, Bye became the inheritor of the most painful and precious part of her brother's broken life: the infant Alice. "Her aunt can take care of her better than I can," Roosevelt morosely wrote a friend. "She would be just as well off without me."[35]

The baby had been christened the day after the funerals. Alice Lee Roosevelt was held by her dazed father and wore a smocked gown, "the one her sweet Mother liked more than anything else," Aunt Gracie recalled. The vicar poured water over her forehead from the family's heirloom silver bowl, the newly baptized infant also wore a locket with Sunshine's "golden hair in it."[36] The family usually called her Baby Lee when she was very young, Sister or Sissy when she was a child, and Auntie Sister when she was an adult. Although these are common enough names to give to the eldest daughter in a Southern household, the Roosevelts—with the exception of Mittie—were Northerners. It is more probable that Theodore found it painful to hear the name Alice. It is also curious that Alice was called Baby Lee, and not Baby Roosevelt, as though Theodore could not claim her.

Indeed, he did not act as a father to her for the first three years of her life. Bye moved with Alice into a new house on Madison Avenue, and although Theodore stayed there when he was in New York, he was not often in the metropolis. Theodore, in May, attended the Republican national convention in Chicago, but in the fall he went back to Medora, seeking the solace of the empty spaces and the hard, physical labor that running a cattle ranch entailed. His thoughts turned inward. He tried to put the brief time of happiness with Alice Lee into perspective. The last words he ever wrote about her came in the form of a memorial, penned in the Dakotas and privately published: "Her life had always been in the sunshine; and there had never come to her a single great sorrow; and none ever knew her who did not love and revere her for her bright, sunny temper and her saintly unselfishness. Fair, pure, and joyous as a maiden; loving, tender, and happy as a young wife; when she had just become a mother, when her life seemed to be but just begun, and when the years seemed so bright before her—then, by a strange and terrible fate, death came to her. And when my heart's dearest died, the light went out from my life forever."[37]

With these words, Theodore Roosevelt resolutely closed the book on Alice Hathaway Lee Roosevelt. Ten weeks after she died, he wrote bleakly in a "sketch" of his life: "I married Miss Alice Lee of Boston on leaving college in 1880. My father died in 1878; my wife and mother died in February 1884. I have a little daughter living."[38] Alice Lee Roosevelt does not appear in his published autobiography. Theodore did not speak of her again. His own daughter clearly did not substitute for his "heart's dearest." Even when Bye reminded her brother, "You have your child to live for," Theodore stayed out West.[39]

Anna Roosevelt was three years older than her brother and possessed of the same intelligence, intensity for life, and internal strength. She had overcome infantile paralysis that left her with a hunched back and a hearing problem. As an adult, Alice always held that "if Auntie Bye had been a man, she would have been president."[40] Bye kept the family together throughout its crises. She had been the apple of her father's eye, and the family treated Bye with awe and deference, which she earned through being wise, capable, organized, and less judgmental than Theodore. Bye handled Theodore's finances after Alice Lee's death (although not his investments). She and TR were very close. Bye believed firmly that TR should stay in politics, and she supported friendships and career moves that kept him there. Theodore consulted with Bye, not Elliott's wife, when the family finally had to make decisions about Elliott's wastrel lifestyle. Bye was the logical choice to raise Baby Lee.

Alice filled a deep void in Auntie Bye's life. Except for part of the summers, which Alice spent with her Lee relatives in Boston, the girl lived with her aunt steadily for three years and sojourned there regularly in her youth.

Alice thought Bye "the single most important influence on my childhood," and "the only one I really cared about when I was a child." Bye called Alice her "blue-eyed darling."[41] The bond between Alice and Auntie Bye was deep, strong, and lasting.

Bye's home presented a marked contrast to the one Alice would soon inhabit. Her aunt was outgoing and warm, witty and charming, passionately interested in civic affairs, able both to soothe and to scorn. From Bye Alice learned how to preside over tea and how to butter bread, *then* cut it into the thinnest slices. From Bye Alice studied the art of leading conversation. And from Bye Alice knew that there could be few taboo topics among those truly interested in the world and all its possibilities. With Bye there was, as Alice later put it, "a wonderful feeling of warmth and ease and hospitality."[42] Bye spoiled Alice, just as her Lee relatives did. Until she moved into the White House, Alice's later surroundings as a young girl were devoid of the sophisticated elegance that made a lasting impression on her at Bye's.

Her aunt held a special place in Alice's heart because she told her stories of her mother. Bye assured Alice that her Alice Lee was beautiful and charming, and Alice needed to hear that, for as an adult she recalled:

My father never told me anything about this. In fact, he never ever mentioned my mother to me, which was absolutely wrong. He never even said her name, or that I even had a different mother. He was so self-conscious about it. And my maternal grandparents, with whom I stayed every year in Boston, never mentioned her either. Nor my aunts. Finally, Auntie Bye did tell me something very revealing, such as that she had been very pretty and attractive. And she gave me some of her things . . . from my father I suppose. The whole thing was really handled very badly. It was awfully bad psychologically. There was I, laden with photographs of my late lamented mama, which I had to stick on my dressing table and on the wall above the bed. And I was always being exhorted, particularly by my Irish nurse, to 'say a prayer for your mother in heaven.' It was all quite awful.[43]

It helped, no doubt, that Bye and Alice Lee had been friends. Sensing Alice's pain and the confusion about her absent father and her deceased mother, Auntie Bye channeled all her resources to compensate for Alice's losses, to create a happy home filled with entertainments and interesting people, and to prove to Alice that she was deeply loved. Aunt Gracie remembered young Alice's joy in Anna's presence and how the two-year-old "was prone to laughing until 'her little sides shook.'"[44]

Under Bye's care, Alice experienced warmth, love, and undivided attention for the only time in her life. For the rest of her days, Alice sought, unsuccessfully, to duplicate that unconditional love.

Chapter 2

"Sissy Had a Sweat Nurse!"

W HEN THEODORE ROOSEVELT returned to reclaim his daughter, he did so at the insistence of his new wife, Edith Kermit Carow Roosevelt, already pregnant with their first child. Theodore felt guilty about his first wife's death, ambivalent about his remarriage, and irresolute about his daughter. Alice longed for Theodore's time—what three-year-old doesn't crave her father's undivided attention?—but she never got enough of it. Edith freely admitted that she was not the best kind of mother for a spirited child like Alice. Relinquished by her beloved aunt, Alice grew up a virtual orphan in a clannish family. She was plagued by self-doubt and a haunting sense that she never compared favorably to her siblings or her girlfriends. This would be the theme of her childhood—and the reason for her rebelliousness—which was part self-protective armor and part desperation caused by feeling she had little to lose. The strong-willed young woman who ultimately evolved delighted onlookers as much as she exasperated her parents.

Edith Kermit Carow always knew she would marry Teedie. When he went off to Harvard and fell in love with Alice Lee, no one was more surprised than she. In the small world of the American East Coast elite, Edith and Alice became social acquaintances. They all traveled in a group together to Canada. Edith even hosted a party for Theodore and Alice just after their wedding.

When Alice died, however, Theodore went out of his way to avoid Edith because of the Victorian moral code that dictated a long mourning period, and that he interpreted also to mean that he should be faithful to his wife until death. In 1885, after a nineteen-month separation, TR and Edith accidentally bumped into each other. They fell cautiously but thoroughly in love. TR had to tell his sisters, especially Bye. She and Corinne had long been skeptical of Edith's influence on their brother. They worried that she would try to isolate him from them. While Edith and Corinne had been best friends in their youth, Edith was always more standoffish and private than the Roosevelts. This was hardly surprising, given her father's alcoholism and death, and the family's reduced circumstances. Corinne told Alice years later that she and Anna "feared" that Edith would "come between" the sisters and their brother. "She did in a way," Alice conceded. To soften the blow for the one who would take it the hardest, Theodore wrote Bye a letter of appeasement: "As I have already told you, if you wish to you shall keep Baby Lee, I of course, paying the expense."[1]

Theodore assumed that Edith would not want the lively, toddling reminder of his first marriage around, or perhaps *he* did not want Alice with them. In any event, Roosevelt failed to ask his future wife's opinion before he wrote to Anna. "He obviously felt tremendously guilty about remarrying," Alice believed, "because of the concept that you loved only once and you never loved again." In his attempt to try to forget that he had ever been married, Theodore considered cutting himself off from its most obvious sign. Edith, it turned out, had decided feelings about her duty toward Baby Lee and wanted to bring her into the new family. It was all his fault, he wrote Bye sheepishly, and pleaded with her not to blame Edith.[2]

On December 2, 1886, in England, Theodore and Edith were wed. Bye accompanied TR across the Atlantic, leaving Alice in Aunt Gracie's care. Bye returned alone, as Edith and Theodore explored Europe until March 1887. Forever after, Edith mistily recalled her "honeymoon days, and remember them all one by one, and hour by hour." From abroad, Theodore had to write Bye an embarrassed letter: "I hardly know what to say about Baby Lee. Edith feels more strongly about her than I could have imagined possible. However, we can decide it all when we meet."[3] The newlyweds returned to New York City on March 27. Edith's wishes prevailed. Alice remembered being dressed in her best frock, handed a bouquet of pink roses, and being sent down the stairs of Auntie Bye's home—her home—to welcome Mother, as Edith insisted upon being called.

Bye had seen Alice's first steps, heard her first words, dressed her, fed her, tended her through her sicknesses—including an illness that deformed her legs—for three years. The whole family knew Alice as "Bye's Baby Lee."[4] Now, Theodore, the brother she admired, was coming home with a woman she mistrusted to take "her" child away from her. Almost thirty years later, Bye empathized with the parents of a bride-to-be, "for," she recalled achingly, "it is hard to face parting with one's daughter." In her memoir, Bye explained that "it almost broke my heart to give her up. Still I felt perfectly sure that it was for her good, and that unless she lived with her father she would never see much of him, and as my father and I had had such a close relationship, this would have been a terrible wrong to her...."[5]

Did Alice feel Bye's sadness or Edith's nervousness? Alice remembered Bye telling her, "Remember darling, if you are very unhappy you can always come back to me."[6] The child barely had time to adjust to her situation, for after a week, on April 4, TR and Edith left again to go on holiday, not to return until May, when they finally claimed her. This time, Bye was not present for Alice's final move away from Madison Avenue. She could not bear another wrenching parting as Alice, Theodore, and Edith left for Sagamore Hill (the new name for Leeholm) to live together as a family for the first time. Alice felt abandoned by the woman who had served as both mother and father for her profoundly important first three years.

After only a fortnight at Sagamore Hill, however, Edith shipped Alice off to her Lee grandparents for the annual summer visit. At least Chestnut Hill and Grandma and Grandpa Lee and her Lee aunts were familiar. Alice was their first grandchild and particularly special because she was what remained of their daughter. Alice remembered loving the "three enchanting weeks with everyone trying to make me deliriously happy. I was treated there as *belonging*. Everything belonged to me. I would come in and jump up and down on the sofa, hoping the springs would break, and they would merely smile indulgently."[7] Alice played with her mother's dollhouse and her mother's dolls, perhaps providing her with the sense of continuity that she lacked at Sagamore Hill. Alice romped with the children of the Brahmins, would make her debut alongside them, and continued the friendships into her old age. It is hard to know what some of them thought about her robust Roosevelt upbringing. Mary Lee recalled that Alice and another friend were great pranksters who delighted in upsetting the schoolroom routine from which they were exempt: "The 'fiend and the pirate' of my youth were Alice Roosevelt...and Molly Lowell. I remember one warm spring day when voices arrived in our schoolroom, coming apparently from nowhere, laughing voices shouting remarks not calculated to keep our minds upon our studies. The [schoolmistresses] deployed as usual around the school house.... At last the culprits were discovered, dirty but cheerful, crammed into the air box in the cellar."[8]

Throughout her childhood, Alice understood that in Boston she had her own separate relatives, her own grandparents, her own friends, and her own time with them. Although she later thought of the Lees as rather stuffy, "at least they were *mine* and I didn't have to share them with my siblings."[9] Alice felt an ambivalence: *different* meant "strange," but it also meant "special." The two feelings warred for the upper hand in her childish understanding.

Caroline Haskell Lee and George Cabot Lee provided for their granddaughter out of their substantial wealth. Alice received her mother's portion of her inheritance in a lump sum, from which she was given an allowance. The money was doled out by her grandfather Lee. When Alice was young, TR and Edith used to joke about the imperative of being nice to her. Edith was grateful for the infusion of Lee funds, since she had to stretch the tight Roosevelt family budget. A note Edith wrote to Bye gives some idea of the workings between the Lees and the Roosevelts: "Thank you for your letter which came today enclosing Mrs. Lee's. The green [coat] is exceedingly shabby and only fit for the country. The faithful Jacob brought me the little dresses [from the Lees] tonight. They are very pretty. Will you send a postal asking Tiffany's to forward Alice's gold beads to Boston...." At another time, Edith sought Bye's help because "I could not trust any one here with Alice's lace dress which is the reason I had to bother you. You will judge what it requires as you know money is no object."[10] Despite their ability to turn Alice's head with extravagant gifts, and whatever their feelings about Theodore's remarriage, the Lees never tried to win Alice away from Edith. Their letters consistently referred to Edith as "your Mother."

Yet the Lees wanted their granddaughter to appreciate her Lee ancestry. Accompanying a gift, Grandma provided a genealogy lesson: "I sent yesterday... a present from Mr. and Mrs. F. E. Haskell. In acknowledging it, they are your Mother's Uncle Fred and Aunt Margaret. I write this, as you seem to have no knowledge of your relatives on our side of the family."[11] Grandma Lee sent this letter in 1906, when Alice was no longer a child but still lacked the appropriate grasp of her mother's kin.

Rejoining the Roosevelt family entailed a mental readjustment. The first time she returned from the Lees' to Sagamore Hill, in late summer 1887, Alice had to reacquaint herself with her new situation—no comfortable, well-loved Auntie Bye (for anything more than a visit)—and a stepmother who was expecting a baby and preoccupied. Edith had suffered a miscarriage with her first pregnancy, and she and TR were understandably apprehensive about her health that summer. Of course, Theodore also had the specter of his first wife's mortal pregnancy before him. He responded with a severe asthma attack. Alice distracted her father by monitoring his morning shaving ritual, by waylaying him for rides on his shoulders, and, in her four-year-old way, forcing him to remember that life goes on.

On September 13, 1887, Edith safely delivered a boy, Theodore Jr. Aunt Gracie came over to care for the infant. Despite Theodore's urging, Edith did not want Bye's assistance. That meant Bye could not be there to help Alice with yet another profound transition. Edith slipped into postnatal depression, as she would do to varying degrees after each of her children's births. She accordingly devoted less of her time to Alice, at exactly the moment her stepdaughter most needed reassurance about the security of her place in the family. There is no evidence that Theodore compensated to help his daughter.

Alice pronounced her brother "a howling polly parrot" and was interested in watching him, "especially when he 'eats Mamma.'" After he was born, Alice sat by his bassinet, guarding, "lest someone should take baby brother away."[12] This fear was rooted in her own experiences. Life was precarious, unpredictable—a mother "taken away" by an incomprehensible thing like death, and herself "taken away" from her home with Auntie Bye just a few months earlier. Ted and Alice grew to be "boon companions," as Alice phrased it, and remained so until Ted's death. Other pregnancies followed: Edith had a miscarriage in 1888, gave birth to Kermit in 1889, Ethel in 1891, Archie in 1894, Quentin in 1897, and had miscarriages in 1902 and in 1903. Alice's own needs had to fit within the spiral of her stepmother's confinement, pregnancy, postnatal depression, and decreased attention. Nursemaids and eventually governesses tended the growing brood since Edith was frequently emotionally withdrawn and Theodore was physically absent. He continued his annual autumn hunting trips, regardless of domestic upheavals.

Even when Theodore was at home his burgeoning political career meant spending more and more time away from his children. In 1889, President Benjamin Harrison appointed him civil service commissioner. Alice was "distressed" that her father wasn't home for Ted's birthday—and Edith wasn't having an easy time without him either. She wrote to TR, away in the Rocky Mountains, "I am trying to make Alice more of a companion. I am afraid I do not do rightly in not adapting myself more to her. . . . I wish I were gayer for the children's sake. Alice needs someone to laugh and romp with her instead of a sober and staid person like me." But, Edith suggested flatly, "I am not myself when you are away."[13]

Alice also needed attention and guidance to help her understand why she felt like the outsider in the nursery. What Alice craved was recognition of her differences, open discussion of the events of her birth, and reassurance of her place in the family. She was confused at one point about Edith's identity, thinking that she was "Papa's sister," just as Auntie Bye and Auntie Corinne were. "My brothers used to tease me about not having the same mother. They were very cruel about it and I was terribly sensitive," Alice recalled as an adult. Young Ted taunted her because the infant Alice had had a wet nurse. In her seventies, Alice remembered this childhood hurt: "So this horrid little cross-eyed boy of about five would go around to all and sundry exclaiming, 'Sissy had a sweat nurse! Sissy had a sweat nurse!' It was frightfully wounding to the character!"[14]

Theodore and Edith actively contributed to Alice's sense of unease. Theodore's silence about Alice Hathaway Lee complemented Edith's acerbic comments. Alice remembered Edith making it plain to the family that she and Theodore had been in love long before TR ever met Alice's mother. Once, in a fit of pique about Alice's behavior, Edith told Ted that if Alice Hathaway Lee had lived, she would have bored Theodore to stupefaction.[15] Ted lost no time in telling his half sister. The story is unfortunate enough, but it becomes sinister if Edith phrased it as a comparison: Alice took after her dull, empty-headed mother. Alice insisted that incidences such as these accounted for her attitude in later life: "It's not surprising that early on I became fairly hard-minded and learnt to shrug a shoulder with indifference. I certainly wasn't going to be a part of everyone saying, 'the poor little thing.' "[16]

As an adult, Alice thought that Edith resented being second choice, and had never forgiven TR his first marriage. Alice's later remembrances of Edith are unsympathetic: "In many ways she was a very hard woman... and she had almost a gift for making people uncomfortable." She had a "withdrawn, rather parched quality.... My stepmother made an enormous effort with me as a child but I think she was bored by doing so ... [and] she could be mean."[17] Alice dutifully called Edith Mother when she was alive. After Edith's death, however, she referred to her as "my stepmother," as though the latter term more adequately reflected Alice's feelings. Letters during Alice's childhood show a warmer version of Edith. Once Edith was past childbearing, the two settled into a relationship that had fully as much mutual fondness and respect as it had tension. But the crucial years of Alice's childhood were fraught with her need for love and attention, neither of which she received in sufficient quantity. Edith wrote to Bye about the nine-year-old Alice's attempts to comprehend her situation: "I do feel quite as sorry for the poor child as for myself and the other inhabitants of the nursery, for she realizes that something is wrong with her, and goes through a real mental conflict trying to get straightened out."[18] If Edith looked at her nine-year-old stepdaughter as though something were "wrong" with her, it adds another layer of ambivalence where there would have ideally been unstinting love. It all made for parlous times as a teen.

Glimpses of the troubles between them can be seen in Edith's and Alice's contrasting attitudes toward convention. A Roosevelt cousin wrote that "Edith was relentless in her disapproval of transgressors of the established code of morals and conduct." He viewed it as a personality—perhaps a generational—clash: "To a brilliant stepdaughter who at the turn of the century was imbued with the same kind of revolt against parental authority that has been widespread among teen-agers of the last half-century, the cold and detached insistence on standards of conduct by the wife of her adored father must have been trying—all the more so in that Edith Carow had a gift of seeing through people, old or young."[19]

It was at that moment in Alice's life that Auntie Bye married. Bye's friendship with a naval attaché serving at the American embassy in London, Lieutenant Commander William Cowles, had blossomed into a love affair. Bye left for England at Christmastime in 1894. Alice could not stop crying long enough to see her off. In England Bye spent her time taking care of cousins Helen and James Roosevelt, whose mother had recently died. Helen was nearly a teenager when Bye arrived, and Alice could not have helped feeling jealous at the attention Helen received full time from Bye—even though Helen and Alice were warm friends at various points in their lives. But even Helen and James could not block the effect of the lieutenant commander on Bye. Though some in the family suggested the middle-aged Bye married Cowles so that she could stay in London rather than because she passionately loved him, their wedding, on November 25, 1895, began a solid and affectionate partnership. And while it was Ted who said it, all of the children habituated to Bye's attention must have felt it: "Aunty Bye won't love us as much now."[20]

Alice had to look elsewhere. By all but her own adult accounts, Alice worshipped Theodore. "I loved my father but I was never particularly close to him," she told reporter Sally Quinn late in life. When she was forty-three years old, journalist Charles Selden interviewed Alice and her best friend, Ruth Hanna McCormick, about their famous fathers. He concluded that Alice was a chip off the old block, who had "what the modern psychologists call 'the father complex.'" Alice thought of her father as her hero, according to Selden, which she denied.[21] When she was a child, Alice seems to have loved her father in the extravagant way many girls do. She could, then, only have sensed how TR's Victorian code became entangled in his feelings for her. "My father," Alice contemplated, "obviously didn't want the symbol of his infidelity around. His two infidelities, in fact: infidelity to my stepmother by marrying my mother first, and to my mother by going back to my stepmother after she died."[22] Alice and Theodore's relationship was complicated by nineteenth-century morality, by the physical distance between them for the first years of her life, by Edith, by the addition of five half siblings, and later by Theodore's ineptitude in the face of Alice's teenage rebellion. Perhaps Alice's intelligence—evident as a child—highlighted the similarities between them. TR was so like her, intellectually and temperamentally, that in Alice he saw his own faults mirrored.

One of Alice's earliest memories of her father occurred when she was still living with Auntie Bye. For the first time in months, Alice was about to see her father. The two-and-a-half-year-old waited at Auntie Bye's side by the stables at the Meadowbrook Hunt Club to greet TR when he completed the fox hunt. Theodore had ridden furiously that day, and returned with a broken arm, torn clothing, and a bloody face. As he ran toward his daughter, Alice screamed. He caught her tightly. Helpless in the grip of the bloodied, sweaty man who did not look anything like her father, Alice screamed again. Theodore shook Alice to quiet her. She screamed louder. He shook harder. "It was a theme," Alice commented wryly, "which was to be repeated, with variation, in later years."[23]

Where TR had been an asthmatic child, Alice labeled herself a physical coward as a girl. She wore a brace on her legs, the result of undiagnosed polio as a child, which contributed to her unease around the strenuous life at Sagamore. The contraption worked, and Alice eventually walked perfectly, but the memory of it stayed with her. At eighty-three, she recalled feeling "like a tenement child...deformed with my legs...and I was always very conscious of that." When Alice was eight or nine, she had to wear braces to keep her feet from turning out. Edith stretched Alice's Achilles tendons each night, spending five minutes on one leg and seven and a half on the other. Edith explained the device to Bye, who had suffered from a similar childhood disease: "They reach half way up her leg, and consist of two iron bars screened to the bottom of her shoe and connected by a leather strap around her leg. They have a hinge so she can move her foot freely up and down, but not sideways." Two weeks later Edith wrote again, with a dismal progress report: "Alice suffers far less with her foot but I fear it will be a long, long time before there is any permanent relief—one day she will walk quite easily and the next can hardly hobble. The Doctor thinks she does not have enough cartilage but I feel there may be rheumatic pains beyond the muscular trouble which he recognizes."[24]

Alice referred to the apparatus as a medieval torture instrument that made her self-conscious. She could not take walking for granted, for even on level ground the braces would lock up and throw her to the pavement. The braces did make good weapons, though, when employed to clunk her little brothers over the head. A more positive update on Alice came later: "She does not mind her braces the least bit in the world. Evidently they give her rather a distinction than otherwise among the children." This was another example of Alice learning to shrug her shoulders with indifference—and another case of *strange* simultaneously meaning *special*, just as it had done for TR when he suffered from childhood asthma.[25]

Shy because of her braces, Alice used to "spend hours of time pretending that I was a fiery horse, preferably cream colored, like Cinderella's horses, able at a bound to cover vast regions of the earth, and also at will to turn into something quite different, such as a princess with very long hair, or an extremely martial prince." All of these imaginary roles involved legs that worked: legs that bounded over the earth, danced like a princess, or fought in battle like a prince.[26] As an adult, Alice had little sympathy for people who wallowed in their illnesses. She had the example of Auntie Bye, who suffered pain every day of her life but never complained. Alice also had the opposite image of her stepmother. More than once, Alice's routine was disrupted and she was sent away because of Edith's various conditions. It was a point of pride with Roosevelts to bear physical ailments stoically.

Alice did not enjoy competing with her siblings and cousins at noisy, outdoor games, but she loved horses and was an excellent rider. She threw herself into nursery pillow fights, played with her dolls, and spent wonderful hours reading in the hayloft. In 1891, Edith described Alice and Ted with a new gift: "Alice liked the Buffalo Hunt better than anything she had.... Ted's sharp eye noted what excellent horse blankets the cotton wadding in which it was packed made, and Alice ... became absorbed for the rest of the afternoon in helping him construct them." A formative memory was of being carried up the hill at Sagamore on the shoulders of Auntie Bye's tall butler, seeing the sunset and thinking she'd never seen anything so exquisitely beautiful. She dreamed about sunsets after that.[27]

When Alice was six, on a trip with the family, her stepmother wrote to Auntie Bye: "The children were asleep but Alice waked from a doze in a state of joy, and was up at an unheard of hour next morning to get her new horse and cart in bed to play with. She looks splendidly, very clear, which means she feels well, and so bright and happy. She has improved much in her riding and seems to have more elasticity and spring of health than I have ever known." Nine-year-old Alice scrawled to her stepmother with creative spelling: "Yesterday morning all of us went up to see Ethel. I had a very nice time plying with her. In the afternoon we went to the centtrel park. I brought my houp with me. I know how to role it quit nicely now. We are going out driving this morning in Auntty Byes little yeller wagon." In 1891, Edith had reported: "The afternoon was stormy but Alice was happy as possible playing with Kermit. It is most lucky for her that she has such a flair for little children! She is so well and happy and really enjoys her lessons." As the eldest, she was occasionally pressed into service as a babysitter while Edith was away. Alice wrote sagely about a squabble she had overseen between Archie and Ethel: "She knocked him down but the thing he hurt was his feelings."[28]

The children played together frequently, but they did not study together often. Alice received sporadic tutoring when she was young and occasional lessons when she was older, but did not attend a formal school. Theodore and Edith provided Alice's first education. They taught her how to read and instilled intellectual discipline by having Alice recite her lessons to them. They read to her from *Grimm's Fairy Tales*, *Tales from the Arabian*

Nights, Milton, Scott, Dickens, Twain, Longfellow, Kipling, the *Nibelung-enlied*. She belonged to, she said, "the Andrew Lang period of the Blue Book. He translated these lovely folk tales... from every known language." Theodore acted out tales of George Washington, the Revolutionary War, the War of 1812, Davy Crockett and the Alamo, the Civil War, and Custer and the Indian wars. Edith instructed Alice in the Bible, which Alice read from cover to cover more than once, just to say she had. Alice inhaled books, as all Roosevelts did. She was given free rein in the library at Sagamore Hill, and was the only child allowed to interrupt her father when he was closeted there.[29]

A related love was wordplay. From riddles to anagrams, Alice enjoyed the intellectual delight of manipulating letters and phrases. Her papers are punctuated with examples of diversions such as illustrated limericks and acrostics. Alice was fluent in French, and had been introduced to German. Latin she swore she never liked "because I was <u>made</u> to do it." She recalled a "marvelous little book called *La Grecque Sans Larmes*, which of course meant we dripped with larmes getting through it...." History delighted her, too, and she wrote to her father proudly of the time she soundly beat her cousins at a game they created of writing down "as many names as we could in history of mythology beginning at A, and going through the alphabet, spending two minutes on each letter."[30] She also studied music, geography, and some of the sciences, particularly astronomy and geology. Alice later regretted the lack of formal schooling, but her intellectual curiosity lasted her entire lifetime.

Just once, in 1898, Alice enrolled in school. A letter from a classmate remains from that time that gives an indication of how well the fourteen-year-old socialized with other children:

Most adorable Alice: This just shows how <u>devotedly</u> I love you—wasting my valuable time in school writing to you. Our hearts are all broken—mine especially—to small bluggy fragments over your leaving us. I forward some valentines that were in the box for you, I know who they both came from too, so I labelled them. I have the "itsy bitsy turtles" done up tight in a handkerchief to keep them from crawling out and getting squashed and broken like our hearts. Send me a bottlefull of your tears, if you please.... I feel quite sure I will break down and blubber at roll call to-morrow when your sweet name isn't called. In other words, "A place is vacant in our school, which never can be filled" (until you come back). Weepingly, sufferingly, hastily, Patty.[31]

Other letters written by childhood friends attest to her popularity. Alice did not detail her school experiences, but was adamant about the one school she did *not* want to attend: "The summer before Father was in Cuba I had been told that I was to be sent to boarding school in New York at Miss Spence's school. I had seen Miss Spence's scholars marching two by two in their daily walks, and the thought of becoming one of them shriveled me. I practically went on a strike. I said that I would not go—I said that if the family insisted, and sent me, I would do something disgraceful."[32]

The stubborn streak in Alice had been strengthening throughout her childhood. She might have quaked inside, but on the outside, Alice stood firm. Edith wished she would evince the proper, docile behavior of a Victorian girl. However, by the time Alice was fourteen, she was entering the turbulent waters of young womanhood where boys turned from adversaries to heartthrobs, and families became a place to run from rather than to. A portrait of "the model girl," common in etiquette books of the time, may have been Edith's ruler by which to measure her stepdaughter's shortcomings. Alice did not adhere very closely to the ideal—Ethel did. As a young teenager, Alice had learned to live for herself, and she preferred fun to duty. Bye, the independent salon mistress, was Alice's role model.

When Bye and Will Cowles returned from England in 1897, they moved into their Madison Avenue house. Will docked with his ship, the gunboat *Fern*, in Hampton Roads, Virginia, leaving TR and Bye time in New York to catch up. During the winter of 1897 to 1898, brother and sister were together a good deal, discussing the navy, its war readiness, and politics in general, often with congenial guests around Bye's dining table. Since 1895, TR had served as head of New York City's Board of Police Commissioners, and the family alternated between Sagamore Hill and the city. Roosevelt continued to make a name for himself among reform-minded Republicans.

While at Bye's, Theodore came to appreciate once more the salubrious effect that the calm and straightforward Anna Roosevelt Cowles had on all those around her. In April 1897, TR became assistant secretary of the navy and moved the family to Washington, D.C. The change, according to her parents, was not good for Alice. When she became too difficult to handle, TR thought immediately of his sister. Preoccupied with the tumultuous decisions leading up to American entry into the Spanish-American War, TR could not manage Alice. Edith could not control her either, for after Quentin's birth, she was sick in bed for weeks. Then around Christmastime, Ted grew ill. In the ensuing absence of parental guidance, Alice reacted to Edith's withdrawal from the family and the temporary loss of her "boon companion" with anger. She disobeyed curfew, rode up and down the hills of Washington on her bicycle with her feet on the handlebars, and fearlessly led a gang of boys—she was the only female member—into local mischief. When one of the boys dressed as a girl and knocked on the door asking for Alice, Theodore reached his limit. He and Edith despaired of Alice's attitude and her actions, called her a "guttersnipe," forbade her to communicate with her co-conspirators, and sent her to New York. Auntie Bye would have to work a miracle.[33]

A letter written in turns by Alice and Helen R. Roosevelt to their relative Franklin Delano Roosevelt in 1897 gives a sense of Alice's spirits. Helen began:

Alice spent last night here, and we sat out on the doorstep till nearly 10 o'clock, and whistled and made remarks to the passers by, some of which they heard!... Yesterday we went out alone in a cab and winked at all the men we passed....Alice is going to write now, as she has a few important questions to ask you. HRR

I want to know the name of the girl who James told me you were stuck on instead of me. Have you pro[posed] and has she acc[epted]? Please write and tell us her name as we are very anxious to know....I suppose

James told you all the pleasant little things I said about you, they are all true. A.L.R.

Isn't she bad? Have you <u>really</u> given her up or not? Please answer <u>all</u> these questions carefully, they are <u>so</u> important, and we are curious. HRR

I hope you have given me up, if not you had better. Have you seen the piece of poetry that James wrote.... It is dedicated to me and is perfectly horrid and silly, that is if he means it. A.L.R.

Of <u>course</u> he means it! He wouldn't have written it otherwise. For fear you have <u>not</u> heard it, I am sending it to you: "A noun has got a meaning too. / It's verb I'd like to do to you. / If I succeed, why there I'll see / That you shall never part from me." Isn't it beautiful? Alice sings it all the time to the tune of "Ta ra ra boom de ay." Affectionately, Helen R. Roosevelt.[34]

This letter of youthful flirtation and general silliness contrasts with a note to her father a month earlier, showing that Alice was perfectly capable of acting the ideal eldest daughter. She described the riding lessons she was giving Ethel and Kermit, her discovery of a nest of baby raccoons "in the tree where you shot Ted's 'coon,'" and the menacing weasel that escaped her pitchfork at Sagamore.[35]

The headstrong Alice was sent to live with Bye the day after her fourteenth birthday, two days before the battleship *Maine* exploded in Havana's harbor. She spent the rest of the winter and all of the spring with her favorite aunt. Uncle Will left shortly for Cuba, to investigate the ill-fated *Maine*. Alice had become accustomed to her freedom and enjoyed being a tomboy. Under Bye's ministrations an extraordinary transformation occurred. Alice became more tractable, polite, and agreeable. Theodore could not understand how Bye had wrought such a change, but Alice always behaved better with someone's undivided attention. And it helped that Bye was one of those remarkable adults who never forgot her own youth: "Have you shocked [cousin] Elfrida," Bye wrote to Alice conspiratorially after she left, "by telling her any of the bad things we did?" She could enter into their little love affairs, too. Bye was certain, for example, that James Roosevelt was "madly gone on" Alice, not another girl—and she was sure that Teddy Robinson, Auntie Corinne's son, was pairing up with Helen.[36]

Bye was great friends with all the young nieces and nephews, and because she understood them, she could also gently teach and enforce the rules. There was no "running riot" with Bye. Previsit instructions in 1897 consisted of these stiff lines and a nocuous comparison: "Now darling, I am too happy you are coming, but, there will be a few rules and regulations.... You know dearie Auntie does not believe in a great party just tearing around all day and so you and Helen will have a couple of hours music and reading." She expected them "to put everything nicely in order whenever you all have put it wrong, hats etc all must be put in their places and you girls have to try and help Auntie about everything. Helen understands and I would not for all the world feel that she was more help and more careful and dependable than you."[37]

Alice's dutiful updates amazed TR. "Her letters are really interesting and amusing," he wrote his sister gratefully. "Evidently you are doing her a world of good and giving her exactly what she needed. I quite agree with what you say about her; I am sure she really does love Edith and the children and me; it was only that running riot with the boys and girls here had for the moment driven everything else out of her head." Meanwhile, TR kept his daughter apprised of family matters—the boys' flying squirrels, Edith's health, Ted's recovery, his own romps at the Lodges' home, where the children stayed while Edith was recovering. When Edith was well enough, she wrote, too, although she couldn't resist a good swipe. Alice's last letter, Edith bantered, was so lovely she "thought it must have been done by Helen...."[38]

Perhaps war fever added to Edith's edginess. The constant talk in Washington, Edith wrote on April 14, was of war. It came one week later, to the whoops and hollers of the Roosevelt children. Thinking of the *Maine* blown up by Spanish imperialists, and patriotically taking on the cause of the Cuban freedom fighters, Theodore quit his desk job at the navy, declaring, "I have a horror of people who bark but don't bite."[39] He and his friend Colonel Leonard Wood formed the First U.S. Volunteer Cavalry, nicknamed the Rough Riders. Because Edith was recovering from surgery and could not take care of Ted, he joined Alice at Auntie Bye's—who by this time was coming to grips with the astounding fact that, at age forty-three, she was pregnant. Bye, Alice, and Ted made a happy household.

Letters flew thick and fast among the family members. Alice wrote TR about her lessons and regaled him with accounts of goldfish on the roof, a riotous game of follow the leader until Archie cut his lip and howled ("I told him that his teeth were crying red tears [the blood, you know], that made him laugh and then I gave him a ball"), and Archie's excessive repetition of songs on the hand organ until they all became "quite sick of those tunes...." In response TR sent what the family called "posterity letters"— ostensibly intended for his children, but really addressed to future readers. For example, this from the battleground to his fifteen-year-old daughter: "I have had a hard and dangerous month. I have enjoyed it, too, in a way.... My own men are not well fed, and they are fierce and terrible in battle; but they gave half they had to the poor women and children. I suppose a good many of them thought, as I did, of their own wives or sisters and little ones. War is often, as this one is, necessary and righteous; but it is terrible."[40]

Meanwhile, the family (including Bye) had migrated back to Sagamore to await the return of the heroes. Alice passed the time teaching herself to ride astride on her father's saddle, until she could do it "almost as easily as I can girls' way." Girls generally rode sidesaddle, not astride, but that made the boys' way more interesting. After the battles, Colonel Roosevelt led his men, quarantined for yellow fever, to Long Island. The family visited him there. Alice particularly enjoyed that, for she was allowed to see her father's tanned and handsome troops on review. "If I was in love with one Rough Rider, I was in love with twenty, even though I did have a pigtail and short dresses," Alice later sighed.[41]

That fall, Alice turned philosophical and decided to "keep a diary or journal or whatever you wish to call it." She thought it would "amuse" her when she was older. The catalyst was her tremendous sorrow at leaving Sagamore Hill for Boston for the summer. She said good-bye to all the relatives and then to all the animals. She was diverted slightly from her sadness by the Dewey Naval Parade in New York City featuring veterans of the Spanish-American War. She got to ride in one of the boats, just behind her father on the *Monmouth*. The day was exciting, culminating in fireworks over the dark river that reminded her of Romantic poet Thomas Hood's "a lake and a fairy boat."[42] New Yorkers were glad to celebrate Admiral George Dewey, victor of Manila Bay—but just as pleased to get a look at the conqueror of Kettle Hill, whose next adventure was the race for governor of their state. Colonel Roosevelt's campaign kicked off in the fall of 1898 with a speech at Carnegie Hall. Edith, aware of the "many forces at work in New York politics," cared only that her husband was "safe at home."[43]

Winning the governorship of New York was relatively easy for the newly minted war hero. His Rough Riders helped him campaign, swearing earnestly that they would have "gone to hell with him." Everyone was caught up in TR's charisma and the excitement of the race, even Alice's teenaged friends who eagerly requested his "signature." Alice assisted Edith and TR's secretary, Amy Cheney, with the mounting correspondence. All efforts paid off. A Roosevelt cousin celebrated by naming her new guinea pig "Governor Roosevelt—Gov. for short."[44] Alice attended the swearing in, flanking Edith in Albany's assembly chamber.

"We have never been happier in our lives than we are now," Edith wrote six months into TR's tenure. Perhaps part of their contentment was a result of the good relations with their eldest daughter. Theodore boasted to a friend about his nearly sixteen-year-old child: "My big girl is a very big girl indeed now, almost grown up, and yours must be, too. I wish they could be together. Alice, I am sorry to say, does not show any abnormal activity, but is a good rider, walker and swimmer, and has an excellent mind and I think I could say that she is by no means bad looking." Edith concurred. She told her friends Alice was indeed "pretty and she is certainly intelligent."[45]

Their time in Albany was Alice's last fling at childhood, and she enjoyed being a governor's daughter. The executive mansion was commodious and full of interesting nooks and crannies calling out to be explored. Alice participated in some of the younger children's pranks, such as sneaking out of the bedrooms for a pajama-clad snowball fight. Under the watch of her omnipresent governess, Miss Young, her days were spent lunching, walking, shopping, writing letters, playing tennis and basketball (she was captain of her team), ice skating, and horseback riding. Alice was "fired by reading *Antigone* with a desire to study Greek," and pondered taking up Latin again, too. She loved the opera *Faust* and judged a play, *The Colonial Girl*, "quite amusing and good for an entirely second rate company."[46]

She was still the big sister, and she wrote often to homesick Ted, who was then attending Groton School in Massachusetts. He filled pages with his exploits, mostly football and visiting during half holidays, or "half hollerdays" as he more colorfully put it. When her parents were away Alice stood in for Edith. In letters to her absent parents she faithfully chronicled all the children's activities—from new pet lizards to art lessons. With some enjoyment, Alice shared that "Quentin now has a trick of whenever he sees me, of putting his thumb in his mouth and then taking it out and offering it to me to suck! I don't think it's at all nice, so I offer him mine to disgust him, whereupon he grows quite infuriated and beats his hands up and down at me and yells, 'Do you want my thumb? Do you want my thumb?' It's as good as a circus." As First Daughter of New York, she helped her mother in various capacities, for example, serving tea and cakes to the great lace-bedecked phalanx from the "State Association of Mothers."[47]

In 1900, to Edith's dismay, as a result of the enthusiasm of midwestern and western Republicans and to the relief of party bosses in New York State, Theodore was tapped to run for vice president on William McKinley's ticket. Alice loved Washington, D.C., and was thrilled at the prospect of returning, but Edith did not wish to lose the good life they had in Albany. The long campaign trail took TR away from the family. This made all of them, including the candidate, "melancholy." He wrote to Alice from Fargo, North Dakota, that he enjoyed "meeting these crowds of funny old farmers and cowboys," because he felt "thoroughly at home with them." "West Virginian republican supporters" sent Alice a "small bear" that the family named Jonathan Edwards, "partly because we think he shows a distinctly Calvinistic turn of mind." It was all very exciting, but Alice, who had a deep sense of family honor, was offended at Theodore's second-place spot. Edith, too, did not relish the thought of her husband stuck "in such a useless and empty position."[48]

Nevertheless, after the electoral victory, the new vice president and his family arrived in the nation's capital on March 2, 1901, just before McKinley's inauguration. They stayed with Bye and Will at their rented home at 1733 N Street, for Edith wanted to spend the summer at Sagamore as usual and move into Washington properly in the fall. The family (minus young Quentin), surrounded by friends and relatives, attended the swearing-in at the Senate chamber. Quentin rejoined the others in the room above Thompson's Drug Store that Edith had rented for its view of the inaugural parade. The day concluded, for Alice and the adults, with a seat in the presidential box at the inaugural ball, held at the Pension Office Building. Alice envied the girls there who nonchalantly wore old dresses, and not the "excessively new white point d'esprit" gown Edith had made for her. Absorbed in watching the dancers, Alice perched on the arm of a chair until admonished not to, because First Lady Ida McKinley was sitting in it. That fact had escaped Alice. At sixteen years of age, Alice had only just begun to take an interest in politics beyond her father's fortunes. She considered the McKinleys "usurping cuckoos," but that night Alice had eyes only for the dance floor.[49]

The next morning, they returned to Oyster Bay, with its delights of berry picking, swimming, picnics, and general family togetherness. The summer was tainted by a painful abscess in her jaw that would trouble her intermittently for years. Alice, growing more impatient for Washington, enjoyed watching dancers perform the newest fad called the hootchy-kootchy. Always a quick study, she would tuck that away in her repertoire of actions to cause parental consternation.

A family vacation to the Tahawus Club in the Adirondack Mountains was rounding out the summer when news of an assassination attempt on President McKinley, in Buffalo, arrived. At the confirmation of his death, Alice and the rest of the children did a little selfish jig of happiness at their elevated status. She wrote when she was an adult that she was "not particularly elated" in the knowledge of her father's assumption of the presidency. "I was having a delightful time with a band of cheerful young people; greedy for sensation, centered upon myself, I was not merely an egotist, I was a solipsist."[50]

At the time, however, the local newspaper carried a story that probably gave a truer flavor of Alice's feelings than she admitted to as an adult. Alice and her friend Sarah Boneditch were driven forty miles in a buckboard by Michael F. Cronin, the proprietor of the Alden Lair Lodge, where TR had paused on his way from Tahawus to Buffalo. The girls wanted to follow Roosevelt's path toward the beautiful Wilcox mansion in Buffalo, where he was sworn in as president on September 14, 1901. "At the request of Miss Roosevelt," Cronin revealed to the reporter, he "retold the story of [TR's] midnight ride." Upon hearing the thrilling tale, "Miss Roosevelt asked the driver to give her one of the eight shoes worn by the horses that night." Cronin had already given the horseshoes away. Another guest overheard the request and recognized the appellant. He generously surrendered his trophy to Alice. Asking for the story and the historic horseshoe demonstrates an involvement in the events swirling around her that her later memories contradict. Perhaps the seismic battles that take place within a teenager's psyche in the war for personal independence explain the contradiction. When she was eighty-four, she told an interviewer that her response to the news of McKinley's shooting was "sheer rapture." She began, in what she later called an "amiably ghoulish" way, to let her finger fall on calendars at random, hoping to predict the day McKinley would die.[51]

The teenaged Alice might be forgiven for harboring a partly jaded view. After all, she had been the daughter of the governor of New York and the daughter of the vice president. So, although her sense of family honor was assuaged by Theodore's assumption of the presidency, Alice had no reason to think that her life would necessarily be any more fun. The McKinley White House had been a somber one. Because of the First Lady's illness, the McKinleys hosted few lavish gatherings. Further, Alice heard Edith fretting over the impending loss of privacy. Alice may have felt that her new position would circumscribe her ability to do as she pleased, but the possibility of a White House debut was promising. As an intelligent, well-read member of a political family, Alice had some idea of the opportunities that would occur as the Roosevelts became the First Family. Her childhood had ended with President McKinley's death. She lamented neither.

Chapter 3

"Something More Than a Plain American Girl"

IT WAS THE START of a new age; the first year of the twentieth century and less than two weeks after Theodore Roosevelt assumed the nation's highest office, his rambunctious family members hurled themselves into the White House. The Roosevelts' excitement was at odds with a nation grieving for its fallen president. Among the family, only Alice wore the subdued mien of a mourner, but McKinley wasn't the cause. Alice felt a characteristic isolation from this tremendous family event. She lingered with friends, she went to Auntie Bye's, and then to Chestnut Hill. By letter Edith tried to keep her stepdaughter informed of family news. "Father looks very serious—naturally—but is not at all nervous," as he took up his new duties. Thinking ahead, she suggested to Alice that "in one way you will find this a hard position, but in others it will be delightful, and I can do much for you that would have been financially impossible otherwise" because of TR's salary increase.[1] This was a considerate note from a busy woman. The spotlight was about to be fixed relentlessly on the First Family, and Alice would need guidance and support from Edith. When they clashed, Alice felt shy and alienated and turned to friends who did not always meet with her parents' approval. Yet none of them could have predicted Alice's rapid rise to international celebrity, nor what it would mean to the teenager struggling to mature.

Alice remembered the first time she realized her father was truly the president. She had been staying with Auntie Bye at her Connecticut home throughout September and October, and when TR was on his way to Yale University's bicentennial celebration, he stopped for a day with his sister and his daughter. "I had not expected him to be changed and, of course, he was not," Alice recalled. "There was no atmosphere of worry about his new responsibilities; not a trace of the solemnity that so often seems to afflict those in high position. He was, as always, full of the buoyancy and zest that swept everything along with it. However, much else was very different since I had last seen him at Sagamore in the backwater of the Vice-Presidency—the stir that accompanied his arrival, the crowds of politicians, newspapermen, and other visitors." She would soon enough know what it was like to attract the same stir, the same newspapermen, and similar crowds. Alice concluded in those early weeks that she, in fact, rather liked the "feel" of the ruckus caused by traveling with the president.[2]

By mid-October Alice had entered fully into the spirit of things. The new First Lady made the room assignments in the White House, and then decided to renovate the historic mansion, which she had found in "disarray." Alice occupied the large bedroom on the northwest side. Ethel's was next to hers, and they both overlooked Lafayette Square and the palatial homes of John Hay and Henry Adams across the street. Alice disparaged the furnishings of the White House when the Roosevelts arrived as "late General Grant and early Pullman," both "ugly and inconvenient." Her bedroom held "cumbersome black walnut pieces and two brass beds."[3] Compared to her cheery room at Sagamore, decorated as it was with floral wallpaper and chintz curtains, her bedroom in the White House was spartan.

But the White House was a paradise for children, and teenaged Alice could occasionally be convinced to join in games with the younger set. She careened down the main stairway on the large tin trays borrowed from the pantry, and raced along the upstairs hall on stilts and bicycles.[4] Boisterous games of hide-and-seek and tag spilled into every room. Leaping out of the circular upholstered seats in the East Room to scare visitors was a favorite pastime. Uproarious pillow fights made the White House attic ring with laughter. Many of the children's animals took up residency, too. The blue macaw, Eli Yale, ruled the conservatory.

The children loved living in the Executive Mansion, and their antics were soon widely reported. Americans found them a fascinating family, especially after the McKinleys, whose daughters had died in infancy. "Baby Ruth" Cleveland was a distant memory, and while the Lincoln boys were well known in their day, they had left the Executive Mansion four decades earlier. American voters liked to know that their president was one of them, and that their elected leader shared an empathetic understanding of the joys and sorrows of raising children. In January 1902, Edith's candid letter to a friend assessed her children's first half year in the White House: "Alice is exceedingly pretty, and has a remarkable steady head though in some ways very child like. Ted is a good boy and stands well at school. Kermit is odd and independent as always, and Ethel is just a handful. She is a replica of Mrs. Cowles. Archie we call 'the beautiful idiot' and Quentin is the cleverest of the six."[5]

The much-needed renovation was one of Edith's initial acts as First Lady, and although she carried off a widely acclaimed transformation, it meant moving her family into, out of, and then back into the White House. For Edith, it was worth it. The First Lady likened the old Executive Mansion to "living over the store," because when the Roosevelts arrived, the main floor of the White House consisted of public rooms and executive offices. The family would never have the privacy that Edith treasured unless some significant steps were taken, but the conversion from "gilded barn to comfortable residence" would not be completed until November 1902.[6]

Despite the upheaval, life took on a pattern for Alice. She began to perceive great possibilities in being First Daughter of the land. Added to her social calendar would be occasions of state, visits with dignitaries, and special perks yet to be discovered. She continued to see Auntie Bye at the Cowleses' comfortable N Street home, where President Roosevelt held his first cabinet meetings and where he met with members of Congress whose morals or reputations did not measure up to Edith's standards.

Alice similarly used the sympathetic Bye when she wanted to entertain friends. She had no sitting room of her own at the White House. Moving back to Washington meant reunions with particularly congenial friends, especially a group calling itself the Gooey Brotherhood of Slimy Slopers. Comprised of young women and men, the Slopers all went by nicknames.

Agile Ali was president, and her comrades included Dusky Dick, Betty Bright, Bill the Lizard, May Merrylegs, Presumptuous Pete, Jerky Jake, Sami the Sloper, and perhaps others. The only Slopers who signed their names to extant letters were Roger Alden Derby and Richard Derby. They had tongue-in-cheek meetings with matching minutes, and a newspaper spoof entitled *The Sloping Gazette*. The latter included such bits of nonsense as this:

> Three Slopers went off on a sloop
> But one slipped while ascending the poop
> Now in torment he lies
> Giving vent to sad cries
> Why?
> Because he can't be with his troop.

When they gathered at Auntie Bye's for "slopes," they shared tea, literary allusions, and dancing. They met up frequently at Washington entertainments. Their letters to each other were full of inside jokes and references to each other's suitability as Slopers—but, as Dusky Dick wrote, " 'Tis better to have sloped and slipped than never to have sloped at all."[7] He may have been referring to a Sloper who married, for once that happened, the Sloper was cast out of the ranks. May Merrylegs gave a sense of the Sloper attitude when she wrote to Agile Ali: "Alice—I loff you! I feel like a champagne cork with the wire taken off—If I don't do something or write something I shall burst. You are a congenial soul.... I shall shortly repair to my room and dance. I am quite mad. And it is Sunday evening too. (How shocking)."[8] While she took pleasure in her friends, Alice could not enter fully into society until her debut.

First Lady Edith Roosevelt had officially ended the mourning period for William McKinley by throwing open the White House doors for the traditional New Year's Day Reception. From 11:00 a.m. until 2:00 p.m. on January 1, 1902, President Roosevelt and the First Lady received the brilliantly dressed line of foreign ambassadors, Supreme Court justices, senators, representatives, military officers, and other dignitaries. On the night of the second of January, Theodore and Edith presided over their first cabinet dinner. The following evening, the Roosevelts introduced their daughter into society. Alice's was the first debutante ball ever held at the White House, and Washington society considered it the most distinctive dance at the Executive Mansion since the days of legendary hostess Dolley Madison.[9]

Edith and Alice had been planning for months. Alice could hardly wait. She was "enchanted" by the thought of a Washington debut, and "to come out at the White House made it something to look forward to with even more excited anticipation," she explained in her autobiography. The coming-out ball was a defining moment in every debutante's life. For Alice, this was certainly true, as it began her rapid rise to national—ultimately, international—prominence. Her debut turned her into a celebrity, which then both complicated and enhanced her life. Celebrityhood threw into question family relationships. It circumscribed her actions while it presented opportunities. It made her courtship and marriage laborious. It made it harder to form new friendships and more difficult to trust the friends she had. By the time she left the White House, the *Richmond Times-Dispatch* insisted, "There have been few young women in America, or for that matter in any other country, who have received so much newspaper attention as has Miss Roosevelt."[10]

Debutante balls were a traditional rite of passage among the elite, symbolically demonstrating that the young woman was grown up and eligible for marriage to the right man. The social season provided numerous opportunities for striking, well-bred women to shine, but at the debutante's own ball the spotlight was hers alone. Alice's cousins Corinne Robinson (Auntie Corinne's daughter) and Eleanor Roosevelt (her uncle Elliott's daughter) made their debuts around the same time Alice did. For them, coming out was "a terrifying ordeal." As an adult, Corinne remembered that a debutante "was simultaneously made aware of the great and depressing obligations that family and social position imposed upon her. Society was a serious business and upon entering it a girl lifted her share of the city's poor, beleaguered, and untidy masses upon her fragile and well-bred shoulders."[11] Once a young woman debuted, she was automatically placed on the roll of the Junior League, a charitable organization begun by Alice's friend Mary Harriman in 1901 when she was nineteen.

Most parents of debutantes impressed upon their daughters the importance of aiding those less fortunate, but few eighteen-year-olds took to the selfless grind of charity work like Corinne and Eleanor. Alice dismissed such social obligations. The education in national and international politics she eventually received as First Daughter more than replaced visiting settlement houses and teaching dance to immigrants, as Eleanor did. As there existed no tradition of First Daughters taking up benevolent causes, Alice did not labor under a national expectation to devote herself to charity. And that simply wasn't her personality. She had no qualms about dedicating her young life to more pleasurable pursuits.

Normally, a Knickerbocker daughter would debut at Delmonico's in New York City at age eighteen. For Alice, there would be a second coming-out dance in December 1902 at the Assembly Ball as one of the "Magic Five" Roosevelt women. A debut en masse in a crowd of cousins did not suit her. Instead, she scheduled her White House ball for early January 1902 to take advantage of the Christmas holiday when enough young men could attend without shirking their schooling. The First Lady was willing to go along with Alice's wishes—although perhaps Edith was motivated by the chance to marry off her stepdaughter a year early. It was also a perfect vehicle for announcing the tone of entertainments hosted by the new First Lady. Staging such an important evening required great attention to details. Edith Roosevelt hired Isabelle "Belle" Hagner to help. The competent and charming Belle Hagner had worked for Auntie Bye and would become Edith Roosevelt's indispensable social secretary. Hagner was "the first salaried government official answering to the First Lady as her boss," and so presaged the extensive East Wing staff enjoyed by modern First Ladies.[12]

Even with the help of a secretary, the debut preparations were staggering. A guest list had to be drawn up, invitations issued, and décor and food planned. At least the U.S. Marine Band was an obvious choice, but a list of dances had to be chosen and ordered. Alice's expectations for every moment were understandably high. "A young girl should be treated like a bride when she makes her debut into society," social critic Ward McAllister decreed. "Her relatives should rally around her and give her entertainments to welcome her into the world which she is to adorn."[13]

As plans commenced, it became clear that Alice could not have everything she desired. The most alarming problem was the dance floor. Because of the White House renovation, the ballroom lacked a proper wooden dancing floor. The alternative to hardwood was a makeshift floor of coarsely woven linen "crash" laid over the old mustard-yellow carpet. Unlike other debutantes, who had to negotiate only with their parents for the fulfillment of their debutante dreams, Alice had to seek the approval of Congress. Thus, at one of the first White House dinner parties, Edith gave the First Daughter the task of charming the monies for the hardwood out of the redoubtable Congressman Joseph G. Cannon. Alice remembered that she "worked every ploy [she] knew on him, including Auntie Corinne's 'elbow-in-the-soup' treatment." Alice rather enjoyed this early taste of lobbying, but she was unsuccessful. The First Daughter made do with linen crash. Alice found it "personally humiliating."[14]

Not having a cotillion was worse. A cotillion was a formalized dance that entailed an elaborate concatenation of steps and a series of partners, with the debutante leading off. Cotillions usually included the presentation of flowers or favors for the dancers paid for by the hosts and could include expensive baubles, such as jewelry, watches, combs, purses, or stickpins made of gold and silver. Eleanor Roosevelt remembered that "your popularity was gauged by the number of favors you took home." Cotillions were de rigueur for debutante balls: the White House debutante could not fail to have one. But Edith, always anxious about money, said no.[15]

Adding insult to injury, for Alice, was the embarrassing substitution of punch for champagne. At the elegant New York debutante balls, champagne was served, Alice reminded her stepmother, and she thought it was terrible for the Roosevelts to be so rustic. The First Lady may have had an eye to cost or to pro-temperance Republican voters. Aping the sophisticated customs of New York might increase the status of the capital city, or it could be perceived as unseemly. For Alice, it was the ultimate disgrace. She offered to pay for the cotillion favors and the champagne out of her Lee allowance, but her stepmother forbade it. Edith maintained that the debutante ball was the duty of the parents. Thus Alice must make do with what the Roosevelt budget would allow.

What Alice's debut lacked in the accoutrements of maturity, it made up for in White House ball tradition. Approximately six hundred people attended the unofficial White House event.[16] The receiving line began at the customary time of 10:00 p.m. Edith and Alice stood in the Blue Room to greet the guests, a combination of her friends such as Helen Cutting, Robert Goelet, Arthur Iselin, Edith Root, Alice Warder, Robert Gerry, and Daisy Leiter; her relatives—Auntie Corinne and Uncle Douglas, Auntie Bye and Uncle Will, cousins Helen and James Roosevelt, Franklin Delano Roosevelt; and political and diplomatic officers who were also friends of the Roosevelts. "Miss Ruth Hanna," daughter of Republican Senator Marcus Hanna, attended wearing a gown of "liberty pink." The Blue Room boasted potted palms and the bright green leaves of smilax vines wrapped around the chandeliers and wound across the ceiling, decorating the pictures of George and Martha Washington, Abraham Lincoln, and Thomas Jefferson in the East Room. Holly graced every lintel. More than two thousand flowers—roses, carnations, hyacinths, and narcissus—completed the lavish decorations.

The First Daughter wore a traditional pure white taffeta gown with a white chiffon overskirt and a bodice appliquéd with white rosebuds. Around her neck hung a simple diamond pendant. One of Alice's guests, her soon-to-be friend Marguerite Cassini, thought Alice underwent an apotheosis: "Under the lights of the heavy chandeliers in the East Room, the tomboyish-looking girl I have seen around Washington is transformed into an assured, sparkling young woman in a stiff white satin gown and long white gloves ruffled on her arms. Her hair is of an indefinite blond and her skin lacks color but her eyes are a queer, attractive long shape, a phosphorescent grayish blue, changing color according to her mood, edged by long black lashes. Her smile curls up in mischief." The *New York Tribune* concluded: "A more charming debutante has rarely been introduced in Washington. She was as attractive in her dignified simplicity and natural grace as she was beautiful. Tall, with a striking figure, blue eyes, and a fine fair complexion, she is certainly one of the prettiest girls in Washington."[17]

The Marine Band struck up the first waltz, "The Debutante," at 11:00 p.m. Lieutenant Gilmore of the Artillery and Major Charles McCauley of the Marine Corps vied for the honor of dancing with the White House debutante for the first german. Lieutenant Gilmore won—a victory the artillery celebrated manfully. After dancing, the guests enjoyed a buffet supper that one of Alice's girlfriends called "sumptuous." Couples could then promenade in the White House conservatories or recommence dancing. Auntie Corinne thought that "Alice had the time of her life, men seven deep around her all the time." Franklin D. Roosevelt, an enthusiastic dance partner of Alice's, called it "glorious" from beginning to end.[18]

Alice, much later in life, admitted only to "enjoy[ing] it moderately."[19] Perhaps she remembered the crash, the punch, the absence of a cotillion, and the next day's newspaper coverage. In its front-page article, the *New York Times* called Alice's debut "one of the most charming social events Washington has ever seen," but declared that the decorations "seemed extremely simple." Adjectives suited to the innocence of a debutante ball, no doubt, but for Alice, hardly satisfying. The *New York Tribune* perhaps thought its article complimentary when it called the ball "a homelike affair, with an entirely unofficial air," but guessing Alice's response to this review is not difficult. Ironically, besides the debutante herself, the only thing the press was effusive about was the crash, "waxed so perfectly that dancing on it was a delight."[20] Small comfort, no doubt. The First Lady, too, must have resented being damned with faint praise. Six years later, when Theodore and Edith sponsored their second daughter's debutante ball at the White House, Alice couldn't help comparing. Ethel Roosevelt danced her cotillion on a hardwood floor while her guests refreshed themselves with "buckets of champagne."[21]

The front-page coverage introduced the First Daughter to America. She became known everywhere as Princess Alice. It was undemocratic, but spoke to her unique position. Alice received the first of hundreds of requests for her autograph and photograph. Americans had a taste for sensational journalism that did not go unnoticed by those assigned to report on the First Daughter's activities. Charging into the new century, Alice seized her chance. She was the first White House teenaged daughter since the demure Nellie Grant had graced Washington twenty-five years earlier, and that was enough to cause a stir. Soon, however, Alice's distinctive temperament manifested itself, and the press corps knew it was watching someone—something—brand new.

Alice was the first female celebrity of the twentieth century. Her name had "attention-getting, interest-riveting, profit-generating value."[22] In print, Alice Roosevelt was seldom identified as "daughter of the president." Her name—sometimes only her first name—was sufficient; an early Cher or Madonna. Americans recognized her face from the rotogravure section of the newspapers. Of all the Roosevelt family members outside the president, it was Alice who monopolized the dailies. By mid-1902, crowds gathered wherever she went. Alice's entrée to the larger world was through the doorway of celebrityhood, foisted upon her not-unwilling self, beginning with her White House debut.

Fans provided a market for Alice-inspired goods. She was the subject of popular songs that were turned into sheet music with her picture on the cover. "The Alice Roosevelt March" featured a lithe Gibson girl drawing of her. "The American Girl" was "respectfully dedicated to the First Young Lady of the U.S.A.," and on the cover her photograph was patriotically flanked by two buglers.[23] She became famously linked with the color "Alice blue," the blue-gray of her eyes, which became the most popular shade for dresses and gowns. Alice's face gazed steadily out from a French chocolate card—an early-model baseball card—tucked inside a Guerin-Boutron candy bar. Many different photos of the First Daughter were made into postcards sent by admirers and collected—then and now—by postcard aficionados and autograph seekers.

It was awkward for Alice to walk the fine line between her parents' desire for privacy and her own need for attention. She did not always enjoy being pursued by reporters and photographers. She worried that people liked her only because she was a daughter of the president. As she traversed the rocky years of young adulthood and the relationship with her parents temporarily worsened, choosing public approbation over parental approval became easier. As a young woman, Alice was confused by Edith and Theodore's attitude:

> The whole attitude toward publicity was so ridiculous. I was brought up on the principle that "nice" people didn't get their names in the papers except when they were born, when they married, or when they died. We were always being enjoined not to talk to reporters and to avoid photographers. At the same time there was all this interest in our every move. The family was always telling me, "Beware of publicity!" And there was publicity hitting me in the face every day.... And once stories got out, or were invented, I was accused of <u>courting</u> publicity. I destroyed a savage letter on the subject from my father, because I was so furious with him. There was he, one of the greatest experts in publicity there ever was, accusing me of trying to steal his limelight.[24]

Edith was not at all ambivalent about publicity. She cherished her privacy. Her feelings were well known to Alice and everyone else. Edith remodeled the White House in part to cut down on the number of citizens trooping through their new home. She responded to certain types of mail with form letters to discourage the formation of an entourage. She gave no interviews and was never tempted to write her autobiography. Edith took care to see that her family was similarly sheltered—as much as was possible for a woman who once complained, "Not one of my children ever wants to be told or directed about anything whatever!"[25]

Edith knew that she could not protect her children from publicity once they left the grounds of the White House, and she was unable to stop the press from writing about her family. Quentin penned a letter to Alice with a telling postscript: "05¢ five cents for the signature please."[26] For a twelve-year-old, he had a cynic's understanding of First Family fame. One way Edith could exercise control was to monitor the photographs of the children that the press printed. Edith hired Frances B. Johnston and other professional photographers to take still shots of them. She vetted Alice's choices. These became the official photographs released upon request. Alice's were always the most sought after, both by individuals and newspapers.

Theodore believed that there were appropriate and inappropriate times for publicity. He was masterful at manipulating the media, and his daughter learned everything she knew about the subject from him. As an adult, Alice quipped only half jokingly that her father had to be the bride at every wedding, the baby at every christening, and the corpse at every funeral. Alice, as strong-willed as her father, absorbed but did not always adhere to his definitions of acceptable and unacceptable. A battle of wills ensued. Alice did as she pleased, and took the consequences when the press reported it. "Do not like the advertisements of you appearing at portrait show," TR once wrote her sternly. "They distinctly convey the impression that any person who wishes to pay five dollars may be served tea by you and Ethel Barrymore. I cannot consent to such use of your name and must ask you not to serve tea."[27] But Alice wanted to participate in this charity event for the New York Orthopedic Hospital. She telegraphed sweetly to her father that his note had arrived too late.

Torn between her family's accusations of courting publicity and her own assimilation of her father's tactics, Alice's young adulthood was complicated in a way that her peers could not fathom. The subtle dynamics of Theodore's lingering guilt over his remarriage, Alice's fears of abandonment, and Edith's distant mothering made the relationship between Theodore and Alice precarious. Alice competed for TR's attention with her half brothers and sister, and with all his constituents. Unlike a father who leaves home to work, Roosevelt's office was partly their home: the governor's mansion, the White House. The boundary between home time and work time was fluid, with office seekers, politicians, private citizens, diplomats, and cabinet members in various combinations over for dinner nightly.

Despite her parents' objections, Alice made her own rules. "Being the offspring of a very conspicuous parent, I wasn't going to let him get the better of me," Alice remembered.[28] She did engage the press even if she couldn't help at least some of what was written. Reporters followed her. They invented stories about her. Their attention constrained her actions. As a young woman, Alice was both typical and exceptional. She was a normal teen, with periods of depression and rebellion alternating with phases of longing for parental guidance and family togetherness. Of course, most of her friends had not lost their mothers and none were daughters of presidents. In Alice, these tensions left her sometimes moody and morose, sometimes feeling lighthearted and giddy. It was the self-possessed, daring young woman with a zest for living who became the role model for young Americans.

Alice's first diary entry for 1902 explained the effects of the sudden and continuing press coverage. She lamented that the congressional daughters who lunched with her had the "pleasure of meeting (not me, but) the 'President's Daughter.'" With unconscious irony, Alice noted afterward she went to Auntie Bye's to talk over plans for her invitation to the coronation of Edward VII. As she had in Albany, Edith requested Alice's help for official events such as "a card reception where however, the people only passed through, Mother and I shaking hands with them...." About this same time, Alice's name first appeared as an enticement for charity purposes. "To the lucky drawer of this prize will also go Miss Roosevelt's card," the article in the *New York Tribune* promised.[29]

In early February, after Alice's debut, the focus of the family turned to Ted Jr., who became very ill with pneumonia at Groton School. Edith went to nurse him, and Theodore soon joined his wife and eldest son. Alice worried because TR would not take her to stay with her "own darling Teddy Brother." Edith sent her long letters from Ted's bedside, with details of the patient's pulse, respiration, medications (morphine and milk with whiskey), and temperature—and how "in his sleep he called loudly for 'Sissie.'" Only the little children and Auntie Bye and Uncle Will were around as Alice turned eighteen on February 12, 1902. On the fourteenth, TR returned from Groton and had lunch with Alice, Auntie Bye, Secretary of War Elihu Root, and Attorney General Philander Knox, Alice recorded, but she left immediately after dinner—finally—to see her brother. Upon her reaching Boston, the *New York Tribune* featured a story on the Roosevelts at Groton. The title concluded triumphantly: "Miss Roosevelt Arrives." For the next week, Alice devoted herself to the care of her stepmother and brother. "I do love that boy," Alice worried.[30]

Private concerns yielded to Alice's public service debut when she christened Germany's American-made imperial yacht the *Meteor*. The initial overture came from Kaiser Wilhelm II through American ambassador Andrew D. White.[31] Roosevelt immediately saw diplomatic advantages and gave his consent. If Roosevelt ever thought of his daughter's role only as an attractive accompaniment to the christening, it is certain that the French knew that the *Germans* did not. The French ambassador to Washington, Jules Cambon, wrote with a mixture of envy and apprehension to the minister of foreign affairs, Theophile Delcasse, on January 15: "It is the completion in a series of acts [by Germany] calculated to win over the public opinion of the country." The Russians worried that the event would crystallize German Americans into a force that would eventually support the fatherland.[32]

For all her bravado, Alice was shy and nervous at the actual event. Prince Henry, representing his brother the kaiser, arrived in Washington on February 23, 1902. Alice spent part of that day practicing by smashing bottles in Auntie Bye's backyard. Alice met the prince the next afternoon and thought him "a most cheerful soul."[33] That night, President Roosevelt gave a stag dinner for the prince and other foreign dignitaries who had gathered for the yacht's launch. The First Lady had the East Room decorated with thousands of tiny red, white, and blue electric lights in the shapes of anchors, ropes, and other nautical emblems. The menu consisted of duck, terrapin, and "filet de boeuf Hambourgeoise," enhanced by punch served in little boats that flew the *Meteor*'s flag. Dessert was a coup: colored ice cream molded into fruit shapes and served in spun sugar seashells with the German eagle on one side and American insignia on the other.[34]

The morning of the twenty-fifth, the participants and the observers made their way to the ceremony. Alice relished the day, evident in her effusive diary entry:

Got to Jersey City at almost seven, had breakfast in the car. Then we all, the Prince, Father, Mother, myself and the parties got on the ferry boat to go to Shooters Island. Had bully fun going over. [C]hatted... with the Prince. Got to Shooter's Island about 10.30. I christened the yacht. First I smashed the bottle of champagne on the bow saying "In the name of his Majesty the German Emperor I christen this yacht *Meteor*," then I cut the last rope which held it. . . . Everyone says I did well and successfully. The Prince then gave me a bunch of pink roses, and when he congratulated me both shook and kissed my hand. . . . [W]ent over to the *Hohenzollern* (the Emperor's yacht) and had lunch. The Prince gave me (from the Emperor) a bracelet with a miniature of the Emperor set in diamonds. Got more roses from the officers of the boat. Also a book of views of Berlin from the Emperor and a cable at lunch from him too. I sent him one directly after launching the boat. At lunch sat on the Prince's left, his Admiral von Eisendech on my right. He drew a picture for me on the back of his lunch card. The Prince made a speech to Father then Father one to him and then he made one about me. I should say toast, not speech.[35]

The newspapers chronicled the day in even more detail. The front pages of the *Washington Post*, *New York Tribune*, and the *New York Times* cleared column inches for sprawling diagrams of the *Meteor* and the *Hohenzollern*, descriptions of the women's dresses, Alice's comportment, and exactly how often the prince took Alice's arm. For her part, the *Times* commented, "Miss Roosevelt was the most self-possessed person on the stand."[36]

Alice enjoyed the prince, the publicity, and the diamonds. Henry Adams acerbically commented, "Of Prince Henry I know next to nothing except that he brought damnable weather and left diamond bracelets galore, with his dear brother's self-satisfied face on them. Alice Roosevelt wore hers to a . . . dinner, and excited the derisive howls of my niece Elise for its hideousness."[37] The *New York Tribune* editorial was kinder: "It is only a few weeks since Miss Roosevelt left the schoolroom and in a day she has become one of the most regarded women in the world, replacing the young Queen of Holland in popular favor. She is seeming unaffected by the sudden notoriety thrust upon her, but stands in the glare of the footlights without flinching." Because the ship was the private yacht of the kaiser and the sponsor was the daughter of the president, the "gala affair" was newsworthy. Half a world away, Frenchwomen could purchase a stylish cloak named the " 'Miss Roosevelt' Wrap," by Beneson of Paris. "Alice," Marguerite Cassini conceded, "became a star overnight. The country fell in love with her."[38]

The only unhappy segment of the American population was the Women's Christian Temperance Union (WCTU). "It does not seem necessary to say what I am going to write to the daughter of the President, who is herself such a reformer," the national general secretary wrote to Alice. She claimed to represent the wishes "of the fifty thousand young women in the country who wear the white ribbon" of the temperance pledge. They begged Alice to use a nonalcoholic substitute for the christening champagne.[39] The good women of the WCTU were destined to be disappointed in Alice.

After the christening, Roosevelt's friend Whitelaw Reid, owner of the *New York Tribune*, watched Alice's deportment with approval and commended the president on the larger effects: "I fancy that the Prince's visit has been internationally useful, and I am sure it has given almost wholly unmixed pleasure in this country. Of course, you had no thought of political advantage in it anymore than the Prince had; yet I believe that it will also be found to have been of great political use."[40] It was the first example of the First Daughter's usefulness in foreign relations, the side of politics she found most absorbing as an adult, and the first time Alice's fame proved a boon to her father's presidency.

Immediately after the prince's departure, a tempest in an English teapot beset the president. Alice received an invitation from Whitelaw Reid, TR's special ambassador, to attend Edward VII's coronation. The idea thrilled her. She had never been overseas, and by the time her father was her age, he had been through Europe and East Asia. Alice and her aunts excitedly discussed appropriate attire. Then word came that England wanted to seat the famous daughter of their ally in Westminster Abbey with the rest of the world's royalty. The *Literary Digest* reported Europeans believed that Alice should be thought of as "a princess of the blood" who deserved "the honors due to the oldest daughter of an emperor."[41]

The Irish-American population wielded its considerable clout by inundating the White House with complaints about the anticipated trip. The

Sons of Erin believed that Alice should not go unless she took with her a petition signed by a million American mothers in protest of the English treatment of Ireland and South Africa. Irish-American societies across the United States condemned Alice's proposed attendance at the coronation as an unacceptable show of support for England. The chair of the Republican National Committee at the time, Marcus Hanna, dragged a bag of "several hundred letters [from] Irish organizations and individuals" to the White House. After hearing the first few, Roosevelt knew he could not send his daughter.[42]

TR cabled Britain and refused the invitation. "It is . . . likely," the *New York Times* suggested, "that the President on reflection became disinclined to have his daughter placed in a position where necessarily she would be regarded as something more than a plain American girl visiting London on a sightseeing trip." In fact, as TR explained to Ambassador Joseph H. Choate, he decided that "both the attentions which through courtesy would be shown her, and the fact that other attentions could not be shown her, would be misunderstood." Roosevelt allowed that his daughter's instant celebrity status took him by surprise. Reid frowned on the "misrepresentations and falsehoods" told by the press about Alice just "to make a political point."[43]

Alice was crushed. She confided to the back of her diary—the place she wrote her most secret vows so the maids wouldn't see—"I swear by all I believe in that if it is any way feasible I will go to the coronation of the next king, he who comes after the present Edward the seventh. [signed] Alice Lee Roosevelt." Half a year later, Alice had not forgotten her lost opportunity. When Edith would not permit Alice to accept an invitation to visit Jamaica, she complained, "Mother says I can't [go], as it is English territory and they would make a fuss about me. I don't give a hoot if they did. It's all because the newspapers kicked up such a row about my going over to the coronation in the spring."[44]

This seating question at Edward VII's coronation marked the first time that Alice became a pawn of pro- and anti-administration newspapers. Roosevelt's fans took great pleasure in the First Daughter's internationally recognized status, while his detractors accused TR of undemocratic aspirations and suggested that Princess Alice's father would soon proclaim himself king. London's *Daily News* gloomily recalled the cancellation of fetes planned in Alice's honor and England's disappointment at her absence. But the paper understood that the "fuss" over Miss Roosevelt "would seem to be not in accordance with the simplicity which marks American republicanism, and, if permitted, it might excite some unfriendly remarks in circles in America which the President would desire to conciliate."[45]

After that unsuccessful foray into the international spotlight, in early March, Alice embarked on a month-long consolation trip to Cuba. She packed six dozen photographs of herself. Former Rough Rider Leonard Wood communicated to Roosevelt that he and his wife would happily entertain Alice as their guest in the governor's palace over Easter. The Woods's gesture significantly cheered her. Wood had been the military governor in Havana since December 1899. American occupation of the island would end in May 1902, a month after Alice left. Once in Cuba, she was a faultless First Daughter. Although Cubans expressed ambivalence toward the American troops, Alice encountered only well-wishers. She viewed exercises at a school for orphans; presided over a charity reception; attended teas, parties, balls, and a cavalry review given in her honor. She also had her fortune told, an outgrowth of her enduring fascination with Romany culture. Another American visitor to the island at the same time vouched, "There was always plenty doing wherever Alice appeared—like her father, she was a center of activity." Alice's diary displayed her delight: "Several awfully nice Cuban men and girls out there. Had bully fun as I always enjoy meeting them."[46]

Alice and her chaperone shopped, ate spicy Cuban food, and followed jai alai games closely. Alice knew that "as the daughter of the President, I was supposed to have an intelligent interest in such things as training schools, and sugar plantations, the experiments with yellow fever mosquitoes." But the young men—and the betting—on the jai alai fields were never far from the teenager's mind.[47] As she left the island, Alice received a telegram from the governor of Matanzas asking for her help in revoking the death sentence of a local man convicted of murder, and a letter from a prisoner in Havana's "City jail" pleading for her intercession. The historical record is silent as to whether or not Alice assisted these men, but her celebrity status clearly preceded her. The condemned man and his allies surely hoped that their public appeal—it was the subject of a *New York Times* article—and Alice's proximity to the U.S. president would bring about their pardons.[48]

Alice began in earnest her life as the First Daughter upon her return. In that role, she had to balance the self-absorption of an eighteen-year-old with the demands of celebrity. She, and thousands of other Americans, read about herself in an illustrated, page-long *Ladies' Home Journal* article where she was described as "warm-hearted, impulsive and demonstrative," "gracefully slender," "an excellent horsewoman," fond of "outdoor exercise and all forms of wholesome athletic sport," in short, "the typical American girl of good health and sane ideas."[49]

On April 13, 1902, Alice made a confession to her diary: "I dressed up this evening in my Spanish white lace mantilla and wound my hair and dress with brilliant pink roses. No one saw me, I simply paraded up and down and looked at myself in the glass. This, I think, is a case of 'confession is good for the soul.' 'Vanity of vanities,' saith the preacher, 'all is vanity.' And I have absolutely no reason at all to be vain. These last remarks are decidedly in the school girl 'my diary thoughts,' my opinion on life and that sort of thing. I have decidedly fallen."[50] It was a Sloperesque dance, but framed in guilt. Only to her diary could Alice, raised by a famous father and a puritanical stepmother, confide her confused attempts to understand what the rest of the world suddenly saw in her.

Chapter 4

"I Tried to Be Conspicuous"

ALICE ROOSEVELT'S INABILITY to trust wholeheartedly created a potent and troubling mix when added to the celebrity status that caused her to question the intentions of friends and suitors. Her ferocious desire to be free of confining rules may have been a test: who would love her even when she pushed the furthest boundaries? Alice's teenage years predated the 1920s and the 1960s, two eras famous for youth rebellions. In the first decade of the twentieth century, a woman's goal was marriage, which required behavior beyond reproach. But Alice had a special worry: she could never trust that any man loved her for herself. The more she gave in to her fears and became a female caricature of her father's most criticized traits—impetuosity, stubbornness, insensitivity—the more she alienated some men, and perversely, the more she also became a hero to others. The end result would be a woman who fit no mold. The journey to that late-life, serene self-possession was painful; all the more so because so much of it occurred in public.

The First Daughter could turn to neither her father nor her stepmother for help in making sense of her situation. While he could find a moment for the occasional Highland fling with his daughter, TR was unavailable for the heart-to-hearts that she craved. And Edith, Alice recorded on April 30, 1902, was "in bed all day with a headache and dead tired." Tensions were high in the Roosevelt household. On May 8, Alice noted that she had a "foolish temper fit this morning with Mother. A newspaper paragraph saying [two different men] in love with me." Edith, unbeknownst to Alice, was pregnant—this explained her ongoing "headaches." But the next day, Edith miscarried, and remained in bed and downcast for a fortnight.[1]

Throughout her four years there, Alice served as White House hostess on various formal occasions, just as she had assisted at Auntie Bye's functions. The First Lady found Alice so useful that she vowed that she would "not have a big dinner till you are here to help me again." Edith was ill when an illustrious French commission visited the capital to unveil a statue of General Jean de Rochambeau, the French nobleman who fought beside George Washington. Lying on his back on the sofa in the Executive Office, energetically "kicking his heels in the air," TR accepted the invitation of the French ambassador Jules Cambon by shouting, "All right! Alice and I will go! Alice and I are toughs!" On the morning of May 22, 1902, Alice stood proudly beside Theodore to receive their visitors. In Edith's stead, the commission presented Alice with a pair of exquisite Sevres figurines. The next day, a host of Washington dignitaries, including the president and First Daughter, went to Annapolis to admire the French ship *Gaulois*. Before the commission departed, Alice attended a dinner at the French embassy and sat next to Charles de Chambrun, a man she found particularly handsome.[2]

In early June, she left for Boston and her summer visit to her Lee relatives. Alice had three good weeks in Chestnut Hill, watching country club boat races, dining with friends, flirting with Harvard men, and driving to the Pops concert in an automobile. What really helped her vacation was the announcement from Grandpa Lee that he would raise her allowance by five hundred dollars, to two thousand dollars a year. This increase represented a figure greater than the yearly salary of the average American worker in 1902. "I am happy!" Alice exclaimed to her diary, and used the funds to shop "madly."[3]

Despite her relatively substantial income, Alice worried about money. When her allowance arrived at the beginning of each month, she, like her friends, paid her bills and bought new clothes. Alice occasionally exceeded her budget, but living within her means was not arduous at first. In October 1902, for example, she noted that two days before the end of the month, she was "so far only about fifty dollars over my allowance." That did not curtail a spree on the thirty-first, when she "shopped all morning at three different stores." Nevertheless, she never felt she had enough money. Her diary is full of promises to marry only very wealthy men, and plans as to how she would spend a lot of money, if she only had it. "I pray for *money*!" Alice confessed as she watched her bills mount.[4] It became less feasible to meet her desires on two thousand dollars a year when she broadened her circle of friends to include wealthy Washington socialites such as Eleanor "Cissy" Patterson and Countess Marguerite Cassini. Theodore and Edith criticized Alice for her choice of friends, while Grandma and Grandpa Lee lectured their granddaughter on her financial profligacy.

National interest in the First Daughter amplified as her socializing increased. The "Alice Roosevelt Waltz" by composer Ferdinand Sabathil debuted on Independence Day 1902.[5] Newspapers were particularly interested in who might be dancing with the First Daughter. On July 19, the *New York Times* had to retract an earlier story claiming to announce Alice's engagement, only one of several incorrect guesses by newspapers. She told family friend John Greenway in December 1902 that she had "been reported engaged five times in the last eight months!" But the fact that the rumors were printed at all made her parents uncomfortable—and so did her summer of parties, boat races, dances, and other frivolities. "Got a talking to this evening at having no interests in life from Mother and Father. Not at all unexpected nor yet in the least undeserved; only I am afraid I just about care. I wish I did. No hope for Alice."[6] Alice's tone wavered from sarcastic to penitent, but the next day she left for Newport, the resort city of the very wealthy—where few other Roosevelts, save Auntie Bye, ever went.

The Vanderbilts and similarly monied families escaped from the heat of Boston and New York to play the whole summer long on the beaches of Rhode Island. Alice enjoyed Newport—even though she knew that she did not have the income to keep up with its inhabitants. Betting was a prime sport at Newport. Women gambled at bridge, tried their luck in the casino, and played the odds on yachting races. Vacationers spent their time battling at croquet, driving cars, having their horoscopes read, dining, picnicking, sleeping late, dancing, horseback riding, playing tennis, and sailing. In the summer of 1902, Alice created a mild scandal when she and her friend Ellen "Lila" Paul drove unchaperoned from Newport to Boston in Lila's automobile. The *New York Tribune* covered the news in a tone of astonishment on its front page: "In a big red automobile which snorted and bounced its way along the country roads leaving a cloud of dust in its wake, Miss Alice Roosevelt traveled yesterday afternoon from Newport to [Boston]. Miss Ellen Drexel Paul, of Philadelphia, was her companion and drove the machine. Tired, but thoroughly delighted with automobile riding, Miss Roosevelt arrived last evening at the home of her grandfather, George C. Lee."[7]

Alice's pleasure in the new sport led her to purchase her own touring car in 1904, an expensive, long, sleek, $2,500 "red devil" automobile. Alice loved driving cars—fast. Whenever she could she drove a car rather than a horse-drawn vehicle. More than once Alice paid fines for excessive speed while driving. "It must be great fun to run an auto," Auntie Corinne wrote dryly, "but <u>do</u> think of the life and limbs of your victims." Yet it was the unchaperoned drive from Newport to Boston that made the biggest impression on America. A writer for *Motor* magazine in 1907 asserted, "It needed only this edict from the White House to completely establish [women's driving] among those whose puritanical scruples had kept them reluctant lest in some occult manner this highly masculine pleasure should reflect against them."[8] The First Daughter thus added a legitimacy to the heretofore risqué combination of women and automobiles, and opened the avenues for women drivers.

Alice returned to Washington, where the remodeling of the White House continued. She did not shake her Newport schedule immediately. "Drank three cups of coffee for breakfast and then had a scrap with Auntie Bye," Alice noted in early September 1902. On the third, Theodore Roosevelt's carriage was hit by an electric trolley in Massachusetts. Roosevelt appeared unhurt, but the accident killed a Secret Service agent of whom the younger Roosevelt children were particularly fond. Alice's diary entry was strangely unemotional. However, the accident must have shaken her, for her diary is full of her father's activities for the next few weeks. Alice noted that "Father very busy writing the speeches for his western trip," on September 16, and the next day that "Father and the Senators yesterday were going over the revision of the tariff. He is having a pretty hard time." She even changed her habits to be able to see her father, having been reminded horribly of his mortality: "Have begun to get up for breakfast." Theodore did not approve of his daughter's increasingly busy social schedule. It prohibited her from breakfasting with the entire family, the one meal that the Roosevelts tried to eat alone together. It was not Alice's style to wax sentimental about her feelings for her father. However, she did try to prove to herself that she was capable of loving him. She feared that she was not capable of loving anyone.[9]

About this time Alice also broadened her talents in another area of which TR disapproved. "Read a lot about draw poker and poker dice throwing," the First Daughter wrote. The next day she "dealt [her]self poker hands all morning." Later in her life, Alice intimated that she learned to play poker only after she was married.[10] Although others may have helped to hone her skills, Alice taught herself while still a teenager. Poker was a way for Alice to enter the men's sphere, to prove that she was a good sport. Alice preferred to be on the inside of any group of men, and she knew that she would never be happy simpering on the outside, especially if their activity looked amusing. It didn't matter to her that the fun—playing poker and betting, in this case—was considered an unacceptable pastime for women in 1902. Ladies bet on bridge discreetly. Alice bet on poker and bragged about her winnings.

At the end of September, Theodore Roosevelt had to undergo a procedure because of an abscess caused by the trolley car accident. Alice supported her father by sitting with him through the trying ordeal of the doctor scraping the bone of his left leg. She wrote he was "getting on splendidly" after the operation.[11] Father and daughter must have talked together about the overarching domestic crisis of the moment as the physician operated, for Alice's diary entry contained what was for her then an unusual statement of position on a political issue. The anthracite coal strike, begun in Pennsylvania, threatened to cause a shortage of home heating fuel across the nation. Opinions warred as to whether the miners' rights, in such a case, could outweigh the specter of Americans freezing to death. Alice understood that her father "of course has no legal rights. But," she continued, "I think it is time that the government should have something to say about a thing which so much concerns all the 'people' as the great coal industry does." Alice wrote this down in her diary because she was trying to take an interest in something outside herself, as her parents suggested she should. Alice confided the aftereffects of such a parental lecture in an undated entry: "I am bored to extinction by nearly everything down here at Oyster Bay at home. I ought to take an interest in politics. I mean to, but I simply can't. I might if I were not always thinking about what I wish I could do, about what I would do if I have the wherewithal."[12] Or perhaps she commented on the coal strike because TR impressed upon her the seriousness of the problem. Either way, it warranted no further comment in her diary. Instead, the end of the month found her shopping and worried about lacking the "wherewithal."

In Chestnut Hill with the Lees, Alice's life accelerated as the fall social season opened. She attended parties, dinners, and balls. She bought a "pocket pistol" and "had great fun with it." Alice moved from house to house in Boston and New York, taking advantage of all invitations. Parental complaints mounted: "Family putting the hoof down about my staying at several very amusing places," Alice sniffed. She returned home, made up her accounts to Edith, and felt sorry for herself. On December 13, she had an "at home," but: "No one ever came to see me. What wouldn't I give to be a most marvelous belle and be more run after than any other girl."[13] Since Alice had a habit of seeing those whom she wanted to see, it is hard to tell whether complaints such as this were absolutely true. Did "no one" really visit or did only people for whom Alice didn't care appear?

December promised her first Christmas in the White House, but her diary suggests she felt thwarted in her current crush, ignored at Christmas parties and dances ("No one paid very much attention to poor Alice"), and grumpy about having to spend most of the month with relatives. On the twenty-fourth, she slept until 12:30 p.m., shopped until midafternoon, and stopped in at Auntie Bye's. After a family Christmas Eve dinner, Alice skipped church to play with "a most fascinating baby pistol," her Christmas present from TR.[14] On Christmas Day, the Roosevelts celebrated in their traditional manner, beginning with stockings and concluding with dancing. Alice did not share most of the rest of her day with the family. "Got up about quarter before seven," she recorded. "Archie had a surprise Christmas tree for the family. Then we had our stockings on the bed in Father and Mother's room. Breakfast at eight and then our big presents. $305.00 all together from Mother, Grandma and Grandpa. Most of my other things were stupid but I had great amusement... for the benefit of the family. Mr. [Robert Munro-] Ferguson gave me some very nice lace. Lunch at Auntie Bye's.... Called on Marjorie Nott and won fifteen dollars from Freddie Hale.... Of course we all danced afterwards in the East Room."[15] Her teenager's cynicism, coupled with a bad case of the doldrums, seemed to blight most of the holiday season. She left as soon as she could to see friends in New York City.

The 1903 winter weighed heavily upon Alice. For weeks in a row she was dejected and unable to enjoy her social rounds. She slept late almost every day. She compared herself unfavorably to other women. In mid-January, she revealed part of the source of her pain. She was trying to recover from her crush on Arthur Iselin, a process that took well into the spring.

She slept the days away, but nights were no better. At a dance at the Italian embassy, "No one paid any attention to me and I really am beginning to feel absolutely despondent about ever having a good time again." She was not meeting the men she found attractive, and she seemed to be without a best girlfriend as well. Alice missed the kind of friend in whom she could confide her feelings. After a series of unhappy days, Alice couldn't help comparing herself with two acquaintances: "They are both so attractive and everyone likes them so much. It is very hard to have friends like them and be one's self a perfectly nondescript sort of a person. I don't think I have made an impression on anybody, and no one really cares to play with me, or to dance with me. Oh *how* I wish I were a most marvelous belle."

Theodore, observing his eldest child, complained to Ted: "Sister continues to lead the life of social excitement, which is I think all right for a girl to lead for a year or two, but which upon my word I do not regard as healthy from the standpoint of permanence. I wish she had some pronounced serious taste. Perhaps she will develop one later."[16] Alice concluded her diary entry, written the same night TR wrote to Ted, in a way that would have given Roosevelt hope, had he known. "How I hate going out," she groused. "What is the good in it anyway. A crowd of vapid people almost all of them no good whatsoever in the world. I feel dead tired."[17]

Like the parents of many teenagers, Edith and TR approved of some of their daughter's friends, but not others. Alice was not allowed to accept invitations until Edith had sanctioned them. But there were many times that Edith herself organized Alice's schedule, presumably filling it with suitable associates. "I've arranged for you go from Phil. to Orange on the 2nd as there is a dance there that night. There is also one on the 3rd. Cousin Mamie . . . has asked you to dinner on Saturday night and I have accepted, and on Monday you can come home—I only hope you may have as good a time as I used to have," Edith concluded with a touch of wistfulness in a letter full to the margins with scheduling details.[18]

Alice consistently penned "no hope for Alice" in her diary, echoing Edith or Theodore, or both, and eventually Edith noticed her stepdaughter's depression. Beyond carping letters to Ted, Theodore made no attempt to address Alice's pain. Both TR and Edith attributed Alice's excessive sleeping and her unhappy moods to either an infelicitous social life or some sort of high dramatics. One Sunday evening in January, Alice wrote up a description of the mother-daughter talk that Edith, at least, seemed to find comforting: "This evening Mother said that she too had been noticing the queer worried expression that I have been acquiring by long months of patient practice in my eyes and my handsome carriage. The poor dear Lamb was afraid she had hurt my feelings and came back to my room and told me that she didn't want me to think that she thought that the expression came from worried feelings inside, because she knew that it didn't. My feelings hadn't of course been in the least hurt, but how little can she imagine what really naughty thoughts I have, and what fascinatingly 'darling' things I do, though these all are probably temporary, and only because I am so very youthful."[19] Edith did not take Alice seriously. The First Lady was preoccupied once again with becoming pregnant. Perhaps she was happiest with young children who loved her uncritically and could never talk back.

The holiday spate of White House receptions didn't particularly enliven Alice's downcast state. The Roosevelts held the big, traditional New Year's Day reception in the renovated White House, and Theodore and Edith stood to welcome the crowds of admirers. Alice found the Judicial reception "exactly like all the rest only queerer people if possible." But she was good at receiving lines and official dinner parties, and had become a practiced social chameleon. Alice could switch on her First Daughter bearing and manners whenever necessary. One European visitor commented that Alice had "a brilliant manner and a friendly conception of her duty to her father's guests...very competent, thoughtful, picturesque, with an inexhaustible stock of pleasant surprises." This is in direct opposition to Alice's own self-image: "I [stand] by, looking on with open mouth. I am a fool. I can't join in repartee of any kind." She told her diary that she didn't think she would go to New York for any of the social life at all in 1903.[20]

Alice's unhappiness reached a denouement at the end of January. She tried to explain her sense of desperation to Edith, but wound up in a deeper morass of sadness and self-pity:

Mother had early tea with the children and I went down and sat with her and wept madly all through it. Because I can't go abroad— because I can't go to Jamaica, because I can't do a great many very unimportant things that my own selfish self wants to do. I also said that Father doesn't care for me, that is to say one eighth as much as he does for the other children. It is perfectly true that he doesn't, and Lord, why should he. We are not in the least congenial, and if I don't care overmuch for him and don't take a bit of interest in the things he likes, why should he pay any attention to me or the things that I live for, except to look on them with disapproval. Of course he loves me in a way because I am one of his children, and he certainly does possess his much-prized "sense of duty." Heaven knows I am perfectly well aware [that I haven't] got it in my commonplace self to love anyone overmuch, except Alice, but I certainly do love him with all the love that I am so far capable of.[21]

Alice clearly signaled her estrangement from her family, her need for attention from Theodore, her desire from compassion from Edith, and her belief that her father loved her less than her siblings and then only out of a sense of duty. Are the words in Alice's diary her own, or are they Edith's? Did Edith say crushingly to Alice, "Well, Alice, what do you expect? You don't take an interest in your father's life. Why should he automatically take an interest in yours?" What did Edith respond when Alice accused her father of not loving her? Could Edith have said, "Of course he loves you Alice. You are his daughter." The ambivalence in Alice was profound.

Her position often forced Alice to endure such inconsistencies. In an interview at the time of her ninetieth birthday, Alice recalled that she thought she was "a rather pathetic creature, terribly homely and that they were just saying I was pretty because I was the President's daughter." "Sometimes," the nonagenarian continued, "I look at pictures of myself then, trying to see what they thought was pretty. But then I determined not to be a pathetic creature. I decided to defeat it so I became resistant, contrary and I tried to be conspicuous."[22] Alice had two choices. She could turn inward and be tractable, conformist, and "good." That is what her parents exhorted her to do, pointing out the model of cousin Eleanor Roosevelt. Or Alice could resist. She could make of the world what she wanted. This option had the advantages of going against her parents' wishes, and of guaranteeing attention—good or bad—for Alice, who never took attention for granted. Choosing at an early age to "be conspicuous" meant that she was ripe for the celebrity role. Alice Roosevelt became bigger than life—no matter how hollow or lonely she may have been—as a self-defense mechanism.[23]

Edith was unable to comprehend her stepdaughter. As a girl, Edith had

been serious minded and solemn. No doubt she believed that she was trying to help Alice shape up or grow up, or both. But the incongruity between Alice's needs and Edith's attempts to meet them frustrated both
women. "Alice," TR wrote to Ted not long after Edith's talk, "has been
just as good as gold of late."[24] Perhaps Edith's methods really were temporarily effective; arguments with her parents almost always preceded re-
morseful promises to change. Or perhaps Theodore had no idea of his
daughter's emotional state.

Travel was the remedy for Alice's depression, just as it had been for her
father's asthma, and her mood perked up in mid-February 1903, when she
was allowed to experience a New Orleans Mardi Gras. Edith Root, the
daughter of TR's secretary of war, accompanied her. En route to Louisiana
by rail, Alice noted that "reporters at all the stations were most skillfully
rushed off by the porters."[25] Newspapers announced Alice would be queen
of the Comus Ball, sponsored by New Orleans's oldest and most prestigious club. It was only a rumor—the local debutantes commanded all the
royal thrones—but she still had an excellent time. They stayed on Avery
Island with former Rough Rider and Tabasco sauce entrepreneur John Mc-
Ilhenny and his family, and "for a week we went nearly every evening to a
carnival ball, the Atlanteans, Momus, Proteus, and Comus, and to a small
dance, the Carnival German, and to a benefit opera as well!" She was welcomed by the king and queen of the Comus Ball in a tribute that brought
her a standing ovation. Alice also found time to bet money on a race of
some sort, where she "came out ten ahead." Alice worried, as usual, that
she was not as popular as her friends. "Edith Root is having a very swell
time, I am afraid better than me. Anyway she gives me the impression that
she is.... Oh why aren't people devoted to me?" Nevertheless, she wrote in
superlatives to thank Mrs. McIlhenney: "It was all *too* marvelous and I
don't ever expect to have quite such a good time again." To Alice's credit,
the New Orleans newspapers lavished a similar praise on her: "Never did
[a] young girl wear her honors more sweetly and with such unaffected
grace...."[26]

Upon her return home in early March, Alice spent more time at Auntie
Bye's, her refuge after lectures from TR and Edith. Perhaps in response to

the publicity surrounding the Mardi Gras trip, Alice recorded that "Mother says it is unfortunate in my station in life that I am born with a [penchant] to make myself conspicuous and that I should have been an actress." Alice's response to Edith's criticism was deceptively jaunty: "Heigh Ho! Wait until I am 21!" However, that same day, in the most private back of her diary, Alice demonstrated that Edith's comment did hurt her: "All that I want is to have a large fortune, next to that to have a change of ideas. I can't force it to come but suppose I am merely passing through a phase."[27] "Passing through a phase" was Edith's phrase, echoed by the teenage Alice in sad parody.

An imminent trip to Puerto Rico also served to increase Alice's immunity to parental disapproval.[28] A gratifyingly large crowd gathered on March 14 in New York Harbor to see her off. Policemen, detectives, and Secret Service officers circulated among the hundreds of people who waved the First Daughter good-bye. Alice found the three weeks with Governor William H. Hunt's daughter Beth were great fun. She laid a cornerstone, reviewed the troops, stood in a receiving line for two hours, christened a fire engine, and visited an industrial school and a sugar plantation. She watched as WELCOME TO MISS ALICE ROOSEVELT was spelled out "in different colored fireworks... going off with loud cracks" in the dark. She was on her "best official behavior." "I am really trying to be very good," she wrote Edith. "Every other word I say is 'me gusto mucho Puerto Rico' with a beautiful smile." Crowds gathered to cheer her. Her conduct made her presidential father happy. "I am very much pleased that you found the visit so interesting," TR wrote, "and it was a good thing in more ways than one. You were of real service down there because you made those people feel that you liked them and took an interest in them and your presence was accepted as a great compliment."[29] Although Alice in later life recalled that she did not often do "something in a public way" within the United States, where her father held the political limelight, she conceded that "it was a little different when I was overseas. In places such as the Philippines and in Puerto Rico and Cuba I was called upon to fill a far greater number of public engagements."[30]

Nothing she did escaped censure or comment. As a behavioral model

Alice was fair game, newspaper editors felt. In 1903, the First Daughter went as a guest of Mabel Gerry to the Chicago Horse Show "for a week of being stared at." John McCutcheon, of the *Chicago Tribune,* drew a cartoon—that Alice loved—in which spectators, judges, and horses all craned their necks upward to Alice's box. The center of attention was the First Daughter, and the band played "Alice, Where Art Thou?"—yet another song written in her honor.[31] But the gods of publicity take as well as give. About the same time as McCutcheon's cartoon, a rival Chicago paper printed a much less flattering editorial accusing her of " 'chanking' vigorously" at the theater and elsewhere in public and warned "the soubrettish young women who copy the peculiar characteristics of the daughter of her strenuous sire" not to emulate her gum chewing. While Alice, "never pausing in her violent mastication," gambled at the racetrack, the "young horsemen" bet on whether she would "choke herself or fracture her jaw."[32]

In the spring and summer of 1903, Alice also began a new, headline-making friendship, and despite Edith's desire for a female support system in Alice's life, the thrill-seeking Russian countess Marguerite "Maggie" Cassini, was not the type of woman Edith had in mind. The friends became experts at escaping their chaperones. Alice's spending habits worsened as she tried to keep up with the seemingly unlimited budgets of Maggie and Cissy Patterson, who often joined the pair. Together, their audacity was compounded. Alice taught Maggie how to gamble. Maggie taught Alice how to smoke. Cissy taught them both to dance the newest, raciest dances. They all flirted with the same men and defied the same barriers of social etiquette.[33] The "Three Graces," as newspapers called them, scandalized New York and Washington with their disregard for proper behavior. "Our friendship," Maggie recalled in her memoirs, "had the violence of a bomb, the duration of a skyrocket." She and Alice shared "a common taste in fun and pranks, a delight in flouting the conventions, in mockery, in outrageous behavior generally." Maggie described her relationship with Alice as "two badly spoiled girls set only on their own pleasure," imposing "a veritable reign of terror." Theodore and Edith were certain they squandered their days and nights in frivolous pursuits and demoralizing pleasures.

When she was older, Alice contextualized her father's frustration: "Most of these society friends were the offspring of his own childhood friends, whom he had spurned. He was very self-conscious about it.... My father was always taking me to task for gallivanting with 'society' and for not knowing more people like my cousin Eleanor." But even Eleanor was envious. "Alice was so much more sophisticated than *I* was," she admitted.[34]

But cousin Eleanor would never have behaved as badly as Alice and Marguerite did toward those who entertained them. George Westinghouse gave a ball for the pair and told the two friends to create the guest list. Their desired invitees numbered so many that Westinghouse had to build an annex to his ballroom. Even though the workers put in overtime, the extension was not completed by the day of the dance. "So," Maggie recalled, "the imaginative Mr. Westinghouse ordered orchids, carloads of orchids, and with these he completely blanketed the unfinished walls. On the night of the ball we seemed to be dancing in a room hung with exquisite velvet coverings of mauve and purple and violet. Such a prodigal and extravagant gesture!"

Unfortunately, as the orchids wilted, they reminded Alice of "a cemetery after a huge funeral." So Alice and Maggie left long before the ball was over. Another generous host, Knickerbocker James Hazen Hyde, also gave a ball in their honor. This, Alice and Maggie did not condescend even to attend. The day of the Hyde ball, they received an invitation to dine alone with the dashing bachelor Congressman Nicholas Longworth in his private club. The women cabled last-minute regrets to Mr. Hyde, who never forgave them.[35]

Alice's lifestyle as celebrity First Daughter annoyed Theodore when it became apparent that she could use her position to gain special treatment from people such as Westinghouse and Hyde. Alice was furious with her father when he put a stop to her traveling for free on the railroads, a traditional benefit of the presidency. "Horrid father won't let us travel anymore on the passes. I am so mad at him. My train bill so far this season has been $176.25!"[36] Roosevelt saw such opportunism as unfitting in a democratic society. On the other hand, the things he most abhorred caused the greatest admiration in young women around the globe. The *New York Tribune* re-printed an article entitled "Gleanings" from a British newspaper:

> Miss Alice Roosevelt, says an English society writer, seems to possess a good deal of the indefatigable spirit of her Presidential papa. Socially she is certainly one of the most strenuously active young women of her time. She is almost as much *en évidence* at fashionable functions in New York as she is in Washington, and thinks nothing of making the trip back and forth between the two cities (it takes five or six hours) simply to be present at the entertainment of some friend....It would astonish English girls to see how this daughter of the ruler of the great republic makes these flying trips. She seldom travels with a maid, and when alone carries her own jewel case and dressing bag. When she reaches her destination she calls up her own cab and makes arrangements in regard to any luggage she may have. Miss Roosevelt is a remarkably healthy, bright looking girl, and does not show in the least the hard work that must be the result of being a belle in two cities. Late hours, six out of seven nights a week, combined with a series of receptions, luncheons and dinners, to say nothing of innumerable train journeyings, are apt to prove a bit fatiguing, but the indefatigable young woman from the White House shows no sign of flagging in her pursuit of pleasure, and is evidently enjoying herself enormously.[37]

President Roosevelt only slowly came to appreciate the importance of his eldest daughter as an image management tool. It was an opportunity lost; putting her to work cutting ribbons, laying cornerstones, or leading parades in the United States would have been a public relations asset for his administration. It would simultaneously have distanced her from the daughters of "the malefactors of great wealth" such as Grace Vanderbilt and Cissy Patterson or even unhealthier influences such as the countess Cassini. More important, Alice would have felt loved and needed by her father. If Roosevelt had somehow found a way to make his daughter more of a partner, capitalizing on her assets, both their relationship and his administration would have benefited.

Alice continued her rebellions. When Roosevelt said that no daughter of his would smoke under his roof, Alice climbed on top of the White House roof and smoked. "I smoked on the roof, outdoors, and in everyone else's house," she recalled. "I naturally...smoked to annoy the family." Alice was the first American woman to smoke openly in the nation's capital. She carried cigarettes in her compact and delighted to shock those around her by dropping it so that they would spill out. An uncle tried to cure her by making her smoke two big black cigars. "I smoked them both through with enjoyment," she said. "He was sure I'd be sick, but I wasn't."[38]

Cigarettes were occasionally found in the hands of "gentle and distinguished foreign women," but never American women, whose male relatives loathed the idea. Once again, the First Daughter changed the rules. The *Washington Mirror* blamed her for the increased use of cigarettes by women in public and suggested, "Probably if this habit of the Lofty were known to those in Parental Authority, there would be an exhibition of the strenuous life which has never found its way into the standard works of the Author." Parental Authority knew. By 1905, they had given up and could even joke about it. The remodeling of Sagamore Hill was nearly complete, but, Edith quipped, "We can't have a fire there because the chimney smokes like a daughter!" And Theodore drew a cartouche of cigarette-smoking Alice, the cloud of smoke reaching as high as her pompadour. Perhaps if they knew that Alice and young Kermit swapped tobacco and corncob pipes, they wouldn't have been so sanguine.[39]

Alice rebelled against the humiliation of her father's attitude toward, as she put it, "Large Families, the Purity of Womanhood, and the Sanctity of Marriage." She founded the Race Suicide Club, so named because of TR's speech condemning white Anglo-Saxon Protestant women who were derelict in their primary duty of producing sufficient numbers of children to keep America strong. Alice and three friends had great fun with this secret club, as a surviving letter attests. "In view of certain rumors which have reached me," the "Chairman of the Committee on Orthodoxy" wrote, "concerning a prominent member of the R.S.C. I feel it my bounden duty...to recall to your memory certain clauses of the catechism which I am afraid you may be in charge of forgetting at this crisis—viz: 'What is the object of the same'? (The question preceding this answer you may possibly recall?) Also—'What will thou submit to in return for the golden token'? If these two articles are faithfully adhered to you will still be considered an honorary member of the R.S.C." The answer to the second question was, "I will submit to all but the token will not be forthcoming." The Golden Token was Alice's idea, and the club and its meetings made, she admitted, "the rudest game" of TR, who would not have enjoyed the parody.[40]

Other peccadillos were more public. Alice was also known to slide miniature bottles of whiskey into her elbow-length gloves and smuggle them into teetotaling houses so she could present them to her male dinner partners. In her purse, she could be counted on to carry four essentials: cigarettes, a fertility image (no doubt sanctioned by the R.S.C.), her green snake named Emily Spinach (after her thin aunt), and a copy of the Constitution. Justification for her reputation as a wild thing mounted. She convinced the daughter of the secretary of the navy to duck out of an official troop review and gallop down the nearby dunes instead. She went aboard one of America's first submarines—and may have been the first woman to do so.[41] The German navy named a boat after her and requested her portrait as its eponym. The *New York Herald* calculated—only partially tongue-in-cheek—that in fifteen months Alice had graced 407 dinners, 350 balls, 300 parties, 680 teas, 1,706 social calls, and 32,000 people by shaking their hands. She had to ask Belle Hagner to order "two dozen more...photographs of that charming young creature Alice Lee Roosevelt," which, she figured, "had better all come to me first so I can put my spider tracks across them." Alice gambled at Newport, at the racetrack, and in foreign countries. Once a journalist snapped pictures of the First Daughter at Benning racetrack, outside of Washington, as she handed money to a "betting commissioner." Friends of the president suppressed the sale of the photographs to the newspapers, and Theodore had "a serious talk" with his daughter. That did not stop her.[42]

One of the most retold stories of the wayward First Daughter originated as family friend and western novelist Owen Wister tried to carry on a conversation with the president. Thrice a supremely unselfconscious teenager flung herself into their midst, burst out with a question, then receded. "Alice," her exasperated father threatened, "the next time you come in, I'll throw you out the window!" He turned to Wister and shrugged, "I can be President of the United States—or—I can attend to Alice. I cannot possibly do both!"[43] Continued diatribes from Edith on her "extravagance" and her "uselessness" made no headway. Grandma Lee's stern admonishments had little effect. "[I] trust you will profit by my lecture, and keep your good resolutions and be careful what you do when on your many visits, as reports get so exaggerated," the doughty woman cautioned.

Even warnings from her friends did not dissuade Alice once she had a taste of the freedom of behaving exactly the way she wanted. "Really, I envy you all the interesting side[s] of the life you lead, only...," a friend predicted, "you'll wake up some day and realize it all too late. Why not postpone some of the playing 'till later, and see now what you can make out of your position. Imagine having the entire world open to you—to be the girl in it so to speak. You ought to follow your Father's example—he leads the men of the country—you ought to [lead] the women."[44]

Alice sped toward the worst of her money woes after teaming up with Maggie, Cissy, and the other big spenders in their circle. Alice's allowance went to clothes and gambling debts. Ball gowns were very expensive, and Alice had rejected the earlier practice, enforced by Edith, of making over her dresses. In order to keep up with her new friends, she expended an increasing amount on a greater number of dresses. "I am in a pretty bad way," she confessed in October 1903. The next month, she had to ask her grandpa Lee for the thousand dollars she had run over budget. Her grandfather had a special place in his heart for Alice, and it was lucky that he did. His response makes one wonder what, precisely, she told him about her situation. "Under the terms of the trust, the trustees [Grandpa Lee and her uncle George Lee] are authorized to pay over to you, at any time, a portion of the income if in their opinion they think it is necessary to do so. Your uncle and I consider that it would be right and proper, under the circumstances, to pay you the money, therefore we send it." Further, Grandpa Lee admitted, "Your Uncle George and I are the only ones who know anything about this financial operation and we won't tell Grandma." Alice seems to have promised to change her ways in return for his assistance. Even so, he couldn't resist a mild lecture, but it was one of the more loving rebukes that Alice received from an adult: "You say that you don't really think that you are as bad as you seem. You are not bad at all in my estimation, but you lead such an exciting, undomestic life that you will come to grief, physically, before you are 21 years old. Of course it is all right 'to go it whilst you are young,' but I am afraid that you are overdoing it and will regret it later. You go with people who have money to burn and, I fear, lead you into extravagances. But as you are going to turn over a new leaf and reform I won't find any more fault with you now." Grandpa was concerned. The historical record suggests that he threatened to cut her off from free access to her funds should she prove unable to reform. To test her, he gave her a thousand dollars. He told TR and Edith that if she spent it in less than four weeks and came asking for more, he would put her on an allowance for the rest of her life, which is precisely what happened. As a consequence, Alice never had unlimited access to her inheritance, and to the day she died, she received a quarterly stipend.[45]

Alice spent most of 1904 in a perpetual whirl of parties and musicales at embassies, teas and receptions at friends' houses, and balls and dances. She attended the St. Louis World's Fair in late May and participated in official events. A group of "thousands" of women gathered around to see their idol arrive. Alice remembered "a tremendous crowd at the station rubbernecking quite a good deal," that followed her all around the fairgrounds. The *New York Times* corroborated her description, trumpeting that Alice was "fairly mobbed" by "an enthusiastic crowd" of five thousand women, all shrieking, "There she is!" and "Hurrah for Miss Roosevelt!" Ted was amused to note, when he visited the fair after his sister, that her "trail over the fair is still visible." He found a Ferris wheel car and a camel named for her. The press noted that three hundred women exactly copied the First Daughter's "dress and manners."[46]

Alice's increasing fame—and the sheer number of letters she received—prompted the family to deem it necessary for a White House secretary to open Alice's mail, read it, and then pass it on. This hampered Alice's flirtations. "Alice dear," wrote one male friend, "[I] didn't realize that Royalty underwent so many trials, at least that their friends did! I shudder to think my scrawl had been opened and perused by a masculine eye! and a strange one at that! Of course now I feel tongue-tied—what can you expect? Now that he finds I'm not begging for your money—or [angling] for your...handkerchiefs, perhaps he will [let] you read them first.... Can't I get up a signal with you—to write on the envelope and let me within the Golden Gates?" Another joked, "Hope the Secretary doesn't read all of this letter—or his hair will fall out."[47]

Alice's friends had to learn to cope with her celebrity status, and most did so cheerfully. Charles McCauley wrote, tongue-in-cheek, "I want you to have this little 'jewel' so that when the *N.Y. Herald* of Feb.18th appears the article will read something like this: From the King of England a diamond brooch; the German Emperor, a diamond and emerald necklace; [from] Mrs. Astor a diamond tiara; Miss Vanderbilt a turquoise and diamond bracelet; Major McCauley a pin of diamonds and rubies, etc." At least her fame allowed Alice's friends to monitor her doings: "I saw a *Paris Herald* and February 11th [sic] was recorded as Miss Alice Roosevelt's birthday." Another friend "saw in the paper that you were here to go to Chicago for the Horse Show." But sometimes even her hosts couldn't keep up with her: "Reporters of [Boston] *Transcript* just called to know when you are coming, where are you going to stay, and who is coming with you. I couldn't enlighten them," Grandpa Lee wrote in despair.[48]

Coming to terms with her fame was not easy for anyone connected to Alice, least of all the First Daughter herself. Less than a month after he assumed the presidency, Roosevelt wrote to Owen Wister: "[A]s for the children, we spend no small part of our time in doing our best to prevent them becoming self-conscious through being talked about. They lead exactly the lives led by any other six children who live in a roomy house with a garden and go to school, and are on the whole pretty good, and are not always good at all."[49] This attempt at normality obviously did not last long. Alice's debut began a process the end result of which no one could truly foresee. It became harder to control the media interest; "camera fiends" planted themselves expectantly at the front door of the White House.[50] If Edith and TR were committed to the ritual that launched their daughter into society, they were ambivalent about her propulsion into the hearts and drawing rooms of America—while still unmindful of her growing need for guidance and attention.

Chapter 5

"Frightfully Difficult Trying to Keep Up Appearances"

I<small>N ONE SENSE</small>, at least, Alice Roosevelt adhered to the conventions of her age. Her motives, though, differed from her peers'. Finding the perfect spouse was her top priority. While her friends desired the social approbation that came from being a wife, for Alice marriage meant—she hoped—independence and wealth. As with so much else, she inverted the expectations of the day, turning them to her own advantage. But courting was not easily accomplished in the public crucible of the White House.

When she was fourteen, she confessed that she was "planning hard about everyone in the matrimonial line of course!"[1] To this pursuit she devoted much of her time. To find a husband, a young Knickerbocker woman looked first within her own social circle, and second, if family ethics permitted, to titled Europeans. That avenue was not open to the First Daughter. Theodore Roosevelt thought it abominable to marry off the cream of America's women to foreign men. He was responding in part to the many daughters forced to marry against their wills by scheming parents who needed money or sought to improve their social status.

Alice was not opposed to marrying a rich man. In fact, she sincerely hoped she would. Given the elaborate social rules under which elite Progressive Era lovers labored, she was more likely to meet a man of substance than not. Conventions governed how and where and when one met a potential beau. The New York winter season began in November with the Madison Square Garden Horse Show, continued throughout the holidays, and ended with the approach of Lent. A few intimate parties and one or two larger affairs such as the Tuxedo Ball preceded it, but the first place to see and be seen was circulating among the boxes at the horse show. Dinners, receptions, dances, cotillions, suppers, plays, operas, and parties of all sizes and themes sustained the season. The Assembly Ball was the most important event of the winter. At this glamorous gathering of American elites, proud parents formally introduced their daughters to society. Usually held in mid-December, the Assembly Ball and its parties segued into the New Year's balls given by wealthy society leaders such as the Astors, the Millses, the Gerrys, the Reids, and the Goelets. These events began and ended with dancing, included a five-course supper and a cotillion, and stretched until the wee hours.

Wealthy New Englanders courted according to an elaborate and intricately prescribed system. Class absolutely dictated the social system, the social ladder, and the social season with its hierarchy of greater and lesser events, all of them exclusive. Alice Roosevelt, as the product of a marriage between the Brahmin Lees and the Knickerbocker Roosevelts, had entrée to the best parties and balls of both Boston and New York, including the gatherings of the Four Hundred. Ward McAllister coined this term in 1888 from the maximum number of people who could fit into the Astors' formal ballroom in their Fifth Avenue mansion. The Four Hundred differed from Knickerbockers and Brahmins; it included industrialists who had become rich virtually overnight. Because it was such a diverse group, these newly rich shared little but "social insecurity."[2]

Theodore Roosevelt cautioned his daughter that some captains of industry, such as Cornelius Vanderbilt and Edward H. Harriman, were really Robber Barons whose ostentatious wealth disguised the absence of business ethics and personal morals. Alice considered the Four Hundred a livelier group than the tradition-bound Knickerbockers, and therefore a great deal more fun. Theodore found such taste appalling. Alice's insistence upon including the sons of the Four Hundred among her circle of acquaintances (thus adding them to the pool of her potential husbands) was a continuing source of discord between Alice and her parents. "Got in a row with dear father this afternoon," Alice complained to her diary in 1904, "all about Maggie, my friends, my taste, etc." When Alice settled upon Nicholas

Longworth, TR's relief over the bridegroom's sterling midwestern lineage may have tipped the scale of parental approval, despite the incongruity of the First Daughter's choice. Nick had a sense of humor about the Four Hundred and as a student at Harvard, coauthored a stinging parody of McAllister: "Ward McAllister—Wow! Wow! Wow! Were hit not for that vulgar hupstart, George Washington, we might still be livin' under the rine of 'er grycious majesty Queen Victoria! Ward McAllister—Wow! Wow! Wow!"[3]

Nick was charming and funny but was neither Alice's first love nor her last. Alice had been smitten with a few other young men, but only two of them, Edward Carpenter and Arthur Iselin, were anything more than infatuations. Alice fell into and out of teenage crushes with the same frequency and intensity as the rest of her girlfriends. The status of their hearts was a popular topic of correspondence, and marriage the foremost occupation of Alice and her friends whenever they gathered. "If you can come [visit] we will try and get some men over for Sunday to captivate your fancy," promised one friend. The letters from Alice's women friends repeatedly mention affairs of the heart—speculations on engagements, commentaries on party guests, and knowing references to men who "send their love." Sometimes their letters had virtually one topic: "Write me a few times and tell me all about yourself and [your] lovers.... Is there any immediate chance of your becoming Mrs. John Greenway?" asked one friend. "I wonder how many dukes H.R.R. has in tow? Do write me if you know," a Newport girlfriend commanded. H.R.R. herself—Helen Rebecca Roosevelt, the daughter of Franklin's older half brother—queried Alice, "How's the handsome young doctor? You certainly are the very most fickle female I have _ever_ known." Helen could accuse Alice of capriciousness because she had been stuck on the same beau, Theodore Douglas Robinson, for ages, and they would wed. Helen also didn't have newspapers reporting whatever they chose about her—if she had been as "fickle" as Alice, no one would have known. But if Alice danced twice with the same man, she would find her engagement announced in the next day's papers. The resulting storm of protest at home always exasperated Alice: "Had a foolish temper fit this morning with Mother. A newspaper paragraph saying...[Henry] Cushing is in love with me. I tell you, the papers can make [it] up absolutely out of the whole cloth."[4]

Discretion was a highly prized virtue. Edith Roosevelt, born as the Civil War began, deplored many modern trends. In her generation, courting happened in the drawing room under the watchful care of a chaperone. She and Theodore were so circumspect that they went abroad to marry, in deference to the memory of TR's first wife, and they stayed in separate hotels before their wedding.[5] Edith could not help that her stepdaughter was a celebrity, and both parents believed independence should be cultivated in children, but Edith lectured Alice on the impropriety of being too well known. Edith feared—justifiably—for Alice's reputation, as reporters trailed her and crowds congregated at the sight of her.

The most derogatory insinuations about Alice appeared in the slanderous paper *Town Topics*. Socialites paid to make sure it never published their names, and they certainly never admitted to reading it. Publisher William D'Alton Mann implied that the First Daughter's morals were suspect. "From wearing costly lingerie to indulging in fancy dances for the edification of men was only a step," Mann wrote. "However, it is admitted that she is a smart girl, and smart girls are supposed to be clever enough to take care of themselves without the aid of chaperones."[6] This item suggested four major missteps: expensive intimate wear, dancing for men, being clever, and going without a chaperone. These charges against the First Daughter were so serious that the publisher of the very respectable *Collier's Weekly* took Mann to court in protest.

Alice generally reveled in the (flattering) publicity, but her stepmother believed, with the etiquette arbiters, that "the very essence of good manners is self-possession, and self-possession is another name for self-forgetfulness."[7] This impasse between mother and daughter caused them both much anguish. As Alice's prominence grew, Edith approved less and less of what she did. The two did not discuss Alice's feelings about men as she entered marriageable age.

Alice's diaries and letters provide a sketchy but revealing chronicle of her "affairs," as she called them. In her strong and distinctive script, Alice recorded her attendance at lunches and balls and listed who "took her in" to dinner, the party favors she received, and sometimes the men with whom she danced. A large part of Alice's teenage journal consisted of a running tally of what she labeled her "crushes." She indicated these by drawing a thick heart in her customary black ink and usually inserting a number inside of it. Often she labeled the heart with a name. This was not her system alone, as certain friends' letters utilized the same shorthand. "Dear 76" is what Alice called Edward Carpenter on April 24, 1902. Eight days later, she penned, "Have broken 6 [hearts] now it reaches about 87. Daniel, Leonard, Nelson, Holden, Walker, and Pryor." When she reached her one-hundredth crush, William Burden, she added, "Last?" This was a triumphant fashion in which to consider men, suggesting a competition, serious or not, among Alice's circle as to how many hearts they could break. "How many little heartlets have you had since I last heard from you?" inquired Helen Roosevelt once.[8]

Deciphering the emotional code is not an easy task. Measuring her desirability to various suitors was surely akin to gauging her approval rating from her parents. Perhaps Alice simply relished her outward success at the game of romance, with its exhilarating exertion of command over the opposite sex. There were few other ways a woman's power could exceed a man's in the early twentieth century. Once married, she lost that power as the husband became the legal head of the household. Certainly Alice Roosevelt displayed the shifting passions that were often the hallmark of those newly entered into society. She understood the strict moral and social codes, but she also had the typical teenager's confusion when trying to understand herself in relation to men and to assess her talents in comparison to other women of her age.

Alice absorbed at least three different interpretations of the maxims governing courtship. Her earliest came from Edith's and Theodore's firm opinions on the place of young ladies in society. Edith had a reputation for intolerance toward people considered sexually promiscuous, and had been known to bar the White House door to anyone who did not measure up to her strict behavioral code. Theodore linked marriage and childbearing with the good of America, calling motherhood—strictly, of course, within the sacrament of marriage—a "primary duty of life."[9]

A second view came from the older and world-wise cousins and friends Alice met and overheard at Auntie Bye's sophisticated salon. Divorce was rare, but among elites nearly any conceivable accommodation between husband and wife was discussed. The third approach to courtship Alice read about in the popular novels and prescriptive literature of the times, such as *Godey's Lady's Book*, *Leslie's Illustrated Weekly*, and etiquette books. Such periodicals, often pocket size, advised young people on appropriate ways to greet, call on, and write to each other, and how to observe the traditions of christenings, debutante balls, weddings, receptions, teas, and funerals. Gender-specific duties were emphasized: how to take a man's arm and when, how to coordinate your menu with your ballroom decorations according to season, and what to do with your chaperone at a party. Weekly magazines filled their pages with serialized fiction moralizing on the perils of ignoring the rules. In these stories, good women fell because they had been seen alone with a man, or with too many men, or with the wrong man. The etiquette manuals provided delicate guidelines on courtship that were sometimes all the more confusing because of their vagueness. For instance, this sentiment sounds self-evident, until one tries to apply it: "No well-bred woman will receive a man's attentions, however acceptable, too eagerly; nor will she carry reserve so far as to be altogether discouraging."[10]

The proper age for marriage, according to contemporary authority Dr. Elizabeth Blackwell, was between twenty and twenty-three for men. The average age of marriage for women around this time was twenty-two. The idea that a woman's physical weakness indicated her spiritual superiority still lingered in the early 1900s, while health concerns for the childbearing woman dictated much thinking about the ideal marriage age. Contradictory notions of sexuality in the late nineteenth and early twentieth centuries were expressed in a dialogue among ministers, doctors, and social critics. Social-purity crusaders kept the issues—masturbation, prostitution, the duties of wives and husbands, age of consent laws, the white slave trade, family limitation, and pornography—alive. The one thing all three groups had in common was a dislike for society's "heartless discriminations in favor of the rich and the influential." Alice declared publicly that sex was never spoken about in her family. She claimed to have gleaned her information from the "'begat' series" in the Hebrew Bible and observing the farm animals at Sagamore Hill, but she informed historian Elting Morison in the 1950s that her father "had told her the facts of life."[11]

Alice knew that for men part of her interest was that she purposefully broke some rules. Her devil-may-care attitude incited heated debate among family and friends, but they need not have feared. Though etiquette books warned "Those who defy the rules of the best society, and claim to be superior to them, are always coarse in their moral fibre, however strong they may be intellectually," Alice had an uncanny sense of how far she could push.[12] She had seen the punitive potential of society—she had to look only as far as her friend Marguerite Cassini's exile for an example of how quickly a person could be ostracized because of rumors. Alice remembered, too, the warning about a girlfriend who wore an embroidered dress that buttoned up the back to go driving with a group of friends. Upon their return, her buttons were askew. "I was told," Alice recalled later, "I wasn't to see her in certain houses after that."

The rules Alice broke were never the inflexible laws that would have meant her expulsion from society. They were not maxims dealing with sex or romance. Looking back on her youth, Alice once explained to an interviewer: "The restrictions came more from the social conventions of the day. One was never allowed out with a date and one had to go to a dance with a chaperone. One could never give a man a lift, not even a White House aide. There were always enough watchful eyes to check on one. Woe betide the girl who emerged from the conservatory at a dance with her hair slightly disheveled. As one's hair tended to fall down at the best of times it was frightfully difficult trying to keep up appearances."[13]

Alice suffered the wrath of Washington commentators who damned her for eating asparagus with her gloves on, jumping fully clothed into a swimming pool, betting in public, and shooting her pistol off the back platform of a train—all of which she did—but her joie de vivre was always carefully constrained within the most important societal boundaries. None of these misdemeanors was sufficiently serious to risk her position in society or with her parents. Alice's sharp sense of family loyalty would not allow her to incur her father's mistrust, and that is one reason that, as president, he could send this astute daughter overseas as his goodwill ambassador.[14]

Alice's ability to conduct herself with social ease was amazing when compared with that of her cousin Eleanor. In December 1902, at the prestigious Assembly Ball, Eleanor and Alice were two of the "Magic Five" Roosevelt cousins who made their collective debut. The eighteen-year-old Eleanor Roosevelt was nervous, fearful of not being asked to dance, and afraid of saying or doing something to embarrass herself or her family. Even years later she remembered that night with repugnance: "There was absolutely nothing about me to attract anybody's attention. I was tall, but I did not dance very well. . . . I do not think I quite realized beforehand what utter agony it was going to be or I would never had had the courage to go. . . . [B]y no stretch of the imagination could I fool myself into thinking that I was a popular debutante! I went home early, thankful to get away. . . ."[15]

Making the social codes fit her, instead of the other way around, was both Alice's defense and her gift to other women. Theodore's early absence and Edith's ambivalent mothering resulted in one of Alice's greatest strengths: her sublime public self-confidence. Alice never forgot that she was a Roosevelt, and the longer she served as First Daughter, the more of an asset her aplomb, her certainty of place and of station, became. As a young woman, Alice learned the importance of having a protective mask to wear when necessary.

Just before Christmas 1902, Alice, then eighteen years old, confessed some of her goals to her diary: "I should like after going to New Orleans for Mardi Gras and Carnival, to travel South through Puerto Rico and Jamaica, come home about Easter and then go abroad [to] take in a London season . . . and the . . . Regatta. Come home for the house I have [built] at Newport and then have large parties on the *Mayflower* everyday for the international races [and] to have parties during the fall. Later in the [season attend the] Horse Show then . . . get proposed to by the only man I ever loved and marry him. How's that for a programme?" she concluded jaun-tily.[16] Missing is any interest beyond elite society, just as TR feared. Nelson Aldrich called such casual poise part of "the values of belongingness and order," and attributed it to "the haven of Old Money," which gives to its members a lineage, a recognizable name, a destiny, a place in the world, potentially boundless love, and social security, as well as a shortcut to iden-tity. Alice's sense of belongingness allowed her to cultivate her insouciance. Cousin Eleanor, by contrast, almost wholly absorbed the etiquette-book standards. "I remember one afternoon rowing on the river at Farmington with Eleanor," Alice told an interviewer later in life. "For some reason or other she started lecturing me on the sort of presents one could receive from gentlemen—flowers, books, cards, were all possible, I was assured, but jewelry of any kind, absolutely not. I listened to her earnest discourse, fingering all the while a modest string of seed pearls that an admirer had given me the week before."[17]

When it came to finding a husband, Alice's consistent contravening of the social code had side effects. Carrying a snake with her to parties—as she frequently and gleefully did—distinguished her in an immediate and, Alice hoped, fascinating way from other young women. This may have been another attempt to define herself apart from the role of First Daugh-ter, as well as to test her acquaintances to see if they really liked her. One, she thought, was "awfully nice and I hope he won't dislike me anymore. It's all about the difference between 'The President's Daughter' and 'Alice Roosevelt,'" she fretted. A full two years after her father assumed the pres-idency, Alice wrote that "I am afraid the only attention I get is just out of curiosity to see what I am like on account of my position." Whenever her friends did something notable, Alice got top billing, and even when there wasn't much newsworthy, their activities were still reported because of the First Daughter's participation.[18]

Alice had girlfriends of every disposition, but she easily and rapidly dismissed men who could not stand the test of public display as well as she did. Caspar Milquetoasts were no match for Alice's quick wit or the Roose-velt family lifestyle. Only a man with Theodore Roosevelt's strength—as defined by a daughter—would be a compatible life partner. "Why don't you cultivate [Mr.] Hare? ... Try him—he is fierce enough to suit even you," wrote a friend, only half in jest. Such men were less likely to conform to the moral codes and hence less likely to be immediately accepted by Mother and Father. Alice had long spurned the companionship of those her age, acknowledging that "attraction for me had very little to do with sex. It was more closely connected with a certain vitality, a sense of humor, and a mental affinity. That was when the mayhem started."[19] Mayhem is exactly what Edward Carpenter caused in Alice's teenage heart.

Alice met Carpenter, as she called him—defying convention—on her 1902 visit to Cuba. Between official duties, Alice and her women friends flirted with the men of the American military who had been invited to the balls as dance partners. Carpenter and his best friend, Frank R. McCoy, were career army officers serving as aides to Major General Leonard Wood. Alice liked Carpenter's sense of humor and his uniform. Her diary of the trip consists almost solely of the ups and downs of her relationship with Carpenter, and an ongoing log of how much money she won or lost betting on jai alai.

Alice and Carpenter had a stormy relationship. She related having "almost literally groveled in the dirt at his feet last night begging him to ... send me a message by McCoy. I have never been so humiliated before and never intend to be so again. I suppose it is just good discipline but all the same it is uncomfortable and loathsome. ... I shall never get over the turn down. It has been my first and I trust my last. I must ... retaliate." This sentiment did not last long. The next day, she "[b]ought silly little charms for Carpenter. ... He came to lunch and we 'had it out' afterwards. I really have a ... temper." Apparently the reconciliation did not meet with success. Whether prompted by her temper or Janet Lee, Alice's competitor for Carpenter's heart, the next night, Alice scratched dolefully, "Carpenter has absolutely thrown poor Alice over."[20]

Things were looking up by the time Alice left Cuba two days later. A crowd of friends came to see her off, but Carpenter, she exulted, "stayed in the boat after the others left. ... He gave me some photographs [of himself]. ..."[21] Upon her return to Washington, Alice happily carried on a regular exchange of letters and gifts with Carpenter for almost two months.

Carpenter began one lengthy letter without a salutation. Instead, in a manner that would have caused society arbiters to feel faint, he wrote, "Don't you DARE!!! to do it. If you do I'll haunt you, I swear I will. And when I get rigged up to haunt I'm a holy horror and no mistake." He recounted his invitation to a friend: "Do me the favor of punching my head three times," because he had been, in an attempt "to be funny, and to show off," foolish enough to suggest to Alice in his last letter that she take a photograph of herself with another man and put it in a locket. "And," Carpenter panted, "instead of saying 'Never!' or 'Not in a thousand years,' or some other comforting sentence, [you] had said instead that it was a charming suggestion which [you] would follow out at once and would give the locket to the man!... But oh, if you do! If you do! Well—you'll see me roused." Apparently Alice was not attempting to make him think that he was her only love interest, for he rather plaintively asked her, "What ever did you dance that cotillion with him for? In your heart I believe you are fond of him." He signed his letter FAITHFULLY, YOUR, L.A., shorthand for Alice's nickname for him: Lazy Ape.[22]

The two were reunited briefly when Carpenter and McCoy visited the First Daughter at the White House on May 27, 1902, but by that time Alice had turned her attentions to the Knickerbocker heir J. Van Ness Philips and a dashing relative of General Lafayette, Charles de Chambrun. Alice wrote on the twenty-third that she loved de Chambrun, her ninetieth crush, but this affair was short-lived. On May 28, during what must have been an uncomfortable, or perhaps titillating, dinner, Alice was seated between Van Ness and Carpenter: "J.V.N.P. took this occasion to tell me that the only way for me to cure him would be to marry him. I simply yelled and laughed so. Then we, Van Ness, McCoy, Carpenter and myself went down to Chase's.... Van Ness again made his remark to which it goes without saying I said no." Van Ness had the worst of it that night, because Carpenter and McCoy accompanied Alice and Edith Root home.[23]

Hearing Van Ness Philips's intention bothered Carpenter, who came to see Alice the next day. It took him two and one half hours to communicate what was on his mind to the by-then unreceptive Alice. "He started off by saying that he was in love with me and then he asked me to marry him. He said he would give me a year and a half to think about it for then he would be a captain of artillery and in command of a light battery. He wants to call me 'Alice' when we are alone together. On the whole, he behaved like two idiots.... I positively said no." The following day, Alice "received notes from Carpenter and Philips—It's very foolish."[24]

Alice took her first two marriage proposals in stride. Had Alice consulted the advice literature rather than her own sense of romance and fun, she would have been chastened. *Ladies' and Gentlemen's Etiquette* cautioned, "The prerogative of proposing lies with the man, but the prerogative of refusing lies with the woman; and this prerogative a lady of tact and kind heart will exercise before her suitor is brought to the humiliation of a direct offer. She should try, while discouraging him as a lover, to still retain him as a friend." Ward McAllister warned ominously that a woman should "be cautious how she refused the first offers of marriage made her, as they were generally the best." If Alice felt remorse at having received the proposals or regret at turning them down, she did not confide it to her diary.[25]

Although Alice did "retain them as friends," Carpenter and Philips virtually disappeared from her diary—and her heart. The latter wrote hopefully but unsuccessfully in July. Because they traveled in Alice's social circle, she was not overtly rude to Carpenter and Philips. *Practical Etiquette* warned, "A young lady ought to be very careful how she mentions offers of marriage that have been refused by her." Society expected a forward course for the man: "The duty of the rejected suitor is quite clear. Etiquette demands that he shall accept the lady's decision as final and retire from the field. He has no right to demand the reason of her refusal. If she assign it, he is bound to respect her secret, if it is one, and to hold it inviolable. To persist in urging his suit or to follow up the lady with marked attentions would be in the worst possible taste."[26] Alice thought both men ultimately foolish for their persistence—and looked on them both with disdain.

And, by midsummer, her heart was once again preoccupied. Alice fell for Arthur Iselin, a long-lasting infatuation that would eventually make her miserable enough to swear that she would never marry. In October 1903, Delancey Jay, the scion of one of America's oldest families, confessed to Alice that he thought of her often and "I . . . also find myself using your picture, barbarian that I am, like an idol—it hangs by my bed like an up to date Madonna or Saint of some kind! You really look quite serious and nice in it." But he knew that his suit was shaky for "I'm not Arthur Iselin!" By July 1902, four of Alice's friends cornered her at dinner and "gave me fearful lectures this evening because I like Arthur Iselin so much. They are trying to 'open my eyes as to his character.'"[27]

If Iselin's character aroused the suspicions of Alice's crowd, at least his lineage would have made her parents happy. In 1924, Mrs. John King Van Rensselaer approvingly described his family as one "whose ancestors have directed the social life of New York for ten or more generations [and who] still continue to entertain and be entertained without the blare of publicity."[28] As with Carpenter, Alice had a stormy and uncertain affair with Arthur, in spite of the fact that Alice seemed to care deeply for him. Initially, it appeared that the relationship would be reciprocal. Arthur wrote to her in April, when they were only beginning to enter the flirtation stage, "Dear Alice, I saw the enclosed in today's *Herald* and thought it might be from you—[signed] Arthur I." He had glued a clipping to the top of a page that read, "Sweetheart, I will call Saturday, 8:45 or 9; do not refuse me, darling. I love you, love you, love you." Arthur had underlined the last part and appended "Madly! Madly! Madly!" This was a sense of humor to compete with her own. Despite her diary entry of July 19, 1902, vowing, "I swear by all I believe in that if Arthur Iselin ever asks me to marry him I will," the coveted proposal never came.[29]

In early August, Arthur's affection showed signs of waning. Alice saw him at a party, "but it was very stupid. Arthur is very much in love and intends to marry a beautiful Southern girl . . ." Diary references to Arthur continued unabated throughout the month, sprinkled with examples of her frustration, such as "poor Alice" and "no hope for Alice."[30]

By late 1902, Alice's desire to marry had intensified. It had been a year since her debut, and as family troubles and budget woes worsened, the combination had an unfortunate influence on her self-esteem. Her diary for this period often alluded to how unattractive she was and how much nicer

other women were. On November 18, as the social season began at the
Madison Square Garden Horse Show, Alice made another promise to herself: "Saw Robert Goelet. They say he is engaged. If he is not I will try to
love and marry him. I pray to God that he asks me to marry, cares for me
and me alone love[s]." Three weeks later, Alice had dinner with friends
and remarked that it was "frightfully rude" that "Arthur Iselin—the
beast—never turned up." Arthur's lack of response saddened Alice. The
next night found her making her second debut at the Assembly Ball. Arthur's absence was all she noted. After the ball she confessed her fear that
"he will soon be engaged to someone or other and I don't know how I will
stand it. I pray God make him love me." Then, seeking solace, she wrote
his name over and over: "Oh Arthur, Arthur, Arthur, my love and my life."
This Alice would do seriously with only one other man: Nick Longworth.[31]

Suitor Arthur Bredon was a brief distraction. But he did not compare
with *her* Arthur. "I would be absolutely fascinated by him," Alice reflected,
"if I allowed myself to be, but I have just gotten over my feelings for Arthur
Iselin and I really believe I was rather in love with him. I don't want to go
through another experience of the same kind, unrequited affection, etc.,
for it was really very unpleasant." In mid-January, Alice cast about for
friends to divert her. She received a teasing and not very comforting letter
from a girlfriend: "Are Arthur [Iselin]'s classic features still too much for
your peace of mind[?] I hope you have recovered your sanity by this time."
Even parties with the Four Hundred failed to help lift her sense of gloom.
"Arthur Iselin simply hates me," she concluded sadly. She resolved, "I
should never get married, anyway not for a long time and then only for
love."[32] The desolation over Arthur caused the excessive sleeping and moping her parents had ignored.

Eventually, Alice felt more like herself. In one very full evening, she
attended a reception at the British embassy and another at the Italian embassy. She "played madly round" with Arthur Bredon and Van Ness Philips and "had really quite a good time." Soon after, she danced a cotillion
with Philips, admitting, "I led him on, so he proposed more or less all over
again." Alice never enumerated his faults in her journal, but they were
probably not connected with money. Marrying into the Philips family

would have erased her financial woes. At any rate, Alice could never be happy with a man whom she could manipulate into a marriage proposal, refuse, and then remanipulate—regardless of his wealth.[33]

Her mind never strayed far from marriage, for the night before Philips's second proposal she had received important news from a friend: "Helen tells me that [illegible] told her this evening at dinner that he liked six girls very much and that he could fall in love with one of them and that one of them was me Alice Lee Roosevelt. Resolved: that I shall make him propose to me."[34] The name of the young man is illegible because Alice didn't want her maid to read it—she had once caught her maid reading her diary and ever after, in order to hide confidential information, Alice slanted her handwriting to an extreme and unreadable degree. It didn't matter, in some respects, who the man was. It was important that he be wealthy, fun, of good family, and able to fall in love with her—soon. Alice's wording allows for some latitude in interpretation: did she intend to have him propose for the sake of keeping score, or because she really would have said yes despite her earlier vow to marry "not for a long time and then only for love"?

What she did want—and badly—was to escape the constraints of family life and to have more money. She imagined herself somewhere between Auntie Bye's popular political salon and her good friend Grace Vanderbilt's footloose, cosmopolitan, and unimaginably wealthy life. The most enticing characteristics of such an existence were heaps of money and immediate independence. Popularity was desirable, but ran a remote third. Alice knew she would have to depend upon her husband for riches, and that once she said "I do," she would at least be free of parental control. Popularity was something that any intelligent and witty woman could manage on her own in high society, especially given enough money. If Alice's husband-to-be was socially accepted in his own right, so much the better. As she reached the marriageable age of nineteen, she spent her birthday with a group of friends and noted, "After supper we all sang and Nick played. Nick Longworth [and] Bredon...were the stars. Perfect marvels." Congressman Nicholas Longworth—wealthy, sought after, and utterly charming—the bachelor representative from Cincinnati, would soon oust all thoughts of Arthur Iselin.[35]

In the White House, Alice Roosevelt was the First Daughter of the land: a role model, a symbol of the times, a source of national pride. It took her father a while to learn how to capitalize on Alice's "well-knownness," but once Alice stepped onto the foreign stage, Roosevelt saw his opportunity. By sending Alice overseas, he added to the prestige of his administration, kept his daughter and his wife happy, and reclaimed the limelight for himself. And so overseas is where Alice would go. The "perfect marvel," Nick Longworth, went, too.

Chapter 6

"He Never Grew Serious About Anything"

NATIONAL PREOCCUPATION with the First Daughter's unmarried state reflected Alice's pensive, private deliberations. Arthur Iselin's proposal eluded her, and she had turned down Edward Carpenter and J. Van Ness Philips. Time was growing short. Society's arbiters recommended that a woman marry within three years of her coming of age. Alice never evinced any real desire to remain single, never displayed a distaste for the institution of marriage or worried that being coupled would infringe upon her independence. In TR and Edith, she had a loving model. When she conceptualized marriage in her writings, she thought of it as a method of increasing her monthly stipend and allowing her to be with the man she loved. Her pragmatism precluded any dreamy thoughts about bridal showers, honeymoons, or walking down the aisle on her father's arm. Alice wanted to marry, sooner than later—but her problem was finding the right man. But then when she found him, she was never really sure of him.

The sons of diplomats, politicians, businessmen, and the idle rich constituted the large array of potential husbands from which Alice could draw. The president's eldest child might have married into the elite American military establishment, perhaps a graduate of West Point or nearby Annapolis, given TR's fondness for the navy. Alice could have followed the example of four of her relatives and married within the family.[1] No matter how large the theoretical pool, the actual pursuers for Miss Alice's hand had one thing in common: courage. The famous First Daughter scared away all but the most intrepid souls.

The paradox of Alice Roosevelt was that she should have been able to marry anyone. But because she was the president's daughter—with its visibility, political power, and her own attention-seeking, autonomous living—few men actually approached her. Edward Carpenter may have spoken for the many when he wrote to her: "Do you know I can't think of a blessed thing but the cold eye of your secretary reading this—it is enough to freeze the fingers off anybody."[2] Neither could Alice marry beneath her socially—and not only because she swore never to be poor. A titled European or a Democrat would not have gained the family's acceptance; the former because of her father's well-known aversion to marrying off Columbia's daughters to the sons of foreigners, and the latter because that would have been harboring the enemy. Nick Longworth's combination of bravery, political ambition, age, personality, and lineage thrust him to the forefront of her suitors.

The advice manuals warned women against men "much older than themselves, licentious men, drunkards, gamblers, cold-hearted tyrants, those whose work took them away from home frequently, and 'despisers of the Christian religion.'"[3] Alice chose a man who embodied at least five of these fatal flaws. Nick was much older, a womanizer, a lover of alcohol and gambling, and given to long hours on the floor of the House or on floors of houses other than his own. TR and Edith were conservative parents who believed that marriage was sacred, intended for procreation, and best done between a man and woman of similar backgrounds. Edith once warned Alice against Nick. "Your friend from Ohio," Edith told her, "drinks too much."[4]

By the turn of the nineteenth century, most Americans chose their own mates and married for love. The late 1800s saw a resurgence of the upper-class rage, begun in 1785, of marrying into aristocracy, one that did not taper off until after the 1956 union of Grace Kelly to Prince Rainier of Monaco.[5] While some people found the idea of an American girl becoming a real princess quite charming, others, especially Theodore Roosevelt, found the custom deplorable. "My father," Alice said, "wanted me to meet all sorts of people but not to marry them. A foreigner would have been bad, except perhaps an Englishman."[6] As long as his daughter married in the general realm of the society to which the family belonged, TR had no cause to fear the dissolution of Alice's inheritance through marriage. He knew the premium Alice placed on the things money could provide.

Plagued by mounting debts, Alice confided to her diary in 1902, "I swear to literally angle for an enormously rich man.... I cannot live without money." A year later, she pledged, "Vow. That I will accept the next man who proposes to me. I have run over a thousand over my allowance." More than enough money for the average American never stretched far in the company she kept. Love was most significant when she wished for reciprocity. "Please love me," she wrote over and over in secret diary letters to her various beaus. Alice implored Arthur Iselin, "Please, please love me.... Would you not love me enough and ask me to marry you?" And later she would write, "Nick love me be kind to me."[7]

How well did the twenty-year-old Alice understand love? Arguably, not at all. Much of love was a game of possession to her, even as late as the beginning of her relationship with Nick. After a date with a beau one evening in 1904, she wrote, "The moment he was gone I suddenly went crazy about him, about the same old feeling, and I treated him like a dog, that is to say I ignored him absolutely and I am sure he won't fall in love with me—and of course I want him to."[8] Despite the capriciousness of her youth, Alice had an internal scale of measurement that she called love, and this must be considered when evaluating the role it played in her decision to marry. Long after her husband's death, Alice said, "One of the reasons I married was because I felt I had to get away from the White House and my family. I didn't want to stay there. I wanted a place of my own...."[9]

These statements belie the intense feelings of love for Nick Longworth that Alice committed to her diary. She married him because he was much different from the Groton and Harvard "boys" she disparaged. His age—he was thirty-six years old in 1905—made him attractive, in part because of her own intellectual precocity and her admiration of the sophistication she saw at Newport. As Alice neared her twenties, her troubled relationship with her father stood as a poignant accent to the love she sought from her male friends. Edith and Theodore thought that a more mature man would settle their daughter down, so they fostered Alice's penchant for fatherlike figures. The press mirrored to Alice her place in society, and from it she received the approbation she rarely got from her father. Half of the clippings in her voluminous wedding scrapbook are about Theodore Roosevelt—having nothing whatsoever to do with Alice or her wedding—mute testimony to a daughter's admiration. Only there, in between its pages, could she fully capture her father's attention. She looked for a substitute in someone like Nick, fifteen years her senior, who would surely lavish her with unconditional love. How much of Nick's attraction for the First Daughter was based on age is hard to know, but that dynamic surely contributed to what even Alice later acknowledged as her "father complex."[10]

Alice also married Nick because he was a politician. She often castigated herself for not taking a serious interest in politics, but Alice underestimated her acumen. The political arena was the world she knew best. As a girl, Alice had met President Benjamin Harrison and decorated nursery chairs with flowers picked with British diplomat Cecil Spring-Rice. As a woman, she would thrive in the very middle of the national political scene from the Bull Moose years through Watergate. Nick spoke the language Alice had heard all her life, but this time, the mouthpiece was handsome and dashing. A eulogy for Nick summarized how Alice eventually came to feel about her husband: "He never grew serious about anything and his anger was only peevishness. He ate and drank abundantly and well, dressed in luxurious elegance, and viewed his political career as a source of amusement and a means of keeping himself occupied. . . . He was too intelligent and self-respecting to be blatant or hypocritical, or to have had any illusions about politics."[11]

This, however, was hindsight. Alice married Nick in part because of his derring-do, because he had lived his young life with a renegade spirit similar to Alice's, because it appealed to Alice's vanity to win the man who had unsuccessfully wooed her good friends Marguerite Cassini and Cissy Patterson, and because he was both wealthy and strong. Unlike the "Groton boys," Nick knew his way around politics, high society, and women. He stood up manfully under the derision of those members of the Fourth Estate who claimed he would always be Mr. Nicholas Roosevelt, playing second fiddle to his headstrong and famous wife. As many a younger competitor for Alice's favors had already discovered, her sharp tongue and disregard for social conventions augured poorly for a wife who should maintain and remain in her own separate sphere. Nick had the energy, intellect, and more than enough money to keep up with his intended.

Representative Longworth probably also had, as the press insinuated, a keen idea of the political mileage to be gained from marrying into the First Family. Alice enjoyed her position as First Daughter. There was no reason to believe she wouldn't also love being First Lady. In 1906, it was not a far-fetched idea that Nick might someday win the presidency, especially with the backing of his popular father-in-law. If Nick had to suffer through inti-mations that he only married Alice for her political worth, Alice, too, heard whispers that she wed Nick solely because he was the fastest ticket back into the White House.

Alice and Nick met, according to the most widely held story, about the time that Nick was introduced to Marguerite Cassini, probably during the winter season of 1903. Alice maintained that her father first told her about the "new congressman" from Ohio, who was "Harvard and the Porc," and who he thought "might amuse" her. Alice initially mentioned her future husband to her diary on her nineteenth birthday, in 1903, noting his pres-ence at a dinner she attended. He became a permanent fixture in Alice's diary around her twentieth birthday.[12]

Nicholas Longworth was born November 5, 1869, in Cincinnati, Ohio, the eldest child and only son of Nicholas and Susan Walker Longworth. The Longworth family moved imperturbably and confidently among other leading citizens: the Wulsins, the Tafts, the Graydons, the Fleischmanns. These were the founding families of Cincinnati's art, music, and charitable institutions, and social clubs such as the Pillars and the Queen City Club. Nick's father, Judge Longworth, had served briefly on the Supreme Court of Ohio and loved all outdoor sports. He invested in the relatively new pastime of amateur photography and dabbled in writing. His novels, *Silas Jackson's Wrongs* and *The Marquis and the Moon*, if not best sellers, at least secured his place among Cincinnati's men of letters. After his death from pneumonia at age forty-seven, the elder Longworth was remembered as someone who would "literally take the fur coat off his back for a friend whom he thought was in need...."[13]

Nick was the fourth generation of Longworths in Cincinnati. The family fortune accrued through real estate, viniculture, and the law. Appropriate to his station, Colie—the name the family used to distinguish Nick from his father—attended the opera and the theater, learned to speak fluent French, and received tutoring in the classics. Rookwood, the family estate, offered skating and fishing ponds, a herd of cattle, and apple orchards alongside the riding stable. Nick did not come of age in cosmopolitan New York or Washington as did his bride-to-be, but his education lacked for little nonetheless. The Longworth family summered at Newport and toured Europe in the autumns. They created a stir when they installed the first indoor arc lights in the area. Nick enjoyed the best his family could provide, aided by his mother and sisters, whose lives revolved around his needs. His youngest sibling, Clara, who as an adult became an accomplished Shakespearean scholar, wrote that "all that was best in life must be reserved for Colie," to whom the family referred adoringly as "the first born of Israel."[14]

When he was five years old, Nick began to study the violin. It became his lifelong avocation, and he was widely recognized as a gifted violinist. Cincinnati prided itself on possessing the most sophisticated musical community in the Midwest. The annual Cincinnati May Festival, begun in 1873, continues today. The festival brought some of the world's best talent to the city—composers, musicians, and conductors—and many of them stayed for part of the summer to teach at the Cincinnati College of Music. Nick absorbed the cultural atmosphere and likely took lessons from visiting professors; Leopold Stokowski called music Nick's "natural element."[15] Nick also played the piano expertly, composed pieces for violin and piano, and sang—often with lyrics he made up on the spot. Nick loved classical music best, especially Mozart, Vivaldi, Beethoven, and Brahms, but also enjoyed contemporary popular songs. In later life, Nick served as president of the Washington, D.C., Chamber Music Society and founded the Friends of Music in the Library of Congress.[16]

After preparatory school, Nick entered Harvard and graduated in the class of 1891. Scholarship was not his strong suit. Alice admitted that Nick "didn't quite gobble books the way we did."[17] He made friends easily, and the Porcellian Club welcomed him, making him a brother "Porc" to his future father-in-law. Alice recalled the premium her father placed on this. As a brotherhood of patrician white men, the club offered its members entrée to social and business opportunities later in life. During the college years, the Porc was the unexcelled leader among Harvard's many clubs, and as such, acceptance was the measure of the man. As "legacies," TR's sons Ted Jr. and Kermit were admitted. The Brotherhood of the Porcellian rejected the lanky undergraduate Franklin Delano Roosevelt, despite the fact that FDR's own father was a member. FDR called this exclusion the "greatest disappointment of my life."[18] Even though Nick was a midwesterner, his charm and his wealth—not to mention his solid C average—made him Porcellian material. He was also a gentleman athlete—rowing, riding, fencing, and playing tennis.

Nick spent one more year in Boston, at Harvard's law school, but returned as all good Buckeye sons did, to earn his LLB from the College of Law of the University of Cincinnati. He gained admittance to the bar in 1894, at age twenty-two. Nick's first legal problem was attending to his father's tediously tangled estate, and he soon found the conviviality of politics more to his liking. His political career began in 1897, when he joined the Young Men's Blaine Club, under the tutelage of Cincinnati political boss George B. Cox. After serving on the Cincinnati school board and the Republican National Committee, he spent two terms in the Ohio House of Representatives and another two in the state senate. He won election to Congress in 1902 and took the oath as a member of the Fifty-eighth Congress on March 4, 1903, just as the famous Alice Roosevelt was returning from Mardi Gras. Unlike Alice, Nick seldom challenged the rules. As *Leslie's Illustrated Weekly* put it in 1906, "His path has been lined with roses because of his money and family influence.... He turned to politics for diversion."[19]

Alice was not initially struck by Representative Longworth; after all, meeting him was her father's idea. Or perhaps it was that Nick was engaged to a hometown girl. In fact, Nick seems to have been deeply involved with several different women before Alice. Nick's reputation as Cincinnati's Don Juan was so well known that the city's matrons were watchful. One of his flames warned Nick: "Oh Boy, you've got a horrid lot to live down—so don't lose a minute's time in denying it. I've been fighting four battles here at home for my mother has been informed by many 'well wishers' of your 'past' and she pleads with me to see you in your true light."[20]

Nick was simultaneously involved in a longer and more significant liaison with Miriam Bloomer, whom he called Little Hooty. Their connection involved a level of intimacy impossible for Alice, living as she was in the public eye. The usual meeting place for Nick and Miriam was the Pillars, another private Cincinnati club. Nick cared enough for her to be seen in public with her on his home turf—but also to be vulnerable with her, to care about having hurt her (he sent her roses in apology), to be jealous of her, and to confess that he was "thoroughly swizzled. I have no doubt but that this state of mind makes me seem very ridiculous in your eyes; but you must try to treat it with the same philosophy as the Frenchman who, being informed that an acquaintance was desperately in love with his own wife, said— 'Tiens—C'est bizarre mais ce n'est pas un crime.'"[21]

Their relationship continued after Nick took up his place in the U.S. House of Representatives, and in the *New York Times* in 1907, she was described as "a former fiancé of Nicholas Longworth." "I'll come," Miriam promised Nick, "on the 4.30 train and you can meet me and we'll dine quietly any old place—for I'll have on a street dress and then if you like you can come out here with me and stay all night...." They remained friends even after Nick was married—Little Hooty was present at his White House wedding and the postnuptial dinner—but not long after she watched Nick marry Alice, Miriam suffered "a severe nervous collapse."[22] Habitual clandestine meetings in Washington and elsewhere put Nick in a league wholly apart from Alice. He had mastered the art of deception in relationships long before he knew the First Daughter.

The romance between Nick and Alice had to wait for both of them to fall in and out of love with other people. The 1903–1904 social season marked the creation of the Alice, Maggie, Charles, and Nick quartet. By January 1904, Alice had targeted a new crush in Charles de Chambrun. Unfortunately, so had Maggie Cassini. This ill-timed complication tried the friendship between the two women, which underwent further testing when Maggie swept Nick off his feet—after she was through with de

Chambrun. The society press and the Washington rumor mills made much of this intriguing set.

"Charly" de Chambrun was the new secretary at the French embassy. In her memoirs, Maggie painted a picture of the felicitous Frenchman: "He was the greatest fun...long as a rainy day and quite handsome except for an awkward walk. He had a crazy giggle which made you think him a fool till you discovered he was brilliant with an encyclopedic memory....When we danced he stepped on my toes. At tennis he never watched the ball, at bridge he failed to follow suit, always too busy laughing at some joke, his own or another's. And lazy! But he was charming, amusing, a promising diplomat, and soon was the center of our parties."[23] The four of them—the president's daughter and the Russian ambassador's daughter, the representative from Ohio and the French diplomat—made up a clique both powerful and exotic even for the capital city.

The month of January 1904 decided Alice's fate where the Frenchman was concerned. Even as she awarded him a heartlet in her journal, Alice watched as his relationship with Maggie deepened until she could not deny it. Her January 20 entry explains much about the state of her feelings:

Called on Mag Cassini and found her upstairs in a lightly scented bedroom in her wrapper, a gorgeous Chinese one. Dinner at Nick Longworth's. Mr. Aggasiz took me in. Nick Longworth on the other side. Chambrun talked to me afterwards. He doesn't feel a bit for me anymore—Not that he ever really did and when I am so devoted to him. John...and N.L. played and sang. We went on about 11:30 to the... dance. Auntie Bye receiving.... The men who were at dinner had a corking table.... I won fifty dollars from Nick whether Walter Luckerman had on a wig or not. He said I couldn't find out but I did. But the family heard and I got into hot water. Poor "lil" A. Danced madly until the finish. Really enjoyed myself. But I wish C de C would care for me. <u>dear</u> Charly.[24]

The next day's entry continues the tale. She had lunch with Nick at the House of Representatives then "went back to N.L.'s for an hour or so and then to tea at Mag Cassini's—great fun. . . . Had such a nice talk with C. de C [at a reception] . . . Mag sat next to N.L. at dinner and had talked to him afterwards until about 11:30. I am very much afraid he is quite devoted to her. And then she had nabbed C. de C. for a half hour conversation. He is so funny about her. Oh <u>dearest</u> Charly."[25]

There was still a bit of competition involved in her response to the situation, as though she were beginning to be torn between the men, or as though she were unhappy that either would be more interested in her girlfriend. Even as Charly held her interest, Nick spent an ever-increasing amount of time with them. Charly and Maggie quarreled when her father discovered the seriousness of Charly's intentions. Maggie then turned her gaze to Nick. At least Cissy was out of the picture, after her earlier flirtation with Nick. Cissy married the dashing womanizer Count Joseph Gizycki of Poland, thirty years her senior, in April 1904. The small wedding at her parents' Dupont Circle house was an indication of their disappointment in Cissy's choice.[26]

The trio of Alice, Nick, and Maggie beguiled the press and Washingtonians who enjoyed speculating which woman Nick would choose. They played together throughout the 1904 winter season, attending dinners, cotillions, skating and sleighing parties, taffy pulls, and sight-seeing trips to the House of Representatives, usually chaperoned by Nick's mother, Susan Longworth. By February, competition between the two young women for Nick's attention had intensified. "Once when within the same week," Maggie recalled, "we gave two dinners at the [Russian] Embassy with Nick at one and Mrs. Longworth, his mother, at another, the hullabaloo was really something. The papers rushed into stories about the marked devotion of 'the brilliant young Cincinnatian to the fascinating Countess Marguerite Cassini.' . . . Then Alice went out to Cincinnati for a visit and bang, around swung the weathervane again."[27]

In twos, threes, and fours they enjoyed great times through the spring of 1904. They spent many happy evenings about the town, ending often at Nick's Washington club, the Alibi, where, over the dinners he prepared, they dissected the evening's gossip. Nick's culinary specialty was "Toothsome Terrapin," and his hobby was wines—natural, given the Longworth family fame for the Catawba grape wines produced at Rookwood in his great-grandfather's time. The four of them developed their own private language, full of inside jokes and innuendoes. Nick and Alice, though, shared "a slashing wit," which bound them together appreciatively. In March, de Chambrun left for Paris. He wrote to Alice to remind her that the odds were uneven while he was gone. "Tell Nick, for goodness sake, to turn his attention to his Cincinnati constituents and that, when I come back in three weeks, I trust to find him exerting his energy and application to a closer attention to business." De Chambrun couldn't make up his mind about his favorite flirting partner: "Tell Mag she is a daisy, and please say many pleasant things to yourself from me," he encouraged Alice.[28]

The women quarreled before Alice's trip to Ohio. "I really like Margarite [sic] Cassini—but I don't think she knows what the words truth, honor and loyalty mean." Alice left out the details of the battle, but gave a hint of the cause in a later diary entry. "Why am I such a failure? I am not so much less attractive than many girls I know who have a very good time, and with my position as my father's daughter... I should have a more marvelous success but I certainly do not. Oh how I wish I did. Oh for money and self-assurance." Three days later, Alice was pining for something else. "How crazy I am about Nick," she wrote, putting words to the source of her altercation with Maggie. The Countess Cassini, for her part, explained, "It became more and more fun to tease my friends by trying to take their beaux away from them." Alice was falling in love with Nick, and Maggie failed to see or chose to not see. In her autobiography, the Russian attributed it to her penchant to view "only her own fun." Alice repeatedly asked Maggie whether or not Nick had proposed to her, and was placated in receiving a negative response from her friend. By May of 1904, though, the halcyon days were over: "Nick and Maggie out to Country Club again. She is going with him instead of riding with us.... I am sure she has him. N.B. Revenge on her.... Oh nasty Maggie I'll get even yet, see if I don't."[29]

The picture became more and more bleak. "Maggie was to have come and seen me this evening. I telephoned for her. They said she was at the Boardmans and when I telephoned there Josephine said she was out walking with Nick. She had met him in some square or other. In the first place I think it is a very cheap thing to do: to go out walking at night with a man. In the second place she should have let me know she wasn't coming...and thirdly...and not least importantly, I am furious with him for having misled her." Then she closed by swearing the same oath against Nick that she had against Maggie: "<u>Revenge</u>, N.L. <u>Retaliate</u>."[30]

Alice hedged her bets. One of her friends had been untrue to her, but she was protective of both of them just in case—until the next day brought devastating news of what had transpired in that park. As they sat and smoked up on the roof of the White House, Maggie confided to Alice that Nick had proposed to her. Although Maggie rejected him, Alice was hurt but philosophical. "Heigh-ho. He is the second person (French Charlie was the first) that I have vowed to have and she has reft from me so I suppose there will be a third....I don't think he should have been as nice to me as he has been, well, well, well." Theodore Roosevelt's daughter kept her sorrows to herself. No matter how deeply she felt her rejection and her sadness, she continued as though nothing had happened. The following day, she had lunch with Nick at the Alibi, and by the end of the month, the countess was stopping by for tea at the White House again. Maggie remembered that after her disclosure, "the inseparable twosome was no longer so inseparable.... We were still friendly, we still saw each other here and there. But the old intimacy disappeared."[31] Perhaps it is a measure of Alice's pain, or the revenge she swore, that she never once mentioned Marguerite Cassini in her own autobiography.

Alice tried to move on. Nick disappeared from her journal as she went about the business of being First Daughter, but she mentioned only one other, short-lived, crush. No other man caught her attention. Christmas Eve 1904 marked a turning point in their relationship. Nick telephoned the First Daughter, and they breakfasted together. Alice had "a delicious time" because "Nick...the liar said he loved me." The hopeful tone of her diary was justified, according to her chronicle of Boxing Day: "[H]ad a long talk with Nick...he made violent love [to me] all day long. Well! Well! Nick!" "Violent love" did not mean the same a hundred years ago as it does today, so it is difficult to know precisely what Alice meant, especially in light of a later—but suspect—statement that she had never kissed a man before she

Alice Hathaway Lee Roosevelt, Alice's mother, near the time of her engagement to Theodore Roosevelt

—◆—

BELOW: Auntie Bye and her "blue-eyed darling"

First Lady Edith Kermit Carow Roosevelt, Alice's stepmother

✦

Theodore Roosevelt, Alice's politician father, in a characteristic pose for the cameras and the crowds

The Roosevelt
family: Quentin,
TR, Ted, Archie,
Alice, Kermit, Edith,
Ethel, at Sagamore
Hill in 1903

Alice's bedroom at
the White House,
where she confided
her secrets to her
diary

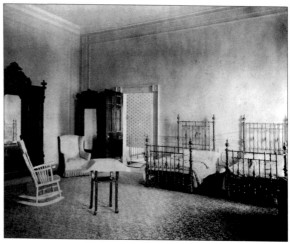

OPPOSITE: First Daughter
Alice Roosevelt

⊱◆⊰

Prince Henry of Prussia and Alice
at the launching of the kaiser's yacht,
the *Meteor*, Washington, 1901

A popular figure on
sheet music, Alice appears
in this selection as a Gibson
girl; patriotically flanked by
Rough Rider-like buglers;
and sharing billing with
Marguerite Cassini

Alice's trademark large hat is just visible in the center of the cameras in this newspaper cartoon.

A French chocolate card featuring the American Princess

A hand-tinted postcard of the First Daughter from 1904

Alice and Nick Longworth enjoying each other's
company on the Far Eastern trip

Watching the Sumo wrestling exhibition in Japan

Alice, parasol at her side, observing events in Japan

Eligible bachelor Representative Nicholas Longworth

ABOVE: Rookwood, the Longworth house in Cincinnati—Alice could never quite call it home.

Willard Straight, Alice's dear and witty friend

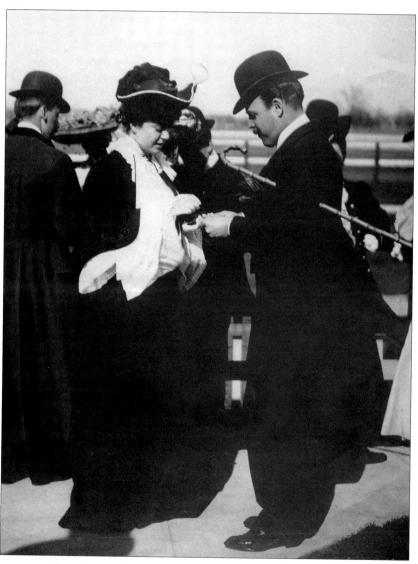

The First Daughter counting her winnings at the racetrack with
Representative Longworth, one of the series of photographs TR censored.

The White House bride with Manchu on her lap

ABOVE: The addictive
excitement of the Chicago
Coliseum during the 1908
Republican National
Convention

⊷◆⊶

Alice, age twenty-four,
resisting the effort to start
a draft for her father at the
1908 GOP convention

The Longworths keeping tabs on the enemy at the Democratic convention in Denver, 1908

—◆—

BELOW: Alice and Nick in 1911, stepping out as young swells in the nation's capital

Purchasing war bonds from the Girl Scouts, 1917

◈

BELOW: Quentin Roosevelt posing with his airplane, before his death behind enemy lines in France during World War I

TR without his glasses, as his family would have seen him.

had married. A diary entry for January 19, 1905, read, "Nick had a supper at his Alibi. . . . Nick and I in a very dark corner afterwards. It was quite wonderful but I know that I will wish I hadn't. I know he doesn't <u>really</u> care for poor little me."[32] Like most women, Alice governed herself by an internal scale. If she knew he truly loved her, she could allow more physical intimacy.

After that, Alice expected their relationship to be different. A woman named Beatrice caught Nick's fancy—or so Alice thought—and this threw her into a depression. She worried he was only "trying to be nice" to her and that he didn't care for her anymore. On the last day of January 1905, Alice concluded: "I know that Nick does not love me anymore—if he ever did—which I am not sure of, and he has made me love him. Oh, I love him so much."Alice swore revenge on Beatrice, but the same day she "reverted" because her "dear lamb" had come to tea at Auntie Bye's and taken her for a drive to explain the misunderstanding.[33] Such an explosion of fear, followed by a reconciliation, would become the pattern for their courtship and marriage. Their wooing was dazzling, destructive, seductive, and not unlike a roller coaster in its giddy ascensions and conspicuous declines.

"Dearest Little Alice," Nick wrote as she turned twenty-one in February 1905, "May I be permitted to call you 'Little Alice' this last time, for tonight at twelve o clock you will become of age and be an heiress and then I suppose you won't be little anymore." He included a photograph of himself as a birthday present, "scarcely an 'objet d'art' and cavilers might say by no means an 'objet de vertu' but at least it may serve to remind you sometimes of your devoted Nick."[34] Soon the couple had quarreled again. Alice was no longer sure she wanted to marry him. Was there an understanding between them at this point? Her fears battled with her professions of love: "Oh Nick I love you passionately Nick—I want to see you—have you with me always for every moment of this day and night for ever and ever." For months, she filled her journal with page after page of unsent letters to her beloved, concluding them all with "My Nick."[35]

In the late spring they were apart, but Nick's letters were mostly reassuring. He wrote in April of the "so many things I want to tell you and so many things I want you to tell me" that were difficult to commit to paper.

He wrote, too, that he was "wild to know what the President said of me," which was worrying despite his disclaimer: "not perhaps so much because he is the biggest man in the world as because he is the father of the most charming girl in the world." Alice wanted details of his social life. "I have not amused myself very much," Nick wrote from Cincinnati, "principally because the person I want to see is not here." By the end of April, he swore he was "longing to see you, honey. I keep missing you more and more all the time."[36]

In early June, Alice went to stay with Nick and his family. Their glorious time together marked another turning point in their relationship, evident in Nick's prose:

> My darling girl: It is useless for me to try to tell you how I miss you. It really seems as though the light had gone out of the world. I am in the depths of despondency and if it was more than three weeks longer I don't know what I should do. As it is I can't pull myself together a bit. You were more charming than ever here. You were sweet to everybody and everybody was crazy about you. There wasn't a minute that we were together that I didn't wish was an hour and not an hour that I was away from you that I didn't wish was a minute. It was a beautiful world when you were here....[37]

"I love you and I always shall," he concluded, and three days later, Alice "practically told Charlie [McCauley] that I am engaged to Nick." Earlier in the week she began an entry noting that "Father is making peace between Russia and Japan," and then went to matters more pressing: "With Nick and [a friend] at dinner—after the people left as usual I put on another [illegible] my pink wrapper and Nick when he was kissing and feeling me did an evil thing—but it was my fault. I have let him do so much . . . But it was terrible. We are actually engaged though of course we have been for some time practically so, and I love him more than anything else in the world."[38] Was whatever he did terrible because it hurt her in some way, or did she mean that it flew in the face of convention? Was it terrible because it happened before they had an officially announced (and therefore less likely to be retracted) engagement? What was different this time, when her last notation called what they did in the dark corner "wonderful"?

Throughout her adult life, Alice Roosevelt Longworth maintained that she did not like to be touched, hated to be kissed, and didn't particularly enjoy dancing because it put human bodies in too-close proximity. Perhaps when she was young she did enjoy it. If so, then somewhere in her later life she had a change of heart. It is possible that Alice suffered from what so many late-Victorian physicians warned of: "the brutal and impulsive behavior of husbands on their honeymoons."[39] If she built a resentment against Nick, borne of his selfishness, then this might explain some of the mistrust and unhappiness that would come to characterize their marriage.

Alice was sensitive enough to protocol that the terrible nature of the June event prompted her to write that she would regret it. Whatever they did was clearly not advocated by the social arbiters—mother and father uppermost—either because Nick would lose respect for her and then never marry her or because they were not properly engaged. Whatever it was, the evening of June 11, 1905, was a second instance of something physical between them that escalated the stakes. After the first, six months earlier, Alice considered whether or not she could or should marry Nick. After this June night, she felt herself engaged to be married—and he must have actually asked, and she must have responded positively, reading between the lines of his letter to her of June 20:

> My darling little girl: Your letter was the sweetest thing that ever came to me. I had been waiting for it so long that I almost feared it was not going to be like that.... But O Honey, when I did get it it made me feel prouder than anything in the world that you should say what you did, for it makes me think that I must be a pretty decent sort of a person when the most charming girl that ever lived really cares for me.... Alice, darling, I simply can't tell you in a letter what I want to. I am simply wrapped up in...love of you....[40]

While President Roosevelt monitored the peace process between Russia and Japan, his daughter kept a close watch on her fiancé as he went home to Cincinnati. "I am so desperately sorrowful—he is going to see all his old girls. I know [he] is—I can't bear it. He said he wouldn't the brute.... I can't live without him." To Alice's great relief, Nick returned to her without asking for a separation. They had much to discuss, for preparations for the East Asia trip had begun.

Alice wrote Auntie Bye all about her talk with the Tafts and their good advice as to what she ought to pack.[41] Her separation from the family began when Edith and TR left for Oyster Bay in late June. As she foundered in the unknown waters of emotional and physical love, and embarked upon a long, stressful tour halfway around the globe as her father's special emissary, Alice was without parental support. Because of her nervousness about Nick and the trip, she lost five pounds and suffered alternately from indigestion, toothache, and eczema. Nevertheless, Edith and TR went about their lives unconcerned: "My parting from my family...was really delicious," Alice wrote sardonically, "a casual peck on the cheek and a handshake, as if I was going to be gone six days. I wonder if they really care for me or I for them."[42] In Nick, Alice believed she had found someone who proved that he truly loved her, and gave her evidence of his affection. At least Auntie Bye seemed to approve of him, even if Edith did not.

Chapter 7

"When Alice Came to Plunderland"

THE TUMULTUOUS RELATIONSHIP between Alice and Nick took an unusual turn when President Roosevelt decided to take full advantage of his daughter's nascent diplomatic skills. In 1905, he was engaged in mediating peace between Russia and Japan, recently at war over lands they both claimed. The president wanted to send a high-level delegation to East Asia (the Far East, as it was then styled by Westerners), and decided to attach Alice as a goodwill ambassador. When Nick was chosen for the political junket, Alice readily consented. The trip would prove successful professionally—Alice charmed her hosts—and personally, for the trip cemented Alice and Nick's engagement. The last act of this journey was played out in the White House on February 17, 1906, with the wedding of Princess Alice to Congressman Longworth.

In 1905, President Theodore Roosevelt asked his daughter to be part of a multipurpose delegation from Washington to East Asia. Alice was thrilled.[1] Roosevelt wanted this mission to be part fact finding, part goodwill, and part saber rattling. Led by Secretary of War William Howard Taft, the assemblage left Washington with a large party of congressmen and their wives, newspaper reporters, and Alice. The group was bound ostensibly for an inspection tour of the Philippines but, because the trip coincided with Roosevelt's mediation of the Russo-Japanese war, Taft traveled to Japan to confer unofficially with Tokyo about the peace process.[2] TR directed Alice to continue to China in the midst of an anti-American economic boycott in order to reassure Peking personally of his goodwill. The First Daughter would have audiences with the mikado in Japan and the dowager empress in China. The delegation of seventy-five people included, among others, Senator Francis G. Newlands and Representatives Frederick H. Gillett, Herbert Parsons, Charles Curtis, Bourke Cochran, and most important of all for Alice, Nick Longworth.[3]

Alice spent all of 1904 in the United States, and so she looked forward to seeing new lands and being away from home for the four-month-long journey. Auntie Bye cautioned her before she left, "Don't just for the sake of a sensation carry your complications too far! There are plenty of excitements that will come to give interest and not leave regrets so be careful."[4] The admonition seems not to have been ignored, for Alice amazed everyone with her generally polite and considerate behavior on the trip.

Alice, her chaperone Mrs. Francis G. Newlands, Secretary Taft, her friends Mabel Boardman and Amy McMillan, and a few others left Washington early on July 1, 1905. They stopped first in Chicago, where they received the news of the death of the venerable secretary of state, John Hay. Alice worried the journey would be canceled because TR might need Taft back in Washington, but President Roosevelt assured Taft that the delegation must continue. The train rolled on toward the coast. It was the first time Alice had been west of the Mississippi.

Californians were interested in the First Daughter, and she was ready for adventure. She met influential San Franciscans and lunched under the giant redwoods as a guest of the Bohemian Club. Alice played poker in the evenings, and papers reported that she escaped her chaperone for a brief excursion through the fringes of infamous Chinatown—although she wrote to her father after sailing for Hawaii, "I did not go to Chinatown in San Francisco and treated with scorn all invitations to do so." She didn't need to go there to seek adventure because, as she told TR, there was "an opium den" and "a gambling place" on board ship. She promised him that she had frequented "neither one of them!" Taft seconded her good behavior, telling his wife, Helen, "Alice conducts herself very well. She is modest and girllike. I quite like her."[5]

Helen Taft was sharper-edged than her affable husband. She found his assessment difficult to take. Her hands were full journeying across Europe with their sick children rather than on the junket with her husband, where she would much rather have been. Adding insult to her daily lot of frustration was the time she tried to hold a train for the late arrival of her luggage and could not do it on her own. "I am Mrs. William Howard Taft of Washington.... My husband is the Secretary of War of the United States." The stationmaster only looked at her blankly. It was not until she said, "You must have heard of him. He's traveling now with Miss Alice Roosevelt," did the stationmaster spring to attention, hold the train, accompany her out, and carry her luggage aboard. Her friends teasingly referred to her afterward as "<u>The</u> Mrs. Taft whose husband was traveling with Miss Alice Roosevelt." From that moment on, the only references Helen Taft made to her husband about the First Daughter were derogatory.[6]

Elsie Clews Parsons, wife of Representative Herbert Parsons, shared Mrs. Taft's feelings about the delegation's most famous member. In her memoir, Parsons recalled "rubberneck" crowds anxious to see Alice. "We had a chance fully to appreciate for the first time what an attraction for the American public Alice, as everybody called her, was. To many, perhaps to most, Alice <u>was</u> the party. This was so outside as well as inside the country, before the trip, during the trip, and after the trip. Many times after our return, the only question that was asked me of experiences and impressions was 'How did you like Alice?' "[7]

After joining with the rest of the delegation, the party sailed on the *Manchuria* on July 8. Alice reported to her father that they had a "very cheerful time" on the way, with good companions at their table, including Nick Longworth. Alice gave the inside scoop to TR about her fellow passengers. She wrote him that she invited "the congressional dames" to tea in her room "to placate them and make them love the trip. They are pretty terrible, most of them," Alice confided, especially one woman "whose color comes in a box and she always wears a dainty ribbon tied here and there to match it."[8] After days, they docked at Honolulu and, Alice wrote Edith, were met by boats "with bands of such fascinating Hawaiian music." They toured a sugar plantation ("just like the ones I had seen in Cuba") and refinery, went sight-seeing, "swimming and surf riding" ("which was great fun"), and danced the hula. Alice loved the "strenuous day," despite being "nearly suffocated" in thirty to forty leis "reaching from my neck to almost my knees—and for politeness sake I couldn't take them off." Back on board the *Manchuria,* the delegation began the ten-day trip to Tokyo to pay their respects to the Japanese. On July 24, they docked in Yokohama, which was, Alice enthused, " *'banzai, banzai, banzai'* all the way."[9]

The American minister to Tokyo, Lloyd Griscom, met the excited travelers. He considered "the pick of Congress crossing the Pacific to survey our outlying possessions" astonishing. "Ten years ago," he mused, "this would have seemed a fairy tale."[10] Griscom, an able and tactful diplomat, intercepted the Japanese plan of having Alice stay at the Shiba Rikyu, one of the royal palaces, because "it might be embarrassing for the President of a democracy to have his daughter accorded the honors of a royal princess," and instead made sure that Alice stayed at the embassy. Griscom believed that "the Japanese were firmly convinced that Alice was the Princess Royal of America" and so, he wrote, "Our journey to Tokio was a triumph." The Japanese lined the roads, waving American flags and cheering for Alice, "while the women bowed double again and again. Alice clutched my arm," the minister recalled, "and exclaimed 'Lloyd, I love it! I love it!' " A host of Japanese officials met them in Tokyo, including Prince Tokugawa, and members of the war department. Taft wrote his wife that they dined that night with the prime minister at a banquet given by the Nagasakis "in honor of Alice and me."[11]

Alice enjoyed seeing the lands she had read about as a girl materialize before her eyes just as much as she liked the attention. She wrote her father that "we have seen Geisha dancing, wrestling, jiu jitsu, fencing, and acting—I don't think it would be possible to see more in six weeks than we put into six days!" In her memoirs, she described the cycle of diplomatic entertaining: lunch with Prince and Princess Fushimi, a reception for Count Matsukata and Count Inouye, a dinner given by the businessmen of Tokyo, lunch with the minister of war, standing in a reception line with Princess Nashimoto and Princess Higashi-Fushimi where the Japanese women filing past curtsied to her as well. Baron Albert d'Anethan, the Belgian dean of the diplomatic corps, recorded this incident: "At a garden party given at the American Legation, the daughter of the President was paid homage next to and on the same level as the Princesses Fushimi and Hashimi." At the same garden party, Alice presided over a table at which sat Prince Fushimi, Princess Higashi-Fushimi, Marquis Oyama, Count Inouye, and Baron d'Anethan. Regardless of the demands that leading such a gathering made on the twenty-one-year-old, in later years, Alice always remembered the amusing sight they made: "All the Japanese ladies wore big floppy hats and carried parasols.... We look[ed] like a slightly stoned version of the Ascot scene from *My Fair Lady.*"[12]

Alice recognized that the ebullition of Japanese officials sprang from their high expectations of the peace talks: "Not only the Government, but the man in the street was interested in and friendly to the Americans as well. Crowds followed us everywhere.... They cheered when the American Secretary of War went out on the balcony to wave good-bye—they cheered the daughter of the American president when she appeared—and then they cheered us all over again." It was, for the Japanese, an "unparalleled opportunity to cultivate American good will," Griscom thought.[13] Japan counted on America to meet its demands for control over Korea, the Manchurian railways, and the island of Sakhalin. In early May, when Taft and TR cemented the itinerary, Roosevelt knew that the Russian ambassador to the United States, Count Arturo Cassini, was "having a fit about Taft stopping at Japan on his way to the Philippines."[14] Roosevelt hoped the peace settlement would gain a balance of power in East Asia, but his sympathies lay more with Japan than Russia.

The Americans met the mikado on July 26, the morning after they arrived in Tokyo. Presented to the emperor in groups, they bowed three times and repeated the procedure in another room, where the crown princess received them in place of the ailing empress. After a luncheon given by the emperor, Taft informed his wife that "Alice Roosevelt, Griscom and Mrs. Griscom and I went up and were received by the Emperor and the Princess, and the Emperor seemed to be in a very great good humor."[15] The emperor sought to influence the outcome of the peace treaty through his hospitality toward the American guests. He seated Alice on his right, "although, of course," Alice told her father, "the conversation was chiefly about you...." The emperor's desire to impress his important American guests explains the rare honor he accorded them by allowing them to see his private garden, "hitherto never exhibited to foreigners." It also explains why, according to Taft, "the Prime Minister said that he was very anxious to have an interview with me...." The unplanned meeting resulted in "virtually a secret treaty whereby Roosevelt agreed that Japan was to absorb Korea."[16]

Leaving Tokyo for Kyoto, the delegation enjoyed more admiring Japanese crowds. Taft recounted the scene for his wife: "I have never seen such a popular tumult and gathering.... Every member of the party was cheered to the echo, especially Alice...there were cheers and cheers and cheers... from Tokio to Yokohama...whenever we stopped at a provincial capital they brought in presents for Alice Roosevelt and me and that continued until 1:00 the next morning when we reached Kioto."[17] Alice was showered with so many gifts that her friend the interesting Willard D. Straight referred to her as "Alice in Plunderland."[18]

The importance the Japanese and Chinese placed on family and tradition made Alice a particularly effective goodwill ambassador. Griscom remembered the bouquets thrown to "the daughter of the Peacemaker," and he believed that "never had there been such a demonstration for foreigners." Other members of Griscom's staff wrote privately, "[T]he Japanese did wonders for them and the whole show was a very great success. Miss Roosevelt did her part very well and made a great big hit with both Japanese and foreigners. I never saw the Japanese crowds loosen the manner they did this time—wild cheers and great crowds everywhere." Alice conceded, "No people have ever been treated with greater consideration and kindliness than we were by the Japanese, not only Mr. Taft and myself, but the entire party." "I don't know what would be left of you," Alice wrote TR, "if you had come out here!"[19] The First Daughter wore "the Japanese national costume" on her visit to the wife of Marshal Oyama, further endearing her to her host country.

After the signing of the Treaty of Portsmouth on September 5, 1905, a Japanese newspaper commented on the significance of the trip to Japan: "Miss Alice Roosevelt, upon whose intelligence and resolute character the Americans pride themselves, frequently renders assistance to the President in delicate missions where tact and diplomacy are required. Some months ago Miss Roosevelt...was received in Tokio by the Emperor and Empress with the highest honors. This visit must be considered as one of the happy preliminaries of a peace so swiftly concluded."[20]

Amid more cheering crowds, the delegation left Japan for the Philippines—and Taft's real reason for the trip. His mission was an inspection tour of the Philippines, but he also hoped to influence the legislators who accompanied him. He had spent almost four years as the civilian governor of the islands and was consequently an advocate of Philippine advancement. Taft wanted to lower the 1902 Philippine tariff and grant a greater measure of self-governance to the American protectorate. To facilitate their education, the travelers listened to shipboard lectures on Filipino economy and history. Mr. Taft sincerely hoped to enlighten the congressmen so they would vote to "support measures of benefit to the archipelago." Taft realized that Roosevelt wanted to inspire the Filipinos by sending Alice, so "that he might show to the people of the islands his interest in them and his confidence in their hospitality and cordial reception of his daughter."[21] She won international praise for her conduct in the Philippines where, as a representative of the U.S. government, she spent most of her time in semiofficial tasks.

Alice and Taft spent much of their ten days in Manila on the familiar round of receptions, banquets, speeches, balls, and information-gathering side trips. For the people they met, though, their visit was something special. One American soldier stationed there wrote his mother that he was expecting "to have a swell time for a few days" because of the Taft party and "big naval parade" in their honor.[22] Ten thousand people marched past the reviewing stand and attended a reception at the Malacañan Palace where the First Daughter "stood for hours with the [Governor Luke E. and his wife] Wrights and Mr. Taft, all of us literally dripping, while we shook hands with the hundreds of guests."[23] Students at various schools showed off their accomplishments to President Roosevelt's daughter. With some of the women of the delegation, Alice sat in on a meeting of the island's women's club. Before they left Manila for a two-week tour of the other islands, the Filipinos hosted a ball for Alice. "The eyes of the whole world are upon her," according to the *Washington Post*, "representing as she does not only the Chief Executive of our nation, but the typical American girl." The *New York Times* confirmed that Alice wore a native gown to "the most elaborate affair in the city's history ... which was presented to her by several Filipino women, who were occupied three months in making it."[24]

On August 14, Taft made mention to his wife of yet "another important entertainment," that he attended, "a dance and reception given by the Filipino ladies to Alice Roosevelt." Taft wrote that "Alice was promptly on time at nine o'clock and was gracious and courteous." Rear Admiral Enquist of the Russian navy and his staff made unusual and no doubt insistent guests at the ball. Enquist was there to lobby Taft concerning his ships, which were being forcibly held in Manila after a battle with Japan. The attention to the First Daughter caused the *Washington Post* to note slyly, "It is a little trying on the limelight artist to keep a focus on Oyster Bay and Manila at the same time."[25]

Alice spent the next fortnight spreading American goodwill around remote areas of the Philippine Islands. On Panay, the delegation toured a sugar mill and listened to appeals from the local populace to remove the high U.S. tariff on sugar. They dined in Iloilo and left the next day for Bacolod on the island of Negros. There, Alice and the other women brave enough to have traveled through the rough waters drove around the island with the local governor's wife. Sailing southward, the party reached Sulu, where it was rumored that the sultan proposed to Alice, declaring "that his people wished her to remain among them." As it meant joining his harem, Alice declined.[26] At Camp Keithly, Alice stayed with the officers' families in their bamboo houses before leaving at dawn the next morning to journey eighteen miles to Camp Overton in "mud to the horses' knees, ruts to the hubs of the wheels, and miles of bamboo corduroy that consisted mainly of holes."[27] After more island-hopping, the excursion returned to Manila, from there to sail for Hong Kong.

Episcopalian Bishop Charles H. Brent of the Philippines, who met with the Americans to discuss the fate of church lands and to argue for greater self-governance for the Filipinos, believed that Alice's visit helped to cement the ties between the two peoples: "The very fact that our democratic system forbids the transmission of hereditary glory, or the reflection of official character even from parent to child, made the incident even more striking in the minds of a people who hold domestic ties in high esteem, and who were ready to be influenced by the daughter of her father...."[28] Although the bishop appreciated the visitors' earnestness and their willingness to learn from and about the Filipinos, it was not enough to propel Congress into action on behalf of the islands.

The delegation left Manila on August 31 and disembarked to the cheers of crowds in Hong Kong three days later. While she visited the British colony, Alice decided that she wanted to see Canton, despite the Chinese boycott of American goods that threatened Sino-American relations. The embargo damaged U.S. trade and worried Washington. President Roosevelt attempted to mitigate the excesses of the American Immigration Bureau officials, as the Chinese blamed the unequal enforcement of U.S. immigration laws for their woes. The boycott had originated in that port city. Anti-American sentiment was violent in Canton at the time, and so the women of the party were prohibited from landing.[29]

It is unclear whether Alice actually ventured into Canton. In her autobiography she maintained that she coaxed an American gunboat captain to take them to the island of Shaneen, just across the narrow canal from Canton. There, she wrote, "only an occasional coolie on the opposite bank shook his fist at us." Her friend, actor and official photographer Burr McIntosh, recalled that the women were "strongly advised" to stay on British soil. "At Hongkong there were rumors of bitterness against the party at Canton, where already the city was placarded with signs bearing the Portrait of Miss Roosevelt in a sedan chair, being carried by four Turtles in place of coolies. This is a threatening insult...but Miss Alice wanted to see Canton and that settled it." According to Alice, she, Nick, and a few other intrepid travelers made it back from Canton unscathed.[30]

The poster was an attempt by the boycott organizers to convince the rickshaw drivers, who were of the coolie (or laboring) class, not to transport Alice. The turtles stood for henpecked husbands and were meant to shame the drivers into refusing to carry the Americans. Alice's visit had an important effect on the boycott, for it led to a split among the ranks of organizers. Some argued for increasing their visibility while the American press was present to report it. Others believed they would sooner win their demands if they ceased demonstrating in honor of the First Daughter. Their disagreement allowed American Foreign Minister W. W. Rockhill to win from Prince Ching an edict calling for an end to the boycott. The poster showed the strength of Alice's symbolism, for there was no doubt that the woman in the placard was Alice Roosevelt. Nothing daunted, Alice brought a copy home as a souvenir, after she intervened to save the lives of the poster artists for their ridicule of a foreign visitor.[31]

The delegation left Hong Kong safely. Taft and most of the party boarded a return ship to the United States. Alice, her chaperone and friends, Nick Longworth and a few other congressmen—with the inevitable reporters—continued on to China, where President Roosevelt calmed the diplomatic and economic waters by sending his daughter to visit Tz'u Hsi (Cixi), the formidable dowager empress of China. In Peking Alice stayed with the Rockhills for one night, then left the next afternoon for an audience with the dowager empress at her summer palace, followed by lunch featuring "Snow-flake Shark's Fins." Alice spent the night in Prince Ching's palace and had an entire hall to herself. The audience with the dowager empress occurred early the next morning. The rest of the delegation had to drive out from Peking at dawn, arrayed in their best clothes, and even then, only the highest ranking members of the group were allowed to see the aging and powerful Tz'u Hsi.[32]

Mrs. Rockhill presented Alice first. After she and the others had made their three curtsies (or bows), the women of the party left to dine with the Empress of the East and the Empress of the West. Tz'u Hsi joined them after lunch to distribute expensive presents. She spoke through an interpreter, Dr. Wu Ting Fang, the international attorney and scholar who served as foreign minister to the United States from 1897 to 1902 and 1907 to 1909.[33] Suddenly, Alice recalled, Wu "turned quite gray, and got down on all fours, his forehead touching the ground." He continued to interpret, lifting his head only to speak. Theodore Roosevelt, when questioned about it later by Alice, decided that Tz'u Hsi might have humiliated Wu "to show us that this man whom we accepted as an equal was to her no more than something to put her foot on—that it was a way of indicating that none of us either amounted to much more than that in her opinion."[34] After Tz'u Hsi left, the party strolled through her gardens. All except for Alice, who led the way seated in a royal sedan chair held aloft by eight bearers. She laughed as her friends teased her.

The American newspapermen showered the First Daughter with exorbitant praise, despite the perilous proximity to "undemocratic" behavior. The *New York Times* rhapsodized, "It is all very well to preserve the majesty of the law, which knows no distinction of persons; of the social conventions, which leave no room for an American Princess. But even among us there are public and private persons of both sexes and the President's daughter has an individual quality which the most rabid Americanism must recognize." The American Princess spent the rest of her time in China entertaining diplomats and high-ranking Chinese so that Alice's only complaint was the lack of time for sightseeing.[35]

Alice and her party traveled next to Korea on the battleship *Ohio*. The American minister, Edward Morgan, took them by special train from the coast to Seoul. Alice's memories were of a Korea "reluctant and helpless...[and] sliding into the grasp of Japan. The whole people looked sad and dejected, all strength seemed to have been drained from them." Alice lunched with the Korean emperor and the crown prince, received the Korean cabinet, and was entertained "industriously" by Korean and Japanese officials. According to her friend Willard Straight, vice consul and secretary to the American minister in Seoul, they "came, saw, and conquered....[They] were treated with more consideration than has ever been shown visiting royalty before....These people are looking for straws just now and the Roosevelt trip looked like a life preserver...." The Koreans hoped the United States would compel the Japanese to keep their promise of Korean independence. It was not to be. Alice stayed in the peninsula ten days and by the time she left was "more than fed up with official entertaining, with being treated, one may say, as a 'temporary royalty.'"[36]

Straight, a talented amateur artist, tried his hand at doggerel in an attempt to capture something of Alice's visit. The poem also conveyed his feelings of righteous fury as the Japanese "murdered" Korea, his simultaneous vexation at the Koreans' inability to overcome internal corruption enough to help themselves, and his conviction that Alice represented their last chance:

> When Alice came to Plunderland,
> The Crown Prince sought her lily hand,
> The Emperor had a pipe
> Dream that this was where his native land
> Could shake the Japs forever and
> Secure a friendship ripe
> With father.
>
> But now there's trouble brewing, for
> The Emperor doth reign no more,
> The Japanese are out for wealth,
> They're not in business for their health.
> The Koreans wail, "What can we do?
> Our clothes is picked, our watches, too
> Our country's in receivers' hands.
> We've neither graft nor fees,
> Since Alice came to Plunderland
> We've nothing left to 'squeeze'."[37]

Alice and her companions returned to Japan on September 28, 1905, three weeks after the Treaty of Portsmouth that ended the Russo-Japanese War had been signed. This time they stayed almost fifteen days, long enough to tour the national shrines and historic sites. Official entertaining decreased because the Japanese blamed President Roosevelt for the unsatisfactory conclusion of the peace treaty. While they retained control of Korea, the Japanese returned Sakhalin to Russia without receiving an indemnity. This, a colleague wrote to Straight, the Japanese blamed on the United States because "caricatures of Roosevelt were displayed in the street" and the anti-American sentiment exploded in a series of riots. There was "not a *banzai* to be heard. I have never seen a more complete change," Alice recalled. "We were told that if anyone asked, it would be advisable to say that we were English." Plainclothes policemen accompanied Alice and her friends during this return trip.[38]

Not everyone displayed anger, however. Alice shrewdly noted that the anti-American feeling was strongest with the Japanese people, not the government officials. And it wasn't universal. She received a reassuring note from a girls' school: "To our great regret, we have learned that during the recent riot in Tokyo some of your countrymen were insulted, and also some Christian churches were burned by the mob. But the fact is that they did not know what they were doing, and we sincerely hope that your countrymen will not misunderstand us on account of incidents of this nature." Certainly this letter represented the views of only some Japanese citizens. The writers made a comparison that other denizens of the Land of the Rising Sun would have found repulsive: "We all appreciate with gratitude what America has done for us since the coming of Commodore Perry. What your distinguished father has done at this time will be remembered forever in Japan."[39]

The letter she received from "Russian women" was more fervent. "We, Russians, love you dear Miss Alice, with all our heart, as the daughter of the one who does all his best to get peace and give us the peace of soul and of mind!" Patriotically, they asserted that "Russia is not exhausted and would find means to continue this war, but we are morally tired of this blood being shed on the fields of the far East." They wanted Alice to pass along their thanks for President Roosevelt's assistance. The Russians, who had lost militarily at Port Arthur and at Mukden, were aided in their peacemaking efforts by the fact that Roosevelt's overarching goal was a balance of power.[40]

Those observers not watching the foreign diplomacy were keeping an eye on a certain Ohio congressman. Nick, seeking privacy, was not always easy to find. At the first port of call—Hawaii—he and Alice, the Newlandses, and a few other junketeers lingered and had to scrounge a skiff to take them out to the *Manchuria* before they were left behind. Mr. Taft and Mrs. Newlands occupied an uncomfortable position. They were charged with looking after the President's daughter. Taft had the job because he was head of the delegation and because TR was a friend. Mrs. Newlands was an experienced chaperone, acceptable both to First Daughter and First Lady. The secretary of war also controlled, to the extent possible, the publicity surrounding the trip. Taft's longtime acquaintance with the Longworth family and his role of elder statesman made him further responsible to fellow Cincinnatian Susan Longworth, Nick's mother, for any potential shipboard scandal.

Alice knew that the East Asia congressional junket would serve as an alembic: so much time together in an unfamiliar setting would solidify her relationship with Nick or dissolve it. She worried about their behavior and was "terribly afraid that it will get out about my being too obviously with Nick." Nick was along because of his seat on the House Foreign Affairs Committee. He said he wanted a firsthand look at the tariff situation, the Hawaiian labor problem, and the U.S. occupation of the Philippines. The press and most of America were hoping to see Nick's commitment to a different sort of foreign affair. REPRESENTATIVE LONGWORTH TO GO ALONG—TROPICAL ROMANCE ANTICIPATED, one headline blared.[41]

International reporters chronicled all of her movements during the trip, but no journalist wrote as frankly about the relationship between the First Daughter and the congressman as William Taft did to his wife, Helen. No reporter had Taft's inside position, nor could anyone writing for the public allow themselves Taft's candor about the relationship between his two fellow travelers. Taft had a better news source than journalists: Alice's traveling companions Mabel Boardman and Amy McMillan. They gathered information on the indefatigable First Daughter's emotional state for the secretary. He then wrote to his wife: "Mabel Boardman told me that Alice told her sister that she and Nick were engaged; they are a great deal together but Nick impresses no one with his sincerity. I don't think the engagement is much more binding than a Kentucky engagement. I quite like Alice—she is . . . straightforward and does not appear to be spoiled. In certain respects she is younger than her years. She is quite amenable to suggestion and I have seen nothing about the girl to indicate conceit or a swelled head. A broader, better man than Nick could wield a very beneficial influence over her. Certainly his is not for her good."[42] As Taft noted, "Alice likes to smoke cigarettes—indeed she is quite nervous unless she has a chance after a meal. She likes strong drink occasionally and Nick always helps her, though such a habit ought not to be formed in one as highly strung as she is."[43]

Taft liked Alice, and she for her part was "really quite devoted" to "Uncle Will," at least then. He exercised very little discipline over her and was seldom out of sorts. She remembered never having "the least awe of him. I always felt that I could 'get away with' whatever it was he objected to." Taft did rein in Alice in protocol matters, insisting once that she host a ladies' luncheon for the congressional wives of the party. Taft also delivered one or two "curtain lectures" to the First Daughter, "more in sorrow than in anger," and only because he felt keenly his responsibility to the president.[44]

Alice lived a fine line between being consumed with (as yet unannounced) love and being the First Daughter. She still doubted Nick's constancy. Her worries about his behavior and about public and familial reaction, considering the rocky course of their courtship en route to Asia, were well founded. She faced the daily temptation to be alone with Nick, but then she would abrogate her duties as her father's ambassador. Because she was not a private person on the East Asia junket, it was doubly difficult to court and be courted. The intimate task of finding out whether or not she and Nick could make agreeable lifemates had to be conducted, out of necessity, under public scrutiny, which, given their status, may have been the best possible rehearsal. They spent a great deal of time together, but her journal does not specify how much of it was alone. They had Spanish lessons one day; the next, they and some other shipmates played cards before the evening dance; the following morning was filled with the official photograph shoot. The difficulty for Alice was clear to Taft, as he complained to his wife: "It has not always been easy to secure from Alice the graciousness that our treatment here deserves, because she seems to be so much taken up with Nick. She becomes absorbed in him and pays but little attention to anybody else. She is however amenable to persuasion and has quite winning ways when she devotes her attention."[45]

There were enough mornings and afternoons and evenings with Nick to make the secretary of war uneasy. Had they been aware of Taft's severe misgivings, Edith and TR would have flinched. "Nick and Alice are doubtless engaged," the secretary wrote Helen Taft. "They occasionally quarrel—Alice enjoys the society of some college boys in the interval and then they make up. Nick has much control over Alice but I can't think either is so in love with the other that there is any assurance of their happiness in married life. Alice is not a bad girl—she has good generous impulses but she lacks discipline greatly."[46] If Alice portrayed the woman without a care for Nick's sake, inside she felt melancholic. When the couple fought, Alice, despite her outward appearance, had the worst of it, for she had the most invested in the relationship.

Taft's astute comment on Nick's control over Alice was borne out by her keening in late July: "Oh my heart, my heart, I can't bear it. I don't know what is the matter with me. Nick...looked at me...as if he didn't like me, and said he wouldn't play with me tomorrow morning and I feel as if I might die. He will go off and do something with some horrible woman, and it will kill me. It can't make any difference, I can forgive him anything, anytime, but it hurts like it hurts. Nick, love me, be kind to me—I am crying—I am crazy with grief. Oh my blessed beloved one, my Nick." Alice, stoic daughter of stoic parents, pushed aside her own grief in public to assuage Taft's fears that her divided attention would undermine the elaborate protocol necessary to their endeavor. On her conduct in Japan, a Nagasaki newspaper reported, "Miss Roosevelt charmed us all, as she seems to have a way of doing wherever she goes; simple and unaffected in dress and manners, she reminds me of her father, and she has the same cordial handshake, the same way of giving you her undivided attention for the time that you are speaking with her."[47] What such a double existence cost Alice emotionally is impossible to measure.

By mid-August, there was nothing Taft could do. The engagement, while not officially announced, was recognized by the congressional travelers as authentic. Taft still hoped it might be a short-lived tropical romance, but, of course, the truth is that Alice had fallen for Nick months before the ship set sail. Still, Taft maintained that Nick liked the "prestige" of being coupled with the president's daughter more than anything else.[48] The press speculated on the courtship, but wrote little, as it could secure no confirmation. Instead—a picture being worth a thousand words—newspapers published photographs from the junket, always careful to print those in which both Nick and Alice appeared.

Alice's diary grew ever more sparse throughout the trip, until she stopped writing altogether. One more piece to the puzzle of their relationship exists, though—a letter from Alice to Nick while they stopped in Korea. Because neither left the delegation for any length of time, Alice probably wrote to Nick because they were not speaking. The letter, dated Thursday, September 1905, is on letterhead that reads AMERICAN LEGATION, SEOUL, KOREA.

> Your losing your temper and getting these uncontrollable dislikes for me has got to stop. You say that it is because I get on your nerves by doing and saying foolish and rather conspicuously common things— if that is the case it is very decidedly the pot calling the kettle black as no one could accuse you of over-refinement in any direction—either in words or deeds. [When] you left this morning and I asked if you felt any better about me you said "no I do not" in a tone of such frank dislike and with an expression of such active disgust that if I did not love you so much would make me never wish to see you again. Indeed I can not help feeling hurt in what you are trying to bring about— trying... something which will give you an excuse to [get] out in as gentlemanly a manner as possible of what you consider a most unpleasant hole. I shall not give you that excuse unless you consider this... sufficient. But your behavior has been ridiculous and most contemptible—I am disappointed.[49]

This is a unique letter. Her rare display of force was in stark contrast to Nick's second thoughts. If Nick wanted to be released from the engagement, Alice was not ready to let him go regardless of the fact that she thought he disliked her and was disgusted by her. Perhaps the vision before her eyes was her stepmother's unmarried sister, Aunt Emily Carow, whom Alice called "a horrid old maid."[50] Maybe the immaturity of which Taft wrote met the specter of spinsterhood on that trip. For all his faults, Nick would save her from being an "old maid" and, if she gambled right, might return her to the White House as First Lady. Alice had told Griscom she wanted to marry a man who would be president and prominent politically for she hated to look forward to the obscurity into which she would fall after her father ceased to be president. But the content of the letter and the tone pervading it prove how deeply the wounds ran. In comparison to her parents, Alice feared she lacked the moral fiber to contribute to a marriage like theirs. Nick dominated Alice's emotions, unhealthily, Taft thought. He swore that he would "never believe that they are permanently engaged until I hear that they are married."[51]

The diplomatic mission of the trip had been a success in more ways than one, as had been Theodore Roosevelt's efforts to mediate peace between Russia and Japan. TR summed up his position on his handling of the Russo-Japanese War in a posterity letter sent to Alice in Tokyo on September 2, 1905, the day the peace treaty was signed. The president maintained he did not seek the prominence that came to him because of the settlement, but that in the end it was a good thing he had chosen to moderate the peace. Further, TR complained to Alice, "It is enough to give anyone a sense of sardonic amusement to see the way in which the people generally, not only in my country but elsewhere, gauge the work purely by the fact that it succeeded. If I had not brought about peace I should have been laughed at and condemned. Now I am over-praised." This letter foreshadows the role that Alice would play in her father's life after her marriage, when he increasingly sought her advice and discussed political situations with her. Edith, meanwhile, had been sending Alice letters full of political news ever since she stepped on board the *Manchuria*.[52]

The First Daughter and her entourage sailed for the United States from Yokohama on October 13, enduring "a rough passage." As the trip wound to its close, two stories inspired national gossip. Newspapers circulated a rumor that American railroad magnate E. H. Harriman had made a bet with millionaire Robert Goelet that he could beat the fastest recorded Japan-to-New York time.[53] Goelet took the bet. Harriman, his wife, their daughter Mary (a good friend of Alice's), and Robert Goelet had been visiting Japan to consider the possibility of rail lines through China, which is how they came to return on the *Siberia,* with Alice and her party. The *Siberia* was already ahead of schedule, so Harriman seemed to have the odds in his favor. When he summoned his private railway car to meet them in San Francisco, the junketeers lost no time embarking from boat to railroad. Harriman's train raced across the country until it was officially slowed by an urgent telegram from President Roosevelt. TR feared for his daughter's safety on the speeding train—and he was offended by her having accepted a ride from one of the "malefactors of great wealth" against whom he had spent a large part of his presidency railing. TR's brief order to Harriman to "slow down" succeeded, but it did not impede the free publicity that Harriman gained by chauffeuring the First Daughter. Indeed, when TR's telegram reached the newspapers, his fatherly concern for the speed at which Alice rocketed across the plains solidified in the popular mind that Harriman's railway was fast—and comfortable enough for a princess.[54]

While Taft may have had his own reasons for not wanting to hear of Nick and Alice's engagement while abroad, the rest of the nation was breathlessly waiting to learn of an Edenic conclusion. Furious speculation began as soon as the steamer docked in California. The *New York Times* suggested that Alice was "closely attended by Congressman Nicholas Longworth. Both she and Longworth laughingly declined to discuss their reported engagement, but she called him Nick."[55] Before any confirmation could be released to the press, however, the couple had to ask permission of the bride-to-be's parents. Alice put off this chore because she felt "shy and self-conscious" for fear that they might be " 'sentimental' about it." Finally, Alice cornered Edith in her bathroom "and told her the news while she was brushing her teeth, so that she should have a moment to think before she said anything." Meanwhile, Nick, "with great formality was announcing it to Father in the study."[56]

Alice did not record Edith's and TR's responses to the proclamation. Victorian etiquette had suggested that the suitor ask for his intended's hand in marriage—but in the twentieth century, securing the father's consent was not as crucial.[57] On the other hand, the father was the president of the United States. Nick and Alice informed her parents because they already had the eyes of the nation on them; parental disapproval would have come up against a storm of protest from a nation of romantics hungry for happy endings. But even if the Roosevelts had wanted to prevent their daughter from marrying Nick Longworth, they could not have. Years of controlling the nation rather than Alice meant they could not dictate, or even suggest, a more appropriate suitor. But perhaps Nick's flaws were not so evident at the time. The First Lady was "well satisfied" with the engagement, allowing her concerns about Nick's drinking and the age difference to be outweighed by his inheritance, intelligence, and obvious desire to succeed in politics.[58]

NASUM NANDA read Nick's mysterious cable to his sister Clara. In the siblings' special code NASUM meant an engagement was about to be announced. But NANDA was not in their lexicon. After applying "imagination and a small amount of concerted effort," Clara decoded NANDA as Nick and Alice. The bride-to-be was similarly busy trying to write her relatives before the journalists got wind of the news. Correspondents vied for the scoop, but it was the editor of the *Chicago Tribune* who, soon after the couple reached the capital, wired his Washington office asking whether or not they were engaged. "She went out driving with Nick Longworth this afternoon without a chaperone," came the reply. "If they are not engaged, they ought to be." The careful surveillance paid off. The *Tribune* divulged the engagement a half day before the family did. Then the floodgates opened. Alice's scrapbook contains more than two hundred clippings from papers across the United States and Europe announcing the engagement. Her celebrity status overshadowed the wedding details. She relished the publicity, while TR and Edith simply threw up their hands, powerless against the onslaught of demands for details of the engagement, the invitations, the wedding dress, the decorations, the music, the celebrant, and on and on. Alice called the two months between the engagement and the wedding "a turmoil."[59]

The newspapers first wanted to know when Nick had proposed. He told the *New York Evening World*: "I did not know officially that I was engaged until the announcement." This could not have thrilled his fiancée, who had already expressed fears about his complacency. One skeptical but enterprising journalist prodded the weary congressman—Was it on the steamer on the way back from the Philippines, he asked? "I don't really know," Nick responded. "I've been in what you might call a trance for so long that I am somewhat mixed as to dates." Another paper placed a premium on creativity: "Rumor says that the fateful question was put as they were entering the door of the Empress Dowager's palace in Peking, and that the affirmative came at the same spot as they emerged!" Burr McIntosh wrote in the *Literary Digest* that Alice's courage and pluck in the Philippines made Nick's heart "bump around at a rather lively rate." McIntosh speculated, "If anything was necessary to cement a love match already begun, those wild rides among the hills did it."[60] All of these stories are highly romantic and completely false. Alice never pinpointed a specific time, and neither she nor Nick ever released explicit details to the press. Their engagement grew out of their intellectual and physical passion until it was simply understood. Perhaps Alice, so desirous of the marriage, never pressed him for an actual proposal.

Americans expected a good marriage from Alice Roosevelt. The representative of American womanhood finally embarked upon her "destiny," with ambivalent feelings as her baggage. Alice went to great lengths to win and keep Nick. She compromised her heart, her integrity, and possibly her body to win him. The First Daughter never allowed her fans to see even one tiny glimpse of her confused emotions. She and Nick, used to standing consistently in the spotlight, presented a mostly united front to the world.

Alice had superstar status in an age before film stars. Her dash across the country was daring and exciting, and more than one young American must have sighed in disappointment to hear of the paternally enforced slowdown. As Alice passed through their hometowns, children lined the streets and waved the American flag. Women and men jostled one another at the stations to get a look at the First Daughter. Brass bands played in her honor from the Pacific to the Atlantic. Alice stepped off Harriman's train in New York at the height of her popular acclaim. She was "an American girl who has not been spoiled," despite her great successes overseas, according to the *Richmond Times-Dispatch*. Ordinary citizens agreed that the important thing about Miss Roosevelt was that she was emphatically American and truly her father's daughter. The *New York Times* remarked that she looked "as chic and as full of spirits as when she left several months ago with Secretary Taft. Homage she has received in the Orient apparently had not turned her head." The *Times* quoted Alice's brief speech to the reporters: "You may say for me, I am more than ever convinced there is no country like our own."[61] Alice understood politics.

One delicate question surfaced after the East Asia trip. Did the presents given her by foreign leaders—rolls of costly Chinese fabric, jewelry, expensive clothing, national works of art, even a little black dog named Manchu—legally belong to the federal government or to Alice? A Canadian newspaper suggested that foreign officials "looked upon Miss Alice as an American Princess, as a daughter of the Government, as a representative of the nation—or they never would have given her such presents. Mr. [William Jennings] Bryan is in the Orient, but it is not likely that he will be loaded down with any such shower of gifts." As she sailed home, reporters estimated their worth. Theodore and Edith heard bloated claims that MISS ROOSEVELT'S EMBARRASSING PRESENTS necessitated twenty-seven crates and a $60,000 duty. TR sent her a warning telegram: "Do not bring in any present that you do not really value, and if the presents are of much money value leave them in storage at Custom House until we can talk over method of paying duty. I know nothing about the presents excepting what I see in the papers which I take for granted is a wild exaggeration but I send this telegram by way of precaution."[62]

Alice was grateful her father had taken her side. Articles in her defense claimed she "was placed in a position where she could not decline any of the presents...without placing the Government in the attitude of rejecting friendly overtures." A *Times* editorial posited that if the Congress passed a bill exempting Alice from import duties, "we do not believe that there would be a score of Americans who would object." At a press corps interview in late October, Alice emphasized, "The gifts I received in the various places we visited I accepted as a compliment to my country and not in the nature of a personal tribute." Whether the gifts were for America, its president, or its First Daughter, most people felt that she deserved them, because as a Chicago daily claimed, "She did much to cement friendship between the United States and foreign countries." Alice eventually paid $1,026 in duties. While still a hefty sum, the outcome vindicated Alice. The press had exaggerated the number and the value of the gifts.[63]

Theodore Roosevelt's private diplomat had carried herself with aplomb overseas. She continued to receive interesting gifts—such as a "large brass shell which was used during the siege of Port Arthur last winter."[64] More important, tremendous praise came from her own family, including a precious note from Auntie Bye written after a fellow junketeer had told her approvingly about Alice's behavior; it concluded: "My little Alice that was really mine for four years. [H]ow perfect how dear you are to the old Aunt."[65]

Her trip resulted in the enrichment of the administration, the nation, the Roosevelt family name, and Alice's own character. Her visit spurred citizens to ask questions about the tariff situation in the Philippines, the Chinese exclusionary laws, and the future of Korea. After Alice's journeys, Roosevelt's admirers and his detractors tried to define the line between the nature of royalty and the nature of celebrity in a democracy. Alice's visits were looked upon as an honor by most of the people of Hawaii, the Philippines, Korea, Puerto Rico, Cuba, China, and Japan, and they hoped that Alice's goodwill missions would encourage stronger diplomatic ties with the United States.

Alice's ambassadorial spunk served as a role model for Progressive Era women, because of a fame rightfully earned. She was neither a Victorian woman nor a New Woman, but rather something else entirely: a modern celebrity. The First Daughter had the prestige of the White House attached to her and not the taint of the theater, from whence sprang the other legendary women of the day. President Roosevelt learned by the time he sent Alice to East Asia that her fame would increase with each stop on the itinerary. By 1905, TR knew both that his daughter's celebrity status was inevitable and that it could help his administration. As the newspapers noted, "There have been few young women in America, or for that matter in any other country, who have received so much newspaper attention as has Miss Alice Roosevelt."[66] TR might have worried privately about the effect of Alice's prominence on her own life, but he did not have to fear the results of her fame on his administration when she functioned as his good-will ambassador.

Chapter 8

"To Bask in the Rays of Your Reflected Glory"

A CONFUSING WELTER of details and decisions filled the two months of turmoil between the official announcement of the First Daughter's engagement on December 13, 1905, and the wedding, set for February 17, 1906. Congratulatory notes showered onto the White House staff. Wedding gifts began arriving shortly after the nuptial date was made public. The *New York Tribune* described Alice as "overwhelmed with congratulations," and "almost buried in flowers" from well-wishers around the world. The crew of the German "torpedoboat-destroyer" *Alice Roosevelt* sent their hopes for the future happiness of their "patroness." Many of the notes mentioned the months of publicity she and Nick had endured. Alice knew that the attendant hoopla had ended the American guessing game for, as she wrote to tell her cousin Eleanor, "I hope you are surprised but I am much afraid you are not!"[1]

Her wedding occasioned a national celebration. Alice represented the ideal of true American womanhood—she had grit, poise enough to keep up with Europeans, good breeding, unostentatious wealth, attractive looks, athletic ability, common sense unspoiled by too much education, and charitable impulses (if one looked hard enough). As Anne Ellis wrote in her memoir, aptly titled *The Life of an Ordinary Woman*, "We felt very near to her. You see, this was Romance, and having none of our own we took part of hers."[2] Americans from all walks of life sent Alice congratulations, written laboriously by hands not used to holding pens, hasty notes scrawled on postcards showcasing the bride and groom, letters from women and men sighing at the wonderful conclusion to the grand saga.

.   .   .

After five years of continuous journalistic coverage, Americans had exempted Alice from the standard of female impropriety attached to having one's name in the newspapers more than thrice—especially since it now appeared she would follow the acceptable path to the altar. Alice Roosevelt personified the female side of her popular father: she led the strenuous life. If it was in a manner of which TR sometimes disapproved, what matter? Americans generally didn't. Seldom did newspapers criticize Alice by calling her or her actions unladylike. At the turn of the century, she was helping to change the definition of proper behavior for women. Newspapers attributed her hijinks to the exuberance of youth.

Being eldest daughter of a charismatic and much-loved president allowed her unmatched freedom—balanced by the drawbacks of public life. Alice joined no reform movements, unlike so many of her Progressive Era sisters. Women's clubs and benevolent societies, including the Junior League, taught elite women important lessons in how to maneuver through public spaces—whether legislative corridors, ethnic ghettos, or hometown battlegrounds—but Alice learned by living in public. Newspaper reporters and cameras taught her to act efficaciously and becomingly in the masculine public sphere. Her fame as First Daughter might have been a hindrance to participation in settlement homes, while her temperament kept her away from causes that TR, at least, labeled noble, such as the Newsboys' Lodging House of his own youth.

But now, Alice stood on the threshold of what most of the world at that time considered a woman's noblest calling. Marriage was right and good—and after her stormy public adolescence, Alice appeared finally to be settling into a seemly adulthood. The nation breathed a sigh of relief along with TR and Edith at the proper conclusion to Alice's youth. She had chosen, to all appearances, a creditable man—a politician like her father; a solid midwesterner. No effete easterner, no foreign royal would claim Princess Alice. With fondness, Americans set about commemorating her wedding. The Roosevelt-Longworth marriage became an emblem of national pride. One Californian encapsulated all the themes of Alice's time as First

Daughter: the worthy daughter of the worthy sire, the spirit of democracy, the importance of marrying an American, the subtle reminder that her fame eclipsed Nick's:

> Here's to Alice Roosevelt,
>   Who's won a home with Nick,—
> The lad who failed so many times,
>   But finally made it stick.
>
> We wish her health and pleasure
>   Throughout a long, good life,
> And we are glad no stranger
>   Has won her for a wife.
>
> 'Tis not that she is better
>   Than many a handsome maid;
> 'Tis not that she is brighter,
>   Or of a finer grade,—
>
> But just because she's Alice
>   Of strenuous, square-deal hue,—
> An ordinary mortal,—
>   (Although her blood is blue).
>
> We send this greeting, Alice,
>   From California state;
> And trust you'll long live happy,
>   And make a loving mate.[3]

As congratulations flowed in, Alice systematically pasted them into her scrapbook. They were happy reminders of the affection of friends, relatives, and anonymous well-wishers. TR's friend Owen Wister jokingly asked Alice "How could you increase your poor father's duties by adding to them the duty of being a father-in-law?"[4] The funniest and one of the most loving congratulations came from Alice's confidant, Grandpa Lee. He wrote that her Boston relatives were overjoyed at the news of her engagement to "Nick Longworth, 'Harvard, 1891.'" He continued in his kindly and prepossessing way:

> I was not surprised in the least as I had read of it for at least 365 days in the newspapers. You have raised the old nick for quite a long time and now you have decided to settle down for life with a young Nick. Good! I hope that he has a good, kindly disposition, but with sufficient strength of character to make you:
>
> 1st Get up in the morning and breathe the fresh air.
> 2nd Make your breakfast off something besides lemon juice.
> 3rd Leave off cigarettes, cigars and cocktails.
> 4th When traveling leave at home the dog and snakes.
> 5th Conduct yourself so as to be happy and make him happy too.
>
> But you are all right and I congratulate [you] again and feel that you have done the right thing. Uncle George has just been in here and says "That Nick is a first rate fellow." So that point is settled.[5]

Meanwhile, Nick's friend Julius Fleischmann sent the groom a note attesting to the change love made in him: "Your friends [in Cincinnati] now knew it all, when you were home this fall, they say now that you were not the Nick as of old but a very tame sort of 'eat out of your hand' individual. Well I did not know it but I hoped it for I felt that it was the goal you most deserved to reach...."[6]

Like her mementos from the East Asia trip, Alice's wedding gifts caused comment. In combination with her Asian loot, MISS ROOSEVELT COULD OPEN A MUSEUM WITH THESE PRESENTS, one journalist suggested. Alice groused that there was "fantastic exaggeration" about the number and type of gifts she received—but she cast doubt on her own statement by asserting, "I had about the sort of presents that any girl gets from her relatives and friends and friends of the family; with the exception of a few from foreign potentates." Indeed, she later chortled, "The one thing I really relished about my wedding was the presents." In 1900, the limited range of acceptable gifts included silver boxes, cloisonné, picture frames, hand mirrors, belt clasps, and "pins of every conceit for the hair." Usually wedding presents were for the bride specifically. The other option was gifts for the bride's new home. Appropriate here were vases, tea caddies, apostle spoons, "embroidered table-cloths, doyleys, and useful coverings for bureau and wash-stands."[7]

While Alice did receive conventional gifts, she also received heirlooms, such as the priceless memento from her uncle Francis H. Lee. Uncle Frank sent "a silver can belonging probably to your great great great grandfather Joseph Lee who was a privateersman in the Revolution [and] furnished models for the Navy of that period, was a partner and brother-in-law of George Cabot[,] President of the famous Hartford Convention, this can according to the hallmark was made in London in 1751." From the White House aides, Alice and Nick received a cut-glass cake dish, which she used every day. Their fellow congressional junketeers sent Alice an aquamarine and diamond pendant. John Greenway sent her a deer's head, "quite one of the nicest things that I got," Alice wrote to thank him.[8]

Among the most glamorous presents were an invaluable Gobelin tapestry from the French government, a mosaic from Pope Pius X, a bracelet with a diamond-ringed miniature of Kaiser Wilhelm of Germany to match the one he gave her when she christened the *Meteor,* and an enamel snuff box from King Edward of England, with his miniature on the lid, also set in diamonds. The king of Italy gave Alice what she described as a "rather hideous" inlaid mosaic table, too big ever to be used in any of her homes. Her very favorite present came from the Cuban government. Old friend Senator Henry Cabot Lodge suggested to the Cuban legislature that pearls might be rather more to the bride's taste than the bedroom suite inlaid with semiprecious stones upon which they had tentatively agreed. So, in grateful remembrance of Colonel Roosevelt's part in the 1898 war of liberation from Spain, Cuba presented the First Daughter with a string of pearls from Boucheron in Paris worth twenty-five thousand dollars. She wore those pearls the rest of her life, and had them on when she died. The Japanese government sent gold cloth embroidered with the royal kikumon—a stylized chrysanthemum pattern—the badge of the imperial family. The empress dowager and emperor of China gave Alice the most exorbitant gifts, including eight bolts of Chinese silk brocaded with gold, a jade "ornament," a "pair of gold earrings, set with pearls and precious stones," "one pair of bracelets, set with red and green jewels," and "a white fox robe." Monitoring the proceedings, one British foreign officer concluded that "no sovereign's daughter could have had more tremendous to-doings than this Republican young lady."[9]

Commemorating the wedding became a national pastime. "Just now the fashionable fad is the presentation of some kind of a wedding present to Miss Alice Roosevelt," the Medford *Patriot* affirmed. Westerner Anne Ellis and her friends, vicariously living the romance, all chipped in fifty cents apiece for a special-order centerpiece of Battenberg lace. "We inserted a paper—we had no cards—with all our names on, and sent it, then waited, reading the papers to see what other people had sent."[10] In the outpouring of popular affection, she received a number of unusual presents—hand-made and home-baked goods, feather dusters, washing machines, books, bales of hay, a hogshead of popcorn, live and stuffed animals of many sorts, and a "large linen centerpiece" from the children of the Colored Industrial Evening School, in thanks to the president for "his attitude toward ne-groes." The United Mine Workers of America gave Alice a railway car full of coal as a wedding present, in appreciation for the president's services in settling the anthracite coal strike of 1902. Because they "consider[ed] themselves children of the amiable President" the Abenaki tribe also sent a gift.[11] Many Americans wrote songs in their honor, for example, "Alice, the Bride of the White House," "Love's Happiness (A Wedding Song)," and "The Wooing of Alice and Nick," which concluded with a lullaby. Reporters meticulously listed the presents as the country took pride that a daughter of Columbia was worthy of such worldwide attention.[12]

Anyone could read about Princess Alice's wedding presents, but few were able to view the gifts. After the turn of the century, a bride decided whether or not to display the wedding presents, though the trend was away from displaying gifts. Instead, presents were shown to best friends only for the purpose of celebrating the love and good wishes of the bride's circle. Social arbiters warned women against parading their treasures for crassly comparing one giver's choice (and financial outlay) to another's. In the First Daughter's case, it would have been impractical to show the wedding presents to all visitors, because of the sheer numbers of people who could claim a right to view the gifts, and because of the incalculable worth of her presents. Alice enjoyed the ritual of the "excitement of gifts coming in, of opening them and then arranging them in the library over the blue room," where she let only her closest friends see them.[13]

Wedding etiquette further stipulated that the bride-to-be must recognize the graciousness of the giver by sending thank-you notes written in her own hand. This Alice did not do. She "skimmed unconcernedly along the surface," in her own words, writing only a few notes in between the congratulatory parties. Edith Roosevelt, who considered good manners the measure of a person, took it upon herself to marshal the forces of propriety. She and Belle Hagner, her social secretary, wrote many of Alice's thank-you notes, while Alice remembered that "even guests and younger members of the family were pressed into the service." There were so many gifts to be numbered and acknowledged that Edith had to cancel her usual luncheon with the cabinet wives in February.[14] Edith and Belle thus relieved Alice of one of the most onerous chores connected with the event.

While Alice enjoyed the prewedding whirl, Nick confronted unusual pressures. Two controversies erupted in his home state. First, the national Women's Christian Temperance Union was "up in arms" because the Ohio delegation wanted to give Nick and Alice a crystal punch bowl. Although the good women prayed for a change of heart, the delegates were not swayed. They sent an enormous punch bowl that stood—on its glittering pedestal—nearly two feet high, ornamented with pears and apples, and came with a dozen matching cups. The bowl was so large that its velvet-lined shipping box was the size of a writing desk. But not everyone caught wedding fever. Nick heard that half of the Ohio state senate balked at passing a House-authorized joint resolution of wedding congratulations. The fractious Buckeye senators declared the resolution "undignified" because "too much publicity had already been given to the coming nuptials." They defeated a motion to suspend the rules and vote on the resolution. The reason—a Midwestern condemnation of "too much publicity"—was likely of little consolation to the bridegroom in the face of the undeniably lukewarm support from his former colleagues.[15]

Just at that time, some of President Roosevelt's western friends arrived to comfort the beleaguered Nick. A group of ten Ponca Indians marched down Pennsylvania Avenue bearing a wedding gift of a buffalo skin for Nick, for they reasoned, "Can a man be boss of his own wigwam if it is so that all the ponies, the beads, the buffalo hides, belong to his wife?" Representative Longworth hid. The determined delegation proceeded to the White House, where they asked the president to present the skin to "Shining Top."[16]

The newspapers included everything but the buffalo skin as they calculated Nick's worth. Would Alice's money problems now be solved? Estimates of the Longworth fortune varied widely. One newspaper had him "heir to $300,000," while another stated that "the realty part of the estate alone will go to the $2,000,000 mark," and a third claimed that he was "worth about $15,000,000."[17] The Longworth family fortune accrued decades earlier when the first Nicholas Longworth accepted land in payment for his legal services. Eventually he invested in more land, and then in grapes and a winery, producing an average of 150,000 bottles of wine a year. He is often credited with beginning the wine industry in the United States and with having produced the first sparkling wines in the country. When the first Nicholas died in 1836, his fortune was estimated at $15 million. Whatever the exact figure in 1906, it was enough for Alice—who had already visited Rookwood and seen the Longworth holdings—and it was acceptable to Edith, who approved of Nick's "comfortable income according to our not over-ambitious ideas."[18] Nick was, however, never able to keep up with the friends from Alice's youth. Her dream of being "fabulously wealthy" eluded her.

Susan Longworth lunched at the White House on December 13, 1905, the day the engagement was formally announced. Traditionally at this meeting the families would have discussed the formalities of the match. Alice remembered Susan Longworth as "rather a formidable lady who was better dressed and straighter-backed than anyone in Cincinnati. . . . I enjoyed her in a way," she recalled, but "was never able to play the part of the dutiful daughter-in-law."[19] No doubt this was influenced by Alice's iconoclastic lifestyle. Mrs. Longworth, a traditional, conservative Ohioan who thought of herself first and foremost as Nicholas's mother, did not wholly approve of Alice—but it was the simple fact of Nick's marrying that put her off balance. Writing to her friend Katharine Wulsin, Nick's mother confessed:

> I was utterly unprepared for the announcement—having made up my mind (in the comfortable way that mothers have) that I knew more about my son than any one else did. The President has given a most cordial consent & seems very much pleased. Mrs. Roosevelt sent for me to come to see her a few days ago and she said Alice was the most charming person to live with on account of her sunny temperament and thoughtfulness for others—that in spite of her irresponsibility and impractical ways she was the most punctual person (in which she differed from the President who wasn't) and she said "When Nick tells her to be ready at a certain time she will never keep him waiting a minute."[20]

Another friend tried to comfort her by suggesting that the president's daughter might be the only young woman who could keep "Nicky's" interest, "for instance as we know that he was in deadly terror of getting sick of his wife at the breakfast table and that the 'stat d'aime' involved in this fear would be apt to make him tire of any usual nice girl. In this case I really believe that the 'six white horses' as represented by the celebrity of the princess will do much to cast a glamour over the situation and create an illusion around his domestic life which he might not have in any other way...."[21]

At the time this letter was written, "Nicky" was already thirty-six years old. But the writer certainly had his measure. Alice knew she was marrying into a close family. Clara, her future sister-in-law, recollected, "The mutual and tender link which bound [mother and son] was at the base both of his ambitions and their fulfillment. Nothing could have been deeper or more complete than his filial veneration, but, aside from this essential fact, he treated her more as a sister than a parent...."[22]

Once Nick's engagement was announced, Susan Longworth receded to the background. Though she lived with him in Washington some part of the year, she was absent from journalistic and firsthand accounts of the wedding. In terms of public interest, the Roosevelts topped the dowager from Ohio, just as newspaper articles featuring the bride outnumbered those on the bridegroom. Susan, fiercely protective of her son and his career, could not have been unaware of the imbalance.

Approximately one thousand invitations were sent out, but this number excluded the majority of those who wanted to come. A longtime Washingtonian explained, "Social America was on tiptoe, hoping for an invitation. The Has-Beens tried resuscitation, and the Never-Wasers resorted to novel tricks to break in. Many people, quite unknown to the Roosevelts, sent expensive presents and then brazenly asked for invitations. Their gifts were promptly returned." Having the right connections in a political town like Washington meant that even private parties were only as private as the limits to one's social or political network. White House receptions could be crashed with relative ease. One insider wrote that "almost any well-mannered white person could still wangle an invitation to a White House reception except during the weeks of preparation for the marriage of 'Princess Alice' to . . . Nicholas Longworth." Lottie Strickland—one such well-mannered white person—made it all the way from New Orleans to Cincinnati before she was apprehended as a stowaway. Strickland and her friends had come to the momentous decision that she should represent the common folk at the White House wedding. "I hid in [railroad car] sleepers," she said, "but the passengers helped me. I started from home with ten cents. We thought that a working girl ought to be at the wedding, and I am sure if I get to see President Roosevelt and tell him what I want he will allow me to attend."[23]

Everybody wanted to go to the wedding. It was the biggest social event of the season, maybe of the Roosevelt presidency. Washington insiders' social standing was in jeopardy. "Such wire-pulling as is going on here fills even the oldest politicians with awe. . . . Some matrons are already negotiating with Florida hotel keepers," so that they could be out of town—a last-minute, face-saving excuse, according to the *Washington Post*. The *Times* suggested that requests for invitations were limited by neither class nor gender: "So widespread has been the interest in the marriage, and so prevalent the mistake as to its social and official significance, that Miss Isabelle

Hagner, Mrs. Roosevelt's secretary, and Mr. Loeb, private secretary to the President, have been sorely beset for the past two weeks with communications from men high in official circles all over the United States, with requests that are almost commands for invitations to the wedding."[24]

Despite the Roosevelts' disclaimer that the ceremony was a private function, one's proximity to the seat of power was measured by the receipt of the coveted invitation. One Washingtonian remembered that she and her family were lucky enough to be included, but after their invitation arrived they faced a different sort of problem: all of their friends begged them to "use their influence" with the Roosevelts to extract more tickets. Finally, the demands forced Theodore and Edith to issue a public statement explaining the criteria used in issuing invitations: "The capacity of the White House required that under existing circumstance invitations be limited to the closest kinsfolk, the personal friends of Miss Roosevelt and Mr. Longworth, and certain classes of officials in Washington. No friends of the President and Mrs. Roosevelt are being asked unless they also come within one of these classes, and even with these limitations the number of guests threatens to overtax the capacity of the White House." The invitation list redefined Alice's own group of peers. The *New York World-Telegram* reported the disappointing news that some of Alice's dearest friends could not secure an invitation.[25]

A colder cut awaited. Alice was interviewed just before the wedding, as reporters searched for clues as to the bride's plans. " 'Why aren't you having any bridesmaids?' they asked Alice. 'I'd love to. Yes, I'd just love to,' she replied, 'but I'd have to have at least 150 if I had any. It's too bad I can't have any, but I can't make my friends jealous, and how could I ever choose six bridesmaids from among them all? I'd want them all, and I must say,' with a bewitching smile, 'that I think they'd like it.' "[26] It is possible that Alice wanted to be the center of attention and so chose to have no competition from friends she feared were prettier than she. It is certainly true that Alice got to be a "most marvelous belle" on her wedding day. Perhaps this was her symbolic public revenge on those who had gossiped about Nick's prior womanizing. Many of her friends were already married, and hence could not serve as bridesmaids. However, it is worth noting that "the fashion of bridesmaids has gone out temporarily," the author of *Manners and Social Usage* asserted, while another etiquette guide took it for granted that the option of dispensing with bridesmaids existed: "In America, if there are no bridesmaids...."[27] Further, not one of the many memoirs mentioning the wedding comment on Alice's decision to approach the altar unattended. If it had been truly unusual it would have drawn note, especially as many of them were written by women of her own class who would have recorded any exceptional circumstances.

In late January, Alice set about shopping for her married life. This task consisted of acquiring a trousseau, "a complete stock of apparel sufficient to last [the bride] during the first few years of her married life." New York thrilled that MISS ROOSEVELT TO BUY TROUSSEAU HERE, as the *New York Herald* proudly proclaimed on Christmas eve. Nick and Alice spent a week shopping—or trying to shop—but nothing, including "private" luncheons, escaped the notice of the press. Alice began at Kurzman's, a Fifth Avenue clothing importer frequented by elite New Yorkers (including Alice's grandmother Mittie). Well-wishers crowded the streets and surrounded their car as the couple, joined at times by Nick's sister Clara, went from store to store attempting to make their purchases. Alice recalled that she and her fiancé were "dogged by reporters, [with] inquisitive crowds following when I went shopping; to some extent [it was] the sort of thing a royalty or a move star endures, or enjoys." Alice and Nick stopped their car to run into a millinery shop, and as they did so, the long line of photographers and reporters that followed behind them blocked the street. "Traffic," the *New York Times* revealed, "came to a standstill until Roundsman Thompson of the mounted squad with the assistance of half a dozen hastily summoned policemen stepped in, cleared the crowd away, and established police lines on either side of the entrance to the store."[28] Alice, Nick, and Clara had difficulty getting to the boat that would ferry them to Long Island because of the crowds. Once aboard, they good-naturedly posed for pictures and waved good-bye to their fans.

Alice did enjoy the fuss. She accepted her role as America's First Daughter and understood that reports of her actions and words were likely to appear in the newspapers. The push-pull of being raised by Theodore and

Edith—who faced each other from opposite ends of the publicity spectrum—resulted in Alice's having few private days. By this time, Alice could joke easily with journalists. "[T]here is one secret you will not learn," she teased, "and that is where we are going immediately after we are married."[29] To a degree, Theodore reconciled himself to his daughter's fame. Edith never did. The First Daughter—caught in the middle—mostly did what she wanted to do, always conscious of whether her father was watching. When he was not, she filled in the sadness with cameras and reporters. Eventually, Alice would try to use Nick for the same ends.

Nick was ambivalent about how much he enjoyed being the companion of a woman whose very presence could draw a crowd of one thousand. Nick had luxuriated in Alice's limelight while they toured East Asia and could escape when necessary. But now he was firmly and officially part of her entourage. He wrote her in October that he was "snatching a few moments between newspaper reporters to tell you that I have gotten home alive and 'have nothing to say' from which you can see that being in love with a celebrity is not altogether a bed of roses." In another letter to her he confessed that he "simply love[d] to bask in the rays of your reflected glory."[30] The *Washington Mirror* had accurately predicted Nick's challenge, even before they left on the congressional junket: "Princess Alice will be in her glory in an Oriental environment, with bowing and salaaming at every turn. She has withstood more adulation, flattery, and throwing of bouquets than perhaps any woman in America. She will get all this to her heart's content, but what will she do when she gets back to the Land of the Free. 'Nick' had better learn a few steps, how to leave the room backwards and how to ko-tow . . . or he will find himself out in the cold when the Princess enters her Washington palace."[31]

Nick apparently knew how to "ko-tow." Alice remained the country's foremost female celebrity, the closest thing the nation had to royalty, and the typical young woman all at once—no doubt a trying combination in one's fiancée. He stood a distant second in media interest, but he did inspire curiosity. *Leslie's Illustrated Weekly* hastened to add, "It is no discredit to Mr. Longworth to say that he suddenly has become an important public personage by reason of the fact that he is the White House bridegroom and son-in-law of the President." Not discrediting perhaps, but embarrassing. Visitors to the House of Representatives viewing galleries pointed to Nick and whispered, "There's Alice's husband."[32] Nick must have been counting the days until Alice receded from public view and he could settle into married life with the certain knowledge that his bride's patrimony—and *past* fame—could assist his career.

At the time, however, Nick continued to send loving letters when they were apart, assuring Alice he was living "the life of an anchorite so far as food, drink and other alleged temptations of the flesh are concerned." He told her he was sad without her: "I don't like anybody here and its simply because a foolish (sometimes) little person called Baby Lee has wound herself into the very inmost convolutions of my soul and I can't get rid of her for a moment, even if I wanted to." "You are just a part of my life," he wrote passionately, "that nothing and nobody else can fill." In the midst of the wedding preparations, Nick also had to keep his constituents happy and pay attention to his House seat. Alice was learning about it all. "Far from being bored by your discussion of politics as she is played in Ohio," Nick wrote her with enthusiasm, "I love you all the more for taking an interest in it." He laid out his predictions for the upcoming electoral campaign and promised, "I will talk more about politics with you next month, and I would honestly rather have your advice about people and things than anybody's I know."[33]

When they were reunited, festivities continued apace at the White House. Two thousand guests attended the congressional reception on the first day of February 1906, where Alice and Nick were the center of attention. Her celebrity status intact, the First Daughter "was kept almost as busy bowing and smiling as was her father." On Sunday, February 11, the *New York Times* pointed out, Alice did not attend church, but stayed home to write thank-you notes before she and Nick dined with Susan Longworth. The next day, Alice's twenty-second birthday, TR and Edith gave a larger dinner at the White House, followed by a musicale in her honor.[34] Willard Straight was invited to both. Carpenter was in town, too, and Goelet—all three former flames attended the wedding.

Two days before the ceremony, Nick threw a party for his ushers at the

Alibi Club. Theodore Roosevelt attended the stag event but left before the merriment reached a level unseemly for a president.[35] One more congratulatory party was held that week—the night before the wedding—lending credence to White House usher Ike Hoover's observation that "for at least two years before her marriage there was never an evening when there was not some party being given in her honor."[36] Finally, Alice's dream was coming true: she had found a wealthy man, made him love her, fell for him in turn, and gloried in the culmination of her days as a single woman in the White House. Alice was toasted, congratulated, gifted with fabulous presents, remarked upon, photographed, followed by crowds, and almost entirely free from parental control.

Alice and Nick were seen alone every day when Alice drove Nick to work. The *Philadelphia Record* detailed the habits of the two they called "not coy lovers." "They drove to the Capitol this morning in the smart high trap the President gave his daughter a year ago, Miss Roosevelt holding the reins and wielding a whip like the clever horsewoman she is. At the House end of the Capitol she stopped for an instant to allow her fiancé to alight, then drove leisurely back to the White House."[37] Grandpa Lee would have been proud—Nick had the commendable effect of making Alice rise in the morning and breathe the fresh air. He would have looked askance, though, at the fact that it was she who held the reins. Another habit the couple had developed would upset him more: "The bride elect became the central figure [at White House functions], and so often after a brief appearance, she would quietly disappear—she and Nick."[38]

On the tenth, Nick came down with tonsillitis or the grippe.[39] Alice lost weight and suffered from another attack of eczema. The tensions normal to any wedding could have caused the couple to take to their respective beds, but the concentrated publicity was fierce and may have contributed to second thoughts. A series of letters written by Alice to Nick prior to their wedding helps to give some clue as to the couple's relations.

From these letters the capricious nature of their relationship is plain. They did love each other. To suggest otherwise is contradicted by the documents. "I ought to know it is too wonderful to last," Alice wrote Nick resignedly. "Don't lose your head about anyone please don't, Nick. Think of me. I love you so very much I am so jealous, my darling please." Her closing to that note was fatalistic: "No matter what happens I have been happier than I ever imagined anyone could be my darling."[40] In another letter she cried, "I didn't really think you would write to me, but oh why didn't you? I fear you care for someone else...." At times, Alice's worries about his constancy made her angry:

> Nick—[Someone] has told me all sorts of things about you this evening that makes me fearfully unhappy. He says that Katherine Elkins means to have you before the winter is over, that she will marry you and that you will really want to marry her. You are a cur and a cad if this is so—now don't you really think you are. When you telephoned to me today your voice didn't have a very sincere ring when you talked about Monday night. Or does it only seem that way to me in the light of subsequent conversations. I have had letters from friends and then Josephine told me that she lunched with you on Tuesday and that you were very cross—evidently had a bad attack of remorse on account of the night before. Oh darling lamb, so you really regret it all so much. I am just more of a philosopher—What is done is—well, just done—a fact not to be gotten around, but at least not to be thought and worried about. I am afraid that I wish you [would] die, rather than marry anyone else but me.... Beloved—love me and marry me—Alice.[41]

This letter has the same protean tone that William Howard Taft attributed to Alice and Nick's shipboard romance. Her letter began in ire and ended in a plea. This time it appeared that Nick went off with other people to punish his fiancée after a tiff, whereas in East Asia Alice had gone elsewhere to console herself.

On the other hand, Alice did communicate to Nick her happiness in the relationship. "My own beloved Nick," she wrote once, "today has been very dull and tiresome because I haven't seen you once. And I haven't been able to think of anything else. Last night when...you kissed me, I was so happy, so wonderfully, marvelously happy. I love you darling...." Her letters speak often of missing him: "My darling, darling, darling Nick, if you don't come soon I shall go quite mad.... My own darling, I love you more every moment though I don't think it's possible to love any more than I do now already love."[42]

A letter from Nick to Alice is worth quoting in length in part because it is one of the very few of Nick's extant courtship letters, and because it gives a good sense of the workings of their relationship from his perspective. "My darling little girl," it began—a salutation suggesting both a cognizance of their age difference and a comfort with it:

It's no use. I simply can't stay away from you any longer and I am coming on Saturday night so that I shall be in Washington at 12:40 on the B&O on Sunday. Buck is coming with me but we can send him in another hack and you and I will drive back to my home for lunch, yes? Then if you like we will go to Nat's party at the Alibi and if we get tired we can adjourn to my well-furnished study. I think it would be nice to go to Mrs. Norman's for lunch on Tuesday so let's accept. Everything has come out nicely, even better than I expected so that I can come back to you conscientiously. I don't see any reason why you should not be the lady representative from the East half of Cincinnati for some years to come. I went out in Society last night and stayed up at a ball at the Country Club till 4:30 a.m. It wasn't so much the dancing that kept me there as it was listening to the thousands of nice things that were said about my Alice. You are really the most popular person in the world not even excepting my *"pere-au-loi perspective"* and I simply love to bask in the rays of your reflected glory and it isn't only the people in Society that say nice things about you but everybody including all my really toughest friends—perhaps that's the nicest thing about it.... We'll never be away from each other so long again. I can't and won't stand it so you will have to make up your mind to be right by my side from now until I become a senile and decrepit old man. But the last thing that will ever be left in me when everything else is gone will be the wholly absorbing love for you Alice....[43]

While Alice may have held the reins, Nick was firmly in control. He began with a possessive diminutive. By accepting the Norman invitation and assuming that Alice would want to retire to his study, he made up his mind and Alice's. He informed her that he stayed out until early in the morning, but sweetened that news with compliments. The relatively strict gender roles of the Progressive Era were mitigated by Alice's independent spirit and strong personality, but this letter suggests Nick was more patriarch than partner.

Alice was not a typical woman of the age. Once given a taste of the freedoms brought to her as First Daughter, she would have found it difficult to play the traditional wife. But at age twenty-two, Alice had neither the experience nor the desire to step far outside prescriptive norms. In fact, she actively sought a conventional path. Her overall lack of doubt concerning her own desire to marry Nick must have meant that she was comfortable with Nick's taking charge.

Finally all the wedding preparations were finished. The couple secured their wedding license. Edith released the wedding program to the newspapers on February 14. The invitation turmoil had died down. The majority of the presents had been received. Grandma and Grandpa Lee, Auntie Bye and Uncle Will, Auntie Corinne and Uncle Douglas had arrived, along with various cousins. Susan Longworth presided over the last days of her son's bachelorhood from their rental home on Eighteenth and I streets. Nellie Grant Sartoris, daughter of former president Ulysses S. Grant and a White House bride herself, was on hand for the festivities.[44]

At that time, Edith took Alice aside to have the traditional premarital mother-daughter talk. Alice remembered later, "Anything to do with sex or childbirth was just not discussed. Yet it was curious how much surreptitious attention was paid to the consequences of sex in those days. For instance, I never discussed such matters with my stepmother when I was a teenager, although she did come to me before I was married and said, 'You know, before you were born, your mother had to have a little something done in order to have you, so if you need anything, let me know.' "[45] Although Alice was not as naïve about sex as she would have later generations believe, her confusion at this announcement was understandable. There wasn't a lot to go on. Perhaps it was a surgery necessary for her mother to become pregnant. Edith did not habitually speak about sex—nor about Alice Lee. While she discharged a distasteful duty, she added to the overall edginess of the bride.

The day before the ceremony was filled with an East Room rehearsal, minus only the minister and the president, who was engaged in matters of state and could not be pulled away. Then all of the attendants followed Nick and Alice to the Alibi Club for an informal dinner hosted by Charles McCauley. As she wrote her name in the Club book, Alice grandly proclaimed "that hers should never again be written as Alice Lee Roosevelt." At 10:00 p.m., the party moved to the Keans, where they joined the large contingent of out-of-town guests staying at the senator's home.[46]

At last, the day of the wedding dawned. The morning of Saturday, February 17, 1906, started early for the White House staff, but the bride did not arise until 11:00 a.m. The father of the bride spent the morning writing letters about election fraud and the U.S. Naval Academy, while Edith knitted and chatted with Grandma Lee—to keep her mind off the chastisement she really wanted to give her dallying daughter.[47] At least the First Lady could remain calm in the knowledge that Ike Hoover had everything else under control. Out of curiosity, Grandpa Lee mingled in the assembling crowds of onlookers who gathered to get a glimpse of illustrious wedding guests.[48] Alice watched the throng as she dressed quickly. Her American-made gown was white satin, high-necked, and trimmed with point lace from Alice Lee's wedding. She wore elbow-length white kid gloves. The dress had a very long train of silver brocade woven especially for her in New Jersey. Alice adorned herself with the pearl necklace from the Cuban government, a diamond brooch from her parents, the kaiser's diamond bracelets, and Nick's wedding present to her, a diamond and pearl necklace. Her long hair was ordered with difficulty on top of her head in a pompadour. It held the lengthy tulle veil and traditional orange blossoms that completed her wedding ensemble.

At 11:30, the East Room was packed full of invitees. On a makeshift platform in front of the east window sat the altar, adorned with white Easter lilies. American Beauty roses, white rhododendrons, and pots of azaleas

disguised the cavernous state room. Isabel Anderson watched as a "prominent society leader with a penchant for associating herself with the family
at every wedding which she attended" tried to bully her way into the circle
of relatives in the front rows. A White House aide barred her admittance
"and the lady returned, baffled." Just before noon, Edith, wearing a russet
brocade dress, entered on Ted's arm. They walked up the aisle, cordoned
off from the guests, and sat down with the rest of the family. Nick waited
at the altar with his best man, Nelson Perkins. Precisely at noon, under the
direction of Lieutenant William Santelman, the United States Marine Band
broke into the "Wedding March" from *Lohengrin*. Alice picked up her bouquet of white orchids. Father and daughter slowly progressed to the altar.
As the bride met her intended, the Episcopal bishop of Washington, the
Right Reverend Henry Yates Satterlee, intoned the marriage rite from the
Book of Common Prayer.[49]

Clara Longworth de Chambrun felt the wedding "bristled with 'officialdom,'" since so many members of the Supreme Court, the Senate, the
House of Representatives, and the senior officials of the diplomatic corps
were in attendance. "My impression," Nick's sister recalled, was that everyone invited appeared, "also that whether those who came did so as a
matter of duty, right or friendly inclination, each of the three categories
appeared equally convinced of possessing a 'superior claim' over the rest."
Sara Delano Roosevelt told her daughter-in-law Eleanor that "Alice
looked remarkably pretty and her manner was very charming." Eleanor,
who was pregnant then, could not accompany Sara and FDR since social
morés dictated that she stay in confinement. Eleanor was probably relieved
to avoid the White House, which at that time always made her "'rather
nervous.'"[50]

The wedding service was over in fifteen minutes. Alice and Nick processed out to take the only photographs of the day. It was unusual—and
Alice would say later, regrettable—that so few pictures were taken, but for
once the newspaper reporters' cameras were not allowed in. Before the official photograph, cousin Franklin stepped forward to help adjust her veil,
which had slipped because of the weight of her pompadour. The cameras

clicked, gave off a puff of smoke, and recorded for posterity the fourth White House wedding of a president's daughter.[51] One photograph froze Alice in time between the two most important men in her life. She stood in the center, ramrod straight, hands at her sides. Her new husband was close to her on her right. To her left, Alice's father leaned away from the couple, jamming his hands into the pockets of his coat, unconnected from the event. Most photographs of the new bride showed her looking tired—her eyes are puffy—and just a tad overwhelmed by the morning's experiences. "I am told," Alice commented later, "I fluctuated between animation and grimness on my wedding day."[52]

After the picture taking, the parents of the newly married couple received guests in the Blue Room, as the bride and groom collected their intimate friends for a private wedding breakfast. The other invited guests gathered in the State Dining Room for a larger celebratory meal featuring heart- and wedding-bell-shaped sweets. The bride's cake was the source of one of the most talked-of episodes of the day. Finding that the knife provided by the caterer insufficient to cut the cake, Alice asked White House aide Major Charles McCauley if she might borrow his sword. Thus she cut the first piece with a flourish and handed it round.[53]

"The Brothers Immediate" of the Porcellian Club met in their time-honored send-off of one of their own to his married life. The other guests were startled to hear male voices singing the traditional club and school songs above the popping of champagne corks. The Porc allowed no one but members in good standing to enter the male sanctuary. While the Brothers toasted Nick and reminisced, Alice changed into her traveling dress and said private good-byes to her family. Edith's exhaustion showed. "Mother," Alice told her, "this has been quite the nicest wedding I'll ever have. I've never had so much fun." Edith leaned close to her and retorted, "I want you to know I am glad to see you leave. You have never been anything but trouble." Alice remembered that it was "quite fantastic. It just came out like that." She took it in stride. " 'That's all right, Mother. I'll be back in a few weeks and you won't feel the same way.' And I was and she didn't. Well, I don't *think* she did." While it is true that Alice had been troublesome for

Edith, it is not true that she was only trouble. There was a great deal of warmth between the two women that would grow as Alice moved into adulthood. The tone is not unlike that used, even today, by many Eastern elites with their children in public. And, of course, Edith was exhausted. She confided to her diary that at the cabinet dinner three days later she was "so tired" she "nearly fainted."[54]

Nick and Alice began their secret exit around 4:00 p.m. Even though the day was chilly, hundreds of well-wishers remained on the White House grounds hoping to see the famous pair. The White House staff had planned the escape in elaborate detail. Rumors had been purposefully spread among the crowd as to which door the couple would use, and these were heightened when an automobile appeared at the West Gate on Executive Avenue. At the same time, another car drove up to the Southwest Gate. The anxious crowd divided in two, and as they were moving to surround the cars, a third auto slowed to a stop directly in front of the White House. Finally, completing the confusion, a fourth car appeared at the East Gate. Two of the four cars belonged to Nick. One at a time and in pairs the cars started their engines and honked to each other. Finally, Nick and Alice climbed out the window of the Red Room and onto the south portico of the White House, and one of the cars drove up to whisk the couple away. Friends and family members pelted Nick and Alice with rice (although Alice's youngest brothers switched to beans when they ran out of the traditional hymeneal token) as they raced away to their honeymoon. Their immediate destination was Friendship, the country estate of John R. McLean.

Alice Roosevelt became Mrs. Longworth on paper, but to journalists, photographers, and the average American citizen, she remained Princess Alice. Media coverage had extended to every facet of her life—clothing, schooling, friends, activities, family—and inevitably to the rite of passage that marked her adulthood. The last burst of media enthusiasm released Theodore and Edith from the compelling bonds of their daughter's turbulent lifestyle, just as it signaled Alice's final freedom from parental control. As Nick and Alice escaped to Friendship and their future, a journalist claimed the ultimate summation:

After the wedding is over, Teddy
And they sail on the honeymoon train,
Then you can shoulder your big, big stick
And get in the spotlight again.[55]

As a national event, the wedding of the First Daughter was a great success. The French, along with other nations, mused, "Doubtless our gallantry toward Miss Roosevelt will serve to knit closer the ties of friendship which unite us to the great republic." However, the *Journal des Debats* also recognized that while friends, the two countries still stood divided by cherished cultural norms. Jumping through a window was "novel…judged by French standards, for the irresolute women of our climate need under such circumstances the support of strong arms in which to be carried off. They do not know how to take themselves off…."[56] If Alice were irresolute, it was only about the quality of Nick's love. She might crave his attention, but Alice Lee Roosevelt Longworth possessed the inner strength to take herself off when Nick, in a sadly familiar and devastating move, would also abandon her.

Chapter 9

"Alice Is Married at Last"

THE PROMISE of spring in the air on their wedding day might have been an omen of good fortune for their marriage. It was too early to tell. The Roosevelt family prepared to enjoy life without the high-maintenance Princess Alice around while destitute Washington journalists cast about for a replacement for their best headline maker. The *New York Times* gave a weak effort with THE NEW BELLE OF THE WHITE HOUSE. Buried on page two of the magazine section, the article tried to drum up some interest in fourteen-year-old Ethel, an entirely nice girl who was celebrating, as younger sisters do, the fact that she could move into the big bedroom Alice vacated.

Ethel lacked Alice's penchant for notoriety, and the press, finding little newsworthy in the staid Cathedral School girl, soon returned to more fertile ground.

> Alice is married at last. The sod torn up in the scuffle has been replaced. The store teeth and suspender buttons and tufts of hair that marked the scene are gathered up.... The earth has resumed its course around the sun.... Ever since she debuted into society...there has been constant danger that she would stampede the cabinet with her poodle and pet garter snake or demoralize the senate with one of her skirt dances and acrobatic stunts. With proposals enough to paper her bedroom and suitors so thick on the steps that guests had to crawl in and out of the pantry window, she was fast becoming a menace to the Mormon church.... It rejoices me that Alice is wed. I trust it will settle her nerves.[1]

The editorial's epic tone was about right.

The *New York Evening Mail* theorized that "American men and women all look upon the President's daughter as in a sense their daughter, feeling 'a paternal solicitude for her future happiness.'" It had not been just a wedding, according to the *Philadelphia Press*. Alice and Nick did a national good deed: "The thoughts of countless young and single hearts have been turned toward the bliss of wedded life by this happy event.... For the number and kind of marriages in the land has more to do with the happiness and prosperity of the United States of America than the tariff, the Panama Canal, railway rate regulation or any other one of the big questions that engross the attention of the nation's lawmakers."

Others took a different tack. In the sensible heartland, the call was for normality. The *Springfield Republican* was glad that Alice was now "the wife of her husband," a fact rendering her "beyond the clutch of international diplomacy; the last camera shot is fired, and she becomes that finest of American figures...'a regular woman.'"[2] Fans who had made her their hobby regretted the change in Alice's status. One wrote: "We who have watched Alice Roosevelt and learned to love her, think it as a great mistake in her leaving her Father until he was out of office, especially as there is no one left in the White House to take her place. How we shall miss her! Now she has dropped down the line into plain 'Mrs. Longworth.'"[3] That remained to be seen.

Meanwhile, the focus of this continuing attention had quietly slipped away to Friendship, the seventy-five-acre oasis of millionaires Ned and Evalyn Walsh McLean in northwest Washington. Secluded and luxurious, there were beautifully landscaped grounds for wandering, and a private golf course and swimming pool. This Eden served as Oyster Bay had for Alice Hathaway Lee and Theodore Roosevelt on their honeymoon. At Friendship the newlyweds could be alone together to discover the intimacies that chaperones and social conventions had postponed until the vows were exchanged. The kind McLeans took Bye's role and provided for the Longworths' every whim. Theodore Roosevelt had confided to his diary, of his 1880 honeymoon with Alice Lee, "our intense happiness is too sacred to be written about."[4] Their daughter likewise refused to divulge her thoughts on her own honeymoon, but she did save a letter she received at Friendship that must have desacralized their joy.

"You are without a doubt the happiest woman on earth today," the anonymous female writer began, continuing:

> I have thought so many times that I would not undeceive you.... I believe you to be all that is honest and pure; therefore I do not believe that "Nick" told you before he led you to the altar that "he" is the "*Father* of a beautiful child, *our* child. *My* child." You are a wife but not a Mother, and could you know the intense love I bear the Father of my child you could not but know that it is *reciprocal*. Dear girl he *loves* me in a way in which he and you do not share that love, for *I* am the *Mother* of his child. Until three years ago he was contentent [*sic*] to remain away from everything pertaining to marriage, but Ambition seized him, he met you dear girl and decided to win you at any cost, for he had wealth a (small portion) and he desired "notoriety," which he has obtained at the sacrifice of his love. I lived in Washington where I frequently saw you together until he desired me to return to this city. He has made arrangements whereby I may travel and meet him when you start on your tour. He has liberally provided for us. I am not dependent. I have promised him not to reveal this for the love of him but think you should know the man you are to perhaps spend your young life with. Sometime *you* shall see *his* image and *likeness*— and then I will reveal to you *my* identity as I am far too heart-broken to say more.[5]

We can only speculate on the discussion that must have arisen in the wake of this shattering letter, and the hollowness Alice must have felt. No other such letter exists among Alice's papers. Why she saved this one is a mystery. Nick's Don Juan reputation was well known to Alice—and to everyone else in Washington—and so the letter may have been nothing more than the horrible act of an unbalanced mind. It is also possible that the author really was involved with Nick, and if so, her timing was cruel.

While the affair seems believable, one thing about it does not: the child. Rumors of Nick's philandering both before and after his marriage to Alice were regnant, but there was never a whisper of a child. Add to that the fact that Alice never became pregnant by Nick, and it is plausible to conclude that he was infertile. Of course, the tragedy for Alice is that she could not have realized that on her honeymoon when she was deeply in love with him. Unless Nick knew he was infertile because of some childhood illness or injury and told her so, that letter was a serpent in the garden. Whether this felt like abandonment or deceit, it planted more doubts in the very midst of what should have been a time of bliss. Alice thus never had Nick to lean upon, wholly and without reservation. If she somehow took the woman's allegations in stride, it was not long before Nick's attentions truly did stray, just as she had feared. In the same way that Eleanor Roosevelt had to depend upon her own strengths because of her parents' early deaths and her husband's infidelity, Alice was denied her last hope for a relationship based on unconditional love and shared trust. Mother, father, surrogate mother, and husband all abandoned her in real and profound ways. This last betrayal reinforced early lessons about self-reliance.

Alice could hardly have contemplated separation from Nick in the wake of the letter. What would her father, the president of the United States, have said, had his daughter backed out of the international event that was her wedding, only days after its conclusion? The wedding gifts weren't even all opened at that time. Alice had chosen her own bed, and in the stalwart Roosevelt tradition, she was doomed to lie in it. Or maybe she was so utterly in love with Nick that she, who herself had been the recipient of censure from the press and the public, convinced herself that the letter was a hoax. In this way Alice could preserve her sanity and allow her marriage to start off on the best possible footing.

Whichever it was, the Longworths carried on with their plans. They left amid the expected fanfare for the next phase of their honeymoon: a three-week trip to Cuba to see for themselves the site of TR's heroics during the 1898 Spanish-American War. The Cubans had presented Alice with her favorite wedding gift, her trademark pearl necklace, and she was delighted to say her thanks in person at the reception at Havana's Presidential Palace.[6] Support for America was strong but not shared by everyone. Nevertheless, the Longworths enjoyed the goodwill of all they encountered, especially "ancient Cuban Generals who came in with bouquets to tell the Lady that they had fought with her father," as Willard Straight observed.[7] He was there serving as secretary to their old friend Edward Morgan, then the U.S. minister to Cuba.

Straight had just been posted to Cuba and had the unenviable task of finding a suitable place for the Longworths to stay, once he discovered—in the week before they arrived—that no one had seen to it. Eventually, Straight located a house, but then had to equip it with everything from furniture to silverware and linens, hustling along those who told him, "Mañana." Once the Longworths arrived there were "balls and many grand parties." "They killed off two on their first night here," Straight recounted to a friend, "one at the American Club and one at the Palace." He thought "it seemed to bore [Nick and Alice] to be by themselves for any length of time." Straight, always very affectionate toward Alice, may have seen what he wanted to see, or perhaps discord appeared because of Nick's roving eye or his trysts with the bottle.

In Cuba, the Longworths met the vacationing Florence and Warren Harding. Warren, the new lieutenant governor of Ohio, was a friend of Nick's, but the women did not know each other. It might have done Alice good to unburden herself to Mrs. Harding, who was the stoic victim of Warren's ongoing marital infidelity. Alice and Florence would be great friends for a time, both appreciating in the other their determined personalities, their mutual interest in astrology and the occult, and their shared position as political wives. While the friendship eventually unraveled, it began beside the blue Caribbean waters when both women were trying to relax, one after a wedding and the other after an electoral campaign.

En route to Santiago, the Longworths took "a nice leisurely train that stopped when Nick or Willard or Edward Morgan wanted to shave." On board, Straight noted, "we spent most of the day with our feet in the windows, Longworth and myself experimenting and attempting [creative concoctions] with whiskey, gin, vermouth and limes and sugar. It was a successful party." From there they took a boat trip to Daiquiri, where a ship's flags spelled out WELCOME HERE. It was, a military guide noted dryly, "a much more courteous reception than your father got when he landed there in 1898."[8] At Daiquiri, they mounted horses and rode along the "Rough Rider trail" to the site of TR's battlefield valor. Alice was unimpressed. The hills were "mildly sloping" and the whole scene seemed "on as small a scale as the war itself had been." The disappointment colored their trip back to Santiago and may have contributed to what Alice called a "heated argument" with Nick against the trunk of the Peace Tree that was, of course, captured by photographers.[9]

Alice was in for a cruel shock about her groom. Sometime during the honeymoon, she came upon Nick, "drunk and on the floor." She was "revolted." It was the first time she thought with any seriousness of Edith's warning about Nick, but by the time the two returned home the fight was forgotten, or at least put aside for the press.[10] The new husband called the trip "the most delightful I ever had . . . one of endless delight." The piece was notable less for Nick's superlatives than for the fact that Alice was not quoted (she "smiled her approval") and was referred to only as "Mrs. Longworth" or, by Nick, as "my wife."[11] Was her unusual reticence a result of travel weariness, Nick's dictum, or the work of a reporter schooled not to speak to wives when husbands were present? This curious silence began a pattern of Alice standing, or trying to stand, in Nick's shadow. It didn't last long. One journalist wondered whether "society is to have a princess royal" or whether "Mrs. Nicholas Longworth intend[s] to conform to the etiquette which applies to the wife of a junior member of Congress?"[12] Although she made a policy of not granting interviews, Alice's irrepressible nature and her wit—more brilliant than Nick's—made obscurity unthinkable.

First on her agenda, unpredictably, was family. "With the perversity of human nature," Alice recounted in her autobiography, "having become removed from them by marriage, I became aware of how delightful families are, of what good times they can have together. So, late every afternoon, I went over to see them for an hour or so between tea and dinner." She and Nick returned to Washington on March 4 and dined that noon with the president and the First Lady. Edith's diary that month is full of lunches with Alice, or Alice and Nick. Kermit joined them because, he acknowledged, "I can't imagine Sister as a stately married lady. . . ." Their father opined, "I think Sister is much improved by her marriage."[13]

Alice and Nick moved to 831 18th Street in Washington, which had been Susan Longworth's home.[14] Susan had taken up residence there with her son when he joined Congress so that she could be close to her darling "Nicky." She reluctantly returned to Rookwood in Cincinnati, loath to leave her son and her adopted city. A letter to her from a fan of her new daughter-in-law warned her against staying:

> We saw by the paper you were to make your home with her. This will be a great mistake as everyone likes to be head of the house, especially a bride likes to be alone with her husband without his mother.... More unhappy marriages have come from a man taking his wife to his mother's. It was bad enough for 'our Alice' to marry a man so much older than she without having an old lady always around.[15]

Susan's *harrumph* at the unsolicited polemic may be assumed.

Alice tried to settle into married life. This was not easy, as postwedding parties continued unabated, the desire to host gatherings of her own was strong, and tourists found their home an irresistible stop. "For awhile," Alice remembered, "I tried to have 'days at home,' but soon had to give them up, as they amounted to keeping open house for the passers-by. Sightseeing stages actually used to stop and let off their passengers, who would come in, wander around, have tea, and occasionally depart with a souvenir such as a doily or a small spoon."[16] Like Kermit, her friends wanted to see whether there were any changes in the new married Alice. One Sloper wrote, "You probably know all sorts of interesting things including 'how to be happy though married.'" Still, her friend charged, Alice had been seen at the horse races with a male friend. "Really Agile," ran the tongue-in-cheek sermon, "you are still as mad as ever I hear and bet quite recklessly. Don't you realize what a shocking example you are setting to your innocent little friends like me—and being at the races with Mr. Hitt! I was of course scandalized but have recovered in spite of the shock."[17]

Alice scandalized more than just old friends when she gave up the custom of calling. Calling was an institution in Washington where the roster of politicians and their wives changed every few years. Calling protocol was strict. Calls lasted usually less than thirty minutes. The one who was "at home" and receiving the calls ensconced herself in her drawing room and her butler or maid announced each new arrival. Callers sized each other up over their teacups and moved on. If someone was not at home, callers left their calling cards according to an elaborate system of particular corners folded down, which conveyed information about the caller. Given the central role of politics in daily life, social calls in the capital were unlike those anywhere else. Because politics is about power and calling is a custom in which the realities of power—social and political hierarchies, changing configurations of power, the identities of those with and those without political influence—are laid bare, the masks evident elsewhere are eliminated.[18]

"Virtuously," she thought, Alice began calling. But she came quickly to believe that "no sane human beings should let themselves in for" such an ordeal. This break with tradition caused gossip across the District. Cousin Eleanor was "appalled" by Alice's "independence and courage." One newspaper editorialized, "If young Mrs. Longworth takes the lead and flings these customs to the winds there will be great rejoicing in the Dupont circle contingent.... Hitherto in Washington officialdom has ruled with an iron rod.... Now, according to the dream of Mrs. Longworth, the statesmen must feel the power of social rank.... This will, of course, be an innovation and, no one except the daughter of the chief of the Executive would dare to start such an enterprise."[19]

Alice never looked back. One function of calling was to climb the social ladder. She was already at the top. Regardless of the job Nick held, Alice Roosevelt Longworth would always be a Roosevelt and the president's daughter (even when Theodore Roosevelt was no longer president; even when he was dead). She needed no acceptance from the cave dwellers (long-term residents in the capital city), for although she had not been born in Washington, she had lived there much of her life, and showed every sign of staying.

Alice was entering her political apprenticeship when discussions with her husband and her father gave her a serious interest in politics. Her desire for the story behind the political story, for the nuances of a political relationship, the journey of a bill in Congress, or the actions of a Supreme Court justice could not be satisfied by fifteen minutes of stilted and public conversation. Uniform calls failed to showcase her wit. She was the master of the personal. Time and time again acquaintances commented that she could best be understood in person, where the arched brow, the subtle display of the canine, the graceful motions of her hands, the trailing sentence, provided innuendo understood by an alert audience.

In May 1906, Alice had a chance to compare the Washington traditions she was overthrowing with Cincinnati's customs when she accompanied Nick to the music festival, "a somewhat formidable experience for one who is not musical," she recalled. Although she saw British composer Edward Elgar conduct his own work, she did not wax rhapsodic about the festival. She was pleased that she'd "weathered it fairly well." Nick took pity on her and whisked her away for a sanity break during an intermission. This backfired. They "returned very late," and, according to the *Cincinnati Enquirer*, the city's elite "frowned deeply."[20] It had not been her first trip to the Queen City, but it was her first time in Susan Longworth's home as the daughter-in-law. It was never an easy role for Alice. Nick's dutifully tender care of his mother made him into a different man in Cincinnati. Despite calling Susan "Mummy," he ruled the roost so sublimely that Alice referred to him as "the eagle." Her nickname for Susan—"Bromide"—encapsulated Alice's dismissal of her dull, conventional mother-in-law. "My conduct is pleasing in the eyes of the eagle," she penned sardonically. "Altogether thus far I have amused myself much for there is nothing like the joy of leading that little life of my own. . . . It is quite frantically entertaining—this business of getting both eagle and bromide to stand without twitching and feed from the hand. I fully expect them by the end of the week to be in strong leading string and quite house broken. The eagle suddenly became amenable (more so than the other—but it is more important that he should)."[21]

However, Alice's relationship with the Longworths would disintegrate until by 1912 they were barely speaking. Strongly held political differences, as well as more mundane disputes, would annihilate the initial sweetness of their encounters. Susan, at bottom, considered no woman good enough for her son. Alice accepted a fragment of the blame: "I was not...one who 'merged' with the family she married into; not by a long shot, I fear. Besides being an egotist, I was far too much one of my own family...."[22] But that was all in the future. By the end of the month, Alice and Nick were happily and haphazardly, Auntie Bye thought, embarking upon the final phase of their honeymoon.

Europe presented tremendous opportunities for the president's daughter and the Ohio representative. They were guests of Ambassador Whitelaw Reid at Dorchester House in London. "In confidence, strictly, [the Reids] told me," wrote Bye to Alice, "the King is to dine with them and when they spoke of your coming the King said he would come while you were there! He really is an old dear and how he would have loved you. It is well for Nick that he is old now," Bye said flatteringly.[23] The Reids planned for the Longworths to meet all the most brilliant people in Great Britain, and Alice looked forward to seeing family friends, too.

The European honeymoon was fraught with international implications. The same position of First Daughter that made King Edward VII want Alice for a dinner partner made her itinerary potential dynamite for U.S. foreign policy. President Roosevelt advised them that if they planned to visit Austria, they must also go to Budapest, "so that you shall not seem to ignore Hungary and pay heed only to Austria. If you go to Austria and Hungary I should avoid stopping either at Vienna or Budapest, or else I should stop at both; and if you do go...you and Nick listen smilingly to anything that any one from an Austrian archduke to a Hungarian count says about the politics of the dual empire, but, as I need hardly add, make no comment thereon yourselves."[24]

They sailed on June 1, 1906, on an American ship, the *St. Louis*, as "it was considered 'better politics,'" than sailing on a foreign-owned ship. Eight days later, they arrived at Victoria Station, London, to the acclaim of "a small crowd of well-behaved newspaper men." They were met by the Reids and taken to Dorchester House, where a much larger group and "a perfect battery of cameras" appeared. Then began a dizzying whirl of amusements among the British "smart set." Ambassador Reid wrote Edith in excruciating detail, including explanations of which princess was which and who the various duchesses and ladies "used to be."[25]

The long-awaited dinner with King Edward was on June 12 at the ambassador's residence. Alice was the first person presented to the king and made "her prettiest curtsey." She was seated by him at dinner and he "stayed much longer for the supper after the music than he had planned to do." The king was complimentary about Alice, who "enjoyed herself very much." The party was made up chiefly of Britons, "on the theory that Alice had come to England to see English people...." After this event, Roosevelt wrote his daughter, "I took sardonic pleasure in the fearful heartburnings caused the American colony in London, and especially among the American women who had married people of title, by the inability of the Reids to have everybody to everything. Nothing was more delightful than the fact that some of the people who were not asked to the dinner, but who were asked to the reception, hotly refused to attend the latter."[26] Cutting off one's nose to spite one's face elicited from TR, and from Alice, too, only the thinnest of sneers—especially when it concerned Americans who married into foreign aristocratic families.

The next night produced more evidence of Alice's celebrity. The Reids hosted a lavish reception—dinner and dancing—for eighteen hundred people at Dorchester House that Alice found "all so like the parties during the London season that one reads of...." America's Princess stood cheerfully in the receiving line. The ambassador and the king were pleased. An invitation to tea with the queen at Buckingham Palace arrived next. Alice remembered the occasion as "all very informal." Only the queen, Mrs. Reid, Alice, and a lady-in-waiting were present, until the queen of Greece arrived. Queen Alexandra was hard of hearing, but she carried on in a style any Roosevelt would admire, for "it didn't seem to worry her much. She kept up a fluttery irrelevant conversation." Alice, accustomed to fame, "felt very much at home with her...."[27]

Nick and Alice also found time to be tourists at Blenheim Palace and Covent Garden. They viewed a debate in the House of Lords and another in the House of Commons. Alice sat in the Speaker's gallery, and Nick saw the "procession with which the Speaker every day enters the House to open the proceedings." MP Sir John Henniker Heaton had them to tea on the terrace, a mixed blessing, Alice thought. "With the Houses of Parliament behind you and the Thames in front, and with half the men who govern England strolling about, it is a thing to remember. On this particular afternoon, however, it was as cold as Greenland. The tea was late in coming, we were all shivering, and would have given a good deal to be comfortably inside instead of romantically on the terrace."[28]

Because they were more than tourists, the Longworths also lunched with the Speaker of the House of Commons, had tea with the Duchess of Albany, and were the guests at a gathering where Lord Curzon spoke. George N. Curzon, author and statesman, had returned recently from India and his controversial partitioning of Bengal, and was about to become chancellor of Oxford University. Lady Curzon, whose Washington wedding had awed Alice as a child, glimmered in Alice's memory. One of the events Ambassador Reid tried to decline—the luncheon for three hundred members of the Society of American Women in London—turned out to be "really rather agreeable." Reid had been outmaneuvered by the society's president, who asked Nick to speak, which he did "with dignity and grace."

The remainder of the day would have tried the endurance of a professional athlete. From tea the ladies went to dinner, while Ambassador Reid and Representative Longworth attended the official Foreign Office dinner in honor of King Edward's birthday. The women intended to rejoin the men for the after-dinner reception, but were literally carried away by the crush. Finally, in "the small room where the supper for the Royalties and the Ambassadors was laid," they found each other again. After "a rather weary time struggling with the crowd to get hats and overcoats," they went on to "an early ball" at the home of the Duke and Duchess of Devonshire. This was to begin with a supper, but none of them could find room for it. Instead they left after thirty minutes for the Duchess of Westminster's. Alice danced at the insistence of her host, but she resisted the offer of yet another supper.

While Alice enjoyed mingling with so many different people, she was particularly thrilled by lunching with the king at his Ascot pavilion because she sat next to Archibald Phillip Primrose, the Fifth Earl of Rosebery. She thought him "one of the most brilliant and engaging figures in English political life." As she had read many of his books, mostly historical monographs, she was intensely interested in him. Lord Rosebery had been foreign secretary under Gladstone, whom he had replaced as prime minister. His service was short-lived, and his transformation from statesman to author was complete by the time the Longworths met him. But as an aristocrat of long bloodline, he commanded respect, and the luncheon was notable for the presence of "half a dozen Royalties."

Throughout the continuous rounds of official duties, Alice, according to Mrs. Reid, "has really had an enormous success and people everywhere have been charmed with her. Her natural frank manner and quickness of repartee please everyone." Nick also met with approval: "We all like Mr. Longworth so much too and the men feel he has such clear views about the questions at home and discusses them so well."[29]

The only unfavorable press came from American newspapers as they reported what can best be described as the knee-breeches flap. Some felt Representative Longworth had acted undemocratically when he wore knee breeches for his formal court presentation. The Longworths felt that wearing such attire was "of no more consequence" than "taking off one's shoes when one goes into a temple in Japan." In fact, they thought it "a mere matter of manners." And, as Alice pointed out, Nick had worn his breeches before the king at their first meeting, the dinner on the twelfth. Yet something about Americans bowing to the head of another country, especially the old Mother country, smacked of injudicious toadying. Alice, properly attired in her wedding dress, escaped journalistic censure. On every other subject, though, the American press praised the couple. "I don't care what the foreign papers say about Alice," Edith confided to Belle Hagner at home, "as long as the American papers continue to behave as they are doing."[30]

Among the private joys of their time in England was their introduction to English country life at Wrest Park, the Reids' country home in Bedfordshire. It was Alice's first encounter with the legendary peacefulness of the English countryside. A large number of congenial people gathered, including Delancey Jay, Katherine Barney, Ogden Mills, Gladys Vanderbilt, and the Reids' friend famous cricketer F. G. Menzies. The weekend whiled happily away in bridge, golf, lawn tennis, "automobiling," and some church-going on Sunday.

On the twenty-second, the Longworths moved on to Germany to pay their respects to King Edward's nephew, Kaiser Wilhelm, and to watch some yacht racing. The dinner on board the kaiser's ship, the *Hamburg,* was entertaining. The kaiser was a good host, asking many questions about their journeys and their concerns for the United States. Alice, an astute judge of character, drew a comparison between the two leaders: "King Edward had great dignity and impressed one as having reserves of strength that would always be there when the occasion called. The Kaiser, though one could not say that he was undignified, was restless, loquacious; he would take up a subject, rattle it about, express an arbitrary opinion that he appeared to think disposed of it, and then go on to something else. Yet it is stimulating and amusing to talk with that sort of character."[31]

The Longworths returned briefly to London for another ball before starting for Paris, where, according to the local newspapers, they were "everywhere welcomed with genuine sympathy. The congenial couple have elicited what in France is called excellent *'presse.'* Their portraits in straw hats and travelling attire are a feature of the front pages of over a dozen morning papers." Their hosts in France were Ambassador Robert McCormick and his wife, Katherine Medill McCormick. The McCormicks were great collectors of European art and first editions of French literature. They were also the parents of Medill and Robert. The former would go on to the U.S. Senate, while the latter would become the formidable "Colonel" McCormick, owner and publisher of the *Chicago Tribune.* Alice had once viewed Bert McCormick with an eye to engagement. All that was in the past, and as the ambassador and his wife met the Longworths, the newspapers raced to describe the visiting dignitary: "Mme. Longworth, with the grace of a true Parisienne, gave a nervous shake to her skirt, [and] adjusted her straw hat, tipped to the front according to the latest fashion.

There was no trace of fatigue on her bright, fresh face as she daintily alighted to the platform. She is exceedingly captivating," the *Petit Parisien* enthused. "Her countenance has an expression of graceful refinement, blended with shrewd, sly, good natured humor, and her attractive face finds a delightful framework in her luxurious locks of blonde hair."[32] And Monsieur Longworth? He was not mentioned.

Official gatherings were interspersed with visits to Nick's family in Paris, with dress shopping at Worth's and sightseeing at Versailles and Rochefort. Nick's sister Clara and brother-in-law Adelbert de Chambrun ("dear Charly's" brother) joined them for dinner at the Elysée Palace, hosted by French president Armand Fallieres. Alice sat between Fallieres and Georges Clemenceau, then minister of the interior. She enjoyed Clemenceau, who regaled her with stories of his youth in America. Clara remembered the couple being "taken up as the latest novelty by the 'Monde Chic,' just as they had been in London."[33]

There followed a leisurely trip to Bayreuth. This was Nick's week of the honeymoon, a pilgrimage stop for many music lovers then and now. Bayreuth, located in southeastern Germany, was the result of composer Richard Wagner's dream to unify Germany by showcasing its art. In the 1870s, Wagner oversaw the creation of a festival and the construction of a *festspielhaus* to replace the crumbling eighteenth-century baroque opera house built by German royalty. While Wagner's theater and its special effects were absorbing, the real draw was the music. It fed Nick's soul, but Alice found the sixteen-hour Ring Cycle "something in the nature of an endurance test." At least she could amuse herself with the many Americans present, some of whom were presumably just as bored as she.[34]

After viewing the medieval cities of Nuremberg and Munich, the Longworths returned to Paris to stay once more with Nick's sister Clara and her husband. Relations between the two couples would never be perfectly close, because Clara, like all the Longworth women, found Nick's marriage to Alice incomprehensible. No woman would be good enough for Nick, but the jejune First Daughter seemed an odd match for her distinguished brother. Impeccable manners triumphed on the honeymoon tour, however, and Alice and Nick contentedly played tourist in the Bois de Boulogne and the Champs-Elysée, seeing French theater and sampling local cuisine. At one café, Alice recalled, the patrons were engaged in the disconcerting pastime of "singing a song with rather ribald verses about the King of Spain's marriage and about ours."[35]

As July wound down, the two prepared to depart. Willard Straight wrote from Cuba asking Alice to meet him in New York, for fear he wouldn't see her for a long time. "The days of the Daiquiri are numbered and I am pulling out of this station very shortly," he informed her. President Roosevelt had helped transfer Straight to China, a larger field for his talents. Straight teased that he wanted to greet Alice upon her return "bearing liquor, lacquer and lunacy—which is an ode still incipient." He knew to make prior arrangements because "it would be a hopeless thing to try and break the cordon of secret police. I might simply want to offer you a nosegay and I'd be arrested as an anarchist with a little bunch of greenhouse bombs."[36] His charming offer was probably refused, if only because the Longworths were not lingering in New York City. They planned to collapse temporarily at Sagamore Hill for a debriefing from President Roosevelt.

The couple also needed time to sort out some problems. Perhaps Nick was bothered by the intimate nature of Straight's note or his wife's inability to appreciate Wagnerian opera. Maybe there had been a heated discussion about the fact that Alice was not pregnant, as so many Americans, the chief executive especially, hoped. Theodore Roosevelt had been "delighted" to learn of the birth of his niece Eleanor's baby, and shared the national disappointment over the absence of similar news from his daughter. Maybe Alice and Nick disagreed about his political future, as the headlines from home were reading LONGWORTH FOR GOVERNOR, a position Alice never really desired for him—or her.[37] Or more likely Nick had overindulged in alcohol or flirting—the two often went together with him—causing Alice's withdrawal.

Whatever its exact nature, some cloud had darkened their honeymoon sky, and the *St. Paul*'s passengers eagerly tattled about the couple's apparent estrangement to the ubiquitous journalists: LONGWORTHS IN SILENT MOOD ON VOYAGE HOME: DINED ALONE AND SPOKE TO ONLY THREE PERSONS the headline read. Their shipmates "confessed...that the President's daughter and her husband, who were naturally enough quite tired from the strain of nine steady weeks of going about, were somewhat of a social disappointment....Mrs. Longworth looked tired and even angry when she came aboard at Cherbourg....Mr. Longworth also participated in this silent mood, and for three days the bride and bridegroom were not seen or heard to address one word to each other. They sat on deck passing the time, each with a book." Only the steerage passengers, who presumably had not seen much of the Longworths, cheered when the couple disembarked.[38]

The Roosevelts met Alice and Nick at the docks nearest to Sagamore Hill. After a brief respite in the bosom of the family, the still-smarting Alice retreated to Newport, where she would often go for surcease from pain caused by Nick's drinking. Alice amused friends there with tales of her European exploits and willed away the hurt.[39] Nick went to his mother's home, ready to meet with labor leaders who were courting him.

Politics called. The Longworths needed to present a united front for the voters in Ohio, which is where the leader of the Republican Party suggested they go posthaste. "Tell Nick," TR wrote Alice in a letter full of fatherly advice, "I think his people will like to feel that you have a genuine interest in the city and come out there to make yourself one of Nick's people."[40] And eventually to Cincinnati went the president's daughter and her husband. Marriage and honeymoon had changed neither Nick nor Alice. He remained true to the bottle and happy in the company of other women, while she learned anew the virtues of self-reliance. Alice, at age twenty-three, loved Nick, but she wore her wariness like a protective shield.

Chapter 10

"Mighty Pleased with My Daughter and Her Husband"

WHEN ALICE AND NICK appeared at Oyster Bay "full of all sorts of amusing stories" from Europe, it was time to plot election strategy and for Nick and Alice to put their divisions aside. TR found no evidence that the glamorous European honeymoon had "hurt Nick at home," but warned them that Nick's opponents "will do all they can to make it injure him." Representative Longworth's first job was to reconnect with the Republican Party.[1]

Alice really wanted to return to Washington while she was still the president's daughter. But taking TR's advice, the Longworths made their obligatory trip to Nick's Ohio district, after visiting Sagamore for political and psychological sustenance. "Sister has improved an awful lot," Ethel confided to Belle after seeing Alice, "and I think that Nick has too. They are perfectly sweet together. Sister simply worships him."[2] The whole family agreed.

The Longworths were the picture of contentment upon their return to Rookwood. Met by reporters who wondered about Princess Alice's plans, she laughingly told them, "I would willingly try to assist my husband to return to Congress if he would allow me to do so." While Alice was young and devoted to Nick, she enjoyed Cincinnati—to a point. As Ethel put it, "Sister loves Cincinnati, but is a little ashamed to love it too much, I think." Alice herself allowed, "I never stayed very long at a time in Cincinnati in those days. I should say I went East on an average of two or three times a month, to stay at Sagamore, or at Newport with Grace Vanderbilt, and always to visit Auntie Bye at Farmington."[3] When she left, it was solo. Nick stayed at Rookwood with his mother. Alice was as ambivalent about Susan Longworth as she was about Cincinnati.

Bucolic and peaceful, the Queen City also had an unctuous side, covering the predictably vicious politics of an important town in an important state. In that year's election the labor vote was testy and demanding of both parties. Nick had told Alice about how he had been "made sick" in 1905 by the "nasty mud-slinging campaign in Ohio," and how "conditions were such that I couldn't bring myself to speak for the whole ticket." In that year, he was "heartily glad" to see that "the old order of things has definitely ceased and [political boss] George Cox has definitely retired from politics." Nick's assessment of Cox would prove to be premature. While it wasn't on a national scope like her father's political scene, Alice found that learning about the history of Ohio politics and who supported Nick and why could be moderately diverting.[4]

In September, the Longworths' visit to Columbus caused a stampede that nearly cost them their lives. Alice tried to unveil a statue of Ohio's martyred hero William McKinley on the Capitol grounds. Local authorities lost control of the crowd, numbering more than fifty thousand, and two people were taken away in an ambulance. Others fainted in the squeeze. In an effort to stave off pandemonium, Alice pulled the ribbons to unmask McKinley's statue early. As she did so, the streamers were quickly seized by souvenir seekers. The crowd dashed forward and the Longworths escaped through a window behind them into the governor's office. They tried to fight their way into a waiting car but failed, and bolted themselves behind the door of a nearby office building. There they stayed until the police came to extricate them. "It was the worst crush I ever witnessed," Alice said to reporters. She told them she had been "terrified" and had "seen nothing like it in my trip around the world." However, she confessed to her hosts privately that "it was the most exciting experience of my life," confirming that Alice knew precisely what the press wanted a well-brought-up young woman to feel in the middle of a raging crowd—and it wasn't excitement. After reading the frightening newspaper reports, Edith wrote her daughter that she "felt it was a bad day for Roosevelts when I saw that you had had to steal out of town as if you were escaping from a lynch mob."[5] That's one time it was a relief to board the train for Cincinnati.

It was an even greater relief to learn that Nick had been renominated for Congress without opposition, despite rumors of his break with the weakened but not powerless George Cox, and the frustration of labor union members who knew Nick was not their friend. Nick's acceptance speech made Alice happy. "Stripped of all unnecessary verbiage," Nick declared, putting the unions in their place, "the issue in this campaign is plain and clear—stick by Roosevelt.... Upon questions of party policy, I am first, last, and all the time a follower of President Roosevelt. Not because he is my friend and counselor in many things; not because we are of near family connection; not because of my admiration for him as a man, but because upon great, public questions I believe that he is right, and because I believe that by following his leadership I shall be doing that which is right."[6]

The campaign officially opened on October 7 in Cincinnati, and Alice arrived early to the kickoff. She was met with a standing ovation. She bowed and waved to Nick, who returned her smile from his place on the platform. Throughout the campaign season, her presence swelled the size of crowds that came to hear him and see her. Alice sat on platforms while Nick spoke; they shook hands all over the district. She opened the Cincinnati fall festival. In Marietta, she laid a cornerstone while her father's vice president, Charles Fairbanks, spoke. Alice left nothing to chance in the 1906 election, hiring a spiritualist to provide her with an "occult formula" to guarantee Nick's victory. It was her first campaign with Nick, his first attempt at reelection since their marriage. Her popularity was "Longworth's strength," and she wanted to be a useful campaigner.[7]

Their victory was sweet. The press recognized their partnership: "Mrs. Longworth is the great issue in her husband's campaign. She accompanies him to his political meetings, and probably makes more votes by her presence than he does by his oratory." Even Edith had to admit, "You must have enjoyed campaigning. I used to love to go with Father, and the papers have said such really nice things." Then, from her father, the note that crowned her efforts with glory: "Let me congratulate you and Nick with all my heart upon the successful way in which both of you have run your campaign. I tell you I felt mighty pleased with my daughter and her husband...." Edith, too, wrote with praise: "Last night they put on one of the bulletin boards here [at the White House] 'Alice and Nick have won' and the crowd called out 'Hurrah for them both.'"[8] Nineteen hundred six also propelled another interesting man into office: William E. Borah was elected to the U.S. Senate from Idaho.

After the victory parties were over, Alice and Nick, violin and the dog, Manchu, in tow, headed to Oldgate, Auntie Bye's Connecticut home. Although Bye worried about the dearth of excitement there, she had nonetheless pelted Alice with invitations in the weeks after the honeymoon. Bye hoped the visit would wash away the muck of the campaign, as they gave her all the latest election news. Of course, Bye was never really out of the loop. The more political of TR's sisters, Bye kept in close touch with him, even when she was away from D.C. It was to her house the president went to relax. Her circle of acquaintances was wide. She considered her friend (and nephew) Joseph W. Alsop's successful race for the Connecticut senate "preliminary steps" to national prominence. She placed great faith in Alsop's prediction that Nick's seat was secure because of Alice. "I cannot begin to say how empty the house seems without you and Nick," Bye wrote plaintively to her favorite niece after a November visit.[9]

In the middle of the campaign Alice had received, through a diplomatic pouch, a letter from Willard Straight. He wrote from Russia, where he was a warfront correspondent with Reuters and the Associated Press. Straight sent details about the events since Bloody Sunday, January 22, 1905, when the czar's troops had opened fire on starving workers protesting the despotism that caused their hunger. Straight chronicled a government attempting to implement civil reforms. The anger of the peasants still simmered, he wrote, and it was "open season for Czars and policemen." His letter described the terrible conditions of the peasantry, the amazing differences between Russia and the Europe of Alice's honeymoon, and some memorable characters he encountered. "You who are fond of the game would love it here. Servants are accepted universally as spies. At the Embassy they keep all secret codes . . . in a time lock safe. . . ." Russia was quiet, and

"Warsaw is the storm center at present—but there are constant uprisings and burnings in the provinces." Straight was right; Alice was fond of the game—and fonder still of those who played it wittily and well. His conclusion and his postscript are intimate, suggestive, but inconclusive: "For the rest—all that need not be said—you know. Thief. For which I am very glad." A postscript introduced an acquaintance to her who was on his way to Washington: "I like that he will have a chance to see something of you. It is a very wonderful world this in which we live—isn't it?"[10] Alice's difficulties with Nick were tempered by a long-distance flirtation with the up-and-coming Straight.

Nick, meanwhile, was dealing with the effects of having wed a hobbled heiress. He learned that Alice, while moderately wealthy, did not have access to all of her mother's legacy. A series of letters from Grandpa Lee to Nick made plain the older man hoped Nick would oversee his willful granddaughter's finances. "There is not much use in writing to Alice about it, as her knowledge regarding money and property is limited to the quickest method of 'blowing' it in, so I leave it to you to talk the matter over with her." He suggested that her property be held in trust for her, realizing that "the income from this property, say $2500 more or less, and the $2000 which I allow her are all her present income...."[11]

Alice received a $500 allowance from Grandpa Lee quarterly, and occasional income from her Boston property. She never ceased wanting more, as her grandfather well knew. "I am," he wrote her sadly, "aware that if you have any monies...you are very uneasy till you start it into circulation." Alice grew increasingly conscious of her poverty compared with her wealthy friends, especially Evalyn Walsh McLean, eventual owner of the Hope diamond. Grandpa Lee also controlled stocks and bonds for Alice, but he called them "local securities." She asked him to send the "money" to her, which made Lee remonstrate with her. While he professed to be happy to be "relieved of all contingencies regarding the investments," he also wrote that neither she nor Nick "would know anything about them." "If you elect to have the money," he cautioned, "you must not invest it except with the sanction of Nick and under his advice. Don't undertake to speculate unless your advisor will assume all loss. Women generally lose every cent, playing that game. You let it alone." And, he commanded, "Show this to Nick." In the end, the decision was made to sell some of the stocks (Massachusetts Gas Company and American Telephone and Telegraph) in order to send her $8,000 in May, leaving $515.55 in her account.[12] It isn't clear what she wanted the $8,000 for, or exactly how much remained of the stocks, which Lee continued to oversee.

Since Alice's funds were so tightly controlled, very little went to charity. Alice frequently received letters asking for money from people from all over the world, and as the veracity of such cases was difficult to establish, she generally did not respond. Alice felt that she could ill afford to be lavish in her giving. Beyond Nick's salary as a representative he had his own dwindling fortune, which he spent lavishly on clothing, food, drink, and his club life. In 1906, there was still a certain amount of money. But already, as Alice noted, "Nick was not sufficiently well-off to keep up more than the house in Washington."[13] Worsening financial troubles were still in the future.

For the moment, there was the start of the new House session and the holiday with her family. Alice sat up in the executive gallery for the opening of the House of Representatives on December 3, taking it all in and watching Nick below her reacquaint himself with his colleagues. She received alongside Edith at the annual diplomatic reception. "I think that I saw more of the family during the three winters after I was married . . . than I did during the entire time that went before. During the five winters in Washington that I was grown up, I spent much time seeing my friends in less stiff surroundings than the White House provided. I had no sitting-room of my own. . . . So I used to meet them at their own houses or at my aunt's. . . . But as soon as I had a house of my own, I began to realize that I had a particularly pleasant family."[14] And her marriage to Nick was not the refuge she had hoped it would be.

The relationship between Alice and her parents improved. While visiting the White House, Alice holed up with Edith, the three youngest children popping in. Theodore Roosevelt joined them frequently to "talk about the people he had been seeing during the day, the public questions that were up, or [to] discuss . . . latest news of the boys from school . . . my activities in the world of 'society,' people and things generally." Alice usually stayed until "the last possible moment" and then rushed home to dress for dinner. At least the family no longer reproached her for ignoring them.[15]

Nick's first Christmas as a member of the family was "ideal," TR proclaimed to his sister Corinne. He "joined easily and naturally in every detail of the celebration," the president reported, including the traditional stocking opening in TR and Edith's bedroom. Alice, he thought, "enjoyed it...more than she has any Christmas since our last one at Sagamore six years ago—for this is our sixth Christmas in the White House." The holiday celebration continued as the entire family went to the German embassy to exchange presents with the Baroness and Ambassador Speck von Sternburg, old family friends.[16]

The question on everyone's mind that holiday was who would succeed TR when his term expired. Roosevelt desperately wanted to stay in office another four years, but he had announced at his 1904 election that he would serve only two terms—the remainder of McKinley's and his own. He regretted having made such a promise, but he had to keep it. The press considered Nick an inside source since he was both the son-in-law of the president and a good friend of Republican front-runner and fellow Buckeye William Taft. Nick took his cue from his father-in-law and reiterated to reporters that TR would not run again, no matter how much he might personally desire it.

While Alice stuck close to the family, Nick was glum about his failure in the House to procure higher pay for U.S. diplomats. Success in that endeavor was still some years in the future. In February, Nick had more bad news: Roosevelt was set to appoint an African-American man named Ralph Tyler to be customs surveyor at the Port of Cincinnati—a thing Nick's constituents told him in no uncertain terms that they deplored. Nick was "at the White House three times a day pleading desperately with an Exalted Personage to keep Ralph Tyler away from Cincinnati so that the son-in-law can continue to come from there." Some solace returned in the celebration of his first wedding anniversary, but even more when Roosevelt eventually selected someone other than Mr. Tyler.[17]

After Easter, the Longworths returned to Cincinnati. Alice interpreted the local scene for her father as the "Taft movement" got off the ground. Despite whispers of a third-term draft for TR, Nick publicly announced his support for his friend Taft. That instantly made him an enemy of Taft's opponent for the Republican presidential nomination, Joseph B. Foraker, and simultaneously angered Boss Cox by his coming out for Taft before Cox wanted him to. Nick was carefully quoted as saying, "Personally—and speaking only for myself—I am for Taft for president."[18] Alice was well-enough schooled in politics to know that an attempt by her father in 1908 was not in his best interests. At least she knew that intellectually.

Alice escaped to see her Lee grandparents in Boston and to visit everyone in Washington. That spring, she frequented Benning racetrack near Washington. She was the society headliner and often in the company of wealthy brothers Perry and August Belmont, the first a former Democratic congressman and the latter an investment banker and racehorse owner. The absence made Nick's heart grow fonder. "Darling little Bubby," he wrote in May: "I've just gotten back from the Pillars where I had a very quiet and respectable evening playing bridge.... And now I am about to go to my lonely beddy without my sweetest bubby to put her head on his shoulder. I've missed you all day my darling, and I'm going to miss you more tonight."[19]

Some Cincinnati friends joined the Longworths on a two-day drive to the Kentucky Derby, where the crowd greeted Alice with "an ovation of hand clapping, waving handkerchiefs and cheers." Local reporters were uncharacteristically sensitive: "It must be awful to be a President's daughter and not be able to draw a natural breath without an extra being published about it. And the great mass of people expect a celebrity to do something unusual every minute of her life, so the calm, 'jelly regular, splendidly null,' perfectly bred conduct of the lady of the day yesterday came as a great blow to the populace, who would have preferred having her do some interesting stunts."[20]

As the summer heated up, Nick and Alice returned to Hawaii. Their last visit had been in 1905 as part of the congressional junket. Then they had spent barely a day on the main island, "Just enough to whet my appetite," Alice recalled. On the way, the couple luxuriated in a five-week western holiday—after a setback. Alice fell headfirst into the red, oozing muck in Yellowstone. Nick, "instead of displaying his customary gallantry," doubled over in "a most provoking laugh." Friends took Alice to the hotel to wash off the sticky clay; Nick "preferred admiring the scenery to facing his wife's pique." After visiting San Francisco, the couple considered exploring Alaska. But the siren call of Honolulu could not be denied.[21]

They stayed in a cottage at Waikiki, swam daily, feasted on Hawaiian delicacies, and were shown the sights by friends and local elites. On Maui, the breathtakingly beautiful Haleakala, which rises straight out of the sea to jab upward toward the heavens, made her feel "like a rather vigorous lotus eater," right out of Tennyson's poem. They rode horseback up a volcanic mountain at midnight, reaching the edge of the crater just as the sun did. They spent the next two days ambling down the mountain and along the cliffs above the coastline, interrupted only by well-wishers who greeted them with leis. Their exploration ended with a luau in the Iao Valley, its lush vegetation and peaceful stream hiding the memory of the fierce battle won there by King Kamehameha.

Alice was enthralled by the entire Hawaiian experience, as she told a friend in a wistful letter: "We had the most delicious time this summer in Honolulu—Living in a frivolous cottage in a palm grove beside a marvelous ocean. Quantities of…human beings ready for anything at any moment and the most wonderful riding and bathing you can imagine. I hated to leave and I am homesick for it the whole time." It was not all sight-seeing, for they greeted five thousand people at a reception hosted by Governor George R. Carter. For that duty, they were reunited with the secretary of commerce and labor, Oscar Straus, who had sailed to Hawaii on their ship. Straus told reporters that Alice "charmed everyone who met her," and she was styled "Mrs. Longworth, Woman Diplomat."[22]

Election activities accelerated throughout the fall, as did election rumors. Nick was variously mentioned as Ohio's next governor and its next senator, as Cincinnati's next mayor, and as America's next ambassador to Germany. Meanwhile, TR embarked on a speaking campaign through the Midwest, down the Mississippi River, and then south through Tennessee, Louisiana, and Arkansas. Edith sent her daughter an advance copy of the president's schedule with instructions not to show it to anyone, so that Alice could plan to meet TR in Canton, Ohio.

President Roosevelt's popularity was so great that he was able to hand-pick his successor in the White House, and after some deliberation, chose William Howard Taft. Taft, from Nick's congressional district in Cincinnati, had been a family friend of both the Longworths and the Roosevelts for years. Taft had served in various capacities in TR's administration, including governor-general of the Philippines and secretary of war. Taft idolized Roosevelt but was not, as TR deluded himself, an exact political duplicate. On the eve of the 1908 presidential election, the two friends lived in a mutual admiration society. In fact, the only real critics of the transition from TR to Taft were Alice—who hated to see the family vacate the White House—and Helen Herron Taft. Mrs. Taft had an abiding suspicion of the charismatic Theodore Roosevelt, and found fault all through the 1908 campaign. She thought that TR should have announced for Taft earlier than he did and could be warmer in his public appeals. Helen Taft's misgivings began a sad series of events that led to the breakup of the Taft-Roosevelt friendship and TR's ultimate challenge of Taft's incumbency four years later.

Alice and Nick traveled between Washington and Cincinnati all fall, gathering information, tracking the campaign, and keeping an eye on Nick's district until Alice came down with appendicitis. For several months she had suffered mysterious on-again, off-again pains, the "mulligrubs," as she called them. At Nick's insistence, she reluctantly missed her grandparents' golden wedding anniversary. She had to have her "appendix plundered," as she put it to her friend Eleanora Sears. Assisting the physician on the appendectomy was Dr. Sophie Nordhoff-Jung, who would become Alice's most trusted doctor. Alice holed up in the White House for the surgery. The rooms were larger and more comfortable than any hospital. Edith could shield her from the prying eyes of the media. The chance to be within the circle of the family again was too much to pass up. Nick wrote his mother that during Alice's surgery "the President and I sat hand in hand, so to speak, in the library and heard the reports."[23]

Surgery was not taken lightly in 1907. Auntie Bye's tender letter from

Connecticut made clear her own feelings: "My darling big girl, I hate you to have had even a threatening of appendicitis and not to have been near to look in. Sweetheart you are so far from me that my heart often has a sore spot at not seeing you, and you never forget, do you dearie that the old Aunt is always ready to fly to you literally at any moment were you ailing and needing me."[24]

The greatest benefit of convalescing in the White House was being close to the hub of the political news. Alice cooked up a plan with her father to attempt to discover what the phlegmatic Mr. Taft intended for the subject of a critical speech, his first upon his return from the Philippines. Alice and the president hoped for a real curtain-raiser, a speech to galvanize and unify Republicans. The two men came to Alice's room, where Taft found TR's energy overwhelming. "Finally," Alice recalled, "I propounded my question. I can see the Secretary, perfectly enormous, sitting in a solid wing chair, his hands clasped on his middle, saying with a slow rumbling chuckle, 'Well, I thought I would talk about the Philippines,' whereat there was a roar of protest and ironic mirth from Father and me. Indeed I was so emphatic that one of the stitches in my scar broke."[25]

The Christmas holiday barely interrupted politics. Nick's best present came in mid-December from Speaker of the House Joseph Cannon: appointment to the powerful Ways and Means Committee. Nick wrote his "Dearest Mummy" that he had been "having a very busy time quite different from what I had expected after election when I thought I was entitled to a good loaf. But the Fates have decreed that I am to sit practically every day . . . with the Ways and Means committee from 9:30 in the morning until 5:00 in the afternoon absorbing facts and figures about the most abstruse and difficult subjects before congress nevertheless it is most interesting and I am enjoying it."[26]

Amid the celebration, there was time to see to the important niceties of life that Alice often found so easy to ignore. "Thank you most deeply for your thought to send me the joyful tidings of the birth of your blessed Baby boy! . . . and a very merry Christmas to you both and the two little ones" she wrote to Franklin and "Eleanor-dear."[27] Everyone enjoyed the traditional Christmas at the White House. Alice, Nick, and the other children came in to TR and Edith's room on Christmas morning and opened their stockings. After breakfast came a tableful of presents for each child, then a three-hour horseback ride for some members of the family—but not Alice, lest she pop another stitch.

That January was the start of the last full year of Roosevelt's presidency. He fought more and more frequently with congressmen who felt his protection of the "poor, ignorant, and turbulent" was at the expense of businesses he believed went too far in their search for profit. The beginning of a rift within the Republican Party could also be seen in debates over the tariff, a complicated bill guaranteed to alienate as many members as it would please. TR had managed to avoid it for seven years. By the time the GOP had committed itself to a review of the current tariff, the progressive half of the party favored increasing it, and the conservative half preferred the status quo. While the tariff would be left to TR's successor, other bills would be seen as anticorporation—such as the Pure Food and Drug Act and the meat inspection rider—and would push conservative Republicans to back Taft. The quarrelling in Congress occurred during a brief economic downturn that had all Americans, even wealthy bankers such as Grandpa Lee, "hoping for better times."[28]

Better times, for Alice and her family, were not on the immediate horizon. They shared an overwhelming sadness at leaving the White House. Fame was wearing but addictive. Even the youngest among them understood its value. Alice confessed that "no one will ever know how much I wished, in the black depths of my heart, that 'something would happen' and that Father would be renominated. It was against human nature, against mine anyway, not to feel that the prospect of all those great times coming to an end was something to be regretted, though most secretly." One of Franklin Roosevelt's favorite stories, told by his "Uncle Teddy," was TR's response when pressed to run for the third term: "They are sick of looking at my grin and they are sick of hearing what Alice had for breakfast."[29]

The winter provided political interest, but everyone agreed that Taft was certain to be nominated—unless TR changed his mind. In Taft's own state of Ohio, during a civic celebration in the tiny town of Norwood, the spontaneous applause at the mention of Roosevelt's name went on so long that it disrupted the speaker's address. Nick defended Theodore Roosevelt frequently and publicly. Thanks in part to his marriage to the First Daughter, he, too, seemed certain to maintain his House seat. He was rewarded when delegates to Ohio's Republican convention in early March lauded Roosevelt but voted for hometown favorite Will Taft as the party's next standard-bearer.[30]

Alice tried a different form of public activity that year when Ruth Hanna McCormick become the national director of the Women's Committee of the National Civic Federation (NCF) in May. Since TR had forced her to attend Ruth's wedding to Medill McCormick, Alice and Ruth had become lifelong best friends. Ruth's father was the first president of the NCF, founded by wealthy businessmen in 1900 to promote harmonious relations between labor and capital. Prominent women joined the cause. Because of Marcus Hanna's position, his daughter, who shared many of his views and was politically active in her own right, was the logical choice to head the Women's Committee.

Women's suffrage was emphatically not on the agenda, but there were early attempts to include working women on the committee. "The professional woman agitator has misrepresented her sex. Who ever heard of a mother with seven children wanting to vote? But who is more competent to suggest improvements in her own and her working husband's condition than such a mother?" asked one of the Women's Committee members. Daisy Harriman exhorted listeners at the organizational meeting to form a local chapter of a women's division in New York City by reminding them of the influence they have over the "owners and stockholders," and asserting that since they "spend the money which the employees help to provide," they should "take a special interest in their welfare, especially in that of the women wage earners."

In order to see for themselves, female elites such as J. P. Morgan's daughter Anne Morgan, Sarah Platt Decker, Corinne Roosevelt Robinson, Maude Adams, Daisy Harriman, Gertrude Vanderbilt Whitney, and Alice Longworth attended NCF meetings to hear working-class women, union representatives, and others speak about ameliorating the lives of the working poor. The May meeting delegates were welcomed to the White House by Theodore Roosevelt, and one can speculate on the role of Alice in this coup for Ruth's fledgling committee.[31]

Alice attended meetings and undoubtedly discussed labor problems with Ruth, but she never cared for working in a group. While Alice didn't mind lending her name to an organization whose goals she shared, *Robert's Rules of Order* and fund-raising were not her style. Those smacked too much of the earnest reformer whom one admired but didn't emulate. Alice preferred to be closer to the seat of power.

Alice attended her first national political convention that year when the Republicans met in Chicago. It gave her "a taste for that form of entertainment that I do not think I shall ever get over," she wrote in her memoir. In fact, from 1908 on, Alice went to the conventions of both parties. They were usually spellbinding, sometimes heartbreaking, almost always full of action. "The real fun," she knew, was "outside the convention hall—at the headquarters of the national committee and of the candidates—in the conferences that are peppered through the various hotels and are going on day and night—at the all-night sessions of the committee on resolutions which has the drafting of the platform." And there were festivities, including Julius Fleischmann's theater party where "we were cheered and made much of," many lunches and dinners out with friends, and all of Chicago to explore. Ruth and Medill—a local—were her guides around the Windy City. Auntie Corinne, Uncle Douglas, and cousin Corinne accompanied them. The French ambassador Jules Jusserand and his wife, and the British ambassador James Bryce and his wife, also made fascinating companions.[32]

The June convention was full of the hurly-burly that became so addictive for Alice. Nick and Alice, Ruth and Medill, and Auntie Corinne and Uncle Douglas monitored the events together. Setting a precedent that drew a standing ovation, Alice made sure that others could monitor events as well. With "a simple act of courtesy," Alice took off her trademark large hat. "Fancy women," she puzzled, "deliberately putting an obstacle in any one's way to the enjoyment of a thing so big and important." After her

thoughtful act, "There was a noticeable absence of large millinery crea-
tions in the house." The same held true four years later.[33]

Even though he wasn't there, Theodore Roosevelt's progressive ideas
infused the platform, and his name set off a fifty-minute cheer. Alice jeal-
ously counted the length of the Taft demonstration—twenty-five minutes,
half of her father's. She heard every speech and maintained the Roosevelt
family line on her father's third term. "I was given the usual amount of
publicity, which consisted largely in attributing to me many pert remarks
and actions of which I vow I was never guilty—such as ... waving a fan
with 'Third Term for Teddy' on it, and being generally boisterous. I really
do not believe I was boisterous." "Keen, interested," she agreed, but not
boisterous.[34]

Surely part of the difficulty lay in defining *boisterous*—and in the continuing desire of her adoring public to see her misbehave. In May, for example, Alice had placed a tack on a chair in the diplomatic gallery in the
House of Representatives and watched, laughingly, as her dupe impaled
himself. This earned her some fan mail:

> Last week cute Alice Longworth
>   Placed a tack upon a chair
> In the gallery of Congress
>   And let some one sit down there.
> The victim muttered "I am stuck,"
>   And gave a little spring,
> Then used some pointed language
>   About the pointed thing.
> Of course, 't was only "just a joke"
>   (And not a tactless one),
> But it started a new fashion
>   For the dudes of Washington.
> Those who listen from the gall'ry
>   While some windy statesman rants
> Are wearing anti-puncture
>   Tire-protectors on their pants!

"I want to say," her pro—third term admirer wrote, "the world laughs with you and you become more popular than ever...." Mail like this Alice assiduously tucked away, as it balanced out continuing warnings from the family to avoid "too much newspaper notoriety."[35]

The 1908 convention did nominate Taft. New York congressman "Sunny Jim" Sherman got the vice presidential slot. Alice had tipped off reporter William Allen White with that insider news. The culmination of the convention for the president's daughter came when she held an "impromptu" reception for "hundreds" of convention goers. MRS. LONGWORTH WELCOMES CROWD: PRESIDENT HIMSELF COULD NOT SURPASS DAUGHTER'S HANDSHAKING ACHIEVEMENT blared the *Chicago Tribune*. A friend inadvertently started the reception by shaking Alice's hand good-bye, and suddenly a queue of strangers appeared behind her, hands out. One woman complimented her: " 'Mrs. Longworth, you are the dearest girl in America,' to which she responded, 'I am glad to have you say that.' " The *Tribune* reported, "No one, not even Senator Lodge, has attracted the attention in the Coliseum that has been given Mrs. Longworth, and a queen could not have received it more modestly or more graciously. The oldest men, as well as the youngest, went much out of their way to see 'Teddie's' daughter, and she could have started a furious ovation at any time by simply rising and bowing to the public."[36] She also could have started a third-term stampede for her father.

After a brief holiday in a Chicago suburb, the Longworths and the McCormicks hopped the train to Denver to "see how the Democrats did it." There, in the heat of a Colorado summer, Alice also measured the demonstration for William Jennings Bryan, which aimed to top TR's in Chicago. "As yelling, sweating delegates tramped past our box, we noticed that they had watches in their hands and heard them occasionally inquire of one another if it had 'gone over the time yet.' " It was visibly difficult for Alice to hear the Democrats slander her father, but she generally maintained her composure.[37]

Alice did make an interesting acquaintance in Denver: Ruth Bryan Leavitt, Bryan's daughter, who would become the first woman elected to Congress from the South. Alice confessed to a "fellow feeling" for her. The three politicians' daughters found themselves "trotted out" from their unobtrusive box at a pro-suffrage rally. Alice was "unmistakably, distinctly, and undisguisedly bored," as "all the vice-presidential candidates in town," spoke earnestly on the necessity of women's suffrage, "and did not appear to observe that the subject was a rather dreary one as far as most of the listeners were concerned." Rather than being able to listen unobserved, an efficient soul—knowing trophies when she saw them—herded Alice and the two Ruths onto the stage quite against their wishes. "Nice, gentle quiet little Mrs. McCormick" gave a speech to promote her work with the National Civic Federation. Stirring music, with nearly everyone joining in, followed her talk, and through it all, "Mrs. Longworth sat, a monument of astonished and bewildered boredom." Of course, whether other women stifled yawns and shifted in their seats was not publicized. If the daughter of William Jennings Bryan—Bryan was fated yet again to be the Democratic Party's unsuccessful presidential nominee in 1908—were to fidget, the *Denver Post* could not allude to that, as that would have been impolite of the main journalistic organ of the town hosting the Democratic convention. To the attendees it didn't matter, as Alice "was crushed, torn, jammed, pushed and almost trampled to death" in admiration.[38]

In the early years of her marriage, Alice seemed to be trying out different roles for herself: involved political wife, NCF reformer, charter member of the Washington Congressional Club (for wives of congressmen), dutiful daughter (better late than never), style setter (she was on the best-dressed lists and famous for her "Alice Longworth picture hat"), and the irrepressible Princess Alice. Her sense of humor remained intact through it all. A carload of tourists looking for Sagamore Hill had their chauffer pull alongside Alice, Ethel, and Quentin, who were shopping. "I wonder," said one, "if the President's daughter, Mrs. Nick something or the other, is there and if we can get a peep at her and the other daughter, Miss Ethel." And Alice, "with features as immobile as a graven image," replied, "To the best of my knowledge they are not at home just now." A local Democratic Party leader overheard the exchange, flagged down the car full of disappointed celebrity hunters, and explained the joke.[39]

Nick and Alice appeared to be much in love. While Alice was mocking the sightseers, she received a touching note from Nick in mid-August:

"Manchu and I had a rather panting and fitful slumber. It having eschewed its basket for a distinguished and at times audible position beneath my bed whence I had not the heart to drive it because we both missed our Bubbie so much." Nick sent Alice two dozen red roses in Oyster Bay. Every day she was away from him, she told reporters, he sent her flowers. His devotion, she averred, was evidence of the happiness of their marriage. By month's end, Nick joined her for a fortnight at Sagamore.[40]

The Roosevelt family spent the fall beginning the sad task of packing up the White House. Edith longed for the quiet of Sagamore, but worried about her husband's transition to retirement. She confided in Cecil Spring-Rice, after the temptation of a third term had passed, that TR's "mind is full of his African trip. He is to start next April and take Kermit who will be nearing the end of his first year in college. They expect to be gone a year and Theodore has promised to write an account of his trip for *Scribner's*, and as this means a book afterwards I hope he may be busy and interested for the summer after he comes home."[41] Roosevelt's African safari was to be part scientific expedition, part spiritual renewal, and part a way to take himself out of the limelight so Taft could act without journalists claiming TR was the puppet master guiding hapless Will.

Alice alternated between distaff duties in Cincinnati and politics in Washington. Nick gave a "eulogy and a defense of the president's administration" in Rock Island, Illinois, wherein he proposed that Theodore Roosevelt should return to the presidency after two Taft terms. His idea was tremendously popular. Nick was the man in the middle that year, trying to celebrate his father-in-law, elect his constituent Taft, and keep the way open for his own advancement. His visibility increased as he rode the election trail with vice presidential candidate Sherman, giving speeches and riling up the crowds. While he was away, Alice told reporters that she would stay at the White House with her parents. "Then she added, with a sort of wistfulness that was never a part of the old Alice Roosevelt, 'the house is so big and I would be so lonesome by myself with Mr. Longworth away.'" When he worked for Taft inside Ohio, Alice campaigned with him, usually a silent but compelling draw on the platform. In Pittsburgh, she took part in a parade and a five-hundred-dollar fund-raising dinner in her honor, and led the applause later that night as the speeches began.[42]

Nick—in a statement about either his loyalties or his ambitions—made sure that he and Alice spent the election night at the Tafts' Cincinnati home. There, with the extended Herron and Taft families and Nick's sister Nan Wallingford, they waited to hear the results. The outcome for Taft was clear by midnight. Crowds gathered outside, bands played "Hail to the Chief," and the people's choice ambled from his easy chair to acknowledge his victory. Happily Nick's election had the same ending and, as Alice wrote John Greenway, "by a larger margin than was expected." Alice shared in the congratulations: "We are credibly informed [that] you largely contributed," wrote Edwin Morgan.[43]

While Alice anticipated it and had indirectly worked for Taft's victory, she resented the crowing of her in-laws. Their constant glorifying of Taft made Alice "indulge a proclivity toward malice that occasionally comes over me." Whenever the Longworths suggested they owed little to her father, Alice became furious. When the election details arrived, the Longworths "gloated" as they compared them with TR's 1904 returns. "The stage was set," Alice shrugged, "for the first steps that led to the 'breaking up of a beautiful friendship.'"[44]

More than one friendship disintegrated after 1908. Alice never quite felt the same about her in-laws, and Roosevelt and Taft experienced the dissolution of their comradeship as well. Taft was not another TR. His personality was cautious, judicious, and vapid. TR was the personification of energy.[45] Despite what the Roosevelt family considered his promise, Taft did not retain TR's cabinet. Nor did he continue Roosevelt's policies unbroken—any more than TR had carried on McKinley's policies. Helen Taft and Edith Roosevelt even clashed over the best way to run the White House.

As the end of her father's presidency became real, Alice herself "helped to make bad blood" by doing a scathing but hilarious impersonation of the new First Lady. She contorted her visage into what she called her "hippopotamus face" to sneer, "this, my darlings, is what is coming after you."

Receiving a ticket from Helen Taft to let her into the White House for the inaugural luncheon was the final straw: "Instead of taking it as obvious routine," Alice recollected, "I flew shouting to friends and relatives with the news that I was going to be allowed to have a *ticket* to permit *me* to enter the White House—I—a very large capital I—who had wandered in and out for eight happy winters! Indeed, I gave myself over to a pretty fair imitation of mischief-making."[46] There was no relief in sight for Nick. He remained the man in the middle.

Chapter 11

"Expelled from the Garden of Eden"

ALICE ROOSEVELT LONGWORTH closed out the election year of 1908 with an act of uncharacteristic sentimentality. She and TR's aide Archie Butt walked through the White House: "We went from room to room and each one had some sweet memory for this girl whose career in the White House has been the most dramatic of any in its history. 'Princess Alice,' she was called, and she ruled over her kingdom as no other woman has ever done there.... To me she is far more attractive now than she was as a young girl, for she has developed not only physically but mentally and in poise. She was sad this afternoon, for she seemed to realize just what the change would mean to her. She was not complaining, for she has too much of her father in her for that, but she did not hesitate to give voice to the note of sadness."[1]

Alice could not escape being changed by her time as First Daughter. As Archie Butt noticed, she grew up under the gaze of the public, just as Susan Ford, Amy Carter, and Chelsea Clinton would do at the end of the century. And like theirs, her blossoming was accompanied by moments of parental despair. But Alice remained utterly independent and protective of her inner self even as she gave generously of her public persona. If observers were correct, she enjoyed the status of her position enough to hope that Nick would carry her back into that historical house once again. Nineteen twenty-four, in fact, was the year suggested by some members of the GOP during the election: Taft for two terms, then TR back again for eight years, then a seasoned Nick Longworth ascending to the presidency in 1924.[2] That was a long time away.

Before any dreams of returning, there was the inexorable march of awful "lasts" to endure: the last Christmas, the last birthday celebrations, the last receptions, balls, and dinners, the last guests, the last day, the last night. "Nobody likes to leave the White House, whatever they say. We were no exception," Alice stated emphatically years later. Each member of the family marked the looming change in his or her own way. Alice found time to bury a voodoo figure in the White House garden, a hex on the next occupants.[3] Ethel prepared for her debut. Young Quentin led his "White House Gang" on merry chases and lived in the present. Edith packed systematically, hoping for a smidgen of normality to come. TR gave away mementos—White House china, photographs, trinkets.

Christmas at the White House was a large family affair. Nick and Alice plucked gifts from a Christmas tree burdened with surprises for sixty revelers. The Roosevelts wanted to make the holiday especially memorable. Try as they might to keep it at bay, melancholy lurked among the tinsel. Alice thought a photograph taken at the time showed the family looking "as if we are being expelled from the Garden of Eden."[4]

Ethel's debut returned effervescence to the winter social season. Wine, aging since the 1905 nuptials, buoyed the 440 guests, who danced continually on a floor so shiny that it reflected the chandeliers above. Even the "tottering ancient" older sister Alice found it "one of the prettiest parties I have ever seen at the White House." Butt oversaw the details of the ball, and wrote that the White House looked "far more beautiful than it was even at Alice's wedding."[5]

Alice had the hardest time keeping up a happy appearance. Eleanor and Franklin had been invited to the traditional January diplomatic reception at the White House. They saw cousin Alice only briefly. She had "a cold and a headache etc. but she looks lovely and very well and so quiet!" Eleanor reported. ER—who never knew quite how to approach her cousin—also mentioned cattily that Ethel didn't appear spoiled by her foray into adult socializing the way her older sister had, and pronounced Ethel "not along Alice's lines at all!"[6]

President Roosevelt warded off sadness by surrounding himself with congenial dinner guests. Nearly every night, Butt chronicled, "Mrs. Roosevelt starts out to have family dinner and by 1 o'clock the President has asked so many as to make it almost a state affair. He is certainly the soul of hospitality. He dearly loves a great number of people around his table. He is just as happy with a lot of schoolboys as he is with a lot of statesmen, a little bit happier, I often think."[7] At that particular time, the schoolboys were a useful antidote to the terrible daily feuds dished up by conservatives in the Republican Party, some of whom looked forward to March with a joy as intense as the family's sorrow.

Lively reports of the titanic clash of wills on Capitol Hill poured from reporters' pens: "The last annual message of President Roosevelt and the last session of the 60th Congress came together with a crash. It was not quite a case of an irresistible force and an immovable body, but it was near enough to make things interesting for awhile. Every session of this Congress has during the last two years furnished, at its opening, an exhibition of some such conflict with the President." By the time of his last annual address in 1909, Congress and the president had reached a parting of the ways. The final session was a battle about presidential power centered on the Secret Service, an ideological clash that eventually gave birth to the Federal Bureau of Investigation. Alice called it "one long lovely crackling row between the White House and the Capitol," but she had observer status.[8] For those involved, the price was dear.

Nick navigated the middle, fast becoming his chosen place. At the same diplomatic reception where Eleanor sized up Alice, Butt observed many absences among the congressmen who "showed their resentment toward the President by remaining away."[9] But "Old Nick," Butt thought, looked anxious about House matters. "He is very popular there and members tell me that he conducts himself with wonderful discretion. But to be a member of the body which feels itself insulted by the President, and yet retain his temper when that body attacks his father-in-law, is a difficult task, especially to one who is as devoted to Mr. Roosevelt as he is. As he said goodnight to the President last night, the President hit him on the back and said: 'Poor old Nick! What is he not suffering for love's sake these days!' Nick laughed and said, 'I think I am enjoying it about as much as you are, Mr. President.' "

Nick escaped to the Metropolitan Club. He skipped out on the House debate over the tone and the wording of Roosevelt's last message. He thought, for everyone's sake, he ought not participate in the conversations where he'd have to stick up for TR or defend himself. Nor did he want to "embarrass some [of his] personal friends there who may want to hit back for home consumption." Nick tried not to feel impatient. He hated sitting on the edge of his seat so he could "skin out of the House to prevent voting to censure [his] own father-in-law." Alice avidly followed the recalcitrant Congress, her husband's awkward position, and her father's "spanking" by the intractable politicians. While neither man in her life was particularly happy, she was thrilled to be at the center of things. "I suppose what you don't know about politics by this time is not worth knowing," her mother-in-law wrote her.[10]

On Alice's twenty-fifth birthday, the Longworths concentrated on politics in Grand Rapids, Michigan, where Nick gave a Lincoln's Day speech and Alice laid a cornerstone for a new federal building, "with all the solemn rites of the Masonic ceremony." Thousands cheered her as they sang one of her father's favorite hymns, "Onward Christian Soldiers."[11] The extravagant attentions paid them were a reminder that their lives would continue in the pattern imposed by Nick's service in the House and Alice's celebrity.

The family proudly circled round TR for a last moment of glory to watch the Great White Fleet make its magnificent return from around the world. The twenty-six white battleships sailed past slowly, each booming a twenty-one-gun salute. The president toured the flagship, greeted the officers, and basked in triumph. Roosevelt had sent the fleet out to exhibit American naval strength. It was the capstone of his efforts to build a more efficient navy and one of his greatest accomplishments.

Inevitably, the last evening in the White House arrived. The president and First Lady hosted a small dinner for the Tafts, who were staying overnight on the eve of the transfer of power. Alice and Nick, Auntie Bye and Uncle Will, Belle Hagner, Henry Cabot Lodge, Archie Butt, the Roots, and the Tafts' good friend Mabel Boardman took part in what Alice considered a "curious occasion." The Tafts, she recalled, were trying to stifle their "natural elation," while TR was already assailed by doubts concerning Taft's abilities to carry on the Rooseveltian vision. Butt "was frankly emotional," and the devoted Root dropped tears into his soup. Helen Taft's insistence on having things her way in the White House meant she was, in Edith's opinion, overly aggressive and unconscionably early in making hurtful changes. "It was," Alice wrote, "a singularly hushed and cheerless dinner." The only thing that made the night bearable for her was the roiling snowstorm that shook the shutters and kept the Tafts awake. It presaged a miserable inaugural. Her voodoo was working.[12]

Indeed, the snow continued unabated, temperatures dropped, and the sun shone the next day only long enough to create a "loathsome slush." Taft's well-wishers braved the storm, but futilely, as the administration of the oath of office took place in the Senate, out of public sight. Alice, Edith, Bye, Quentin, and Belle skipped the swearing-in and went instead to console themselves over lunch at the Longworth home. The other family members were at school or work, except for Quentin, who remained to sit in the president's box and watch the inaugural parade with his pal from the White House gang—the new presidential son, Charley Taft. TR exited immediately after the inaugural address, as audience members wept quietly.[13]

Edith's famous restraint finally gave way on the train. In her thank-you note to Belle for the thoughtful farewell gift of terrapin—TR loved it and ate "every last morsel"—Edith confessed that TR "did not get any sherry for I drank it all, and found it most comforting." Looking for the positive, Edith thought the flowers from well-wishers festooning their carriage made them "feel as if we were on a honeymoon journey." They were optimistic about their futures. Both said they longed for private life. While Edith had no real regrets at departing, she feared TR was conditioned to the publicity. She told his military aide that Roosevelt, despite his professed desire for it, had "forgotten" how to be "the simplest American alive." "My future is in the past, save as I may do the decent work that every private citizen can do," Roosevelt wrote stoically. Yet Edith knew that TR received letter after letter suggesting that 1908 was not the end of his political career. This is exactly the sort of idea Alice relished. A return of the Roosevelts to power was her ideal. Meanwhile, she didn't miss the chance to check out the new regime at the inaugural ball, where she was gratifyingly "gulped over." Archie Butt knew, if Alice couldn't admit it publicly, that the Princess wanted to maintain her distinctive place in Washington society.[14]

Taft's inauguration forced Alice into a different relationship with the new inhabitants of the White House. Alice survived the first visit to what had been her home, but not without bitterness. It was a small gathering of congressmen and their wives, and it ended early. Mary Borah, the wife of Senator William E. Borah of Idaho, recalled President Taft filling the room with his "hearty roar," as a result of something Alice said. But when Mrs. Taft loudly told a guest that she had "found the [White] [H]ouse in a very bad condition," Mary Borah looked sympathetically at Alice, who directed her attention elsewhere. "Your visit must have been trying poor child," Edith wrote, "though your account of it was most amusing. I don't think you need call [at the White House] again until next month, but you will surely be invited before then to some feast or function and remember for Nick's sake to be really careful what you say for people are only too ready to take up and repeat the most trivial remarks."[15]

As her father and Kermit departed for Africa, Alice embarked on her own journey—an intellectual journey. Officially without a title (beyond wife of a representative—and she was one among hundreds of those) and without the outsized presence of her father, Alice forged an identity different from the footloose First Daughter. Reading far into the night, she cultivated her wide-ranging interests. She began a lifelong and serious study of human evolutionary biology, a topic that also fascinated her father. She read about the latest developments in astronomy. The Philadelphia author Mary Cadwalader Jones gave Alice her first volume of the *Oxford Book of English Verse*, a book she consulted so regularly that it was held together with string by the end of her life.[16] Alice educated herself more systematically about politics. Slowly but surely she laid the groundwork for the real presence she would become in Washington. Made from her father's mold, she could speak on nearly every subject and charm people from many different backgrounds. She was charismatic, fun, daring, and fascinated by politics and politicians, by the ebbs and flows of Washington society, and by whatever was new or amusing. The few topics she found tedious, she sidestepped. The tariff was one such subject.

As the former president readied to depart "in a roar of cheers," the new president called Congress into special session on March 15, 1909, to address the tariff.[17] High protective tariffs had been a GOP cornerstone, but progressive Republicans advocated reform in light of the great profits made by barely regulated trusts and monopolies. With TR's approval, the 1908 Republican Party platform promised some action on the Dingley Tariff of 1897. The party was committed to revision, but the platform did not stipulate whether tariff rates would be revised up or down. Taft found, to his sorrow, that a unified Republican stance was a thing of the past. The tariff, and Taft's handling of it, exacerbated the fissure in the GOP ranks opened during TR's presidency.

In Taft's special session to address the tariff, the Republicans had a large congressional majority, but within the GOP there existed a progressive faction called the Insurgents. These men, led by George W. Norris of Nebraska, were generally supportive of Roosevelt's ideals, and they worked with Democrats to weaken the power of the office of Speaker Joseph G. Cannon, a Republican from Illinois. Cannon—so conservative that it was said of him that at the creation of the universe he'd have voted for chaos— led up the Progressive agenda in the House. "I am god-damned tired of listening to all this babble for reform," he raged.[18] The first salvo in the Insurgents' war against the broad and autocratic powers of the crusty House Speaker was the adoption of the Calendar Wednesday rule. It allowed committee heads to call up bills not passed by the Rules Committee, which was in the Speaker's control, thus sidestepping his power.

The House discussion on the tariff bill gave the Insurgents another chance to flex their muscles as they pushed toward the traditionally Democratic position of low tariffs. Nick Longworth championed high tariffs. He was from the home state of both Taft and William McKinley. Many Republicans thought of the high McKinley Tariff of 1890 as the acme of tariff legislation and anything connected to the name of the sainted McKinley was dear.

From the time of his appointment to the Ways and Means Committee,

Nick's intellectual absorption with the tariff had deepened. The representative felt "that no protective tariff law of itself, ever closed a factory, ever mortgaged a farm or caused an American working man to lose his job; and no free trade law failed to do all three."[19] Reflecting McKinley's influence, Nick worked to create a permanent tariff commission to remove politics altogether, and he was willing to use reciprocity—an agreement with foreign nations to lower the U.S. tariff if they lowered theirs—to make adjustments in tariff schedules. It was a stimulating subject for Nick, and he enjoyed the feinting and the sparring of the sprawling tariff bill.

The representative's wife believed "there is nothing I forget quite so quickly as details of a tariff bill, and even when one is up I enjoy it principally for the passions it arouses in the rate advocates and rate makers. . . . I spent hours listening to the [1909] debates, yet all recollection of them is as completely gone as if my ears had been stuffed with cotton-wool and my eyes blindfolded." What Alice did keenly note is how Insurgents were "making themselves felt"; more evidence of the strength of her father's vision.[20]

From the gallery, Alice happily followed the House battles. From his seat on the floor, Nick watched nervously. Only Theodore Roosevelt paid no attention at all. He resolutely ignored the political situation in the United States during his safari until, that is, the wounded and self-righteous Gifford Pinchot turned up bearing tales of Taft's betrayal. Pinchot, retained in Taft's administration as chief forester, had been fired for questioning the integrity of Taft's secretary of the interior. The seeds Pinchot planted then grew slowly but steadily to flower in 1912.

Taft's tariff bill was a contentious one, backed fully neither by the Democrats nor the Republicans. When he made support for the tariff a test of party loyalty, Taft increased the risks to his party. The Payne-Aldrich Tariff was bitterly fought and in the end made no one perfectly content. President Taft signed the bill in August 1909. The Insurgents became convinced that Roosevelt's handpicked successor was not made from the stern stuff of their standard-bearer. Taft's suspicions of the Insurgents deepened to a steely dislike. Meanwhile, dissatisfaction with Speaker Cannon seethed sub rosa.

While Nick toiled in this poisonous atmosphere, Alice escaped. Long captivated by the vision of air travel, Alice led the newest Washington craze. The first successful human flight had occurred in late 1903, at Kitty Hawk, North Carolina. In 1909, Orville and Wilbur Wright and their sister, Kathleen, appeared at Fort Myer to try to get their airplane into the air for sustained periods. Day after day for months, Alice and other Washingtonians went to learn about flying machines and were taught, she thought, with "unfailing patience" by the "modest, self-effacing" Wrights. Orville Wright spent half an hour one day showing Alice how the airplane worked from top to bottom. She was fascinated. She pleaded with him to take her flying, to no avail. From President Taft to cabinet members, congressmen to military observers, the grass filled with dreamers. "When the machine actually left the ground and circled the field, a hundred feet or so up, it gave us a thrill that no one in this generation will ever have," Alice recalled. Taft was there on July 27, to see Orville stay up in the air for a record-breaking seventy-three minutes. Even the slightest wind would ground the attempts and entail long periods of waiting for the propitious moment. Since Alice's boredom threshold was low, she took to entertaining the crowds by running "a most popular 'lunch wagon.'" From a dozen vacuum bottles she poured iced tea and the newly fashionable gin, club soda, and lemon juice concoction called a Tom Collins.[21]

Her curiosity about flight had been aroused in part by a frequent visitor to Sagamore Hill when she was a child, the aviation pioneer Samuel P. Langley, an astronomy professor, secretary of the Smithsonian Institution, and an airplane inventor. In the 1890s, Langley experimented on the banks of the Potomac with his "aerodromes." By the time Alice was watching the Wrights, Langley had been dead three years. He never achieved his goal of building a flying craft capable of carrying people, but Alice remembered his zeal as he spoke over dinners with the Roosevelts about the future of flight.

Busy with the tariff, Cannon, and the Wrights, neither Alice nor Nick found time to write to their mothers until August. "I always know in their case," Edith wrote Susan Longworth resignedly, "that the old proverb is true and I should be told any bad news very quickly." When she wasn't listening to the "boring" tariff debate, Alice was reading in the heat of the day, walking in Rock Creek Park in the late afternoon, playing cards with such friends as Ned and Evalyn Walsh McLean, and having dutiful dinners with the "political lights of Ohio and their wives." Between the Wrights' flights, she had been a patroness of a production of Oscar Wilde's controversial play *Salome*.[22]

Nick was troubled by stomach pains, probably brought on by stresses in the tariff battle, which was rapidly turning into a war, between Taft Republicans and Roosevelt Republicans. In such a conflict, Nick would always be trapped midway. As it was, he and Alice spent a good deal of time with President Taft that summer while the First Lady and the children were vacationing away from Washington. Alice was less than reverential. She arrived very late to one of his parties and made such an outrageous apology that "everyone laughed. The President took her hands in his and said: 'Alice, if you will only stop trying to be respectful to me, I believe you would become so.' 'And then I would bore you to death as the other women do,' " Alice countered. Nick was glad, he finally wrote his mother when the "agony" of the tariff bill was past, "that Alice has found diversion in the aeroplane flights—'*Sans ca*' she would indeed have had a dull summer."[23]

In late June, Edith, Ethel, Archie, and Quentin took a steamer to visit Edith's sister Emily Carow in Italy. Alice, staying behind, wrote Ethel that rather than going through the "unsatisfactory" ritual of waving a dockside good-bye, she'd prefer that the two of them "wilt in the hole of a fortune teller and then have nice cool drinks" as a farewell. Alice was not well while her family was away. Worse even than the month she spent exercising her restraint in Cincinnati was a flare-up of pain in her jaw from the old childhood injury that necessitated frequent trips to a specialist in Boston. Alice looked for sympathy from Edith, but it was not forthcoming. Edith's letter attests to her own difficulties: traveling with children, a good friend's death, six months away from TR. "It was very nice to get your letter and to hear about your successes even though it has not been an amusing one." After reminding her stepdaughter of her duties concerning Susan, Edith continued, "I do hope you can meet me when I land, and will have arranged to go wherever I am going."[24] It was always this way—Edith's love for her stepdaughter was real, but generally communicated with asperity.

While TR was a little out of the spotlight, in Africa, Alice jumped in. She participated in a fund-raiser for the Anti-Tuberculosis Society of Cincinnati. Still trying to figure out her post–First Daughter role, she agreed to sell flags on the society's behalf, and sold the most flags and the highest-priced flag. This was front-page news in the *New York Times,* especially as the paper could report some of the intimate details of the Longworth marriage: "Her first flag was bought by Thomas Pegan, a business man, who paid her with a $100 bill. The second one she took herself, emptying her purse of its $15. Congressman Longworth said his wife was receiving entirely too much attention, so he hunted out one of the society girls who was in an obscure doorway and gave her $50 for a little strip of white cloth. Mrs. Longworth did $1,000 worth of business in a half hour."[25]

If Nick felt it necessary in this case to squelch Alice's fame—which also nicely resulted in some publicity for him—he found himself defending her honor shortly afterward when a minor scandal erupted with the publication of Emma Kroebel's memoirs. Kroebel was Germany's "chief mistress of ceremonies" in Korea when Alice and Nick ventured there with the congressional junket in 1905. Kroebel told of behavior so shocking that few could believe it, even of Alice:

The emperor [of Korea] finally decided to bestow upon the daughter of the president of the United States the highest honor at his command, namely, a reception at the graveside of his departed consort, the empress. An imposing suite of dignitaries and flunkeys were accordingly dispatched to the grave in a picturesque and secluded spot a mile outside Seoul.... As the diners gathered, into their midst roared "a cavalcade of equestrians...." At their head rode a dashing young horsewoman clad in a scarlet riding habit beneath the lower extremities of which peeped tight-fitting red riding breeches stuck into glittering boots. In her hand she brandished a riding whip and in her mouth was a cigar.

It was Miss Alice Roosevelt. We were flabbergasted.... Everybody was bowing and scraping in the most approved Corean court
fashion, but the rough rider's daughter seemed to think it all a joke.
As the mistress of ceremonies I stammered out a few words of greeting, and the guest of honor mumbled a word of thanks, but nothing
more. She was mainly interested in the colossal figures of gods and
the mammoth stone images of animals which hold watch over the
graves of the departed members of the Corean dynasty.

Spying a stone elephant which seemed to strike her fancy, Alice
hurtled off her horse and in a flash was astride the elephant, shouting
to Mr. Longworth to snapshot her. Our suite was paralyzed with horror and astonishment. Such a sacrilegious scene at so holy a spot was
without parallel.[26]

Kroebel charged that Alice was uninterested in all formal entertainments, and after this imbroglio at the tomb of the empress, never attended
another; instead, she forced Nick to attend in her place.

The next day's paper carried Nick's defense of his wife: "It was too
preposterous to be taken seriously, he snorted, as nothing of the kind took
place or could have taken place. He said he never knew or heard of the author of the story, but complimented her upon her vivid imagination and
said it had afforded the subject of it a great deal of amusement." Whether
Nick did not permit Alice to speak on her own behalf or whether she asked
him to respond to Kroebel is unclear. Perhaps, since one of Alice's credos
at the time was "there is nothing so satisfactory as a lie that is accepted immediately for the pure truth—but also nothing so barren as one that is
unbelieved," she could not respond for fear of that barrenness.[27]

As she herself admitted at the time, in Korea Alice had reached her sat-
uration point with official appearances. As Taft had suggested, she may
have been punishing Nick for any romantic slight by pairing up with Willard Straight. In 1905, just after the junket ended, Alice had penned a
thank-you to Straight: "Those photographs are excellent, but please oh
please don't ever let anyone see the one of 'Nick' in my nice but abbreviated
[illegible]. I don't think my family would ever forgive me if once they
learned the truth—and astride the guardian angel at a martyred Empress'

tomb—it would be almost too much!"[28] Straight kept her confidence. Nick upheld the Roosevelt name in print, and the story died down.

December brought some of the Roosevelts together for their first fractured Christmas. Alice was battling jaw pain, walking six miles a day, and leading "a most decorous existence," when she and Nick—who had turned forty in November—journeyed to Sagamore Hill. Ted was present for Christmas Day. TR was still abroad with Kermit, confessing in a letter to Arthur Lee that while the trip "has been a great success, I am now an elderly man, not fit for very hard exertion," and "only a fair shot." TR brooded in Africa and the others had "not much" of a Christmas. Edith decided to sail for Egypt in mid-February to rejoin TR. "I can scarcely wait and yet I am torn asunder to think of leaving three boys behind to say nothing of Alice," Edith acknowledged to a friend.[29]

She need not have worried about her stepdaughter. Part two of the battle to oust Speaker Cannon commenced while Edith was readying to leave, providing a handy distraction for Alice. Insurgent leader George Norris opened the winter session with a resolution to increase the size and the power of the Rules Committee, while simultaneously barring the Speaker of the House from membership. Democrats supported him and after "a continuous rough and tumble on the floor," involving a filibuster and every other possible ploy to delay the vote, the standpat Republicans lost. "Mr. Cannon," a progressive newspaper screamed in justification, "is personally opposed to every reform that is now being advocated by any political party." Nick, longing above all to see harmony prevail, regretfully joined the Insurgents. Cannon lost his position and his reputation and, Alice winced, "was greeted with jeers and cat-calls" instead of the "fear, respect, and even some degree of affection" that he had known before progressivism swept the land. The lesson of Joe Cannon's fall was not lost on Alice: Nick was considered for the new Rules Committee, but not ultimately selected because of his role in toppling Cannon and threatening the Old Guard Republicans.[30]

Alice's increasing dislike of the assertive and caustic First Lady, Helen Taft, did not help things. For her part, Helen, mirthless and unable to match Princess Alice for sheer dramatic appeal, found much to criticize in the other woman. Alice's blasé response to societal restrictions was well known to Helen Taft. She would have heard of Alice's demonstration of the new dance craze, the Turkey Trot, at a ball in Washington. As one observer put it, Alice lit a cigarette first, "to give zest to the performance." Her male partner was forgotten, but Alice "sailed down the middle of the room, puffing little jets of smoke at the ceiling, to the horror of the women." One of them thought "Alice looked like a steam engine coming down a crimped track."[31]

Events reached a climax for Helen Taft at the president's diplomatic reception in January 1910. Alice watched with interest the expressions on Washington faces as the wife of the Russian ambassador began to smoke. She joined in. The courtly Taft bent down to light Alice's cigarette. The other European women then took out their cigarette cases until the room was full of a sight few Americans had ever seen: a bevy of women smoking. The First Lady was not amused. Alice smirked. Taft's biographer considered this a terrible faux pas: "The only person [Alice] could not charm out of disapproval after one of her escapades was the President's wife and she underestimated Mrs. Taft's influence—or did not care. It was Nellie who kept Nicholas Longworth from being appointed minister to China, a post he coveted, because she thought that Alice might stir up storms in the Celestial Kingdom."[32]

Whether Alice would have liked the position of diplomat's wife, especially in a place as remote as China, was unlikely. She did enjoy her visit there in 1905, and there were friends of hers in different capacities in East Asia, but China wasn't exactly the Court of St. James's. Like Cincinnati, China was too far away from Washington. With her father about to return, and increasing numbers of people sharing her frustration with Taft's administration, the capital was more enticing. It was hard to remain angry at Taft. For Christmas that year, the president, who had a sense of humor, gave Alice Longworth a cigarette holder![33]

In May, Alice sailed alone for England to meet the rest of the family gathered around TR, fresh from his successful safari and an invigorating scuffle with Britain's protectorate Egypt, which he suggested was not fit to rule itself. The English gave him a warm welcome. Nick was chained to Congress that spring, but Alice amused herself shipboard with Harry Emery, then chairman of the tariff board. Emery was perfectly congenial: "an economist, a philosopher, and all-'round scholar and the most delightful companion for long stretches of cards, poetry, or general chatter." The two of them had lunch with Tammany boss Tim Sullivan. Alice saw right through him: "I think he was as straight and well-intentioned and genuinely sympathetic in his personal relations and humanitarian enterprises, as he was callous and corrupt politically."[34] She also met another Democrat: longtime TR foe William Randolph Hearst, the newspaper tycoon who had spent the last decade printing critical articles about Roosevelt.

Kermit, Ethel, and the faithful Willard Straight met Alice at the dock. That night she and TR and Kermit huddled together exchanging news. Alice analyzed the past year's political battles. TR, listening, became ever more certain that he could not campaign on behalf of Taft and his policies in the looming congressional elections. But first Roosevelt had other public duties. At President Taft's request he represented the United States at the funeral of Britain's King Edward. He gave a series of prestigious lectures, including the Romanes lecture at Oxford University. In that address, "Biological Analogies in History," Roosevelt distilled a lifetime's thoughts on human evolution and history. This particularly interested Alice. But so did the Derby—this year socialites were swathed in black mourning crepe. Alice amused herself with friends such as the Astors and the Arthur Lees in London, and "three days of plays, restaurants, and races" in Paris, where her luck held. She won enough on the horses to pay for her entire trip— including spending money.[35]

The trip home passed quickly because Ruth and Medill were on board to dissect the political situation in the United States. None of the party underestimated the meaning of the exuberant greeting awaiting TR. Alice stood beside her father as New Yorkers met him with a happy riot of noise and color from a flotilla of boats in the harbor and a dockside teeming with well-wishers. Nick came aboard the ship with the welcoming committee.

The reunited couple joined the Roosevelts trailing behind TR, who thoroughly enjoyed being the star of the confetti-sprinkled parade in his honor.

Duty beckoned:

> Teddy, come home and blow your horn,
> The sheep's in the meadow, the cow's in the corn.
> The boy you left to tend the sheep
> Is under the haystack fast asleep.[36]

The allusion in the newspaper doggerel to President Taft's frequent naps pointed to the larger problem of deteriorating relations within the Republican Party. Nick filled in TR on the House side of things. Roosevelt could no more stay away from the fracas than he could refrain from criticizing his former friend Taft who, he had decided, had "not proved a good leader, in spite of his having been a good first lieutenant...."[37]

In the spring of 1910, Alice turned twenty-six, Ted's marriage to the thoughtful and kind Eleanor Butler Alexander was announced, and Nick and Alice were leaders in a new society craze: roller skating from door to door picking up friends as they went and "winding up at somebody's house for supper."[38] Also that spring, Alice's good grandfather, George Lee, passed away. His death left her much sadder and a little wealthier. His bequest to her was $5,300 a year, the same amount that his children would receive. This made her happier than the recurring proposition that Nick might become governor of Ohio, an idea that bloomed with the Washington tulips.[39] Alice nixed it, but it was a difficult idea to kill.

It was unthinkable to live in Ohio, so far from the center of power. And the balance of that power kept shifting. The Republican split was on everyone's mind. TR's progressive legislative program—explained by him as the morally correct action of providing an equal playing field, or a "square deal," for all citizens—was interpreted by conservative Republicans as undue governmental shackling of corporate America. Because of the bumbling way Taft handled the Payne-Aldrich Tariff—for example, excluding progressive congressmen's states in his tour to drum up support for the bill—doubts about Taft increased. Meanwhile, Americans read the serialized epic of TR's gallant African expedition from his own pen. Then the newspapers filled with fulsome reports of Roosevelt's visits with the crowned heads of Europe. The average citizen had never stopped admiring the larger-than-life "Teddy," and the grand welcome he received made the contrast between the beleaguered Taft and the heroic Roosevelt even greater.

By 1910, the vise that squeezed Nick Longworth tightened. His friendship with Taft and other conservative Ohio politicians caused him much worry. His camaraderie with the Tafts predated his marriage. While Nick was not entirely a creature of Boss Cox, he still needed hometown support to stay in the House. Cincinnati had been the butt of a muckraker's sharp pen in 1905, when Lincoln Steffens denounced the powerful Cox and his Byzantine methods, which resulted in cries for reform in the widely read *Cincinnati Post*. Nick was not especially committed to reform, but not especially *not* committed to reform either. He was committed to retaining his seat in the House of Representatives.

Nick tried to make his position unambiguous to his volatile father-in-law, who saw Nick's dilemma clearly. Despite his disgust with Taft and his "lawyers' Administration," TR told Nick, "Of course you must stand straight by Taft and the Administration. He is your constituent, and, as you say, while the situation for you was awkward enough while I was President it [is] even more awkward under the actual conditions." Roosevelt lobbied gently: "But in standing straight for the President, do keep yourself clear to stand for progressive policies." TR was full of advice. He saw only "doubtful . . . wisdom" in the governorship because it was unlikely to serve as a stepping-stone to the White House. But Taft thought it a good idea. In the "hot fight" at the 1910 Columbus convention, the Ohio GOP finally settled on Warren G. Harding as its gubernatorial candidate. Florence and Alice watched the proceedings together, with entirely different agendas for their husbands. Both women got their wish that July. In her autobiography, Alice claimed that Nick was relieved: "He enjoyed the work in Congress and year by year was gaining in experience and seniority. The governorship was not in line with his plans."[40]

It definitely wasn't in hers. Taft wrote to his wife in late September 1910 about an evening spent at the Longworths' with Archie Butt and some others. He noticed Alice "drawing away from" him because of the "situation between her father and me, though she professes to be very affectionate still. The whole evening," Taft mused, "was one suggestive of sadness in that there was little sympathy between Alice and her mother-in-law. She dislikes her mother-in-law extremely, and her mother-in-law dislikes her extremely … Clara and de Chambrun have very little to do with Alice, and form such a contrast that the mother sympathizes with them. Nannie, I believe, is the [sister-in-law] with whom Alice gets along the better. Alice is very unhappy here, calls it Cincin-nasty, and is only too delighted when she can get away."[41]

Theodore Roosevelt, meanwhile, had some difficult decisions to make. Still enormously popular, lobbied by those who felt Taft was not upholding progressivism, and uncertain that his original plan of spending a couple of years writing would sustain him financially and emotionally, TR felt compelled to help his party in the off-year congressional elections. While some Republicans were thrilled to have the charismatic Colonel Roosevelt beside them at the podium, others—the standpatters, Taft's men—searched for ways to avoid joint appearances in their hometowns. Roosevelt set off on an elder statesman's tour. In Osawatomie, Kansas, on August 31, 1910, Roosevelt gave a landmark talk. Labeled "The New Nationalism" by historians, and considered "the most radical speech ever given by an ex-president," it sounded suspiciously like a presidential platform. It presented a clear challenge to Taft's leadership. "The truth is," TR confided to Henry Cabot Lodge that August, "we have had no National leadership of any real kind since election day 1908." In the 1910 off-year election, Democrats took over the House of Representatives, which may have signified the electorate's impatience with the president, or it may have been a vote of support for TR's progressivism.[42]

Nick and Alice avidly followed Roosevelt's actions, even as they "slept, ate, and breathed Schedule K," of the Canadian reciprocity bill when the Sixty-first Congress reconvened on December 5, 1910. Alice remembered the last day especially, after Nick's bill to establish a permanent tariff commission failed. While Nick dealt with the sine die deluge, she couldn't keep away from the excitement. "I stayed up at the Capitol until I got hungry, when I would hop into the electric [automobile], taking one or two friends with me, others following, and go back to the house to cook eggs and drink buckets of coffee; then to the Capitol again; a few hours there, and back we would go to my house to the pantry. I claimed to have a record that averaged an egg an hour for twelve hours," she recalled.[43] The reciprocity bill passed in 1911 but failed when Canadian voters rejected it in their election shortly thereafter. By that time, it was just one more insult for Taft, amid mounting cries for Colonel Roosevelt to declare himself a candidate for the presidential nomination in 1912.

In late September 1911, the Longworths visited the Panama Canal, a project irrevocably linked with the man with the Big Stick—which is why Alice wanted to go. The *New York Times* announced, CONGRESSMAN SAYS TAFT IS DOING GREAT THINGS QUIETLY. But Nick adroitly hedged his bets. When the *Times* asked him about the presidential race, "It was pretty far ahead to guess, he said, but he conveyed the impression that in his opinion the best man to succeed Taft was Taft. As to insurgents, the Ohio Congressman thought a majority of them were actuated by patriotic motives, though some were no doubt playing politics." While Nick smoothly doled out compliments to both sides, his friendship with Taft had been deepening. That year Taft had celebrated his birthday over lunch with Nick—just Nick—at the White House.[44] One can only imagine the shipboard discussions that must have taken place as Nick and Alice examined all the potential scenarios for 1912.

As a break from the political worries, the Longworths enjoyed Panama. They accompanied Colonel George Goethals, the man in charge of building the canal. They met with the colonel's aide, West Point graduate Robert E. Wood, who was in the middle of his decade of service in Panama. Alice was fascinated by the "color and the atmosphere of those early mornings, those torrid days, which we spent watching the work at the locks and at the Gatun dam; the machinery, and the thousands of men digging the Culebra cut."[45] Breathtaking in size and scope, Alice never lost her enthusiasm for the project. She treated with disdain all later suggestions that

Panama be given control of the canal. It was TR and the United States who had brought to fruition the dream of a canal; it was the United States that should control it.

In October, Alice was an honored guest in Pittsburgh, where she christened a reproduction of the *New Orleans,* a steamboat built in 1811 by her ancestor Nicholas Roosevelt. Taft was there, too. Alice scrutinized him through narrowed eyes, "meditatively—speculatively," wondering about his likely moves.[46] Taft had always wanted a seat on the Supreme Court. He was not enjoying the presidency. A bare few months into his term, his beloved spouse had suffered a paralyzing stroke. Anguished about his wife's condition and deeply wounded by the animosity shown him by progressive Republicans, Taft was not a happy man. Might he, Alice wondered, step down after just four years?

The 1912 election was one of the most important in American history. Four strong candidates staked out very clear positions on issues that touched every voter. The outcome of the race, while wholly unsatisfactory to the Roosevelts, resulted in profound transitions in both major political parties and a sea change in national politics. And it culminated in betrayal for Alice: political abandonment by the husband who had promised to stand by her forever.

Chapter 12

"Quite Marked Schizophrenia"

THE 1912 ELECTION was a defining event in Alice's life. She watched angrily as her husband, whose loyalties were stretched to the breaking point, chose his friends over his wife and in-laws. In Alice's mind, he opted for expediency over integrity. Nick had every reason to be pragmatic about his career—third parties rarely won. But in pledging himself to William Taft rather than to Theodore Roosevelt, Nick Longworth underestimated his wife's devotion to her father and the Progressive cause. Alice's and Nick's assessments of the importance of progressive politics, of a united family front, and of what would be best for them as a couple clashed. In the end, the election was a disaster for everyone: Alice, Nick, TR, the Tafts, and the Republican Party.

Alice Longworth earnestly shared the convictions of her father's Bull Moose Party, including his support for women's suffrage, but not his controversial belief in judicial recall. The complicating factor, of course, was that also running for reelection in 1912, as a committed standpat Republican, was the husband she truly cherished. It was a very real contest with difficult personal consequences. Alice loved her husband, but she idolized her father. She knew "it was particularly hard on [Nick] that I was, of course, single-minded in enthusiasms for anything that Father decided to do."[1] While Alice managed to hold her marriage together despite the tempest of the election, the shock of Nick's betrayal drained her last reserve of trust. It was this political betrayal that drove them apart, rather than Nick's dalliances with other women. Unlike her cousin Eleanor, whose life shattered in 1918 with the knowledge of Franklin's adultery, Alice—the

politician—was devastated in 1912 by Nick's political infidelity. Like Eleanor, Alice would use this disappointment to build a stronger public self and
to go in a direction more independent of her husband, pursuing her own
ends.

In early 1912, Theodore Roosevelt stood poised on the brink of announcing that he would enter the Republican primary against incumbent William Howard Taft. He desperately wanted the presidency again. He longed
to complete some of his initiatives, undo a few of Taft's, and fulfill the
promises he made in the New Nationalism speech. But it would be risky.
While Theodore Roosevelt was an idol of many Americans, he lacked the
backing of the powerful Republican National Committee (RNC). TR
would be accused of hubris, of royal ambitions. He knew that he could not
be perceived as actively seeking the nomination; it had to fall to him as the
natural result of the voters' unhappiness with Taft. Roosevelt also knew
that should he win the nomination, he might lose the national election. He
understood the complications. As he wrote to his son Ted, "...I feel as
Nick Longworth strongly feels, and as most of my best friends feel, that for
me personally the nomination would be a veritable calamity, and I do not
want to take it if it can possibly be avoided."[2] Yet Roosevelt had a strong
sense of duty. He came to believe that Americans wanted him back in the
presidency to enact his progressive agenda. His political enemies called it
self-deception.

Yet it was clear that even in President Taft's home state, TR had supporters: OHIO LEADER WANTS ROOSEVELT IN 1912, read the headline in early
December 1911. Nick leaped into the fray. LONGWORTH SAYS FRIENDS WILL
OPPOSE ANY BOOM FOR PRESIDENT, the newspapers blared two days later.
Nick issued a statement saying he'd just returned from Oyster Bay and that
he, "like all of Mr. Roosevelt's real friends," was discouraging any TR
draft. Nick spoke with the authority of the insider—he was on his way to
open Christmas presents with the Roosevelts on TR and Edith's bed.[3]

Like Nick, Alice counseled her father against his seeking the Republican nomination:

Don't much like it. Hate to have him get it by a fight...[I]f he does declare himself a candidate he must make it clear that it is not because of a demand for him on the part of the many people to whom he makes a picturesque appeal. Nor to satisfy those also [who] are pretty dissatisfied with the present administration—nor must he be deceived by the clamor for him by those who are running for office and feel that with him at the head of the ticket they will pull through even though he is defeated. He must make it clear that he is a candidate because he considers his policies the right policies and his remedies the right remedies for existing wrong conditions. He should lay unmistakable emphasis on the difference in what he stands for and [what] Taft stands for....It must be because he is convinced that the people wish his views carried out. His motives for being a candidate are his convictions. This must be clear to all....It would be harmful to his party or country were he defeated for the nomination and more seriously harmful to party and country were he defeated for election.[4]

Ignoring both daughter and son-in-law, by mid-February 1912, TR had finagled an "extemporaneous" tide of support from the group of pro-Roosevelt governors who called for him to "put his hat in the ring." Just before TR went public, Nick wavered. TR assured him, "I think you are right as to your saying that you are for Taft. In my judgment, it would be a mistake for you not to say so. You have definitely declared yourself, and I think it was the only thing you could do." This assuaged Nick's fears temporarily, as did TR's promise to "soak it to 'any Roosevelt creature' who dared to worry him in Cincinnati."[5]

The object of this protection wasn't comforted for long. The next day, Alice wrote, "Nick feels it a tragedy. If I can only keep him cheerful, sober and moderately contented. I've begun to have a desperate feeling again. That lost feeling of being absolutely alone. Darling Nick, I love him so much." Later that night, she followed up with, "I have just been in Nick's room again talking with him. He says that if Father comes out he will probably declare that he will not run again. I can hardly bear it. I shall do my utmost to persuade him not to. I can see how he feels. He says he can 'wobble' no longer—if it came to choosing between Father and Taft—certainly he is for nearly all that Father stands for . . . [but] that poor fat man has been courting him. Only must [Nick] sacrifice us for that lump of flesh? It is Nick's district. . . . I can't decide whether Nick has the conviction or the morals. It is bitterly hard."[6]

Alice believed that Nick truly was on the progressive side of the Republican Party and so should follow his conscience and declare for TR. His idea of pulling out of his own House race would consign them to living at Rookwood, being "sacrificed" for Taft, who had come a-wooing. Her private anguish was trying to weigh his "convictions" and his "morals." Nick and Alice were troubled by the political possibilities long before TR announced that he would run. And as for her "lost feeling of being absolutely alone," that was the feeling of abandonment from her youth washing back over her when Nick drank and flirted with other women—or with other political beliefs.

Nick's inability or unwillingness to remain sober concerned Alice because she despised drunkenness. Alice especially detested sloppy drunks. The loss of control, the surrender of one's command over one's self, and the ugly personalities that alcohol could awaken repulsed her. Whispered conversations about her uncle Elliott's sad death and Grandfather Carow's alcoholism swirled around her childhood. Alice took on the stern disapproval of her parents on this subject. An inebriated man was by definition feeble, lacking self-discipline and drive. Alcohol weakened Nick's judgment and made him reckless in social situations. When he drank he was indiscreet with her female friends. Whether he meant it to or not, it hurt. The extent of his dalliances is impossible to recapture, but Washington rumors circulated consistently. In Nick's defense, if ever there was the temptation to seek an escape with alcohol, the 1912 campaign was it.

They had another "gloomy talk" the next day, February 17, 1912, but followed it with a "really splendid" conversation, she recorded. "He asked me to state my side. I think I made a very clear and serious presentation of my views. I can only pray that he is guided by what I say." The stakes were high. If Nick committed to the wrong campaign, he could jeopardize his political future. Roosevelt would not have disowned him for backing Taft, but it was likely that the party regulars would pull their support if he switched to the progressives. Alice left for Oyster Bay to speak directly with her father. "We talked the whole thing over," Alice enthused. "He says Taft's chances are 3 to 1 against him (F.) for the nomination. He was more wonderful than ever." Roosevelt was clear-eyed about the race. Huge crowds flocked to see him that spring, and he told a reporter, "It's my past that brings them; not my future—a trap for politicians like myself." The difficulty of combining progressive principles, victory at the polls, and family harmony vexed Alice daily. One morning she "had a talk with Nick and was a fool and wept. . . . If he will only have a serious talk with Father." Alice knew the persuasive power of TR, "such a persistent talker," as Taft put it cynically, "that he can keep up the courage of his followers far beyond any justification for it." The next day things were better again as she talked "on the telephone this morning with my darling Nick." "I love him so," she confided to her diary.[7]

Instead of joining her as she asked, Nick went to see Taft. Alice recounted what he said. Taft was sympathetic and told Nick to "do whatever he pleased. Rather hard to say anything else, it strikes me."[8] With Taft's reassurance secured first, Nick only then took the midnight train to Oyster Bay. TR promised there would be no pro-Roosevelt competitor in Nick's district. Alice was cautiously happy. Nick was miserable. Despite both TR's and Taft's approval of his course, Alice noted that "his nerves [were] on edge," he was "still gloomy and [had] a pain in his interior."[9]

On February 21, 1912, Roosevelt formally announced that he would be a contender for the Republican presidential nomination. The Longworth family was predictably furious. Alice joined Nick on March 8 in Cincinnati where Clara had been publicly excoriating Roosevelt. Alice was livid. "Clara said she was justified in her opinion of Father. Always has said he was a man of overweening personal ambition. I got furious and told her that Father was entering in it for the principle—Poor Nick angry—Says I must 'shut up.' I am not going to take any more than I have given but if anyone has the impertinence to cast doubt on Father's good faith before my face—I shall certainly hurl the truth at them. . . . I am in this fight for all I am worth and we must and will win." The relationship between Clara and Alice was permanently damaged. Not long after this Alice's diary fills with epithets such as "Those hateful people. How I dislike and despise them."[10]

As March wore on, and the primaries and state conventions began, Alice stepped up her study of the issues. She had to be armed with arguments from both sides. She was finding it difficult to maintain her composure. As TR wrote Kermit, "I think [Alice] felt she just had to see me because of course all respectable society is now apoplectic with rage over me." Auntie Bye understood, as she, too, found it "wearing to live in a non sympathetic atmosphere when most of one's so-called friends differ in public beliefs from oneself." Alice thought Ruth and Medill were "the only people I can 'rant and rave' and really talk to." Even Edith was sending Alice "strong and unsympathetic letter[s] about Father," cautioning her to consider Nick's position. "I don't care," Alice fumed.[11]

Meanwhile, her in-laws never paused in their jibes. Alice remembered the toll this took on her: "We all managed to keep the peace to a surprising extent, though I was so full of bottled-up savagery that I very nearly became ill. Food choked me and I existed principally on fruit and eggs and Vichy [water]. I had a chronic cold and cough, indigestion, colitis, anaemia, and low blood pressure—and quite marked schizophrenia."[12]

Political bulletins and exclamations of hope that she could not express to her husband tumbled together in Alice's diary. "How I want to sock it to the other side!"—for example. Sagamore Hill was awash in political advisers, congressional hopefuls, men and women lobbying for various favors. The Roosevelt home had always been swimming in political ideas: "A daily dish of the household," Alice called it. And there is no overestimating the influence of the one sitting at the head of the table, serving the main course. Alice spent her time at Sagamore Hill, in close contact with Roosevelt National Committee campaign leaders, especially Chairman Joseph M. Dixon and Vice Chairman Frank Knox. A great deal of her news came from other Roosevelt workers, particularly Ruth and Medill, John O'Laughlin, George Perkins, and Gifford Pinchot. Dixon and O'Laughlin were in the habit of telephoning her with early predictions and ultimate reports of the primary tabulations. This must not have been easy for Nick Longworth to stomach—made all the harder as evidence of TR's great popularity with the average voter was inescapable. As a couple they worked it out. "Nick pleased me so," Alice noted in her diary, "by saying... that he was pleased about Illinois," where TR swept the primaries.[13]

Nick worried about being tarred with his father-in-law's brush. He wondered whether to repair to his home state to campaign for the Ohio primary. "If he goes he probably will be asked... questions and if he stays he will be taunted with having preferred the flesh pots of Washington to his home town. Hard either way, dear lamb," Alice wrote.[14] They decided jointly that he should go to Cincinnati. The couple was close that spring, dining alone together often, discussing politics, dancing, enjoying Nick's violin and their friends. But politics eventually called him to Rookwood. Two weeks remained before the Ohio primary.

Alice missed her husband, but was thrilled with her father's important primary victory in California. Once TR announced, Alice never wavered in her loyalty. No real criticism of TR appears in her writings. Nick, knowing he could not ask her to be objective, suggested his wife not join him in Ohio, especially during the convention. He told her that "the feeling there was unbelievably bitter." Alice knew that he really meant "particularly in his own family." He also requested she not go to hear TR speak at the convention. "It would be sure to get in the papers," Nick warned, "and it would not appear well...." She did as he wished, but not joyfully. Instead she took herself off to Sagamore to find comfort with her clan. Meanwhile, the Rough Rider himself was predicting a victory on the first ballot to the cheering conventioneers. Despite the deep divisions in Ohio, Roosevelt added that state primary victory to his earlier wins. Luckily, Longworth also won his primary race. The papers described Nick as maintaining a "complacent, if not altogether pleasant neutrality."[15]

In early June, TR informed Alice that should he lose the Republican nomination, he would create his own political party and go toward the national election regardless. "Father and I walked around.... He is so adorable. I love him so very much that I don't see how I can bear it if all does not go well. I told him all I have heard—and he talked about everything in his own wonderful way...." The likelihood of the new party brought

Nick's simmering frustration to a boil. He "wished he had followed his instincts and withdrawn for then he could speak out freely." Alice tried to comfort him. "He will be a great man," she mused, "he is so really clearheaded and right minded, but so sensitive, my darling precious lamb."[16]

The great question prompting Roosevelt's decision and Nick's annoyance occurred because of the decision of the Rules Committee concerning contested delegates in the run-up to the national caucus. By the time the Republican convention began, Roosevelt had 411 committed votes, Taft had 201, and the fiery Wisconsin progressive, Senator Robert LaFollette, had 36. One hundred thirty-six delegates were coming to the convention "uninstructed" and could cast their vote in Chicago any way they pleased. There was a critical mass of 254 contested votes. The Rules Committee, packed with Taft's men, handed 235 to Taft and only 19 to Roosevelt. TR reacted with outrage. Flinging aside tradition, he vowed he would personally attend the convention and fight for the votes he considered stolen from him. The Roosevelts arrived in Chicago the night before the convention opened. TR put it succinctly to a friend: "The Republican Party [has] become pretty nearly hopeless. Either it had to be radically regenerated from within, or a new party had to be made. I attempted regeneration. By simple swindling, the party bosses (as I cannot help thinking, rather fatuously) defeated the attempt."[17]

The long-anticipated Republican convention convened on June 16 in Chicago with crowds of people pushing against one another to catch a glimpse of the Roosevelts and the Longworths. Alice was in the thick of things. She and Nick had separate rooms at the Blackstone Hotel because of their chaotic schedules. Alice tried to mill about to get a sense of the crowd, but was "besieged by cameras" and had to retire to TR's room. Her days consisted of viewing the proceedings at the convention and plotting strategy with the Roosevelt campaign leaders, including Ruth and Medill. Alice and Nick spent the morning of the seventeenth going over his speech, and she "marked what he might cut."[18] The eighteenth they were together all day again, while Nick went out at night.

On the nineteenth, Nick alternated between excitement and mournfulness. At his side, Alice was by turns elated by the enthusiasm shown for TR, worried about Nick, and angry at the "hoards of creatures taking [her] picture...." It was probably elation that induced her to try *again* to convince Nick to support Roosevelt. She really believed he was, in his heart of hearts, a progressive, but Nick could hardly retract his public vows of support for his fellow Ohioan.[19] Alice never stopped attempting to get her husband to see that his policies were more like Roosevelt's than Taft's— and she never lost the feeling that Nick was somehow wrong not to fall in line with the family, blood being thicker than water.

It was certainly her strong "tribal feeling" and her anger at the Republican regulars for depriving her father of the nomination that prompted Alice to reject their proposition of making Nick governor of Ohio. Warren G. Harding sidled up to the couple in the Chicago Coliseum and offered to support Nick in a run for the governorship. Alice's impatience with the Ohio GOP's "strong-arm tactics" got the better of her. Before Nick could answer, she shot back: "I [do] not believe that Nick would accept anything at the hands of the Columbus convention...one [can] not accept favors from crooks." Nick begged her to apologize. She never did.[20]

Ultimately, the president's control of the party machinery was too firm for Roosevelt to dislodge. On the twenty-second, as Nick and Alice sat together, stone-faced and unsmiling, Harding nominated Taft, calling him "the greatest progressive of the age." Taft supporters roared. Roosevelt branded the whole thing a sham and insisted it was "in no proper sense any longer a Republican convention."[21] On June 23 just before midnight, Theodore Roosevelt and his followers shook the rafters of nearby Orchestra Hall chanting, "Thou shalt not steal," as they announced the creation of the Progressive Party, soon dubbed the Bull Moose Party, to challenge both the Republicans and the Democrats for the presidency in 1912. "Such spirit, buoyancy, and enthusiasm," Alice noted to her diary. She was there, with Edith, Ethel, Kermit, and Archie, waving to the well-wishers. Nick was not at her side. He was off making celebratory toasts with the Ohio delegation. Hurt and saddened, Alice avoided him the next day. Reporters noted that Nick "wore a dejected look," while Alice "breathed defiance."

"He will do," Alice told reporters threateningly, "what he thinks is right, regardless of how it may affect his political career." And, she could have added, his marriage. Nick chose the Republicans over the Progressives. He chose alcohol over Alice. She wanted a divorce. At a hasty but firm family tribunal, her parents talked her out of it.[22]

The train to Washington was "crowded," Alice recalled, "with enemies and deserters." Alice lobbied for converts to the Progressive Party. She turned her charm and intelligence to Idaho's Senator William Borah. He had come to Washington, D.C., six years earlier, a handsome, TR-worshiping, maverick Republican. Borah listened as Alice tried every political inducement she knew. But in 1912, his conscience told him to stay with the GOP. He had attended the convention as a Roosevelt supporter and had wavered, believing the Republicans had unfairly chosen Taft. With unassailable logic, Alice reminded the senator that he had once before left the Republican Party, then to follow a lesser man than her father. But Borah's experience in the 1896 election and his support of silverite William Jennings Bryan had taught him the futility of third-party attempts. Across the aisle of the Pullman dining car, Alice Longworth and Bill Borah squared off. Her well-marshaled arguments, personal magnetism, and Roosevelt mystique did not prevail. The senator won. Borah kept TR on a pedestal but would vote for Taft in 1912. Next time they met, he would not be able to resist her.[23]

On the twenty-fifth, Nick and Alice traveled to Baltimore with the McLeans to take in the Democratic convention. It did not bring good news. As Alice sat near cousins Eleanor and Franklin, the Democrats nominated progressive New Jersey governor Woodrow Wilson. TR's supporters hoped the Democrats would put forward a right-leaning Democrat, leaving voters to choose from among TR and two conservatives. Eleanor told her friend Isabella Greenway that Alice was looking well and bubbling over about the "wonderful" Chicago convention. But Nick, Alice worried, was "gloomy" and "despairing," and she said she herself felt "so tired and depressed."[24] She was not close enough to Eleanor to confess the personal toll of the GOP decision.

Still, TR's speaking tours proved his popularity undimmed. As his fortunes eclipsed Taft's, Nick's fell. Progressives in Ohio threatened to "smoke out" Nick and work doubly hard for his defeat if he didn't declare for Roosevelt. "His wife is progressive," the Ohioans mused, "but every act he has ever done in Congress stamps him as a reactionary." Alice was sorry for him. "My darling helpless Nick... I do love him so much," she wrote. The aftermath of the conventions and the realization that Wilson would probably take the presidency gave Alice another cold. Nick's turmoil made him reassess his course. After a consultation with President Taft, Alice recounted, Nick "talked, quite calmly; he said he had three choices—to withdraw and do nothing; stay in and be an active Republican; or stay in and do nothing except for himself—and if I can't see [it] I am lacking in sense and am a 'woman.' The latter anyway is true! But I will not betray him, darling Nick." Nick felt the best he could do was to "stay in and do nothing except for himself."[25]

Alice left for her annual summer visit to the Lee relatives in Boston, protesting that she hated to leave her precious Nick. They met up afterward at Sagamore Hill, where an important decision was made for her, against her will. On the wide veranda looking out over the bay, Theodore, Nick, and Alice sat rocking and strategizing. The men laid down the law: Alice could not attend the Progressive Party convention in Chicago. "I could scream," Alice stormed, "but if N. was defeated, as he probably will be, and I felt I have done anything he hadn't wanted in a political line I should feel frightfully." Her presence at the convention might cause Nick to lose votes, but it surely would have helped her father. In her autobiography, Alice described the depth of her unhappiness: "I used to have ignoble thoughts of goading Nick into doing something that would justify me in packing my bag and hopping a train to Chicago—something reprehensible, such as making a display of friendliness to the unfortunate Mr. Taft. That was the unattractive frame of mind that I was in for days at a time during those dementing months of the campaign!" She loyally but reluctantly stayed out of the spotlight. Her father approved of her resolution. He described Alice to a friend as "a most ardent, intelligent and uncompromising progressive."[26]

More than one thousand "serious, earnest, almost fanatical men and women" converged on the Windy City for the opening of the convention on August 5, but MRS. LONGWORTH NOT THERE, the papers noted. She was at home being "rather unpleasant this morning to Nick. It suddenly came over me in a rush what I was missing." To add insult to injury, her mother-in-law came for a visit. Alice could hardly remain civil. She was imagining an escape, to "Egypt and India and China and the Great West and South America and the South Seas. I felt as I could burst unless I went to one of my distant lands."[27]

The Progressive Party convention was, Edith thought, "like a great religious meeting with deep seriousness beneath all the enthusiasm." TR was in his element, greeting supporters, plotting strategy, exuding enthusiasm and confidence. His speech was apocryphal and stirring, repeating the famous closing of his Orchestra Hall oration: "We stand at Armageddon, and we battle for the Lord." His "confession of faith" sent legions of campaigners off to their home states on fire to spread the gospel of progressivism. Alice kept up through phone calls and telegrams, and kicked against the fate that denied her a front-row seat at that historic convention. To Auntie Bye she confided, "It was a bitter disappointment and I don't think I shall ever get over not having seen it. But poor Nick is having a dreadfully hard time and being such a dear about it all and he felt very strongly and was back[ed] up by Father."[28]

As the fall wore on, Alice consulted with headquarters and visited her father regularly. She heartily approved of the Bull Moose ideal: "The platform is the best thing I've read for ages. I in fact read it again and again today and am 'for it.' I am getting active pleasure out of it—not an atom too radical." Still, Alice hated to be sidelined by the combination of her own celebrity and by the expectation that she show outward loyalty to her husband's cause. In her autobiography she lamented how "my sister-in-law and everyone I knew were busy working for Taft." Auntie Bye expressed the same desire Alice had: to "help campaign for Father, or do any work for him." Everyone was feeling the strain. Her stepmother confessed to Belle Hagner, "There is such a hard time ahead that I can scarcely keep a stiff upper lip. I wish I could see you but Washington is the forbidden city for me."[29]

The subject of a three-day parley at Sagamore was whether or not to run a Progressive in Nick's Ohio district. Roosevelt had earlier ruled that the Progressive Party would support slates in every state possible while protecting Nick. By August, the matter was out of his hands. The Progressive Party in Ohio chose to run A. O. Zwick against Nick. Alice's anger was tinged with pragmatism. "I can see [both] sides and it won't do to talk. But I feel rather betrayed and as if it might easily go to the devil. My precious Nick. I am so homesick for him." Nick worried that what might happen in the national election—the Progressive Party would facilitate a Democratic victory—would now happen to his detriment in his own district. Alice summed up her fears for her husband's election and her loyalty to them both: "I am with Father heart and soul—and with Nick heart and body (I suppose that is about it) and altogether [it] is one of the most unpleasant situations conceivable and I have to face it and do *my* best to make the best of it."[30]

It was a terrible time for them both. Grace Vanderbilt invited her to a costume ball in Newport, the playground of the aristocracy. Nick forbade her. Alice escaped anyway. The ball would make the front pages, Nick seethed, and Alice's photo splashed across the country would provoke an outcry in his district. It didn't help that Grace contributed financially to TR's campaign. "I feel," Alice penned sullenly, "it would be ridiculous to stay away for political purposes. It is not going to be a debauch," she asserted to her diary, and she thought it crazy "to give up going" for fear of "what 'people' will say." She and Eleanor Sears left for the Vanderbilt "cottage," the Breakers, on the twenty-second and turned her attention to the rehearsal for the quadrille. After dinner with Senator Aldrich—she could not leave off politics for long—the ball opened. Alice and Grace "led the cotillion at 4:30 a.m. down around the ocean." She danced happily until breakfast at 7:00 a.m. and fell into bed an hour later.[31]

The next day, she received a telegram that made her furious. In a vengeful mood, Nick had gone to Ilesboro, Ohio, to play golf and see a woman of whom Alice disapproved. When the couple reunited, Alice wrote: "He hates me and I him—don't like his politics or his personality but I hate feeling as I do at the moment that our life together is...a failure and on the verge of breaking up." Alice's tone was ominous. "Things will never be the same again," she thundered. "He knows what I feel about his going to Iles-boro, unreasonable and unwarranted as it was." Nick took to drinking, and Alice didn't stop him. The tit-for-tat injuring "wounded [her] deeply."[32]

Things only very slowly returned to normal. Alice's commitment to the Progressive cause deepened. She promised to "get names for" the woman's finance committee to help with the fund-raising. Nick's position remained untenable. Newspapers made much of it. LONGWORTH STILL FOR TAFT, the headline read, followed by BUT DECLARES THAT ROOSEVELT POLICIES MUST BE CARRIED OUT. "I am what I have always been, a Republican," Nick repeated wearily, but, "at the same time I want it understood that as a Republican I am a Progressive." "There is much merit in 'but,'" one editor joked.[33]

In mid-September 1912, the Longworths went to "Nick's place"—in her anger disavowing all personal connections to Rookwood—to await the election. Cincinnati bored Alice, and the anti-Progressive sentiment there angered her. She took refuge in reading. She consumed *First and Second Maccabees* in the Apocrypha, biographies of Alexander the Great, and Os-car Wilde's poems, but continually interrupting her was the realization that TR "stands for everything that is upright and Progressive and inspired and how sad it will be for the people if he is not made president."[34] So strongly did she feel that she defied both her husband and her father to attend a Pro-gressive rally in Columbus, where TR's vice presidential nominee, Hiram Johnson, spoke. She was the focus of intense interest even though she tried to remain an onlooker. Buckeye Progressives made much of having lured Princess Alice out of hiding.

Nick faced a serious political crisis. He told his sister, "I would go down the street during the campaign and meet first one of my intimates and then another. The first would say 'I cannot vote for you Nick, because your father-in-law is running for President at the head of the Progressive Party and I am not a Progressive.' The next would say: 'I am sorry Nick, but since you are for William Howard Taft as President, I can't vote for you, I am for Roosevelt." Alice stayed off those Cincinnati streets, playing cards with Nick's sister Nan and reading until late the plays of Franz Wedekind and August Strindberg, and James Frazier's classic *The Golden Bough*. Alice longed to go to Washington, but decided against it as Nick "seems to want me very much here. He is so dear and nice now, but I always know something will happen, sooner or later and that it won't last."[35] They were living in a public pressure cooker.

Alice did go—alone—to Chicago on October 12 to hear TR's big speech at the Coliseum. Ever the politician's daughter, she circulated among the train conductors and porters, taking the pulse of the voters, and was thrilled to find them all avowed Progressives. Thousands more supporters gathered to meet TR with "the most wild enthusiasm." She, Medill, and a pregnant Ruth dined with TR afterward, when he was supposed to be resting his throat. While in Chicago, Alice did a little passive volunteer work for the campaign by watching the sales at the Bull Moose store. It was the last day to register to vote, and she drew attention to the cause by her presence. She wouldn't actually get behind the cash register to sell items, probably because she had "asked again if my doing any professional political work would be objectionable," and TR told her it would be. He had requested she not be present in Cincinnati when he gave a talk in Nick's backyard. Even her appearance at an event could be misconstrued, but she had to be in the thick of things at least sometimes. "It was torture," she wrote, "not to be doing something." She did give money: six hundred dollars to her father's campaign, and four hundred to her husband's.[36]

On October 14, Alice was interrupted at dinner by a terrifying telephone call from the *Philadelphia Inquirer*. In Milwaukee, her father had been shot. An unbalanced fanatic who claimed he was opposed to Roosevelt's having a third term in the presidency aimed at TR from six feet away. The bullet slowed on impact with the triple barrier of Roosevelt's heavy overcoat, his lengthy, folded speech, and his steel glasses case. But the bullet did not exit his body. That did not stop the Bull Moose. He gave his scheduled speech before going to the hospital. Ruth telephoned to confirm the details and reassure Alice that TR would be fine.

Alice left for Roosevelt's Chicago hospital room on the morning train. She joined the rest of her family already there, except for Kermit, who was in Brazil. Nick arrived on the sixteenth as the physicians were debating whether to remove the bullet, which had lodged close to his heart. Nick went to the hospital to see TR, but was, according to Alice, "a little intoxicated" at dinner. "Of course [he] was tired but it is discouraging," to have him yet again unavailable to support her in such an awful time. Nick left for Cincinnati on the midnight train. He was making several campaign speeches a day.[37]

TR's opponents (Taft, Wilson, and the Socialist Eugene Debs) graciously called a temporary halt to the mudslinging in the presidential campaign as he healed, but Bull Moose strategy making continued uninterrupted. Alice was thriving; in the thick of it, taking care of her father and plotting tactics with the campaign leaders. Ruth was her mainstay during these worrisome days. The McCormicks were staunch Progressives, and Ruth had added her pleas to Alice's, trying to persuade Nick to join them. Officially, Medill headed the Bull Moose campaign activities in the West, while Ruth chaired the Chicago Committee of 100. Ruth was "a cracking success" at her job, Alice thought, and as a friend she was "the good angel."[38]

Leaving TR in competent hands, Alice reluctantly returned to Cincinnati on the twenty-third. Energized from the time with her family, she was critical of Nick. She attended a rally and heard him speak on the tariff. "He still pulls his mouth down . . . and opens it so affectedly and with such terrible . . . sounds. Middle western to a degree," she wrote, dismissively. She stayed away from the big hometown celebration of Taft, where Nick gave a flattering address. "I am not for any more of such," she wrote from her bed.[39]

A week later, Alice attended TR's best speech of the year, at Madison Square Garden. She had helped him write it. Sitting together, "he would pass over the first draft of every sheet . . . as he finished writing it" to her. Despite the huge and adoring crowd, according to her autobiography, they had "no illusions. . . . It was depressing to realize that the spirit, the enthusiasm, and the conviction of the righteousness of our cause were about to go down before the vastly greater number who did not believe in the issues as we saw them or who did not care."[40] Nick was similarly downcast. "Not a spark of life in him," Alice wrote. Just two days before the election, Alice recounted the wages of stress:

> Nick and I had a tremendous row after lunch on account of me not being for him, not "standing by" him, and I am so hurt and angry. I had prided myself on my self control and what is the use? Talking about going to Ruth in Chicago [for the election night] brought matters to a climax.... He suggested that I should not be [in Ohio] this autumn but I thought he wanted me to come and he seemed to like my being here—and now when I have been away for five days he seems to resent my interest and hopes in and for the Progressive Party.... Of course I am disappointed [in] him infinitely more I fear than he is in me. He is so "sensitive" in his political feeling but also I am heartily proud of the campaign he has made. And of course earnestly desire his success—but we are surely drifting decidedly far apart.[41]

By the next day, they were "on better terms," but Nick was "fatigued" and Alice's "thoughts [were] very far away." She mused again at length in her diary, and her loyalty is clear: "As for Father and his Progressive Party, I don't dare hope.... Everything is against us, but his fight is the fight for all that is great and advanced and human...."[42]

Election day 1912 was stifling. The Democrats carried the presidency as progressive New Jersey governor Woodrow Wilson won. Alice tried to put a good spin on it, looking toward the future and marveling at Taft's paltry eight electoral college votes to her father's eighty-eight. She thought TR's concession statement was "wonderful" and although her "heart ache[d]," she vowed she would hold her "head high."[43]

At least Nick won. Or so it seemed. But two days later it became clear that Nick lost his House seat by ninety-seven votes to the Democratic contender. Were those ninety-seven votes lost when Alice defied her father and her husband to attend the Progressive rally in Columbus? In later life, Alice thought so. At the time, she knew it was "terribly hard on my poor Nick. He looks so crushed, and I know he feels bruised and betrayed. He is

so painfully sensitive about things that really matter to him and no one realizes it. He seems such a nice matter-of-fact object, but I know how deeply
hurt he feels, and it is desperately hard to have been buoyed by false
hopes. . . . It is all hideous and if we can only keep happy together. . . ."[44]

Ever the pragmatist, Alice closed her diary entry with: "Now Nick
must become a real Progressive. These are quickly moving times and one
must be not only alert, but have firmly rooted ambitions and resolve to
keep in the current." One wonders how sympathetic Nick found her. She
railed to herself about how awful it would be to live in Cincinnati with the
"dull little people." Her admitted self-absorption might have had something to do with Nick's big debauch, what Alice called one of the ten worst
days of her life: "We dined at the Crosstown . . . Nick got very drunk—we
stayed interminable hours and when we got home he completely broke
down. I have an infinite sorrow and pity for him which I tried to make him
feel, but it was very terrible. I want him to realize that I have the greatest
faith in him and that this is only a temporary setback and it leaves him the
most free to pursue his own line of action. . . . It is desperate but unless I
go to the devil or go to pieces I will pull him through to a successful
ending."[45]

While Nick's banishment from the House of Representatives lasted
only one term, the effect of the divisive battle of 1912 on the Longworth
marriage would be more profound. Less than a month into her plan of pulling Nick through, Alice confessed to being "absolutely at sea as to the
course I should pursue," given the "rather derogatory thoughts" she felt
Nick was having about her. His mother and sisters apparently felt the same,
as they suggested that the couple ought to purchase their own house rather
than live at Rookwood. Nick would not hear of it. First electoral defeat,
then turned out of his own home by his own family. His reaction was evidence of his despair. "He says," Alice recounted in her diary, "it is a question of divorcing and that he chooses me over all the rest including politics.
He simply must not mean it. I try to make him feel that I am willing and
delighted to be anywhere he wants but it is decidedly discouraging and I so
dread his . . . breaking down again."[46] Susan Longworth and Alice Long-

worth were never close, and the thought of living with her for two years was shriveling. How his depression, and his "moments," which "exhausted" her, coupled with her general arrogance toward the Midwest would play out remained to be seen. Alice took refuge in Christmas at Sagamore Hill—but she knew the demons would be waiting when she returned.

Chapter 13

"Beating Against Bars"

ALICE HAD TO WILL HERSELF to call Cincinnati home. Small-town politics were of only middling interest to her. She had no real friends there. Ruth Hanna McCormick lived in Chicago, but that was as far away as Washington. Worse, Alice and Susan Longworth were forced into close, daily proximity at Rookwood. Nick, their buffer, returned to his law firm but was more interested in potential constituents than clients. For the first ten months of exile, Nick suffered, according to Alice, with not even one "unreservedly cheerful political moment."[1] He had every intention of being reelected in 1914—and that was the only game afoot for his wife. The Longworths' misery did not draw them closer. In fact, their marriage devolved into one of tolerant and usually amused—but distant—affection. It was characterized by lengthy separations, occasional jealous outbursts, and a joint commitment to keeping up appearances. Curiously loving letters held them together, as though they liked each other much better apart.

Alice found three ways to escape from Cincinnati: she left as often as she could for visits to Sagamore Hill; she went to parties; she devoured books and newspapers. For his part, Nick had his usual trio of diversions: wine, women, and song. A comfortable and liquid conviviality formed the backdrop for Nick's ongoing relationships with Ohio politicians, local women, and society friends. Cincinnati's biannual May music festival brought great artists to his doorstep, and he could indulge his love of music. Alice mistrusted the politicians and liked few of his friends. She ignored the women as much as she could, but sometimes she stumbled on them. Out walking one day, Alice came upon Nick and a young Cincinnatian curled about each other in the park. Looking up, the woman unblushingly called out, "Hullo, Mrs. Longworth."[2] At least the music was tolerable.

"I'm approaching my 29th birthday," Alice wrote to her sister. "I've added for you and me a verse of my own" to a poem Ethel had mentioned:

> For seven long years I've been wed
> I've had some assorted emotions,
> but frankly when all's done and said
> In spite of my fears which depress me,
> and in spite of the life that I've led
> I'd sooner have 'sparkling' occasions,
> than find my heart ruled by my head.

"Excellent sentiments, what!"[3] An excellent self-defense, as well.

Alice delayed the inevitable departure from Washington for as long as possible by staying on for the last months of the Taft administration. "Did you hear," she wrote to her sister, "that Mrs. Taft had a Turkey Trot class at the White House[?] To see her doing the Aviation Slide is said to be a very rare sight. I have made a beautiful imitation of it." Of course the best reason to linger was to see the change. "[I]t was almost impossible to believe that those odd beings called Democrats were actually there in the offing about to take things over. . . . It was not nearly so subduing as I thought it would be to be among the Lame Ducks," she recalled with glee. "We were busy with plans for a comeback." One who returned early was Belle Hagner. She had been asked by the new First Lady, Ellen Axson Wilson, to serve as her social secretary, and her continued employment made all the Roosevelts glad for her.[4]

Another interesting feature of the Wilson administration was the new assistant secretary of the navy, Franklin D. Roosevelt. TR wrote of his pleasure in the appointment: "It is interesting to see that you are in another place which I myself once held. I am sure you will enjoy yourself to the full . . . and . . . do capital work." But he promised to caution his niece to be "nice to the naval officers' wives. They have a pretty hard time, with very little money to get along on, and yet a position to keep up...."[5] Roosevelt knew the pity that his sister Bye, wife of Admiral William Sheffield Cowles, took on wives of men junior to her husband. Characteristically, this was only the *first* letter of unasked-for advice to reach the new secretary's desk from Uncle Ted.

Alice and Nick made sure to invite Eleanor and Franklin over. Never warm cousins, Eleanor and Alice had guardedly nice things to say about each other—despite the vast difference in their personalities and interests. Eleanor told her friend Isabella Ferguson about the Longworths' entertaining, where "one of the lady guests had a cocktail, 2 glasses of whiskey and liqueurs and 15 cigarettes before I left at 10:15. It was a funny party but I'm glad I'm not quite so fashionable! Alice looks fairly well though and is very nice." Even though it's a safe guess that the thirsty "lady guest" was Nick's friend, Alice nevertheless had a difficult time with the "rather fine and solemn little Sunday evenings" at her Democratic cousins' home, "where one was usually regaled with crown roast, very indifferent wine, and a good deal of knitting." Alice and Nick once took Susan Longworth with them. Susan knew that as Alice became bored, she "appeared to swell up" so that her "face becomes fat." That night she thought her daughter-in-law "was going to lose [her] eyes" altogether. Alice found her cousins hard to take and very tedious as a couple. But FDR on his own "asserted himself" and was much more fun.[6]

Franklin loved people and thrived on social interaction, but Eleanor was, she herself admitted, a "slave of the social system," making as many as thirty calls between lunch and teatime. ER's son believed that "tallying the number of calls she made and adhering to her rigid timetable were what counted with her, not the conversations she could have had with those she called on." Even Lucy Mercer's secretarial help didn't alleviate Eleanor's fears, which grew as she observed her cousin's seasoned socializing. Eleanor remembered Alice's as "a center of gaiety and of interesting gatherings. Everyone who came to Washington coveted an introduction to her and an invitation to her house." In 1913, Eleanor wanted most of all to blend in.[7] Such a timid response to the cosmopolitan and fascinating nation's center could only cause one cousin to look on with dismay and envy while the other peered back with disdain.

As the curtain rose on Wilson's term, Nick exited Washington first. Alice left her card at the White House with Belle, and "a day or so later went to a perfunctory and formal tea there." Nick wrote Alice newsy letters from Cincinnati with reassurances masking past troubles: "You may compose yourself in peace," Nick wrote, "with the knowledge that Margaret leaves on April 1. She is to marry a young doctor.... Possibly it will relieve your mind to know that Virgie and Hilda are in New York, and I haven't seen any women folk." Her response made no mention of the "women folk," but did make plain that she was "really slaving" at home packing up the house, taking "ammonia baths" for physical sustenance, and stepping out only to attend charity events and dine with Judge Learned Hand and writer Herbert Croly. "Good night my precious one," she concluded. "Your letter sounded cheerful and I am so glad."[8]

No other delaying tactic in sight, Alice eventually said her last goodbyes. She hated to leave Washington—and would return only once while Nick was out of office—but upon reflection she was pragmatic: "It was an excellent thing for both of us to be out for a term. It gave him time in the district he had not had for many years, and it was most salutary for me to be removed for a while from the easy, agreeable existence that I was accustomed to in Washington." That was an echo of the Rooseveltian fear that an effortless life lacked the necessary character-forming challenges. And every now and then she could find something good about the peacefulness of Cincinnati. She once recorded pastorally that she "sat on the porch after dinner and said poetry and hymns and whistled and looked at the earth and the stars. Very blessed me."[9] Cincinnati was also good for walking. As she did throughout her life, Alice walked miles at a time for exercise and meditation.

In the spring, Edith and Ethel were busy planning the latter's wedding to Dr. Richard Derby, a surgeon friend of Kermit's. Theodore later called Dick "one of the most efficient, high-minded, loyal and fearless men I ever met." Nick and Alice arranged to meet up with each other at Sagamore Hill for the ceremony on April 4. Alice went on first, but then terrible rains drenched Cincinnati. Nick's first report was sobering. "The situation here is about as bad as it can be.... The center part of Ohio is a vast lake." He feared that Dayton would be entirely "wiped out" by floodwaters and uncontrollable fires, and thought "what may follow from disease and starvation is awful to contemplate." One can imagine Alice's reaction to such a missive, received while at the Ritz-Carlton hotel in New York City, where, with her maid, she was readying for the ride out to Oyster Bay. She had not seen Nick in weeks, and there were worries on her part about his straying. Now the rains brought these considerations to a halt while Nick responded as a leading politician from the stricken state. He had two boats out ferrying people and "helping wherever we can."[10]

Nick's next letter was less frightening—the loss of life was not as bad as he originally predicted. North of Cincinnati the floodwaters were retreating, but conditions were worsening in the Queen City, where "thousands of houses and factories are under water." "I am so thankful," Alice wrote, "that we live in a sort of Ararat." She wrote on the thirty-first, still thinking that he would be able to get to Sagamore for the wedding. In New York, she went to the opera, saw dressmakers, and dined with her aunts. At Sagamore, she caught up on family news. But these were diversions. "I hate not being in Ohio when there is so much to be done," she wrote Nick, "but I couldn't risk going out and not being able to get back in time for Ethel's wedding.... Darling precious Bubbet, I wish I could see you."[11]

The 1913 flood was one of the worst natural disasters in Ohio history. Governor James M. Cox declared martial law and called out the National Guard in the hardest hit areas around Columbus, Dayton, and Zanesville. Nick could not extract himself. Alice missed him: "It was the best wedding I've ever been to, at least when you weren't the bridegroom! For nothing can quite touch ours." Their letters professed sorrow at not seeing each other, and consistently used the nicknames they developed for each other, Bubbie for her, Bubby for him, with variations. "Precious Bubbet I do want to see you! I am pretty forlorn at times and your letters have been such a comfort," Alice wrote. Nick reciprocated. "I want my Bubbie back badly," he wrote twice in one letter that April.[12]

Despite her outward behavior, the family knew Alice's life with Nick was not ideal. Kermit, with troubles of his own in Brazil, wrote sensitively to Ethel: "I am feeling awfully depressed about Sister. Here's a hard outlook. She's tied down, and has most of the things which theoretically ought to make you happy, but which actually really have so very little to do with it." News of friends and family helped to divert Alice from the grind of Cincinnati, where she had gone once the waters receded. In March 1914 came the joyful tidings of the birth of Dick and Ethel's first baby, Richard Derby Jr. Travel always helped Alice, too. With Edith at Sagamore, the older woman observed how much Alice "enjoys a little change from family in law."[13]

A quarrel erupted in September, when Nick broke his foot doing the Turkey Trot in Cincinnati with someone not his wife. He was laid up on crutches for weeks. While he was hobbling around at the Myopia Hunt Club, watching golf tournaments and squiring about various women, Alice returned to her parents. "Tell me what the Puppuk thinks of the Maine election," Nick begged, but most of his letters were full of names that could only have made Alice unhappy. "Last night I had a dinner and a musical party here. Meyers, Ags, Shaws, Goodriches, Lucy, Mary, Amory, Betty Hig, Edith and her brother (Reynold with cold)."[14]

Willard Straight, who had married Dorothy Whitney in 1911, was one of the visitors to Sagamore Hill, but the distraction of an old friend was not enough to quench her desire for Nick, despite his wandering eye: "Darling Bubby. I love you so very much. You are so much nicer and more attractive and more everything than any one else in the world. . . . I'm getting a terrible longing to hear your voice so I may call you upon the telephone from town," Alice wrote feelingly. On the other hand, her letter outlined all the various obstacles to his joining her at Oyster Bay early—servants leaving, her planned visit to Auntie Bye, some shopping she had to do—despite Nick's desire to talk about the 1916 election with TR before he left the country. Alice's conflicted emotions disrupted the family. Edith wrote, adding with some aggravation, "This Sunday she spends with E. Ellis, a relief to the family for her temper is vile—no doubt she has trouble enough, poor soul, but not to be justly visited on us."[15]

Fretting about Nick's infidelities, Alice watched her parents wave good-bye to the large crowd gathered in their honor as they set sail for South America in early October 1913. TR had concocted a plan to explore an uncharted Brazilian river. He called it his "last chance to be a boy." Edith, a game traveler and a concerned wife, determined to go with him for the first two months as he made an elder-statesman's tour of Chile, Argentina, Uruguay, and Brazil. Edith insisted that Kermit postpone his planned wedding to Belle Willard to escort his father into the wilderness.[16] At fifty-four, Theodore's strenuous life had given him malaria, rheumatism, a blind left eye, and more. Charting the River of Doubt would very nearly finish him off.

Christmas 1913 thus found the Longworths apart again. Nick joined his mother in Cincinnati. Alice, Quentin, Ted and Eleanor, and Ethel, Dick, and their baby got together at Oyster Bay for part of the holidays. Alice spent Christmas eve with Ted and Eleanor—both of whom she always enjoyed—filling stockings, cooking eggs in the kitchen, and having "a nice, silly time." Christmas dinner was a prodigious affair. She ate, she told Nick, "five helpings of roast pig," after which "Ted and I went on, when the family left, to Birdie Vanderbilt's to a party—dozens of people there, who appeared glad to see me and bemoaned your absence." She had a marvelous time. The next days involved shopping, plays, a lunch where "all the ladies but me were ardent and active suffragists," and another where she met Giuseppe Garibaldi II. Alice found the son of the famous Italian nationalist-in-exile "a most perfect combination of both dreamer and fighter—very interesting about Mexico, but not the charmer I had been led to expect."

She told Nick that she was off to a New Year's celebration at the Long Island home of Willard and Dorothy Straight. "I love you very, very much," she assured Nick in closing. "Nice, snowy Cincinnati sounds very attractive, far more so than New York, which has a hard dry cast iron aspect and cold and blowy besides," she wrote before leaving for Long Island. More plays, *Der Rosenkavalier* ("nothing but German buffoonery on the stage, though some of the music was quite pretty"), and an interesting gathering where British suffragist Vera Laughton Mathews impressed her. She, Alice told Nick, "really knows quite a lot on the subject and expresses herself clearly and well." Alice concluded with a 1914 wish for her husband: "All I hope is that it will not be my fault if the New Year is not a happy one for you. Your devoted, Bubbie."[17]

The separations between the Longworths allowed Alice to play with her friends, who, unlike Nick's, were younger, uncritically fond of her father, and from the Eastern establishment. He had known his pals, especially the Cincinnati coterie, from his youth. They all grew up immersed in the Queen City's musical and political traditions. During Alice's absences Nick continued his philandering, which seems to have paused in the early days of their marriage and returned sometime after 1912. One longtime Cincinnati resident remembered that "Nick loved to kiss pretty ladies, which my mother was, and he loved to kiss her." Nick, she summed up, "could get away with anything."[18] Nick was generally discreet. Who knows but that, in certain quarters, it may have helped his political career to have been seen with local Cincinnati women—a sort of "take that, TR and Eastern progressives." In an era when one measure of a man's virility was his female conquests, Nick's womanizing, after his electoral loss, could offer constituents subtle but real proof of his prowess—and evidence that he was not under the thumb of his famous father-in-law, either.

Alice rejoiced when Nick pulled out of his depression to tell her in January 1914 that he would resume his political career. Perhaps the dissipation of her Newport parties was troubling her buried New England conscience: "You can't know how happy I am that you are going to run again— I suppose the governorship would be impossible to try for under the circumstances though how I should love to see you beat both Cox and Garfield—I am sure you have been able to decide all this much more easily without seeing me around and as you told me not to dodge any amusing things I am taking you at your word and staying until Tuesday or Wednesday—by that time I will be surfeited and I doubt if you will be able to force me away from Cincinnati again until the spring!" Politics were never far from Alice's mind. So anxious was she to see him reunited with his career that she wrote approvingly of the Ohio governorship. But Nick's situation would continue to be troubled by divided loyalties. As TR left to explore the River of Doubt in Brazil, his dedication to the Progressive Party had not wavered: "I am with you for this cause, to fight to the end," he vowed to his supporters.[19]

Before she and Nick could discuss matters in person, Alice had to attend the funeral of her grandmother Caroline Lee. It was a "very depressing" event, and Alice promptly came down with the mumps. Grandmother Lee's death was a break with her mother's side of the family. Alice felt extremely sad. She went to recuperate briefly at Auntie Bye's in Connecticut, so as not to "come home a green shadow to the arms of my Bubby." She thanked Bye for taking her in, writing, "My brief moment with you has the kind of joy that I can't even begin to tell you.... You don't know how hateful it is not to see you and have you near ... for there is no one in the world like my own Auntie Bye." Because of her grandmother's death, Alice was also "a little more prosperous."[20] Healed and a thousand dollars wealthier, she rejoined Nick in Cincinnati in mid-January 1914.

Rookwood seemed dreary and parochial. It was Susan's home, full of Longworth heirlooms and mementos of Nick's premarriage life. Because Nick was averse to the idea, the couple never established their own home in Cincinnati. Alice felt trapped. It reminded her of the First Daughter years when she had nowhere of her own to entertain. She went along to Nick's picnics, which gave him an excuse to "repair to the Shrine of the cellar and with appropriate ceremonies do Bacchic reverence...." As often as thrice weekly they hosted "musical parties" of trios or quartets. "[T]here never were more delightful evenings," Alice later reminisced. She learned to be a better listener, once even helping Nick edit an opera he composed.[21] Music never became her avocation but her diaries attest to her enjoyment.

While Alice joined in, these were really Nick's avocations. She kept from Nick knowledge of the one thing she really came to love in Cincinnati: Joseph S. Graydon. A tall, handsome, erudite attorney, Joe Graydon and Alice embarked upon what can best be termed an intellectual affair. Possibly, but probably not, consummated, their mutual affection is clear in his letters to her, and attested to in Graydon family stories.[22] Joe was eight years older than Alice, a Class of 1898 Harvard graduate who had attended Harvard Law and then the University of Cincinnati. His professional and civic careers were exemplary. He was a senior founding partner in Graydon, Head, and Ritchey, a member of the Cincinnati Bar Association, and a supporter of the fine arts in the Queen City. He was a horseman and a tennis player—but it was his mind Alice loved.

Joe Graydon was intoxicated with Immanuel Kant, René Descartes, Edward Gibbon, and William Shakespeare. His letters to her were liberally sprinkled with quotations. He cited long passages of Sir Thomas Browne. The windows in his home library were etched with figures from Geoffrey Chaucer's *The Canterbury Tales*. Though not an academic, he belonged to the Modern Languages Association of America, the Early English Text Society, the Medieval Society of America, Cincinnati's Classical Round Table, and the Historical and Philosophical Society of Ohio, among others. He owned a twelve-volume set of the 1911 *Oxford English Dictionary*. One of Graydon's heroes was Charles Russell, Lord Chief Justice of England. Alice asked him to send her Russell's writings; she wanted to know Graydon's mind.[23]

He called her Seraphina, "One beating against bars." That was rather more nicely than how Robert Louis Stevenson drew her in his novel *Prince Otto*, from whence the allusion came. The pet name was not an exact fit, but it pointed to Graydon's own intensive study of his new friend. Like Alice, Stevenson's Princess Seraphina was a politician. The fictional princess ably ran the country in the absence of her milquetoast husband. She was equally at ease commanding and philosophizing. By the end of the novel Prince Otto and Princess Seraphina have lost their country in a republican coup d'etat. They live out their lives happily if a bit aimlessly, united in love and writing their memoirs. But there was another side of the princess: "Chafing that she was not a man, and could not shine by action, she had conceived a woman's part, of answerable domination; she sought to subjugate for by-ends, to rain influence and be fancy free; and, while she loved not man, loved to see man obey her."[24]

Joe Graydon's nickname was probably a paean to Alice's political acuity. Yet which Princess Seraphina? The coldhearted, bloodless pawn of the prime minister or the exiled but sadder and wiser princess, penning "dull and conscientious" *poésies?*[25] Perhaps Graydon meant to convey that he understood Alice's frustration with her milksop husband, her banishment to Cincinnati, her unspoken ambitions for political influence and intellectual ferment. Maybe he saw himself as the prime minister: her motivator, her muse, but never quite her lover.

One reason that the literary friendship between Alice and Joe may have not crossed into physical realms was the existence of Mrs. Graydon. Marjorie Maxwell had married Joseph Graydon in 1901. They had two children. In his letters Joe never referred to his family by anything other than "madam and the two tall daughters." Alice could not have missed knowing the entire Graydon family, as their paths would have crossed at any number of important Cincinnati events. The Longworths and the Graydons were May Festival organizers and communicants of the Episcopal church; both Nick and Joe were members of the same bar and alumni associations, as well as the Pillars, the exclusive Cincinnati social club where Nick had been meeting women friends for decades. Auntie Bye knew and entertained Marjorie Graydon. Yet, according to her grandson, Graydon DeCamp, Marjorie was "the antithesis of Alice! As wide as the overstuffed chairs she sat in and not very charming or pleasant, by many accounts." In fact, Alice had helped Marjorie in some way with a favorite chair of hers. "Madam," Graydon noted sardonically, "sits and sits."[26]

Alice and Nick spent part of every summer in Cincinnati, and she usually joined Nick at Rookwood after Christmas at Sagamore. There would have been ample occasions for Joe and Alice to commune. Perhaps it was during a railway journey that they first discovered their common intellectual proclivities. Joe reminisced about a "trip to N.Y. via Washington... with cigarettes, stateroom and a taciturn Seraphina sitting on her feet in the corner."[27] The two tried to get together in Chicago, in New York, in Washington. When they were apart, they telephoned and wrote of books they had sent to each other, of poets they loved. Joe's letters show a man desirous of impressing Alice. "I would rather have you angry than uninterested," he emphasized.[28]

Joseph Graydon liked to portray himself as a simple Cincinnati attorney, the human antidote to the corruption and cynicism she complained of in Washington. "What you need," he told her, "is not Kant and the categories, nor Browne and incomprehensibles, but the association of people who are simple, child-like and free from guile—I was about to say—like me." But he was also a man of strong feelings, one who could match her passion. He loathed "statesmen who do not govern. Lawyers who have not the common law in their blood. Poets accentuating content, disregarding form. People who deny themselves that primary source of inspiration—their fellow man.... [It is i]n the minds of children and plain folk we are likeliest to find that spirit of truth and justice, which make us, not only as [Heinrick] Ibsen says 'Pillars of Society,' but possibly also members of that choir invisible that shall sing when human society is not."[29] The Bull Moose himself would have approved of such populist sentiments. Alice did.

Graydon saw the two of them as set apart and "refus[ing] to live in time and space...." He drew graphs for her to illustrate infinity. They took pleasure in differential calculus, Bishop Berkeley's "ghosts of departed quantities." They discussed Kant—and on that subject Graydon was the humble expert, she the willing student. Space, time, God, immortality, intellect, materialism, natural law—all topics of his penetrating mind. "Seraphina, I don't believe anybody but you would stand for this...it is because you have a catholicity of interest which is unique...."[30]

They shared a skepticism for traditional religion. Alice did not discuss her superstitions with most people, and the fact that she did with Joe Graydon speaks volumes about their intimacy. They enjoyed challenging each other. His letter to her in June 1918 began, "For clever Alice: In adopting free will as an acceptable item of table talk, why scoff at original sin?" He wrote four and a quarter pages on the topic, and then enclosed some of his philosophy, written a year earlier—another five legal pages' worth. Graydon's Episcopalian upbringing did not stop him from questioning the very fundamentals of Western religion, but he did so with a charity that Alice did not always share. This irritated him. Alice's diary in October 1915 found her musing, "Gnostics, their remains. Jewish life in [ancient] times. Must find if the difference between the Sephardim and Ashkenazim is not a difference in caste as well as ritual.... [S]urvival of life not being survival of memory. Return to the stream of life, having no recollection of 'ourselves' at age of two, yet nevertheless lived. Yet at age of two we have been so impressed subconsciously that it influenced our whole future life...."[31] Their relationship inspired Alice to reflection—always a satisfying exercise for her.

As his closing changed to "ever yours," his letters become more loverlike: "See that any attention you pay him remains vicarious—that adjective in your note, my dear Seraphina, was worth a great deal." He wondered whether her missing earring had been located, confessing that he "might be found hunting for it by night, to keep as a souvenir." Graydon could be vulnerable with her, admitting to depression ("a lapse into shadowland," he termed it), and "Machiavellian subterfuges, outbursts of simulated frankness, casuistical reticences; all the torturous devices denoting *not* an humble and contrite heart. Beware that man who with an owl-like countenance recounts old saws and modern instances to you, advising how you should order and direct your ways. He is not better than he should be, but a broken reed to hang upon."[32]

At one point, Joe could not see her as planned: "I have been forced to the conclusion that it were best I should not visit in Washington in absence of affairs requiring my presence there. Please do not think I should not like to—or that I am unappreciative of your asking me: nor must you think any other whatsoever suspicious or horrid things as the cause why I am, I hope, disappointing you."[33] A wife's distrust keeping him away Alice could forgive, but not his absence from the same political camp. In April 1916, Graydon's letter contained a warning for their relationship, had he but known it. Concerning the 1916 presidential race he wrote: "I want it thoroughly understood that I am not for T.R. from any consideration of principles, but only through the powerful not-to-be-denied influence of a member of his family. That is to say I am your personal convert."[34] But that was before the United States entered the Great War. Graydon was convinced of the righteousness of the Allied cause, and made plans to enter the army's intelligence branch. Alice was busy denigrating Woodrow Wilson and his handling of foreign affairs. Joe lashed out at Alice for her unpatriotic attitude. "I can find you at least 1000 ex or prospective Republican office holders who would be glad to get your news criticizing the Administration," he wrote. "Why, oh why, do you insist, at first insidiously and then more boldly, in venting it at me[?] You behaved very well about it when you were here, and, as I supposed, recognized the fact and my right to entirely disagree with you. But something has got you started again. Please refrain—I am backing the President and administration for the course of the war. Afterwards can take care of itself."[35]

He wrote next of his own attempts to join the military. At forty-one he was too old for officers' camp. Instead, he "negotiated for a commission in the Intelligence Branch" and was hoping to see it come through. Given the Roosevelt family's shared understanding of "the battlefield as a place of honor, fulfillment, and robust democracy," and Joe's clear sensitivity to his cerebral nature when compared to the model of her celebrity sportsman father ("You may think I never killed a lion or sat for a Sargent sketch, but the velocities of the banishing increments are mine"), Alice surely approved of Graydon's intended sacrifice, regardless of her fears for his welfare.[36]

Perhaps it was their still-diverging politics, or maybe it was the influence of "madam and the two tall daughters," but by late 1919 the affair was abating. While the philosophy nurtured her, the relationship could ultimately never satisfy her. Joseph Graydon did not share her passion for politics. Every time she tried to engage him on the subject, he begged off. His mind preferred to play with Kant's antinomies rather than with others' political destinies. Alice's true soul mate would be a man who combined Graydon's erudition with a political obsession. That man was still in her future. Nonetheless, when Joe was in his sixties and seventies, she was still sending him birthday remembrances—and Alice Longworth was not known for her sentimentality.[37]

Joe Graydon was Alice's first mature love. How much Nick knew is unclear. Alice's love for Graydon was based on an intellectual magnetism and a physical allure. If not sexually consummated, their relationship nevertheless was Alice's first real independent step away from Nick and her father. After Joe, she would be able to envision a man who could match her intellect and share her love of politics, and a man with whom she could take the next physical step. Married to Nick out of habit and for appearance's sake, Alice lived ever more a life on her own terms—fond of her husband and at his side for important political events, and even free to play with him when it suited her, Alice could distance herself from his boozing and womanizing. And she could keep her eyes open for a man who appreciated the political game in all its nuances.

It was the war that came between Joe Graydon and Alice Longworth. Foreign news dominated the lives of all Americans, although most were not as ardent about foreign policy as Alice. The possibility of war against Mexico loomed in the autumn of 1913. Early in that year, military leader Victoriano Huerta's successful coup ended Mexican president Francisco Madero's administration and Wilson extended support to the constitutionalists, a faction committed to democratic policies and the overthrow of Huerta. Alice tracked the Wilson administration's handling of Mexican affairs. She read widely from several different newspaper subscriptions, dined with politicians, and quizzed Nick. Information came from Kermit in South America, who wrote to tell her that war with Mexico *and* Japan looked "pretty likely." It was the Mexican situation that caused Idaho's Senator William E. Borah to warm to foreign affairs.[38] Alice could not have helped noticing him as she read about the congressional debates every day. Ruggedly striking, Senator Borah already had a reputation as a renegade in the GOP. He was a man to watch.

Alice also had her inside sources such as George Goethals, director of the Panama Canal project. Together at a dinner at the Wilson White House, they perched "on the uncomfortable little gold chairs...muttering maledictions on the Administration." Goethals wrote to her in March 1914 that Colonel Leonard Wood believed "intervention is a sure thing in Mexico." Thus it came as no surprise to her when, on Tuesday, April 21, 1914, Wilson dramatically requested Congress to send the U.S. Navy to occupy Vera Cruz. "War is practically a fact today," Alice mused from Rookwood. She followed the turn of events closely, expressing her mistrust of Wilson and his motives. "His message was entirely against Huerta [seemingly] making his personality the issue. The resolution as passed didn't go quite his way.... I would wage a good deal that Wilson is privately communicating with [Pancho] Villa etc. and no wonder as he has given them the arms they will use against us. If Wilson puts this thing through on his own my hat is off to him—but if he fails his shortsightedness is murderously criminal."[39]

Two days later, she knew she was right: "12 Americans killed and 50 wounded at Vera Cruz.... [Wilson] has practically asked the constitutionals for approval of his message and the joint resolution.... At least they are stopping the arms from going across the border." The newspapers were full of the story, including Wilson's invitation to Argentina, Brazil, and Chile to mediate. For Alice this meant Wilson "has made us the laughing stock of the world and if this is true it is unbearably humiliating.... To have this whey blooded schoolmaster at the head is very bitter. I can only hope for some violent out break on the border which will make war imperative—and he will get into it and come out of it discredited."[40] War was an instrument of foreign policy for Alice, who seldom spared ink on its victims.

Another conflagration appeared on the horizon in early 1914. Ruth McCormick was hard at work on preparedness as head of the woman's section of the Navy League. Medill, recently returned from Europe, believed war there was looming. Like all the Roosevelt men, Medill felt that if peace were shattered, it would be his duty to fight. He was clear-eyed about it. He wrote his wife presciently that "while, in Mexico, there might be adventure out of proportion to agony, in Europe, the agony outweighs the adventure."[41]

The assassination of Archduke Franz Ferdinand was the catalyst for the war that Medill foresaw. As Alice drank Napoleonic brandy with Neil Primrose and the Rothschilds, her family raced toward the conflict. Dick Derby left in September 1914 to tend to the wounded in Europe, and Ethel accompanied him. Their five-month-old infant remained with his grandparents. The news from abroad was troubling. Nick's sister Nan Wallingford wrote from France to a Cincinnati friend about Italian workers who had cut telegraph wires to stop Parisians from communicating with anyone outside the city, about rampant fears that funds would become inaccessible, about horses and chauffeurs having been requisitioned for the military, and "hysterical women servants who have quite gone to pieces."[42]

When Alice visited Oyster Bay in mid-September, all the talk was of the future. "The war is so terrible that I can think of little else. All Europe seems to have returned to barbarism," Edith fretted. Ted was involved in establishing training centers for soldiers-to-be for the inevitable (as all Roosevelts believed) day that the United States would enter the war.[43] TR's family would be prepared despite President Wilson's insistence on Americans being "too proud to fight."

For Alice, the election of 1914 temporarily topped the war in Europe as it represented a chance for redemption and a return to Washington. She wrote in her diary for November 3, 1914, "It's not quite one this morning—and election day—hope he gets it.... It will be nice to be in Washington again—and an active part of the government again." But on the whole, Alice noted, the election seemed "trivial" compared to the war. Nick won back his seat easily and without much campaigning by Alice. They were both glad to return to D.C. in March 1915 for the Sixty-fourth Congress. Family and friends celebrated for them. When Alice and Nick dropped by Sagamore Hill before Thanksgiving, Edith thought they looked "well and happy." "Isn't it fine that Nick has got in again?" Kermit enthused. "It will make a lot of difference to Sister."[44]

Tempered by exile in Cincinnati, buoyed by her dalliance with Joe Graydon, Alice resolved to be her own person once again. She would stand separate from her husband's lack of self-discipline and her mother-in-law's disapproval. She was ready to be thoughtfully immersed in political debates in the midst of the international crisis. She tried to persuade Joe to visit her in Washington and, until the war interfered, she attempted to hold on to that most interesting piece of Cincinnati. Alice missed him. But, in the end, it was a relief to return to the capital city, to the life she had grown to love at the hub of the nation's political system. After the war, Alice Roosevelt Longworth would evolve into a Washington statesman. Not limited by a constituency as were elected politicians, she could go anywhere, talk with anyone. Her power came to be greater than any lobbyist's or social maven's because her home was the place to be, to see and be seen, to spill secrets, to meet people, and to broker deals that could not be made in Congress. Alice's drawing room became a required stop on the path to political prominence.

Chapter 14

"To Hate the Democrats So Wholeheartedly"

T HE WORLD WAS AT WAR and the president of the United States did nothing, the Roosevelts fumed. When a German torpedo sank the British passenger liner *Lusitania* in May 1915, killing 128 U.S. citizens—not the first Americans to fall victim to German U-boats—Wilson and the Democrats made no military response. Nick's election returned the Longworths to a Washington on edge as the European conflict entered the bloody stalemate of trench warfare. Alice would come to feel that "all our lives before and after have just been bookends for the heroic, tragic volume of the Great War."[1]

Theodore Roosevelt led the charge against vacillating Democrats and called for military preparedness and, eventually, for U.S. involvement in the war. Alice was never more in accord with her father than over the issue of war in Europe. She thought about the U.S. situation this way: "To look always for the best yet to be alertly ready to deal with the worst in mankind is not a bad working scheme. Recognition of interdependence and mutual responsibility without losing individuality is crucial. Elevate the least without setting limitations to the total, and the only individual who can, who understands, is Father." She felt he was "the great personage of these times. Of all time for me."[2] Military preparedness and the election of 1916 dominated the headlines and family discussions. Alice assisted sporadically in the war effort, refined her political convictions, and sharpened her skills as a salon hostess. She and her father were close companions during the war years, though by the end, drastic changes had occurred: Quentin was dead, Theodore Roosevelt was mortally ailing, and Alice was falling in love.

Led by Theodore Roosevelt, the family advocated military preparedness. The United States should build up its armed forces and stay on the alert, because the conflagration overseas might require immediate involvement. After Germany invaded neutral Belgium on August 4, 1914, TR urged President Woodrow Wilson to commit American troops to stop Kaiser Wilhelm's immoral conquest. No one knew better than Roosevelt the German military capability, having seen it firsthand in 1910. He found the kaiser "an able and powerful man" with a "curious combination of power, energy, egotism, and restless desire to do, and to seem to do, things." But TR didn't trust the kaiser and suspected him then of promising peace while preparing for war.[3] His reservations proved correct.

As 1914 wore on, Alice and TR discussed Germany's relationship with England. Father and daughter conversed "steadily" on horseback for hours at a time. Roosevelt told Alice of his doubts about the kaiser. He believed the German atrocity stories flooding the American press and eventually abandoned his belief that the United States should remain prepared but neutral. Instead, TR supported American entry in the European war for two reasons: to check further German evils and to be a player in the postwar balance of power. As president, Roosevelt had seen "how far Germany is willing to go in doing what she believes her interest and her destiny demand, in disregard of her own engagements and of the equities of other peoples." When Ethel returned from the hospitals in France with somber accounts of German troops firing intentionally on the Red Cross and allied soldiers mutilated by their sadistic attacks, he sprang into action.[4]

TR spearheaded universal military training. To help move Americans off their neutral center point, he churned out didactic books and articles blasting Germany, President Wilson, and American pacifists. He worked with the National Security League, the American Defense Society, and the Army League. He wholeheartedly supported Leonard Wood's creation of the Plattsburg volunteer military training camp and reviewed the troops there, inspiring a martial spirit that the country's real commander in chief could not. Alice wondered how "anyone with common sense [could] hesitate to work for universal military training, far less talk of world disarmament. Poor oafs, poor fools, and Japan with her million men."[5]

A deep loathing for the administration ran through the Oyster Bay Roosevelts, who saw Wilson as idealistic, weak, and out of touch. TR did not mince words: "I despise Wilson," he told his sister. Alice called Wilson a "slimy hypocrite." Edith wrote furiously to a friend, "There is no mistake that could have been made that has been neglected in Washington. The veiled prophet of the White House cares only for his political future and is totally unconcerned as to the futures of the nation and the lives of those we love."[6] Sending one son after another off to fight, Edith felt she hated war as much as she loathed the commander in chief.

All the Roosevelts heard the call "to take their own part." Edith felt herself to be "a horrid example of the pariah woman, for I have not been able to take up any war work as yet. Quentin has his orders for active duty, and when he sails I will try to help the Oyster Bay Red Cross." Eventually she supported national "home charity work" through the Needlework Guild.[7] Richard Derby wrote to Belle and Kermit that they "talk of nothing but preparedness these days." His address to the Harvard Club was "a plea for national service. This morning's paper," he went on, "tells us that the House's bill contemplates a federalization of the National Guard and an increase in the army of up to only 135,000. They are so hopelessly on the wrong track, that it is discouraging. If they could only be made to see that universal service is the only rational and democratic method of defense." From Europe, Edith's sister Emily Carow, soon to be decorated with two Italian Red Cross medals, confessed, "I love my work and have been repaid a thousandfold by every soldier I have nursed." Women on the American homefront patriotically made clothing for soldiers. "No one moved," cousin Eleanor Roosevelt asserted, "without her knitting."[8] No one except Alice. She never knitted a stitch in her life.

Alice did, however, economize consciously during wartime in at least one characteristically outrageous way. She wore slacks in public. She was fifty years ahead of her time and pushing a firm social boundary. Men wore slacks. Women wore skirts. As the *Ladies' Home Journal* later asserted: "Without ever joining anything, she had a trick of doing things on her own account a year or so before other women would organize some sort of social crusade to enable them to do the same things without being talked about." Alice's action was another example of her insouciant independent streak where she pleased herself first. Despite the newspaper coverage, Alice was blasé. "I urge all the ladies to wear pantalettes," Alice said. "They're comfortable, economical and save considerable cloth."[9]

Nick was too old to be in uniform but was fighting the good fight in Congress. His "True Preparedness" speech appealed for federal support to the dye industry. He knew that the United States had only two dyestuff plants that could be converted into factories for high explosives. This was not enough. Readying other factories should begin immediately: "It can be done in the same plant, with the same machinery, and by the same men." He won House approval for the government to spend $180,000 on land to build a nitrate plant in Cincinnati. Despite calling himself a "militant" Republican, Nick was cautious. He and his father-in-law tempered their speeches during election season, going no further than criticizing Germany and calling for American entry in 1916. Nick limited his public excoriation of Wilson in deference to his large German-American constituency. Nonetheless, he warned Americans from the House floor that if war came, the country could not protect itself. Douglas Robinson called his speeches "a real service." "No one," cousin Douglas emphasized, who "has stood for adequate defense has committed political suicide...."[10]

In August 1915, Ted advocated a "comprehensive reserve system" and was among the first to join Wood at the Plattsburg camp. Archie signed up for Harvard's military training program. Sheffield Cowles, Auntie Bye's son, would join Princeton's military camp. The patriarch approved: TR eventually had four sons and one son-in-law fighting in the war, one son-in-law fighting Wilson in Congress, one daughter-in-law marshaling women's involvement in the preparedness campaign, one daughter serving beside her husband in Europe, and the other—Alice—by his side being "a real help to me politically." They were all, he crowed, possessed of "the dauntless spirit we ought all to have."[11]

As to traditional war work, Alice wrote in her autobiography that "one, of course, did that sort of thing too—washed dishes, scooped ice cream, cut pies, peddled Liberty Loan bonds, and made clumsy attempts at first aid." She posed in a Girl Scout uniform for wartime publicity. Her real contribution came from continuous entertaining. "I think," she recalled, "it pleased the Washington that went to and gave dinners, to feel that entertaining the representatives of the Allies had a recognized part in 'winning the war'!" It was for her, she readily conceded, "a far pleasanter form of 'war work' than canteens and Red Cross classes." This allowed her to "send...all the political news" when she wrote to soldiers.[12] It also perfected her considerable talents as a salon hostess.

Soldiering on among the "Washington that went to and gave dinners" was Alice's gift: bringing together those who planned strategy and made policy. Her home became TR's address whenever he traveled to the capital city. The Longworths socialized at this time with a combination of policy makers, the moneyed elite who backed the GOP, foreign dignitaries, and many out-of-town visitors. Mary Borah recalled that after Alice's guests strategized over soup and debated during dessert, she "always had lots of couches and...we'd settle ourselves on these and Nick would take out his violin and play for awhile." Sometimes virtuosi such as Jascha Heifetz and Efrem Zimbalist joined him.[13] Then "conversation would begin [again], usually about politics. Alice was intensely interested in politics." The political topics over teas and dinners and poker games were always the same that year: preparedness, party politics, and "what an ass Wilson is." By February 1916, Alice, Nick, and TR "had decided that there was nothing left for the President to do but resign." But Alice held out little hope for any sort of push from Congress. "On the whole they are such a stagnant lot, our 'statesmen,' that it is," she sighed, "pretty depressing."[14]

Acquaintances failed to notice the developing political concerns of the woman they still referred to as Princess Alice. Isabella Ferguson recounted to ER that she had met Alice in Cincinnati in 1916, where the latter was "filled with noisy exuberance [and] no reality—She was nevertheless refreshing [and] *un*changed (after not seeing her for eight years!). I had looked for strict dignity from numerous tales—but met old time lightness—She seemed to appreciate that you do your job in Washington a little bit better than anyone else."[15]

Turning aside the compliment, Eleanor passed judgment on her cousin:

Of course [Alice] isn't a bit changed [and] it is always entertaining to be with her but now that I am older [and] have my own values fixed a little I can only say that what little I saw of her...life gave me a feeling of dreariness and waste. Her house is charming, her entertainments delightful. She's a born hostess and has an extraordinary mind but as for real friendships and what it means she hasn't a conception of any depth in any feeling or so at least it seems. Life seems to be one long pursuit of pleasure and excitement and rather little real happiness either given or taken on the way, the 'blue bird' always to be searched for in some new and novel way.[16]

It was not Alice's modus vivendi to show a deeper side to her censorious cousin Eleanor.

In the midst of preparedness discussions, the 1916 election loomed. Contemptuous of the Democrats and still convinced that TR could make Americans see the light, Alice attended the Progressive Party convention in Chicago in June. TR instructed the delegates not to nominate him "unless the country has in its mood something of the heroic." He was the unanimous choice of the Progressive Party but gave them a "conditional refusal" as he waited to see what the Republicans did. Edith wrote a friend, "I cannot but feel that the Progressive Party has done great good in forcing its ideas of humanity and justice—that is really what it comes to—upon political machines. I must confess horror that in regard to its founders it has been a car of Juggernaut" under which she could see her husband being crushed.[17] Like her parents, Alice was ambivalent. She wanted her father back in the White House, but easily—cleanly. Instead of dragged along by the Progressive Party "juggernaut," she'd rather he be acclaimed by enthusiastic Republicans as he stood a better chance of victory with an established party.

At the Republican Party convention Alice's hopes dimmed as the GOP chose Charles Evans Hughes. She was devastated. She vowed she had "no feeling of personal chagrin at the result, only a sense of waste that the one man most qualified to cope with the intricate and appalling problems of this time, should have been refused the chance to serve, and what is more to lead, as only he can lead. This is no filial squeal, only my very sincere opinion. It is unnecessary to say how much I hope for the success of Mr. Hughes." TR believed the third party could not win. He withdrew his name, asking all Progressives to vote for the GOP, thus dooming the party he created.[18] One of Alice's friends ran on a state-level Progressive ticket. Alice wrote, "I was delighted to hear of your nomination. . . . Now go ahead and be elected and we will make things hum to a different tune in Washington," starting with "the impeachment of that white-livered coward in the White House." Whether the Republicans or the Progressives won was less important for all the Roosevelts than that someone defeat, as Edith put it, the "vile and hypocritical charlatan," Wilson.[19]

In the 1916 race Nick had to balance his zeal for military preparedness with his sensitivity toward the German-American voters in his district. Alice obliquely referred to the campaign as "unpleasant." For the November election, the two were in Nick's Cincinnati office, where Alice found listening to the returns a depressing business. "I became," she recounted, "increasingly a combination of Poe's Raven and Cassandra, with a dash of malevolent political observer." Nick went to bed, but she sat up alone all night, phoning her journalist friends to get the returns from the West Coast. With the wounds inflicted by her in-laws in 1912 still so raw, it was with "malicious pleasure" the next morning that she trumpeted the blow of Wilson's victory—even though she was fiercely disappointed in the outcome, too.[20] At least Nick's tactful campaign had worked. His constituents sent him back to the House of Representatives.

After repeated challenges to U.S. neutrality, Germany finally pushed President Wilson to a declaration of war on April 2, 1917. Alice was both triumphant and heartsick, as she knew "so well that we are on the edge of inevitable grief and tragedy." She followed war news avidly. She habitually spent afternoons in the House or Senate, listening to the debates and the speeches. The publisher of the *Washington Post* was so impressed with Alice's assessment of the European situation that he begged her to write a column on that topic. Though flattered, Alice professed herself "too aware of my quarter horse limitations."[21]

While Nick visited his mother, Alice read the rationalist writings of

British foreign secretary Arthur James Balfour. His Balfour Declaration of November 1917 gave hope to Zionists, calling for a Jewish homeland in British-held Palestine. Alice found Balfour so persuasive that she "got much excited and somewhat religious after an agnostic fashion." She chatted with him in April, when she also had met Joseph Joffre, the architect of the French war plan. By the spring of 1917, the latter was in Washington to request rapid mobilization of U.S. troops to France. Alice found Joffre likable and quick to confess France's dire position. By contrast, Balfour was "earnest" and charming. He loved to hear Nick play his violin, and she loved to talk foreign policy and philosophy with him. He became a friend to both Longworths.[22]

Spellbound by global events discussed around her table, in the middle of reading her father's latest contentious book, *The Foes of Our Own Household,* and helping Nick with his speeches, Alice felt moved to prophesy in October 1917: "The war will continue until sometime in April. Then Germany having arranged and maneuvered with Japan and Russia to consolidate her Russian gains and her Balkan conquests, will offer such terms that the allies cannot refuse...Belgium vacated. Alsace-Lorraine returned. Certain colonies to be self-governing. She will then set herself to the task of consolidating.... We meanwhile will have had men on the fighting front and will share in the face-saving 'victory.' Wilson will be a portentous and sorry fixture in the peace terms. And then when the war measures lapse, calamity and disintegration in this country. Mexico aflame once more. European influence threatens. The campaign of 1920 F. elected; appealing to all that is noblest.... Let us see. I have spoken."[23] Alice's prognostication on the foreign front were borne out with more accuracy than her domestic predictions. She was deeply concerned about the postwar situation, and continued to ruminate.

Alice took some friends to the newly established Camp Meade in Maryland to see her friend Ned McLean—by then Lieutenant Colonel McLean—in the 312th Artillery. It was her first look at "one of the immense conscript camps." The sight was riveting. She found the "streams" of men in khaki and all the bustle uplifting. Alice identified with the soldiers: "Am proud to be one of them," she penned. The stirring sights of Camp Meade redoubled her feeling that all men who avoided military service were "unalterably contemptible."[24]

She eventually made her way to Cincinnati to join Nick and left from there to travel to Oyster Bay for Thanksgiving. Ethel saw the toll that visiting Susan had taken on her sister: "She looks rather tired after a month in Cincinnati, but is as delightful as always. Much interested in the way political things are shaping themselves." TR reported to Ted, "As usual I talk politics at length with her." Alice had much to say about Wilson as she had been watching Senate Republicans introduce a series of investigations that she hoped would help unseat him.[25]

Alice followed international events closely. "[French prime minister Paul] Painlevé out, [Georges] Clemenceau in. [David] Lloyd George tottering. Everything is a mess. Perhaps, soon, Father will play the big part," she wrote. Contemplating TR as president in 1920 made Alice deliriously happy—so much so that she confessed to feeling "almost friendly to Harding" when he told her he'd overheard others saying "TR is the only man in sight for 1920." Whatever sort of scheming she and her father were doing about 1920, Alice wished she could spill the details to her best friend. After tea with Ruth McCormick, Alice recorded how "as soon as she knows as much as I do about plans for Father it will be easier talking. She is the best fun.... My father president again and my husband speaker would be absolutely satisfactory, even to me."[26]

But the immediacy of war interrupted dreams of 1920. Influenced by a patriotic desire to support the Allied effort, Alice participated in the democratic process to the extent that women were allowed in 1917. She voted. "My first vote cast against German in the public schools."[27] She was one of many Americans who succumbed to a jingoistic response to German militarism. While not as bad as those who called publicly for the elimination of German language programs or the curtailment of civil liberties for German Americans, Alice's sentiment was private, but clear. For the next several days, she dissected the elections in her diary: suffrage might have passed in New York, and Ohio would probably embrace prohibition, but these were "nothing of consequence in comparison to the fact that... Hylan elected" as mayor of New York City. She thought attorney John F. Hylan, a Tammany Hall insider, "the tool of the most corrupt and adroit creature in the country, the exposed candidate of the German propaganda.... There are no words to express my angry contempt for the [Wilson] administration in not supporting [reformer John Purroy] Mitchel.... It was a straight out issue between sedition and patriotism, and that cur in the White House took no part." She soon recorded how she awoke at 2:20 a.m. "consumed with political venom that endured until the clock struck 6." The following day, she "lost [her] temper with Nick" over whether the Red Cross or the YMCA was the more worthy recipient of their financial donation. Nick came down on the side of the Red Cross—an institution governed at that time by Cincinnati native and Taft confidante Mabel Boardman. But that fight was not about benevolence—Alice had spent part of the previous day making compresses for the Red Cross. It was caused by her continued rage against Wilson that sat like a thundercloud over their home.[28]

For distraction, she was staying up late "wallowing in" paleontologist Henry Fairfield Osborn's just-published *The Origin and Evolution of Life: On the Theory of Action, Reaction and Interaction of Energy,* which she found "thrilling."[29] The study of theories of evolution was a lifelong fascination for Alice. In 1917, Osborn was in the forefront of a movement referred to as "the New Biology," which called into question older ideas about the pre-eminence of environment in shaping human nature and actions. Experimental biology, based on laboratory observations and testing hypotheses, came to replace natural history during Alice's twenties and thirties, when she deepened her study of evolution and refined her ideas about social Darwinism.

One of the centers of the New Biology was the Station for Experimental Evolution, located in Cold Spring Harbor on Long Island, not far from Sagamore Hill. It was more than just a neighborly interest that kept Alice enthralled. She shared with her father a passion for biology; the sciences had been TR's first choice of study at Harvard. Theodore was writing a review of Osborn's book at the same time that Alice was reading it. Perhaps some of her absorption had an even more solipsistic source. To one who never knew her mother and admired her father, who grew up with stories of the heroic acts of ancestors, it seems logical that Alice might find the topic of heredity inherently engrossing. And the efficacy of either creating a better environment or in "breeding a better race" is one that engaged many Progressive Era reformers.[30]

Political activism retained its primacy in her life, however, and she rejoiced when her father announced he would visit Washington in January 1918, "as he alone can steer and eventually lead the Republicans." Alice had wanted to invite him herself, so that he could dole out advice on the congressional campaign in person, but she was relieved when other politicos prevailed upon the colonel to come. "He talks on nearly every side of the situation.... He can get the party [together] and crystallize their course of action, show up the present wrong doing as no one else can; and he must be in Washington to see certain people," Alice promised her diary.[31]

Over the early months of 1917, Theodore Roosevelt had hatched a plan to resurrect the Rough Riders to fight in France. He privately announced he stood ready to die in battle. His old friend Elihu Root gently teased that if he truly promised to die, President Wilson would doubtless agree to the plan. Nick tried to help the cause by sponsoring legislation empowering Wilson to create four special volunteer divisions just as TR described. But the president said no. The family was positive that "political considerations" were at the bottom of this "bitterest sort of blow" for TR.[32] More likely it was a combination of Roosevelt's poor health, his ongoing criticism of the head of state, and the fact that the weapons of war had changed since 1898.

His own soldiering prospects frustrated, TR looked to his sons as his surrogates. Writing to General John J. Pershing, the commander of the American Expeditionary Force (AEF) in Europe and a fellow veteran of the Spanish-American War, TR asked that Ted and Archie be allowed to serve. They duly embarked for France on June 20, 1917, when Alice was among the family massed to wave them good-bye. In July 1917, Ted took command of the First Battalion of the Twenty-sixth Infantry in the AEF's First Division. Archie, who left behind his new wife, Grace Lockwood Roosevelt, served under Ted. Also in July, Quentin embarked for Europe, a member of the Ninety-fifth aero squadron, the only pilot among the brothers. Kermit gained access to the front through contacts in the British foreign office. He was separated not just from his wife, Belle, but also from their young son, Kim. As a result, Kermit was the least gung ho of the brothers. Brother-in-law Dick arrived in France in November 1917 to join the American Medical Corps. He, too, left a family behind. But overcoming worries and fears was, as Alice recorded in her diary, the appropriate response for Roosevelt men: "I am certainly proud of the way our family has all stepped up to the fore. Without a thought, they were all in the trouble from the very first. Father backed all his sayings, and we have been able to show people that he meant what he said." The family "hung out our flag with four stars" to signal to the world that they had sent four sons off to combat.[33]

Another early entrant into the war effort from among the Roosevelt circle was George Goethals, recalled to active duty as quartermaster general in the army. And "Dear old Willard" Straight came to bid Alice farewell before sailing for battle in France. He left her with "shocking tales... of the incompetency and chaos at Camp Sill."[34] They didn't know it then, but it was their last meeting. Willard Straight fell victim to the terrible postwar influenza pandemic.

In the last months of 1917, American forces joined the Allies in hellish trench fighting as Lenin's socialist government seized power in Russia. Alice mulled this over. "It is desperately bad. The past turn of hideous war may seem merely the general run of things in comparison to what may come...." Christmas celebrations didn't even feel like Christmas. "Just [Father], Mother, Ethel, the Lloyd Derbys & me. A sadly reduced family. I cannot realize that next year the sadness of this may be a persistent and terrible grief," she worried. Nick was miserably stuck in bed fighting a cold, leaving Alice and her sister to put up a tree for the sake of Ethel's young son. On Christmas eve, Alice and TR stayed up late to talk politics. He read out loud to her from his correspondence. She "looked over" a speech he was to give at Princeton, went through his "goodly array of campaign documents," and his review of *Origin and Evolution of Life*. As Nick regained his health, Alice was gladdened that he and TR had many "long talks. They are very good for each other," Alice thought.[35]

The couple's return to Washington meant reimmersion in society. Alice recorded how she and Nick entertained one friend at lunch who "was so pompous about his European experience that I felt like a third rail, casting off sparks. Finally a certain aura emanating from Nick caused me to lapse into platitudinous civility." Nick could still exert some influence over his wife, and their thirteen years of marriage were not without fondness and good humor. The two were together as the new year dawned, part of the throng at Friendship, where they had spent their honeymoon. The McLeans' champagne flowed, but conversation stopped at midnight when a red, white, and blue sign spelling out GOOD LUCK TO THE ALLIES IN 1918 flashed on, amazing even those habituated to the McLeans' extravagance.[36]

Alice missed the joint session of Congress on January 8, when President Wilson laid out his plan for the postwar world. His Fourteen Points called for national sovereignty, a generous settlement of territorial boundaries, a decrease in the world's ability to create war, and, the fourteenth point: the establishment of a League of Nations. It was a noble and nonpunitive document upon which to base the terms of the peace. At its unveiling, even Alice had to "admit ungrudgingly that it is fine." This sentiment would not last. With her "Republican way of thinking," she soon rejected Wilson's idea as strangling the ability of the United States to act unilaterally when necessary in foreign policy.[37]

William E. Borah, powerful member of the Senate Foreign Relations Committee, feared an international peacekeeping league would commit the United States to a military defense of other nations—both unconstitutional and approaching "moral treason." Borah and "his dogged, studious, moralistic approach to political issues," would emerge as the leading isolationist in Congress.[38] Sharing his views, Alice worked for the defeat of Wilson's Fourteen Points—especially the clause to create a League of Nations—as passionately as she had ever done any political work. She was an integral part of a critical struggle that "defined the foreign policy positions of both parties for decades to come."[39]

By late January, TR's anger at Wilson's mismanagement of the country came to a head. The issue took on a decidedly partisan aspect for Alice. She left a House debate one day so inspired by a speech of Medill's that she penned, "It hurts, to hate the Democrats so wholeheartedly." Edith and

TR appeared at Nick and Alice's home "and began lobbying for the assembly of a War Cabinet" on the British model, "to take the management of the military out of the inept hands" of Woodrow Wilson. This was the opening volley against the Fourteen Points, and at the Longworth home Republicans and Democrats met to oppose Wilson and the League. Alice hosted a breakfast of nearly twenty men who had come to see TR, a press conference of thirty-three reporters, a "men's dinner" with a score of politicians who left with "stiffened backbones," and other luncheons, dinners, and receptions. It was a whirlwind of anti-Wilson, pro-Roosevelt activity, and Alice was the center.[40]

Beyond politics, Alice was swept up in the spirit of service as the war ground toward its conclusion. In December 1917, Ruth had asked her to serve on a committee for housing government employees in the District of Columbia. Alice solicited cousin Eleanor to serve with her. In April 1918, Eleanor, staffing a canteen, was surprised to see Alice "twice in two days" volunteering for Red Cross work. ER told a friend she was going to try to find a place for Alice, for, "it is a pity so much energy should go to waste!"[41]

A better line of war work soon beckoned invitingly: espionage. Alice had a small part in the Craufurd-Stuart affair, which changed Anglo-American relations. Motivated by patriotism, anti-German feelings, and love of intrigue, Alice was a willing participant in what became a social and diplomatic scandal with wider foreign policy implications. In the summer of July 1917, Alice met Brigadier General Marlborough Churchill at the McLeans' parties. By 1918, he had become chief of military intelligence in the U.S. War Department and recruited Alice to, in his words, "serve your country."[42]

Major Charles Kennedy Craufurd-Stuart of the British embassy was a bachelor with a variegated résumé of military and personal service. Socialite May Ladenburg, a friend of Alice's, had recently broken off her relationship with the droll major. Stung, Craufurd-Stuart suggested to military intelligence officials that Ladenburg was using her physical attributes to charm secrets out of her new lover, Bernard Baruch, the chair of the War Industries Board, to transmit them to the Germans. Churchill set out to see if the major's accusation were true. After conferring with Assistant Secretary of the Navy Franklin Roosevelt, Churchill sought Alice's help. He asked her to advise him as to the best locations for listening devices in May Ladenburg's home. Alice obliged, suggesting "an upper balcony with a large...kind of mattress on a swing....And then," Alice related, "I and three or four absolutely charming and practically *invisible* Secret Service men went over there and heard the most enchanting conversation between this lady and my old friend Bernie Baruch." May's questions about train movements were punctuated by kisses. "[N]o evidence ever emerged to indicate that Miss Ladenburg was a German spy. But the Baruch record, by later reports, contained almost ludicrous indiscretions...." Suspicions ran high in Washington. Ladenburg suffered social ostracism, and laid plans for revenge on her former lover Craufurd-Stuart. He became tangled in a web that spun far out beyond Alice Longworth and would poison Anglo-American diplomacy. The Craufurd-Stuart affair contributed to the U.S. failure to join the League of Nations—and had Alice known that, she'd have been doubly proud of her work. Eleanor disapproved of Alice's spying, but Alice thought "we were doing a *most* disgraceful thing in the name of looking after the affairs of our country, [and] it was sheer rapture!"[43]

Then in July 1918, the realities of war struck home. On Bastille Day, July 14, First Lieutenant Quentin Roosevelt died "in line of duty," behind enemy lines. The family heard that he had been "instantly killed by two bullet holes in the head...." Frank McCoy, family friend and a colonel with the 165th Infantry, wrote to the Roosevelts with the sad news. TR's response to McCoy epitomized the chin-up attitude of the family: "It was very dreadful to have Quentin die. All I can say is that it would have been worse if he had stayed at home." Privately, both Theodore and Edith were overwhelmed with grief. Adding to their worry was the news that Archie and Ted had been seriously wounded, although both would recover. Alice sought comfort from Joe Graydon. Despite their political disagreements, she asked him to visit her.[44]

Nick, made of different stuff and fighting a different war, was embroiled in congressional negotiations to locate funds to pay for the expensive conflict in Europe. Some of the methods Congress was considering, Nick informed his mother, would affect the Longworth family holdings. He suggested she transfer the title of their vacation home to her children to avoid the coming high taxes. Nick recommended foxily: "If you decide to transfer title it had better be done before the bill passes the House so that it may appear that it's not to avoid taxes, tho heaven knows the Longworth estate has paid its share...." His postscript reaffirmed the dubious legality of his advice: "I wouldn't speak of this to anyone except [our attorneys]."[45]

Alice was sojourning at Rookwood in Cincinnati when the anticipated news of the armistice came. She awoke very early in the morning and walked for an hour along Grandin Road. "There was no light or stir in any of the houses," she remembered. "I was alone in the November night— every whistle in the city five miles away was in full blast. The noise of the whistles was extraordinary—at first it seemed all dissonance, and then one would catch what seemed a wailing melody, or a crescendo of harsh harmonies. It was fantastic—but not ineffable. I recollect that I wanted to feel that the morning stars were singing together and the sons of God shouting for joy, but it was no use—I was sure they weren't."[46] Too many people dead. Too much destroyed. Too little stirring leadership in the country.

Alice and Nick returned to Washington that day, amid talk of Wilson's trip to Versailles to hash out a peace treaty. Harold Nicolson, a British delegate, saw the process as a quest: "We were preparing not Peace only, but Eternal Peace. There was about us the halo of some divine mission.... We were bent on doing great, permanent, noble things."[47] Woodrow Wilson also believed a League of Nations promised eternal peace. Not everyone was so sure. The day before he sailed for France, Henry White—the only Republican Wilson took with him—came to Alice's for tea. He assured her that "there would be no question of 'a League of Nations to enforce peace...A League of Nations perhaps, *en principe*, my dear,' but nothing that we should really have to worry about, he comfortingly insisted."[48] Alice was unconvinced.

Alice spent part of Christmas 1918 at Eleanor and Franklin's home, joined by Edward, Viscount Grey and Sir William Tyrrell, on break from their duties at the British embassy; Sara Delano Roosevelt; and a few friends of FDR's such as Louis Howe. Despite the armistice, it was a sad holiday.

Uncle Douglas Robinson had died of angina in September, Franklin was ill with the flu, and her father had been ailing for much of the fall. He spent forty-four days in the hospital that early winter, but came home on Christmas Day. Alice, Ethel, and Archie were among the family members there to greet him as he returned to Sagamore, the home he loved. After he was settled in, Alice returned to Washington, glad of the time with him. Then, on January 6, 1919, Theodore Roosevelt died peacefully, worn out by a life joyously and strenuously lived. THE OLD LION IS DEAD, Archie's telegram to his brothers in Europe read.[49] Alice's response is best gleaned from her autobiography: she could not bring herself to write about her father's death. It simply does not occur in her life story. She adopted her father's approach to her mother's death—curative, stoic silence.

That emptiness was filled to a degree as Alice continued in the cause to which she and her father were so committed. The emotional upheaval of his death and her own strong feelings against the League of Nations lent a zeal to her political work. That passion inclined her to another lion, Bill Borah, called "the Lion of Idaho" for his shock of thick hair. Although a Republican, Borah marched to his own drummer, and, as a contemporary put it, "hates anything that interferes with free scope for individuality." He was, as biographer Robert James Maddox noted, more like "Idaho's permanent ambassador to the outside world" than a typical senator. "Immune to most political pressures," Maddox concluded, "he cared nothing at all for party regularity and supported the national ticket only when the spirit moved him, which was seldom."[50] Iconoclasts both, Alice and Borah saw an echo of themselves in the other.

Alice was intrigued by the senator, with his "great leonine head" and his "fascinating" conversation—so good that he "could hold one spellbound for hours with tales of labor disputes in Illinois at the turn of the century."[51] Alice sat in the Senate gallery day after day, and soon found Borah's oratorical prowess only the first of many attributes she admired. The two powerful politicians were drawn to each other. They began by valuing each other as intellectual companions, comrades-in-arms, fellow progressive Republicans, and individuals devoted to shared causes. But before the League fight ended, they were lovers.

The first meeting between Alice and Bill Borah may have been during that heady time of the Progressive Party convention in 1912. Unlike Nick, who would not consider public support for Theodore Roosevelt, Bill, known even then for his individualistic approach to GOP tenets, seemed persuadable. He had bolted once before, in 1896, and he was a well-known supporter of TR who backed most progressive legislation. That's why Alice thought she could convince him to change parties in 1912, as she lobbied him on the eastbound train after the convention. Looking to make a convert, Alice "argued with him unavailingly." As he campaigned that memorable season, Borah widely condemned the Taft faction's theft of TR's nomination. But that was not enough for Alice. She would not move him out of her category of "enemies and deserters" because he did not join the Bull Moose Party—but she did respect his principles.[52]

The next time their paths crossed more than briefly, they were allies. The battle against the League brought out the anti-Wilsonian, isolationist side of Alice, who met with sympathetic assistance from the senator. The anti-League fight threw them together in an intense situation. She admired the fine figure Borah cut on the floor of the Senate, giving fiery speeches infused with the righteousness of their cause. For his part, Borah responded to Alice's commitment to their shared campaign, her own flashing mind at work on political strategy, and the way he saw himself mirrored in her appreciative eyes.

The seven years between the Bull Moose and the League controversies had seen a settling of the Longworths' marriage. Rumors of Nick's infidelities continued. Alice, thoroughly disgusted with his excessive drinking, lack of TR-like backbone, and amorous indiscretions, turned her copious talents to her first love: politics. She had forsaken her husband's House of Representatives for a seat in the Senate gallery. Like other political watchers, including her old rival Cissy Patterson, Alice had followed the unusual career of the distinguished and handsome Idahoan. Alice's intellectual affair with Joseph Graydon waned as her fascination with Senator Borah deepened.

In 1906, the year of Alice and Nick's celebrated wedding, an already-famous William Borah won election to the U.S. Senate. Born in Illinois and residing later in Kansas and Idaho, Borah early developed a westerner's anti-eastern sentiment. He lacked the social and academic pedigrees of men like Alice's father, husband, and Joe Graydon. Borah never completed college and read for the law in his brother-in-law's office. He was destined to be an outsider in the exclusive club that was the Senate, and what destiny didn't preclude, Borah's personal quirks confirmed. Forty-two years old in 1907, he arrived in D.C. with Mary McConnell Borah, his wife of twelve years, at the pinnacle of a successful career as a corporate attorney and criminal lawyer. Immediately preceding his swearing-in, Borah was involved in a sensational murder case against the illustrious Chicago barrister Clarence Darrow. Borah was special prosecutor in a trial that pitted him against the laboring men of the Western Federation of Miners, defended by Darrow. It was a difficult trial, for the man who had been murdered was Borah's close friend, former Idaho governor Frank Steunenberg. The accused killer was William D. Haywood, secretary-treasurer of the Western Federation of Miners. Borah lost the case, but Darrow thought Borah "the ablest man he ever faced."[53]

Overlapping the Steunenberg murder case was a potentially devastating lawsuit. Borah was indicted for fraud against the U.S. government. Essentially, he was accused of profiting on the land sales of the Barber Lumber Company whose interests he guarded as their attorney. This was not an auspicious prelude to his senatorial career. The indictment occurred just as the Haywood trial was opening, and the former governor, though deceased, was also indicted. This seemed more than simply bad timing to Borah and his supporters. They suspected a concerted effort by Borah's enemies to sully his political career, or an attempt to derail the murder case—or both. It became more complex when ex–Governor Steunenberg's ties to the mine owners came to light. If the indictment had gone to trial immediately, Borah might have been dropped as special prosecutor and the union men would have faced a less talented accuser. It appeared to be another round of the perennial western drama of mine owners against union men. In this case, the union men were aided by a small group of Borah's political opponents, including the district attorney and the man who had just lost the rancorous senatorial nomination to Borah.

Seeking to begin his Senate career rather than have it unscrupulously and prematurely ended, Borah called in favors from friends such as C. P. Connolly of *Collier's* magazine, Oscar King Davis of the *New York Times*, and his old school chum Kansas journalist and editor William Allen White. White shared Borah's idolization of President Roosevelt and his progressive politics. He also sympathized with Borah's plight: ready to serve in TR's "great administration" but unluckily caught in the land-deal quagmire. Borah asked his friend to intervene: "I feel that I cannot succeed in public life if I am to enter with [Roosevelt's] condemnation... upon me.... I feel if I cannot satisfy the President and the Attorney General of my absolute innocence that I must resign from the Senate." White sought an audience with TR at Oyster Bay. While President Roosevelt declined to pardon Borah for fear that it would lead to rumors of a cover-up, he did move to make certain the Idaho trial would be as clean as possible. The new senator was fully acquitted and took his seat with the Sixtieth Congress in 1907.[54]

Part of what Alice found fascinating about Borah, nineteen years her senior, were these ties to the romantic West of her father's youth. Borah migrated to Idaho in 1890, not long after TR had established his cattle business in the Badlands. Just as TR had to learn cowboy culture when he bought his Dakota ranch, Borah discerned that practicing law on the frontier demanded cunning, bravado, and original thinking to a degree he hadn't seen in relatively sedate, settled Kansas. Roosevelt reared his children on tales that exalted exactly those traits. It is easy to imagine Alice thrilling to Borah's saga of the 1896 conviction of "Diamondfield Jack" Davis, a hired gunman for a cattle company who killed two sheepherders.

Before the trial began, Borah went undercover (just as TR had done as New York police commissioner when Alice was a girl) and rode horseback across the rough terrain of Idaho and Nevada pretending to be a prospective rancher. He spent nights around the campfires with cowboys, swapping tales. Borah finally ran across a ranch foreman who told him of Diamondfield Jack's whereabouts on the night the sheepherders were killed. Other cowboys corroborated how Diamondfield Jack had gloated about the deaths. Satisfied with his fieldwork, Borah traded the cowboy hat for his attorney's chapeau and put the cowboys on the witness stand. Borah won the case. Diamondfield Jack was sentenced to be hanged, and the sheepherders rejoiced.[55]

Borah's bravery triumphed again when he put himself at personal risk in the case of the death of a strikebreaker in an 1899 Western Federation of Miners turnout against the Bunker Hill Mining Company. The man accused of killing the scab was Paul Corcoran, a local union man. Corcoran's friends testified that he was miles from the shooting when it occurred, but Borah had eyewitnesses who swore that they had seen Corcoran riding along on top of a railroad boxcar, carrying a rifle, and jumping to the station platform before the train came to a stop in the town where the scab was murdered. Corcoran's attorneys put railroad engineers on the stand who testified that Corcoran could not have stayed balanced on top of a boxcar through that serpentine stretch of line, nor could he have leaped to the platform unscathed. Borah decided to test the word of the railroad experts. He assembled the same train, packed it with witnesses, and clambered on top of the boxcar, rifle in hand. For six miles Borah rode the train around the curves and down into a canyon. When they reached the platform, Borah jumped off and hit the ground windswept and breathless, but with both legs intact. "It convinced the jury," Borah remembered. "They slept while the defense put forward its case."[56]

This was the stuff of legend. Theodore Roosevelt had fed his eager brood on such adventures, and Borah's past might have sprung from the pages of Alice's children's books. Physical daring, courage, battles of wit, justice triumphant—all set in the Wild West! How could she be immune? Few women were, if the rumors were true.[57] He was a politician cut from the same cloth as her father. Borah, the independent-minded senator with a talent for storytelling and a biography of blockbuster proportions—here was a man who brought to life the very qualities her father celebrated.

In reality, Borah was both more and less than the heroic lawyer driven by a moral vision of himself and the future. According to his wife, Bill Borah was "a very religious man and taught a Sunday school class in Washington year after year.... He never drank or smoked, but he would swear sometimes." He apparently loved horse racing, an enthusiasm shared by

Alice.[58] The contemporary sense of him was more akin to the portrait painted by the author of *The Mirrors of Washington*. This capitol insider suggested that Borah was melancholy, pessimistic, moody, emotional, impulsive, a loner wrapped in an "elusive charm." One could "imagine him as a...university professor, a moral crusader, even a poet...." "He is not a social being," in part because "he neither smokes, nor drinks, nor plays." Yet, despite himself, he was "too much of a personage to be ignored or suppressed, and manages to be a power in a party which has no love for him.... A report that Borah is on the rampage affects Republican leaders very much as a run on a bank affects financial leaders.... Borah knows that most of the men with whom he is dealing are clay and estimates with uncanny accuracy the degree to which he can compel them to meet his demands."[59]

Ohio politician James M. Cox, who lived in the Stoneleigh Court apartment building with Borah in the 1910s, came to understand him from their solitary evenings together. The "depth and quality" of the senator's mind "impressed" Cox, who believed Borah's great ambition was the Supreme Court, a better fit to the "lone wolf" Cox knew than the chummy Senate. Borah could be sociable, though, and enjoyed his afternoons with Idaho constituents at the regular gatherings of the round table at the Idana Hotel back home in Boise. Business and city leaders chewed the fat and solved the world's problems. Borah seldom agreed with everyone present, but he had the ability to remain friends and stay on pleasant terms with those of divergent views.[60]

A large part of Borah's charm for Alice was his love of literature. His formal educational background was as indifferent as hers, yet both autodidacts found solace and elevation in the written word. Their writings are rife with quotations from Shakespeare, Balzac, Kipling, Emerson, Beaumarchais, and Washington, Hamilton, Jefferson, Gladstone, and Pitt. Borah could quote long passages of Dante, Milton, Dickens, Thackeray, and Hawthorne. As a boy he loved recitation and used to make speeches to the mules on his father's farm as he plowed. Literature and history claimed his interest in school, but debate was his favorite pastime. Cox thought it "doubtful whether there was a more omnivorous reader in either branch of Congress."[61]

As a young man Borah had played the role of Mark Antony in *Julius Caesar* for a traveling Shakespearean company. The thespians chose him because he already knew the part by heart. When his father hauled him back to the plow, Bill's acting career ended. One scholar theorized that Mark Antony gave Borah two rules of life: "First, Borah had to assure himself that he was always acting from an unfettered conscience." This helps explain Borah's famous independence of action. "The second duty of the Mark Antony role was that Borah should pursue oratory as a high calling." Borah's father's prohibition against acting pushed him into law and politics, careers that valued an independent conscience and still let him emote.[62]

Bill Borah was recognized as the best orator in the Senate. He wrote his own talks and rehearsed them all carefully and aloud, but no longer to the mules. He read the addresses of Demosthenes, Cicero, Burke, Wendell Phillips, and Lincoln. He kept a notebook of quotes read and overheard so that he could work them into his orations. One friendly analyst concluded the senator's speeches "were not vacuous, and they were free from demagogy and partisan cant. Many of them were notable expositions on constitutional law or ardent declarations on liberty. . . . Borah did not offer oratory as substance; it was his tool."[63]

That tool helped unlock Alice Longworth's heart. "I enjoyed listening to Borah and [Senator James A.] Reed, too," she wrote. "Occasionally I did not entirely agree with what Borah said, or rather with the slant he gave some question, but he had a quality of earnest eloquence combined with a sort of smoldering benevolence, and knew so exactly how to manage his voice, that before he finished speaking I was always enthusiastic. He and Reed were decidedly the drawing cards from the gallery point of view." Daisy Harriman called Borah "a John the Baptist among legislators," who was "easily the most brilliant orator in the Senate . . . [with] a gift for promoting a number of things for which others take credit after he has originated them in his facile brain."[64] Borah studded his speeches with poetry, another passion he shared with Alice. To the day she died she could recite the works of poets from around the globe and across many centuries. Even among their erudite friends, the two were distinctive for the inspiration they received from the classics and the joy they took in wordplay.

They also had in common their adulation of Theodore Roosevelt. One contemporary observer speculated "that his one great desire was to be the successor of Roosevelt." This may explain the inconsistency that was known as Borah's chief failing. It is a fine line between maverick and contradictory behavior—and depends a good deal on the observer. For Alice, in the wake of Joe Graydon's betrayal—his unwillingness to demonize Woodrow Wilson and his inability to commit to a TR campaign in 1920—Borah's veneration of TR must have been balm. Pious, public canonization of her father she dismissed as excessive, but Borah communicated one thing over and over that must have pleased Alice at the most fundamental of all levels: his belief that she was made in her father's image. He told her often that he felt proud "to claim his wonderful daughter as a _dear_ friend of long years."[65]

Alice's political beliefs found a champion in Senator Borah. Upon reaching Washington, he transcended his perceived antiunion stance and embraced a host of reforms including an eight-hour workday, the direct election of senators, and the creation of the Children's Bureau and the Department of Labor. Borah also fought for the 1916 Gore-McLemore Resolution warning Americans not to travel on belligerent ships, and against the espionage and conscription acts as violations of Americans' civil liberties. His resolutions led to the 1923 Dawes Plan to reschedule the German debt from World War I. He supported anti–child labor laws and giving women the vote, but only on the state level.

Alice and Borah did not concur on every issue. For example, Alice thought that the makeup of the Senate deteriorated after passage of the Seventeenth Amendment mandating the direct election of senators. This amendment was one of Borah's successes. Charles Merz, writing in the _New Republic_, characterized Borah as "a better states' rights man than most of his Democratic colleagues." In January 1922, House Republicans passed an antilynching bill that was blocked in the Senate under the leadership of Borah, who saw this as the top of a slippery slope of ever-increasing federal interference in states' rights. Summing up Borah's "maverick" status, Merz concluded, he was "a more liberal Democrat than Wilson" on some issues.[66] Further, Borah's voting record demonstrated a concern for farmers and laborers that Alice would have felt less and less keenly the farther the 1912 battle receded into the distance. Alice sat by Bill at a showing of a D. W. Griffith film, *Orphans of the Storm*, "a big spectacular performance with lurid scenes of the French Revolution...." The senator, she recalled, "behaved as if the scenes had been taken on the spot and became almost emotional about them, blazing with indignation at the cruel behavior of the French 'nobility,' fairly palpitating with sympathy at the vicissitudes of the populace and the heroines." Borah supported "world peace, limitation of armaments, justice for small nations, amnesty for political prisoners, honesty in government, economy, tax reduction, and the preservation of individual liberty."[67]

Borah's own political philosophy was unorthodox. This would not have distressed Alice. Neither of them could be classified as Republican regulars. A staunch defender of the Republican Party in her middle years, Alice nonetheless thought too independently to toe the party line. She had imbibed a heady dose of moral correctness in the 1912 campaign and afterward leaned toward her father's issues, such as conservation of the environment, protecting the rights of labor, and a strongly nationalistic foreign policy. Borah fought against high tariffs, while Nick Longworth championed them. Borah generally thought highly of Woodrow Wilson, and no Roosevelt or Longworth did.

Even when they disagreed they could do so amicably and openly. Borah regarded Alice as an intellectual equal—and he himself was considered an intellectual among senators, chiefly because of the breadth of the allusions in his speeches. But it was politics that bound them. A *Literary Digest* journalist suggested, "Those who love [Washington] are men like Senator Borah, who could hardly exist elsewhere than in the United States Senate; or, to go over to the other sex, women like Mrs. Alice Longworth...to whom it is breath in the nostrils."[68]

And it didn't hinder Alice's relationship with Bill that he was, continued the journalist, "an Apollo in appearance." An observer in the 1920s left some clues to the "real Senator Borah." In person, Borah was "far less austere, far less gloomy" than his photographs. He "frequently smiles and can tell a story gracefully." He had a "sardonic" sense of humor and, "in conversation, he is rarely discreet." He read "voluminously" and was popular because he could discuss "an extraordinary variety of matters." His mind was "alert and facile." Despite appearances, he was not truly a loner, but he did "find his own company excellent."[69] This, of course, could also precisely describe Alice Longworth. At bottom, she and Bill were kindred spirits.

They both believed Wilson's peace plan would compromise American autonomy in foreign affairs. The League of Nations was to be a multinational organization created to keep peace in the world by referring conflicts to its members. The League's Permanent Court of International Justice, known as the World Court, would rule on international disputes so that none would ever reach the battlefield. The League idea drew in many Americans who were tired of war. Roosevelt and other Republicans had initially been warm to the concept. But many people, including TR, Borah, and Alice, came to see the principle of collective action as counter to the tradition of American politics laid out in George Washington's admonition against "permanent alliances with any portion of the foreign world." Borah told TR in 1917 that "if [a league] would work at all it would simply be almost fiendish in its results." The Idahoan had been a member of the Senate Foreign Relations Committee since 1913 and thus was at the eye of the storm when Wilson vowed to make the League a central part of the peace treaty. Even before the details were made public in early 1919, Borah "espoused open warfare."[70]

In the face of the president's call to congressional unity on behalf of his peace treaty, the Republicans dissolved into two groups, varyingly opposed to the League idea. The "strong reservationists" followed Lodge's belief that with major changes a League might be acceptable. The "Irreconcilables," led by Borah, did not support any sort of league at all. On this, Alice was his intellectual twin. She felt they were trying to keep the United States "out of the internationalism that we felt menaced our very existence as an independent nation."[71] Glued to her seat in the Senate gallery, Alice listened to every speech she could. Ruth was right beside her, with the same firm resolve. The two friends worked together to stiffen the will of any politician giving the least sign of capitulating. Laying strategy was an ongoing affair, as the Irreconcilables traded ideas and reviewed one another's points. They met frequently at Alice's and gained the appellation the Battalion of Death for their ferocious tenacity against the League idea. For her leadership role, they christened Alice the "Colonel" of the Battalion of Death.

In early March 1919, Irreconcilables spearheaded the senatorial round robin statement to gather votes against the League of Nations as it was then drafted. They had more names than they needed. Lodge, chair of the Senate Foreign Relations Committee, conveyed the bad news to Wilson. The GOP would take control of the Senate after March 4, 1919, and thus Wilson would have to consult the upper house. Many Republican senators chafed at the section of the League covenant that gave Great Britain the equivalent of six votes to the one granted to the United States. Nor did they like the fact that small countries had the same vote as America. On March 3, Alice went to the Senate to hear the filibuster from Illinois' senior senator, the elderly and near-deaf Lawrence Y. Sherman. Sherman acknowledged that the League had put him in a "savage mood," and that he was "prepared to attack in 'meatax' fashion." He was "tacitly supported" by Wisconsin's Robert M. La Follette and others. After lunch, Sherman continued. Alice went home at 3:00 a.m. and returned "six hours later" to find the senator still on the offensive. He had begun at 8:00 a.m. and went on without interruption until noon, when the Senate adjourned. The filibuster forced Wilson to call the special session he swore he would not, and when the president denounced Sherman, the venerable senator dismissed Wilson as "a superfluous luxury." Alice then rushed to the House, which was full to bursting with spectators viewing "a rag bag of exhausted, frowzy legislators."[72]

While Congress was out of session, Medill, who had won election to the Senate in 1918, masterminded the speaking schedules of the Irreconcilables as they canvassed the nation in late April and spread the news of the destruction they believed the League of Nations would wreak upon the

United States. Alice and Nick went to Cincinnati for six weeks, time she thought "wasted." They arrived back in time for Nick—heretofore anti-suffrage—to vote for the woman's suffrage amendment, to Alice's "great pleasure."[73]

Upon her return, the Battalion of Death sent Alice on a mission to coax the "mild reservationists"—those who sought only minor changes to Wilson's League covenant—to join their side. It was difficult, but she kept at it, spending "more and more time at the Capitol." Meanwhile, Medill "was most amazingly resourceful in producing ideas calculated to annoy," while Bill Borah worked to stall matters by having a leaked version of the lengthy peace treaty read word for word into the record in the Senate. On July 8, the night Wilson returned from Paris, Alice had one of her mild reservationists in tow. She tossed him in her car and drove to the White House to calculate the size of the crowd and the intensity of its support. Needing help from all sources, Alice stood on the curb "fingers crossed, making the sign of the evil eye, and saying 'A murrain on him, a murrain on him, a murrain on him!'"[74] She did not relate whether the experience of hurling imprecations at the president won over her companion.

In an emotional plea before the Senate two days later, Wilson begged the intransigent politicians to pass his treaty so they did not "break the heart of the world." Alice, Frank Brandegee (a good friend and senator from Connecticut), and Medill went for a long drive that afternoon, angrily dissecting the speech and planning how best to invigorate the cause and "capture votes in the Senate." All summer and early fall the peace treaty sat before Lodge's Foreign Relations Committee, which finally released it to the full Senate in September. Seeking to get around the troublesome senators, President Wilson left on September 3 for his own speaking tour of the nation. Borah, Medill, and Hiram Johnson dogged his steps, patiently explaining to great crowds the fallacies in Wilson's logic. They kicked off their anti-League tour at Soldier Field in Chicago, which proved too small for the audience. Borah went on speaking to packed, cheering houses in Nebraska and Iowa.[75]

Meanwhile in Washington, at Lodge's suggestion, Alice wrote a letter to be made public that declared emphatically that TR had not supported the

League of Nations, as Wilson was telling crowds. Just as her stepmother and her brothers—recently returned from the war—were considering making a similar statement, Wilson suffered a paralyzing stroke. Alice's murrain had evidently worked. Her circle, she felt, was "noticeably lacking in the Greek quality of *Aidos*—the quality that deters one from defiling the body of a dead enemy."[76]

Wilson's illness meant no slowdown for the Battalion of Death. Debate over the treaty continued on Capitol Hill. Alice heard all the best speeches in the Senate. In between them she tried her persuasive powers on the undecided and laid plans in the committee rooms and in senatorial offices with her comrades. So used was she to unrestricted access that Borah's secretary, Cora Rubin, remembered that Alice grew distressed the few times she couldn't get into Borah's office. Alice was so regularly in the senators' family gallery that the rules were changed to include "immediate members of ex-Presidents' families," so she wouldn't have to seek out a senator to gain access. On November 19, 1919, the Senate began voting on the Treaty of Versailles—with the reservations written in part by Borah and Lodge—including Article X that would create the League of Nations. Alice and Ruth were there for the ten-hour debate—breaking only to try to influence some reservationists, smoke a cigarette, or snatch a bite to eat.[77]

Bill Borah had the honor of the last speech. The Senate gallery was overflowing with the largest crowd Alice could recall. He was in top form. He charged the senators with nothing less than protecting democracy by voting against the treaty. Democracy, Borah thundered, was "vastly more than a mere form of government.... It is a moral entity, a spiritual force...." And wedding democracy to "the discordant and destructive forces of the Old World" would cause democracy to "lose its soul." "Your treaty," Borah warned, "does not mean peace," but war.[78] His gestures were sure, his voice resonant, his argument convincing. Even his sometime critic Hiram Johnson conceded that Borah had "excelled himself, and made the one great speech of the whole fight." The voting began at 5:30, and the treaty fell to defeat in the Senate, 39 to 55. It was called up again and defeated again, 41 to 51. A third vote, on the treaty without any resolutions, also failed. Finally, at 11:10 p.m., Congress adjourned. The jubilant celebratory dinner was held at Alice's house. Next to her as she drove home that extraordinary night was Bill Borah.[79] She was entranced.

The battle was not over, however. Lodge, the focus of pro-League criticism, decided to seek compromise by holding a conference of mild reservationists. Quite by accident Alice and Ruth discovered their secret meeting at Lodge's home. The Colonel was furious. She confronted Lodge. She made him explain himself. He wanted to try the treaty again, and pass it with his reservations. "I said to myself," recalled Alice, " 'He will have the Irreconcilables to deal with.' " She informed the rest of the Battalion of Death of Lodge's plans. She sympathized with the senator and understood that his job was to find the middle ground even though she believed he was as opposed to the League as she. Nevertheless, she called him Mr. Wobbly.[80]

Alice contributed to insider negotiations. She read unpublished correspondence concerning the resignation of Secretary of State Robert Lansing and had journalists at her door, informing her of scoops before they were printed. She and Frank Brandegee spent hours talking things over. Borah was often their subject. The Idahoan had a tendency to castigate GOP reservationists and to ridicule the very reservations he had helped Lodge to write. Historians, too, have criticized Borah for habitually charting his own course, changing that course unaccountably, and condemning Republicans as well as Democrats. One biographer suggested that "Borah approached true happiness when flagellating his own party."[81] Alice never shied from criticizing members of the GOP, but she had neither constituents nor bills requiring compromise.

When another vote was taken, on March 19, 1920, the Lodge reservations went down to defeat again. Irreconcilables and Democrats loyal to Wilson's version without the reservations teamed up to defeat the proposal. Then the treaty came up for a vote without the reservations. It failed a final time. The United States never joined the League of Nations. Senator Lodge blamed Borah, Alice, and Brandegee for having started the whole fight.[82] Alice's behind-the-scenes lobbying played an indisputable role in this key political event. She knew as much about the issue as diplomats and policy makers. Her knowledge, her presence, her pressure, and her influence over those men were real factors in the battle, and thus she, as Colonel of the Battalion of Death, helped to block U.S. entry into the League of Nations. Borah likened the death of the treaty to the surrender of Robert E. Lee.[83] The Battalion of Death adjourned to the Longworth home again for one more celebratory gathering. It felt somehow anticlimactic. She and the rest of the wary isolationists looked toward the Republican convention, ten months away, and feared a change of heart that would move the GOP to attempt a resurrection. But the gloom could not settle fully on Alice, for she was in love with the towering senator beside her, and carefully contemplating his future.

Chapter 15

"Hello, Hello, Hello"

THE 1920 ELECTION ushered in ten years of Republican supremacy and many political triumphs for Alice and those she loved. She continued to be, as the *New York Times* put it, "a leader in the capital's most exclusive circles, where her astute observance of political developments has made her a confidante of statesmen who value her opinion almost as much as they do her distinguished husband's."[1] The 1920s was also a very satisfying—if tumultuous—decade for Alice. She had fulfilling relationships with a large circle of friends, an ease with her husband borne of twenty years of marriage, a serious love affair with the most powerful man in Washington. And, at age forty-one, Alice Longworth became a mother.

Love cemented the bond that politics created. For their relationship, Bill Borah risked his marriage and his career—the latter based, ironically, on his oft-noted integrity—while Alice, presumably, risked Nick's career. Her code of ethics did not include cheating, but Nick had turned their marriage into an open one because of his years of infidelity. Alice and Borah did not flaunt their affair. They took pains to hide it, although rumors circulated through Washington nonetheless. When they were apart, hundreds of letters from Borah to Alice—spanning the eight years prior to Nick's death—attest to Bill's love for her. He showered her with almost daily notes, a correspondence mixing devotion, politics, appeals for her advice, and compliments on her political acumen. He thought Alice "the dearest one in the world," "instinctively wise," "a wonderful woman," "an inspiration," who helped him plan legislative and electoral strategies, to whom he confessed his melancholy, and who, in 1925, bore his only child. If Alice and Nick stumbled through the haze of an immature love and fatally tripped on the crags of ego, vanity, and unmet expectations, then Alice found a solid relationship based on mutual respect and shared passions with Bill. Her decision to carry their child to term spoke movingly of her love for Bill Borah.

With the defeat of the League of Nations behind them, Alice and her friends turned optimistically to the 1920 election. The 1918 off-year contest had gone their way, but Republicans lacked an obvious front-runner after Theodore Roosevelt's death. Among those names bruited about were Roosevelt family friend General Leonard Wood, Illinois governor Frank Lowden, the irascible Senator Hiram Johnson, and Ohio's Warren G. Harding. The Wilson years had reshaped the Grand Old Party. Gone were Roosevelt-era reforms. Instead the party took up the position of the right and held it solidly for the remainder of the century. During the 1920s, Republican ideals were much closer to Nick's than to Alice's, but she moved rightward, too, and the pair was always hopeful for Nick's advancement.

The Longworths were together for the opening of the Republican convention, held June 8 through 12, in the Chicago Coliseum. Alice and Nick, Ruth and Medill, Henry Cabot Lodge, Frank Brandegee, and Warren Harding took the train together. The conference was all the more interesting for leading up to the first presidential election in which women could vote. Congress had passed the Nineteenth Amendment in 1919, and by August 1920, enough states had ratified it to allow women full suffrage rights. Alice approved. She had "always believed that women should have the vote."[2]

Two days before the convention, Republican women met to lay strategy. Alice and Ruth were active in the Republican Women's National Committee (RWNC), a group with nationwide representation that worked on behalf of GOP causes and women's issues in particular. Alice listened as Auntie Corinne—a member of the RWNC executive committee— encouraged women to put aside personal preferences and work together for the good of the organization, which was in the middle of selecting a new chair. Alice supported Ruth's candidacy and lobbied women for their votes. After a fractious campaign, Ruth won the chair. She stood then on the brink of "the career she believed she was born to, electoral politics." Under Ruth's leadership, the RWNC focused on their real objective: "equal division of power and responsibility" for women in the Republican Party. It was an elusive goal. In 1920, only twenty-seven convention delegates were women. The RWNC began by organizing women in their geographic region. But the immediate task at the convention was women-friendly platform planks. Their cause was aided by Medill, Bill Borah, and a few other male progressives.[3]

At the convention, Alice and the rest of the Roosevelts worked for Leonard Wood, whom one contemporary described as "a big, well set-up man, approachable and with a fine presence."[4] Auntie Corinne gave the speech seconding his nomination. Nick was for fellow Buckeye Warren Harding. There was no love lost between Alice and Harding. She could not forget 1912. Harding wasn't even her second choice—Johnson was because of their shared fight against the League. She had little faith that either Wood or Johnson would win. Long before the convention, Alice and Congressman Bascom Slemp had put their heads together to figure out likely front-runners. That their prognostications were coming true was little consolation.

Alice's sidekicks in Chicago were Ruth and Medill, Borah, Wood, Brandegee, *North American Review* publisher Colonel George Harvey, and the rest of her "old birds" in Suite 404 of the Blackstone Hotel. She had arranged for those Republican power brokers to give her the slate of candidates before the convention opened. Suite 404 was the infamous "smoke-filled room" where Harding had been called before party leaders to confess any reason that he should not be made president. When, over breakfast, Harvey told Alice that her nemesis Harding had gotten the nod, she was furious. Why not some other, better qualified "dark horse," like Frank Knox? At least Harvey could assure her that Harding would "go along" with the anti-League position that he and Alice had hammered out before the convention opened. Alice reluctantly promised that the Roosevelt family would agree to "play ball" with this weak candidate whose best quality was that he could be controlled.[5]

Alice was in the thick of things in Chicago, and newspapers followed her movements. She was one of a small number of people, including the candidates and some lucky New Yorkers, who got hold of the third edition of the *Times* dated June 9 actually on the *ninth*. This made the news because the *Times* was flown to Chicago by airplane—a new, modern means of delivery. Alice was the only woman listed among the fortunate few, and it was clear that her status as an insider merited her the paper. Meanwhile, she must have cringed at the one mention of her husband by the mainstream press. A man from Kentucky, identified as a friend of Nick's, had missed the special delegation train and arrived late because, the *Times* reported, his "liquor had not been made in time."[6] Prohibition had gone into effect in January 1920, giving rise immediately to many alcohol jokes. Not that this troubled Nick. The wealthy in America found ways to slake their thirst for spirits unhindered by the technicalities of the Eighteenth Amendment.

The eventual Republican presidential candidate was among the capital's heaviest drinkers. That was but one reason Ohioans Harding and Nick got on so well. Like Nick, Harding was affable, friendly, and neither intellectually nor constitutionally suited to the nation's highest office. Alice thought Harding looked like "a decaying Roman emperor." Nick and Harding also had in common a penchant for extramarital affairs, a fondness for poker, and a love of golf. The times, Frank Brandegee famously scowled, did not require "first raters." As the GOP nominee, Harding was the compromise who "could carry Ohio . . . had no serious enemies within the party, and . . . made a winning figure on the stump." His running mate, Vermonter Calvin Coolidge—"a precise little object," Alice called him, "a little bit of whalebone, there"—was the exact opposite, in everything but his politics.[7]

Nick held on to Harding's coattails, and Alice understood the importance of pushing down past insults. They jointly signed a congratulatory telegram to the new nominee and were soon making pilgrimages to Marion, Ohio, home of Warren and Florence Harding.[8] A month after the convention Nick and Alice spent the night at the Hardings', talking late about the League of Nations specifically and "the campaign generally." Nick issued strongly supportive statements to the press, promising to deliver his district to Harding. He said that he and the presidential nominee "agree absolutely over the general situation and the issues. The Senator is growing in strength all the time." He promised to dedicate the last ten days of his own campaign to work in any way that Harding or the GOP needed. Before the Longworths left, they strolled along the streets of Marion so Nick could bask in Harding's reflected glory. Then Nick left for the hustings, stumping for Harding in Maine. In mid-August, the couple was back in Marion again, "calling on the senator," as he had decided to conduct a front-porch campaign as the great Republican William McKinley had done so successfully in 1896. Nick shared the porch with Harding, delivering a blistering speech against President Wilson's "reckless methods and [financial] extravagance" and the Democratic Party's ill-advised economic platform.[9]

Alice waved the flag, too: LOOKS LIKE GOOD G.O.P YEAR, SAYS MRS. LONG-WORTH the *Chicago Tribune* headline blared. Because she was in the Windy City, the paper was certain she was "on a political mission." Alice demurred. She was in town only to visit Ruth, she maintained—but shortly after that the *Tribune* snapped a photo of her "conferring" at Republican headquarters.[10] Soon after, no doubt because of Ruth's influence, Alice became "one of the Republican leaders who will direct the fight for the capture of the state of Ohio," by joining the executive committee of the state's Republican campaign committee. Newspapers announced that she would "take the stump for the party when the big speaking campaign opens," as Ruth, Auntie Corinne, and brother Ted were doing. Alice never actually made a speech. She was supposed to have spoken in Jackson, Ohio, at a "barbecue and burgoo," along with Harding and Nick, but there's no evidence that she did. She was as shy before crowds as she was brilliant in small gatherings. The two venues take vastly different skills, and while Alice was glad to appear on podiums, she seldom opened her mouth. She understood the critical need for her presence and appeared at political events and TR memorials. For example, she went—right in the middle of campaign season—to dedicate Roosevelt Road in Wheaton, Illinois, west of Chicago. Like those of his sister, Ted's virtues as a speaker were not as useful as his physical recall of TR for adoring audiences.[11] The Republicans were glad to have Corinne, Alice, and Ted on their side, because the Democrats had their own Roosevelt: in San Francisco in late June, the Democratic delegates had chosen Franklin to be presidential nominee James M. Cox's running mate.

Franklin's last name caused confusion among Americans, and that confusion caused the hackles to rise in Oyster Bay. Too many voters assumed that Franklin was TR's son. To clarify, Republican Party leaders shooed Ted after Franklin on the campaign trail. Ted, using western metaphors, proclaimed FDR "a maverick. He does not have the brand of our family."[12] Speaking to a crowd of Rough Riders, Ted found a warm reception. Franklin and Eleanor were hurt. Alice thought they should have stood up for themselves at that point, but they didn't. This was the first crack in what would become a serious rift between the two Roosevelt branches.

Nick soldiered on with his speech making, through Maine—which the Republicans did win—and elsewhere.[13] Alice had her own part in the campaign. In Marion, she participated in a two-day conference of powerful, politically driven women that included Harriet Taylor Upton, a veteran of the suffrage battle in Harding's state; Margaret Drier Robins, president of the Women's Trade Union League and the International Congress of Working Women; and Auntie Corinne. They joined five thousand women across the nation who were observing Social Justice Day. Some of the women paraded to the Harding home to hear a lengthy speech about how the Republican Party would protect mothers, children, female farm workers, and the American family; support an eight-hour workday for women; speak out against lynching; and uphold Prohibition. Alice had spent much of August and September in Chicago, where party luminaries had gathered. One photographer there snapped pictures of two important politicians as they tried to learn HOW WILL THE LADIES, GOD BLESS 'EM, VOTE? The chair of the women's section of the Democratic National Committee enlightened Franklin Delano Roosevelt, while Senator Borah was double-teamed by Alice and Ruth.[14]

In the end, Alice was right: 1920 was a good GOP year. The presidential election was a landslide. The invalid President Wilson longed to run again and called for Americans to make their votes be "a solemn referendum" on the peace treaty and the work done at Versailles, but his party denied him the nomination. As Nick said smartly, "The President had his wish. A solemn referendum was had...and the League was repudiated." The Democrats were swept away by the tidal wave of discontent that Americans felt in the wake of the Great War, the bitter League battle, wartime incursions into Americans' civil rights, and the taxes levied to pay for World War I.

With a solid majority in the House and in the Senate, and with a Republican in the White House, Nick found himself considered for the speakership. The *New York Times* editorialized that "in spite of the handicaps of hereditary forehandedness and an overshadowingly illustrious father-in-law, he has worked himself up to a position of influence and authority in the House. He has wit, humor, industry, application, a good mind. In spite of a certain modesty, he has made his talents acknowledged. He studies public questions carefully. He can think on his feet as well as in a library," and—no small thing on Capitol Hill—Nick was popular. This was not to be his time, but Nick's day was approaching fast.[15]

Nick settled back to the House Ways and Means Committee where, since 1907, he had been devoting himself to the tariff that so absorbed his intellectual energies. Protectionism was Congress' first order of business. Republicans wanted to replace President Wilson's Underwood Tariff with one better suited to the postwar situation. By September 1922, they would succeed, when President Harding signed the controversially high Fordney-McCumber Act. Nick was of "the belief that the American market is primarily for the American producer" and that the high tariff would guarantee a bright postwar future for the United States. The only Republican in the Senate debate to vote against the tariff bill was Bill Borah. He feared the administration's handling of foreign affairs was "intolerant, shortsighted, [and] prejudiced" and would "keep closed the foreign markets."[16]

The final issue of World War I was settled when the United States concluded a peace with Germany in 1921. But two years later, people imprisoned as a result of Wilson's wartime Espionage Act were still in jail. This prompted Senator Borah to demand their immediate release. Supporting his call were the American Civil Liberties Union, the Women's Trade Union League, Jane Addams, and his old courtroom adversary Clarence Darrow, among others.[17] Some vestiges of war were slow to depart.

Another war-era bill, prohibition of alcohol, became law after the guns were silent. As soon as the Volstead Act passed Congress, lobbying began for its repeal. Alice marveled "that anyone ever thought it possible to legislate an appetite that is part of human nature out of existence." Nevertheless, Alice and Ruth, both plagued by their husbands' tendencies toward alcohol abuse, supported Prohibition. Among congressmen, Alice snorted, "the men who voted dry and drank wet were with us in large numbers." Alice never joined the women who crusaded against liquor and she was realistic about its use in her home. She continued to serve alcohol at dinner parties, as did most other Washington hostesses. Nick's Ohio constituents were "wets" and hoped for repeal, and Nick himself "had the deepest conviction of the folly, futility, and unfairness of trying to eradicate all drink." He also felt strongly that Prohibition was a "denial of the rights of the individual," as Congress should not be allowed to tell people what they could not do in their own homes. Alice and Nick gave their butler the creative task of replenishing their dwindling stock of alcohol. He became adept at making gin out of oranges with the small still they provided. In the Longworth tradition, the couple also tried their hand at wine making, but with less success than Nick's great-grandfather had enjoyed from his vineyards in Cincinnati. The pair proved better at brewing beer, and made a batch Lord Balfour loved.[18]

But Alice soon grew tired of seeing her "friends and acquaintances awash in bootleg liquor, from month to month thinking concentratedly on the next drink." She became a dry. Her decision was based less on a belief in the virtue of abstinence and more on the disgust she felt seeing the drunkenness around her. "If the people I knew got drunk," she averred, "I did not really mind, I merely did not wish to see them and associate with them when they were in that condition" because "tipsy people bored me, they irritated and exasperated me." Alice took to lecturing them on the inviolability of the Constitution and the evils of drink.[19]

Completely in character, though, she'd take the opposite position with any sanctimonious drys. "The fanatics on both sides were just about equally distasteful to me," Alice concluded. But Nick was the real concern. Ted and some of their friends believed that Nick's drinking had reached the stage where it would stop his career. New York congressman Jim Wadsworth told Ted "it would be a good idea for both of us to speak to Nick about his drinking, in view of the fact that he is a probable majority leader of the Republicans next year. Of course this is something that makes one feel like a prig to talk about to anyone, but I do think that Nick physically is going to suffer soon unless he cuts down considerably." Alice's repugnance reached new heights, especially when she contrasted him to that "sincere prohibitionist," Bill Borah.[20]

The *New York Times* front page proclaimed IDAHO LEADER NOW SEEN AS LEADER OF DRY FORCES, as Bill gave speech after speech criticizing the repeal effort. In every address he proudly called himself a teetotaler. Borah also became her champion as he led the opposition to Harding's plan to pay Colombia for the land on which her father built the Panama Canal. "Theodore Roosevelt was not a common adventurer," Borah proclaimed as he defended TR against the old charge of stealing Panama. Alice and Bill stood together against downsizing the navy, giving up too much American freedom of action overseas, making Europe pay its war debts, and remained firmly against continuing attempts to inveigle American entry into the League of Nations. Bill became friends with Ted, who had been rewarded for his campaign support with the post of assistant secretary of the navy. It was that same position that had helped launch TR to fame.[21]

Nick socialized with Alice but could just as often be found with Harding, playing poker in the White House. He was also keeping company throughout the decade with his "girls"—Alice Dows, Laura Curtis, Marie Beale, and Cornelia Mayo. Alice Dows and Nick shared a passion for music, and she could convince Nick to play his violin for her guests, bringing out in him, she felt, "a hidden shyness." But Nick, Ted, and Jim Wadsworth walked together frequently; daily, when bills were pressing. Once a week, they took lengthy hikes through Rock Creek Park and called it "the

Statesmen's Sunday Morning Marching Club." Borah, who rode alone at that time, often crossed their path and endured good-natured joshing about his horse's advanced case of "bog spavin."[22] In various configurations they spent countless hours dissecting the plans emanating from Capitol Hill and laying strategies.

The early years of the decade were absorbed by negotiations over the Washington naval disarmament conference. Borah believed passionately in the duty of the United States to maintain peace around the globe, and after the horrors of World War I, he wanted to assure peace through multilateral disarmament. Borah hated war and regretted voting for it as he had in April 1917. But the League of Nations—no matter how badly its supporters wanted the issue resurrected—was doomed to failure, Borah thought, and also unconstitutional.

Instead of the League, Borah felt the shared goal of decreasing tensions worldwide could be met by a formal agreement among powerful nations. He introduced the bill requesting President Harding to invite representatives from Great Britain and Japan to discuss a five-year plan of reduction of naval armaments. Eventually, nine nations sent delegates to Washington for the three-month-long conference. Borah believed that the naval buildup after the turn of the century had led to the horrible war just past, and without severe cuts in naval budgets across the globe, another conflagration would be upon the world in less than fifteen years. At the very least, he preached, working people would be bled of their paychecks because of the cost of the current naval arms race. The grand orator predicted "economic ruin... moral breakdown... industrial peonage for the masses... wounds and mangled bodies and shattered minds and millions dead...."[23]

The goal of the Washington Conference, which opened on Armistice Day 1921, was to slow the postwar naval race. Nick wrote his mother that during Secretary of State Charles Evans Hughes's opening speech "there weren't more than fifteen people in the audience of whom Alice and I were two, who knew how far the Administration were proposing in naval disarmament and the air was full of gasps."[24] Hughes stunned onlookers when he suggested that the United States should scrap tons of extant warships, told the other nations what they should destroy, and proposed a moratorium on building certain types of ships.

While leaders needed convincing of the Hughes plan, the idea was so popular in the national imagination that President Harding swallowed his scruples and expressed his support. The program expanded to include Far Eastern issues and land armaments. Although angered that the agenda had strayed from his original idea, Borah worked for a positive outcome. He made sure that newspaper reporters had free access to the conference debates and uncensored reporting. While Borah smoldered, more and more topics were added. His research proved that the so-called treaties emerging from the Washington conference were alliances cloaked as treaties, and he could not vote for them. The Four Power Treaty, wherein nations promised to respect each other's Pacific holdings, the senator believed would also bind the United States to defending Britain's island colonies. He and his irreconcilable brothers went on the attack. As Democrats argued for three hours on March 11, Borah, Johnson, and Reed assaulted their logic. Their debate packed the Senate galleries, and Alice was riveted. Though the Senate ratified all of the disarmament treaties to come from the Washington Conference, Borah opposed them on the grounds that the result would give too much power to Japan in East Asia.[25]

After the conference ended, it fell to the new assistant secretary of the navy, among others, to lobby for American adherence. Ted and Alice, who felt similarly on most issues, were together many times a week throughout the early 1920s. Alice was one of her brother's confidantes. He sent her letters marked CONFIDENTIAL and SECRET filled with their shared nicknames for political players, and poetry to illustrate their prognostications. Weekends filled up with poker parties at the Longworths', dinners at the McCormicks', and luncheons at the McLeans'. The circle of friends expanded to include Ethel Barrymore, Eleanora Sears, Lord Balfour, Charles Curtis, and Bill—if not always Mary—Borah.[26]

In 1922, Nick and Ted worked together on the naval appropriations bill wending its way through Congress. There was a move afoot in the House to cut down the size of the navy to sixty-seven thousand men—which Alice, Ted, and Nick opposed. They wanted eighty-six thousand, which conformed with the Four Power Treaty. Frequently, the two men discussed the plans and then, as Ted chronicled in his diary, "In the afternoon we got together and went over all phases of the situation from end to end." In a speech before the National Press Club, which Nick heard, Ted decried this manpower cut. Walking back to the Longworths' afterward, Nick strategized that it might be "a good play to have the entire Ohio delegation at his house on Wednesday where I could speak to them informally."[27]

Ted took up Nick's idea on the evening of April 11. "We had a meeting of the Ohio delegation at Nick's house," Ted wrote. "I brought down two bottles of whiskey to help their conversation, and Sister served them punch made with home made gin. I was in good form this evening and spoke well to them. Nick was much pleased with the results. He told me that there were only two men who were for the 86,000 amendment when they met, [including] himself. . . . When he left he said that with the possible exception of two men we had all those who had been there." That same day, Ted claimed the reduction would be a "national disaster" that would relegate the United States to a second-rate power able to exert "but little influence in the world for peace and justice."[28]

Nick talked Ted into trying to secure a letter of support from President Harding for the appropriations bill, which Harding duly wrote with their input. Ted had steered Harding into a higher dollar amount and away from phrase that suggested that "future international conventions might result in further reductions in naval armament." Nick read the letter in the House and, Ted thought, "made an excellent little speech at the same time. He conveyed just the right degree of solemnity and dignity. There is no question but that it had the right effect." Then, Nick, Medill, Ted, and some other "big navy men" all started calling folks to ascertain their upcoming vote. Eventually, they won "by a handsome majority against all odds and every prediction." House members broke into a spontaneous "Indian war dance" down the center aisle, accompanied by "loud cheers and wild whoops." Ted was ecstatic. He rounded up all "the young naval officers and our best friends" and took them to his home. They shared a bottle of champagne, a gift from family friend Arthur Lee. Ted thought, "It seemed rather appropriate to drink the success of our navy in champagne given to me by the First Lord of the British Admiralty."[29]

Later that summer, Susan Longworth died, on June 27, 1922, after a lengthy illness. Nick and his sister Nan were at their mother's bedside when the seventy-seven-year-old matriarch succumbed to pneumonia. He telephoned the news of his beloved "Mummy" to Alice in Washington, and she left the following morning for the funeral in Cincinnati. Susan and Alice were never close, but Alice knew her place was at her husband's side for the burial rites. The funeral was held at Rookwood, and among the pallbearers was Joe Graydon.[30]

While reconciled to a month in Ohio, Alice must have been of two minds about the letters she was receiving from Ted. "When are you coming back?" he wrote enticingly. "Washington is now the center of real activity and excitement. The railroad strike and the coal strike have pushed everything else into the back-ground." Ted had sought Bill Borah's views on the strike. "As usual, he has some good suggestions," Ted reported. Her brother promised to "go over [the political scene] in detail" when she returned to D.C., and give her the fine points from his dinner with President and Mrs. Harding.[31]

Tragedy visited the family again in October 1922, when Ethel's only son, eight-year-old Richard Derby, died very suddenly of blood poisoning. Christmas at Sagamore was a sad affair. Death continued to hound the Roosevelts. On May 1, 1923, Bye's husband, Will, passed away. The admiral and Bye had been married nearly thirty years. Edith wrote that his death had been "a long breathing away of life—no pain, but hard for Auntie Bye." Isabella Munro-Ferguson gave a heartrending description of Auntie Bye at this time. Her "superhuman courage" of the "great and lasting" kind held her upright, Isabella thought. "Nothing left but the ghost of her once big blue eyes and the defiant toss of her head—upon an entirely crumpled and wasted body—and a mind seemingly more vitally acute than ever before...." Bye suffered increasingly from disabling arthritis and deafness, compounded by worsening eyesight and circulatory problems. In the 1920s, she continued to entertain politicians and society leaders even as she surrounded herself with many lively members of younger generations.[32] Alice wrote loving letters and came to visit as often as she could, while Bye was stalwart in her pain and bore it uncomplainingly.

Then, in August 1923, Warren Harding died. Whispers of scandals had been circulating around the capital, and the president had taken himself off to Alaska and a western speaking tour to ponder his troubles. In California a heart attack killed him. Nick lost a powerful friend, but Alice had never cared for the Hardings. "When he came to Washington after his election," she recalled, "we saw him and discussed with him matters of policy and Cabinet prospects." She "was put up to tell him how ill-advised" Harry Daugherty would be as his attorney general. Harding ignored Alice—perhaps because of the contempt that showed whenever she spoke to him—but she and some of his "supporters" were proven right, as evidence of Daugherty's corruption mounted. Alice also had no patience with the "shocking" disregard in which Harding held the Constitution insofar as Prohibition was concerned. "No rumor could have exceeded the reality," she wrote, of the boozing upstairs in the Harding White House. The secret drinking spot was Harding's study, which had "air heavy with tobacco smoke, trays with bottles containing every imaginable brand of whisky...cards and poker chips ready at hand—a general atmosphere of waistcoat unbuttoned, feet on the desk, and the spittoon alongside." Alice's final words on Harding finished him off: "I think everyone must feel that the brevity of his tenure of office was a mercy to him and to the country. Harding was not a bad man. He was just a slob."[33]

Alice felt similarly about Florence Harding: not a bad woman, but a bit outré. She had known Mrs. Harding for years. Being First Lady had not improved her. Alice would have agreed with journalist Mark Sullivan's assessment of Florence. He found her insecure, jealous, incessantly chatting, and forever losing the battle to keep her unfaithful husband nearby. "In appearance," Sullivan wrote, "she was a little too mechanically marcelled, too shinily rouged and lipsticked, too trimly tailored. Towards her, Harding was always gravely deferential, and his men friends learned to be the same. They, and he always addressed her as 'Duchess' and gave her a deference and eminence appropriate to the fantastic title." Alice thought her "a nervous, rather excitable woman whose voice easily became a little high-pitched, strident."[34]

And yet, once Flo Harding became First Lady, Alice had to put aside her overt disdain. "There is no city in the world perhaps where political rank counts for so much socially" as Washington, and the First Lady was the highest-ranking woman, "shinily rouged" or not. Alice enjoyed having the White House open to her again and she did share at least one interest with the Duchess: the supernatural. Alice's fascination began as a girl after she and Kermit encountered gypsies. The two children visited them frequently enough to learn a certain amount of Romany.[35] She was attracted to the color and mystery of their lives—so very different from her own. As a young woman, she rejected traditional Christianity and refused to be baptized. She had her palm read and her fortune told at various points in her life. As an adult, Alice absorbed all she could find on Romany culture. At her death, those well-worn volumes still occupied an important place in her library. Alice and the Duchess, often accompanied by Evalyn McLean, indulged their interest in having their horoscopes read, but this threesome did not last long. Florence could be paranoid, and she bragged to Alice and Ruth about how she kept score of the slights against her and against Warren in a special little red book.

Thus, when the Coolidges moved into the White House, Alice was pleased. Under the Coolidges', "the atmosphere was as different as a New England front parlor is from a back room in a speakeasy." Grace Coolidge and Alice paired up often. They both loved acrostics, crossword puzzles, and other word games. They enjoyed watching the Senate. Alice often sat alongside the First Lady in the "President's pew" in the Senate chamber. Grace Coolidge had "a simplicity and charm... was amused by all the official functions and attentions, yet was always absolutely natural and unimpressed by it all," Alice thought. Though she liked Coolidge as a dinner guest, he could drive her to fury, for his taciturnity made him a social liability. Once she found him so "bad mannered" that she didn't speak to him for the rest of the evening. Nick had made a "felicitous" little speech—the sort of thing Nick did very well, she thought—and Coolidge, in response, "grunted." "*Poor* Mrs. Coolidge," Alice recalled, "*she* got up" to say a few words. When he wished he were elsewhere, he pursed his lips, folded his arms, and said nothing. He looked then precisely as though he had been weaned on a pickle. Alice gave currency to this phrase, which she said she wished she had originated, but thought that her dentist had.[36]

Nick would work very closely with President Coolidge, if his supporters had their way. As early as February 1923, they were proposing him for the authoritative position of House majority leader. But western congressmen, younger and less conservative in their thinking—those who, the *New York Times* pointed out, would never be caught dead in the spats worn by Longworth—withheld their support. Twenty-five "progressive" representatives assailed what they called the Millionaire Ways and Means Committee on which Nick had served for years, and suggested that the Old Guard controlling it wielded too much power. "Special privilege [has] entrenched itself in legislative power," just as it had during the Joe Cannon years— only back then, Nick had been the insurgent. Progressive congressmen called for a child labor amendment, assistance to farmers and veterans, "government control of necessities of life, when necessary, to prevent profiteering," excessive war profits, "uniform presidential primaries," and amendments to the Federal Reserve Act—but most of all they wanted promises of shared power in order to bring their bills to the floor.[37]

In November, Nick wrote to Republican members of the Sixty-eighth Congress about the possibility of becoming majority leader. Claiming that he did not seek the honor, and would be loathe to give up his place on the Ways and Means Committee, he asserted that "it was only after strong pressure and careful thought that I finally acceded and my candidacy was announced by my delegation. I have asked, and shall ask, no man to support me as a personal favor, and if the leadership comes to me I will undertake it with feelings far less of justification than of a stern sense of the seriousness of the responsibilities which it will involve." Nick, personally popular and backed by influential House members, was elected by voice vote. His task was to tack between the Republican conservatives and the progressive faction, keeping the former happy and the latter from bolting to join the Democrats and tip them the majority. He was an expert compromiser who could persuade without ruffling feelings. During Nick's two years as majority leader, the House "acted on 594 measures, nearly double the number passed in the same period of the previous Congress." Nick maintained that "the individual must sacrifice his own independence for the good of the whole." This belief would serve him well in the future—better than he might have ever guessed—for as Nick was scuffling with recalcitrant representatives, Alice reconnected with Senator Borah.[38]

The relationship between Alice Longworth and Bill Borah was the worst-kept secret in Washington. The two powerful, easily recognized individuals were seen riding in Rock Creek Park and whispering together in the halls of Congress. Borah, who seldom accepted dinner invitations, went frequently to Alice's. His attentions unleashed a side of her she generally kept hidden. Washingtonian Agnes Meyer recalled Alice about this time in a "very carnal sort of mood. She ate three chops, told shady stories and finally sang in a deep bass voice: Nobody cultivates me, I'm wild, I'm wild."[39]

Infrequently, rumors circulated about Borah. Some suggested his Lion of Idaho nickname referred to his record of sexual conquests, most of which occurred in his youth. There was evidence that his relationship with his wife was distant at best. There is little "passion, intimacy, or love" in the "business-like" letters to his wife the senator dictated to his secretary in the 1920s. Borah had been linked with Alice's longtime friend and sometime enemy Cissy Patterson—the same Cissy whom Alice had defeated in the battle for Nick twenty years earlier. At one party at the Longworths', Cissy and Borah supposedly disappeared. Alice, jealous of her rival, the next day sent Cissy some hairpins she said she'd found in the library. "I believe they are yours," Alice's note was purported to have said. "Alice, please look in the chandelier," Cissy retorted, "I think you will find my garter." Such rumors are impossible to substantiate—and Alice later denied that it ever happened—but Cissy moved on to another man and left the field open for Alice. It may or may not have comforted Alice to know that Cissy moved on to Nick. Alice apparently found them once, both drunk and making love on the floor of her bathroom; another time she thought she detected Nick hiding in Cissy's carriage. Later in life, Alice herself was known to recount the tale of how Cissy left her stockings "stuffed down the sofa and her chewing gum...parked under the mantel" at the Longworths'.[40]

Perhaps it was incidents such as that that caused Alice to "just let it happen" when she discovered in the early spring of 1924 that she was pregnant. Bringing the child to term and then giving it up for adoption would not have been done. Abortions were uncommon but possible to get for a woman of her background. They did not have wholly safe outcomes, and perhaps no one knew that better than Bill. One explanation for why he and Mary remained childless is that when he was a strapping youth, moving westward across the country to find a place to make his fortune, his money ran out in Boise, where he eventually became involved in politics. He took a job as secretary to Governor William J. McConnell and soon met the governor's daughter, Mary, "a vivacious, blue-eyed blonde, sociable and attractive, the prize catch in Boise's young social set." Rumor had it that Mary became pregnant, and because the governor couldn't stand the scandal of an illegitimate child—nor even of a child born less than nine months after the wedding ceremony—Mary sought an abortion. It was not performed well and resulted in Mary's inability to bear children. Bill, then, might have insisted that Alice not seek an abortion in 1924 because of the guilt and sorrow and fear attached to Mary's ordeal in 1892.[41]

Forty years old in February 1924, Alice was game to try motherhood. It certainly was a part of the human experience that she had not yet attempted. TR was known for his dire warnings against race suicide among white women, but as a young woman Alice had been the founder of the Race Suicide Club—its only goal to tweak her father's pomposity. Nevertheless, Nick's infertility kept Alice from doing her duty, as her father saw it, and producing scads of children. Even if TR's teachings had lost some of their grip on Alice, perhaps the deep pain caused by abandonment had not. A child of her own might finally be one human who would never abandon her. No matter what, this child would always be hers and, in the way children do, could fill an ancient void inside her. Whatever the reason—tradition, psychology, cultural mores—Alice decided to "let it happen."[42]

The historical record does not provide many clues about when Alice knew she was pregnant or what she told Nick. Alice's granddaughter, Joanna Sturm, believes that Alice never told Nick and managed to cover up Borah's paternity.[43] There is no evidence of what Bill told his wife, if anything. The human element of this pregnancy involved two powerful men, both old enough to be grandfathers. Nick was fifty-six when the child was born, and Bill was sixty. Mary Borah was fifty-five. All four of them must have come to the conclusion, decades earlier, that their marriages would not be favored with children. Although the 1920s was a time of liberation for women—suffrage, flappers, increasing educational and work opportunities—the centrality of marriage and children to a woman's life had not decreased.

If Alice conceived in April it was about the time Nick was being considered as keynote speaker for the GOP convention looming in June. Congress was working hard and Nick was legislating the Bonus Bill, tax cuts, the National Origins Quota Act, and farm relief measures. Business on Capitol Hill ended in June, and the Republican convention opened shortly thereafter, in Cleveland, Ohio. Alice, in what may have been a difficult first trimester, stayed home. She was in Chicago, Ruth noted, "not very well" and under the care of a physician. The last time Alice had missed a convention was 1912, when she had been forced to stay away from the jubilant Progressive Party gathering by her father and her husband. Bill Borah didn't go to Cleveland either.[44]

At least one national magazine had been promoting BORAH AS PRESIDENTIAL TIMBER, a pun on the natural resources of the Idaho senator's state. Borah supporters began a "literary bombardment" urging Borah for president, "which took the form of throwaways and endless chain post-cards," to be sent ideally to millions of voters. Borah said publicly and privately, "We are playing the game . . . far below the intelligence and character of the voter," and declined to run.[45] No matter how badly he might want the nation's highest office, had he run and somehow gained the Republican nod, he would never have been liberated from the fear that nosy journalists might discover his relationship with the majority leader's wife. And her pregnancy would be front-page news as soon as word got out.

At the Cleveland convention, Ted Roosevelt kept notes as he, Nick, and other leading Republicans gathered to hammer out the platform and settle on a vice president. For the latter position, the insiders discussed at least nine names, with no resolution at that first long meeting. The following day the platform was agreed upon, but the vice president was still up in the air. They mulled over the names of six more men, but reached no consensus. Then, Bill Borah's name surfaced, "but all of us," Ted wrote in his journal, "who knew Borah well were positive that he would not take it. Hour after hour passed. . . . The corridors were filled with newspaper men requesting information which we did not have to give them. . . . Longworth expressed a common view when he said he could not make out whether [President Coolidge's personal representative William M.] Butler had some deep laid scheme he was waiting to spring or whether he was simply a plain 'boob.' At shortly after midnight, with all as much at sea as ever, Butler came up to the room and said, 'It is settled. Borah is the Man.' . . . The conference adjourned at once to line their respective delegates up for Borah. We met the newspaper men in the hall and they turned hand-springs."

Ted had recently dined with Borah, who "definitely" said then he wouldn't agree to having his name put forward for vice president. But Butler told Ted that he had information from Washington that Borah would accept. Ted was dubious, but he knew exactly whom to contact for the straight scoop: "I put in a long distance call for sister. . . . I told her what happened. She told us just what we had expected—that Borah had talked to her at nine-thirty that evening on the telephone and would not take the vice presidency under any circumstances. Furthermore, he had not seen Coolidge since Monday. That left us bang up in the air. We did not feel we could tell Butler because that involved sister. We knew that the newspapermen would get hold of Borah at once and thought they would settle the matter."[46]

On the last day of the convention, President Coolidge sent for Senator Borah. Coolidge had been pursuing Borah for the second-place spot for months. On that day, Coolidge himself asked Borah if he would agree to have his name placed in nomination. "In which place?" Borah asked laconically. Coolidge told Borah that the convention would draft him for vice president anyway. Borah said he would decline the draft. Perhaps the president didn't believe him. He should have. The Cleveland convention—

which Ruth Hanna McCormick dismissed as "the dullest I have ever attended"—was enlivened only by the excitement of Senator Borah turning down the vice presidential spot. In the 1920s, the vice president was a nonentity, ignored by the press, party caucuses, and usually the president.[47] When Borah declared that he would be of better use to the country by remaining in the Senate, he was headed for greater things with his autonomy intact. The Republicans had to be content with Charles Dawes.

First, however, Borah had to win reelection in Idaho. Hindsight proves the senator had little to fear, but Borah was always skittish about campaigns. He had feuded so long with the Republican machine in his home state that had he been less popular with the voters and less well known nationally he might have had cause to worry. The campaign also meant his absence from Alice that fall. It could not have been the ideal situation for either of them. Bill and Mary Borah had not maintained a home in Idaho since 1907, and so, except for election years, the senator often remained in the District of Columbia when Congress was not in session. Unfortunately for Alice, her pregnancy coincided with a time of forced separation.

A torrent of letters flew between them. Brief and without context or preliminaries, they were part of a larger dialogue. Borah even wrote from his Senate office across town. The two augmented their notes with the telephone and frequent face-to-face visits, which made unnecessary traditional descriptions and details. Theirs was a correspondence in shorthand. The topics were almost entirely political. Alice saved Bill's several hundred letters to her, but he disposed of hers, despite the joy he took in them. She asked once whether she wrote him "too many letters." "No," Borah insisted. "No you do not—they are most welcome. Let them come in battalions!"[48] Beyond politics, their other favorite topic was themselves.

On the westbound *Portland Limited*, Bill muscled his way to the train's writing desk to reestablish their connection: "Wending my way slowly across the continent reflecting, dreaming, hoping, *believing*...." This was one of his first letters since the campaign had parted them. His tone, now that she was approximately four months' pregnant, was reminiscent of any father-to-be. "Be a good lady," he cautioned, "do not smoke too much—be careful of your eating—take lots of exercise and *remain* beautiful."[49]

Her first trimester over, Alice was then with Nick for part of the Democratic convention in New York. The lengthy contest took 103 ballots before the nominee emerged. Alice kept a gimlet eye on Franklin. He was working hard for presidential contender Al Smith, who eventually lost to John W. Davis. As always, reporters noted Alice's presence, and even they saw a changed woman: "She grows sedate—almost subdued, one would say.... She has been very intent upon the proceedings, following every maneuver with keen eyes—and silently." Of course they didn't know the real reason.[50]

Back in Cincinnati, Alice pored over the bulletins and newspaper clippings Bill sent outlining western thought and giving clues as to how Idaho voters might respond. She posted return envelopes full of her analyses of people and situations. They studied the restoration of the Progressive Party, as Robert La Follette and Burton K. Wheeler ran on that third-party ticket. "I guess your diagram of Wheeler is right and accurate," Borah responded to one such letter. "You are a wonder. I feel awfully proud of myself when I think of having passed safely under your keen analysis."[51]

By early September, the newspapers were announcing BORAH'S ELECTION DEEMED CERTAINTY, and even La Follette gave his support in a strongly worded telegram to Bill (which Bill proudly enclosed for Alice to see). Despite a resurgent Borah-for-president boom, Alice continued to worry about his reelection, and Borah fretted, too. His unease and the solitary traveling he undertook on the campaign made him ache for her: "'What will I do, what will I do with only a photograph to tell my troubles to.' I heard that song last night and thought it beautiful. I fear I am getting sentimental and I know how you dislike sentimentalists." That thought didn't stop him from posting very tender, secret notes: "My own sweetheart, I want to see you. It seems too long to wait but we will be inseparable, won't we. You can never know how dear you are to me."[52]

By the end of the month, things were looking up. Ted entered the race for New York's Republican gubernatorial spot and won the primary. Alice was overjoyed, and Borah "delighted." The West seemed likely to support Coolidge and Dawes, and Borah—with the combined support of Idaho Progressives and Republicans who preferred *him* in the White House—

wondered to Alice about his presidential chances in the wake of Teapot Dome and other misdeeds that shook the government. In the midst of those scandals, the *Literary Digest* championed Borah for the presidency, noting, "One can not talk with any group of Americans, whatever their situation in life, without finding how disgusted with current politics they are and how happy they would be to break away from their past allegiance." A candidate from outside the polluted mainstream was needed, leading this journal that echoed the *Boston Herald,* to conclude that the call " 'Borah for President' has considerable merit."[53]

Such sentiments had never really died down. While Borah was a fighter for clean government, and disgusted at the many outrageous failings of the Harding and Coolidge administrations, the conclusion of his September lament to her must have been extraordinary for Alice to read: "I have about reached my limit of endurance [for governmental scandal]: Lorimer, Stephenson, Newberry, Fall, Daugherty, now Dawes. If there was anyplace to take refuge where one could see a future I should hesitate no longer. But I can see something after next election—do not doubt it. These things, these fearful things feed my desire and enlarge my plans—and you will be there."[54] Bill in the White House! And Alice would be there with him—but how? The implications of the conversations that must have taken place in order for Borah to have written as he did are worth considering. Was this simply an idle lover's dream? Had they discussed divorcing their spouses and remarrying? If that were the case, surely as realists both knew that a divorced and remarried man would never be elected to the nation's highest office. If not marriage, then could Alice have been content with the position of backstage paramour?

Alice had long been used to the roles of president's daughter and congressman's wife, and she lived at a time when the social position for women was behind the throne. She was very good at analyzing people and events, exceptional at running a salon and bringing very different people together for extraordinary results. She had participated in a congressional junket and played a role in foreign policy. Alice Roosevelt Borah might have made the most politically savvy First Lady ever—but this could be only a reverie. Divorce would ruin careers—her husband's and her lover's, and possibly her brother's. But it is an astonishing thing that Alice and Bill must have spoken together of a shared future, and evidence of their ambition that this dream of a future included the White House. Of course, political considerations worked against the reality of Borah as president. His independent views made stalwart Republicans nervous. Idaho controlled too few electoral college votes to matter. But dreaming of happy futures is the lovers' prerogative.

"As the campaign draws to a close," Bill wrote to Alice from Idaho on November 3, "I am wishing a certain lovely lady with her radio were here to receive the returns as she entertained during the New York conventions. But I will be patient." They had managed to meet in Chicago.[55] Alice, approximately five months' pregnant, had the excuse of seeing her obstetrician Joseph DeLee of Chicago's Lying-In Hospital on East Fifty-first Street. Dr. DeLee had delivered Ruth's babies and was skilled in special-care obstetrical cases, and Ruth insisted that Alice allow herself the best physician in the field. Perhaps that September Alice and Bill discussed the timing of the announcement of her pregnancy, which came, not surprisingly, after the elections. Likely it was then that they evolved the secret code enabling them to write about their desire for each other and the awful, constraining reality of being married to others.

Chary of their spouses and anyone else into whose hands a letter might mistakenly fall, Alice and Bill used the innocuous word *hello* to mean all sorts of permutations of "I love you." *Hello* appeared with a purposeful regularity in his letters. Bill always closed with assurances such as "Hello, Hello, Alice, more than you know." The use of their code word was so apparent that even an artless spouse could have decoded the not-so-secret language: "I did enjoy your letters," he wrote in September, "you are a dear—hello. I am sending you some photos from the round up and some scenes—logging, hauling, and wheatfield scenes in my own state. These you are to see in person some time. Hello—again and again Hello." "But I do try to write and I do Hello all the time"; or "Hello every minute. I wish you understood fully how Hello." His usual closing was "Hello, Hello, Hello—Affectionately, Bill."[56]

Hello—even in its variations of meaning—could not convey all he felt for her, so Bill initiated a second clandestine system of expressing his suppressed feelings. He tucked copies of his speeches, newspaper articles, telegrams, and other printed materials pertaining to his career into the envelopes along with his notes to Alice. Then, in miniscule dashes, like sideways exclamation points, Bill underlined stray letters throughout the articles. When Alice put the underlined letters together they spelled out his secret messages. From a *New York Times* editorial entitled "How to Head Off a Third Party," Alice pieced together: "Darling, I am so lonesome. I want my own sweet girl. You are more to me than you have dreamed. I am counting the days until I shall see you." One week later, Borah signaled her, "My darling, I am more lonesome tonight than I can tell. Oh how I long for the dearest one in the world. Do you love me the same? Loved one, I kiss you goodnight." Before their rendezvous in Chicago, Alice read, "My dear, I am coming to see you soon and we will be happy again." Consoling her in their long autumn separation, Borah underlined, "My sweetheart, I love you above all earthly things."[57]

These touches of intimacy, tucked between political commentary, sustained the romance while they were apart. Borah, who was known far and wide as an inscrutable, pragmatic, reclusive, no-nonsense Westerner, sparkled in his secret musings to Alice. Their coded language explains part of her attraction to him. Nineteen twenty-four was the year they most frequently used their underlining code, when the emotional upheaval of pregnancy may have most called for the reassurance that the surreptitious but real reinforcement of their love brought. "Trust me to the end of my days," he willed her.[58]

In early October 1924, Alice, approximately six months' pregnant, left Cincinnati and Nick's reelection campaign to join a family conference in Oyster Bay about the New York governor's race and Ted's future. Bill waited impatiently for the news of her safe travel and for Alice's assessment of her brother's chances. Ted had offered to go west to campaign for Borah, who declined the proposal as it would take Ted away from his own fight, and Borah's victory looked secure anyway. While at Sagamore, Alice fell down the stairs. News of this pushed all thoughts of Ted out of Bill's mind: "I hardly know how to write. I am so uneasy and anxious lest your terrible accident cause you illness. Such falls sometimes injure internally.... About the best message I can hastily send is Hello Hello always and ever hello."[59] Her written assurance turned their attention back to the election.

Physically separated from her lover and emotionally removed from her husband, Alice confided in her best friend Ruth Hanna McCormick. McCormick's diary hints at discomforts and illnesses that Alice endured throughout the fall of 1924. Ruth could be counted on to understand fully the risks to all involved. From her comes evidence that Alice was not initially thrilled about the pregnancy. In early November, when Alice was three months from the birth, she wrote, "Alice arrived.... it has been decided that she tell everyone soon that she is going to have a baby. I haven't even dared to record it in my Diary. Poor Alice. She feels humiliated about the baby and dreads what people will say but I firmly believe she will be a different person after the baby comes and she holds it in her arms."[60] Ruth, the mother of three children, could empathize with at least some of Alice's feelings.

Election day 1924 brought good and bad news. Coolidge was elected. Nick and Bill won reelection, but Ted lost the governorship of New York to Al Smith. Only thirty-seven years old at the time of this defeat, Ted wasn't sure how to restart his political career. Elected to the New York assembly in 1919 and 1920, and appointed assistant secretary of the navy from 1921 until 1924, Ted's gubernatorial campaign was haunted by rumors of his involvement in the scandals that plagued Harding's administration, particularly the Teapot Dome debacle. Ted had weathered calls for him to quit his position at the navy because of his alleged involvement. Alice, protective of her favorite brother, tried to pull strings by asking Calvin Coolidge—unsuccessfully, as it turned out—to intercede on Ted's behalf with the Senate investigation. Nick had defended him on the floor of the House, saying he was "prepared to make a statement" as to Ted's blamelessness. Ted was innocent of any wrongdoing, but his high-profile campaigning for Harding and his past connection with the oil company involved in Teapot Dome made it easy for political enemies to link his name with the scandal. And for the Roosevelt family, one of those enemies was unexpected—and unpardonable. Cousin Eleanor, active as a Democratic organizer in New York State, built an enormous, steaming teapot, hoisted it on top of her car, and pursued Ted all across the Empire State. Her exploit did more damage without any words than did official calls for Ted's removal on the floor of Congress. ER later expressed regret at having played such a "rough stunt."[61] This worsened the bad feelings between the Sagamore Hill and the Hyde Park Roosevelts. Eleanor had violated the "tribal feeling" that Alice—Ted's loyal half sister, the outsider in the nursery—held to so closely all her life. Alice never forgave her.

Edith felt her eldest son had made "a good campaign," but in addition to the wisps of the scandal that clung to him, it appeared that Ted was wholly unacceptable to the temperance vote. As a fan of Alice's wrote to her a decade later, "If your brother Theodore were not an announced wet I would be glad to vote for him," for president.[62] But Ted, pulsing with the example of his father and the courage of his convictions, wouldn't hide his beliefs even if they were contrary to the majority of his constituency. He was one of those who voted wet *and* drank wet. It was morally commendable, but it cost him the governor's mansion.

Bill gloated to Alice, as he could to her and no one else, about his own landslide reelection: "I have a telegram before me which says that Coolidge vote in Ida[ho] was sixty four thousand . . . Borah eighty nine thousand—see how needless for my dear friend to have worried. Hello Hello. I wish very much I could have a long talk with you this evening. We will have many, many affairs of state to talk over in the coming months—and often I will be saying Hello—always saying Hello."[63]

Adding to their reasons to celebrate, Bill received the appointment he coveted and would occupy for the next nine years: chairman of the Senate Foreign Relations Committee. He took over from the redoubtable Henry Cabot Lodge, the Longworths' good friend and a colleague whose death in November 1924 they both mourned. Alice had known him literally her whole life. He first saw her in her cradle. One of her earliest childhood memories was the "rather special" congressman who was "mysterious, important, and powerful," and who defined for her how politicians differed from other men. Lodge reciprocated this affection, writing to Alice in 1921 in a plaintive letter, "I am fortunate in having so many good friends of whom I am very fond but the people I love are few. I do not have the faculty of dispensing my affections. You and yours have been a part of my inmost life and love for many years."[64]

With the elections behind them, Alice, and probably Bill, decided the time was ripe to announce the pregnancy to the family and to the press. It is not clear what role Nick played in any of these decisions, although Alice would have been sensitive to the effect of the publicity on his career. The last thing she would have wanted was for Nick to lose an election, as that would mean exile in Cincinnati—immeasurably worse this time, for it would also mean separation from Bill. So once both men were safely re-elected, and because the slender Alice was showing, it was time.

Alice had kept her stepmother in the dark. Edith's diary of November 12 contained a short, cryptic note: *"Bouleversé,"* which means "overthrown, upset, distressed." Edith elaborated slightly in a letter to her sister-in-law: "Alice's news was rather a blow...." Either Edith worried about Alice suffering the same fate as her mother in childbirth, or, like much of Washington society, she suspected the truth. Two weeks later, on November 29, Edith wrote to Belle Hagner, "The shock of Alice's news is still with me...."[65]

Kermit, touring Ohio with Nick, learned from his wife, Belle, who must have heard it through the women's side of the family grapevine—and heard that Alice characteristically downplayed the importance and her own happiness. "That is the most amazing news about Sister," Kermit replied. "No one here has told me yet, so in accordance with your instructions, I'm still supposedly in ignorance. I think that it's great...." He wrote to Belle the next day: "Yesterday Nick and I wandered around calling on his friends, political and otherwise. He finally told me about the expected arrival. He seems very much pleased about. I imagine Sister is doing a good deal of bluffing when she talks as she does."[66]

Tired of the rumors, an intrepid journalist finally telephoned Alice to verify. "Hell yes," Alice told him, "Isn't it wonderful?" The news was out. "One of the most original, interesting, and charming women in Washington official circles," would give birth in February, and "the country will await the event with scarcely less interest than the principals." First Lady Grace Coolidge passed along the bombshell to her husband. "Yes, I knew that," Cal drawled. "Alice told me a couple of months ago." Grace was stunned. "Imagine a man having a bit of gossip as choice as that and keeping it a secret!" she laughed to her friends. Ruth Hanna McCormick noted in her diary that day: "The morning paper announces that Alice Longworth is going to have a baby! So it is out at last! I have kept the secret so long it seems strange to hear [people] talking about it. Poor Nick will have a hard time of it for awhile and so will Alice. Everyone will gossip about it and then I hope it will be forgotten for awhile." Alice, being Alice, met the implied rumors head on. She told a journalist that she was "always ready to try anything once," and that—an allusion to her age—she was looking forward to the birth of her "gland baby."[67]

Most cave dwellers and politicians felt that the new Speaker of the House was not, could not possibly be, the father. Was it on purpose that the Chicago paper—run by the McCormick family who knew her well—announced that *"Mrs. Longworth"* was expecting the stork—not *"the Longworths"*? Nick's extramarital affairs were notorious to insiders. Fishbait Miller, the longtime doorkeeper for the House of Representatives, called Longworth "one of the greatest womanizers in history on Capitol Hill." One oft-told story happened, according to Miller, when a colleague wanted to have a bit of fun at the Speaker's expense. "Mr. Speaker," the congressman said. "Your pretty bald head reminds me of my wife's behind. Is it alright if I rub my hand across it? Then I'll know for sure." Nick considered this request, and then, hand on his own pate, retorted, "I'll be damned if it doesn't."[68]

Nick's reputation was infamous; but Alice was reputed to be untouchable, and Bill was aloof, serious, Christian, and so dedicated to matters of state that his life precluded mundane dalliances. Borah had a "reputation for integrity in public life," had fought for clean government, and publicly chastised members of his own party for corrupt practices.[69] While there were rumors about Borah's randy youth and Cissy Patterson's assertion that she and Borah were once lovers, no verifiable documentation exists to prove this. Cissy is hardly a credible source because she and Alice were once in competition for Nick—and Alice won—and because there was always a certain tension between the women that might explain Cissy's story of her encounter with Bill in Alice's living room.

Alice, Nick, and Bill were thrust into precarious positions with the announcement of the impending birth, but Ruth continued to worry about Nick. "It is ridiculous when you think of Nick. What will he do with it?" she mused to her diary.[70] No record exists of Nick's immediate response. It is possible that Alice never told him about Borah; and possible that Alice concocted to sleep with her husband around the time she knew she was pregnant in an effort to throw suspicion away from Borah.[71] Still, Alice was not prone to dissembling; she knew about Nick's cupidity; his drunkenness repelled her and precluded much intimacy between them; and despite rumors of many illicit affairs, not one woman ever charged Nick with a paternity suit. Either Nick was infertile or he was able to dissuade his lady friends from going public.[72]

When Alice's pregnancy was announced, she was in Chicago for an appointment with Dr. DeLee. Ruth McCormick was Alice's strength. She knew all about Alice's mother's complications and could talk with Alice to help allay her fears. It was Ruth who accompanied Alice to the hospital to see the doctor. She thought Alice appeared "more cheerful and more at ease about her situation." The physician agreed with her. DeLee, Ruth recounted, said Alice was "very well and in good condition and that she must come back here three weeks before the baby is due." Alice's Washington doctor gave his professional opinion that Alice should leave Washington sooner rather than later. "When do you advise her making the trip to Chicago? Make it early please!" he begged. "It is hard to keep her away from the Capitol and there are steps and psychic shocks!"[73]

One of the shocks was the suicide in October of Alice's very good friend Senator Frank Brandegee. His humor was acerbic, and his politics were very similar to hers. He appreciated her mind, and the two found each other absurdly funny. Brandegee was the only alcoholic Alice tolerated and even assisted when he was inebriated. In December, the opening day in the Senate was cut short out of respect for its deceased members, including

Lodge and Brandegee. After the solemn opening day, the Committee on Committees met and officially elevated Borah to chair of Foreign Relations. Then in the House, Alice watched the members applaud Nick, a perennial favorite among representatives. The drive for Nick as Speaker resurfaced. Borah had noted at election time, "I see the papers today are much about Nick being speaker and you being speakeress." Borah thought Nick "entitled to it." Alice agreed. The Speaker ranked fifth in Washington protocol, and wife of the Speaker of the House occupied a position with significant social clout. In December, Ohio Republicans unanimously endorsed him in a letter sent to all House Republicans. Nick had the assurance of his supporters that they commanded more than the necessary votes for the speakership, and this was borne out at a clandestine meeting in February 1925. At that conference, Republican leaders gave the nomination for Speaker to Nick an "unprecedented" nine months before the Congress was to assemble.[74]

YOU CAN'T HELP LIKING NICK went the title of a complimentary article in the *Literary Digest*. Nick won Speaker for three reasons: longevity, regularity, and personality. In office since 1902 with only one two-year lapse, he had piled up twenty years' experience. He never bolted the party, despite severe provocation in 1912—and in fact, his speakership would be known in part for his swift and stern punishment of the Republican Progressives who, as Nick put it in a Chicago speech, "under Wisconsin leadership showed their true colors at the election. They not only had their own Presidential candidate [La Follette], but worked harder against the Republican candidate than the Democrats did." And Nick was known far and wide as a good guy; a politician who didn't take politics too seriously, who could disagree with the Democrats and then drink with them, and who had as one of his closest friends his antithesis: rural Texas Democratic representative John Nance Garner. Nick was "a Republican during working hours, but he left his partisanship in his office."[75]

His drinking and the womanizing continued, despite cautions from worried friends and family. Auntie Bye's congratulatory note, which never exactly said congratulations, was a masterpiece of subtext: "to become a father and the Speaker of the House seems more than any one is entitled to,

and if you could see your likeness in the *Hartford Courant* you would feel
sure it had gone to your head. I would hardly like you in either position if
it has given you this expression of dissipated good-fellowship."[76]

By the end of January 1925, Alice had settled into Chicago's Drake
Hotel. Borah was more open about his concerns for her health in his letters,
perhaps because he knew Nick could not be there with her and would not
inadvertently intercept her mail. From Washington Bill wrote, "I am wondering how you are getting by with these first days. I am afraid you will be
lonesome but you are so very wonderful—Mistress of all exigencies—that
I am sure everything will come out fine."[77]

His letters arrived daily. He filled her in on political news and wished
she could be with him to talk over topics such as his stance on the French
World War I debt, hearings before the Judiciary Committee concerning
the misdemeanors of two senators, and the status of various bills. Borah
was full of anger toward President Coolidge, who had led him to believe he
would act on the senator's suggestion of appointing Medill McCormick the
new ambassador to Great Britain. But even as Borah was meeting with
Coolidge on that subject, from London another man was named.[78] Bill received news of Alice through her letters, in telephone conversations, in
phone calls from Ruth, and from the newspapers. He wanted to be with
her. He shared Theodore Roosevelt's belief that motherhood was a woman's highest calling. A pent-up longing for progeny spilled out, and as the
due date neared, he grew ever more rhapsodic about her condition:

> I was delighted with your letter today—it seemed to me I could
> hear you speaking. But Alice the next four or five weeks are the most
> wonderful of your crowded and wonderful life. You will allow me to
> say won't you that it would have been truly a great wrong for you—
> so rich in personality—not to have had a child.
>
> Now if you are going to have a child, you are going to pass through
> the miracle hour of giving a being life. Marvel of marvels—so you
> will be careful and listen to your Dr. won't you. I know you will for it
> is you and you are always true to the exigency.

You are not sentimental Alice but in your marvelous being is a profound and beautiful strain of the rarest and richest sentiment. Do not hesitate to cultivate it—do not disown it. It enriches your character and will enrich another life. I feel deeply about you these days and I am writing as a long long time friend—one who wants you to know how worthy you always are and how worthy you are going to be in your supremest days.[79]

Surely one of the points in her letters to which Bill responded was Alice's fear, shared by all first-time mothers, that she might not be up to the task of giving birth. In Alice's case delivery was complicated by the timing. February had been an important but not always happy month for the Roosevelt family. Her own birthday was February 12, but her mother and grandmother had died on February 14, and these dates loomed large in her imagination. Bill's letters of this time contained many more references to God and to his prayers for her, perhaps a response to her own worries. Auntie Bye, seasoned veteran that she was, betrayed no such worry to Alice when she wrote in early February of her longing "for a first glimpse of my second grandchild; you may like it or not," she chaffed, "but my grandchild it will be, though it is rather a horrid thought to be provided with a whole extra inexplicable grandmother."[80]

Edith arrived on the morning of the fourteenth, and learned from Ruth that she had taken Alice to the hospital—so Edith hurried to be by Alice's side. The six-and-one-half-pound baby girl was born, without complications, at 10:30 a.m. on the fourteenth, the very date on which Alice's mother and grandmother had died forty-one years earlier.[81] Ruth, Edith, and Kermit were with Alice, but Bill, like the rest of the world, read about the birth on the front page of every newspaper. He dashed off a letter:

Dear Alice: Just read the evening papers and we are happy beyond the power of words to tell. There are to be two Alice Longworths—did not believe such possible. It is wonderful! Most wonderful. We shall be impatient almost beyond endurance until we lay eyes on that baby girl. I can well understand the wise men from the east who impelled by I know not what sublime faith wandered on until they came to where the divine child was. Well we will be patient—as patient as possible. But I shall be disappointed if it does not talk—I think Alice's baby ought to be talking in one week at most! Isn't it wonderful. I know you must be very happy and proud—gratified that you have measured up to the noblest most divine exertion of women. Hello more than ever Hello. All the evening papers had an account of the coming of the baby. The first I knew of it was when I glanced down and saw your picture. I tremblingly reached for it—fearing that you might be very ill—but when I read the wonderful news I put that old paper in my desk as a memento. Hello Hello—yes Hello.[82]

A night's sleep did not diminish Bill's enthusiasm. He wrote to tell her the fate of a conference report in the Senate, but concluded by admitting that such matters of state were nothing "compared to the Alice Jr. that is now the most important fact in this great country of ours. I will guarantee more people are discussing the latter thing today than farm legislation."[83]

What Alice thought of comparing their baby to farm legislation isn't clear. It is intriguing, however, to speculate on her response to his letter, written upon news of the birth. The letter conveys his fear that she might be "very ill" and his pride that she had "measured up to the noblest most divine exertion of women." While this may be evidence of that deep streak of fatalism that animated the senator, missing from the letter are all of the tender endearments that a lover might whisper at this defining moment in their relationship—particularly one missing the birth of their child. Even though he believed Alice to be unsentimental, this was Bill's first experience of fatherhood. But his letter reads as though it were for public consumption. He used a plural pronoun—was Mary standing over his shoulder as he wrote?—and then switched to "I." He congratulated her for coming through the birth so well (and she had just turned forty-one). This letter was probably followed closely by a phone call in which the two parents could speak more confidentially about the birth experience, the baby, and their feelings.

Nick heard of the baby's birth thirty minutes before the members of the House of Representatives did. As floor leader, he had to stay in the capital. The announcement brought a spontaneous ovation from his peers. He met the infant the day after she was born and told the newspapers ironically that he was "a little bit jealous... because she looks so much more like a Roosevelt than a Longworth, but she's young yet." "Judging by the look on the baby's face," one paper crowed, "she is a true descendant of her famous granddaddy, Theodore Roosevelt." To which Borah wrote to Alice: "Good—like our Roosevelt."[84]

Photos of the infant also bear a distinctive resemblance to Bill Borah's flat, broad face. But by all accounts Nick Longworth took one look at the child thrust into his late midlife and fell irredeemably, irrevocably, head-over-heels in love with her. She, newspapers suggested, would be "the real speaker of the house so far as domination of the Longworth ménage is concerned."[85] And it was true. Nick and the baby became inseparable.

Alice said it was she who named the baby Paulina—pronounced with a long "i"—after her favorite apostle, a decidedly odd act for someone once referred to as "an aggressive atheist," unless she was swayed by the more spiritually inclined Borah.[86] The apostle Paul was credited with tremendous strength of character, a Jew who zealously persecuted Christians until his conversion. He left his philosophy in his letters to the churches he founded, and both Bill and Alice certainly read those that became part of the New Testament.

As a tradition in literature, the name Paulina has a more checkered cast. John Gower's *Confessio Amantis,* written around 1385, has a Paulina who is duped by the mendacity of her husband. In the sixteenth century, Montaigne mentioned a similar topic, with Paulina, the Roman wife who, because of the trickery of the temple priests, found herself lying not with the god Serapis but with "a wanton lover of hers." Gervase Markham's 1609 poem "The Lamentable Complaint of Paulina, the Famous Roman Curtezan" casts her in the role of the savvy courtesan, which was what Paulina referred to thereafter in literature. Fifty years later, Thomas Pecke's "Upon Paulina" has Paulina making a cuckold of her husband: "Paulina her first husband, made a Stag; / Nor had the last, any cause to brag. / She was as hard as horn, to first, and last." In that same year, Richard Lovelace's poem "Lucasta" makes reference to a woman who, like an unfaithful wife, appears to be one thing, but in reality is another. William Shakespeare, in *The Winter's Tale*, has Paulina standing up to the king's authority and defending her mistress from the fabricated allegation of adultery. Ultimately, Paulina emerges triumphantly, with a "behind-the-throne control" over the men in the play.[87] Alice and Bill, who read literature and poetry from all ages, likely knew that the unusual name Paulina was associated with adultery.

Whether Nick liked the name or not, he decided that this new addition to his life was a tremendous gift. There is no reason to think that Alice and Nick were not still fond of each other after their nineteen years of marriage, only that the romance had been long absent. At any rate, if Nick, the soon-to-be Speaker of the House, publicly voiced his suspicions as to Paulina's parentage, or gave a hint of his doubt publicly, he would bring down not just the chair of the Senate Foreign Relations Committee, but ruin his wife's reputation and destroy his own political career. In 1925, a man with several mistresses could be viewed with admiration for his prowess, but a man who was openly cuckolded was weak and foolish, clearly unfit to rule his house, let alone the House.

While Nick became accustomed to being a daddy, Bill kept up a steady stream of letters, professing his love, his desire to see Paulina, and his hope that he could soon talk politics with Alice in person again. Even with the interminable night sessions at the Senate preceding sine die that physically exhausted him, Borah wrote almost daily, if "only to say Hello." On Sunday, February 22, he penned another rhapsody in praise of her giving birth. "It is a beautiful day—one of those days which enriches the soul with aspirations beyond mortal attainment—one of the days which makes one wish for the company of dear friends—Hello yes today so much Hello that it all seems feeble when words alone must suffice. . . . Alice you are a very wonderful woman. . . . What a deep vein of true glorious sentiment in your marvelous being and now to be developed to its full bent. It is great but I expected it. I know down in your deepest feelings you must be very happy—Hello hello. And that will help a little won't it."[88]

While Alice had sent telegrams to inform people of the birth—for example, President Coolidge's secretary, Everett Sanders—the newspapers continued to provide intimate reports of Alice and Paulina. When they ran out of day-to-day news, the papers took to augury. A full-page article entitled "Science and the Longworth Baby" illuminated "Why a Brilliant Career Is Predicted for This New Descendent of King Robert Bruce, Ex-President Roosevelt and So Many Other Famous Ones." Even Edith Roosevelt, Ted told Borah, was "greatly elated over Paulina and thinks she is a wonder."[89] Ted was in the throes of assessing his political future after the gubernatorial loss, and Borah was providing advice.

Into the midst of the celebrations surrounding Paulina's birth came the shocking news of Medill McCormick's death. The coroner listed the cause as "myocarditis," but Medill had committed suicide, just as Frank Brandegee had. For Medill, it was the culmination of a difficult life marked by "self-destructive tendencies" and most recently by his electoral loss. His death devastated Ruth and their three children. Ruth had lingered in Chicago to help Alice through the first difficult month as a new mother, and Medill had purposefully gone away from his family to spare them. Edith found it "such a horrible blow" that she felt she "could not write to [Alice] or to Ruth.... So much of service and interest lay ahead" for Medill, she mourned. Soon after Medill's death, Ruth sought solace in her work. It was not an ideal time for her best friend to be wrapped up in a new baby, but it was Alice who pushed Ruth back into the fray. "When Senator McCormick died," Ruth told a reporter, "my thought was to give up politics myself. Alice knew what I needed better than I did. She told me that I must not only not give up but that I must not get out of politics even temporarily, not even for a day. She was right about it."[90] Work had saved TR upon his widowered state.

Perhaps Medill's death was a catalyst for Borah, a reminder that life is short, for immediately thereafter his letters brim with loving salutations toward Paulina. Even before he had seen her for the first time, he and Alice set aside a special place on Paulina's infant body where they could kiss but no one else would: "Give Paulina a kiss on the back of her little neck," he wrote a fortnight after she was born. "I know what Paulina will get on the neck," Bill crooned in the summer.[91]

In early March of 1925, Alice and Paulina returned to Washington, D.C., the latter clad "in garments of pink and white and blue, gifts of Mrs. Medill McCormick."[92] Bill was finally able to meet their daughter. There is no record of this moment, but it is clear that having the "two Alices" near to him was idyllic: "[A]s I wended my way home about 11:00 a.m. somewhat weary anyway, I looked out the window and as we passed 1733 and said Hello and was deeply thankful I could say hello and could hear the echo Hello. Oh I will certainly be glad to see Paulina and ————." He trailed off at the end of the sentence, as though it were too superficial to call Alice his "dear, dear friend" any longer. Alice, Bill, and Paulina were in Washington together from early March until May, when mother and daughter went to Cincinnati. Nick left on a two-month European trip on May 20 to assess the ramifications of tariffs and the Volstead Act. The 1920s were far removed from current fathering norms, and a two-month trip away from a newborn was entirely consistent with social expectations for the Longworths' class. Perhaps, though, Ruth's predictions of gossip were coming true. LONGWORTH POSES AS FOND FATHER, ran one sly headline in May.[93] And in some circles, Alice had been referred to as "Aurora Borah Alice," for a long time—a phrase that neatly captured Alice's incandescent personality as well as her love interest.

Mary Borah was one of the first people to meet Paulina in Washington. According to Mrs. Borah's memoir, Alice telephoned and said, "Mary, Paulina wants you to come over and have lunch with her." Mary recalled, "Paulina slept through most of my visit but woke up before I left and Alice let me hold her. She was a beautiful baby."[94] The reasons behind this extraordinary invitation are obscure. Assuming that Mary Borah did not fabricate the story, Alice may have been attempting to deflect suspicion caused by the rumors swirling around the capital—for surely not even Alice Roosevelt Longworth could be so brazen as to invite her lover's wife to see their child. On the other hand, it would be exactly the sort of action Alice would take to demonstrate conclusively that she cared not a whit about local gossip.

It is not clear whether either spouse knew for certain the identity of Paulina's biological father. Although long a senator's wife, Mary did not live in the nucleus of power as did the Longworths. "Little Borah," as she was called, had the reputation of being ditzy and scattered, and unable to formulate an original thought. "He never talks politics with me...I hint around a little, but I don't get much from him. I have to buy a paper to learn what he's going to do next," she told a reporter—who described her as "the good humored matron." James M. Cox remembered Mary as a woman who "chided the Senator a great deal about his carelessness in dress" and could tell a good story.[95]

Alice could be vengeful, as her childhood diaries show. She did not suffer fools gladly. She could gloat. But if Alice went to see Mary Borah in order to revel in her dual victory—stealing Borah's affections and bearing his only child—then it apparently went right over Mary's head. Alice was "a frequent morning caller" at the Borahs' apartment. Mary told a reporter that she and Bill became "close personal friends" with Alice and Nick. She accompanied Alice to hear speeches in both houses of Congress. In fact, on December 7, 1925, the day that Nick was elevated to Speaker of the House—and ten months after Paulina's birth—Alice watched from "the speaker's row of the gallery" with her two invited guests, one of whom was Mary Borah. Whether or not Little Borah knew the truth of Paulina's patrimony, she embraced the infant with a tenderness like Nick's, even carrying photos of Paulina and showing them off to friends.[96] Her memoir is full of complimentary references to Alice, from the time she first saw her as First Daughter past her becoming a mother. Its very tone gives rise to another interpretation: Mary, who may have had an abortion and who loved all children, was grateful to Alice for bearing Paulina, seeing her birth in some significant way as redemption.

To spare each others' feelings, or to preserve Bill's paternity from history, the adults involved never publicly confirmed the truth. But Bill could not hide his pride, and in a third code, initiated after Paulina's birth, he asserted his fatherhood. Unlike the previous codes, though, this one was more difficult to crack. On the tenth of July, Bill wrote to Alice from Boise, where he was in the middle of what he termed a "civil war" over water issues: "I know what those farmers and their families have suffered for the last five years and I feel deeply that they are being cruelly pushed by the

Gov. But I must not carry these things to P.F.P.—Hello." Three days later the abbreviation became more clear: "I feel very low in my mind today and thought I could gain advantage by communicating with P.F.P. and through her with P—How deeply I realize as to both—Hello Hello."[97] In the same letter, however, he concluded, "I love your notes about Paulina." This is a difficult point. Why write out Paulina if he was also abbreviating her name as "P"? He did both with no specific consistency or pattern, and often included Paulina in "Hello Hello."

By the end of the month, foreign events had superceded the local water war. Borah sent Alice a copy of a positive letter from a constituent because, "I always must have PFP hear the good news."[98] In August, tired of being away, Borah wrote, "I am getting quite homesick for PFP—Rock Creek Park, P—Jester, ect., ect. All because Hello." In September, he apologized for his monosyllabic responses to her phone call, but he had "three persons in committee" before him and couldn't talk. At least he had their photos: "PFP and daughter sitting here—hello hello." Even as Borah used PFP to refer to Alice and P for Paulina, he rendered the code much less mysterious when he changed one letter—the one letter that verified his role: "Dear Alice, I enjoyed your brief note this morning particularly how Paulina went after the visage of P.M.P. Anyway you must for me say Hello to her. She will in time think more favorably of her M.P."[99] Paulina's Male Parent—Borah's own hand provided the ultimate proof of his paternity— and Alice was P.F.P.: Paulina's Female Parent.

Possibly this cipher was to protect Nick and Mary. Possibly it was simply a generational code of ethics. Kiss, perhaps, but never tell. Paulina's Female Parent had as much to lose as Paulina's Male Parent, but their child would suffer most. There were rumors. Washingtonians shook their heads at the gossip that Alice would name her baby Deborah. A famous joke convulsed cave dwellers: "What do a new parquet floor and the Longworth baby have in common? There's not a bit of a 'nick' in either one." The senator's reputation as a loner helped them keep their secret. Ruth knew; perhaps Ted did. But even Borah's secretary, Cora Rubin—who had been with him since before he left Idaho—certified he had no real close friends.[100]

Alice never told Paulina about Bill Borah. Secure in Nick's love, Paulina found out only before she left for college when she overheard her governess, Dorothy Waldron, speaking with her mother.[101] It was unintentional. Perhaps Alice never meant to tell her daughter so as not to destroy Paulina's good memories. Mary, Bill, Alice, and, most important, Nick went on as though everything was normal, thus giving her the immeasurable gift of a stable childhood. What this cost the adults involved is unimaginable.

Chapter 16

"The Political Leader of the Family"

Bᴇ 1926, Aʟɪᴄᴇ Lᴏɴɢᴡᴏʀᴛʜ was referred to in print as "the political leader of the family." In 1927, her profile graced the cover of *Time* magazine, making her, Gore Vidal asserted, "a permanent, for good or ill, member of the world's grandest vanity fair."[1] Her power extended beyond the Roosevelt clan, and Paulina's birth had not slowed her down. She wielded quiet but real influence over two of the leading politicians of the day, the Speaker of the House and the chair of the Senate Foreign Relations Committee. Alice lived for politics. Her political acumen was so widely recognized that she was even briefly considered for the vice presidency on the Republican ticket at the 1928 convention.

Alice and Nick moved to 2009 Massachusetts Avenue on Dupont Circle after Paulina's birth. There, they played serious poker. Alice claimed to have cleared ten thousand dollars one winter—and that was after she paid Nick's debts.[2] They also threw impromptu lunches and hosted dinners attended by people from the upper echelons of the nation's capital, such as Secretary of the Treasury Andrew Mellon and Senate Majority Leader Charles Curtis.

The public gained a glimpse of Alice's private life when an acquaintance of hers, Nelle Scanlan, anonymously published *Boudoir Mirrors of Washington*, featuring the "singular" Alice Longworth. In an evocative and compelling word portrait, Scanlon insisted that "What she does, unconventional though it may be, is not inspired by a desire to shock, so much as an expression of self-determination, a vigorous protest against irksome customs and restrictions. Her attitude is one of supreme indifference to public opinion."[3]

The press predicted a similar future for Alice's daughter. "If Paulina is like her mother she will like the society of intellectual men; have an innate knowledge of politics and be deeply interested in world affairs. There is no woman in Washington who attends Congress more regularly and who wields a greater influence in official life than Mrs. Nicholas Longworth." The toddler accompanied her mother on social calls, enticed her father home from his Speaker's duties, and loved to hear the organ whenever Nick took her to church.[4] Paulina's first years were happily bounded by her family and her nursemaid.

"The daughter of T.R. is not submerged in the mother of Paulina," the *Ladies' Home Journal* noticed in the mid-1920s, a time of flappers, New Women, and sexual emancipation. In fact, Alice was "one of the most influential women in Washington," according to the *New Yorker*, which insisted that "an invitation to the Longworths is more prized by the discriminating than an invitation to the White House. Mrs. Longworth gives no guest lists to the papers.... Heavy politics are played at the Longworth house and Alice sits in.... She knows men, measures and motives; has an understanding grasp of their changes.... It is too bad for the Roosevelt political dynasty that Alice wasn't a boy. She is the smartest Roosevelt there is left—the old Colonel's daughter in more ways than one. She has a quick, inquiring, original and penetrating mind especially equipped to cope with political situations for which she has an instinctive liking." The *Ladies' Home Journal* interviewed both Alice and Ruth and concluded that both women "play politics for the love of politics, and they prefer to play them with men who run government rather than with women who seek to reform government. Both are frankly and bitterly partisan. They are not without influence on national legislation concerning matters which interest them." Yet Paulina remained central to Alice's daily life. Ruth—well aware of what society expected of mothers—insisted Alice was "even more keen about the welfare and nourishment of Paulina than she was about the welfare and the nourishment of the Senate Battalion of Death that killed the League of Nations."[5]

Alice and Paulina regularly dropped in on the Borahs. By 1929, Little

Borah was spending her days caring for veterans of the Great War and for local boys and girls, some homeless, some orphans. She surrounded herself with neighborhood children, let them into her home, dried their tears, and helped them through their troubles. As a feature article put it dramatically, "Childless herself, [she] has offered herself as mother to the world's motherless."[6] The visits with Paulina must have brought Mary joy—she would have had the power to end them, otherwise. It is impossible to pin down Alice's reasons for taking Paulina to the Borahs, and interpreting this action would be easier if it were clear whether all four adults involved knew Paulina's parentage. The Longworths and the Borahs were friendly. Alice may have been thoughtfully calling on Mary with Paulina because she knew how much Mary enjoyed children. Or Alice might have found such visits darkly amusing. They gave Bill further access to Paulina, although he also saw her at the Longworths', where he could play informally and privately with the child. While Mary Borah had only praise for Alice, a real friendship between the two women seems implausible, given their disparate temperaments and their relationship to Bill. An acquaintanceship based on shared political beliefs, husbands whose work drew them together, and the delight they could take in Paulina is more likely.

Nick continued to take Paulina to the House of Representatives weekly. He indulged her. She played with his typewriter and wrote strings of nonsense letters that were fun to type—a child's love letter sent home in an official envelope marked TO MOT HER. Alice sentimentally preserved it. She worried about a case of trench mouth, which was "tiresome because I had to be very remote with Paulina. She is running all around. Seems fine. Has gained nearly ½ lb. . . ." By the time Paulina was eighteen months old, Alice told Ethel, "I long, I really long to have" Paulina play with her Derby cousins.[7]

First Lady Grace Coolidge was especially fond of Paulina, perhaps because her own children were much older and because she had recently and suddenly lost her son Calvin Jr. to a relentless infection. Just after Christmas 1925, when Paulina was ten months old, she and Alice had called on the First Lady. After tea, the women were irresistibly pulled to the floor to play with the baby. Grace told a friend that Paulina resembled Alice and T.R., and "She seems to have the most real 'personality' of any child that I ever knew at her age. But that may be that she looks so much like her mother that I unavoidably see her mother's personality reflected in her."[8]

While Alice relished motherhood, her absorption in politics continued. Purely social events did not exist for Alice. "So many Congressmen's wives have gone to Washington expecting of course to become intimately acquainted with Mrs. 'Nick' Longworth," one newspaper article chirruped. "They had visions of playing bridge with her, drinking tea at her home and having her and her husband for dinner. But did they? No, indeed. The former Alice Roosevelt felt she had better uses for her time than gossiping with the average Congressman's wife. She would rather be in the Senate gallery listening to the discussion of subjects concerning which she frequently knows more than the speakers. She preferred reading philosophy and poetry to squandering hours at some dull tea table."[9]

Alice played the social game when necessary, releasing her eggplant recipe to the Congressional Club's fund-raising cookbook. Edith contributed her recipe for Indian pudding; Mary Borah gave hers for gingerbread and for marshmallow pudding; and Grace Coolidge's corn muffin recipe stood beside recipes from Helen Taft and Lou Henry Hoover. Alice had been a "charter member" when congressional wives formed the club in 1908 "to lighten the sorrows and increase the joys of official position." Famous for its cookbooks, music, and educational programs, its meetings were socially sanctioned distaff behavior and therefore a bit of a bore for Alice Longworth.[10]

More to her liking was a new adventure in May 1925: Alice posed for a Ponds cold cream advertisement. She sat for the painted portrait featured in the ad. She said she did this for the five thousand dollars to tuck away for Paulina's future. In her usual forthright fashion, Alice divulged the sum and its purpose, to the consternation of Ponds, which wanted customers to assume the ads were the spontaneous—and unpaid—endorsements of enthusiastic women. Alice was one of several famous smooth-skinned women who posed for Ponds: Queen Marie of Romania, Mrs. Marshall Field Sr.,

Anne Morgan, and Little Borah—which may or may not further explain Alice's involvement. After two decades of refusing to be formally interviewed by the press, Alice, by appearing in the cold cream ad, did give "official and social Washington another surprise."[11]

Alice was without peer in the capital city. When the celebrated Queen Marie of Romania visited the White House in October 1926, it was Alice she most wanted to see. The First Lady had been warned about the queen's impulsive nature and love of publicity and told not to leave Queen Marie alone at her reception. Concern for the ladies in waiting diverted Mrs. Coolidge for a moment. Immediately, Queen Marie summoned Alice. Wearing a simply cut dress made of Empress Tz'u Hsi's red silk, Alice sat by Queen Marie's side, who "from then on . . . paid no further attention to the waiting guests." Protocol dictated that the queen decided when the discussion was over, and Queen Marie's absorbed conversation with Alice derailed the White House plans. Bill and Mary Borah were present, and what Mary remembered of "the most important official function given at the White House during my 22 years in the capital" was Alice boldly offering a "cigarete" to the young Princess Ileana."[12]

Alice's unconventional behavior reached its acme at prizefights. "It indicates a primitive interest in a primitive affray," as one *Chicago Tribune* editor put it. "It represents interest in physical well being, skill, courage, and stamina." On Saturday nights, Alice liked to go to the fights with Ted. Nick went infrequently. Calvin Coolidge could also be convinced to accompany her. Alice's friend the fight promoter George "Tex" Rickard kept her apprised of the up-and-coming boxers and sent her tickets for the best fights. Tex orchestrated the celebrated 1921 "Battle of the Century" between U.S. heavyweight Jack Dempsey and French boxer Georges Carpentier. Alice was one of the few women crowded into Boyle's Thirty Acres in Jersey City, New Jersey, that night. Alice bet on the Manassa Mauler, because she thought it "a bit disloyal" to do otherwise. Her patriotism paid off. Dempsey dropped the Frenchman in the fourth round.[13]

While Alice enjoyed the nation's attention, her husband was entering the prime of his professional life. Well groomed and carefully dressed,

Nick cut a dapper figure. Legendarily cheerful, he could "find lovableness in his most pronounced political opponent." But there was more to him, for in Nick the House would have a new kind of Speaker, one who "will have to be reckoned with in his party councils. His is the gloved hand, but beneath the glove is an iron grip." His pride in the House bordered on the chauvinistic, and Washington watchers expected him to be a powerful Speaker.[14]

Nick had demonstrated his ability to play hardball in 1925 when he publicly repudiated thirteen GOP progressives and denied the La Follette supporters their committee seats. That fall, he and Alice traveled to Chicago, where in two different speeches he made clear that he would deal firmly with the "Radicals." "They have shown their colors . . . ," he said, "and they are not entitled to important committee places or seats in the inner councils of the party they fought." Nick played on growing fears of Bolshevism in the wake of the Russian Revolution of 1917 by linking GOP reformers with extremism. When he had led the 1910 charge to defang Joe Cannon, the power shifted from the Speaker to the floor leader. Once elevated, though, Nick carried the power right back to the Speaker's rostrum. "Regardless of the rules," Nick told a reporter, "the Speakership always will be what the Speaker makes of it."[15]

Insiders believed Nick's success was not his alone: "In Alice Longworth he found a rarely accomplished political assistant, one who has been frequently described as the 'best man in the Roosevelt family,' and whose influence in public life, exerted through sheer political common sense, is not less than that of any woman who has ever lived in the capital." Still, marriage to her was not without its perils; the "distinction" of being the son-in-law of Theodore Roosevelt "was not entirely an asset, for there were those who looked upon him in the light of a social curiosity and even today, most of the visitors to the House ask to be shown Alice Longworth's husband." And, of course, Speaker of the House might not be "the final port in the ambitious political cruise of Nicholas Longworth. . . ." Not everyone agreed. In his quarter century in the House, two journalists charged, Nick "never sponsored anything of the slightest importance, and until he was made Speaker in 1925 was known chiefly as the husband of Alice Roosevelt."[16]

Nick ascended to the speakership at the session of Congress that began on December 7, 1925. His opening words included a bit of flag-waving for the House, promising to make it "the great dominant legislative assembly of the World. Thus we may rest assured that the Republic of the United States shall forever live and that popular government shall never die...." And while Nick noted that the listening representatives were united in their hope to reduce taxes, he knew he faced challenges. He griped once that Congress is "always unpopular." Congress either "meddled" or "did nothing," in the public's perception. If Congress "follows a President it is likened to a flock of sheep.... On the other hand, if it defies the President then it becomes a bunch of factionists and demagogues." And, Nick insinuated, oftentimes when Congress did the hard work and hammered out a bill, the president reaped the praise. But Nick liked the challenge of bringing order through collaboration: "When Congress is making up its mind what to do there are 531 minds going through the process. In consequence there is much quibbling, and many poor arguments and foolish debates are heard by the country at large, for there is no secrecy about our deliberations.... In spite of all that I like my job. I know that without cooperation it could become the most unpleasant position in the world."[17]

Nick had the ease of manner that endeared him to everyone. He paused to shake hands and discuss a shared love of music with African-American House doorman Harry Parker. Ambassador Walter Evans Edge believed that "rich or poor, Jew or Gentile, Catholic or Protestant, presented no distinction to Nick." Nick saw the best in others, even Democrats. One of his best friends was his political enemy, John Nance Garner, a self-styled "plebian" who had served with Nick on the Foreign Affairs and the Ways and Means committees and rose to become House minority leader. "Cactus Jack" was not everyone's model legislator. One Senate insider called him "a chain drinker." Labor leader John L. Lewis memorably labeled Garner "a labor-baiting, poker-playing, whiskey-drinking, evil old man."[18]

But Nick and Garner understood each other. They shared the conviction that the Senate had nothing on the House. Cactus Jack and Nick used to linger long after the House adjourned, rehashing the day's business and strategizing for the morrow. They disagreed often and occasionally bitterly, but their friendship prevailed. "Keeping the Democratic leader informed, out of a true appreciation for his verve and his political acumen, was good leadership—but it went beyond that for Speaker Longworth," according to his House colleague Lewis W. Douglas. Douglas thought Nick an "excellent parliamentarian, and an able and colorful legislator," who got "high marks" from both sides of the aisle for his "impartial governance." Will Rogers made the Speaker's office his headquarters when he was in Washington because he knew that between Nick and Garner, he'd "get the real 'lowdown' on what the government wasn't doing."[19]

It was said of Nick that his aristocratic nature generally rubbed off on others. An editorial at the time of his death suggested that this happened in private, as part of the business of knitting together an obstreperous body of legislators. During World War I, Nick, Cactus Jack, and a few fellow collaborators, along with an occasional journalist friend, used to retire to sip a few companionable drinks. The "Board of Education," a room beneath the Capitol Dome, became their favorite haunt when Nick was Speaker. This space was stocked with illegal alcohol that greased the wheels of compromise. Garner said the room got its name because its use gave them an education: "'Well...you get a couple of drinks in a young Congressman and then you know what he knows and what he can do. We pay the tuition by supplying the liquor.'" The Board of Education expedited legislative matters and smoothed over differences by coming to compromises in private, where misunderstandings could be avoided. Garner's access to Nick assured Democrats that they were being heard.[20]

In the Senate, Borah presented a marked contrast in his modus operandi. He often took the lead on an issue and, for opaque reasons, dropped it. One critical journalist described Borah as "individualism in all its glory and in all its futility," yet called him "without equal in the country to-day in arousing popular enthusiasm and delivering telling blows." Borah was condemned more each year for not living up to his leadership potential. His stubbornness got in the way, and he wore the "maverick" label with pride: once his ideas entered the mainstream, he often renounced them. Calvin Coolidge sized up Borah riding in Rock Creek Park one day and wondered "if it bothers the Senator to be going in the same direction as his horse."[21] Both those who loved him, such as Senate page Richard Riedel, and those who didn't, like journalist Drew Pearson, recognized his strengths. Pearson called him "the great advocate. Scintillating of thought, and enthralling of expression, he is without peer as the passionate pleader. He has raised his voice for many splendid causes, peace, disarmament, anti-imperialism, Russian recognition. He has stirringly denounced infamy, demagoguery, incompetence, and corruption in high and low places." Ultimately, he thought Borah was no organizer, no "commander, but a scholar."[22] Nick stood in the trenches; Bill dreamed from the mountaintop.

Alice knew that part of Bill's reluctance to fight every battle to the finish came from his ambivalence about politics. Time among his constituents always made Borah wistful. It is true the senator loved the adulation of Idahoans—he was always careful to send Alice laudatory editorials about himself. Yet the long bucolic drives, the days on horseback, the afternoons leaning on pasture fences listening to human stories made him rue the rural life he abandoned. On the campaign trail the rough but honest Idahoans gave it to Borah straight, and he admired them. He also felt for them. "I am moved to tears for these farmers," he confided to Alice. "After ten years of adversity, after the pledges of the last campaign, after six months of the farm board, after two years of Hoover, they are getting less for their wheat than it costs to harvest it. I could weep with them." After a hard day among the bitter yield, he wrote her, "It is h— to campaign with broken pledges scattered about you."[23]

Bill was also prone to bouts of depression. "I am very blue, no reason, just blue," he confessed to Alice soon after the 1930 election. His preferred remedy was a solitary horseback ride to "think out what it is all about." But when he was in Washington, in the thick of it and trading "spanks and spit" with senators and reporters, it was easier to summon the reasons he chose politics. "I wonder if God is going to be good to me," Borah mused to Alice, "answer my prayer and give us a real political upheaval, sweeping over party lines, over old traditions and recording for once the voice of an outraged people." Borah's passion was most evident in such utopian plans as his attempt to banish warfare.[24]

The outlawry of war had been a topic of interest to the senator since the days of the League battle, and by 1927 it had the additionally interesting property of being the issue that could propel him into the White House. Borah never lost his mistrust of international organizations like the League, or his dislike of Europeans. Nevertheless, when, in April 1927—to mark ten years since U.S. involvement in World War I—French minister for foreign affairs Aristide Briand suggested that France and the United States join together "to outlaw war," Borah eventually made the issue his own. Lobbied hard by original members of the outlawry movement such as Chicago attorney Salmon O. Levinson, Borah conquered his suspicion of the French idea and modified it to suit his own purposes. It took the senator most of 1927 before he could find a way to back the plan fully.[25]

Taciturn President Coolidge made his famous, terse, and perplexing statement that he "did not choose to run" for reelection in 1928. Those who admired him put a favorable interpretation on this and stated boldly their champion was simply too modest to campaign but would accede to a draft. Those hoping for a change in the White House silently blessed Coolidge for his brevity and fought to bring their own men to the front. Bill, who seemed to want the presidency, but never quite enough, grabbed onto the outlawry issue as a campaign centerpiece. Earlier, he had made plain—in part to thwart the presidential aspirations of easterner Charles Evans Hughes—that the 1928 election could not neglect the farm problem and tougher Prohibition enforcement, two topics urbanites found uninspiring. Borah won a highly publicized debate on the question "Should the Republican National Platform of 1928 Advocate the Repeal of the Eighteenth Amendment?" He argued against Columbia University president Dr. Nicholas Murray Butler in front of more than three thousand listeners at the Roosevelt Club. A better rallying point than Prohibition for his rural base, he thought, was the outlawry of war. He hastened to spread the word. One Idaho newspaper duly explained: "If Europe spends a disproportionate share of its limited funds in military preparation it will have little left for

American wheat and corn."[26] Ultimately, Borah was wrong. The outlawry of war as the bridge between peace and prosperity never caught the imagination of westerners.

The presidential nod did not come his way in 1928, but he did play an important role in the Kellogg-Briand Pact, the idealistic treaty that made war illegal. In February 1928, Borah put forth Levinson's idea in a *New York Times* article—enlarging Briand's bipower treaty: *all nations* of the world should be invited to sign the pledge to outlaw war. This was swordplay with blunted tips. Borah had just cornered the French—whom he suspected of seeking special friend status with the United States through the originally conceived bipower treaty—while simultaneously evading the vexing diplomatic discussions of which types of war, exactly, were to be outlawed. Insisting that all nations promise to make all war illegal, Borah stood above the petty semantic squabbles of the diplomats, grandly offering a sweeping and simple solution, while capturing the moral high road. He became the "political mentor of the American peace movement."[27] Borah used the power of his position to promote the Kellogg-Briand Pact to his Foreign Relations Committee and to the country at large. Sixty-three nations ultimately signed. It was a brave and optimistic moment.

As history would prove, the treaty had one fatal defect: it contained no enforcement provisions. Whether it was realpolitik or inability to commit fully to a battle, Borah quit the fight before the critical enforcement provisions could be included. Proud to have foiled the French in their attempt to entangle the United States, Borah hoped the presidency would follow. Levinson and others saw the Kellogg-Briand Pact without the enforcement clause as only a beginning to their new world, but Borah saw it as an end. This was "gall and wormwood" to Levinson. Nevertheless, the attorney gratefully funded and chartered the William Edgar Borah Foundation for the Outlawry of War, still in existence today.[28]

Borah's supporters had been struggling for two years to make his case for the 1928 presidential race. Borah felt the GOP was controlled by harmful "industrial and financial combinations" that needed to be "purged." Maintaining his independence, Borah announced that this party reform could be done "under the auspices of any political body . . . [and] his speeches will be made in response to invitations of organizations willing to sponsor the reforms he will indicate." In part because he truly loathed the illegal activities of businessman Harry Sinclair and Secretary of the Interior Albert B. Fall in the Teapot Dome oil lease scandal, and perhaps because he had an eye to publicizing his moral credentials, Borah came up with the idea of soliciting donations to get the GOP out of debt. He sought to replace the $160,000 conscience money that Sinclair had given, earned out of the bribe he had taken from Standard Oil. Bill believed that once good Republicans understood that Sinclair's money was tainted, they would do the right thing. If not, "I know of no defense for Republican morality. For myself, I am not willing to sit quiet while this stigma remains upon the escutcheon of the party."[29]

At the same time that Borah was trying to find an issue for 1928, Ethel reported to Belle Hagner, "There is real talk—an undercurrent—of Nick as a Presidential possibility! Can you believe it?" Nick could attract bipartisan support. Reporter Frank B. Lord suggested in early 1927 that "if the Democrats of the House of Representatives were required to name the next Republican president of the United States, you would be perfectly safe in laying a wager of 100 to 1, which would be about the proportion in which they would vote, that Ohio would have another of her distinguished citizens in the White House. . . ." But Nick was happy where he was. He told his sister that he had "realized *more* than I ever hoped for in the way of ambition. There was a time, I might have wanted to be in the Senate," but Speaker of the House "is much better and more in line with my aptitudes." Nick averred he had "a horror of the Presidential bee; I have seen it ruin too many good men."[30] He was content with the House and his daughter.

He suffered Paulina to make powdered sugar pies on top of his bald, indulgent head. He went to every French and piano lesson with her. She accompanied him to the Capitol Saturday afternoons and held court for the favored congressmen who came to spoil her. Alice thought taking her on to the floor of the House would "exploit" the child, so even though Nick wanted dearly to do so, he kept those chamber appearances to a minimum. Paulina concluded her Saturday ritual with a visit to Cactus Jack, who made much of her. Photographers loved to snap pictures of the Speaker and "Kitz," as Nick called her, who loved the attention. She was growing apace. Kermit told Ethel in January 1928: "I saw Sister in Washington, as much wrapped up in Paulina as ever. The latter was in good form. She is more advanced than [her cousin], indeed does not seem like a baby at all."[31]

In the end—and to Alice's great disappointment—neither Nick nor Bill earned the nod for 1928. The battle lines were drawn by the end of June. In Houston, Franklin Roosevelt walked to the podium leaning on his son Elliott to name "the happy warrior," Al Smith, the Democratic Party's choice. Two weeks earlier, the GOP convention had been held in steamy Kansas City, where Republicans selected Herbert Hoover on the first ballot. Bill Borah "delivered himself up, influence, statesmanlike presence, magnetic voice and all, to the nomination of the Great Engineer—much to the annoyance of some of his progressive friends." The platform contained strong planks on Prohibition, the outlawry of war, labor, and farm relief based upon Borah's ideas.[32]

As conventions go, this one lacked drama, though Alice's celebrity status drew attention. For a memorable few hours, her name was mentioned for the vice presidency. It was supposed to be a "hoax 'boom'" made by the editor-in-chief of the Western Newspaper Union, but it was taken seriously by some of the delegates present—evidence both that the significance of women's participation in politics had made such an idea possible and of Alice's own credentials as a canny, intelligent, and serious politician.[33]

Though Alice believed Herbert Hoover was not "politically seasoned," she nonetheless put party before persona and in 1928 took to the campaign trail. She liked Lou Henry Hoover, a Stanford geology graduate with a broad range of concerns. Herbert Hoover was an engineer by training, keyed to details and often seeing the big picture only at the last minute. For Alice, the real excitement in 1928 was Ruth Hanna McCormick's campaign for the U.S. Congress. She ran as a delegate at-large for a seat in the House of Representatives. Ruth undertook a sixteen-thousand-mile campaign across Illinois, speaking to farmers and miners of the economic assistance she would find for them if elected. She was a supporter of the outlawry of war and of Prohibition. The latter Ruth actually considered "a mistake, but it was the law and the government 'either ought to enforce it or repeal it.' "[34]

She beat her six opponents in April, campaigned all fall, and won more than one million votes to become "the first woman congressman from Illinois" and "the first woman elected state-wide to a national office." Alice was overjoyed. The two rented a house in Kansas City during the convention and even though Alice herself would never run for office, Ruth recognized Alice's talents. "Alice," she put it, "is a statesman and I am a politician.... She has no patience for the drudgery of details, but she has wonderful intuition as to where this or that tendency in politics is going to carry us, has an uncanny certainty in predicting results, and she dearly loves a fight." To Alice's delight, Ruth moved to Washington, D.C., to start work even before the special session of the Seventy-first Congress opened in April 1929.[35]

While Alice and Ruth worked hard for Hoover's election, one of Borah's biographers insisted that "no man did more than the Senator from Idaho to make Herbert Hoover President of the United States." It was Borah who saw to it that skittish middle western and far western voters cast their votes for the GOP. In return for Hoover's espousal of Borah's ideas in the platform, the new president expected Borah to orchestrate a compliant Senate into accepting the resultant legislation. Hoover underestimated Borah's independence. Over lunch on January 19, 1929, Hoover asked Borah if he would become his secretary of state. Borah declined, saying he had not campaigned for Hoover seeking a quid pro quo; nor did he have the financial wherewithal to move into the cabinet. And, Borah told the president, he prized his work in the Senate, especially his ability to disagree with Hoover—a liberty he would not enjoy as secretary of state.[36]

Just after Hoover's inaugural, politics took a backseat to the protocol war labeled the Alice Longworth–Dolly Gann affair. It set Washington abuzz. Dolly Gann was Vice President Charles Curtis's sister. Curtis had lived with his sister and brother-in-law since his wife had died in 1924, and Dolly had been his recognized hostess during his senatorial career. Large, blond, and assertive, she campaigned expertly for her brother, speaking to women's groups in particular. Mrs. Gann was well known to Washington society and could be found at all manner of parties and occasions. She was recognized as "having an excellent knowledge of national politics and the questions of the day."[37] The war began when her brother, Charles Curtis, became vice president.

In Washington society, protocol matters. "Protocol is the rule book by which international relations are conducted," asserted the chief of protocol during the Truman administration. One purpose of rules of protocol is "to create an atmosphere of friendliness in which the business of diplomacy can be transacted." In Washington protocol, the vice president—who also presided over the Senate when necessary—and his wife ranked second behind the president and the First Lady. Third ranking was the chief justice of the Supreme Court and his wife, then the Speaker of the House of Representatives and his wife followed by the ambassadors. Trying to ascertain the protocol for their functions, the august Senate Ladies Luncheon Club pondered the ramifications of an unmarried vice president. In February 1929, the Senate Ladies decreed that "an official hostess" could be only "the wife of the official." Thus, they chose the wife of the president pro tem of the Senate to be president of their organization—making her the second-ranking woman in the United States—and not Dolly Gann.[38]

Their opinion did not trouble Mrs. Gann, who played a major role in the Hoovers' inaugural ball. MRS. GANN ACTS AS 'FIRST LADY,' proclaimed the *New York Times,* and noted that the ball "formally opened with the arrival of Vice President Curtis and Mrs. Gann." But on March 30, outgoing Secretary Frank Kellogg at the State Department seconded the Senate wives' decision, stating "that in State social functions Mrs. Edward Gann . . . is to be seated after the wives of Ambassadors."[39] Secretary Kellogg made the clarification in response to Curtis's notification to the State Department that his sister would be his "official hostess." The vice president's response was swift and furious. He swore he would not accept Kellogg's pronouncement and made a formal and public statement requesting a reversal of the decision—the first vice president ever to do so.

The newspaper coverage of this protocol question was serious and thorough. Page one of the *New York Times* gave the full text of Curtis's disputation. Trying to demystify the trouble, the *Times* explained that since the president did not accept dinner invitations to private homes, the vice president was the nation's chief "diner out." If Kellogg's ruling were to remain intact, it would mean that Helen Taft, wife of the chief justice, and Alice Longworth, wife of the Speaker of the House, would both outrank Dolly Gann, as would the wives of the ambassadors.[40]

After Kellogg's departure, Henry Stimson, the new secretary of state, inherited the problem. He responded with dogged, official silence while Washington hosts and hostesses clamored for an answer. Stimson's footdragging obstructed the whole social season. Nothing daunted, the British chimed in with their own tradition, where their Speaker of the House of Commons had his sister as his official hostess. She sat "at the head of the table in his household, but has no official precedence outside." In the meantime, the diplomatic corps spent two full hours considering the controversy. No fools they, the diplomats said they would rely on the wisdom of the "Ladies of the Senate," who had "refused to accept Mrs. Gann as ranking with the wife of the Vice President."[41]

While Stimson stalled for time, opposition to the Kellogg decision multiplied. It became a mark of patriotism to support the vice president. Senator J. Thomas Heflin of Alabama proclaimed that he would fight on the vice president's behalf because, "It's decidedly against American principles to put Mrs. Gann off in a corner and make her step down for these foreigners." Senator Borah could not be drawn into the fray and refused to comment on Heflin's threat that the Senate should decide the whole matter. Opinions came from around the country. Philadelphians saw it as a matter of honor. Republican women there vowed that " 'no semblance of slight' to the vice president should go 'unrebuked before the world,' " and they chided Stimson for his "evasive position."[42]

Evasive or clever, Stimson ultimately decided not to decide. He said the State Department "would not rule on or arbitrate problems of official-social precedence." That sent the question right back to the dismayed diplomatic corps. A *New York Times* front-page article declared Dolly Gann a winner in the first round. And the next day's similarly placed story "scored a complete triumph" for Mrs. Gann when the dean of the diplomatic corps announced that she would be accorded the status Mr. Curtis requested "until we can obtain some definite ruling on this point from a constituted American authority." But this left a door open, and while some Washingtonians disliked the decision of the diplomatic corps—especially Washington's Old Guard—others didn't see any real loophole as there was no such "authority." So, as the spring social season began, Dolly Gann ranked second, in the place of the vice president's wife, a custom established in practice by an April 11, 1929, dinner given by the Chilean ambassador.[43]

Thanks to Alice, the calm did not last. GANN SOCIAL WAR REOPENS IN CAPITAL: ALICE ROOSEVELT LONGWORTH IS CREDITED WITH INITIATING NEW STAGE, read the headlines in early May. The Longworths refused to attend a dinner given by Agnes and Eugene Meyer, former chair of the Federal Farm Loan Bureau, because Dolly Gann was to be seated ahead of Alice. Mrs. Meyer had hoped to sidestep the controversy by having several round tables with a ranking host or hostess at each. Unfortunately for her, "Mrs. Meyer reckoned without Mrs. Longworth. The daughter of the late Theodore Roosevelt is undoubtedly the most popular lady in Washington. She not only dictates many of the political whims of 'Bill' Borah and other Senators, but when she takes the trouble she sets social precedent. Most of the time she is too busy either with politics or Paulina, but on this occasion Mrs. Gann apparently aroused her social ire."[44]

Editorial writers were quick to comment: "Precedents in official society have never meant anything to her. Details of etiquette which she... found boring she rarely troubled to observe....A witty and forceful commentator on public affairs, Mrs. Longworth has for years made her own social laws; to challenge her freedom was to risk being barred from her brilliant salon.... But before she is through with her campaign logic will have been forgotten in the play of tactics and the fire of repartee." Alice apparently suggested that during her father's administration she had inspired "Alice blue," but the contemporary administrative color seemed to be "Gann green."[45]

But both women always insisted that there was no "battle." Alice acknowledged that Nick cared about precedent, but she attributed their refusal to attend the Meyers' party to his fondness for alcohol. At lunch with Agnes Meyer the day before the Longworths were to dine at their house, Alice learned that their hosts had decided to seat Lady Isabella Howard, the British ambassador's wife, on Eugene Meyer's right, and Dolly Gann in the place of honor on his left. Alice told Agnes, "Ha, ha; you will be in trouble with Nick. I will tell him this thing, you see." Alice couldn't resist, as she said, "making trouble," which she wryly admitted later rebounded on her, because Nick said, "Don't want to go to dinner with Eugene anyway. Comes to my house and he drinks. I go to his house and I don't get a drink. He's obeying the law, and I'm disobeying the law, but he takes advantage of my disobeying the law and has plenty of drinks with us. I will not go to his house if he's going to put Dolly Gann ahead of the wife of the British ambassador." Alice phoned Agnes Meyer to say, "Nick won't go, but we all laughed about it. And we said he's using [the protocol issue] as an excuse...to avoid going to a dry dinner and having to drink heavily at home before and when he gets home afterwards." Alice insisted "it was a wet and dry row, really...."[46]

The following day, Alice recounted, Nick hosted a luncheon in the Speaker's dining room and "went around telling everyone how smart he was to get out of a dry dinner with his dear friend Eugene. They were all friendly about it. There was no bad feeling. But from then on they decided to pin it on Dolly Gann and myself." But, as she concluded, "Obviously, there never was any row; any one who knew me was aware that rank and conventionality were things I always fled from and shirked. I could not very well tell the true story—that Nick had seized a straw to avoid a dry dinner...." And when Alice and Dolly walked into the Senate gallery together, and sat in the same row—the vice presidential row—on May 14, they caused all heads to turn away from the speech on farm relief. The two women laughed and talked together, enjoying the disbelief etched in the faces around them.[47]

Yet, there are reasons to believe that Alice herself felt strongly that the sister of the vice president should not occupy the position of "second lady." Alice was untraditional. She did break rules. As she grew older, she became more conservative in some ways, and Nick certainly placed great importance on the traditions of his House—which would include the social rank of the wife of the Speaker. By fighting for the appropriate rank she would be "standing up for the dignities of the Speaker's office." And while her heart may have been in the Senate with the Lion of Idaho, outwardly she had a duty to support the House. The *New York Times* stated that "when she appears at any official function she is no more likely now [as wife of the Speaker] to allow herself to be outranked by those over whom she considers she has precedence than previously she would have dreamed of attempting to precede those who officially outranked her." Alice understood politics and respected the code, and while she later protested to an interviewer, "It had nothing to do with me," she amended her statement by noting, "Well I would come into it, you see because the wife of the speaker should go ahead of her...."[48]

It is also the case that Alice was not overly fond of the vice president. Charles Curtis cheated at poker. "We all said, 'Well we just don't come in when Charlie deals,'" Alice remarked once to an interviewer. "And Charlie would say to me 'Stay in, stay in,' when I said I was going to drop out, and then he would give me an ace to make me happy." To make matters worse, Curtis had a reputation as a political lightweight. One journalist at that time described him as "mediocre—a nice, genial, little fellow, but basically a run-of-the-mine Kansas politician."[49]

Alice did not change her ways when Nick became Speaker of the House. Averse to making official calls, a "penalty" of public life, as she called it, she refused to adhere to that social tradition. "He and I," Alice wrote, "had long before decided that I was more a liability than an asset to him along those lines, that if the wives of his fellow politicians were going to be affronted by my inactivity in assuming 'social obligations' he would have to make the best of it. He did not think, any more than I did, that a successful political career depended on such perfunctory and conventional activities."[50]

Dolly Gann gave an interview to the *New York Times* in July and suggested that as the vice president is a symbol of the nation, "it is his duty to see that both he and his official hostess are accorded 'every respect that the symbol of our government should receive from all right-minded people.' " Ultimately, Dolly Gann did gain her position as Washington's "second lady." Whether or not the January 1930 sacking of James C. Dunn, the chief of the protocol division at the State Department, was connected is not clear. The newspapers continued to report any sightings of Alice and Dolly Gann together. Their acquaintance lent credence to Alice's assertion that the Longworth-Gann feud was really about Nick's impatience with the Meyers' dry dinners. Dolly Gann went out of her way to pay tribute to Alice in her autobiography, writing that she admired Alice's independence, her ability to do "what she chooses and cares not a snap of her finger what anybody thinks of her." They were, after all, both Republican women working for GOP goals. Dolly thought that no one topped Alice for charm, erudition, or interesting experiences. "A law unto herself," she called Alice—apparently without irony—and thought she understood "how a woman of Alice's brilliancy might find it more satisfying to ignore less scintillating humans than to endure them."[51]

Profoundly absorbing at the time, the protocol episode passed into history and became a cultural reference point. Assistant Secretary of the Treasury Seymour Lowman had the best word on the affair. At a White House reception one night, President and Mrs. Hoover descended the stairs, followed by Vice President Curtis and his sister, then Secretary of State and Mrs. Stimson. At the bottom of the stairs, Mrs. Stimson inadvertently stepped on and ripped Mrs. Gann's train, causing Lowman's irreverent quip: "Now at last we will see where Dolly Gann sits."[52]

One story dated the end of the Alice Longworth–Dolly Gann feud to July 1950—twenty years later—at a political gathering at the home of

Peter and Ruth "Bazy" McCormick Miller. Bazy, the daughter of Ruth Hanna McCormick, was the editor of the *Washington Times-Herald*. Senator George W. Malone of Nevada brought Alice and Dolly to the front, and intoned, we "recognize no hostilities today, either of a political or private nature," at which time Alice and Dolly shook on it.[53]

Chapter 17

"An Irresistible Magnet"

B<small>Y</small> 1930, N<small>ICK AND</small> A<small>LICE</small> occupied the center of Washington society, which, in that federal city, was generally synonymous with the political. "Society, in truth, came to them," the *New York Times* marveled, "the pick of anybody's party being likely to desert early and in considerable numbers to join any group assembled, however informally, at the Longworth home, or got up on the spur of the moment by Mrs. Longworth anywhere else." When British novelist Rebecca West sojourned in Washington in 1935, she noticed, "The city is dominated by the last good thing said by Alice Longworth...."[1]

Alice's significance for national governance resided in her ability to bridge the social and political. Henry James called the nation's capital " 'the City of Conversation,' " writing that "Washington presented two faces, 'the public and official' " and the inhabitants of the city spent their time talking, mostly about "Washington—almost nothing else." Even Nick's sister Clara, never fond of Alice, admitted that the Longworths' home "was always a center where personal friends and men of all parties met and mingled as they did nowhere else. Alice's vivid conversational talent made the dinner parties particularly memorable." The *Washington Times* asserted that "every man prominent in the politics of the last quarter century passed through the Longworth drawing rooms, irrespective of party. Nick's popularity and Alice's wit and charm combined to form an irresistible magnet."[2] A permanent fixture in Washington by then, Alice chose how to use her time, unconstrained—as much as she ever would be—by social expectations.

Nineteen thirty gave Alice an enormous political opportunity: Ruth Hanna McCormick was making a race for the U.S. Senate. Her delegate-at-large position was likely to be a victim of Illinois redistricting, and by May 1929, she had made up her mind to try for the Senate seat. It wasn't until September 22—a month and a week before the stock market crash—that Ruth formally announced. Alice and Bill were happy to have the publicity she brought to their continued noninterventionism as she campaigned against U.S. involvement in the League of Nations' Permanent Court of International Justice. All three saw it as a "back door" entrance to the League. The fact that such a position came from the first woman to make a "creditable attempt" at the Senate was all to the good. In April, Alice was with Ruth as Illinoisans cast their ballots in the primary. The grand tension of the vote counting made Alice shout, "Oh, I just can't stand it!" when an early prediction had Ruth winning by 175,000 votes.[3] Her victory was attributed to her World Court stance, though Ruth herself credited the support of female voters and the clean campaign she waged. Nick celebrated Ruth's nomination by handing her his gavel and inviting her to sit in his Speaker's chair. Next came the hard work of winning the general election.

By then, Cissy Patterson had become coeditor of Randolph Hearst's *Washington Herald*. Making her own kind of mischief, Cissy used her new platform to assail Alice. Bested in the competitions for Nick and for Bill, Cissy attacked with a page-one editorial. The opening salvo was entitled "Interesting But Not True":

Reports that Mrs. Alice Roosevelt Longworth will manage the Senate campaign of Mrs. Ruth Hanna McCormick are interesting, but not true.

Mrs. McCormick takes no advice, political or otherwise, from Mrs. Longworth.

Mrs. Longworth could not possibly manage anyone's campaign being too lofty to speak to newsmen and too aristocratic for public speaking.

Mrs. Longworth gives no interviews to the press.

Mrs. Longworth cannot utter in public.

Her assistance, therefore, will evolve itself as usual into posing for photographs.[4]

Alice called it "very amusing," but the rumor mills erupted, boosting sales of Cissy's paper considerably. That may be why she published a second editorial on the same topic entitled "Will She? Can She?"

Some weeks ago, I wrote that Alice Longworth had no real gifts to bring to Ruth Hanna McCormick's campaign. Ruth McCormick is Alice Longworth's close friend.

I was in error. I spoke hastily.

Senator Borah, another *close* friend of Alice Longworth, has said that if Ruth McCormick is elected, he will vote to unseat her because of her excessive campaign expenditures. Mrs. Longworth may now present her real gifts. She may use her political influence, of which the country has for so long heard so much. She may soften this decision of the frugal gentleman from Idaho.

But it is for Alice to come now bearing her offerings. Will she? Can she?[5]

This second editorial was brazen. Cissy, in the aftermath of her marital troubles, had published a novel in 1926 that her grandniece called "a deliberately bitchy book."[6] *Glass Houses* told the barely camouflaged story of Cissy's unrequited love for Bill Borah, and Alice's competition in the lists. The novel received good reviews, but her newspaper columns reached many more readers. Linking Alice and Bill so publicly and suggesting that Alice's only useful political service to her best friend was to influence Bill kindled more gossip. Cissy calculated none of it to assist the three principals, but to assuage her pain and sell her paper. It cost her something she really regretted, however: Nick's friendship. She wrote him a lengthy letter explaining, without details, that Alice had been "treacherous and vicious about me behind my back" and had struck first in the off-again, on-again relationship between them. Cissy blamed her column on the 102-degree weather, her loneliness, and the momentary loss of her "newspaper sense" that caused her not to see "that the story would burst like a bomb around the world." She told Nick that had she known, she might have hesitated—not with regard to Alice ("I haven't any"), but "on your account." Cissy told him sadly that she knew he'd have to stick by his wife and regretted that she had "lost your friendship." "But remember, my dear," she closed, "that if ever I can help you or your friends, or do anything for you, I'll be right there. You know that."[7]

Ruth was, as Cissy suggested, in the midst of tough times. Ruth's campaign expenditures were being publicly scrutinized by the Senate Campaign Fund Investigating Committee headed by Senator Gerald P. Nye. The impetus for this may have been nothing more than one senator's crusade to keep the Senate free of women. Nye wasn't the only man anxious to keep women out of the "most exclusive club," though. Hiram Johnson, their old friend from the League days, opined to his son that he had "mixed emotions" about how Ruth's opponent in the primary "had been outsmarted by a woman...." Johnson thought the "thorough breakdown and demoralization [of the Senate] will come with the admission of the other sex." He found women politicians in general lacking in "patriotism, morality, altruism, and idealism." Alice could not help Ruth with the vindictive Nye Committee, which instigated a smear campaign that included a spy in her closet, wiretaps on her telephone line, and a break-in at her offices.[8] After surviving all that, Ruth—and the rest of the country—turned to the election in the fall.

Bill left Washington in September to rustle up Idaho votes, writing to Alice sometimes twice a day, enclosing clippings about their political friends and enemies. His campaign rolled along in its usual fashion. On the way west in early September, he was "holding levees on the train all day, everybody seems interested to get a close up. I could get along with less of it." Alice was traveling that fall—to Rhode Island and then to Cincinnati to enroll "Princess Paulina," as one newspaper called her, in a private school. Alice confessed she was "all of a twitter watching her learn to read." Between receptions and an unsuccessful attempt at a dude ranch vacation, the restless Borah confessed, "I wish I could have had a talk with you about politics. I should like to hear you 'illuminate' on some of the things now happening." He was feeling "so blue" that he was "afraid of" himself, while cogitating on the election in Germany: it "may mean much. Germany may present us some morning with a repudiated treaty."[9] Borah's prescience about the 1930 German election, which gave an alarming percentage of votes to Adolph Hitler's National Socialist German Workers Party, and his suspicion that Germany might repudiate the Versailles treaty, would prove to be true in three short years.

En route to yet another small campaign stop, Bill poured out his frustration with the platform adopted by eastern Republicans. "Is there no clear cut courage left?" he cried. "They sincerely do not stand up against the thirsty cry of the wets and dare not face the evils of repeal." He lamented again in early October: "Wish I had remained on the farm as father willed me to do." Part of his gloom came from his sympathy for his constituents, caught in the Great Depression. Yet he could still see humor—if a bit grim—around him. "Did you notice Coolidge in one of his essays suggest that the League of Nations take a hand in settling Brazil's <u>internal</u> war? My God, I think ours is the greatest gov. on earth, having survived certain presidents."[10]

Alice and Bill avidly followed Ruth's election fight in Illinois, where she was tangled up in the Prohibition quandary. The *St. Louis Post-Dispatch* poked fun at her dilemma: "And Ruth said to the dry voter and to the wet voter in Illinois, 'Entreat me not to leave either of thee or to return from following after either of thee: for howsoever thou believest, I will believe; and where thou markest thy ballots, there would I have my name; thy votes shall be my votes and thy office my office. When thou wouldst abstain or drink, then would I have thee do the same; the god of politicians help me if aught but death part thee and me.' " Ruth was a dry. Her opponent was a wet. Facing an Illinois referendum on the Eighteenth Amendment, Ruth promised to abide by the voters' wishes. This cost her support among the strong Prohibitionists, many of whom were women and her core of supporters.[11]

But it wasn't the World Court or Prohibition that counted most for

American voters in 1930; it was the Great Depression. Every week more banks closed, more people lost their jobs, homes, and farms, all while cheerful but hollow bulletins issued from the Hoover White House. The day before the election, Bill wrote to Alice, "I know how you are scanning the political horizon; bad year to bet." He was right. The Democrats routed the Republicans in 1930, and Ruth's attempt at the U.S. Senate failed. Bill loyally blamed the poor organization of the Illinois GOP. If she still "wants to do the big thing she still has a great chance to do so," he penned to Alice.[12] But he could afford to be generous—as he was only one of a handful of Republicans returned to office that Democratic fall. Nick was also re-elected, but it was clear he would lose his position as Speaker. Overall, eight new Democratic senators and fifty-one new representatives took their seats in Congress in 1930. Both Houses were almost exactly divided between the parties.

In the wake of the disaster, Alice mused to her sister, "What an election! I thought we'd have the House by 8 or 10—I never believed the reports from the headquarters that we'd have at least 25—or that there would be a real democratic sweep, giving it to them by 30 or more. We'd said piously all along, 'if there isn't an undercurrent.' There was one, but not a Simon-pure democratic one. So behold us, probably not sure of how long the House, or Senate, will organize until the next Congress meets! Isn't it fantastic, but it will be all kinds of fun—for anyone with a taste of chaos." Bill Borah's funk continued unabated. After the campaign, he stayed a week in Idaho giving speeches on foreign policy subjects. "I have literally," he complained, "never been so torn and driven. I am leaving now with a half dozen demands behind but I am more than weary, worse than the campaign." Alice sent him a long, typed discursive letter on the election, and some of Paulina's first attempts at writing, which Borah teased "looked better" than Alice's own handwriting.[13]

Unlike Borah, who, though prone to depression, was physically vigorous and politically powerful, the other man in Alice's life was in decline. Nick was losing his speakership. The end of the Seventy-first Congress had been a sentimental affair. Nick set the tone by playing reflective tunes on the piano in the House chamber. The representatives who lingered last sang "Carry Me Back to Old Virginny" in mournful harmony. Nick had made his good-bye earlier, saying, "Perhaps this is the last time I will address you from this rostrum.... If I am to retire from this office, I do so with profound gratitude to my colleagues ... for the esteem and confidence you have had in me." One of Nick's staff members, Lucile McArthur, cried as she watched the overwhelming display of fondness for Speaker Longworth on the part of his whooping and applauding colleagues. Members on both sides of the aisle gave Nick a standing ovation, and she remembered how Nick grew "redder and redder with pleasure and gratification."[14]

A group of people closest to Nick gathered for a private luncheon after adjournment. According to Nick's secretary, Alice, "the human dynamo," was present. "She was all over the place all the time; talking vivaciously to newspapermen who poked their heads in the door every once in a while and then oozed in to see what the party was about; to members who dropped in to say good-by to Nick ... and even to an occasional tourist who opened the door out of curiosity."[15]

But when the parties were over and the gavel banged down, Nick grew sad. He was suffering from a head cold he'd had for a fortnight and couldn't shake. Seeking congenial company, he made his fourth journey to Aiken, South Carolina, in as many years. He left Washington on March 30, 1931, to stay at the winter home of Laura and James F. Curtis. Though the Curtises had been described as "old and intimate friends" of Nick's, that was only half correct. *Laura* was his intimate friend. They shared, among other things, an ardor for music, high-stakes poker, and "wringing wet" parties.[16] At his mistress's home, weakened as he was by years of alcohol abuse, and worn out by the duties of the House, Nick's cold turned into pneumonia. The Curtises sent for Alice, who arrived on April 8—the first time she had been in Aiken since before her wedding. Alice allowed one of the attending physicians to release a confirmation of the pneumonia. When she heard, Cissy Patterson arranged for an oxygen tent to be flown to Aiken. President Hoover, also fretting about the health of his lieutenant, wrote that day to Alice, saying, "We share your anxieties and your confidence...."[17]

Confidence faded as Nick took a sudden turn for the worse. Ever mindful of the status of the Speaker, Alice kept the papers informed. The pneumonia overwhelmed Nick's worn body. He died that day, April 9, just before 11:00 a.m., attended—as it turned out—neither by wife, lover, nor, as he had desired, the transcendent measures of Beethoven's Seventh Symphony.[18]

Whatever mixture of grief or anger Alice was feeling, she turned not to her hosts for solace, but to her family. Kermit and Archie flew to be with her in South Carolina. Colonel Campbell Hodges, Hoover's military aide, was personally sent by the president to help. Once in Aiken, Hodges reported back that the widow had everything under control. Mildred Reeves, Nick's secretary, attested that in characteristic fashion, Alice had "retained her self possession and was actively directing arrangements for the burial."[19] Under Alice's direction, Reeves oversaw the competent staff that arranged the special train to take Nick's body back to Ohio. Speakers of the House were not entitled to lie in state; nor, since Nick was not a veteran, was he permitted to be buried in Arlington Cemetery.

Perhaps as a last sign of respect for Nick and the independent but loving life they had worked out, Alice invited Laura Curtis to accompany his body on the train to Rookwood, which she duly did. James Curtis did not go to Cincinnati nor was he one of the honorary pallbearers as the coffin was carried from his home to the train station for a brief memorial by the citizens of Aiken. Alice Dows, another of Nick's mistresses, also accompanied Nick's body to Ohio. She told Gore Vidal later that "we went in a private train, like *two* widows." Alice Dows had poured out her love, presumably for Nick, in reams of suggestive poetry. "Thy Gift" begins, "I love thee with no vow or ring / Without an outward sign; / Yet I am chained by everything / To keep me wholly thine." In 1927, she published her first volume, replete with poems such as "When He Comes": "Flutters of expectancy / Fill the room— / Cries my soul in secrecy, / 'Will he come?'" And when "he" does come, Dows concluded, "Then earth's transformed / Into heaven."[20] Alice had entered her marriage to Nick without bridesmaids, but she was flanked by black-gowned grieving women at his funeral. Joe Graydon also was there, one of the honorary pallbearers.

Meanwhile, in the Capitol the Speaker's gavel lay draped in black and surrounded by lilies. This was the idea of doorman Harry Parker, who had especially fond memories of Longworth. A special service was conducted at Washington Cathedral, broadcast simultaneously on nationwide radio. The sympathy telegrams began arriving that day too. Among the first was a brief one that Alice kept all her life. Signed W E AND MARY BORAH, it read, "Our deepest sympathy." Secretary of War Patrick Hurley and others broadcast their tributes to Nick on NBC Radio. President Hoover eulogized his fallen Speaker in a statement issued to the national press: "Mr. Longworth served his fellow countrymen in state and nation for over thirty-three years—nearly the whole of his adult life. In his service he contributed greatly to the welfare of the American people. His happy character, his sterling honesty, his courage in public questions, endeared him and held the respect not alone of his myriad of friends but of the country at large. His passing is a loss to the Nation." Hoover's personal telegram to Alice echoed the same themes, that Nick was "entitled" to the "honors which he bore so modestly and yet so worthily."[21]

The president and the First Lady led the list of notables who trekked sadly to the Midwest, past the flags Hoover had ordered to fly at half-mast. Their nine-car presidential train followed that of Vice President Curtis and the congressional delegation. Eleven members of the Senate and a representative from every state came to pay their respects. First among them was Cactus Jack Garner, there to mourn the man he called "my closest and best-loved friend."[22]

The Right Rev. Henry Wise Hobson conducted the ceremony at Cincinnati's Christ Episcopal Church. In the front pews with Alice were Roosevelt women (Edith, Ethel, Belle, and Grace); her sister-in-law Nan Wallingford; Mildred Reeves; the despondent Laura Curtis; and presumably Alice Dows. Archie and Kermit were pallbearers. Six-year-old Paulina remained at Rookwood with her nanny. Thousands of mourners lined the streets of Cincinnati as a two-mile-long funeral procession made its way through Eden Park—a gift to the city by the Longworths—out to Spring

Grove Cemetery, Cincinnati's most prestigious burial ground.[23] Rt. Rev. Henry Wise Hobson read the order for the burial of the dead as the flower-draped coffin was lowered into the ground on the sunny, blue-skied day.

Alice's "boon companion," brother Ted, was serving as governor general of Puerto Rico. He and his wife, Eleanor, were too far away to make the journey home. But the Roosevelt spirit came through clearly across the distance in their notes of sympathy. "What a wonderful time for Nick to go," Eleanor wrote characteristically, "at the height of his popularity...." Ted enthused, in an otherwise loving letter, "It is a tragedy but it might well have been worse." Perhaps he was thinking of their alcoholic uncle Elliott, who had died scandalously in the home of his mistress. Ted was glad that Kermit and Edith were with Alice. "Oddly enough," he mused, "I should think K. and Mother would be the most comfort [to you]." Like the rest of the family, Ted implored her to change her scenery and come visit with Paulina.[24]

Newspaper columns swelled with quotes from friends about Nick's leadership qualities, his sociability, his good humor, his steadfast conservatism, and his effects on the House. Nick reestablished the power of the Speaker and ruled just as firmly as Cannon, whom he had helped to unseat in 1910. Longworth engineered several important innovations. He allowed radio broadcasts of House debates—the quality of which had improved as a result of the better work ethic and collegial tone he established. Speaker Longworth, influenced no doubt by his friendship with Ruth Hanna McCormick, did away with the trivializing term of address used to call upon female representatives, "the gentle lady," and insisted that all members of the House use the more acceptable "gentlewoman," the mirror of "gentleman." Further, Nick provided a rest room for the three female legislators in the House, a welcome change that beat the Supreme Court's installation of a lavatory for women attorneys by more than half a century.[25]

Longworth streamlined the functioning of the House. His reforms made it more efficient than the Senate. The contradictions abounded: he was Speaker of the House but referred to as Nick; he enjoyed the grubby side of politics but saw true dignity in his calling; he loved Bach but could play "The Pants of Queen Lil"; he wore spats but his good friend was a

Texas roustabout. Nick used his even temper, his amiability, and his wide friendships to lead by persuasion. Contemporary commentators realized that "even when he was bludgeoning the House he was never disagreeable about it." A "genial czar" was Nick—and it is perhaps the highest praise to recall that his passing was mourned by Democrats and Republicans alike. Will Rogers wrote that he'd "been told many times by Democrats that [Nick] was the most able and popular man in Congress." Nick summed up his approach in 1928 by saying, "I know of no nobler profession than the profession of politics, and by politics I mean the holding of office for the benefit, not of one's self, but of the public. Of course as a career it does seem precarious. Real success appears very remote. Moreover, there can be no hope of large money returned. No honest man has ever grown rich in the profession of politics. But there is another recompense which, to my mind, is the greatest of them all. I can think of no satisfaction greater than the knowledge that one has served one's country honorably and well."[26]

Alice did not grieve in public. Though sad, she was not debilitated by Nick's death, as Ruth Hanna McCormick's absence from his funeral suggests. If Alice had truly needed Ruth, she would have been there. While Alice wasn't mourning overtly, Laura Curtis was. Nick's lady friend looked to Lou Hoover for sympathetic understanding, "I know you realize how unhappy I have been," she wrote to the First Lady. Alice knew, too. She and Laura developed a close friendship in the wake of Nick's death.[27]

Ohio faced the pressing question of filling Nick's term. Several politicians thought it was time Alice evolved from a behind-the-scenes politician to an elected one. Representative John C. Schafer of Wisconsin stated publicly that Alice was "eminently qualified. She long has been interested in public affairs and knows intimately the problems which face Congress and the inside of legislations...." He volunteered to campaign for her as "one of the best informed women in the country on politics and Congressional life."[28]

Ohio state senator Robert Taft felt only Alice could unite the two disparate factions in Cincinnati and actually get elected. Although Alice was "very reluctant," he believed he could persuade her. Taft told President Hoover that she would be "the strongest person" the GOP could snag, and "while she will not always be easy to handle...a strong personality like that who is regular would be far better than to run the risk of being defeated." A guaranteed Republican victory would be ideal, as Nick's death turned the House Democratic. The necessity for a stalwart Republican was critical, as the House stood at 216 Democrats, 215 Republicans, and 1 Farmer-Laborite. But Alice insisted she was too shy to campaign, and she did not want to be one of the women who, as she put it, used their husbands' coffins for a springboard. As a friend pointed out, Alice lacked the "faculty for suffering fools gladly, so essential in political life. Indeed, she did not possess the faculty for suffering them at all."[29] By December, the Republicans had lost the House, and Cactus Jack picked up the Speaker's gavel that Nick had laid down.

Nick provided for his family in his will, written nine months after Paulina's birth. He left his estate to Alice and made her his executrix. Original estimates placed his wealth at more than $16 million, which surely caused Alice to hope that the newspapers knew something she didn't. Nick, as one family member recalled, "had spent his money as though he owned the mint." His worth was eventually figured at $825,000 in personal property and $800,000 in real estate, mostly his share of Rookwood and the ever-dwindling surrounding lands. In December 1932, the Cincinnati probate court ordered Alice to pay a $25,919 inheritance tax—this after almost $200,000 went to pay Nick's debts.[30] Alice and Paulina were not left with a king's ransom, but then Nick said no honest man ever got rich in politics.

Alice did not linger at Rookwood. By the end of May, she had resumed life in Washington, where family visited in various configurations to check on her. Clara stayed with her into May, and the two reminisced with Lou Hoover at the White House. The First Lady had been especially considerate toward Alice during Nick's illness and death, and Alice truly appreciated her "rare and remarkable gift of sympathy." Ted and Eleanor left Puerto Rico to confer with President Hoover, stopping in to see Alice and Paulina. Of all her family, Ted understood the permutations of the Longworth marriage because brother and sister had been so close and so often together in the 1920s. "I know," Ted soothed, "just how hard it is for you under all the circumstances."[31]

America expected Alice to act the grieving widow—and in part, she was. She and Nick were longtime intimates and comfortable friends, and his death brought sorrow as well as release. Yet the routine of her days, the ebb and flow of her years, would have to be reconfigured. Their marriage had been so open for so long that Alice and Nick had come to an easy place. The baby brought them closer together. Nick really did love Paulina. If he had his suspicions about Borah, he adhered to the gentleman's code: he never cast aspersions; he never made insinuations. He stood up for his wife during the Dolly Gann flap and the Cissy Patterson newspaper editorials. The timbre of their conversations during the pregnancy is lost, but Nick's letters after the baby's birth included a resurgence in his use of their early-marriage nicknames. Jointly caring for the infant brought out a tenderness and a vulnerability that had not existed between them for years. After Nick's death, uppermost in Alice's mind was Paulina, and how much she would miss her father.

Alice, in the prime of life, was pragmatic, self-absorbed, and apparently happy without a husband. But her daughter was turning out to be as shy as her mother, yet without the gumption to push past it. A Cincinnati native, Angela Meeske, met Paulina at a debutante party and found her "a very *receding* person. . . . She was just—there. She never contributed very much." A close friend of the family sighed that "Alice doted on Paulina. But what I always thought was key was that she never let Paulina finish a sentence. She would feed her a line. Wanted her to learn repartee. . . . The pressure made her stammer."[32] Of course, finishing a sentence for a child who stutters is a counterproductive but natural impulse. Today, a parent might seek out a therapist for a child whose father had died when she was six and who later developed a stutter and a painful shyness. But at the time, therapy was not a common option.

Alice's role models for motherhood were Edith and Bye. Had Alice stayed with her outgoing and charismatic aunt rather than growing up with her introverted stepmother, she may have been a different parent to Paulina. Alice had the ideal of Bye—warm, engaged, and conspiratorial—but the reality of Edith. Bye could not give her much childrearing advice, because she died not long after Nick. In August 1931, Bye succumbed to the multiple physical troubles that assailed her. The blow was great to Alice. Bye's "blue-eyed darling," Alice was present at Bye's simple funeral service, along with brothers Kermit and Archie. Auntie Corinne was there with her son. Eleanor Roosevelt and her mother-in-law Sara Delano Roosevelt were also among the mourners.[33]

As the cherry trees blossomed in Washington a year later, Alice's dear friend Ruth Hanna McCormick married Representative Albert Gallatin Simms. Simms was a banker and a rancher and a former U.S. congressman from New Mexico. The wedding took place in Colorado Springs, but Alice did not attend, perhaps because she had rather a different take on Simms than did Ruth: "Marry Albert Simms!" Alice was dumbfounded. "Sleep with him—one thing. But never marry him—how could she have done it!"[34] Ruth moved into her new husband's home in Albuquerque, which was beyond the political pale. Between the Simmses' cattle business, and her involvement in local political and civic affairs, Ruth—and her advice—seemed far away.

Yet Alice needed her. Ruth had been described as a woman who "always had a solution for every problem," and she had once faced Alice's terrifying problem: a kidnap threat. In late March 1932, guards surrounded Alice's home to protect the seven-year-old Paulina.[35] She had received two different notes, two weeks apart, directing her to deliver fifteen hundred dollars or the child would be taken. The police believed the letters were inspired by the tragic kidnapping of Charles and Anne Morrow Lindbergh's son. The heartbreaking disappearance of the Lindbergh baby on March 1, 1932, was sensational news across the globe. Front-page updates appeared daily on the too-slim body of knowledge officials were compiling on the captors. Rumors circulated about a kidnapping ring eying high-profile children, including Alice's daughter.

The first note Alice received commanded her to take a taxi to a specific place in the country, then drive eighteen miles an hour to a spot where a signal would be given for her to place the money one foot from the edge of the road. Alice sent a go-between, and although they followed the directions, there was no signal and no one picked up the cash. Alice asked that the guards be removed from her home, and she and Paulina left for New

York. Two days later, guards were posted at Ruth's sister's home to protect her six-year-old niece.[36] Eventually, the scares passed, and life returned to normal despite the unanswered questions about the whole ordeal.

Memories crowded Alice's spring, as the House of Representatives paid tribute to its late Speaker and to all members of Congress who had died during the previous year. Alice was present on May 25, for the first time since the closing day when Nick brought down the gavel. She listened as Burton L. French, from Borah's state, eulogized Nick as a "man of ability," "a man of strength," a man who "commanded the attention of his colleagues." On the one-year anniversary of Nick's death, the House adjourned in remembrance. As a mark of their love for him, friends created the Nicholas Longworth Foundation of the Music Division of the Library of Congress. Many donors remained anonymous, which may mean that "Nick's girls" wanted to remember the evenings spent together with Nick serenading guests on his violin.[37]

His widow carried on. She continued to be involved in politics and reportedly had "forty lawmakers" to her home as an audience for the German ambassador. Her name appeared with regularity in the newspaper columns. Alice watched Bill's press coverage wax in the months leading up to the 1932 political season. Their correspondence continued, festooned still with "Hellos." *Collier's* magazine proclaimed Borah "Idaho's gift to America," a "legend," "something of a Paul Bunyan." To interviewer Beverly Smith of the *American Magazine,* Borah castigated critics who called him inconsistent and destructive. In spite of being "in an extreme minority," Borah countered, laying out his accomplishments for voters, "I have been able to help with work which I think is unquestionably constructive: The fight for the eight-hour day. The creation of the Department of Labor. The creation of the Children's Bureau. The amendment providing for the election of senators by popular vote. My resolution calling for a disarmament conference which resulted in the naval disarmament treaty. My resolution calling for an economic conference which led to the Dawes Plan. My resolution, as early as 1923, calling for the outlawry of war." Besides, Borah told Smith, "constructive and destructive" mean different things to different people. "Blocking the entry of the United States into the League may be called destructive. To my mind it was one of the most constructive victories in our history." And as for his having blocked anti–child labor and woman's suffrage bills, Borah reiterated that these were matters best left to the states—but that he had "always favored" such legislation.[38]

The Democratic Party caused Alice distress. That year brought the alarming possibility of Alice's feather-duster cousin attaining the Oval Office. Alice used all the weapons at her disposal—news media, the radio, dinner parties—to defeat FDR and reelect Hoover. Although she liked Franklin personally, she loathed his politics, especially his foreign policy. She believed that she "really could have had a lot of fun with Franklin if only the damned old presidency hadn't come between us." His ascension was an affront to family honor, dating back to the bad blood created when Franklin ran for vice president and Ted jeered that he didn't "wear the brand of our family." Alice thought Franklin should have snapped back, " 'I wear no man's brand, not even the brand of my cousin to whom I was devoted, for whom I once voted.' Instead of that, he took it seriously and was frightfully cross about it. It hurt, you see." In 1924, Eleanor had heated up the trouble with her steaming teakettle giving the false but unforgettable impression that Ted had participated in the Teapot Dome scandal. "It was a pretty base thing for her to do," Alice felt, that "not unnaturally continued the bad feeling." But she admitted that her branch of the family "behaved terribly. There we were—*the* Roosevelts—hubris up to the eyebrows, *beyond* the eyebrows, and then who should come sailing down the river but Nemesis in the person of Franklin."[39]

The thought of FDR in the White House so appalled Alice that she served on the board of directors of the women's division of the GOP in 1932. Lou Henry Hoover asked her to work in other ways, including on an advisory panel that boasted notable women such as Ruth Hanna McCormick Simms, tennis star Helen Wills Moody, three former First Ladies, and several college presidents.[40] Alice's friendship with the educated and multitalented First Lady had reached the point where the latter was sending floral remembrances of Paulina's birthday and presents for Christmas. Many of the leading Republican women were friends. Dolly Gann served as president of the Republican Women's League in 1932 and spent a cold January on a campaign speaking tour for Hoover. Her task was to defend him against charges that he had caused the economic crisis. Ruth was concentrating on her new marriage, but found a breathtaking two hundred thousand dollars to donate to Hoover's cause.[41]

Beginning on June 14, 1932, the Republicans gathered in Chicago—Alice's favorite convention city—in order to choose their presidential nominee. From her base at the Blackstone Hotel she was in her element. "Look, there's Alice," people called as she made the rounds of the Coliseum floor, assessing support for vice presidential hopefuls. Newspapers noted that Alice was the only dignitary sitting in reserved boxes "who dared leave the enclosure of the sacred elite and walk about with democracy."[42]

The prohibition amendment was a topic of great interest, as the rumor that the Democratic platform would commit to repeal made Republicans scramble for a middle ground. From the NBC studio Alice listened in to the radio debate between her journalist friend William Allen White and Columbia University president Nicholas Murray Butler on June 14. At the Republican convention headquarters, the resolutions committee was busy looking for the path congenial to the greatest number of voters.[43] Bill Borah did not tread it. The appellation Enigma stuck to Borah, a bundle of contradictions. "Whether I am a Republican or not... is an issue between myself and my constituents," he blustered. Public sentiments like that helped to seal his fate. The Republican Party passed him by in 1932—again. Herbert Hoover and Charlie Curtis were renominated without fuss on a platform that opposed direct handouts to counter the effects of the Depression, and put its faith in the tariff, federal belt tightening, and voluntary efforts to alleviate local financial distress.

Later that month, Alice returned to her Blackstone suite for the Democratic national convention. Because of her interest in conservationism, delegate Dudley Field Malone suggested that Alice should be appointed secretary of the interior, as flattering as it was unlikely. She found much to interest her, especially the moment when William Gibbs McAdoo released the California and Texas votes, putting Franklin Roosevelt over the top. Cactus Jack Garner won the second-place spot on the ticket. Alice and former New York governor Al Smith—who lost the presidential nomination to Roosevelt—shared a bitter, two-hour discussion about the outcome.[44]

The platform committed Democrats to the repeal of Prohibition, in a charge led—not surprisingly—by Garner. It also called for federal relief programs, help for farmers, an old-age pension, and a constricted tariff. But Democrats pledged themselves to more conservative measures: a balanced budget, "sound currency," "removal of government from all fields of private enterprise," and, like the Republicans, more federal budget cuts. FDR flew to Chicago to accept the nomination from convention delegates personally. He bucked the tradition that kept the nominees away to prove that, despite his polio, he was physically able to do the job. He walked laboriously but proudly to the podium on the arm of his son and promised all Americans "a new deal."[45]

After the Chicago hoopla was over, the Hoovers hosted a garden party for Republican leaders, prefatory to the official notification that Hoover had the GOP's backing. The First Lady invited the "real" Roosevelts to the White House garden party. Edith, Alice, and Ethel were the "center of interest." Alice, dressed in black and white—symbolic of the political differences between the two branches of the family—and Ethel held their own informal reception with the Marine Band for accompaniment. In the Blue Room, Edith stood supportively beside the presidential couple but wouldn't give a statement: "I haven't talked for the press, not in seventy-one years, and it's too late to begin now," she said mildly.[46]

The three Roosevelt women were near to President Hoover when he gave his acceptance speech that night in Constitution Hall. Edith sat on the platform, holding a bouquet of roses. Alice and Ethel sat in a box to her right. The speech opened the campaign season, and Alice threw herself into it. She joined Edith, Grace Coolidge, Helen Taft, Carrie Chapman Catt, and other notable women in signing an appeal to female voters, urging them to cast their ballots for Hoover in 1932. Alice published an article, "Some Reminiscences," in the widely read *Ladies' Home Journal*, explaining how her aid for Hoover did not come at the expense of "any personal feeling" against her fifth cousin FDR.[47]

Alice and the First Lady toured the Midwest, heading up parades in Indianapolis, where Alice was slated to speak, sharing platforms with state and local Republican leaders, catching bouquets, waving from the backs of trains, and greeting voters. "I'm glad to see my fellow buckeyes," Alice told an excited crowd in Cincinnati. In Columbus, she made a longer speech—thirty-one words. She explained that she had gotten "so carried away with the . . . spirit of the meeting that I just had to talk."[48]

That was a warm-up for her first real political speech, broadcast over national radio and given in Cincinnati. The importance of the battle was obvious, and family honor was at stake as well.[49] Alice's fear of speaking in public was legendary, yet she stood close to the microphone and let her cousin have it: "It seems to me that, regardless of the result, when we look back on this campaign, two things will stand out. The first of these is the extra-ordinary extent to which the Democratic party has based its fight upon the discontent of the people, bred of the world-wide depression. The calculated effort to capitalize on this condition without anything remotely resembling a sound plan for its relief, strikes me as an unusually ignoble policy for a great party and one of which its more high-minded members must, in their more candid moments, be completely ashamed." She found it particularly gruesome that Democratic propaganda suggested Hoover created and then prolonged the Great Depression, and stated that such efforts take "first rank among examples of conscious and unscrupulous partisan dishonesty." She charged that the record in the Democratic-controlled House was so bad that even they wouldn't talk about it:

> On the contrary, it muzzles those who were largely responsible for that record, tries to forget that the record was made, and its spokesmen denounce Mr. Hoover as preaching the doctrine of fear when he points out in detail what would have happened to the country had the Democratic proposals prevailed.

Why should we not shudder at the idea of putting the Democratic party in complete control of the government in these critical times? I hope those who are listening to me will let their memories go back to the last session of Congress. The Democrats in the Senate, with no program of their own, had to support Mr. Hoover's reconstruction recommendations, which they now denounce. In the House the Democrats scuttled their own program in a way that alarmed and appalled their own leaders, in and out of Congress. If not thwarted by the President's vetoes, they would have plunged us into the chaos of national insolvency. When you consider this record, the promises and pledges that they now make with such prodigal abandon for campaign purposes, seem fantastic and absurd.

Her ringing conclusion was a small-*d* democratic one, suggesting that voters should not be misled by their financial woes or the glamour of Franklin Roosevelt. "I do not believe in talking down to the voters. That is precisely what the Democrats do believe in doing. They belittle the intelligence of the average citizen, and I, as an average citizen, resent it. There is no more impressive sight than a great free people flocking to the polls. This year we face a test. Are we truly free; free from prejudice, from resentment, from blind bitterness, free within ourselves to cast our vote with patriotism, with intelligence, with faith? If we are we will vote for Herbert Hoover."[50]

Edith applauded. The two saw eye to eye on this topic. "I suddenly thought today," Edith wrote to Belle Hagner, "what Franklin D. stood for. It is not Delano but Depression." Energized by her behind-the-scenes battles against FDR's presidential bid, septuagenarian Edith became the honorary chair of the F. Trubee Davison for Governor Women's Republican Club in New York. Ethel agreed to serve as the active chair of the committee. Edith gave a Hoover campaign speech in Madison Square Garden. As she complained to a friend, "These are trying times for us, and the confusion of names does not help. Continually letters [arrive] congratulating me on my distinguished son the Democratic nominee. His line parted six generations ago from my husband's." Alice coped with the same confusion, receiving letters about "her brother's nomination to the presidency."[51]

The Oyster Bay Roosevelts were disappointed in 1932. The Great Depression had ravaged Americans for nearly three years, and voters blamed the party in power. Anxious for change, they voted overwhelmingly for Franklin Roosevelt and the Democrats. Ted, who had been appointed governor-general of the Philippines in January 1932, took to telling those who asked about his relationship with the new president that he was FDR's "fifth cousin, about to be removed." Alice said often that she "wasn't so much for Hoover, than against Franklin, in a *nasty* way."[52]

Chapter 18

"The Washington Dictatorship"

IN JANUARY 1933, Alice Longworth had lunch with British diplomat Harold Nicolson. His subsequent description captured the essence of the mature, widowed Alice—in her prime and at her fighting best—nearly the age of fifty: "My word, how I like that woman!" he wrote to his wife, Vita Sackville-West. "There is a sense of freedom in her plus a sense of background. That, I feel, is what is missing in this country. Nobody seems to have anything behind their front. . . . But Alice Longworth has a world position, and it has left her simple and assured and human. It was a pleasant luncheon: you know, the sort of luncheon where one feels mentally comfortable and warm."[1]

About this time Alice's relative Joseph Alsop arrived in Washington. Joe was a sportswriter who moved on to news and became a syndicated columnist for the *New York Herald Tribune*. A pro–New Deal Republican, he amused Alice, and he regularly lunched at the F Street Club with her and the "then-famous, extremely conservative, and sharp-tongued" *Baltimore Sun* columnist Frank Kent, whom Alsop called "Mrs. L's admirer." "The object of these lunches," Alsop recalled, "was the destruction of political characters and political pretenses." Alice's impatience with pomposity was legendary, and government service, especially elected service, seemed to draw pretension like no other career.[2]

From Alsop's memoirs, a fuller picture of Alice in the 1930s emerges. Joe, nearly thirty years younger than Alice, described her as "very beautiful in a fine-boned way." He found her courageous, "witty, intelligent, and tough minded, [with] a mortal horror of anything or anyone with the least savor of gush or sentimentality, earnest dullness or overly ostentatious virtue. Such persons she enjoyed shocking, sometimes profoundly, as she had done to Eleanor Roosevelt since they were children together."Alsop, like so many others, enjoyed but had a hard time defining Alice's distinctive wit: "No one I have ever known had a wit like hers. It depended on extreme precision of language, combined with the wildest fancy which produced the most astonishing combinations. When [utilities executive and attorney] Wendell Willkie was nominated as the Republican presidential candidate at Philadelphia in 1940, I remember foolishly saying that the movement for Willkie came from the grassroots. Mrs. L gave a loud snort and said, 'Yes, from the grassroots of 10,000 country clubs.' "[3]

Alice Longworth did not confine herself to witticisms during the years of Democratic rule, for it was then that she really began looking on the world with detached malevolence.[4] The problem was, she cared too deeply about the future of the country to be entirely detached. But the malevolence she directed full force at her cousins. Attacking her archrivals was satisfying because she truly felt that the Democratic Roosevelts were making mistakes that carried profoundly disturbing political and global ramifications. Yet her malice was tempered by ambivalence. This is evident in the kinder things she said later, especially about Eleanor. During the 1930s and 1940s, though, Alice became known for the pitiless precision of the verbal daggers she could aim. When the New Deal years were over and the other Roosevelts gone, that reputation remained.

The day before Franklin Delano Roosevelt was inaugurated as president of the United States, Alice Longworth had taken her daughter to the White House to wish Herbert and Lou Hoover bon voyage. "Oh, it was grim," Alice recalled. The presidential couple "sat like waxworks, all stiff, bruised, and wounded." Those same words might have applied to her. FDR's ascension to the nation's highest office opened a new chapter for Alice. The previous decade of close ties to the party in power and easy access to the White House and the legislative halls ended. She continued to draw powerful policy makers to her, but in the 1930s, they were the outs. Instead, "hovering around" her, as she put it, were the "sufficient number of people who didn't like Franklin." That included her brother Ted. He tendered his resignation as governor-general of the Philippines to the new president and had it accepted. Borah retained his senatorial seat, but his was now the minority party. Alice was angry about the election results—she had worked hard to reelect Hoover, and FDR was in the place her brother ought eventually to have occupied—but she nonetheless watched the inaugural ceremonies from a ringside seat, thanks to the invitation sent her by cousin Eleanor. She then dined with the new First Family afterward.[5]

Friends occupied her days now that Paulina was eight years old and in school full time. Alice socialized with the Pinchots, whose presence brought back memories of her father, and with Sinclair Lewis and his wife, Dorothy Thompson, a fascinating couple whose writings she enjoyed. She was closest to columnist Frank Kent, humorist Will Rogers, and longtime Washington cronies like Evalyn McLean. In a gossipy 1931 book, society commentators characterized Alice as "brilliant if not gifted, who through the prestige of her position and the vitriol of her tongue dominates Washington's ultra-fashionable official group more completely than any other whip-cracker in the capital." Alice had a circle of friends in New York City centered around theater critic and raconteur Alexander Woollcott. Though not officially associated with his Algonquin Round Table, a group of luminaries from the worlds of arts and letters, Alice moved among the Algonquin members on her frequent visits to New York City.[6]

Friends such as these were invited to teas and dinners at her 2009 Massachusetts Avenue home. Joe Alsop described Alice's house in the mid-1930s as "a large, hospitable, remarkably ill-kept establishment." Mrs. L—as he and others called her—"stuck to the old way" of entertaining, especially concerning her table. He outlined a typical spring dinner: "The best creamed crab soup I have ever had or else a consommé so strong one felt one could skate on it. If the start was consommé, this was followed by soft-shell crabs, perfectly sautéed, without any of the carapace of crumbs that deviant chefs in those days had begun to give them. The accompanying salad contained tomatoes sliced paper thin and skinned, and cucumbers properly soaked in salt, and therefore, limp and less bitter to taste. The main course was usually a saddle of lamb—enough so that guests could eat as many slices as wanted—with glorious fresh vegetables. All this was followed by crème brulée, which her cook knew how to make better than any other in my experience."[7]

The talk was always political, and the tone grew increasingly intolerant of Democratic plans as President Roosevelt unveiled the package of legislation he hoped would heal America's domestic problems. In his first inaugural speech, Roosevelt famously told Americans that "the only thing we have to fear is fear itself." He quickly called Congress into session, and the "first hundred days" of legislation began. Bills for banking reform, agricultural assistance, and relief measures poured out. As FDR's New Deal programs attacked the financial problems most Americans faced, the Roosevelts, insulated from the worst of it by their wealth, attacked FDR. Edith had taken to referring to "the Republican Roosevelts" to differentiate her family from the Democrats in the White House. (Alex Woollcott called them the "out of season Roosevelts.") Archie's politics were moving further to the right than anyone else's in the family, and he could not even talk about the New Deal with some of his friends. "Shooting and fishing... seem to be the only pleasant things we can discuss together," he wrote grumpily to one New Deal administrator.[8]

Not all of the Democratic Roosevelts felt unalloyed happiness at FDR's election. Though in sympathy with her husband's policies, Eleanor nonetheless mourned the loss of privacy and the freedom of movement she feared would accompany her rise to First Lady. Her model for the position was Aunt Edith, who had treasured most the rare private times with her husband and family. But Eleanor would construct the role differently. In the crisis of the Depression, she soon picked up where she left off as First Lady of New York. There, she had taken leading positions in organizations such as the League of Women Voters, the National Consumers League, and the Democratic Party. In part, Eleanor had channeled the hurt and betrayal of FDR's extramarital affair with Lucy Mercer into a productive agenda, returning to the type of service she had performed in the Rivington Street settlement house and the Junior League at the time of her marriage. She worked with social activists such as Maud Schwartz, Rose Schneiderman, and Frances Perkins. Her circle in the 1920s and 1930s also came to include many women-identified women, like Elizabeth Lape and

Esther Read, Marion Dickerman and Nancy Cook, and Mary Dewson and Polly Porter—all but the last activists in related causes. Alice referred to them as Eleanor's "female impersonators," but Franklin could be just as cruel, joking about her " 'squaws' and 'she-men.' "[9]Alongside these reformers, Eleanor gained valuable experience that she put to use as she and Franklin evolved a working partnership. Eleanor became her husband's eyes, ears, legs—even a prototype spin doctor through her various published writings. Together the presidential couple assessed the impact of the Great Depression on the United States.

Republicans had been at a loss and uncertain about how to turn around an unemployment rate of nearly 25 percent and bank closures in every state. Roosevelt thus enjoyed a honeymoon period with some Republicans. Not Borah. Though in poor health, the senator managed to launch an attack on the National Industrial Recovery Act almost as soon as New York Senator Robert Wagner introduced it in June 1933. Borah played a very small role in the "first hundred days' " legislation of the New Deal because of painful "serious intermittent hemorrhages." Debate over the National Industrial Recovery Act went on without him. He was forced to enter Johns Hopkins Hospital for surgery. The cause of his pain was a significantly enlarged prostate, and while the operation was successful, the recuperation was slow, and he celebrated his sixty-eighth birthday from his hospital bed.[10]

Alice kept up the fight. She engaged in guerrilla warfare—stealthy, persistent, devastating. FDR announced that the United States should abandon the gold standard, and Alice was sitting in the Senate gallery next to Will Rogers as the bill passed. In "the Roosevelt tradition," Rogers reported, she "took it right on the chin and smiled." Behind the smile lurked anger. Like other Republicans, she saw this step as a foolhardy abandonment of sound money principles. Not long after the vote, Alice sauntered into a White House reception wearing her ideology. She was bedecked in gold: a golden pendant hanging on a gold necklace, a gold watch, gold hair combs. A crowd quickly gathered around her. Then, according to the *Chicago Tribune*, "she did her stunt" of "wiggling her ears in a truly professional way, causing the huge golden eardrops to dangle and jump." Alice made her point, and it was all the more striking because she seldom wore extravagant jewels. Humorist Cal Tinney joked, "If F.D.R. could have taken her to the Treasury and deposited her, the deficit would have turned into a surplus."[11]

At another White House reception President Roosevelt told Alice smugly that he was poised to sign a bill that would save the ailing country fifty million dollars. "That's a drop in the bucket," she leveled at him, "compared to what you are costing the country." Part of her calculated campaign was never to refer to Franklin as President Roosevelt. She enjoyed this, because it made him "wince."[12] Only in her published writings did she use his legal title, but in private it was always his first name.

Some of her most memorable one-liners were aimed at her cousins. She damned them both by suggesting that Franklin was "one-third mush and two-thirds Eleanor."[13]As the New Deal wore on and more and more legislation came pouring out of Washington, Alice huffed that the pants ought to come off Eleanor and go on Franklin. Since she believed that the New Deal was limiting the country, Alice drew an analogy: she said, "Nobody should ever underestimate the way he behaved when he had infantile paralysis, and how he had managed to adjust himself to a permanently crippled condition. I maintained that in the same way, he was trying to adjust this great lusty country into the same condition as his own." Even she admitted later that "that was pretty nasty." At a different time, she called Franklin a " 'Mollycoddle,' with a 'Mollycoddle Philosophy.' " These sorts of cuts went to the heart of her cousins' private weak spots: Franklin's paralysis and Eleanor's lesbian friends. It was humor of a sort only a relative could deliver.[14] Alice's "Eleanor face" was both a good likeness and very cruel. As she had with her "Mrs. Taft face," Alice did the Eleanor impersonation with the least encouragement. She contorted her mouth to mimic ER's prominent teeth, and copied Eleanor's high voice, ending her exclamations in a screech. Eleanor, who turned her pain inward—the opposite of her cousin—once asked Alice for a demonstration. It apparently hurt.

Alice might not actually have had the effect she intended, though. According to Eleanor's particular friend former journalist Lorena Hickok, Alice suffered some "discomfort" as she watched the effect of her Eleanor face on its inspiration. Mary Borah claimed that Eleanor "seemed to enjoy it.... [And a]fter that no one worried about their not getting along." The cousins could put aside their differences for the children; Henrietta Nesbitt, the Roosevelts' housekeeper, stated that Paulina "came over quite often to play with her White House cousins." ER generously offered to look after Paulina and included her in White House dinner invitations. She sent notes to Alice telling sweet stories about their young relatives. Both of them signed their letters "affectionately." Eleanor had lunch with Alice at Rookwood in 1938. "We never allow politics to come between us," Alice told a columnist. On more than one occasion a friend of Alice's heard her tell of how very beautiful she thought Eleanor was as a young woman, and how she admired her cousin for having overcome such a truly horrible childhood. Upon serialization of Eleanor's autobiography, *This Is My Story*, Alice exclaimed, "Did you realize Eleanor could write like that? It's perfect; it's marvelous...." One biographer asserted that Alice "could and did damn the new President, but let anyone outside the family say a single word against him and she would glare icily and remind the offending speaker that... members of her tribe were not to be spoken of in a derogatory manner." For example, Alice maintained that Franklin and his secretary, Missy LeHand, were not lovers, and did not hesitate to tell people that.[15]

Nevertheless, Alice's vituperation toward Franklin and Eleanor during the years they inhabited the White House, and even after, was relentless. Friends have suggested that Alice had been profoundly frustrated with Nick, because the apex of his ambition was only Speaker of the House; with Borah, who could not seem to curb his contrariness at those crucial four-year intervals; and with Ted, who failed to take her advice to return from Puerto Rico in time to resume his climb up the GOP ladder to the presidency.[16] Alice was a gambler used to winning, but she did not seem able to pick a man to whom she could hitch her star. Then, when Eleanor—she of little humor, grace, or wit—and Feather Duster Franklin made it to the White House instead of her, the reason behind the sharpness of the jabs at her cousins came into focus. If Alice was the smartest of TR's children, she was also stunted by her shyness and barred by her gender from the nation's highest office. "Nemesis in the person of Franklin," she said often. "We were out. Run over."[17]

The Roosevelts were not the only topic of interest to her. In the midst of the Great Depression, cave dwellers turned their energies to establishing the Washington National Symphony Orchestra. Alice sat on the national campaign committee and handwrote notes to potential subscribers.[18] She helped in an unusual way, too. Newly arrived Polish immigrant and virtuoso violinist Roman Totenberg made his American debut in November 1935 with the symphony. Before a glittering audience, Totenberg played Beethoven's Concerto in D minor on Nick's violin. One of Nick's former infatuations, poet and music patron Alice Dows, had convinced Alice that the young violinist would be worthy of the instrument. To keep it in good shape, and to help further the career of the already-decorated musician, Alice loaned the violin to Totenberg. Alice Dows paid the insurance "as long as Totenberg uses it," because, Dows told her, "You are doing a very generous and grand thing in letting him have it and I am eternally grateful." Two months after his debut, Totenberg played at the White House. The violinist recalled the president telling everyone, "That's the violin that [belonged to] old Nick," and joking, "I hope Mr. Totenberg plays it better than Nick did!" Alice was not invited that night, but Bill and Mary Borah were there to hear.[19]

Nick's violin was not, as was commonly assumed, a Stradivarius. Like nearly everyone else, Totenberg and Dows thought it was made by Antonio Stradivari, the seventeenth-century master violin maker. Around 1945, Totenberg queried a representative from London's W. E. Hill Company about the instrument. It was the Hill Company's opinion that Nick's violin "was a very good copy by [Giuseppe] Rocca," Totenberg recalled. Alice had the violin appraised by Rembert Wurlitzer in 1957 for tax purposes. Wurlitzer concluded that Nick's violin was "the work of some skilled copyist and is definitely not an original Stradivari." He placed its value at five hundred dollars. He thought it an excellent copy and felt it would have been hard for most people to tell it was a replica. Roman Totenberg's fame increased, and he eventually acquired a Stradivarius of his own in the early 1950s. At that time, he returned Nick's violin to Alice over a "very nice" tea at her home. Totenberg felt Alice expressed no more than an average interest in classical music. She was in the habit of attending the symphony in the afternoons in the 1930s and 1940s, and the popular riparian concerts along the Potomac. In 1957, Alice loaned Nick's violin to another violinist. The incomprehensible rumor that later emerged that Alice burned Nick's valuable Stradivarius is thus trebly incorrect.[20]

Alice was not immune to the economic downturn caused by the Great Depression, and no New Deal program existed for her. Nick's death had meant a substantial decrease in her income. Of course, poverty was relative. Like Alice, Evalyn McLean suffered from both the loss of her husband and the Depression. Looking one day for commiseration, Evalyn arrived on Alice's doorstep in tears and bearing her itemized budget. "Alice, what will I do?" Evalyn wailed, "I simply can't get my budget below $250,000 a year. Flowers, $40,000; household, $100,000; travel, $35,000...." Past her initial shock, Alice, a good friend, "knew what was expected of her. 'Evalyn,' she said, 'you are quite right. You simply can't shave it one cent.'"[21]

Alice was never destitute, but she did take the advice of friends who suggested she capitalize on her continuing fame by writing a memoir. Alice embarked on the task in the fall of 1932, but soon found that writing bored her. Still, she managed to produce the required pages. She called it *Crowded Hours*, a title borrowed from her father's description of his exciting Rough Rider days. The book was published by Charles Scribner's Sons, which paid Alice a five-thousand-dollar advance. They promoted the book nationally with newspaper advertisements focused on the holiday gift-giving season. Parts of *Crowded Hours* were serialized in teasers for *Ladies' Home Journal*. Alice wrote as she liked, sparing no one, though the editors, she complained, took out the "hardest cracks." Alice enjoyed nothing about the book writing but the publicity. "By the time the proof reading was over," she told Belle Hagner, "on top of months of unaccustomed work, and that work writing—think of me writing, my angel!—I was so bored by it that I could see no shred of worth in it." She went to recuperate with Laura Curtis.[22]

The *Ladies' Home Journal* articles ran through the fall of 1932, while the presidential race was underway, which allowed her to use them as a way to puff Hoover. *Crowded Hours* was published in October 1933. Alice reveled in the revival of her fame. Like her cousin Eleanor, Alice received "a smattering" of votes in a magazine poll of the women who contributed to American progress in the past century. She even attended an Author's League fund-raiser for "needy authors," where she was embarrassed to find that she'd pulled her own name out of the hat for the prize of a first edition of Charles Dickens's *Pickwick Papers*. Her autobiography was on the best-seller list for weeks. ALICE ROOSEVELT SEARS NOTABLES OF FORMER DAYS, the *Chicago Tribune* headline read. "A sparkling flood of reminiscences," crowed a *New York Times* reviewer. Strangers and old friends—such as John McCutcheon, Frank Lowden, and Samuel McClure—sent congratulatory notes. Speaking requests poured in, most of which she declined. She gave a lecture entitled "I Believe in America" in Chicago in November 1938. The program chair from a Republican women's club pleaded for her to send "a short note, a challenge to inspire us...." The Dwinell-Wright Company asked Alice to update and complete *The Story of the White House and Its Home Life,* which she did. This was a fifteen-cent book, sixty-three pages long with her signature scrawled across page 61. She wrote the last eleven pages in first person, covering presidential families from her own to the Franklin Roosevelts. Charming and complimentary, her stories were calculated for the broadest possible audience and were not objective. The Hardings merited only one paragraph, while her friends the Coolidges were awarded seven. Even Mrs. Taft fared better than Florence Harding, who was dismissed in half of a sentence.[23]

To exploit her resurgent fame, Ponds cold cream reissued its previous advertisement. "Today Mrs. Longworth guards her skin's freshness with the same two creams she used and praised seven years ago," read the ad. It showed the photo of Alice in 1925 alongside a photo of "Mrs. Longworth today—fresher, more vital looking." "I never use makeup," Alice swore. "I never use anything on my face that I am not absolutely sure of." Ponds called her "one of the most vital figures in political and diplomatic circles in Washington."[24]

When Ted and his wife, Eleanor, returned home from the Philippines in early September 1933, Alice was thrilled to see them. It was not long before she and Ted launched their next project—one free of politics: a book of poetry that would be called *The Desk Drawer Anthology*. Alexander Woollcott was the inspiration. Sunning themselves at Woollcott's lakefront home in Vermont, Ted and Woollcott idly discussed all the poets whose works were good but "somehow escaped the accident of fame," and how most anthologies were little more than the favorite poems of the editor. They wondered whether an anthology could be created for which all of America did the selecting. If Ted and Alice would edit the entries, Woollcott promised to use his popular *Town Crier* radio show to ask listeners to send in their favorite poems for consideration—the ones they'd cut out and tucked in wallets or desk drawers so they'd have them to read again and again. More than forty thousand poems appeared as a result of his plea. It took Alice and Ted many months to read through and compile the poems, and the book was published by Doubleday, Doran just in time for Christmas 1937.[25]

Alice was also making a name for herself as a columnist. Although her policy was never to give interviews, she did feel free to express herself in print. "What Are the Women Up To?" she asked in a *Ladies' Home Journal* guest column in 1934. "Why haven't there been more than nineteen in Congress since they won the suffrage?" In this article the public glimpsed the political philosopher so well known to her friends. Alice wrote about the "unprecedented" women in government, such as "the best Secretary of Labor we have ever had," Democrat Frances Perkins; U.S. minister to Denmark Ruth Bryan Owen; and National Mint Director Nellie Tayloe Ross. "The fact remains, however," Alice mused, "that though women compose nearly half the vote, this is still a man's government...." She analyzed all the women in Congress, including Ruth Hanna McCormick and Isabella Greenway. She highlighted the role of women in the earlier temperance and suffrage battles. She suggested that "it took more power to achieve the suffrage than women have shown since the achievement," but that it would still take "a few more campaigns" until women's power was commensurate with their past successes. Alice noted that men generally called upon women as consumers and moral watchdogs of New Deal legislation. And she wondered slyly, why "as [women] are such an important part of domestic economics, more of their sex have not been sent to Congress to help frame and pass the measures which it is claimed so vitally concern them, and about which they are supposed to have such practical knowledge in their business as managers of the family's budget." Women's interest in politics, Alice concluded, "is undoubtedly more alert and intelligent than it has ever been before." It was an optimistic conclusion and a sophisticated read of the way male politicians were attempting to disenfranchise women since suffrage and to shift their power from the ballot and the statehouse to the home.[26]

The First Lady did not merit mention in Alice's article, presumably because she was not an elected official. Alice and Eleanor remained in contact, but temperamentally and politically they were no closer than they had been a decade earlier when ER was a shy political wife frustrated by the vexing tradition of calling. Eleanor once explained to Corinne her view of herself as First Lady: "I never think of myself as mistress of the White House with casual people, much less with my family." Her informality meant a more permeable barrier than the president desired with their cousin. Alice and her criticisms drove him to the breaking point. FDR told his son once, "I don't want anything to do with that woman!"[27]

In her autobiography, Eleanor insisted that "neither Franklin nor I ever minded the disagreeable things my cousin Alice Longworth used to say during the various campaigns. When the social season started after the third campaign, in which Alice had been particularly outspoken, she was invited as usual to the diplomatic reception." FDR, who should have known better, bet an aide that she wouldn't have the courage to appear after damning him every which way for the previous nine months. Alice did show up: politics was politics, family was family, and she was always game for a battle—or a party. Jim Farley, standing in the reception line with the President and the First Lady while Alice was making her way toward them, overhead FDR say, "Eleanor, *your* relative, not mine, is fast approaching." She set him off with public displays of her criticism. ALICE FAILS TO APPLAUD COUSIN FRANK, the headline read in January 1934, after Alice—prominent in the Speaker's gallery—never once clapped throughout Roosevelt's State of the Union address. Republican women stood up for their chief, stoutly maintaining that Alice could not clap because she had to hold her lorgnette so she could see.[28]

"Wary" would characterize the relationship between Alice and her presidential relatives. Alice enjoyed attending White House functions to get a view from within the enemy's camp. Eleanor was both driven by duty and in a highly conspicuous position. Not including Alice in White House functions would be an affront to ER's sense of family duty and would give reporters the satisfaction of confirming their suspicions about an undignified family feud. "We were going to see a lot of" her, Mrs. Nesbitt affirmed.[29]

It wasn't until late in the second term that the First Lady pushed aside her tribal feelings. As Alice told the story, a rumor circulated suggesting that she loathed going to the White House and attended only because a presidential invitation—from a relative or not—was a command. Eleanor thereupon wrote Alice saying that she and Franklin never wanted Alice to feel uncomfortable, and she should only come when she really wanted to. "How disagreeable people are, trying to make more trouble than there already is between us...." Alice fired back. "I *love* coming to the White House. It couldn't be more fun and I have always enjoyed myself immensely." Eleanor publicly denied such a letter: "'There is nothing to that,' she said. 'Long ago I told all those, including Alice, to whom invitations to all White House functions go regularly as a matter of routine, that I wanted them all to feel under no compulsion to accept all of them. But this alleged conversation with, or note to, Alice simply never happened.'" Alice was still summoned to important, high-profile gatherings such as the visit of King George and Queen Elizabeth of Great Britain in 1939—where she wore a "beige lace gown," her "wide brimmed brown hat," and carried "a shooting stick." Nevertheless, she received fewer and fewer invitations on the recognizable heavy white card stock. Alice regretted this. "Perhaps it gave them pleasure not to have me," she said, "but they should have been better winners. They could have said, 'Look here, you miserable worm, of course you feel upset because you wanted this. You hoped your brother Ted would finally achieve this, and now he hasn't. But after all, here we are.

Just come if it amuses you.' But they took it all seriously. They took the meanness in the spirit in which it was meant."[30]

And it was mean-spirited. "Eleanor," Alice scowled, "is a Trojan mare." The double jab—the First Lady's popularity as a front for the nefarious New Deal legislation, and a poke at Eleanor's lack of beauty—was a palpable hit. New Dealer Harold Ickes thought that Alice's allusions to her cousin "would have been in better wit if they had been in better taste." He put it down to jealousy. Whatever it was, it was obvious. Alice appeared the day after Eleanor did at a crowded 1939 art exhibit for the benefit of Polish war refugees. She discovered that her cousin had posed in front of a Picasso. "Very well, then," Alice said as she moved to a Renoir, "I'll take this one."[31]

Perhaps the cruelest treatment of Eleanor was Alice's encouragement of FDR's relationship with Lucy Mercer Rutherfurd, ER's former social secretary whose love letters ER had found in 1918. As the responsibilities of governing took their toll, President Roosevelt reached out to his former mistress, whom Alice described as "beautiful, charming, and an absolutely delightful creature. I would see her out driving with Franklin," Alice recalled of their early days, "and I would say things like, 'I saw you out driving with someone very attractive indeed, Franklin. Your hands were on the wheel but your eyes were on her.' " FDR kept the relationship a strict secret from Eleanor—and he brought Lucy to dine at Alice's home at least once. Not until Franklin's death did ER learn of the liaison, from cousin Laura Delano. During the rapprochement between Lucy and FDR, Alice may have tried to warn Eleanor, but the latter wouldn't hear it, saying primly that she "did not believe in knowing" what one's husband did not want one to know. It is not clear when or if Eleanor ever learned of Alice's complicity. But Alice was unrepentant. She believed that Eleanor "had so little enjoyment, so little amusement" and "she always seemed to manage to hold Franklin back from having a good time." That was the context for her oft-quoted "Franklin deserved a good time. He was married to Eleanor."[32]

Yet Alice and Eleanor had much in common beyond their shared family ties. Both women married men who sought out other women. As it would turn out, both men had mistresses by their sides at their deathbeds. The shock, humiliation, anger, and sense of betrayal commonly felt by spouses so deceived might once have made for a bond between Alice and Eleanor. But Alice, as one interviewer suggested, was very prickly in public and very warm in person, while Eleanor was the opposite. Even for those closest to her, Eleanor couldn't be affectionate. Eleanor confessed that she suffered from "Griselda moods" during which she played the silent and sullen martyr, making living with her at these times very difficult. Michael Teague, a close friend of Alice's in her last decades, heard her acknowledge she knew "why Eleanor was the way she was, but her way of dealing with it didn't make it any easier for the rest of us."[33] The Roosveltian ability to protect interior sorrows with a steel exterior was deep in both Alice and Eleanor. The wounds inflicted by Nick's drinking were painful, but Alice did not bleed in public. Alice and Eleanor had such different personalities that they could not help but respond to their situations differently—Alice by erecting a wall of witticisms and Eleanor by taking refuge in duty.

Another reason that their husbands' infidelity failed to make the cousins into confidantes was the era. Society rewarded men and punished women for engaging in the same behavior: a woman had to be "good" enough to keep her husband, but men were considered more virile if they had mistresses. A sort of mystery attached itself to men who attracted scores of women—film heroes Rudolph Valentino or Douglas Fairbanks, for instance. Men who had such an insatiable appetite seemed to draw women to them, and if that were the case, no real blame could be attached to the wife, because clearly, no one woman could keep such a man happy within the confines of their home. Still, because the initial assumption would be that there was a flaw in the wife, women did not confess their husband's infidelities—especially not to their peers. Such secrets were hidden; not at all the sort of thing made public, even among public men. If a vast segment of the American citizenry did not know about President Roosevelt's withered legs, even fewer knew about the lighthearted women who could revive his spirits despite the domestic and international troubles that plagued him.

So while Alice knew about—and probably abetted—Franklin's affair,

Eleanor would likely have heard only unconfirmed rumors about Nick's. But even had they known the details of each other's private lives, it is highly unlikely that they ever would have wept on each other's shoulders. Alice didn't weep. Just like her cousin, she found friends to sustain her and threw herself into political causes. While Alice lived with Nick's straying for many years, Eleanor did not know about FDR's reunion with Mrs. Rutherfurd until after his death. And for Alice, Nick's unforgivable sin was his drunkenness, not the other women. It was alcohol that damped his political ambitions. Temperamentally, the cousins were just too unalike to be drawn together, despite their similarities. Alice didn't care for what she saw as Eleanor's kind of preachy, saccharine, do-goodism. At the time, Alice was only one of Eleanor's critics. In the 1930s and 1940s, she didn't have the image of the heroic Eleanor that exists today. Nearer to the end of her life, Alice softened about Eleanor. She could comment for posterity on Eleanor's "really remarkable achievements," and how, "of all the Presidents' wives, none used her position in quite the same effective way that Eleanor did."[34]

Meanwhile, Alice was assisting Nick's former lover Laura Curtis. Laura's financial status was so precarious as a result of the Great Depression that she was on the verge of selling her house at 1925 F Street, NW. Friends decided that it would be a terrible waste to dismantle the home, sell the antiques, and dismiss the efficient staff, so they convinced Laura to convert her home into a social club. The F Street Club, as it became known, was created when Laura's friends, including Alice, contributed their money and bought a membership. Founded in April 1933, the F Street Club became the spot for wealthy Republicans to air their grievances over turtle soup, filet mignon, homemade biscuits, and dessert. Its membership broadened slightly in later decades, but it remained the place, as one newspaper put it, to "hob nob with the people who make the political wheels turn in Washington."[35] Alice frequented the F Street Club, as did Ruth, as would other luminaries such as author and politician Clare Boothe Luce.

The Roosevelts were effecting real change nationwide through their activist policies by 1935. Looking for a change of scenery, Alice took ten-year-old Paulina on an extended European trip, primarily to visit

Longworth relatives in France. Alice, recently named one of the twelve "great women of today" by columnist Elsa Maxwell, waved from the deck of the *Manhattan* to reporters and to her brother Kermit, who came to see them off. The trip did not ease her mind about the course on which Franklin had set the country. Upon her return, she continued to watch him closely. She sat in the Senate gallery monitoring debates. She maintained her broad reading of newspapers. She was present at events like presidential vetoes, even when they turned out to be Democratic victories. And she wrote about her observations. She thought the government itself was becoming a "menacing" trust, because "under the New Deal, the Government has moved to join hands with private monopoly to control the entire Nation.... That is the clear objective of a large part of all New Deal policy; control and regimentation of resources and individuals...." Events overseas added to her qualms. Benito Mussolini had been in control of a resurgent Italy since 1922. Adolph Hitler ascended to power in Germany a decade later. As fascism spread across Europe, militarism and fear trailed menacingly behind. On October 3, 1935, Mussolini invaded Abyssinia (now Ethiopia). Poet Ezra Pound wrote perversely, "7 million of subjected population in Abyssinia will be benefited," but Alice did not share Pound's fascist tendencies, and she knew that FDR's "moral embargo" was an insufficient response benefiting neither U.S. businesses nor Ethiopians.[36]

Alice's very real concerns with her cousin's policies (and her own financial worries) led her to take up journalism in a more consistent fashion. She began writing a daily column for the McNaught Syndicate in late 1935. Her column had various names: "The National Scene," "Capital Comment," "Alice Longworth Says," and "Alice in Blunderland," among others. It was carried by papers that included the *Washington Star*, the *Los Angeles Times*, the *Cincinnati Times-Star*, the *San Francisco Chronicle*, and the *Ft. Worth Star Telegram*, and read in cities from Honolulu to Boston. Alice's column was a shot glass–size comment on contemporary events intended to go straight to the bloodstream. The topics were wide ranging, from the evils of living under Hitler's tyranny to the abdication of Great Britain's Edward VIII, the U.S. Good Neighbor policy toward Central and South America, to the U.S. farm problem. The columns, one enthusiastic reader thought, would "do more to set the world straight than many political speeches."[37]

Alice had rich fodder in the 1936 election year. Her editors hoped that her political savvy and wit would create a readership on the right, or steal readers away from the sugary chat that passed for comment—especially in the early days—of cousin Eleanor's "My Day" column. Eleanor really did chronicle her day's doings, but Alice generally kept herself out of her writing. Both women occasionally exhorted their readers to action, and Alice was not above giving advice to politicians such as Alfred Landon, the Republican Party's lackluster 1936 presidential nominee. She also used the column to continue her digs at Franklin. "You can always tell," she wrote, "when Mr. Roosevelt is feeling at the top of his form by his tendency to identify himself with the great. Last January he completely identified himself with Andrew Jackson, and on occasions he has confused his personality with that of Thomas Jefferson." He would run for a third term, Alice predicted that year: voters must be wary.[38]

She maintained a critical watch over the White House. Following is a typical sort of censure from her pen:

> The balanced budget plank in the Democratic platform, if any one has the nerve to propose one, is going to look fairly sick. Along comes [Secretary of the Treasury] Mr. Morgenthau asking for another two billion mortgage on the future, in addition to the hundreds of millions of current cash called for by the tax bill. On the theory that "there's gold in them thar hills" the administration evidently believes there is money to spare in "them thar taxpayers."
>
> Mr. Roosevelt sees automobiles running, airplanes flying, relief checks fluttering to their recipients, people generally going about their usual avocations. He is apparently convinced that everything is lovely, so he still talks in financial hyperbole, and makes another peacetime record for the national debt.
>
> Moreover, the one and a half billion dollar relief fund is now to be turned over to him, to be disbursed under his personal direction. That

will keep the privy purse well lined and should enable him to satisfy his itch for spending for at least a few months longer.[39]

Like a dagger, "The National Scene" could inflict a rapid and telling wound. Roosevelt's court-packing scheme she called "a direct move to tighten the Washington dictatorship." On giveaways to farmers in the election year, she quipped, "American agriculture never faced a more promising season, so far as the political fruit crop is concerned." Alice warned about the "black soil magic" of the administration's attempt to evade the Supreme Court in the first Agricultural Adjustment Act by passing a second AAA after the first was ruled unconstitutional. In three swift sentences, Alice exposed Harold Ickes's lust for power while simultaneously condemning the totalitarian turn of the Revolutionary Party in Paraguay: "The Paraguayan 'liberators' have outlawed politics for a year. They have also put capital and labor under the jurisdiction of the secretary of the interior. That must make Mr. Ickes' mouth water." Ickes had been a Bull Mooser before becoming FDR's secretary of the interior.

Like Borah, Alice did not spare her own party. She could be critical of Republican National Committee decisions and chastise individual politicians, even, as it turned out, when she loved them. Of Borah, she wrote that he spoke "with a fevered vigor. But it was not the same voice that has crowded the Senate galleries for so many years. Possibly it suffers in radio transmission." She attended the 1936 Republican convention as a delegate, but sought to keep the feet of the faithful to the fire. Alice's columns called for responsible and moral conduct by politicians and urged a more forcible Republican challenge of the Democratic hegemony.

While Alice's columns were journalistic jabs—sharp, short, and to the point—Eleanor's began as diffuse peregrinations across the scenery of her life. Readers told Alice their preference: "As for Mrs. Roosevelt's pathetic attempts to write[,] what she writes and the way she writes it is an offense to any discriminating literary palate. Why occupancy of the White House warrants foisting that sort of tripe on the public is beyond my comprehension. I presume I am just one of the millions of Democrats who are literally fed up to the teeth with sanctimonious New Dealers all talking and acting like God." Margaret Cobb Ailshie, an old friend of Alice's, then publisher of the *Idaho Statesman,* vowed her paper would carry Alice's column despite the expense, because "with all due respect to your cousin, I think her column on 'coughing at concerts' is the Ne Plus Ultra of what not to write and how not to write it." A reader brainstormed, "We have been paying our farmers for not raising hogs, cotton, corn, etc. I wonder if...there is not some way of paying Mrs. Roosevelt for not writing...." One fan letter came from a man born in 1856 who commended her for her "keen and clear cut grasp...on our political and economic conditions and ability to put it on paper." Others made suggestions for columns, and one helpful reader, answering his own question, wrote, "Why am I writing you this legal treatise? Just because you have the ear of many who have influence...."[40]

Her columns moved some readers to civic involvement: "I can not afford to contribute money" to politics, one woman wrote, "but I am a good secretary and would be glad to give my services gratis after business hours if I could ally myself with a sane and just man or organization." She asked for Alice's suggestions. "The National Scene" prompted one reader to put aside a bit of his misogyny: "When I find myself liking a woman columnist better each day really, it shocks me.... You see, frankly speaking, my appreciation of what women can do and how well they do it, has been and is, in the majority of cases, very, very low. You bring it up a little bit for WOMEN...."[41]

She did receive many fan letters from female readers. They wrote to tell her how they admired her "courage" and her "use of the sacred market of free expression." One woman enthused, "I have always thought of you as: Being good for The United States of America." More than one fan suggested her father would be proud of her, as "a chip off the old block, alright, a living counterpart of our own beloved T.R." or one who was "hitting them 'between the eyes' just like your father." Several readers suggested that she become vice president or president of the United States. One booster was specific: "I have my candidates all picked out for the [1936] Cleveland convention. It is not Hoover or Borah, it is Gov. Landon for president and Alice Longworth for Vice President."[42]

Alice's columns were based on her intimate knowledge of Washington politics—but as one of FDR's most vocal critics, she was no longer a White

House insider. Nevertheless, at her parties and in her columns she gave currency to speculations and considerations that bespoke a wide range of sources. "Two dramatic possibilities were much discussed during the Winter and Spring," her column pointed out in June 1936: that the Republicans would choose a Democrat for their vice presidential candidate, and that the anti–New Deal Democrats would stage a walkout at the GOP convention.[43] In her own circle of friends, Alice kept up a spikier criticism. She had fun circulating this parody of Edgar Allan Poe:

> From the White House of the Nation
> Speaking without hesitation
> Comes the voice of unchecked knowledge
>   From the lady, Eleanor.
> In the limelight gaily basking
> Speaks the lady, without asking;
> Like the brook that rushed onward,
>   Ever onward, evermore.
> Speaks the expert on great problems:
> Home and children, love and war:
> Speaks the lady,
>   Eleanor
>
> And this expert ever flitting,
> Never sitting, never quitting,
> Gives her pills of fancied knowledge
>   Wisdom from her stock and store.
> And we hear the painful sighing,
> Hear a population crying
> For the stilling of the ringing
>   Sound of Eleanor.
> But the voice still keeps advising,
> Criticizing and chastising,
> Moralizing, patronizing, sermonizing,
>   EVERMORE.[44]

Columnist James Reston remembered Alice's "collection of anti-Roosevelt speeches, newspaper clippings, and jokes, which she read out to her guests with boisterous laughter and spiteful comments of her own." For example, among her papers was a cutting poem entitled "Rejected." It tells the story of the devil meeting FDR at the gates of hell and challenging the president's credentials to enter. Franklin replied with a long list of his misdeeds ("I paid them to let their farms lie still / And I imported stuffs from Brazil"), and his meanness ("I furnished money with government loans / When they missed a payment I took their homes"), and his enjoyment of it all ("When I wanted to punish the folks, you know / I put my wife on the radio"). At the end of this litany, the devil sent FDR away from hell, telling him firmly, "For once you mingle with this mob, I'll have to hunt another job."[45]

Alice certainly had her own critics. A representative of the Gannett newspapers wrote to Alice's publisher wondering how "so colorful an individual as…Mrs. Longworth…can produce such conventional and uninteresting copy."[46] That was the main complaint about *Crowded Hours* as well: that she didn't write as well as she spoke. Alice's columns started soundly, and the asperity was fun to read. Even cousin Eleanor could admit to a friend that Alice "certainly writes well. I wish I were as free as she, though I do not wish ever to be as bitter." But Alice's columns lost their sparkle, even as Eleanor's gained in depth of analysis and seriousness of purpose, and Alice's was discontinued while Eleanor's ran until 1962. An editorial entitled "Eleanor vs. Alice" was not particularly complimentary to either woman, but it condemned Alice for being "strictly a Tory in character" and having "all of her father's self-assurance, but little of his discernment." The irony is that she may well have had her father's discernment, but because of her father, what Alice lacked was precisely self-assurance. It is difficult to remember that despite the column, and regardless of her reputation as a wit, Alice was "terribly shy," as she put it, and supremely self-critical, too. All this she hid from the public that found her "so charming and so <u>gloriously</u> <u>alive</u>."[47]

Though unafraid to aid her friends and attack her enemies, Alice could only watch helplessly as the Republicans lost in 1936. That election represented Bill Borah's last chance at the presidency, but his candidacy was doomed from the outset. The senator had a dedicated but powerless following. As one observer wrote in 1936, "Borah's chief handicap is Borah, and a lifetime of non-allegiance to those groups which he now needs to make him President." His determination to follow his own course drew to him unusual supporters such as fellow Idahoan Ezra Pound. The poet wrote to Senator Borah from Italy with some frequency in an attempt to convert him to fascism for the moment that Borah would assume the presidency. While the poet's dislike for FDR and for England resonated, Borah was not tempted by Pound's cant and kept his replies noncommittal. "I suggest," Borah wrote Pound, "that you come back to Idaho and to the United States. . . . I can talk better than I can write. So drop in when you get home and see me."[48]

Many of Borah's backers saw him as Theodore Roosevelt's heir. In a 1936 word portrait, Bill Hard, a journalist friend, compared Borah to bedrock. The name called up the simplicity of western life and the red rock hills that helped create Borah, and the fact that he—unlike the effete easterner Franklin Roosevelt—knew how to get down to fundamentals. Hard came upon Borah sitting behind a newspaper, but surrounded by Mary Borah and her friends at luncheon:

> As usual, by himself. As usual, reading. As usual, making no festivity whatsoever of eating.
>
> And who, indeed, could possibly make any sort of festivity out of his sort of eating? Unaccompanied by any malt, vinous or spirituous liquors. Unaccompanied by tea or coffee. Unfinished by cigars or cigarettes or even a pipe. Just food. Consumed, apparently with the sole desire of acquiring enough strength to do some more reading.
>
> I am struck by his amazing withdraw-ness from other human beings, and by his equally amazing lack of upstage-ness in his dealings with them. He is both as "homey" as an old shoe, and as far away as the moon.[49]

Hardly the sort of thing to inspire the undecided voter.

As her column gained adherents, Alice could have used it to promote Borah's candidacy. She did not. Perhaps their relationship was cooling. Their letters taper off in the early 1930s, but they may simply have switched to the telephone with Nick gone. Other party members sought Alice's endorsement, and she received letters from elected officials such as Frederic C. Walcott of Connecticut, who wanted to "explain my vote to override the President's veto of the Independent Offices Appropriation bill." The Women's National Republican Club made her a guest of honor at their fifteenth anniversary celebration in January 1936 at the Hotel Astor. Senator Robert A. Taft and President Ulysses S. Grant's granddaughter, the Russian princess Julia Grant Cantacuzene, spoke before an audience of eighteen hundred stalwarts who craned their necks to see the famous Alice Longworth. Two weeks later, she attended the massive anti–New Deal Liberty League dinner, whose two thousand guests included a who's who of politics and business. Ohio Republicans were proud to have Alice sit on the State Central Committee to choose the slate and the voting agenda for the fifty-two Buckeye delegates to the national convention. In the end, Alice and the others chose Ohio's "favorite son" Robert A. Taft, rather than Borah, who was running his own full slate in Ohio.[50]

The campaign loomed. Alice went as a columnist and as a Cincinnati delegate to the GOP national convention to vote as instructed for the son of her former enemy, Taft, rather than for the father of her child. If she felt a moral quandary, she was publicly jaunty. She and Ruth were inseparable, two among nearly sixty female delegates in Cleveland and members of the preliminary platform committee as well. Ruth, able and prepared, told reporter Kathleen McLaughlin that she expected that three women were likely prospects for the GOP's committee on resolutions: Alice, Corinne, and herself. Alice was not chosen for that influential committee "for no reason," as veteran political reporter Arthur Krock put it, "that seemed significant in the larger convention sense." Instead, Mildred Reeves— Nick's former secretary—won that seat.[51]

The Cleveland convention turned out to be Borah's last stand. Seventy years old and fighting for the Republican nomination against Landon, Frank Knox, and Arthur H. Vandenberg, Borah never mustered the enthusiasm necessary to push him to the front. His support was confined to the western states and the party was trying desperately to seek voters nationwide as it faced the undeniable popularity of Franklin D. Roosevelt. Landon became the GOP's standard-bearer, with Knox as the vice presidential candidate. That "had a strong appeal," Alice told her readers, because Knox had been "with my father in the Rough Riders and followed him into the Progressive party in 1912."[52]

Alice and Corinne were two of the women the RNC called to serve that year on the recreated Women's Council of 100, whose job was tracking national electoral challenges. Alice asked novelist Mary Roberts Rinehart to join. Ethel Barrymore and other friends also added their names to the list.[53] The first incarnation had been organized in 1919 with the goal of returning a Republican to the White House. All of the original members were summoned back to "active duty." Their main job in 1936 was to get Alfred Landon elected.

Alice kept up the drumbeat in her columns as she surveyed the Democratic convention from her seat in the press section. She accused Senator Joe T. Robinson of alchemy when he told the faithful in Philadelphia that FDR had "complied with the spirit of" the 1932 Democratic Party platform. "If the spirit of black is white," Alice blasted, "if the spirit of sour is sweet, then the Senator is using his words correctly. But never, outside of metaphysical speculation, has the word spirit been called upon to bear such a burden." The Democratic Party could corrupt the English language, and Roosevelt could allow such chicanery. But that was mild compared to some of her charges: "The determination of Mr. Roosevelt," she wrote caustically of his acceptance speech, "to assume a leadership comparable to that of the Fuehrer in Germany and the Duce in Italy is more than ever revealed.... The intention of the Executive is clear: To continue to arrogate to himself the power that the Constitution distributes among the three branches of the government." She warned that Franklin was still laying the ground for an unparalleled third term and dared him to refute it. On June 30, she put it more succinctly by repeating what was being said "around Philadelphia": F.D.R. really stood for "Fuehrer, Duce, Roosevelt."[54]

Somehow putting politics aside, in July the family gathered to pay one last homage to Quentin Roosevelt with a memorial service and a dinner commemorating his life and career. Representing the Oyster Bay Roosevelts were Edith, Alice, Ted, Archie, and Kermit. President Roosevelt and his mother came from the Hyde Park side. Family friend Frank McCoy, New York City mayor Fiorello La Guardia, and General John J. Pershing, under whom Quentin had served in France in 1918, also attended. Kermit and Alice had grown apart, separated by their politics, as he leaned leftward. In 1921, Kermit had memorialized his brother with the publication of *Quentin Roosevelt: A Sketch with Letters*. Fifteen years later, Kermit had already passed the apex of his career. An adventurer at heart and an author like his father, Kermit lacked TR's moral fiber. His marriage to Belle seemed happy, but he increasingly found enjoyment in liquor and his mistress. The alcoholism that ran through the Roosevelt clan claimed Kermit: by the mid-1930s, "He was in the habit of having whiskey for breakfast."[55]

The Sagamore Hill Roosevelts also shared a soft spot for Alf Landon because he had backed TR in 1912. Landon was glad to claim that association. "As a mark of his enduring respect for the man on whose behalf he first entered active politics," Landon made a pilgrimage to Roosevelt's grave at Oyster Bay. He had a fifteen-minute, closed-door meeting with Ted before they set out to drive from New York City to Sagamore. Once there, Landon laid a chrysanthemum wreath on TR's grave, took tea with several Roosevelts, and then boarded a train for Topeka, where he would await the election results.[56] Landon's final campaign act was a radio address sponsored by the RNC. Also speaking on the hour-long program were representatives of various constituencies the GOP hoped to reach: African Americans, teachers, union members, and farmers. Alice Longworth spoke—for two minutes—to *her* constituency: all of America. On national hookup, Alice told listeners forcefully that her cousin's New Deal had "undermined civil service"—civil service reform was a goal of the League of Women Voters that year—and "that the merit system supported by her father [was] going through its 'darkest days.'" She urged Americans to turn away from irresponsible spending and put a "sane and orderly government" in the White House.[57]

Alice was so certain that Americans would not reelect a man she had been referring to as a dictator in her columns that she parlayed a hundred dollars with Woollcott on Landon's success. She lost. FDR achieved a landslide. The electoral college vote was 523 to 8. Alex Woollcott voted for FDR because, he gloated privately, "I want to disassociate myself from the swine who, almost in a body, are out for Landon." The Republican loss was so devastating "that there was talk of their imminent demise as a party."[58]

Two months after the election, Alice tried to bury the hatchet with the now-hundred-dollar-wealthier Woollcott at a fiftieth birthday party Joe Alsop threw for the theater critic. Woollcott told his radio audience, "The lovely Alice Longworth was so incautious as to make an election bet with me. Her check has just arrived with a suggestion that I give it to my favorite charity. I shall. It may console her to know that the entire sum will be devoted to providing food, clothing, shelter and medical attention for a poor broken-down old newspaperman named Alexander Woollcott." Humor patched up their friendship. They served together as two "book connoisseurs" who, for New York publishers, helped choose a list of five hundred indispensable books for every home library.[59]

It was probably her friendship with the radio star that led to one of the most unusual decisions of Alice's life—when she agreed to be part of a radio advertisement for Lucky Strike cigarettes. The "Lucky Strike Hit Parade" was a thirty-minute show that involved a sweepstakes. Listeners guessed which songs would be the "top ranking" songs on the program. The winner won "a prize of fifty fine-tasting Lucky Strike Cigarettes." As the musical countdown began, "With Plenty of Money and You," coming in at number three on February 3, 1937, the radio announcer broke in to introduce "its own 'Roll of Honour'—the men and women famous in many different fields who prefer Luckies over any other cigarette." Describing Alice as "one of the keenest observers of the political scene," the announcer and Alice had a scripted conversation that centered on her attendance at House and Senate debates ("Those...can get pretty heated, can't they?") and her absorption in the issues that kept her rooted in the building even during lunch in the Senate restaurant ("It's so convenient. They can have lunch and a cigarette and be back on the floor in no time."). Alice then explained why so many congressmen smoked Luckies: "All the speaking that goes with their careers means a continuous strain on their voices and throats—they really <u>need</u> a cigarette that is considerate of their throats—a light smoke." And, of course, for the finale, Alice herself admitted to using them, "off and on."[60] Her radio appearance was unusual, because Alice, though so voluble in private settings, still hated public speaking.

Smoking she did with greater ease. As a girl, it was a rebellion against her parents' rules and society's norms. Her example allowed other American women to light up. Alice Longworth contributed something else to the history of smoking, too. Ironically, it was she who gave Franklin Delano Roosevelt the long cigarette holder that became his trademark.[61]

Chapter 19

"I Believe in the Preservation of This Republic"

BY 1940, WHEN their daughter turned sixteen, Alice and Bill Borah were old friends. She had known him nearly half her life. He was seventy-four and she was fifty-six as the calendar turned to the new year—both of them old enough to have known great joy, made and lost friends, and contemplated their own mortality. They had had their squabbles and were no longer as close as they once had been, but Paulina remained their connection.[1] The senator, embarking upon his thirty-third year in Congress, missed the heady days of Republican rule when his words were scrutinized around the globe. Borah knew that the Supreme Court seat he desired would probably never come, but his doctor proclaimed him in excellent health and ready to remain a guardian of American democracy for years. Thus, his death, on January 19, came as a shock to everyone.

Borah's final battle had been to warn FDR against assuming the power to seize American businesses, war emergency or no. The senator lectured the president, invoking documents he believed were the basis for representative democracy. "The glory of the Bill of Rights," he stormed, "is that it is a restraint upon government as well as upon individuals." And if the United States were to abrogate its lofty position, countries trying to "fight their way back to civilization" from fascism and bolshevism and nazism would not be able to "look to this Bill of Rights as embodying their hopes and ideals."

Getting ready for work on Tuesday, January 16, Borah was stricken by a brain hemorrhage. He hung on to life for the next three days, coming out of his coma only briefly. The president was one of many who phoned to inquire about the senator's health. The physicians told reporters on the seventeenth, "There is no hope whatever." Bill Borah died, with his secretary and a nurse by his side, at 8:45 p.m. on the nineteenth.[2]

Newspaper boys from Washington to San Francisco hollered the news from street corners. The next day, Senator Arthur Vandenberg delivered his friend's eulogy by radio, a powerful tribute:

> He grew in stature with each succeeding year.... He grew in the talents which made him the greatest advocate and orator of his time. He became the Senate's dean—not alone in years of service, but equally in the personal prestige of a unique and mighty character which was worthy of the Senate in its richest tradition since this Government was born. He loved America and America loved him.... He believed in America with a passion that was the touchstone of his life. America—whether it always agreed with him or not—believed in him. It knew his courage. It knew his shining probity. It knew his soul-deep sympathy with human needs. It knew his deathless dedication to representative democracy.[3]

Seven years later, at the unveiling of a statue honoring Borah in the Rotunda, Vandenberg added, "Being human, he was not infallible. But he never hedged; he never was in doubt. He never sought the easiest way.... He wrote the honest verdict of his conscience upon every major issue that arose for nearly half a century, and ... in every instance it had its powerful impact upon the affairs of men." Vandenberg drew a parallel with the first Republican president, noting of Borah that "there was something of Lincoln in him. He was the humanitarian who practiced what he preached."[4]

Franklin Roosevelt called Borah "a unique figure," "fair minded, firm in principle, and shrewd in judgment," a man who "sometimes gave and often received hard blows." These were softened by his "great personal charm and a courteous manner which had its source in a kind heart." Like many others who offered encomiums, Roosevelt praised Borah's mind, his integrity, his seriousness of purpose, and his commitment to Emersonian nonconformity during his thirty-three years in the Senate.[5]

Ruth McCormick Simms and cousin Eleanor flanked Alice during the funeral in the Senate. Ruth was one of the very few who understood Alice's grief. The First Lady represented her husband and the nation, but it was also a gracious family gesture to support Alice. They sat in the Senate gallery where Alice had so often cheered on Borah, where she had fully appreciated the nuances of his speeches, discussed in draft while they were alone together in Rock Creek Park or shoulder-to-shoulder in her sitting room. Few realized the truth of their connection. Friends who mentioned his passing in their letters could not know to offer her comfort, and commented on his death as just one more Washington event. It was Little Borah who accompanied the body on the funerary train to Idaho as crowds silently lined the track, who saw his body lie in state in the capital, and who attended the interment in Boise.[6]

The full contours of Bill Borah's love for Alice will always remain obscured by the clandestine nature of their relationship. Yet from the early 1920s until the day he died, Bill found in Alice a kindred spirit and a sympathetic sounding board. Her agile mind aided the formation of his political thoughts, and he found solace in the fact that a woman he held in such esteem returned his love. "I have a frightful struggle with the 'blues' on such a day," he wrote her once. "Actually my thoughts have been of you—one who is always an inspiration—who can dispel doubt and gloom and inspire hope and instill courage as no living creature can. I was thinking this morning if an aeroplane would unload you here the whole town would be different in an hour—you are a wonder." Alice took the edge off Borah's perpetual loneliness. She gave him political advice and worked on his behalf—a partner in his political career. Bill Borah never made it to the White House, and it isn't clear whether that highest position was Alice's hope for him. She swallowed her criticisms of Bill for the most part, and she understood his iconoclasm—she who had received such a large portion of that troublesome gift from her own father. In the end, to comprehend fully the relationship between Bill Borah and Alice Longworth, as political confidants, as lovers, and as parents of Paulina, one must, as Borah directed Alice, "read in my message much more than I have written."[7]

·   ·   ·

The 1940 presidential campaign was hard fought by Republicans, who assumed they would pick up Democratic voters made nervous by the thought of Roosevelt's controversial third term. "I am more interested in politics than ever," Alice told the newspapers, "because it is more necessary that people vote and vote intelligently today than it ever has been, because democracy is in such peril all over the world." Alice saw ominous international trends. Anti-Semitism and fascism were on the rise in Europe, and she believed demagoguery characterized the Roosevelt presidency. "We must get the power of decision in foreign affairs back into Congress. The power to make war back to the House, the power to make treaties—foreign agreements—back to the Senate.... Send warning that our government is a representative democracy, not only in form but in fact.... The center of our government has changed in 8 years to a hardly concealed authoritarianism," she mused.[8]

By late 1939, Alice thought that Ohio's Bob Taft was the Republican Party's best choice for a standard-bearer. One contemporary described Taft as "nothing less than a portable university. The campus was plain but the faculty first-rate. His exceptionally brilliant mind had the computerlike qualities of speed, accuracy, and utter thoroughness." Alice agreed. Flattered, Taft was "most anxious" for Alice to attend the convention as a delegate, as he knew that Ted had already come out for Thomas E. Dewey. Meanwhile, Republican nominee Wendell Willkie went after the Democrats from another angle: "Every time Mr. Roosevelt damns Hitler and says we ought to help the democracies in every way we can short of war, we ought to say: 'Mr. Roosevelt, we double-damn Hitler and we are all for helping the Allies, but what about the $60 billion you've spent and the 10 million persons that are still unemployed?'"[9]

But Alice was not a great fan of Wendell Willkie's. She threw her thoughts down on paper, contemplating the European situation and laying out her isolationism:

The identical views of the 2 candidates have served to trick the people into believing that you can "aid Britain short of war"—and keep out of war. All out aid means war—is war—undeclared or declared. The people had no choice. The Anglophiles—the Hitler haters—nominated their candidate Willkie— From that moment there was no choice—no alternative—to all the steps "short of war"—up to the brink—and over—in to war. So with regard [to] the scene . . . Japan is against us—Germany smashing Br. and Br. munitions transports and ours too. Smashing Suez—with the Spanish and French smashing Gibraltar. It ought to be a full . . . drawn war before many months have gone by—no "appeasing" by either side of the other—a fight to utter exhaustion. Administration has asserted that every measure that has been taken is for the purpose of national defense—to defend U.S.—to keep us out of war—the draft is . . . necessary to defend U.S.—IF ATTACKED— It is openly stated now that we are organizing an army for EVERY PURPOSE—for the purpose of defending Br because Britain is between U.S. and . . . German victory. . . . [This] year our . . . first line of defense . . . is the British navy.[10]

The summer of 1940 was a disquieting time. The news from Europe and Asia was relentlessly bad. After the German invasion of Poland on September 1, 1939, and the Allied declaration of war against Germany, Europe had settled into what Senator Borah labeled a "phony war." But that turned out to be a time of regrouping for Hitler, and in April 1940, the Nazi blitzkrieg began again. By the summer, Italy was in the war, and Germany had conquered France. England stood alone. Japan had announced the creation of the Greater East Asia Co-Prosperity Sphere, its term for the empire it wished to create across Asia. To protect this endeavor, Japan entered into the Tripartite Pact with Germany and Italy in the fall of 1940. This set the stage for the Japanese invasion of French Indochina. While some Americans believed that President Roosevelt should prepare for the inevitability of U.S. engagement, polls continued to show that the majority of citizens preferred not to get involved militarily.

Alice and other isolationists came to the same conclusion. They took a long view of history, noting that Europe had survived its battles for thousands of years. While even today we find Hitler and his campaign of genocide and enslavement incomprehensible, at the time most Americans did not understand the depth nor the breadth of evil in his plans. Consequently, isolationists believed the man in the White House seemed determined to bring the United States into a war of misguided nobility to protect the British. Alice feared this would bring political, social, and financial disaster to America. Worse, it would simultaneously increase the power of the president while providing a screen for the continuation of the New Deal programs she had been publicly criticizing. Alice had written to Ted in August of 1939, "I'm fascinated by Franklin's note to . . . Hitler. To use the phraseology of the Covenant of the L[eague] of N[ations] to Hitler! Clanking the ball and chain of the Versailles treaty, which is Hitler's red rag, bloody shirt—the reason with a big R for everything he does. It can't have been inadvertent—mere stupidity. It must have been deliberate. 'Needling' the Führer. It's proof to me that Franklin's trite pieties mean nothing. That he wants war. That he realizes that war is the only way he can retrieve his power which has been slipping so rapidly—that only war can divert attention from his sweeping failures."[11]

Everyone had an opinion. Women and men of good heart disagreed about the best role for the United States, and argued endlessly the potential outcomes. Representative Hamilton Fish urged all candidates for the presidency to declare their stances on "collective security, entangling alliances, military and naval pacts, armed intervention, secret diplomacy, war commitments and delegating to the President discretionary war-making powers." Congress had outlawed certain types of assistance to belligerent nations in an effort to protect U.S. neutrality. President Roosevelt wanted to have the power to decide when and against which countries the acts would be used. This was unacceptable to isolationists and constituted a potential abuse of presidential power. Conversation grew heated in the capital city. Alice fueled the debate. After a dinner at the home of Senator Burton K. and Lulu Wheeler, Alice and the six other guests "rose to depart, determined to do whatever they could to avert involvement in war."[12]

Alice had studied George Washington's farewell address, and it became her starting point: "I know well that a prescription given to a small nation of three million people need not be the right direction for a world power.

But the lasting validity of Washington's exhortation would become apparent if people did not forget to remember how he qualified it: 'The nation which indulges towards another an habitual hatred or an habitual fondness is in some degree a slave.' This is my credo." Borah fervently shared that credo. He went to his grave regretting that he could neither stop Congress from repealing the arms embargo nor the president from wanting to cozy up to England.[13]

In November, voters responded to President Roosevelt's campaign promise that American "boys are not going to be sent into any foreign wars," although critics were quick to point out what he knew himself, that once the United States was involved, it would no longer be "a foreign war." The third-term issue turned out to be less important than Americans' desire to stay out of the tragedies unfolding overseas, and FDR's pledge soundly defeated Wendell Willkie in 1940.

It is worth remembering now the lack of public support for war that existed in this country until Pearl Harbor. In hindsight, and after more than fifty years' clarity about Japan's aggression in the Pacific and the atrocities in Hitler's Germany and Stalin's Russia, it is difficult to believe that people such as Herbert Hoover, Robert Taft, John L. Lewis, Lillian Gish, Charles A. Beard, Charles Lindbergh, Ted Roosevelt, Robert Frost, Charles Ives, John Dewey, Van Wyck Brooks, e. e. cummings, and Oswald Garrison Villard honestly felt that assisting the British-led Allies would threaten the very roots of democracy in the United States. The despair of the noninterventionists deepened as they felt President Roosevelt took step after unconstitutional step to drag the United States closer to military engagement and circumvent Congress's prerogative to make war.[14]

Kansas journalist William Allen White put together a group to encourage FDR's support for Great Britain: the Committee to Defend America by Aiding the Allies (CDAAA). White's committee was closely aligned with FDR's own outlook.[15] White intended to limit his support to lobbying for supplies and moral encouragement to the Allies, but he was forced to resign because he was outnumbered by more zealous members who felt that aid should involve full military commitment.

An organized opposition to the program of the CDAAA arose in the late summer of 1940, as Germany launched the Battle of Britain. Four Yale law students, including a young Gerald Ford and future Supreme Court justice Potter Stewart, wrote a petition they hoped would inspire other collegians to band together in a national, noninterventionist pressure group. This was the start of the America First Committee (AFC). "We demand that Congress refrain from war, even if England is on the verge of defeat," their petition declared. "But," as America First founder Robert Douglas Stuart Jr. put it, "it became pretty clear to all of us that we needed some heavies to make an impact." The four students sought these "heavies" at the Republican national convention. There sympathetic Senator Taft directed them to General Robert E. Wood. Later, at the Democratic national convention they picked up the support of noninterventionist senators Burton K. Wheeler and Champ Clark, who also suggested they contact Wood.[16]

Wood, born five years before Alice, is best remembered today for his long tenure as president of Sears & Roebuck. In 1940, he had just become chair of its board of directors. Wood was a West Point graduate, a veteran of the Philippine-American War, and an important aide to General Goethals in the Panama Canal building endeavor. In World War I, he rose to brigadier general and was a decorated acting quartermaster general of the army. Securing Wood was a coup.

The first executive committee meeting of the AFC occurred on September 21, 1940. Alice Longworth was a charter member of the national board of directors and of the Washington, D.C., chapter. In these capacities she accepted the AFC creed, which stated, in part, "I believe in an impregnable national defense.... I believe in the preservation of this Republic. Embroiled again in European affairs, we shall lose it.... Sympathetic as we all may be with unfortunate nations overseas, we must remember that we stand alone. Europe and Asia cannot be expected to fight our battles."[17] The organization stressed the protection of the American way of life by heeding the admonitions of Washington and Jefferson to avoid permanent or entangling alliances.

Support for the new organization poured in, from such young people as John F. Kennedy (who sent money and was a "chapter chairman" at Harvard) to farmers, celebrities, industrialists, former Populists, and Progressives. New members included Chester Bowles, Jay C. Hormel, Frank O. Lowden, Eddie Rickenbacker, and Lessing Rosenwald. The Amos Pinchots, former New Dealer Hugh S. Johnson, author John T. Flynn, journalist William H. Chamberlain, and Hoover's undersecretary of state William Castle joined the Washington branch, where Lulu Wheeler served as treasurer. Nonmembers like Senator Wheeler and socialist leader Norman Thomas gave speeches at AFC events. Songwriter "Reidy" Reid penned a ballad, "America First," which made clear that joining was a patriotic act: "The skies are bright, and we're all right / In our Yankee Doodle way / But it's up to us, every one of us / to stand right up and say / AMERICA FIRST! AMERICA FIRST! AMERICA FIRST, LAST AND ALWAYS!"[18] The AFC was the first major noninterventionist organization to oppose vocally the CDAAA. The AFC believed that the CDAAA had the advantages: President Roosevelt's actions were interventionist, the press was largely interventionist, the anti-Hitler emotional appeal was theirs. But the AFC had the majority of Americans believing as they did. That asset was one of only two things uniting the 850,000 individual America Firsters, that and their diversity—they shared no common "economic doctrines, social bases, or political affiliation."[19]

Any number of sympathies might have moved noninterventionists to join. For example, those with a profound abhorrence of war, including parents of potential soldiers and potential soldiers themselves, were likely to sign on. The AFC, however, generally distanced itself from radical pacifists. Those who mistrusted Great Britain—Alice, like many Roosevelts, had a case of this—and some Americans of German descent had an interest in America First. The belief that another world war threatened American democracy and capitalism motivated many members. They already worried, as Bob Taft did, about "the complete unsoundness of the New Deal theory of democracy." Taft particularly excoriated Roosevelt's Lend-Lease, destroyers-for-bases deal, and the methodical repeal of the cash-and-carry law, which pushed the United States closer to direct intervention. That alarm was sounded on all America First literature. " 'The path to war is a false path to freedom,' " was the first principle of the America First

Committee. The preamble to the organization's Statement of Principles and Objectives insisted that the freedoms guaranteed in the Bill of Rights "inevitably will be sacrificed if we enter this war."[20] The passionate belief that America stood most to lose should it enter the war was a consistent caution of America Firsters.

It proved, however, a difficult thing to keep AFC membership separated in the public mind from anti-Semites and fascists who supported Nazi ideology. "There is no room in our program," AFC bulletins insisted, "for persons with leanings that place the interests of any foreign country or ideology ahead of those of the United States. We do not countenance anti-Semitism nor political partisanship." The national committee dropped Henry Ford's membership because "the Committee could not be sure that . . . Mr. Ford's views were consistent with the official views of the committee."[21] Ford was known for having given credence to the fallacious *Protocols of the Elders of Zion,* and as General Wood readily admitted, they had made a mistake inviting him to serve in the first place.

Communists left the organization voluntarily as a result of the Nazi invasion of the Soviet Union in June 1941, which meant—for them—that American military efforts to help defeat the Germans and protect the Comintern became imperative. "Should America Fight to Make Europe Safe for Communism?" America First asked rhetorically. AFC literature insisted that "Communists who really desire to destroy our Government" were as unwelcome as fascists and "ultra-pacifists."[22]

Alice and other America Firsters watched in dismay as U.S. destroyers escorted British merchant ships carrying war materiel across the Atlantic after President Roosevelt repealed the "cash" and then the "carry" sections of the 1937 Neutrality Acts. They found FDR's definition of neutrality preposterous. Once Roosevelt used the loss of American lives from the unintentional German sinking of U.S. convoy ships to issue his "shoot on sight" directive of September 11, 1941, fifty-eight AFC members released a statement asserting that the president had usurped the powers of Congress. Among the signers were Alice and Ruth McCormick Simms, whose *Chicago Tribune* had been publishing anti-intervention editorials.[23]

Alice referred to herself as an "overage destroyer" in reference to yet

another unconstitutional step of FDR's—the destroyers-for-bases deal of
September 3, 1940, in which the United States traded "overage" U.S. destroyers for British naval bases. Many Americans shared her concerns. Just
two months before Pearl Harbor, 80 percent of Americans polled rejected
U.S. entry into the European war. These were the people the AFC lobbied,
preaching nonintervention through speeches, letters to Congress, public
debates, posters, press releases, newspaper advertisements, and rallies such
as Women United, a "spontaneous nationwide expression from members of
54 cooperating women's organizations." Ted's wife, Eleanor, was "honorary chairman" of the event.[24]

The America First Committee canvassed celebrities to get the word
out. Hollywood star Lillian Gish—who occasionally stayed with Alice on
visits to Washington—was a popular AFC orator. By AFC count, thirty
thousand people came to hear her speak in May 1941, and she reached larger
audiences during a radio debate with a CDAAA representative. "Just a
note of thanks for your valiant efforts to keep our flesh and blood from rot-
ting in Europe, Africa, or Asia," wrote one man succinctly. But Hollywood
bosses listened to fans who opposed Gish's view, and she resigned from the
AFC rather than face unemployment. Alice was a comfort to Gish, who
felt, in Alice's presence, that she could talk freely and in so doing, make
sense of the political issues and her troubles. Lillian Gish thought Alice
"much better than a dream come true. We regret," Gish wrote, "all the
years we didn't know you."[25]

Charles Lindbergh, who knew Alice well enough to visit her home not
long after his celebrated solo flight across the Atlantic, was another renowned America Firster. Lindbergh generated a massive backlash against
the organization when he gave a speech many considered anti-Semitic in its
message that Jews were calling for war with Germany. Speaking on September 11, 1941, in Des Moines, the aviator told Iowans that he understood
why: "The persecution they suffered in Germany would be sufficient to
make bitter enemies of any race. No person with a sense of the dignity of
mankind can condone the persecution of the Jewish race in Germany. But
no person of honesty and vision can look on their pro-war policy here to-

day without seeing the dangers involved in such a policy, both for us and for them." Like other groups who called for war, Jews, Lindbergh cautioned, should fight to avoid it, "for they will be among the first to feel its consequences." While he stated he was not "attacking" Jews, he did single them out by suggesting that "their greatest danger to this country lies in their large ownership and influence in our motion pictures, our press, our radio, and our government."[26]

Despite Lucky Lindy's professed admiration for Jews, the response to his words was overwhelmingly negative. Revulsion, disbelief, and anger spilled across editorial pages nationwide. Alice Longworth was one of eleven members of the AFC national committee who met at the Chicago headquarters to assess the damage and consider a remedy. Six days later, to give time for absent committee members to vet the statement and to continue monitoring public response to Lindbergh's speech, the AFC released a one-page statement. It reiterated the national committee's concern that it was the interventionists who "sought to hide the real issue by flinging false charges" and "inject[ing] the race issue into the discussion of war or peace."[27] It stressed that neither Lindbergh nor the AFC was anti-Semitic.

The document did not censure Lindbergh. The organization did not force him to resign. The national committee did "condemn his speech and declare that 'his act must bring upon him the condemnation of all believers in democracy and peace.'" The committee maintained that its members were not in the habit of inspecting speeches before they were given, and the mail coming in to headquarters showed "89 percent supported Colonel Lindbergh's views and 11 percent were in disagreement." Included in the support was a strong letter from Hyman Lischner, who wrote to second the "farsighted words—aye, prophetic words of that courageous and robust American." Lindbergh had thought long about his speech, written six months before he gave it. A *Chicago Tribune* editorial emphasized that "it is better to handle the subject in public discussion than to leave it to the savagery of irresponsible private conversations." The America First Committee contained noninterventionist Jews among its members and leadership. While AFC directors felt Lindbergh's speech was "politically unwise" they nonetheless believed that American Jews were an important constituency to persuade, though difficult because of the rationale for their interventionism.[28]

The AFC used Alice's name as a guarantee that the group was neither anti-Semitic nor pro-fascist. When one interventionist called America First "the greatest Nazi propaganda movement that has ever flourished in this country," John T. Flynn of the AFC countered: "Does anyone believe General Robert E. Wood or...Alice Longworth or Governor Lowden... or any number of others are capable of representing the interest of so unspeakable a system as that of the Nazis?"[29]

Alice's friends and family were puzzled by her zealous noninterventionism. Kermit, who had briefly abandoned the bourbon for a commission in the British army and was fighting the Nazis in Norway, wrote to Ethel: "I can't quite make out what's the matter with Sister." He mused, "Of course she always is agin the Government and it may be that; but I wouldn't like having her mayhem fall into my hands in the fortunes of war, or perhaps I would." Kermit clearly understood the issue differently, and had congratulated Wendell Willkie for having made a "magnificent answer to Lindbergh." Alexander Woollcott wrote to a friend on February 25, 1941, "Alice Longworth has become such an isolationist that she no longer cares to meet me...." Donald Maclean, who worked for the British embassy and was secretly spying for the Soviet Union, accused Alice Longworth of being "fascist and right-wing...[and] everything that's awful." On the night of FDR's third inauguration, Joe and his mother, Corinne Roosevelt Alsop, were guests at Alice's dinner party. Among the isolationist guest list, Joe, an interventionist, "felt 'like a mongoose in a whole nest-full of cobras.'"[30]

Alice was not the lone Roosevelt in the AFC. Ted and his wife were active—attending an executive committee meeting on April 8, 1941, in New York City—although Ted did not share Alice's commitment. Getting tangled up in the world's wars did not appeal to him, but "if and when we are committed, then I feel that every last one of us have got to do all he can to bring the war to a successful conclusion." He took up command of his old WWI unit in early 1941 and was promoted shortly thereafter to brigadier general. Family friends also participated. Ruth joined the AFC national committee by November 1941, and had donated at least four thousand dollars to the cause. Ruth's daughter (Alice's goddaughter) Katrina McCormick Barnes was a financial backer of the AFC, as was cartoonist John R. McCutcheon.[31]

Was Alice's time wasted in such an effort? The AFC did not keep America out of World War II, but noninterventionists "definitely affected the strategy" of FDR's administration. They kept their position, which, they were proud of recalling, was the view of a large majority of the population, in front of the president—an important role in a democracy. Secretary of War Henry Stimson "felt that the non-interventionists had fought the President almost to a standstill near the end of 1941 when the Japanese attack on Pearl Harbor took the decision out of American hands."[32]

Alice followed her isolationist convictions, but the price for activism was high. The AFC never lost the taint of anti-Semitism. To an extent, all its members became tarred with that brush—despite their having joined for more than a dozen other reasons. Alice Longworth's own writings do not indict her as a virulent anti-Semite. Like most Americans of her class and time, she could display a complete lack of sensitivity toward Jews, while at the same time counting among her friends Jews both prominent and not so well known. "It is hardly fair," she wrote in a 1941 draft column, "to criticize Jews as a group. Persecution has been the difficult breath of their being for too many centuries to expect them to ignore their so-called racial sympathies and merge into the nations of which they are citizens. Their national citizenship is secondary to their age long blood ties." Even Belle Roosevelt, Kermit's wife and a friend of First Lady Eleanor Roosevelt's—and generally farther to the left of the political spectrum—could be insensitive, mourning "the note of bitterness" the narrators "injected" into the 1943 "Jewish Memorial and protest" she attended with ER.[33] Very, very few Americans were without prejudice.

The Japanese attack on American soil in the early morning hours of December 7, 1941, and the resultant deaths of 2,344 Americans extinguished the AFC. Just after Pearl Harbor, General Wood stated the case: "The principal purpose to which the AFC was dedicated and which bound together its members throughout the country no longer exists. As patriotic Americans, loyal to their government, the members of the AFC now have no alternative but to disband, cease their activities, and dedicate themselves to the job at hand—winning the war." Even the *New York Times,* no friend to the isolationists, could "salute the leaders of the America First Committee who have taken [this] patriotic action without a moment's loss of time."[34]

After the tragedy at Pearl Harbor, America Firsters became pariahs. Ted's wife, Eleanor, complained to Alice, "I went over to the Island last week for two nights and did they all walk round me like I was a swamp! I had told Alec [Woollcott] I would not come because it was nauseating to me to see people who screamed for war with no intention of interrupting their lives to take part in it." Eleanor felt she had a right to be angry, as she and Ted had been volunteering their time to assist Chinese refugees. Alice helped her by appearing at a charity sale in New York to benefit Madame Chiang Kai-shek's Fund for Chinese War Orphans.[35]

The war came closer when Alice's nephew Quentin, Ted's son, was wounded in Tunisia, North Africa. The newspapers gave the sanitized version, but from Ted—writing from the battlefront—came the real story of a bullet lodged forever between Quentin's kidney and liver. The promotion that followed was some solace, and Quentin was soon writing the family cheery missives again. Alice's brother Archie also joined the war effort. His service in World War I had earned him full disability, but that didn't stop him. Archie and his wife, Grace, stayed with Alice in Washington before he shipped out.[36]

Alice continued her denigration of FDR's administration. In April 1943, Kermit's wife, Belle, dined with Alice and Frank Kent. Alice was, Belle confided to her diary, "disarmingly loving to me, but my goodness, the accumulation of bitter criticism is hard to take, and Kent's antagonism (he was never, himself, an isolationist), I found intolerable—not one word of praise of anything or anybody." They talked politics, of course, and Alice's candidate at this early stage of the 1944 presidential election was Ohio's conservative governor John W. Bricker. Of the current crop in Washington, Belle reported, Alice and Kent "tore down everything and everybody.

Alice said she was sickened by the self-righteous attitude of those attempting to form a fine new world. I asked if she didn't think it a worthwhile objective, and she said frankly, no, it was impossible, and it was anyhow, only a cloak to throw over the desire and intent to remain in power."[37] Alice had watched efforts at innovation after World War I with the League of Nations and the World Court—and still thought she had been right about the futility of that task.

The two friends shared Alice's aversion to FDR. Kent was the well-known author of a syndicated daily column for the *Baltimore Sun* entitled *The Great Game of Politics*. It had been running since 1922, the year he went to London as a political correspondent. Joe Alsop thought him "by far the best of the vigorous political columnists in Washington." But his true calling was congressional muckraker. He wrote half a dozen books, most of them, such as *Political Behavior* (1928), exposing the customs—both conscientious and unsavory—of Washington politicians. Kent's letters to Alice demonstrate his infatuation with her. Kent, who was married, addressed Alice as "Darling," boasted to her of his successes, and professed his undying antipathy toward the New Deal.[38]

Another Roosevelt hater became even more important to her: president of the United Mine Workers John L. Lewis. Big, rugged, handsome—"a man of great physical presence," according to one who knew him.[39] Lewis was not, in fact, that different from Bill Borah, physically and temperamentally, Alice herself pointed out. She found them possessed of "the same large, shaggy heads and they both alternated between being very stimulating or very taciturn. They were *never* boring." Lewis was astute, powerful, recently widowed, and the preeminent domestic thorn in FDR's side, as he proudly led a controversial wartime coal strike. Journalist Elsa Maxwell wrote a flaming column in support of Lewis and the right of American workers to strike. Her paean to workers concluded with a characterization of Lewis as "that weird cross between William Jennings Bryan and Machiavelli, who was discoursing learnedly on Milton." She told him that at the cinema his picture was hissed more loudly than the pictures of Hitler or Hirohito. "Lewis' face grew solemn. 'Alas,' he said, 'the public forgets too quickly.'" "In my private opinion," the journalist confessed,

"John L. Lewis is the most fascinating, DANGEROUS, soft-voiced, gentle-mannered, blockbuster in the whole Labor Blitz." It's no wonder that Alice kept this column among her papers. And, as happened with Bill Borah, political sympathies couched in elegant language kindled the fires—and he amused her. "Humor was the great bond between us," she said.[40]

"Dear Aquarian," Lewis called Alice, in honor of their shared birthdays on February 12. The two exchanged books—it was she who had sent him the Milton—literary references, insider knowledge, and compliments. "Assuredly we should propitiate the gods," he wrote. "Verily, you have a deft touch with the Greeks. Perhaps I can aid with the Norse school and the Celtic spirits." She understood his cryptic messages: "Bread and butter, conceivably. The roses—the telephone—never! I vow it." And while he respected her boundaries, he found ways to insinuate: "I suspected the leaves would turn and secretly desired to remain and watch the event. [Yet] meek spirit and the conventions and duty prevented. A word, Alice, [about] these October nights. Beware of spells cast by the waxing hunters moon. If perchance you should become bespelled write me before you are dis-spelled. . . ." He let her know exactly where his mind was. He recounted a boring afternoon visit: "As my host droned on my roving literary eye was reading titles. It came to one and stopped. 'Crowded Hours.' The world he ees not too beeg, no."[41] From vacation he wrote, "You, compañero, have oft been in my mind. You have truly met your recent troubles bravely as I knew you ever would. Thanks for your superb letter from Grandin Road. Have read it oft—but shall burn it today. No other eye should ever see—. . . Later we will laugh again at many things, which only we can see." And his signature line for that letter: "The things unsaid. We know them. Juan." [42] He addressed her as ALL and signed himself JLL. "Dear friend," he also called her, and sometimes wrote letters with no content, perhaps for the sake of contact only, such as this one:

> Mon Ami: The night falls, the wayfarer needs must rest. 'Tis a cheerful inn at a crossing of the Camino Real. Mine host does one well, if one but carry a bulky purse that clanks anon. I supped well and was fain content save for one rude fellow to who I was sore put to be civil.

'Twas his head and not his heart. Albeit he should mend his manners, else he come afoul some gentleman less patient and more bold than this 'parfait gentil knight.' The elements weary the traveler but the inns refresh and help shorten the leagues that lie between. The Yuletide wanes and the old year with it. May the New Year be more to your wish, gentle lady, and all good fortune attend thee and thine."[43]

Alice enjoyed this wordplay. It was a language shared by few, and indulged in by even fewer.

Respecting her opinions, Lewis imparted Alice's "words" to a colleague, attributing them to "a well informed source."[44] She brought him into her inner circle of Washington politics and society, although he had already breached the walls of Washington's elite. Lewis, famous organizer of the working class, appeared in the *Washington Social List*. He was not, however, among the Harvard and Yale networks in D.C. Access to journalists and politicians in the informal venue of Alice's home was invaluable, as hers remained the hub of anti-administration gossip.

Alice and John Lewis had much in common. He became disenchanted with the New Deal and came to share her enmity toward Roosevelt. They had worked together on the America First agenda, and they shared a "love of strategy for its own sake." Even during the important 1941 strike, when the FDR White House favored the miners and convinced operators to negotiate with the union, Lewis, like Alice, had the gumption to "humiliate the president publicly for inept leadership." Lewis reported the progress of the strike to Alice. "The chess game which is coal is satisfactory at this exact moment of writing. I detect some signs of weakness in my noble opponent.... We can move either way we choose, later."[45] As war came, Lewis's reputation diminished. Americans desired unity—and Lewis did not obediently rally 'round the president. When Hitler invaded the Soviet Union in June and Stalin joined the Allies, Communist sympathizers in the labor movement shifted their support to Roosevelt. Always working the angle he thought best for labor, Lewis didn't care how people perceived him.

Alice and John L. Lewis also shared a horror of a fourth term for FDR.

Eleanor Roosevelt herself "doubted whether Franklin [could] be reelected" in 1944. ER saw only two likely candidates for the Democrats: John G. Winant and Henry A. Wallace, and she preferred the former. The president also preferred Winant, reported Belle Roosevelt after a forty-five-minute conversation with FDR. He said Winant "brushes aside all the inessentials with one gesture—and he can handle the English, which is a very important part of the set-up."[46] The ability to bring the war to a successful close, and to maintain the appropriate relationship with the British while doing so, was uppermost in Roosevelt's mind and a driving factor in his consideration of a fourth presidential term.

And then, in June 1943, came the sad news of Kermit's death. He had been stationed with the U.S. Army at Fort Richardson in Alaska, far from the battlefront and the glory. He was not well. Hard drinking and malaria had taken their toll. Unable to escape a series of personal failures, Kermit put a bullet through his head. Archie was philosophical about his brother's descent into liquor and aimlessness. "Of course, intellectually, I know it's the best thing that could happen," Archie wrote to Ethel, "but it is a real break with the past. Two of our generation have now gone, both in time of war." Archie's opinion was ultimately a cold one: that in dying when and where he did, Kermit "saved many a heart break and many an uncomfortable and a complicated time for those who were nearest and dearest to him."[47] Edith could not see it as Archie did. Kermit was always a happy and free spirit, the most like TR in many ways, and to know that he could not recover his joy and live a full life was a crushing realization for his mother.

Edith felt her age keenly. She had never stopped missing Theodore, and she longed for more time with her children. Her body showed signs of the years passing by, never so much as when she had fallen and broken her hip just before Thanksgiving in 1935.[48] She had been confined in a heavy brace, which helped the healing but made walking difficult. Heart trouble complicated her eighth decade. But it was Kermit's battle with alcoholism that hurt the most. World War II might have been Kermit's salvation—hard work and a noble cause—but his body was too far gone.

Ted, fifty-six years old, also had to overcome physical challenges to do his part in the war. A brigadier general with an arthritic hip who commanded his troops with the aid of a cane, Ted's career and his life ended in a blaze of glory. On June 6, 1944—D day—Ted led the U.S. Army Fourth Infantry Division from the first boat that went ashore on Utah Beach. Under enemy fire, he got them inland. Then he went back and did it again— leading wave after wave upon the beach. Three days later "the most decorated soldier to serve in World War II" died from a heart attack. He was awarded the Congressional Medal of Honor posthumously "for gallantry and intrepidity at the risk of his life above and beyond the call of duty" that "contributed substantially to the successful establishment of the beachhead in France." When a son dies a hero's death, the son dies nevertheless. Edith wept through the first church service she attended after she heard the news.[49]

Lieutenant Colonel Archie Roosevelt remained at his post, battalion commander with the 162nd Infantry in New Guinea, until a grenade and malaria sent him to a hospital stateside to recover. All of Theodore and Edith's boys had served in World War I. Quentin did not return. The remaining three served in World War II. Only one, Archie, came home to see his mother and his sisters and to try to pick up life as before.[50]

Chapter 20

"Full Sixty Years the World Has Been Her Trade"

ALICE LONGWORTH's public drubbing of the New Deal created her reputation as the leading political wit in Washington. Her epigrams encapsulated concerns some Americans felt about the Roosevelts' leadership. They were repeated endlessly. Alice became identified with her one-liners—so much so that her other contributions to American political discourse faded from public memory. People forgot that such wit is possible only when upheld by a broad intellect, insider status, and years of political and legislative expertise. For the two long decades of Democratic rule, Alice inspired the Republican troops with her constant barrage. She was part court jester, part Machiavelli. She had access and power and institutional memory. More and more the media referred to her as Princess Alice again (a title she thought "*too* utterly revolting" at that stage of her life).[1] Eventually, she embraced the celebrity role of acerbic political analyst. The general public paid her sustained attention; politicians could not ignore her, even though as the cold war began Alice was still an "out of season" Roosevelt.

Not until 1952 would Dwight D. Eisenhower's presidential victory shatter the Democratic hegemony. The World War II hero defeated Alice's candidate, Robert Taft, who had failed in his White House primary attempts in the 1940s, too. The cynical satisfaction of watching the man who defeated him, Thomas Dewey, lose to both Franklin Roosevelt (in 1944) and Harry S Truman (in 1948), hardly made up for Taft's losses. Though she was able to celebrate the emergence of a new champion in Richard Nixon's election to the House of Representatives in 1947 and to gain satisfaction from a groundswell of posthumous critical press for Franklin Roosevelt,

Alice Longworth remained largely isolated from the White House during the Truman years.

Mitigating her sense of being outside the center of power was the ongoing success of Alice's dinners. Alice's salon continued at the heart of Washington entertainment, helped by the fact that First Lady Bess Truman was not known for her brilliant diversions.[2] Darrah Wunder, longtime executive secretary of the Cincinnati League of Women Voters, wrote about Alice in her memoir. "I loved Alice Longworth's dinner parties, although one had to do detective work to find out who the guests were. Alice would say, 'Bob you know Darrah Wunder, or Bunny or Archie of course you know Darrah.' Of course they didn't, but I knew Bunny de Chambrun, married to [Pierre] Laval's daughter, and Archie Roosevelt, and I hunted up a good friend who briefed me on the ones I didn't know. It was at Alice's that I met John L. Lewis for she invited anyone that amused her." And everyone seems to have reciprocated, either by showing up or by inviting Alice to their parties. Wunder, who served as Martha Taft's private secretary, recalled how "Alice was wonderful to me and a great help, for when we were having some newly elected Senators and their wives to dinner and I feared the party wouldn't get off the ground quickly, I'd suggest we'd ask Alice and Bob would always agree."[3]

Personal losses continued in the 1940s. Her household and her circle of intimates would shrink when her daughter married and Ruth and Edith died. Union business and national politics frequently called John L. Lewis away from Washington. Alice turned sixty on February 12, 1944, without those closest to her. Joe Alsop remembered Alice caricaturing herself at that time as Atossa, from Alexander Pope's "An Epistle to a Lady" (1735). It was one of the countless bits of poetry Alice could recite from memory:

> But what are these to great Atossa's mind?
> Scarce once herself, by turns all womankind!
> Who, with herself, or others, from her birth
> Finds all her life one warfare upon earth:
> Shines, in exposing knaves, and painting fools,
> Yet is, whate'er she hates and ridicules.

> No thought advances, but her eddy brain
> Whisks it about, and down it goes again.
> Full sixty years the world has been her trade,
> The wisest fool much time has ever made.
> From loveless youth to unrespected age,
> No passion gratified except her rage.

Alsop thought that Alice's use of Pope's misogynistic writings to describe herself was evidence of an unhappy life, but she would hardly recite a positive poem about herself—that would be boasting—and to do so would elicit the fawning she so despised. Yet this poem reverberates with some of the criticism leveled at Alice, especially the indulgence in passionate rages. It held some bitter truth for her, too. "War is an inevitable thing," Alice philosophized, "peace is the interlude."[4] As a child she did feel "loveless"; as an adult she did enjoy exposing knaves and fools. "The world had been her trade" all her life. Alice had "gratified . . . her rage" against Franklin and Eleanor Roosevelt. In so doing, the reputation of her "eddy brain" had brought her new admirers and wider fame. As the cold war advanced, Alice Longworth retreated to the role of "the wisest fool." She was impatient with the Republican Party's inability to defeat Harry Truman in 1948, and less than thrilled about the anti-intellectual Dwight D. Eisenhower. In her sixties, Alice conformed—to the public, at least—to that sketch of Atossa.

But that mantle was not all that she wore. She often quoted another smidgen of "Epistle to a Lady:"

> 'Twas thus Calypso once each heart alarm'd
> Aw'd without Virtue, without Beauty charmed;
> Her tongue bewitch'd as oddly as her Eyes,
> Less Wit than Mimic, more a Wit than wise.

Alice had not lost the ability to "alarm" men's hearts. John Lewis was a steady companion throughout the 1940s and 1950s. Her tongue certainly "bewitched" legions of Americans, but she herself was often her own target. Though she might suggest she was "more a wit than wise," acquaintances and friends knew of her superior intelligence. She had stopped keeping up with current fiction in the late 1930s. She concentrated instead on contemporary history and current events, including the scientific news that fascinated her, such as Edwin Hubble's discovery that the universe contained more than one galaxy. During a trip to Pasadena, she, Paulina, and two friends trekked up the San Gabriel mountains to the Mount Wilson Observatory. Alice spent the night listening to the lawyer-turned-astronomer demonstrate the Hooker one-hundred-inch telescope. They gazed into the depths of space, just as Alice had done so often as a girl at Sagamore Hill. Hubble thought he'd "never spent a better night in a telescope" than he'd had with Alice, fueled as it was by her endless curiosity and enthusiasm.[5]

Her fascination with biology continued as well. After all, she had studied social Darwinism for thirty years. She had watched as evolution had been used by New Dealers who believed that some Americans were genetically incapable of caring for themselves. Then Adolph Hitler viciously twisted the field to justify his murder of those he deemed "sub-human." In the postwar years, Alice followed the research being done at Cold Spring Harbor Laboratory and studied the evolving field of molecular genetics. She read avidly about the work of Linus Pauling, James Watson, and Francis Crick. She read paleontologist Louis B. Leakey and maintained her interest in primate behavior. Alice enjoyed *The Sea Around Us* so much that she telephoned Rachel Carson to tell her so.[6] Politics and science were the background for the rest of her reading, which included several newspapers every day—always the *New York Times,* the *Washington Post,* and the New York *Daily News.* Bill Walton, a *New Republic* journalist and Kennedy intimate, called her "one of the best read, best educated women I've ever come across."[7]

Alice's schedule was idiosyncratic and structured by her reading habits. Washington parties generally broke up early, as legislators had to be to work in the mornings. After such gatherings, Alice retreated to her bedroom on the third floor of the Massachusetts Avenue house and read far into the night—sometimes straight through until dawn. "It's intoxicating for me," Alice insisted. She read and reread books. She read book reviews. "I got no education and I'm rather glad I didn't," Mrs. L took to saying in the 1960s, "as it saved so much excitement for my antiquity."[8]

Alice's bedroom resembled a Dickensian shop, with books stacked upon books, spilling out of the revolving bookcase she kept by her bedside. When she wanted to look up a passage and could not locate the book she sought, she bought another copy. Proprietors knew her tastes and set aside volumes for her to consider. She frequented local bookstores, such as Olsson's on Dupont Circle, and the Saville in Georgetown, walking out briskly in the early afternoons. When she was forced to part with some of her books, one book buyer, novelist Larry McMurtry, described them as "excellent books, in several languages."[9] Friends learned not to telephone until after 1:00 p.m. Before then, a maid would answer and take a message. After 1:00, Alice would pick up herself and bark her fierce hello—more a statement than a question.

Such hours were difficult with a child, even one in her teens. Half a year after Alice's sixtieth birthday, and one month after Ted's death in France, nineteen-year-old Paulina announced her engagement to Alexander Sturm. Sturm was the son of Katherine McCormick Sturm, who was distantly related to the *Chicago Tribune* family, and businessman and artist Justin C. Sturm. Alex attended Yale, wrote and illustrated two books before he turned twenty, but was, Alice thought, not good enough for Paulina. She saw in him the thing she had most despised in her own husband: addiction to liquor. Paulina had mercifully grown up without the specter of alcoholism. While not a perfect childhood, at least it was free of alcohol-related traumas. She attended school in Cincinnati, and Alice took her to spend the summers in Wyoming at the Dewey Riddle Ranch. Paulina's debut was held at Cincinnati's exclusive Camargo Club, attended by hundreds of Washington and Ohio acquaintances.[10] Paulina had attempted Vassar College, which she disliked and from which she did not graduate.

Alice and Paulina did not have an idyllic relationship. Some friends suggested that Alice wanted her daughter to be just like her. Paulina was certainly as shy and as intelligent as Alice. But Alice grew up surrounded by half siblings, whereas Paulina was an only child with few playmates. Alice put her daughter on display, as doting parents do, but when Paulina resisted or withdrew, Alice finished her sentences and drew the spotlight back to herself. Kermit, who had good insight into Alice, once referred to Paulina as "Sister's competition." Paulina's stutter, fairly unusual in girls, may have been a result of anxiety or stress. For all her other talents, Alice was not an ideal mother. It's true that Edith's example of mothering was far from perfect, but Alice had also had her rambunctious and adoring, if distracted, father. Nick had died when Paulina was six, and all of the parenting duties then fell to Alice. She encouraged Paulina's horseback riding and even once fought Andrew D. Mellon's plan to raze Paulina's riding school. Alice was not demonstrative with Paulina, nor was she the sort of mother to whom a child readily went for comfort, physical or emotional. Paulina's nanny, Dorothy Waldron, did not wholly make up for it. She was strict and distant, a "dragon" to one friend's way of thinking, although another considered "Waldie" "a very nice person" who was close to Paulina."[11]

The difficult relationship with her mother may be what pushed Paulina toward Alex Sturm. After a brief courtship, they declared their intention to marry. As one of Alice's friends commiserated, she knew Alice would "be sad to lose her." And good Joe Graydon wrote at this juncture of Alice's life, offering solace about Ted's recent death and congratulations on Paulina's engagement. He "hope[d] not so much that she may have a happy life as that she may have a useful and interesting one which in the end is bound to be the most satisfactory." Was that a comment from an old friend who read in Alice's own choices "a useful and interesting" but not a happy life? Or was it a twinge of regret about his own choices?[12]

Paulina's wedding plans were made as the 1944 campaign unfolded. New York Governor Thomas E. Dewey was the Republican whipping boy, running against President Franklin Roosevelt's fourth-term attempt. Dewey, a dapper dresser, whom Alice found to be otherwise "incompetent" and "a frightful bore," looked "like the little man on the wedding cake." This dandy dismissal alone did not bring about Dewey's defeat at the polls, but some people gave it that much credit. From the vantage point of 1960, Clayton Fritchie wrote, "Politicians are agreed that such scornful quips hurt Dewey in the election."[13]

While the maxim was attributed to Alice, she regularly denied having formulated it. Not until 1968 was her confusion about how she came to be credited with it cleared up, when she received a letter revealing the true author. Isabel Kinnear Griffin wrote to say that twenty years earlier she was "working with Helen Essary Murphy on the *Democratic Digest*, [a] publication of the Democratic National Committee." An "unflattering picture" of Dewey that needed a caption prompted Murphy to pop out with, "He looks just like the little man on the wedding cake!" The two women loved the line so much they didn't want it to go unnoticed and felt the *Democratic Digest* was not a large enough forum. "We plotted," Griffin wrote Alice. "At the British embassy reception that afternoon we asked each person we met: 'Is it true Alice Longworth said Governor Dewey looks like the little man on the wedding cake?' As we had anticipated, it spread like wildfire, only now it had become: 'Have you heard Alice Longworth's description of Governor Dewey?'"[14] Such was a mark of Alice's stature as a wit.

The 1944 Republican convention was held in June in a swelteringly hot Chicago. Alice checked into the Blackstone with Paulina. The two watched the show with Ruth and her daughter Bazy. Unlike 1936 and 1940 when Alice was a delegate, in 1944, she had no official role. Paulina was a page and Ruth was a member of the resolutions committee from New Mexico. Ruth supported Dewey and as the owner of six thousand cattle and ten thousand sheep in Colorado, she told reporters she was "interested in the agricultural plank." Just for the record, she stated, "I was a member of America First, and I don't approve of alliance with Britain." Alice was hoping to see the GOP promise to provide "a big navy, and strong air power." The only public remark Alice would make about the contest that would pit the Republican nominee against cousin Franklin's fourth attempt was succinct and devastating: "The Republican party is here to elect a President and not retain a dictator." Privately, she thought sterner measures ought to be taken: "Amending the constitution to set a limit on presidential terms is long overdue."[15] Like many other Americans, she disliked any man's ability to serve in an unending presidency, too reminiscent of a dictatorship in those World War II days, and contrary to the aims of the founders, Alice thought.

Dewey won the GOP nomination, with John Bricker (whom Alice had damned with faint praise by calling him "an honest Harding") receiving the vice presidential nod. Taft was Alice's first choice in 1944, but the erudite Ohioan could never surmount his lack of charisma to win a nomination. Although "he could outthink almost everyone," Bob, unlike his genial father, hated to kiss babies and attend pancake suppers. Neatly nailing both Taft's personality and her loathing for FDR, Alice said, "Having the Senator replace FDR in the White House would be like a glass of milk after a slug of Benzedrine." Had Taft won in 1944, Alice's life would have been much different. He had called her "an intimate friend" since 1938. Alice truly liked Martha Taft, who was well educated, fun, and devoutly interested in politics. [16] Because of their friendship, Taft's election would have made Alice a political insider again.

Perhaps it was the disappointment of seeing Dewey triumph over Taft in the primary that gave impetus to the *Chicago Tribune* interview entitled "Politics Losing Hatred's Spice, Alice Laments." In 1944, the journalist wrote, "Everyone is so terribly amiable. No one really hates any one else. . . . Various combatants in the political arena today may think it pyramided with hate, but Mrs. Longworth scoffs at it. . . ." Alice compared the "feeble" disagreements of the 1944 political scene to 1912 and found them "tepid." " 'But then,' " Alice declared, " 'then one really felt violent. I had heard of seeing red, but I didn't merely see red. Things danced redly before my eyes. O, it was wonderful.' Who hated? The other faction, she was asked. 'No, no, no,' [Alice] cried in excitement. 'We all hated! We hated. They hated. Everyone hated.' And you enjoyed yourself? 'A great many people didn't, but I did. It was a bath of hate and fury. There hasn't been anything like it since.' With that," the journalist concluded, "she sat back and smiled and smiled and smiled." Though Alice proclaimed it animated her, as one friend put it, "everyone always pretended to be nice and she pretended to be unpleasant."[17] Malevolence was becoming part of her persona.

The postconvention letdown was tempered that year by Paulina's wedding, which took place in Magnolia, Massachusetts, on August 26, 1944. Because Ted's wartime death had occurred only about a month earlier, the wedding was simple. Ethel Barrymore stood by Alice, and Ted's son, young Cornelius Roosevelt, gave the nineteen-year-old bride away before their two hundred guests. As her engagement photos attest, Paulina had grown into a beautiful young woman. She wore her mother's stunning pearl necklace, given to her by Cuba on the occasion of her own wedding, and a lace veil from Russia, a gift to Alice from the Romanovs. Justin Sturm played the organ for the seven-minute wedding ceremony led by the Right Reverend Oliver J. Hart. Paulina's grandmother Edith Roosevelt, her aunts and uncles, including Mrs. Ted, Ethel and Dick Derby, and Belle, were there to see her wed. Alex's mother was pleased with the event. She thanked Alice and called it "real perfection...all beautiful—well timed—well carried out and with great taste and charm!"[18] Alex and Paulina settled near his parents in Southport, Connecticut.

Ruth, suffering from pancreatitis, could not attend the wedding. Her health was failing, but surgeons delayed operating and her pancreas ruptured. Ruth had been in Chicago seeking votes for Dewey. She died there, with her daughters, Triny and Bazy, by her side. Alice's sorrow can only be imagined. Ruth had been her best friend since they were young women. She and Ruth had attended each other's weddings, buried husbands, raised children, plotted strategy, and fought side by side for shared causes. Alice had supported Ruth's career in electoral politics and allowed Ruth to cajole her into active work for which Alice frequently and fondly called her "B.D.—Benevolent Despot." With Ruth, Alice could be at her silliest and most playful. Ruth's family remembered the astonishing loud monkey impressions the two friends did, perching on the backs of the sofa, screeching, and picking imaginary lice off each other. The two could chitchat about "Freud and religion and sex...."[19] Mourning Ted and Ruth, whose deaths came so close together, must have taken an incalculable emotional toll on Alice.

Then, on April 12, 1945, she and a stunned world received news of the death of Franklin Roosevelt. Alice conveyed her sympathies to Eleanor.

The suddenly-former First Lady admitted to her that she was "shocked" by Franklin's death, but "grateful that Franklin suffered no pain and was spared a long illness." While Alice and Eleanor retained what Joe Alsop called the "suitable gestures of cousinhood," Franklin's death—with mistress Lucy Mercer Rutherfurd in the house—did not spur either woman to confessional confidences.[20] The spleen and duration of Alice's public condemnation of Roosevelt's New Deal had been too great.

Friends, lovers, family, enemies—all dying. The 1940s was a decade of loss. When death keeps such close company, the survivor's chill can spur some to work with renewed vigor, conscious of fleeting time, and others to sink into bitterness or melancholy. Alice kept in fighting trim, but just barely, if Isabella Greenway King's picture of Alice that August 1945 was true. "I had a marvelous time with Alice Longworth," she wrote to her son:

Drove myself down to the Ritz... at 5:30 and remained till 10. We had a cozy dinner in her room. The visit will fill a whole letter. The high spots are that all is well with Paulina and Alex—but Alice's fingers are crossed and she knocks on wood as she speaks.... Alice is in bad shape with a deep rattling bronchitis which she can't shake and somewhat jolted from falling down her Washington stairs in the dark—and being generally battered and bruised and cutting her nostril open on the balustrade. She called the Dr who said he'd come in 3 hours. "If you can't come now don't come at all" was Alice's answer. So the cut healed of itself—when it should have been sewed—but doesn't show because as Alice says "It's in a wrinkle!"... A package was delivered during the evening. It was 2 detective stories ordered by Alice—for herself—there you have the picture except her extraordinary appearance which I felt—let her down rather shamefully.... She was charming, heart warming—and I do love her....[21]

Contemporary events soon replaced the detective stories. Alice had been paying attention to the "ceasefire reaction" in the press and the news from the Pacific as the atomic bombs brought an end to World War II. In the wake of the Allied liberation of Europe and the clear need for assistance to the war's survivors, Alice became an honorary chairman of Associated Relief for Austria (ARA). Its goal was "to distribute clothing, food and money to the peoples of that country 'who need it most, regardless of party affiliation, race or religion.'" Shoring up Austria with assistance from the non-Communist West to gain an ally in the upcoming cold war was a secondary but real goal.[22]

In the spring of 1946, Alice learned she would be a grandmother. What should have been unalloyed good news was tempered by her knowledge that her fears about Alex's drinking had been realized. Unable to assist her daughter or control her son-in-law, Alice continued to grow apart from Paulina. Alice was not close to Alex's family either. "The relationship between Mrs. Longworth and Mrs. Sturm," thought David Mitchell, a friend of the younger Sturms, "was very complicated and quite difficult at times...." It was to John Lewis that Alice confessed her concerns for the mother-to-be. "I know how hard it is to wait," Lewis reassured her.[23] A healthy granddaughter, named Joanna, arrived on July 9, 1946. Hers would be an unhappy and chaotic childhood, but Alice, kept at arm's length by her daughter, was unable to help for the first decade of Joanna's life.

Joanna was born a week before family matriarch Edith Kermit Carow Roosevelt turned eighty-five. Edith missed Alice. "It is so long," Edith sighed, "since we have had a family gossip...." After the deaths of Ted and Kermit, Edith had not often ventured far from Sagamore Hill. Age was telling on her, but she kept her sense of humor. She called herself "a battered old Mother, but still on deck!"[24] When Paulina was at Vassar, Alice had seen more of Edith. In Washington, Alice became a magnet for another generation of Roosevelts, as Bye had been earlier. Alice's nieces and nephews sought her out as their studies or jobs took them to D.C. Nephew Archie Roosevelt wrote in August 1950 to tell her about his upcoming marriage to Selwa Showker ("I know you will like her," he promised). One niece found Alice "a relation who is a real and understanding friend," while her new husband was "appreciative" of "the warmth of your welcome to us in Washington—and he does not say these things easily." And this particular relation was something unusual, as the niece, Edith, had married Alexander Barmine, described in the gossip columns as a "former Red

Army General," and by his wife as one who "incidentally happens to belong to a family of Russian nobility that dates only five hundred or so years
back!" Alice bucked cold war convention and made a point of dining with
them, signaling, according to journalist Cholly Knickerbocker, that the
couple was "not only socially acceptable, but are always welcome in her
home," and as a result, in others. Archie and Selwa ("Lucky") Roosevelt
echoed this, because they knew Alice's "stamp of approval meant that [we]
were also *persona grata* in the salons of the 'three Bs'—Mrs. Robert Woods
Bliss, Mrs. Robert Low Bacon, and Mrs. Truxton Beale."[25]

Alice didn't just introduce young relatives around, she folded them in
with an extraordinary group of friends. Her poker parties, which were
good sources of news, included, over the years, people as diverse as film
star Constance Bennett and her husband, Brigadier General John Theron
Coulter; Lawrence Spivak; Secretary of the Treasury Ogden L. Mills;
Mary Brooks, assistant chair of the RNC; "Wild Bill" Donovan, head of
the Office of Strategic Services; Maryland GOP powerhouse Louise Gore;
and Bazy and her husband, Peter Miller. Other friends, like philosopher
Isaiah Berlin, attended luncheons, teas, or dinners. In between visits, So-
licitor General Philip B. Perlman kept Alice apprised of interesting proceedings in court by "preparing a schedule of cases for your, well, if not
edification, certainly for your amusement during the fall and winter. For
instance, the Supreme Court willing, there will be two cases involving the
famed [alleged Soviet spy] Judy Coplon...." He filled his letter with Justice
Department news written "very, very confidentially." With another frequent luncheon guest, Supreme Court Justice Felix Frankfurter, Alice discussed Benjamin Franklin, the U.S. Constitution, and the books they sent
each other. Chief Justice Charles Evans Hughes was a special friend, as was
Justice William O. Douglas. A profile in the November 1950 *American
Weekly*, when she was sixty-six, depicted Alice as "a living, vital legend in
a city where famous figures are legion. People still turned to look at her
erect, almost military bearing as she walked the streets—to gossip of
her headstrong actions, her famous feuds. Beneath the picture hat which
she almost invariably wore, her gray-blue eyes were still level and direct.
Her hair, once a light brown, was peppered with gray, but her posture made

her seem taller than her five feet, three inches and belied her age."[26] New hostesses made their appearance in the cold war years—like Perle Mesta and Gwen Cafritz, for example, but Alice's house remained the destination of choice for journalists and policy makers.

Alice ran "a political drawing-room" and like a diplomat, brought leaders from many different fields to her home on Massachusetts Avenue. She could be, as *Die Weltwoche* put it, "just as benevolent as malevolent." Trying to capture the essence of Alice for his readers, the columnist described her "tremendous influence by the subtle means which are only at the disposal of intelligent women.... However large a party, Alice Longworth is its natural center. This is due to her inexhaustible vivacity, her great art of imitation, the grace of her attitude and movements, but first of all to her ruthless intellectual honesty. She gives lavishly without stint, and does exactly the same without an audience. A stupendous memory enables her to recite, like Winston Churchill, not only Keats and Milton and the *Nibelungenlied*, but also the most exotic modern poetry. She is very angry with her compatriots because they have lost the habit of reading, and lives with her books until three o'clock in the morning. They, she says, are my best company."[27]

That company always included journalists and authors. She received a copy of Sir Richard Burton's *The Kasidah,* from C. D. Batchelor, a political cartoonist. Batchelor was the creator of one of Alice's favorite cartoons: "All this and Truman, too," which showed great, looming heads of ER and FDR, and down below, a miniscule Harry Truman. Intrepid travel writer and photographer Freya Stark came, as did Walter Trohan, conservative journalist and chief of the *Chicago Tribune* Washington bureau from 1949 to 1969. He and Alice shared strong opinions about U.S. foreign policy. They were both furious when President Truman relieved General Douglas MacArthur of his command in Korea. Trohan had the additional lure of being one of Truman's poker buddies, and so could bring back insider dirt. With journalist Malcolm Muggeridge, Alice exchanged views of his *Winter in Moscow.* "One or two chapters are amusing, I think," he wrote her modestly, "but I blush for some of it."[28]

While most of Alice's friends were men, she did have many women in

The dazzling Colonel of the Battalion of Death

ABOVE: The erudite Cincinnati attorney, Joseph Graydon, whose mind delighted Alice

⋯◆⋯

LEFT: The Lion of Idaho, Senator Bill Borah

⋯◆⋯

OPPOSITE: Alice with her infant daughter, Paulina, born in 1925

ABOVE: Nick and baby Paulina

---◆---

Alice appeared in a Pond's
cold cream advertisement as
an investment for her
daughter's future

MRS. NICHOLAS LONGWORTH
on keeping one's appearance up to the mark

Ruth Hanna McCormick shaking hands with a constituent, while Alice looks on

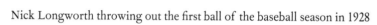

Nick Longworth throwing out the first ball of the baseball season in 1928

Ted and Alice sharing a laugh during the 1920s

Alice on the cover
of *Time* magazine
in 1927

—◆—

A dapper
Nick Longworth,
c. 1925

A formal photo of Nick
and Paulina

❖

Alice and Paulina and
their shared love
of reading

Alice Roosevelt Longworth

tells how Senators choose a light smoke...
considerate of their throats

"*I often lunch in the Senate restaurant at the Capitol. Nearly every Senator and Representative there smokes, and the number I see take out a package of Luckies is quite surprising. Perhaps surprising is not the word. Because off and on, ever since 1917, I myself have used Luckies for this sound reason: They really are a light smoke—kind to the throat. It's simply common sense that these Senators and Representatives, whose voices must meet the continuous strain of public speaking, should also need a cigarette that is considerate of their throats . . . a light smoke.*"

Alice Roosevelt Longworth

In a recent independent survey, an overwhelming majority of lawyers, doctors, lecturers, scientists, etc., who said they smoked cigarettes, expressed their personal preference for a light smoke.

Mrs. Longworth's statement verifies the wisdom of this preference and so do leading artists of radio, stage, screen and opera, whose voices are their fortunes, and who choose Luckies, a light smoke. You, too, can have the throat protection of Luckies—a light smoke, free of certain harsh irritants removed by the exclusive process "It's Toasted". Luckies are gentle on your throat.

THE FINEST TOBACCOS—
"THE CREAM OF THE CROP"

A Light Smoke
"It's Toasted"–Your Throat Protection
AGAINST IRRITATION–AGAINST COUGH

ABOVE: Mary Borah (second from left) and Alice (third from left), spectators at the Capitol while Native Americans perform a snake dance, May 1926

≈◆≈

Attesting to senators' smoking habits

ABOVE: A smiling Alice
(back row, second from left) and
a pensive Paulina (front row, third
from left), with Vice President
Charles Curtis

Labor leader John L. Lewis,
testifying at a public hearing about
the 1943 miners' strike

Bride Paulina Longworth and groom Alexander Sturm take center stage for a day

Alice with her infant granddaughter, Joanna Sturm

❖

BELOW *(left to right)*: Katharine Graham, Felix and Marion Frankfurter, Joe Alsop, and Alice Longworth

The famous pillow, at her home in Dupont Circle

BELOW: Charming Robert Kennedy who, Mrs. L thought, could have been "a revolutionary priest"

Making a point
to Richard Nixon

❖

BELOW: The "elbow-
in-the-soup"
concentration on
cellist Pablo Casals's
return to the
White House

Joanna Sturm with her grandmother—two women with lightning-quick
and curious intellects who loved and respected each other.

A family favorite photograph of Mrs. L, paused in her reading,
sitting by the phone she always answered herself

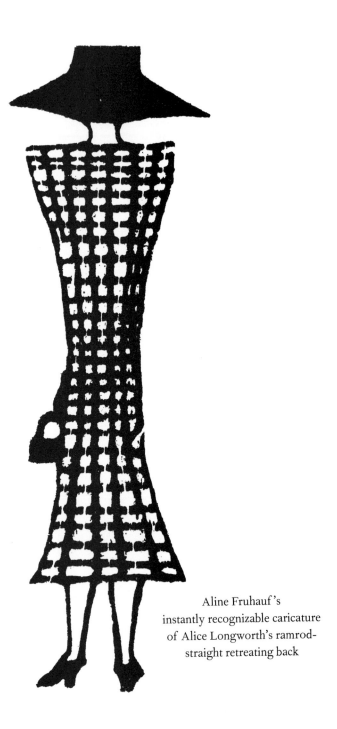

Aline Fruhauf's
instantly recognizable caricature
of Alice Longworth's ramrod-
straight retreating back

her circle, too. Nick's former lover Laura Curtis Gross was a longtime pal. There had been an attempt at a rapprochement with Cissy Patterson before the latter died.[29] Alice was close to Evangeline Bruce, Tish Alsop, former Office of Secret Services operative and columnist Kay Halle, and *Vogue* columnist Susan Mary Patten. A frequent visitor for poker and tea was the intelligent, straight-talking Bazy. She and her husband, Peter Miller, had purchased the LaSalle, Illinois, *News-Tribune* in 1946. In 1949, she took over the editorship of the *Washington Times-Herald*. Shortly thereafter Bazy and Miller divorced and she wed *Times-Herald* city editor Garvin E. Tankersley. Divorce was so uncommon in 1951 that the couple could hardly find a minister to marry them. Disregarding social custom, Alice attended their wedding and often invited Bazy and "Tank" to her home, shocking Washingtonians. After the sale of the *Times-Herald* to the *Washington Post*, Bazy became a successful columnist for the *Chicago Tribune*, writing "Sidelights from the Nation's Capital," for almost twenty years. She shared Alice's conservative political views and was very fond of the older woman.[30]

Edith Hamilton, the popular historian of the ancient world, traded books with Alice, who also sponsored a friend of Hamilton's for membership in the F Street Club. Alice became very good friends with the multitalented and erudite Huntington Cairns and his wife. Hamilton and Cairns worked together to edit and publish Plato's *Dialogues,* and Cairns was also the editor of one of the most dog-eared books in Alice's library, *The Limits of Art: Poetry and Prose Chosen by Ancient and Modern Critics.* He was an attorney with the U.S. Treasury who, during WWII, had an engrossing position on the U.S. Commission for Protection and Salvage of Artistic and Historic Monuments in War Areas. Cairns was connected to the new National Gallery of Art in Washington. He also, for more than two decades, advised the federal government on censorship issues. He knew as many people as Alice did, in as many fields. Through contacts such as these, in 1947, Alice was able to help John Lewis locate a publisher for one of his books.[31]

That year, Alice assisted the career of another author. Her broad reading brought her into contact with a book she thought worthy of the Pulitzer Prize. She put *Tales of the South Pacific* by a then-unheard-of author named

James A. Michener into the hands of her friend *New York Times* columnist
Arthur Krock, who was on the prize committee. *Tales of the South Pacific*
was an "unusual" book, she averred, and very unlike Krock's own choice—
which Alice felt had "no vitality!" The committee agreed with Alice. She
congratulated Michener years later when she met him, saying, "I'm proud
of the fact, Michener, that you didn't let us down." The Pulitzer helped to
launch James Michener's career. He went on to write more than forty bestselling books, run (unsuccessfully) for Congress, and earn many other
awards, including the Medal of Freedom in 1977.[32]

At her home and at the F Street Club, Alice entertained these and other
writers. One political spouse emphasized how such parties were "an essential means of communication." David Mitchell experienced this firsthand.
Mitchell came to dinner as a friend of Paulina and Alex's. He was a young
banker, just stepping into his career. Thinking of his interests, Alice told
him, "We must get a banker for you!" Mitchell was grateful at her considerate gesture, but later stunned when he found the other "banker" was Bill
Martin, the head of the Federal Reserve Board![33]

But politicians were the mainstays of her get-togethers. Because "she
could draw people out masterfully and she was interested in nearly everything," as one guest said, almost anyone could turn up for dinner. In the
1940s, if they were politicians they were usually fellow conservatives such
as the Robert Tafts and the Richard Nixons. In later years she would enjoy
inviting guests with diametrically opposed viewpoints and seating them
next to each other—just because it was fun.[34] She was not the only hostess
who did that, but in the immediate aftermath of the Franklin Roosevelt
years, as her political leanings then were decidedly rightward, she preferred the company of kindred spirits.

Dean Acheson was one such. The son of an Episcopal bishop, an author, attorney, and secretary of state in the Truman administration, Acheson once resigned as undersecretary of the Treasury under Franklin
Roosevelt. He objected to the president's decision to take the United States
off the gold standard—the same thing Alice had protested when she draped
herself in gold at the White House reception. Acheson was Alice's powerful contact in the State Department. He enjoyed her teas and found her

difficult to resist. Acheson confessed to Joe Alsop once, Alice "tempts me to spice my talk." Alice was fond of pointing out to sundry visitors her five-foot-tall wall hanging of a prowling tiger that she thought looked just like the stylish and well-groomed secretary of state. The painting especially captured the subtle menace of his mien—right down to the eyebrows. Acheson's had "a prowling quality" and were "just like a cat's whiskers," Alice said; they "reacted involuntarily."[35] The secretary of state had the cold war to battle and was one of the authors of the U.S. policy of containment toward Communism. Alice shared Acheson's anxieties about the Soviet Union, and for her there was a historical continuum that explained the position of the United States in 1946:

> I think history has borne out my conviction that the first World War should have ended without victors and vanquished. Today it seems that even a German victory early in 1914 or 1915 would have been better than what we got eventually. At least there would not have been a Hitler and not a Russian frontier on the River Elbe. I have often wondered what would have happened to the German character if the Germans had had less misfortune in their past. But that's merely conjectural. Let us speak of the last war. People call me anti-British. That's absurd. I only insist that our relations with the British must not be ruled by a "habitual fondness." Our own interests first, and if they coincide with British interests, all the better. Franklin just as Wilson mismanaged our diplomacy. Of course, Britain's defeat would have imperiled our own security, but as the price of our assistance we should have imposed upon Churchill the spirit of compromise—not with Hitler and his fellows, but with the German opposition. To help Stalin unconditionally was sheer lunacy. What's the use of having Russian imperialism as the successor of both German and Japanese [imperialism]?[36]

Alice honed her opinions by talking with people such as Secretary Acheson, reading methodically, and attending congressional sessions. She was still one of the "regulars" who "habitually frequent every klieg-lighted congressional hearing." Alice was "on hand" for hearings on topics as diverse as candidates for the position of undersecretary of the navy (for which she was spotted wearing black and "daintily waving a long, red cigarette holder"), hearings on "Greek-Turkish loans," and the improprieties in government contracts during the war in the Senate War Investigative Committee.[37]

She herself became a topic in a Senate investigative committee in 1946. In a pamphlet written as part of a "smear campaign" to defeat Alice's friend Senator Burton Wheeler, Alice was accused of unduly influencing senators' votes as the leader of a powerful interest group, the so-called "social lobby." The acrimonious congressional debate began with Senator Wheeler denying that he knew the social lobby. "Well," the *New York Times* reported his interrogator as charging, "I saw the Senator dining with it in the restaurant of the Senate." "What silly nonsense," the Montana senator retorted. "To show the Senators the type of mind that is speaking I will say I had lunch, yes, with Alice Longworth, and I am proud of the fact that she asked me to go to lunch.... She never mentioned this bill. That is the social lobby." Wheeler was an old friend who would not have considered Alice's interest in legislation as *necessarily* lobbying for one outcome or another— and he was a canny politician who wouldn't have admitted it had it occurred. The whole notion would have caused Alice great amusement, but her power did not go unnoticed.[38]

In 1947, she had personal reasons for attending Senate Committee on Labor and Public Welfare hearings. Bob Taft—"Mr. Republican"—was the powerhouse in the GOP-controlled Eightieth Congress that opened on January 6. He and his colleagues set about undoing entrenched New Deal legislation, with varying degrees of success. They wanted to "restore those principles of freedom which had been the foundation stone of America's historical development," as Taft put it.[39] Leading the charge were young conservative legislators, like Ohio's John Bricker, Wisconsin's Joseph McCarthy, South Dakota's Karl Mundt, and California's Richard Nixon. Taft cosponsored the Taft-Hartley Act, designed to replace important sections of the New Deal pro-labor bill, the Wagner Act. For ninety minutes in the Committee on Labor and Public Welfare, Taft led the grilling of John L. Lewis. The labor leader was getting the better of the senator, and applause and laughter greeted some of Lewis's "sallies," the *New York Times* reported:

> "You think you are an average man, Mr. Lewis," remarked Mr. Taft. "It is practically up to you to decide what your union does." "I wonder why you make such an inaccurate statement, Mr. Senator," remarked Mr. Lewis in a drawling voice as he smiled. The chamber echoed to laughter. Mr. Taft persisted. He said the union was run by "powerful" men, not "average men." "I, too, have read in the papers that you are pushing the Republican party around and making the decisions," commented the witness. Quickly Mr. Taft replied that "in this Congress nobody can boss anybody else." "Methinks the Senator doth protest too much," parried Mr. Lewis. The audience tittered.

Alice listened to this wordplay sitting "behind the committee members." After Lewis made clear his opposition to "any amendment of the Wagner Act," he gallantly "extended his hand to her across the table as he left the witness chair."[40]

Family and friends wondered about John Lewis and Alice. The two depended upon telephone calls and visits when they were both in Washington, but their summertime and holiday correspondence gives a sense of their affinity. They exchanged Christmas presents and books; Alice gave him the edited volumes of her father's papers, which John professed he would "treasure." He read them with his daughter, Kathryn, both of whom had admired TR. John's notes echoed her concerns, chiefly Paulina. He worried about Alice's health. He devoted four pages in one note to ideas about when and where they could meet. Her letters, he assured her, "gave a lift to a tired man." The pair were co-conspirators when John Chamberlain of *Time* magazine begged Alice to use her influence over Lewis in the selection of a leader for the United Mine Workers fund: "We know that John Lewis has a great respect for your political acumen." Alice sent Chamberlain's letter on to Lewis, who gave her instructions as to what to say back and how to phrase it.[41] In the 1970s, Alice told a reporter she felt "lucky in my middle age, to find a new delightful companion." When the journalist asked whether they had discussed marriage, she admitted, "I think it was in the wind. But I didn't take it seriously. I wouldn't have married anybody. Once is enough, but, for me, he was the best company there ever was." Like Borah, John was a Renaissance man. He could discuss politics and poetry and family and foreign affairs spiritedly while making her feel she was the only one in the room. And she liked his philosophy for dealing with obstreperous elected officials: "Be subtle. Lure him with the rapier and then cleave him with the axe."[42]

The old causes had new incarnations. In 1947, her isolationism led her to unite with eighty other "prominent Americans" to champion a United States of Europe. She joined an appeal to all Americans for their support. It read, in part, "Twice within our lifetime...the national interest of this country demanded that we participate actively in wars resulting mainly from Europe's disunion. A third World War, springing from the same causes, lies as a threat to our peace and prosperity as long as Europe remains split up into isolated national units." The signers called for an economic union "dedicated to liberty and peace," governed by a "federal police force" that would "release the nations of Europe from the crushing burden of competitive armament." The American group was headed by Arkansas Senator William J. Fulbright and based on the pan-European ideas of Count Richard N. Coudenhove-Kalergi. Alice became a member of the national board, which included Herbert Hoover, Louisiana Democratic representative Hale Boggs, Clare Boothe Luce, James Farley, Allen Dulles, and Norman Thomas. They hoped to support "a common foreign, economic, and military policy and a common 'bill of rights.'" In fact, the organization they wanted sounded very much like the European Economic Community initiated in 1957. This project had something of the outlawry of war in it—a chief concern of Borah's, and perhaps for Alice a way to carry on in his memory. It also was an alternative to the United Nations, a brainchild of Franklin Roosevelt that held its first meeting in 1945. The United Nations involved the United States, but the United States of Europe would not similarly entangle America.[43]

Such foreign policy concerns dominated the 1948 presidential election.

As the cold war unfolded and the iron curtain divided Communist from non-Communist Europe, Republicans applauded President Truman's containment policy and his loyalty programs to locate and purge "subversives" from the civil service. The GOP hit hard at Truman's domestic agenda, suggesting that New Deal–type reforms such as a minimum wage and farm support had outlived their usefulness. Then the Democratic Party, with "one foot in the grave and the other on a banana peel," according to New Dealer Harold L. Ickes, split three ways.[44] President Truman gained a reluctant nod from the Democratic regulars. Southerners opposed to his civil rights initiatives offered their own candidate, South Carolina governor J. Strom Thurmond, on their own ticket, the States' Rights, or Dixiecrat, Party. Iowan Henry A. Wallace, one of FDR's former vice presidents, made a bid with his Progressive Party.

Republicans thus seemed likely to capture the presidency regardless of whom they selected. Alice was one of many celebrities actively working for Bob Taft. She was joined by film star Gary Cooper, poet John Dos Passos, humorist Dorothy Thompson, and columnist and Soviet expert Freda Utley, among others. And it wasn't just celebrities who came out for Taft in 1948. Paulina Longworth Sturm and Bazy McCormick Miller, "two young women, girlhood friends, whose grandfathers made political history," as the *New York Times* described them, founded Twenties-for-Taft. This organization began when the pair gathered twenty-five hundred names of women between the ages of twenty and twenty-nine who pledged to work on behalf of Taft's nomination. It was to no avail. The convention in June passed by Taft again and settled on Thomas E. Dewey, again. Alice was not surprised at Dewey's subsequent defeat. She didn't even vote for him. "You can't," she sniffed, "make a soufflé rise twice."[45]

On September 30, 1948, as the maples at Sagamore Hill dressed themselves in orange and red, Edith died. The end of the former First Lady's life was bitter. "I don't at all like living in this world," she wrote to Alice in 1944—as WWII raged, Franklin still held the presidency, and TR had been gone for twenty-five years. Survived by Alice, Ethel, Archie, and many grandchildren and great-grandchildren, Edith had seen too many years pass in conflict. The recent deaths of Kermit and Ted deepened her sorrow. She had traveled widely as a widow, and had lived a life rich with literature, friends, and family. She never lost her interest in politics. But at the end of her life the normally busy Edith had few plans. "Indeed," she wrote, "my strength is to sit still." But one of the last letters she penned was a thank-you to Alice in a hand shaky with her eighty-seven years. It contained a palliative—straight from the heart of a strong and complex woman seasoned but not broken by life's vicissitudes. "Dearest Alice," she began. "You came to me as a little child and have been a good daughter and I have many happy memories." Alice must have been touched. "Do come to see me when the first trees are blooming and Long Island at its best," Edith urged, "and I shall refuse to let the family sit upon our backs!"[46] It was a tender conclusion to their long relationship.

After Edith's death and with the continued political failings of the Republican Party, Alice found solace in the poetry of Ezra Pound. On her sixty-fourth birthday, she claimed a new "fitting" poem for herself: a stanza of Pound's "The Return":

> SEE, they return; ah, see the tentative
> Movements, and the slow feet,
> The trouble in the pace and the uncertain
> Wavering!
> See, they return, one by one,
> With fear, as half-awakened;
> As if the snow should hesitate
> And murmur in the wind,
> and half turn back;
> These were the "Wing'd-with-Awe,"
> Inviolable.
> Gods of the Wingèd shoe!
> With them the silver hounds,
> sniffing the trace of air!
> Haie! Haie!

These were the swift to harry;
These the keen-scented;
These were the souls of blood.
Slow on the leash,
pallid the leash-men![47]

In 1949, Huntington Cairns took Alice to visit Pound in St. Elizabeth's Mental Hospital in Washington, D.C. They met his wife, Dorothy Pound, "who really took care of him," Alice thought. Joe Alsop, Edith Hamilton, Robert Lowell, and Alice's friend painter Marcella Comes Winslow went to visit the poet. They remembered how his "beard was divided into three parts" and how Pound "used to wear three hats piled on top of each other. Alice thought "At the time it seemed quite natural...."[48]

Ezra Pound fascinated Alice. She owned several inscribed volumes of his poetry. But in Italy he had grown increasingly anti-Semitic. Pound made radio broadcasts condemning the United States as "illegally at war," because of FDR's "criminal acts." When the Allies conquered Italy, American forces jailed Pound, returned him to the United States, and indicted him on several counts of treason against America. When he was found mentally incompetent to stand trial, he was sent to St. Elizabeths.[49]

The mental hospital, one of its physicians averred, "had become a sacrarium for savants," and by the 1950s, visiting Pound "became a status symbol among some circles...a sort of conservative chic." While Alice may have gone for that reason, there were additional attractions: they could bash FDR together, she liked iconoclasts, Pound was a TR fan, and the poet may have reminded her of her days with Bill Borah. In short, as her granddaughter put it, "She had fun with him." Alice and Pound planned to coedit an anthology of poetry from around the world.[50]

A compassionate recognition of Pound's genius and artistic courage made it easier to overlook the fascism and the anti-Semitism and what poet Charles Olson called "the vomit of his conclusions." In 1949, a stellar list of poets saw past Pound's prejudices and awarded him the Library of Congress Bollingen Prize for the *Pisan Cantos*, written during Pound's incarceration in Italy. Established with Cairns's help (Cairns was a trustee of the Bollingen Foundation), the award brought tremendous controversy to the poet, but not freedom.[51] That took another nine years. In 1958, Pound's friends brought about his discharge from St. Elizabeths. Ernest Hemingway, Robert Frost, and T. S. Eliot organized the effort. Alice gave credit to Archibald MacLeish. They won their case in part because they charged that Pound's hospitalization was "intellectually damaging" to the United States, and in the cold war era such a suggestion carried weight. Pound was released into the care of his wife, who returned with him to Italy. The extent of Alice's influence is not clear. She was friendly with those who spearheaded the movement, and it's conceivable that she talked up the cause of his release to politicians and members of the Justice Department at her dinners. She thought Pound was mentally disturbed, but "not a danger to the country" and thus should not be locked up.[52]

One man whom she concluded *was* a true danger to the country was Alger Hiss. Hiss graduated from Harvard Law School and became a model New Dealer, devoting his professional life to governmental service in the Justice and State Departments. In 1947, he was president of the Carnegie Endowment for Peace. His impeccable career made it very hard for most Americans to believe the sensational charge leveled at him in 1948 by Whittaker Chambers, a confessed former Soviet spy. In front of the House Un-American Activities Committee (HUAC), Chambers accused Hiss of being a Russian agent who had worked with him in the 1930s—precisely the years he had served in Roosevelt's administration. Hiss denied it, and he denied knowing Chambers. Representative Richard Nixon, a member of HUAC, was one of the very few who took Chambers's allegation seriously. When Hiss and Chambers both came before the House committee, Alice was there. The case was thrilling and convoluted, and it had everything—duplicity, denials, wild goose chases, microfilm hidden in pumpkins, handwriting analyses, psychological profiling, and allegations of homosexuality. Nixon looked to be a strong cold warrior whose intellect and determination helped him unravel the threads of deception between Hiss and Chambers. After the HUAC hearings, in New York City, Hiss—to protect his name—sued Chambers for slander. He continued to deny that he was a Communist spy, and claimed that he was only a casual acquaintance of Chambers's.

Her friends at the Justice Department sent Alice an "unrestricted pass" for that dramatic case. She was fascinated, and could "hardly bear to leave New York and the trial," when she had to make a trip to Washington. She and her sister-in-law Eleanor were both absorbed in the whole process. Eleanor was reading *The Art of Cross-Examination,* and both of them felt "that any time we spend talking to people about other subjects is wasted!" Eventually, Hiss was sentenced to five years in jail. The public was divided as to Hiss's guilt, but the trial did convince most Americans that Franklin Roosevelt and the Democrats had not been vigilant enough about Communist espionage. When Klaus Fuchs, a Manhattan Project scientist, was found to have given the Communists secret information from the atomic bomb project, Nixon and other hard-liners appeared more reliable than those who advocated a dovish line on the U.S.S.R. After the Hiss trial ended, Alice sent around copies of Victor Lasky's *The Seeds of Treason.* One friend wrote gratefully, "I'm completely satisfied at last that [Hiss] and [his wife] Priscilla are guilty as Hell—and perhaps of a great deal more than has been revealed. Tell Mr. Nixon that he's my new hero—a stunning job he did. Wish they could send <u>him</u> to be your beau on the next big party instead of the infamous Mr. McCarthy."[53]

"The infamous Mr. McCarthy" was Wisconsin's Senator Joseph McCarthy, who capitalized on the fears of Communist infiltration to get himself reelected. In the 1950 campaign, McCarthy intimated that he knew of hundreds of current employees of the federal government who were Communists—and worse, that Secretary of State Dean Acheson knew who they were and allowed them to continue in their positions. Initially, McCarthy looked like an honest crusader. His anti-Communist rhetoric was not unlike Nixon's. Taft and other leading Republicans encouraged McCarthy or copied his talking points in their campaigns.[54]

It was a tense time. China had just "fallen" to Communism. The Soviet Union had recently exploded its first atomic bomb, ending the U.S. monopoly on atomic power. Events in Korea would erupt into a civil war in June, with U.S. soldiers involved there in the United Nations' first ground war. A reporter asked Alice's opinion of the Korean conflict as the U.N. forces were having little success stopping the Communist North Korean advance. "Maybe this will wake people up," Alice commented sharply, "and make them realize how they were sold out" by FDR's wartime diplomacy."[55] Her statement was both a slam at FDR's leadership and evidence of the way she thought of the world.

McCarthy's language influenced the 1952 election as Republicans and Democrats scrambled to prove their anti-Communism. According to Taft's election committee, Taft would "turn our country away from socialistic trends and will restore the free competitive economic system which made America great." Taft's campaign literature in the 1952 election listed Alice Longworth as 1 of 101 names of "The Citizens Crusade for TAFT." Alice continued fund-raising for Taft through the summer, right up to the eve of the 1952 convention in Chicago. She enjoyed her usual suite at the Blackstone Hotel and her usual publicity at the convention. She broke away from the Taft boosting to note that press appreciation of her clothing "will bring cheers" from Paulina, "who insisted upon and selected the wardrobe...."[56] Even Paulina's approval could not compensate for her disappointment that Taft quickly lost his position as front-runner and was denied the nomination yet again.

"Eisenhower was a pleasantly avuncular figure, ideal, I suppose, for the times, but there were certainly no sparks there," Alice said once, but that didn't stop her from being delighted to have a Republican back in the White House. She had worked for the GOP victory, made all the more exciting because her friend Nixon wound up in the vice presidential slot. He claimed that he never really considered seriously the possibility of his nomination for the second spot on the ticket until one of those "behind the scenes conversations" with Alice. She scolded him and told him to discuss it with his wife. "For the good of the party," Alice urged Nixon, "you should take it if you have the chance."[57] When he did, she was pleased. Alice handed out absentee ballots at the Eisenhower-Nixon headquarters in Washington, and donated money to the campaign to help spread, in Eisenhower's words, "the message of our Crusade." Alice must have cackled a bit to learn that John A. Roosevelt, Eleanor and Franklin's son, had crossed the party line and was also out campaigning for Eisenhower and Nixon. She urged her sister, Ethel, to come visit her in Washington and "take a look at Our Side as soon as they move in. Ike is doing well, don't you think?"[58]

She was moved to excesses of praise for Eisenhower: "Today for the first time since 1909," Alice wrote him after the State of the Union address, "I glowed with pride and enthusiasm for a speech by a president not only for what you said but for how you said it. I've looked at politics and government for a long time (it's 63 years this winter that I first came to Washington) and I want to tell you it's mighty pleasant to feel pride and confidence in the leadership which you have shown you possess." Alice was also pleased that the Eisenhowers reestablished the OLD SOCIAL WHIRL, as Bess Furman headlined in the *New York Times,* and Republicans were happy to showcase TR's daughter. Eisenhower told Alice that her favorite John Singer Sargent portrait of TR "occupies the dominant spot in the Cabinet Room these days."[59] The fact that a Republican was back in the White House also facilitated a resurgence in the Theodore Roosevelt industry.

Alice was very involved in the monuments established to honor her father. While the three remaining Roosevelt children did not always agree among themselves on the details, overall the siblings shared a vision of apposite memorializing. In 1919, the Theodore Roosevelt Memorial Association (TRMA) had been born to preserve the memory of the president. After Edith's death, the TRMA purchased Sagamore Hill and turned it into a "presidential shrine." President Eisenhower opened Sagamore Hill to the public in 1953 with a live national radio speech. On the veranda where the Roosevelts had spent so many happy summers were twenty of TR and Edith's grandchildren, wiggling loose teeth, coloring pictures, and waving to the visitors.[60]

Several books had marked the ongoing interest in the nation's twenty-sixth president, spurred by Harvard University Press's eight volumes of the *Letters of Theodore Roosevelt.* In the early 1950s, they were edited by Elting E. Morison and a young historian named John Morton Blum, author of the influential biography *The Republican Roosevelt.* The TRMA threw a party to launch the *Letters,* held at the TR birthplace in New York City. Blum recalled evocatively: "We had all assembled for cocktails when Mrs.

Longworth appeared in the archway...A hush fell as she stood there, a cigarette holder in her mouth, exactly like the holder Franklin Roosevelt had so often used and at exactly the same angle. She had on her head a diamond tiara and she wore a shimmering evening gown of 'Alice blue.' Mrs. Longworth was about seventy then and I was thirty, but I had never seen a sexier woman." She "projected," Blum felt, "the charisma attributed to her father...."[61]

The Republican landslide of 1952 made Bob Taft Senate majority leader, but he did not live long enough to enjoy it. Senator Taft died in July 1953 after a brief but devastating bout with cancer. He was sixty-four. In his memory, friends established the Robert A. Taft Memorial Foundation "to promote the advancement and diffusion of knowledge and understanding." Alice agreed to serve as a trustee, as did Bazy Tankersley and a number of senators who had worked closely with Taft. Had he lived, Taft would have supported another of Alice's causes that year: an alternative to "United Nations Day" called "United States Day." Governor J. Bracken Lee of Utah boycotted, for the second year in a row, United Nations Day. Backed by Alice, General Mark Clark and *Chicago Tribune* publisher Colonel Robert McCormick—members of the advisory committee to "United States Day"—the governor objected to the inclusion of the Soviet Union in the U.N.[62]

Communist Russia's insidious infiltration of American institutions, especially the federal government and even the U.S. military, was the "red flag" Senator Joe McCarthy waved before voters in 1952. His constituents reelected him handily in the Republican rout that year, which served to encourage him to heights of extremism. In his investigations—which ranged broadly across education, media, and government—McCarthy alleged that such men as Secretary of State Dean Acheson and Secretary of Defense George C. Marshall were soft on Communism. When McCarthy accused the U.S. Army of harboring Communists, the army struck back. In the televised Army-McCarthy hearings that spring and summer of 1954, it became clear that there was no low to which the senator would not stoop. His badgering provoked attorney Joseph N. Welch to ask, "Have you no sense of decency, sir?" as Americans watched on new television sets a man who seemed to be without scruples or morals.

Alice attended the Army-McCarthy hearings, sitting sometimes with wife of the vice president, Pat Nixon. When asked by a reporter who saw her there for the third time what side she was on, "She replied: 'I maintain my usual viewpoint of detached malevolence.'" Alice's lifelong isolationism made her inclined to worry about Soviet infiltration, and McCarthy fed her love of spectacle and appreciation for political drama. But Alice saw a side of the senator she did not like at all. As her friends attested, she was a good judge of people and could see right through them. While she had initially enjoyed him "because he was so wicked," the moment McCarthy slid into alcoholism, "that ruled him out," stressed Bill Walton. "Now *there*," Alice said about Joe McCarthy, "was a cheap creature. He had the easy manners of a perfect jay." One friend remembered that Alice "hated" McCarthy and displayed on her mantel a devastating cartoon that made fun of him. At a party in 1950, while at the height of his notoriety, McCarthy draped his arm around Mrs. Longworth. "With a kind of yokel jocularity, he brayed, 'Ah, here is my blind date. I'm going to call you Alice.' She leveled her gaze at him and said, 'No, Senator McCarthy, you are *not* going to call me Alice. The truckman, the trashman, and the policemen on the block may call me Alice but you may not.'"[63]

Nixon's stature grew among conservatives, and Alice found him very interesting. He was "competent," and she liked him. Before and during Senator McCarthy's "sin of pride," as he called it, Nixon came often to her salon. He told stories from inside the battle, like the time he broke up a fight between McCarthy and Drew Pearson, just after the senator slapped the journalist in the cloakroom of the Sulgrave Club. "When Nixon sought your company he probably thought that it was a political advantage," one interviewer suggested to Alice. "I'm certain that he did," she responded. "We took it for granted that it probably was." As she championed him, he became something of a champion to her. A loyal supporter from his earliest days in the House, Alice swept up Nixon, his wife, and their two daughters. Their friendship was well known, and others went to her asking for her help in securing the Nixons for dinner parties. In 1955, papers noted that the vice president "took time off for a long private luncheon at the home of Mrs. Alice Longworth...." In 1959, Nixon appeared on her appointment calendar for at least eight tête-à-têtes. Her friendship lent both social and political cachet. Invitations to her dinners would have been very useful to him, as "political 'inside-dope' stories, rumors, tips, reports of personal feuds, and party intrigue are...favorite topics of conversation."[64]

As Nixon toiled in President Eisenhower's shadow, the U.S. economy roared. The baby boom was at its height—Alice's own granddaughter was a part of that demographic phenomenon—and the first strums of bubble-gum rock were being played. The modern civil rights movement began as Barbara Johns and Linda Brown called the country to task for an unjustifiable system of separate but equal education. Eisenhower personally went to Korea to end the Korean conflict, as he had promised. While there was no real victor in that war, no atomic weapons were used, and the cold war remained the backdrop against which legislative decisions were made. Overall, the country was happy with Eisenhower's administration. When he announced his bid for renomination by the GOP in 1956, Alice cracked, "Well, I see he's thrown his halo in the ring again." She wrote to congratulate President Eisenhower on his reelection, and told him in person at the inauguration festivities. One week later, Alice's world shattered when her daughter died.[65]

Paulina's marriage had been brief and rocky. Alex never really found his stride as a writer, but in 1949, he and his friend William B. Ruger founded Sturm, Ruger & Company. Alex's fifty thousand dollars and Ruger's tool-making skills created what would become "the largest firearms company in the United States." Ruger had "perfected a design for a .22-caliber automatic pistol," which was their starting point. Paulina and Katherine Sturm's secretarial abilities helped launch the company. It was an optimistic time in the family, and Joanna was thriving. According to her grandmother, at three she could "talk glibly on every conceivable subject and she never forgets anything she is told. She adores Paulina and I think tries to be especially good on that account—Her father and his factory are also pretty grand." But two years later, when his daughter was only five years old, alcohol-related hepatitis killed Alex.[66]

Paulina turned to the Roman Catholic Church for solace. Encouraged by friends who thought that the stability and ritual of the mass and the church year would help her, Paulina took to her new religion with zeal. After Alex's death, Paulina and Joanna had moved back to Washington, D.C. She bought a small house at 1220 Twenty-eighth Street, about a mile from Alice's home. Paulina volunteered with Dorothy Day's Catholic Worker social justice organization, but she was plagued by persistent migraine headaches, and the grief caused by Alex's death would not lift. Paulina took nightly refuge in alcohol. Her physician prescribed sleeping pills and pain killers, and on January 27, 1957, an overdose of the medicines, coupled with alcohol, led to her death. Day wrote a poignant panegyric for Paulina, about whom she suggested "there was always something child-like and shy" but "she was valiant, too."[67]

Alice believed that the overdose was unintentional. Paulina had Joanna to live for. Just as important, a newly converted Catholic would never succumb to suicide, given the church's teachings. The church's official position was that suicide was "unlawful," a "most atrocious crime" wherein a human took to himself God's "dominion over life." Some friends expressed a different opinion about Paulina. Bill Walton thought that such accidents occur only when one is "wooing death." He admired Alice for her tenacious crusade to make sure that her daughter was not deprived of the ecclesiastical burial that she would have been denied had her death been ruled a suicide. Other friends blamed the doctor for prescribing the sleeping pills, because in combination with the other drugs, they were lethal. On the day of her death, Paulina's neighbors recalled that she had been in very good spirits and looking forward to an upcoming trip. They saw no reason for concern.[68]

As usual, Alice kept her deepest sorrows to herself. No matter how poor a mother she may have been, Alice did love Paulina very much. Her nickname for her daughter was "Presh," short for Precious. One note from Alice to "Presh my darling," scribbled in pencil and in haste, concluded,

"Remember only that I love you—my darling Presh. I love you. Mother."
Janie McLaughlin, who worked for Alice from 1958 until 1980, recalled
that Alice always kept photographs of Paulina in her bedroom. Alice, at age
seventy-four—and recovering then from a radical mastectomy—took in
her ten-year-old granddaughter. Even though there were others who
wanted Joanna to live with them, Alice stood firm. Paulina had left Joanna
in her care, and Alice wanted to honor that. Alice told Bazy, in an unusually
emotional exchange, that she felt she had "been given a second chance."[69]

At her Dupont Circle home, Alice created for Joanna "an aerie on the
fourth floor" and said the two would live as " 'free spirits' together." Looking for playmates for Joanna and support in the raising of her granddaughter, Alice reached out to her sisters-in-law and other family members. She
wrote to cousin Eleanor in July 1957, and ER promised to visit her and Joanna in Washington. Alice turned most of all to Ruth's daughter Bazy
Tankersley, who had a daughter, Kristie Miller, almost Joanna's age. The
two became close friends. Joanna would come to call Kristie her "pseudo-
sister." Both girls—especially Joanna—loved horses, and the Tankersleys
owned a horse farm in Maryland where Bazy bred and sold Arabians. After
school, Joanna frequently went to their Al-Marah Farm to ride.[70]

Joanna reaped the benefits of being Alice Longworth's granddaughter—such as having tea at the Eisenhower White House—but Alice and
Bazy also worked hard to provide stability and a life with routines and
schedules that had been missing. Every summer, for example, Alice
and Joanna returned to Wyoming, where Alice had taken Paulina as a girl.
Grandmother and granddaughter rode together at the Sunlight Ranch and
relaxed. The rest of the year, Joanna attended school, went riding at Al-
Marah, returned home for dinner with "Grammy," did her homework, and
went to bed. Alice and Joanna would find they were kindred spirits, and
their relationship would become extremely close.

But in the aftermath of Paulina's death, Ethel worried about her sister.
Ethel wrote eight months after the tragedy: "Is it all as beautiful and satisfying as ever? And do you listen to the wind and watch the shadows and
love it all? I am sure Joanna is busy and happy, which...[is]...good...for
grandparents....Are you yet able to sing on your charred limb? I keep

thinking about you and yr agony of spirit over what is past and gone—and I hope that it is lessening. Such terrible blows take time to bud up the wound—it never heals of course. But some people's bandages seem wonderfully durable. Mine aren't." Then she quoted Yeats, from "The Ballad of Father Gilligan":

> He Who hath made the night of stars
> For souls who tire and bleed
> Sent one of His great angels down
> To help me in my need.

Ethel, always gracious, used Yeats as a bridge to connect Alice's sorrows with hers—both their souls tired and bled, but they could be "great angels" to each other. Her husband, Dick, was not well, and, as she told Alice gently, "I don't agree with you about not telling the bad things to the special ones, so I tell you all this."[71]

Chapter 21

"The Most Fascinating Conversationalist of Our Time"

THE 1960S OPENED with a thrilling presidential race. Alice Longworth was personally fond of both contenders, so she could not have been happier. She preferred Richard Nixon's Republican politics, but the whole Kennedy clan delighted her. Either outcome augured well for the upcoming four years. Nixon thought Mrs. Longworth "the most fascinating conversationalist of our time." Both he and his opponent, John F. Kennedy, pronounced Alice their favorite dinner partner. Mrs. L, as she was generally called then, was in her seventies and a recognized Washington icon. Should anyone outside the new Capital Beltway have forgotten, her national reputation was solidified by media coverage of her eighty-fifth and ninetieth birthday parties and the trip she and her granddaughter took to Asia, where she hadn't been for sixty years. Admirers there recognized her as "Alice Blue Gown." At home, her teas, like the hostess herself, had a legendary quality, and journalists, friends, politicians, and family came to entertain and be entertained as they had for the past fifty years. Katharine "Kay" Graham watched Alice for a model of aging gracefully. "Read a lot and not drink" was her summation of Alice's secret.[1] Even as Dupont Circle filled with multistory buildings and amusing hippies, Theodore Roosevelt's daughter remained engaged in current events and opinionated about the passing political scene, as feisty and independent a celebrity as ever.

The Eisenhowers had been good to Alice Longworth, but they were not dear friends. Nor, as it turned out, was President Eisenhower particularly close to his vice president. During the 1960 presidential race, Eisenhower informed reporters he could not think of a single instance when Nixon's ideas had been so compelling that he had adopted them. Alice had a higher opinion of Dick Nixon. She stood by him throughout his phoenixlike career, losing patience only at the bitter end of Watergate. She emphasized frequently to reporters that Nixon was "exceedingly level-headed," a man who "knows what goes on in the world."[2]

Alice avidly watched Nixon's performance in America's first televised presidential debate. Joe Alsop phoned Alice for her opinion. He considered her a brilliant "political handicapper" ever since she had told him, on election eve in 1948, that she didn't think Truman was beaten. "Well, Joe," Alice told him glumly in 1960, "your man's in, my man's finished. I don't see why they bother to go on with the election. Dick has finished himself off." Even though Alsop believed, like Alice, that "the real Nixon was vastly more interesting, impressive, and formidable than his popular image," he lost the election by less than one percentage point—a 118,000 popular vote difference—in one of the closest presidential races in U.S. history. The Nixons retreated to California. Dick and Alice kept up a running exchange of books, and Pat lamented the absence of their "famous 'sessions' which were always so stimulating." When Nixon ran for the California governor's seat, Alice sent him what he considered a "more than generous" financial contribution, but he lost and seemed destined for obscurity. However, she vowed publicly that Nixon would "continue to have my company, because this is a real personal friendship."[3]

As the Nixons left, the charismatic Kennedys moved to the center of Washington politics and society. "I like *all* Kennedys. I've a real feeling for them," Alice said. She called President Kennedy a "literate man of action," just like her father. While she thought that President Kennedy had a fine mind, she saw a kind of fire in Attorney General Robert "Bobby" Kennedy and felt he could have been "a revolutionary priest, a member of Sinn Fein." She also thought that Bobby would have made an excellent president or elder statesman. She told an interviewer in 1967 that Nixon and Bobby were "two of the trickiest politicians I've known—and I like tricks." Bobby had a sense of humor, which Alice appreciated. "I liked Bobby," she affirmed; they shared "a real feeling of amusement and empathy." Alice swore that, when together, they never discussed politics, but that they "would gossip about things." "We strive to amuse the other," she said, "as scrupulous and splendid guests—both of us . . . a hostess's delight!"[4]

As a friend of the Kennedys since the president's senatorial days, Mrs. L attended the inauguration. John Kennedy's address centered on foreign policy, warning that the United States was willing "to pay any price, bear any burden" to fight the threat of Communism. Alice, who was always more attuned to foreign policy than domestic, approved of his hard line on Communism, and she enjoyed all of the vivacious, optimistic, intelligent, passionate young people clustered around his family. She had been to "oh, lots" of the seminars at Hickory Hill, the estate of Robert and Ethel Kennedy. Home to a large and loving clan, Hickory Hill reminded Alice happily of Sagamore Hill, with its children and animals and air of informality. But Alice felt the Hickory Hill seminars were unique. Those invited to "Hickory Hill U." came to eat, drink, and discuss current events— from politics to psychology—under the leadership of experts such as Harvard historian Arthur Schlesinger Jr. and MIT economist Walter Rostow. Philosopher Mortimer Adler cotaught a session in 1962, for example, with Notre Dame's Father John J. Cavanaugh on "whether the Declaration of Independence makes America a Christian country." While this could have been intellectuals trotting out their pie-in-the-sky notions to show off, Alice concluded, "There was nothing precious" about the Hickory Hill gatherings; it was "not snobbery." She thought Schlesinger was "*so* good; he really was a pleasure to listen to." In turn, he found Alice "really quite witty and entertaining," which he didn't expect, as he had supported FDR. Other guests might include Secretary of Defense Robert S. McNamara, United States Information Agency head Edward R. Murrow, Secretary of the Treasury Douglas Dillon, economist John Kenneth Galbraith, Secretary of the Interior Stewart Udall, Ambassador Averell Harriman, and White House press secretary Pierre Salinger. Alice, with her typical modesty about her intellect, claimed she was "too self-conscious" ever to ask a question and usually sat "looking, listening, delighted to be there." Kennedy chronicler David Halberstam reported that at the Hickory Hill seminars, "the women had to be either very pretty, or Mrs. Longworth."[5]

Kay Graham, who became the influential publisher of the *Washington Post* after her husband Phil's death in 1963, described Mrs. Longworth during the Kennedy era as occupying "an established position in Washington as an older prominent figure whom we all adored. She was so established that she was known as 'Washington's other monument.'...Mrs. L had a distinguished aquiline face and long hair tucked up somehow, but not neatly. She was highly intelligent, witty, sharp, and irreverent. She had a caustic and quick wit....She was everybody's favorite dinner guest." In February 1963, British socialite Lady Diana Cooper, visiting Joe and Susan Mary Alsop, was the honoree at a party with a guest list that included Robert and Ethel Kennedy, Edward and Joan Kennedy, Douglas Dillon, Senator John Sherman Cooper, Ambassador David Bruce, and Alice Longworth. The "singular focus of the conversation," Lady Diana remembered, was "politics, politics."[6] And that remained Mrs. L's avocation.

Alice was in her element during the Kennedy era, as the president and First Lady sparked a renaissance of gracious entertaining. Invitations to her salon had always been "a passport to the President's ear" and, as one hostess noted, "Even presidents came to her parties." One analyst's opinion was that Alice's "flattery prompted politicians to repay her graciousness by taking her aside and divulging juicy classified tidbits." On the other hand, old friend Justice Felix Frankfurter was always glad to give her his opinions because, he told her, "you use your tongue for truth-speaking and not for blarney." In 1966, Robert E. Kintner, powerful president of NBC, rated Alice "a fund of accurate information...." Part of the appeal of dining at the Longworth table was a guarantee of confidentiality for all those present. For example, Alice's niece Lucky Roosevelt, then a *Washington Star* journalist, remembered, "We had a tacit understanding that I would never report anything about Mrs. Longworth's dinners, but thanks to her I came to know the Washington establishment."[7]

Alice Longworth's dinners were unaffected by the fads of younger hostesses. Lucky Roosevelt recalled, "We must have dined with Mrs. Longworth dozens of times, and the menu was always the same—crab soup, roast filet of beef with tiny potatoes and a vegetable or two, miniature biscuits, salad and cheese, and the best crème brûlée in the world. Delicious

French wines always accompanied the meal, and the long table was laid with a lace cloth, enough silver to stock Tiffany's and the finest Baccarat glasses." Alice's sister, Ethel, complimented her: "I don't think anyone entertains as well as you do. Everything about it is perfect—food and flowers and silver and china as well as the people you have." Alice Longworth's dinners were such an institution that she apparently didn't even alter her menu for the Catholic Kennedys. "You are a temptress—our Eve of the New Frontier," Ethel Kennedy wrote impishly. "It's always jolly eating meat on Friday." Alice also resisted the social innovation called the cocktail party, which she dismissed as "a Shriner's convention," where the liquor interfered with business.[8]

Her afternoon teas were traditional, too. They involved "tea from a small Dutch silver caddy; a shallow kettle bought half a century ago in London at the Army and Navy stores." Alice lit the burner herself and served Earl Grey tea from the venerable firm Jacksons of Piccadilly. Mrs. L preferred her tea Russian style—sweetened strongly with brown sugar and served in a tall glass that sat in a silver holder. The kettle on the table boiled loudly, but hostess and guests ignored it if the conversation was engrossing. With the tea, Alice served crisp homemade sugar cookies— sometimes with cinnamon—chocolate cake, and bread and butter. Alice Longworth had tea every afternoon, by herself on occasion, more often with one to a dozen other people. Generally, Alice phoned to invite friends, but every now and then people simply dropped in, as her name was in the local phone book.[9]

Those who gathered around her commented on how attractive Mrs. Longworth was. "Her face is mobile, always registering thought and emotion," one interviewer observed. Many friends praised her striking bone structure and the clear blue of her eyes, but Alice had grown very thin. Still lithe and flexible enough to put her toes behind her ears or stand on her head—both of which she did frequently—she was diagnosed with emphysema around 1960, the result of decades of smoking. She had quit by the time Janie McLaughlin came to work for her in 1958, but the illness left her short of breath and made her cough. Alice's greatest fear was that the emphysema would force her to slow the rapid pace of her conversation, which would be "absolute hell on earth." In the Roosevelt tradition, few people knew about the emphysema—but her sister did. "What a nice visit," Ethel wrote in 1962. "I feel all caught up and as ever, enchanted and bemused by you.... You have what is very rare—a way of disregarding, never mentioning, troubles and doubts and pains and aches—which surround us— you down them in a way that is an example."[10]

Even though she was frailer, Alice commanded center stage. John L. Lewis remained part of her life until his death in 1969. Austrian actor Oskar Werner, Johnson adviser Jack Valenti, producer of *Meet the Press* Larry Spivak, and Ambassador Sol Linowitz found their way to her table—her poker table, in the cases of Spivak and Linowitz—and the artist "Andy" (as he signed himself in cards to her) Wyeth and his wife, Betsy. Otto von Habsburg, legatee of the Habsburg dynasty, thanked her for the "charming luncheon." MacGeorge Bundy claimed Alice had overcome his "extremely strong prejudice against Sunday brunch," because hers was "sheer fun."[11]

Alice recalled the long-ago lessons from Auntie Bye. Bye was remembered not for her debilitating arthritis or her deafness, but for her ability to bring together all sorts of people, "all ages...and all kinds." A friend asserted that Bye had "a great gift for mixing people up and yet making everything go perfectly well. She had, in the finest meaning of the expression, a perfectly wonderful, extraordinary social sense." At Bye's home in Connecticut, "there were piles of books on tables and chairs—she read everything in the world—and her comments were extraordinary about all topics of the day."[12] That precisely described Alice as well. As television made inroads, Alice used it as another news source. She watched an occasional television drama like *Ben-Hur*. Her scientific, philosophical, political, and poetical reading continued.

Mrs. L earned her reputation for a caustic and quick wit, but she was also charming and full of good stories. She went out of her way to include bashful guests and to set them at ease. And she was a Roosevelt. This sense of self, and sense of self-in-history, was part of it. She was mellowing, but as Joanna's friend Kristie Miller asserted, Mrs. L still "did not suffer fools lightly. If you crossed her of course you were going to feel the lash." She could be impatient. Bill Walton called her "wicked," and "naughty," but Robert Hellman, who styled himself "Joanna's close friend and male alter ego," said he'd never seen Alice be cruel to anyone who was defenseless. More than anything, Alice was interesting and fun to be with, especially because of her mordant humor and her comprehensive intellect. Mrs. L was a polymath, able to discuss nearly any topic with more than passing knowledge. Walton remembered how entertaining it was to hear her quote great passages from various authors. "It would be something apropos, politically, that she thought fitted. And she'd just *rip* through it. She had," Walton summed up, "the goddamnedest memory of anyone I've ever run across." She could also laugh at herself. Once a dinner partner stopped her short with, "Alice, you say things with more finality to less foundation than anyone I know." She hooted "harder than he did."[13]

Alice thought no one had "a drier, more delightful, humorous, ironic view of life" than President Kennedy and she regularly enjoyed his company. She found him "an engaging character of great ability who needed no window dressing." She respected his mind, what she called "his natural bent for knowledge." She applauded First Lady Jacqueline Kennedy's attempts to restore the White House and support the fine arts. Alice was present in November 1961 when Spain's virtuoso cellist Pablo Casals played for the second time in the White House. The first appearance had been in 1904, when Alice was First Daughter. After the hour-long concert, in front of the other 152 guests, the president presented Mrs. Longworth to Casals. Mrs. L dined with the first family before the pre-Broadway opening of Irving Berlin's musical *Mr. President*, which she viewed from the presidential box—along with Kennedy matriarch Rose Kennedy and Bill Walton—at the National Theatre. The same summer of 1962, Alice, looking "spry and chic in a wide-brimmed, black straw hat," stood by the Kennedys in the White House at the unveiling of the restored "bison mantel," a TR era adornment. Alice was pleased when Kennedy signed a bill to name the Longworth House Office Building after Nick. In October 1963, she dined with the president and the First Lady at the White House as preparations for the 1964 presidential campaign were being laid.[14]

One month later, John F. Kennedy was assassinated in Dallas. Joe Alsop took it very hard, "sobbing uncontrollably" at the confirmation of Kennedy's death. Alice was not shocked—her own father had been shot by a madman—but she was deeply saddened. She thought Joe was being too "boy stood-on-the-burning-deckish." Alice especially decried any attempt to turn Kennedy into a martyr. The potential for assassination, she believed, came with the job of president, and she found it rather pathetic that Americans needed to deify Kennedy. "The moment he died," she mused, "the desire to have a god to worship was extraordinary."[15]

This is not to say she didn't mourn Jack Kennedy. She attended the funeral mass at Saint Matthew's Cathedral with the Alsops, and Ted Kennedy telegraphed to ask her to the East Room of the White House to "join in paying him respects." Alice's condolence letters were heartfelt. To Jackie, she wrote: "Your fortitude through those cruel hours in Dallas and after is unforgettable. I think you know my affection for you and Jack and how I appreciate the unique luster of intelligence, of beauty, of gayety you two imparted to the Presidency. Should you sometime care to see me you need only say so. Love from your affectionate old friend." And to Bobby she asserted: "You Kennedys have an epic quality, of the sort that legends are made of. I don't believe that any family has [ever] taken a brutal tragedy of personal loss with such unflinching courage. Especially you. Because I've always thought that you and Jack had a kinship, a like sense of purpose, beyond the fact of being brothers. I want you to know how truly sorry I am. Love to Ethel and to you."[16]

Alice knew what it was to lose a beloved brother. She was still mourning hers. Ethel Roosevelt Derby wrote in 1964, twenty years after their eldest brother's death: "Dearest Sister:—The Ted. I never forget when you called me the day we heard nor do I ever forget how brave you are, in more ways perhaps than anyone now, but I know." Ethel felt that "the years would not have brought him great satisfaction. What would he have done—," she asked rhetorically.[17] Thoughts such as that didn't much decrease the pain of the living.

When Senator Robert Kennedy was assassinated in June 1968, in the midst of the presidential nomination season, Alice had no public reaction. But she grieved Bobby's death as keenly as she had his brother's. At the time, she was having her portrait painted by Marcella Comes Winslow. Winslow remembered how pictures of Bobby decorated Alice's house and asked compassionately whether she wanted to pose that day, Alice replied, " 'Well, yes, what's wrong with you?' She liked to put on that nothing could really bother her," Winslow thought.[18] Alice was invited to the requiem mass at Saint Patrick's Cathedral in New York City and to the funeral train that took mourners to the interment in Arlington National Cemetery. But she passed up the offer to contribute to *That Shining Hour*, a book of recollections about Senator Kennedy put together by his sister Patricia Kennedy Lawford. Alice abhorred the public need to enshrine either Kennedy after death.

Alice supported former First Lady Jacqueline Kennedy's remarriage to Greek shipping magnate Aristotle Onassis. Not all Americans were pleased to see the iconic First Lady remarry. Alice knew what life on the pedestal felt like and congratulated Jackie for doing just as she pleased: "I've always thought that the delightful damsel at the right on the bull leaping frescos at the [Palace at] Knossos was a Minoan YOU—so now you are returning to the lands and seas of your forebears and Mr. Onassis' names should be Minos and Odysseus instead of those overworked classicals, inappropriate for the Mycenaen he most surely is. This is just a line to tell you what a great pleasure you are and to wish you happiness...." In her return note Jackie "marvel[ed]" at Alice's "original and penetrating way" of seeing and sensing things. "I always did want to live in the Minoan Age," Jackie confirmed. And she closed with her hope that Alice would someday soon meet "Ari."[19]

By the time Jackie Kennedy was planning her wedding, Lyndon Johnson's presidency was winding down. Vice President Johnson had assumed the office in 1963 upon Kennedy's death. Alice thought highly of the whole Johnson family, and they treated her as a national treasure. President Johnson used to introduce her as "the closest thing we have to royalty." She considered him "a lovely rogue elephant," with whom she "had great fun." Alice felt "Lyndon had real flavor. He was not all tight and buttoned up." LBJ may have reminded Alice of Nick's old partner in the House, another Democratic Texan, Cactus Jack Garner, or it may have been Johnson's policy on Vietnam, but his wife, Lady Bird, thought that "they both recognize[d] in each other a strong untamed spirit." For whatever combination of reasons, in 1964, Alice crossed party lines and voted for Johnson. She had taken to calling herself a Bull Moose, not a Republican.[20]

During the Johnson administration, Mrs. L received invitations to banner White House events such as the large musicale in honor of Italy's prime minister Aldo Moro, where American opera diva Leontyne Price sang. The First Lady enjoyed Mrs L. After a lengthy tea, Lady Bird wrote in her diary that "one of the main things I like about Alice Longworth is her spirit and vitality at seventy-nine or thereabouts." Mrs. Johnson encouraged Alice to reminisce about her days as First Daughter once when daughter Lynda joined them for tea. Alice thought Lynda "a nice, serious creature," which was high praise. Lynda and Mrs. L continued their conversation at Alice's home, where they agreed that as a First Daughter "you were damned if you do and damned if you don't." A year later, Alice returned with Joanna for another tea with Lynda and Lady Bird. The First Lady found Alice, age eighty-one, "fiercely undaunted by old age, bristling with the quality of aliveness," telling stories about how she had to escape the White House for Auntie Bye's if she wanted gentlemen callers.[21] Lynda was probably sympathetic, given media interest in her and her sister, Luci.

As the Johnson daughters announced their engagements, that attention reached frenzied proportions. Lady Bird wanted to bring about "a meeting of the bride of half a century ago with the bride of 1966," and so she invited Alice—"an explosion of vitality and interest"—to tell Luci about her escapades. Lynda was also present to hear Mrs. L discuss how much less invasive the press was then, and how she and Nick were never bothered on their honeymoon by inquisitive journalists.[22]

Lady Bird Johnson was an activist First Lady whose cause, environmentalism, was called "beautification" then. Her interests resonated in Alice, who had inherited her father's concern for environmental conservation. Alice told an interviewer that the First Lady "was working so hard to make things better and pleasanter for people; she has unfailing good humor and knows what goes on with politics...." Mrs. L called on Lady Bird to give her tickets to a movie premiere to support the World Wildlife Fund. Alice's philanthropy was nearly always done quietly, and was frequently on behalf of environmental causes. One regular visitor to her home in her later decades was British naturalist Gerald Durrell, author of *My Family and Other Animals,* whose brother, novelist Lawrence Durrell, came occasionally as well. Alice often sent Gerald Durrell away fortified with a donation for the Wildlife Preservation Trust, which he founded.[23]

The Johnsons also had an admiration for Theodore Roosevelt in common with Alice. In January 1965, President Johnson hand delivered to Alice's door a remembrance of the forty-sixth anniversary of TR's death. "Yours is a proud heritage," LBJ wrote in a letter released to the public, "and I would like on this day to express to you something of the gratitude which our nation feels for the wise and vigorous leadership into the twentieth century which President Roosevelt gave us." Alice, giving credit where she thought credit was due, wrote to her friend MacGeorge Bundy to thank him for putting LBJ up to it. Bundy denied it, and suggested kindly that LBJ himself wrote the letter "because it so precisely reflects his own feeling about your father and about you." Regardless of its origin, Alice was "profoundly touched," she wrote to Johnson, "by your knowledge and estimate of what he was." Two years later, Alice helped President Johnson dedicate the giant statue of TR on Roosevelt Island in Washington, D.C. Alice seldom turned away an opportunity to showcase her father and his legacy. She and her sister, Ethel, took Lady Bird and Lynda on a personalized one-hour tour of Sagamore Hill, and one of the gifts Alice presented to LBJ was a biography of her father.[24]

Mrs. L also appreciated the Johnsons' concerns about the preservation of national history. She was a guest of honor at Mrs. Johnson's luncheon for "prime movers in historic preservation projects." Since she was not a member of the National Trust for Historic Preservation, Alice laughed to reporters that she must have been invited because they were interested in the "preservation of a national s-i-g-h-t." By then, Alice herself was regularly called "more of a landmark than the Washington monument."[25]

When Lyndon Johnson declined to run for reelection in 1968, Alice sent him a letter of support: "I want you to know how grateful I am for your splendid, faultless stand on Vietnam." By 1967, before the North Vietnamese Tet offensive, which halved U.S. public support for the war, Alice had begun to lose faith in the war effort. "We have not rushed into this god damned thing. We've taken a long time to get where we are and apparently we're going to take a long time to get away from it...," she complained to a friend privately.[26]

Events in Vietnam neither dampened Alice's enthusiasm for the Johnsons nor quenched her desire to revisit Asia when the chance presented itself in 1965. Alice decided to return to the sites she had visited in 1905 when, as she put it, "China was still Cathay" and she "saw it with the eyes of Kipling and Conrad."[27] Accompanying her was her granddaughter, Joanna, in college then, and her good friend Joan Braden. The three went by way of Honolulu, just as Alice had done sixty years earlier. Joanna's friend Kristie Miller joined them in Japan. Mrs. L's companions were amazed at her recall of the details of locales that she hadn't seen in more than half a century.

The highlights of the 1965 trip for Alice included a visit with her old friend Charles Lee, who owned a hotel in Hong Kong, and an interesting time at the Japan Monkey Center. There she indulged her lifelong fascination with primate evolution and was given a special tour of the center's extensive facilities. The Monkey Center had opened less than a decade earlier and had already established an excellent reputation as a research facility. Mrs. L found the many different monkeys more interesting than the current emperor and empress of Japan, having, she said, "met the Emperor the last time I was here." Nevertheless, Miller remembered, the Japanese people "liked her very much and were flattered by her having made the trip."[28]

In between excursions, Alice visited with Dorothy Emmerson, wife of the Charge d'affaires at the American Embassy in Tokyo. Emmerson recalled the eighty-one-year-old Alice sitting in the lotus position—taught to her, along with other yoga positions, by TR—on the veranda of one of the temples they visited. Mrs. L much preferred the temple architecture to the peaceful swept sand of the famous Tokyo rock gardens. The latter was Alice's "idea of hell." She "hated it, just hated it.... She said, 'That's my idea of nothing at all.' She got very angry. She got very passionate about how sterile and boring [it was], and she really liked lots of stimulation.... Meditation was not her strong point."[29]

Just as in 1905, Alice was the center of attention wherever she went. Kristie and Joanna remembered Alice's characteristic ability to transcend hunger, weariness, and her desire for privacy. She was, Joanna described, "a fire horse falling into harness." Anytime anyone "staggered up and said, 'Aren't you Alice Blue Gown?' she very graciously pulled herself together and was so nice...she just made [people's] day." Apparently, Alice's age was not a predictor of her energy level for, as Joan Braden remembered, "Mrs. L was up every morning at the crack of down, rearing to go. I was a python by comparison." Alice enthused, "We had such fun," and contemplated a trip to Moscow.[30]

New York called first. In 1966, Truman Capote threw his famous Black and White Ball at the Plaza Hotel for his friend Kay Graham. The event generated excessive publicity. Alice, Lynda Bird Johnson Robb, and Margaret Truman Daniel—three former First Daughters—converged and chatted. Hollywood fixtures such as Frank Sinatra, Mia Farrow, Anita Loos, Claudette Colbert, and Lauren Bacall attended the masquerade. Partygoers spent magnificent sums on their designer attire—but Alice's stole the show: a simple black dime-store mask held on by elastic. Alice characterized the ball as "the most exquisite of spectator sports," a line the *New York Times* borrowed for its headline.[31]

As Capote's ball unfolded in New York, a burglar was vandalizing Alice's home in Washington. The guest list had been published, so he knew the house would be empty. He took mostly jewels, many of which had been wedding presents. They were so distinctive that they were recovered quickly from a Chicago smelting firm. Authorities had been alerted by Windy City jewelers who were offered pieces engraved with Alice's name. Alice received a box of "gold scraps" that turned out to be the "historic mementos" she had gathered over seven decades. Most of the gemstones— such as the diamonds set in the bracelets from Kaiser Wilhelm—were gone. The one piece left whole was a locket that contained a snip of her father's hair.[32]

Social divisions in the 1960s ran deep. The rise of the counterculture, the African-American civil rights movement, and increasing unhappiness with American involvement in Vietnam generated a response from conservatives who Nixon, campaigning in 1968, would call the "silent majority." Alice Longworth straddled the divide. *Boston Sunday Herald* readers learned of a woman who "likes the Beatles, 5 o'clock tea, Theodore Roosevelt, Republicans." "I'm glad," Alice said, "to have had a taste of the Edwardian, but I like it now. It's exciting."[33]

She hung an "African tribal mask" on the small bronze Statue of Liberty that had been a wedding gift from the sculptor's family. "I hang this mask right on the Goddess of Liberty," Alice told an interviewer. "It symbolizes black power in a free land. America's black citizens are not only winning liberty; they're discovering a wonderful heritage in art such as this. Don't you find that exciting?" she asked. Among Alice's acquaintances was Portia Washington Pittman. The two women saw each other "quite often," Alice told another interviewer in 1968. "She's my contemporary, Booker Washington's daughter. She brings her grandchildren here." As she watched the changes around her—including Washington, D.C.'s first elected mayor, African-American Walter E. Washington—she said, "If I were younger I'd be delighted to run for vice-mayor of a ticket with a black mayor." Mrs. L had been attending prizefights with her chauffeur Richard Turner ever since he began to work for her in the 1950s. The two shared an appreciation for the local pugilists. Once when Turner was taking her somewhere in her ancient limousine, a car sideswiped them. The other driver then had the temerity to yell out his window, "Watch where you're going, you black bastard." Whereupon Alice rolled down her window and spoke precisely: "Shut up, you white son-of-a-bitch."[34]

As an octogenarian, she claimed Gloria Steinem as "one of my heroines," and feminist congresswoman Bella Abzug asked Alice to serve as "one of the Honorary 'Chairpeople'" for a fund-raising event. At age ninety, Alice told a reporter that her lifelong preference as a nonjoiner kept her away from the women's liberation movement—and the fact that she "feels she has been treated by men as an equal." But Alice had "followed women's movements all her adult life." "I'm enormously interested and wish them well. I think it's high time women are getting somewhere." In

1977, one month before the National Women's Conference was held in Houston, Joanna said that her grandmother "certainly is a feminist. But she'd never admit it. She feels it's tacky to identify yourself with a group, and to become overemotional. It's a question of esthetics." Guided by her "extremely feminist convictions," Joanna joined the National Women's Political Caucus, sought out a female stockbroker, and shunned marriage as "a sexist institution." Alice wanted it made clear that her own interest in feminism wasn't "borrowed from her granddaughter."[35]

Alice was very sympathetic toward the gay liberation movement. "I'm amused that some people are so shocked, as if they thought homosexuals and lesbians never before existed. That has never bothered me." Her insouciance in the face of the rest of the nation's anger and fear moved one gay rights group in Washington to make her an "honorary homosexual," which pleased her enormously. She attained cult status among some populations of gay men.[36]

Mrs. L enjoyed Joanna and her acquaintances, especially Robert Hellman, who spent considerable time with Mrs. L in her last decade. One friend of theirs who had tea with them on several occasions thought that Mrs. Longworth "had a keen sense of Washington fraudulence and enjoyed the company of young people who were fairly free from those pretensions...." Another loved Mrs. L's "fantastic imagination," and approved of how her conversations didn't "move in a straight line.... Almost like someone flipping out on drugs." Alice thought this idea was "too much fun" and wondered whether after she "outgrew her hormones," she "started manufacturing LSD." She said frequently that "the secret of eternal youth is arrested development." When the tear gas from protest marches came through her windows, she joked that it "cleared my sinuses." She took to referring to herself as "a withered Twiggy," a reference to the era's slim superstar model.[37]

In an interview at the time of her ninetieth birthday, television commentator Eric Sevareid told her of the newest movement: "to liberate the old." "That *is* fun!" Alice interjected. Its purpose, Sevareid continued, was "to make people understand that old people have feelings, and that they even have sexual passion.... Are you for all that?" She smilingly shot back, paraphrasing Queen Victoria, "Well, as long as they don't do it in the streets." At another time, when asked her opinion of the sexual revolution, she said she'd always lived by the adage "Fill what's empty, empty what's full, and scratch where it itches."[38]

At the height of the counterculture revolution came the 1968 election, pitting Lyndon Johnson's vice president, Hubert Humphrey, against Richard Nixon. George Wallace of Alabama ran on a third-party segregationist platform. With Joanna, Alice attended the GOP convention in Miami that year, but found it "the dullest thing I've ever seen." The Republican Party stressed the orderliness of their gathering compared to the fisticuffs outside and inside the Democratic convention in Chicago. Alice reverted to her Republican roots. She spent the election eve phoning friends to remind them to vote for Nixon and sent him an encouraging telegram: "Here is to simply overwhelming returns tomorrow! It was such fun seeing Pat and the girls for a moment at Miami. Love to them and many recollections of earlier days."[39] His success almost didn't happen. Democrats held the House and the Senate.

Alice loaned her name to local charities. She had served as a member of the opening night committee for the six-day-long Washington International Horse Show at the D.C. Armory in 1965 and held the same position in 1968. She gave "one of the first top level dinners following the election," just before a fund-raiser for the John F. Kennedy Center. The best party of all, though, occurred after the inauguration, and she was the star. On February 12, 1969, Alice Longworth turned eighty-five. Guests included dignitaries of all sorts. President Nixon came and reminisced for forty-five minutes. Throughout the evening, a recent interview conducted for British television by Jonathan Aitken blazed. The interview showed Alice at her best—smart, funny, with a wide-ranging repertoire of topics. For Aitken, she did her celebrated mimicry of cousin Eleanor and showed off the Chinese tiger wall hanging that looked like Dean Acheson. Alice's birthday cake was topped by a confectionary replica of her trademark hat.[40]

President Nixon had earlier sent her a greeting, declaring, "Your valor has always been an inspiration, and your infectious good humor has given even the most serious of men and women the ability and courage to laugh at their foibles and appreciate the lighter side of life." His was one of many felicitations she received. Perhaps the most interesting began thus: "I think it 'fitting and proper' that you have a note from one of the members of the Borah tribe on the anniversary of your 89th [sic] birthday." From Texas, Lyndon Johnson saluted her: "Happy birthday from a long-time admirer. I don't know if there is such a thing as a social lioness, but all of us cubs think you're the best. One thing I want from history is for tomorrow's generation to regard Lynda and Luci with the same affection all Americans hold for you. And Lady Bird and I hope they'll be as beautiful." The Eisenhowers' telegram wished a happy birthday to "the youngest 85 year old we have ever known." With self-deprecating humor, she called herself "a loathsome combination of Marie Dressler and Phyllis Diller," but no one would have agreed with her comparison to the two disheveled celebrities.[41]

At this time in her life, Alice acquired yet another admirer—another man gifted with words and a sublime intellect: scientist, philosopher, and dreamer Buckminster Fuller. "At age 73," he wrote her, "the frequency at which one falls in love with other than one's grandchildren approaches zero. Therefore, I was astonished to find myself 'knocked for a loop' by you. So I hasten to send to you my abstract bouquet." This literary posy consisted of three of his books, *No More Second Hand God, Education Automation*, and *The Unfinished Epic of Industrialization*, as well as offprints from his articles on topics from computers to women's status. Borah-like, Fuller also included testimony from *Saturday Review* editor Norman Cousins praising Fuller as one of the "ten or twelve men in the world...whose influence transcends geography and language. Among these men are Albert Schweitzer, Bertrand Russell, E. M. Forster, Paul Tillich, and you."[42]

Many men appreciated Alice Longworth's amazing mind. Among her devotees was the "father of the nuclear navy," Hyman Rickover, who called her an "outstanding female scientist." He and Alice had one conversation that prompted him to send her a letter distinguishing the specifics of parsecs and astronomical units, and attaching some illustrations of measurement. Bazy Tankersley knew her to be a self-taught expert on nuclear fission. After one White House dinner the other guests wanted to know what topic had she broached that so intensely interested the royal visitor with whom she had been absorbedly speaking. "Astronomy," she told them. "Stars, galaxies, and where we are in the little corner of the galaxy." After that their discussion moved to "genes and the chromosomes.... Then," she said, "we branched into molecular genetics and things of that sort. He couldn't have been more fun." The study of quasars and quarks was "intoxicating for me," she told an interviewer happily. When good friend Harvard professor, attorney, author, and Supreme Court Justice Felix Frankfurter died, Alice was one of the few friends to attend his private memorial service. Frankfurter was a Democrat who helped start up the *New Republic* and assisted Zionist causes.[43]

Alice's bookshelf was filled with many tomes from Princeton University's prestigious Bollingen Series, launched in 1943, particularly on scientific and philosophical subjects. She read and reread books, "to fix them in my head," she said. Journalist Betty Beale found Alice in her mid-eighties reading Mario Puzo's novel *The Godfather,* John Birmingham's *Our Time Is Now—Notes from the High School Underground, The Treasure of Sutton Hoo—Ship Burial for an Anglo-Saxon King,* Nigel Calder's *Violent Universe, The World of Bats,* a book about Trinidad called *The Loss of El Dorado, Nixon* by Earl Mazo, as well as Voltaire (in French), Kipling, Pindar, Homer, Pope, Hawthorne, Whitman, and "dictionaries like Fowler's *Modern English Usage* because she 'loves words.'"[44]

Robert Hellman seldom found a subject on which Mrs. L was not conversant, and in many cases, an adept. He spent a great deal of time with her while finishing his doctoral degree in modern German intellectual history from Columbia University. They frequently discussed his topic, the left-wing pupils of Hegel and their scientific examination of the four gospels. Hellman attested to the fact that Alice had read Arthur Schopenhauer's *On the Four-Fold Root of the Principle of Sufficient Reason.* There was nothing an intellectual historian could teach her, he said, about Schopenhauer, Nietzsche, or Kant. She'd been studying them all her life. According to Hellman, "The most salient thing about her was her intellect."[45] Yet what most Americans saw was the wit.

The Nixons, like the Johnsons and Kennedys before them, were generous with their invitations. Alice went frequently to the Nixon White House to meet important guests such as the Shah of Iran, the Duke and Duchess of Windsor, and British Prime Minister Edward Heath. She attended a black-tie dinner given by the Brazilian ambassador in honor of her acquaintance Mauricio Nabuco, Brazil's ambassador to the United States from 1948 to 1951. Richard Nixon's favorite minister was the Reverend Billy Graham, and Alice could not help but encounter him at the White House. A dinnertime conversation once prompted her to send the cleric a book entitled *The Steel Bonnets*, which Graham, no more immune to Alice's sparkle than anyone else, promised to "always treasure." "What a marvelous woman you are," Graham gushed, "even if you don't believe."[46]

During the summer of 1970, Alice Longworth had a second mastectomy, prompting her to call herself "Washington's topless octogenarian." Generally, however, she preferred to keep quiet about the surgery. Later, when First Lady Betty Ford suffered from her historically public battle with breast cancer, Alice cheered her on with get-well wishes. When Alice felt up to hosting again, Henry Cabot Lodge Jr. exclaimed afterward, "The company and the food were, of course, superlative, but what made it so unique was you—as you have always been. Notwithstanding the vicissitudes of which you told me, you look marvelous—vivid and beautiful. Through the years you have generously extended your hospitality to Emily and me and it has always been something to look forward to and to look back on with joy.... You will always be for me the most stimulating, witty, and utterly delightful of companions."[47]

In 1971, according to journalist Dorothy Marks, Alice's social life had not let up much. Describing what Marks called a usual week, she said the eighty-seven-year-old began with service as the honorary chair of a charity ball celebrating the District of Columbia's "Age of Innocence, 1900–1910," the era when she was First Daughter. She attended the Washington Press Club's dinner welcoming new members of Congress, and stopped by a ball at the Spanish embassy for Prince Juan Carlos and Princess Sophia of Spain. "Two nights later she joined in the singing to help Soviet Ambassador Dobrynin and his wife harmonize '*Que Sera, Sera*'" at a private dinner party.[48]

The wedding of Patricia Nixon and Edward Cox on June 12, 1972, meant another opportunity for the nation to recall Princess Alice's nuptials. Later that year at a White House dinner honoring Presidential Medal of Freedom winners, she sat between conservationist Horace M. Albright and Bob Hope. "Conversation," Albright remembered, "was on many subjects and, at times, hilarious, mainly initiated by Mrs. Longworth and Hope." The topic turned to current fears about the overpopulation of the planet, and Alice reminded the dinner guests that when she was young, large families were praised. "She quoted her father's favorite lines which, in turn, created quite an uproar at our table:

> Teddy, Teddy, Rough and Ready,
> Hear his battle cry!
> Get the habit.
> Be a rabbit.
> Multiply!"[49]

During the summer of 1972, Alice attended the Republican Party convention, but it's not likely she knew how desperately and illegally President Nixon was scrambling to win reelection with the big margin of victory that had eluded him in 1968. She did know how he agonized about the election, and was fascinated by the contour of his career: "It's really amazing to see what has happened to Dick. There he was defeated by Kennedy and then by Pat Brown for Governor of California and he made that whin[ing], snarling speech. He's come through all that. . . . I didn't think that it was the end of him at the time and that he would get back, but I was one of the few who did. I <u>knew</u> that he would try again because he has that great quality of persistence. I'm not so sure though about his judgment, but I don't think he's ruthless," she mused. She thought Nixon's biggest handicap in the 1972 campaign was that he "is apt to bore people."[50]

Americans did "mind" Nixon personally, but his campaign tapped into the conservative backlash, and Nixon achieved the landslide he craved, although the Democrats maintained their congressional majority. Alice was invited to several inaugural festivities for President Nixon; however, she did not attend because she was under the weather. Nixon, who knew that she "could never resist anything political," sent her a handwritten note of concern.[51]

A distracting flurry of press interest in Alice's past occurred when *Washington Post* journalist Maxine Cheshire broke a story that horrified Mrs. L: "Was Alice Roosevelt in Love with FDR?" Eleanor Roosevelt's biographer, Joseph Lash, had interviewed a Roosevelt relative who swore that Alice had set her hat for Franklin. Alice adamantly protested to Lash. To ensure her denial would endure for posterity, she tape-recorded it—a tape, Cheshire wrote, "punctured frequently by outbursts of laughter." Alice feared that "her decades of outspoken disdain for FDR's New Deal politics may be interpreted as the pique of a jealous woman." In a later interview, Alice said, "I was no more likely to marry Franklin than I was someone's second footman." She meant every word, even though she had a sense of humor about it. When replying to the letter sent by a teenaged admirer of TR in the mid-1960s, for example, she used the stamp sold at that time—with Franklin's face on it—but she "placed the stamp upside down, so that Franklin was, in effect, standing on his head." And she told interviewer Jean Vanden Heuvel, "Franklin was great fun. I used to see him when he was a boy, always liked Franklin, was amused by him." Alice, who knew good politicians from bad, characterized Franklin as "an able politician...and...an engaging character!"[52] Her ambivalence toward Eleanor was well-known, and after ER's death in 1962, Alice got tremendous currency from repeating Eleanor imitations and quips.

But even the sardonic joy of reliving the Hyde Park Roosevelt years had to halt as Dick Nixon's administration crumbled under the weight of Watergate. At first Alice took the scandal in stride: "Everyone is hypnotized by Watergate. One hangs on the boob tube all day long. But depressed? I'm not depressed at all....I don't think in those terms." Alice had seen scandal. She had lived through false accusations toward her father, she had watched Teapot Dome unfairly taint Ted's career. But Capitol Hill denizens lacking Alice's longer view were troubled. "The future of the Nixon administration dominates conversations. No dinner party is complete without a resident Watergate expert," noted one social-pages reporter. When the ad hominum attacks on Nixon started, Alice compared his attackers to Rudyard Kipling's Bandar-logs, the Monkey People who kidnap Mowgli in *The Jungle Book*. Kipling described how "they boast and chatter and pretend that they are a great people about to do great affairs in the jungle, but the falling of a nut turns their minds to laughter and all is forgotten."[53]

But as Watergate discoveries mounted, Alice found it difficult to countenance Nixon's actions. Still, she telephoned him in June—about the time the televised Watergate hearings led to the startling discovery of the secret tapes of Oval Office conversations—to assure him, as he put it gratefully, "of your continuing friendship and support. It has always been my experience in my political career," Nixon continued stentoriously, "that you learn who your real friends are—not when the road is smooth but when it is sometimes rocky. That is why Pat and I are so deeply grateful to be able to include you in our list of oldest and dearest friends." When Nixon refused to hand over the tapes to the Senate investigative committee and did away with the office of the special prosecutor, Alice remarked memorably, "My shoulders are in a constant state of shrug." That fall, after Nixon's declaration that he was "not a crook," Alice had to admit that while she had "'known and liked Dick Nixon for years,'...he has done 'some asinine things.'" She told another reporter, "He's an old friend and I'm sorry he's having a hard time. Of course, there are things we disagree about." She said archly that Nixon's "potential clock keeps dick, dick, dicking away."[54]

Because of Watergate, one of the last times Alice saw the Nixons was at her ninetieth birthday party in February 1974. "'So, the old crone had a birthday!' she chortled." The party at her house was front-page news, and guests came from all walks of life. Her sister, Ethel, helped her celebrate. They had become great friends in their old age, exchanging frequent phone calls and visits. "I think about solitary pleasures," Ethel wrote once, "and how you and I like them." She knew a different side of her sister than did others, and shared a similar love of and knack for poetry. Ethel took no joy from the limelight, whereas Alice reveled in her party. The long list of guests included old friends and newer acquaintances from political Washington: Mayor Walter E. Washington, Henry Kissinger, broadcasters David Brinkley and John Chancellor, S. Dillon Ripley of the Smithsonian, Art Buchwald, Sargent Shriver. She served champagne and rum cake. The Nixons gave her Iranian caviar, which she loved and ate with a spoon right out of the jar. "I'll wallow in it...let others wallow in Watergate," she said puckishly. So many reporters clamored for interviews that she took to calling it her "goddamned birthday." One cajoled her into reminiscing: "I loved [politics] around me, but had no temptation to run for office. I was too shy, that's the uncomfortable thing—I was always hideously shy, and I still have spurts of it. I'm not one for causes particularly...I was for the cause when my father was running—he was a cause for me. I'm very old fashioned, essentially, I'm for fun, a good old hedonist—interested, very interested in politics, and I like a lot of things."[55]

Many of the stories written about her featured a pillow Alice had been given earlier by Bazy Tankersley. Alice was very fond of it, and said laughingly, "It can be taken as nasty as you want!" The pillow read "If you haven't got anything good to say about anyone come and sit by me." She adopted it as her signature statement—not one most people could get away with, but as William Wright wrote in his study of Washington, "People who are spontaneous, uninhibited, and oblivious to their surroundings are not greatly admired in Washington, unless they have the enormous clout of an Alice Roosevelt Longworth...."[56]

Six months after that happy occasion, Nixon was forced to resign. He and Alice remained friends. She did not think much of his farewell speech, in which he quoted from Theodore Roosevelt's diary at the time that her mother, Alice Hathaway Lee, died. TR wrote, "When my heart's dearest died, the light went from my heart forever." Nixon used that, and a much longer passage preceding it, to suggest, as he said, that Roosevelt "only thought the light had gone from his life forever—but he went on. And he not only became President but, as an ex-president, he served his country always in the arena, tempestuous, strong, sometimes wrong, sometimes right, but he was a man." It was "not particularly pertinent," Alice snorted. The validity of comparing a grieving widower in his twenties with his life ahead of him and a man in his sixties with a career clearly behind him escaped her. At that stage, Alice felt "the Watergate story 'had gone on long enough.' It was getting to the point where it was about to become very boring.... I feel sorry for the people involved," she said. Alice was clearly conflicted about Nixon and Watergate. She called it "good, unclean fun" just as often as she expressed support for the outgoing president.[57]

Bill Walton summed up Alice's later years by saying that "her dotage wasn't like others." She wanted an "outrageous old age," and he could "never think of her as an unhappy widow." Alice, he emphasized, "*loved* her life."[58] She shared her home at this time with Cat, a large Siamese who kept her company when she read and who amused her with its haughty, feline demeanor. "Darling Puss-Cat, every gesture a small reproof," she said ruefully to it once. Kristie Miller and her husband, William Twaddell; Larry Spivak; Tish Alsop; Susan Mary Alsop; Evangeline Bruce; Michael Teague; Susan Weld; Sandy Roosevelt; Teddy Weintal; Lynn Magruder; Robin Roosevelt; and Lucky Roosevelt continued to see her frequently. Out-of-town friends called. No one wrote much, because Mrs. L seldom opened letters—or bills—which would accumulate among the books.

The greatest happiness of her old age was her granddaughter. Joanna and she had a relationship so close it defied description. Author Michael Teague thought they "were very good friends [with] a healthy respect for each other's independence and idiosyncrasies." Robert Hellman recalled that the two were very affectionate and "touching." He meant that Mrs. L, who was well known for not liking physical contact, touched and let herself be touched by Joanna. Bazy Tankersley felt that they had overcome much to reach a relationship of deep devotion to each other. Alice's niece Alexandra Roosevelt Dworkin thought Alice and Joanna were "perfectly evenly balanced."[59]

Poetry remained a great source of comfort and intellectual engagement, a shared joy between grandmother and granddaughter. The two recited reams of poetry together from memory. The amount of poetry Mrs. L knew and loved cannot be overstated. G. K. Chesterton's "Lepanto" was a favorite. Its subject is the 1571 battle between Don John of Austria's Catholic forces and Ali Pasha's Ottoman Turks in the Gulf of Lepanto. The poem is martial and full of brilliant imagery, and reads beautifully aloud because of Chesterton's musical cadences. Alice and Joanna could recite all nine

stanzas at a rapid clip. One memorable night, Hellman brought his friend
James K. Galbraith to visit Mrs. L. Galbraith, whose father had been ambassador to India, loved Kipling's poem "Christmas in India." To Alice's
enthusiastic delight, Galbraith recited the entire poem from memory and
the three had a glorious evening talking poetry and politics. Poetry "was
the operative currency of Mrs. L's world" with guests, but especially with
Joanna.[60]

When Nixon left for California and Vice President Gerald Ford assumed the presidency, Alice's political interests flagged. President Ford
was a longtime member of Congress, but not an acquaintance of hers. Still,
he invited her to the crowning social event of his administration: the visit
of Britain's Queen Elizabeth II to Washington, D.C., during the American
bicentennial. When Mrs. L received an invitation to the State Dinner, to be
held on the White House grounds, Lynn Magruder encouraged Mrs. L to
go, suggesting that Joanna's friend Robert Hellman escort her. After he
scrambled all over town for a tuxedo, the two set off. A very professional,
young female Marine assigned to Mrs. Longworth swept her right to the
front of the line to meet the queen and Prince Philip. They exchanged
pleasantries about the diamond-rimmed purse that Mrs. L carried, which
had been a wedding gift from King Edward VII in 1906. After chatting
with the Fords, Alice moved on. When Lady Bird Johnson came their way,
Mrs. L inquired of Hellman, "Shall I ask her how Lyndon is?" "You can't
do that," he whispered, "because he's dead." "Oh"—she glanced at him,
not missing a beat—"then I shall ask her how Lyndon *was*."

Not far away from the festivities, in his Georgetown home, Joe Alsop
was pouring cocktails for Mrs. Longworth's friend the young British editor
of the *Economist*, Dudley Fishburn. Alsop was bemoaning the fact that
Alice Longworth was in her nineties and just not getting out much anymore.
Fishburn pointed silently at the television. There was Mrs. L on the lawn
of the White House, surrounded by Cary Grant, Bob Hope, and Senator
Fulbright.

When dinner was over and the toasts had been made, Mrs. L and Hellman made their way to the limousine. A White House employee tapped
him on the shoulder. "We have someone," he said, "who worked in the

White House when Mrs. Longworth lived here." Hearing this, Alice turned to greet a tall, distinguished, silver-haired African-American man who asked if she remembered him. She did. They launched into tales of White House life "when all the world was young." She responded to his laughter with peals of her own. And when they were through, he inquired gravely if he might escort her to her car. She gave him her elbow, and the two walked slowly away.[61] It was Alice Roosevelt Longworth's last visit to the White House.

Epilogue

ALICE ROOSEVELT LONGWORTH died peacefully at home on February 20, 1980, after a brief bout with pneumonia. Joanna and Robert were by her side. Cat kept a vigil beside her on the bed. True to form, Mrs. L's last action was to stick out her tongue playfully at Robert. "I'm an old fossil, a cheerful fossil," she had said not long before. "I have no contemporaries."[1] Nor did she have an equal.

Fittingly, Alice Roosevelt Longworth came into the world in an election year and went out in one, too. She was not the only First Daughter to die in 1980. Esther Cleveland Bosanquet was born in the White House and married spectacularly in Westminster Abbey, but her death failed to make the same headlines. Alice was the first born and the last to die of Theodore Roosevelt's children—and she is the longest lived of all presidential children.[2] But her fame was never merely that of having been First Daughter. While those 1,616 days in the White House placed her in a rare position, she used it to become an American icon. She remains one to this day.

Few First Daughters stay in the limelight after they leave the White House, but Alice Longworth did. She went from feeling like "an extra piece of baggage in relation to the family" to the nation's most-watched female, and she colluded in the creation of that role.[3] It fed her desire to stand out among the growing Roosevelt brood and catch her father's attention. Launching the *Meteor*, releasing Emily Spinach past unsuspecting diners, racing the red touring car, or shooting off her "cunning" little pistol helped her to be noticed—gratifyingly—beyond the circle of the family. International recognition came after the 1905 Asian congressional junket. The Roosevelt-Longworth "wedding of the century" might have led right up the aisle to wifely obscurity, but she was already too famous. Instead, Alice shaped the female ideal of the era. Unaffected yet dignified, lively and unspoiled, Alice was the personification of the American girl at the opening of the twentieth century.

The men in her family helped keep the Roosevelt name before the public after her marriage. In 1912, her dilemma as Nick Longworth's wife and TR's daughter shone a sympathetic spotlight her way. While she began her resistance to Woodrow Wilson's League of Nations as a partner with her father, she ended by making a name for herself among Washington politicians quite apart from his. Her quick mind, her endless curiosity, her love of the game were assets to powerful men—and women, especially Representative Ruth Hanna McCormick—seeking passage of legislation and elected office. Until she was ninety, Alice Longworth cultivated politicians just as they courted her.

Her animus to Franklin Roosevelt's New Deal, coupled with her tribal fury that he had gained the nation's highest office instead of her brother or her husband, put her at the center of Republican detractors. It was less a reinvention of herself than an embracing of the inevitable that occurred somewhere in the post-FDR years. Alice saved her severest scorn for Franklin and Eleanor. She could criticize them as no one else could, for she was family, and no matter what she said, she would always be family. Franklin was a powerful president whose many years in office gave Alice time to build a comprehensive stock of scorn and consolidate her position as gadfly-in-chief. Newspapers played up their rivalry because it made good copy and boosted circulation. Alice knew the most powerful members of the fourth estate. She had learned from her father the importance of press control. Journalists had always mingled with politicians at her house. She appreciated those who made a profession of ferreting out and selectively making public the inner workings of the government. Alice Longworth was a passionate believer in democracy, including freedom of the press. As democracy's detectives, journalists protected the country. She found journalists entertaining and joined their number briefly. They shared secrets with her and kept her name before the public. Even as she hated to see Richard Nixon fall from grace, she could not help but admire the role played by her friend Kay Graham's reporters—so like the muckrakers of her father's era.

Columnists from Will Rogers in the 1930s to Sally Quinn half a century later printed Alice's pithy comments. And the more her verbal conceits were repeated, the more her reputation as a wit spread. The more it spread, the more people sought her out for her comments. Lady Bird Johnson knew that "in any gathering where she is present, Alice Roosevelt Longworth was one of the stars of the occasion, a natural magnet for everybody hoping to hear something spicy...."[4] And that particular talent relegated all of her accomplishments to the background. It did so at the culmination of a series of blows during the Roosevelt and Truman years that would have crushed a lesser spirit: the deaths of her lover, two brothers, stepmother, and best friend. When emphysema and a mastectomy bracketed her daughter's death, it is perhaps no wonder that, thus reminded of her own mortality and in her seventies, Alice refortified the protective wall of "detached malevolence." It was a tactic similar to the one she had used to turn her youthful rebellion into a barricade to avoid further abandonment. That she could allow her granddaughter to breach that wall is a poignant reminder that Alice Longworth was a complex and intelligent woman. Had she been less, she would not have drawn people to her for eight decades. "Tell, tell!" she would demand of those who came to see her. "Tell" of other worlds, of privileged information, of governmental plans, of news of loved ones, of battles, of catastrophes, of scientific discoveries. It is ironic that Alice Longworth really couldn't pick a presidential winner. On Nick, Ted, Borah, and Bob Taft she bet and lost. By the time her betting finally paid off, in the election of Richard Nixon to the nation's highest office, Mrs. L was eighty-four and rather blasé. In the end, he let her down—twice, first by his underhanded dealings in Watergate and second by the sloppy way he dealt with defeat.

Alice made a career out of being Theodore Roosevelt's daughter. But she was no more bound by tradition than he. Eschewing her step-mother's early-to-bed early-to-rise sensibility, Alice stayed awake until the wee hours, reading, studying, prowling the house—she called it "kicking the tentpegs"—in search of more books, her main source of nutrition in her last decade. She opened her home to the city's School Without Walls, where Kristie Miller taught writing classes. One of the students, Glenn Kowalski, wrote a song about the rather surreal experience of analyzing the plot development of literature while sitting in "Alice Roosevelt's House." Another young Washington resident, Anita Wilburn, remembered how in the 1960s she would "hang out around Dupont Circle hoping to get a glimpse of her." Wilburn thought of Alice Longworth as "history on the hoof."[5]

Like an actor, Alice was adept at telling important stories for the umpteenth time as though they were new. She was frequently interviewed in the 1960s and 1970s by historians and other writers seeking to understand the changes in the nation's capital throughout the twentieth century. "Shall I tell that one again?" she would ask, and interviewers always said yes. Mrs. L could recall the time of gaslights and phaetons. She remembered presidents Benjamin Harrison and Calvin Coolidge. When she was First Daughter, there were only a handful of embassies in Washington, D.C. She was around when the Panama Canal was dug and before Mount Rushmore was carved. She could reduce interviewers to fits of laughter when she told about sneaking into the White House or jumping into the ship's pool fully clothed. They wanted to know if she, like Luci and Lynda Johnson or Tricia and Julie Nixon, had dated as First Daughter. Only kitchen maids went on dates then, Mrs. L said archly, and it was called "walking out."

Presidential children are inspected and judged today just as she was a century ago. But Alice expanded the sphere of activities for young women by choosing to ignore codes of behavior that had been standard for those of her background. Half of America was appalled, but the other half applauded as she smoked, bet, drove unchaperoned, played poker,

and shunned organized charity work. As a young wife, the scrutiny continued when she gave up the custom of calling, wore slacks, and decided
not to play the victim when Nick retreated to alcohol and other women.
Dropping out of sight as some presidential children did was never a real
option for Princess Alice. Therefore, better to make the best of it, to be
amused by it. When even her meanest thoughts were counted as marks
of her cleverness, she learned that if you can't say something nice, say it
wittily.

"I can be serious, but I can't be solemn," she declared. That's why
she could get away with popularizing a wincing put-down of President
Truman's nemesis, General Douglas MacArthur: "Never trust a man
who combs his hair straight from his left armpit." Or saying of childbirth—at a time when motherhood was near to sainthood—that "having
a baby is like trying to push a grand piano through a transom." She claimed
of the oversized purse she carried that it was "half filing cabinet, half psy-
chosis." Near the end of her life, she allowed poison ivy to take over
her front yard because she found it rather funny. Upon watching President Johnson bare his stomach on television to show off the scar from his
gall bladder surgery, she deadpanned, "Thank God it wasn't a prostate
operation."[6]

As a celebrity, Alice Roosevelt Longworth had a unique style. To the
public, she was Princess Alice, or Mrs. L, or just Alice. No less than her
father's, hers was an instantly identifiable "look." The rolls and rolls of
gold-threaded cloth given her by the empress dowager of China in 1905
lasted until the end of her life. They became distinctive gowns cut from a
similar pattern—unfitted, long-sleeved A-lines that allowed her maximum freedom of movement and showed off the fabric to perfection. Everyday dresses featured the same silhouette. She topped these off with
her signature hat. She had worn hats ever since she was First Daughter
and had made large-brimmed hats fashionable. They bothered LBJ,
who complained he couldn't kiss her because of the brims. "That, Mr.
President," she told him drily, "is why I wear them." Even after such
habiliment had declined in popularity, Mrs. L maintained the custom.

Hers were wide-brimmed black or brown hats made for her by Washington milliners. This was the look that artist and caricaturist Aline Fruhauf captured so perfectly in 1971: the hat, the silhouette, and the ramrod-straight posture, hands jammed into the pockets of her dress. The image would have been instantly recognizable to most Americans, in and out of Washington.[7]

Alice, like Bill Borah, was sometimes accused of inconsistency, yet much was constant throughout her life: books; her intellectual curiosity; the need to be at the center; her conviction that the United States should not become entangled in the business of foreign countries; her dismissal of whiners, complainers, and those who indulged in regrets; her belief that what a later generation would call self-fulfillment, and what she called "an appetite for being entertained," was just as viable a path as "do-gooderism"; her support for conservative national fiscal policy; her loyalty to her friends; her shyness; her loathing of drunkenness; her fear of losing control; her commitment to independence. Being contrasted to her cousin Eleanor bothered her not one bit. Robert Hellman said Alice liked being "the un-Eleanor." There was—there is—no valid comparison with the longest-serving First Lady and the enormously powerful national platform that accompanies that position. Alice and Eleanor were friends, after all, and more than that, they were of the same tribe.[8]

One interviewer quipped that Alice Longworth had "a low boring point." She came by it honestly. Theodore Roosevelt once complained to his sister about a dinner companion: "I hated myself for being so bored to extinction by him. But there are very many honest people whom one sincerely respects but cannot associate with. I never can like, and never will like, to be intimate with that enormous proportion of sentient beings who are respectable but dull. It is a waste of time. I will work with them, or for them; but for pleasure and instruction I go elsewhere." Alice Longworth was lucky and intrepid enough to be able to choose from among the world's most talented citizens for dinner companions. Alexandra Roosevelt Dworkin remembered her great-aunt as "very outspoken—and on a basis of equality with presidents and authors, and so the communication was direct—the dialogue may have been beneficial to them. There was no kowtowing or dissembling to presidents and politicians because they were equals."[9]

Alice Longworth's life can tell us much about the Roosevelt presidency, the larger Roosevelt family, the role of women in nonelective politics, conservative politics in the twentieth century, even Senator Borah. But at the end of the day, Alice Longworth herself doesn't fit into any neat category. Progressive, New Woman, politician, political organizer, Washington insider—she was all of these but more. Perhaps statesman is closest to her role. Just as a diplomat studies the issues, gathers information, carries it to lawmakers, brings together important constituents so that they can create legislative change, and does so with tact, discipline, gravitas, and savoir faire, Alice was a statesman. Her close friend Bazy Tankersley affirmed that Mrs. L "always made you feel important and was interested in what you had to say. This was the secret of her great social success."[10] Because Alice was so avidly interested in politics and foreign policy, her role transcended that of the social hostess. She was interested in power, hers and others', and at ease with it as well. She had more power in her dining room than the one vote suffrage gave her. Politics was a deadly serious game, played at a time when manners mattered and statesmen were integral to the governmental process.

Alice did not take the world on its own terms. It wasn't all under her control, nor did everything work out as she would have liked, but she made of it what she wanted. That was part of the appeal of the prizefights—the blood, the gore, the strenuous athleticism, but also the fighter uncomplainingly getting up again and again. In 1955, a fractured hip didn't keep her from going with Turner to see an important boxing match.[11] She fed off the spectacle.

Alice Roosevelt Longworth was one of a kind: an autodidact known for her wit, an iconoclast who valued tradition, a celebrity whose influence was often private, a conservative who started and ended her life as a progressive (or at least a Bull Moose). For all her "detachment," no politician was more connected; for all her "malevolence," no hostess had a larger circle of friends or a more-sought-after salon. She didn't call herself a feminist, but no life could have been more dedicated to freedom of choice and individual empowerment. She never lost the rebellious streak that she nurtured in her youth and that propelled her to international fame. As one reporter summed up, "Mrs. Longworth has gone thru life doing what struck her fancy, leaving the conformists awash in her wake."[12]

Acknowledgments

Writing a biography is an impertinent task. It takes a certain audacity to believe that one can come to know another human being well enough to commit their life to the historical record. Luckily, over the many years of this project, I have been the grateful recipient of wisdom and encouragement from many wonderful people who have given me the courage to see this task through. To thank them publicly is a joy.

My work and my thinking have been molded by professors at the University of Texas: Robert Abzug, Oscar Brockett, John Brokaw, Robert Divine, Hafaz Farmayan, Peter Jelevich, Patricia Kruppa, Amarante Lucero, Richard Pells, Thomas Philpott, and Philip White.

Colleagues beyond Texas have contributed to my understanding of Alice Longworth through their writings and their conversations: Thomas H. Appleton Jr., Charles Calhoun, Willard Gatewood, Sandra Harmon, Richard Jensen, Theresa Kaminski, Karen Leroux, Kris Lindenmeyer, Judy MacArthur, Deborah McGregor, April Shultz, Amanda Smith, John Weaver, and Elliott West.

I am conscious always that I stand on the shoulders of giants—Roosevelt biographers and historians on whose fine scholarship my work leans: John Morton Blum, James Brough, Betty Boyd Caroli, Blanche Wiesen Cook, John Milton Cooper, Kathleen Dalton, John Allen Gable, Lewis L. Gould, Joseph Ornig, Edmund Morris, Sylvia Jukes Morris, Edward Renehan, Michael Teague, Howard Teichmann, and Geoffrey Ward.

A special word of thanks to the Borah scholars who kindly assisted me with interpretive issues: LeRoy Ashby, John Milton Cooper, Marian McKenna, Robert James Maddox, and Keith Miller. In addition, Professor Ashby located a critical document for me in the Claudius O. Johnson Papers.

I have been fortunate in my Monmouth College colleagues who possess specialized and extremely helpful knowledge that enabled me to solve various intellectual and technical mysteries: Dan Barclay, Marcie Beintema, Marlo Belschner, Daryl Carr, Ken Cramer, Rob Hale, Petra Kuppinger, Steve Price, Jeff Rankin, Anne Sienkewicz, Ira Smolensky, Shawn Perry-Giles, Douglas Spitz, William Urban, Mark Willhardt, and especially Bev Scott. With uncomplaining good humor scads of Monmouth College students have heard about Alice Longworth in classrooms, hallways, and my office. To all of you who keep asking, "how's Alice?"—and you know who you are—thanks a million.

Friends and colleagues have munificently shared their ideas, their expertise, or sources with me: Samuel Brylawski, Daniel Byrne, Aaron Cluka, Judi Doyle, Glen Elsasser, Jennifer Goedke, Sarah (Sally) Hunter Graham, Robert T. Grimm Jr., William H. Leckie, Nick Miller, John Milton, Stefan Rinke, Emily Roane, Michael H. Rubin, Larry Rudiger, Lisa Smith, Roger Smith, Henry Tsai, and Nancy Beck Young, I am indebted to Jerome Klena and Phillip Saeli for help with document retrieval and to Alexis Zanis for superlative organizing of the Borah letters.

This book, like all others, owes much to the unselfish assistance of archivists, curators, and librarians whose knowledge of their institution's holdings often results in the gift of hidden gems of information: Lenora M. Henson, Theodore Roosevelt Inaugural National Historic Site; David C. Alan, Lauinger Library, Georgetown University; Dennis Northcott of the St. Louis Historical Society; Tina Bamert and Margaret Yax of the Cincinnati Historical Society; Evelyn M. Cherpak of the Naval War College Library; Joseph R. O'Neill of the Joseph Cardinal Bernardin Archives and Records Center, Archdiocese of Chicago; Jane Keskar of the Kipling Society, London; Carol A. Leadenham and Ronald M. Bulatoff at the Hoover Institution Archives, Stanford University; Lesley Martin of the Chicago Historical Society; Andrea Cantrell, Special Collections, University of Arkansas Libraries; Darryl I. Baker and Sue Lemmon of the Mare Island Naval Shipyard; Michael Mohl of Navsource.org; Tomas Jaehn of the Fray Angélico Chávez History Library, Santa Fe; Troy Reeves at the Idaho State Historical Society, Boise; Jewell Fenzi of the Foreign Service Spouse Oral History Project; and the staffs at Churchill Archives Center, Churchill College, Cambridge; the Courtauld Institute, London; the Indiana Historical Society; the Newberry Library, Chicago; the Southern Historical Collection, University of North Carolina at

Chapel Hill; the University of Chicago Special Collections; the University of Vermont Special Collections; the Franklin D. Roosevelt Presidential Library; the Herbert Hoover Presidential Library; the Abraham Lincoln Presidential Library, Springfield; National Archives, London; and the Library of Congress. Especial thanks to two people whose passion for and knowledge of their subjects and their collections are unsurpassed: Anne B. Shepherd of the Cincinnati Historical Society and the peerless Wallace Finley Dailey, Curator of the Theodore Roosevelt Collection at Harvard University's Houghton Library.

Closer to home, the Monmouth College Library staff, past and present, has cheerfully fulfilled interlibrary loan requests and helped with arcana: Matthew Antoline, Elizabeth Cox, Lynn Daw, Sarah Henderson, Irene Herald, Lauren Jensen, Patricia Pepmeyer Launer, Rita Schnass, Sue Stevenson, and particularly Rick Sayre.

To have been taken under the wing of the ever-gracious Sterling Lord is surely some sort of miracle. He and Robert Guinsler at Sterling Lord Literistic have proven patient and kind beyond expectation. At Viking, executive editor Wendy Wolf has made what should have been a painful process of paring down the manuscript an interesting and shared intellectual puzzle. I am very grateful to Maggie Payette for the stunning cover design, to Francesca Belanger for the text and interior layout, to production editor Noirin Lucas and to publicist Sonya Cheuse for their dedication to this project.

My sincere gratitude to those who shared their memories or stories of Alice Longworth with me. They played an integral role in my learning about Mrs. Longworth: Susan Mary Alsop, Stephen Benn, John Morton Blum, Ann Catt, Gary Clinton, Anita Wilburn Darras, Sherrie DeCamp, Alexandra Roosevelt Dworkin, James K. Galbraith, Robert Hellman, Glenn Kowalski, Lynn Macgruder, Janie McLaughlin, Angela Meeske, Kristie Miller, Frances Mitchell, David Mitchell, John Pope, Mary Reed, Robin Roosevelt, Selwa Roosevelt, Alice Sturm, Joanna Sturm, Michael Teague, Jeanne Tomb, Roman Totenberg, and William Walton. Graydon DeCamp responded to my inquiry about his grandfather with enthusiasm while David Mitchell kindly helped me understand the Sturm family. Bazy Tankersley spent hours recalling critical details about her friend Alice Longworth, gave me valuable insight into Washington society, and magnanimously provided all manner of other support as well.

So many friends and acquaintances have been generous in their encouragement and support over the years: Rajkumar Ambrose, George Arnold, Margaret McAndrew Beasley, Steve Buban, Katie Cogswell, Hillary Lee Dickenson, Laura Duncan, Kathleen Fannin, Gayle Fischer, Richard Giese, Virginia Hellenga, Susan Holm, Doug Jansen, Pat Joe, William Julian, Sandy Kyrish, Peter Linder, Linsey McDanel, Bev McGuire, Leah McLaren, Paula Nuckles, Mary Helen Quinn, Steven Reschly, Alisa Roost, Hannah Schell, Salise Shuttlesworth, Thomas J. Sienkewicz, N. J. Stanley, Jacqueline Urban, William Wallace, and Andrew Weiss.

Karen Cates, Simon Cordery, Lewis L. Gould, and Kristie Miller went above and beyond by reading the manuscript in an *extremely* long draft form. Their suggestions and criticisms materially improved the book.

Thanks are just not enough for the crucial support that took the form of continuous chocolate, champagne, and cheerleading from Paula Barnes, Brad Brown, Karen Cates, Simon Cordery, Karen Gould, Krissi Jimroglou, Evelina Lipecka, Kristie Miller, Danielle Nierenberg, Mary Lou Pease, and Stacey Robertson.

There are some people to whom my debts are so profound that they can never be fully repaid. This project began under the tutelage of Lewis L. Gould at the University of Texas. He first suggested that I think like a historian and set me on the road to my future. Lew Gould's professionalism is threaded through with such generosity of spirit. He continues to personify for me the ideal scholar, teacher, and mentor.

Kristie Miller's cheerful and sociable self led me to the enormous cache of primary documents held by Alice's granddaughter. The real treasure, though, was Kristie. I remain grateful for her tangible and intangible support. She shared her sources with me, allowed me to use her grandmother's diary, introduced me to the people and places in Mrs. L's world, and most of all kept faith that the book would do Alice Longworth justice.

Joanna Sturm made this book possible by allowing me free and unfettered access to the documents that helped to tell the story of her grandmother's life. This book would have been very different if not for her multifaceted generosity. Like Joanna Sturm, Robert Hellman answered countless questions and challenged me to seek a more nuanced view of Mrs. L. His tour of Alice Longworth's library proved vital to my interpretation.

Every author must feel helpless contemplating how to thank one's family for the magnitude of their contributions. I do. For every good thing, thank you: James and Agnes Rozek, Ned and Mary Cordery, Doug and Larissa Rozek, Stuart and Annie Rumens, Adam Dix and Sara Rumens. In his autobiography, Theodore Roosevelt wrote that children are better than books. He was right. Gareth Cordery's lovely distractions have made it all worthwhile. Finally, I am blessed in my partnership to an extremely patient man who is also a brilliant historian. Simon Cordery's unflagging support was always at the center. But really, for Simon, there are no sufficient words. I hope the celebrations have outweighed the sacrifices.

Notes

Abbreviations

ARLC   Alice Roosevelt Longworth Collection, Library of Congress

ARLD   Alice Roosevelt Longworth Diary, Library of Congress

ARL Diary   Alice Roosevelt Longworth Diary, Joanna Sturm Papers

ARL Har   Alice Roosevelt Longworth Family Papers, Theodore Roosevelt Collection. Houghton Library, Harvard University

ARLPF   Alice Roosevelt Longworth Princeton File, Cincinnati Historical Society

ARP   Amos R. Pinchot Papers, Library of Congress

CH   Alice Roosevelt Longworth, *Crowded Hours* (New York: Charles Scribner's Sons, 1933).

CHS   Cincinnati Historical Society

EKR Diaries   Edith Kermit Roosevelt Diaries, Theodore Roosevelt Collection, Houghton Library, Harvard University

ERDP   Ethel Roosevelt Derby Papers, Theodore Roosevelt Collection, Houghton Library, Harvard University

FDRL   Franklin Delano Roosevelt Presidential Library

Greenway AHS   Greenway Collection, Arizona Historical Society

HHPL   Herbert Hoover Presidential Library

JSAP   Joseph and Stewart Alsop Papers, Library of Congress

JSP   Joanna Sturm Papers, privately held

KBR   Kermit and Belle Roosevelt Family Papers, Library of Congress

LC   Library of Congress

LHHP   Lou Henry Hoover Papers, Herbert Hoover Presidential Library

LLF   Lord Lee of Fareham Papers, Cortauldt Institute, London

Morison, *Letters*   Elting E. Morison, *The Letters of Theodore Roosevelt,* 8 vols. (Boston: Harvard University Press, 1951–1954).

NLIII   Papers of Nicholas Longworth III, Cincinnati Historical Society

NLP   Nicholas Longworth Papers, Library of Congress

NLPF   Nicholas Longworth Princeton File, Cincinnati Historical Society

NYT   *New York Times*

PHP   Peter Hagner Papers, Southern Historical Collection, University of North Carolina at Chapel Hill

RFPH   Roosevelt Family Papers, Theodore Roosevelt Collection, Houghton Library, Harvard University

RHMcC   Ruth Hanna McCormick Papers, Library of Congress

TR Diary   Transcript of Theodore Roosevelt Diary, Joanna Sturm Papers

TRJR Diary   Theodore Roosevelt Jr. Diary, Library of Congress

TRJRP   Theodore Roosevelt Jr. Papers, Library of Congress

TRP   Presidential Papers of Theodore Roosevelt on microfilm

WEBID   William E. Borah Papers, Idaho State Historical Society

WEBLC   William E. Borah Papers, Library of Congress

WHTP   William H. Taft Papers, Manuscript Division, microfilm edition, Library of Congress

WSP   Williard Straight Papers on microfilm, reel 1, Cornell University Library

Abbreviations of personal names in the notes

AHL   Alice Hathaway Lee

AHLR   Alice Hathaway Lee Roosevelt

ALR   Alice Lee Roosevelt

ARC   Anna Roosevelt Cowles

ARL   Alice Roosevelt Longworth

EKR   Edith Kermit Roosevelt

ER   Anna Eleanor Roosevelt

HHT   Helen Herron Taft

JLL   John L. Lewis

JSG   Joseph S. Graydon

LHH   Lou Henry Hoover

NL   Nicholas Longworth

RHMcC   Ruth Hanna McCormick (Simms)

TR   Theodore Roosevelt

TRJR   Theodore Roosevelt Jr.

WEB   William E. Borah

WHT   William H. Taft

Preface

1. Alice Longworth said Joseph Alsop gave her that appellation: "Princess Alice Is 90," *60 Minutes* transcript, 17 February 1974, Papers of Eric Sevareid, LC. See also "Alice Roosevelt Longworth," *Theodore Roosevelt Journal* 6, 2 (Spring 1980): 6.

2. Michael Teague, *Mrs. L* (Garden City, N.Y.: Doubleday, 1981), xviii.

3. Paul Horgan, *Tracings* (New York: Farrar, Straus, and Giroux, 1993), 172; ER to Isabella Ferguson, 21 June [1916], Greenway AHS.

4. Mary Hagedorn interview with Mrs. Richard Aldrich, 30 March 1955, Hermann Hagedorn. Interviews relating to Roosevelt women, Harvard University.

5. Author's interview with William Walton, 27 May 1994.

6. Winifred Mallon, "Mrs. Longworth

Sets Tongues Wagging," *NYT*, 26 May 1929, 15.

7. Author's interview with Lynn Magruder, 14 October 2001.

8. Kristie Miller to author, 1 March 2001.

Chapter 1: **"It Was Awfully Bad Psychologically"**

1. Alexandra Roosevelt Dworkin feels strongly that the Roosevelts were not "aristocracy." "We're all," Dworkin explained, "just part of a large amorphous bourgeoisie, which is very different from the aristocracy." Author's interview with Alexandra Roosevelt Dworkin, 7 October 2001.

2. Michael Teague, *Mrs. L* (Garden City, N.Y.: Doubleday, 1981), 19.

3. For a comparison, consider Cornelius van Schaak Roosevelt's investment in the Illinois Central Railroad (ICRR): he loaned more than $2,000 to the ICRR in the form of a bond. In 1888, the railroad paid him back $450 plus $34.08 interest— nearly the average annual wage earned by a laborer. See C. V. S. Roosevelt's note in the Papers of the Illinois Central Railroad Company, N 1.5, 1856–1888, Newberry Library, Chicago.

4. Gore Vidal, "Theodore Roosevelt: An American Sissy," Random House Web site: http://www.randomhouse.com/boldtype/0501/vidal/essay_us.html

5. TR Diary, 30 June 1878.

6. Michael Teague, "Theodore Roosevelt and Alice Hathaway Lee," *Harvard Library Bulletin* 33, 3 (Summer 1985): 230 (Hereafter cited as "TR and AHL).

7. TR Diary, 18 April 1878.

8. TR Diary, 1 January 1878.

9. TR Diary, 21 August 1878.

10. Sylvia Jukes Morris, *Edith Kermit Roosevelt* (New York: Coward, McCann & Geoghegan, 1980), 58.

11. "Summer house," TR Diary, 22 August 1878; "dog," 24 August 1878.

12. Except for "I met Miss Lee Barry," in early September.

13. Typescript of letter from TR to "Old John," 25 February 1880, JSP.

14. TR Diary, for the old school, 27 November 1878; for the theater party, 30 April; for the walk, 4 May 1879.

15. TR Diary, 13 May 1879.

16. TR Diary, for pretty girls, 24 June 1879; for Edith, 16 November 1879.

17. TR Diary, 31 December 1879 and 1 January 1880.

18. TR Diary, for happy, 25 January 1880; for first love, 30 January 1880.

19. Anna Roosevelt to AHL, 1 February 1880, ARLHar.

20. AHL to TR, 13 July 1880, and TR to AHL, 15 August 1880, both ARLHar.

21. AHL to TR, 10 October 1880, ARLHar.

22. For 79 presents, AHL to TR, 10 October 1880; for ring, AHL to TR, 16 October 1880, both ARLHar.

23. Sarah Booth Conroy, "Rough Rider's Romantic Side," *Washington Post*, 10 May 1995.

24. AHLR to Anna Roosevelt, 3 November 1880, ARLHar.

25. AHLR to TR, 5 April [1881], ARLHar.

26. For "so kind to me," AHLR to TR, [4?] April 1881; for "at night, AHLR to TR, [30?] March 1881, both ARLHar.

27. Vidal, "Theodore Roosevelt."

28. Theodore Roosevelt, *An Autobiography* (New York: Charles Scribner's Sons, 1926), 80.

29. AHLR to Anna Roosevelt, 22 July 1883, ARLHar.

30. Teague, "TR and AHL," 236.

31. Teague, "TR and AHL," 237–38.

32. The doctor did not diagnose her with Bright's disease until just before she

gave birth. Anna Bulloch Gracie, "Account of the Birth of Alice Roosevelt and Death of Alice Hathaway Lee Roosevelt," 25 March 1884, ARLHar.

33. Edmund Morris, *The Rise of Theodore Roosevelt* (New York: Coward, McCann & Geoghegan, 1979), 240. See especially footnote 69. Also, Wallace Finley Dailey, curator, TR Collection at Harvard, e-mail to author, 10 September 2001.

34. For "go mad," David McCullough, *Mornings on Horseback* (New York: Simon & Schuster, 1982), 286; for "more we work," Lillian Rixey, *Bamie* (New York: David McKay, 1963), 50.

35. Rixey, 54.

36. Gracie, "Account of the Birth of Alice Roosevelt."

37. TR, *In Memory of My Darling Wife Alice Hathaway Roosevelt and of My Beloved Mother Martha Bulloch Roosevelt...* (New York: G. P. Putnam's Sons, 1884).

38. TR to "Dear Sir," 1 May 1884, TR 1858–1919 Collection, Chicago Historical Society.

39. S. J. Morris, 77.

40. Rixey, v.

41. Teague, *Mrs. L*, 12 and 10.

42. For bread, Betty Boyd Caroli, *The Roosevelt Women* (New York: Basic Books, 1998), 392; for warmth, Teague, *Mrs. L*, 28; for "wonderful feeling," Caroli, 392.

43. Teague, *Mrs. L*, 4–5.

44. Caroli, 62.

Chapter 2: "Sissy Had a Sweat Nurse!"

1. For "come between," Michael Teague, *Mrs. L* (Garden City, N.Y.: Doubleday, 1981), 36; for Baby Lee, Sylvia Jukes Morris, *Edith Kermit Roosevelt* (New York: Coward, McCann & Geoghegan, 1980), 91.

2. For "love once," Teague, 5; for "his fault," Betty Boyd Caroli, *The Roosevelt Women* (New York: Basic Books, 1998), 81.

3. For honeymoon, Sarah Booth Conroy, "Rough Rider's Romantic Side," *Washington Post*, 10 May 1905; for "Edith feels more strongly," Morris, 102.

4. See, for example, Elliott Roosevelt to Anna Roosevelt, 22 March 1886, Papers of Elliott Roosevelt Sr., FDRL.

5. For "one's daughter," ARC to Belle Willard, January 10, 1914, KBR; for "a terrible wrong," Caroli, 84.

6. Teague, 12.

7. Teague, 13 (emphasis in original).

8. Mary Lee, *A History of Chestnut Hill Chapel* (Chestnut Hill, Mass.: The History Committee of the First Church in Chestnut Hill, 1937), 35.

9. Teague, 16, 18 (emphasis in original).

10. For "gold beads," EKR to ARC, n.d.; for "no object," EKR to ARC, Thursday [1890?], both from RFPH.

11. Caroline Lee to ALR, n.d., 1906, ARLC.

12. For "eats mamma," Morris, 112–13; for "take baby brother," EKR to ARL, n.d. [1948], JSP.

13. EKR to TR, 15 August 1889; for Alice's being "distressed," see EKR to TR, 31 August 1889, both ERDP.

14. For "Papa's sister," Morris, 133; for "sensitive," Sally Quinn, "Alice Roosevelt Longworth at 90," *Washington Post*, 12 February 1974, B3; for "sweat nurse," Teague, 18.

15. Teague, 36–37.

16. Teague, 18.

17. Teague, 30, 36, 37. In *Crowded Hours* (New York: Charles Scriber's Sons, 1933) written while Edith was alive, Alice treats her stepmother more kindly than in her interviews with Teague. Alice most often

affirmed Edith's version of Alice Lee; see, for example, Dorothy McCardle, "Comparison with Teddy Puzzles Mrs. Longworth," *New York Post*, 10 August 1974, ARL Clipping File, Harvard University. See also Teague, 30. Alice does not mention Edith and Theodore's youthful romance in her autobiography.

18. EKR to ARC, fragment, n.d., RFPH.

19. Nicholas Roosevelt, *Theodore Roosevelt* (New York: Dodd, Mead, 1967), 24–25.

20. TR to Anna Roosevelt, 18 November 1895, in Anna Roosevelt Cowles, *Letters from Theodore Roosevelt to Anna Roosevelt Cowles* (New York: Charles Scribner's Sons, 1924),163.

21. Quinn, B3; Charles Selden, "The Father Complex of Alice Roosevelt Longworth and Ruth Hanna McCormick," *Ladies' Home Journal*, March 1927, 6. For the denial, see Henry Brandon, "A Talk with an 83-Year-Old Enfant Terrible," *NYT Magazine* 6 (6 August 1967): 8. Ruth Hanna McCormick, daughter of powerful Senator Marcus Hanna, would become an elected politician in her own right.

22. Teague, 36.

23. *CH*, 4.

24. For "tenement child," Quinn, B3; for "two iron bars," EKR to ARC, [26 January 1893?], RFPH; for "Alice suffers," EKR to ARC, 3 February [1893?], RFPH.

25. For "lock up," *CH*, 18; for "she does not mind," EKR to ARC, 25 February [1893?], RFPH; for "asthma," David McCullough, *Mornings on Horseback* (New York: Simon & Schuster, 1982), 106–7.

26. *CH*, 3.

27. For "Buffalo Hunt," EKR to ARC, n.d., 1891, RFPH; for sunset, ARL preservation tape, ICD 16021, 21 June 1967, JSP.

28. For "the children," EKR to ARC, 30 September 1890, RFPH; for "yesterday morning," ALR to EKR, 12 May 1893, JSP; for "the afternoon," EKR to ARC, 2 July 1891, RFPH; for "she knocked," ALR to EKR, 3 July 1896, JSP.

29. For "Andrew Lang," "Education," unidentified typescript (ts), JSP; for Theodore, *CH*, 29–30. See also TR to ARC, 26 April 1891, RFPH; for library, John Morton Blum to author, 2 April 2005.

30. For Latin and Greek, Unidentified ts, JSP, and Teague, 46; for history, ALR to TR, 10 August 1898, JSP.

31. Patty [?] to ALR, [February 1898?], ARLC.

32. For other letters, see, for example, Edith A. Clark to ALR, 14 February 1898, JSP; for Miss Spence, *CH*, 26.

33. See *CH*, 18; Lillian Rixey, *Bamie* (New York: David McKay, 1963), 113–14. See also Theodore Douglas Robinson to ALR, 9 March 1898, JSP.

34. Helen R. Roosevelt and ALR to FDR, 10 September 1897, Roosevelt Family Papers, FDRL.

35. ALR to TR, August 1897, JSP.

36. ARC to ALR, 21 August 1897, JSP.

37. ARC to ALR, 27 July 1897, JSP.

38. For "running riot," TR to ARC, 23 February 1898, Morison, *Letters*, 1:783; for "done by Helen," EKR to ALR, 14 April [1898], JSP.

39. For talk of war, EKR to ALR, 14 April [1898], JSP; for "bark," TR to Douglas Robinson, 2 April 1898, Morison, *Letters*, 2:809.

40. For "sick of," ALR to TR, 10 August 1898; for posterity correspondence, ALR to TR, 12 July 1898; TR to ALR, 19 July 1898, all JSP.

41. *CH*, 24–25.

42. ALR Diary fragment, 28–29 September 1898, JSP.

43. EKR to Mrs. William Dudley Foulke, n.d., 1898, Papers of William Dudley Foulke, LC.

44. For "gone to hell," V. C. Jones, "Before the Colors Fade: Last of the Rough Riders," *American Heritage* 20, 5 (August 1969): 95; for "signature," ALR to Carolyn Postlethwaite, fragment [1898] letter and Carolyn T. Postlethwaite to ALR, 16 October 1898, both JSP; "Gov.," Christine K. Roosevelt to ARL, 8 October 1900, JSP.

45. EKR to Cecil Spring-Rice, 15 December 1899, F.O. 800/241-242/9/1, National Archive, London; TR to Martha Selmes, 10 October 1899, Greenway AHS; EKR to Cecil Spring Rice, [c. 1899], F.O. 800/241-242/9/1, National Archive, London.

46. For basketball, see ALR to John Greenway, 14 April 1900; for ice skating, see ALR to John Greenaway, 11 March 1900, both ALR Folder, Greenway AHS; for the opera, ALR Diary Fragment, 14 October 1898; for the play, 15 October 1898, both JSP.

47. For one example of Ted's letters to Alice, see the "hollerday" letter: n.d.; for "thumb," ALR to EKR, 10 March 1900; for tea and cakes, ALR Diary Fragment, 18 October 1898, all JSP.

48. For "farmers," TR to ALR, 14 September 1900, JSP; for "bear," TR to Cecil Spring-Rice, 19 November 1900, Morison and Blum, eds., 2:1424; for "empty position," Morris, 206.

49. *CH*, 36–37. See Morris, 207–209 for the family and the inaugural.

50. *CH*, 41–42.

51. For "at the request," clipping included in William K. Verner to ARL, 28 February 1974, JSP; for response to news, "The Reporters: Jonathan Aitken Interview with Alice Roosevelt Longworth," Yorkshire Television, [January 1969].

Chapter 3: **"Something More Than a Plain American Girl"**

1. "Mrs. Roosevelt Moves Into the White House," *NYT*, 26 September 1901, 6; for "I can do much for you," EKR to ALR, 17 September 1901, ARLC.

2. *CH*, 43.

3. EKR to ALR, n.d. [1901], JSP; see Sylvia Jokes, Edith, Kermit Roosevelt (New York: Coward, McCann, and Geoghegan, 1980), 222–23, for the configuration of the second floor; for Alice's remarks about the interior design, see *CH*, 44–45.

4. William Wright, *The Washington Game* (New York: E. P. Dutton, 1974), 19.

5. EKR to Cecil Spring-Rice, 27 January 1902, Churchill Archives Center, Papers of Sir Cecil Spring-Rice, CASR, Churchill College, Cambridge, England.

6. The phrase is Ellen Maury Slayden's in her *Washington Wife* (New York: Harper & Row, 1962), 46. On the renovation, see EKR to Charles McKim, 9 September 1902; William Loeb to McKim, 13 September 1902; EKR to McKim, 15 September 1902; "Questions Referred to Mrs. Roosevelt," by McKim, n.d.; EKR to McKim, *n.d.* [Sunday]; EKR to McKim, 5 October 1902; all JSP.

7. Richard Derby to ALR, 1 October 1902, JSP.

8. "May" to ALR, 19 October 1902, JSP.

9. "Miss Alice Roosevelt Introduced to Society," *NYT*, 4 January 1902, 1; "White House Ball," *Washington Post*, 4 January 1902, 1.

10. For "planning for months," EKR to ALR, n.d. [1901], JSP; for "enchanted," *CH*, 47; Truman L. Elton, "Daughter of the President and Her Reputed Fiancé," *Richmond Times-Dispatch*, n.d., reel 461, TRP.

11. Stephen Birmingham, *The Right People* (Boston: Little, Brown, 1968), 123–124.

12. Carl Sferrazza Anthony, *First Ladies* (New York: Morrow, 1990), 296, 298.

13. Ward McAllister, *Society As I Have Found It* (New York: Cassell, 1890), 243.

14. For "elbow-in-the-soup," Michael Teague, *Mrs. L* (Garden City, NY: Doubleday, 1981), 76; for crash, *CH*, 47.

15. ER, *This Is My Story* (New York: Harper & Brothers, 1937), 37; EKR to ALR, n.d. [1901], JSP.

16. "Carloads" is Alice's description of how many of her friends attended (CH, 47). The *New York Tribune* reported 370 people, while Wilbur Cross and Ann Novotny (*White House Weddings* [New York: David McKay, 1967], 136), and Marie Smith (*Entertaining in the White House* [Washington, D.C.: Acropolis Books, 1967], 150) both stated there were "some seven hundred" guests in all. The *NYT* suggested that three hundred young women attended and nearly as many young men. See "Miss Alice Roosevelt Introduced Into Society," *NYT*, 4 January 1902, 1.

17. Mary Randolph, *Presidents and First Ladies* (New York: D. Appleton, 1936), 187; Marguerite Cassini, *Never a Dull Moment* (New York: Harper Brothers, 1956), 166; "Miss Roosevelt a Debutante," *New York Tribune*, 4 January 1902, 10.

18. Charles Seldon, "The Father Complex of Alice Roosevelt Longworth and Ruth Hanna McCormick," *Ladies' Home Journal*, March 1927, 72; Randolph, 190; Lillian Rixey, *Bamie* (New York: David McKay, 1963), 187; Ted Morgan, *F.D.R.* (New York: Simon & Schuster, 1985), 81.

19. *CH*, 47.

20. "Miss Alice Roosevelt Introduced to Society," *NYT*, 4 January 1902, 1; "Miss Roosevelt a Debutante," *New York Tribune*, 4 January 1902, 1.

21. Teague, 76.

22. Irving J. Rein, Philip Kotler, and Martin R. Stoller, *High Visibility* (New York: Dodd, Mead, 1987), 15.

23. Walton and Cripe, "Alice Roosevelt March" (Chicago: Victor Kremer, 1902); Harold L. Frankensteen, "The American Girl" (Detroit: H. A. Sage, 1905).

24. Teague, 70, 72 emphasis added by Teague. She did not destroy the letter. In it TR accused her of "courting notoriety," with "bizarre actions" that were "underbred and unladylike," TR to ALR, 28 August 1904, JSP.

25. Morris, 268.

26. Quentin Roosevelt to ALR, 14 December 1909, RFPH.

27. TR to ALR, telegram, 19 November 1903, TRP.

28. Teague, 108.

29. For Edward VII, 27 January 1902, ARLD; for card reception, 4 February 1902, ARLD; "Named by Miss Roosevelt: Benefit of Pascal Institute," *New York Tribune*, 5 February 1902, 7.

30. For "Sissie," EKR to ALR, 10 February 1902; for birthday, EKR to ALR, n.d. [1902], both JSP; "Groton Boys Gaining," *New York Tribune*, 16 February 1902, 9; *CH*, 47–48; for "love that boy," 15 February 1902, ARLD.

31. Andrew D. White to TR, 4 January 1902, TRP.

32. Cambon to Delcasse, 15 January 1902, in *Documents Diplomatiques Francais* II (Paris: Imprimerie Nationale, 1931), 32–33.

33. Christening practice, 23 February 1902; appraisal of the prince, 24 February 1902, ARLD.

34. Smith, 153–54; Morris, 234; Ona Griffin Jeffries, *In and Out of the White House* (New York: Wilfred Funk, 1960), 276–80.

35. 25 February 1902, ARLD.

36. "The Kaiser and Miss Roosevelt," *New York Times*, 26 February 1901, 1.

37. Worthington Ford, ed., *The Letters of Henry Adams* (New York: Houghton Mifflin, 1938), 375.

38. For the *Tribune* quote, see "Kaiser's Compliment to American Women through Miss Roosevelt," 26 February 1902, 2:4; "The 'Miss Roosevelt' Wrap," *New York Herald, Paris Edition*, 14 September 1902, 11; enclosed in Edith [Root] to ALR, 14 September 1902, JSP; Cassini, 169.

39. Clara Parrish to ALR, 6 February 1902, ARLC.

40. Whitelaw Reid to TR, 12 March 1902, TRP.

41. TR to Joseph H. Choate, 3 February 1902, Joseph H. Choate Papers, LC; "The 'Fuss' Over Miss Roosevelt," *Literary Digest* 24, 15 (12 April 1902), 509–510.

42. Selden, 72.

43. "Miss Roosevelt Will Not See Coronation," *NYT*, 8 March 1902, 8; *CH*, 50; TR to Joseph H. Choate, 3 March 1902, Choate Papers, LC; Whitelaw Reid to TR, 12 March 1902, TRP.

44. 21 June 1902, (written on inside back cover of diary); 27 January 1903, ARLD.

45. "The 'Fuss' Over Miss Roosevelt," 509–510.

46. Isabel Anderson, *Presidents and Pies* (New York: Houghton Mifflin, 1920), 68; 26 March 1902, ARLD.

47. *CH*, 52; "Miss Roosevelt Starts for Cuba," *New York Tribune*, 10 March 1902, 2; 13 March–7 April 1902, ARLD.

48. 6 March 1902, ARLD; "Appeal to Miss Roosevelt," *NYT*, 13 March 1902, 1; Alejandro Mendez Plasencia to ALR, 22 March 1902, JSP.

49. Clifford Howard, "The President's Daughter," *Ladies' Home Journal* 19, 5, (April 1902), 5.

50. 13 April 1902, ARLD (emphasis in original).

Chapter 4: "I Tried to Be Conspicuous"

1. For Highland fling, Martha Selmes to Julia Dinsmore, 10 January 1902, Dinsmore Family Papers, AHS; 25 April–11 May 1902, ARLD. For the miscarriage, see also Sylvia Jukes Morris, *Edith Kermit Roosevelt* (New York: Coward, McCann & Geoghegan, 1980), 237.

2. For "help me," EKR to ALR, n.d., JSP; for "toughs," Edmund Morris, *Theodore Rex* (New York: Random House, 2001), 108; for Edith's indisposition, 22–23 May 1902, ARLD, and *CH*, 53.

3. 30 June 1902, ARLD.

4. 28 and 31 October 1902, ARLD. "I pray for money!" 26 October 1902, ARLD (emphasis in original). See also 21 December and the undated entries at the end of the 1902 diary.

5. Manhanset House (Shelter Island, New York) program, 4 July 1902, JSP.

6. "Mr. and Mrs. Roosevelt Enjoy an Outing," *NYT*, 19 July 1902, 8; ALR to John Greenway, 29 December 1902, Greenway AHS; for "Got a talking to," 20 July 1902, ARLD.

7. 2–18 August ARLD; "Alice Roosevelt Loses a Game of Tag with the Camera," *New York Journal*, 17 August 1902, n.p., TRP; "Miss Roosevelt's Hand Read," *Philadelphia Press*, 19 August 1902, TRP; "Miss Roosevelt Loses Her Way," *New York Tribune*, 19 August 1902, 1.

8. Unidentified, clipping n.d. ("Miss Alice Roosevelt, who will soon summer at the Summer White House...."); Corinne Roosevelt Robinson to ALR, 25 May 1903, both from JSP; Luellen Cass Teters, "Fair Woman as Motorist," *Motor* magazine, January 1907, 19, quoted in Virginia Scharff, *Taking the Wheel* (New York: Free Press, 1991), 71–73.

9. For "coffee," 6 September 1902; for accident, 4 September 1902 and *CH*, 54;

for not loving, 1–17 September 1902, all ARLD.

10. For poker, see 17, 18 and 22 September 1902, ARLD; Henry Brandon, "A Talk with an 83-Year-Old Enfant Terrible," *NYT,* 6 August 1967, 69; and *CH,* 169–170.

11. 23 and 30 September 1902, ARLD.

12. N.d., at the back of the 1902 diary. See also 1 October 1902, ARLD.

13. "Hoof," 30 November 1902; "no one ever came," 13 December 1902, ARLD.

14. 23–24 December 1902, ARLD.

15. 25 December 1902, ARLD.

16. For the embassy dance 8 January; for "both so attractive," 11 January 1903, ARLD; TR to TRJR, 20 January 1903, reel 330, TRP. See also TRJR to ALR, 3 February 1903, JSP.

17. 20 January 1903, ARLD.

18. For Edith's sanctions, EKR to ALR, 9 November 1902; for scheduling, EKR to ALR, undated, both JSP.

19. 18 January 1903, ARLD.

20. For Judicial reception, 12 January 1903, ARLD; for European visitor, S. J. Morris, 273; for "I am a fool," 30 January 1903, ARLD. On 23 and 25 January Alice vowed not to go to New York anymore.

21. 27 January 1903, ARLD.

22. Sally Quinn, "Alice Roosevelt at 90," *Washington Post,* 12 February 1974, B3.

23. Author's interview with Joanna Sturm, 25 April 2005.

24. TR to TRJR, 9 February 1903, reel 330, TRP.

25. 16 February 1903, ARLD.

26. *CH,* 55. See also "Chosen Queen of Comus Ball," *New York Tribune,* 1 February 1903, 2; "Welcome to Miss Roosevelt," *NYT,* 1 February 1903, 1; "Miss Roosevelt Honored," *NYT,* 18 February 1903, 1; "Miss Roosevelt Charmed," *NYT,* 19 February 1903, 1; "Alice Roosevelt's Debut in Carnival Wonderland," *New Orleans Daily*

Picayune, n.d. [1903], JSP; for betting and Root, 21 February 1903, ARLD; ALR to Mary E. McIlhenny, n.d. [1903] JSP; for "wear her honors," untitled article, *New Orleans Daily Picayune,* n.d. [1903], JSP.

27. 8 March 1903, ARLD.

28. ALR to EKR, 24 March 1903, JSP.

29. For "official behavior," *CH,* 56; for "very good," ALR to EKR, 20 March 1903; for "fireworks and gusto mucho," ALR to EKR, 24 March 1903, both JSP; "Miss Roosevelt's Ovation," *New York Tribune,* 4 April 1903, 5; TR to ALR, 27 May 1903, TRP.

30. Michael Teague, *Mrs. L* (Garden City, N.Y.: Doubleday, 1981), 73.

31. For "stared at," *CH,* 59; ALR to John McCutcheon, 29 November 1903, John McCutcheon Papers, Newberry Library, Chicago.

32. Helen Rebecca Roosevelt to ALR, n.d., ARLC. Helen pasted the unidentified clipping to her note. See also 24 October 1903, ARLD; "Miss Roosevelt Eager to See Horses Start," *NYT,* 4 April 1905, 9.

33. See Ethel Barrymore's *Memories* (New York: Harper & Brothers, 1955), 131, for an example of Maggie and Alice in competition over Nick. See also Ira R. T. Smith, *Dear Mr. President* (New York: Julian Messner, 1949), 60–61.

34. Marguerite Cassini, *Never a Dull Moment* (New York: Harper & Brothers, 1956), 188; for "gallivanting," Teague, 77; for ER quote, Geoffrey Ward, *A First-Class Temperament* (New York: Harper & Row, 1989), 45n7.

35. Cassini, 189.

36. 16 February 1904, ARLD.

37. "Gleanings," *New York Tribune,* 9 March 1903, 5.

38. Frances Spatz and David Camelon, "Legendary Ladies: Rebellious 'Princess Alice,'" *American Weekly,* 12 November 1950, 24–25. "To annoy the family," ARL preservation tape, ICD 16037, n.d., JSE.

39. "Smoking in Public," *Washington Mirror*, 3 June 1905, JSP; EKR to ALR, n.d. [1905], JSP ("I am distressed to hear..."); TR to ALR, 21 July 1905, RFPH; Kermit Roosevelt to ALR, 15 November 1905, JSP.

40. "S. Shakespeare" to "the Chairman of the 'More-Light-in-the-Darkness' Committee," 15 December 1905, JSP, and Teague, 82.

41. For purse, Sarah Booth Conroy, "Rough Rider's Romantic Side," *Washington Post*, 10 May 1995; for troop review, Walter Evans Edge, *A Jerseyman's Journal* (Princeton: Princeton University Press, 1948), 64; and "Mrs. Goelet in Submarine," *NYT*, 27 July 1911, 2. Alice wrote to journalist Samuel McClure two decades after the event to clear the record. She was usually credited with having gone to the bottom of the sea in the submarine. Not so, she told McClure. At Newport she "did go aboard a submarine." But, "it was hitched to the dock the whole time, obviously. I have a dim recollection that we were told we were a couple of feet underwater, if that is possible with the boat tied to the dock." She was happy to set the facts straight: "I don't in the least mind a 'story' on myself, when it is a true one, but this most certainly is not!" ARL to Samuel McClure, 18 June [c. 1925], McClure Manuscript, Manuscripts Department, Lilly Library, Indiana University, Bloomington, Indiana.

42. *CH*, 59–63; "Miss Roosevelt's Exciting Ride, " *New York Tribune*, 30 May 1903, 9; "Miss Roosevelt at York Harbor," *New York Tribune*, 29 July 1903, 8; "Miss Roosevelt Sinks in the Boat," *New York Tribune*, 11 September 1903, 9; "Miss Roosevelt's Photograph: Presented to Officers of Dispatch Boat Named for Her," *New York Tribune*, 4 November 1903, 6; "White House Brides," *New York Herald*, 5 January 1906, TRP; ALR to Belle Hagner, 23 July 1903, PHP; "Miss Roosevelt at Races," *NYT*, 12 April 1904.

43. Owen Wister, *Roosevelt* (New York: Macmillan, 1930), 87.

44. For examples of Edith's lectures, see 10 January 1904 and 10 May 1904, ARLD. This lecture from Grandma Lee is from Caroline Lee to ALR, 20 July 1903, ARLC. Unidentified author [signed "E———" to ALR, n.d., ARLD.

45. 8 October 1903, ARLD; George C. Lee to ALR, 5 November 1903, ARLC; Quarterly stipend: George C. Lee to ALR, 1 January 1904, JSP.

46. 26–31 May 1904, ARLD; *CH*, 64–65; "Women Mob Miss Roosevelt," *NYT*, 27 May 1904, 1; "Miss Alice Roosevelt," *World's Fair Bulletin*, June 1904, 34; July 1904, 40; TRJR to ALR, *n.d.*, JSP; copied the First Daughter, "Miss Roosevelt Gives Up Pike Trip," *St. Louis Republican*, 2 June 1904, 1, Francis Collection, St. Louis Historical Society.

47. For "Alice dear," unidentified author [signed "E———"] to ALR, n.d.; "Hair will fall out," Libby Lawrence to ALR, n.d., both ARLC.

48. Charles McCauley to ALR, 12 February [n.d.]; for *Paris Herald*, Gwendolyn [unknown] to ALR, n.d.; for Horse Show, Unidentified author, n.d.; George C. Lee to ALR, 20 June 1904, all ARLC.

49. TR to Owen Wister, 2 November 1901, TRP.

50. EKR to ALR, n.d., JSP.

Chapter 5: **"Frightfully Difficult Trying to Keep Up Appearances"**

1. ALR Diary, fragment, 14 October 1898, JSP.

2. Ward McAllister, *Society As I Have Found It* (New York: Cassell, 1890); "social insecurity" Kathleen Dalton, from "Theodore Roosevelt: Knickerbocker Aristocrat," *New York History* 67, 1 (January 1986), 46.

3. 20 May 1904, ARLD; Joseph Alsop, *I've Seen the Best of It* (New York: W. W. Norton, 1992), 33.

4. For "captivate your fancy," Margaret [unknown]to ALR, n.d.; for "Mrs. John Greenway," Gwendolyn [unknown] to ALR, n.d.; for dukes, Helen [Douglas] to ALR, n.d.; and Helen R. Roosevelt to ALR, n.d.; all ARLC; for "temper fit," 8 May 1902, ARLD.

5. Sylvia Jukes Morris, *Edith Kermit Roosevelt* (New York: Coward, McCann & Geoghegan, 1980), 98.

6. Mark Sullivan, *The Education of an American* (New York: Doubleday, Doran, 1938), 211.

7. Nora C. Klein, *Practical Etiquette* (Chicago: Flanagan, 1888), 8 and 61.

8. Number 76 was 24 April, 87 was 2 May, and 100 was 26 September, all 1902, ARLD. Helen R. Roosevelt to ARL, n.d., ARLC.

9. Carl Sferrazza Anthony, *First Ladies* (New York: William Morrow, 1990), 1:305–306. The TR quote is from "Message of the President of the United States Communicated to the Two Houses of Congress at the Beginning of the Second Session of the 59th Congress," *Congressional Record* (Washington, D.C.: Government Printing Office, 1906), 29, reel 427, TRP.

10. Klein, 21.

11. For men, Ronald G. Walters, ed., *Primers for Prudery* (Baltimore: Johns Hopkins University Press, 2000), 95; for women, Harvey Green, *The Light of the Home* (New York: Pantheon, 1983), 21; "heartless discriminations," Sondra R. Herman, "Loving Courtship or the Marriage Market? The Ideal and Its Critics 1871–1911," *American Quarterly*, 25, 2 (May 1973), 242; "begat series," Michael Teague, *Mrs. L* (Garden City, N.Y.: Doubleday, 1981), 57; John Morton Blum to author, 2 April 2005.

12. Abbey B. Longstreet, *Social Etiquette of New York* (New York: D. Appleton, 1887), 9.

13. Buttons askew and restriction quotes, Teague, 66.

14. For the asparagus, see Dabney Taylor, "Idaho's 'Little Borah' Looks Back on Her First 99 Years," *Idaho Statesman*, 19 October 1969, 14. Asparagus may be eaten with ungloved fingers. For overseas trips, see Chapter 7, below.

15. ER, *This Is My Story* (New York: Harper & Brothers, 1937), 37. Alfreda, Christine, and Dorothy Roosevelt rounded out the Magic Five.

16. 21 December 1902, ARLD.

17. Teague, 151.

18. "Awfully nice," 12 January 1903 and "I am afraid," 8 November 1903, ARLD; for top billing see, for example, "Led Newport Dance with Alice Roosevelt," *Washington Post*, 14 August 1902, and "Miss Roosevelt's Hand Read," *Philadelphia Press*, 19 August 1902; both TRP.

19. "Fierce enough," Libby Lawrence to ALR, n.d., ARLC; "attraction for me," Teague, 77.

20. ARL wrote about Carpenter every night in her diary from the first through the seventh of April 1902. The retaliation quote is from the third, the charms quote from the fourth, and the "poor Alice" quote from the fifth.

21. 7 April 1902, ARLD.

22. Edward Carpenter to ARL, 3 May 1902; and n.d., both ARLC.

23. 23–28 May 1902, ARLD.

24. Carpenter proposed on 29 May, and ARL received their notes on 30 May, according to her diary.

25. Eliza Bisbee Duffey, *Ladies' and Gentlemen's Etiquette* (Philadelphia: Porter & Coates, 1887), 125–26; McAllister, 242.

26. J. Van Ness Philips to ALR, 22 July

1902, ARLC; "A young lady," Klein, 18; "rejected suitor," Duffey, 135–136.

27. Delancey Jay to ALR, 29 October 1903, ALRC; 9 July 1902, ARLD.

28. Mrs. John King Van Rensselaer, *Social Ladder* (New York: Holt, 1924), 33. By 1924, when Mrs. Van Rensselaer wrote, the Mrs. Arthur Iselin to whom she referred was the former Eleanor Jay, sister of Delancey Jay.

29. Arthur Iselin to ALR, 16 April [1902], ARLC.

30. "Very stupid," 8 August 1902; "poor Alice, 3 August 1902; "no hope," 7 August 1902, ARLD.

31. "Me alone loves," 18 November 1902; "the beast," 10 December 1902; "oh Arthur," 11 December 1902, ARLD.

32. "I would be," 10 January 1903, ARLD; Margaret [unknown] to ARL, n.d., ARLC; "Arthur...hates me," 20 January 1903; "never get married," 21 January 1903; both ARLD.

33. Receptions, 26 January 1903; cotillion, 28 January 1903; "I led him on," 10 February 1903, all ARLD.

34. 9 February 1903, ARLD.

35. 12 February 1903, ARLD.

Chapter 6: "He Never Grew Serious About Anything"

1. Helen R. Roosevelt married her sixth cousin Theodore Douglas Roosevelt in 1904. ER married her fifth cousin once removed, FDR, in 1905.

2. Edward Carpenter to ARL, n.d. 1902, ARLC.

3. Sondra R. Herman, "Loving Courtship or the Marriage Market?" *American Quarterly*, 25 (May 1973), 239.

4. Karl Fleming and Anne Taylor Fleming, *The First Time* (New York: Simon & Schuster, 1975), 181.

5. Cleveland Amory, *Who Killed Society?* (New York: Harper, 1960), 227–46. Amory maintained that by 1900 "no less than 500 of America's '400'" had married foreign titles (229).

6. Michael Teague, *Mrs. L* (Garden City, N.Y.: Doubleday, 1981), 129.

7. "I swear," ARLD back of the 1902 diary; "vow," 3 October 1903, ARLD. To Iselin, n.d., ARLD, from the back of the 1902 diary; to Nick, 27 July 1905, ARLD.

8. 7 February 1904, ARLD.

9. Teague, 129.

10. Fleming and Fleming, 177 and 183.

11. Drew Pearson and Robert S. Allen, *The Washington Merry-Go-Round* (New York: H. Liveright, 1931), 230–31.

12. "'Tis True That They Are to Wed," *Cincinnati Enquirer*, 12 December 1905, clipping, ARL Scrapbook, LC; Marguerite Cassini, *Never a Dull Moment* (New York: Harper & Brothers, 1956), 190; "new congressman," Teague, 129; 14 and 17 February 1904, ARLD.

13. On Nicholas Longworth Sr., see his obituary, 1890 and "50 Years Ago in Cincinnati," *Cincinnati Enquirer*, 19 January 1940, in the Judge Nicholas Longworth Princeton File, CHS; and "Nicholas Longworth, Esq., of Cincinnati, and the Vineyards of Ohio," *Harper's Weekly*, 2, 82 (24 July 1858), 472–74.

14. Clara Longworth de Chambrun, *The Making of Nicholas Longworth* (New York: Ray Long & Richard Smith, 1933),115.

15. De Chambrun, 222.

16. Constance McLaughlin Green, *Washington* (Princeton: Princeton University Press, 1963), 301.

17. Teague, 137.

18. Geoffrey Ward, *Before the Trumpet* (New York: Harper & Row, 1989), 236.

19. Llewellyn Thayer, "The White House Bridegroom," *Leslie's Illustrated Weekly*, 1 March 1906, 174.

20. Helen Hay to NL, n.d., NLIII.

21. NL to "My Darling" [Miriam Bloomer], n.d., NLIII. Miriam Bloomer lived in the Hotel Alms with her family. See *Mrs. Devereux's Blue Book of Cincinnati Society,* 1906, CHS.

22. "Former fiancé," "Miss Bloomer Not Burned," *NYT,* 29 September 1907, 2; "I'll come," Miriam Bloomer to NL, n.d., NLIII; at the wedding, Eleanor Adams, "Chit and Chat About This 'n That," *Cincinnati Enquirer,* 19 January 1964, ARLPF. See also Wilbur Cross and Ann Novotny, *White House Weddings* (New York: McKay, 1967), 139; "collapse," "Miss Bloomer Not Burned," *NYT,* 29 September 1907, 2.

23. Cassini, 180–81.

24. 20 January 1904, ARLD (emphasis in original).

25. 21 January 1904, ARLD (emphasis in original).

26. "American Bride for Count," *NYT,* 15 April 1904, 5; "Count Gizycki Hastens Wedding Preparations," *NYT,* 7 April 1904, 9.

27. Cassini, 199. See also "Mr. Longworth to Marry Miss Alice Next February," n.d., unidentified clipping, ARLPF.

28. Charles de Chambrun to ALR, 25 March 1904, ARLC.

29. "I really like," 27 January 1904; "Why am I," 12 March 1904, ARLD; "tease my friends," Cassini, 181; "only her own fun," Cassini, 200; "Nick and Maggie," 1 May 1904, ARLD.

30. 2 May 1904, ARLD.

31. 3 May 1904, ARLD. In Cassini's memoir, the story is different—so different, in fact, that it is likely that Nick proposed to Maggie twice (Cassini, 200).

32. "Had a long talk," 26 December 1904; "Nick had a supper," 19 January 1905, ARLD (emphasis in original).

33. 29–31 January 1905, ARLD.

34. NL to ALR, [11 February 1905], JSP.

35. From 15 January through 21 April, every entry ends with "My Nick."

36. "So many things," NL to ALR, 8 April 1905; "I have not," NL to ALR, 19 April 1905; "Longing to see you," NL to ALR, 25 April 1905; all JSP.

37. NL to ALR, 14 June 1905, JSP.

38. "Practically told Charlie," 17 June 1905; "Father is making peace," 11 June 1905, ARLD.

39. Charles E. Rosenberg, "Sexuality, Class and Role in 19th-Century America," *American Quarterly,* 25, 2 (May 1973), 140.

40. NL to ALR 20 June 1905, JSP.

41. "Desperately sorrowful," 1 June 1905, ARLD; ALR to ARC, n.d. [1905], ARLHar.

42. Lost five pounds, Sylvia Jukes Morris, *Edith Kermit Roosevelt* (New York: Coward, McCann, & Geoghegan, 1980), 297; "parting," 26 June 1905, ARLD.

Chapter 7: **"When Alice Came to Plunderland"**

1. WHT to Luke E. Wright, 17 March 1905, WHTP.

2. Henry F. Pringle, *The Life and Times of William Howard Taft* (New York: Farrar and Reinhart, 1939) 1:297–98.

3. Complete list of junketeers in "Personnel of Secretary Taft's Party," Mabel T. Boardman Papers, LC. See also "Taft and His Party Start," *NYT,* 1 July 1905, 1

4. ARC to ALR, 20 June 1905, JSP.

5. ALR to TR, n.d. [1905], JSP; WHT to HHT, 10 July 1905,WHTP.

6. HT, *Reflections of Full Years* (New York: Dodd, Mead, 1914), 292–94.

7. Elsie Clews Parsons, "Congressional Junket in Japan," *New-York Historical*

Society Quarterly, XLQ, 4 (October 1957), 338 (emphasis in original).

8. ALR to TR, n.d. [1905], JSP.

9. ALR to EKR, n.d. [1905], JSP; for "banzai," Michael Teague, *Mrs. L* (Garden City, N.Y.: Doubleday, 1981), 84.

10. Lloyd Griscom to Willard Straight, 21 April 1905, WSP.

11. Lloyd C. Griscom, *Diplomatically Speaking* (Boston: Little, Brown, 1940), 257–58; WHT to HHT, 26 July 1905, WHTP.

12. ALR to TR, 30 July 1905, JSP; George A. Lensen, ed., *The d'Anethan Dispatches from Japan, 1894–1910* (Tallahassee: Diplomatic Press, 1967), 206; Teague, 87; and *CH*, 84, for Alice's more contemporary and irreverent recollection of the event.

13. *CH*, 85 and Griscom, 257.

14. TR to John Hay, in Elting E. Morison and John Morton Blum, eds. *The Letters of Theodore Roosevelt* (Cambridge, Mass.: Harvard University Press, 1951–1954) 4:1168.

15. WHT to HHT, 31 July, WHTP; The newspapers claimed the empress was ill. ALR thought her "out of town" (*CH*, 80).

16. ALR to TR, 30 July 1905, JSP; WHT to HHT, 31 July 1905, WHTP; Parsons, 402; Griscom, 258 and 298.

17. WHT to HHT, 31 July 1905, WHTP.

18. Teague, 91.

19. Bouquets, Griscom, 260; "The Japanese did wonders," Martin Egan to Willard Straight, 14 August 1905, WSP; "No people," *CH*, 86; "I don't know," ALR to TR, 30 July 1905, JSP.

20. ARLC, undated and unsigned letter file; "national costume" from the same source.

21. WHT to Luke E. Wright, 17 March 1905, WHTP.

22. Fred Leith to his mother, 4 August 1905, Fred Leith Ms. Coll. 89, Naval Historical Collection, Naval War College, Newport, Rhode Island.

23. *CH*, 87; "Pageant for Taft,' *Washington Post*, 5 August 1905, 1. See also "How Miss Roosevelt was Greeted by the Little Brown Filipino," *Brooklyn Daily Eagle*, 3 September 1905, TRP, reel 461.

24. Mabel T. Boardman, "A Woman's Impressions of the Philippines," *Outlook*, 82 (24 February 1906), 435–46; "Miss Roosevelt's Reception in the Philippines," *Washington Post*, 6 August 1905, sec. 4, 6; "Miss Roosevelt's Ball Closes Manila Visit," *NYT*, 13 August 1905, 4.

25. WHT to HHT, 14 August 1905, WHTP; The Oyster Bay quote is from an untitled blurb in the *Washington Post*, 6 August 1905, sec. II, 4.

26. "Sultan of Sulu Offers to Wed Miss Roosevelt," *NYT*, 22 August 1905, 7. See also "Taft Party at Iloilo," *Washington Post*, 15 August 1905, 1. For an assertion that the sultan never proposed, see "Miss Roosevelt's Embarrassing Presents," *Literary Digest*, 4 November 1905, 644.

27. Boardman, 444.

28. Charles H. Brent, "The Visit to the Philippines of Secretary Taft and His Party," *Outlook*, 81 (14 October 1905), 371.

29. "Miss Roosevelt's Plans," *Washington Post*, 16 August 1905, 2; "Taft Party at Hong Kong," *NYT*, 3 September 1905, 1; TR to Victor H. Metcalf, 16 June 1905, in Morison and Blum, eds., 4:1235; TR to Herbert H. D. Peirce, 24 June 1905, in Morison and Blum, eds., 4:1251; "Boycotters Heavy Losers," *Washington Post*, 6 August 1905, 1; and "Extends the Boycott," *Washington Post*, 11 August 1905, 4.

30. *CH*, 91; McIntosh, "Mrs. Longworth's Pluck in the Face of Peril," *Literary Digest*, 32.9 (3 March 1906), 346; and

"Alice Roosevelt Defies Chinese," *Washington Globe,* 4 September 1905, reel 461, TRP.

31. CH, 92; "Gunboat for Miss Roosevelt," *NYT,* 4 September 1905, 1.

32. Menu, JSP; *CH,* 95–99.

33. Henry Tsai, *China and the Overseas Chinese* (Fayetteville: University of Arkansas Press, 1983), 100–103.

34. *CH,* 99–100; Paul A. Varg, *Open Door Diplomat* (Urbana: University of Illinois Press, 1952), 59–60.

35. "The Young Lady of the White House," *NYT,* 19 October 1905, 8; for part of the extensive media coverage of Alice in China, see "Miss Roosevelt at Peking," *NYT,* 13 September 1905, 4; "Miss Roosevelt Visits Empress," *New York Tribune,* 16 September 1905, 2; "Guests of Dowager Empress," *Washington Post,* 16 September 1905, reel 461, TRP. "Rides on Royal Palanquin," *NYT,* 20 September 1905, 1; "Empress Dowager and President's Daughter," *New York Herald,* 24 September 1905, magazine, 1.

36. *CH,* 103 and 104; "come, saw," Willard Straight to Frederick Palmer, 3 October 1905, WSP.

37. "To Miss Roosevelt," reel 1, WSP, #1260, Division of Rare and Manuscript Collections, Cornell University Library.

38. Frederick Palmer to Willard Straight, 24 September 1905, WSP; "not a banzai," Teague, 87; "if anyone asked," *CH,* 106; policemen, Lloyd Griscom to ALR, 19 September 1905, JSP.

39. The Girls of the Kamibe Higher Elementary School to ALR, 6 October 1905, ARLC.

40. "Russian women" to ALR, 14 August [1905], JSP; Lewis L. Gould, *The Presidency of Theodore Roosevelt* (Lawrence: University Press of Kansas, 1991), 181.

41. 29 June 1905, ARLD; headline, *CH,* 71.

42. WHT to HHT, 10 July 1905, WHTP. On Mabel Boardman and Amy McMillan, see WHT to HHT, 31 July 1905, WHTP. According to Kentucky historian Thomas H. Appleton Jr., a Kentucky engagement is a May–December romance. Appleton Jr. to the author, 8 December 1991.

43. WHT to HHT, 1 August 1905, WHTP.

44. "Congressional wives' luncheon," 71, the "curtain" (or private) lectures, 69, *CH.* For ALR's assessment of the luncheon, see ARLD, 3 July 1905.

45. 9–11 July 1905, ARLD; WHT to HHT, 3 July 1905, WHTP.

46. WHT to HHT, 25 July 1905, WHTP.

47. 27 July 1905, ARLD; Nagasaki newspaper quoted in "Miss Roosevelt in Japan," *New York Tribune,* 28 September 1905, 5.

48. WHT to HHT, 14 August 1905, WHTP.

49. ARL to NL, n.d., September 1905, ARLC. It is impossible to know whether or not Alice ever gave this letter to Nick.

50. ARL to NL, n.d. [1905], JSP.

51. Alice had told Griscom, WHT to HHT, 26 July 1905; "never believe," WHT to HHT, 31 July 1905, both WHTP.

52. TR to ALR, 2 September 1905, ARLHar; for example, EKR to ALR, 10 September 1905, JSP.

53. For the "rough passage" and the bet, see F. Palmer to Willard Straight, 20 November 1905, WSP.

54. *CH,* 106–7; "To Break All Records," *New York Tribune,* 24 October 1905, 1; "Miss Roosevelt Lands," *NYT,* 24 October 1905, 1; "Harriman's Race Stopped," *NYT,* 25 October 1905, 1; "Miss Roosevelt Here from Eastern Trip," *NYT,* 27 October 1905, 1; Harriman won the bet when the *Siberia* beat the *Korea*'s record by 27 minutes.

55. "Miss Roosevelt Lands," *NYT*, 24 October 1905, 1.

56. *CH*, 108–9.

57. Mary Elizabeth W. Sherwood, *Manners and Social Usages* (New York: Harper, 1897), 96–98.

58. Morris, 303.

59. De Chambrun, 193; "Alice Roosevelt to Become Mrs. Longworth," *Chicago Tribune*, 13 December 1905, 1; *CH*, 109.

60. "Longworth Didn't Know He'd Won," *New York Evening World*, 15 December 1905, and "Longworth Says He's in a Trance," *Brooklyn Times*, 14 December 1905, both from the ARL Scrapbook, LC; "rumor says," Thayer, 174; McIntosh, 346.

61. Truman L. Elton, "Daughter of the President and Her Reputed Fiancé," *Richmond Times-Dispatch*, n.d. 1905, reel 461. TRP; "Miss Roosevelt Lands," *NYT*, 24 October 1905, 1.

62. Untitled clipping, *Montreal Daily Star*, 18 October 1905, reel 461, TRP; TR telegram to ARL, 17 October 1905, JSP. See also "Miss Roosevelt's Embarrassing Presents," *Literary Digest*, XXXI, 19 (4 November 1905), 643.

63. "Six Months in the Strenuous Life of Miss Roosevelt," *Indianapolis Sunday Star*, 1 October 1905; and "Miss Roosevelt to Pay $25,000 Duty on Gifts," *NYT*, 18 October 1905, from reel 461, TRP. *NYT* editorial, 21 October 1905, 8, was entitled "Miss Roosevelt's Presents." ARL's quote to the press is from "The President's Daughter," *Indianapolis Morning Star*, 31 October 1905, reel 461, TRP; *Chicago Record Herald*, 17 October 1905, n.p., reel 461, TRP; "1,026 on Oriental Gifts," *NYT*, 17 December 1905, 1.

64. Thomas Sammons to ARL, 14 September 1905, JSP.

65. ARC to ARL, 31 October 1905, JSP.

66. Elton, "Daughter of the President," reel 461, TRP.

Chapter 8: "To Bask in the Rays of Your Reflected Glory"

1. "At the White House," *New York Tribune*, 14 December 1905, 16; Robert Toapp to ARL, 13 January 1906, JSP; ARL to ER, 8 December 1905, ER Papers, FDRL.

2. Anne Ellis, *The Life of an Ordinary Woman* (Boston: Houghton Mifflin, 1999 [1929]), 241.

3. V. V. Pittman to ARL, 17 February 1906, JSP.

4. Owen Wister to ARL, 17 December 1905, JSP.

5. George Lee to ARL, 7 December 1905, ARLC.

6. Julius Fleischmann to NL, n.d. [1905], NLIII.

7. "Miss Roosevelt Could Open a Museum with These Presents," unidentified clipping, n.d., reel 461,TRP; "I had about the sort," *CH*, 109–110; "the one thing," Michael Teague, *Mrs. L* (Garden City, N.Y.: Doubleday, 1981), 128–29; Mary Elizabeth W. Sherwood, *Manners and Social Usages* (New York: Harper, 1897), 197 and 118.

8. Francis H. Lee to ARL, 30 January 1906; ARL to John Greenway, n.d., [1906], both JSP. For the junketeers' gift, see "The President a Guest at Longworth Dinner," *NYT*, 16 February 1906, 1. Alice expressed her gratitude for the cake plate in *CH*, 111.

9. "Cubans Love Mr. Roosevelt," *Kansas City Star*, 6 February 1906, JSP; Thomas Henry Sanderson to Cecil Spring-Rice, 20 February 1906, FO 800/241, microfilm, National Archive, London. For the gifts from China, see the letter from the Chinese legation, Washington, to ARL, 27 January 1906, JSP.

10. "Gift from Negro Children," *NYT*, 15 February 1906, 2; [untitled] *Medford Patriot*, 8 February 1906, JSP; Ellis, 242.

11. Joseph de Gonzague to TR, 14 February 1906, JSP.

12. Anita Comfort-Brooks, "Alice the Bride of the White House" (New York: N. Weinstein, 1906); "Wooing of Miss Alice," *Washington Post*, 8 February 1906, JSP; for presents, see Nelle Scanlan, *Boudoir Mirrors of Washington* (Philadelphia: John C. Winston, 1923), 32–33; *CH*, 109–111; Irwin Hood Hoover, *Forty-Two Years in the White House* (New York: Houghton Mifflin, 1934), 34–35; Mary Randolph, *Presidents and First Ladies* (New York: D. Appleton-Century, 1936), 187–91; "A Car of Coal as a Present," *New York Tribune*, 28 December 1905, 1; "Gowns and Gifts for Miss Alice," *Philadelphia Press*, 29 December 1905, reel 471, TRP; "Beautiful Presents for Miss Roosevelt," *NYT*, 11 February 1906, 1; "Dowry Chest of Empress for Miss Roosevelt," *NYT*, 15 February 1906, 1.

13. For gift display traditions, Sherwood, 118 and 126; *CH*, 111.

14. *CH*, 111; 12 and 13 February 1906, EKR Diaries.

15. "W.C.T.U. Up in Arms," *NYT*, 11 February 1906, 1; "Ohio Senate Divided," *NYT*, 16 February 1906, 2.

16. "A Gift for Mr. Longworth," *NYT*, 16 February 1906, 2.

17. The $300,000 estimate is from "Miss Roosevelt's Wedding on February 14," *Brooklyn Times*, n.d. The $2 million estimate is from "Transferring Realty Estate of Longworths," unidentified typescript, n.d. The $15 million estimate is from "Longworth Didn't Know He'd Won," *New York Evening World*, 15 December 1905; all ARL Scrapbook, LC.

18. Gustavus Myers, *History of the Great American Fortunes* (New York: Random House, 1936), 186; Sylvia Jukes Morris, *Edith Kermit Roosevelt* (New York: Coward, McCann, & Geoghegan, 1980), 302.

19. Morris, 302. See also Sherwood, 125; "rather a formidable," Teague, 138.

20. Susan Longworth to Katharine Wulsin, 9 December [1905], Wulsin Family Papers, Mss844, CHS.

21. "Wigeon" to Susan Longworth, n.d., JSP.

22. Clara Longworth de Chambrun, *The Making of Nicholas Longworth* (New York: Ray Long & Richard R. Smith, 1933), 154.

23. The number of reported or remembered invitations ranges from seven hundred to eleven hundred. "Social America," Scanlan, 31; "almost any well-mannered," Constance McLaughlin Green, *Washington* (Princeton, NJ: Princeton University Press, 1963), 191; Lottie Strickland, "Tramping to the Wedding," *NYT*, 7 February 1906, 1.

24. "White House Their Goal," *Washington Post*, 22 January 1906, reel 462, TRP; "Longworth Ill Abed," *NYT*, 10 February 1906, 1.

25. "Use their influence," Randolph, 204; "capacity of the White House" from "Longworth Ill Abed"; "Close Friends of Miss Alice Not Invited," *New York World Telegram*, 14 February 1906, reel 461, TRP.

26. "Miss Alice Buys a Gown," *New York Post*, 2 February 1906, reel 461, TRP; and Wilbur Cross and Ann Novotny, *White House Weddings* (New York: McKay, 1967), 154.

27. Sherwood, 119.

28. Trousseau, Eliza B. Duffey, *The Ladies' and Gentlemen's Etiquette* (Philadelphia: Porter & Coates, 1877), 193, 292–294; "Miss Roosevelt to Buy Trousseau Here," *New York Herald*, 24 December 1905, reel 471, TRP; "Kurzman's Is Bought by Arnold, Constable," *NYT*, 8 May 1932, 4; "dogged by reporters," *CH*, 109; "traffic," "Miss Roosevelt Goes

Back to Washington," *NYT*, 1 February 1906, 9.

29. "Miss Roosevelt Goes Back to Washington," *NYT*, 1 February 1906, 9.

30. NL to ARL, 26 October 1905, JSP; NL to ARL, n.d., ALRC.

31. "Miss Alice Roosevelt Will Leave Washington," *Washington Mirror*, 3 June 1905, JSP.

32. Llewellyn Thayer, "The White House Bridegroom," *Leslie's Illustrated Weekly*, 1 March 1906, 174; Ellen Maury Slayden, *Washington Wife* (New York: Harper & Row, 1962), 90.

33. "Anchorite," NL to ARL, 23 November 1905, JSP; "far from being bored," NL to ARL, 5 November 1905, JSP.

34. "Bowing and smiling," "Reception to Congress at White House," *NYT*, 2 February 1906, 1; "Miss Roosevelt's Quiet Day," *NYT*, 12 February 1906, 1; "Miss Alice Is 22 Today," *New York World*, 12 February 1906, ARL Scrapbook.

35. Alice remembered this party happening at the Alibi Club (*CH*, 112), and Nick's sister recalled the same party occurring at "his mother's house" (de Chambrun, 195). Nick had eight ushers: Ted Jr; his brothers-in-law Buckner Wallingford and the Viscount Charles de Chambrun; a cousin, Larz Anderson; Guy Norman; Quincy Adams Shaw Jr.; Francis R. Bangs; and Frederick Winthrop. Nick's best man was Harvard classmate Thomas Nelson Perkins. See Cross and Novotny, 155–156; and "The President a Guest at Longworth Dinner," *NYT*, 16 February 1906, 1.

36. Hoover, 34.

37. "Gems for Miss Alice," *Philadelphia Record*, 15 December 1905, ARL Scrapbook.

38. Scanlan, 31.

39. "Longworth Ill Abed," *NYT*, 10 February 1906, 1.

40. ARL to NL, n.d., RFPH.

41. ARL to NL, n.d., RFPH.

42. "My own beloved Nick," ARL to NL, 15 February 1905, RFPH; "My darling, darling, darling," ARL to NL, n.d., JSP.

43. NL to ARL, n.d., ARLC.

44. "All in Readiness for the White House Wedding," *Washington Post*, 17 February 1906, ARL Scrapbook; Nellie Grant married Algernon Charles Frederick Sartoris on 21 May 1874.

45. Teague, 55 and 57.

46. "Wedding Eve Party for Miss Roosevelt," *NYT*, 17 February 1906, 1.

47. Lady Bird Johnson, *A White House Diary* (New York: Holt, Rinehart and Winston, 1970), 65.

48. Corinne Roosevelt Robinson, *My Brother Theodore Roosevelt* (New York: Charles Scribner's Sons, 1921), 238–39; and Morris, 304.

49. Isabel Anderson, *Presidents and Pies* (Boston: Houghton Mifflin, 1920), 33–34. For a few of the primary sources on the wedding, see "Miss Roosevelt's Wedding Plans," *New York Herald*, 13 December 1905; "Miss Roosevelt Weds in February," *New York Herald*, 14 December 1905; "A White House Wedding," *Middletown* (New York) *Daily Times*, [n.d.] 1905; all reel 471, TRP. See also "All in Readiness for the White House Wedding," *Washington Post*, 17 February 1906, 1; "The White House Wedding," *New York World*, 17 February 1906, 1, JSP.

50. De Chambrun, 196; "Alice looked," Joseph Lash, *Eleanor and Franklin* (New York: W. W. Norton, 1971), 221; "rather nervous," Geoffrey C. Ward, *A First-Class Temperament* (New York: Harper & Row, 1989), 45n7.

51. Preceding Alice Roosevelt were Maria Monroe in 1820, Elizabeth Tyler in 1842, and Nellie Grant in 1874. The latter

two, like Alice, were married in the East Room.

52. Teague, 123.

53. Ona Griffin Jeffries, *In and Out of the White House* (New York: W. Funk, 1960), 281–82; *CH*, 113.

54. "Mother," Teague, 128; "nearly fainted," EKR Diary, 20 February 1906. Kristie Miller, a friend of Alice Longworth's, believes that the public denigration of elite children by parents "counterbalances the swell-headedness that can come with being a Roosevelt," and that it further helps not to tempt fate. "If you compliment, the gods will smite you." Miller emphasized that such parents absolutely love their children, despite the language that is culturally specific.

Joanna Sturm, Alice Longworth's granddaughter, however, believes that Edith Roosevelt really meant what she said, and that this was an example of Edith's meanness, probably exacerbated by her exhaustion. (Author interviews with Kristie Miller, 17 August 1989 and with Joanna Sturm, 11 April 2006.)

55. Unidentified newspaper clipping, n.d., ARL Scrapbook.

56. "A Princess of America," *Literary Digest*, XXXII, 11 (17 March 1906), 414.

Chapter 9: "Alice Is Married at Last"

1. Unidentified clipping, n.d., JSP.

2. All newspaper quotes from "Post-Nuptial," *Literary Digest*, 3 March 1906, 310.

3. Unidentified author to Susan Longworth, 28 February 1906, JSP.

4. 27 October 1880, TR Diary.

5. Anonymous letter to ARL, 19 February 1906, JSP.

6. Invitation from President Estrada Palma to the Longworths, 22 February 1906, JSP.

7. Straight's observations in the following four paragraphs are from Willard Straight to "Paddock," 31 March 1906, WSP.

8. Jennings Stockton Coxby to ARL, 13 March [1906], JSP.

9. *CH*, 115–16. The quotes are from page 115.

10. The information about the honeymoon comes from the author's interview with Joanna Sturm, 11 June 2006. Her memory is that the incident with Nick drunk on the floor was on board a ship.

11. "A Delight, Says Longworth," *NYT*, 4 March 1906, 1.

12. "Mrs. Longworth on Social Etiquette," *China Times*, 7 September 1906; clipping included in Mary Harriman to ARL, 27 January 1907, JSP.

13. "With the perversity," *CH*, 137; March 1906, EKR Diary; Kermit Roosevelt to Belle Hagner, 18 March 1906, PHP; "Sister is much improved," James Brough, *Princess Alice* (Boston: Little, Brown, 1975), 198.

14. For photographs of the home as Susan Longworth decorated it, see "Miss Roosevelt's Future Home at the Nation's Capital," *Leslie's Illustrated Weekly*, 15 February 1906, JSP.

15. Unknown author to Susan Longworth, 28 February 1906, JSP.

16. *CH*, 116.

17. "Maggie" to ARL, 8 April 1906, JSP.

18. Catherine Allgor, *Parlor Politics* (Charlottesville: University Press of Virginia, 2000), 121.

19. "Virtuously," *CH*, 116; "appalled," ER, *This Is My Story* (New York: Harper & Brothers, 1937), 206; "Mrs. Longworth on Social Etiquette," *China Times*, 7 September 1906, clipping included in Mary Harriman to ARL, 27 January 1907, JSP.

20. "Formidable experience," *CH*, 116;

"returned very late," Eleanor Adams, "Tea with Washington's Grande Dame," *Cincinnati Enquirer*, 2 January 197[?], ARLPF.

21. ARL to Marjorie [Ide], n.d. [1906], JSP.

22. *CH*, 134.

23. ARC to ARL, 28 May 1906, JSP.

24. TR to ARL, 24 June 1906, reel 342, TRP.

25. "Better politics," *CH*, 117; Whitelaw Reid to EKR, 17 August 1906, ALRC. All unattributed quotes on the honeymoon come from this lengthy letter.

26. "Curtsey," Elisabeth Mills Reid to ARC, 29 June 1906, JSP; "enjoyed herself," *CH*, 119; TR to ARL, 24 June 1906, reel 342, TRP.

27. "So like the parties," *CH*, 120; "very informal," Teague, 142; "didn't seem to worry," Teague 150; "felt very much at home," *CH*, 123.

28. "The Longworths at Blenheim," *NYT*, 3 July 1906, 4.

29. Elisabeth Mills Reid to ARC, 29 June 1906, JSP.

30. "Of no more consequence," *CH*, 123; "I don't care," EKR to Belle Hagner, [19 July 1906], PHP.

31. *CH*, 122.

32. "French Opinion of Mrs. Longworth," newspaper clipping, 7 July 1906, from Herman Hagedorn, interviews relating to Roosevelt Women, Harvard University.

33. Clara Longworth de Chambrun, *The Making of Nicholas Longworth* (New York: Ray Long & Richard R. Smith, 1933), 197.

34. *CH*, 127. See also "Longworths Go to Bayreuth," 17 July 1906, 2; "Longworth Auto Accident," 24 July 1906, 1; "The Longworths at Carlsbad," 25 July 1906, 1; all *NYT*.

35. *CH*, 128.

36. Willard Straight to ARL, 28 June 1906, JSP.

37. TR to FDR, 7 May 1906, reel 341, TRP; "Longworth for Governor," *NYT*, 11 July 1906, 1.

38. "Longworths in Silent Mood on Voyage Home," *New York World*, 12 August 1906, clipping in JSP; steerage passengers, "The Longworths Home," *NYT*, 12 August 1906, 1.

39. EKR to Belle Hagner, 12 August [1906], PHP. See "Longworths Leave Oyster Bay," *NYT*, 18 August 1906, 1; and "Longworth at Home Again," *NYT*, 19 August, 1. Both suggest that the Longworths together stayed at Oyster Bay for three days and then they traveled together to Cincinnati.

40. TR to ARL, 24 June 1906, reel 342, TRP.

Chapter 10: **"Mighty Pleased with My Daughter and Her Husband"**

1. "Full of all sorts." EKR to Belle Hagner, 15 August 1906, PHP; "hurt Nick," TR to ARL, 24 June 1906, reel 342, TRP; "injure him."

2. Ethel Roosevelt to Belle Hagner, [17 August 1906], PHP.

3. "Longworths at Home Again," *NYT*, 19 August 1906, 9; Ethel Roosevelt to Isabella Ferguson, n.d. 1907, Greenway AHS; *CH*, 154.

4. NL to ARL, 31 October 1905 and 9 November 1905, JSP.

5. Betsy Greiner, "The Day Alice Came to Town," *Timeline* 4, 1 (February–March 1987), 16–25; EKR to ARL, 18 September [1906], ARLHar; "Mrs. Longworth Is Cause of Panic," *Chicago Tribune*, 15 September 1906, 1; "Mrs. Longworth Mobbed," *NYT*, 15 September 1906, 1.

6. "Longworth Renominated," *NYT*, 16 September 1906, 1.

7. "She bowed and waved," "Ovation to Mrs. Longworth," *NYT*, 7 October 1906, 1; "occult formula," [Illegible; last

name maybe Fife?] to ARL, 17 August 1906, JSP; "M" to ARL, 30 October 1906, JSP; "Longworth's strength," "Unions Against Longworth," *NYT*, 26 September 1906, 1.

8. "The great issue," "Longworth off Blacklist," *NYT*, 21 October 1906, 1; "enjoyed campaigning." EKR to ARL, 24 October 1906, JSP; "Let me congratulate," TR to ARL, 7 November 1906, in Morison and Blum, eds., 5: 488; "Last night," EKR to ARL, 8 November 1906, JSP.

9. Alsop's prediction, ARC to ARL, 29 October 1906, JSP. Joseph W. Alsop was the father of columnists Stewart and Joseph Alsop; "how empty the house," ARC to ARL, 22 November 1906, JSP.

10. Willard Straight to ARL, 13 September 1906, JSP. An earlier letter (28 June 1906, JSP) alludes to a "Thieves Guild."

11. George Cabot Lee to NL, 15 March 1906, JSP.

12. "Uneasy till you start," George Cabot Lee to ARL, 8 October 1907; "show this to Nick," George Cabot Lee to ARL, 30 March 1906; stock sales, George Cabot Lee to ARL, 13 September 1906, all JSP.

13. See, for one example of a charity letter, Bela Horvatz to ARL, 12 January 1907, JSP; "Nick was not," *CH*, 134.

14. "Uproar in the House," *NYT*, 4 December 1906, 2; diplomatic reception, "In the Society World," *NYT*, 13 December 1906, 11; "saw more of the family," *CH*, 136–137.

15. *CH*, 137–38.

16. TR to Corinne Roosevelt Robinson, 26 December 1906, Theodore Roosevelt Papers, American Antiquarian Society, Boston, Mass.; "Roosevelt Family at German Embassy," *NYT*, 27 December 1906, 2.

17. "Longworth's Plan Fails," *NYT*, 23 January 1907, 6; "Roosevelt May Cost

Longworth His Seat," *NYT*, 5 February 1907, 4. "Longworths a Year Wedded," *NYT*, 18 February 1907, 1; "Roosevelt Names Foraker's Choice," *NYT*, 1 March 1907, 3.

18. TR to ARL, 10 November 1907, in Morison and Blum, eds., 5: 836–37. "Longworth Is for Taft," *Chicago Tribune*, 11 April 1907, 5; and "Longworth for Taft," *NYT*, 11 April 1907, 5.

19. "Steel Millionaire Ross Must Pay for Banquet," *Chicago Tribune*, 31 March 1907, A1; "Society Stake is Won by Ardette," *Chicago Tribune*, 7 April 1907, A1; NL to ARL, 20 May 1907, JSP.

20. Jean Howerton Coady, "Alice's Derby: 1907 Winner Lost to Mrs. Longworth," *Louisville Courier-Journal*, n.d., clipping in JSP.

21. "Just enough," *CH*, 141; "Wife's pique," "Mrs. Longworth in Accident," *Chicago Tribune*, 15 August 1907, 4; "Longworths to See Hawaii," *NYT*, 9 July 1907, 1.

22. "Lotus eater," *CH*, 142; "Most delicious time," ARL to Beatrice [Bond], 8 November 1907, JSP; Carter reception, No title, *NYT*, 5 August 1907, 4; "Mrs. Longworth, Woman Diplomat," *Chicago Tribune*, 7 September 1907, 4.

23. "Mulligrubs," *CH*, 146; "appendix plundered," ARL to Eleanora Sears, 31 December 1907, ARLC; "hand in hand," NL to Susan Longworth, 13 December 1907, JSP.

24. ARC to ARL, 15 November 1907, JSP. See also "Mrs. Longworth Under the Knife," 12 December 1907, 1; "Operate on Mrs. Longworth," 13 December 1907, 1; "Mrs. Longworth Is Better," 14 December 1907, 9; all *NYT*.

25. *CH*, 147–48.

26. The *NYT* asserted that Cannon had to put Nick there because TR leaned on him. See "Longworth Placed on Ways and Means," 17 December 1907, 3. The

article also suggested that Alice and Nick's "teas" helped to reconcile the Ohio delegation with Cannon's choice. NL to Susan Longworth, 1 November 1908, NLIII.

27. ARL to ER and FDR, 23 December 1907, ER Papers, FDRL.

28. George Cabot Lee to ARL, 19 February 1908, JSP. See also *CH*, 146.

29. "No one will ever know," *CH*, 148; "sick of hearing," Kristie Miller to the author, 6 September 1989.

30. Spontaneous applause, "Fighting Spirit Was Aroused," unidentified clipping, 1 September 1908, JSP. The man speaking was TR's rival, Senator Joseph B. Foraker. For Nick's defense, see for example, "Defends Roosevelt's Acts," *NYT*, 23 February 1908, 10; Ohio convention, "Ohio Republicans Instruct for Taft," *NYT*, 5 March 1908, 4.

31. "Women in Society Unite to Help Labor," *NYT*, n.d. For ARL's presence, see "Women's Department of the Civic Federation," *NCF Review*, September 1908, 7–8, both RHMcC Papers, LC; "White House meeting, "Women in a Secret Crusade for Labor," *NYT*, 6 May 1908, 7; Ruth's role, author's interview with Ruth "Bazy" McCormick Miller Tankersley, 31 May 2006.

32. *CH*, 149 and 151.

33. "'No Millinery,' Convention Rule," *Chicago Tribune*, 6 June 1912, 3; and "Patriots Feel Hunger's Pains," *Chicago Tribune*, 20 June 1912, 7.

34. *CH*, 151–52.

35. "Meddlings," by Howard Saxby Jr, otherwise unidentified newspaper clipping enclosed in A. E. Robinson to ARL, 12 May 1908, JSP. See also "Mrs. Longworth's Joke," *NYT*, 12 May 1908, 1. For family warning, see George Cabot Lee to ARL, 21 May 1908, JSP.

36. William A. White, *The Autobiography of William Allen White* (New York:

Macmillan, 1946), 401; "Mrs. Longworth Welcomes Crowd," *Chicago Tribune*, 20 June 1908.

37. "How the Democrats did it," *CH*, 152; "Mrs. Longworth in Denver," *Chicago Tribune*, 7 July 1908, 5; "yelling, sweating delegates," *CH*, 152; "Mrs. Longworth Lost Temper," *Chicago Tribune*, 10 July 1908, 9; see "Alice and Ruth Described," *Chicago Tribune*, 8 July 1908, 9, for a gentler treatment of both women.

38. "Princess Alice Bored at Reception," *Denver Post*, 8 July 1908, 3.

39. "Hats Are Nearly as Big as Cartwheels and Grow More Freakish in Style," *Chicago Tribune*, 5 July 1908, E-1. She also made the list of "loveliest-dressed" women: "Loveliest Gowns in the World Worn by Women of America," *Chicago Tribune*, 5 July 1908, E-1. On the Congressional Club, see "Congressmen's Wives Clubs," *NYT*, 15 March 1908, 9; "No Clubhouse Yet for 'Congressionals,'" *NYT*, 6 April 1908, 7; for joke, "Mrs. Longworth's Joke," *NYT*, 22 August 1908, 1.

40. "Manchu and I," NL to ARL, 18 August 1908, JSP; roses, "Entertain Mrs. Longworth," *NYT*, 20 August 1908, 7; fortnight at Sagamore, "Longworths at Oyster Bay," *NYT*, 25 August 1908, 7.

41. EKR to Cecil Spring-Rice, 13 July [1908], F.O. 800/241-242/9/1, National Archive, London.

42. Distaff duties, Ethel Roosevelt to ARL, 30 September [1908], JSP; "eulogy," "Views of Congressman Longworth," clipping with a Rock Island dateline, 2 October 1908, Hermann Hagedorn. Interviews relating to Roosevelt Women, Harvard University; election trail, "Sherman's Western Tour," *NYT*, 20 September 1908, 3; "Sunny Jim Comes to Aid Uncle Joe," *Chicago Tribune*, 28 September 1908, 3; "house is so big,"

"Drops Politics for Styles, *Chicago Tribune*, 29 September 1908, 6; fund-raiser, "Honor Mrs. Longworth," *NYT*, 7 October 1908, 1. The five-hundred-dollar tab caused trouble for the local Republicans later. See "Longworth Dinner Costly," *Chicago Tribune*, 27 November 1909, 2.

43. ARL to John Greenway, 27 November [1908], Greenway AHS; Edwin Morgan to ARL, 9 November 1909, JSP.

44. *CH*, 156.

45. Archibald Butt to his mother, 19 June 1908, in Lawrence F. Abbott, ed., *The Letters of Archie Butt* (Garden City, N.Y.: Doubleday, Page, 1924), 43.

46. *CH*, 159 (emphasis added).

Chapter 11: **"Expelled from the Garden of Eden"**

1. Archibald Butt to Clara Butt, 28 December 1908, in Lawrence F. Abbott, ed., *The Letters of Archie Butt* (Garden City, N.Y.: Doubleday, Page, 1924), 258.

2. "President Singed By Abbot's Irony," *Chicago Tribune*, 7 October 1908, 4; "Abbot Skeptic on Longworth Story," *Chicago Tribune*, 10 October 1908, 4.

3. Michael Teague, *Mrs. L* (Garden City, N.Y.: Doubleday, 1981), 140.

4. Memorable holiday, Archibald Butt to Clara Butt, 26 December 1908, in Abbott, ed., 254; "expelled," Teague, 140.

5. "Tottering ancient," *CH*, 161; the details of Ethel Roosevelt's debut can be found in the series of letters from Archibald Butt to Clara Butt (26 December, 28 December, and 29 December 1909) in Abbott, ed., 254–261; "Miss Roosevelt's Debut," *NYT*, 28 October 1908, 1.

6. Eleanor Roosevelt to Isabella Ferguson, 8 January 1909, Greenway AHS.

7. Archibald Butt to Clara Butt, 29 December 1908, in Abbott, ed., 261–62.

8. Annual message, *Current Literature*, XLVI, 1 (January 1909), 12–13; "crackling row," *CH*, 160.

9. For Butt quotes in next two paragraphs, see Archibald Butt to Clara Butt, 8 February 1909, in Abbott, ed., 277–78.

10. "Spanking," *CH*, 162; Susan Longworth to ARL, 31 December 1908, JSP.

11. "Mrs. Longworth at Cornerstone Laying," *NYT*, 13 February 1909, 6; "Mrs. Longworth, Bricklayer," *Chicago Tribune*, 12 February 1909, 2.

12. *CH*, 164–65; "Tafts as Guests in White House," *Chicago Tribune*, 4 March 1909, 3.

13. "Loathsome slush," *CH*, 165; inaugural, Sylvia Jukes Morris, *Edith Kermit Roosevelt* (New York: Coward, McCann & Geoghegan, 1980), 343–44.

14. Terrapin, EKR to Belle Hagner, 4 March 1909, PHP; "simplest American," Archibald Butt to Clara Butt, 1 February 1909, in Abbott, ed., 323; "future is in the past," TR to Paul Morton, 2 March 1909, in Morison and Blum, eds., 6: 1541; "gulped over," *CH*, 166; distinctive place, Archibald Butt to Clara Butt, 1 February 1909, in Abbott, ed., 322–23.

15. Mary E. Borah, *Elephants and Donkeys* (Moscow: The University Press of Idaho, 1976), 49; EKR to ARL, n.d. [1909], ARLHar.

16. ARL preservation tapes, ICD 16022, 28 June 1967, JSP.

17. "Roosevelt Sails in Roar of Cheers," *NYT*, 24 March 1909, 1.

18. Lewis L. Gould, *Grand Old Party* (New York: Random House, 2003), 157.

19. Clara Longworth de Chambrun, *The Making of Nicholas Longworth* (New York: Ray Long & Richard R. Smith, 1933), 200.

20. *CH*, 166.

21. Ishbell Ross, *The Tafts* (New York: World Publishing, 1964), 225; "Officer's

Wife Flies with Wilbur Wright," *NYT*, 28 October 1909, 4; "Wright Sets New American Record," *NYT*, 21 July 1909, 1–2; "lunch wagon," *CH*, 167–69.

22. EKR to Susan Longworth, 14 June 1909, JSP; for Alice's days, *CH*, 169–72; "'Salome' at Magnolia," *NYT*, 25 July 1909, 7.

23. For Nick's stomach trouble, see EKR to Belle Hagner, 22 June 1909, PHP; "bore you," Ross, 225; "Alice has found diversion," NL to Susan Longworth, 1 August [1909], ARLC.

24. ARL to Ethel Roosevelt, 24 June 1909, ERDP; EKR to ARL, [September 1909], ARLHar.

25. "Mrs. Longworth Is First," *NYT*, 17 October 1909, 1.

26. "Book Hits Alice Roosevelt" *Chicago Tribune*, 17 November 1909, 1. See Emma Kroebel, *Wie ich an den Koreanischen Kaiserhof kam* (Berlin: Verlag von R. Jacobsthal, 1909), 162–67.

27. "Longworth Denies His Wife Insulted Ruler of Corea," *Chicago Tribune*, 18 November 1909, 5; Alice's credo, ARL to Ethel Roosevelt, 13 December 1909, ERDP.

28. ALR to Willard Straight, 12 October 1905, WSP.

29. "Decorous existence," ARL to Ethel Roosevelt, 13 December 1909, ERDP; "an elderly man," TR to Arthur Lee, 6 October 1909, LLF; "not much" of a Christmas, *CH*, 173; EKR to Mark Sullivan, 14 December 1909, Mark Sullivan Papers, LC, states that Edith will sail in mid-March. EKR to Belle Hagner, 13 December 1909, PHP, states that she will sail mid-February to meet TR in Khartoum on 15 March, as does EKR to Cecil Spring-Rice, 17 December 1909, F.O. 800/241-242/9/1, National Archive, London; for "I can scarcely wait," see EKR to Cecil Spring-Rice, 17 December 1909, F.O. 800/241-242/9/1, National Archive, London.

30. Newspaper clipping, Cannon Scrapbook, Joseph Cannon Papers, Abraham Lincoln Presidential Library, Springfield, Illinois; Nick joined the insurgents, Joseph Cannon to Edward Denby, 5 October 1910, Box 8, Cannon Papers; "jeers and cat-calls," *CH*, 174; Nick not selected, "Longworth Not Snubbed," *NYT*, 27 March 1910, 16.

31. Nelle Scanlan, *Boudoir Mirrors of Washington* (Philadelphia: John C. Winston, 1923), 22.

32. Ross, 236–37.

33. Ross, 246.

34. "Mrs. Nicholas Longworth Sails," *NYT*, 12 May 1910, 16; Tim Sullivan, *CH*, 176.

35. *CH*, 178.

36. Poem from *Life*, in Nathan Miller, *Theodore Roosevelt* (New York: William Morrow, 1992), 511.

37. TR to Gifford Pinchot, 28 June 1910, in Morison and Blum, eds., 7:95.

38. "Roosevelt, Jr., to Wed Miss Alexander," *NYT*, 11 February 1910, 1; Ted and Eleanor (whom the family called "our Eleanor" or "Mrs. Ted") were wed on 20 June 1910. Roller-skating, "Society at the Nation's Capitol," *Chicago Tribune*, 5 May 1910, 8.

39. "Bequest to Mrs. Longworth," *NYT*, 29 March 1910, 1, suggested Alice would inherit $10,000; "Alice Longworth an Heiress," *Chicago Tribune*, 28 May 1910, 12. The latter article states that she was to inherit one twelfth of $975,500. Finally, the reports settled on $5,300: "Mrs. Longworth's Legacy," *NYT*, 27 July 1910, 1. For governor idea, see "A New Longworth Boom," *NYT*, 9 May 1910, 18.

40. "Lawyers' Administration," from TR to Henry Cabot Lodge, 11 April 1910, in Morison and Blum, eds., 7:74; "of course you must" from TR to NL, 11 July 1910, in Morison and Blum, eds., 7:101; for Taft's idea, see "Taft Said to Favor Long-

worth in Ohio," *NYT,* 26 June 1910, 4; Ohio convention, "Ohio Convention Faces Hot Fight," *Chicago Tribune,* 26 July 1910, 5; Nick's relief, *CH,* 180.

41. WHT to HHT, 24 September 1910, WHTP.

42. New Nationalism, George E. Mowry, *Theodore Roosevelt and the Progressive Movement* (Madison: University of Wisconsin Press, 1946), 144; TR to Henry Cabot Lodge, 17 August 1910, in Morison and Blum, eds., 7: 117; 1910 election, Hoyt Landon Warner, *Progessivism in Ohio* (Columbus: Ohio State University Press, 1964), 262.

43. *CH,* 181.

44. "Longworths Off to Panama," *NYT,* 22 September 1911, 7; "Taft Begins Trip on 54th Birthday," *NYT,* 16 September 1911, 12.

45. *CH,* 183.

46. *CH,* 184. See also "A Roosevelt Pilot on Ohio," *NYT,* 9 October 1911, 1.

Chapter 12: **"Quite Marked Schizophrenia"**

1. Women's suffrage, *CH,* 282 and 339; Elaine L. Silverman, "Theodore Roosevelt and Women" unpub. Ph.D. diss., UCLA, 1973, 73; judicial recall, "Roosevelt Answers Cry of Revolution," *NYT,* 27 February 1912, 1; "hard on Nick," *CH,* 186.

2. TR quoted in James Brough, *Princess Alice* (Boston: Little, Brown, 1975), 215.

3. "Ohio Leader Wants Roosevelt in 1912," *NYT,* 3 December 1911, 16; for Nick's statement, John Callan O'Laughlin, "Politics Leading Issue in Capitol," *Chicago Tribune,* 5 December 1911, 5; for Nick's authority, see "Longworth Cheers Taft," *NYT,* 27 January 1912, 2.

4. 13 February 1912, ARLD.

5. TR to NL, 7 February 1912, in Morison and Blum, eds., 7:497; "soak it," 15 February 1912, ARLD.

6. 16 February 1912, ARLD.

7. "Gloomy talk," 17 February 1912, ARLD; "talked the whole thing over," 19 February 1912, ARLD; "my past," Lewis L. Gould, "The Price of Fame," *Lamar Journal of the Humanities,* X, 2 (Fall 1984), 14; "was a fool and wept," 21 February 1912, ARLD; Taft's sentiment from WHT to HHT, 20 July 1912, WHTP.

8. 22 February 1912, ARLD.

9. Longworth's meeting with TR was on 26 February. Nick's gloominess and "pain" from 27 and 28 February 1912, ARLD.

10. "Clara said," 8 March 1912, ARLD. When Clara de Chambrun wrote her biography of her brother, Alice received barely a mention—not even a photograph. See *The Making of Nicholas Longworth* (New York: Ray Long & Richard R. Smith, 1933), 203; 31 May 1912, ARLD.

11. Both sides, Augustus P. Gardner to ARL, 1 March 1912, JSP; "apoplectic with rage," in Brough, 216; "wearing to live," ARC to ARL, 11 July 1912, JSP; "rant and rave," 15 March 1912, ARLD.

12. *CH,* 192.

13. "Sock it," 17 March 1912, ARLD; "daily dish," ARL, "Some Reminiscences," *Ladies' Home Journal,* November 1932, 3; "Nick pleased me," 10 April 1912, ARLD.

14. 1 May 1912, ARLD.

15. "Feeling...bitter," 15 May 1912, ARLD; "to get in the papers," *CH,* 194; "Victory Surely His, Roosevelt Boasts," *NYT,* 16 May 1912, 1.

16. "Father and I walked," 8 June 1912, ARLD; "followed his instincts," 4 June 1912, ARLD.

17. TR to Arthur Lee, 14 August 1912, LLF.

18. 17 June 1912, ARLD.

19. "Hoards of creatures," 18 and 19

June 1912, ARLD; Nick really a progressive, 13 August 1912, ARLD.

20. "Longworth for Governor," *NYT*, 29 May 1912, 4; "strong-arm tactics," *CH*, 202–203.

21. Lewis L. Gould, *Grand Old Party* (New York: Random House, 2003), 189. For Nick and Alice, see "The Day's Sessions" and "Harding Nominates Taft," both *NYT*, 23 June 1912, 2.

22. "Such spirit," 22 June 1912, ARLD; "Roosevelt Delegates Go from the Regular to Rump Convention," *NYT*, 23 June 1912, 1; "Longworth in Trouble," *NYT*, 24 June 1912, 6; divorce, Michael Teague, *Mrs. L* (Garden City, N.Y.: Doubleday, 1981), 158, and author's interview with Michael Teague, 3 August 1989.

23. Arguing with Borah, *CH*, 204; "Borah Refuses to Join the Third Party," *La Follette's Weekly Magazine*, 28 September 1912, 8, 14, 15. For a sense of Borah's role in TR's inner circle at Chicago, see Nicholas Roosevelt's "Account of the Republican National Convention at Chicago, June 1912," compiled from notes taken on the spot, 93M-11, Harvard University.

24. "Delegates Storm Baltimore," *Chicago Tribune*, 24 June 1912, 5; the cousins together, ER to Isabella Greenway, 8 July [1912] and ER to Isabella Greenway, 9 July [1912], both Greenway AHS; Nick "gloomy," 25 and 26 June 1912, ARLD.

25. "To Smoke Out Longworth," *NYT*, 25 June 1912, 6; 8 July 1912, ARLD.

26. "I could scream," 28 August 1912, ARLD; "ignoble thoughts," *CH*, 212; TR to Robert Ferguson, n.d., Greenway AHS.

27. "Hail New Party in Fervent Song," *NYT*, 6 August 1912, 1; 6 August 1912; 7 August 1912, ARLD.

28. EKR to Belle Hagner, 9 August [1912], PHP; ARL to ARC, 10 August 1912, RFPH.

29. "The platform," 8 August 1912,

ARLD; "my sister-in-law," *CH*, 214–215; "help campaign," ARC to ARL, 11 July 1912, JSP. See also 27 March 1912, ARLD: "Only wish I could do anything to help along the work"; "stiff upper lip," EKR to Belle Hagner, 10 March [1912], PHP.

30. "Both sides," 19 August 1912, ARLD; "heart and soul," 20 August 1912, ARLD.

31. 14–25 August 1912, ARLD. For Grace Vanderbilt's contribution, see 1 November 1912.

32. 26 August 1912, ARLD. For Nick's drinking, see 1 September 1912. Alice recorded that he "behaved disgustingly."

33. "Get names," 8 September 1912, ARLD; "Longworth Still for Taft," *NYT*, 19 September 1912, 11; "Humors of the Campaign," *NYT*, 20 September 1912, 10.

34. 10 October 1912, ARLD. For Alice's reading, see 14, 15, and 16 September 1912.

35. "I cannot vote for you," de Chambrun, 204; Nick "seems to want me," 2 October 1912, ARLD. The titles of what she's reading are sprinkled throughout the Cincinnati days in her diary.

36. "Wild enthusiasm," 12 October 1912, ARLD; Bull Moose store, "Mrs. Longworth at Store," *Chicago Tribune*, 14 October 1912, 2; "asked again," 12 October 1912, ARLD; "torture," 4 October 1912, ARLD; campaign donations, 10 October 1912, ARLD.

37. 16 October 1912, ARLD.

38. Kristie Miller, *Ruth Hanna McCormick* (Albuquerque: University of New Mexico Press, 1992), 53; "good angel," 14 October 1912; "cracking," 19 October 1912; both ARLD.

39. "Middle western," 23 October 1912, ARLD; "I am not for," 26 October 1912, ARLD; see also "With Torches Honor Taft," *NYT*, 27 October 1912, 4.

40. "First draft," Teague, 112; "no illusions," *CH*, 221.

41. 3 November 1912, ARLD.

42. 4 November 1912, ARLD.

43. 5 November 1912, ARLD.

44. "'Nick' Longworth Beaten in Ohio?" *Chicago Tribune*, 8 November 1912, 5; "Longworth Is Beaten," *NYT*, 8 November 1912, 1; Jean Vanden Heuvel, "The Sharpest Wit in Washington," *Saturday Evening Post*, 238, 24 (4 December 1965), 32; "terribly hard," 7 November 1912, ARLD.

45. "A real progressive," 7 November 1912; "dull little people," 9 November 1912; "dined at the Crosstown," 13 November 1912. For Alice's self-absorption, see 10 November 1912, all ARLD.

46. "At sea," 5 December 1912, ARLD; "a question of divorcing," 17 December 1912, ARLD.

Chapter 13: **"Beating Against Bars"**

1. To will herself, ARL to NL, 31 March [1913], JSP; "unreservedly cheerful," *CH*, 223.

2. This story appears in many places. See, for example, Howard Teichmann, *Alice* (Englewood Cliffs, N.J.: Prentice Hall, 1979), 96.

3. ARL to Ethel Roosevelt, 30 January 1913, RFPH.

4. Turkey trot, ARL to Ethel Roosevelt, 30 January 1913, RFPH; "odd beings called Democrats," *CH*, 225; Belle's job, EKR to Belle Hagner, 5 March 1913, PHP.

5. TR to FDR, 18 March 1913, TRP.

6. ER to Isabella Ferguson, 12 December [1915], Greenway AHS; evenings at the FDR's, Michael Teague, *Mrs. L* (Garden City, N.Y.: Doubleday, 1981), 156–157.

7. Elliott Roosevelt and James Brough, *An Untold Story* (New York: G. P. Putnam's Sons, 1973), 69; "a slave," and blend in, from ER, *This Is My Story* (New York: Harper & Brothers, 1937), 206.

8. "Perfunctory...tea," *CH*, 226; NL to ARL, 24 March 1913; ARL to NL, [25 March 1913], both JSP.

9. "An excellent thing," *CH*, 223; "sat on the porch," ARL Diary, 10 September 1917, JSP.

10. Richard Derby, TR to William Crawford Gorgas, 11 September 1917, in Morison and Blum, eds., 8:1238; "Ohio is a vast lake," NL to ARL, 27 March 1913, JSP.

11. NL to ARL, 31 March 1913; ARL to NL, 31 March [1913], both JSP.

12. ARL to NL, 4 April 1913, and NL to ARL, 5 April 1913, JSP.

13. Kermit Roosevelt to Ethel Roosevelt Derby, 2 June 1913, RFPH. EKR to Belle Hagner, 24 March 1914, PHP.

14. "The Puppuk," NL to ARL, n.d. [1913]; "dinner and a musical party," NL to ARL, 22 September 1913, both JSP.

15. ARL to NL; undated, JSP; EKR to Belle Hagner, 14 September 1913, PHP.

16. Joseph R. Ornig, *My Last Chance to Be a Boy* (Baton Rouge: Louisiana University Press, 1994), 37; Kermit Roosevelt to Ethel Roosevelt Derby, November 1913, ERDP.

17. ARL to NL, 27 December 1913, JSP.

18. Author's interview with Angela Meeske, 19 April 2004. Meeske was born in 1923, and her mother would have been nearer to a contemporary of Nick Longworth's.

19. ARL to NL, fragment, 8 January 1914, JSP; TR quote, Ornig, 39.

20. "Very depressing," EKR to Belle Hagner, 17 January 1914, PHP; recuperate, ARL to ARC, 31 January 1914, Anna Roosevelt Cowles Papers, Harvard

University; "a green shadow," ARL to NL, 16 January 1914, JSP; "my brief moment," ARL to ARC, 31 January 1914, RFPH. "More prosperous," ARL to NL, 16 January 1914, JSP.

21. "Shrine," *CH*, 230; "delightful evenings," ARL Diary, 24 April [1914], JSP.

22. Joseph S. Graydon's grandson, Graydon DeCamp, attests that "considerable family lore and speculation surrounds Joe Graydon's 'friendship' with Alice Longworth. We grandchildren have long suspected that they were something more than just friends. Or at least that they wished that were so. The only time I ever met Alice, at her house on Massachusetts Avenue in 1969, she welcomed me with a warmth that quite took me aback. I felt instantly like family, and was right at home in that big old house hidden behind a two-story tangle of massive honeysuckles. I am not only Joe Graydon's only grandson, I also resemble him [physically]." DeCamp, e-mail to author, 29 March 2004.

23. Graydon DeCamp to author, 2 April 2004; JSG to ARL, 23 November 1915, JSP, and Lewis Alexander Leonard, ed., *Greater Cincinnati and Its People* (Chicago: Lewis Historical Publishing, 1927), 4: 425–26; "Rites Wednesday for J. S. Graydon," *Cincinnati Post and Times-Star,* 25 February 1963; and "Graydon Will Is Filed," *Cincinnati Enquirer,* 14 March 1962, clippings in Joseph S. Graydon Princeton File, CHS; W. T. Semple to Mr. Greve, 22 April 1924, Classical Round Table, MssVF2434, CHS.

24. "Seraphina," JSG to ARL, 9 December 1915, JSP; Robert Louis Stevenson, *Prince Otto: A Romance* (New York: Charles Scribner's Sons, 1925 [1905]), 80–81.

25. Stevenson, 224.

26. Graydon DeCamp to author, 2 April 2004; JSG to ARL, 4 January 1917, JSP. See also ARL to ARC, 17 January 1917,

Anna Roosevelt Cowles Papers, Harvard University, for Alice's handwritten postscript, thanking her aunt for "being so kind to Marjorie Graydon."

27. JSG to ARL, 6 March 1916, JSP. ARL told Graydon's great-grandson, Stephen Benn, that she and Graydon went to New York together. Author telephone interview with Stephen Benn, 2 August 2004.

28. JSG to ARL, 29 July 1916, JSP.

29. JSG to ARL, 16 March 1916, JSP.

30. "Time and space," JSG to ARL, 6 March 1916; "departed quantities," JSG to ARL, 16 March 1916; "catholicity of interest," JSG to ARL, 25 April 1916, all JSP.

31. JSG to ARL, 14 June 1918; ARL Diary, 29 October 1917, both JSP.

32. "That adjective," JSG to ARL, 15 April 1916; "souvenier," JSG to ARL, 7 July 1916; "a broken reed," JSG to ARL, 25 March [1916], JSP (emphasis in original). The "shadowland" quote is from his letter to her of 7 July 1916.

33. JSG to ARL, 19 January [1918], JSP.

34. JSG to ARL, 15 April 1916, JSP.

35. JSG to ARL, 7 June 1918, JSP.

36. "Intelligence Branch," JSG to ARL, 23 August 1918, JSP; "honor, fulfillment," Edward J. Renehan, *The Lion's Pride* (New York: Oxford University Press, 1998), 4; "banishing increments," JSG to ARL, 29 July 1916, JSP.

37. JSG to ARL, 21 October 1943 and 23 October 1946; both JSP. JSG's birthday was 19 October.

38. Kermit Roosevelt to Richard Derby, 31 August 1913, RFPH. Robert E. Osgood, *Ideals and Self-Interest in America's Foreign Policy* (Chicago: University of Chicago Press, 1953), 250.

39. Goethels, *CH*, 226; "War is practically a fact," ARL Diary, 21 April 1914, JSP.

40. "12 Americans," ARL Diary, 23 April 1914; "laughing stock," ARL Diary, 25 April 1914, both JSP.

41. Kristie Miller, *Ruth Hanna McCormick* (Albuquerque: University of New Mexico Press, 1992), 103.

42. Nan Wallingford to Katherine Wulsin, 1 August 1914, Katherine Elizabeth (Roelker) Wulsin Correspondence, CHS.

43. EKR to Belle Hagner, 10 September 1914, PHP; military training centers, TRJR to John McCutcheon, 2 August 1915, Papers of John McCutcheon, Newberry Library, Chicago.

44. EKR to Belle Hagner, 20 November 1914; Kermit Roosevelt to Belle Hagner, 3 December 1914, both PHP.

Chapter 14: **"To Hate the Democrats So Wholeheartedly"**

1. Edward J. Renehan Jr., *The Lion's Pride* (New York: Oxford University Press, 1998), 5.

2. "To look always," ARL Diary, 1 November 1915; "great personage," ARL Diary, 3 October 1915, both JSP.

3. Elting E. Morison and John Morton Blum, eds. *The Letters of Theodore Roosevelt* (Cambridge, Mass.: Harvard University Press), 7:394, 397. See also Lawrence F. Abbott, ed., *Taft and Roosevelt* (Garden City, N.Y.: Doubleday, Doran, 1930), 1: 421–23.

4. Kathleen Dalton, *Theodore Roosevelt* (New York: Alfred A. Knopf, 2002), 443–45; TR's attachment to his letter to Lyman Abbot, 3 April 1910, in Morison and Blum, 7:358–399. The quote is found on page 396.

5. ARL Diary, 29 July 1917, JSP.

6. TR to ARC, 23 July 1916, in ARC, *Letters from Theodore Roosevelt to Anna Roosevelt Cowles, 1870–1918* (New York: Charles Scribner's Sons, 1924); ARL Diary, 9 October 1917, JSP; EKR to Mrs.

James Garfield, n.d., James R. Garfield Papers, LC.

7. "Pariah woman," EKR to Mrs. Garfield, 2 July [1916?], James R. Garfield Papers, LC; Needlework Guild, see EKR to Edith Wilson, 4 March 1918, Harold Ickes Papers, LC; EKR to Daniel Beard, n.d., Daniel C. Beard Papers, LC.

8. Richard Derby to Belle and Kermit Roosevelt, 22 February 1916, KBR; Emily Carow to Belle Roosevelt, 7 January 1918, KBR; ER, *The Autobiography of Eleanor Roosevelt* (New York: Harper & Row, 1978), 89.

9. Charles Selden, "The Father Complex of Alice Roosevelt Longworth and Ruth Hanna McCormick," *Ladies' Home Journal*, March 1927, 74; for Alice's quote, see Howard Teichmann, *Alice* (Englewood Cliffs, N.J.: Prentice-Hall, 1979), 100. See also "Her Pantalette Gown," *NYT*, 25 September 1915, 11.

10. Speech of Hon. NL, "True Preparedness," n.d., NLP; "Tie Vote on Buying Big Wright Plant, *NYT*, 13 November 1919, 2; Douglas Robinson to NL, n.d., JSP.

11. "Comprehensive reserve," TRJR to John McCutcheon, 2 August 1915, McCutcheon Papers, Newberry Library, Chicago; ARC to Belle Roosevelt, 10 July 1917, KBR; "A real help to me," quoted in Dalton, 463; "dauntless spirit," TR to Edith Franklin Wyatt, 5 December 1917, Edith Franklin Wyatt Papers, Newberry Library, Chicago.

12. *CH*, 258. For the Girl Scout publicity photographs and more "war work" by Alice, see also James Brough, *Princess Alice* (Boston: Little, Brown, 1975), 246; "All the political news," Joseph J. Kerrigan to ARL, 1 October 1919, JSP.

13. *CH*, 258; ARL Diary 16 July 1917; 29 July 1917; ARL Diary, 31 October 1917, JSP. See also Gladys Brooks, *Boston and Return* (New York: Athenaeum, 1962), 193.

14. "Conversation would begin," Mary Borah, *Elephants and Donkeys* (Moscow: University Press of Idaho, 1976), 67; see ARL Diary for 1917; Wilson "an ass," 3 August 1917, JSP; "President...resign," ER to Isabella Ferguson, 24 February [1916], Greenway AHS; "a stagnant lot," ARL to ARC, 17 January 1917, RFPH.

15. Isabella Ferguson to ER, [late spring 1916], ER Papers, FDRL.

16. ER to Isabella Ferguson, 21 June [1916], Greenway AHS.

17. Patricia O'Toole, *When Trumpets Call* (New York: Simon & Schuster, 2005), 291; EKR to Mrs. Garfield, 2 July [1916], James R. Garfield Papers, LC.

18. "No feeling of...chagrin," ARL to Fred [?], 22 June 1916, JSP. When TR withdrew his name it was "committing infanticide" according to John Milton Cooper in "If TR Had Gone Down with the *Titanic*," in *Theodore Roosevelt: Many-Sided American*, Natalie A. Naylor, Douglas Brinkley, and John Allen Gable, eds. (Interlaken, N.Y.: Heart of the Lakes Publishing, 1992), 507.

19. ARL to Fred [?], 22 June 1916, JSP; "vile and hypocritical," Lewis L. Gould, *Grand Old Party* (New York: Random House, 2003), 209.

20. *CH*, 241–42.

21. "Grief and tragedy," ARL Diary, 1 July 1917; "quarter-horse limitations," ARL Diary, 15 July 1917 and 23 September 1917, JSP. The *Washington Post* editor was Ned McLean.

22. "Agnostic fashion," ARL Diary, 13 September 1917, JSP; Balfour as friend, *CH*, 249–50.

23. ARL Diary, 1 October 1917, JSP.

24. ARL Diary, 23 September 1917, JSP.

25. Ethel Roosevelt Derby to Belle Roosevelt, 29 November 1917, KBR; TR to TRJR, 29 November 1917, in Morison and Blum, 8:1257; ARL Diary, 11 December 1917, JSP; and *CH*, 264.

26. "Father will play the big part," ARL Diary, 16 November 1917; "almost friendly," ARL Diary, 19 October 1917; "as soon as she knows," ARL Diary, 7 December 1917, all JSP.

27. ARL Diary, 5 November, 1917, JSP.

28. ARL Diary, 7 and 8 November 1917, JSP.

29. ARL Diary, 18 November 1917, JSP.

30. Hamilton Cravens, *The Triumph of Evolution* (Baltimore: Johns Hopkins Press, 1988), 19.

31. ARL Diary, 28 November 1917, JSP.

32. *CH*, 246.

33. Ted and Archie, Renehan, 132; Kermit, Cecil Spring-Rice to TR, 19 April 1917, F.O. 800/241-242/9/1, National Archive, London; ARL Diary, 11 August 1917, JSP; "flag with four stars," TR to Archibald Roosevelt, 8 September 1917, in Morison and Blum, 8:1237.

34. ARL Diary, 1 November 1917, JSP.

35. "Desperately bad," ARL Diary, 12 December 1917; Christmas, ARL Diary, 24 December 1917, both JSP.

36. Pompous friend, ARL Diary, 5 January 1918, JSP; McLeans' party, *CH*, 266.

37. ARL Diary, 8 January 1918, JSP, and *CH*, 267–68.

38. John Milton Cooper, *Breaking the Heart of the World* (Cambridge: Cambridge University Press, 2001), 19.

39. Gould, 216.

40. "It hurts," ARL Diary, 7 January 1918, JSP; "War Cabinet," Renehan, 171; gatherings at Longworths' home, *CH*, 268.

41. Housing committee, ARL Diary, 21 December 1917, JSP; to serve with her, or perhaps to ask Eleanor to take her place on the committee—the document isn't clear, ARL Diary, 22 December 1917, JSP; ER to Isabella Ferguson, 2 April 1918, Greenway AHS.

42. George Egerton, "Diplomacy, Scandal and Military Intelligence: The Craufurd-Stuart Affair and Anglo-American Relations, 1918–1920," *Intelligence and National Security* 2, 4 (October 1987): 110–134; meeting Churchill, ARL Diary, 1 July 1917, JSP; "serve your country," Michael Teague, *Mrs. L* (Garden City, N.Y.: Doubleday, 1981), 162.

43. "Upper balcony," Teague, 162; "no evidence," Egerton, 113; "Ladenburg suffered, Egerton," 127; "sheer rapture," Teague, 162. For ER's disapproval, see Teague, 163.

44. "In line of duty," "Record of Transfers and Changes, Quentin Roosevelt," JSP; "instantly killed," ER to Isabella Munro-Ferguson, 28 June 1918, Greenway AHS; TR to Frank McCoy, 12 September 1918, copy in JSP; JSG to ARL, 31 August 1918, JSP.

45. NL to Susan Longworth, 22 August 1918, NLIII.

46. *CH*, 275.

47. Barbara W. Tuchman, "Woodrow Wilson on Freud's Couch," in *Practicing History* (New York: Knopf, 1981), 147.

48. *CH*, 277.

49. Renehan, 217–22.

50. Robert James Maddox, *William E. Borah and American Foreign Policy* (Baton Rouge: Louisiana State University Press, 1969), xiii, xiv. The contemporary's account is Clinton W. Gilbert, *"You Takes Your Choice"* (New York: G. P. Putnam's Sons, 1924), 192.

51. Teague, 179, 187.

52. *CH*, 204.

53. Beverly Smith, "The Lone Rider from Idaho," *American Magazine*, March 1932, 96. Smith is probably quoting from Oscar King Davis, "Borah Insists on Conspiracy," *NYT*, 27 July 1907, 3.

54. "I feel that I cannot succeed," Marian C. McKenna, *Borah* (Ann Arbor: University of Michigan Press, 1961), 73; *The*

Autobiography of William Allen White (New York: Macmillan, 1946), 374–75.

55. Dave Grover, "Diamondfield Jack," *Idaho Yesterdays* 7, 2 (1963): 8–14. See also McKenna, 24–27.

56. Quoted in McKenna, 30.

57. See Claudius O. Johnson, "Very Personal Notes on Senator William E. Borah," April 1939, cage 214, Claudius Osborne Johnson Papers; Washington State University Libraries.

58. Doug Baker, "Oregon Writer Visits with Mrs. W. E. Borah," [1966], clipping, WEBID; horse racing, McKenna, 9.

59. Gilbert Clinton, *The Mirrors of Washington* (New York: G. P. Putnam's Sons, 1921), 251.

60. James M. Cox, *Journey Through My Years* (New York: Simon & Schuster, 1946), 100; transcript of Westerman Whillock interview by Jeffery G. Seward, Boise: Idaho State Historical Society, 8 January 1974, 21.

61. Smith, 40. For the list of politicians quoted, see Henry F. Pringle, "The Real Senator Borah," *The World's Work* 57 (December 1928): 135; Cox, 100.

62. John Milton Cooper, "William E. Borah, Political Thespian," *Pacific Northwest Quarterly*, October 1965, 146–48.

63. Claudius O. Johnson, "Comment," *Pacific Northwest Quarterly*, October 1965, 145.

64. "I enjoyed listening," *CH*, 300; Daisy Harriman, *From Pinafores to Politics* (New York: Henry Holt, 1923), 359, 358.

65. "One great desire," Clinton, 255; "to claim his wonderful daughter," WEB to ARL, 24 September 1924, JSP (emphasis in original).

66. Alice and Seventeenth Amendment, *CH*, 338–339; Charles Merz, "The Idaho Minority of One," *New Republic* 43 (3 June 1925): 39, 40; "Borah as Presidential Timber," *Literary Digest*, 7 April 1923, 11.

67. *CH*, 319; "world peace," Pringle, "The Real Senator Borah," 134.

68. "Current Magazines," *NYT*, 8 March 1925, 25.

69. "Apollo," "Borah as Presidential Timber," *Literary Digest*, 7 April 1923, 11; Pringle, "The Real Senator Borah," 138–140. "Variety of matters" on page 144.

70. George Washington's Farewell Address, 17 September 1796, in Henry Steele Commanger, ed., *Documents of American History*, 4th ed. (New York: Appleton-Century-Croft, 1948), 174; Borah quotes from Maddox, 51 and 55.

71. *CH*, 277. The other Irreconcilables were Medill McCormick (who entered the Senate in May 1919), Robert M. La Follette of Wisconsin, California's Hiram Johnson, Frank Brandegee of Connecticut, Philander Chase Knox from Pennsylvania, George Moses of New Hampshire, former Progressive Miles Poindexter of Washington, and James A. Reed, Democrat from Missouri.

72. Ralph Stone, "Two Illinois Senators Among the Irreconcilables," *Mississippi Valley Historical Review* 50, 3 (December 1963): 451 and 454; "rag bag" *CH*, 281.

73. *CH*, 282.

74. *CH*, 285.

75. *CH*, 286, 287; Cooper, *Breaking the Heart of the World*, 167, 168.

76. *CH*, 288.

77. Transcript of Cora Rubin Lane interview by Jackie Day-Ames, Boise: Idaho State Historical Society, 25 May 1976, 19; "immediate members," *CH*, 296; 19 November, Maddox, 67; Alice & Ruth's presence, "Humor, Satire, Wit, and Spoofing Help to Kill the Treaty," *Chicago Tribune*, 20 November 1919, 2.

78. Cooper, *Breaking the Heart of the World*, 265. All the words in quotes are Borah's, except for "lose its soul"—that phrase is Cooper's.

79. Hiram Johnson to Hiram Jr. and Arch Johnson, 21 November 1919, in Burke, ed., *The Diary Letters of Hiram Johnson*, vol. 3; next to her was Borah, *CH*, 292.

80. *CH*, 295; Mr. Wobbly, Brough, 262.

81. Maddox, 67.

82. *CH*, 309.

83. Maddox, 68.

Chapter 15: **"Hello, Hello, Hello"**

1. "Longworths Await Stork," *NYT*, 20 November 1924, 19.

2. GOP convention, Kristie Miller, *Ruth Hanna McCormick* (Albuquerque: University of New Mexico Press, 1992), 124–25; "always believed," *CH*, 339.

3. Leola Allard, "Women Want Friend as Head of Convention," *Chicago Tribune*, 8 June 1920, 4; "the career...born to," Miller, 123. For Ruth McCormick as chair of the committee, Miller, 125; RWNC objective, "Seek Successor to Miss Hay," *NYT*, 8 June 1920, 4; cause was aided, Miller, 125–26.

4. Harold L. Ickes, *The Autobiography of a Curmudgeon* (New York: Reynal & Hitchcock, 1943), 226.

5. *CH*, 311; "Republicans Confer on Chicago Planks," *NYT*, 19 May 1920, 2.

6. "Chicago Sidelights on Day of Oratory," *NYT*, 12 June 1920, 3; "*Times* in Chicago on Day of Issue," *NYT*, 10 June 1920, 1; "New York Crowds Cool Toward the Ticket," *NYT*, 13 June 1920, 6.

7. "Decaying Roman emperor," "The Reporters: Jonathan Aitken interview with Alice Roosevelt Longworth," Yorkshire Television [January 1969]. "First raters," William E. Leuchtenburg, *The Perils of Prosperity* (Chicago: University of Chicago Press, 1958), 86; Harding as compromise, Lewis L. Gould, *Grand Old Party* (New York: Random House, 2003),

222; "precise little object," ARL preservation tape, ICD 16025, 20 September 1967, JSP.

8. "Callers Flood Harding," *NYT*, 15 June 1920, 1.

9. "Harding Accepts League as Issue," *NYT*, 14 July 1920, 1; "Longworth to Stump in Maine Campaign," *NYT*, 6 August 1920, 3; "calling on the Senator," Philip Kinsley, "G.O.P. Majority in Congress to Grow, Fess Says," *Chicago Tribune*, 15 August 1920, 5; "reckless methods," "Harding to Speak at Minnesota Fair," *NYT*, 15 August 1920, 3.

10. "Looks Like Good G.O.P Year, Says Mrs. Longworth," *Chicago Tribune*, 17 August 1920, 19; "T.R.'s Daughter at G.O.P. Headquarters," *Chicago Tribune*, 25 August 1920, 7.

11. "Mrs. Longworth to Help," *NYT*, 26 August 1920, 3; "Mrs. Longworth Enters Campaign," *NYT*, 27 August 1920, 4; "T.R. Jr. Cancels Talk," *Chicago Tribune*, 5 September 1920, 1; "Harding Goes South on Speaking Tour," *NYT*, 13 October 1920, 3, states that Alice was going to be a speaker; "Harding Demands Proof He Changed," *NYT*, 21 October 1920, 3, covers the Jackson rally, but doesn't list Alice among the speakers; "T.R.'s Daughter Helps Dedicate Roosevelt Road," *Chicago Tribune*, 3 October 1920, 3; "Republicans Count on Maine Victory," *NYT*, 9 September 1920, 3.

12. Charles W. Snyder, "An American Original: Theodore Roosevelt, Jr.," in *Theodore Roosevelt: Many Sided American*, Natalie A. Naylor, Douglas Brinkley, and John Allen Gable, eds. (Interlaken, N.Y.: Heart of the Lakes Publishing, 1992), 97.

13. "Cox Coming East for Final Appeal," *NYT*, 18 October 1920, 2; "Houston's Plans on Tax Changes Anger Kitchin," *Chicago Tribune*, 10 December 1920, 11.

14. "Harding Proposes a New Department," *NYT*, 2 October 1920, 2. "How Will the Ladies, God Bless 'Em, Vote?," *Chicago Tribune*, 26 September 1920, C-7.

15. "President had his wish," "White Undismayed by Result in Maine," *NYT*, 15 September 1920, 4; "The Next Speakership," *NYT* editorial, 15 January 1919, 10; "Turn to Longworth in Speakership Fight," *NYT*, 13 January 1919, 6; "Mann Opposition Gaining Strength," *NYT*, 19 January 1919, 6; and "Longworth for Gillette," *NYT*, 28 January 1919, 8.

16. NL, "Traffic and Trade Agreements Speech" to the House of Representatives, 21 December 1920, made just before the tariff came up for revision in January 1921, NLP; Marian C. McKenna, *Borah* (Ann Arbor: The University of Michigan Press, 1961), 191–93; "intolerant, shortsighted," WEB to RHMcC, 28 July 1923, Hanna-McCormick Papers, LC.

17. Francis Ralston Welsh, "Truth Versus Treachery: Senator William E. Borah," [1923], Commerce Papers, HHPL.

18. *CH*, 314 and 315.

19. *CH*, 316.

20. "Fanatics on both sides," *CH*, 316; Wadsworth's view, 7 May 1922, TRJR Diary; "Sincere prohibitionist," Thomas L. Stokes, *Chip Off My Shoulder* (Princeton: Princeton University Press, 1940), 228.

21. "Not a common adventurer," McKenna, 175; "tee totalar," Richard V. Oulahan; "Address Stirs the Capital," *NYT*, 31 May 1926, 1.

22. "Girls," Robert Allen and Drew Pearson, *Washington Merry-Go-Round* (New York: Blue Ribbon Books, 1931), 24; Music, "Washington Society," *Chicago Tribune*, 3 March 1927, 27. Dows is quoted in Clara Longworth de Chambrun, *The Making of Nicholas Longworth* (New York: Richard R. Long & Ray Smith, 1933),

220; "Marching Club," De Chambrun, 286–87.

23. "Borah Amendment Adopted by Senate," *NYT*, 26 May 1921, 1; "economic ruin," "Open Arms Parley Is Borah's Demand," *NYT*, 30 August 1921, 13.

24. NL to Susan Longworth, 13 December [1921], NLIII.

25. McKenna, 179. Evans C. Johnson, *Oscar W. Underwood* (Baton Rouge: Louisiana State University Press, 1980), 319–20; Robert K. Murray, *The Politics of Normalcy* (New York: W. W. Norton, 1973), 61.

26. TRJR to ARL, 21 July 1923, JSP; for their friends see TRJR Diary, entries for spring and summer 1922; Charles Curtis was no relation to Laura Curtis.

27. "In the afternoon," TRJR Diary, 9 April 1922; a good play, TRJR Diary, 10 April 1922.

28. TRJR Diary, 11 April 1922; Arthur Sears Henning, "Battle to Save Navy for U.S. Is Begun in House," *Chicago Tribune*, 11 April 1922, 1.

29. TRJR Diary, 13–16 April 1922; "Harding Wins Fight Against 'Pygmy' Navy," *Chicago Tribune*, 16 April 1922, 1; for Nick's letter, see "86,000 Adopted as House Passes Bill," *NYT*, 16 April 1922, 1.

30. "Pneumonia Victim," *Chicago Tribune*, 28 June 1922, 10; "Mrs. Nicholas Longworth," *NYT*, 28 June 1922, 12; "Mrs. Longworth Died After a Long Illness," *Cincinnati Times-Star*, 27 June 1922; "Simple Service for Funeral of Mrs. Longworth," *Cincinnati Times-Star*, 29 June 1922, both Susan Longworth Princeton File, CHS; De Chambrun, 268.

31. "When are you coming," TRJR to ARL, 26 July 1922; "go over . . . in detail," TRJR to ARL, 31 July 1922, both JSP.

32. EKR to Belle Roosevelt, 1 May 1923, KBR; "Admiral Cowles Dies in 77th Year," *NYT*, 2 May 1923, 19; Isabella

Munro-Ferguson to John Campbell Greenway, 11 August 1923, Greenway AHS; on Bye's infirmities, see Betty Boyd Caroli, *The Roosevelt Women* (New York: Basic Books, 1998), 128–131.

33. "When he came," 322; Alice's contempt, 323; "shocking" disregard, 324; "Everyone must feel," 325, all *CH*.

34. Mark Sullivan, *Our Times: The Twenties* (New York: Charles Scribner's Sons, 1935), 6:97–98; *CH*, 323.

35. "There is no city," Maurice Francis Egan, "Washington, Past and Present," *NYT*, 15 August 1920, 38; Romany interest, Teague, 43.

36. "Atmosphere was as different," and "a simplicity and charm," *CH*, 326; for the dinner party, see ARL preservation tape, ICD 16025, 20 September 1967, JSP; for the dentist, see Teague, xiv.

37. "Fight on Longworth Angers Penna. Drys," clipping in a letter from Ethel Roosevelt Derby to Belle and Kermit Roosevelt, 4 February 1923, KBR; Western congressmen, "Diplomacy of Organization," *NYT*, 30 November 1923, 14; "Progressives Call for Radical Laws," *NYT*, 1 December 1923, 1.

38. NL to Republican members of the Sixty-eighth Congress, 24 November 1923, NLP; "acted on 594 measures," Donald C. Bacon, "Nicholas Longworth: The Genial Czar," in *Masters of the House*, Roger H. Davidson, Susan Webb Hammond, and Raymond W. Smock, eds. (Boulder, Colo.: Westview Press, 1998), 130.

39. Katharine Graham, *Personal History* (New York: Knopf, 1997), 27.

40. Sexual conquests, Claudius O. Johnson, "Very Personal Notes on Senator William E. Borah," April 1939, cage 214, Claudius Osborne Johnson Papers; Washington State University Libraries; "passion, intimacy, or love," LeRoy Ashby, e-mail to author, 23 May 2006; for two versions of this Cissy story, see Alice

Albright Hoge, *Cissy Patterson* (New York: Random House, 1966), 72; Ralph G. Martin, *Cissy* (New York: Simon & Schuster, 1979), 189; for Alice denying it ever happened, see Paul F. Healy, *Cissy* (Garden City, N.Y.: Doubleday, 1966), 9; for the bathroom incident, see Martin, 190; for the carriage, Kristie Miller, e-mail to author, 19 October 1999; for the stocking and chewing gum, see Alsop, *"I've Seen the Best of It,"* 92.

41. "Vivacious, blue-eyed blonde," McKenna, 23; pregnancy rumor, Johnson, "Very Private Notes." Marian McKenna, author of *Borah* (Ann Arbor: University of Michigan Press, 1961), interviewed Mary Borah's personal physician, Dr. Ralph Falk. During one of their lengthy conversations, Professor McKenna asked Dr. Falk why the Borahs never had children, and asked specifically about the abortion rumor. Dr. Falk cited "doctor-patient privilege" and said that he "could neither confirm nor deny the fact of the alleged abortion." McKenna believed "it was a weak assertion." Had there been no abortion, it is reasonable to assume that Dr. Falk would have said so, especially as he was a good friend of the Borahs and because Mrs. Borah was still living. Marian McKenna, e-mails to author, 26 and 29 May 2006.

For Mary Borah's story of her earliest days with Bill Borah, see the transcript of her oral history at the Idaho Historical Society. (Mary McConnell Borah, interviewed by Rosita Artis, Boise: Idaho State Historical Society [OH #0013], 18 October 1969.) She tells the tale of a very brief courtship, truncated when Borah had to go to Washington for a case. They married instead of being separated, according to Mrs. Borah. For another version of how Mary met and married Bill Borah, see the transcript of Mary McConnell Borah, interview by Maureen Bassett, 15 October 1971, Oral History Project, Latah County Museum Society, Moscow, Idaho.

There is another piece of evidence to support the abortion theory. Ann Catt, curator of the Latah County Historical Society and Mary Reed, former curator at the McConnell Mansion Museum, both in Moscow, Idaho, where Mary McConnell was born, pointed out that there is very little in Mary McConnell Borah's memoir, *Elephants and Donkeys*, about her family. Her Moscow years are virtually ignored. Both Catt and Reed suggested separately how odd it is that Governor McConnell's daughter would fail to elaborate on her father, also one of the most prominent men in Idaho. His virtual absence from Mrs. Borah's memoir made them suspect some sort of falling-out. As Ms. Catt said, though, after Senator Borah's death, Mary Borah went to live with her sister in California—so any hard feelings didn't seem to have been directed at her sibling. (Author's telephone interview with Mary Reed, 30 May 2006; author's telephone interview with Ann Catt, 30 May 2006.)

42. In response to my question about why Alice allowed herself to get pregnant, Alice Longworth's granddaughter said she "just let it happen." Joanna Sturm believes emphatically that Alice Longworth would never have had an abortion. (Author's interview with Joanna Sturm, 12 June 2005.)

43. Robert Hellman, e-mails to author, 21 and 22 May 2006.

44. Alice stayed home, "Old Party Leaders Take Back Seats," *NYT*, 11 June 1924, 4; RHMcC Diary, 21 August 1924, courtesy of Kristie Miller; Borah not at Cleveland, McKenna, 208.

45. "Borah as Presidential Timber," *Literary Digest*, 7 April 1923, 11; WEB to RHMcC, 28 July 1923, Hanna-McCormick Papers, LC.

46. Ted's memories from his "Summary

of Republican National Convention, Cleveland, Ohio, June 10, 11, 12, 1924," TRJRP.

47. "In which place?" Charles Merz, "Borah's One-Man Party," *New Republic* 43 (10 June 1925): 67; "dullest," Miller, 145; vice-president, Richard Langham Riedel, *Halls of the Mighty* (New York: Robert B. Luce, 1969), 189.

48. WEB to ARL, 28 September 1924, JSP.

49. WEB to ARL, 11 July 1924, JSP.

50. "Roosevelt Is Happy as Smith Passes McAdoo," *Chicago Daily Tribune*, 8 July 1924, 2.

51. WEB to ARL, 25 September 1924, JSP.

52. "What will I do?" WEB to ARL, 16 September 1924; "My own sweetheart," Underlined in "The Neglected Farmer," clipping in WEB to ARL, 25 September 1924, both JSP.

53. "Borah and a Third Party," *Literary Digest*, 26 August 1922, 14.

54. WEB to ARL, 26 September 1924, JSP.

55. WEB to ARL, 3 November 1924, JSP; meet in Chicago, RHMcC Diary, 5 September 1924, courtesy of Kristie Miller.

56. "I did enjoy your letters," WEB to ARL, 23 September 1924, JSP; Hellos, WEB to ARL, 25 October 1924, 7 November 1925, and 4 October 1924, all JSP.

57. *NYT* editorial (14 September 1924) enclosed in WEB to ARL, 18 September 1924, JSP; "my darling," "At the Mercy of Congress," clipping, n.d., in WEB to ARL, 26 September 1924, JSP; "My dear," "Pot and Kettle Politics," *New York Journal of Commerce*, 18 August 1924, unattached clipping, JSP; "My sweetheart," "The Magic Power of Campaign Words and Phrases," clipping, n.d., in WEB to ARL, 23 September 1924, JSP.

58. Secret message in "Speaker Scores Party Leaders in Bad Faith," in WEB to ARL, 5 August 1924, JSP.

59. WEB to ARL, 8 October 1924, JSP.

60. RHMcC Diary, 6 November 1924, courtesy of Kristie Miller.

61. Uncertain future, "Roosevelt Rests," *NYT*, 6 November 1924, 3; Alice's intercession, William Allen White, *A Puritan in Babylon* (New York: Macmillan, 1958), 270n18; "prepared to make a statement," "T.R. Should Quit Navy, Democrat Says in Hot Row," *Chicago Tribune*, 16 March 1924, 3; "Demands TR Shall Leave Navy," *NYT*, 16 March 1924, 1; "rough stunt," ER, *This I Remember* (New York: Harper & Brothers, 1949), 32.

62. EKR to James R. Garfield, 15 October 1924, James R. Garfield Papers, LC; Katherine Edmondson Callaway to ARL, 20 January 1936, ARLC.

63. WEB to ARL, 6 November 1924, JSP.

64. "Rather special," *CH*, 1; Henry Cabot Lodge to ARL, 24 April 1921, JSP.

65. EKR Diary, Wednesday, 12 November 1924. Definition from *Cassell's Dictionary* (1971), 104; "Alice's news," Sylvia Jukes Morris, *Edith Kermit Roosevelt* (New York: Coward, McCann & Geoghegan, 1980), 462–63; "the shock," EKR to Belle Hagner, 29 November 1924, PHP.

66. Kermit Roosevelt to Belle Roosevelt, KBR. Both letters are dated 14 November 1924. The first was from Rookwood, the second from Zanesville.

67. The journalist was Robert Bender from the United Press bureau, James Brough, *Princess Alice* (Boston: Little, Brown, 1975), 275; "One of the most original," "Longworths Await Stork," *NYT*, 21 November 1924, 19; Coolidges, Brough, 274, 275. RHMcC Diary, 21 November 1924, courtesy of Kristie Miller; "Mrs. Longworth Expecting Stork," *Chicago Tribune*, 21 November 1924, 1; "gland

Notes to Pages 315–22   *527*

baby," "Princess Alice," *New Yorker,* 28 February 1925, 9.

68. William "Fishbait" Miller and Frances Spatz Leighton, *Fishbait* (Englewood Cliffs, N.J.: Prentice Hall, 1977), 103–4.

69. Robert James Maddox, "Keeping Cool with Coolidge," *Journal of American History* 53, 4 (March 1967): 776.

70. RHMcC Diary, 6 November 1924, courtesy of Kristie Miller.

71. Joanna Sturm, Alice Longworth's granddaughter, and Robert Hellman, Sturm's partner, feel very strongly that Alice "duped" Nick. "A woman as smart as Mrs. L. could have finessed that with a fellow who drank as much as Longworth," Hellman wrote. (Robert Hellman, e-mail to author, 22 and 21 May 2006.) Mrs. Longworth disclosed the truth about Joanna's grandfather when Joanna was an adult, and when all the other principals were dead.

72. Angela Meeske, a lifelong resident of Cincinnati, maintains that Nick Longworth was the father of a son, the result of an affair with a Cincinnati woman. The son, according to Mrs. Meeske, never tried to hide his connection—in fact, sitting by his chair in his living room was "an oversized portrait" of Nick. (Author interview with Angela Meeske, 19 April 2004.) This is the only rumor I've ever heard of Nick's fathering a child, except for the malicious letter Alice received while on her honeymoon.

73. RHMcC Diary, 24 November 1924 ("more cheerful") and 7 November 1924 ("Dr. DeLee"), courtesy of Kristie Miller; "When do you advise," Morris Fishbein, *Joseph Bolivar DeLee* (New York: E. P. Dutton, 1949), 156.

74. "Congress Begins Its Final Session in a Cheerful Mood," *NYT,* 2 December 1924, 1; WEB to ARL, 6 November 1924, JSP; "Longworth Campaign Started by Ohioans," *NYT,* 17 December 1924, 44.

See also "Wants Longworth in Chair," *NYT,* 20 December 1924, 17; "Longworth Is Confident," *NYT,* 24 December 1924, 5; Bacon, 131.

75. "You Can't Help Liking Nick," *Literary Digest* 87, 8 (21 November 1925), 46; "Flags at Capital at Half-staff," *Washington Times,* 9 April 1931, 2.

76. ARC to NL, 28 February 1925, JSP.

77. WEB to ARL, 23 January 1925, JSP.

78. RHMcC Diary, 27 January 1925.

79. WEB to ARL, 2 February 1925, JSP.

80. ARC to ARL, 3 February 1925, JSP; Caroli, 414.

81. See "Daughter Is Born to the Longworths," *NYT,* 15 February 1925, 1; "Longworth Cheered in the House," *NYT,* 15 February 1925, 1.

82. WEB to ARL, 14 February 1925. Borah usually did not use a plural pronoun. Either Mary Borah was reading over his shoulder or he wanted to make sure that his note was suitable should Nick read it. However, the transparent Hello, Hello code makes it likely that Borah was simply too transported by the news to be thinking clearly.

83. WEB to ARL, 15 February 1925, JSP.

84. "A little bit jealous," "Longworth Meets Infant Daughter," *NYT,* 16 February 1925, 5; "Miss Paulina Has Real Roosevelt Face" and "A Chip Off the Old Block," newspaper clippings, n.d., JSP. The quote is from the latter. WEB to ARL, 16 February 1925, JSP.

85. Untitled clipping from [*Chicago*] *Tribune,* 15 March 1925, JSP.

86. Alsop, 91.

87. Elizabeth Brunner, "The Battle for Feminist Approval: Paulina in Shakespeare's *The Winter's Tale,*" 1995, (http://members.tripod.com/~ElizBrunner/Scholar/PaulinaWinters.html).

88. WEB to ARL, 22 February 1925, JSP.

89. ARL, telegram to Everett Sanders; Everett Sanders, telegram to ARL, both 14 February 1925, Everett Sanders Papers, LC; "Science and the Longworth Baby," newspaper clipping, n.d., JSP; WEB to ARL, 24 February 1925.

90. "Self-destructive tendencies," Miller, 151, 152; EKR to ARL, 27 February 1925, JSP; "when Senator McCormick died," Selden, 76; "Mrs. Longworth Leaves Hospital," NYT, 28 February 1925, 2.

91. WEB to ARL, 28 February and 1 July 1925, JSP.

92. Untitled clipping, [Chicago] Tribune, 15 March 1925, JSP. See also "Longworth Baby Quits Chicago Today," NYT, 6 March 1925, 23; and "Paulina Visits Father," NYT, 8 March 1925, 2.

93. WEB to ARL, 1 March 1925, JSP; "Longworth Poses as Fond Father," NYT, 16 May 1925, 21.

94. Mary Borah, Elephants and Donkeys (Moscow: University Press of Idaho, 1976), 113.

95. " 'Little Borah' Has to Read the Papers to Keep Track of Noted Husband," Lewiston Tribune, 3 August 1936, WEBID; James M. Cox, Journey Through My Years (New York: Simon & Schuster, 1946), 100.

96. "Frequent morning caller," "Little Borah is Confidant of Ex-Servicemen," Capital News, May 1929, WEBID; "close personal friends," Suzanne Dabney Taylor, "Little Borah at 101," newspaper clipping, 29 October 1971, WEBID; Mrs. Borah as guest, "Washington Society," Chicago Tribune, 8 December 1925, 25; photos of Paulina, WEB to ARL, 18 July and 10 July 1925, both JSP.

97. WEB to ARL, 10 July 1925; WEB to ARL, 13 July 1925, both JSP.

98. WEB to ARL, 28 July 1925, JSP.

Sometimes Bill Borah used periods (P.F.P.) and sometimes he did not (PFP).

99. WEB to ARL, 5 August 1925, JSP. WEB to ARL, 17 September 1925, JSP. P.M.P. WEB to ARL, 16 October 1925, JSP. Alice herself referred to her father as "my parent," and this can be heard throughout the ARL preservation tapes.

100. Cora Rubin Lane, interviewed by Jackie Day-Ames, Boise: Idaho State Historical Society, 25 May 1976. See especially page 20 of the transcript.

101. Robert Hellman, e-mail to author, 20 May 2006.

Chapter 16: **"The Political Leader of the Family"**

1. "The 'Battalion of Death' in New Onslaughts," Kansas City Star, 24 January 1926, C-1; Time magazine, 7 February 1927, cover; Gore Vidal, "The Woman Behind The Women," New Yorker, 26 May 1997, 73.

2. Henry Brandon, "A Talk with an 83-Year-Old Enfant Terrible," NYT, 6 August 1967, 69.

3. Nelle Scanlan, Boudoir Mirrors of Washington (Philadelphia: John C. Winston, 1923), 17.

4. "Little Miss Paulina Longworth," Louisville Courier-Journal, 19 September 1926, 9; JSP; Clara Longworth de Chambrun, The Making of Nicholas Longworth (Ray Long & Richard R. Smith, 1933), 283.

5. Charles A. Selden, "The Father Complex of ARL and RHMcC," Ladies' Home Journal, March 1927, 6; "Princess Alice," New Yorker, 28 February 1925.

6. "Little Borah Is Confidant of Ex-Servicemen," Capital News, May 1929, undated clipping, WEBID. For Mary Borah's explanation of her involvement with veterans, see her oral history at the Idaho

Oral History Center, pages 6 and 7 of the transcript, tape 2.

7. Letter to "mot her," n.d., JSP. The only other legible word is *Paulina;* ARL to Ethel Roosevelt Derby, postmarked 14 August 1926, RFPH.

8. Grace Goodhue Coolidge to Mrs. Dwight Morrow, 28 December 1925, quoted in Ishbel Ross, *Grace Coolidge and Her Era* (New York: Dodd, Mead, 1962), 168. Or, the timing may have been just before Christmas: see "Longworth Baby at White House," *NYT,* 16 December 1925, 52.

9. "Little Miss Paulina Longworth," 9.

10. "Mrs. Coolidge Writes Cook Book Recipes for Congressional Club's Favorite Dishes," *NYT,* 16 September 1927, 25; "Kitchen Secrets in New Cookbook," *NYT,* 20 November 1927, 22; for Alice as charter member, see "Congressmen's Wives Club," *NYT,* 15 March 1908, 9, and *The Congressional Club Cookbook* (Washington, D.C.: Congressional Club, 1927), 428, 437.

11. "Mrs. Longworth's Portrait to Advertise Beauty Cream," *NYT,* 1 June 1925, 1; Cornelia Bryce Pinchot to Bessie Dobson Altemus, 7 April 1927, Papers of Cornelia Bryce Pinchot, LC; for other women who posed, see Stanley Walker, *Mrs. Astor's Horse* (New York: Frederick A. Stokes, 1935), 93–94; "official and social Washington," "Mrs. Longworth Joins Royalty in Beauty Ads," *Chicago Tribune,* 1 June 1925, 9.

12. "From then on," Ross, *Grace Coolidge,* 199; Mary McConnell Borah, "Entertaining Royalty," clipping, n.d., WEBID.

13. "Who Goes to Prize Fights—And Why?," *Chicago Tribune,* 1 July 1921, 8; ARL preservation tape, ICD 16025, 20 September 1967, JSP. See also "Notables to See the Title Match," *NYT,* 14 September 1923, 14.

14. George Authier, "The New Speaker of the House," *National Republic,* January 1926, NLP.

15. Nick quoted in "You Can't Help Liking Nick," *Literary Digest* 87, 8 (21 November 1925), 46; "regardless of the rules, Authier, NLP.

16. "In Alice Longworth," Authier, NLP; "never sponsored anything," Robert S. Allen and Drew Pearson, *Washington Merry-Go-Round* (New York: Blue Ribbon Books, 1931), 230.

17. Nick's opening speech in de Chambrun, 293; Congress, "is always unpopular," S. J. Woolf, "Speaker of the House and Proud to Be," *NYT Magazine,* 12 February 1928, 3.

18. Harry Parker, "Recalls Longworth Smile," *NYT,* 10 April 1931, 18; Edge, De Chambrun, 285; "chain drinker," Richard Langham Riedel, *Halls of the Mighty* (New York: Robert B. Luce, 1969), 192. Riedel made this observation of Garner when Cactus Jack had become vice president. John L. Lewis quote from Anthony Champagne, "John Nance Garner," in *Masters of the House,* Roger H. Davidson, Susan Webb Hammond, and Raymond W. Smock, eds. (Boulder, Colo.: Westview Press, 1998), 146.

19. Robert Paul Browder and Thomas G. Smith, *Independent* (New York: Knopf, 1986), 52; "Will Rogers Says Longworth Was Both Able and Popular," *NYT,* 11 April 1931, 18.

20. Garner quote from Neil MacNeil, *Forge of Democracy* (New York: David McKay, 1963), 82; for more on Board of Education, see Champagne, in Davison, Hammond, and Smocks, 162; and MacNeil, 81–84.

21. Jules Abels, *In the Time of Silent Cal* (New York: G. P. Putnam's Sons, 1969), 36.

22. Allen and Pearson, 211–214. For

Richard Riedel's loving treatment, see *Halls of the Mighty,* especially pages 272–82.

23. WEB to ARL, 9 October 1930, JSP.

24. "I am very blue," WEB to ARL, 10 November 1930, JSP; "I wonder," WEB to ARL, n.d. [1930], JSP; banish warfare, Lewis L. Gould, *The Most Exclusive Club* (New York: Basic Books, 2005), 101.

25. For Salmon O. Levinson and Robins and their interests in having Borah as their spokesperson for the outlawry movement, see especially Robert James Maddox, "William E. Borah and the Crusade to Outlaw War," *Historian,* 29 (2), 1967: 200–220.

26. "The Roosevelt Club Borah-Butler Debate" (Boston: The Roosevelt Club, 1927); Idaho newspaper quoted in Charles DeBenedetti, "Borah and the Kellogg-Briand Pact," *Pacific Northwest Quarterly* 63(1), January 1972: 24.

27. DeBenedetti, 28.

28. Maddox, 220; Claudius O. Johnson, *Borah of Idaho* (Seattle: University of Washington Press, 1936), 405–406; "Idaho Varsity Takes Levinson $55,000 as Giving Honor to Borah," *Chicago Tribune,* 12 April 1929, 41.

29. "Borah Will Start Two-Year Campaign for New Party Deal," *NYT,* 12 June 1926; "Whooping It Up for Borah in Idaho," *Spokane Review,* 15 September 1927, JSP; WEB to Evan Evans, 21 March 1928, WEBID.

30. Ethel Roosevelt Derby to Belle Roosevelt, 14 January 1926, KBR; Frank B. Lord, "A 'Close Up' of Longworth," [*Movie* magazine] draft, spring 1927, NLP; Nick quoted in de Chambrun, 289.

31. Lucile McArthur, "Idle Moments of a Lady in Waiting," *Saturday Evening Post* 204, 12 (19 September 1931), 5; Kermit Roosevelt to Ethel Roosevelt Derby, 3 January 1928, ERDP.

32. "Delivered himself up," Thomas L. Stokes, *Chip Off My Shoulder* (Princeton: Princeton University Press, 1940), 228; platform, Johnson, 421.

33. Vice-presidency, Edward Anthony oral interview transcript, 12 July 1970, 35–36; hoax boom, Gene Dulin to Herbert Hoover, 8 August 1928, Campaign and Transition Files, both HHPL.

34. Preston Wolfe oral interview transcript, 18 August 1967, 14, HHPL; Robert Silvercruys oral interview transcript, 9, HHPL; "a mistake," Miller, 187, 191. For McCormick's campaign, see Miller, chap. 7.

35. "First woman," Miller, 196; "Alice is a statesman," Miller, 192.

36. "No man did more," Johnson, 408; lunch with Hoover, Johnson, 432–33.

37. "Senator Curtis Aided by Sister in Capital," *NYT,* 16 June 1928, 5; "Sister Speaks for Curtis," *NYT,* 8 August 1928, 3; "Mrs. Gann Is Hostess," *NYT,* 4 March 1929, 2.

38. Stanley Woodward, "Protocol: What It Is and What It Does," *Department of State Bulletin* reprint, 3 October 1949, 501; "Mrs. Moses Heads Senate Ladies' Club," *NYT,* 6 February 1929, 11.

39. "Inaugural Ball Largest Ever Held," *NYT,* 5 March 1928, 2; Kellogg's quote from "Mrs. Gann's Social Rank," *NYT,* 30 March 1929, 22.

40. "Curtis Protests on Social Ranking," *NYT,* 4 April 1929, 1 and 14. See also "A Man Who Must Dine for His Country," *NYT,* 15 March 1931, 81.

41. "At the head of the table," "Silence Enjoined on Curtis Status," *NYT,* 5 April 1929, 4; "Diplomats Confer on Curtis Hostess, But Refuse to Act," *NYT,* 9 April 1929, 1; "Stimson Won't Rule on Mrs. Gann's Case," *NYT,* 10 April 1929, 4; "Diplomats Accord Rank to Mrs. Gann as Curtis Hostess," *NYT,* 11 April 1929, 18.

42. Heflin quote from "Diplomats Confer on Curtis Hostess, But Refuse to Act,"

12; "Protest in Philadelphia," *NYT,* 10 April 1929, 4.

43. Stimson quote from "Stimson Won't Rule on Mrs. Gann's Case," 1; "scored a complete triumph," "Diplomats Accord Rank to Mrs. Gann as Curtis Hostess," 1; Chilean ambassador's dinner, "Mrs. Gann as Guest Has Honor Place," *NYT,* 12 April 1929, 1.

44. "Gann Social War Reopens in Capital," *NYT,* 5 May 1929, 23.

45. "Social War at the Capital," *NYT,* 8 May 1929, 25.

46. ARL preservation tape, ICD 16024, 20 September 1967, JSP.

47. ARL preservation tape, ICD 16024, 20 September 1967, JSP; see Jonathan Daniels, *Washington Quadrille* (Garden City, N.Y.: Doubleday, 1968), 233–35, which has a story that matches best with Alice's interpretation. "Obviously, there never was any row," *CH,* 32; "Mrs. Gann and Alice Longworth Sit Together in Senate Gallery and Chat in Friendly Vein," *NYT,* 14 May 1929, 2.

48. Winifred Mallon, "Social Battle Rages Anew in the Capital," *NYT,* 12 May 1929, 22; ARL preservation tape, ICD 16024, 20 September 1967, JSP.

49. Curtis cheating, ARL, "Of Politics and Politicians," n.d., JSP; "mediocre—" Robert S. Allen interview, 1970, 3, HHPL. But Curtis did love his sister. When he died, Charlie Curtis left her $25,000. See "Footnotes on Headliners," *NYT,* 23 February 1936, E2.

50. *CH,* 329.

51. "Mrs. Gann Defends Right to Social Precedence as Hostess to 'Symbol of Our Government,'" *NYT,* 31 July 1929, 24; "White House Changes Master of Ceremonies," *NYT,* 10 January 1930, 29; "Curtis and Speaker Guests in Box Party," *NYT,* 14 February 1930, 25; "'Alice' Greets 'Dolly' at White House Fete," *NYT,* 9 December 1930, 36; Dolly Gann, *Dolly Gann's Book* (Garden City, N.Y.: Doubleday, 1933), 121–22.

52. Addenda to Transcript of F. Trubee Davison, Oral Interview with F. Trubee Davison, 14 September 1969, 14, HHPL.

53. Frances Spatz and David Camelon, "Legendary Ladies: Rebellious 'Princess Alice,'" *American Weekly,* 12 November 1950, 25.

Chapter 17: **"An Irresistible Magnet"**

1. Winifred Mallon, "Mrs. Longworth Sets Tongues Wagging," *NYT,* 26 May 1929, 5; Rebecca West, "The Kaleidoscope That Is Washington," *NYT,* 12 May 1935, SM3.

2. James quoted in Constance McLaughlin Green, *Washington* (Princeton: Princeton University Press, 1963), 190; Clara Longworth de Chambrun, *The Making of Nicholas Longworth* (New York: Ray Long & Richard R. Smith, 1933), 283–84; "Nick Longworth's Political Career Colorful," *Washington Times,* 9 April 1931, 3.

3. Kristie Miller, *Ruth Hanna McCormick* (Albuquerque: University of New Mexico Press, 1992), 203. For the "back door," see John Milton Cooper Jr., *Breaking the Heart of the World* (New York: Cambridge University Press, 2001), especially 399–401; "I just can't stand it," Miller, 218.

4. Ralph G. Martin, *Cissy* (New York: Simon & Schuster, 1979), 275. See also Robert Allen and Drew Pearson, *Washington Merry-Go-Round* (New York: Blue Ribbon Books, 1931), 14–15.

5. Alice Albright Hoge, *Cissy Patterson* (New York: Random House, 1966); Martin, 276.

6. Hoge, 73.

7. Cissy Patterson to Nick Longworth, n.d., JSP. For the end of the feud between

Cissy and Alice, see Paul F. Healy, *Cissy* (New York: Doubleday, 1966), 238–239.

8. Hiram Johnson to Archibald M. Johnson, 9 April 1930, *The Diary Letters of Hiram Johnson*, vol. 5 (New York: Garland Publishing, 1983); Miller, 228–29.

9. "Holding levees," WEB to ARL, 5 September 1930, JSP; "Princess Paulina Takes Up the Three R's," clipping, n.d., in WEB to ARL, 17 October 1930, JSP; "all of a twitter," ARL to Ethel Roosevelt Derby, 23 December 1930, ERDP; "I wish I could have had," WEB to ARL, 19 September 1930, JSP; "so blue," WEB to ARL, 23 September 1930, JSP.

10. "No...courage," WEB to ARL, 27 September 1930; "remained on the farm," WEB to ARL, 3 October 1930; "Brazil's...war," WEB to ARL, 10 October 1930, all JSP. Emphasis in original.

11. "Whither Thou Goest I Will Go," clipping enclosed in WEB to ARL, 23 September 1930, JSP; Miller, 229–30.

12. "I know how you are scanning," WEB to ARL, 1 November 1930; "wants to do the big thing," WEB to ARL, 5 November 1930, both JSP. Ruth's loss, Miller, 233–34.

13. ARL to Ethel Roosevelt Derby, 23 December 1930, RFPH; WEB to ARL, 10 and 11 November 1930, JSP. For the long letter, see WEB to ARL, 12 November 1930. For "Presh's figuring," see 24 November 1930, JSP.

14. Donald C. Bacon, "Nicholas Longworth," in Roger H. Davidson, Susan Webb Hammond, and Raymond W. Smock, eds., *Masters of the House* (Boulder, Colo.: Westview Press, 1998), 139; de Chambrun, 317–18.

15. Lucile McArthur, "Idle Moments of a Lady in Waiting," *Saturday Evening Post* 204, 12 (19 September 1931):142.

16. Allen and Pearson, 24; Jonathan

Daniels, *Washington Quadrille* (Garden City, N.Y.: Doubleday, 1968), 235–38.

17. Alice's confirmation, "Rep. Longworth's Right Lung Infected," *Washington Times*, 8 April 1931, 1; Cissy Patterson to Laura Curtis, n.d., JSP. "When I heard that Nick probably had pneumonia I instantly telephoned your house," Cissy wrote—but not Alice's home. See also "Death of a Speaker," *Time*, 20 April 1931, from their online archive: http://time-proxy.yaga.com/time/archive/printout/0,23657,741406,00.html. It attests to the fact that the oxygen tent arrived. Herbert Hoover to ARL, 8 April 1931, LHHP.

18. "Longworth Sinking," *NYT*, 9 April 1931, 1; "Death Ends Career of Speaker Longworth," *Cincinnati Times-Star*, 9 April 1931, 1, states that both Alice and Laura were at his bedside. See also "Longworth Is Dead," *NYT*, 10 April 1931, 1.

19. "Rites Will Be at Rookwood at 2 P.M. Saturday," *Cincinnati Times-Star*, 10 April 1931, NLPF.

20. "Longworth's Body Starts Back to Ohio for Funeral Today," *NYT*, 11 April 1931, 1; Gore Vidal, *Palimpsest* (New York: Penguin Books, 1995), 263; "The Gift," Alice Dows, *Illusions* (Philadelphia: Dorrance Publishers, 1931), 50; "When He Comes," Alice Dows, *Idle Hours* (Philadelphia: Dorrance Publishers, 1927), 55.

21. "Speaker's Gavel Draped," *NYT*, 12 April 1931, 24; see also "Recalls Longworth Smile," *NYT*, 10 April 1931, 18; W[illiam] E. and Mary Borah, telegram to ARL, 9 April 1931, JSP; Herbert Hoover, Executive Order, 9 April 1931, President's Personal File, HHPL; "Hurley Pays Tribute Over Radio to Speaker," *NYT*, 10 April 1931, 19; Herbert Hoover to ARL, 9 April 1931, President's Personal File, HHPL. See also "President Lauds Long-

worth for Service to His Country," *NYT*, 10 April 1931, 1.

22. "Cincinnati Grieves for 'Man of the People,'" *NYT*, 10 April 1931, 18; for the list of the pallbearers, see "Funeral Rites to Be Simple," *NYT*, 11 April 1931, 12; "Garner Mourns for Friendly Foe," *NYT*, 10 April 1931, 18.

23. Graydon DeCamp, *The Grand Old Lady of Vine Street* (Cincinnati: Cincinnati Enquirer, 1991), 87.

24. Eleanor Butler Roosevelt to ARL, 10 April 1931; TRJR to ARL, n.d., [1931], JSP; "oddly enough" TRJR to ARL, 12 April 1931, JSP.

25. See, for example, "Curtis and Cabinet Eulogize Speaker," *NYT*, 10 April 1931, 18; "Loss of Longworth Stirs Sorrow Here," *NYT*, 10 April 1931, 18; Arthur Krock, "The Week in America," *NYT*, 12 April 1931, E5; Longworth's career is assessed by Donald C. Bacon, "Nicholas Longworth," in *Masters of the House*, Roger H. Davidson, Susan Webb Hammond, and Raymond W. Smock, eds. (Boulder, Colo.: Westview Press, 1998).

26. John Q. Tilson, "The Late Hon. Nicholas Longworth, of Ohio, Memorial Address," *Congressional Record*, May 1932, NLPF; *NYT* editorial, "Speaker of the House," 12 April 1931, E1; and "Curtis and Cabinet Eulogize Speaker," *NYT*, 10 April 1931, 18; "bludgeoning the House," Allen and Pearson, 231; the term "genial czar" is Donald C. Bacon's; "Will Rogers Says Longworth Was Both Able and Popular," *NYT*, 11 April 1931, 18; for Nick's interview, see S. J. Woolf, "Speaker of the House and Proud to Be," *NYT Magazine*, 12 February 1928, 23.

27. Laura M. Curtis to LHH, 27 April 1931, LHHP; Kristie Miller, e-mail to author, 18 April 2004, quoting Ruth's daughter Bazy Tankersely.

28. "Mrs. Longworth Is Urged to Run for Congress," *Washington Times*, 10 April 1931, 3; see also "Death of Longworth Gives House to Democrats," *Washington Times*, 9 April 1931, 2.

29. Memorandum of Lewis Strauss's telephone report of Robert Taft's conversation, 28 April 1931, Lewis L. Strauss Papers, HHPL; "Republican Majority Narrowed by Death," *Cincinnati Times-Star*, 10 April 1931, NLPF; Frances Parkinson Keyes, *Capital Kaleidoscope* (New York: Harper & Brothers, 1937), 24.

30. "As though he owned the mint," Joseph Alsop, unpublished draft of his memoirs, 127 (in the author's possession); for assessments, see "Longworth's Estate All Left to Widow," 17 April 1931, 28; "Longworth's Estate Is Put at $825,000," 23 April 1931, 18; "Longworth Inheritance Tax $25,919," 8 December 1932, 15, all *NYT*.

31. ARL to LHH, 20 May 1931, LHHP; Mildred Hale to ARL, 15 May 1931, JSP; "rare and remarkable gift," ARL to LHH, 14 April 1931, LHHP; for Ted's return, see "Plans to Aid Porto Rico," *NYT*, 26 May 1931, 19. See also TRJR to LHH, 20 April 1931, LHHP; TRJR to ARL, n.d., JSP; "I know just how hard," TRJR to ARL, n.d., JSP.

32. Author interview with Angela Meeske, 19 April 2004; Kristie Miller's interview with Bazy Tankersley, 17 August 2004, in e-mail to author. Paulina Longworth was forced to use her right hand, even though she was left-handed. Some theories suggest that this forced right-handedness contributes to stammering.

33. "Mrs. Cowles Buried after Simple Service," *NYT*, 28 August 1931, 11. See also "Mrs. W. S. Cowles Dies at Age of 76," *NYT*, 26 August 1931, 16; Caroli, 130–31.

34. Miller, 238.

35. Kristie Miller, e-mail to author, 17

August 2004. Miller wrote that her father so characterized Ruth Hanna McCormick Simms, who was Miller's grandmother. "Alice Longworth Home Is Guarded," *Morning News* [Danville, Pennsylvania], 25 March 1932, 1; Genevieve Forbes Herrick, "Mrs. Longworth Reveals Threat to Seize Paulina," *Chicago Tribune*, 25 March 1932, 3.

36. "Longworth Home Guarded by Police," *NYT*, 25 March 1932, 3; "Kidnapping Threat Again Stirs Capital," *NYT*, 28 March 1932, 3.

37. "Late Speaker," *Cincinnati Enquirer*, 25 May 1932, NLPF; Memorial Address of Hon. Burton L. French, 25 May 1932, clipping from *Congressional Record*, NLIII; "House Mourns Longworth," *NYT*, 10 April 1932, 2; Friends' tribute, "Washington Society," *Chicago Tribune*, 4 April 1932, 19.

38. "Friends of the German People to Organize New Chicago Group," *Chicago Tribune*, 3 April 1932, G1; Walter Davenport, "The Man Who Grew Up," *Collier's*, 10 September 1932, 10, 11; Beverly Smith, "The Lone Rider from Idaho," *American Magazine*, March 1932, 100.

39. "Had a lot of fun," Teague, 159; "I wear no man's brand," Jean Vanden Heuvel, "The Sharpest Wit in Washington," *Saturday Evening Post* 238, 24 (4 December 1965):33; "Nemesis," Teague, 159.

40. ARL telegram to LHH, 24 October 1932, LHHP; "Noted Women Are Active in G.O.P. Campaign," *Chicago Tribune*, 12 October 1932, 6.

41. ARL telegram to LHH, 17 February [1932?], LHHP; for the Christmas present, see ARL to LHH, n.d., LHHP; "Mrs. Dolly Gann to Take Stump," 23 January 1932, 2; "Mrs. Gann Praises Hoover in Omaha Talk," 27 January 1932, 8; both *NYT*; Ruth's donation, Miller, 239.

42. "Look, there's Alice," "Women Delegates Noisier than Men," *NYT*, 15

June 1932, 13; "dared leave enclosure," "Keynoter Gives Women a Place—in Nine Words," *Chicago Tribune*, 15 June 1932, 3.

43. "Butler and White Debate Prohibition," *NYT*, 15 June 1932, 14.

44. "Two Feminine Notables Here Offer Contrast," *Chicago Tribune*, 27 June 1932, 3; "Society Draws No Party Lines When It Comes to Conventions," *Chicago Tribune*, 29 June 1932, 3; "Young for Nominee Is Urged by Malone," *NYT*, 11 April 1932, 3; "Mrs. Longworth and Smith Meet for First Time," *NYT*, 23 July 1932, 2.

45. Arthur M. Schlesinger Jr., *The Crisis of the Old Order* (Boston: Houghton Mifflin, 1957), chap. 28; Geoffrey Ward, *A First-Class Temperament* (New York: Harper & Row, 1989), 784–85.

46. EKR to LHH, 6 August 1932, LHHP; "Notification Made a Social Occasion," *NYT*, 12 August 1932, 1; "700 Dine with Hoover on Lawn at White House," *Chicago Tribune*, 12 August 1932, 8.

47. "President's Speech Is Cheered Wildly," *NYT*, 12 August 1932, 5; "69 Women Appeal in Hoover's Behalf," *NYT*, 26 October 1932, 13; "Mrs. Longworth for Hoover, She Says in Article," 14 October 1932, *NYT*, 4; "Nemi Tale Recalled by Alice Longworth," *NYT*, 14 October 1932, 14.

48. "Republicans Poised for Intensive Drive," *NYT*, 30 September 1932, 11; Genevieve Forbes Herrick, "Women's Angle in Politics Is Amusing, Original, and Quixotic," *Chicago Tribune*, 9 October 1932, G1; "fellow Buck-eyes," "Mrs. Hoover Hailed by Mid-West Crowds," *NYT*, 29 October 1932, 9; "Makes 31-Word Speech," *NYT*, 2 November 1932, 13.

49. "Here's a Sample of Conscious and Unscrupulous Dishonesty," *Cincinnati*

Times-Star, 4 November 1932, clipping from NLPF; see also "Republicans Fight to Hold Woman Vote," 3 November 1932, 17; "Democrats Scored by Mrs. Longworth," 4 November 1932, 10; both *NYT.*

50. "Here's a Sample of Conscious and Unscrupulous Dishonesty," NLPF.

51. EKR to Belle Hagner, 8 August [1933], PHP. In 1932, Edith told Belle, "I feel as she does. . . ." EKR to Belle Hagner, 26 August 1932, PHP. "Women to Aid Davison," *NYT,* 30 August 1932, 4. EKR to Alice French, 6 July 1932, Alice French Papers, Newberry Library, Chicago. For a record of Edith's speech, see Caroli, 206. "Headline Footnotes," *NYT,* 23 October 1932, XX2.

52. "Fifth cousin," Ethel Roosevelt Derby to LHH, undated [1933], LHHP; "The Reporters: Jonathan Aitken Interview with Alice Roosevelt Longworth," [January 1969], Yorkshire Television; "against Franklin," ARL preservation tape, ICD 16024, 20 September 1967, JSP. Alice recalled on this tape that Edith went on to the White House to stay with the Hoovers, to make clear she was for Hoover and not for Franklin Roosevelt. Later in her life, Edith would soften about Franklin.

Chapter 18: **"The Washington Dictatorship"**

1. Harold Nicolson to Vita Sackville-West, 16 February 1933, in Harold Nicolson, *Diaries and Letters, 1930–1939,* Nigel Nicolson, ed. (New York: Athenaeum, 1966), 137.

2. Joseph Alsop, *I've Seen the Best of It* (New York: W. W. Norton, 1992), 91.

3. "Very beautiful," Alsop, 91; "a wit like hers," Alsop, 93.

4. She frequently used "detached malevolence" to describe herself. For an early use of it, see Franz Klein, "Alice Roosevelt

Longworth," 12 June 1946 Draft, for *Die Weltwoche,*" 1, JSP.

5. "Oh, it was grim," ARL preservation tape, ICD 16025, 20 September 1967, JSP; Michael Teague, *Mrs. L* (Garden City, N.Y.: Doubleday, 1981), 170–71. "Hovering around," James Brough, *Princess Alice* (Boston: Little, Brown, 1975), 295; TRJR to FDR, 4 March 1933, TRJRP; Inaugural invitation, 4 March 1933, JSP.

6. Drew Pearson and Richard S. Allen, *Washington Merry-Go-Round* (New York: Blue Ribbon Books, 1931), 11; Samuel Hopkins Adams, *A. Woollcott* (New York: Reynal & Hitchcock, 1945), 176.

7. Alsop, 93.

8. EKR to LHH, 12 August 1933, LHHP; Archibald Roosevelt to Carter Harrison, 8 November 1933, Carter H. Harrison Papers, Newberry Library, Chicago. Harrison was on the New York State advisory board of the Federal Emergency Administration of Public Works.

9. See Peter Collier, *The Roosevelts* (New York: Simon & Schuster, 1994), 271, for "female impersonators"; Doris Kearns Goodwin, *No Ordinary Time* (New York: Simon & Schuster, 1994), 208, for "squaws and she-men." Both authors insist that FDR was fond of these friends of Eleanor's, and Collier drives home the point that they could be "resources" for his career.

10. Marian C. McKenna, *Borah* (Ann Arbor: University of Michigan Press, 1961), 306–307. See also the following *NYT* articles: "Senator Borah Goes Under Knife," 27 June 1933, 19; "Borah Reported Better," 28 June 1933, 23; "Borah Out of Hospital," 30 July 1933, 8. During the fall of 1932, Mary Borah had been seriously ill with "parrot fever," which she was said to have caught from one of the many birds that flew freely around their Washington apartment. See "Mrs. Borah

Afflicted with Parrot Fever," *NYT*, 22 September 1932, 12; "Mrs. Borah Improves After Getting Serum," *NYT*, 25 September 1932, 3.

11. The analogy to guerrilla war is from Brough, 292. "Mr. Rogers Finds Senate 'Fine Bunch of Fellows,'" *NYT*, 29 January 1934, 17. Alice liked Will Rogers. When he died, she agreed to be on a memorial commission to help establish a monument to him in Oklahoma. See "Organize to Build Rogers Memorial," *NYT*, 23 September 1935, 19; Alice's "stunt," "Bureau Chiefs Are Received at White House," *Chicago Tribune*, 2 February 1934, 19; Tinney quoted in Howard Teichmann, *Alice* (Englewood Cliffs, N.J.: Prentice Hall, 1979), 163.

12. "Drop in the bucket," Teague, 161; "wince," Henry Brandon, "A Talk with an 83-Year-Old Enfant Terrible," *NYT*, 6 August 1967, JSP.

13. Brough credits the phrase to EKR not ARL; see his biography, 290. Most other sources credit Alice with it. The percentages vary depending upon the source—but in a backhanded way (because of the era), this is a sort of compliment to ER.

14. These are famous stories, and they appear many places. See, for example, Collier, 345, 387–388; and Teichmann, 156. Brough, 200–298, also contains many of these tales. The first-person quote is from Teague, 161. For the "Mollycoddle" source and ER's response, see Blanche Wiesen Cook, *Eleanor Roosevelt* (New York: Viking, 1999), 2:385–386.

15. Hickock tale from Belle Roosevelt Diaries, 16 April 1943, KBR; Mary Borah, *Elephants and Donkeys* (Moscow, University Press of Idaho, 1976), 141; Henrietta Nesbitt, *White House Diary* (New York: Doubleday, 1949), 172; dinner invitation example, ER to ARL, 7 December 1934, JSP; see also Alice's letter to ER, dated

from the New Deal years, in which Alice thanks ER for volunteering to "look out for Paulina" while Alice was not in Washington (25 October, [?], JSP); "never allow politics," "First Lady Hits Hatreds," *NYT*, 15 November 1938, 12; horrible childhood, author's interview with Kristie Miller, 21 July 1996; "Did you realize," Brough, 298; "could and did damn," Teichmann, 156. If Missy LeHand and FDR were lovers, Alice "insisted" that she "would have heard about it," Brough, 308. Historians have come to different conclusions as to the specifics of an FDR-LeHand relationship.

16. For this last idea, see Collier, 331, 333.

17. Teague, 159.

18. See the handwritten note to "Alma" by ARL at bottom of I. J. Roberts to Alma Zimbalist, 9 March 1936, ARLC, for an example of her symphony work.

19. "Totenberg Hailed in Capital Debut," *NYT*, 8 November 1935, 18. In this article, the violin is identified as a Stradivarius. Alice Dows to ARL, n.d., JSP ("Here is the insurance for a year on the violin...."); "That's the violin," Author's interview with Roman Totenberg, 24 March 2005. Borah's presence, "Garners Honored at White House," *NYT*, 3 January 1936, 22. The occasion was the president's dinner in honor of the vice president, Nick's old friend Cactus Jack Garner.

20. Author's interview with Roman Totenberg; "the work of some skilled copyist," Rembert Wurlitzer to ARL, 31 May 1957, JSP. See also Scott Simon's interview with Roman Totenberg, 22 June 1996, www.npr.org/news/specials/fatherday/. Alice at concerts, Brough, 289. See also Blair Bolles, "Symphony on Potomac," *NYT*, 30 July 1939, X5. Alice did not "hate" Nick, nor was she "hurt" by him at the time of his death (Carol Felsenthal, *Alice Roosevelt Longworth* [New York: G. P.

Putnam's Sons, 1988], 168). Loaning the violin to a protégé of Nick's former lover is more her style. The name of the violinist who borrowed the violin is Charles Tuger or Luger (?). See his thank-you letter to ARL, 17 June 1957, JSP.

21. J. Timberlake Gibson, "The Million Dollar Drop-Out," *Washingtonian*, April 1976, 43.

22. "Book Notes," *NYT*, 23 September 1932, 20; Teague, xvi; Charles Scribner's Sons to ARL, 9 December 1932, JSP. See Loring A. Schuler to ARL, 15 March 1935, for the column ideas; 22 June 1934 for the editing, both ARLC; ARL to Belle Hagner, 6 December 1933, PHP.

23. "Mary B. Eddy Voted 'Greatest Woman,'" *NYT*, 21 December 1932, 21; "Mrs. Longworth Wins Prize Drawn by Her," *NYT*, 18 December 1933, 17; "Alice Roosevelt Sears Notables of Former Days," *Chicago Tribune*, 28 October 1933, 3; Robert Van Gelder, "Books of the Times," *NYT*, 28 October 1933, 13; Edward M. Kingsbury, "Alice Longworth's Vivid Story," *NYT*, 5 November 1933, BR 1; ARL to John T. McCutcheon, 6 December 1933, John T. McCutcheon Papers; Newberry Library, Chicago. Lowden thought the book "full of interest and charm from cover to cover." Frank O. Lowden to ARL, 17 October 1940, Papers of Frank O. Lowden, Special Collections Library, University of Chicago. McClure, founder of the magazine that bore his name, said that he "enjoyed the book very much." Further, he thought her articles "could render a very great service to the country." Samuel McClure to ARL, 3 February 1936, McClure Manuscripts, Manuscripts Department, Lilly Library, Indiana University, Bloomington. See the scanned flyer on http://sdrc.lib.uiowa.edu/traveling-culture/chaul/jpg/longworth/1/1.jpg, courtesy of the Special Collections Department, University of Iowa Libraries; GOP women, May S. Baldwin to ARL, 21 January 1933, ARLC; Mayme C. Althouse to ARL, 21 January 1936, ARLC; Wayne Whipple and ARL, *The Story of the White House and Its Home Life* (Boston: Dwinell-Wright, 1937).

24. The advertisement can be found on page D7, 16 October 1932, *Chicago Tribune*, and on X8 of the same day's *NYT*.

25. TRJR, "Foreword," in *Desk Drawer Anthology*, Alice Roosevelt Longworth and Theodore Roosevelt Jr., eds. (New York: Doubleday, Doran, 1938), xiii–xix.

26. ARL, "What Are the Women Up To?," *Ladies' Home Journal*, 51 (March 1934): 9, 120, 122. ARL's journalist writings pale in comparison to the hundreds of articles her cousin Eleanor wrote.

27. ER to Corinne Alsop, 15 January 1936, reel 1, ER Papers on microfilm; "I don't want anything," Brough, 292.

28. ER, *This I Remember* (New York: Harper & Brothers, 1949), 219–220. See also Cook, 2:416. James A. Farley to ARL, 15 February 1974, JSP; Genevieve Forbes Herrick, "Alice Fails to Applaud Cousin Frank," *Chicago Tribune*, 7 January 1934, E3.

29. Nesbitt, 29.

30. "How disagreeable," ARL preservation tape, ICD 16020, JSP; "There is nothing to that," "First Lady Tells of Joining Guild," *NYT*, 6 January 1937, 16; royal visit, "Simplicity Marks the Garden Party," *NYT*, 9 June 1939, 1; "miserable worm," Brough, 292.

31. Harold L. Ickes, *The Autobiography of a Curmudgeon* (New York: Reynal & Hitchcock, 1943), 244; art exhibit, undated, untitled clipping, JSP.

32. "Beautiful, charming," Teague, 157–58; "did not believe in knowing," Brough, 247; "had so little enjoyment," Teague, 160; for Laura Delano, see Goodwin, 611; "The Reporters: Jonathan Aitken Interview with Alice Roosevelt

Longworth," Yorkshire Television, [January 1969]. In this interview, ARL recalls FDR and Lucy at her home.

33. ER could not be affectionate, author interview with Michael Teague, 3 August 1989. Teague thought that "Mrs. L understood Eleanor better than ER understood herself—or cared to understand herself." For Griselda moods, see ER, *The Autobiography of Eleanor Roosevelt* (New York: Harper & Row, 1978), 59–60. Kenneth S. Davis's description is useful here: "Her tendency to withdraw wholly into herself when hurt, assuming the role of martyr as she raised a wall of silence against those she thought responsible, refusing all their efforts to communicate. She called it her 'Griselda mood.' It was cruelly vengeful. For all its seeming passivity, it was the most devastating kind of psychological aggression when focused upon people of sensitive conscience who deeply cared for her." Kenneth S. Davis, *FDR: Into the Storm, 1937–1940* (New York: Random House, 1993), 303.

34. Teague, 160.

35. Robert L. Mason, "Capital Club Welcomes Chosen Few," *Bethlehem (Penn.) Globe-Times*, n.p., from the George Washington University Alumni Web site, http://www.gwu.edu/~alumni/images/photo/retro. See also "Mrs. J. F. Curtis to Become Club Hostess in F St. Home," 9 April 1933; and Mary Van Renssalaer Thayer, "Though Cozy, It Is Important," *Washington Post and Times Herald*, 2 March 1955, from the same Web site; see also "The F Street Club, 'a Nice Quiet Place,'" *NYT*, 26 April 1983, B6.

36. "Alice Longworth Sails for Europe," *NYT*, 18 July 1935, 21; "Thousands in Rush to Hear Roosevelt," *NYT*, 23 May 1935, 2. ARL, "The National Scene," unidentified newspaper, 4 June 1936, JSP. Ezra Pound to WEB, 10 October 1935, in Sarah C. Holmes, ed. *The Correspondence of Ezra Pound and Senator William Borah* (Chicago: University of Illinois Press, 2001), 42.

37. Fred W. Carpenter to ARL, 9 January 1936, ARLC.

38. "You can always tell," ARL, "The National Scene," unidentified newspaper, 11 June 1936, JSP.

39. ARL, "The National Scene," unidentified newspaper, 28 May 1936, JSP. For quotes in the following two paragraphs: "a direct move," 15 February 1936; "American agriculture," 9 January 1936; "black soil magic," 11 January 1936; Paraguay, 13 March 1936, all JSP.

40. "As for Mrs Roosevelt's," Edith Dickey Moses to ARL, 10 January 1936, ARLC; Margaret Cobb Ailshie to ARL, 21 January 1936, ARLC. Idahoan Ailshie was a friend of Alice's from the First Daughter days. "We have been paying," James Telfer, letter to the editor, undated and unidentified; attached to Paul Block to ARL, 23 January 1936, ARLC. This document was also attached to E. C. Vandyke to ARL and identified by Vandyke as being from the *Milwaukee Journal*, 22 January 1936, ARLC; "keen and clear cut," A. H. Clambrey to ARL, 24 January 1935, ARLC; "why am I," William D. Sohier to ARL, 23 January 1936, ARLC.

41. "I cannot afford," Elizabeth T. Cedergren to ARL, 20 January 1936, ARLC; "woman columnist," James E. Coleman to ARL, 22 January 1926, ARLC.

42. Several letters remark upon Alice's courage. See, for example, Catherine Burton Spenser to ARL, 16 January 1936, ARLC; for "good for" the U.S.A., Laura Winans McDaniel, 31 January 1936, ARLC. For comparisons to TR, see Fred B. Jacobs to ARL, 29 January 1936; Arthur R. Atkinson to ARL, 22 January 1936; J. T. McGuire to ARL, 18 January 1936; all ARLC; "candidates picked out," James H. Throop to ARL, 30 January 1936, ARLC.

43. ARL, "The National Scene," 18 June 1936, unidentified newspaper, JSP.

44. Unidentified poem, sent to ARL from "R.C.," 20 November 1943, JSP.

45. James Reston, *Deadline: A Memoir* (New York: Random House, 1991), 104; the poem "Rejected" was attributed to James Knupp, n.d., JSP.

46. M. V. Atwood to V. V. McNitt, 19 February 1936. See also George Fergus Kelley to ARL, 16 April 1936. Kelley wanted to see her "get more punch" in her articles. "This seems to be the universal criticism," he wrote. Both letters are in the ARLC.

47. "Certainly writes well," Cook, 2:433; "Eleanor vs. Alice," unidentified clipping, n.d., NLP; "terribly shy" is from ARL preservation tape, ICD 16022, 28 June 1967, JSP; Elise French Linn to ARL, n.d., ARLC (emphasis in original).

48. Jonathan Mitchell, "Borah Knows Best," *New Republic*, 29 January 1936, 334; WEB to Ezra Pound, 3 January 1934, in Holmes, ed., 4; Tim Redman, *Ezra Pound and Italian Fascism* (Cambridge: Cambridge University Press, 1991), 89.

49. For Borah as TR's heir, see, for example, the poem written by Joe Butin, 25 February 1936, WEBLC; William Hard, "Foreword" in William E. Borah, *Bedrock: Views on Basic National Problems* (Washington, D.C.: National Home Library Foundation, 1936), 5, 6.

50. Frederic C. Walcott to ARL, 6 April 1934, JSP; "15th Anniversary to Be Marked Saturday By Women's National Republican Club," *NYT,* 12 January 1936, N8. See also Kathleen McLaughlin, "New Year Finds Women's Organizations Planning Many New Activities," *NYT,* 5 January 1936, N7. For Liberty League dinner, "National Figures Among the Guests," *NYT,* 26 January 1936, 37. "R. A. Taft Is Named Ohio 'Favorite Son,'" *NYT,* 28 February 1936, 2.

51. "Mrs. Longworth a Delegate," *NYT,* 14 May 1936, 6; " 'Princess Alice' Arrives and Doubles in Brass as Delegate and Writer," unidentified clipping, 5 June 1936, JSP; Kathleen McLaughlin, "Women Outnumber Men at Roll-Call," *NYT,* 7 June 1936, 33; Arthur Krock, "Steiwer Avoids Rifts," *NYT,* 10 June 1936, 1; for Reeves, see Kathleen McLaughlin, "Women Maintain Leading Roles in Many Phases of the Convention Activities," *NYT,* 11 June 1936, 16.

52. ARL, "The National Scene," unidentified newspaper, 15 June 1936, JSP.

53. Mary Roberts Rinehart to ARL, 5 April 1936, ARLC; "Republicans Summon Women's 1919 Council," *NYT,* 19 August 1936, 13.

54. "Spirit of black," ARL, "The National Scene," unidentified newspaper, 26 June 1936, JSP; "to assume a leadership," and "Fuehrer, Duce, Roosevelt," ARL, "The National Scene," unidentified newspaper, 30 June 1936, JSP; dare, ARL, "The National Scene," unidentified newspaper, 25 June 1936, JSP.

55. "Services Here Honor Quentin Roosevelt," *NYT,* 15 July 1936, 21; "whiskey for breakfast," Edward J. Renehan, Jr., *The Lion's Pride* (New York: Oxford University Press, 1998), 229.

56. "Oyster Bay Shrine Visited by Landon," *NYT,* 30 October 1936, 17. At tea were Edith; Ethel and Dick and their daughter Edith; Belle; and Ted and Eleanor.

57. "Citizens Join Broadcast," *NYT,* 3 November 1936, 14.

58. Alexander Woollcott to Ralph Hates, 28 September 1936, in Woollcott's *The Letters of Alexander Woollcott* (New York: Viking, 1944), 171. For the gloating, see his letter to Stephen Early, 20 October 1936, 172. "Imminent demise," Lewis L. Gould, *Grand Old Party* (New York: Random House, 2003), 274.

59. Edwin P. Hoyt, *Alexander Woollcott* (New York: Abelard-Schuman, 1968), 283. "Notes of the Fair," *NYT*, 18 November 1937, 21.

60. American Tobacco Company: Your Hit Parade and Sweepstakes, 3 February 1937, JSP.

61. June Bingham, "Before the Colors Fade," *American Heritage*, February 1969, 76.

Chapter 19: **"I Believe in the Preservation of This Republic"**

1. Alice was unable to forget the role she thought Borah played in bringing Harding to power in 1920. See ARL, "The National Scene," unidentified newspaper, 3 June 1936, JSP.

2. Borah's speech appears in Marian C. McKenna, *Borah* (Ann Arbor: University of Michigan Press, 1961), 370. The rest of the information here comes from McKenna, 370–372. See also "Borah Dies," *Chicago Tribune*, 20 January 1940, 1; "William E. Borah, Senator 33 Years, Is Dead in Capital," *NYT*, 20 January 1940, 1.

3. *Acceptance of the Statue of William Edgar Borah Presented by the State of Idaho* (Washington, D.C.: Government Printing Office, 1948), 25.

4. *Acceptance of the Statue*, 26, 27.

5. "President Pays Tribute to Dean of U.S. Senate," *Chicago Tribune*, 20 January 1940, 12.

6. Mary Borah, of course, received all the formal sympathy notes, such as the one from former First Lady LHH, n.d., LHHP; for funeral train, see "Idaho Plans Day of Mourning," *NYT*, 23 January 1940, 12.

7. "Frightful struggle," WEB to ARL, n.d., JSP; "read in my message," WEB to ARL, n.d., JSP.

8. "Alice Roosevelt Longworth's Political Intensity Grows," unidentified clipping, n.d., JSP; ARL, pencil fragment, n.d. ("We must get the power of decision..."), JSP.

9. "Portable university," Richard Langham Riedel, *Halls of the Mighty* (New York: Robert B. Luce, 1969), 149; Robert A. Taft to ARL, 7 December 1939, in Clarence E. Wunderlin Jr., ed., *The Papers of Robert A. Taft, 1939–1944* (Kent, Ohio: Kent State University Press, 2001), 2:95; Willkie quote from Lewis L. Gould, *Grand Old Party* (New York: Random House, 2003), 280.

10. ARL, pencil fragment, n.d., JSP.

11. ARL to TRJR, 26 August 1939, TRJRP.

12. Fish quote from Harold B. Hinton, "Borah Declares Real Neutrality Impossible for Us," *NYT*, 22 April 1939, 1; Elizabeth Wheeler Colman, *Mrs. Wheeler Goes to Washington* (Helena, Mont.: Falcon Press, 1989), 177.

13. Robert Ingrim, "Alice Roosevelt Longworth," draft, 12 June 1946, for *Die Weltwoche*, 3, JSP; Robert James Maddox, *William E. Borah and American Foreign Policy* (Baton Rouge: Louisiana State University Press, 1969), 226.

14. Arthur Schlesinger Jr., *A Life in the Twentieth Century* (New York: Houghton Mifflin, 2000), 238.

15. Wayne S. Cole, *America First* (New York: Octagon Books, 1971), 7–8.

16. "We demand that Congress," Justus D. Doenecke, ed., *In Danger Undaunted* (Stanford, Calif.: Hoover Institution Press, 1990), 7; Bill Kauffman interview with Robert Douglas Stuart Jr. in Ruth Sarles, *A Story of America First* (Westport, Conn.: Praeger, 2003), 208; see also Colman, 193–96.

17. "America First Creed," in Sarles, lv–lvi.

18. Robert Douglas Stuart Jr. interview in Sarles, 211; for members, see "Contribution Card" and 1940 stationery in the

Papers of Frank O. Lowden, Special Collections Library, University of Chicago and Colman, 194; Bernard K. Johnpoll, *Pacifist's Progress* (Chicago: Quadrangle Books, 1970), 228–31; "Reidy" Reid, "America First" (New York: Dixie Music Publishing, c. 1941), Papers of Frank O. Lowden, Special Collections Library University of Chicago.

19. Sarles, 4; Doenecke, xii. For the number of members, see Wayne S. Cole, "The America First Committee," *Journal of the Illinois State Historical Society* XLIV, 1 (Spring 1951): 312.

20. Robert A. Taft to Robert Hunter, 20 November 1940, Robert Hunter Papers, Indiana Historical Society, Indianapolis; "America First Committee: Aims and Activities," ARP; Robert L. Bliss, America First Cmmittee [hereafter AFC] Bulletin #281, Robert E. Wood Papers, HHPL.

21. "How to Organize Chapters of the AFC," 4, ARP; the 3 December 1940 resolution concerning Ford can be found in Sarles, 65.

22. "How to Organize Chapters of the AFC," 1.

23. R. E. Wood, America First press release, n.d., Robert E. Wood Papers, HHPL. In fact, the AFC felt so indebted to the *Tribune* that Stuart wrote to Lillian Gish suggesting that she write a letter of thanks to Colonel Robert McCormick. See Robert Douglas Stuart Jr. to Lillian Gish, 22 July 1941, Papers of Lillian Gish, LC.

24. James Reston, *Deadline* (New York: Random House, 1991), 103–104; see AFC Bulletin #190, 9 April 1941, AFC; Geraldine Buchanan Parker to "Dear Fellow Citizen," n.d., Robert E. Wood Papers, HHPL.

25. J. H. Reis, M.D., to Lillian Gish, 30 March 1941, Lillian Gish Papers, LC. See Lillian Gish's thank-you to ARL, n.d., JSP.

26. Lindberg at the Longworths, Betty Beale, "Mrs. Longworth Can No Longer Resist the Temptation!" clipping, n.d., JSP; Charles Lindbergh's speech is printed in full in Sarles, 65–69. The quote begins on page 67.

27. The meeting was held on 18 September. Lindbergh was also present. Sarles, 56. ARL appeared to have missed more National Committee meetings than she attended. She was not present at the March 1941 meeting, the 28 November 1941 meeting, or the 11 December 1941 meeting. See Frank O. Lowden Papers, Special Collections Library, University of Chicago. News release, "Chapters Please Release Immediately," 24 September 1941, Robert E. Wood Papers, HHPL.

28. "Condemn his speech," quoted in Johnpoll, 231; "89%" Sarles, 56; Hyman Lischner's letter is printed in full in Sarles, 64–65. On page 49, Lischner is described as a "physician of Los Angeles and former president of B'nai B'rith at San Diego." Lindbergh's speech written six months earlier, Sarles, 57; "Lindbergh, Willkie, and the Jews," *Chicago Tribune*, n.d.; text in Robert E. Wood Papers, HHPL; For a list of noninterventionist Jews see Sarles, 49–50; "politically unwise" Cole, "The America First Committee," 321.

29. "Lindbergh Views Hotly Assailed," *NYT*, 31 August 1941, 18.

30. Kermit Roosevelt to Ethel Roosevelt Derby, 7 February 1941, RFPH; Kermit Roosevelt to Wendell K. Willkie, 3 May 1941, KBR; Alexander Woollcott, *The Letters of Alexander Woollcott* (New York: Viking, 1944), 275; Maclean story from Katharine Graham, *Personal History* (New York: Knopf, 1997), 156; Alsop quote from Robert W. Merry, *Taking on the World* (New York: Viking, 1996), 90.

31. For Ted and Eleanor, see "Minutes of a Meeting of Executive Committee of New York Chapter America First, 8 April

1941," ARP; Ted and WWII, Edward J. Renehan, Jr., *The Lion's Pride* (New York: Oxford University Press, 1998), 228–29; for Ruth's involvement, see AFC Bulletin #691, 19 November 1941, Robert E. Wood Papers, HHPL. For Ruth's donation, see Cole, "The America First Committee," 315. "America First Group Names Some Donors," *New York Herald Tribune*, 12 March 1941; clipping in the Robert E. Wood Papers, HHPL, lists Barnes and McCutcheon.

32. Henry L. Stimson and McGeorge Bundy, *On Active Service in Peace and War* (New York: Harper & Brothers, 1947–1948), 375; Cole, "The America First Committee," 305.

33. "It is hardly fair," typed fragment, n.d. ("The result of the election last November…"), JSP. Belle Roosevelt Diaries, 16 April 1943, KBR.

34. Robert E. Wood to John T. Flynn, 12 December 1941, ARP; "The Debate Is Over," *NYT*, 13 December 1941, ARP.

35. Eleanor Butler Roosevelt to ARL, 2 August [?], JSP; Eleanor Butler Roosevelt, *Day Before Yesterday* (Garden City, N.Y.: Doubleday, 1959), 399–400.

36. Harold V. Boyle, "Lt. Quentin Roosevelt Wounded in Action on Tunisian Front," unidentified clipping, JSP. For the bullet story from the family, TRJR to Richard and Ethel Roosevelt Derby, 29 March 1943; TRJR to Ethel Roosevelt Derby, [?] March 1943; both RFPH; TRJR to Ethel Roosevelt Derby, 10 February 1943, ERDP, for the promotion. For a cheery letter to Alice, see Quentin Roosevelt to ARL, 29 March 1943, JSP; Grace Stackpole Roosevelt to EKR, 25 January 1943, Archibald Bulloch Roosevelt Family Papers, Harvard University.

37. Belle Roosevelt Diaries, 16 April 1943, KBR.

38. Joseph W. Alsop, *"I've Seen the Best of It"* (New York: W. W. Norton, 1992),

120; Frank Kent to ARL, 21 October 1944, and 9 July 1944 JSP; "Frank R. Kent, 80, Columnist, Dead," *NYT*, 15 April 1958, 33.

39. Bill Walton knew John L. Lewis and said this about him. Author's interview with Walton, 27 May 1994.

40. See Michael Teague, *Mrs. L.* (Garden City, N.Y.: Doubleday, 1981) 187, for Alice's quotes in this paragraph; Elsa Maxwell, "Elsa Maxwell's Party Line," *New York Post*, 21 January 1944, 12, JSP.

41. All quotes from JLL to ARL, 8 October 1943, JSP. The "Dear Aquarian" salutation is 17 July 1943, JSP.

42. JLL to ARL, [n.d. 1944], JSP.

43. JLL to ARL, 26 December 1944, JSP. Lewis was in a high-rise hotel in Indianapolis; Alice was home. ALL stood for Alice Lee Longworth.

44. JLL to ARL, 16 October 1943, JSP.

45. Melvin Dubofsky and Warren Van Tine, *John L. Lewis* (Chicago: University of Illinois Press, 1987), 285; JLL to ARL, 16 October 1943, JSP.

46. "Doubted whether Franklin," Belle Roosevelt Diaries, 29 March 1943; FDR's view of Winant, Belle Roosevelt Diaries, 20–21 March 1943, KBR.

47. Archibald Roosevelt to Ethel Roosevelt Derby, 26 June 1943, RFPH.

48. "Mrs. Roosevelt, Sr., Gains," *NYT*, 17 November 1935, 17.

49. Sylvia Jukes Morris, *Edith Kermit Roosevelt* (New York: Coward, McCann, & Geoghegan, 1980), chap. 38; "Services Are Held for Gen. Roosevelt," *NYT*, 25 July 1944, 9; Renehan, 233–240; *Medal of Honor Recipients, 1863–1978* (Washington, D.C.: U.S. Government Printing Office, 1979), 668; "Brig. Gen. Roosevelt Dies," *Chicago Tribune*, 14 July 1944, 1.

50. For Archie's service in WWII, see Renehan, 232–33.

Chapter 20: "Full Sixty Years the World Has Been Her Trade"

1. "The Reporters: Jonathan Aitken Interview with Alice Roosevelt Longworth," Yorkshire Television, [January 1969].

2. William Fulton, "Wives of Eisenhower's Aides Are Busy Buying New Plumage for Capital Whirl," Chicago Tribune, 8 December 1952, B2.

3. Darrah Wunder, "A Funny Thing Happened to Me on the Way to the White House," Leeword (September [?]), 4, MssVP2386, CHS.

4. "War is an inevitable thing," "Alice and Ruth Are Here!'" unidentified clipping, 22 June 1944, JSP. Alsop on Mrs. L from Alsop's unpublished memoir, author's possession.

5. ARL preservation tape, ICD 16031, 20 September 1967, JSP. Alice's evening with Hubble, her daughter, and her friends Mildred and Robert Bliss and Mary Beale took place around 1939. By that date, Hubble had published three books of lectures. Alice likely read The Realm of the Nebulae (London: Oxford University Press, 1936).

6. Rachel Carson to ARL, 15 June 1951, JSP.

7. Author's interview with Bill Walton, 27 May 1994.

8. ARL preservation tape, ICD 16031, 20 September 1967, JSP.

9. Larry McMurtry, Walter Benjamin at the Dairy Queen (New York: Simon & Schuster, 1999), 138.

10. Hope Ridings Miller, "Capital Whirl," Washington Post, 18 June 1942; "Paulina Longworth Makes Her Debut at Cincinnati Club," unidentified clipping, [1942]; "Paulina Longworth Makes Bow Tonight at Cincinnati," Washington Evening Star, [1942], all JSP. Angela Meeske, a contemporary of Paulina's, recalled that on the night of the debut, "Alice was mighty imposing, but very agreeable." Angela Meeske to author, n.d. 2004. On the engagement, see "Engagement of Interest," Cincinnati Enquirer, August 1944, Paulina Longworth Sturm Princeton File, CHS; Judith Cass, "Ex-Chicagoan to Wed Miss Longworth," Chicago Tribune, 7 August 1944, 13.

11. Kermit Roosevelt to John C. Greenway, 28 November 1924, Greenway AHS. "Alice Longworth Asks Mellon to Spare Building," NYT, 16 February 1936, 28. It was the Hunt and Riding School, at Twenty-second and P Streets in Washington, D.C. Author's interview with David Mitchell, 26 October 2001; and with Bazy Tankersley, 19 July 1996. Mrs. Tankersley thinks that Paulina's stutter may have been the result of her having been forced to use her right hand when she was innately left-handed, as mentioned earlier. Like her godfather, David Mitchell, Joanna Sturm believes that her mother was very fond of "Waldie" (Dorothy Waldron), and that the affection was returned. Author's interview with Joanna Sturm, 11 June 2006.

12. Margaret [Blake?], 10 August 1943, JSP. See also Herbert Bayard Swope to ARL, 18 August 1944, JSP; JSG to ARL, 10 August 1944, JSP.

13. Howard Teichmann, Alice (Englewood Cliffs, N.J.: Prentice Hall, 1979), 189. For more about "Dewey was a frightful bore—an incompetent little man," see ARL preservation tapes, ICD 16035, [summer 1968], JSP; Clayton Fritchie, "A Politician Must Watch His Wit," NYT, 3 July 1960, SM8.

14. Isabel Kinnear Griffin to ARL, 13 November 1968, JSP. For an example of Alice denying the quip, this one from her ninetieth year, see Norma Milligan, "She Says What She Thinks," Modern Maturity, June–July 1974, 10. Alice told Michael Teague that she thought she had overheard

it at a party. See Michael Teague, *Mrs. L* (Garden City, N.Y.: Doubleday, 1981), xiv.

15. Taft helped Alice find hotel rooms. See Robert A. Taft to Katharine Kennedy Brown, 18 May 1944, in Clarence E. Wunderlin Jr., ed. *The Papers of Robert A. Taft, Volume 2, 1939–1944,* (Kent, Ohio: Kent State University Press, 2001), 548; "Alice and Ruth Are Here!' " For Paulina as a page, see Thalia, "Chicago Host to Many Noted G.O.P. Women," *Chicago Tribune,* 2 July 1944, E1; Penciled draft, n.d. "There seems to be at least a serious...," JSP.

16. For Bricker, see Lewis L. Gould, *Grand Old Party* (New York: Random House, 2003), 296; Richard Norton Smith, *Thomas E. Dewey and His Times* (New York: Simon & Schuster, 1982), 278–279. Benzedrine is an amphetamine. "Outthink almost everyone," is from Richard Langham Riedel, *Halls of the Mighty* (New York: Robert B. Luce, 1969), 150. See Robert A. Taft to Henry F. Pringle, 4 March 1938, in *The Papers of Robert A. Taft, Volume 1,* (Kent, Ohio: Kent State University Press, 1997), 559. See also "Taft Takes Critic on Congress Tour," *NYT,* 16 June 1944, 21; Marcia Winn, "Front Views & Profiles," *Chicago Tribune,* 30 June 1944, 10.

17. "Politics Losing Hatred's Spice, Alice Laments," *Chicago Tribune,* 23 June 1944, 9; Author's interview with Robert Hellman, 25 April 2005.

18. "Miss Longworth Becomes Bride in East Today," *Chicago Tribune,* 26 August 1944, 13; Katherine McCormick Sturm to ARL, 28 August 1944, JSP.

19. Ruth's health failing, Albert Simms to ARL, 16 February 1945, JSP; Bazy McCormick Miller to ARL, 8 March 1945, JSP. See "Mrs. Simms, G.O.P. Leader, Dies in Sleep," *Chicago Tribune,* 1 January 1945, 1; "Ruth Hanna Simms, Republican

Figure," *NYT,* 1 January 1945, 19. Triny was Ruth's eldest daughter—Katharine Augusta McCormick. She married Courtlandt Barnes Jr. and became publisher of *Common Sense.* Ruth and Alice as monkeys, author's interview with Bazy Tankersley, 31 May 2006. See also Kristie Miller, *Ruth Hanna McCormick* (Albuquerque: University of New Mexico Press, 1992) 132. "Freud and religion and sex," 2 August 1917, ARL Diary, JSP.

20. ER to ARL, 18 April 1945, JSP; Joseph Alsop, *I've Seen the Best of It* (New York: W. W. Norton, 1992), 91.

21. Isabella Greenway King to John Selmes Greenway, 20 August 1945, Greenway AHS. For more on Alice's worries about Paulina and Alex, see JLL to ARL, 21 August 1945, JSP; JLL to ARL, 12 August 1945, JSP.

22. "For Relief to Austria," *NYT,* 1 November 1945, 25.

23. David Mitchell, Alex Sturm's college roommate, said the "marriage was in terrible trouble because of alcohol." Author's interview with David Mitchell, 26 October 2001. JLL to ARL, n.d., 1946, JSP.

24. "Mrs. Edith Roosevelt 85 Years Old Today," *NYT,* 6 August 1946, 35; EKR to ARL, 27 August 1946, JSP.

25. Archie Roosevelt to ARL, 6 August 1950, JSP; Edith Kermit Roosevelt Barmine to ARL, 25 September 1948, JSP. Clipping enclosed, Cholly Knickerbocker, "The Smart Set," 23 September 1948, *New York Journal-American*; Selwa Roosevelt, *Keeper of the Gate* (New York: Simon & Schuster, 1990), 159.

26. Philip B. Perlman to ARL, 24 August 1951, JSP; Felix Frankfurter to ARL, n.d.; 15 January 1955; 15 July 1955; 3 December 1955; all JSP; Frances Spatz and David Camelon, "Legendary Ladies: Rebellious 'Princess Alice,' " *American Weekly,* 12 November 1950, 25.

27. Robert Ingrim, "Alice Roosevelt Longworth," draft, 12 June 1946, for *Die Weltwoche*, 5, and 6, JSP.

28. C. D. Bachelor to ARL, n.d., JSP; for a reproduction of the cartoon, see Teague, 192; online transcript of Walter Trohan interview by Jerry N. Hess, 7 October 1979, 61, 62; Harry S Truman Presidential Library, Independence, Missouri, http://www.trumanlibrary.org/oralhist/trohan.htm#transcript. See also "Walter Trohan to Head Staff at Convention," *Chicago Tribune*, 6 August 1956, 4. Malcolm Muggeridge to ARL, 24 August 1947, JSP. Muggeridge's conversion to Christianity was a quarter century in his future.

29. See, for example, "These Charming People," *Washington Times-Herald*, 4 June 1944, for a photograph of Senator and Martha Taft, and Cissy and Alice, who are holding hands and smiling. See also Ralph Martin, *Cissy* (New York: Simon & Schuster, 1979), 293–294.

30. Author's interview with Bazy Tankersley, 19 July 1996. See also the following articles from the *Chicago Tribune*: "Ruth Elizabeth McCormick to Be Married," 24 June 1941, 15; "Miss Ruth Elizabeth McCormick Wed in Little Country Church," 30 August 1941, 11; "Ruth McCormick Miller and Husband Buy a Paper," 12 October 1946, 13; "Illinois Judge Grants Divorce to Mrs. Miller," 13 January 1951, 10; "Newsman Wed to Mrs. Miller in Washington," 1 June 1951, 4.

31. Edith Hamilton to ARL, 28 January 1947 and 8 February 1951, both JSP; JLL to ARL, 9 February 1947, JSP.

32. For this story, see James A. Michener, *The World Is My Home* (New York: Random House, 1992), 287–288. For a competing story, see Peter Khiss, "Hemingway Lost Pulitzer in 1941," *NYT*, 20 April 1966, 49, which states that Krock, in response to ARL's telephone call, "forcefully relayed the opinion" to the rest of the committee, which then resulted in Michener's winning the prize.

33. William Wright, *The Washington Game* (New York: E. P. Dutton, 1974), 21, 20; author interview with David Mitchell.

34. "Draw people out," Bazy Tankersley quoted in Kristie Miller e-mail to author, 22 May 2003; "It was fun," author interview with Janie McLaughlin, 26 May 1994.

35. Dean Acheson to Joseph Alsop, 26 May 1947, JSAP. On Acheson's resemblance to the tiger, see Page-A-Day Notes to author from Joanna Sturm and Kristie Miller, n.d. 2003, and "The Reporters: Jonathan Aitken Interview with Alice Roosevelt Longworth," Yorkshire Television, [January 1969].

36. Ingrim, 4.

37. Ruth Montgomery, "D.C. Wash," *Chicago Tribune*, 10 March 1951, 7. Alice and Martha Taft were photographed in 1947, for example, at the hearings on "Greek-Turkish loans," and the Senate Education and Labor Committee. See "Personalities," *NYT*, 6 April 1947, SM8 and 16 February 1947, SM24. William Moore, "Invite Yourself Out, A Senator Advises Pauley," *Chicago Tribune*, 21 February 1946, 11; Phillip Dodd, "Leahy Helped on Plane Deal, Kaiser Claims," *Chicago Tribune*, 30 July 1947, 1.

38. "White House Wins on Reorganization," *NYT*, 19 March 1938, 1; Willard Edwards, "Urges Horse Whipping of Wheeler Smearers," *Chicago Tribune*, 18 July 1946, 1.

39. Gould, 311.

40. Louis Starr, "Hits Government," *NYT*, 8 March 1947, 1 (for "extended his hand") and 3 (for the "wordplay").

41. JLL to ARL, 16 January 1952 and 31 December 1957; "tired man," JLL to ARL, 27 November 1945; John Chamberlain to ARL, 21 August 1949 and; JLL to ARL, 7 September 1949, all JSP.

42. ARL quoted in James Brough, *Princess Alice* (Boston: Little, Brown, 1975), 192. The original source is a *Boston Globe* interview, 17 August 1975, JSP; "Be subtle," JLL to ARL, 17 May 1948, JSP.

43. The information in this paragraph comes from "Our Backing Asked for U.S. of Europe," *NYT*, 18 April 1947, 12, and "New Group Backs Federated Europe," *NYT*, 24 April 1947, 3.

44. Harold L. Ickes to Joseph Alsop, 21 July 1948, JSAP.

45. "Film Stars, Writers, and Artists Promise to Work for Taft," *Chicago Tribune*, 27 April 1948, 8. "Women in their 20's Organized for Taft," *NYT*, 23 April 1948, 16; "Spur 'Twenties for Taft,'" *Chicago Tribune*, 24 April 1948, 2. Ruth's daughter Bazy Tankersley has no memory of Paulina being meaningfully involved with the campaign, or interested at all in politics. Author telephone interview with Bazy Tankersley, 1 June 2006. Didn't vote for Dewey ARL to Joseph Lash, 27 January 1972, JSP; "Soufflé" "New New Deal," *NYT*, 14 November 1948, E1. In 1945, when Truman ascended to the presidency, Alice Longworth may have said, "Henry Wallace talked about the common man, and lost the Presidency. Harry Truman was the common man, and got it." It would have been just as appropriate in 1948. Charles Poore, "Common Man-Hunt," *NYT*, 19 September 1948, BR5.

46. "My strength," EKR to ARL, 27 April 1944, JSP; "Dearest Alice," EKR to ARL, n.d. [1948], JSP.

47. ARL, scrap on The Ritz-Carlton's stationery, 12 February [1948], JSP.

48. Dorothy Pound to ARL, 4 April 1949, JSP; Joseph Alsop to Robert Lowell, 11 March 1949, and Robert Lowell to Joseph Alsop, n.d. [1949], JSAP. For Marcella Comes Winslow, see Teresa Moore, "A Washington Life," *Washington Post Magazine*, 9 July 1989, 27. For Alice's

memories, see Jean Vanden Heuvel, "The Sharpest Wit in Washington," *Saturday Evening Post* 238, 24 (4 December 1965), 32.

49. This background information comes from Nathaniel Weyl, *Treason* (Washington, D.C.: Public Affairs Press, 1950) and Tim Redman, *Ezra Pound and Italian Fascism* (Cambridge: Cambridge University Press, 1991). Redman clearly exposes the racism and anti-Semitism of both Ezra and Dorothy Pound.

50. E. Fuller Torrey, *The Roots of Treason* (New York: McGraw Hill, 1984), 219, 239; author's interview with Joanna Sturm, 25 April 2005. Poetry anthology, see J. J. Wilhelm, *Ezra Pound* (University Park: The Pennsylvania State University Press, 1994), 280.

51. Catherine Seelye, ed., *Charles Olson and Ezra Pound* (New York: Viking, 1975), xv. For Olson's phrase, see page 18; for the list of judges instrumental in awarding Pound the Bollingen Prize, see Wilhelm, 277–278. For the controversies, see the rest of that chapter, especially page 280, which also explains that it was Cairns who first brought ARL to see Pound.

52. "Intellectually damaging," Anthony Lewis, "Poets Carry Day for Ezra Pound," *NYT*, 20 April 1958, E7. For Pound's release, see Wilhelm, 308–311; Torrey, 253–60; "Not a danger," Author interview with Robert Hellman, 25 April 2005.

53. For pass, Mary A. Cassidy to ARL, 14 November 1949, JSP; Eleanor Butler Roosevelt to "Lloyd," 17 December 1949, Lewis L. Gould Collection, Monmouth College Archives, Hewes Library, Monmouth College, Monmouth, Illinois; the book Eleanor was reading was probably written by Francis L. Wellman (New York: Macmillan, 1946); "Emily" [no last name] to ARL, 5 November 1950, JSP.

54. Drew Pearson, *Drew Pearson Diaries, 1949–1959* (New York: Holt, Rine-

hart, and Winston, 1974), 171. The entry for 19 June 1951, called Taft, "a great pal of McCarthy's."

55. "Visits Chicago," *Chicago Tribune*, 4 August 1950, 5.

56. "Turn our country away," "Wedemeyer Hails Taft as 'Realist,'" *NYT*, 6 May 1952, 23; "You know where TAFT stands," advertisement, *NYT*, 26 May 1952, 15; Eleanor Page, "Arlington Races Share Spotlight with Visitors," *Chicago Tribune*, 5 July 1952, A3; Eleanor Page, "Meet the Women Leaders at the Convention," *Chicago Tribune*, 7 July 1952, B7; Elizabeth Rannells, "Have You Heard?" *Chicago Tribune*, 20 July 1952, E3.

57. Eisenhower quote, Teague, 194; Richard M. Nixon, *RN*, (New York: Warner Books, 1978), 103–104; the quote is on page 104.

58. "Daughter of a President Helps Eisenhower Drive," *NYT*, 4 October 1952, 8; Dwight D. Eisenhower to ARL, 15 January 1953, JSP; Doug Wead, *All the Presidents' Children* (New York: Atria Books, 2003), 357. According to Wead, John Roosevelt also campaigned for Richard Nixon; ARL to Ethel Roosevelt Derby, 23 December 1952, ERDP.

59. ARL draft of a letter to Eisenhower, 2 February 1953, and Dwight D. Eisenhower to ARL, 14 February 1953, both JSP; Bess Furman, "White House Plans Old Social Whirl," *NYT*, 4 October 1953, 62; Dwight D. Eisenhower to ARL, 14 February 1953, JSP.

60. From Ethel's letter to Alice it appears that the two sisters most often stood opposed to Archie when dissention arose concerning their father. Ethel Roosevelt Derby to ARL, 1 August 1957, JSP. Ruby Douglas Evans, "Sagamore Hill, Old Home of 'T.R.,' Soon May Be a Presidential Shrine," *NYT*, 19 March 1951, 28; Edith Evans Asbury, "T.R.'s Descendants Stir Echo of Past," *NYT*, 15 June 1953, 1;

"The Texts of Eisenhower Speeches at Dartmouth and Oyster Bay," *NYT*, 15 June 1953, 10.

61. John Morton Blum, *A Life with History* (Lawrence: University Press of Kansas, 2004), 89–90.

62. "Hoover to Head Foundation Set Up as Taft Memorial," *Chicago Tribune*, 14 July 1954, 16; "Utah Snubs U.N. Day," *NYT*, 7 October 1954, 7.

63. "With Pat Nixon," Anthony Leviero, "Stennis Asserts McCarthy Poured 'Slime' on Senate," *NYT*, 13 November 1954, 1; "Detached malovelence," unidentified clipping, Hermann Hagedorn, Interviews Relating to Roosevelt Women, Harvard University; Author interview with Bill Walton. See also Teague, 197, for "perfect jay" and 199 for "truckman." The "friend" mentioned was Robert Hellman; author interview with Hellman, 25 April 2005.

64. Richard M. Nixon to ARL, 28 December 1954, JSP. See "The Tragedy of McCarthy," *Los Angeles Times*, 9 December 1954, which Richard Nixon included in his letter to Alice and called "just about the best analysis which has been written with regard to the unhappy ending of the McCarthy affair." For the McCarthy-Pearson fight, Nixon, 170; "political advantage ARL preservation tape, ICD 16021, 25 May 1967, JSP; for invitation assistance, Laura Gross to ARL, 7 February 1951, JSP; "took time off," "Nixon Is Briefed on Key Subjects," *NYT*, 2 October 1955, 49; ARL appointment calendar, 1959, JSP. And the summer months are virtually empty, as Alice would have been out of Washington then. The conversation is about Washington parties in general, but would apply to Longworth's dinners. The quote is from Donald R. Matthews, *U.S. Senators and Their World* (Chapel Hill: The University of North Carolina Press, 1960), 74–75.

65. Halo, Milligan, 11; Dwight D.

Eisenhower to ARL, 21 January 1957, JSP; "The Eisenhowers Star at 4 Dances," *NYT*, 22 January 1957, 18; "Paulina Sturm, Grandchild of T.R., Dies at 31," *Chicago Tribune*, 28 January 1957, 1.

66. See Paul Lewis, "William B. Ruger, 86, Founder of Gun Company," *NYT*, 10 July 2002, A18; Alan Farnham, "He Knew Quality," *Forbes* 170, 4 (2 September 2002), 206–207; "Mrs. Justin Sturm, Novelist's Widow," *NYT*, 8 May 1971, 32, states that Mrs. Sturm "backed her late son, Alexander, in founding a firearms company, the Sturm Ruger Company, in Southport"; Katherine Sturm to ARL, postmarked 28 September 1949, JSP; "Alexander Sturm Dies," *NYT*, 14 November 1951, 31.

67. Dorothy Day, "On Pilgrimage, *Catholic Worker*, 23, 7 (February 1957), 1, 7.

68. Charles G. Herbermann, et al., eds., *Catholic Encyclopedia* (New York: The Gilmary Society, 14:1912), 326. See also Stanislaus Woywod, *A Practical Commentary on the Code of Canon Law* (New York: Joseph F. Wagner, 1957), 545–546. Author's interview with Bill Walton. The information on Paulina Sturm comes from several interviews with Joanna Sturm, Robert Hellman, Bazy Tankersley, and Kristie Miller. See also "Mrs. Longworth [*sic*] Daughter Dies," *NYT*, 28 January 1957, 23; "Paulina Sturm, Grandchild of T.R., Dies at 31," *Chicago Tribune*, 28 January 1957, 1; and "Death Is Ruled Accidental," *NYT*, 7 March 1957, 44. The neighbors at 1222 Twenty-eighth Street, NW, were the late Gertrude Kirkland and Ann Caracristi. The former was an intelligence operative and the latter was deputy director of the National Security Administration and recipient of the Distinguished Civilian Service Award given by the department of defense.

69. ARL to Paulina Longworth Sturm, n.d., JSP; author's interview with Janie McLaughlin, 26 May 1994; Alice Longworth kept the mastectomy quiet. For get-well wishes, see Herbert Hoover to ARL, 20 September 1956; Dwight D. Eisenhower to ARL, 21 January 1957; JLL to ARL, n.d. ("Wed—26—56"), all JSP; "Second chance," author interview with Bazy Tankersley, 19 July 1996.

70. "Aerie," author's interview with Kristie Miller, 10 October 1990. The "free spirit" quote is from Teichmann, 199. ER to ARL, 5 July 1957, JSP; author's interview with Kristie Miller, 10 October 1990.

71. Ethel Roosevelt Derby to ARL, 1 August 1957, JSP.

Chapter 21: **"The Most Fascinating Conversationalist of Our Time"**

1. "Nixon's Favorite Dinner Partner," clipping, [12 February 1974], JSP. See also "Alice at 90 Rated as No. 1 Dinner Partner," *Alexandria* [Va.] *Daily Town Talk*, 13 February 1974, C2, JSP. For John F. Kennedy, see Ethel Kennedy to ARL, 20 January 1967, JSP; and Myra McPherson, "Trio of Individualists Revamp the GOP Image," clipping *Washington Post*, 27 October 1968, JSP. Katharine Graham, *Personal History* (New York: Knopf, 1997), 391.

2. ARL preservation tape, ICD 16021, 25 May 1967, JSP.

3. Joseph W. Alsop, *"I've Seen the Best of It"* (New York: W. W. Norton, 1992), 430; Patricia Nixon to ARL, 18 January 1962, JSP. For examples of the books, see Richard Nixon to ARL, 28 November 1960; Rose Mary Woods to ARL, 12 January 1960; Richard Nixon to ARL, 13 March 1962, all JSP; "more than generous," Richard Nixon to ARL, 24 September 1962, ARL; Henry Brandon, "A Talk with an 83-Year-Old Enfant Terrible," *NYT Magazine*, 6 August 1967, 72.

4. ARL preservation tape, ICD 16037, 26 September 1967, JSP.

5. Arthur Schlesinger Jr., *A Life in the Twentieth Century* (New York: Houghton Mifflin, 2000), 378. See also Arthur Schlesinger Jr. to Joseph Alsop, 9 December 1949, JSAP. See "Random Notes in Washington: Schlesinger Now Half of Faculty," *NYT*, 11 December 1961, 37; "Random Notes in Washington: Fall Term at Hickory Hill U.," *NYT*, 24 September 1962. Alice Longworth's quotes on Schlesinger come from the ARL preservation tape, ICD 16034, 19 August 1968; all other Hickory Hill quotes are from tape ICD 16037, 26 September 1967, JSP. David Halberstam, *The Best and the Brightest* (New York: Random House, 1972), 292.

6. Katharine Graham, *Katharine Graham's Washington* (New York: Random House, 2002), 131–32. Robert W. Merry, *Taking on the World* (New York: Viking), 397.

7. "Passport," Henry Brandon, "Visitors' Guide to the White House," *Sunday Times* (London), 16 July 1967, 13; "even presidents came, Selma Roosevelt, *Keeper of the Gate*, (New York: Simon & Schuster, 1990), 159; James Brough quoted in Howard Teichmann, *Alice* (Englewood Cliffs, N.J.: Prentice Hall, 1979), 197; for the "classified tidbits," Felix Frankfurter to ARL, 19 December 1960, JSP; Robert Bob Kintner to ARL, 20 July 1966, JSP; Kintner to Joseph Alsop, 7 February 1950, JSAP; Roosevelt, 159.

8. Roosevelt, 159; Ethel Roosevelt Derby to ARL, [1950], JSP; Ethel Kennedy to ARL, [1962], JSP; A. Robert Smith and Eric Sevareid, "Washington After Five," *Chicago Tribune*, 20 February 1966, S28.

9. Jean Vanden Heuvel, "The Sharpest Wit in Washington," *Saturday Evening Post* 238, 24 (4 December 1965), 30; her recipe was quoted widely: "Take a loaf of good unsliced bread.... Butter with sweet butter. Cut a thin slice with a sharp knife. Repeat." It can be found in the *Kennedy Center Performing Artists Cookbook* (Washington, D.C.: Museum Press, 1973), 169. For the loudly boiling teapot, see Michael Teague *Mrs. L* (Garden City, N.Y.: Doubleday, 1981), ix and x. Teague makes the point that Mrs. L and guests could ignore the boiling water, and one can hear it on the preservation tapes; for teas, author's interview with Janie McLaughlin, 26 May 1994.

10. "Face is mobile," Nicholas Von Hoffman, "Snap-Shots at the Hot Shoppe," *Washington Post*, 26 February 1967, 7. Henry Brandon called her beautiful in his August 1967 article "A Talk With an 83-Year-Old Enfant Terrible," 8; author's interview with Janie McLaughlin; "Hell on earth," ARL preservation tape, ICD 16037, 26 September 1969, JSP; Ethel Roosevelt Derby to ARL, 19 May 1962, JSP.

11. Andrew and Betsy Wyeth to ARL, n.d., JSP; Otto Von Habsburg to ARL, n.d., JSP; McGeorge Bundy to ARL, 21 August 1961, JSP.

12. Transcript of Mary Hagedorn interview with Mrs. Richard M. Bissell, 23 May 1955, Harvard University.

13. Bashful guests, James K. Galbraith, e-mail to author, 29 June 2006; author's interview with Kristie Miller, 15 February 2005; author's interviews with Bill Walton, 27 May 1994, and with Robert Hellman, 26 June 2006; Graham, *Katharine Graham's Washington*, 131.

14. Alice's views of Kennedy, Vanden Heuvel, 31, 32; "Cellist Pablo Casals Feted by Kennedys," *Chicago Tribune*, 14 November 1961, B7; "Casals Plays at White House," *NYT*, 14 November 1961, 1; "Washington Steps Out to Greet 'Mr. President,'" *Chicago Tribune*, 26 September 1962, D3; "Mr. President Seen in

Capital," *NYT*, 26 September 1962, 36; "Kennedy Unveils a Marble Mantle in White House," *NYT*, 3 July 1962, 10; "Building Honors Speakers," *NYT*, 23 May 1962, 28.

15. "Sobbing," Merry, 406–407; "boy stood-on-the-burning-deckish," Page-A-Day Notes to author from Joanna Sturm and Kristie Miller, n.d. 2003; Brandon, "A talk," 74.

16. Edward M. Kennedy telegram to ARL, 23 November 1963, ARL to Jacqueline Kennedy (draft), 12 December 1963; ARL to Robert Kennedy (draft), 3 March 1963; all JSP.

17. Ethel Roosevelt Derby to ARL, 12 July 1964, JSP.

18. Teresa Moore, "A Washington Life: Marcella Comes Winslow," *Washington Post Magazine*, 9 July 1989, 27.

19. ARL to Jacqueline Kennedy, 14 December 1968; Jacqueline Kennedy to ARL, 10 January [1969], both JSP.

20. "Royalty," Dorothy Marks, "A Long, Colorful Life," *Deseret News* [Salt Lake City, Utah], 10 February 1971, C1, JSP; "rogue elephant," Norma Milligan, "She Says What She Thinks," *Modern Maturity*, June–July 1974, 11; Lady Bird Johnson to ARL, 31 October 1964, JSP; Lady Bird Johnson, *A White House Diary* (New York: Holt, Rinehart, and Winston, 1970), 394–395; "Alice Longworth Will Cast a Vote for Johnson Today," *NYT*, 3 November 1964, 23; "Bull Moose," ARL Preservation tape, ICD 16021, 25 May 1967, JSP.

21. Johnson, 65, 263. Alice Longworth's story on ARL preservation tape, ICD 16034, 19 August 1968, JSP.

22. Johnson, 394–95.

23. ARL preservation tape, ICD 16024, 20 September 1967, JSP; unidentified clipping, 23 March 1966, JSP; Author interview with Robert Hellman, 25 April 2005. Alice Longworth gave mostly to environ-

mental causes, but her childhood sense of never having enough money never left her. Her Lee inheritance still trickled in as a monthly allowance, and she had investment income, which was based upon what Nick left her—including the odd railroad lease that came due—and from the proceeds of the sales of one hundred acres of land around Rookwood in 1950. The land had been sold to the Myers Y. Cooper Company and subsequently turned into suburbs, which grew apace in the postwar decades.

See Eleanor Adams, "Tea with Washington's Grande Dame," *Cincinnati Enquirer*, 2 January 1977; "Old Longworth Lot Now Being Cleared," *Cincinnati Post*, 1 May 1956; both ARLPF. For the railroad lease, see Landon L. Wallingford to ARL, 9 January 1969, JSP. Alice received $1,413.15 from a one-third share of railroad leases during 1968.

24. Lyndon B. Johnson to ARL, 6 January 1965, JSP. That letter and Jack Valenti to Lyndon B. Johnson, 5 January 1965; the press release of 6 January 1965, and ARL to Lyndon B. Johnson, 6 January 1965, all Folder FG 2/Q-T, Lyndon B. Johnson Library, Austin, Texas. See also McGeorge Bundy to ARL, 9 January 1965, JSP. LBJ's letter was really written by aide Eric Goldman. "Memorial to Theodore Roosevelt Dedicated October 27, 1967," *Theodore Roosevelt Association Newsletter* 2,1 (January 1968), 1; "Mrs. LBJ and Lynda Tour Teddy's Home," unidentified clipping n.d., JSP; for the biography, Johnson, 770.

25. "S-i-g-h-t," Betty Beale, "Prime 'Preservers' Feted," clipping, *Washington Evening Star*, 16 October 1969, F6; McPherson, "Trio of Individualists," both JSP.

26. ARL to Lyndon B. Johnson (draft), [July 14], JSP; Alice Longworth on Vietnam, ARL preservation tape, 16026, 28

September 1967, and ICD 16028, 10 October 1967, JSP. The latter contains the quote. In speaking, Mrs. Longworth drew out the two "longs."

27. Vanden Heuvel, 30.

28. Transcript of Jewell Fenzi interview with Joanna Sturm and Kristie Miller, 9 September 1989, 50 and 54 (hereafter called Fenzi interview).

29. Fenzi interview, 49. See page 54 of that interview for Kristie Miller's memory of Alice in the lotus position, trademark hat on head. See the diary of Mrs. George Dewey for evidence that TR knew yoga. Dewey Diary excerpts, 28 October 1907, JSP.

30. Fenzi interview, 50; Braden and "such fun," typescript of an interview, entitled "Return to the Far East," n.d., JSP; Moscow, Llewellyn E. Thompson to ARL, 10 July 1967, JSP.

31. Katharine Graham, *Personal History* (New York: Knopf, 1997), 391–95; quote on 394; for the headline, William F. Buckley, "The Politics of the Capote Ball," *Esquire*, December 1967, 159.

32. "Guilt Admitted in Longworth Theft," unidentified clipping; "Smelter Bares Longworth Loot," unidentified clipping; Jim Mann, "Mrs. Longworth in Court," *Washington Post*, 26 July 1972, JSP; *Auflick v. Longworth*, complaint for damages; *Auflick v. Longworth*, civil action no. 1650–72; all JSP.

33. "Beatles," *Boston Sunday Herald*, 6 June 1965, B49; Hermann Hagedorn, Interviews Relating to Roosevelt Women," Harvard University; "Edwardian," "The Grande Dames Who Grace America," unidentified clipping, JSP.

34. Mask, David Bowes, "In Search of Cincinnati," *Cincinnati Post*, 30 November 1973, 19; Portia Washington, ARL preservation tape, ICD 16034, 19 August 1968, JSP; Turner story, Nicholas Von Hoffman, "Snap-Shots at a Hot Shoppe," *Washington Post*, 26 February 1967, 7–8.

35. "Conversations on the Phone," typescript, n.d., JSP; Bella S. Abzug to ARL, 24 March 1972, JSP; Milligan, 10; Grandaughter's insight, Susan Watters, "Here's a Capital Denizen Who Pooh-Poohs Politics," *Chicago Tribune*, 9 October 1977, D10; Alice's views, Sally Quinn, "Alice Roosevelt Longworth at 90," *Washington Post*, 12 February 1974, B3; Joseph P. Duggan, "A Tea Party, Just a Trifle Mad, with 'Princess Alice' Longworth," unidentified clipping, n.d., Papers of Huntingon Cairns, LC.

36. Milligan, 10. See Sally Quinn's interview at the time of ARL's ninetieth birthday when she responded, "I don't think that's nasty, why I think that's lovely, so nice. I'm so glad to hear she is," when told that Alice Barney was "claiming to be in love with Alice"; Quinn, B3; Teague, 81; GayPatriot.Net, a politically conservative blogspot, lists her as "one of our divas." See GayPatriot.Net: http://gay-patriot.net/2005/12/11/who-are-our-conservative-divas.

37. The friend at tea was James K. Galbraith, e-mail to author, 29 June 2006; "outgrew her hormones," June Bingham, "Before the Colors Fade," *American Heritage*, February 1969, 43, 73; "secret of youth," Teague, 199; tear gas, Milligan, 10; Twiggy, Marks, C1.

38. Quoted in Don Hewitt, *Minute by Minute* (New York: Random House, 1985), 74; Teichmann, 237.

39. "Dullest thing," ARL preservation tape, ICD 16034, 19 August 1968; draft of telegram to Richard Nixon, 4 November 1969, both JSP. Phoning friends, Teichmann, 211.

40. "'65 Horse Show Opens on Nov. 4," unidentified clipping, n.d.; McPherson, "Trio of Individualists"; "Alice Roosevelt Longworth at 85 Retains Impishness,"

and "'Lady Alice's' Wit Still Sharp at 85," unidentified clippings, n.d.; "Alice a Sensation on TV," *San Francisco Sunday Examiner & Chronicle*, 23 February 1969, 7, all JSP.

41. Richard Nixon to ARL, 12 February 1969; Grace Frances Borah to ARL, 13 February 1969, JSP; Lyndon B. Johnson telegram to ARL, 12 February 1969; Mamie and Ike Eisenhower telegram to ARL, 12 February 1969; For examples of her self-depreciating humor, See "'Lady Alice's' Wit Still Sharp at 85," unidentified clipping, n.d.; Peter Hurd to ARL, 1 June 1969; the Achesons to ARL, 15 February 1969, all JSP.

42. R. Buckminster Fuller to ARL, 21 March 1969, JSP; Norman Cousins to F. Buckminster Fuller, 17 March 1965, JSP.

43. Hyman G. Rickover to ARL, 11 December 1969; ARL preservation tape, ICD 19021, 25 May 1967, both JSP. The precise "royal visitor" is unclear. Quarks and quasars is from tape ICD 16031 [n.d.], JSP; "Lyndon Attends Frankfurter's Private Service," *Chicago Tribune*, 25 February 1965, B12.

44. Betty Beale, "She's Witty, Elegant—She's the Grooviest," June 14, 1970, unidentified clipping in Papers of Huntington Cairns.

45. Hellman's dissertation was entitled *"Die Freien:* The Young Hegelians of Berlin and the Religious Politics of 1840 Prussia" (Ph.D. diss., Columbia University, 1977); author's interviews with Robert Hellman, 25 April 2005 and 26 June 2006.

46. Ymelda Dixon, "A Former Envoy Returns," clipping, *Washington Evening Star*, 16 May 1969, JSP. The only photo accompanying this news story is of the former ambassador and Alice. Invitations for all of the other events are in the JSP. Billy Graham to ARL, 30 April 1973, JSP.

47. For "Washington's topless octoge-

narian," see Teichmann, who quotes a letter from Mrs. Longworth's physician (on page 229). Jane Howard, "Forward Day by Day," *NYT,* 8 December 1974, 324. Betty Ford to ARL, 4 October 1974, JSP; Henry Cabot Lodge Jr. to ARL, 13 November 1970, JSP.

48. Marks, C1.

49. Horace M. Albright, "Memories of Theodore Roosevelt," *Theodore Roosevelt Association Journal*, n.d., 5, JSP.

50. Ann Wood, "Just One of the Roosevelt Showoffs," *Sunday News,* 29 October 1972, 91, JSP; "Of Politics and Politicians," unidentified typescript, 4, JSP.

51. All invitations in JSP; Richard Nixon to ARL, 9 January 1973, JSP. "Mrs. Longworth could never resist anything political...." in Richard Nixon, *RN* (New York: Warner Books, 1978), 210.

52. Maxine Cheshire, "Very Interesting People," unidentified clipping, JSP. This happened in the mid-1960s, as several of the ARL preservation tapes make mention of it; "second footman," ARL preservation tape, ICD 16020, 7 February 1967, JSP; for stamp, Gary Clinton, e-mail to author, 17 February 2005; Vanden Heuvel, 32–33, 33.

53. "Capital's Grande Dame Laughs Off Those Watergate Blues," unidentified clipping, n.d., JSP; "Alice Longworth Marks*%$& Birthday," unidentified clipping, n.d., JSP.

54. Richard Nixon to ARL, 21 June 1973, JSP; "Asinine things," David Bowes, "In Search of Cincinnati," *Cincinnati Post*, 30 November 1973, 19; "an old friend," Milligan, 11; "state of shrug" and "dick-dick-dicking," Page-A-Day notes, JSP.

55. Milligan, 11, for "old crone," and cavier; Ethel Roosevelt Derby to ARL, 12 July 1964, JSP; guest list from "Alice Roosevelt Longworth, GOP Grande Dame, Is Dead," *Houston Chronicle*, 21

February 1980; Louise Le Claire, "Princess Alice Still Reigns," unidentified clipping, 8 September 1974, 24, both JSP.

56. The pillow still exists, but in a second incarnation. The first one may have read slightly differently, probably "If you can't think of something nice to say, sit right down here by me." That wording is from her reading off the pillow on 10 October 1967 on an ARL preservation tape, ICD 16029, JSP. The second version of the pillow has a Siamese cat's face in needlepoint at the bottom curl of the initial "I." Jean Vanden Heuvel first gave the pillow publicity in her 1965 *Saturday Evening Post* interview, "The Sharpest Wit in Washington." William Wright, *The Washington Game* (New York: E. P. Dutton, 1994), 60.

57. For one historian's suggestion that Nixon chose that quote to refer to happier days with his wife, see Fawn M. Brodie, *Richard Nixon* (New York: W. W. Norton, 1981), 143–44. Richard Nixon to ARL, 21 January 1974, JSP, and Dorothy McCardle, "A Daughterly Advantage," unidentified clipping, n.d., JSP.

58. Author's interview with Bill Walton, 27 May 1994.

59. Teague, viii; author interviews with Robert Hellman, 25 April 2005, Bazy Tankersley, 1 June 2006, and Alexandra Roosevelt Dworkin, 7 October 2001. "Darling Puss-Cat," also from Hellman, 2005.

60. Author's interview with Hellman, 26 June 2006.

61. Author's interviews with Hellman, 25 April 2005 and 26 June 2006. Hellman thinks that Mrs. Longworth "really remembered" the White House employee. I have tried unsuccessfully to track down his name. It is possible that he came back to the White House for that event, either to assist in the dinner and reception, or to reconnect with former White House employers, Alice Longworth among them. See also "State Dinner for Queen Elizabeth," *NYT*, 7 July 1976, 49.

Epilogue

1. Author's interview with Robert Hellman, 26 June 2006. He said she "was just being funny." "Alice Roosevelt Longworth Dies," *NYT*, 21 February 1980, 1.

2. Doug Wead, *All the Presidents' Children* (New York: Atria Books, 2003), 350. Esther Cleveland was born in the White House in 1893. Alice's sister, Edith, died in 1977, and her brother Archie died in 1979. Helen Taft Manning was very nearly Alice's age when she died (1 August 1891–21 February 1987).

3. "An extra piece of baggage" is how Alice Longworth characterized it to Bill Walton. Author's interview with Walton, 27 May 1994.

4. Lady Bird Johnson, *A White House Diary* (New York: Holt, Rinehart, and Winston, 1970), 486–487.

5. Books—along with oysters and maple sugar, according to Kristie Miller. "The Procession" (Glenn Kowalski); "Alice Roosevelt's House," on Haunted By Memories (Flaming Disk, 1987). See www.flamingdisk.com for the song. Anita Wilburn Darras, e-mail to author, 11 April 2006.

6. "Serious," In Search of Cincinnati," *Cincinnati Post*, 30 November 1973, 19; MacArthur, Teague, xv; childbirth, Teague, xiv–xv; purse, Jean Vanden Heuvel, "The Sharpest Wit in Washington, *Saturday Evening Post*, 4 December 1965, 30; poison ivy, Susan Sheehan, "Washington's Wittiest Woman," *McCall's*, January 1974, 64; LBJ, William Wright, *The Washington Game* (New York: E. P. Dutton, 1974), 231.

7. Ann Wood, "'Just One of the Roos-

evelt Showoffs," *Washington News*, 29 October 1972, 91, JSP; ARL's dresses were also cut loosely because of the double mastectomy, according to Kristie Miller and Bazy Tankersley.

8. Author interview with Joanna Sturm, 25 April 2005.

9. June Bingham, "Before the Colors Fade," *American Heritage*, February 1969, 43; TR to ARC, 10 April 1890, in ARC, *Letters from Theodore Roosevelt to Anna Roosevelt Cowles, 1870–1918* (New York: Charles Scribner's Sons, 1924), 108–9; author interview with Alexandra Roosevelt Dworkin, 7 October 2001.

10. Author interview with Bazy Tankersley, 19 July 1996.

11. Joseph M. Sheehan, "Fight to Protect Diamond Is Lost," *NYT*, 22 September 1955, 37.

12. Louise Hutchinson, "White House Weddings" Famous Brides Reminisce About Their Ceremonies," *Chicago Tribune*, 13 July 1966, B1.

Selected Bibliography

Manuscript Collections

American Antiquarian Society, Boston, Mass.
  Theodore Roosevelt Papers
Arizona Historical Society, Tucson, Ariz.
  Dinsmore Family Papers
  Greenway Papers
Chicago Historical Society, Chicago, Ill.
  Theodore Roosevelt Collection
Churchill Archives Center, Churchill College, Cambridge, England
  The Papers of Sir Cecil Spring-Rice
Cincinnati Historical Society Library, Manuscript Division, Cincinnati, Ohio
  Papers of Nicholas Longworth III (Mss801)
  Wulsin Family Papers (Mss844)
  Katherine Elizabeth Roelker Wulsin Correspondence (Mss589)
  Darrah Wunder Autobiographical Sketch (MssVF2386)
  Princeton Files:
    Judge Nicholas Longworth
    Nicholas Longworth
    Alice Roosevelt Longworth
    Paulina Longworth Sturm
    Susan Longworth
    Joseph S. Graydon
Cortauldt Institute, London, England
  Lord Lee of Fareham Papers
Herbert Hoover Presidential Library, West Branch, Iowa
  Commerce Papers
  President's Personal File
  Lou Henry Hoover Papers
  Lewis L. Strauss Papers
  Westbrook Pegler Papers
  Robert E. Wood Papers
Houghton Library, Harvard University, Cambridge, Mass.
  Theodore Roosevelt Collection

Anna Roosevelt Cowles Papers (bMS Am 1834.1)
Alice Roosevelt Longworth Family Papers (bMS Am 1541.9)
Archibald Bulloch Roosevelt Family Papers (bMS Am 1541.3)
Edith Kermit Carow Roosevelt Family Papers (*87M-101)
Ethel Roosevelt Derby Papers (87M-100)
Herman Hagedorn. Interviews Relating to Roosevelt Women (R200.H12i)
Roosevelt Family Miscellaneous Papers (bMS Am 1834.2)
Theodore Roosevelt Miscellaneous Papers (*93M-11)
Alexander Woollcott Papers
Idaho Oral History Center, Boise, Idaho
Idaho State Historical Society Library and Archives, Boise, Idaho
William E. Borah Papers (MS605, MS608)
Indiana Historical Society, Indianapolis, Ind.
Robert Hunter Papers
Library of Congress, Washington, D.C.
Joseph and Stewart Alsop Papers
Daniel C. Beard Papers
Mabel T. Boardman Papers
William E. Borah Papers
Huntington Cairns Papers
Joseph H. Choate Papers
William Dudley Foulke Papers
James R. Garfield Papers
Lillian Gish Papers
Harold Ickes Papers
Alice Roosevelt Longworth Papers
Alice Roosevelt Longworth Scrapbook
Nicholas Longworth Papers
Evalyn Walsh McLean Papers
Amos R. Pinchot Papers
Cornelia Bryce Pinchot Papers
Archibald Roosevelt Papers
Kermit and Belle Roosevelt Papers
Theodore Roosevelt Jr. Papers
Everett Sanders Papers
Eric Sevareid Papers
Ruth Hanna McCormick Simms Papers
Mark Sullivan Papers
Robert A. Taft Papers
Manuscripts Department, Lilly Library, Indiana University, Bloomington, Ind.
Samuel McClure Papers
Abraham Lincoln Presidential Library, Springfield, Ill.
Joseph Cannon Papers
H. H. Kohlsaat Papers
National Archives, London, England
Papers of the British Embassy (F.O 800/241-242/9/1)

Naval War College, Naval Historical Collection, Newport, R.I.
    Fred Leith (Ms. Coll. 89)
Newberry Library, Chicago, Ill.
    John T. McCutcheon Papers
    Carter H. Harrison Papers
    Alice French Papers
    Edith Franklin Wyatt Papers
    Papers of the Illinois Central Railroad Company
Privately held
    Joanna Sturm Papers
Franklin D. Roosevelt Library, Hyde Park, N.Y.
    Eleanor Roosevelt Papers
    Elliott Roosevelt Sr. Papers
    Roosevelt Family Papers Donated by the Children
Southern Historical Collection, Wilson Library, University of North Carolina at Chapel Hill, Chapel Hill, N.C.
    Peter Hagner Papers
University of Chicago, Special Collections Library, Chicago, Ill.
    Frank O. Lowden Papers
    Salmon O. Levinson Papers
University of Vermont, Special Collections, Burlington, Vt.
    Grace Goodhue Coolidge Collection
Washington State University Libraries, Manuscripts, Archives, and Special Collections, Pullman, Wash.
    Claudius Osborne Johnson Papers

Other Media

"The Reporters: Jonathan Aitken Interview with Alice Roosevelt Longworth," Yorkshire [U.K.] Television. [January 1969].

Microfilm Collections

Willard Dickerman Straight Papers, Division of Rare and Manuscript Collections, Cornell University Library, Ithaca, N.Y.

Presidential Papers of Theodore Roosevelt, Library of Congress, Washington, D.C.

William H. Taft Papers, Library of Congress, Washington, D.C.

Eleanor Roosevelt Papers, Franklin D. Roosevelt Presidential Library, Hyde Park, N.Y.

Oral Interviews

Allen, Robert S., transcript. Interviewed by Raymond Henle. 11 November 1966. Herbert Hoover Presidential Library.

Alsop, Susan Mary. Interviewed by author. 24 May 1994.

Benn, Stephen. Telephone interview by author. 2 August 2004.

Borah, Mary McConnell, transcript. Interviewed by Rosita Artis. 18 October 1969. [OH#0013] Idaho Oral History Center, Boise, Idaho.

Borah, Mary McConnell, transcript. Interview by Maureen Bassett. 15 October 1971. Oral History Project, Latah County Museum Society, Moscow, Idaho.

Catt, Ann. Telephone interview by author. 30 May 2006.

Davison, F. Trubee, transcript and addenda to transcript. Interviewed by Raymond Henle. 14 September 1969. Herbert Hoover Presidential Library, West Branch, Iowa.

Dworkin, Alexandra Roosevelt. Telephone interview by author. 7 October 2001.

Emmerson, Dorothy, transcript. Interviewed by Hope Meyers. 28 September 1987. Association for Diplomatic Studies and Training, Arlington, Va.

Hagedorn, Mary, transcript. Interview with Mrs. Richard Aldrich, 30 March 1955. Interviews Relating to Roosevelt Women, R200.H12i. Houghton Library, Harvard University, Cambridge, Mass.

Hawley Jr., Jess, transcript. Interviewed by Barbara Pulling. 14 November 1989. [OH#1042] Idaho Oral History Center, Boise, Idaho.

Hellman, Robert. Interviewed by author on several occasions, 1993–2007.

Lane, Cora Rubin, transcript. Interviewed by Jackie Day-Ames. 25 May 1976. [OH#0905] Idaho Oral History Center, Boise, Idaho.

Longworth, Alice Roosevelt, Preservation Tape Collection. Various Dates. Library of Congress, Washington, D.C.

Macgruder, Lynn. Interviewed by author. 14 October 2001.

McLaughlin, Janie. Interviewed by author. 26 May 1994.

Meeske, Angela. Telephone interview by author. 19 April 2004.

Miller, Kristie. Interviewed by author on several occasions, 1992–2007.

Mitchell, David. Telephone interview by author. 26 October 2001.

Mitchell, Frances Binger. Telephone interview by author. 26 January 2007.

Reed, Mary. Telephone interview by author. 30 May 2006.

Roosevelt, Robin. Interviewed by author. 27 May 1994.

Roosevelt, Selwa. Interviewed by author. 13 October 2001.

Silvercruys, Robert, transcript. Interviewed by Raymond Henle. 7 November 1968. Herbert Hoover Presidential Library.

Sturm, Joanna. Interviewed by author on several occasions, 1993–2007.

Sturm, Joanna, and Kristie Miller [Twaddell] transcript. Interviewed by Jewell Fenzi. 9 September 1989. Association for Diplomatic Studies and Training, Arlington, Va.

Tankersley, Bazy. Interviewed by author. 19 July 1996. Telephone interviews by author. 31 May and 1 June 2006.

Teague, Michael. Interviewed by author. 3 August 1989.

Tomb, Jeanne. Telephone interview by author. 24 February 2007.

Totenberg, Roman. Telephone interview by author. 24 March 2005.

Walton, William. Interviewed by author. 27 May 1994.

Westerman, Whillock, transcript. Interviewed by Jeffrey G. Seward. 8 January 1974. [OH#0147] Idaho Oral History Center, Boise, Idaho.

Wolfe, Preston, transcript. Herbert Hoover Presidential Library.

Books and Articles

Abbott , Lawrence F., ed. *The Letters of Archie Butt, Personal Aide to President Roosevelt.* Garden City, N.Y.: Doubleday, Page, 1924.

———, ed. *Taft and Roosevelt: The Intimate Letters of Archie Butt, Military Aide.* 2 vols. Garden City, N.Y.: Doubleday, Doran, 1930.

Abels, Jules. *In the Time of Silent Cal.* New York: G. P. Putnam's Sons, 1969.

Acceptance of the Statue of William Edgar Borah Presented by the State of Idaho. Washington, D.C.: Government Printing Office, 1948.

Adams, Samuel Hopkins. *A. Woollcott, His Life and His World.* New York: Reynal & Hitchcock, 1945.

Aldrich, Nelson. *Old Money: The Mythology of America's Upper Class.* New York: Knopf, 1988.

Allgor, Catherine. *Parlor Politics.* Charlottesville: University Press of Virginia, 2000.

Alsop, Joseph. *I've Seen the Best of It: Memoirs.* New York: W. W. Norton, 1992.

Alsop, Stewart. *Stay of Execution: A Sort of Memoir.* Philadelphia: J. B. Lippincott, 1973.

Amory, Cleveland. *The Proper Bostonians.* New York: E. P. Dutton, 1947.

———. *Who Killed Society?* New York: Harper & Brothers, 1960.

Anderson, Isabel. *Presidents and Pies: Life in Washington, 1897–1919.* New York: Houghton Mifflin, 1920.

Anderson, Judith Icke. *William Howard Taft: An Intimate History.* New York: W. W. Norton, 1981.

Anthony, Carl Sferrazza. *First Ladies.* vol. 1. New York: William Morrow, 1990.

———. *Nellie Taft: The Unconventional First Lady of the Ragtime Era.* New York: William Morrow, 2005.

Ashby, Leroy. *The Spearless Leader: Senator Borah and the Progressive Movement in the 1920s.* Urbana: University of Illinois Press, 1972.

Auchincloss, Louis. *The Vanderbilt Era: Profiles of a Gilded Age.* New York: Charles Scribner's Sons, 1989.

Bacevich, A. J. *Diplomat in Khaki: Major General Frank Ross McCoy and American Foreign Policy, 1898–1949.* Lawrence: University Press of Kansas, 1989.

Bacon, Donald C. "Nicholas Longworth: The Genial Czar," in *Masters of the House: Congressional Leadership Over Two Centuries.* Roger H. Davidson, Susan Webb Hammond, and Raymond W. Smock, eds. Boulder, Colo.: Westview Press, 1998.

Bailey, Thomas A. *Theodore Roosevelt and the Japanese-American Crisis.* Stanford, Calif.: Stanford University Press, 1934.

Baker, John D. "The Character of the Congressional Revolution of 1910." *Journal of American History* 60, no. 3 (December 1973): 679–691.

Barrymore, Ethel. *Memories: An Autobiography.* New York: Harper & Brothers, 1955.

Beal, Merrill D. "'Instructing the People:' Recollections of William E. Borah." *Rendezvous: Idaho State University Journal of Arts and Letters* 18, nos. 1–2 (1983): 43–46.

Beale, Howard K. *Theodore Roosevelt and the Rise of America to World Power.* Baltimore: Johns Hopkins University Press, 1956.

Beran, Michael Knox. *The Last Patrician: Bobby Kennedy and the End of American Aristocracy.* New York: St. Martin's Press, 1998.

Berlin, Isaiah. *Flourishing: Letters, 1928–1946*. London: Chatto & Windus, 2004.

Bingham, June. "Before the Colors Fade: Alice Roosevelt Longworth." *American Heritage*, February 1969: 42–43, 73–77.

Birmingham, Stephen. *The Grandes Dames*. New York: Simon & Schuster, 1982.

———. *The Right People: A Portrait of the American Social Establishment*. Boston: Little, Brown, 1968.

Blum, John Morton. *A Life with History*. Lawrence: University Press of Kansas, 2004.

———. *The Republican Roosevelt*. Cambridge, Mass.: Harvard University Press, 1954.

Boardman, Mabel T. "A Woman's Impressions of the Philippines." *Outlook* 82 (24 February 1906): 435–446.

Boehle, Rose Angela. *Maria Longworth: A Biography*. Dayton, Ohio: Landfall Press, 1990.

Boorstin, Daniel. *The Image: A Guide to Pseudo-Events in America*. New York: Atheneum, 1962.

Borah, Mary E. *Elephants and Donkeys: The Memoirs of Mary Borah*. Moscow: University Press of Idaho, 1976.

Borah, William E. *Bedrock: Views on Basic National Problems*. Washington, D.C.: National Home Library Foundation, 1936.

Braden, Joan. *Just Enough Rope: An Intimate Memoir*. New York: Villard Books, 1989.

Braden, Waldow W. "Some Illinois Influences on the Life of William E. Borah." *Journal of the Illinois Historical Society* 40, no. 2 (June 1947): 168–175.

———. "William E. Borah's Senate Speeches on the League of Nations, 1918–1920." *Speech Monographs* 10 (1943): 57–68.

Bradlee, Ben. *A Good Life: Newspapering and Other Adventures*. New York: Simon & Schuster, 1995.

Brands, H. W. *T.R.: The Last Romantic*. New York: Basic Books, 1997.

Braudy, Leo. *The Frenzy of Renown: Fame and Its History*. New York: Oxford University Press, 1986.

Brent, Charles H. "The Visit to the Philippines of Secretary Taft and His Party." *Outlook* 81 (14 October 1905): 369–372.

Brodie, Fawn M. *Richard Nixon: The Shaping of His Character*. New York: W. W. Norton, 1981.

Brooks, Gladys. *Boston and Return*. New York: Atheneum, 1962.

Brough, James. *Princess Alice*. Boston: Little, Brown, 1975.

Browder, Robert Paul, and Thomas G. Smith. *Independent: A Biography of Lewis W. Douglas*. New York: Knopf, 1986.

Bulkey, Barry. *Washington Old and New*. Washington, D.C.: W. F. Roberts, 1913.

Burchett, Richard Lee. "The Political World of Nicholas Longworth III: 1887–1903." PhD diss., University of Cincinnati, 1971.

Burke, Arthur M., ed. *Prominent Families of the United States of America*. New York: Heraldic Publishing, 1975.

Burke, Robert E, ed. *The Diary Letters of Hiram Johnson, 1917–1945*. Vols. 1–7. New York: Garland, 1983.

Burns, James MacGregor, and Susan Dunn. *The Three Roosevelts: Patrician Leaders Who Transformed America*. New York: Atlantic Monthly Press, 2001.

Burton, David. *Cecil Spring-Rice: A Diplomat's Life.* Rutherford, N.J.: Fairleigh Dickinson University Press, 1990.

Butler, Nicholas Murray. *Across the Busy Years: Recollections and Reflections.* New York: Charles Scribner's Sons, 1939.

Cairns, Huntington. *The Limits of Art: Poetry and Prose Chosen by Ancient and Modern Critics.* Washington, D.C.: Bollingen Foundation/Pantheon Books, 1948.

Caroli, Betty Boyd. *The Roosevelt Women.* New York: Basic Books, 1998.

Cassini, Marguerite. *Never a Dull Moment.* New York: Atheneum, 1956.

Champagne, Anthony. "John Nance Garner," in *Masters of the House: Congressional Leadership Over Two Centuries.* Roger H. Davidson, Susan Webb Hammond, and Raymond W. Smock, eds. Boulder, Colo.: Westview Press, 1998.

Chanler, Margaret. *Autumn in the Valley.* Boston: Little, Brown, 1936.

Cincinnati: A Guide to the Queen City and Its Neighbors. Cincinnati, Ohio: Wiesenhart Press, 1943.

Clapper, Olive Ewing. *Washington Tapestry.* New York: McGraw Hill, 1946.

Clinton, Gilbert. *The Mirrors of Washington.* New York: G. P. Putnam's Sons, 1921.

Coker, William S. "The Panama Canal Tolls Controversy: A Different Perspective." *Journal of American History* 55 (1968): 555–564.

Cole, Wayne S. *America First.* New York: Octagon Books, 1971.

———. "The America First Committee." *Journal of the Illinois State Historical Society* 44, no. 1 (Spring 1951): 305–322.

Coletta, Paolo E. *The Presidency of William Howard Taft.* Lawrence: University Press of Kansas, 1973.

Colman, Elizabeth Wheeler. *Mrs. Wheeler Goes to Washington.* Helena, Mont.: Falcon Press, 1989.

Collier, Peter. *The Roosevelts.* New York: Simon & Schuster, 1994.

Collin, Richard H. *Theodore Roosevelt, Culture, Diplomacy, and Expansion: A New View of American Imperialism.* Baton Rouge: Louisiana State University Press, 1985.

Commager, Henry Steele, ed. *Documents of American History,* 4th ed. New York: Appleton-Century-Crofts, 1948.

Contosta, David R., and Jessica R. Hawthorne. "Rise to World Power: Selected Letters of Whitelaw Reid, 1895–1912." *Transactions of the American Philosophical Society* 76, no. 2 (1986): 1–171.

Cook, Blanche Wiesen. *Eleanor Roosevelt.* 2 vols. New York: Viking, 1992, 1999.

Cooper, John Milton. *Breaking the Heart of the World.* Cambridge: Cambridge University Press, 2001.

———. *The Warrior and the Priest: Woodrow Wilson and Theodore Roosevelt.* Cambridge, Mass.: Harvard University Press, 1983.

———. "William E. Borah: Political Thespian." *Pacific Northwest Quarterly* 56, no. 4 (October 1965): 145–158.

Coudenhove-Kalergi, Richard N. *Crusade for Pan-Europe: Autobiography of a Man and a Movement.* New York: G. P. Putnam's Sons, 1943.

Cowles, Anna Roosevelt. *Letters from Theodore Roosevelt to Anna Roosevelt Cowles, 1870–1918.* New York: Charles Scribner's Sons, 1924.

Cox, James M. *Journey Through My Years.* New York: Simon & Schuster, 1946.

Cravens, Hamilton. *The Triumph of Evolution: The Heredity-Environment Controversy, 1900–1941.* Baltimore: Johns Hopkins University Press, 1988.

Croly, Herbert. *Willard Straight.* New York: Macmillan, 1925.

Cross, Wilbur, and Ann Novotny. *White House Weddings.* New York: David McKay, 1967.

Dalton, Kathleen. *Theodore Roosevelt: A Strenuous Life.* New York: Knopf, 2002.

———. "Theodore Roosevelt: Knickerbocker Aristocrat." *New York History* 67, no. 1 (January 1986): 39–65.

Danforth, D. N. "Contemporary Titans: Joseph Bolivar DeLee and John Whitridge Williams." *American Journal of Obstetrics and Gynecology* 120, no. 3 (1 November 1974): 577–588.

Daniels, Jonathan. *Washington Quadrille.* Garden City, N.Y.: Doubleday, 1968.

Davis, Kenneth S. *FDR: Into the Storm, 1937–1940.* New York: Random House, 1993.

Davis, M. Edward. "Joseph Bolivar DeLee, 1869–1942: As I Remember Him." *Lying-In: The Journal of Reproductive Medicine* 1, no. 1 (January–February 1968): 33–44.

Davis, Oscar King. *Released for Publication: Some Inside Political History of Theodore Roosevelt and His Times, 1898–1918.* Boston: Houghton Mifflin, 1925.

Deacon, Desley. *Elsie Clews Parsons: Inventing Modern Life.* Chicago: University of Chicago Press, 1997.

DeBenedetti, Charles. "Borah and the Kellogg-Briand Pact." *Pacific Northwest Quarterly* 63, no. 1 (January 1972): 22–29.

DeCamp, Graydon. *The Grand Old Lady of Vine Street: A History of* The Cincinnati Enquirer. Cincinnati: The Cincinnati Enquirer, 1991.

De Chambrun, Clara Longworth. *Cincinnati: Story of the Queen City.* New York: Charles Scribner's Sons, 1939.

———. *The Making of Nicholas Longworth.* New York: Ray Long & Richard R. Smith, 1933.

———. *Shadows Like Myself.* New York: Charles Scribner's Sons, 1936.

Ditzen, Eleanor Davies Tydings. *My Golden Spoon: Memoirs of a Capital Lady.* New York: Madison Books, 1997.

———. *The Hero: Charles A. Lindbergh and the American Dream.* Garden City, N.Y.: Doubleday, 1959.

Documents Diplomatiques Francais II. Paris: Imprimerie Nationale, 1931.

Doenecke, Justus D., ed. *In Danger Undaunted: The Anti-Interventionist Movement of 1940–1941 as Revealed in the Papers of the America First Committee.* Stanford, Calif.: Hoover Institution Press, 1990.

Donn, Linda. *The Roosevelt Cousins: Growing Up Together, 1882–1924.* New York: Knopf, 2001.

Douglas, William O. *The Court Years, 1939–1975: The Autobiography of William O. Douglas.* New York: Random House, 1980.

Dows, Alice. *Idle Hours.* Philadelphia: Dorrance Publishers, 1927.

———. *Illusions.* Philadelphia: Dorrance Publishers, 1931.

Dubofsky, Melvin, and Warren Van Tine. *John L. Lewis: A Biography.* Urbana: University of Illinois Press, 1987.

Duffey, Eliza Bisbee. *Ladies' and Gentlemen's Etiquette.* Philadelphia: Porter & Coates, 1887.

Duncan, Bingham. *Whitelaw Reid: Journalist, Politician, Diplomat*. Athens: University of Georgia Press, 1975.

Edge, Walter Evans. *A Jerseyman's Journal: Fifty Years of American Business and Politics*. Princeton, N.J.: Princeton University Press, 1948.

Egerton, George. "Diplomacy, Scandal and Military Intelligence: The Craufurd-Stuart Affair and Anglo-American Relations, 1918–1920. *Intelligence and National Security* 2, no. 4 (October 1987): 110–134.

Ellis, Anne. *The Life of an Ordinary Woman*. [1929] Boston: Houghton Mifflin, 1999.

Esthus, Raymond A. *Theodore Roosevelt and the International Rivalries*. Claremont, Calif.: Regina Books, 1970.

Fausold, Martin L. *James W. Wadsworth, Jr.: The Gentleman from New York*. Syracuse, N.Y.: Syracuse University Press, 1975.

Felsenthal, Carol. *Alice Roosevelt Longworth*. New York: G. P. Putnam's Sons, 1988.

Fenzi, Jewell. *Married to the Foreign Service: An Oral History of the American Diplomatic Spouse*. New York: Twain, 1994.

Ferrell, Robert H. *The Presidency of Calvin Coolidge*. Lawrence: University Press of Kansas, 1998.

———. *Woodrow Wilson and World War I: 1917–1921*. New York: Harper & Row, 1985.

Fishbein, Morris, with Sol Theron DeLee. *Joseph Bolivar DeLee: Crusading Obstetrician*. New York: E. P. Dutton, 1949.

Fleming, Karl, and Anne Taylor Fleming. *The First Time*. New York: Simon & Schuster, 1975.

Ford, Worthington, ed. *The Letters of Henry Adams*. New York: Houghton Mifflin, 1938.

Freidel, Frank. *Franklin D. Roosevelt: A Rendesvouz with Destiny*. Boston: Little, Brown, 1990.

Fruhauf, Aline. *Making Faces: Memoirs of a Caricaturist*. Washington, D. C.: Seven Locks Press, 1977.

Gable, John Allen. *The Bull Moose Years: Theodore Roosevelt and the Progressive Party*. Port Washington, N.Y.: Kennikat Press, 1978.

Gamson, Joshua. *Claims to Fame: Celebrity in Contemporary America*. Berkeley: University of California Press, 1994.

Gann, Dolly. *Dolly Gann's Book*. Garden City, N.Y.: Doubleday, 1933.

Gardner, Joseph L. *Departing Glory: Theodore Roosevelt as Ex-President*. New York: Charles Scribner's Sons, 1973.

Garraty, John A. *Henry Cabot Lodge: A Biography*. New York: Knopf, 1953.

Garrett, Wendell, ed. *Our Changing White House*. Boston: Northeastern University Press, 1995.

Gibson, J. Timberlake. "The Million Dollar Drop-Out." *Washingtonian*, April 1967: 40–43.

Godfrey, Donald G., and Val E. Limburg. "The Rogue Elephant of Radio Legislation: Senator William E. Borah." *Journalism Quarterly* 67, no. 1 (Spring 1990): 214–224.

Goll, Eugene W. "Frank R. Kent's Opposition to Franklin D. Roosevelt and the New Deal." *Maryland Historical Magazine* 62, no. 2 (1968): 158–171.

Goodwin, Doris Kearns. *No Ordinary Time*. New York: Simon & Schuster, 1994.

Gould, Lewis L. *Grand Old Party*. New York: Random House, 2003.

———. *The Most Exclusive Club*. New York: Basic Books, 2005.

———. *The Presidency of Theodore Roosevelt*. Lawrence: University Press of Kansas, 1991.

———. "The Price of Fame: Theodore Roosevelt and Celebrity, 1909–1919." *Lamar Journal of the Humanities* 10, 2 (Fall 1984): 7–18.

Graham, Katharine. *Katharine Graham's Washington*. New York: Random House, 2002.

———. *Personal History*. New York: Knopf, 1997.

Graves, Louis. *Willard Straight in the Orient*. New York: Asia Publishing, 1922.

Green, Constance McLaughlin. *Washington: Capital City, 1879–1950*. Princeton, N.J.: Princeton University Press, 1963.

Green, Harvey. *The Light of the Home*. New York: Pantheon, 1983.

Green, Horace, ed. *American Problems: A Selection of Speeches and Prophecies by William E. Borah*. New York: Duffield & Company, 1924.

Green, Marguerite. "The National Civic Federation and the American Labor Movement, 1900–1925." Ph.D. dissertation, Catholic University, 1956.

Greenbaum, Fred. *Robert Marion La Follette*. Boston: Twayne, 1975.

Greiner, Betsy. "The Day Alice Came to Town." *Timeline* 4, no. 1 (February–March 1987): 16–25.

Griscom, Lloyd. *Diplomatically Speaking*. Boston: Little, Brown, 1940.

Grover, David H. "Borah and the Haywood Trial." *Pacific Historical Review* 32, no. 1 (February 1963): 65–77.

———. *Debaters and Dynamiters: The Story of the Haywood Trial*. Corvallis: Oregon State University Press, 1964.

———. "Diamondfield Jack A Range War in Court." *Idaho Yesterdays* 7, no. 2 (1963): 8–14.

Hagedorn, Hermann. *Leonard Wood: A Biography*. 2 vols. New York: Harper & Brothers, 1931.

———. *The Roosevelt Family of Sagamore Hill*. New York: Macmillan, 1954.

Halberstam, David. *The Best and the Brightest*. New York: Random House, 1972.

Harbaugh, William H. *The Life and Times of Theodore Roosevelt*. New York: Oxford University Press, 1975.

Harlow, Alvin F. *The Serene Cincinnatians*. New York: E. P. Dutton, 1950.

Harriman, Daisy. *From Pinafores to Politics*. New York: Henry Holt, 1923.

Hathorn, Guy B. "The Political Career of C. Bascom Slemp." Ph.D. dissertation, Duke University, 1950.

Healy, Paul. *Cissy: The Biography of Eleanor M. "Cissy" Patterson*. New York: Doubleday, 1966.

Helm, Edith Benham. *The Captains and the Kings*. New York: G. P. Putnam's Sons, 1954.

Henderson, Amy. "Media and the Rise of Celebrity Culture." *OAH Magazine of History* 6, no. 4 (Spring 1992): 49–54

Herbermann, Charles G., et al., ed. *The Catholic Encyclopedia*. vol. 14. New York: The Gilmary Society, 1912.

Hewitt, Don. *Minute by Minute*. New York: Random House, 1985.

History of Medicine and Surgery and Physicians and Surgeons of Chicago. Chicago: Biographical Publishing Corporation, 1922.

Hoge, Alice Albright. *Cissy Patterson.* New York: Random House, 1966.

Holmes, Sarah C., ed. *The Correspondence of Ezra Pound and Senator William Borah.* Urbana: University of Illinois Press, 2001.

Homes for Ambassadors. New York: American Embassy Association, 1910.

Hoover, Irwin Hood. *Forty-two Years in the White House.* New York: Houghton Mifflin, 1934.

Horgan, Paul. *Tracings: A Book of Partial Portraits.* New York: Farrar, Straus and Giroux, 1993.

Hoyt, Edwin P. *Alexander Woollcott.* New York: Abelard-Schuman, 1968.

Hurd, Charles. *Washington Cavalcade.* New York: E. P. Dutton, 1948.

Ickes, Harold L. *The Autobiography of a Curmudgeon.* New York: Reynal & Hitchcock, 1943.

Jeffries, Ona Griffin. *In and Out of the White House.* New York: Wilfred Funk, 1960.

Johnpoll, Bernard K. *Pacifist's Progress: Norman Thomas and the Decline of American Socialism.* Chicago: Quadrangle Books, 1970.

Johnson, Claudius O. *Borah of Idaho.* Seattle: University of Washington Press, 1936.

Johnson, Evans C. *Oscar W. Underwood.* Baton Rouge: Louisiana State University Press, 1980.

Johnson, Lady Bird. *A White House Diary.* New York: Holt, Rinehart and Winston, 1970.

Johnson, Robert David. *The Peace Progressives and American Foreign Relations.* Cambridge, Mass.: Harvard University Press, 1995.

Jones, V. C. "Before the Colors Fade: Last of the Rough Riders." *American Heritage* 20, no. 5 (August 1969): 42–95.

Kasson, John F. *Rudeness and Civility: Manners in Nineteenth-Century Urban America.* New York: Hill and Wang, 1990.

Kelly, Frank K. *The Fight for the White House: The Story of 1912.* New York: Thomas Y. Crowell, 1961.

Keyes, Frances Parkinson. *Capital Kaleidoscope.* New York: Harper & Brothers, 1937.

Kerr, Joan Paterson. *A Bully Father: Theodore Roosevelt's Letters to His Children.* New York: Random House, 1995.

Klein, Nora C. *Practical Etiquette.* Chicago: A. Flanagan, 1888.

Kohlsaat, H. H. *From McKinley to Harding: Personal Recollections of Our Presidents.* New York: Charles Scribner's Sons, 1923.

Kroebel, Emma. *Wie ich an den Koreanischen Kaiserhof kam.* Berlin: Verlag von R. Jacobsthal, 1909.

Lahr, John. *Automatic Vaudeville.* New York: Knopf, 1984.

Lane, Jack C. *Armed Progressive: General Leonard Wood.* San Rafael, Calif.: Presidio Press, 1978.

Lash, Joseph. *Eleanor and Franklin.* New York: Signet, 1971.

Lee, Mary. *A History of Chestnut Hill Chapel.* Chestnut Hill, Mass.: The History Committee of the First Church in Chestnut Hill, 1937.

Leonard, Lewis Alexander, ed. *Greater Cincinnati and Its People: A History*. Vol. 6. Chicago: Lewis Historical Publishing Company, 1927.

Lensen, George A., ed. *The D'Anethan Dispatches from Japan, 1894–1910*. Tallahassee, Fla.: The Diplomatic Press, 1967.

Leuchtenburg, William E. *The Perils of Prosperity*. Chicago: University of Chicago Press, 1958.

Levin, Phyllis Lee. *Edith and Woodrow: The Wilson White House*. New York: Scribner, 2001.

Lindbergh, Charles. *Of Flight and Life*. New York: Charles Scribner's Sons, 1948.

Longstreet, Abbey Buchanan. *Social Etiquette of New York*. New York: D. Appleton, 1887.

Longworth, Alice Roosevelt. *Crowded Hours*. New York: Charles Scribner's Sons, 1933.

———, with Theodore Roosevelt Jr. *The Desk Drawer Anthology*. New York: Doubleday, Doran, 1938.

Looker, Earle. *The White House Gang*. New York: Fleming H. Revell, 1929.

McAllister, Ward. *Society As I Have Found It*. New York: Cassell, 1890.

McCarthy, Michael P. "The Short, Unhappy Life of the Illinois Progressive Party." *Chicago History* 4, no. 1 (Spring 1977): 2–12.

McCullough, David. *Mornings on Horseback*. New York: Simon & Schuster, 1982.

McHale, Francis. *President and Chief Justice: The Life and Public Services of William Howard Taft*. Philadelphia: Dorrance & Company, 1931.

McKee, Delber L. "The Chinese Boycott of 1905–1906 Reconsidered: The Role of Chinese Americans." *Pacific Historical Review* 55, no. 2 (May 1986): 165–191.

McKenna, Marian C. *Borah*. Ann Arbor: University of Michigan Press, 1961.

McLean, Evalyn Walsh. *Father Struck It Rich*. Boston: Little, Brown, 1936.

McMurtry, Larry. *Walter Benjamin at the Dairy Queen*. New York: Simon & Schuster, 1999.

MacNeil, Neil. *Forge of Democracy*. New York: David McKay, 1963.

Madaras, Lawrence H. "Theodore Roosevelt, Jr., Versus Al Smith: The New York Gubernatorial Election of 1924." *New York History* 47 (1966): 372–390.

Maddox, Robert James. "Keeping Cool with Coolidge." *Journal of American History* 53, no. 4 (March 1967): 772–780.

———. *William E. Borah and American Foreign Policy*. Baton Rouge: Louisiana State University Press, 1970.

———. "William E. Borah and the Crusade to Outlaw War." *Historian* 29, no. 2 (1967): 200–220.

Maney, Richard. *Fanfare: The Confessions of a Press Agent*. New York: Harper & Brothers, 1957.

Manners, William. *TR and Will: A Friendship That Split the Republican Party*. New York: Harcourt, Brace, 1969.

Margulies, Herbert F. *Reconciliation and Revival: James R. Mann and the House Republicans in the Wilson Era*. Westport, Conn.: Greenwood Press, 1996.

Marie, Queen of Roumania. *Ordeal: The Story of My Life*. New York: Charles Scribner's Sons, 1935.

Martin, Asa E. *After the White House*. State College, Penn.: Penns Valley Publishers, 1951.

Martin, Ralph G. *Cissy: The Extraordinary Life of Eleanor Medill Patterson*. New York: Simon & Schuster, 1979.

Matthews, Donald R. *U.S. Senators and Their World*. Chapel Hill: The University of North Carolina Press, 1960.

Means, Marianne. *The Woman in the White House*. New York: Random House, 1963.

Merry, Robert W. *Taking on the World: Joseph and Stewart Alsop—Guardians of the American Century*. New York: Viking, 1996.

Merz, Charles. "Borah's One-Man Party." *New Republic*, 10 June 1925: 66–70.

Michener, James A. *The World Is My Home: A Memoir*. New York: Random House, 1992.

Miller, Karen. *Populist Nationalism: Republican Insurgency and American Foreign Policy Making, 1918–1925*. Westport, Conn.: Greenwood Press, 1999.

Miller, Kristie. *Ruth Hanna McCormick: A Life in Politics*. Albuquerque, N.M.: University of New Mexico Press, 1992.

———. "Ruth Hanna McCormick and the Senatorial Election of 1930." *Illinois Historical Journal* 81 (Autumn 1988): 191–210.

Miller, Nathan. *The Roosevelt Chronicles*. Garden City, N.Y.: Doubleday, 1979.

———. *Theodore Roosevelt: A Life*. New York: William Morrow, 1992.

Miller, William "Fishbait," with Frances Spatz Leighton. *Fishbait: The Memoirs of the Congressional Doorkeeper*. Englewood Cliffs, N.J.: Prentice Hall, 1977.

Miller, Zane L. *Boss Cox's Cincinnati: Urban Politics in the Progressive Era*. Columbus, Ohio: Ohio State University Press, 2000.

Mills, C. Wright. *The Power Elite*. New York: Oxford University Press, 1956.

Mooney, Booth. *Mr. Speaker: Four Men Who Shaped the United States House of Representatives*. Chicago: Follett, 1964.

Morgan, Ted. *F.D.R.: A Biography*. New York: Simon & Schuster, 1985.

Morison, Elting E., and John Morton Blum, eds. *The Letters of Theodore Roosevelt*. 8 vols. Cambridge, Mass.: Harvard University Press, 1951–1954.

Morris, Edmund. *The Rise of Theodore Roosevelt*. New York: Coward, McCann & Geoghegan, 1979.

———. *Theodore Rex*. New York: Random House, 2001.

Morris, Sylvia Jukes. *Edith Kermit Roosevelt: Portrait of a First Lady*. New York: Coward, McCann & Geoghegan, 1980.

Mowry, George E. *Theodore Roosevelt and the Progressive Movement*. Madison: University of Wisconsin Press, 1946.

Murray, Robert K. *The Harding Era: Warren G. Harding and His Administration*. Minneapolis: University of Minnesota Press, 1969.

———. *The Politics of Normalcy*. New York: W. W. Norton, 1973.

Myers, Gustavus. *History of the Great American Fortunes*. New York: Modern Library, 1936.

Naylor, Natalie A., Douglas Brinkley, and John Allen Gable, eds. *Theodore Roosevelt: Many-Sided American*. Interlaken, N.Y.: Heart of the Lakes Publishing, 1992.

Nesbitt, Henrietta. *White House Diary*. New York: Doubleday, 1949.

Nicolson, Harold. *Diaries and Letters, 1930–1939*. New York: Atheneum, 1966.

Nixon, Richard M. *RN: The Memoirs of Richard Nixon* New York: Warner Books, 1978.

Ornig, Joseph R. *My Last Chance to Be a Boy*. Baton Rouge: Louisiana University Press, 1994.

Osgood, Robert E. *Ideals and Self-Interest in America's Foreign Policy*. Chicago: University of Chicago Press, 1953.

O'Toole, Patricia. *When Trumpets Call: Theodore Roosevelt After the White House*. New York: Simon & Schuster, 2005.

Page, William Tyler. "Mr. Speaker Longworth." *Scribner's Magazine*, March 1928:272–280.

Parsons, Elsie Clews. "Congressional Junket in Japan: The Taft Party of 1905 Meets the Mikado." *New-York Historical Society Quarterly* XLI no. 4 (October 1957).

Patterson, James T. *Mr. Republican: A Biography of Robert A. Taft*. Boston: Houghton Mifflin, 1972.

Pearlman, Michael. *To Make Democracy Safe for America: Patricians and Preparedness in the Progressive Era*. Urbana: University of Illinois Press, 1984.

Pearson, Drew. *Drew Pearson Diaries, 1949–1959*. New York: Holt, Rinehart and Winston, 1974.

———, and Robert S. Allen. *The Washington Merry-Go-Round*. New York: Blue Ribbon Books, 1931.

Peters Jr., Ronald M. *The American Speakership: The Office in Historical Perspective*. Baltimore: Johns Hopkins University Press, 1997.

Pinchot, Amos R. *History of the Progressive Party*. New York: New York University Press, 1958.

Pincus, Anne Terry. *Kennedy Center Performing Arts Cookbook*. Washington, D.C.: Museum Press, 1973.

Ponder, Stephen. "The President Makes News: William McKinley and the First Presidential Press Corps, 1897–1901." *Presidential Studies Quarterly* 29, no. 4 (Fall 1994): 823–836.

Powell, E. Alexander. *Yonder Lies Adventure!* New York: Macmillan, 1932.

Pringle, Henry F. *The Life and Times of William Howard Taft*. 2 vols. New York: Farrar & Reinhart, 1939.

———. "The Real Senator Borah: Twenty Years in Washington Has Not Weakened Him." *World's Work*, December 1928:133–144.

———. *Theodore Roosevelt*. New York: Harcourt, Brace, 1931.

Randolph, Mary. *Presidents and First Ladies*. New York: D. Appleton-Century, 1936.

Ratliff, Lucy Graydon. *The Graydons of Cincinnati, 1850–1984*. Cincinnati: n.p., 1984.

Redman, Tim. *Ezra Pound and Italian Fascism*. Cambridge: Cambridge University Press, 1991.

Rein, Irving J., Philip Kotler, and Martin R. Stoller. *High Visibility*. New York: Dodd, Mead, 1987.

Renehan Jr., Edward J. *The Lion's Pride: Theodore Roosevelt and His Family in Peace and War*. New York: Oxford University Press, 1998.

Reston, James. *Deadline: A Memoir*. New York: Random House, 1991.

Rhodes, Edward J. M. *China's Republican Revolution: The Case of Kwangtung, 1895–1913*. Cambridge, Mass.: Harvard University Press, 1975.

Riedel, Richard Langham. *Halls of the Mighty: My 47 Years in the Senate*. New York: Robert B. Luce, 1969.

Rixey, Lillian. *Bamie: Theodore Roosevelt's Remarkable Sister.* New York: David McKay, 1963.

Robinson, Corinne Roosevelt. *My Brother Theodore Roosevelt.* New York: Charles Scribner's Sons, 1921.

Rollins Jr., Alfred B. *Roosevelt and Howe.* New York: Knopf, 1962.

Roosevelt, [Anna] Eleanor. *The Autobiography of Eleanor Roosevelt.* New York: Harper & Row, 1978.

———. *This I Remember.* New York: Harper & Brothers, 1949.

———. *This Is My Story.* New York: Harper & Brothers, 1937.

Roosevelt, Archibald. *For Lust of Knowing: Memoirs of an Intelligence Officer.* Boston: Little, Brown, 1988.

Roosevelt, Eleanor Butler Alexander. *Day Before Yesterday: The Reminiscences of Mrs. Theodore Roosevelt, Jr.* Garden City, N.Y.: Doubleday, 1959.

Roosevelt, Elliott, ed. *F.D.R. His Personal Letters: The Early Years.* New York: Duell, Sloan, and Pearce, 1947.

———, and James Brough. *An Untold Story.* New York: G. P. Putnam's Sons, 1973.

Roosevelt, Felicia Warburg. *Doers & Dowagers.* Garden City, NY: Doubleday, 1975.

Roosevelt, Nicholas. *Theodore Roosevelt: The Man as I Knew Him.* New York: Dodd, Mead, 1967.

Roosevelt, James, with Bill Libby. *My Parents: A Differing View.* New York: Playboy Press, 1976.

Roosevelt, Robert B. *Is Democracy Dishonesty?* New York: Journeymen Printers' Co-operative Association, 1871.

———. *Progressive Petticoats.* New York: G. W. Carleton, 1874.

———. *The Washington City Ring.* Washington: F. & J. Rives & G. A. Bailey, 1873.

Roosevelt, Selwa. *Keeper of the Gate.* New York: Simon & Schuster, 1990.

Roosevelt, Theodore. *An Autobiography.* New York: Charles Scribner's Sons, 1929.

———. *In Memory of My Darling Wife Alice Hathaway Roosevelt and of My Beloved Mother Martha Bulloch Roosevelt Who Died in the Same House and on the Same Day on February 14, 1884.* New York: G. P. Putnam's Sons, 1884.

———. *Letters from Theodore Roosevelt to Anna Roosevelt Cowles, 1870–1918.* New York: Charles Scribner's Sons, 1924.

Rorabaugh, William J. *The Alcoholic Republic.* New York: Oxford University Press, 1979.

Rosenberg, Charles E. "Sexuality, Class and Role in 19th-Century America," *American Quarterly* 25, no. 2 (May 1973), 131–153.

Ross, Ishbel. *Grace Coolidge and Her Era.* New York: Dodd, Mead, 1962.

———. *The Tafts: An American Family.* New York: World Publishing, 1964.

Rothman, Ellen K. *Hands and Hearts: A History of Courtship in America.* New York: Basic Books, 1984.

Russell, Francis. *The Shadow of Blooming Grove: Warren G. Harding and His Times.* New York: McGraw Hill, 1968.

Sands, W. F. "Korea and the Korean Emperor." *Century Magazine* 69, no. 4 (February 1905): 577–584.

Sarasohn, David. *The Party of Reform: Democrats in the Progressive Era.* Jackson: University Press of Mississippi, 1989.

Sarles, Ruth. *A Story of America First*. Westport, Conn.: Praeger, 2003.

Saxbe, William B., with Peter D. Franklin. *I've Seen the Elephant: An Autobiography*. Kent, Ohio: Kent State University Press, 2000.

Scanlan, Nelle. *Boudoir Mirrors of Washington*. Philadelphia: John C. Winston, 1923.

Schacht, John N., ed. *Three Faces of Midwestern Isolationism: Gerald P. Nye, Robert E. Wood, John L. Lewis*. Iowa City: Center for the Study of the Recent History of the United States, 1981.

Scharff, Virginia. *Taking the Wheel: Women and the Coming of the Motor Age*. New York: Free Press, 1991.

Schickel, Richard. *His Picture in the Papers*. New York: Charterhouse, 1973.

———. *Intimate Strangers: The Culture of Celebrity*. Garden City, N.Y.: Doubleday, 1985.

Schlesinger Jr., Arthur M. *Learning How to Behave: A Historical Study of American Etiquette Books*. New York: Macmillan Company, 1946.

———. *A Life in the Twentieth Century*. New York: Houghton Mifflin, 2000.

———. *The Crisis of the Old Order*. Boston: Houghton Mifflin, 1957.

Schmidt, Richard T. F. "Stokowski in a May Festival Coup." *Cincinnati Historical Society Bulletin* 25, no. 2 (April 1967): 130–135.

Schriftgiesser, Karl. *This Was Normalcy: An Account of Party Politics During Twelve Republican Years: 1920–1932*. Boston: Little, Brown, 1948.

Schwartz, Abby S. "Nicholas Longworth: Art Patron of Cincinnati." In *The Taft Museum: A Cincinnati Legacy*, Dottie L. Lewis, ed. Cincinnati: Cincinnati Historical Society, 1988: 18–32.

Seagrave, Sterling. *Dragon Lady: The Life and Legend of the Last Empress of China*. New York: Knopf, 1992.

Seale, William. *The President's House: A History*. 2 vols. Washington, D.C.: White House Historical Association, 1986.

Seelye, Catherine, ed. *Charles Olson and Ezra Pound: An Encounter at St. Elizabeth's by Charles Olson*. New York: Viking, 1975.

Selden, Charles A. "The Father Complex of Alice Roosevelt Longworth and Ruth Hanna McCormick." *Ladies' Home Journal*, March 1927: 6–7, 72–74.

Sherman, Richard B. "Republicans and Negroes: The Lessons of Normalcy." *Phylon* 27, (First Quarter 1966): 69–71.

Sherwood, Mary Elizabeth W. *Manners and Social Usages*. New York: Harper, 1897.

Silverman, Elaine L. "Theodore Roosevelt and Women: The Inner Conflict of a President and its Impact on his Ideology." Ph.D. diss., UCLA, 1973.

Slayden, Ellen Maury. *Washington Wife*. New York: Harper & Row, 1962.

Slemp, C. Bascom, ed. *The Mind of the President as Revealed by Himself in His Own Words*. Garden City, N.Y.: Doubleday, 1926.

Smart, James Getty. "Whitelaw Reid: A Biographical Study." Ph.D. diss., University of Maryland, 1964.

Smith, Marie. *Entertaining in the White House*. Washington, D.C.: Acropolis Books, 1967.

Smith, Ira R. T. *"Dear Mr. President...": The Story of Fifty Years in the White House Mailroom*. New York: Julian Messner, 1949.

Smith, Richard Norton. *The Colonel: The Life and Legend of Robert R. McCormick, 1880–1955*. Evanston, Ill.: Northwestern University Press, 1997.

————. *Thomas E. Dewey and His Times*. New York: Simon & Schuster, 1982.

Stenehjem, Michele Flynn. *An American First: John T. Flynn and the America First Committee*. New Rochelle, N.Y.: Arlington House, 1940.

Stevenson, Robert Louis. *Prince Otto: A Romance*. New York: Charles Scribner's Sons, 1925.

Stevens, Harry R. "The First Cincinnati Music Festival." *The Historical and Philosophical Society of Ohio History Bulletin* 20, no. 3 (July 1962): 186–196.

Stimson, Henry L., and McGeorge Bundy. *On Active Service in Peace and War*. New York: Harper & Brothers, 1947–1948.

Stokes, Thomas L. *Chip Off My Shoulder*. Princeton, N.J.: Princeton University Press, 1940.

Stone, Ralph. "Two Illinois Senators Among the Irreconcilables." *Mississippi Valley Historical Review* 50, no. 3 (December 1963): 443–465.

Sullivan, Mark. *The Education of an American*. New York: Doubleday, Doran, 1938.

————. *Our Times: The Twenties*. Vol. 6. New York: Charles Scribner's Sons, 1935.

Taft, Helen H. *Recollections of Full Years*. New York: Dodd, Mead, 1914.

Teague, Michael. *Mrs. L: Conversations with Alice Roosevelt Longworth*. Garden City, N.Y.: Doubleday, 1981.

————. "Theodore Roosevelt and Alice Hathaway Lee: A New Perspective." *Harvard Library Bulletin* 32, no. 3 (Summer 1985): 225–238.

Teichmann, Howard. *Alice: The Life and Times of Alice Roosevelt Longworth*. Englewood Cliffs, N.J.: Prentice Hall, 1979.

Torrey, E. Fuller. *The Roots of Treason: Ezra Pound and the Secrets of St. Elizabeth's*. New York: McGraw Hill, 1984.

Ts'ai, Henry. *China and the Overseas Chinese in the United States, 1868–1911*. Fayetteville: University of Arkansas Press, 1983.

Ts'ai, Shih-shan. "Reaction to Exclusion: The Boycott of 1905 and Chinese National Awakening." *Historian* 39, no. 1 (November 1976): 95–110.

Tuchman, Barbara W. *Practicing History*. New York: Knopf, 1981.

Van Rensselaer, Mrs. John King. *The Social Ladder*. New York: Henry Holt, 1924.

Vare, Daniele. *The Last Empress*. Garden City, N.Y.: Doubleday, Doran, 1938.

Varg, Paul A. *Open Door Diplomat: The Life of W. W. Rockhill*. Urbana: University of Illinois Press, 1952.

Vidal, Gore. *Palimpsest*. New York: Penguin Books, 1995.

Vinson, John. *William E. Borah and the Outlawry of War*. Athens: University of Georgia Press, 1957.

von Dakke, John F. "Grape Growing and Wine Making in Cincinnati, 1800–1870." *CHS Bulletin* 25, 3 (July 1967): 197–212.

Wagenknecht, Edward. *The Seven Worlds of Theodore Roosevelt*. New York: Longmans, Green, 1958.

Waldrop, Frank C. *McCormick of Chicago*. Englewood Cliffs, N.J.: Prentice Hall, 1966.

Walker, Stanley. *Mrs. Astor's Horse*. New York: Frederick A. Stokes, 1935.

Walters, Ronald G., ed. *Primers for Prudery*. Baltimore: Johns Hopkins University Press, 2000.

Ward, Geoffrey. *Before the Trumpet: Young Franklin Roosevelt, 1882–1905*. New York: Harper & Row, 1985.

————. *A First-Class Temperament*. New York: Harper & Row, 1989.

Warner, Hoyt Landon. *Progressivism in Ohio, 1897–1917*. Columbus: Ohio State University Press, 1964.

Warner, Marina. *The Dragon Empress: The Life and Times of Tẓ'u-Hsi*. London: Weidenfeld & Nicolson, 1972.

Wead, Doug. *All the Presidents' Children: Triumph and Tragedy in the Lives of America's First Families*. New York: Atria Books, 2003.

Weyl, Nathaniel. *Treason*. Washington, D.C.: Public Affairs Press, 1950.

Whipple, Wayne, and Alice Roosevelt Longworth. *The Story of the White House and Its Home Life*. Boston: Dwinell-Wright, 1937.

White, Ralph. "The Europeanism of Coudenhove-Kalergi." In *The European Unity in Context: The Interwar Period*. Peter M. R. Stirk, ed. London: Pinter Publishers, 1989.

White, William Allen. *The Autobiography of William Allen White*. New York: Macmillan, 1946.

————. *A Puritan in Babylon: The Story of Calvin Coolidge*. New York: Macmillan, 1958.

Wilensky, Norman M. *Conservatives in the Progressive Era: The Taft Republicans of 1912*. Gainesville: University of Florida Press, 1965.

Wilhelm, J. J. *Ezra Pound: The Tragic Years, 1925–1972*. University Park: The Pennsylvania State University Press, 1994.

Willets, Gilson. *Inside History of the White House*. New York: The Christian Herald, 1908.

Wister, Owen. *Roosevelt: The Story of a Friendship*. New York: Macmillan, 1930.

Woodward, Stanley. "Protocol: What It Is and What It Does." *Department of State Bulletin*, 3 October 1949: 501–503.

Woollcott, Alexander, Beatrice Bakrow Kaufman, and Joseph Hennessey, eds. *The Letters of Alexander Woollcott*. New York: Viking, 1944.

Worthington, C. Ford, ed. *The Letters of Henry Adams*. New York: Houghton Mifflin, 1938.

Woywod, Stanislaus. *A Practical Commentary on the Code of Canon Law*. New York: Joseph F. Wagner, 1957.

Wright, William. *The Washington Game*. New York: E. P. Dutton, 1974.

Wunderlin Jr., Clarence E., ed. *The Papers of Robert A. Taft*. 2 vols. Kent, Ohio: Kent State University Press, 1997 and 2001.

Young, Nancy Beck. *Lou Henry Hoover: Activist First Lady*. Lawrence: University Press of Kansas, 2004.

Zieger, Robert H. *John L. Lewis: Labor Leader*. Boston: Twayne, 1988.

Index

Praise for

Judith Frank

and

All I Love and Know

"In this wonderfully rich, absorbing novel, Frank sheds light on gender and identity, the anguished politics of the Middle East, the limits of love and one family's struggle to stay intact."
—*People*

"The considerable power of Judith Frank's second novel, *All I Love and Know,* comes from two sources not always found in combination: first, the seriousness of the social issues it takes on, and second, its psychological, nearly Jamesian style. . . . Like upmarket Jodi Picoult. . . . Judith Frank even writes her gay characters beautifully—she even writes gay male sex well. . . . From the darkest moments to the lightest, Frank's empathy for her characters transforms front-page news into literary fiction."
—*Newsday*

"This beautiful novel is old-fashioned in its approach, taking its sweet time to tell a tender love story between two flawed, good-hearted people, and yet it feels wholly fresh. . . . This is a compassionate, utterly compelling story of how family members, torn apart by tragedy, must reach deep within themselves to meet their greatest challenge."
—*Booklist* (starred review)

"*All I Love and Know* is a tender novel that deals with the emotional riptides left by an act of terrorism long after the headlines have faded. It is a brave, moving, and deeply compelling book, written with grace, about the ways even love and family devotion are challenged when the worst occurs. It makes for hugely rewarding reading."
—Scott Turow, author of *Identical*

"[A] timeless story . . . beautiful, expansive, and deeply humanistic . . . Frank is a perfect storyteller, creating vivid landscapes and characters and events. . . . We have little choice in how we, or those whom we love, die. But when it comes to life, we can choose. Judith Frank shows us how."
—Huffington Post

"Deeply moving . . . Frank shows profound empathy for her characters, making this book heartbreaking, yet jubilantly hopeful."
—*Publishers Weekly*

"I loved it! Read it non-stop. These people catch you by the heart so powerfully you can hardly believe it is a novel. I've already had to loan it to a friend."
—Dorothy Allison, author of *Bastard Out of Carolina*

"A young couple must deal with both grief and transformation when one of them becomes the guardian of an orphaned infant and a 6-year-old. The fact that the new parents of this instant family are two gay men is a secondary element of this emotional saga and that is part of the brilliance of Judith Frank's *All I Love and Know*. . . . Frank delves into politics, both on the Israeli/Palestinian conflict and on gay rights. The first is handled with a deft hand, the second, with almost a sleight of hand, making the impact of this novel, which is ultimately about the resilience of love, all the more powerful."
—*Boston Globe*

"What a refreshing, impressive novel. That Judith Frank has managed to weave a story about queer partnership and parenting together with an exploration of the moral complexities of the Israeli/Palestinian conflict is rather stunning. This tender, intricate domestic drama both engages and informs what is arguably one of the critical issues of our time. It feels quite revolutionary, not just in the political sense, but in terms of the kind of stories we value."
—Alison Bechdel, author of *Fun Home*

"It seems quite possible the men's relationship will not survive these stresses, which Frank explores in depth and without reassuring sentimentality. . . . [It's] moving to watch them work through to reconciliation. [This is] strong storytelling driven by emotionally complex characters: first-rate commercial fiction."

—*Kirkus Reviews* (starred review)

"This is a big American story, a tapping into the zeitgeist that few other novelists have really traveled—taking the life of gay American couples beyond the struggle for marriage equality and giving a look at the usual challenges of any relationship." —Bookreporter.com

"A powerful novel about love, loss and the will to endure after inconceivable tragedy." —*BookPage*

"Frank's deftly balanced tale of grief and redemption simultaneously asks how the American-Jewish left might negotiate religion and identity in the face of Israeli violence toward Palestinians, and how gay parents might raise children in a country still suspicious of them. Frank wraps these big themes around an intimate, fraught family setting; after the funeral in Israel, Daniel and Matthew return to their New England home, a 6-year-old and a baby in tow, and they're forever changed. After reading this book, one of the best of the season, you may be, too." —*Out* magazine

"Brilliant, thoughtful, [and] unexpectedly funny."

—*Lambda Literary Review*

"The relationship between Daniel and Matt is central to this moving story, which is told with a deep sensitivity. I am not gay, but I never doubted the love between these two young men, or the love and concern that everyone feels for the bereaved children. . . . This is a wonderful book." —Bookloons.com

"It's so good you won't want it to end. Frank writes with insight and authority. . . . It's both an engaging read and utterly believable. Even minor characters are fully drawn and compelling. With plenty of plot twists and characters you can root for, it is, at its heart, a good old-fashioned page-turner."   —*Jewish Daily Forward*

"An excellent and gripping read."   —*Western Massachusetts Jewish Ledger*

"A thoughtful look at how grief isolates survivors and how families may, or may not, come together in crisis."   —*Library Journal*

"Judith Frank does a masterful job of letting readers feel what the protagonists feel. . . . It all rings true, from the deeply psychological personal struggles and the ways children mourn, to the question of how to feel and respond to the terrorist act. This issue-packed novel repeatedly moved me."   —*Psychology Today*

"Between tackling issues like same-sex marriage, the rights of Palestinians versus those of Israelis and frank depictions of sex between two men, *All I Love and Know* is sure to provide plenty of fodder for book groups."   —*Jewish Exponent*

"The best novel I've read in eons. . . . Judith Frank is an exciting new author and *All I Love and Know* is to be treasured."
—David Rothenberg, WBAI

"This is such a riveting book—so vast in its emotional scope, but also very straightforward in its storytelling. . . . It's timely, but it's timeless too . . . in the emotional resonance."   —Bill Goldstein, NBC New York

ALL I LOVE AND KNOW

ALSO BY JUDITH FRANK

Crybaby Butch

ALL I LOVE AND KNOW

Judith Frank

WILLIAM MORROW
An Imprint of HarperCollins*Publishers*

FIRST WILLIAM MORROW PAPERBACK EDITION PUBLISHED 2015.

Designed by Lisa Stokes

Library of Congress Cataloging-in-Publication Data has been applied for.

ISBN 978-0-06-230289-2

15 16 17 18 19   OV/RRD   10 9 8 7 6 5 4 3 2 1

But these three cubic feet of bone and
blood and meat are all I love and know.

Loudon Wainwright III, "One Man Guy"

ALL I LOVE AND KNOW

CHAPTER 1

H E HAD THOUGHT that watching a movie would agreeably dis-
tract him, but the images unspooling on the tiny screen and the
tinny sound coming through the headphones were an irritant, like an
inexpert touch between a tickle and a scratch. Matt sat back in his seat
and took off his headphones, crammed a pillow behind his head and
shoulders, closed his eyes. The events of the past day came streaking
toward him, and he opened his eyes again quickly. He stole a glance
at his partner, Daniel. But there too he had to look away, the sight was
so shocking. Daniel's head hung, his chin touching his chest; Matt had
called the doctor and gotten some Ativan, and Daniel was far gone on
it. His lips were slack, his eyes cratered and bruised. In a single day his
dark hair and beard stubble had become streaked with gray, something Matt had always thought was a horror story cliché. Daniel was all
of thirty-eight and looked ancient and decrepit, Matt thought, and was
immediately ashamed of himself.

Matthew Greene was six years younger than his partner, tall and
thin, with a head of thick brown hair that lightened in the summer
sun. He had a handsome angular face, and a grin that placed a perfect
demonic dimple in his cheek, so that his smile looked more wicked than
he intended. Now his eyes were grainy with exhaustion. They were a

few hours into their flight to Tel Aviv, and meal carts were starting to be rolled down the aisle, bringing with them the smell of cooked meat. The Ativan was in Daniel's bag in the overhead, and he contemplated getting up and fishing it out. He hadn't till now, because somebody had needed to be on the ball, but now he felt wasted, his mind humming and strung out.

Was it only yesterday that the call had come from Daniel's father? Time seemed bundled and knotted, and when he tried to calculate the hours backward, they evaporated before his eyes. When the call came, he had been sitting at the computer in his study, watching a chickadee make restless, shivery passes at the bird feeder in the bare backyard. After he ended the call, he put the phone back into its charger very carefully. He stood and looked around, then sat down on the floor. The room was thunderously quiet, and he was bewildered to be alone with this information. He wondered, When did an event like this actually *take*? If he sat there very quietly, could he prevent it from coursing out into the wider world, where it would happen to other people instead of just to him and Daniel's father? The dog ambled up and he clutched its big head, trembling, thinking that every moment that passed without his breaking the news to Daniel would remain a happy moment from Daniel's old life.

Twenty minutes passed. He was conscious of his bare feet getting cold, of the dog's sigh, and of the study darkening as clouds passed over the weak March sun. Finally, the image of Daniel working tranquilly in his office, innocent of the knowledge that his world was about to be destroyed, became even more unbearable than the idea of telling him, and he stood. He went into the bedroom and put on a sweatshirt, found his coat and keys, and went out to the car. As he drove, he let his mind deliberate but forbade his heart to register, practicing fiercely how to say it, how to build up to it gradually without torturing Daniel with suspense. He had made Daniel's father promise not to call him at work, to let Matt break the news himself; he was glad he could be the one to tell Daniel but agonized over it too, wondering if Daniel would ever forgive him for being the one to tell him his twin brother, Joel, had died.

He pushed back to recline his plane seat. He remembered getting to Public Affairs and going into the office of the director, Daniel's boss, April, so Daniel could make a quick exit without having to excuse himself. Matt stood before her and made his first attempt at saying the words out loud: *Daniel's brother and sister-in-law were killed in a café bombing in Jerusalem.* April cried out and clutched her heart; he had never uttered words before that had so much sheer physical power. They gave him an embarrassing sense of self-importance, as though he were bragging, or exaggerating, and his body was spastic with apology, even though he knew, as she was telling him, that there was no need.

It was weird, he mused. As a kid, he'd dreamed of being famous, as an artist or an actor. Those dreams had subsided as he'd gotten older. But here all that dream-energy had come rushing back, like a floodlight dazzling him. His mind buzzed unpleasantly around those feelings, knowing that he wasn't really culpable for whatever weird feelings came to him in crisis, but also wondering if they said something definitive about his personality. He stood, took down Daniel's bag from the overhead compartment, found the pill bottle he'd been looking for, and shoved the bag back in. He sat down with a thud and a sigh, and put one of the tiny pills on his tongue.

By the time he'd opened the door to Daniel's office, he'd hardly been able to breathe. Daniel had been sitting at his desk with a manuscript in front of him, scratching his head with a big pensive scowl, and at the sight of Matt his face had broken into a smile whose sweetness Matt was certain he would never recover from. He'd breathed "Dan," and "Honey," and burst into tears. Daniel had rushed around the desk, banging his leg and swearing, and Matt choked out the words as they clutched each other, his head over Daniel's shoulder and his eyes squeezed shut because he couldn't bear to see. He felt Daniel slip through his arms to the floor. Kneeling beside him, his fingers twined through Daniel's dark hair, his throat seizing, Matt had raged against the hard fate of this man who so didn't deserve it, and wondered whether

Daniel's face would ever light up again at the sight of him. Certainly it hadn't since.

He remembered the minutes passing, and he remembered growing drowsy, and his mind beginning to drift. He'd listened to the sounds of office life outside the door, made out a phone conversation between one of the secretaries and what seemed to be her daughter complaining about her husband. They spent so much of that day down on the floor— not only because it was hard to stand, it seemed to him, but also because they were trying to cringe low to the ground to make themselves as inconspicuous as possible, like terrified animals. Finally, Daniel lifted his head and whispered, "Take me home." He let Matt help him to his feet. "Easy, baby," Matt murmured as Daniel stood unsteadily, looking at him with wide, shocked eyes.

After he'd gotten Daniel home, he'd been on the phone nonstop. First with Daniel's father, who was channeling all of his horror into obsessing over whether they should fly El Al or Continental. And then with Continental, trying to get a bereavement rate for a next-day flight. Trying to figure out, without bothering Daniel about it, how they'd get a death certificate in Israel. Finding the passports and ascertaining with relief that they hadn't expired. Logging onto Weather.com to see what the weather would be like in Jerusalem this time of year, and, seeing that it fluctuated wildly, overpacking. Calling their friend Cam to take the dog. Interrupting that conversation when a call came in on call-waiting from the president of the college, offering his condolences and his services. Matt thanked him repeatedly, burdened by his windy solicitude; Cam was crying on the other line and he wanted to get back to her.

All the while, Daniel had been lying on the bed, shaking, his knees drawn up and his arms thrown over his head; his jacket and tie and shoes were strewn on the bedroom floor, and he ran periodically to the bathroom to vomit. Matt kept approaching the edge of the bed, and then, overwhelmed by a sense of his own irrelevance, turning away. He picked up Daniel's jacket from the floor, brushed it off, and hung it in the closet. Finally, he lay down carefully beside Daniel, enveloping him with his arms and drawing the stockinged soles of his feet up his calves, trying to still his shaking with his own bigness, his warm body. Daniel's shirt was cold and damp from sweat, and his teeth were chattering. "Honey, you're chilled," Matt had murmured, "let me get you into the shower." But Daniel had let out a moan and blindly thrown an elbow that struck Matt in the cheek, and Matt had stumbled off the bed and ran out of the room. In his study, he stared out the window at the yard, which was blurred and somber in the fading light, and fought back tears of fury. He touched his smarting cheek, which hurt all the way to his teeth, and told himself not to be such a big pussy. There was a pack of Camel Lights stuffed in a drawer; he took one out and lit it, blowing smoke forcefully out the open window. He knew he was being stupid and childish. And yet, fury coursed through him, and on its heels, a terrifying intimation of the suffering to come.

MATT REACHED FOR THE in-flight magazine, flipped through it looking for the crossword and saw that someone had already done it. He studied the map of Continental's flights, and then the floor plans of various European airports, and then he read an article on how to respect and handle the customs of foreign businessmen. He hoped Daniel's father, up in business class, saw it, because he knew he'd like it. He was a corporate executive, and from the time they were teenagers, Daniel and Joel had bought him, as birthday and Father's Day and Chanukah presents, books on how to be effective, how to motivate others, how to think outside the box. Sam's total immersion in the corporate mind-set was something Matt found both alienating and adorable, and he related to Sam like a fascinated anthropologist, getting him to talk about company retreats where they did relay races based on army training exercises, or used their teamwork to build a jet engine out of matches and cardboard and nail polish. It was Rosen family lore that Sam once read a book about how to utilize humor to defuse difficult interpersonal relations. When his wife, Lydia, saw it, she'd smacked her forehead with her palm. She called him the only Jew in America without a sense of humor.

Matt stuffed the magazine back into the seat pocket and opened his tray table. Around him were the shuffle of newspapers, the drone of the engines, the metallic sound coming through people's earphones, the murmur of *beef or chicken?* Across the aisle from them, in the three middle seats, sat a religious family with a fat baby and a toddler in a frilly dress who was peeling stickers off a sheet and laying them carefully on her armrest. Exploded all over their seats and the floor were wet crumbs in smashed Baggies, crayons, plastic pieces from games, empty yogurt containers, Goldfish crackers. The mother was kerchiefed and red-cheeked, joggling the baby with an expression of hassled professionalism, and the father pale, with blond ringlets down the sides of his face, reading a small prayer book. There was something a little hot about the guy's detachment, his look of being above it all.

Matt needed to pee, but he'd waited too long; the food cart was blocking the aisle behind him. He wondered what Daniel's parents were eating up in business class—probably not something called "beef" or "chicken." They were probably drinking heavily, too. The four of them had found one another in the security line in Newark, where Daniel's parents, looking like ghosts in expensive travel coats, had pulled Daniel toward them with a cry and clung to him while Matt dragged their bags and gently herded the huddled group forward, ignoring the curious glances of other passengers. He was sweating and winded by the time they settled in at the gate. It pained him to see how shock had blunted the normally ingenuous features of Daniel's father; Matt could see the tiny webs of capillaries around his nose, and when Sam put his and Lydia's passports and boarding passes into the inside pocket of his jacket, his hands shook. Lydia had sat huddled in the crook of Daniel's arm, from time to time grasping his sleeve and whimpering, "Those poor babies," and "Why didn't God take me instead?" Her dramatic dark eyes were bloodshot, her face dusted over with recently reapplied face powder. Matt felt terrible for her, but her behavior made him think that she had seen one too many Anna Magnani movies. Since when did she even believe in God? He had gladly gone off to perform helpful tasks, buying a neck pillow and some Tylenol for her, and two new luggage tags for his and Daniel's bags, and *Time* and *Entertainment Weekly* for himself.

Now, as a tray was set in front of him, he had the sudden thought: Maybe Lydia's response was a Jewish form of expression? Maybe the Jews were one of those howling or keening peoples, their mourning a residue of the customs of their often-bereaved peasant ancestors? Matt's fingers grew still over the silverware packet he was trying to open. He was destined to be ashamed of himself, he was learning; since yesterday's call, there was virtually no thought that came without recoil. So, believing it was always better to face his demons, he made a mental list of all the thoughts he was ashamed of:

1. Was grief going to make Daniel look old and shriveled?
2. And if so, would they ever have halfway decent sex again?
3. He clearly wasn't going to make the Rufus Wainwright concert on the twenty-sixth: Could he just let that go?
4. Would his, Matt's, needs and aspirations ever be considered important again?
5. Would he ever get to just be a normal, young, shallow queen again, or would tragedy dog him for the rest of his born days?

But Matt knew these questions were bullshit, that he was evading the real issue: If Joel and Ilana had really done what they said they were going to do, he and Daniel would be returning home with their kids, and the life he knew would open up into dark seas he couldn't even begin to chart.

. . . . .

THREE MORNINGS AGO, MATT had awakened singing Gershwin:

> They laughed at me wanting you—
> Said it would be Hello! Goodbye!
> But oh, you came through—
> Now they're eating humble pie.

He lay smiling next to Daniel in bed, with his hands folded behind his head, singing to the ceiling in a husky morning voice. It was their fourth anniversary; four years before, Matt had come up to Northampton to visit the shy Jewish cutie he'd met at a party in New York. He knew Daniel had never imagined being with him for so long; he'd thought of Matt as an amazing sexual windfall, and continued insisting that it was just an affair even after Matt moved permanently to Northampton, even after Daniel's friends began to tease him that his "affair" had begun wearing Birkenstocks with socks, a virtual guarantee that he'd never be allowed back in the city. Daniel just couldn't believe—and sometimes Matt couldn't believe it himself—that a young gay man would choose to leave New York to live in Northampton, which the *Enquirer* had once called, in an effort to shock, Lesbianville, USA.

That morning he turned to Daniel, stuffing a pillow under his neck. "Remember how you thought I was just some shallow hottie, but then you couldn't help falling in love with me?" he asked.

The memory of that morning made Matt clench his teeth, and as he picked at meat in gravy with peas and carrots, his partner still unconscious beside him, his mind cautiously turned over the question of what the terrain was like in Daniel's head. Like a tornado, he imagined, whipping trees up from their roots and slamming them into cars. He remembered an educational segment he'd recently seen on the Weather Channel, where the quiz question was: *During a tornado, where is the safest place in a mobile home?* After a commercial break they returned with the answer: *NOWHERE; leave immediately.* It had shocked him, the cruelty of the trick question; wasn't it bad enough that these people had to live in mobile homes? They were advised to go outside and find a regular house—*some wealthier person's decent home*, he had acidly glossed to Daniel—and failing that, to find a ditch to lie in. He had been indignant. "'Yeah, you pathetic trailer trash, go lie in a ditch!'—that's basically what they're saying, isn't it?"

He set aside his roll and piece of chocolate cake for Daniel, hoping he'd be able to choke down food that was mild and sweet. He looked at Daniel's sagging head. *NOWHERE*, he thought, *that's where it's safe to be*. Leave immediately, go lie in a ditch.

AFTER DINNER AND A long wait in the bathroom line, Matt read the movie and TV reviews in *Entertainment Weekly* and drifted off with the magazine in his hands. He was awakened by murmuring voices and the jingle of a bracelet. Lydia was standing over them, bringing in the sweet musky smell of her perfume, which Matt always smelled on his ears and collars for a few days after they spent time with her. He looked at Daniel and saw that he'd awakened too, and had a cup of ginger ale on his tray table. He pressed his hand, which lay on the seat between them, against Daniel's knee, in a discreet hello.

"Darling," Lydia was saying to Daniel, with a hollow trace of her old intensity, "for the shiva, I think we should pick up some *bourekas* at that little bakery on Joel's street."

Daniel laid his head back. "Okay, Mom," he said. His voice was hoarse, and he brought his fist to his mouth and cleared his throat. His shirt was open at the neck, the curls in the back of his head flattened.

"It's just that Ilana's parents are utterly useless in this regard."

"Okay," Daniel said. His gray face shifted into something like its usual life as an idea came over it. "Actually, I think the visitors bring the food—the mourners aren't supposed to have to cook. And are we even sure the shiva's going to be at Joel and Ilana's? Maybe the Grossmans will want to have it."

Lydia blinked. "That's out of the question."

"Why?" Daniel asked. "Wouldn't it be better for the kids to have a place to come home to where there aren't a million people sitting around?" Gal and Noam were with their *sabba* and *savta*, Ilana's parents, now, but the plan was to bring them to their own house when their uncles and other grandparents arrived.

Matt could see the struggle break out on Lydia's face, and the stubbornness. "Don't you think the people who loved Joel and Ilana will want to gather one more time at their home?"

Daniel shrugged, and Lydia's eyes welled up. "And don't you think I'm thinking about those children?" she hissed. "I think of nothing else!"

"What are *bourekas*?" Matt asked.

Lydia looked down at him incredulously, and Matt was sorry for the silly question. In front of Lydia, he was a chronic blurter, and he knew that she didn't like him very much. Apparently she'd loved Daniel's first boyfriend, Jonathan. Matt—much younger than Daniel, eye candy, a goy, a lover of television rather than art or opera—was clearly the inferior and less appropriate partner.

"They're small triangular pastries in filo dough," she said.

"Oh."

"They're savory, not sweet. They're filled with cheese or spinach. They're a very popular finger food in Israel."

"I see," Matt said.

"Mom," Daniel said, "why don't we wait till we get there, and maybe this shiva thing will just work itself out." He closed his eyes.

Lydia nodded, drew herself up, and said to Matt with a strange pride, "The place down the street from Joel's house has some of the best *bourekas* in the city."

When she headed back to the front of the airplane, Matt said, "Well, *that* was a surreal little exchange."

Daniel's eyes were still closed. "She's trying not to have to imagine how much of her son's body has been blown to bits."

Matt bit his lip, scalded.

Daniel opened his eyes and looked at him with a weak appeal, laid a hand on top of his. "Forgive me if I'm an asshole, okay?"

"Okay," Matt whispered, squeezing Daniel's cold fingers, unspeakably grateful for the gaze that seemed to recognize him for the first time since the news had come.

"Do we have a piece of paper and a pen?"

"Sure, baby."

Matt fished them out of his travel bag, and Daniel sighed, then bent over the paper and began writing in Hebrew. Matt looked at the round strong veins on Daniel's working hand, which passed rapidly from right to left. "What are you writing?" he asked.

"A eulogy for my brother."

Daniel covered the page and then stopped and gave Matt a stricken look. He set the pen down, took off his glasses, and started to cry. Matt gripped his hand. He had never seen Daniel cry until last night, and he was a little scared he'd cry like that now, in public. He'd seen him well up once or twice, and that was shattering enough to witness. But not really crying, and certainly not crying like that, writhing, screaming his brother's name, his teeth bared and his face sealed off and unseeing so that he seemed like one of those creatures, like otters or monkeys, whose faces lie on the disconcerting boundary between human and animal. Now Daniel was quiet, tears streaming down his face. *Oh,* Matt's heart clamored, *what should I do?* How could he be a comfort to this man who had been such a comfort to him? And those kids! Noam was only a baby! He wasn't up to it, he knew it. He would blow it again, the way he had with Jay, with all of the bad-mouthing and posturing, and his boycotting the memorial service, and the crushing fear that he had failed to be there for his best friend in the right way.

Oh poor poor Joel, Matt thought, and Ilana's face too flashed into his mind, big and raucous, and her sloppy ponytail, and tears rushed, hot and brutal, into his eyes.

· · · · ·

SEVEN HOURS LATER THEY stood at the airport curb, huddled around a small, curly-haired woman—Yemenite, Daniel would later tell him—holding a walkie-talkie and wearing a neon-green vest marked with bold Hebrew lettering. Her name was Shoshi, and she was the social worker sent by the city of Jerusalem. The Middle Eastern morning sun was bright and penetrating, and they had taken off coats and jackets and put on sunglasses. Around them, cars jostled and honked, and trunks slammed shut. Taxi drivers in open-necked shirts and Ray-Bans jingled keys in their hands as they approached exiting travelers. While Shoshi and Daniel spoke in Hebrew, nodding rapidly, Matt bent over and pulled down his right sock, his heart still thrumming with excitement and indignation at the lunatics in baggage claim. People had bumped into him and shouldered in front of him, and an elderly man on a fanatical push to the conveyor belt had jammed his luggage cart into Matt's heel, knocking his shoe clear off. Matt had wrestled it back on, surprised by the rage surging up his throat, and the rude old prick hadn't even apologized. Now Matt gripped the handle of his own cart with renewed, glowering concentration. He heard a lot of English spoken in American accents with strange glottal emphases. Their language sounded self-important and bullying to him, as though they were talking to children or foreign servants, and thinking that many of them were probably settlers, he felt a strong antipathy for them. Daniel loathed them. Each time they saw one of them interviewed on television, he would shout, "What's the matter, the U.S. isn't fundamentalist enough for you?!"

Matt's heel was chafed, but not bleeding, and he pulled up his sock and straightened. The sun was warming him to the bone, and there was the smell of something sharp in the air, like citrus or guava, mixed with exhaust fumes. This country seemed to him to be a different earthly element than his own, and he found that both exciting and a little frightening. He wasn't well traveled; his only trip outside the U.S. had been to Amsterdam with Jay years ago, right out of college. Here, under a cloudless sky, people were smoking and gesticulating; everyone had a cell phone attached to his or her ear, even the children. Although Matt was shocked by the open display of assault rifles, and officially disapproved of the soldiers in uniform, he found them beautiful. They were short and brown-skinned and very young.

He began to notice that passersby were casting curious and compassionate glances at Daniel's family. He stepped closer to Daniel, laying his hand on the small of his back, and bowed his head into the conversation. The social worker had switched to English, and was telling Daniel's parents that a van would arrive shortly to take them to the morgue. She touched their elbows as she spoke. She projected an aura of gentle authority, and looked into their faces in a way that was somehow both searching and undemanding. Matt had a powerful impulse to sidle up and confide in her. *I'm the gay boyfriend! I'm the goyfriend! I'm in a foreign country where I don't speak the language!*

At that moment Sam frowned and pointed into the distance, where a small group of photographers were snapping pictures of them with zoom lenses. "What are they doing?" Shoshi's face darkened and she took off toward them with her arms outstretched; when she got near them, she wagged her finger in their faces, barking commands. They gave her a short argument, and then walked away, one of them turning to utter a final deprecation.

The family had instinctively turned their faces away, and when Shoshi returned, panting and apologizing, they moved their bodies to gather her within the pack. A white van pulled up to the curb, and a driver wearing a yarmulke got out and put their luggage in the back as they climbed inside, Daniel helping Lydia into the front seat. Daniel sat with the social worker in the middle seat, leaving Matt and Sam in the back. They settled into the air-conditioning, wound up by the unexpected fracas with them at its center.

"What was that all about?" Sam asked.

"Joel was a minor celebrity," Daniel reminded them; he'd been the host of an English-language television interview show.

There was a pause. "How did they know we were . . . ?" Sam trailed off as Shoshi pointed to Daniel's face. "And my emergency gear," she added.

As the van pulled through the guard stations at the airport exit, Shoshi twisted to sit sideways and told them that the ride to Abu Kabir would take about twenty minutes. Her English was proficient but heavily accented, and from time to time she hesitated and said a word in Hebrew to Daniel, who translated it for his family. She told them that Ilana, Joel's wife, had been identified by her parents, but the other body had been held so that, if it was Joel, he could be identified by his immediate family. She pronounced Joel "Yo-*el*," its Hebrew version.

"*If* it is Joel?" Lydia asked sharply.

"If it is," Shoshi said, giving her a steady look.

"Why do you say *if*?" Lydia's voice was rising.

"Mom," Daniel murmured.

"We cannot say for sure until he is identified."

"Are mistakes ever made?" Lydia insisted. She had twisted around in her seat, and was trying to pin Shoshi to the wall with a single flashing look.

Shoshi was quiet.

"My wife is asking you a question," Sam said sharply from the back. Matt started. He had never heard Sam talk like that; his authority was normally genial. Watching Shoshi's sad and patient look, Matt surmised that they did in fact know it was Joel, but that she wasn't allowed to say so until his body was officially identified.

Finally, Shoshi said, "It is very rare."

Lydia's mouth quivered, and she turned stonily toward the front. Matt looked out the window at long fields, a flat and hazy stretch to the horizon, where he imagined the ocean to be. Irrigation pipes sent up a fine glinting spray. Until that moment, as they'd moved busily through passport control and baggage claim and customs, there had been a faint sense of reprieve. There was the unreality of being in a foreign country, the disorientation of a different time zone. And then the weird and unexpected excitement of being the targets of paparazzi. But now, a crushing silence fell over them. Sam exhaled next to Matt, giving off a smell of alcohol, morning breath, dry cleaning.

No one spoke until the van pulled off the highway onto a smaller road and Shoshi turned again. They were there; a sludge of anxiety seeped through Matt and turned him cold. "I want to tell you a little bit about what will happen inside," Shoshi said. "You will be brought into a room where police will ask you questions about Joel's body. I will come with you." She paused, trying, Matt imagined, to give them time to comprehend these barbaric sentences. "They will ask you questions about his body from his toes to the tips of his hair. Then you will be brought into another room to wait. And finally, you will be taken to what is called the separation room, to identify the body there."

The van stopped, and an electric gate was opened. Matt read the English part of the sign, *Institute of Forensic Medicine*, saw photographers bunched outside the gate, getting shots of the van with zoom lenses. They pulled in and parked in a small lot beside another van, and the driver turned off the engine, leaving them sitting there in silence. "I can't move," Lydia whispered. Matt knew the feeling; his legs were numb, and it felt as though the force of energy required to lurch into movement would require a strength way beyond him. It was Daniel who pressed down the latch on the door; it slid open with a roar. "Let's get this over with," he said.

THERE WAS A BRICK path leading to an unobtrusive entrance. There was a hall with white chairs. Around them, people babbled and wailed. The smell was awful—a combination of what? Formaldehyde, for sure, and burnt hair, but other smells too, hideous ones for which Matt had no olfactory memory or vocabulary. They were urged to wash their faces, and to drink some water. Before Matt knew it, Daniel was stuffed in a chair between his parents, his hands thrust helplessly between his knees. Matt slunk around like the loser in musical chairs. Finally, Lydia snapped, "Sit already, would you?" A horrible wave of righteous indignation rose in his throat. But he sat in a chair beside Sam and stuffed it down, his throat cramping with the effort.

He ran his hands over his face. The sound of crying roared in his ears, and his mind worked at the sound until it smoothed out, became an abstract pattern.

They didn't have to wait long to be ushered into the office with the police; Matt learned later that, except for Joel and an Arab dishwasher, the other fourteen victims had been identified already, and that the remaining mourners in the hall were identifying the bodies of victims of a massive pileup that had occurred the previous night, outside of Tel Aviv. He touched the social worker's sleeve. "Should I go with them?" he asked.

Her look was kind, but doubtful. "The room is quite small," she said.

"Oh, okay then," he said in a quick, anxious display of cooperation that he immediately regretted when the door closed behind them.

He thought he could safely leave the building for a little while and be back by the time they emerged, so he wandered outside. He stepped out of the sun into the shadow of pine trees, gravel crunching beneath his shoes, grateful for air that didn't stink of mayhem. His dress pants were damp at the seat and thighs. An old man was sweeping pine needles off the paths that ran between the stuccoed buildings, a lit cigarette in his mouth, and Matt wondered if he dared ask him for one. He felt shy; he didn't know if this dark-skinned fellow was Jewish or Palestinian, and didn't in any case know either language. He slowly walked toward him, and when he met the man's eye, he mimed smoking a cigarette, his eyebrows raised inquiringly. The old man rested the broom handle against his armpit and fished out a rumpled pack from his breast pocket, extended it toward Matt, and Matt drew one out. With a leathery hand, the man gave him his own stub of a lit cigarette to light it with. Matt inhaled deeply and blew two thin streams from his nostrils.

"Thank you," he said, nodding, in this act of bumming a smoke, without social class or nationality, a man among men.

He strolled back to the building, holding the cigarette in graceful fingers. He leaned against the stucco wall, closed his eyes, and rested. Instantly, his peace was shattered by the vision of Joel's body being torn apart, and he opened them again, found himself laboring to breathe. Inside, they were talking about every inch of Joel's body. Matt felt an overwhelming tenderness toward it. Joel looked a lot like Daniel, but with the slight beefiness of the straight man. Matt and Daniel had been together for a year before Matt met him, and he'd refused to believe that Joel was straight. When Daniel said, "He's *married*," Matt asked, "To a woman?" He quizzed him suspiciously. Had Joel gone to Israel to *try* to be straight? Did he think a macho culture would straighten him up? Was Daniel sure they were *identical* twins? Then one summer, Joel came to visit them in Northampton and brought his wife, Ilana, and Matt took one look at the butch with the booming voice and bruising handshake and shot Daniel a look: *Why didn't you tell me?*

Joel was all *ta-da!*—he had a strong sense of entitlement, but mostly in a nice way. He was a child who had madly flourished under the praise he received when he brought home his accomplishments. He acted as though he believed he was handsome, and that *made* him handsome, although in fact, Daniel was much more so. He was the best dancer Matt had ever seen in a straight man. He flirted with Matt, as though Daniel's gayness gave him a delicious permission; he was even a little inappropriate sometimes, maybe coming on too strong as the cool and gay-affirmative straight twin. He pretended that he was dominated by his giant wife.

Matt crushed the cigarette under his shoe, suddenly sickened by it, and went back inside.

Two big, loutish sons were muttering in Russian, bent over their keening mother, who wore a shapeless housedress and a scarf on her head. The sounds she made seemed to come from some hideous marshy place inside her, and the men winced and muttered, patting her shoulder with stiff paws. Matt took a seat and closed his eyes. An hour passed. He opened his eyes to see Daniel's ghastly face; the Rosens had returned. He patted the seat next to him, and when Daniel sat, he took his arm, but Daniel moved it away. Matt looked around at the hall: For Christ's sake, who was capable of crawling out of their own misery to notice they were queers? He told himself: *Daniel can do anything he wants right now, don't get mad.*

They waited. They were taken outside to a different white house, and led into another office, where they waited some more. "Why must we wait so long?" Lydia moaned, and then her eyes fluttered and she fainted. *"Hello!"* they called, and there was noise, and shuffling, and curt instructions. Daniel and Matt knelt, cradling her head; Shoshi ran out and came back with a wet paper towel, with which she patted Lydia's forehead. They brought her staggering to her feet, her dark hair limp around her face, and pressed a water bottle to her lips. Sam paced around her, swatting at the fabric of her suit where it had become dusty from the fall. The door opened, and Shoshi said, "Now we will go into the separation room, to see the body. I'm sorry to say that the body must not be touched, since it has been prepared for Jewish burial."

They stared at her dumbly. Matt felt goose bumps shiver along his forearms. They heaved themselves to their feet and followed the social worker down a hallway. Matt stopped at the door. When it opened, he could see into the bare room where a man in a lab coat stood beside a covered body on a pallet. He had a sudden passionate urge to say good-bye to Joel. Could he go in? But Daniel and his parents glided toward the pallet without looking back, the door swung closed in front of him and Shoshi, and he felt that without an explicit invitation, he couldn't.

His eyes were dry and itchy, red-rimmed; he rubbed them furiously with his fists. He'd been kept from Jay, too. That officious little prick Kendrick had neglected to inform him that Jay was on a respirator, and the following afternoon Matt had heard from a different friend altogether that Jay had died that morning.

He pressed his forehead against the glass of the small window in the door.

Lydia and Sam stepped back, and Matt got a glimpse of Joel. His eyes galloped over the covered body to see if it looked intact, and it did, he thought, except for maybe in the middle; he squinted and blinked hard, until his mind reassured him that the whole body was there. Joel's face was white, his dark hair swept stiffly back off his forehead as if by a sweaty day's work. Daniel looked somberly at him, then bent and murmured something into Joel's ear. The doctor was speaking to Daniel's parents with a serious and patient look, as though he wanted his words to be remembered. He stopped from time to time, waiting for them to nod. Beside him, Shoshi spoke. "He's saying that Joel was killed on the spot, and didn't feel anything."

Part of Matt's mind caught that, and he wondered if the doctor said that to everybody. But mostly he was watching Daniel, and something was coming over him that took his breath away. He squared his shoulders. At that moment he knew the answer to the question with which he'd often secretly tormented himself: whether he would be loving enough, selfless enough, to fling himself into the path of an oncoming car to save Daniel. He would, he suddenly knew he would. He felt stern and important, for all that he was the one left unnoticed outside the door. History had entered their lives with a sonorous call, and it was up to him to shepherd Daniel, and the children too, through this dark flood and onto higher ground. There was no room to ask whether he could do it or not. He had to.

"Good-bye, Joel," he whispered. "I love you."

Shoshi placed a gentle hand on his arm. He was trembling.

BEFORE THEY COULD GO, they had to sign. Shoshi brought them a form in Hebrew and Daniel perused it. "It says that you identified Joel, and that the body is his," she told Lydia and Sam, handing Daniel a pen.

"They wouldn't let me touch my own son," Lydia murmured.

Daniel put the form down on a table and leaned over it with straight arms. He stared at it for a long time. Matt stepped up to him and laid his hand on his back, and felt it heave. Finally, Daniel turned toward his father, his face crumpling like a child's. "Dad," he whispered.

Sam stepped forward and took the pen from him and ran his finger down the page, which was mercifully indecipherable to him, found the blank line, and signed.

And with that, Joel was dead.

CHAPTER 2

I T WAS FOUR years earlier, and Matt was taking the bus from New York to Northampton, his temple pressed against the cold window. He wore a T-shirt and a leather jacket, and a small overnight bag sat on his lap. On the streets of his neighborhood, the late-March wind whipped around corners, making storefront gratings rattle, and pedestrians picked their way around slush and garbage and discarded flyers for clubs. When Matt left the gym in the mornings, showered and dressed for the office, the morning sun gleamed in his face and made him squint. He'd take the train from Chelsea to midtown, and when he got to work he'd go to the men's room and wet a paper towel, then scrub at the dirty splotches on the calves of his pants.

Spring was on its way, and Matt felt it as a ripping sensation in his chest. He was suffering from insomnia for the first time in his life, and had had a few anxiety attacks that made him fear he was having a heart attack. His best friend, Jay, was dying, and he was fighting with Jay's partner Kendrick, who had been with Jay all of a year while Matt had been his best friend since forever. Kendrick, whom he privately referred to as Shmendrick, was bad-mouthing him to all their friends, claiming that when Matt was around Jay, it was like having to take care of *two* patients. Matt knew that wasn't true, knew that when he was with him, a little more of Jay's soul showed.

The night before, at around three, when he'd returned home from the clubs, he had rummaged through his desk looking for the stub of a joint he'd left there, and found the matchbook with Daniel's name and number on it. He took it to bed with him and sat there inhaling smoke, contemplating, until the tiny ragged joint burned his fingers. Once he had the idea that he could leave town, he could hardly wait for morning to come so he could call. He lay in bed imagining a quiet, orderly house in the New England countryside with a guest bedroom that his imagination formed out of a bed-and-breakfast he'd once stayed in: a fluffed-up bed with a dust ruffle and an iron headboard, a painting of English hunters on horseback hanging above. And then, even as he was laughing to himself for being stoned and silly, his mind attached itself to that image with a surprising passion.

Why Daniel, he wondered later, when he had at least three other friends who lived within a few hours on a bus or train, and when he hardly knew the guy? Later, when he told the story at dinner parties, he insisted he'd had some secret intimation. But at that point, it was just a panicked need to flee the drug scene and the whole circus surrounding Jay, who was back in the hospital with pneumonia, and being sick of his friends, whose eyes were starting to glaze over at the whole topic because, he thought savagely, of their own terror at the risks they were exposing themselves to every day. "I gotta get out of here," he told Daniel on the phone the next morning, at ten A.M. sharp, the first moment he felt he could call. He'd reminded him that they'd met at a party, and endured the terrifying moment of pause before Daniel said, "I remember." When Matt asked if he could visit, panic made him lose his breath, and after a long silence that he read as either cold or thoughtful, Daniel said, "Sure, come on up, I have a spare room."

Somewhere in Connecticut, it started to snow, big early-spring flakes spreading over the bus windshield, melting as soon as they hit the asphalt. By the time they crossed into Massachusetts, the trees lining the highway were drooping with snow, and the blinking lights of the salt trucks pierced the blurry dusk. The guy sitting next to him had fallen asleep with his head thrown back and his mouth open. Matt wondered if he would even recognize Daniel, and tried to bring his image into his mind. He didn't remember the conversation they'd had at the party very well—he'd been more than a little drunk—but he remembered feeling drawn to him, and after all, Daniel *had* given him his phone number. He mulled over Daniel's words on the phone, *I have a spare room*, amused and insulted by Daniel's presumption that he was dying to sleep with him. But he knew that he'd have said the exact same thing, just to protect himself.

As the bus pulled slowly into the Springfield station, he looked out the window and recognized Daniel immediately; he was standing under a small overhang, his hands in the pockets of a parka, his face a study in moderate, noncommittal welcome. Matt stood and brought down his backpack from the overhead rack, worried suddenly that his arrival was a chore for Daniel, imagining him complaining to his friends that he had to host some guy he'd met at a party. When he stepped off the bus, he approached awkwardly, smiling. Daniel looked older and more ordinary in the winter dusk than he had in the glow of alcohol and party music, and Matt felt a small pang of disappointment. Daniel proffered his hand, then laughed self-consciously and kissed him on the cheek. That laugh crinkled his eyes and lifted Matt's spirits. They walked out through the station's slush-covered floors. It was snowing hard now, and Daniel brushed the snow off the windshield and back window of his Camry as Matt shivered in the cold front seat, shaking snow out of his hair and wondering what he'd gotten himself into.

It took them forever to get to Daniel's house, visibility was so diminished. "Remind me what you do again?" Daniel asked. He was sitting forward, straining to see the road. When Matt spoke he had to raise his voice over the din of the defroster. "I'm a graphic designer," he said.

"Shit," Daniel said; he had gotten himself stuck behind a snowplow, and clumps of snow and dirt were pelting the car. Matt hugged himself and slouched down into his jacket.

By the time Daniel pulled into the driveway of a small Cape house in Northampton, Matt had lost his bearings and had no idea where Northampton even was. The walk was still unshoveled, and the wind howled in their faces, and when they got inside they stamped their feet, shouting. Matt shook his head, spraying cold drops everywhere; Daniel laughed "Hey!" and took off his glasses and wiped them on the T-shirt under his sweater. A yellow Labrador barged into the mudroom, its tail banging against the walls. "This is Yo-yo," Daniel said, as the dog pressed himself up against Matt's thigh with a crazy, tongue-lolling smile.

The house had pine floors with wide, soft boards. Daniel took him up a creaking flight of stairs to the guest room, where Matt had to stoop under a sloped ceiling. The bed was made up in maroon sheets and a gray comforter, the effect both masculine and warm. Daniel left the room and returned with a sweatshirt and some wool socks. "Thanks," Matt said, peeling off his wet socks and cupping his hands around his cold toes. Daniel said, "Well, we can't go out, so I'm going to see what I have for dinner. Come on down whenever you want."

After he left the room, Matt looked at the dog and said, "Well, my friend, this is quite awkward." Yo-yo pushed his muzzle into Matt's hand, and he scratched the dog's forehead with two fingers, grinning as a faraway expression gathered in Yo-yo's eyes. He lingered shyly up there for a little while, looking at the photos on the dresser. There were yellowing photos, in old-fashioned silver frames, of Jewish-immigrant grandparents. Color photographs of handsome, well-heeled, coiffed parents. And one of Daniel, probably in college, hugging or wrestling with a boy whom Matt surmised was his brother, possibly his twin. Matt smiled. Daniel was delicious in it, his cheeks fuller and smoother, his hair long and wild. He was clearly a little annoyed by his brother's wild grasp. The brother was pretty hot too, even though he looked like a goof with his hammy smile, as if saying "Cheese!" better than anyone had ever said it before.

When Matt came into the kitchen, Daniel was closing the refrigerator with his elbow, his hands full of eggs. "Sorry," he said, "I meant to take you out." On the stove sat a frying pan, of good quality and heavily used, Matt noted. As Daniel cracked eggs and put a slab of butter in the pan, he became quiet, and Matt said, "Listen, thanks for having me. It's nice to get away. I'll probably head back to New York tomorrow." He sat in a kitchen chair and watched as Daniel deftly sliced onions and grated cheese. Snow was gathering silently along the bottoms of the windows. "How do you live out here?" he asked Daniel, with perfect cosmopolitan snobbery. "I gotta be honest, I'm feeling a little like Shelley Duvall in *The Shining*."

Daniel looked at him and raised his eyebrows. "Who does that make me?" he asked. "A dull boy?" Matt laughed; he could tell he was making himself obnoxious. "I like it here," Daniel shrugged. "In the city, everyone's trying to be cooler and more stylish than everyone else. To me, that's a huge waste of time. And I can't handle the crystal thing."

Matt nodded sagely; he couldn't handle the crystal meth thing either—the extent of it scared and horrified him—but he was also taking in the rebuke. He was remembering his initial attraction to Daniel, something he didn't know how to put his finger on. Certainly part of it was the whole Jewish intellectual vibe, the high forehead, curly dark hair, black-rimmed glasses that gave his face a touch of owlish severity. He looked as though he should be chain-smoking in a French café, devising a philosophical system that explained everything in the universe. He was soft-spoken, his voice slightly nasal, with a nelly sibilance to his *s*'s. The blend of masculine and feminine in him was exact, and perfect. His house was well tended without being fussy. Matt watched him stir the frying onions, and, being a restless person himself, was drawn to what seemed like a talent for immersion in the task at hand.

At dinner, Matt noticed that he was feeling self-conscious eating in front of Daniel, which surprised him a little. You could think in your head that you weren't into a guy, but there were certain signs that infallibly told you otherwise, such as being superaware of how you were chewing. He asked Daniel how he'd gotten to that party anyway, and they talked about the couple who had thrown it, their mutual friends

Mitchell and Bruce. Mitchell was an old friend of Daniel's from Oberlin, and Matt knew Bruce from the gym. They dished about their relationship, agreeing with delighted shouts that the two of them were irritatingly symbiotic. "They're all, 'We like the Chilean sea bass,' 'We're good friends with the proprietor,'" Matt mimicked, making Daniel laugh, which broke his face into an utterly charming sweetness. "Dude, get a mind of your own!" Matt shifted, leaned a little closer over the table, getting confidential. "Enough about them," he said. "What did you think of me?"

Daniel laughed again, and his eyes shifted in a way that amused Matt; he was clearly rapidly editing his response. "Well, that you were attractive," he said, stiff with shyness.

"Really! Say more," Matt joked. "Wait, did I come out with some big drunken confession? I have the vague memory that I did."

Daniel cleared his throat. "You said that being as good-looking as you are proved to be a curse sometimes."

"Shut up. I said that?"

"Yup. You even choked up a little when you said it."

Matt groaned. "Was there at least some context . . . ?"

"Not really."

"Christ, what an asshole." It was coming back to him. He remembered now that he'd been trying to encourage Daniel, because he recognized on him the diffident look of a man who thought Matt was out of his league. "What did you say?" he asked.

Daniel shrugged, a glint in his eye. "I said that that must be really hard for you."

Matt guffawed. "I'm sorry," he said, shaking his head. "I'm a weepy, and apparently quite conceited, drunk."

He helped Daniel clear the dishes, wanting to tell him that he had thought Daniel was hot too, but not being able to find a way out of their conversation, and not sure what message he wanted to give him. They moved to the living room, where Daniel made a fire in the woodstove. "Do you like hot cider?" he asked. He disappeared into the kitchen for a while, and Matt picked up the magazine Daniel edited, browsing through stories of Amherst College alumni who were doing DNA sequencing and building affordable housing for the homeless. Daniel emerged from the kitchen and handed a tall steaming glass to Matt. It had a cinnamon stick in it. When Matt told the story in years to come, he'd say that, between the fire and the hot cider, he was remembering every sitcom episode he'd ever seen where the wife drags the reluctant husband to a cozy, romantic weekend in a Vermont inn. But when Daniel settled beside him, and the sweet cider coated his throat, and Daniel asked him why he'd needed to get out of New York so badly, Matt found himself choking up. "Oh God," he said, waving his hand in front of his face, and he told him about Jay, his best friend since high school. "We started our school's first gay-straight alliance," he said, his eyes gleaming with pride and self-irony. "We spent every Halloween together for ten years." He took two pictures out of his wallet and showed them to Daniel: one from their first year of college, when he and Jay had dressed up for Halloween as the Id and the Superego, and one from their junior year, when they'd gone as Nature and Nurture. Daniel looked at the pictures of the boys in preposterous costumes, and Matt was rewarded by his appreciative laughter. "I was a poli-sci and fine arts major," Matt said, "so these Halloweens really combined all my interests."

"I see that you managed to be the one who went as Nature and the Id," Daniel said.

Matt laughed. "Anything to show off bare-chested." He sighed shakily. "Anyway," he said, "last week there was a misunderstanding about who was going to bring Jay dinner, and Kendrick reamed me out for not being there when it counted. And then, when Jay tried to intervene, that little fucker told me I was upsetting Jay and making him sicker. Can you believe it? *I* was upsetting Jay! This is the guy who made Jay move out of his apartment after his first hospitalization because Kendrick was allergic to mold!"

He sat back on the couch cushion and sighed. "It was all very *Angels in America: The Next Generation*," he said.

Daniel leaned toward him and kissed him, his forehead touching Matt's, his breath sharp, like apples. The dog approached and shoved his muzzle between their knees, and Daniel said, "Yo-yo, don't be rude." He stood and led Matt to his bedroom, where they made out for a while, straining against their clothes like teenagers. Matt kissed him and nibbled him and worried whether this shy and quiet man could give him what he needed. Wind gusted against the windows, and a critter skittered overhead along the attic floor. Then they undressed, and Daniel took Matt's arm and turned him on his side. Matt gasped and tried to make a joke, but Daniel didn't laugh; he leaned over the bed and fumbled for the pants that lay on the floor, reached into the pockets, and pulled out a condom. *You dog*, Matt thought, but then Daniel was gripping his hips with surprising authority. Matt closed his eyes and fell, soaring, into himself, while the world bucked and spun. His orgasm thundered through him, and he passed out. He slept for fourteen hours, and when he awoke the next afternoon, the sun was shining and his body was aglow. He could hear Daniel moving around downstairs and the trickle of water in the gutters. He propped himself up on his elbows and looked outside; the snow had almost entirely melted.

IT WAS LATE AFTERNOON when they began their ascent to Jerusalem. Shoshi had had the driver stop at a roadside pizza and falafel stand and rousted them out of the van, insisting that they try to eat, but the smell of deep-fried and spicy food made everyone indecisive and nauseated. The smell of the morgue clung to them; Matt sniffed Daniel's hair and shuddered. Finally, Shoshi ordered a basket of pitas and some Cokes, which they took into the van. Matt looked out the window, chewing a warm pita, as the highway began to ascend. He was sitting next to Daniel now, his knee pressed against his, wondering what was going to happen next. He thought about seeing Gal, who was almost six years old now; she was a quick, intense child who they all were sure was gifted. Noam he barely knew; the baby had been only a few months old when he had last seen him. He was a cheerful, easy baby with legs that came in fat segments, like dinner rolls. He'd been born after two miscarriages following Gal's birth, and was considered such a gift by his parents that they were, as if amazed out of every expected impulse, completely mellow around him. Matt remembered that last visit, Noam sitting placidly in his bouncy chair in the corner of the dining room as they ate supper; midmeal, Ilana looked over and joked, "Hey, someone should pay attention to that baby over there." The name Noam, Daniel had explained to Matt, came from the word *na'im*, which means "pleasant," or maybe "pleasing"—"nice," but without the banality that word carried in English.

He looked fiercely out the window, deliberately blocking from his mind any thoughts of the future—of those kids living in his house, of himself as the guardian of two children. He thought about playing Uno with Gal, and what a sore loser she was, how she stormed out of the room when she lost and her father had to go speak with her. And almost from the time she learned to talk, if she was in the room, you couldn't tell other adults about the cute thing she'd said or she'd pitch a fit.

She was scathing about American accents, and imitated with withering accuracy the way Matt said her name till he learned to make not just the *ah* sound in the middle, but also the *l* sound at the end, pronounced not with a thick American tongue lazing at the bottom of the mouth but with a sharper tongue tapping the middle of the upper palate. For all that, Matt adored her and couldn't resist pushing the limits with her, making her giggle and howl in protest at the same time. He knew she adored him, too; she greeted him by rocketing into his arms, and he'd make loud strangling noises when she gripped him around the neck. Ilana and Joel had instilled in her a good sense of humor; they were the kind of parents for whom that was a value. Since she was tiny: *Is this my nose?!* they'd ask, pointing to their chin, eyes wide and incredulous. *Naaahhh.* He thought of the look she got on her face when she sensed something was a joke: a hilarious parody of slyness, eyes darting.

They were climbing now; the driver shifted into lower gear and the van paused and then surged. The sky had become both bluer and more cloudy; they drove in and out of the shadow of pine forest. "Look," Daniel said, pointing, leaning toward the window till his face touched Matt's. "Memorials. From the battle for Jerusalem in the '48 war." Matt began noticing the rusty remnants of trucks and tanks scattered among the rocks and pines at the side of the road. "See? There's another one." Matt nodded, impressed by the somber and rustic memorial. They continued to climb; he yawned to pop his ears. In the distance he began to discern, on a series of forested and terraced hills, clustered masses of white stone buildings bathed in late-afternoon light. The van turned and then rose again, and the populous outskirts of Jerusalem began to spread before them. It was called Jerusalem stone, Daniel had told him. Draped over the hills like necklaces made by a primitive hand, the neighborhoods conveyed a sense of inevitability, a rugged majesty. "Wow," Matt breathed, stunned. "Is that occupied territory?"

Daniel raised his eyebrows and turned away. Matt's stomach seized. He hadn't intended the question to be controversial or insensitive. Hadn't Daniel once told him that something like 75 percent of occupied territory was in the area of Jerusalem? His mind scrambled to remember what Daniel had said, and what he'd read, to reassure himself that it hadn't been a stupid question. The van swerved one way and then the other, and a nauseous headache began to gather behind Matt's eyes. They were engulfed by the noise of engines in low gear and the smell of gasoline fumes. They plunged into shadow as they rounded a curve, a towering stone wall on their right. They were rising to Jerusalem, the stench of death on their clothes and hair. His eyes smarted, and he felt profoundly alone, a pebble kicked along by a boot.

They wound around a road on the edge of a hill, then through the twisting narrow streets, all one-way, of Beit Ha-Kerem. Joel and Ilana's apartment building was at the end of a cul-de-sac circled by apartment buildings. Cars were parked everywhere, and every which way; laundry hung from windows, whipped by the wind; when they got out, two cats sprang out of a Dumpster and raced away. The Rosens ran into the dark hallway and up the stairs, while Matt and Shoshi and the driver lugged out the suitcases. The driver held the elevator door open by propping a suitcase against it, and they dragged in the rest of the luggage till the elevator was full, Matt pinned in by suitcases.

He went up the slow, creaky elevator alone. When it stopped, he dragged all the luggage out, and straightened. He grabbed a suitcase and entered an apartment full of crying, huddled adults and a burnt coffee smell. Lydia and the woman he took to be Malka, Ilana's mother, were hugging and rocking with high, keening cries. Daniel had Gal in his arms, her legs swung around his waist and gripping. His eyes were squeezed shut, his mouth pressed against Gal's hair. Matt wondered if he should stand there until introduced; he waited awkwardly for a moment, and then began dragging in the rest of the suitcases. The apartment had tile floors throughout, and windows that slid open to the sun and wind and the dark flapping-crow sound of laundry on the lines. Its furnishings were the cheap hodgepodge of people whose main business is raising children; nothing on the walls but framed family photos, taped-up children's drawings, and a few framed posters from museum exhibits of Impressionist painters. He figured out which was the master bedroom and dragged Lydia's and Sam's suitcases into it, then sat down on the bed. He thought about a novel he'd recently read that depicted an epidemic of blindness, in which only one woman could see. That would be him now, he thought, the one functioning person in a family blinded by grief.

The mattress sat on a low wood frame, and the bed was neatly made. From the little adjacent bathroom he could smell Joel's scent, his aftershave. He ran his hand over a pillow, noticed several long brown hairs. Ilana's. He closed his eyes, thinking about the skin sloughed off all over the bed and floor and windowsills, and the hair on the pillows and in the shower drain. Someday, someone—maybe even him—would clean this apartment, and in doing so they'd eradicate all the earthly remaining traces of Joel's and Ilana's bodies. He stood and opened the door of one of the closets that lined the front wall and thrust his head into Ilana's blouses and skirts and blazers. When he emerged and shut the closet door, he saw a small figure standing in the doorway. Gal's cheeks were a hectic red and she was sucking her thumb. She wore purple leggings and a purple-and-white-striped T-shirt; he remembered Joel saying that purple was apparently young girls' color of choice when they outgrew pink and got snobbish about their previous lack of sophistication. He folded his long legs into a crouch. "Hey there, Boo," he said. "Wanna come give me a hug?"

She came to him and allowed him to hug her, with an obedience that hurt his feelings a little; he picked her up and sat down on the bed with her on his lap. He tucked her hair behind her ear. She pushed him and reared away from him. "*Ichsah,*" she said in the universal guttural expression of disgust of Israeli children. "You smell bad." Then she whispered, "Ema and Abba died."

He thought: *She's seeing if it's true in English, too.* "Yes," he said, squeezing her and kissing the top of her head so she wouldn't see his tears. She wiggled loose and looked searchingly into his face, then put her two hands on his cheeks. Matt tried to return her gaze as honestly as he could. Her features were thinning and becoming more defined as she passed out of her babyhood and into childhood, and her brown eyes were weirdly fierce, as if she were trying to look into his soul. "Has anybody brushed your hair in a while?" he asked, raking his fingers lightly through the tangled mass. "Go get me a brush, and I'll brush it."

She hopped off his lap and went into her parents' bathroom, and emerged with a hairbrush. She stood patiently between his knees with her back to him. He hastily tore Ilana's hair out of the brush and looked at the little nest of hair in his palm, then stuffed it in his pocket.

Her hair was dark, and slightly shorter than shoulder-length. He removed the headband that held it off her face and brushed for a while, bringing out its gloss, thinking that this was as good a place to be as any. Gal was compliant; when he tugged too hard, she let out a quiet whimper that broke his heart because he knew what a shrieky little beast she could be. He wondered if he should be saying something to her, emphasizing how many adults loved her and reassuring her that she'd be taken care of, but he was frightened of saying something that would cause permanent damage. He could hear talking and crying from the other room, and then Lydia's raised, angry voice and the sound of shushing and whispering because the baby was still asleep. Someone turned on the shower. He brushed for what seemed like a long time, until static made the fine hairs crackle around the brush. Then he heard the quick clack of Lydia's footsteps, and she burst in, her lips tight. "Honey," she said to Gal, "go get something to eat, okay? Your *savta* will find you something."

When Gal had gone, Lydia opened her suitcase, releasing a waft of her scent, and began rummaging through the neat piles of knit clothing. "Those religious fanatics are insisting Joel and Ilana be buried tonight," she hissed at Matt. "The funeral is in two hours."

"You're kidding," Matt said.

"No, I'm not," she said, her face livid. "According to Jewish law you're supposed to bury the bodies as soon as possible, and they've already held them so we could get here to identify Joel."

"Wow," Matt said.

He rose and went in search of Daniel, bumping into Ilana's father in the narrow hallway. Yaakov looked at him, bewildered.

"Shalom," Matt said.

"Shalom."

"I'm Matt, I'm Daniel's friend," Matt said, and stuck out his hand, which Yaakov gripped. Yaakov had a strong, broad face, lined from years in the sun. He was wearing a white oxford shirt, the sleeves rolled up to his forearms. His belly strained over his belt. "I'm very sorry about Ilana," Matt said. "I knew her, and she was a wonderful person."

Yaakov nodded with moist, puzzled eyes.

Daniel was in the shower. Matt went up to the bathroom door and hovered there for a moment, then gently tried the handle. The door was unlocked, and after a quick look around, he stepped into the tiny, steamy room, and locked the door behind him. "Hey, baby, it's me," he said, unbuttoning the top two buttons under his open collar and peeling his shirt off over his head. "Can I come in?"

Daniel stuck his wet head out from behind the curtain. He was virtually blind without his glasses, but managed to cast a disapproving look in Matt's general direction. "I don't feel comfortable cavorting naked with you when my in-laws are out there," he said.

Matt looked at him. *"Cavorting?* Honey, believe me, the last thing on my mind is a cavort."

Daniel turned off the water and stepped out, and Matt handed him a towel.

"And I'm worried my parents won't have enough hot water. The boiler's on, but hot water isn't unlimited here."

Matt looked at his foul-smelling shirt. "I'm putting this back on," he said.

Daniel looked nervously at the door and bit his lip.

"Shit," Matt said. He threw the shirt angrily onto the pile of Daniel's soiled clothes and slipped out the door, walking shirtless through the apartment to their room. There was food out on the kitchen table—sliced bread, cold cuts, hummus, olives—and an argument under way between Lydia and her in-laws about whether the baby should be taken to the funeral. It was conducted in English without the benefit of Daniel's mediation, so it was occurring in its crudest form. Lydia was struggling to express the idea that when Noam grew up, he'd regret not being at his parents' funeral. Sam was leaning against a counter, ripping out huge bites of a sandwich, his eyes darting anxiously back and forth, his Adam's apple convulsing as he swallowed.

Matt went into their room, a tiny guest room/office off the kitchen with a sliding door that rumbled when rolled open and shut. He perched on the bed and folded his hands. Maybe he would never get to shower; maybe it was his destiny to reek of death from now on. He sat there for a while, hearing outside the door the noises of raised voices straining to remain polite, staring at his hands till they blurred, trying to recall himself to his life but unable to imagine the details of his friends and his work and the house he lived in. Where had he felt this before, his stomach yawning into an abyss of despair, feeling so implacably plunged into another's dark reality? The closest he'd come was family holidays when he was a child, when he had to dress in a shirt and tie and be ostracized by his cousins because he was a big sissy. One Christmas when he was about ten, he had stolen his cousin Teddy's brand-new toy soldiers, doused them with lighter fluid he found out in the garage, and set them on fire. "Napalm," he explained with a steely look at his cousin as his mother gripped his arm and a big black, rancid fire smoked. Teddy cried "You freak!" and burst into tears, which Matt remembered to this day with satisfaction.

He heard Daniel come out of the bathroom and join the fray, speaking quickly in Hebrew, and then he heard the baby's cry, and silence fell over the apartment.

BY THE TIME IT was his turn to shower, the water was cold. He stood shivering and swearing, turning off the water and furiously rubbing his head with shampoo till the suds ran down his wrists and arms, then rinsed, then soaped himself up again, all over. His nipples were as hard as pebbles, his dick shrunk back like a turtle's head. He scrubbed himself so hard his arm muscles hurt. He got out and toweled off, pushing his dirty pants and underwear into the corner of the bathroom with his toe, and stopped dead when he realized he hadn't brought any clean clothes in with him. He thought for a second, then thought, *Fuck it*, and wrapped the towel securely around his waist. He tiptoed quickly back to his room through the apartment, his toweled-off hair standing straight up and dripping down his neck—passing through the living room where Daniel, dressed in black pants and a white dress shirt, was nuzzling the baby, and his mother was crying. "Don't mind me," Matt waved, with a grimace. As he was closing the bedroom door behind him, he heard Yaakov ask, "Who is that?"

He picked through the open suitcase on the floor, found underwear and his white shirt, only slightly wrinkled. He was pulling on his pants when the bedroom door slid open gently, and Daniel eased in with the freshly diapered baby in his arms, baby clothes clamped under his armpit, and slid the door firmly closed again. "They want to know why you're always half-naked," he said. Matt ignored him and approached the baby. Noam had wispy brown hair, dark eyes in a moon face with multiple chins. "Hey, little baby," Matt said softly, looking at his lover's face and suddenly seeing the handsome dad, which made his heart hurt. "I'm Matt," he told the baby. He took Noam's hand and shook it gently, and the baby's face broke into a smile so crooked and goofy, his little tongue sticking out between his teeth, that Matt laughed out loud.

Daniel laid Noam on the bed and began pulling pants over his fat legs, while Matt leaned over Noam's face and nuzzled him, and Noam grabbed onto his hair. "Ouch," he said, and extricated himself. He looked at the baby's fuzzy tulip skin, the purple shadow of his nipples. "Almost a year, huh. Can he talk?" he asked Daniel.

Daniel straightened and stared at him, his eyes narrowed in thought. "Beats me," he said, shrugging, and they both laughed. Matt pulled Daniel into his arms, and Daniel cried "Don't!" and pulled away. "I can't do this right now," he whispered. "I'm sorry, baby."

"Okay," Matt said. Daniel turned back to Noam, removing his glasses and wiping his eyes with his forearm. As Matt finished dressing, Daniel pulled the waist of the pants over Noam's diaper; he scrunched up the shirt to the collar and pulled it over the baby's head, and stuffed his arms clumsily into the sleeves.

"There," he said, and picked Noam up. "Are you ready?" His lips grazed the baby's cheek.

"Why isn't he crying?" Matt asked. His fingers grew still over the buttons of his shirt as a thought occurred to him. "How do babies mourn, anyway?"

"I have no idea," Daniel said.

Matt considered. "You don't think we'll ruin them, do you?"

Daniel looked at him wearily. "I think somebody has already done that for us."

. . . . .

THE FUNERAL WASN'T THE way Matt had feared it would be—not at all like the settler funerals he saw on television, armed and bearded civilians roaring with bombastic song. But dignitaries had arrived in long Mercedeses, and they and their bodyguards stood, their hands clasped before them, at the front of the crowd clustered under the strong lights set up to illuminate the cemetery. There were photographers, too: Matt couldn't see them, but he heard the clicking of camera shutters. The mourners were gathered on an outcrop of rock on a mountainside, huddled in overcoats, hundreds of people crowded around them. The wind was strong and noisy, and the sound of weeping reached up and was taken by it, bobbing on the wind. Gal stood behind her Grampa Sam, wrapped around his leg, while Daniel held the baby, who was crying, joggling him and cupping his head. Headstones stretched out far ahead of them, and Matt could see that there were graves set into the rock wall as well. He had a sudden memory: Ilana at their house in Northampton, packing to go back home, sighing, calling Israel "that sad piece of rock." Ilana hated Jerusalem, the city in which she'd grown up; she hated the religious people, the city's fraught status as a symbol for three religions. She was a teacher, and her work took her close to abused and neglected and hungry children. She had named her daughter Gal, which meant "wave," to evoke her beloved Tel Aviv, which was on the ocean.

They had been taken to the cemetery in the van, and herded first into a large, crowded hall. When they entered, a hush fell over the crowd. Matt walked self-consciously behind the others to the front. He towered above most of the people there, and Daniel had taken a large yarmulke from a box at the door and pinned it to Matt's hair, so he felt like a big beanpole in Jewish drag. The family held their heads high—asserting, he imagined, that they had dignity even though their destinies had turned them into every other person in the room's worst nightmare, to be pitied and avoided, or maybe fetishized in some creepy way, from this point on. They reached the front and sat in seats that had been reserved for them. It was so clear, he thought, who were to be honored and supported here; he had a sudden and unexpected flash of sympathy for Kendrick's loudmouthed partnering of Jay: he was trying to make himself *count*. Before them, the bodies were laid out, wrapped in white sheets draped with cloths with fringes and Stars of David on them.

A man approached Daniel, bent, and murmured something in his ear. Daniel cleared his throat and rose, and removed the folded eulogy from his overcoat pocket. The coat was Joel's; he'd taken it because he hadn't brought a warm enough jacket, and in the van, he kept sniffing at the lapels and fighting back tears.

The paper crackled under the microphone as Daniel smoothed it with shaking fingers. He cleared his throat and neared his face to the microphone and said, "Shalom." He said, "I'm Daniel Rosen, Joel's brother." His voice was hoarse; he cleared his throat. "I have a big strawberry birthmark on my back," he said. "I've always thought that Joel was in such a hurry to get out and take the world by storm, he shoved me aside, right there." There was a wave of low laughter. "But I loved Joel more than anybody in the world."

Matt took in the complicated message and stored it for future rumination, when he was less exhausted and more mature. That was the last thing he understood, because Daniel delivered the rest of his eulogy in Hebrew. Daniel had learned Hebrew in Jewish summer camp and during the year he spent in Israel; he had learned it quickly—he had a facility for languages, spoke French and German as well—and was vain about it. Out of the corner of his eye, Matt saw Lydia whisper in Sam's ear and wring the handkerchief she held in both hands, and he thought it was sad that they weren't able to understand the eulogy. But as Daniel spoke and got into it, Matt found he didn't mind. The actual words might have destroyed him. Instead, he heard a Jewish man speaking the language of Jewish prayer. It was weird: Speaking Hebrew, Daniel seemed somehow more authoritative. More masculine, even—the microphone took his everyday tenor and wove it in rich, colored strands. He gripped the sides of the podium. His mouth moved in ways Matt had never seen before, his lips and tongue making all the consonants juicy. His language was leaving the mundane world of the queer everyday, and elevating itself to the universal. Matt looked on, enthralled, conscious in a tiny part of his mind that he was idealizing his partner's speech, that it was, after all, coming from the same mouth that kissed him and sucked him. But watching Daniel, he felt proud to belong to him.

There were tears, and the honks and sniffles of people blowing their noses. The baby had fallen asleep on his Israeli grandmother's shoulder. He heard Daniel say in Hebrew, "I love you, Joel"—*Ani ohev otcha*, words he had taught Matt long ago, and uttered from time to time when they were in bed, after sex or right before falling asleep. He whispered a few last broken words, and stepped down. He looked over the crowd, blind and disoriented; Matt stood so Daniel could see him, and he stumbled over to his seat.

He sat beside Matt with his face in his hands, sobbing freely. In the swing of crying, he'd picked up the rhythm of marathon crying rather than sprinting, his sobs low and regular and inconsolable. A box of Kleenex was passed their way, and Matt fed tissues to Daniel, and took the used ones off his lap, laying them on the floor between his own feet. The air was chilly, but damp with body heat. Up on the podium, Sam was sighing into the microphone, making a shuddery crackling sound. He was saying that Joel had never hurt anyone, that he had many Arab friends and colleagues, that he didn't deserve to be claimed by this terrible conflict. "What kind of person," he pondered, "blows himself up in order to harm innocent people?"

Matt bit his lip and looked down at the floor. Sam was gripping the podium and looking out into the sea of mourners as though waiting for a reply. He spoke, Matt thought, as if he was the first person to ponder this problem. As if the fact that he—a wealthy and powerful American man—didn't understand was supposed to mean that nobody could, that it was utterly unfathomable. Sam sighed heavily and shook his head. "I just don't get it," he said. "I just don't get it."

Matt shifted. A rancor was rising in him that he wanted to shake off. *Have some respect*, he told himself furiously. The man was mourning his son, talking about his death the best way he knew how; he had no right to criticize him. Matt's ruminations were interrupted by a squeeze of his hand. Daniel was cutting his eyes toward him. His mind tumbled rapidly over the meaning of this communication, and his spirit lifted a little.

It seemed to have been agreed upon in advance that Malka would not speak. And at the last moment, Lydia didn't rise to the podium either; her arm grew rigid against Sam's hand, and a look of terror came over her face. "I can't," she whispered. Yaakov spoke, in a manner so dazed that Matt wished several times that someone would do him a favor and lead him away from the podium. His head and lips sagged like a stroke victim's; it was hard to tell when he'd finished, he trailed off so many times. Finally, he sighed and turned away, walking in the wrong direction; a man jumped to his feet and led him back to his seat. There was a long respectful pause. Then a friend of Joel's named Shmulik, a man with a round droll face and a very slight lisp, got up and told some story in a rapid-fire delivery that sent waves of laughter over the hall. Matt watched Daniel's face break and redden, taken by surprise, and hearing the peal of his laughter made Matt love him so much he could hardly stand it.

There was a brief speech by a fat honcho. And then a bunch of Hasids came and took hold of the pallets the bodies lay upon, and the mourners walked out to the cemetery through the chilly night air, Lydia clutching Daniel's arm, up a long paved incline and onto this hillside. The Hasids swayed and prayed over the bodies, and Matt gazed at their long beards and side curls, thinking that if Ilana was standing beside him, she'd have something sarcastic to say. They laid the bodies straight into the ground without coffins, and each person shoveled dirt over the grave. He looked quickly at Gal, hidden behind her grandfather's leg. She was crying, her eyes darting around, as if trying to alight upon the person who would save her; the wind was whipping at her face, making her hair fly. Matt burst into tears. He cried through the singing of the national anthem. The women's voices rose tearfully at first, tinny and a little shrill, then took strength in numbers and grew in beauty and texture. The sound of voices in unison, men and women an octave apart, in the cold night air, with the stars shining fiercely, pierced him through with grief and something like joy. He looked at Gal and saw that her lips were moving too, even as tears ran down her face. He told himself to remember that singing would bring her solace.

WHEN THEY GOT HOME they were quiet. Ilana's parents had gone to their own house, leaving the children with the Rosens. The baby was fast asleep in his car seat; Daniel reached in and eased him over his shoulder, carried him in. "Should I change him?" he murmured to his mother.

"No," she said. "Never wake a sleeping baby."

Daniel laid him in his crib without waking him. Lydia went into the bathroom to wash up for bed. In the kitchen, Sam was taking a Ziploc bag out of his briefcase. "I just remembered this," he said, and then looked up to see whom he was talking to. His eyes fell on Matt, who sat down with him at the table. Sam sat heavily in one of the kitchen chairs and pondered Joel's effects. He removed Joel's wedding ring and slipped it over his pinkie, where it caught on the second knuckle. Matt saw that his fingers had thickened over the years and his own wedding band was now a tight squeeze. There was a filthy wallet. Sam went through it and took out dirty cash, tiny wrinkled photographs of Ilana and the kids, and laid them on the table. And then Joel's cell phone, still in its holder. Daniel came into the room. "What's that?" he asked.

Sam undid the Velcro fastener and pulled out the phone. Two small black nails clattered onto the table. Sam inhaled sharply. The three of them stared at one another. Daniel reached down and picked them up, brought them to his face, and sniffed them.

"What are you doing?" Sam asked.

"I don't know," Daniel said, stuffing the nails into his pocket.

They fell out later, when he and Matt undressed and folded their pants over the tiny guest room's desk chair. Matt stooped and gathered them off the floor, and suppressing a strong desire to throw them in the trash, set them on the desk. Daniel was taking the pillows off the foldout couch and laying them in a stack in a corner of the room. He slid the bed open and went in search of sheets. At the other end of the apartment, Lydia and Sam were putting Gal to bed.

The window was slid open to the chilly night air, and a lovely smell was wafting in. Matt tried to place it. When Daniel came back into the room, he looked at his still face and closed eyes. "Yeast," he said. "The Angel bread factory is right across the valley."

They were so tired, they crawled into the small double bed without brushing their teeth. Daniel let out a sigh and turned his back to Matt, curling into a ball. Matt gently spooned him, careful to make his touch feel like solace and not a demand. Daniel was hot and sticky from sweat and tears, the air cool and yeasty, and a kind of sensuous peace came over Matt. They fell asleep within minutes.

But two hours later, Matt awoke to find Daniel lying awake beside him. "Hey," he said.

"Hey."

They lay in silence for a while, the only sound the ticking of the desk clock. Matt drifted off for a few minutes, then awoke again, looked over at Daniel and saw his eyelids blinking. "Do you want to tell me what you said about your brother in your eulogy?" he asked.

Daniel continued to stare into space. Matt heard the dry sound of his chapped lips opening. "I said," he whispered, "that Joel and Ilana would not want their deaths to be used as an opportunity for another wave of violence. They would not want people killed in their name. They were people who worked for social justice."

"You said that?"

Daniel nodded.

"That's beautiful, honey. And brave to say."

Daniel shrugged. His face twitched. "A lot of good it'll do," he said.

Matt fell back asleep, and when he awoke two hours later, he found that Gal was in their bed, between them, breathing raucously, one arm flung over his neck. He removed her arm gently and turned toward her and Daniel. Daniel was awake; Matt could see the movement of his eyelids blinking. He fell asleep again and awoke exactly two hours later, grief and jet lag seeming to have planted in him a diabolically precise clock. As the night crawled on, he dreamed ponderous dreams about problems with the designs he was working on back home. He woke again, got up and went into the kitchen, opened the refrigerator and explored the leftovers: pea soup in a pot, some baked chicken in a dish covered with foil, a tiny bit of rice in a Tupperware container. Ilana's food, he thought; the prospect of eating it seemed deeply symbolic of something, but he was too tired to figure out what. He took out some milk, closed the refrigerator door, and fixed himself a bowl of Honey Nut Cheerios from a box with Hebrew writing on it. He sat down at the table where Joel's wedding ring and tattered wallet sat, along with Sam's watch, some worn and folded pieces of paper, the social worker's business card. He picked up the wallet and opened it, and found another two tiny nails caught in the lining. He got up and threw them in the garbage.

The cereal was sweet and comforting; he ate in big mouthfuls, wiping milk off his chin. He wondered if he and Daniel would be the kind of parents who gave their kids apples or grapes for dessert instead of chocolate pudding, and sent them to school with horrible *Little House on the Prairie* sandwiches on organic whole wheat bread. He thought that if your parents had been blown up, a Ho Ho probably wasn't the worst thing that would ever happen to you. He went back to bed as dawn was breaking, hearing a donkey's strident bray from down below. In the dim light, Gal was blinking at him, sleepy and solemn. She reached a hand toward his face as he settled in beside her, and he kissed it, and her eyes filled with tears. "I want Ema," she said in a tiny voice. The sound of those words, her wish aloud in the air, made her face crumple. Her grief, Matt thought, already seemed weary and resigned.

"I know, Boo," he whispered. He sat up and pulled her limp body onto his lap, kissed her wet face, and rocked her.

WHEN HE AWOKE in the mornings, there was a moment when Daniel's spirit felt light. Then a vague unsettled feeling came over him, and a sense of dread that hardly got its footing before his awareness broke over him and crushed him with such ruthlessness he could only cower and whimper before it. The morning after Joel's funeral, he lay in bed, his arms thrown over his head, whispering the only word he could think of in any language: *Please*.

He could sense that he was in Jerusalem, and that it was warm. His undershirt stuck to his back. He tried to bring Joel's face to his mind, but he couldn't. His throat cramped with the effort not to cry and awaken the sleeping man and child beside him.

He lay there for a while, his breathing ragged, the sound of sobbing roaring in his ears. His consciousness began to wash over the sound *Joel*; and the idea of Joel, Joel's shining essence, came to him. Joel as he was, all at once, gorgeous in full, imperfect personhood, and not as Daniel, swayed by his own ego and needs, had thought of him over the years, as too this or too that. He imagined himself holding his brother, their hearts clamoring against each other, and the mayhem in his mind became something clearer and sweeter, a grief that pierced him through.

He lay there till it subsided, till he felt himself to have been washed ashore, half-dead, panting. He felt the living bodies beside him sigh and stir. His ears made out the rush of traffic on the far side of the valley, and closer, the voices of neighboring women talking over their balconies. And then the baby's sharp wail.

He rose quietly and closed the bedroom door behind him, walked barefoot to the kids' bedroom. His mother was up, walking around the small cluttered room in a housedress with the baby over her shoulder, patting him and murmuring, "I know, I know, honey, I know." Noam was wearing only a diaper, and his red face was covered with tears and snot.

"How long has he been up?" Daniel asked, his voice hoarse. He cleared his throat.

"Since about five. Close the door, will you? The whole house will wake up."

Daniel closed it. "Has he eaten?"

"I tried to give him some Cheerios, but he wouldn't eat. I'm trying to get him to at least take a bottle," Lydia said.

"Did you change him?"

"Of course," she said. "I have some experience at this, in case you've forgotten."

An old skepticism wormed its way up Daniel's throat. He knew that twin babies had been hard for her; she loved the idea of mother-hood better than the actuality. He and Joel had always joked that she couldn't relate to them till they were speaking in sentences with sub-ordinate clauses. Her own mother had died suddenly during Lydia's pregnancy—one of those unlucky people who go into a hospital for a simple procedure and never come out again—and by the time he and Joel were born, Lydia was wrung out by months of grief.

"Could you pick up some of this crap on the floor?" she asked. "There seems to be the entire contents of a toy ark. I've already stubbed my toe three times."

Daniel stooped and began collecting Lego pieces and small animal figures fused together in male and female pairs, tossing them into a big plastic toy box in the corner of the room. Above the crib was one of those black-and-white mobiles that were supposed to be good for a baby's development in some way, but whose elemental faces made Daniel shudder. Noam was screaming and arching backward, and Lydia was struggling to hang on to him.

"Do you want me to take him?" Daniel asked.

"No," Lydia said over the baby's crying. "Thank God Ilana weaned him already. That would have been an utter horror." She sat down on the rocking chair in the corner, wrestled him into a reclining position on her lap, and offered him the bottle again. He twisted his face away. "I know, bubbie," Lydia said softly, her eyes becoming shiny with tears.

Daniel straightened, his eyes filling, too. "You're nice with him."

"One is easier than two," she shrugged, laying the bottle's nipple against Noam's lips. "Nothing can prepare you for two." She slipped it in his mouth and he grasped the bottle and began to suck, sighing and shuddering. "There," she crooned. "What a clever boy." She looked evenly at Daniel. "Grandchildren are easier than your own, too," she said.

She was conceding something, Daniel realized. He fixed his eyes on Noam's working cheeks, arms hugging his chest. "Mom," he whispered. "How am I going to survive this?"

Her face broke and sagged, and then composed itself. She spoke to him sharply. "By getting up every morning and putting one foot in front of the other, that's how. By faking it, until it gets real again. That's what we're all going to do."

"Okay," Daniel said in a small voice.

"And by taking care of these children. Listen." Her voice had lowered, become conspiratorial. "We will not let those Grossmans take them. I won't have them raised in that house."

"One step at a time, Mom," Daniel said. "Let's get through the shiva." He was suddenly dying to get away from this conversation before it got too specific. "There's no milk in the house. I'm going to go out and get some."

Lydia nodded. "And while you're out, see if you can find something better than that awful Nescafé, okay?"

"Okay."

"And what about some cookies, at least, for the shiva?"

"I don't think so, Mom," he said. "We have to trust Shoshi on this one." She had told them—as Daniel had assumed—that, according to custom, the family doesn't provide food for the shiva, that the visitors feed them instead.

He found his sandals and wallet, and looked for the key to Joel and Ilana's car for a long time, rummaging through every kitchen drawer, thrumming with the memory of Ilana's periodic tantrums, her bellowing, "I can't go on living in such a shit hole!" It occurred to him that Joel must have had their car keys with him, and there followed a moment in which Daniel tried and failed to ward off the thought that the bomb's impact had driven the keys through Joel's pockets and into the flesh of his thighs, mashing them into his bones. A little starburst of horror went off in his chest, and he had to sit down. A few minutes passed, and he stood again and looked into the open drawer, which was spilling over with lightbulbs, batteries, hair ties, stamps, pens, and paper clips. Suddenly, his eyes lit miraculously upon a single car key, marked with a tag that said *extra car key*. He held it up with two fingers, a smile twitching at the corners of his mouth.

He closed the front door quietly on his way out. He was glad to leave his mother with the baby; she was being a marvel of strength, he thought, but if she didn't have the children to take care of, she'd probably never be able to get out of bed again. She clearly assumed that she and Sam were going to take them, and for a moment Daniel regretted that Joel and Ilana hadn't made that happen. And yet it was hard to imagine that she and Sam would be thrilled to take on two little kids at their age. He considered calling Joel's lawyer, Assaf Schwartz. He, Daniel, sure as hell wasn't going to be the person who broke the news. Let his parents' wrath descend upon a neutral person. He looked at his watch, and then realized he'd see Assaf at the shiva.

· · · ·

HE DROVE DOWN THE narrow street toward the center of the neighborhood, flooded by sense memory—sun, stone, squeaking iron gates, narrow streets, little stores like caves crammed with goodies. Last September, he'd spent ten days with Joel and Ilana, having come to Jerusalem to interview and shadow an alumnus who was now a member of the Knesset. At the time, Noam was tiny and Ilana was staying home with him, and Daniel, pulling some of his tastiest recipes out of his hat, cooked for her and Joel and Gal to great applause. It was the best time he'd ever had with his brother. They'd spent much of their lives pulled away from each other in the interest of differentiation, beginning in high school, where being referred to as "one of the Rosen twins" had been a dagger in the heart of teenage boys trying to define themselves. They scoffed at the clichéd schemes people liked to egg them on to do, like switching classes to fool the teacher, or taking each other's exams, and when they co-won the senior prize for best student in English, having to share the prize ruined it for them both. When Joel started getting good at track, Daniel quit sports altogether and began focusing on music, becoming first violinist in the regional youth orchestra and picking up acoustic guitar. They thought of themselves as anti-twins, and during college, where they split up for the first time—Joel to Princeton and Daniel to Oberlin—they invented the semifacetious idea of *twinsism*: the act of stereotyping or fetishizing twins, into which fell such things as Doublemint commercials, fantasizing about having sex with twins, Mengele's experiments on twins, and Diane Arbus photographs.

They spent their junior year in the same overseas program in Jerusalem, deciding, after many negotiations, that after two years apart they could risk venturing into a program that put them in the same place. They lived in the dormitories up on Mount Scopus that looked out over the pale hills all around, which were attached by bus route to the small neighborhood of Givat Tzarfatit and then to the great apartment buildings of Ramat Eshkol. That was Daniel's mental map of the area in which he had lived. It was only much later that his reading brought to his attention that this area was surrounded by Arab villages and a large Palestinian refugee camp. They had been utterly invisible to him.

It was a year of great transformation for them both. They had grown up in a Jewish suburb of Chicago and had spent summers at a Jewish camp they both adored, where they had learned Hebrew and had Israeli counselors, and been steeped in Israeli culture. For Joel, there was a deep feeling of coming home. He lucked out by having a genial and outgoing roommate, and he became friends with his group of friends, thereby winning the unspoken contest in his program for best assimilation into Israeli culture.

For Daniel, the feeling of living in Israel was harder to describe. He had been struggling to accept that he was gay, and when he looked back on it years later, he realized that going to Israel was an attempt to shore up his manhood, which felt compromised among his sexually active college friends. But instead, aroused by sensory Israel—the heady sunshine and cool mountain air of Jerusalem, warm challah and harsh coffee, beautiful men in sandals or in uniform, the language that brought his teeth, palate, throat, and tongue into a new, more vigorous rapport—he was certain for the first time that he was gay. He was also sure that he was the only gay man in his entire acquaintance, and was terrified that anyone would find out.

His own roommate was a neuroscience major who spent most of his time in the lab, and to whom Daniel had nothing to say. During those long, lonely days, he'd sit in his crummy dorm room, listening to Israeli music, learning the chords on his guitar, and then poring over the dictionary to learn the words, many of which came in elevated or archaic constructions. It was how he learned Hebrew, and to this day he loved Israeli folk music: it was hardwired in him as surely as Beatles tunes were, so that when he died and they autopsied his brain, they'd find a marble-sized space for all the information he'd ever learned, and a wrinkly hunk of that matter devoted to the lyrics of Israeli songs. Everybody knew them and who had written them; many of them were poems by the great Israeli poets set to music. They were about beloved places and landscapes—sea, mountain, field—about army life, yearning for peace, clinging to love in the face of craziness. His critique of them became increasingly harsh over the years: he found them baldly nationalistic, staking out biblical and emotional claims to various lands, the songs about longing for peace completely empty and hypocritical. Now when Daniel listened to the playfully simple songs about shoelaces, or thunder, or galoshes, sung by men in childishly flattened nasal voices, he heard them trying to show that they were just boys after all, not part of a highly trained occupying force. But his critique of the songs couldn't prevent them from stirring his heart.

When Daniel came out the following year, back at Oberlin, after he got involved with his first boyfriend, Jonathan, Joel was clumsy and defensive; he wrote Daniel a stiff letter from Princeton in which he said that, while he had some gay friends, he didn't believe any of them were very happy people. Daniel and Jonathan had been scathing about it, imagining him to be threatened by his own sexuality.

Over the ensuing years, though, as he and Joel had moved into their adult lives and inhabited different continents, those conflicts had been forgiven, if not entirely forgotten. Then, last September, Joel had joyfully, and twinfully, stepped toward him. He'd sent him excited emails weeks before Daniel's trip about the things they'd do together if Daniel had time, he'd proudly introduced him to the writers and producers at *Israel Today*, he'd plopped his baby boy in Daniel's arms and marveled at how much Noam and Daniel looked alike. When he took Daniel to the airport to fly back to the States, and the security agent at the entrance to the check-in line asked Daniel how he and Joel were related, Joel grabbed Daniel around the neck and pulled his face close to his, and said, "How do you *think* we're related?!"

It was as though, Daniel thought, they could now finally rest in their twinship, and love and admire each other. It was during that visit that Joel and Ilana told him they were making out their wills, and that they wanted to designate him the guardian of their children if they should die. It was in the morning, on Joel's day off, and Gal was at *gan*; he and Joel were on their third cups of coffee, sitting around the kitchen table, the sink piled with dishes, and Ilana was running a finger across Noam's cheek to keep him from falling asleep at her breast.

"Are you sure?" Daniel asked. Pleasure and surprise and pride had flared up in him, along with a little panic. "We couldn't raise them here, it'd mean taking them to Northampton with us."

Ilana looked down at the sated baby on her lap—his head thrown back, his eyes rolling back in his head, milk dribbling from the side of his mouth—and laughed. She took her giant breast in her two hands and packed it back into her bra, pulled down her shirt. "Look," she said, her face, which was usually tuned toward the comic, becoming brooding. "I grew up in a very, very sad house. I don't want my children to grow up in a house like that. If we will die, take them away from here. Enough is enough." She flicked her wrist, her hand flying out in a gesture of dismissal.

Daniel looked at Joel, who was sitting back in his chair, a hand resting on the table. He switched to English. "And the whole being-raised-by-homos thing? You don't worry that Noam will turn into a big sissy?"

They shook their heads. "In fact," Joel said, his face lighting up with a bright idea, "you're welcome to take them both right now!"

"No, really," Daniel said, laughing.

"No," Joel said, "we're not worried about that."

THE GUY BEHIND THE counter at the *makolet* did a bewildered double take when he saw Daniel, who murmured, "His twin brother." The grocer told him that he participated in his sorrow, the Hebrew way of expressing condolence. Daniel laid milk and bread on the counter, stood pondering the different kinds of coffee on the shelf and hesitantly selected one labeled for a French press. Before paying, he stepped back outside to pick up a paper from the newsstand. The front page of *Ma'ariv* made his heart jump. There was a picture of Matt, handsome and imperious, his face wrapped in dark glasses, his hand on Daniel's back. It had been taken outside the airport; the rest of the family was huddled with the social worker, only the backs of their heads visible. He picked up a copy of the *Jerusalem Post*, which ran the same picture, only beneath the fold, and went back in to pay.

As he got into the car, the driver's seat already hot in the morning sun, he thought about his prickliness, his lack of generosity, around Matt these days. An ethic of rigorous self-examination had made him ask himself over the years whether he had just jumped at the chance of having *any* boyfriend, living as he did in a town that was a mecca for lesbians—a town that posted on the municipal parking garage a sign reading *Northampton: Where the coffee is strong and so are the women*—but something of a wasteland for gay men. Over and over, he had come to the position that while Matt wasn't the man he'd expected to love, life sometimes sent you something wonderful you'd never imagined. Now all he could think was that, given the choice between Joel dying and Matt, he would have chosen Matt to be the one to die. It was a thought that had come to him more than once, and its randomness, its sheer primitiveness, bewildered and horrified him. How could you think that about the man you loved? What did it mean about the quality of his love for Matt?

When he returned home, Matt was up, sitting with Lydia at the kitchen table, eating a piece of toast. Daniel felt his heart hurtle toward him in compensatory love and remorse. "Check this out," he said, tossing the *Ma'ariv* onto the table. Matt looked at it and his eyes widened. "Shit," he breathed.

"What?" Lydia asked. He turned the paper toward her and she studied it for a moment. "You look like a movie star caught by paparazzi," she said.

Matt flushed. "What does the caption say?"

Daniel stooped over the paper. " 'Television personality Joel Rosen's family arrived at Ben Gurion Airport from Newark, New Jersey, yesterday, en route to identifying his remains.' " His finger dropped to a headline under the fold. "Wait, there's a little story here about Joel and his show. There's apparently going to be a profile of him in the Friday paper." He looked toward the guest room. "Where's Gal? Still sleeping?"

Matt nodded.

"We're going to have to get her up for the shiva," Lydia said.

Sam came in wearing chinos and a white shirt, his eyes bruised and hollow-looking. He peered down at the paper on the table and frowned. "Is that Matt?" he asked. He bent over, squinting, then looked up. "Look, Matt, you made it into the newspaper."

Matt looked at Daniel, who looked up from the paper and gave him a shrug. "I didn't do it on purpose," Matt said lamely. He was thinking how bummed they must be to have his be the face of the Rosen family.

Daniel's fingers were running under the lines of a story in the paper, his lips moving. He tsked, suddenly irritable, and looked up again. "These profiles of the dead," he said. He read, " 'Aviva was always smiling, always happy.' Why do they always have to turn the dead into grinning idiots? What if Aviva was really depressed, went around moping all the time? Would she deserve to be blown up? And here's another one," he said, warming to his theme as they all raised their heads in surprise. "A sixteen-year-old survivor of the *shuk* bombing, who's going to have half a kilo of shrapnel remaining in her body. She says, 'My hopes? Everybody wants to get married and have a family—I want to live like everybody else.' Why do they always want to be like everybody else? Why is that the most complimentary thing you can say about someone in this goddamn country?"

They were silent. Then Sam clucked, "They're just traumatized kids, Dan."

Matt, meanwhile, was suppressing a grin, thinking, *That's my boy.* He tried to catch Daniel's eye, but Daniel pushed his chair back and went into the bathroom, closing the door behind him.

And there was Lydia looking at him with her big, probing brown eyes. Matt composed his face and cleared his throat. "You know, honey," she said. "Daniel is going to need a lot of support."

Matt blinked at her, not knowing how to answer, the statement was so insultingly obvious. Support was an understatement: Did she know he was going to be a parent of her grandchildren? "I'm aware of that, Lydia," he finally said.

THE APARTMENT WAS PACKED all day with people who had come to sit shiva. They all recognized Matt from the newspaper. He was introduced over and over as Daniel's "friend." In their mouths, his name was pronounced "Mett." He noted that Israelis seemed to favor the limp handshake over the muscular American one. He continued to find them beautiful, with their blend of Middle Eastern and European looks, the women with stylish hair with henna highlights, the men hunched forward to talk with their cell phones in their fists, sunglasses perched on top of their heads. Many people seemed to be avoiding him, though, and he couldn't tell if they were shy, or rude, or uncomfortable speaking English, or homophobic. One guy, a friend of Ilana's, had "closet case" written all over him. He had turned away just as Daniel introduced Matt, but he kept staring at Matt and looking away, and whenever Matt drifted in his direction, he scurried off under some invisible pretext. It could be amusing, Matt thought, to spend the entire shiva chasing after the poor guy. Instead, he stood against a counter, which was crowded with coffee cakes and casseroles, his palms resting on it, with the aim of looking as though he was in charge of something.

A reporter was making his way around the room, nodding sympathetically to the people he was talking to and taking discreet notes on a little pad without looking down at it. Ilana's parents were seated on the couch, and Matt watched them with a heavy heart. They were Holocaust survivors; their lives had pretty much sucked from beginning to end, he thought. He had heard a lot about Malka, things he wasn't supposed to know. She was one of the few children to survive Auschwitz, and her mother had saved her by hiding her in a pile of corpses, where Malka had remained for several days. She suffered from bouts of severe depression; Ilana had once told Daniel that, in those moments, it seemed as if she was returning to the pile of bodies, pledging her loyalty to them by being dead herself. But she didn't look like the wreck Matt had been led to expect she'd be. In fact, he found her kind of lovely. Her posture, bent forward in courtesy or deference or an inability to hear well, expressed a kind of polite earnestness. Her blue eyes were washed out to their faintest color, and reddish-silver hair hung down to her shoulders, one side held back with a barrette—a girlish effect on a woman in her seventies, but not in a weird Baby Jane kind of way. Matt wondered what she had made of her bruising, loud-mouthed daughter, and imagined many a migraine requiring lying on the couch with a cold compress on her head. She had a way of narrowing her eyes that made her look chronically puzzled, or a little dim. Lydia, he knew, thought Malka was stupid. But maybe, he thought, she narrowed her eyes to let everything in more slowly, until her nervous system could stand it.

He knew that taking her grandchildren to the States would be the last straw. Even thinking about it made him have to close his eyes against the awfulness of it. He heaved himself off the counter and went out onto the tiny balcony.

The social worker was there, leaning meditatively over the railing with a lit cigarette in her fingers. "Shalom, Shoshi," he said, glad to see her. "May I bum a cigarette?" He gestured toward the small table her cigarettes and lighter lay upon.

"Sure."

"I'm an ex-smoker," he confided, after lighting up and exhaling.

She shrugged comically. "So am I," she said. "Until there is a *pigua*."

He had heard that word enough times to know that it referred to a terrorist attack. Daniel had explained that it came from the root "to hurt," so that literally it meant something like an injury.

They smoked for a little while, leaning over the railing and looking down at the street, where a cluster of little girls with backpacks was coming home from school, all of them chattering at once. Matt shot a sideways glance at Shoshi. She wore patterned pants and a short-sleeved shell, small gold hoop earrings; she was well put together, if not particularly stylish. He pondered what to say to her, and settled upon, "You must see a lot of horrible things."

She turned and bestowed upon him the gentle, steady gaze he was coming to love. "Yes," she said. "But for me, it's the smell that is the worst."

"Tell me about it," Matt drawled, sniffing his arm and making a face.

"At home, when I call to say there has been a *pigua*, my husband turns on the boiler. But even after many long, long showers, the smell stays with me for about a week."

"How do you keep on going?"

"We don't work all the time. Each unit is on duty for only three months."

He nodded. "How many social workers are there per unit?"

"It's depend," Shoshi said, making a translation error Matt was getting used to. They always went out in pairs, she told him, and had a support team checking in with them. The entire unit met at the very end to assess their performance and to talk through their feelings. "That night, I can't sleep, but I go to work the next morning. I feel sick, weak, nauseated."

She spoke with the openness of the social workers he knew, which to his ear, bordered on the burlesque; if she were American, she'd be mentioning "sharing" a lot. He imagined that there was probably an Israeli equivalent to that language that was a little blunter. He could tell that her frankness came partially, but not only, from her training— and the part that came from her personality felt immensely touching to him. He had been used to feeling outrage that suicide bombings in Israel were widely televised in the U.S. while the bombings upon Palestinian civilians never were. But her struggle to help grieving and traumatized people brought into relief everybody's vulnerable humanity. It pressed upon his worldview and scrambled it a little.

He said gently, "Well, you're very good at what you do. We're lucky we got you."

"Thank you," she said gravely. "I must leave you today. Now it's become the work of the social worker from Bituach Leumi."

They struggled for a while over how to translate that—"national security"?—until Matt understood that it was something like the Israeli version of Social Security. He put his hand on his pained heart. Maybe he was romanticizing her, but she seemed to understand how much he felt like an outsider.

"Won't you check up on us at all?" he asked. "We'll need a lot of checking up on. We're a big mess."

She nodded without smiling. "Sure I will," she said.

IN THE LIVING ROOM, Daniel was listening to talk of revenge. *They just don't want peace! They don't understand peace.* The same old words. Ilana's father and the principal from Ilana's school were huddled together, comparing the moments each had known that Arafat was not a viable bargaining partner. For Yaakov it was Camp David, where Arafat was offered a state on a silver platter and walked away from it—Daniel could have uttered the exact cliché before it came out of Yaakov's mouth. But the principal, an overbearing and pompous man with a knitted *kipa*, whom Yaakov clearly deferred to, clucked and shook his head; naturally, he had known way before that point. Daniel heard from other conversations that the army was already engaged in a retaliation operation called Righteous Sword. It made him miserable.

He looked around for Matt and saw him out on the balcony, talking with the social worker. He knew how to make himself at home; Daniel never had to worry about that, which was a big bonus in a boyfriend. Matt would come home from parties where he'd known no one, and report things to Daniel about his friends that Daniel had no idea about. He watched him now, holding a cigarette away from himself so the smoke wouldn't get into his hair, and nodding as Shoshi spoke earnestly to him. His hair was shaggy—they'd left just before he was due for a haircut—and somehow looked beautiful; he looked most beautiful when careless about his appearance.

The familiar sense of strange marvel that he was with a man like

Matt came over him now. Daniel had always imagined himself with someone more like Jonathan, who was moderately good-looking and with whom he shared a love of George Eliot and John Donne, and who, when they left a movie together, always had a corroborating opinion of it. Matt's judgments were very strong, but always a little weird. He judged the performances of the actors in movies, instead of the narrative or the images.

But for all of Matt's love of crappy movies and reality TV and the same hunky movie stars every other gay man in America had a fetish for, he had excellent instincts about fairness and social justice. Unlike Daniel, he had grown up as a pretty queeny kid, unable to conceal his difference from the other boys, and that had forced him to hone his ability to sniff out piety and hypocrisy, and the violence underlying them. Matt was a political animal. He woke up and read the paper cover to cover; he read political memoirs and contemporary books about politics as avidly and indiscriminately as he did the memoirs of movie stars. His favorite person in the whole world was Bill Clinton, whom he called Shakespearean.

If Matt understood these conversations, he'd rip them apart with indignation and incisiveness. But, Daniel wondered, was that even what he needed? Even thinking about it made his hackles rise.

He looked around the living room at the sober conversations, checked on his parents to see whether they needed any translation help. They were sitting stiffly on the couch, ignored by the other mourners either because of the language barrier or because the guests couldn't face talking to Joel's mother. Lydia had her gracious, attentive social face on—her game face, Daniel thought, and it broke his heart. He went and perched on the edge of the sofa next to her, and she reached up and rubbed his arm. A small group of people from Joel's work was gathered in the corner talking to the reporter, who seemed like a decent enough guy. He had asked Daniel about what Joel was like as a boy growing up, and Daniel had struggled to describe his brother without using cheesy clichés—the last thing he wanted was for Joel to come off as the all-American Jewish boy, likable and popular, a lover of sports and of his adopted country. But whenever he tried to get a little complicated, he found he risked sounding critical. The reporter was very interested in their being twins, and asked him if he felt a part of him was now gone. Daniel had stared at him and said, "Of course. But wouldn't I feel that way if he was just a regular brother?"

Daniel rose when Gal's best friend, Leora, came in with her parents, shyly, edged forward by them, her hair in immaculate braids. Gal came up and seized her hand, pulled her out of the room to her bedroom, and shut the door behind them. Daniel watched them go. He'd be taking Gal away from Leora. He knew and liked her parents; he hugged them, and they murmured in his ear. Leora's mother, Gabrielle, was tearfully saying how much they loved Gal and how happy they'd be to take her anytime, when Daniel's eye caught a man behind them, waiting to get in and looking at him expectantly. Was he supposed to know him? He thanked Gabrielle, and said in Hebrew, "Will you speak to my parents? They're sitting alone." All the while racking his brain to see if he remembered this man.

"I won't stay long," the man said hurriedly, in a confidential half whisper. He was a middle-aged man with disheveled, graying hair and a knitted *kipa* pinned askew on his head. "I just wanted you to have this." He had taken Daniel's hand and was placing something in it. Daniel looked down, and back at the man. It was the nut to a medium-sized bolt, a loosely woven gold chain threaded through it.

"*Ma zeh?*" he asked sternly. What is this?

"My daughter was killed in a *pigua*," the man told him. "Sbarro." He was referring to the pizza place in downtown Jerusalem, which had been destroyed a few years earlier. "The police told us that what ultimately killed her was a nut driven into her neck."

Daniel took a step back, his heart quickening.

"At the funeral, all of her friends from her class wore nuts around their necks, as a tribute to her. And when I heard of your brother's death, I thought you might want to share this tribute with us. To become part of our large family."

"Thank you," Daniel said automatically, his throat constricting.

"I brought some for his children too, in case they wanted to remember their parents by something." He was extending two additional, smaller necklaces.

"No," Daniel said, backing away.

"I understand your feelings," the man said with a look of eager compassion. "May I come in and talk for a moment?"

Just then Daniel felt a touch on his back. It was Matt, standing behind him, big and warm. "Do you need help getting rid of this guy?" he was murmuring.

Daniel turned toward him and nodded helplessly.

"I'm sorry," Matt said to the man, not knowing whether he even understood English. "Family only." He closed the door as the man took an uncertain step backward. "There!" he said brightly. "What did he want?"

Daniel held out the necklace. "His daughter was killed in the Sbarro bombing, apparently by one of these to the neck."

"You're kidding," Matt said. "What a freak."

Daniel gave a surprised huff of a laugh. "How did you know I needed rescuing?"

"You staggered backward and clutched your chest."

"I did not."

Matt looped a finger through the necklace. "Why don't you give that to me."

"No," Daniel said, suddenly uncertain, pulling it back.

Matt raised an eyebrow. "So it's going to join those nails in your pocket?"

Daniel flashed him an angry, self-conscious look. They had pocked his palms and thighs with tiny bloody marks.

"Okay," Matt said gently. "Sorry."

They returned to the living room, and when Daniel noticed that Leora's father was perched on the arm of the couch, talking to his parents, he went over to join them, still a little flushed. His mother had learned that Moti was a builder, and was telling him what a huge impression it always made on her to see an entire city built of stone the color of the hillsides. "Rising to Jerusalem," she was saying, translating the Hebrew verb used to convey the word *going*, when applied to Jerusalem. "It's as though you really are rising, being uplifted—it feels almost spiritual."

"That's the idea of Jerusalem stone," Moti said with a faint smile. He was a big, wide-faced, genial guy; he and Joel had played racquetball together, and Daniel remembered something about his cooking a mean osso buco. "It's supposed to convey a sense of earthiness, but also of holiness." His voice was husky, and he stepped delicately over the English consonants. "The directive to build with Jerusalem stone goes back to the British Mandate. But after the '67 war, when Israel annexed an enormous territory around Jerusalem, the first priority of the city planners was to prevent it from ever being repartitioned. So they used Jerusalem stone to make occupied territory look like an integral part of Jerusalem." He shrugged with a self-deprecating grimace. "Please forgive the lecture. If Gabrielle heard me going on about this she'd be flashing me warning looks."

"No, it's fascinating," Lydia said. "I had no idea."

"The stone mostly comes from quarries in the West Bank now, because stone dust is an environmental hazard."

Daniel had become alert, his sense of Moti shifting and complicating. "So Palestinians produce the stone that's designed to make Jerusalem Jewish forever," he said. "And get sick doing so."

"Exactly."

"That doesn't seem right," Lydia said, and they all laughed uncomfortably at the understatement.

"I'm surprised the supply lasts, there's so much building," Daniel said.

"Oh, they hardly ever use it as a construction material anymore," Moti shrugged. "Now it's usually just used as a facade."

Daniel clutched his chest. "Are you going to destroy *all* our illusions?" he cried.

Lydia sighed and smoothed her dress over her knees, her rings gleaming off creased knuckles. "Of course, I don't know when we'll come back here—that'll depend. Certainly, rising to Jerusalem will never feel the same." She looked up and grimaced apologetically, and Moti took her hand.

WHEN JOEL AND ILANA'S lawyer called at about four thirty, Daniel suddenly felt seized with urgency to open the will. He could continue no longer in this suspended state, with people asking about the kids. His father had cornered him in the guest bedroom, where he'd gone to take a breather, and said, "Your mother is very concerned about the Grossmans. Apparently, Malka told her how glad she was that the children could spend some time with their American family before coming to live with them."

So when Assaf called, Daniel asked him to come over in about an hour. There was a lull in the shiva. Gabrielle had asked if they wanted her to take the kids home with her family for dinner, and after some hesitation, looking at Gal's hopeful face, and at Noam in Gabrielle's arms playing with her necklace, Daniel had asked if she was sure she wanted to take the baby too, and she had said sure, Noam was her favorite cutie-pie.

Assaf Schwartz was a paunchy, middle-aged man with unfashionably large glasses. He shook hands with and offered grave condolences to the whole family, in both English and Hebrew. Daniel remembered that Joel and Ilana had told him about Assaf; they believed that he was a true mensch. Ilana had dealt with him in her work, seen him preside over the divorces and custody fights of her students' parents.

Daniel began to herd them into the master bedroom. Matt headed that way and Daniel caught his arm. "Matt," he said. "I think it's better that you not come in. It'll freak everyone out even more." He lowered his voice. "If they imagine that the kids have been left only to me, instead of to us together, it might prevent a firestorm."

"Oh," Matt said. "Okay." That sounded reasonably strategic to him for all of two seconds, and by the time his outrage surfaced, they were all inside, the door closed behind them. He'd come all this way, he thought, only to have door after door closed in his face. He stood there, his chest heaving. Where could he go? His mind cast around for options. He didn't know where he was, and there wasn't an English-language map in the house as far as he knew, and he didn't know where the car keys were. If he could take the car, he'd just drive and drive along the winding narrow streets till he was good and lost. Or find himself a bar—were there bars in Jerusalem? There must be—and get good and hammered. And pick up some dark-skinned soldier with peach fuzz and traces of acne, and blow him silly.

But he didn't even know what the address was here, to find his way back. He pondered that, his own severe infantilization.

The living room had emptied out, at least for now. He went into the kitchen and started opening cabinets, trying to find a liquor stash. He finally found a bottle of scotch among the vinegar and soy sauce bottles, and poured himself an enormous shot into a coffee mug. He downed it, shuddering. Then he slipped out the front door and stumbled out into the street, squinting from the low, cutting western sun. He walked down the street, stray cats scattering before him. To his left was a narrow flight of stone stairs, leading up; he began to climb them, walking past little gardens, profusions of flowers falling over stone walls, and shadowed doorways into apartment buildings, some with old, creaky iron gates. At the top, a bus roared by on a wide and busy street. He ran across and turned up another flight of stairs, where again he felt sheltered from the warm and busy city. He could smell some type of wild plant. The loveliness of the neighborhood made him want to cry, and the alcohol hit him then and made him stagger. He found a small raggedy playground where a lone grandma, a scarf on her head, sat near a stroller as a toddler played in the sand. He sat down on a bench and closed his eyes, feeling his head spiral. He would sit there till it got dark. If Daniel needed him, he wouldn't be there.

The conversations he'd had at the shiva bubbled in his mind. What were the names of that couple he'd been stuck in a corner with? The guy was the son of Yaakov and Malka's best friends. Natan Fink, that was his name. And his haughty, elegant wife, whose name Matt couldn't dredge up. Natan had apparently played with Ilana as a kid. When the conversation with Matt faltered, he'd gestured toward the baby gate that normally blocked off the kitchen and now leaned unused against a cabinet, as if to say that he'd just noticed it. "When we were young, they didn't have childproofing, and shmildproofing; they didn't believe that a kid would die if he ate a peanut. Do you understand? These people had survived the biggest catastrophe that could happen, they were trying to begin a new life, they didn't waste their time with nonsense. So we kids ran wild; we played on construction sites, in wadis, we rode bikes—without helmets!" He made a shocked face. "All over Jerusalem, into the Arab parts, where the Arabs all knew us and liked us and gave us rolls with *zatar*." He stopped and laughed. "Not that we weren't a little messed up! If you ever hurt yourself, or felt bad, you looked into your parents' eyes and felt ashamed to think of that as suffering." He looked at his wife and said complacently, "But I turned out okay, right?"

His wife patted his arm. "Sure, sweetie," she said.

Natan's eyes moved over the living room and then rested fondly on Yaakov. "They all helped each other. If one lost a job, the others pitched in. If one had, God forbid, to be hospitalized, or had a nervous breakdown, the others were there to help. And Malka and Yaakov! Well. To this day, my parents say that they wouldn't have made it without them. They got on the same boat to Palestine as Malka. None of them were married yet, of course. They'd all lost their parents, brothers, sisters. So they had to be a family to each other."

They were silent for a while, then Natan heaved a mighty sigh. "He's a hero, Yaakov. A true hero. And now—*ach.*"

Sitting on the park bench, Matt wrapped his arms around himself and rubbed. The sun had lowered behind a building and it was suddenly cold. He thought about how he'd tell Daniel this story, about this obnoxious man who worshipped Yaakov. He was sure that by now he knew more about some of these people than Daniel did. Anger rose sullenly in him again. He knew Daniel was grieving, but didn't he, Matt, deserve a little recognition, deserve to be seen as part of the family? As a participant in this drama?

IN THE BEDROOM, THE four parents perched uncomfortably at the edges of Joel and Ilana's bed. Malka, whose feet didn't quite reach the floor, smoothed down the bedspread on either side of her; Lydia had picked up a small framed picture of Joel and Ilana hiking up north before they got married, and was rubbing the dust off the glass with the hem of her blouse. Daniel was crouching at the side of the bed, his pulse racing, ready to get this over with. His mother and Malka kept insisting that he come on up and sit down. "I'm fine," he said, and "There's no room!" till his mother pressed closer to his father, bumping the line of bodies, which moved in a small series of sighs and grunts. Daniel sat, the mattress drooping under half his butt, his mother folding his hand in hers and rubbing it. He pulled it away. "I'm falling off!" he said, and stood.

Assaf stood awkwardly in front of them with a manila envelope in his hand. He twisted and looked behind him at the floor, as though contemplating sitting there, then turned back toward them and cleared his throat. "Is everybody . . . ?" he murmured. He read the opening language of the will, and explained to Daniel's parents that it was just the everyday legal stuff about Joel and Ilana being the parents to Gal and Noam, and being of sound mind. Then Assaf peeked at them over the paper and cleared his throat again. "'It is our wish,'" he read, "'that our children's uncle, Daniel Rosen, be designated the guardian of Gal and Noam, to live with them wherever he wishes.'" He read it once in Hebrew, and then translated it into English.

There was silence. Anxiety gaped in Daniel's chest as he waited for the information to take. Yaakov's face was reddening. Malka looked at him, bewildered, for an explanation. Then she looked at Daniel. "But you'll live with them here, in this house."

Daniel tried to look at her, but it was too hard to meet her stupefied gaze, her sagging mouth. "No, Malka," he said, "I'm going to have to take them to my home, in the States."

"*Lama?*" she asked. Why?

He began to speak, but his parents were staring at him, pulling his attention back. "Have you known this all along?" his mother asked, eyes blazing.

"For a while," Daniel hedged.

"How could you not tell me?" she cried. "I feel like such a fool! I never anticipated this." Her hand was gripping Sam's sleeve hard, and he was murmuring, "Honey."

"I must tell you something important," the lawyer said, raising his voice over the clamor of distress and incomprehension. "In Israeli wills, the disposition of property is always upheld. But not necessarily the disposition of children." He spoke in Hebrew.

Daniel saw understanding slowly dawn over Yaakov's face, and a flash of hope. "What are you talking about?" he demanded.

"The government considers what is the good of the children, in family court."

"What?" Daniel cried. "Their own *parents* wanted this for them. The court would go against the parents' wishes?"

"I'm afraid so," Assaf said gently. He stood with the papers dangling in his hand, and Daniel suddenly hated him, this hypocritical pose of gentle advocacy, his big sorrowful eyes blinking out of those ridiculous glasses. "If they thought it was for the good of the children."

His mother had Daniel by the sleeve; there was the clamor for translation, and he shook it off, he was trying to think. "You can't be serious," he said to Assaf, and then whirled at his parents and spat out an irritated translation. "And I'm sure," he said, his lips curled, "that living with two queers is exactly what the Israeli state thinks of as for the good of the children."

"Daniel," his father said.

"What are my chances?" Daniel demanded in Hebrew, ignoring his father, fixing Assaf with a cold look. He remembered something. "They're American citizens; doesn't that count for something?"

"Not necessarily, Daniel," Assaf said. "You'll still need a court order to take them out of the country." He reached forward and clasped Daniel's shoulder. "But don't assume anything, either good or bad. There are many factors."

His father gripped his elbow. "Don't worry, son," he said softly. "We'll fight this."

Daniel shook his arm free. "I don't understand this," he said. "The *parents* decided what was for the good of the children." He felt he was about to cry and, mortified, covered his face with his hands. "Poor Joel and Ilana," he moaned. "It's what they *wanted*."

"This is crazy," Lydia was saying, looking to Sam for corroboration.

The lawyer crouched and tried to take them all in with his gaze. "Everybody, please be calm," he said, first in English, then in Hebrew. "Look. We are shocked by these terrible deaths. When we recover a little bit, I know that we'll all do our best to make sure that Gal and Noam have lives that are as safe and normal as possible."

Normal? Daniel burst into tears.

Malka was clutching at Yaakov and asking him how Ilana could do this to them, and he was urging her, with increasing impatience, to calm down, to try to understand that the court would surely be on their side.

CHAPTER 4

H E COULDN'T FIND Matt anywhere. Their bedroom was empty, the sofa bed made up, with the bed pillows, in worn pillowcases, stacked upon it. The window was open and the curtain billowing. He checked the bathroom and the balcony, and went back into their room and sat down on the sofa. He unbuttoned the top buttons of his shirt and stared at the desk till his vision blurred. There was a knock on the door frame; Yaakov stood there with his jacket on. "Malka doesn't feel well," he said. "I must take her home."

Daniel nodded numbly.

Yaakov turned away, and Daniel's parents came to the door of his room. His mother's face was tight; she was demanding, "How long have you known about this?"

His father leaned heavily on the desk.

Where the hell was Matt? The thought of not bringing the children home made Daniel sick; the prospect of caring for them was the only thing that had kept him from going off the deep end. He buried his head in his hands.

"Daniel, I want to know how long you've known about this," Lydia said.

"Not long, Mom," he lied, his voice muffled through his fingers, "just for about a month."

"It was Ilana's idea, wasn't it." She had a difficult relationship with Ilana, whom she perceived as constantly policing the boundaries between them; she'd been furious when Ilana had asked her to wait a month before visiting, after Gal was born. They all spent a lot of energy denying that this was true, but Daniel knew that it was. Still, leaving him the kids hadn't been Ilana's idea, not hers alone.

"No," Daniel said firmly, looking up. "It was both of them. We had a conversation about it."

There was silence. Finally, Lydia said, "I have trouble believing that."

"Why?" he demanded. "I find that offensive. You think Joel wouldn't trust me to raise his children?"

"Daniel," his father said. "Please don't escalate this any more than necessary."

Lydia began to cry. "I feel so betrayed," she said. "It's as though Joel were killed all over again."

"Oh, please!" Daniel said. "His having a desire of his own means he was killed all over again?"

"Daniel," his father barked.

"I can't help the way I feel," his mother said. "Do not tell me how I can and cannot feel."

Daniel's hands were sweating on the knees of his pants. This new legal hitch made him feel desperately undermined, as though his bid to be an adult had failed right in front of them. He knew that, to his father, he'd always been the perplexing twin, given every opportunity but lacking in the kind of ambition Sam understood. He'd always suspected that Sam thought of his homosexuality itself as a form of sloth, something that put him in the disappointing category of people without a work ethic. And now—any cachet he'd had, any way he'd been ennobled by the prospect of rescuing the children, had vanished.

His father closed his eyes, and when he opened them again he said, "At least in Massachusetts the kids would be closer to us."

Lydia looked at him sharply, and he shrugged. "Look," he said, "we might have to be realistic about this." He looked steadily at her as her eyes widened with incredulity and outrage, her mascara thickened with tears. "Honey, we're in third place," he said. "For whatever reason, Joel and Ilana clearly wanted Daniel to take the kids, and the state is going to lean toward keeping them here, with their other grandparents."

"That's out of the question," Lydia said. "Malka is mentally disturbed, she can't even keep her house clean. And how old are they? They must be in their seventies!"

Sam shrugged again and gestured toward Daniel, as if to suggest that he was a better option, and Lydia's face, rigid with shock and rage, crumpled. "It's as though he were killed all over again," she cried.

"Mother, would you stop saying that?"

"How are you going to raise these children!" she demanded. "And with whom? With *Matt*?" She gave an ugly laugh.

And then, when Daniel couldn't stand it for one more moment, Matt walked into the room, red-cheeked, bringing in with him the bracing chill of the night wind. "How's it going?" he asked.

Daniel looked up. Matt looked like a miracle, handsome and tousled. Daniel wanted to fling himself into his arms. But instead, he found himself saying accusingly, "We're not going to get the kids."

"What?"

His parents' eyes swiveled heavily toward Matt, and Daniel saw for the first time just how much Lydia disliked him. Sam explained what had happened, with Daniel interrupting to gloss the situation in the bleakest light. "The good of the child," he snapped. "Since when has a religious state considered it the good of the child to be placed in the care of queers?"

His father made an admonishing sound, and Lydia winced. "Don't say that," she said. "I hate that word."

"It's what we are, Mother," he said. "No matter how respectable we are, how well-behaved, to them we're just *queers*."

Matt sat next to him on the couch and put a hand on his arm. Lydia rose frostily and took Sam's hand, and said, "I'm not going to listen to this. We'll let you calm down."

When they'd left, Matt slid the door shut.

"It's true," Daniel insisted.

"You're preaching to the choir, honey," Matt said. He tried to take him into his arms, but Daniel shook him off.

"Where *were* you? I looked all over for you." His face was exhausted and ashy, crusted with layers of dried tears, and Matt's heart went out to his poor, tired spirit.

"I'm sorry, baby," he said gently. "I left the house for a little while and went for a walk." He was proud of himself for not mentioning that Daniel himself had sent him away.

"A little while?! I'm sitting here getting tortured by my parents, who can't believe I'm capable of raising a child, and on top of that facing *losing* the kids . . . Have you been *drinking*?" He paused, letting out a shaky sigh. "It's just that I have to know if I'm going to be able to depend on you."

Matt's face contorted with disbelief. "What are you talking about?" he cried. "That's so unfair!"

"It isn't about fair or not fair, Matt," Daniel said. "It's about being there to help."

Matt's hand was gripped over his heart, wrinkling his shirt. "Hey, I'm a nice, helpful guy, but I'm not a magician," he protested. "I can't be sent away and be there for you at the same time." There was no reply. "You've hardly let me near you in the past couple of days. You've hardly even acknowledged me! Ilana's father asks who I am every time he lays eyes on me. And you know what? This is my life, too; you're not the only one who's going to be raising those kids." He was thinking, *If we even get them*—and he had no idea how he felt about the prospect of not getting them. He remembered Daniel's return from Israel last year, and how, as he unpacked, his hands paused over the opened suitcase on his bed and his face took on a solemnity that Matt had never seen before, and which was so much the cartoon essence of solemnity—his eyes shining and his face drawn long—that Matt thought at first that he was about to joke about something. When Daniel told him that Joel and Ilana wanted their kids to live with them if something happened to them, Matt's heart had tumbled all over itself to join him in the sense that a wonderful honor had been bestowed upon them. And he had felt that all along, on Daniel's behalf, but also on his own. It seemed a sign of tremendous trust and love, and he had a sense of how subversive it was too, how deeply it went against the grain of the Israeli ideology of populating the land with Jewish children. He had never imagined that it would come to fruition; and when it did, he veered madly between excited pride and dread.

"It's my name in the will," Daniel countered, "and I'm the one who will have to go to court."

"And no doubt you'll keep me as far away from those proceedings as possible," Matt said.

Daniel stood and smacked his pants to smooth them. "You know what?" he said, drawing himself up. "I'm not having this conversation."

"Come on, Dan," Matt pleaded, standing between Daniel and the door. In the tiny room he could hear the labored breathing of his partner, could feel stress and sweat radiating off his body. "I don't want to fight."

Daniel refused to meet his eyes. They stood like that for a minute, and then Matt spoke. "This is awful," he said. "This is the most awful time in our entire lives. So let's be friends, okay? Otherwise, we're not going to survive this."

Daniel looked quickly at him, thinking, *We?* He took a shaky breath. "It's just that . . . I looked all over for you," he said, his eyes filling with tears.

Matt leveled him with a stare, knowing he should put his arms around him, even if he got pushed away again and again. But how much could you get blamed for not being there before you decided to just stop being there?

Daniel sat back down and covered his face with his hands. "I just wish I could talk to you," he said. "I come to bed wanting to curl up and talk to you. But I can't. You just don't get it."

Matt sat back down. "What don't I get?" he asked softly.

"The whole thing," Daniel said, waving a hand helplessly.

Matt shut his mind down, like a computer on sleep mode, and waited a few beats, willing himself to be patient. "What whole thing?"

Daniel looked at him. "I know how you feel about Israel, and about Joel and Ilana living here."

"And?" Matt asked, knowing that Daniel was referring to arguments they'd sometimes had, in which Matt had argued that Joel and Ilana should leave the country as long as it was an occupying power. He'd written his senior thesis on South Africa during apartheid, under a South African professor he admired who had gone into exile; and even though Daniel insisted over and over that the comparison didn't hold, South Africa was Matt's model for what the Israelis were doing. "In exile!" Daniel would exclaim. "I'm sorry, but who are you to tell people where to live?" It was the biggest bone of contention between them, and Matt thought it was stupid and a waste, since he and Daniel actually felt pretty much the same way about Israel, and because, when it came down to it, why should he be that invested in it anyway?

"I know you don't really feel this," Daniel said now, "but sometimes I think you might feel they deserved what they got."

Matt inhaled sharply. "Are you kidding me?" he said. *"Are you kidding me?"*

"I know it's not really true," Daniel said.

"You know it's not *really* true, but you think it may be a *little* true? Is that what you're saying?"

"Well, is it?" Daniel asked, looking up with a sudden challenge.

"Stop projecting, dude," Matt said, giving him a cool look. "Stop taking out your fucked-up feelings about this country on me."

Daniel flushed and sank onto the couch. He shot Matt a look of mingled anger and confusion. "I don't know what the hell I'm supposed to be feeling. I mean, I know what I'm *supposed* to be feeling. Righteous indignation at the terrorists for killing innocent people, and all of that." He looked quickly at Matt, then down again. *Aha*, thought Matt, *that's what he's mad about.* If you believed that the Occupation was itself a form of constant terrorism—because what else could you call humiliating Palestinian civilians, subjecting them to a thousand petty and infuriating regulations, stealing their land, depriving them of their livelihood, blowing up their homes? If you believed that, what the hell *were* you supposed to feel at this moment?

But it wasn't fair to take out his anger on him! Matt called it pulling the goy card. Because Matt wasn't Jewish, Daniel always claimed that he couldn't understand the depth of Daniel's misery over it, over the historical irony that his people had overcome oppression by becoming an occupying force. Once, a few years ago, he had made Matt read Leon Uris's *Exodus.* "Every Jewish kid of my generation read it," he'd told Matt. He wanted him to get a sense of Israel's prehistory, however distorted it was by the novel: how it came into being in the wake of the Holocaust, and how Jewish warriors smuggled into Palestine the refugees no other nation would save. He also wanted Matt to feel the romance of Israel, which Daniel had learned to feel in Jewish camp as a teenager, and which he thought the book would evoke in a passionate gay man. The Jewish soldiers were so manly and self-reliant, and there were many scenes of beautiful Jewish teenage warriors dancing the hora around campfires, eyes flashing. Matt gulped the book down, and reported that it gave him a total boner. "But do you get what I mean about what Jews love about Israel?" Daniel insisted as Matt nibbled his neck, whispering, "You be the handsome, emotionally damaged underground fighter, and I'll be the haughty girl in charge of the refugee camp in Cyprus." And then, when Daniel, laughing, pushed him, "Yes, I get it, I get it!"

Now Matt nodded warily. He knew that if Daniel couldn't have this conversation with him, he couldn't have it at all. He reached for Daniel's shoe, removed it, and took his foot into his hands, began massaging it gently over the sock.

"When my dad started talking about how innocent Joel and Ilana were . . . I mean, they *were* innocent. But you know what I mean. . . ."

"Yeah, I've been thinking about it. That whole innocence thing," Matt mused. "It kills me." His lip curled a little. "Your dad—you know, he was just doing his thing, he's devastated. But do you think anyone ever called Jay innocent when he died?"

Daniel snorted.

Matt's hands stopped.

"Don't stop," Daniel said. He opened his eyes. "What?"

Matt's eyes were blinking very rapidly, and his lips were pressed together.

"It's not the same thing," Daniel said.

Anger wormed into Matt's throat. Daniel's tone was so final and derisive. He sat still, fuming, and Daniel propped himself up on his elbow.

"Oh, come on, Matt," he said, incredulous. "It's not."

"Why?" Matt asked. "Because Jay was just fucking without a condom, while your brother was heroically drinking a latte?"

That stunned them both into silence. Then Daniel scrambled back into a sitting position and shouted, "Go to hell!" He glanced in the direction of the kitchen, where his parents were sitting, and lowered his voice to a vicious whisper. "Go to hell! I knew I couldn't talk to you!"

"You *can* talk to me," Matt cried. "Just don't insult my friend! Why do you have to insult him? I know you think he was just a silly queen, but he was a good person, Dan." He sat on the couch, his chest heaving, ashamed that he had insulted his partner's dead brother, and yet so hurt and furious he couldn't help it. For some reason, he remembered going to the movies with Jay, and how Jay always made Matt be absolutely quiet—not even a whisper or a snide comment here and there—even though when they'd watch TV together they could talk as much as they wanted. It was a rule. Jay hadn't had any long-term relationships till Kendrick, and he wasn't a breeder, and he didn't live in a majestic holy city at the center of a world-historical conflict. But did that make him unimportant? And why did Daniel have to be such a huge homophobe?

"This isn't about Jay! This isn't about you!" Daniel hissed.

But it had an impact on him! How could he say that? Just then the door slid open and Gal came in. She was chewing on a piece of bread wadded in her hand, and wore a bead necklace around her neck. The hair around her face had been pulled back and tied with a fancy hair band, clearly Gabrielle's work. She looked at them curiously as they quickly wiped their eyes and tried to compose their faces.

"Hey, Boo," Matt said, his voice hoarse. "Did you play with beads at Leora's?"

"Yeah," she said faintly, being cooperative with an interrogating adult while she eyed Daniel, who had turned his back to them and was wiping his eyes with his forearms. "Why Uncle Dani crying?" she asked.

Matt looked at Daniel. "He's sad," he told her. "He misses your *ema* and *abba*." He hoped it was okay to bring it up when she was having a break from mourning.

She shot Daniel a suspicious look, then backed up till she was standing against the doorjamb. "Why did the bad man hate the Jews?" she asked.

Daniel looked at Matt sharply and sat down beside him. "Who told you that?" he asked.

"Savta."

Matt waited, bitter mirth surfacing in his nose and sinuses; this one was *so* up to Daniel.

"Some Arabs hate the Jews," Daniel said, clearing his throat, "because when the Jews came to Israel, they lived on land that the Arabs say was theirs."

"Was it theirs?"

"Lots of it was," Daniel said. "The Israelis and the Arabs are not good at sharing."

She considered this. Then she asked, without looking at Daniel, "Is that why he killed Ema and Abba? Did they live on his land?"

Daniel and Matt looked at each other, eyes still, minds racing.

"No," Daniel said, "they didn't. He was just a very bad, angry man."

Gal gnawed off another piece of bread. "Leora's scared of taking a shower by herself," she reported to Daniel in Hebrew.

"Really? How come?" he asked, shrugging at Matt when her eyes darted away for a moment.

"She's afraid that water will go up her nose. She doesn't know how to breathe through her mouth," Gal said, and slipped out of the room.

Daniel and Matt sat there, looking at each other stupidly, until Matt rose and slid the door shut. "That was pretty lame," he said. "We better get our story straight."

Daniel laughed a little, and sighed a wide-eyed, shuddery sigh.

"I liked the part about the Jews and the Arabs not being good at sharing," Matt said, and when Daniel looked sharply at him, he protested, "No, really, I'm serious. What did she say there at the end?"

Daniel told him about Leora's fear of the shower, and they shrugged and laughed.

Matt snuck his hand onto Daniel's knee and pressed lightly. When Daniel looked into his face, his eyes were bright and intense. "Dan," he said, "I'm sorry."

Daniel breathed in and then out again, his breath like a small parcel he was picking up and putting down. He wasn't sure what Matt was saying—whether he was apologizing for what he'd said or just expressing general sorrow about the whole sad situation. And he did not forgive him. But it was hard, because Matt looked beautiful as feeling suffused his face and lent radiance to his eyes and mouth, and because, for better or for worse, he was the safest harbor Daniel knew.

Daniel got up to wash his face. Gal had gone into Joel and Ilana's room with his parents; a low TV sound came from behind the closed door. He swallowed a few sleeping pills. When he returned to the bedroom, Matt had opened up the bed. Daniel took off his pants and shirt, crawled under the covers in his underwear, and turned his face to the wall.

LYDIA EMERGED FROM BEHIND that closed bedroom door the next morning with her eyes red and her mouth set, and told Daniel that she was working very hard to accept that Ilana hadn't trusted her to raise the children. When Daniel opened his mouth to protest for the hundredth time that it wasn't just Ilana, she held up her hand and stopped him. "I'm trying to accept it," she said firmly. "She was entitled to her opinion." She heaved a great sigh. "And that's all I want to say."

It rankled, but he decided to let it go. He told himself that she had lost her son and was coping with this renewed injury, trying to be a big person the best way she could.

As it became clear that it would take at least three months for the custody issue to be worked out, Matt began making plans to go home. Daniel would stay for the duration; he'd have to meet with a caseworker and appear in court, probably several times. He had talked at length with his boss, and they'd worked out an arrangement where he could continue doing most of his story meetings and editing by telephone and email, at least through the next issue of the magazine. He found out that he could rent a cell phone on a monthly basis, and miraculously, Matt, who'd initially decided not to haul along Daniel's laptop, changed his mind on an impulse and grabbed it on their way out of the house. "What made you think to do that?" Daniel asked when Matt pulled it— *voilà!*—out of the closet.

"I don't know!" Matt exclaimed, basking for a moment in being the hero. "I just grabbed everything that I thought might help."

Gradually, a semblance of normalcy settled over the family. In private, they would be shaving or brushing their teeth when their knees would buckle, and they would cry out. Each time it shocked them, to be so thoroughly felled. Joel and Ilana came in and out of their dreams, stunned and bleeding and weeping and begging for help, or miraculously alive and wondering what the fuss was all about. In Daniel's dreams he swept past the yellow police tape and the authorities talking into crackling walkie-talkies and the black-coated Chevra Kadisha brushing little scraps of blood and tissue into small plastic bags, into the ruined and burning café, stepping on glass and blood, straining so hard to see his brother through the smoke that he finally did, his enormous effort making the air crystallize into the shape of his brother. He often came out of those dreams when Gal stumbled into their room crying "Ema!"—having dreamed that her mother was angry at her for talking back, or that she'd appeared in her room and smiled at her. He'd sit up, stunned by the still-lingering image of his brother, and hold her and rock her while she sobbed and sobbed, his cheek pressed on her hot, heaving back, trying to take long, even breaths, to soothe her with his body warmth and rhythm. They decided that it would be best for her to get back into her routine as quickly as possible, so Daniel took her to school, where she marched in like such a resigned and compliant trouper he almost snatched her back and took her home.

In the late evenings, after both children were in bed, the adults gathered heavy-eyed in the kitchen, which smelled of soup and dish soap and clementines. Lydia wiped down the counters while Daniel swept and did a *sponga*—using a mop with a soaking, soapy rag wrapped around the squeegee end, he soaped up the floors and then squeegeed the water into a drain in the corner of the kitchen, and then wiped down the floors with the rinsed-out rag. Matt grew accustomed to his disquisitions on the superiority of this method of mopping over the American method of repeatedly dunking the very mop you were cleaning the floors with into dirtied water. The phone rang incessantly, but after a certain point they let the machine in the bedroom take it. They kept the TV and radio, which were reporting the army's incursions into the West Bank, off. They talked about Joel and Ilana's estate, and the money coming to the children from Bituach Leumi; Sam was going over the details of their affairs with the lawyer, and researching the most tax-advantageous ways to invest the money in two countries. And then there was the baby's constipation. They'd done some consulting among everyone who'd changed a diaper—which was all of them—and discovered that he hadn't pooped in three days. Daniel had gone through Ilana's address book until he found the name of the pediatrician, and called and talked to the nurse, who had told him that at Noam's age, not pooping for five days or so was normal, but nevertheless recommended lots of fruit in his diet, plus prune juice, prune juice, and more prune juice.

Matt had made a reservation to return on a Continental flight that would leave in four days. One morning, as he was helping Gal get dressed, he said, "You know, Boo, I'm going back to the States for a while." His heart was heavy; a kind of dull depression had settled over him, like asthma settling upon lungs. It was crazy, but part of him missed those first days of crisis. The tears, the rush from experience to experience, the way being a man in charge filled him with an ennobled feeling, as if he were a hero in a tragic film. But there was something else, too. Once the immediate crisis wore off, you had to admit to yourself that Joel and Ilana really weren't coming back. It was so unfair: They were mourning and mourning, shouldn't they get something in return, some alleviation of their pain?

It was morning and Gal was dressing for school. She was choosing between two purple shirts, and from her intensity, Matt thought, you would have imagined that they were even the tiniest bit different from each other. Gal had taken the shirts out of the drawer, which looked as though a tornado had run through it, and laid them both on her bed, tenderly smoothed them out. She was wearing jeans and a white undershirt, and Matt noticed that the kid's belly he'd blown many a raspberry into had flattened as she grew. She still needed to eat breakfast before Daniel took her to school, and she hadn't brushed her teeth yet either. He sat on the bed next to the shirts and folded his hands in his lap, fighting back the urge to hurry her.

Finally, she looked at him, her face darkening, and said, *"Oof!"*

"What's the matter, can't decide?"

She brought one shoulder up to her scowling face in a pretantrum half shrug.

"Do you want me to decide for you?"

"No!" she said, and began to cry.

He reached out his arms. "Come here, Boo," he said, but she stomped her foot and yelled "I not Boo, I *Gal!*" and ran crying out of the room. When Matt rose to go after her, he found her in the living room, in her grandmother's arms, Lydia murmuring to her and wiping her eyes. Matt shrugged. "She can't figure out which shirt to wear."

"Okay, sweetness, let's go take a look," her grandmother said, rising and holding out her hand. Gal went with her back to the bedroom, a thumb in her mouth, turning to shoot Matt a reproachful look. He sighed and went to get some cereal for her. She refused him a kiss good-bye when she left with Daniel for school. "She gives excellent cold shoulder," Matt said.

That evening, Lydia baked the chicken of Daniel's childhood, with Lawry's salt, garlic powder, and paprika. The chicken slid off the bone. The baby was in his high chair with shreds of chicken on his tray, rubbing grease from his knuckles onto his cheek as he crammed his fist into his mouth. A bottle of diluted prune juice stood on the edge of his tray.

Gal sat at the head of the table, smacking her lips over a drumstick like a tiny tsar. She had spent much of the day at school in tears, her teacher had reported to Daniel when he came to pick her up, but her spirits and appetite were rallying. Matt had noticed that she despaired every day, but not for the whole day. They were discussing the logistics of getting Matt to the airport, when Gal turned to Daniel and asked, "When I go to live with Sabba and Savta, will Noam come with me?"

Silence fell over the table. "Who told you you were going to live with your grandparents?" Daniel asked.

She looked at him, and then away, as though she'd been caught doing something wrong. "Sabba," she whispered.

They broadcast to one another grim, significant looks.

"What did he say, sweetheart?" Lydia asked, and when Gal cast a frightened look her way, she said, "You didn't do anything wrong, baby."

"They asked me do I want to come live with them."

They looked at her expectantly. Here was a new twist, Matt thought. He knew right away that she'd said yes; how could anyone as big-hearted as Gal turn down those sad, sad people?

"Did you say yes?" Daniel asked gently.

She nodded, and he pursed his lips and nodded back solemnly.

"Call the lawyer," Lydia said to Sam in a low, deadly voice, without moving her lips.

"Honey," Sam murmured.

Daniel's eyes were fixed on Gal. He reached out his arms and she climbed down off her chair and slid sideways onto his lap. Matt watched him with a lump of love in his throat. "I'm not sure who you're going to live with," Daniel said, gently turning her face toward him with two fingers. "There are lots of grown-ups who love you."

"Like you?" Gal asked.

A teary laugh burbled up from his throat. "Like me," he said. "And Matt, and Grandma and Grampa, and Sabba and Savta. And who else?"

"Gabrielle and Moti."

"*Nachon,*" Daniel sang; in Hebrew you could sing "Right!" in two happy notes. "*V'mi od?*"

Gal listed all the adults they knew, including all of her parents' friends, and a few they didn't know—a girl who was her friend, Leora's older sister's scout leader, and a man who, after much interrogation and clarification, they decided apparently owned a lightbulb store.

"So many people love you!" Daniel said in mock astonishment. She'd warmed to the project, and was bending backward to dangle off his knees upside down. He heaved her up till she was sitting upright again, and became grave. "Matt and I and Grandma and Grampa and Sabba and Savta all love you so much that you'll always be taken care of. But we don't know who you and Noam are going to live with yet. Either with me and Matt, or with Sabba and Savta."

Matt felt a tremor pass through him, and looked straight down at his plate. It was the first time it had been said aloud that the kids wouldn't be living with their American grandparents.

Gal nestled into Daniel's chest and put her thumb in her mouth.

"I hope you boys know what you're getting into," Lydia said quietly. "You know that you're going to have to make some huge adjustments to your lifestyle."

"Duh," Matt muttered, pushing his chair back and going to the cabinet to forage for cookies. He hated everything about those sentences: the sanctimonious parent shit, the condescension, the word *lifestyle*.

"Can I go play in my room?" Gal asked.

"Sure," Daniel said.

Can I go play in mine? Matt wanted to ask. He returned to the table with a handful of chocolate-covered biscuits.

"I'm going to call the Grossmans," Daniel said. "She has so many important questions, and we need to get our stories straight."

Matt tried to imagine them, the ones she'd asked and the ones she hadn't yet. *Why did the bad man kill Ema and Abba? What happens when you die? Am I going to die? Where am I going to live?* He watched as Daniel picked up a little chunk of cantaloupe and put it in Noam's mouth. It seemed to be on the list of things babies could eat, as opposed to nuts or peanut butter or anything with pits. Matt was sure they'd manage to choke or poison him the moment he got to their house. And then their lifestyle would hardly have to change at all!

"Wait," Sam said. "Before you do anything, let's stop and think. You might want to consult a child specialist, so we can learn the most effective thing to tell Gal. Why don't you call the social worker and ask her for a referral."

The baby started to kick and rub his eyes with his greasy fists. Lydia went to the sink and returned with a wet cloth, took each of his hands, and wiped them off.

"You know, Dad, I don't think it's that complicated. I just want to tell them that they can't promise Gal she'll be living with them, when it's unclear where she'll be living."

Daniel called Yaakov that night, and afterward, he came into the bedroom, where Matt was reclining on the bed reading the *Jerusalem Post* and cackling. "I love this food critic," Matt said, holding up the paper. "He described a certain wine as 'Talmudic without being disputatious.'"

"Listen," Daniel said. "I just have to blow off some steam before I report back to my parents."

"What did he say?" Matt asked, dismayed and fascinated.

Daniel told Yaakov he wanted to talk about Gal. He had worked up to it slowly, aware that even hearing his voice on the telephone could send them into a tailspin. He had heard the click of the other line being picked up, and Malka's breathing. "I told him it didn't seem right to tell Gal she was going to live with them," he said. "I said that it was really important to tell her the truth. And then he became a lunatic. He kept yelling, '*Truth? Truth?* Wait until she learns the truth! Wait until the judge hears the truth!'" He sat down on the bed and put his head in his hands.

Matt sat up and smoothed the hair at the back of Daniel's head. How many terrible conversations had they had in this tiny room with the stacked pillows and sheets, the tiny desk scattered with change and watches and wallets and notebooks, the dry wind sifting through? "You mean the truth that we're godless sodomites?" he said lightly.

Daniel craned his head violently away from Matt's caress. "I want to say, 'Okay, the man's in anguish.' He is! 'Okay, the man's from a different culture than we are.' That too! But how many times am I supposed to excuse homophobic insults because the guy is traumatized? Because I know that the homophobic anger is just a cover for his despair?"

Matt knew the answer. The answer was many, many times. He hadn't told Daniel about how Lydia had cornered him that afternoon, sat on the edge of the couch next to him, and put her hand on his and said knowingly, confidingly, "Matt, be honest with me. You can't possibly want to raise two small children."

He'd asked, "Why not, Lydia?"

She gave him a *Don't kid a kidder* look.

He said, "Look, it wouldn't have been my first choice. But I loved Joel and Ilana, and I love their children, and you know how I feel about carrying out their wishes? I feel *fantastic* about it."

She'd stood and crossed her arms and pinned on him the severe look of the prophet. "See how you feel about it when instead of going out dancing at night you're nursing a vomiting child."

Dancing? Did she *know* where they lived?

And now they were going to be in a supplicating position to get custody of the kids, and that meant they'd have to put up with God knows how much bullshit. He could see it already. It would be implied that their gayness was trivial, a luxury, in comparison with the huge issues of terrorism and orphanhood. They'd be told to shut up about being gay already, as though it was they who were constantly hammering that point home, as though they were children clamoring for a Popsicle in the midst of a typhoon.

Suddenly, Matt couldn't wait to go home.

Daniel left the room to talk to his parents, and Matt closed his eyes as quiet settled around him.

WHAT WERE THEY LIABLE to see at the site of the former Peace Train Café? Daniel knew that all signs of blood and broken glass would be mopped up. He imagined that after just ten days there wouldn't be an official memorial there yet, but that there would be an unofficial one. In bed, he imagined himself there, on the site where his brother had said his last words, breathed his last breath. He saw Joel sitting back in his chair, one hand on the table, playing with a book of matches or a packet of sugar. Was he smiling at Ilana, laughing at something she said? Was he smoking the odd forbidden cigarette? Daniel fiercely hoped he'd gotten in a last smoke. It was Windbreaker weather, and the wind ruffled Joel's sleeve. Daniel imagined the soft, hidden parts of him, his armpits and belly and his cock nestled against his leg. He thought of the pictures of the two of them as children, each marked with a *D* and a *J* under the corresponding child so they could be told apart, in a kiddie pool in the backyard, their kids' bellies, with their outie belly buttons, jutting over their trunks.

When he imagined the bomber, he saw a sweaty, agitated kid in a big coat.

He and Matt walked downtown, on side streets clustered with stone houses, tall trees that looked like palms, with trunks the texture of pineapple skins, and huge furry-brown firs. Plants tumbled over stone walls and through the bars of ornamental iron gates, narrow verdant walkways with stone steps, the occasional small dog barking shrilly from a balcony lined with planters. It was a dry and sunny morning, and despite himself, despite the dread that seeped over him at the prospect of seeing the spot where Joel and Ilana were killed, Matt felt happiness bound into his limbs from the air, the exercise, the quiet companionship of being with his partner. They passed crowded bus stops, the elderly sitting on benches in hats and overcoats, and teenagers huddled together, laughing. Red Egged buses passed them with huge gasps and exhalations of dark exhaust. Traffic got noisier as they approached downtown, and crossing streets they ran between honking cars.

It was the first time Matt had been downtown. It was crowded and dirty—Israelis were huge litterbugs. Daniel stopped to buy a small bouquet of tulips wrapped in plastic from a street vendor surrounded by buckets of flowers. They turned down the pedestrian walkway, looking at stores crammed with jewelry and tourist Judaica—Star of David necklaces, seder plates, menorahs, mezuzahs—middle-aged proprietors standing outside for a smoke in the sun, the smells of pizza and falafel and grilled lamb heavy in the air. People pushed and elbowed past them without interrupting their conversations. Armed soldiers patrolled the streets, and there were guards posted in front of coffeehouses, most of them Ethiopian, in fluorescent yellow vests. Matt suddenly noticed that he was in a crowd, and also that he wasn't afraid. It had nothing to do with the presence of the soldiers, he thought. It was that they had already been touched, and wouldn't be again. At least by something huge, like a terrorist's bomb. He had already begun worrying about the silly, banal ways of dying, like being killed crossing the street, or slipping in the tub and cracking his head open, or one of the kids choking on something. Because if one of them were to die like that, it would just be too hideously ironic.

The café was down by the bottom of the walkway, and he didn't see it till they were almost upon it. It had been called Peace Train Café, after the Cat Stevens song, not translated, just like that, pronounced "Pees Trrrein." It was boarded up, and in front of it lay heaps of flowers, cards, teddy bears, yarhzeit candles with tiny wavering flames. Tourists were stopping to take pictures, and off to the side, two lanky teenagers stood melancholically, their arms draped around each other.

They stopped and stood with their hands in their pockets. Matt lightly rubbed Daniel's back.

Daniel took a breath. He couldn't tell how big the café had been—it was entirely boarded. Smoke streaks stained the building's upper floors, and its windows were blown out. He carefully laid his bouquet on top of a heap of withered roses. At his feet was a piece of pink construction paper with a snapshot of a smiling family taped to it, and the words *Zichronam l'vracha*—May their memory be blessed—written below it. He knew the names of most of the sixteen dead by now, having encountered them over and over in the newspapers, which had run features on many of them. Five of them, almost a full third, were the Golan family, who had taken their three kids out for ice cream at the end of the Sabbath.

Daniel looked at Matt, who had stooped to peer at some of the pictures. Two women in sunglasses, carrying purses, came up and stood next to him, shaking their heads and making tsking noises. *"Nora,"* one of them said. Terrible.

He stood there, leaden, dumb, like a beast being goaded to haul things. He turned around, and turned back, and scratched his jaw. He'd been building up to see something sublime, and this was so banal, the Hallmark version of his lacerating grief. The sublimity was all in his fantasies and dreams, where his mind soared and blacked out from the enormity of what it imagined, the enormity of his love for Joel, of Joel's body being shattered, his shining life obliterated.

Beside him stood Matt, tears running freely down his face.

Daniel thrust his hands into his jacket pockets. He felt that he should stay there till he'd taken it all in, till the image had imprinted itself upon his mind so that years from now he'd be able to call it up, and to say, *I'll never forget the sight of that bombed-out café.* But it was as if the images before him were fake, the way a child's tinkling keyboard is a fake piano, and he felt cheated by them.

Matt was sniffing and making throat-clearing noises as Daniel steered him away by the elbow. He led him into a tiny alley and past stores with ceramics and handcrafted jewelry, and then they went through a dark passageway, up some stairs, and emerged into a pretty café courtyard set up with tables and umbrellas. "It's still here," Daniel said. Inside, the shop was dark and cool, lined with crammed bookshelves. They ordered espressos and brought outside tiny cups rattling on saucers. Matt hiccupped and asked Daniel if he would bum a cigarette for him from a young man who was reading at another table; Daniel went over and returned with one, whispering, in a faint attempt to amuse him, that the kid was reading Heidegger. Matt lit the cigarette and inhaled deeply, blew the smoke into the sky in a thin stream. He touched Daniel's sneakered foot with his own, and Daniel looked at him.

"Dan," he said, looking into his eyes.

Daniel nodded. He was depressed and didn't know what to do with that, except to be angry at Matt for making him come here in the first place. He felt as though Matt had gone for the facile response to the makeshift memorial, and Daniel was angry at him for that too, but was trying to stuff back that feeling because it was ungenerous and judgmental.

Matt wiped his face with the tiny napkin beside his saucer. "I'm going to leave you all of my underwear and socks and T-shirts," he said. Neither of them had packed many clothes, and Daniel would need them.

Daniel nodded. "I'll buy whatever else I need. They have clothes in Israel." And then, with a half-comic yelp, "Don't leave me alone with them!"

"Oh, honey," Matt murmured, and then with a quick anxious pang: "Do you want me to stay?"

"Don't offer what you can't give," Daniel said with a level look. He knew Matt was dying to go home.

"Okay," Matt said in a small voice.

"Really," Daniel said. "It just makes things worse."

Another surge of emotion rushed over Matt's face. "It's just," he said, his voice breaking, "it's just that it's hard to leave you."

"I'll be okay," Daniel said. Even as he had no idea how he would manage without him, he was longing for Matt to leave, so he wouldn't have to worry about him, so he could handle things in his own way.

They sipped the hot, harsh, grainy coffee and felt the cool wind brush their arms and necks.

THE NEXT MORNING, STANDING at the airport curb with Matt's luggage at their feet, they clung to each other, until Daniel broke away.

"I love you," Matt said, eyes glistening, his fist to his heart. "Me and Yo-yo, we'll be waiting for you and the kids."

"If we get them."

"We'll get them."

"I hope so."

"No, really." His forehead was touching Daniel's. "We will. The house will be a total disaster area. It'll be great."

Daniel laughed.

"Okay, baby?" Matt asked.

Daniel nodded, looking at the ground. Suddenly, he couldn't bear to look at Matt's face. He turned away, got into the car, and drove off without looking in the rearview mirror.

Matt went inside and moved quickly through the line, up to the security woman who took his passport, looked him up and down, and asked him what he was doing in Israel.

Matt's mind tumbled over the answers: *partner* or *friend*, *died* or *killed*? What kind of explanation?

"My friend's brother was killed. I came for the funeral," he said, cursing himself. Later, he wondered why he hadn't just said *partner*. The security guard wasn't screening out queers, just terrorists.

"Killed?" She looked at him, her curiosity breaking through her interrogation technique.

"Yes, in the Peace Train bombing," he said.

She looked at him soberly. "I'm sorry," she said, and put a sticker on his suitcase.

He went through passport control and up to the terminal. He had an hour before boarding, so he cruised the duty-free shop, where determined Israeli men with huge watches on hairy arms and women with lacquered nails were throwing enormous boxes of cigarettes and after-shave into shopping carts. He went back outside and bought treats, a stack of Elite chocolate bars and a bag of sunflower seeds. He sat down by the gate, peeling back the crinkly silver lining of one of the bars. He'd been unprepared for the deliciousness of Israeli chocolate. It was a strange and guilty pleasure to be alone, leaving the Rosen family and their trauma behind. Of course, he told himself, he wasn't really leaving them behind, he was resting up so he could be there for Daniel and the kids when they came home.

He broke off another square of chocolate and sucked on it, and reached into his bag for a magazine and his iPod. He put in the earbuds and turned it to shuffle. A murmuring came into his ears.

I'm so tired, so tired of all this drama.

Oh, God. Too perfect. He closed his eyes as Mary J. Blige's voice—and the voices of her sighing, echoing backup singers—swelled into his ears.

No more pain
No more pain
No more drama in my life
No one's gonna make me hurt again

His music. His music! He closed his eyes, and his big, emotional heart throbbed to the beat of pain and survival.

CHAPTER 5

DANIEL GOT BACK from the airport to find his parents feeding the kids dinner. Gal and the baby were sitting nicely in their chairs eating spaghetti, Gal trying to twirl it with a fork, the way Matt had taught her, and Noam grabbing it in his fists, his chin glistening with tomato sauce. His father was working on his own enormous plate, a paper napkin tucked into his collar. Daniel tossed his keys onto the counter.

"Spaghetti?" his mother asked, putting her napkin on the table and pushing back her chair.

"No thanks," he said, "I'm not hungry."

The minute the words came out, he wished he hadn't said them, because he was starving. He stood and looked at the placid family, rubbed his temple with his thumb. He'd thought that things would be simpler once Matt left; no more clamor for recognition, no more having to deal, on top of everything else, with the feeling that he was a bad person because he didn't acknowledge their relationship to Matt's satisfaction. But the whole drive back to Jerusalem he'd dreaded coming home alone to his parents, coming home as he had at sixteen, sexless and unpartnered.

"Are you sure?" Lydia was asking. "Maybe just a little plate?" And Gal was asking, "Is Matt on an airplane?"

He sat down at the table. "Okay, maybe just a little," he told his mother, and turning to Gal, "Yes."

She was blinking rapidly. "Matt's plane won't crash," she said in Hebrew.

"That's right." Daniel leaned over and wiped spaghetti sauce from her mouth with his napkin.

Gal's silky hair rose in wisps, and her eyes were dark. "How do you know?" she asked.

His parents were looking at him inquisitively, and he quickly translated.

"I just do," he told Gal, but that made her face fall, and he could tell he was insulting her. "They have very, very good pilots," he said. "Airplanes almost never crash."

He leaned back as his mother placed a steaming plate in front of him. "Don't indulge her," she murmured.

He whirled on her. "*Indulge* her? Are you kidding me?"

Lydia flushed. "The *fears*, I mean. Not the child."

Gal was asking, "But do they *ever* crash?"

"I meant the *fears*," his mother repeated.

"Daniel," his father said.

"Almost never," he said to Gal, speaking in Hebrew, ignoring his parents. "Really, sweetie, I'm just not worried."

"But do they *ever*?"

"Sweetie," he said. He scooted back his chair and patted his lap, frightened, because he'd used up the extent of his repertoire for comforting her. "Come here."

She was crying now, and there was a sudden sweep of her arm and her plate went crashing to the floor, spaghetti and sauce splashing onto the cabinet bottoms and slithering over the tile.

"Hey!" Daniel shouted.

Gal jumped off her chair and ran into her room, and they heard the door slam. Daniel and his mother looked at each other accusatorily.

"I don't know why you have to be so hurtful," his mother said. "You're not the only one suffering."

"I don't like being corrected when I'm trying to manage something difficult," Daniel snapped.

"Your mother was trying to help," his father said.

Daniel rolled his eyes. "Dad, could you just stop?"

"We'll get this mess," Lydia said. "You get your temper under control and go calm her down."

In her room, Gal was sobbing. Daniel got on his knees and gently gripped her shoulders so he could look her in the face and apologize for yelling at her. She wrenched herself away and threw herself onto her bed, sobbing into the pile of the morning's rejected clothes. He stood, irresolute, knowing better than to touch her again, and watched her shoulders quaking, enduring the long moment when she went still and silent before she caught her breath and let out a shattering scream. He murmured her name, whispered, "Shh, shh."

She screamed again, and he winced, dreading the baby hearing and melting down himself. He went over to the open window, glanced out at the geraniums Joel had planted in the window boxes, which none of them had had the wherewithal to keep alive. He wondered if it would be okay to slip out of the room for just a second and find the watering can. But then he reproached himself for really just wanting to escape the screaming. He thought about Ilana, her fierce competence, how she would hold Gal like a big butch mama-warrior when she cried, and the image made him faint with grief and longing. How would Gal ever survive losing that?

He lowered himself onto the floor. Gal's screaming was becoming hoarse and rhythmic. The minutes passed, and then an hour, and still she cried. Lydia opened the door and peeked in, and Daniel waved her away. He said, "*Oof*, Gal-Gal, so many tears." He tried to think of a story to tell her, but it was Matt who was good at that, not he. Finally, he told her a stupid story about how when Yo-yo was a puppy, he chewed all the handles off the cabinets in the kitchen. But that elicited an outraged howl, as though he had mortally insulted her with his frivolity. Hurt clawed up his throat and stung his eyes. It astounded him how badly she could hurt his feelings. And it scared him how long she could cry. He tried to tell himself that his job was simply to be there while she cried, that when she grew up, she would be strong because someone had sat there with her long ago, steadfast, a witness. He remembered her therapist telling him, "Most people think of children's tears as a bad thing, as something they must make go away." They'd been sitting in her toy-strewn office, where he supposed she got children to reenact their traumas with puppets and dolls. "But that's because the tears upset *them*, not because they're bad for the child. Your job is to think of *her* when she cries, not to think about your own distress. She won't cry forever if you don't try to get her to stop."

He clung to that, but Gal cried for longer than he thought a child could cry. Around midnight she began to hyperventilate, and he panicked a little, wondering whether he should rouse his parents, or call the doctor. Before he could do anything, she fell into a coughing fit and vomited all over her bedding. Daniel picked her up and looked for a place to set her down while he stripped the bed; he finally set her in a tiny rocker in the corner of the bedroom. "Oh, it got on your shirt, sweetie," he said, and pulled gently at the arms, shimmying it over her head. He stood and pulled at the sheets, which gave off the acidic reek of half-digested tomatoes, swearing when they caught on a mattress corner. He took them, and all the soiled clothes, out to the laundry porch and threw them in a corner on the floor. Then he walked softly to Joel and Ilana's room. His parents were in bed, watching TV with no sound. "Sorry, I'm looking for fresh sheets," he whispered as they sat up.

"Turn the light on," his father said.

The light made them blink. Noam was in a diaper, curled against his grandfather's side, sleeping with his thumb in his mouth and a massive scowl on his face. Lydia was sitting up, drawing her nightgown to her throat. "Let me take over, honey," she said.

"No," Daniel said. "Let me see it through." He found sheets in the closet and eased himself quickly out of the room again.

In the kids' room, he'd turned off all the lights except for a little lamp on the desk. Gal sat in the chair, hugging herself and rocking and making an unholy keening sound through clenched teeth. Daniel turned on the little boom box to a CD of Israeli songs he knew she liked. He turned it down low and talked to her as he made the bed, making chitchat about how nice the sheets were and what a comfy bed she had and how it was okay to throw up sometimes, even though it was gross. He told her about how once, when he was a kid, he'd thrown up thirteen times, after eating an entire bag of gummy bears. And then he glanced over at her and she was so desolate and so alone on that little chair—her chest naked and skinny, her hair matted around her small face—that his eyes filled with tears.

He lifted her and set her gently on the clean bed, where she crawled weakly onto her pillow. Her chest was still convulsing, the tears still spilling down her face and into the creases of her neck. He lowered himself to the floor again, laid his head back on the wall. He dozed on and off, more or less, a headachy agitation buzzing through his consciousness, and then he awoke. He looked at his watch; it was 1:30 in the morning. Gal was making a racket breathing through her mouth. He got stiffly to his feet. She was curled on her side, her eyes open, shaking and whimpering. He grabbed a box of tissues from near the changing table and crawled clumsily onto the bed, leaning his back against the wall and wrestling her into a seated position between his legs. He wrapped his arms around her, smelling shampoo and vomit. He took a tissue out of the box, held it to her nose, and said, "Blow," and she did. "Again," he said, and mopped her up the best he could. He reached for the extra blanket at the foot of the bed and wrapped it around her, then gathered her in tight again. For a while he just sat there breathing against her back, hoping that the swell of his chest and the beat of his heart would calm her with their warm and steady animal rhythm. She was hiccupping now.

"Gal," he whispered into her ear. "Something terrible happened to us." He was whispering in Hebrew, and his voice broke. She began crying again, but she was tired now, and limp. "Gali, we'll stick together, okay? We will. We have to live in this terrible world." He didn't know whether that was a horribly wrong thing to say to her, whether it would poison her whole idea of the future. But the night had burned him down to ember and ash. "It's going to be very hard. We're going to have to be very brave. But I love you very much and I'm going to take care of you and Noam. Me and Uncle Matt." It occurred to him that Matt would be home soon, and that they could call him to reassure Gal that he was okay. But then he remembered what his mother had said about indulging her fears and suddenly he understood what she'd meant. Why revive Gal's fears about Matt's plane crashing? Maybe it was better to be matter-of-fact about Matt's arrival, to display a casual confidence in the world's predictability. He'd have to move through the world performing that confidence, for her and Noam's sake, from now on.

Gal sighed and shuddered. The desk lamp cast its warm light on the baby's crib with his stuffed bear crammed between the slats, the random toys that always littered the floor no matter how hard they tried to keep them in their box. Gal was moist and warm inside the blanket. He laid his face against her hair.

Gal turned her face up to him. It was swollen and filthy with dried snot and tears. Her dark lashes were stuck together. "I want *choco*," she said.

"*Choco!*" he breathed. It sounded like the best idea anyone had ever had. He rose stiffly and found her a clean pajama top. His left leg was asleep from the butt down, and he stomped his foot on the floor. "Should we get up and see what the house looks like late at night, when everybody else is asleep?"

She nodded and shuddered again, and he slipped the top over her head and stuffed her arms into the long sleeves. They got up and he extended his hand to her, and they walked down the hall to the kitchen, Daniel's leg woolly and tingling, Gal wobbling by his side. "Do you smell that?" he asked, wrinkling his nose. It was fresh cigar smoke.

Gal looked up at him. "Grampa," she said sagely, with a throaty *r*.

In the kitchen, Sam sat at the table in his pajamas with a glass of milk and the plastic sleeve of a box of plain biscuits with scalloped edges, lined neatly up, one toppled into the empty space he created as he made his methodical way through them. A lit cigar was tipped onto a glass plate at his elbow. He looked up at them and cleared his throat, abashed.

"Rough night, huh," he said. Gal clambered up onto the chair opposite her grandfather, reported that the cigar was *fichsah*, and also bad for him.

"I know, honey," he said gently. "I just have one once in a while."

"We're having hot chocolate," Daniel said, finding the box and spooning generous heaps of powder into two mugs. "Do you want some?" His father shook his head. Daniel opened the refrigerator and took out a plastic pitcher with a bag of milk inside it, poured milk into a pot, and set it on the stove. He stood and turned on the burner and stared at the blue flame. He was so tired he could hardly stand. And yet, there was something curious and light in the feeling. As though he'd been scoured until gleaming, as though he were more soul than body.

His father stood and took his cigar out onto the balcony, and when he returned, it had been carefully put out. He sat down and pushed the plastic sleeve of biscuits toward Gal. She leaned onto the table with her elbows and picked one out, and bit off the scalloped pieces with tiny bites of her front teeth.

"I like dunking them into milk," Sam said.

Daniel checked on the milk to make sure it didn't boil, and looked at his niece. What a wild little creature. One look at her, he thought—in her hodgepodge pajamas and bare feet, crumbs on her mouth, her eyes swollen into slits and her nose red and crusted—and social services would whisk her away. She looked just like the dirty-faced Palestinian refugee children they showed on the news. His mind drifted murkily, like weeds on water. He thought of the bulldozers destroying houses somewhere in the West Bank, possibly at this very moment, and the kids out there who were going through the same thing she was. He hoped they had nice relatives to take them in and hold and rock them.

He thought of the news photographs of small coffins swept along on the shoulders of shouting men. It was always men. Sometimes you saw the women. They were always shrieking, which was alienating. They never showed you the quiet daily grief of the Palestinian moms; you never saw a Palestinian adult rocking and cuddling a child. It made you think they weren't a people who rocked and cuddled.

His mind skipped through some association he couldn't follow to Matt, to how much he hated those *Baby on Board* signs on the back windows of American cars. "We don't have a baby," he'd snap, "so go ahead and slam right into us, we deserve it!"

Daniel turned off the stove, and poured the sputtering milk into two mugs.

"You know," Sam said. "I don't sleep anymore. It's very curious."

"Not at all?"

"Not at all. I don't seem to need it anymore."

"Everybody needs sleep, Dad."

"So I would have thought." Sam's hands were crossed in front of him as he watched his granddaughter.

"Are you scared you'll dream of Joel?" Daniel ventured the question shyly. It was a new way to talk to his father.

Sam looked at him and considered. His face was heavy, his nose a blunt bulb studded with pores, as though grief had rubbed his patrician veneer down to its coarse male essence.

"I don't know," he said. "It's hard to know whether dreaming about him is a positive or a negative."

"I know what you mean," Daniel said, bringing the mugs to the table. "You wake up destroyed, but at least you got to see him."

Gal's eyes were moving between them, in a slow drunken version of their usual sharp darting. Her nose was running, her sniffs a deep, crackling rumble. Daniel looked around for a tissue, but all he found was a roll of paper towels, which he worried would be too painful on her tender nose. "Honey," he said, "could you get the box of Kleenex from the bedroom?"

She slipped down to the floor and left the room.

Daniel sat down across from his father. He brought the hot mug to his lips and sipped the scalding chocolate.

"You know," his father said. "When you and Joel started third grade and were separated into different classes for the first time, Joel got massive school anxiety. He woke every morning crying from a stomachache." He paused, and mused. "It wasn't what we'd anticipated. You, meanwhile, sailed off to school every morning without looking back."

He picked up the cigar and ran his fingers along its stem. "It wasn't what we'd anticipated," he said again. "Your mother wanted to let him stay home, but I felt that it wasn't going to get any easier as you boys grew up, and the sooner he got used to it the better. Nowadays, of course, there's probably some new theory about separating twins into different classrooms."

Gal came back into the kitchen with the Kleenex box and one of her model horses, which she set carefully on the table.

Daniel helped her blow her nose, wincing when she flinched at the tissue's rub on the reddened skin around her nostrils. She climbed back onto her chair, dipped her face down to her mug, and stuck her tongue into her hot chocolate. "I a dog," she said.

"I *am* a dog," Sam said, correcting for the millionth time the translation mistake she always made because there was no "to be" verb in Hebrew.

Gal looked at him. "You a dog, too?" she asked her grandfather in a high, comical voice.

"Ha-ha," Sam said, reaching toward her as though he were going to tickle her.

"Drink your *choco* like a little girl, Gal-Gal," Daniel said, "and then we're going to brush our teeth and go to bed." They sat and waited as she drank. Daniel rested his cheek on his propped hand and thought of his poor brother, scared to go to school without him. He was surprised his father remembered something about him and Joel that had happened so long ago; Sam hadn't been particularly involved in the details of raising them. There was a little gleam of pride: his parents had always considered him, Daniel, the fragile one; he'd been smaller at birth, stranger-shy beyond the usual age, prone to hurt feelings. But he'd obviously been hardier than they'd thought.

But then the image came to him of Joel as a little boy in his pajamas, lying about a stomachache and feeling guilty about lying, and it broke his heart. He'd heard somewhere that mourning was like falling in love, and it was, he was—thinking of Joel came with a strange, painful elation. Oh, he loved him.

THE DOG'S TAIL THUMPED madly against Cam's thigh as Matt held his face in his two hands, scratching his chin, and asking him if he'd been a good doggie. "Were you?" he asked, his teeth clenched in play ferocity. "Were you?" He bent his face down and got a slurp right on the mouth. "You *were*? Oh, what a good boy." He scrubbed his mouth with his sleeve and looked at Cam, who stood there with an indulgent look on her face, her own dog, Xena, staring at Yo-yo from between her legs with intense border collie eyes. Xena was an agility champion, and the boss of Yo-yo. "Was he?"

She laughed her grainy guy-laugh. "Except for an incident with a tampon that I won't go into," she said.

"Gross," Matt said, sorry, as he so often was an instant too late, that he'd let Yo-yo kiss him on the lips. It was good to be around dog energy, though; it made him remember walking Yo-yo on the state hospital trails in the late afternoon of September 11, standing around with the other stunned dog owners watching their faithful, goofy dogs wrestling and playing under that gorgeous blue sky.

"You wanna come in?" Cam asked. They were in the tiny hallway of her house, the dog's bed and bowl, and a bag of his food, stacked in the corner.

"I don't think so," Matt said. "I need to unpack and straighten up." He dreaded going back into that bedroom, but what, he wondered, would he even say to Cam? She was looking at him with big, sad eyes. She was still in work clothes, her black striped oxford shirt tucked into belted pants, a man's watch gleaming on her wrist. The prospect of putting into words what he'd been through made him feel like a third-grader tossed an ink pen and ordered to write an epic poem. On the way home, he'd imagined telling their story to his friends, and found himself struggling with something inchoate and hard, that Israelis had become somehow *real* to him; the lawyer, the social worker, Joel and Ilana's friends, the children. The sound of Hebrew had become at home in his ear. He knew these people would be received sympathetically by anyone who heard his story, and he wanted them to be, he supposed, but he wanted his interlocutors to have to move through the whole deadly political judgment first and then cross over to the other side.

"When's Danny coming home?"

Matt shrugged. "We don't know yet. And I'll probably have to go over there at least once for a parental competency exam. You know, to make sure we're not the type of parents who will have homosexual orgies when the kids are home."

Cam laughed. "Bummer," she said. "No more orgies."

"How was your month?"

She shrugged. "Oh, you know," she said. "Same old, same old. I broke up with Diane."

Matt vaguely remembered, but didn't have the energy to figure out, which of Cam's many short-lived relationships she was referring to. "That's too bad," he said.

"Nah, whatever." She shook her head dismissively. "Compared to what you guys have been through, c'mon."

"Well, that's okay, Cam, it's still your life. What happened?"

She paused, then gave him an apologetic grin. "Too much drama. When they throw a clock radio at you and scream that they're sick of your passive-aggressive bullshit after you've been together for just two weeks, you know it's probably not gonna work out."

Matt laughed, and bent to clip on Yo-yo's leash.

"Come over if you get lonesome," Cam said. "We can get takeout or something."

"I will. And thanks so much, Cam. You're the best."

She reached over and clasped his shoulder, and Matt smiled to himself; he and Daniel liked to pantomime being on the receiving end of one of Cam's alarming handshakes or backslaps, writhing in pain with polite smiles frozen on their faces.

It was getting dark as he led Yo-yo across the tiny lawns, stopping to let him sniff and pee, the cold air encasing his forearms under the sweatshirt he wore. The forsythia and azaleas were in bloom; soon his neighborhood would be fragrant with lilac. He'd left the front door unlocked, and they pushed into the house, which had grown dark in the few minutes he'd been with Cam. He turned on every light he could reach. The answering machine in the kitchen blinked with seventeen messages; just looking at it made him tired. He dreaded going back upstairs, into that bedroom. But he'd have to clean it up sometime, and it might as well be now, while he still had all that weird jet-lag energy. He got out a jumbo-sized garbage bag, found a sprinkle of pot in a sandwich bag and his rolling papers in the stamps-and-matches drawer, and rolled a thin joint. He trudged up the stairs with the lit joint at the corner of his mouth, smoke curling up his face, and at the door of the bedroom, turned on the light. He stood looking at it. The garbage can was brimming with used tissues, the bedclothes were thrown back, the pillowcases still furiously rumpled, the closets open, the cap off the Tylenol bottle on the bedside table. Clothes—discards from his frenetic packing—lay in heaps on the dressers. He took a big drag, held it in, set the joint on the edge of one of the dressers. He sat on the bed. His breath was heavy, his throat scorched.

Gently, his buzz began to run over him, as though someone had cracked an egg on the top of his head and the yolk was seeping down. Daniel's pants were crumpled on the bedroom floor, the still-belted seat atop two accordioned legs. Matt rose and picked them up; they were dirty at the seat, where Daniel, his knees buckling as Matt led him out, had sat on the damp asphalt in front of his work building in his jacket and tie. Matt drew out the belt and stuffed them into the dry-cleaning bag. He took the joint off the dresser and, his hand cupped under it, went into the bathroom to tap off the long filament of ash. Then he finished it in two big hits and doused it in the sink. He emptied the trash in the bedroom and bathroom, threw the rest of the strewn clothes into the laundry hamper, stripped the bed and made it up with clean sheets, unpacked his clothes, ran the empty suitcases up to the attic.

And suddenly he was so tired his legs almost buckled.

He stumbled into the bathroom, shedding clothes, and after washing his face for a long time in very hot water and giving his teeth a quick, vigorous brush, fell into bed, where he turned on the TV and watched the last hour of *Stepmom*, sad for the Susan Sarandon character but identifying immediately with poor Julia Roberts, who was so shallow and thoughtless! Oh, but they came to respect her in the end. He blew his nose, grateful to be alone in his quiet bed, just him, deliciously, no one entering the room with a tear-stained face. If that made him a bad person, he thought, so be it.

CHAPTER 6

I T WAS WILD going through the messages. The New York friends had called! Stephen and Scott, guys he hadn't seen for years. Lindsay Price had called to say he'd seen Daniel's family on the news. The local Fox affiliate had dug up an old picture of Joel, and Lindsay said that he'd been horrified thinking at first that it was Daniel who'd been killed, and then relieved when he realized it was just Daniel's brother. There was a long silence on the tape, then it clicked off, and the next message was from Lindsay again, saying, "Not that that's really any better, it's just . . ." Matt rolled his eyes. He played it again, for signs of whether Lindsay was using, but he couldn't tell. He was sitting at the kitchen table with a cup of coffee for which he'd put milk through the steamer, in celebration of drinking good coffee again. Yo-yo was gobbling down his breakfast, his metal tags clattering against the bowl.

"Anyway," the message said, "if you want to call . . ."

Matt snorted and erased the message. He had a lined yellow pad in front of him and was taking careful notes because he remembered his bewilderment in the months following Jay's death, when he'd been mad at the whole world but actually not sure whether this or that friend hadn't called after all. He wanted to keep track now for Daniel. His stomach rumbled. He had slept, on and off, for seven hours, which he thought was pretty good, and he was determined to be on a Northampton schedule today, and to stay up till nine at the earliest. He lit a cigarette he'd brought downstairs from his stash. Smoking was an indulgence of being home alone, like eating cereal for dinner and not making the bed. He rose to open the kitchen windows, and saw that the tulips along the backyard fence were in bloom, nodding and snoozing in the shade.

He wasn't even your boyfriend, Lindsay had said one night when Matt had come down to visit, maybe a year after Jay had died. He implied, with the significant look of someone breaking a hard truth, that he was speaking for all of them, which had infuriated Matt. But in fact, as it turned out, he had been. After that, every time one of his friends asked "How are you?" it became a huge minefield: If he said he was feeling shitty, their silence implied that he was a leech on Kendrick's grief. It was just like now, when you thought about it—Daniel's loss, not his. Him brooding and lurking along the edges of tragedy, trying his damnedest to be appropriate.

He'd dropped them all because they were bad for his mental health, and because half of them were tweekers anyway and he just didn't want to be part of that scene. It was an unprecedented act for Matt, who thrived in the light of friendship. That first year living with Daniel had been a hard and lonely one for him; Daniel had a lot of nice friends, but even as he'd integrated into their circle he'd felt them to be Daniel's friends, not his. And even though it had been he who had cut off his New York friendships, it wounded him that they hadn't tried harder to bring him back—especially Lindsay, whom he'd supported through meth addiction and rehab. The friendship had briefly flared up again after September 11, when Lindsay had been his point person for checking up on everybody, but even then Lindsay acted as though only New Yorkers could possibly understand the profundity and horror of the whole thing, and Matt was sure he was using again, so after many evenings of complaining bitterly to Daniel, he stopped returning Lindsay's calls. Now the messages on his machine gave him a sense of bitter satisfaction. It was irrational, he knew, but he felt that this new tragedy proved that his sadness was legitimate, even his past sadness. He would never call any of them back. Let them just sit with their horrid fascination, and gossip with one another about how horrible it all was, and go get wasted in club bathrooms, and go to hell.

Brent and Derrick, their best couple friends, had called twice. Derrick was Daniel's steadiest, call-every-day friend—a fine, upstanding fellow, as Matt thought of him. Listening, he smiled; Derrick knew his way around a condolence call. He was a psychologist who taught schools how to introduce diversity programs, so he was trained in acknowledging others' feelings. Then Brent took the phone, and there was his voice, a melodious, demonstrative baritone Matt loved, saying in a big rush, "We can't wait for you guys to come home. Come home soon!"

Matt looked at his watch. It was around 8:30, and Derrick would probably be at work, but Brent, who was a professor, might be home. He picked up the phone and dialed them on speed dial, and Brent picked up on the second ring, saying, "Matt?"

"Hi."

"Matt," he breathed, as though hearing Matt's voice was the culmination of all his desires and he could now rest. "When did you guys get back?"

"Just me," Matt said. "Daniel's still there."

"How was it?" Brent asked. "Wow, what a stupid question. How's Daniel doing?"

Matt shrugged. "You know," he said. "He's completely fucked-up. He's dealing with his twin brother being blown to bits, and his parents are there, which doesn't make it any easier, and then there's the kids."

"What's going to happen to them?" Brent asked.

There was a pause. "We never told you?"

"No." And then, before Matt could say anything, he said, "Oh my God, are you guys taking them?"

"We're trying to," Matt said. "Joel and Ilana wanted that; it was in their will."

"Wow," Brent said.

Matt was quiet, parsing that "Wow." Of all Daniel's friends, Brent was the one whom Matt had immediately clicked with; he was hilarious, and a media scholar at Mount Holyoke, and after Matt had stopped being a little intimidated about being friends with an academic, he loved being around someone so smart, someone who made his mind dance. But Matt had also been the laughing audience for many of Brent's scathing performances about moms with kids, and he worried a little that he and Daniel would become the butt of Brent's breeder jokes. Recently, Brent had stopped going to Woodstar Café, down the street from his apartment, since it had become a hangout for moms with kids in strollers, saying that being there made him want to stick a knife in his eye.

"Does that make us uncles?" Brent asked.

"Absolutely," Matt said, smiling.

"You guys will be all 'Do your homework' and 'Clean your room,' and we'll be the place they go when they run away from home. And who takes them to the doctor when they want to transition. Well, *I* will. Derrick will want to make sure the lines of respectful communication remain open between you and them."

"Dude, they're six and one year old," Matt laughed.

"What are their names again?"

"The girl is Gal, and the little boy is Noam." Matt found he was still smiling. "Look, it's not certain. It turns out that the will isn't binding, and the kids' Israeli grandparents are going to go to court to try to keep them there. And they're Holocaust survivors, and Ilana was their only child. So we're basically trying to take away the only thing they have left. Can you imagine?"

"Shit."

"I know."

There was a long pause. Then Brent said, "How are you feeling about it?"

Matt sighed. "I have no idea," he said. "You *know* I've never wanted kids before. I feel awful about taking them away from their grandparents. But Daniel wants them. And it's what Joel and Ilana wanted."

"Sure."

Matt drained his cup of coffee and put it down. "I think maybe I want them just a little bit," he said to Brent, emotion rushing into his voice and surprising him. "Is that weird? Am I just being a competitive asshole?"

"Probably," Brent said, and they both laughed. "What do you think your chances are of getting them?"

"I'm not sure. Fifty-fifty?"

After another pause, Brent said, "Wanna come over? Since after the kids arrive, I'll never see you again?"

"Oh please," Matt said. He opened the back door and looked down at the stoop, which was coated with pollen. "Let me do some cleaning up around here, and go through the bills, and I'll call you later."

"See?" Brent said. "It starts already."

"Shut up," Matt said. "It does not start already."

After he hung up, Matt swept off the stoop and the steps, propped the broom against the house, and sat down, looking out at the garden. His imagination was very gently entwining itself around the idea of being a father. He was ready for something new. He should learn Hebrew! He wanted to be able to understand his daughter—*his daughter*—when she spoke to Daniel, and it would be important for both kids to know their mother's language. It felt a little weird, setting out to learn the language of the oppressor; it felt a little like learning Afrikaans. His mind worried the comparison for a while, as he hosed out the grime from the birdbath and filled it, dragged out a bag of birdseed from the garage, and filled and rehung the feeders. Then he began imagining himself in a classroom with little wood desk chairs and batik wall hangings of Hasidic fiddlers, with all the bar mitzvah boys—the bored kids with braces and chubby cheeks learning their Torah portion from a severe, bearded man.

It was only an idea that caught his fancy; he didn't intend to act on it, at least right now, when there was so much work to catch up on. But the next day, Brent called him to say that a colleague of his knew an Israeli artist named Yossi-something who was married to a physicist at UMass, who was apparently waiting for his green card and taught Hebrew under the table. Matt kept the paper with Yossi's number on it next to the phone for a few days as he caught up on delinquent projects—a poster for a film festival and a boarding school annual report that accounted for about a quarter of his yearly income and that was, miraculously, only a week overdue. He lingered over the number when he came into or left the kitchen, and each time tender fantasies overcame his awareness that, to some people, Hebrew was the language of the set of byzantine, malicious laws that legitimized blowing up their houses or keeping them apart from their farms, their own spouses and children. The idea of learning Hebrew made him think of Gal and Noam as his daughter and son, he didn't know why.

He didn't tell Daniel about it yet because their official attitude on the phone was a guarded neutrality on the subject of the children, as a way of protecting themselves in case they didn't get them. And when he thought about it, he wasn't really sure how Daniel would react. But finally, he put in a call to Yossi. Yossi was unpleasantly abrupt on the phone, asking midway through Matt's spiel, "Who *is* this?" Which made Matt sigh and have to start over: "My name is Matt Greene." Yossi made him tell him exactly how he'd gotten his number, and when Matt couldn't remember Brent's friend's name, there was a stony silence on the other end that made Matt wonder: *Do I need this crap?*

It occurred to him later that Yossi was being extra careful because he wasn't legally allowed to hold a job. But when Yossi arrived at his door a few days later, he thought that he might just be a prick. He was gorgeous—tall and broad, with closely cut hair, a dark beard shadow, and blue eyes that looked a little washed out from gazing into the sun, perhaps, or inward, at his own weighty thoughts. A lovely sprout of chest hair showed above his shirt where it was open at the neck. Matt suddenly remembered that Brent had reported that Yossi had been an air force pilot. If he had extended his hand, Matt would have gripped it with all his might, but he was spared that display because all he got was a curt nod. When Yo-yo barged at him, Yossi quieted him by taking his head into his two large hands. "Don't mind him," Matt said, taking note of his wedding band. "He's a goof."

"I don't," Yossi said.

Matt got him coffee, which he drank black, and as they sat down at the kitchen table, Yossi asked him in a nonplussed way why he wanted to learn Hebrew. "Are you Jewish?" he asked.

Matt felt himself bristle. As happened with some straight men, Yossi made him feel girly and silly. "No, I'm not," he replied. "But my partner is." He cleared his throat and gazed at the man across the table from him as he digested the word *partner*, enjoying for once the anticipation of telling their story, knowing that it would wipe the dismissive look off of Yossi's handsome face. "My partner—his name is Daniel—Daniel's brother and sister-in-law were killed in a *pigua* in Jerusalem, and there's a chance that we are going to raise the children."

Yossi sat back in his chair and placed his hand on his chest. "Ah," he said gently. "How old are they?"

"Gal is six and Noam is eleven months."

Yossi heaved a sigh. "Terrible. It was the *pigua* at Peace Train Café?"

Matt nodded.

"So your first Hebrew word is *pigua*."

It hadn't been, quite, but Matt didn't correct him, Yossi was so obviously touched by the thought, and it felt delightful to have this Israeli warrior feeling bad for him. "Yes, and the word *ptsatsa*," Matt said, bringing out the Hebrew word for "bomb," and then thinking that he was perhaps working the pathos too hard. "But that's about it. Oh— *buba* and *miskena*, things like that."

Yossi smiled faintly. "*Miskena*. Is there a word in English?"

"I don't think so. 'Poor thing'?"

Yossi shrugged. "*Miskena*, that's for a girl. You must also learn the word for a boy poor thing. *Misken*."

"*Misken,*" Matt repeated.

"*Miskenim,*" Yossi crooned, as though he were actually comforting children. Poor things. "*Im,* that is plural, for masculine."

Matt nodded.

Yossi sighed and got out his books. Then he placed his hands on them and leaned forward. "It's good to learn a language to speak to children."

Matt looked at him, confused, trying to parse the meaning of that sentiment, which seemed either very deep or very cloying, when Yossi added, "Because you will be on a similar level."

"Aha, true."

"I try to think—" Yossi cleared his throat. "What kind of things you might say to children in their situation." He was lost for a moment, lashes fluttering, in tender, brooding thought. " 'Try to sleep,' " he said, turning his glance to Matt. " 'I love you. I will take care of you.' Shall I teach you those phrases?"

They worked on them for a while, and then Yossi opened a workbook with the Hebrew alphabet and lines for penmanship practice, and taught Matt to read a few basic words. He would break each lesson into two, he said, teaching him simple conversation for the first half hour, and reading and writing for the second. He watched as Matt drew his first Hebrew letters, and he gave him homework for the following week. They smoked a cigarette together on the back steps before he left. Matt asked him if he had kids, and Yossi said he did, three boys, one twelve, one ten, and one Gal's age.

"Oh," Matt said. "Maybe they can play together."

"Rafi is deaf," Yossi said bluntly.

"Okay," Matt said. "Does that mean they can't play together?"

"No," Yossi laughed. "Of course not."

"Do you like it here?"

Yossi opened his palms and shrugged. "It's good for my wife, this job. And it's a very good place for Rafi, because of the school for the deaf. But I miss home. People aren't very friendly here."

"Really, you think?" Matt asked. He thought about this town, where men with gray beards and pedantic demeanors, and willowy ponytailed women, and the million and one psychotherapists and, of course, the stocky lesbians with severe and perfect haircuts engaged with one another with great, inculcated civility; civility he'd initially found, after living for years in New York, phony, almost comical.

"At home, you can jump over to someone's house without calling, and they will pull up another chair for dinner."

"Oh," Matt said. "We don't do that in New England."

On his way out, Yossi instructed Matt to say the sentences he'd learned one more time. He lifted his chin sternly, like a father demanding a recitation from a child. "Try to sleep," Matt said, as Yossi raised his eyebrows and nodded. "I love you. I will take care of you."

Yossi gave him an approving clap on the shoulder and said, *"Yofi! Le'hitraot.* That's mean 'See you later.' "

Closing the door, Matt took a huge breath. Yossi's sternness and scrutiny and praise made him feel a little like a sheepish child, but he had a nice glow from that too, from being praised for being smart. He paced around the kitchen, feeding the dog and washing out the coffee-maker and setting water to boil for pasta. He wasn't used to not being the most handsome man in the room. But he'd found that he gladly deferred to Yossi's alpha hunkiness. A Magnetic Fields song playing and replaying in the back of his mind floated up to his consciousness, and he laughed to himself. He dialed Brent and Derrick's number, and when Brent picked up the phone, he sang, without saying hello, "He's amazing, he's a whole new form of life."

Brent laughed, and finished the couplet: "Blue eyes blazing, and he's going to be your wife."

"Well, not quite," Matt said thoughtfully. "It's more like he's going to be my *ward*."

He was having to work until pretty late, but now and then he took a little time to practice his Hebrew alphabet. It pleased him to form the letters; it reminded him of design school, where they made them learn to design by hand, painstakingly drawing the alphabet, or cutting out the listed ingredients from some random product and making a composition out of them. He was enjoying being alone, he found; he turned down invitations to dinner and movies from his friends.

ONE MORNING, WHILE CLEANING the bedroom, Lydia cried out; she emerged waving a DVD and crying, "We can see him again!" She clasped first Sam, then Daniel, looking into their faces with a tearful smile. She had come across the DVDs of Joel's show, which were stored, it turned out, neatly labeled and dated, in a flat plastic tub under Joel and Ilana's bed. When she went back into the bedroom to take out the box, Daniel murmured to his father, "She does understand that it's not *really* Joel, just a film of him, right?"

Sam was making plans to go home, to take care of some business and to visit an old friend they were worried about, who was in the hospital with an undiagnosed ailment that had made him collapse several times. He was on the phone with the airlines, on hold; he took off his glasses and massaged the bridge of his nose.

They couldn't stay away—they had to watch them—but they dreaded it, too. After his father hung up, Daniel got in a few whispered moments on the phone with Matt, who told him he didn't have to watch if he didn't want to, which vaguely annoyed Daniel even though he knew it was sensible, and true.

When the kids were down, his parents sat next to each other on the couch. Daniel checked and double-checked on Gal before putting the DVD into the player; he just couldn't face the idea of her waking up and coming into the living room and seeing an image of her living father. He was well into a second beer, and he fiddled with the remote control while perched on the edge of the recliner. The screen turned blue, and then it was on, *Israel Today*. And there was Joel, sitting behind a desk, welcoming the audience to a show about education in the development towns. He was going to be talking to a teacher from one of the towns down south—a new *oleh* from the U.S. who was agitating to get more resources down there—and to someone from the Ministry of Education.

There was a close-up of his face, and Daniel's heart seemed to stop beating, it was so eerie and so piercing to see the brown eyes alive— alive!—and his light skin, textured and mottled, a freckle here and there. Joel's face looked out into the living room. He was in that world and Daniel was in this one; for a moment Daniel had the sense that they were barely separated at all, that the television was a mere technicality. Joel's presence was there in front of him, in its breathing, thinking, sentient animality. What was the difference, really, between that vivid picture and his actual self?

The camera broke away to a short video about the poor conditions in a dilapidated school somewhere in the south.

"It didn't used to be like this," his father said, his voice hoarse. "It used to be that when people died, they were dead, and you just looked at pictures, or imagined them."

"I can't decide if this is better or worse," Lydia said, her hands in her lap, trembling.

They watched Joel interview his guests, clear, incisive, his voice warm, hunching over his crossed arms and leaning toward the guest in the studio. Daniel finished his beer; his father got up to go to the bathroom, and when Lydia asked if they should pause it, he waved his hand no. He stayed away until the show ended, and when he returned, said, "Is it over?"

"That such a lovely man should be killed for this . . . this, I don't know what," Lydia murmured. "It's senseless. Even if he wasn't my son, I'd be devastated by it. He's a wonderful interviewer, isn't he? He manages to be both hard-hitting and likable—you can tell that the interviewees like and trust him."

"If he was hard-hitting," Daniel remarked, "he'd ask how much the Ministry of Education invests in Arab Israeli education."

There was silence as his parents turned to him in surprise. "I really don't think that's appropriate," Sam said.

"Why not?" he said, unable to stop himself from rushing on. "*That's* the big scandal in Israeli education. They're *citizens*, and they're funded at something like one-fifth the rate of Israeli kids. Their schools are a disaster."

"It's a pity you disapproved of your brother so much," Lydia said bitterly.

"He was a good man with a blind spot," Daniel said. He felt that it was a generous assessment. It had always bothered Daniel that Joel hadn't stepped up; he had a responsibility, he felt, as a public figure.

"And I suppose you alone can see clearly," his mother challenged.

"Not me alone, Mother. But I think I saw more clearly on this issue than Joel did."

"That's pretty arrogant, don't you think?" Sam said. "After all, he lived here, and he had an entire research team at his disposal."

Daniel shrugged.

They were quiet. "I had no idea you felt this way about your brother," Lydia said. "Was he aware of that?"

"A little," Daniel said, thinking about the one argument they'd had that had made Joel blow up, when Daniel had told him that Matt saw many analogies between Israel and apartheid South Africa. Joel had turned beet red and tried to pin Daniel to the wall with heated questions about security and self-defense and what specific techniques he was referring to. He'd asked scornfully if Matt was now such a big expert on the subject because he'd written a paper about it in college. Daniel should have known better: The South Africa comparison was like a red flag in front of a bull to most Israelis. And it was shitty of him to use Matt's name instead of just being upfront about his own feelings. Joel was pissed off at Matt for a long time after that.

He sighed. "I could have worked harder at, I don't know, showing him my point of view. But he lives here. *Lived* here." And what? He hadn't thought it was his place to precipitate a whole moral crisis in Joel. Which was sensitive of him, but also, when he stared it in the face, a little cowardly. When it came down to it, he just hadn't wanted to get into it. They'd had such a great time when he'd come last year, and he loved them so much! And maybe it wouldn't have precipitated a moral crisis at all—if it hadn't yet, why would it now?—and he didn't want to see that.

The blue screen was clear and unblinking; he rose to eject the disc, and discovered he was a little buzzed from his two beers. It hurt to be disappointed in Joel; it made his very soul feel sore. And what about himself, what had he done? Just these last weeks, the Israeli army had killed fifteen Palestinians, three of them children. The Israeli authorities denied it. But he'd been reading the Internet reports by human rights organizations and knew about the terrible toll on civilian life. And worse, this violence was supposedly happening on his family's behalf.

His parents rose heavily, and seeing how perturbed they looked made Daniel feel horrible. He'd attacked their beloved dead son—what good did that do anybody? Had he done it to aggrandize himself? If he had, what kind of infantile impulse was that?

Lydia went into the kitchen to load the dishes in the sink into the dishwasher, and Sam shuffled in his slippers to the bedroom and closed the door behind him. Daniel used the bathroom, then murmured a good-night to his mother and went into his room and got into bed. He lay there for about an hour, his mind jangling busily and unpleasantly. Then he sat up and thought about how to make it stop. He rose and pulled on a pair of jeans and a tight T-shirt, and took his leather jacket off the back of the desk chair and slipped it on. Wearing it felt both protective and sensual; he lovingly treated it with lotion twice a year, at the beginning and the end of the leather-jacket season. He'd had the lining replaced once already.

He found his wallet and slipped it into the inside breast pocket, picked up the car keys. He patted his jeans pockets reflexively and turned off the small desk light.

Gal, he hoped, would sleep through the night. He couldn't tell his parents he was going out, and they had gone to bed by now anyway. But he didn't want them to worry if they found he wasn't there. In the end he left a note on his pillow that said *Be back soon. D.* He looked at it uncertainly, scratching his chin, feeling how very quickly he could regress when left alone with them. It was only two days since Matt had left, and already his mother had begun doing things like telling him to clean up after himself, as though he hadn't cleaned up after himself every day of his life for twenty years. Without Matt, there was nobody to help signify that he was an adult. No one to be more immature than he was.

He closed the front door quietly behind him, trotted down the stairs, and got into the car. He pulled onto the street and nosed his way out of the quiet neighborhood, making the only turns he could down the maze of one-way streets. Cars were parked every which way, on streets and sidewalks. He turned onto Ruppin; the Knesset was yellow and illuminated on his left, the Israel museum on his right. And then he was climbing another narrow street, and heading left down Aza. He turned onto Keren Ha'Yasod and found what he'd hoped he'd find, a small patch of dirt parking lot still untouched by the crazy development that had gone up around the park.

He pulled in, closed and locked the door behind him. He walked silently down the street to Independence Park, his steps quickening as he saw the high lights of the park ahead and, in their light, the crazy flitting shadows of bats. It was many years since he'd visited the old gay cruising ground; he wasn't even sure whether now, in the Internet age, men still cruised here—in fact, whether regular old face-to-face cruising still existed at all. The mountain air was cold on his hot face and hands. He slowed down once he entered the park, put his hands in his pockets. An occasional person passed on the stone paths, and he could smell a verdant, spiny aroma—eucalyptus or cypress. The swoon of sensation and emotion suddenly made his legs watery. He made it to a bench, laid his arms along the top of it, threw his head back and breathed.

He was overwhelmed because it was Joel he wanted. Not like that, of course, but his heart strained for Joel. He closed his eyes, and memories of the summer of Joel's wedding, when he'd come for two months to visit, came easily to him. Joel was reporting for the *Jerusalem Post* and living with Ilana in that apartment on Rehov HaPalmach. There was a ton of wedding hoo-ha, gifts arriving every day, Joel the bright, exotic center of their extended family. It was a time when Daniel's critique of compulsory heterosexuality was especially honed, and it galled him that his brother accepted so comfortably the privilege heaped upon him. Meanwhile, various Rosen relatives were planning tours of the Holy Land, the kind that took tourists to Masada to climb before dawn and thrill to the desert sunrise, the story of Jewish fighters choosing death over capture, the motto *Never again*. And his increasingly keen awareness of the way oppression operated by making certain things invisible to the eye— things like his own emotional life—began to bleed into distaste and anger about the things he himself couldn't see because Israel made them invisible. His relatives' boosterism and romantic idealizing of the Israeli army and unthinking racism galled him; he read Said's *The Question of Palestine*, and it blew him away. He thought about summer camp, which had offered Zionism as a glorious refuge from American suburban life, and his new knowledge made him have to rethink the whole thing.

His temples pulsed as he thought about that uncomfortable, angry, transformative time. It was the first time Joel had been in close quarters with an uncloseted Daniel, and he joked anxiously when Daniel came home in the dawn hours, just as he and Ilana were getting out of bed. It was 1990, and Daniel's lack of knowledge of how to find gay men in Jerusalem was matched only by his determination to find them. He was shy by nature, and sexually diffident, but he'd experienced gay liberation and love and sex with men in the years since his junior year abroad in Jerusalem, and he felt almost driven to transpose the experience of that year into a gay key, as an act of recuperation, of self-assertion. He cruised Independence Park and answered personal ads in the local city papers, playing elaborate games of phone tag by pseudonym, sending letters to post-office boxes, and he had a few flings that summer with men who, it turned out, had felt as clueless as he did about how to find one another. During the day he read, met Joel for coffee or lunch, walked the city. But when he stole out of his bed and left Joel's apartment at night, it was with hunger and anger both; it was a way of being separate from his brother, going off to a place Joel couldn't imagine and had no cachet in. A secret Israel in which Joel couldn't succeed brilliantly, where people defied their culture with their stubborn desires.

And here he was again, same place, only better lit, newly abutted by skyscrapers and by the huge crane omnipresent in busy, expanding Jerusalem, and of all those men, it was Joel, perplexed, disapproving, shrugging—*It's your life*—he yearned for. He considered just going home, but a painful lassitude had settled over him, making it hard to move his limbs and rise. A figure was walking toward him, and his mind played a quick speculating game about what he would find when it materialized.

It was a man with a *kipa* pinned onto his curly hair and a wide ingenuous face. He sat down next to Daniel for a while, his knees cast wide, almost but not quite touching Daniel's own. He wore a delicious scent, which Daniel breathed in with pleasure, and his knee jiggled nervously. The agitated presence of an aroused stranger steadied Daniel. Their knees touched. Finally, the guy stood, and Daniel did, too. He led Daniel through bushes into a small clearing, where he grabbed him and spun him around, breathing hard, his beard stubble scouring Daniel's face. He was big and heavy in a way Daniel liked. He knelt and unbuckled Daniel's belt with trembling hands; Daniel saw the glint of a wedding band. He felt the man's hot breath on him and closed his eyes. The guy was more eager than skilled, but Daniel was excited by his nervousness, by the way the desire must have become intolerable for him to sneak out like this. Daniel clasped his hair, his thumb grazing the clip that held the *kipa* on, and that sent another surge of desire through him, getting a religious man on his knees.

His orgasm was bright and high. After he pulled his pants up, he turned the guy till he faced away from him, unzipped and unbuckled him and stroked him, pressing against his naked ass hard enough to give him pause. He would have liked to fuck him, but that wasn't allowed under the terms of his and Matt's monogamy agreement, which they had made one fine Fourth of July they now called "Monogamy

Tuesday." It allowed oral sex and hand jobs only, and sex with any given man one time only; it prohibited bringing anyone home.

The wind cooled his back where his shirt rose above his jeans. Candy wrappers and an empty paper container blew through the patch of hard dirt they stood upon and jammed against a scrubby bush. The man yelped and shuddered in his arms. He staggered away from Daniel for a moment, fumbling to tuck himself back in. Still breathing hard, he kicked dirt and leaves and cigarette butts over the snail's trail of semen he'd left on the ground. *"Tov,"* Daniel said, indicating he was ready to go. He turned, and then suddenly the guy pulled him back and laid a kiss on him, and too shocked to protest, Daniel met his lips and tongue, closed his eyes and felt the blood rush to his head. The man's breath smelled of a hundred cups of coffee. When he pulled away, Daniel staggered, dizzy, clasped his jacket for balance. *"O-pah,"* the man said, steadying him like the nice husband and father he no doubt was.

Daniel drove home quickly through the empty streets, a smile twitching at his lips. He and Matt had debated the question of kissing other men, because they both loved kissing, but it created a dangerous intimacy. In the end they'd allowed it because it almost never happened with guys you picked up. Daniel ran his hand over his chapped mouth and chin, wondering whether his parents would notice that they looked red in the morning. He reached for the lip balm that was always rattling around in one of the coffee holders—Ilana's, he knew—and ran it over his lips, and then he felt as though he'd kissed her too.

He was home in five minutes; he opened the front door as silently as a burglar and eased it shut behind him, crept into his bedroom and closed the sliding door inch by quiet inch, stripped down to his underwear and got in bed. His legs and groin tingled, and he caught and then lost the rumor of the guy's scent. A sense of drowsy well-being gently washed through him. He placed his fingers on his ribs and felt them expand and contract with his breath. Through the open window floated the heavenly smell of the Angel factory. He listened into the silence and heard no rustle or cry.

MATT AND CAM were hunched in front of his computer, reading a smackdown between two mothers on BabyCenter.com. Matt had found the site a few hours ago, and was so riveted he hadn't heard Cam come in until the frantic scrabbling of claws against the wood stairs caught his attention and Yo-yo and Xena burst in, panting, and crashed against his knees. "Ouch!" he yelled. "Cam?"

"Hey," she said, coming in with a squeak of sneakers and looking around his study. "I brought Chinese and a bottle of wine."

"Check this out," Matt said, rolling in his desk chair to grab another chair and pull it up. "You guys, lie down! That means you too, Yo-yo!" He'd read a mother's diary of her child's first year, and the recalls on the car seats—which it seemed nobody used correctly anyway—and the frighteningly intense debates about the family bed, but he'd had no success finding anything about bereaved children, except for those who had lost a grandparent or a pet. Nothing about how to talk to kids whose parents had been killed by a bomb. But then again, he wasn't sure if he was missing some stuff because he was reluctant to register, because that required reporting his children's genders, something he just balked at, fearing they'd start sending him grotesque special articles about how, even in the womb, little boys naturally reach for trucks while little girls reach for dolls.

Now he was reading the milestone chart "What to Expect from Your

Thirteen- to Eighteen-month-old." "Someone seems to have bragged that her two-month-old was already eating solid foods," he told Cam, "and that really ticked the other moms off." He read aloud: "'Well, well, well. In addition to being mother of the year, you are also more educated than a pediatrician. Just because your daughter *can* eat solids, does not mean that she *should* do so. A two-month-old baby's digestive system is not ready for the onslaught of solid foods. You are probably setting your daughter up for an increased risk of allergies, as well as digestive problems later on. I am sorry that your children have a mother who thinks so little of them that she ignores advice given by pediatricians worldwide.'" He looked at Cam, who was squinting at the screen and murmuring, "Dude, lighten up."

"Signed," he said, grinning, "'Sad in Indiana.'" He pouted his lips. "She's sad because those kids have to have such a bad mom."

"It *is* sad, actually," Cam said, and they laughed.

"I'll tell you, it's a cutthroat world out there for the moms," he said. "Those message boards are brutal! But the good news is, they don't expect jack shit from the dads. I swear, if these women's husbands do anything without being hounded into it, they're total heroes. They call them DH, which it took me a long time to figure out meant 'darling husband.'"

"Gross," Cam said.

"I don't know, Cam," he said, rubbing his face, suddenly depressed by all the arguments, the sheer quantity of *information* parents apparently had to be interested in. "Did you ever want kids?"

"Nope. The thing is, I basically raised my mother"—Cam's mother had had some combination of alcoholism and bipolar disorder—"I don't have the energy to be at anyone else's beck and call."

Matt nodded with a small smile; and yet, the women Cam loved were unfailingly troubled and demanding.

"If you get them, it's not like you're going to have a choice or anything," she said. "You'll just raise them. They'll grow up, and be fucked-up like the rest of us."

· · · ·

DANIEL WAS RUNNING LATE; he'd gone to the supermarket, where he'd been accosted by a woman who thought he was Joel for a moment, and then he'd had to stay with her as she recovered. And just as he pulled out of the parking garage on his way home, he remembered that he'd forgotten eggs, the thing that had sent him shopping in the first place. He stopped at the *makolet* on his block and bought eggs with his last bit of cash, and wound his way home through twisty, clogged streets. Assaf had agreed to be his lawyer, and he had set up this appointment with the caseworker. She was an American with a New York accent named Dalia Rosenblum, who'd made *aliyah* ten years ago, and he had bet his parents a thousand dollars that she was religious.

"You don't have that kind of money," his father had said with an annoying complacency.

"Okay, I'll bet you *two* thousand dollars," Daniel had shot back.

His father had given him the wise nod of the father humoring the impetuous son.

His phone conversation with Assaf had thrown him into a stew of anxiety and fear. First, Assaf had told him that the social worker assigned to do the parental competency hearing would be interviewing him six times over the course of three months. Daniel had said that he couldn't be away from work that long, and begged him to find out if there was any way to do it more quickly. Assaf also said that the courts tended to want to toss the kids around as little as possible, especially after a trauma like this. When Daniel asked him if he thought it would help or hurt to have Matt present at the parental competency hearings, Assaf was silent for a long time.

"That bad, huh," Daniel said.

"No, no—it's that I honestly don't know. I have never experienced such a situation." He weighed it out loud: On the one hand, it wouldn't help that they were gay, and that Matt wasn't Jewish, but on the other, Daniel couldn't lie about his living situation, and Assaf believed that parental competency assessments explicitly mandated assessing the spouse. "I think you will have to acknowledge him, and that therefore he will need to be present," Assaf had concluded.

When Daniel got home, he saw a strange car parked outside and cursed; he was late for the caseworker. He walked into the house, apologizing, laden with plastic bags of groceries. "Don't worry about it," Dalia said. She was a young woman with a covered head; she wore a dress and hose. Daniel swiveled toward his father, who was hovering over the hissing kettle, as he hefted the bags onto the counter, and rubbed his fingers together to signify the money Sam owed him. He had the sudden memory of Ilana calling the cops on the religious people who'd put up a *succa* by her supermarket and played loud music during evenings of the Succot holiday. They'd told her they couldn't do anything about it, which she'd known before she even called. But it had made her feel better to do something rash and mean toward the religious people she— and most of her friends—lived among in simmering animosity.

He put some biscuits on a plate and brought them out, set them on the big nicked coffee table. His mother emerged from the bedroom in a nice dress, freshly made-up, and introduced herself. They sat. Dalia began by emphasizing that she was the advocate for Gal and Noam, and that the court, to which this case would surely go, would settle it according to its best judgment of the best welfare of the children. "You say that in a way that implies that Daniel doesn't want the best for them, that *he's* not their advocate," Lydia said.

"Not at all," Dalia said. "But the custodianship of the children is contested. I have just come from Ilana's parents, and they are quite determined to raise the children as their own, here in Israel."

"You're aware that Joel and Ilana wanted Daniel to be the guardian, yes?" his father said.

"I have seen the will," Dalia replied, implying, to Daniel's ear, that it was somehow open to interpretation. He wished his parents would shut up; they were making it look as though he couldn't speak for himself. Dalia was probably in her midthirties, with dark eyebrows and straight hair slanting across her forehead. She sat with a pad of paper in her lap and a pen in her hands. Her hands were quiet. "I know this must seem arbitrary and wrong to you," she said. "But evidence shows that the mourning process is best facilitated if the child's physical and social environment remain essentially unchanged."

Daniel's heart sank. So not only might he and Matt not get them, but even if they did, they'd be harming their mourning process.

"You live, in the States, with a homosexual partner, is that true?"

"Yes," Daniel said, holding her gaze.

"Will the court have a problem with that?" his mother asked. Daniel leveled a stare at her, and she looked at him, uncomprehending.

Dalia gave an expressive shrug and said she didn't know. "There are two parts to it: the partner and living in the States. How does your partner feel about raising two children who are not his own?"

Daniel made a quick, strategic decision to read her as simply direct, as many Israelis were, rather than as homophobic. He paused; he wanted to get this right. "Matt hardly knows the baby. But he and Gal have always been close. He's devastated by what has happened and wants to take these children in, to help them heal in a loving home." It sounded wretchedly platitudinous when it came out of his mouth, but it wasn't untrue.

"It will certainly be a big change in his lifestyle," his mother said. *Yes,* Daniel thought, *those are the words coming out of her mouth.* Dalia looked at Lydia and then back at him, then at Lydia again. He saw that she was registering that Lydia didn't like Matt. "What do you mean?" Dalia asked.

Seeing all eyes on her, Lydia backtracked. "Oh, nothing dramatic," she said. "I only mean that he's a young man."

"Mom, he's thirty-two. A lot of men have children at that age, and they adjust just fine."

"That's all I meant," Lydia protested.

There was a pause in which the air seemed motorized, whizzing with brainpower, as everybody made a quick decision about how to proceed. Then Dalia asked a series of questions—about their jobs, their income, their house—and the hum dispersed and settled. She asked

Daniel what his town was like, and where the kids would sleep in his house. He gave her the names of references, Derrick and his boss April; and he had the idea of giving her the name of Joel's best friend, Josh Levinson, who'd come over with them in the junior-year program and had made *aliyah* around the same time as Joel. He'd seen Josh and his wife at the shiva, and they'd tearfully urged him to stay in their lives. Dalia wrote the names and numbers on her pad without looking down at it. She asked if he and Matt knew how to take care of a baby, and he said they hadn't before now, but that they'd had a crash course in the past weeks. As if on cue, they heard Noam begin to cry in his bedroom. Daniel and Lydia stood at the same time. "I'll get him," Daniel said, his desire to display parental competence only slightly stronger than his desire to get his mother out of Dalia's earshot before she said anything else that might sabotage his cause.

He went into the kids' room, sighing in a big release of tension, saying, "Hi, mister!" He stopped in his tracks. In his crib, Noam was red and crying and covered in poop. "Holy shit, Noam, you exploded!" Daniel cried, and hoisted him up, holding him at arm's length. "Mazel tov, sweetie!" He planted a big kiss on the baby's red face, and then pulled away in disgust from the smell. It was even in Noam's hair. He laid him on the changing table and peeled off the filthy diaper with his fingertips, fastidious at first, and then realized that if he just accepted the fact that he was going to get covered in shit, things would go a lot more quickly. He dropped the diaper in the pail. There were streaks of shit on Noam's thighs and on the hands he was grabbing his pacifier with. The stench made Daniel gag.

There was a shadow at the doorway and Dalia came in. "I let the baby get covered in feces!" Daniel exclaimed. "Choose me, I'm a fantastic parent!"

Dalia approached with a faint smile. "Sha-*lom*," she cooed, caressing the second syllable. "Did you make a big kaki?"

"He's been constipated since we got here," Daniel said. "This is an event, his first bowel movement in two and a half weeks."

Dalia nodded, reaching to smooth Noam's hair off his forehead, then clearly thinking better of it. "It's very common in grieving babies."

Daniel stared at her. "Constipation? You're kidding."

"No, why would I be kidding?" she asked.

"That makes so much sense! It didn't occur to me . . ."

She shrugged. "How does a baby mourn? He doesn't have a language for what he's lost."

They looked at Noam, who had picked up the wipes box and was turning it around in his hands with great interest.

"I'm sorry about your brother," Dalia said, moving forward quickly to ease the box out of the baby's hands before he could put it in his mouth. "I have a brother too, in New York. He's homosexual, too."

Daniel nodded warily. She said it without looking at him, without any kind of emotional fanfare. She wasn't a particularly warm person, he thought, except maybe to the baby, but all Israelis loved babies and talked to them with warm expressiveness. He wished she had said "gay" instead of "homosexual," which always made him flinch because it made it sound like a medical condition. But she seemed smart to him, and observant, and not unkind.

After dinner, on the phone with Matt, he told him how, in front of the caseworker, he gave the baby the longest, most disastrous bath in modern history. "It had everything," he said, a grin saturating his weary voice. "We ran out of hot water and I'd forgotten to turn on the boiler. The baby conked his head on the faucet and actually bled." He laughed. "Matt, I actually made him bleed. And those scalps, they're still a little soft, it turns out, so he'll probably have a bruise that his maternal grandparents will show to every social service official in the country. But wait. Then he had a second bowel movement—a much much looser one, I'm here to tell you—right in the tub. Which made me vomit. Yes, literally." He held the phone away from his ear a little and waited for Matt's laughter to subside. "We must have used at least twelve towels. Okay, four. By the end, I was soaking wet." He paused. "We *so* shouldn't be allowed to raise children."

"It probably at least broke the ice with the caseworker," Matt said.

"I guess you could call it that. And the baby's pretty happy tonight. We played a rousing game of Napkin on the Head."

"What's that?"

"A game where you put a napkin on your head," Daniel said.

"Aha," Matt said.

"It was hilarious."

"I'll bet it was," Matt said, smiling. "Hey, listen, I've been wanting to tell you something." He paused. "I've started taking Hebrew lessons."

Daniel blinked. "You have?" he asked softly.

"I know that you'll want Gal to continue speaking Hebrew when she grows up, and teach Noam, too," Matt said in a rush. "So I thought I should get in on it. Is that okay?"

"Honey," Daniel said. He knew what a stretch it was for Matt, what a gesture.

They hung together on the phone for a while, not speaking. "I love you," Daniel finally said.

"Me too, babe."

When he got off the phone he went into the kids' room, where Noam was asleep in a clean diaper and shirt, and his mother was supervising Gal as she got into her pajamas. "I just got off the phone with Uncle Matt," he said. "Guess what? He's started taking Hebrew lessons!"

Gal looked at him and considered. "Really?"

"Really! We can help him, right?"

"Yeah!" she said in the fake chipper voice she used when prompted by an adult to be enthusiastic.

He looked at his mother, who wasn't very enthusiastic at all; in fact, she was tight-lipped.

"What?" he demanded.

Her eyes darted toward Gal. *Later*, she mouthed.

A few hours later, after Gal had had two books read to her, a meltdown, and a cup of water, and had finally fallen asleep, they repaired to the kitchen. Daniel asked, "Do you have a problem you want to discuss?"

"I don't have a problem," his mother said.

"Then what was that back there in the bedroom? And what was that with the caseworker earlier, about Matt having to change his entire lifestyle?"

"I didn't say that!" his mother said.

Daniel was quiet. He didn't often fight with his mother, because when he did she grabbed the opportunity to crowd up too close to him with her tears and her drama. Joel had done better with her, their whole lives, exploding easily and making up easily, too; her drama didn't bother him. Daniel preferred to stay away from that. But he had dealt with her undermining of Matt all day long.

"Just say you have a problem with Matt, Mother. Just say it!"

"I have a problem with Matt! There, are you happy?"

Daniel gave her a look, a challenge.

"He's frivolous! He's pretty and shallow! He cares more about the latest styles than he does about these children. I've visited you; I've seen him have a hissy fit because he got a bad haircut, or couldn't find the right shoes."

Daniel snorted in disbelief. Sam came in, asking if anyone was making coffee, but stopped when he saw the looks on their faces. "What's going on?" he asked.

"Mom's busy getting all the homophobia out of her system."

"Daniel!" his father said. "Your mother is not a homophobe." She had been an avid PFLAG member when Daniel came out, so that was the official position.

"I have no problem with you, Daniel," Lydia said, crying now. "I've come to terms with your brother choosing to leave his children with you. It's Matt I have trouble with. The idea that *Matt* is going to raise my grandchildren—Matt! and not me—I can't get over that, I'm sorry."

"Well, you're going to have to get used to it," Daniel said.

"Don't you think I know that?" she cried.

They stood in stricken positions around the kitchen, and then Sam said quietly, "My only problem is that the kids have already been through so much. Being in a gay family, which is so much tougher, seems like a lot to ask of them."

"Oh God," Daniel said, turning to leave the room. Then he stopped and whirled around. "You know, Dad," he said heatedly. "People always say that about being gay. When their kids come out, they say, 'I'm just worried that your life is going to be harder.' But it's *they* who make their kids' lives hard! It's people like them, who don't support their kids because their lives are supposedly going to be harder. It's totally circular, can't you see?"

"Tell me something," his mother was saying, pointing at him. "What happens when Gal needs her first bra, when she gets her period? Can you imagine Matt dealing with that in a sensitive way?"

"Our friend Peter is a very talented drag queen," Daniel said. "I thought I'd let him take care of it."

There was silence. "Is that supposed to be funny?" Sam asked.

"Do *you* think Matt will make a good, committed father?" his mother demanded with a look that challenged Daniel to be honest, that tried to bore into his soul.

"Yes I do," Daniel said. He said it fiercely, thinking about what a goof Matt was, how imaginative and affectionate and funny. If the kids had any shot at having a fun home with them, it would be because of Matt, not him, who couldn't really be called a fun guy under even the best of circumstances.

She leaned back on the counter. "I don't believe you. I don't believe you think that."

It was this kind of shot, Daniel thought, that made him hate fighting with her. A feeling of shame stole over him, and he flushed. She thought that because she had seen him treat Matt like shit over the past couple of weeks.

"I'm through with this conversation, Mom. He's my *partner*. If I get these kids, he will raise them with me. And I'm just hoping—I'm *hoping*—that you're going to help me get them, and not sabotage me."

"Of course I am!" his mother cried. "I'm just being honest with you. Would you prefer I lied about my feelings?"

Daniel groaned. They always asked you this, and you always had to say no, of course you wanted them to be totally honest about how disgusting and inferior they thought you were.

"Enough," Sam said.

Daniel opened his mouth to speak.

"I mean it," Sam said, his voice breaking and his face red. "Enough! Isn't it hard enough? These kids—their lives are *over*! That bastard—"

Lydia stepped up to him and laid her hand on his back. "Shh," she murmured.

"It's okay, Dad," Daniel whispered. It was hard to look at him: emotion was grabbing and contorting Sam's normally equable face and making it grotesque. Daniel stepped up to his father and touched his forehead with his, eyes shut, gripping his shoulder. "Their lives aren't over. Just very challenging."

Sam clutched the back of Daniel's neck and squeezed, nodding, his chest shuddering.

A FEW DAYS LATER, he drove to Yaakov and Malka's to pick up the kids. He'd had a blessedly quiet two and a half days, and had finally caught up with some work, emailing the various writers for progress reports, and having a long phone conversation with April about the various news stories that needed to go in the College Notes section in the front of the magazine. The president of the college had given a speech on the importance of area studies in the wake of 9/11—along with a blistering attack on the reduced grant monies for scholars in those fields—that had been covered in the *New York Times*, and they sat over it for a while, deciding whether to print the whole thing or just portions of it; after they decided to write a story about it instead of simply printing the speech, they went through and chose the quotations they thought most important to preserve and to highlight. When he hung up the phone, Daniel stayed at the kitchen table for a little while, the yellow legal pad beside him covered with notes, basking in that hour or so of quiet concentration and small problem solving, the knowledge of how very good he was at his work.

He had gotten a call scheduling the first parental competency visit for the following week, and had spent some time haggling with various social service administrators about bunching the visits so that Matt wouldn't have to come more than once. Now they had four bunched within a two-week period, and Matt had bought a round-trip ticket for that length of time. The back-and-forth was starting to be a financial strain, and Sam had offered to pay for this flight.

He parked with two wheels on the tiny sidewalk in front of Yaakov and Malka's apartment. He loved Rehavia: it was one of the oldest European neighborhoods in Jerusalem, stone buildings cast into lovely shade by a profusion of plants and trees, climbing plants shooting up the buildings' sides, the occasional professional building—of doctors or small Europe-based companies—marked by modest gold plaques in Hebrew and English. He walked up the walkway and into the cool dark hall, and up the half-flight to their apartment, where he knocked softly on the door.

Malka opened the door and stepped backward in surprise.

"Shalom," he said.

"Shalom. Are you early? The children are at the park with Yaakov." The apartment was dim behind her, and he could smell the sweet mustiness of an old people's house.

Daniel looked at his watch. "No, I'm on time," he said. "But I can wait. Would you like me to wait outside?" The lawyer had forbidden them to discuss the custody case with anyone, especially the opposing parties, and he dreaded the idea of making small talk with Malka.

She blinked nervously, smoothed down her dress. "No, come in," she said.

She led him into the living room; the blinds were half-closed. Over the couch, which had a tasseled cover on it, hung a fanciful painting of a Hasidic violinist, in the style of Chagall. On the side wall hung a batik of the Dome of the Rock and the Western Wall at sunset. He sat on the couch. A huge oak display cabinet that held decorative eggs and birds, spun-glass clowns, and china plates on stands darkened the other side of the room. On the side table next to him stood some black-and-white photos in heavy silver frames. His eye ran along a few faded photos of Yaakov in groups of khaki-clad pioneers with caps and rifles. One had fallen over, and Daniel reached to stand it up again. It showed a young Malka wearing a white blouse and black skirt, her hair pulled back, holding a violin to her chin with a faraway look in her eyes. He looked up; she was hovering at the doorway.

"Did I hear once that you played in the Jerusalem Symphony?"

"Yes," she said, "first violin," with a touch of pride.

"I play violin, too," he said. "*Played*. It's been a long time. I was in the Chicago youth orchestra."

She nodded. "I used to play a lot when Ilana was a baby, because the music soothed her," she said, perching on the arm of a chair.

They talked violin concerti. He felt as though he needed to be very, very gentle around her. He was remembering a conversation he'd once had with Ilana, in which she told him that her mother carried the burden of the Holocaust for all of them—as though if she only carried enough despair, she could spare them. Yaakov, meanwhile, had suffered the same inconceivable losses—of his entire family, his very sense of personhood—but he had remained moving, surviving labor camps and death marches. It was striking, she told him, what a psychological difference it made to be able to move, even if under the constant threat of machine-gun fire, should you falter and slow.

He sat there for a while longer. Malka went into the kitchen, and he heard shuffling, a cabinet opening, a clink of silverware on a plate. He looked around and tried to imagine a teenage Gal in this apartment with her friends. Where would they sprawl around and talk smack in this silent, stuffy place where dust motes turned silently in the few glimmers of light let in from the blinds? He knew the answer immediately: She would never bring her friends here—she would spend her afternoons and evenings at their houses, while Malka made Yaakov call their parents to check up on her, and Noam played endless computer games behind a closed bedroom door.

Malka emerged with a piece of poppy seed cake, the kind sold in grocery stores in long plastic bags. He wasn't a big fan of poppy seed cake, but he ate it politely. She fussed about what might be keeping Yaakov. When they heard voices sound from the hallway, they stood up with relief.

TWO DAYS LATER, MATT was giving Daniel's guitar to a flight attendant to stash and trying not to think about the last time he'd been on this flight to Tel Aviv. The flight was full, and, already feeling greasy from the stale air, he fought his way to the back of the plane, past people aggressively claiming baggage space, blankets, and pillows. Was it anti-Semitic to think of them as aggressive? he wondered.

Flattening himself to pass a Hasidic family, he found his row and stowed his bag overhead after removing his book, a magazine, and a bottle of water. The memory of taking down Ativan for Daniel flashed through his mind and made him feel faint; he steadied himself and tip-toed past the two children seated in his row, who swiveled their knees to the side, and collapsed into his window seat. He sat there with his eyes closed for a few moments, feeling his heart gallop, pulling the plastic bag–covered headphones out from under him and letting them drop onto his lap. His skin was clammy; he wondered whether he was going to have a full-blown panic attack. He began to take con-certed deep breaths, and after a few minutes, aside from the sweat that coated his face, he was able to compose himself.

The plane took off by imperceptible, jumbo jet degrees. Next to him, a little girl was writing in Hebrew, in a Hello Kitty diary with a tiny lock on it. She saw him look at her and ever so slightly slanted the cover so he couldn't spy on what she was writing. The idea that he would want to see how she felt about her best friend's betrayal, or her mother's new boyfriend, cheered him a little. Beside her sat her brother, his eyes narrowed, his thumbs madly mashing a Game Boy.

Matt got up and washed his face. He drank a soda; he napped.

When he awoke he reached for the book in his seat pocket, a book Brent and Derrick had bought him. He had gone over to their house the previous evening. They were in the kitchen, making a late dinner— one of their fancy homemade pizzas—when he arrived; Derrick was slicing pears into slivers while Brent, wearing an apron over his bare torso, rolled out the dough. Matt helped himself to a beer and perched on a bar stool. Brent and Derrick exchanged a significant look, and then Derrick wiped his hands on a towel and said, "We wanted to give you something." He disappeared into the living room and returned with a book. It was called *Gay Dads*.

Matt colored and laughed. "Thanks, guys."

"It's okay if you're ambivalent," Derrick said, standing before him and looking into his face, kind and forthright.

"I know," Matt said, flipping through, looking at the handsome photographs of men and their kids.

"We know one of the guys in the book," Derrick said, "which is how we heard about it."

Now Matt opened the book and leafed through again, and then began to read. It was kind of moving, but kind of horrifying, too. Many of the guys had moved to the suburbs, many had turned into stay-at-home dads, many said that most of their best friends now were straight. Many said that parenthood offered them a connection to their extended families. "We're just a boring normal family," more than one of them said. It horrified him. He *came* from a boring normal family; he wanted something else. If that made him selfish, he couldn't help it.

When he'd read it through, he closed the book, a little pissed at Derrick and Brent for giving it to him. Derrick seemed so invested in him and Daniel being parents. He felt like saying to him, *If you're so into having kids,* you *have them!* And from Brent, it just felt like a setup. He ran his fingers along the spine. The guys in the book went to such lengths to have children. It wasn't at all like his and Daniel's situation, where the children had fallen into their laps. He wondered how his parents would take it, old John and Shirley Greene from Naperville, Illinois. They'd probably say "Gosh" or "Dear Lord" when he told them about these Jewish children whose parents were blown to kingdom come. They already had four grandchildren whom they doted on: his brother and sister were five and seven years older than he was.

They were fine; he just didn't have that much to say to them. It was something Daniel, whose family was so close and intense, had trouble understanding, even after he'd been home with Matt for several Christmases, and noticed that there were no books in the house, and played every game known to creation—from Hearts to checkers to Monopoly to Matt and Daniel's personal favorite, Taboo—and heard the kids tease Matt's dad about the plastic tree he'd bought because he didn't like having to clean up the needles. Each time Daniel was there, Matt's brother, Craig, came into the house and said, "Oh, the scent of fresh pine, nothing like it!" Same joke every time.

DANIEL WAS WAITING FOR him; he picked him out from among the crowd clustered at the exit. He was wearing sunglasses, and hadn't shaved, and looked like the handsomest Jewish man ever. Matt clasped him to him, but they didn't, as was their custom, kiss each other till they were in the car, and even then Matt saw Daniel's eyes darting around to make sure nobody walking by could see.

It had grown hotter, and there was a wavy haze down on the plains; the pale ocean appeared and disappeared between the dunes. "Thanks for bringing my guitar," Daniel said.

"No problem. I stopped off at your office and picked up some stuff, too."

"Did you pay the bills?"

"Yeah, we're good to go till the end of next month. Your salary went in, and I finally got paid for the reunion brochure."

"It's about time," Daniel said, closing the window now that the air conditioner had taken hold.

They didn't speak much as they climbed to Jerusalem, other than Daniel briefing him on what he knew about the parental competency exams that were going to start the next day. They would undergo a battery of tests he'd never heard of, except for the Rorschach. "Yay, tests," Matt joked faintly. Daniel nodded, getting the joke but worrying just a little about how Matt would perform on them. He felt the disconcerting alienation he always felt when they got together after being apart, as though this large man would make demands of him and thwart him from doing what he'd been doing, which was handling things on his own, his own way. On the other hand, it was thrilling to be seated next to a handsome man giving off delicious male smells; they'd been together for four years, and he never got over it.

"They still do the Rorschach?" Matt asked.

"Apparently."

"Wouldn't you think they had something more electronic, or digitized, now? It seems so, I don't know, I'm thinking Elizabeth Taylor in *Suddenly, Last Summer*."

A smile softened Daniel's face, and he reached over to touch Matt's hair. "Hey there," he said.

"Hey there," Matt smiled, taking Daniel's hand in his two hands and kissing the palm. He had a thought. "What do you wear to a Rorschach, I wonder?"

Daniel thought about it. "A solid color, not a pattern."

"Ah, yes," Matt said, stroking an invisible beard.

MATT DRESSED FOR the tests in khakis, a white polo shirt, and loafers, and gelled his hair so that it lay close to his head from a side part. It was his idea of conservative, and it made Daniel laugh because it made him look like the new boy at boarding school, ripe for hazing. The tests were held in one of the labyrinthine municipality buildings, new buildings set around a stone plaza right on the very edge of the Old City. An elderly guard sat at a table inside the shadowed hallway, and made them wait till he called up to verify that they were expected. Dalia met them as they stepped inside a vast room with smoky-blue carpets and dozens of cubicles where city employees did their work. She greeted them in a businesslike manner and told them that she would separate them for the day as the staff interviewed them and did a few diagnostic tests. She introduced them to Dr. Mickey Schweig, the psychologist on their case, a small, elderly man with a morose aspect. He would interview Daniel, and administer both of their tests. As she took Matt's elbow to steer him toward his room, he looked back at Daniel in mock alarm, feeling as though they were suspects who were going to be interrogated separately to discover the discrepancy in their story. He wondered: What *was* their story?

Dalia sat him down at a small round table and offered him coffee, and he said, "That'd be great. With milk?"

She boiled water in a small electric kettle and made him a small glass of Nescafé with milk, and then sat opposite him. She asked him to tell her about himself; she asked if it was okay to take notes. She wanted to know about his parents and siblings, where he grew up, his childhood activities and conflicts. He told her about his parents, friendly midwesterners: how his father glad-handed waitresses, calling them by name and asking them what they'd recommend; how his mother made succulent roasts, meat loaf, Jell-O molds, and ambrosia.

"As for conflicts," he said, looking directly at her, "of course the main one was being a queeny kid."

"Tell me about that," she said.

"I guess I'd like some reassurance that it won't be used against me and Daniel," he said, surprising himself with his ferocity.

Dalia set down her pen, looking mildly surprised herself, and he wondered whether she was just that instant discovering that she should take him seriously. "I can't speak for every actor in this custody process," she said. "But as far as I'm concerned, in my own personal evaluation, I'm less interested in your being homosexual than in the way you handle the conflicts that arise around it."

That made so much sense he thought it quite possibly might be true, and disarmed, he relaxed. "I caught a lot of flak in school. You know, they call it bullying, but let's face it, what goes on in schools is actually child abuse. When kids beat you up and then adults deny your reality, or blame you, that's child abuse. It didn't just happen to me; I saw it happen all the time."

"What do you mean by adults denying your reality?"

"I mean, saying things like, 'Oh, that's just the way boys are,' or 'You must have done something to provoke it.' Yeah," he sneered, "it's my fault I walked the way I walk."

"You feel strongly about this."

"Would you talk to a battered woman that way?" he challenged. "Would you ask her what she did to provoke it?"

"No," she said, and paused. "Would you describe yourself as at peace with your homosexuality?"

"I always have been—it's others who haven't been at peace with it." He said that quickly and belligerently, and then apologized. "I feel strongly about it," he said. "It's about supporting kids when they need support."

"Okay," Dalia said.

"When my best friend, Jay, and I started the gay-straight alliance in high school, things got better. We were still harassed, but there was comfort in numbers. The best day of high school was a demonstration we held—there were maybe twelve of us, and probably half were girls who were 'allies'—against homophobic harassment. These students we'd contacted from the U of I—that's the University of Illinois—came up on a bus to support us. It was covered for eighteen seconds on ABC News in a segment on the new gay activism."

He paused, considered. "Jay died four years ago," he said.

Dalia looked up. "AIDS?"

He narrowed his eyes. Was she stereotyping gay men, or just knowledgeable? "Yes."

"Do you know your HIV status?"

"Yes."

They gazed contemplatively at each other for a few moments.

Dalia looked away first, and cleared her throat. She invited him to talk more about his parents, whom, he hastened to assure her, he was now on good terms with. She asked about his work, his move to Northampton, how he met Daniel. It was close to one o'clock by the time she set down her pen again and pushed back her chair. "Okay, let's break for lunch, and when you come back, Dr. Schweig will administer some personality tests."

Matt stood, wondering if Daniel would be done, too. He opened the door, then turned back.

"Negative," he said.

"Okay," she said. "Thank you for telling me."

Daniel was standing by the elevator. They went downstairs and emerged onto the hot, bright plaza, the sun making them blink and sneeze, and stood uncertainly while people surged around them and buses roared past them with grinding gears. In the near distance rose the craggy walls and golden domes of the Old City. Daniel took Matt's sleeve and steered him toward a falafel stand on the adjoining street that they'd passed on their way in. The street was dingy and shaded. "What did you guys talk about?" Daniel asked.

"Oh, this and that," Matt said lightly.

"Really?" Daniel said. "Us too!"

The falafel stand was manned by a large bearded man in a *kipa*, who was intimidatingly quick and efficient. His spoon flew over pitas, slathering on tahini and eggplant; he turned from the fixings to behind him, where falafel was cooking in baskets dunked into boiling oil, and back to the front. They carried the beautiful warm sandwiches and two bottles of Coke back to the plaza, and found a bench in the shade, where they ate bent forward, so that tahini and hot sauce wouldn't dribble onto their pants. "Wow," Matt said through a burning palate. "Heaven." When he was done, Daniel handed him a napkin and he wiped his hands finger by finger, then took a long swig of Coke.

"I've been thinking," Daniel said, wiping his own face, casting a look at Matt. "You're not going to like this."

"I'm already crazy about it," Matt said. "Go ahead."

"I'm just thinking aloud, okay? Don't jump all over me."

"Dan, just say it."

Daniel reached behind his glasses with a finger and rubbed his eye. He cleared his throat and spoke. "Why shouldn't we just stay here?"

Matt blinked. *You have got to be kidding*: That was his thought.

"I'm not talking forever, just a few years. Think about it. It would make everything so much easier! It wouldn't tear Gal away from her friends, and both kids from their grandparents. We could live here, in the apartment. We could get work here; we both have skills that would make us a good living. For design work, you don't even really need Hebrew."

"Dan," Matt sighed.

Daniel's face was reddening with emotion. "I just can't stand the idea of tearing Gal away from here. It's wrong! It's the wrong thing to do!"

Matt rubbed his face. Maybe if he just let Daniel talk it out, he would work it out of his system.

"What do you think? Don't just have a knee-jerk response."

That was irritating. "We don't live here," Matt said. "Our life is in the States. *My* life is in the States."

"That's not a reason," Daniel said.

"Should I give more?" Matt asked, beginning to heat up. "I thought you were just thinking aloud. Have you decided this?"

"No!" Daniel said.

"It sounds as though you have. You have all the reasons down."

"It's not a decision I can make without you," Daniel said. He was saying the right thing, but Matt, looking at him with narrowed eyes, didn't believe him, and that scared him. Suddenly he had a premonition that Daniel was using this to leverage himself out of their relationship, a premonition that came with such dark fury, he knew it must be true.

"Are you breaking up with me?" he asked.

"No! Jesus!"

"Don't lie to me."

"I'm asking you to do this *with* me!"

"But you know I can't!"

"Why not?" Daniel demanded.

"Do I have to say it?" There was no answer. "Do I? Okay. *Because it goes against everything I believe in to live here*," Matt said, leaning toward Daniel and giving him a gentle piercing look, trying to bring him back to himself. "And everything you believe in too, by the way."

Daniel shook his head. "This isn't about politics," he said. "It's about these children."

"Oh please!" Matt cried. "I don't even know where to start! You're doing just what they do to us all the time, dismissing our politics as though they have nothing to do with real life. You *know* that's not true."

"It's just that, I've been thinking, parenthood means sacrifice, living for someone other than yourself."

Matt looked at him. "Wow, you thought that up all by yourself?" he asked with wide-eyed mockery. "Who *are* you?"

Daniel sat back, resolute. "Maybe I'm not the same man anymore."

Maybe that was it, Matt thought, his heart flailing in his chest. He'd always thought, when wondering whether they'd stay together forever, that no one could be one hundred percent confident. Sure, he'd stay with Daniel through many changes—although, admittedly, some of them might be especially challenging, like quadriplegia, a possibility he'd spent many an hour pondering in some torment. But what if circumstances made Daniel unrecognizable to him?

"You're the same man, Daniel," he said softly, with a silent prayer.

Daniel passed a hand over his face. "It's not as though the U.S. is such great shakes from a moral perspective."

Matt took heart from the weakness of that salvo.

"I just can't stand the thought of tearing Gal away from here," Daniel said, his mouth twisting. "I can't."

"She'll be okay. . . ."

"No she won't!" Daniel cried. "She's going to lose everything she knows! She's such a little trouper, it *kills* me to watch her get up and soldier through her day."

Matt looked at his watch. They had to be back inside in ten minutes. "I can't believe you sprung that on me right now," he said. "We have to go in there now and take personality tests, for Christ's sake. If you've decided you're staying, what's even the point?"

An old Arab woman rolled by, her heavy, lined hand on the shoulder of a young boy, and catching the boy's eye, Matt wondered what he was seeing when he looked at the two flushed, angry American men.

"I haven't decided," Daniel insisted.

"Whatever," Matt said, standing.

They went back in and spent the afternoon associating to Rorschach blots and telling stories about TAT pictures. Matt found the TAT pictures profoundly depressing, not only in their content, but in their style as well. The figures seemed utterly isolated, the cloud formations menacing. The portrayal of gender was taken straight from the 1950s. He kept looking at the psychologist, wondering if this was a joke test, but when he met his eyes he saw no glimmer of connection or humor, just the patient waiting of the diagnostician. He wondered how the hell he'd gotten into this mess, how it came to be that he was sitting in a dingy office in the middle of this hot, teeming, smelly, violent, godforsaken city, being forced to make up stories like a mental patient. For every picture, he wanted to make up a story about deviant gender or sexuality.

When Dr. Schweig finally released him, he was exhausted. He had to wait for Daniel to take his tests, and he didn't want to have to pass through security again, so he sat on a chair by the elevator for an hour, cursing the fact that he hadn't brought something to read, until Daniel came out of a room and closed the door softly behind him. They looked at each other; Daniel crossed his eyes. Then, as Matt raised his eyebrows, Daniel put a finger to his lips and walked quickly to the elevator, his mouth twitching. Only when they burst out onto the plaza did he begin to laugh.

"Were those cards messed-up, or what!" Daniel said. "They were a disgrace!" He started giggling. "Did you get the blank card?" he asked.

Matt began laughing, too. "There was a blank card?"

"Oh yeah," Daniel said. "I said to the psychologist, 'That represents the blankness of God's intent to Man's scrutiny.' I mean, what the fuck?" His mirth was broken through with confused indignation, and that set them off again. People on official business were walking past the giggling men, avoiding them with varying degrees of curiosity and irritation.

"You did not!" It was exhilarating: Daniel had misbehaved, and not him! There was a little bit of hardness to the feeling, for wasn't Daniel a hypocrite for treating him as a fuckup, and then cutting loose himself? Still, it was lovely to watch him seized by the giggles. They went down the steps to the parking garage, Daniel's back shaking in front of him, his shirt damp from sweat. Maybe, Matt thought, the idea of staying in Jerusalem was just a momentary faintness of heart, a streak of crippling empathy for Gal. They passed together into the dark, cool underground, their shoes making soft, clean noises on the concrete floor. "Do you think we could get away with not going straight home?" Daniel asked. He flung his arm around Matt. "Let's ditch the grieving children and stop somewhere for a beer."

"Absolutely," Matt said. Daniel feeling frisky was a treat under any circumstance. "But if you just lost the kids for us because you failed to take this test with the proper seriousness, you're in big trouble."

TWO WEEKS OF FURTHER tests passed. Daniel didn't bring up wanting to stay in Israel again, but a low current of anxiety buzzed through Matt as he waited for the moment he'd have to fight it out again. After they were interviewed and tested separately, Dalia and the psychologist met with them together to discuss their relationship, and then came over to the apartment twice to see them with the kids. It hurt Lydia's feelings that she was asked not to be there for those interviews. "Won't I be a big part of these kids' lives if they go to you?" she importuned Daniel privately, and he knew that it killed her that Matt was being tested as a parent and she wasn't. For his part, Matt noticed that Daniel wore to both interviews shirts that had belonged to Joel, and he wondered if he was trying to channel Joel, or to look like a respectable and upstanding straight man, or maybe enacting some creepy version of those twins who dressed alike well into their adulthood and then married twins, a phenomenon Daniel had spent a lifetime loathing. But it was funny to see how the straightest-looking of clothes—a polo shirt tucked into chinos—got a gay twist when the marvelously delicate Daniel wore them. The interviews themselves—the two of them sitting on the floor, stiff and smiling, among the playing children—were, to his mind, a bit of a charade, although when the psychologist asked Gal what she liked most about Uncle Matt and she said, with a decisiveness that made them all smile, "He's really funny," he felt inordinately proud, both of her response itself and of the fact that he understood the Hebrew.

In Gal, Matt found an even more exacting Hebrew teacher than Yossi—although he didn't have quite the same drive to impress her as he did Yossi—and, as an added bonus, one who was learning to read and write herself. They sat next to each other at the kitchen table, drawing letters and writing simple words onto lined sheets of paper, Gal's eyes darting back and forth from her own paper to Matt's. "You know, Mordechai," she said one day—she had inexplicably begun calling him Mordechai. Why? When he asked, she just shrugged, but when Daniel asked her, she said she thought he needed a Hebrew name. "Your letters are better than mine."

"That's because I'm an artist," he said, "and also, I already know how to write in one language. But often I can't understand what I'm writing, and you can understand everything you write."

She studied her own letters and said, *"Oof!* Let's do a vocabulary test instead." She never tired of testing his vocabulary. She'd call out words she thought of off the top of her head, in English, and he'd have to translate. If he got the word right, she'd ask him to modify it with an adjective like *good* or *bad*, or *big* or *small*, so he could learn its gender. When he got that right, her eyes would widen and she'd give him an indulgent pat on the hand. *"Col ha'cavod,"* she'd say. Good job! or, as the literal translation went, All honor to you!

Lydia came into the room, got out a loaf of bread that Daniel had bought that morning, and set it on the cutting board. "Time to set the table, kidlets," she said.

Matt knew that they wouldn't be eating for another half an hour; this was Lydia's way of making it hard for him to have a relationship with Gal. She'd told Daniel that she felt *horrible* about Matt's learning Hebrew with Gal, because there was no way for her to participate since he'd thought of it first. Daniel had told her that that was silly, that it was a good idea for all of them to know Hebrew. And then she made him facilitate it: He had to ask Matt and Gal if Grandma and Grampa could join them, even though Sam had no intention of doing so. She participated from time to time, and when she did, they always had to say how smart Grandma was, and how good her memory was. "Who got 'window'?" she'd demand.

"You did, Grandma," Gal would say.

Since Matt's return, Sam was busying himself with what he called Joel and Ilana's "effects." He and Daniel went through Joel's clothes, a ravaging experience for both of them; halfway through, Sam sat hard on the bed, his face stricken and drooped, and said, "I can't believe I'm doing this." Daniel kept a lot of them. As for Ilana's clothes, Sam insisted upon calling in Malka to help. He'd become the emissary to the Grossmans; he had a calming effect on them—probably, Daniel imagined, because of the quiet, benign quality of his attention, one of Daniel's own favorite things about his father. He and Malka spent an afternoon in the bedroom with the door closed, and Malka left with an armful of clothes, her face pale and set against the indignity of seeming to slink off with the dregs the victor left behind, as hyenas do. They saved Ilana's jewelry for Gal, except for one necklace that had particular sentimental value for Malka that Sam hadn't quite understood.

Sam made two duplicates of the wedding video, and additional prints of all the negatives he found stuffed into the pockets and between the pages of the photo albums. Then he bought photo albums and compiled them. One set for him and Lydia, one for Malka and Yaakov, one for Daniel and Matt and the kids. He set himself up at the kitchen table, wearing khaki pants and sandals, and an untucked, short-sleeved buttondown shirt, reading glasses perched on the end of his nose. He was solitary, focused, in his element. He had dealt the photos into three piles, like cards, and now he was trying to manage one of the large piles, putting it into chronological order, using Joel and Ilana's album as the key.

When she got home from school, Gal climbed on a chair next to him and studied the piles. "What are you doing?" she asked.

"I'm making three different albums, so we can all have pictures of your parents, and of you and Noam when you were babies," Sam said. "Careful, honey, that belongs here."

Daniel was on the floor, playing with blocks with the baby. He stood and came over; he could tell that Sam was worried Gal would disrupt his piles and his concentration. The photo Sam had taken from her was a wedding picture in which Joel and Ilana were disarranged, drunk, grinning. "They didn't have me yet," Gal said experimentally, craning her neck up at Daniel. Just checking. She picked up a picture of herself as a newborn, held by Ilana, who was touching her nose to hers. Ilana's hair in a ponytail, eyes half-closed. Content, drowsy.

"That's me," Gal said.

"That's you," Daniel said, putting his hand on her head. "You and Ema. Look how much she loved you."

Gal studied it, then placed it carefully on the correct pile.

"Thanks, honey," Sam said.

"Was I a good baby?" Gal asked in a small voice.

"Yes, you were," Daniel said somberly, turning her face to his. "And a good girl, too."

Did she take it in? Who knew? She looked at him with enormous eyes, then got up and opened the snack drawer. The baby squawked and Daniel picked him up and jiggled him.

Matt flew back home to return to work, and another few weeks passed, in which Daniel had to appear in family court twice. The judge seemed taken by the fact that he and Joel were identical twins, which Daniel hoped meant that he was considering that, genetically speaking, the kids could actually be his.

Then one day Daniel got a call from Assaf, who had gotten a call from Yaakov and Malka's lawyer. "They want to settle, Daniel," Assaf said. "They agree to have you and Matt take the children, under the condition that they can visit them once a year, and that you bring them here once a year. That's fantastic news. Of course, the court has to approve."

Daniel sank onto the couch with the cordless phone. "What happened?"

"There was a car accident," Assaf said. "A minor one, but it looks as if Malka blacked out for a second behind the wheel, and that frightened them. The attorney said they simply want the best for the kids. But I have a feeling that they also didn't do too well with the parental competency visits."

Poor, poor Malka, Daniel thought.

Assaf said that he most likely wouldn't be allowed to adopt the children, at least not yet. Adoption, he reminded him, was the most binding form of custody a court could award to a nonbiological parent. But there were other gradations of custody, ones that were more temporary and contingent upon follow-up visits and testing.

Daniel nodded. They had been over this before.

His mother came into the room and saw the expression on his face, and was hovering around him whispering "What? What?" as he flapped his hands at her to shush her so he could hear Assaf.

"I'll call back when I know more about what comes next," Assaf said. "Daniel. I'm glad."

Daniel hung up, told his mother what had happened, hugged her and his father.

"Thank God," Lydia said, clutching her chest. "Thank God."

"I have to call Matt," he said, taking the phone into the bedroom and closing the door. He sat down, placed the phone on the desk, and buried his face in his hands. Then he placed his hands on the desk and took a deep breath. He dialed, and the phone was picked up immediately by a breathless Matt.

"Hey, it's me," Daniel said. "Who were you expecting?"

"Hey!" Matt said. "The woman from the Forbes Library, who might have some design work for me."

"Not your new lover?"

"You mean the young one without the crying children?"

Daniel laughed with a tiny wounded pang. "Speaking of the crying children, Assaf called today to say that Malka and Yaakov have decided not to contest custody."

Matt shrieked.

"It still has to go through the courts," Daniel said. "But who else can they give custody to?" He was listening very hard for Matt's response, but all he could hear was the sound of his breathing on the other end. "Are you hyperventilating?"

"Kind of."

"Do you need to put your head between your knees?"

"Let me just lie down." Daniel heard a grunt and a sigh. "Okay," Matt said. "Phew. How long do you think before we can bring them home?"

"I don't know."

They were quiet for a few minutes. Daniel took off his glasses and covered his eyes with his hand. *Here it is, bucko*, he thought: the moment your bluff is called. "Do you think we can do this?" he asked.

"You're asking if I think *I* can do it, right?" Matt said.

"No, both of us."

"Oh my God, you're such a liar," Matt said. "Absolutely."

MATT LAY ON THE bed for a while after they hung up. It was still morning in Massachusetts, and the bed was unmade; he hadn't had coffee yet. He would have to move his study up to the guest room, an attic refinished by the previous owners. His current study, a big, boxy, sunny room across the hall from their own bedroom, would be perfect for the kids' bedroom. The guest room was smaller, and the roofline slanted down to cut off some of the usable space.

He thought that all in a rush, then felt a pang: No more guest room! Guests would have to sleep in the living room or in his study. And what, he wondered, would they do with the beautiful guest bed? Was it appropriate to put a six-year-old in a double bed, and would it even fit in the room with a crib? Not if they put a little desk in there, for Gal to do her homework. And when Gal got older and needed her own room, she'd want the attic one, a funkier and more private space than the bedroom she'd be sharing with Noam, so he'd have to move his study again. He supposed he'd rent office space in town. Would they have to buy a bigger house? He sat up and placed the phone back on the night table.

He got up and washed his face, then went up the creaky, bowing stairs and stood in the guest room doorway, running his hand through his hair and trying to imagine where he'd put his computer, his printer, his bulletin board. He sighed. When he moved in, he'd poured his energy into trying to put his own stamp on Daniel's house, becoming a regular at the local antique shops, stripping and refinishing tables and benches, repainting the drab conventional white walls in a palette of boysenberry, deep olive, and lemon. He'd put mismatching chairs, of a variety of materials, around the dining room table. Daniel had put up a fight about the changes, arguing that Matt's sleek tastes didn't suit a farmhouse, but Matt convinced him that Daniel needed to expand his *idea* of the farmhouse, and besides, he needed to feel as if the house were his, too. Daniel had come to love the warm colors of the rooms. And now they'd have to remake the house again, only this time, making it uglier. He'd do something nice with these walls, though, which he'd never gotten to. And get a small air-conditioning unit. He looked glumly at the antique two-pronged electrical outlet under the window. And call an electrician.

He went downstairs and made himself coffee, fed the dog. He opened the door onto a sunny day, and late-spring cold surged into the kitchen through the screen door. He got Yo-yo's leash and snapped it onto his collar, a lingering heaviness at his heart over what was about to happen to his house, thinking, *Let it go, it's okay, let it go.*

DANIEL WENT TO COURT the next week, and Judge Fuchs, a man with a flat bowl of black hair and enormous wire-rimmed glasses, awarded him custody of the children, and permission to take them to the U.S. Daniel had come with his father and Assaf, and the whole thing felt a little anticlimactic. What had he expected? he wondered later. For the judge to rehearse the course of this tragic case, sum it up in sonorous Hebrew? To exchange a hearty, moved look with him? After all, he'd been ruling on their case from the beginning, and Daniel had developed a transference attachment. But the judge's eye contact was sporadic and impersonal. There were certain conditions, which he switched to English for the first time to say. Daniel looked at his father. "Excuse me, Judge. May my father come up and listen?" he asked.

"Of course," the judge said.

His father approached and put his hand on Daniel's shoulder. Daniel, the judge said, was to bring the children to Israel once a year to visit their grandparents for a minimum of two weeks, and allow their maternal grandparents to visit in the U.S. at least once a year, also for a minimum of two weeks. They were to be followed by a social worker in the U.S. They were to return to this court after two years, so that it could follow their progress.

"Do you understand?" he asked Daniel.

"Yes."

"The court expresses its hope that you will give the children every opportunity to express and cultivate their Israeli heritage, and will foster in them love of Israel. Do you understand?"

"Yes, Judge," Daniel said. He did understand, but he'd have to think about how to do that later.

And that was that. Nothing about Matt, about the fact that he was awarding custody to two gay men. No comment about how well they'd done on their parental competency exams, and how great the tests showed their personalities were, and how they had confounded the court's expectations. He didn't even give a knock of the gavel. They filed out of the court and Daniel and his father embraced, Sam clutching the back of Daniel's head with his hand. When they let go, they were flushed. Daniel turned to Assaf and took his hand in both of his. "Thank you," he said.

Assaf took them to lunch in the courtyard of the American Colony Hotel, where they sat at an elegant iron table on a flagstone floor, surrounded by a burbling Turkish fountain and olive trees and flower beds. Daniel brought up the fact that there had been no mention of Matt, and Assaf pointed out that the actual custody, after all, was to Daniel alone. "But you're right," he added. "I think he probably left that out so there won't be any gay rights implications to the case."

Sam ordered a bottle of expensive champagne, and when the waiter had ceremoniously poured it, held up his glass. When they'd raised theirs, he said, "To my grandchildren, Gal and Noam. May their lives, which have gotten off to such a terrible start, get brighter by the day."

"*L'chaim,*" Assaf said.

"And to Daniel," Sam said, turning toward his son and contemplating him with a smile bright with love and pain. "Raise them well, son. I know you will."

Daniel bit his lip and tried not to be a total girl in front of his father. "That means a lot to me, Dad," he said.

THEY DECIDED THAT THEY wanted to tell the children that they were going to move to the U.S. in the presence of their other grandparents, to indicate that it was a decision that the family as a whole was making, for their benefit. It was Daniel who called, and he spoke with Yaakov.

"Yaakov, I want you to know how much I appreciate this."

There was a long silence, so he soldiered on, in stiff Hebrew. "I will take very good care of the children, I promise, and we'll work it so you can see them as often as possible. You're very welcome to stay with us when you come to visit them in the States. Have you ever been to the U.S.?"

"No," Yaakov said. "Only to Europe. And Istanbul."

"I think you'll like where we live," Daniel said, resolutely conjuring in his mind the gentle verdant mountains and rippling streams instead of the tattooed lesbians who lounged and smoked and made out on the streets of his town. He proposed to Yaakov that he and Malka come over that evening for dinner, and to talk to Gal. "It'll be good," he said, quietly calculating how to convey that Matt wasn't there, "if all the adults—you and Malka, my parents, me—could tell her together that we've made a collective decision."

There was a long pause on the other end. Then Yaakov said, "I don't know what there is to talk about. You are taking the children. How hard can that be to tell Gal? It doesn't require an international convention."

Daniel bit his lip. "Don't you want to tell her that you and Malka love her, and that we all agreed that this is how we'd take care of her and Noam?"

"She knows we love her," Yaakov said. "There's no need for a formal declaration."

When Daniel hung up, he had a tremendous headache. It was much harder to talk to Yaakov from the position of the victor than from the position of antagonist, because even though Yaakov was being a big prick and not thinking of what Gal needed, he felt horrible for him. He went into the kitchen to report dejectedly to his mother, who said, "You can't expect them to be happy about it, honey. Just to behave well in front of the children."

But the bad feeling persisted through a trip to the supermarket, through picking up Gal from school. Gal had been irritable all afternoon; her teacher took Daniel aside and told him that she had hit another kid pretty hard, and that she'd had to put her in a time-out. On their way home, carrying her backpack and an art project with macaroni glued onto construction paper, Daniel had tried to ask her about what had happened, but she refused to talk, giving him a lot of the shrug/tsk combination that played such a big part in Israeli children's bad moods. "Are you feeling sad?" he asked as they approached the tiny *makolet* near her school for her traditional after-school Popsicle.

"Are you feeling sad?" she said in a mocking voice, her face twisted into grotesque concern.

"Hey," he admonished, and she ran inside, mingling with the other little kids gathered around the square white freezer. He watched her wait obediently in line, then give her coins to the elderly man in a *kipa*, who handed her an orange Popsicle. She brought it outside, struggling to peel off the wrapper without getting her fingers sticky, and then dropped the whole thing onto the grimy sidewalk. Daniel's heart sank. She looked at it and up at him, and he said quickly, "*Ain davar*, we'll get another one."

"I don't want!" she said, and marched toward home, and he followed her the whole way, watching her stalwart, angry back.

At home, Daniel snapped at his mother, and he picked a fight with Matt on the phone when Matt asked if he should come help them pack and fly back with them, by saying, "It's not necessary, we can really manage on our own," and finally, after Matt persisted with further questions, saying, "You're going to have to decide this one for yourself, Matt, I already have two children to deal with."

"Whoa," Matt said.

"Look, I can't talk right now, okay?" Daniel waited. "Let's talk later."

"Sure," Matt said, hanging up the phone before the word was even out.

MATT COOKED DINNER FOR Cam later that evening, and he told her about his dilemma as he cleared the dishes and put them into the dishwasher, spooned the leftovers into Tupperware containers. He wanted to be part of their coming home. He was wondering if he could just show up a few days before they left, or whether that would be unpleasant or unhelpful in any way. But even if it seemed unhelpful, he still wanted to do it! "We really can't afford it," he said. "Already, two round-trips to Israel for me, and one for Daniel, have been about thirty-six hundred dollars, although I think Daniel's father's going to pay for one of those. This would bring it up to almost five grand, and we'd have to float it on a credit card." He paused. "But I just don't think that money should be the issue here."

"Oh, go!" Cam said.

Matt laughed. "Of course you'd say that." Cam was an impetuous girlfriend, a lover of the grand gesture. She loved to do things like spring a weekend trip to Miami Beach on a girlfriend, secretly canceling all the girlfriend's appointments and packing her suitcase, and then, when she showed up for a supposed coffee date, whisking her away in her car to the airport without telling her where they were going. Matt and Daniel privately thought that that wasn't romantic, it was controlling.

"So I should just show up, even though Daniel said not to?"

"Did he say not to, or did he say he doesn't *need* you to?"

Cam was arguing exactly what he wanted to argue, and that made him doubt himself. He wet a sponge and wiped down the counters. It really wasn't a good idea. It would be far more sensible to wait for them at home, to pick them up from the airport, and have everything lovely and welcoming when they arrived. But the impulse to go was persistent, and he believed in listening to your instincts, too.

CHAPTER 9

DANIEL DREAMED THAT he was in the café. It wasn't the Peace Train Café, it was one he'd never seen before, a café with a huge mirror on one wall that made it seem as though there was a whole duplicate café on the other side. A man entered, bulky, his face sweaty, and Daniel knew he was the bomber. He tried to get someone's attention, but the waitress was talking to a group at another table, with her back turned to him. An enormous cappuccino stood steaming on the table before him, crisp brown grains of sugar speckling and staining the foam. Sunshine slashed across one knee, and he scooted his chair over into the shade. Then Ilana was sitting across from him—she must have been there all along—and he felt embarrassed that he was so baldly standing in for Joel. Someone laughed and shouted in Hebrew, "I told you so! Didn't I tell you so?" His chest was knotted, and he was sweating. The bomber had disappeared, but Daniel knew with terrible dream-certainty that the man's fingers were reaching for the cord that hung under his coat. In the spinning chaos of his thoughts, Daniel pictured his flesh blown from his bones, wondered murkily if his brain would register the agony even if his head was blown clear off.

He woke up screaming, and sat up, stunned, his voice echoing in his ears. He'd never produced such a sound, and for a second he thought someone else was screaming. When he realized where he was, he leapt out of bed as though it were on fire, and burst from his room. The house was quiet in the early dawn light: Incredibly, no one had heard him. He sank to his knees on the living room rug, then sat on his heels and bowed his head and breathed, waiting for the panic to stop.

His headache didn't go away; it persisted through the packing, the visits to various government offices to arrange papers and passports, the accelerated pace of bringing the children back and forth from their house to their grandparents'. A *hamsin* moved into Jerusalem, the sky turning white, hot wind whipping up sand and garbage and twisting laundry on the line. His eyes became swollen, the skin under them chafed and tender. They pulled down all the blinds in the apartment, making it into a dark cave, and congregated whenever possible in the master bedroom, which had the apartment's only air-conditioning unit, as the wind rattled the blinds. They ate cold foods, yogurt and salads and spreads on bread. Lydia complained about crumbs in the bed, where Gal was eating her snacks in front of the TV. "Use a plate, honey!" she said, swiping at the crinkled bottom sheet. Even Noam was cranky, shrieking when they took anything sharp, or a choking hazard, away from him. Daniel took him into the bathroom to splash cold water on his pink, sweaty face, and laughed when he saw Noam's thrust-out lower lip in the mirror, it was the very picture of infantile indignation.

Sam had spent the morning at the kitchen table, writing numbers on a pad of paper, with quick punches at the calculator. He called Daniel into the kitchen in the tone he used for important matters, usually financial, and pulled out a chair for him. "Listen, Daniel," he said, "I'd like you to be able to keep the apartment for the next few years, so you'll have a place to be when you bring the children to visit their grandparents. So I'm going to pick up the mortgage and taxes, to make that possible. Maybe we can find someone to manage it and rent it out for the periods when you're not here."

"Really, Dad, are you sure?" Daniel asked, and when his father nodded, he said, "Thank you so much. I can't tell you how nice that is of you." In the past, he'd turned down all of his father's attempts to help him out financially, except for this most recent gift of Matt's plane ticket, because those offers made him feel that his father thought he couldn't make it on his own. But this gift didn't feel like that at all. It felt like an amazing act of understanding and empathy. The apartment felt to him like a living thing, its light and smells, its tiled floors and thick, strong blinds, the sheets they put on the beds, the gas stove that clicked noisily four times before lighting, the nicked and pocked coffee table, the broom closet stuffed with pails and plastic bags, the mop handle falling down every time someone opened the door. Living in it was like loving a middle-aged person who'd been around the block a few times.

And then their departure was only a week away. Gal's class threw her a going-away party, and when Daniel came to pick her up he stood for a few minutes at the edge of the classroom, watching kids say good-bye with varying degrees of social competence and drama, their faces bearing the traces of chocolate frosting. Gal was flushed and wearing a crown, and when she saw him, she came over to him. "Look," she said, thrusting a small, leather-bound book at him. They had taken pictures of themselves, individually and in groups, and had composed a photo album. Daniel flipped through it, trying not to bawl. There were also cards with crazy first-grade writing all over them, and a bag of candy—candy Daniel was sure he'd be finding in corners of his house a year from now. Gal's teacher, Sari, stooped to give her a tearful hug, and Gal, with a pained look on her face, allowed herself to be squeezed. "You'd better come see me when you come visit," she said huskily. "Or else, *oy vey!*"

They walked home quietly. Daniel didn't dare speak. The wind whipped at them and Gal winced as her hair lashed her face. They descended to the cool dark underground walkway that crossed under-neath Herzl Street, their sneakers making cupped muffled sounds on the sidewalk. Daniel's hand sweated onto the photo album. How could he survive all this tiny girl was losing, when he felt her pain so sharply it made him gasp?

When they got home, Gal said she had a headache. Lydia got her to undress and gave her a cool sponge bath, and when Daniel passed by, he saw his mother murmuring to her and running a washcloth over her back as Gal stood, hands limp, turning obediently. Her face and lips had lost their color. After she was dried off, she crawled into bed and faced the wall, and she didn't stir for the next twelve hours.

MATT PAINTED THE KIDS' room, ordered a bed, a crib, a changing table, and a dresser for it. When the furniture arrived, he and Derrick and Brent sat on the bedroom floor holding Allen wrenches and scratching their chins over large unfolded instructions. When they took a break they went out to the backyard and wiped the accumulated dirt and pollen off of the plastic lawn chairs and sprawled in the shade of the big oak, drinking beer. Matt had a heavy feeling about all the grief about to enter his house, and Derrick gave him a pep talk. Derrick was a tall, forthright man with coffee-colored skin, a shaved head, and a neat goatee—not exactly handsome, but a treat to look at, his face was so open and lively. Derrick told him, emotion catching his throat, that he was about to find himself capable of things he'd never imagined he could do.

"I want them to feel safe," Matt said. "How do you make kids feel safe?"

Derrick looked at him gently. "Is that what you're worried about?"

"I don't know, I've been thinking about it. How can you promise a kid she'll be safe when she already knows, better than you do, how dangerous the world is?"

Derrick sat up straighter, narrowed his eyes in thought. "I'm remembering a study done by Winnicott—he was this big English psychoanalyst—with I think it was English children after World War Two, who were evacuated from London, away from their parents, during the blitzkrieg. The ones who were assured that they and their parents and their houses were going to be safe, even though there was no evidence for that—on the contrary, the evidence pointed in the opposite direction—those kids fared better emotionally in the long term than the ones who were told by adults that they honestly didn't know what was going to happen. Which goes against everything we're normally taught, that the most important thing when dealing with children going through trauma is telling them the truth."

Brent got up and set his bottle on the small brick patio, then roamed the borders of the yard, doing miscellaneous weeding. They were quiet for a while, watching him stoop and grip and wiggle gently, bringing up small balls of dirt and root. They commiserated over the political situation, Israel's ravaging of West Bank towns; as a black man, Derrick thought of Israel as a colonial power, but as a social worker he tried to conscientiously examine his own potential anti-Semitism.

"When you're there," Matt said, "it seems really complicated. There are all these Israelis with their funny personalities, kind of assholes but also really human and likable, and no contact whatsoever with the Palestinians who are living through hell just a few miles away. And then you come home and see from here what Israel's doing, and suddenly it seems very simple: it's a nation committing terrible crimes against another people."

They sat for a while longer, directing Brent here and there as though he were their sexy lawn boy.

"I'm going to fly back with them," Matt said. "I bought a ticket."

Derrick looked at him quickly. "Does Daniel know?"

"No. I can't bring myself to tell him; I'm afraid he'll be mad, or tell me not to come. So I'm just showing up. It'll be kind of like a sitcom!" he said brightly, and Derrick laughed.

THREE DAYS BEFORE THEIR departure, Lydia took Gal to the mall to look for a good-bye present for Leora, and they returned with a necklace that said *Friends forever*.

"Good job, guys!" Daniel said as he and his father bent over, looking at it together, Gal nervously holding open the box close to her body, as though the whole thing might be ruined if they disturbed it. He shot his mother an impressed look, and she said, "It's perfect, isn't it."

It fell upon Daniel to help Gal with the card. He sat with her on the living room rug, legs open over construction paper, scissors, and markers. "What do you want to write?" he asked.

Normal summer weather had returned to Jerusalem, and a soft, warm breeze came in through the open windows, ruffling Gal's hair. She was barefoot, sitting between her heels, in shorts and a hideous T-shirt she loved that said *Princess* in curly script studded with rhinestones. "I don't know," she said. "What should I say?"

"Do you want to tell her that you love her and will miss her?"

"Yes," she said gravely. "And also that she should come visit me in Massachusetts." It had taken her a while to be able to pronounce the name of the state, which they still sometimes playfully called "Massachoochay."

"Okay," Daniel said.

"And I want to draw a picture," she said, her energy gathering.

"Good idea."

She bent forward till she was lying on her stomach supported by her elbows, selected a brown marker, and began to draw. Daniel was pretty sure it would be a horse. He sat facing her with his legs crossed, in a posture of watching and supporting as he brushed the newspaper off the coffee table and snuck looks at it.

"*Oof!*" she cried, and violently crumbled the paper.

"Wait," he protested, "let me see!" He unfolded it. "What's wrong with this?"

She gave him a withering look. "The head is all . . . it's disgusting!"

"Okay," he said mildly, taking a new piece of construction paper from the pile, which she carefully folded in half.

She completed the next horse before deciding that it was a failure too, and this time her small fierce face darkened into tears. Daniel snatched at the paper before she could destroy it.

"Sweetie, tell me what you want to do that you're failing at. Because I think this one's really nice."

"You always say that!" she cried. "Even if it's shit! Where will I put the writing?" She sat up and swiped at the markers, which went flying off the carpet and clattering over the linoleum floor.

Daniel looked soberly at the drawing, turned it every which way in his hands. "Can't we put the writing on the back? I think that'd look really nice. And then you could draw even more around the horse, like grass and the sky."

"No! It's a card, so it's supposed to be inside!"

"Not always, people write in all kinds of places," he said. He patted his lap. "Come sit here for a second."

"No! I have to do this!"

"Just to calm down for a second, and then we'll take another look at it."

She stood and he took her wrist to pull her down, and she smacked his arm and ran into her room and slammed the door so loudly the baby started crying.

Lydia and Sam came out of their room.

"Let her stay there for a little while and calm down," Daniel said, meeting them in the hallway. His face was red, and he was trying to calm down himself, to stop being furious at Gal for refusing his help and comfort.

"What happened?"

"Just a fit of anxious perfectionism," he said.

"Do you want me to talk to her?" Lydia asked.

"No, please, Mom, let me, just let her be alone for a little while."

"Let me at least get Noam," she said, venturing into the room. She emerged with the crying baby a few minutes later, her lips pursed. Daniel looked at her, knowing Gal had snapped at her. She caught his eye. "Brat," she said.

He laughed. They went into the kitchen to start dinner. Sam sat the baby at his high chair and, instructed by Lydia, brought out the little containers of shredded chicken and rice. She handed him an apple and a paring knife and he peeled and cut it into careful slices. Lydia glanced from time to time toward Gal's room, and then at Daniel, until he impatiently said, "Mom, stop, I'll get her in a few minutes."

He sat slumped in his chair, and his anger slowly wound its way through glumness and on into sadness so acute he had to rise again. He went into Gal's room. She was on her bed, folded into a rocking ball, murmuring to herself. He picked up some toys and some Noah's Ark pieces and sat on the floor quietly until he almost dozed off. He started awake and reached for his guitar, which stood propped against the wall. From the open window came the sound of a honking car, and of children shouting. "Gal," he said quietly. "It must be so hard to leave your best friend."

She quieted and lay still, alert.

"If I had to leave *my* best friend. *Oysh.* I'd be so mad." *Offer her something positive to hang on to*, he told himself. But he couldn't think of anything. What was there to offer? The promise of new friends?

How could they do this to her?

He sat and tuned the guitar, then softly strummed the mellowest chord progressions he could manage. He found himself humming the words to a Hebrew folk song called "Shores Are Sometimes" that he and Joel had learned together, in Joel's dorm room on Mount Scopus, the Hebrew-English dictionary between them on the floor.

> *Shores are sometimes longings for a stream*
> *Once I saw a shore*
> *deserted by its stream*
> *left with a broken heart of sand and stone.*
> *So may a man*
> *be left abandoned spent and worn*
> *just like the shore.*

He remembered the sound of their voices rising in unison—he could hear it so clearly! Joel had a heartier voice than Daniel's, while Daniel's was richer and more textured. He closed his eyes and tried to press the memory into his mind so he'd never forget it.

Matt sang with him sometimes too, and he had the best voice of all, a lovely tuneful tenor. When they first started living together, he had been embarrassed to join in with Daniel, joking that his irony forbade him to encourage the corny Kumbaya action. But he was drawn irresistibly to the clean, resonant sound of Daniel's guitar, and before long, Daniel had him sitting with him as night fell, softly singing.

"That's a sad song," Gal said around the thumb still in her mouth, and Daniel said, "It sure is." She sat up on her bed and slapped at her eyes the way she wiped them, a gesture that always made him wince, it looked so punishing. She rose and went to the Noah's Ark box, reached in and took out some animal pairs in her fist. "Why don't any of these have a boy and a boy together?" she asked.

He looked up at her, laughing with surprise, and pulled her into his lap for a rough nuzzle.

THAT EVENING, HE TRIED to reach Matt but kept getting the machine. Where the hell was he? It was early morning in Northampton. *He'd better not be having an affair*, he thought—not while his own days were composed of one mind-numbing task after another, among either bureaucrats or children. He thought of calling Derrick's, but it was too early. The need to talk to Matt brimmed and swelled in him, and Daniel cursed him for being absent when he needed him most. He despaired of its success, but he had to run it by him anyway, had to propose again that they stay in Israel, at least for a few years. The reasoning seemed so unanswerable to him. And even if Matt couldn't live here, maybe they could spend a year apart.

When the kids were asleep, he told his parents he had something he had to talk to them about, and told them his idea. They looked at him, stunned.

"We've made all these preparations for leaving, we have unrefundable plane tickets," his father said. "Are you sure you've thought this through?"

His mother's face was pale and taut. "Honey," she said. "I know it's hard to take Gal away from her home—"

"We really don't need to," Daniel interrupted.

"What about your job?" his father asked.

"I'd resign. But I'm sure I could find freelance editing work here." Daniel was eager and rational.

His mother's voice trembled. "I don't think I could lose two sons."

"Mom, please don't be melodramatic. You could come here all the time."

"Daniel," his father said. "We have a plan, a plan that we've made together after a lot of thought, and I think we should stick to it."

They went to sleep troubled, his mother in tears, and in the morning they carried on a coded conversation with the two children nearby. "Let's ask her," Daniel said in a low voice, gesturing toward Gal.

"Don't you dare!" his mother said, steering him out of the room with a pincer's grip on his elbow. When they were in his room, and he'd yanked his arm away, she hissed, "Do not make that child decide. This is an adult's decision. You cannot put the burden on her."

Daniel slumped onto the desk chair and averted his gaze, unable to look at her, she was thrumming with such anger and resolve. He was aware that he had been stupid to suggest they ask Gal, and rankled that he'd lost ground in their argument by doing so. "I thought you didn't want her raised by Matt," he said, sending out his last-resort salvo.

"I don't," she said. And then there was a rustle at the front door and they heard a delighted shout from Gal. Lydia turned; Daniel stood and emerged from the room, stopped in surprise.

It was Matt himself, disheveled and smiling, a small bag slung over his shoulder, which he dropped as Gal ran up and flung her arms around his hips, crying, "Mordechai, you came back!"

He bent and squeezed her, kissed her hair; the baby let out a squeak and banged his spoon on his tray. Daniel and his parents stared at Matt, amazed. "Surprise," he said, with a sheepish shrug.

Daniel was still in the shorts and T-shirt he'd slept in, morning stubble dotting his chin. "I couldn't reach you on the phone," he said idiotically.

"Well, that must be because I was in the air coming to be with you, honey," Matt said, stepping forward. His shirt was damp at the armpits, and he leaned in, his lips approaching Daniel's, then turning to kiss his cheek.

"I really . . ." Daniel said, and then could go no further.

His parents were standing with their arms crossed.

"Hi, Lydia. Hi, Sam," Matt said.

"We were just going to take the kids to the park," Lydia said, and started whisking everyone together as Gal hopped around and yelled, "No! No! Mordechai is here!"

"Was it something I said?" Matt asked comically. His stomach was sinking. He'd clearly walked into something bad; this had been a mistake after all.

"Of course not," Lydia said, her eyes resolutely fixed on Gal, who was being steered by Sam to where her sandals lay on the floor.

"I was just kidding."

And then they were gone. Matt looked at Daniel, whose face was tense and who wasn't meeting his eyes. *Great*, he thought. He walked into the living room and set down his bag, then went into the kitchen to put on some water for coffee. His face was greasy from travel; he ran cold water in the sink, stooped and washed his face. He rose dripping and ripped a sizable piece of paper towel off the roll to blot himself dry with.

"Matt, I can't," Daniel was saying. "I tried to call."

"Can't what?" He turned, his heart pounding. This was it, Daniel was going to break up with him.

"I can't take them back, I can't do that to Gal."

Matt sat on a kitchen chair, letting the words buzz around him without landing. Because once they landed, catastrophe would ensue.

"Matt." Daniel kneeled at his feet and grasped his hands. "Please understand." His face was stricken, his brown eyes huge.

Matt was nodding reflexively.

"That would mean living without me," he said, feeling the words come out of his automaton's mouth, saying the words that logically followed the thing Daniel had said. "Is that what you want?"

"No," Daniel said, tears spilling over his face.

Matt nodded. *Nod, nod, nod:* That was the way you were supposed to respond to somebody's words.

But then he could hold them off no longer; the words landed, and adrenaline surged through him, making him gasp, making him feel like one of those people who could lift cars off of children. "Daniel," he said. He remembered something—see? Adrenaline!—"Ilana asked you to take them away from here if anything happened to them."

"No she didn't," Daniel said.

"She did! You've told me the story dozens of times, and in every version she asks you to! She says, 'Daniel, take them away from here!'"

Daniel sat back on his heels, then crumpled till he was sitting on the floor. "I can't stand it," Daniel cried. "I can't."

Matt stood and carefully turned off the kettle, then sat in the chair above Daniel, bent over him, so that their foreheads touched. "Honey," he breathed.

"How can I leave him behind?"

"What?" Matt whispered. "Who?"

And then he slid to the floor and wrapped Daniel in his arms. He stroked and rocked him for a long time, thinking about Daniel walking around in Joel's clothes, about the two of them in the womb together, how they'd been together since before they were even human. They'd started out breathing that strange element together, their tiny astronaut bodies floating, bumping against each other in silent salutation, and then they came out with their wrinkly, scaly human flesh, and then they grew and filled out. And then their lives and desires drew them apart, and now those two bodies were going to be buried on different continents. The thought gave him chills, and he gripped Daniel tightly, feeling like the slimmest and most inadequate of lifelines.

"It's like . . ." Daniel's voice caught. "It's like, okay, I won. I won, and he lost."

"What do you mean?"

"It's like, Joel was always barging ahead, making all the noise. Now he's dead, and all that's left is me." He closed his eyes as tears overwhelmed him again. The tiny sound with which he said the word *me* made Matt grip his hands.

"That's a lot! A lot that's left!"

Daniel shook his head, his shoulders deflated.

Matt asked, "Do you feel like he abandoned you?"

"No, I feel like I'm abandoning *him*," he said. "I feel like he got punished, and I . . . I could have been like him, I just pulled back and let him step into the limelight so I could have"—his lip curled—"so I could have my precious quiet space by myself."

Matt didn't get it. It sounded as though he were saying that he'd tricked Joel, let him walk into the path of the bomb. He stroked Daniel's hands with his thumbs and tried to sit quietly and just listen, not to say that that sounded crazy to him, not to try to make Daniel think the right thing. Meanwhile, a hope was racing through him, a hope that, whatever Daniel was thinking, realizing it and facing it would help him let go of this craziness about staying in Israel, would help him come home.

"Do you know what I mean?" Daniel said, looking at him with heartbreaking hopefulness, those killer Rosen eyelashes stuck together by tears into dark spikes.

"Not really, baby," Matt said gently. "But I get how hard it must be to leave him here." In fact, once he said that, Matt also felt a searing sadness about leaving Joel and Ilana.

Daniel sighed a long tremulous sigh and staggered to his feet. He told Matt he had to go out, alone, and left the house without telling anyone where he was going, so that Matt had to eat an awkward dinner alone with Sam and Lydia and the kids, in which Lydia fretted over whether, now that he was there, they'd all fit into the cab to the airport.

Daniel came back three hours later, calmer, sunburned. He'd been sitting at Joel's grave, Matt knew, and had forgotten to put on sunscreen. He didn't want to eat anything, and he had a terrible headache. "You're dehydrated, honey," his mother said. "See?"—touching his arm—"Dried salt."

Gal peered at it. "*Och*, Dani, you must drink," she admonished with a grave look, the experienced veteran of many a sun-drenched Middle Eastern field trip.

"Here, Gal," Lydia said, holding a glass of water toward her. "Bring this to your uncle, and make sure he drinks it."

The two of them forced glasses of water on him until there were three glasses sitting in front of him at a time, which made them laugh.

"Is everybody ready to go home?" Daniel asked.

They turned to look at him sprawled in the chair, his eyes swollen by tears and sun but bright and steady. Daniel's eyes.

"Yes," they whispered.

THEY LEFT ON A late-night flight. The Grossmans came over a few hours before, with small, fragile smiles on their faces. Malka was wearing a pretty dress, and makeup to hide the dark circles around her storm cloud–colored eyes. They sat on the couch, holding Noam and talking nonsense to him, as Matt and Daniel and Sam zipped up suitcases and Gal ran manically around the house. Daniel caught her as she ran from one room to another and said, "Gal, come say good-bye to your grandparents."

"Good-bye!" she bellowed.

Daniel laughed, and brought her over to the small hushed space of the couch. "My father gave her a brownie," he told them, "and now she has a sugar high."

"Gal-Gal," Malka said. "I have something for you." She reached into her purse and pulled out a small box.

"Thank you!" Gal said, the gracious gift recipient. "Oh, Savta, this is pretty!" It was a small silver necklace, a *chai*, from the Hebrew word for "life." She turned around so her grandmother could clasp it behind her neck and then fell on Malka and grasped her around the neck. Malka's face was bright over her shoulder. Then, leaning over Noam, Gal gave her grandfather a big noisy kiss on his cheek.

"We have something for you, too," Daniel said, and Gal pulled away saying "Right!" and ran into her bedroom. She emerged shyly, holding in front of her with two hands a gift that Sam had made and Lydia had beautifully wrapped.

"What could this be?" Yaakov asked, while Malka murmured, "You really didn't have to." The baby reached for the shiny ribbon, his eyes glittering.

"No, Noam!" Gal instructed.

"You open it," Malka told Yaakov, and he handed the baby to her and worked delicately at the paper with his big stubby fingers.

Sam had found a picture of the whole family—Joel, Ilana, and the kids—in a pile of pictures that hadn't yet been put into an album. It had been taken at the beach, and they were all in bathing suits, sprawled together on a towel, Noam in a diaper, the kids both caked with sand, Gal chewing a peach that was dripping over her fingers. They all looked windswept and relaxed, but the eye was drawn primarily to Ilana, who was sitting with her legs stretched out, leaning back on her hands, her eyes closed, raising her face to the sun.

Sam had had it enlarged and framed in a gorgeous, simple wood frame.

Gal hovered over them as they took it in. "Doesn't Ema look like a movie star?" she asked.

"Yes, she does," Malka whispered.

"So now you can remember us," Gal said.

"Oh, *motek*, it doesn't take a picture to remember you," Yaakov said, his voice husky.

Daniel was sitting on the edge of the armchair. "We're hoping you'll come visit us for Chanukah," he said. "And we'll be back for Purim."

They nodded, unhearing, looking at the picture.

Leora and her parents arrived, and the Grossmans said good-bye, clutching the children with ashen faces, Gal chirping, "We'll see you soon! Very soon!" Lydia had packed the perishables from the refrigerator and freezer into a box, and she pressed it upon them to take it home, so they left the house bearing leftovers. Excruciating symbolism, Daniel thought.

Gal and Leora disappeared into her room, and Gabrielle hovered around tearfully asking what she could do, until Matt finally dumped the baby into her arms. They'd sent the toys and baby stuff ahead, and they were essentially packed. Finally, after a cup of Nescafé that they drank quietly while standing, Gabrielle holding and nuzzling the baby, Daniel looked at his watch and they decided it was time to roust out the children. When the girls came out, Gal was clutching a small stuffed horse Leora had given her, and she wore the passive, polite expression on her face Daniel was becoming accustomed to—the look of someone accepting a slightly embarrassing prize. "Look, Ema!" Leora demanded, holding up the necklace she had clasped around her neck.

"Wow, that's beautiful, Gal-Gal," Gabrielle said. "What a fantastic sentiment, too."

They stood, nodding, smiling. "Well," Moti finally said. He hugged Daniel's parents, reaching for the easy ones first, and Gabrielle followed. Then he bent and lifted Gal into his arms. "You're a very special girl, Gali. Very special in our hearts."

She nodded solemnly, and he buried his bearded face into her face, looked over her shoulder at his wife with stricken eyes. Gabrielle was standing with an arm around Daniel, crying. She reached for Gal and squeezed hard, then set her down before Leora.

"Bye," Leora said.

"Bye," Gal said. "But it's not really good-bye, not *totally*, because we'll see each other again."

"C'mon, guys," Daniel said, "let me walk you to your car."

Afterward, he came up and checked the kids' room to make sure they hadn't forgotten anything. He picked up a pillow on Gal's bed to fluff it a little, and noticed a scrap of folded paper underneath it. Unfolding it, he saw that it was written in Gal's wavering and uneven print:

> *Dear Ema and Abba,*
> *I and Noam are at Uncle Dani's and Uncle Matt's.*
> *Love, Gal*

He laid it carefully back under the pillow, tears stinging his eyes. She'd learned only recently to write those letters, and some of them were still backward, and the spelling experimental. She'd learned how to address and sign off on a letter. Maybe the words would be magical, Daniel thought, thinking of the surprise that lit up Gal's face when any of them read aloud a word she'd written. Letters were already magical, the way they conjured actual words, which in turn conjured actual things. Maybe if she wrote them very correctly, very neatly, they could conjure her parents.

THEY SAT IN A *sherut* minibus with other families who had been picked up before them. Within minutes they'd skirted their neighborhood and were on the road to Tel Aviv. The sun had disappeared past any lingering glow behind the hills, giving the city an ashy look. Matt sat squeezed between Daniel and his father, Noam on his lap grabbing at this and that, and finally shoving the strap of Matt's carry-on bag into his mouth. *Here we go,* Matt thought, *here we go.* His heart was in his throat, but he thought that, for twenty hours or so, all he had to do was help move everyone from one place to another. He couldn't wait to get rid of Daniel's parents and start whatever life lay ahead for himself and Daniel and the kids.

Daniel closed his eyes until he was sure they'd passed the cemetery; he couldn't bear the idea of passing it in this direction and watching it fade away in the distance. He was surviving, he felt, by warding off, by stiff-arming at least half of what he felt at any given moment. It wasn't something you could afford to feel all at once. He was following Joel and Ilana's wishes: that was the part he let himself feel right now. He looked across at Gal, who sat staring solemnly at the other passengers, and then at his mother, her eyes closed and head held high, her arms wrapped around the purse on her lap.

They drove down and down some more, ears popping. The air on the bus grew warm, and the odors of the passengers—body odor, perfume, the cinnamon of someone's chewing gum—seemed to thaw and spread in the humid air. Noam whimpered, probably carsick, and Matt touched his face with the backs of his fingers. When they pulled up at the terminal, Matt forced his way out first and held the baby away from him, and Noam vomited, looked at what he'd done, and began to cry.

"Well, this is an auspicious start!" Matt said brightly, looking up from where he was squatting with the crying baby.

"I'm not going to throw up," Gal announced.

"Good girl," Sam said.

When they thought Noam was finished, they went into the terminal and got in the security line. It took about fifteen minutes to get to the agent, who asked for their tickets and passports.

They looked around and patted their pockets. "Matt?" Daniel asked. Matt had been carrying the bag with the passports and court papers.

Matt looked frantically at the bags piled onto the cart, and then looked up, eyes wide. He could barely bring himself to say it, contemplated lying for a moment and claiming that Lydia had been in charge of it. Then he said, "I left the bag on the *sherut*."

They looked at him, shocked. "How do I call the *sherut* company?" Daniel asked the agent.

"The taxi companies are over there," she said, pointing beyond the very end of their rapidly growing line.

Matt took off in that direction as she was telling them they'd have to step aside till they had their papers, and as Gal was crying, "My horse from Leora's in that bag!"

Shit shit shit, Matt thought, sprinting past Hasidim with monstrous suitcases, the stout Arab woman handing out fruit slices to her kids, the thousand baby strollers, and the men calling out orders to their families. He vaulted over baggage carts jutting out into his path. He arrived panting at the line for Shemesh cabs and broke to the front over loud protests. "My bag is on a *sherut*, I left it there!" he shouted to the woman in Hebrew.

"Wait a second, sir," she said with firm white-collar authority, giving him the Israeli hand signal for waiting, which he had thought was an obscene gesture before he'd learned what it meant.

"I can't! I can't! My passport, and the papers for the children—" He'd reached the limits of his Hebrew and switched into English, and then reached the limit of his breath altogether, and burst into tears.

"Okay, don't cry!" the woman said in alarm as people started falling back and staring. Someone patted him on the back, and an elderly gentleman in a white shirt came forward, offering to translate. "I can speak English," the clerk said irritably, tossing her long hair back as she put the phone receiver to her ear. "Everybody, please stand back." She looked at Matt. "What was the name on the reservation and what address did you leave from?"

He told her, and she made a call, and someone radioed out, and Matt heard her say, "Is it there?" and the tinny voice respond through the static, "Yes, here it is," and he clutched his hand to his chest and the people in line applauded and asked him teasingly if they needed to call an ambulance for him.

Meanwhile, Daniel had run over. "They found it, they found it," Matt said. "The driver's on his way."

Daniel doubled over in relief. "Jesus, Matt," he said. "Our papers are in there! What were you thinking?"

"I'm sorry," Matt said, steering Daniel off to the side so that this crowd of upstanding Israeli Samaritans wouldn't witness a fight between two hysterical queens. The adrenaline was just burning off; he could feel it prickle his fingers. "I was trying to get the baby out before he barfed all over us and the cab. I'm really sorry. They found it, it's okay now."

Daniel just shook his head. He was still shaking it and muttering to himself when the driver came up with the bag and they wrung his hand in thanks and headed back to Daniel's parents and the kids, who now stood anxiously at the back of a long, winding line. Matt had taken out the colorful patchwork stuffed horse Leora had given Gal, and was waving it in the air grinning, singing, "Ta-da!"

II

CHAPTER 10

O N A HOT day in July, in a Northampton backyard, Gal was hiding. She was being quiet quiet quiet: *"Shhh,"* she whispered, like Dani did when she was crying; the sound reminded her of her mother too, in a part of her mind balanced somewhere against the very back of her palate, rising sometimes like a taste, or like fumes, into her head. She had closed the shed door behind her; a line of fuzzy gray light marked its edge. She reached out her hands, feeling her way forward in the dark; she hit the handle of a lawn mower, and stubbed her sandaled foot on the edge of something else, and when the pain came, tears sprang to her eyes. In the back of the shed was a pile of cardboard boxes, some flattened, some thrown whole onto a sagging tower. She stepped behind it, and lowered herself onto the floor.

She rubbed a spiderweb off her face, once, twice, then a third time, hard. Her toe still smarted, and her arm glowed with the itch of mosquito bites. She pressed a fingernail into a bite on her elbow till the pain was as intense as the itch. *Try not to scratch,* Matt had instructed her as he rubbed ointment on them, squirted a slug of ointment on her finger so she could rub, too. In the yard, the boy, Yossi's son Rafi, crept, looking for her. He was deaf and had a machine in his ears; he spoke Hebrew with a flurry of hands and a muffled foghorn voice, and at first she'd had to try not to stare, knowing it was rude. They said he was her age, but he was littler, with flyaway curly hair almost as big again as his face. Matt said she had to play with him, so she was, even though she couldn't tell if he understood her when she spoke.

It was quiet here, and that felt good. In the daytime there were always people in the house, and Noam was crying because he was fussy or bumped his head, and someone would wave the others off, saying, "I'll get him." Dani and Matt's friends waggled their fingers ruefully at her, and she said, "Hi," and they asked her how she liked her purple room, and told her how excited Matt had been when he was painting it, and how much he couldn't wait for her and Noam to arrive. Most of them were homos—*gay*, Matt told her to say. Like Derrick, who was the first brown person she'd ever talked to, with his shaved head and big kind eyes, earrings that twinkled on both ears, like a girl's. And Cam, who Gal thought was a man until she heard her uncles talking about her; her mistake mortified her, and she kept it to herself. Agility obstacles were arranged throughout Cam's backyard, and Gal liked running through them, jumping over the jumps, weaving through the poles, crawling on all fours through the long cloth tunnel that she had to barge through face-first. Sometimes Cam let Xena out, and the dog would give Gal a scare by running at her heels and nipping; sometimes Gal had to stop because she didn't like it, although when Cam asked if she was scared, she always said no.

There was something draped over her, as though the sky was a different shade. The air was hot and heavy and damp, and she would forever associate humidity, and the infuriating whine of mosquitoes, with grief. The town she lived in now seemed to her like a circus. She walked with her uncles down the streets of Northampton: the square, honest New England brick buildings with their rippling slate roofs and steeples and clock towers ringed with strange and fascinating looming faces, girls with shaved heads and rings in their noses, fat women holding hands, teenagers crouching in doorways smoking and holding puppies with bandannas around their necks by the leash, men with beards and tattered green coats asking for a quarter. And whenever Daniel or Matt introduced her to a new person, that person beamed at her with a lacerating benevolence, and she had to turn her face away.

When she went back inside, Matt's mother would give her lemonade. Gal liked her plump hands and pillowy stomach, and the food she cooked, pancakes and bacon. The skin of her upper chest was blotchy and freckled, and Noam was quiet on her capable shoulder. In the colors Gal's mind formed, these new grandparents didn't stand out with the stark light of her other grandparents; they were paler, plumper, slower. Being around their stolid, warm shapes was like settling back in a beanbag chair. She didn't have to show them that she loved them because otherwise they'd be sad. They didn't pin her down with laser-beam looks and pepper her with questions to make her demonstrate her knowledge or show that she was okay, because even though Matt told them she spoke English, they didn't really believe she spoke it well. Instead, they patted her and said, "There, there." Matt laughed when she asked about this, said that it means "Everything is okay, don't worry."

She heard the clink of Yo-yo's collar and his big snuffling nose at the door of the shed. Fear blossomed in her heart; she hadn't thought of the dog, who would find her, and then the boy would follow him. He would find her and shout *"Boo!"* in his scary foghorn voice, and the prospect of that made her tremble. But what if he didn't, what if he came to the door and then walked away, leaving her alone in this dirty heap of crushed boxes? A gnawing mix of foreboding and shame filled her up till she sighed and closed her eyes. It was stupid, this hiding place, stupid. When he saw her there, he would know that she was just like the boxes, dirty and crushed.

She heard the clank of the latch as Rafi opened it, felt light arch over her, and then a shadow. She peeked up, heart pounding. He was standing over her, grinning, tapping his chest with two fingers. *"Matzati otach,"* he said. I found you.

. . . .

HE HAD A FEW hours to work while his mother tended to the kids and his father was at the hardware store investigating childproofing gadgets, so Matt was sitting at his computer in shorts and an undershirt, a fan stirring the papers beside him each time it rotated in that direction. To his surprise, his bid had won the design work for the new engineering school at Smith College, and he was both grateful for the regular income and panicky about whether he'd have the time to do the work well. He was trying to design a logo that would convey the idea of empowered women engaged in scientific pursuit, but, as he did whenever he had a moment to himself, he was thinking about Daniel, who, since they'd gotten home, had lost it, slowly but surely, like a tire with a tack in it. It was as though he'd realized that after expending a superhuman effort to get the kids in the first place, it wasn't going to stop, he had to continue working even harder to actually *raise* them.

Daniel's arms were thin and bony, and he was letting his beard grow; together with the weight he'd lost, it made him look older and more ascetic, a touch too rabbinical for even a matzo queen like Matt. Once, there had been a lusciousness about him, an offering of lips and belly and nipples, but it had burned off, leaving pure wire. He could hardly stand to be cared for or even looked at; where he used to lower his lashes shyly under Matt's gaze, he now turned away, evasive. When Matt reached out to touch him, he pulled away with a look of being vaguely put-upon.

In the mornings, Matt had to pull him out of bed and lead him to the shower while the kids dug into their heavy morning sleep. He had to keep him going for the family health care benefits; he knew that after a long absence, Daniel had to show up for work in a big way, and sometimes he was frightened because Daniel was forgetful and carried himself a little like a drunk.

His own emotions were in abeyance; he was just moving forward, helping Daniel function. When you were with someone for a long time, he reasoned, you didn't feel in love all the time; your love waxed and waned. He'd been attracted to other guys before, but their monogamy agreement was meant to deal with that, to provide an outlet and to acknowledge that, hey, it was likely to happen and it was okay. On days when Daniel was away and he was alone in the brisk air of his friendships and his work, enjoying the quiet in the house, Matt could imagine that if Daniel were to stay this way, it wouldn't be such a terrible thing.

And still, he tried to remember, to conjure out of thin air, the things he'd loved about Daniel in the first place. He remembered being with Daniel at a Northampton bar a few years ago, for their friend Mark's birthday, and being introduced to Mark's neighbor, a young guy, a kid, really, named Toby. Shy, long-haired, and husky-voiced, he worked with homeless people in Holyoke and was involved in the recent fracas over their tent shantytown. Mark, by way of introduction, had told them that Toby was a "sneaker freaker" and was working on a documentary about sneaker freakers. They had nodded sagely when he told them that, but when Toby turned away for a second, Daniel had leaned in and whispered, his lips touching Matt's ear, "We'll Google it later," making Matt quake with silent laughter. There were about twenty people at a long table littered with bar appetizers, drinking margaritas and beer and gin and tonics, leather jackets and Windbreakers flung on the backs of their chairs. Matt and Daniel had talked to Toby for a while, and found him not only smart and sweet but so beautiful he gave Matt a headache. Toby slipped out early, saying he had to get to another birthday party, and they left shortly afterward. Out on the warmly lit downtown street, Daniel had turned to Matt and said, "Oh my God. Oh my God! Was that the yummiest boy you've ever seen, or what?!" And Matt had hopped up and down and yelled, "I know!"

In bed that night they were having sex in their tried-and-true mode, using the shorthand of lovers who have been together for years, and whose bag of tricks no longer has the capacity to shock and awe. Then Matt had sung "Hello, Toby!" which made Daniel laugh. "Toby's on top of you," Matt whispered, fondling Daniel lazily and feeling his hard-on become urgent, "and I'm there, touching his ass—"

"Too fast!" Daniel panted, swatting away his hand.

"Oh." Matt backed up, and his mind moved quickly over the narrative requirements of this fantasy. Getting them seated in an advantageous arrangement at the bar. Getting everyone else who had been there out of the way. "Mark's gone off to the bathroom," he said. "Toby's feet are up on a chair. Dan, you're admiring his sneakers. 'What great sneakers these are!'" *Or whatever the hell way you're supposed to admire a sneaker freaker's sneakers*, he thought. "You're pulling gently on the laces—"

"Too slow!" Daniel yelped. "Enough with the sneakers!"

An indignant look came over Matt's face. "But it's his fetish!"

Daniel's head popped up from the pillow, his face no longer rapt, just red. "Yeah, but it's not *mine!*"

They had giggled till they were weak, and made love with the remnants of excitement combined with affectionate goofiness. That's what Matt had thought would carry them into the future when the initial passion settled and waned: their affection and gameness, their ingenuity at making fire out of the sparks created by other people. He'd been proud of his willingness to be that way, proud of his own maturity.

From the window he caught a flash of Yossi's kid darting around, peering behind the trellis and looking up into the trees. He wondered whether it was okay in the year 2003 to let the kids out by themselves to roam the neighborhood backyards, but knew that if he called them in, the house would be louder. Plus, it had to be good that they weren't sitting glassy-eyed in front of a PlayStation. He himself had spent entire summers outside. He supposed that if he'd had a different kind of mother, he might have spent his time at her dressing table, in a room where the shades had been drawn against the heat, smelling her various potions, maybe daring to draw her rouge brush lightly across his cheeks. But his mother didn't even possess a dressing table, so instead he'd meandered on his bike around the neighborhood, past the driveways where groups of small boys debated the rules of their games in shrill voices. He remembered the heat shimmering off of the blacktop, feeling superior to them and left out, with equal keenness.

.   .   .   .

THE FIRST WEEKS HOME, it seemed he went daily to Target with the kids to solve some urgent child-gear need while Daniel was at work. Noam whimpered in the shopping cart basket and Gal staggered alongside them, ashen, red-eyed, lips and nose chapped, blinking against the assaultive lights. The other shoppers looked sharply at them and asked if they were okay, and considered him doubtfully—a blond man with two dark-haired children—when he said that they were. Gal asked him anxiously if he'd brought money with him. He thought he should probably buy them clothes, but he was shocked at what he found: the pitiless rigor with which they were divided into girls' clothes, which were all pink and covered with flowers and butterflies and sparkles, and boys' clothes, which were all camouflage or said things like *Future MVP* or *Born to Build*. And the toys too, every one of them sporting a logo or design of a Disney character. He went in wanting to buy the kids something and leaving without one single toy.

And then at home, whirling with chores. He'd known that once the kids came, the house would be chaotic, but somehow that hadn't prepared him for the crap all over the floor, the clothes strewn on beds and over chairs, dishes piled up in the sink. Lydia and Sam had come only a week after their arrival, against both his and Daniel's wishes; they simply hadn't been able to keep them away. And while they meant to help, and were thoughtful enough to stay in a hotel, Matt's experience was constant grocery shopping, making dinners for six people, fleeing into his study to escape the many forms—irritability, exhaustion, compulsiveness—taken by long-term grief, feeling as if he and Daniel were still waiting to begin their real lives with the kids.

Quickly, pausing only briefly for regret, he and Daniel had decided to transform the dining room into a playroom, and moved the long pine table and its mix of chairs into the basement, bought a large area rug from Home Depot, a futon couch, and a wicker toy box, from which random tinkling music emanated at night when they walked by, making them stop in their tracks and put their hands on their lurching hearts. Everywhere he walked, Matt picked something up or washed something. He turned to pick up some shoes, and while he was in the front hall, he charged the cell phones and picked up a cup that'd been left on the hall table. He brought the cup into the kitchen and while he was there, whirled around, emptying the dishwasher and getting the dog water, and finding a piece of a toy Gal had been looking for. He took that into her room and plugged it into the toy, then turned in circles in her room, hanging her pajamas on a hook, making her bed. He took the garbage into the garage, where he noticed a dead mouse in one of the traps; opened up the trash, gloved his hand with a plastic bag, and lifted the trap with the rigid mouse inside it, dumped it into the garbage, wondering, *What the hell will we tell the kids when they start discovering all the dead mice?* And tied up the trash again.

At night, the upstairs hallway was lit up like an airport runway with night-lights. They brought Noam to their bed because it was easier than getting up several times a night and going to him when he awoke to find that his pacifier had dropped from his mouth. In bed they could watch TV and just stick it back in. By morning, everybody was in his and Daniel's bed, including the dog. Their sleep was strenuous, cutting from one demanding dream to another to the rhythm of the air-conditioning unit, which hitched on and off from the whir of the fan to the rumbling vibration of the cooler. The sheets were pulled and wrung into rope. When his eyes opened to the early morning, the first thing Matt took in was a clutter of empty cups and bottles and balls of used tissues on the bedside table, left from the middle of the night when the kids awoke in tears and he fetched them things to drink, set Gal up on a bunch of pillows, and had her relate her complicated and nonsensical dreams to him and Daniel while they sleepily stroked her hair and vowed their undying protection during the scary parts, the parts with the witch or the monster. Matt would get out of bed and lower himself to the floor, his bony knees aching as they pressed on the hard wood, peer underneath the bed with a flashlight for her, and come back up with an all-clear, wiping dust off his feet before getting back under the covers.

Now, looking out the window down to the street, Matt saw two women walking slowly with a toddler swinging between them, and turning up their front path. The house was always full of people come to help—their friends, and now his parents, and the congregation of Beit Ahavah! Their neighbor Val, who lived three doors down on the other side from Cam, and whom they hadn't known at all till now, came over most days of the week with her four-year-old Lev in tow, and brought what seemed like half the Reform shul with her. He wasn't sure which ones these were. The lesbians from the shul all had dark hair, dramatic eyebrows, children adopted from China and Vietnam and Guatemala, or hard-won through various fertility techniques. They brought over coffee cakes, clothes their kids had outgrown, parenting guides as thick as metropolitan phone books. Twice now the house had grown so full it was like an impromptu lesbian party, women on the couch and floor with toys between their hairy legs, Noam catching their eyes and holding out toys to them in a quest for their bewitching *Thank yous*! They dispensed advice to Matt and joked self-deprecatingly about their own initial forays into parenthood, when their own nice houses had become pigsties and they'd become incapable of conducting the most rudimentary adult conversation, so busy were they being locked into power struggles with their two-year-olds, who threw screaming fits because their moms had cut their toast into rectangular halves instead of on the diagonal.

Matt heard the doorbell, a swell of voices downstairs, his mother's polite greeting voice. He should go down and mediate, he thought, but then changed his mind: his mother would just shoo him back upstairs. She'd developed a kind of flair for being around Jewish lesbians, whom she called "the gals." She'd tell him and Daniel about so-and-so's struggle to get pregnant and the strain it had placed on her relationship, and explain the intricacies of in vitro fertilization, which she familiarly called IVF, an explanation that necessitated an air drawing of the cervix and ovaries, which made Daniel and Matt and Matt's father exchange alarmed glances.

He was stunned by this new life, the mess of it, the people—some of whom he knew, some of whom were complete strangers—letting themselves in and out of the house, the front door wide open all day long, people swiping mosquitoes off the open margarine tub in the kitchen, his bare feet sticky from dirt and humidity on the wood floors. Stunned. Home had always been where he went to get *away* from his family. Now his house was blown apart, the wind and the grief blowing through it. But a small part of him felt like a flower. He reveled in the sensuality of the kids' baby skin and their hair and the breath sifting raggedly from their mouths. He wasn't getting laid, but he was finding in himself a new kind of desire, milder and wider and sweeter than libido, that spread out onto all the living creatures under his care.

IT WAS RAFI'S TURN to hide. Gal rested her forehead on her arms, which rested against a tree, shut her eyes, and began counting to forty in Hebrew. The air was still and the shrill buzz of crickets elicited a semiconscious memory of the electric station down the street from her apartment in Jerusalem. Her mind glanced off of this and that till she lost count. An impulse of strict conscientiousness made her decide that the rule was, if you lost count, you had to go back to the beginning. She began again.

When she was done, she stood back and surveyed the yard with a raised head and narrowed eyes. She felt as if she were in a movie about a little girl searching for a hiding little boy.

It wasn't a good yard for hide-and-seek; it was small and neat, the grass trimmed yesterday by Matt's father, who said she could call him Grampa or Grampa John or just John. Its only ornaments were the flowers that grew along the fence and the feeders and stone birdbath that Matt let her fill with the hose, showing her how to hold her finger over the nozzle to direct and intensify the stream. You had to go into the neighbors' yards, the ones that drew closer to the woods, to find the sheds and dense bushes and raised decks you could shimmy under on your stomach, startling the cats sleeping under them. And of course the agility obstacles in Cam's yard, which was the first place Gal headed, ducking into the small opening in the shrubs that divided the two lawns.

There was a lump in the middle of the cloth tunnel. Where was his head? She thought her parents may have been buried without heads. That was a secret thought she had, something that nobody was telling her.

She walked up to Rafi and stopped, her heart pounding. He was lying down, trying to make himself as flat as possible in the space between the round opening of the tunnel and where it trailed on the ground. She knew he couldn't hear her approach. She wondered whether if she tapped him, she could make him jump. She stuck out her finger and held it hovering over his body. Would the little girl be mean and scare the little boy? Then she withdrew it, and instead tugged a little at the cloth, to warn him of her approach. The lump stirred, and she laughed as he thrashed his way out, red-faced.

STARING AT THE COMPUTER screen, his mind going through the motions, Matt heard his father come home and the exchange of voices with his mother. He felt a surge of guilty gratitude for their unhurried, unflappable presences in the house. When he'd called to say the kids had arrived, Shirley made him repeat the foreign names several times ("Let me put your father on. How do you spell that? Wait, let me write it down"). She'd said, "Those poor babies," and "Well, I know you have a lot of tenderness in you, Matt, for all you don't always want people to see it." This shocked him, that she'd seen something about him. And they'd immediately made plans to come out to meet the "little Jewish grandbabies," as his mother referred to them. They slept on an air mattress on the living room floor, and the kids lounged on it during the day, watching *Oprah* or *Judge Judy* with Matt's mother, and dragged the blankets around. He had to acknowledge that his parents were helpful with the kids, but their presence made something catch and strain in his throat. Did this mean that they could now come anytime they wanted to? Did it mean that they were a genuine part of one another's lives now?

He went downstairs when Yossi came to pick up Rafi, and Daniel got home from a late meeting as Matt and Shirley were cleaning up from dinner. They ate dinner at five now, which Matt called "gracious living chez Rosen-Greene." The baby sat on the kitchen floor, and Matt's father was placing Noam's favorite toy just out of his reach to encourage him to walk toward him. It was a plastic playhouse where, when you pressed down one of the buttons, a woman's voice cooed "Hello, Daddy" in a voice so licentious and inappropriate Matt insisted on playing it for everybody who came to visit. John stooped and held Noam's hands with his own thick freckled ones, their arms extended in a bow, and he was chanting, "C'mon, buddy. That's the stuff!" while the toy coquetted, "When Daddy comes home, it's a happy sound. Everyone smiles when Daddy's around. Daddy!"

"Hello, Daddy," Matt said suggestively, sidling up and giving Daniel a kiss on the cheek.

"Honey, not in front of the children," Daniel said with a faint smile. Matt turned away and returned to the sink, where he'd been scraping spaghetti off of plates into the garbage. To him, that comment wasn't funny, it just sounded like another way to brush him off. "Crap," he said, noticing a small splash of spaghetti sauce spots on his white T-shirt.

Daniel set his briefcase down on the floor at the doorway to the hall. "Where's Gal?"

"Off watching TV," Matt said.

Daniel went to the refrigerator and got a beer. He sat down at a kitchen chair pulled askew from the table.

"Let me heat you up a plate," Matt's mother said.

"Thanks, Shirley," he said. "That's nice of you."

"Matt," Daniel said, "Val called me at work today. Apparently, we've been discussed at the Reform shul."

Matt turned. "You're kidding." He wasn't sure he liked that, although he'd warmed to Val pretty quickly, and God knows she was a big help. She and her husband, Adam, were true children of Northampton: Adam was an acupuncturist, and Val a massage therapist and yoga instructor. They were active members of the synagogue and of the local chapter of MoveOn, and Adam was on the board of the Men's Resource Center. They were involved in prayer circles and various rituals for life passages. They were both athletic, and took their kids on a lot of camping and cycling trips; you walked into their house, and the mudroom was crammed with hiking shoes caked with dried mud, hiking poles, snowshoes, cross-country skis, soccer balls, baseball gloves, lacrosse sticks, bike helmets. They were so hooked into nature and community they made Matt and Daniel feel like schmucks who hadn't really made an effort.

"No," Daniel said. "Val and Adam talked to the rabbi and 'informally mentioned'—that's what she said—that we were new friends of theirs, and then the rabbi talked about us in her sermon, or speech . . . what do they call it?"

"Don't ask me," Matt said. He was irritated and intrigued by this news. "What did she say about us? She doesn't even know us."

Daniel took a swig of beer. "It was just a brief mention, young children from a war-torn nation, something like that. I think the message was that Northampton is a peaceful town people can take refuge in, but that it's important to have a greater global consciousness. Anyway, it turns out that the features editor from the *Daily Hampshire Gazette* goes to that shul, and he called shortly after I spoke to Val to ask if he could write a story about us."

"What did you say?" Matt asked, weighing the prospect in his mind, thinking about the candid shot of him on the front page of *Ma'ariv*, which had inadvertently placed him in the center of the family while all the articles erased him completely.

"I said I had to think about it," Daniel said. "Don't you think it'll make everybody in this town feel sorry for us?"

Matt's mother murmured, "No. It's just compassion, that's all, there's nothing wrong with that."

Daniel considered. "Also," he added, "isn't it a little annoying the way everybody applauds fathers for simply raising children? If we were women, women raising children, it'd never be regarded as news-worthy."

"That's so true," Matt said. He and Daniel had both been on the receiving end of many a dazzling smile when they were out in public with the kids, and sometimes it pleased them while sometimes it grossed them out a little. People who'd never given them the time of day suddenly had a lot to say to them.

"I think you're reading too much into it," Shirley said, looking up from where she was bent over the dishwasher, trying to find space for one more sippy cup.

"Mom," Matt said, sounding even to his own ear like a whiny adolescent, the old trapped feeling worming its way into his throat.

"Hello, Daddy," Noam's toy cooed, and they laughed, and through his pacifier Noam laughed too, a big, phony social laugh, as he practiced how to be in a group laughing.

THEY LET GAL GO to bed in underpants and a T-shirt because all her pajamas were in the laundry, and they let her begin the night in their bed because even though it set a bad precedent, she was exhausted and looked as if she were on the brink of a tantrum. She was stretching out on the sheets of the big bed, cooled by the air conditioner, while Daniel closed the blinds against the summer twilight. She watched him as he tended to her, bringing a glass of water to the night table, switching on the bathroom night-light, fishing the book they'd been reading from under the covers at the foot of the bed, and, reacting to the sweetness and intimacy of being alone with him, the way that if she closed her eyes just a little, or just listened to his voice, she could imagine he was her father, said, "You're not my *abba*."

Daniel crawled onto the bed beside her, a little stung, even though he knew she was just experimenting—with the names for their relationship, with how bad or mean she was allowed to be.

"I don't think I'll ever call you Abba," she said speculatively, glancing sideways at him. In the vivid, shadowy landscape of her mind, something had happened to Daniel since they'd come to America; he'd caved in, like the mouth of an old man she'd once seen who had no teeth. When they came toward each other, she had to go soft, nervously avert her gaze, not knowing whether she'd bump into the solid man or walk right through him as if in a dream. Matt was big and spindly and light, and she could fling herself against him, even though his anger was sometimes blistering, and she might be tickled or stung. Daniel, though, was fringed in darkness. He'd sit with a book, staring vacantly into space; sometimes he walked by her without seeming to see her at all. There were moments when, at rest or at play, a strange fearful pressure built in her chest that made her feel as though there was a balloon trapped in there, bumping against her lungs, trying to break loose and take flight—and she had to struggle not to run, or howl.

"What will you call me?" he asked.

"Dani," she said.

"Okay."

The book was *Abba Oseh Bushot, My Father Always Embarrasses Me*. In Israel, it was a special book that Ema read to her, loudly, so Abba could overhear all the embarrassing things the *abba* in the book did to his little boy, Ephraim: singing loudly on the way to school, warning that if he didn't get a kiss when he left Ephraim at school, he'd have to kiss one of the other children, wearing shorts to Aunt Batya's wedding, sliding down in his seat and hiding behind his fingers at the scary parts in movies. They liked to pretend that her *abba* was as embarrassing as Ephraim's dad was.

Daniel read a page, lingered over the last line with his finger under it for Gal to read herself. The witty Hebrew prose pushed a smile behind his eyes and forehead. He loved the portrayal of the dad as a lazy and slovenly writer, the illustrations in which there was always someone looking at him askance, the way the mother was a cool customer, a newspaper reporter in heels and makeup who gave her son a quick kiss on her way out the door and who laughed at the father's eccentricities.

Partly, it was a book about how embarrassing it was to have a stay-at-home dad.

"Good job," he said to her, and turned the page.

It wasn't really a good job, Gal thought, because she knew the book by heart already. But Dani didn't know that because he wasn't there when her mother read it to her. His oblivion to that made her despair, which converted into peevishness. She snuggled more deeply into her pillows, sliding down from Daniel's armpit till his elbow hovered awkwardly around her face. She pushed it away with a put-upon sigh.

Daniel looked down at her slouchy demon self. "Gal, don't push, please; ask if I could please move my arm."

"You smell bad," she muttered.

Daniel closed his eyes. It was a refrain, one with curious power, and he and Matt had consulted about it. Breath? Body odor? Matt would sniff him all over and shrug. "You smell good to me." Recently they'd wondered if she meant simply that he smelled different from Joel.

"Okay, *buba*, I'm going to give you a kiss good-night, and I'll see you in the morning."

"I want to see my album," she said quickly.

Daniel rose and brought over the album her class had made for her before she left. It made a sticky sound as she opened it. She went through it and pointed to every child in every picture, naming him or her ritualistically in a mechanical voice, without lingering or musing. When she was finished, she thrust the book at Daniel and pulled the covers up to her chin.

He remembered the advice of her grief counselor, that he should offer words to her, words she could use to name the different shades of her grief. "You must really miss your friends," he said, aware that this was not his best effort. She'd been wearing on him since they'd gotten home to Northampton, and he was tired, and helping her find words for her feelings was starting to feel overrated. If she'd only let him hold her, as she had in the early days of their loss, he felt sure things would be better. These days when she got upset, her body stiffened and her voice got shrill. "Tell me what you're feeling," he'd say, and she'd shriek in his face or stomp out of the room.

When she didn't respond, he bent down, kissed her cheek, told her he loved her. He left the door ajar. Gal watched his hand slip along the door frame and out of sight, until he'd left her in the cool dark. She swallowed her desire to call after him. She looked toward the bathroom, where the night-light glimmered. Let's say she had to get there without touching her feet to the bedroom floor. Let's say that if she didn't, a terrorist would kill *her*, too. Could she do it? She could certainly climb onto the bottom slats of the bedside table. But how would she get onto the low dresser next to the bathroom door? Her mind worried it; she gazed at the drawers, which had little bits of clothing sticking out of the cracks, like tongues from the mouths of people concentrating hard. She knew that when Daniel and Matt went to bed, Daniel would go around and tuck all those clothes back into his dresser drawers, because he couldn't sleep unless all the closet doors and drawers were nicely shut, which made Matt laugh and call him OCD.

Her eyes scanned the floor. Matt's sandals were lying there, splayed, their buckles open. She could stand on them to get to the dresser; she imagined stepping down on the straps, the ball of her bare foot pressed by the buckle, pulling them out till she stood on the shiny-worn leather soles. She could do that, and then shuffle with them to the dresser, move everything—the coffee mug with spare change in it, the little wood box that held Matt's bracelets and rings, the bibs and rattles and half-full cups of water—carefully to the side, and get onto the dresser, knee-first. And from there, slide down onto the bathroom's tile floor, to safety.

T HEY CALL IT vanishing twin syndrome. The vanishing twin begins as a twin to another fetus, but disappears during the pregnancy, spontaneously aborting and absorbing into the other twin, the placenta, or the mother. It is believed that a significant number of singletons start out as twins.

Metaphorically speaking, he had always thought of himself as the vanishing twin. He knew that when he and Joel were infants, Joel cried for milk while he was a good baby who waited quietly in his crib to be fed. That, in high school, when Joel ran for president of the student council, he ran for treasurer because Joel wanted to be president so badly.

He was so self-sufficient and contained. He always chose the smaller piece—of cake, or of attention. And somewhere, in some tiny, proud place of his consciousness, he'd imagined that he'd be rewarded for it.

But instead there was this grotesque, vindictive punishment of Joel, a punishment straight out of ancient tragedy meted out by a tantrum-throwing god, in which Joel's children would be taken from him and given to Daniel to raise. In which Joel would die and Daniel would be featured in the newspaper, raising Joel's children.

He was in his office with the door ajar, his jacket hung over the back of his chair, his desk a mess of galleys. Looking at the picture of

himself and Matt with Gal and Noam on the front of the features section, Yo-yo's big head resting on Matt's knee, he had an uneasy feeling
that the article was unseemly, almost gloating. The article's headline
read "Children Find Shelter from Terror's Grip." In the picture, Gal was
on his lap, and his chin rested on her head. Matt sat back with one arm
behind him along the back of the couch, his T-shirt riding up; the baby
was on his lap and pressed against his other forearm with both hands
outstretched, trying to grab something—a rattle, Daniel remembered,
a rattle that the photographer, a hassled and stylish woman who had
described herself as "running catastrophically behind" that day, had
grabbed and shaken to get the kids' attention. The gesture had mortally
offended Gal, who was giving her famous petulant shrug.

How did the idea of *dad* carry so much marvelous emotional pull?
He'd always envied the natural masculine authority Joel accrued simply
by virtue of holding his children. So now he had it, too.

Why had he let them write the article at all, if not to gloat just a
little? To gloat about how the kids were his responsibility now, and to
show what a great and thoughtful job he was doing with them, what
a loving home they'd come into? He studied the picture, the intense,
propriety expression on his face. He looked like a patriarch in a yellowing photograph with scalloped edges. He had to admit to himself that a
secret feeling of exultation came over him whenever he called Gal and
Noam "my kids." At home he walked around in shorts and undershirts,
his chest hair curling up through the V of the neck, his upper arms,
hairless with long, light muscles, exposed. When he looked at himself
in the mirror he saw an image of manhood—strong and sweet—that
thrilled him. For a boy who was good at music but bad at sports, a teenager who felt there was a big hole where his sexual cachet should be,
this was a tremendous transformation.

How did the idea of *dad* carry so much marvelous emotional pull?
He'd always envied the natural masculine authority Joel accrued simply
by virtue of holding his children. So now he had it, too.

His stomach growled from a mix of hunger and nausea. Matt had made
him eat two soft-boiled eggs before he left the house. In the days before
Matt's parents had left, Shirley had taken to making him a mash of graham crackers and milk after dinner, into which she slipped a splash of half-

and-half. His pants were belted to the last buckle hole now, and his shirts sagged under the armpits. At night, in bed, he ran his fingertips over the prominent jut of his ribs, feeling them rise and fall with his breath, imagining how easily they could be smashed, shards driven into the soft, moist, pulsing organs underneath. He remembered one of the clichés of twinship that people used to pester him with, asking whether when his brother was hurt, he felt his pain. *No,* he'd scowl; to him, it was a stupid question. But now he could feel his body being ripped out of the world. What happened in your consciousness at that moment? Somehow he imagined it crying out *Whoa!*—bewildered over this thing that had never happened to it before, managing only the most banal and inadequate of responses.

He turned to the opening of the article:

> *Daniel Rosen and Matt Greene never expected their elegant*
> *Northampton home to be the refuge of two small, grieving children.*
> *The life partners of four years were thrown into turmoil four months*
> *ago when Rosen's brother, Joel, and sister-in-law, Ilana, were killed*
> *by a terrorist's bomb in a Jerusalem coffee shop. In their will, they*
> *had designated Rosen the guardian of their children—Gal, six, and*
> *Noam, one—should they predecease them.*
>
> *Rosen admits that he was surprised by that decision, and his*
> *eyes fill with tears when he talks about it. "There's such a powerful*
> *stigma against gay men raising children, especially in Israel, where*
> *it's unheard of. So my brother and Ilana were demonstrating an*
> *unusual degree of love and trust. That's how I see it."*
>
> *It took the couple three months to get the children to the U.S.,*
> *because the custody arrangement had to be approved by the Israeli*
> *courts. Rosen is grateful to be home, and to live in a community*
> *like Northampton, where people are accepting of two men raising*
> *children together.*

There was a passage about Matt; there was a section about Joel being an English-language talk-show host, and about his and Daniel's history at Jewish summer camp, and how that got them initially interested in Israel. "When asked about summer camp, the normally reserved Rosen lights up, and he says, 'I *lived* for camp!' It was there that the boys first learned Hebrew, and their love for Israel was cultivated." The rest of the paragraph covered Daniel's education at Oberlin, and his gradual transformation on the topic of the Israel-Palestine conflict. It got several details wrong, such as his major and the year he graduated. He paused for a minute, irritated, then decided it didn't matter. His eyes skipped ahead:

> *Rosen admits to having complicated feelings about the suicide bomber who killed his twin. "Look," he says, "the safety and prosperity of an entire society is based upon shutting the Palestinians up where they can't be seen. So I can understand trying to violently place yourself within the Israelis' field of vision, in a way they can't ignore. I don't condone it, but I do understand it."*

Reading that, he remembered the reporter sitting back in her chair and contemplating him. "You're a very understanding man," she'd said. "A forgiving one. If someone blew my brother up, I wouldn't be making these fine distinctions, I can tell you that."

Were the distinctions really so fine?

He folded the paper neatly and put it in his briefcase, and turned to the email messages waiting for him in his inbox.

AT HOME, MATT HAD the features section spread out on the kitchen counter, and he and Brent were reading, elbows resting on the counter, pricked by cracker crumbs, shoulder muscles pulsing through their T-shirts. The sun flooded through the kitchen's screen door, and at Matt's elbow, crackers lay cascaded out of a ripped sleeve, beside a container of hummus with its plastic top off. His parents had left the previous morning, and an airy, expansive feeling of being in charge of his own domain was mingling with irritation at Brent, who, before

Matt had brought in the paper, had been telling him a long story about something one of his colleagues had said that had made him anxious about his tenure case, which was coming up in the fall. Brent's book manuscript had been accepted by a great press, and as far as Matt could make out, he was a total rising star in his field. Now that his materials were all in, he had the summer to wait till his case came up. "There's nothing more you can do, right?" Matt had said. "So you might as well try to relax this summer."

Brent had been quiet for a moment, and Matt could tell that he was brooding about how little Matt understood about the complexity and direness of his situation. But he didn't have the energy to draw him out. He knew that made him a bad friend, but honestly, after what he'd been through in the past few months, it was a little hard to listen to Brent obsess over what was clearly a nonproblem.

Gal was upstairs in their bedroom watching *The Parent Trap* for the gajillionth time, and Matt had put Noam in the playpen with every single toy he had. He studied his own face in the picture. It was a good picture; he looked handsome; his gaze into the camera was self-assured and masculine, his hair flawlessly messy. It was a picture he wouldn't mind his old New York friends seeing, which weirdly seemed to be his criterion for what was acceptable and what wasn't, even though he didn't even care about them anymore. The dog sniffed around his ankles for crumbs. "Hey, Yo-yo," he said, "once you're in the public domain, there's no telling what can happen. Next thing you know we'll be seeing your head on a naked Labrador's body."

He scanned down the article to find his name.

Sitting on the floor, his partner, Matthew Greene, looks on with a small smile, his blond hair long and disheveled, and his long legs stretched out on the carpet as he leans back on his hands. He projects the aura of a man who belongs in a West Village nightclub rather than in a New England farmhouse, sitting on a crumb-strewn carpet remnant surrounded by toys and stuffed animals.

Matt tsked, irritated at how the writer was hammering at the urban gay male angle; his sensitive ear heard something smug in it. He put his finger on the paragraph. "She's all, 'Look at the shallow gay man brought down by a dose of the real world.'"

"Oh," Brent said, peering at it and wrinkling his nose. "I hate that."

They grunted, settled down, and read some more. The writer described Noam as "a genial butterball of a toddler," and wrote of Gal:

It was hardest to move the six-year-old, Gal (pronounced "Gahl"), who had the rich social life of the kindergartener in Israel, and who, while raised in a bilingual family, is now living in a new linguistic universe. Gal is full of penetrating questions, the thirty-eight-year-old magazine editor says, about what happened to her parents and about the dangers that she or her new guardians might face as well. "There's nothing you can say to her," Rosen admits, "that can really reassure her. If this happened to her parents, how can I convince her it won't happen to me or Matt? How can I convince her that it won't happen to her?"

THAT WAS AN EXCELLENT quote, Matt thought. Glancing at Brent, who was reading, his face sharp and intent, he had a small feeling of excitement over being in the paper; it brought back those urgent days when he had felt himself to be a rocky pier against which dark and stormy waters pitched. Certainly the storm was still there, somewhere, but it was buried now, somewhere in Daniel's strange disappearance, and indistinguishable from mind-numbing tedium—sitting on the floor, playing endless games of Spit, Chicken Cha Cha Cha, Gulo Gulo, Zooloretto, Tsuro (which Daniel called "Tsuris"), keeping Noam from putting Gal's Legos in his mouth, trying to retrieve the piece that had skittered under the couch without having to heave his whole long body off the floor and then sit down again, so slithering onto his stomach and reaching, fingers outstretched, grunting, spitting dust off his lips, a twinge shooting through his shoulder, while Noam said—mildly, regretfully—"Uh-oh."

There was a loud thump at the bottom of the stairs, then a flurry of pounding feet on the wood floors, and Gal came in, saying in Hebrew with affectionate condescension, "Mordechai, how are you, little uncle?"

"I'm fine, my diminutive niece," he replied. He tilted up her chin to examine the gap where her bottom front tooth had fallen out that morning. Her upper teeth were pushed a bit forward from thumb-sucking, and he wondered whether the adult ones would come in that way as well; he remembered someone once telling him that his kid's braces came with a little payment book, like a mortgage. "Where did you put it?" he asked, and she dug into her shorts pocket and pulled it out, held it out in her palm.

"Can I see?" Brent asked, and she held it out in front of him for a second, then closed her fist protectively. "How much does the tooth fairy give these days?"

"We don't know yet," Matt said. "She's probably off consulting her conversion charts from shekels to dollars right now. Hey, Gal, your picture is in the newspaper."

"Where?" She raised her arms so that Matt could lift her onto the counter beside him, and as he hoisted her he was glad his mother wasn't there to see her bare feet on a kitchen surface, which would put him in the category of people unfit to live in a nice home. "That's me!" Gal looked at him and at Brent with such astonishment they laughed.

"What does it say about me?" she demanded.

"Let's see," Matt murmured. "Try not to scratch." He grabbed her hand gently; her legs and ankles were studded with mosquito bites, some covered with Band-Aids because she'd scratched them till they bled.

He looked at the passage describing Gal again. What should he tell her? Normally, it was Daniel who was in charge of all the official stories about difficult things: where their parents were, where we went when we died, whether he and Daniel would die too, whether the Arabs were bad, why she had to listen to him and Matt even though they weren't her actual parents, why some of the women who came over looked like men. He let Daniel do it because he worried he'd get it wrong and Daniel would be mad at him for screwing up the kids even more. But it was clearly his turn here; her quick eyes were turned up at him, and there was no Daniel to judge his response. "It says," Matt told her, "that it was sad for you to leave Israel, and that you miss your parents very much, but you're adjusting to life in the U.S."

She nodded. "I'm adjusting," she said.

"Yes you are. You're a very brave girl," Matt said, touching her cheek.

"I could never be as brave as you, Gal," Brent said, shaking his head gravely.

She regarded him, taking his measure. "Your parents are alive?" she asked.

"Yes," Brent said.

"Mine are dead," she informed him.

"Honestly, I don't know how you put one foot in front of the other," he said.

Gal's eyes filled with mirth. "It's called walking!" she cried. "It's not very hard to do that!"

Brent laughed. "You're a funny kid," he said.

"Thank you very much!" Gal drawled, with scathing kid sarcasm, a recent acquisition she was enjoying taking out for a spin.

"She hates me," Brent mouthed to Matt.

ONCE THE PARENTS HAD all gone, the summer seemed to ripen and slow and warm. Noam was an urchin in a diaper, his skin warm and damp, dirt and crumbs stuck to the heels of his hands; Gal's tongue was stained purple and red from Popsicles. They enrolled her in swimming lessons with Rafi at the Y, and while a teenager worked with them on the different strokes for forty-five minutes, Matt plopped himself and Noam in the baby pool, holding the baby under the armpits and swirling him in the water to show him what floating felt like. At night they all huddled in Daniel and Matt's bed, the air crisp and cold, where they watched movies selected for their strong images of girls.

Matt enjoyed this, being on the big bed with Daniel, the kids, and the dog—enjoyed it despite the crumbs, despite the fact that before he went to sleep, he lay there thinking over and over, *Don't be a huge princess, it's just a crumb,* till he had to get up and brush off the sheet with long swipes. Just them, no parents, Noam and Daniel falling asleep midmovie, Daniel's light snore, Noam's cheeks working the pacifier, the clicking sound of his sucks, Gal's fierce, silent attentiveness. He'd lie back on the pillows and watch her face in profile, those crazy beautiful lashes of hers, wondering what kind of intense thoughts were churning away in there. One night they watched *Fly Away Home,* which, if Matt and Daniel had known it opened with a car crash that kills a girl's mother, they never would have brought home. Matt grabbed the DVD box and examined the back, where the summary began, "When a young girl loses her mother in a car crash . . . ," and passed it to Daniel, who'd chosen it, an acerbic little feeling brewing inside that it was ironic that *he* was considered the fuckup. Gal froze watching it, and they held their breath; she turned and looked each of them in the face. It was only when the father comes to fetch the little girl in New Zealand to take her to Canada that she spoke. She turned to them and said, "But he was her *real* father."

"Yes," Matt said. "Her biological father."

She blinked sadly at him. "That's really different," she said. She got up a few minutes later and went to bed, and he and Daniel argued briefly, in tight, insistent whispers, about whether to go talk to her, each implying that the other was dealing with her grief irresponsibly. Finally, Daniel got off the bed with a put-upon sigh and went to Gal's room. He came back a few minutes later, shrugging. "She doesn't want to talk about it," he said.

Later, as he brushed his teeth in his boxers, Noam sacked out in the middle of their bed, Matt inspected the small bulge at his stomach in the bathroom mirror. "You're gorgeous, Matt, relax," Daniel said.

"If you say it automatically like that, you lose all credibility," Matt said.

"Has the dog been out?" Daniel asked. They used passive voice to ask each other whether any one of their thousand daily tasks had been done, to avoid sounding accusatory even while they were in fact accusing each other.

"No," Matt said. "I made coffee and emptied the dishwasher."

They looked at each other steadily, with poorly suppressed challenge and irritation.

"Crap," Daniel said, pulling his T-shirt on and going back downstairs.

Noam was wearing only a diaper, his thumb in his mouth. Matt quietly pulled back the covers, punched and arranged pillows, and got into bed. When Daniel came back up, he got in bed on the other side of the baby, facing Matt.

"Are those thighs the juiciest things you've ever seen?" Matt whispered naughtily.

"Oh God, I know," Daniel said with a playful groan. He ran his finger gently across Noam's forehead, his eyes half-closed and soft. "You're all right, right, buddy?" he whispered.

They were a little worried about him; they'd read up on his developmental stage, and learned that at seventeen months, Noam was late walking. He could stand if they lifted him up by the hands and held on to him, but the moment they moved backward to encourage him to take a few steps, he lowered his bottom to the floor, straining at their hands. Nor was he speaking, any words at all save the syllables *da* and *na*, and while his demeanor was uniformly placid during the day, his eyes were evasive and he didn't respond readily to the sounds of his name when they called him. It hadn't occurred to either of them to worry about that—they just appreciated how easy he was, how you could set him in his playpen in the kitchen or Matt's study and he'd play happily with his toys without bothering you. But then, at Val's urging, and galvanized too by the way Noam loved going over to the stereo and turning it up to blasting, they'd taken him to the doctor for a hearing test. His hearing was normal, but the pediatrician had said that they couldn't rule out autism, at the mildest end of the spectrum. Daniel had been furious, and wanted to fire the pediatrician. "That's the most irresponsible thing to say!" he raged. "Noam's a sweet, beautiful boy who's been through unimaginable upheaval, and this jerk jumps to autism!" But they obsessively read everything they could find on autism on the Web anyway, and argued about whether Noam's passy, or growing up in a bilingual household, was responsible for delaying his speech. Matt knew that autism was unlikely. He saw the way Noam got engrossed with a toy and then brought it over to Gal so she'd admire it with him or show him what to do with it; he noticed his drowsy gaze when you rocked him, the way he reached up to hook his fingers over your lips or grasp onto your ear. He thought about the grief held by that little body, wondering whether by now it was anything more than an inchoate, restless drift of the organs, a confusion he'd moved past because it couldn't be settled. To his friends, Matt joked that Noam was "slow," dramatically mouthing the word.

Matt turned off the light and for a few moments the only sound was the lap of the dog's tongue as he washed himself. Then Daniel's voice came through the darkness. "I was talking to my dad tonight, telling him about the businesses on Green Street being uprooted for the new engineering school," he said. "He's certain they're being abundantly compensated."

Matt smiled. "Oh, well that's a relief," he said. It was a running joke between them, Sam's reflexive trust of powerful institutions. They lay with their fists tucked under their chests and chins. Desire stirred in Matt, and for the next hour, thoughts about their sexual future and the cluelessness of the privileged classes rankled him, until the air conditioner finally hummed him to sleep.

AS THE DAYS PASSED, Matt progressed on the engineering school project with decent speed, got his aesthetic groove back for a stretch of five glorious days in mid-August, fortified by patched-together babysitting and Daniel doing extra kids duty at night. A teenager named Michelle from a few streets away had left a flyer in their mailbox, offering babysitting services, and they went over to her house to meet her and her parents; they used her in the mornings when Matt was upstairs working. Val or Adam took the kids for playdate afternoons, above and beyond the call of duty, sending them home with painted faces, or fancy paper hats, beaded necklaces, bracelets, crowns made of flowers—always one especially extravagant item they were instructed to give to Matt.

It was corn season in the valley, and the kids were crazy about corn. Daniel bought half a dozen ears from a farm stand every day on his way home, and they boiled them for no more than three minutes and ate them with salt, because as Gal, quick study that she was, learned to say, "They're so sweet you don't *need* butter." It was her job to shuck, and she picked every single silk strand off and held it in the air to scrutinize it before depositing it in the garbage, or more likely, draping it onto the outside of the trash bag. "A little lesson in Zen mindfulness," Daniel commented to the fidgeting Matt.

The tobacco harvest began, farmers hanging the large, glossy leaves used for fine cigars in weathered and slatted tobacco barns. And the sunflowers were up, like crowds of periscopes sent up by inquisitive aliens, craning this way and that. Daniel and Matt let the machine take most of the calls, unless it was Val calling to offer them some new kind of fabulous favor. Most of the time, they didn't even pick up for Derrick and Brent, which made Matt feel deeply guilty; his friends had once been everything to him, and deserting them because he now had children seemed like an enormous violation of a queer ethical standard. While Daniel cooked dinner, they let Noam pull all the pots and pans out of the cabinet and play with spatulas and wooden spoons, and Matt lay on the floor with a colander on his head and the tea strainers over his eyes, croaking, "Take me to your leader." Then he took up a wooden spoon and, using it as a microphone, sidled up to Daniel as Daniel skewered vegetables for the grill, and sang:

'Cuz I'm a one man guy in the morning,
Same in the afternoon.
One man guy when the sun goes down,
I whistle me a one man tune.
One man guy, one man guy,
Only kind of guy to be,
I'm a one man guy, I'm a one man guy,
I'm a one man guy
Is me.

Daniel shimmied a chunk of purple onion onto a skewer and gave him a quizzical look. "Doesn't it end up that the guy is, like, himself?"

"That's if you keep that last stanza in there," Matt said, in the voice of a teacher energized by a smart student. "Which I don't."

"Aha," Daniel smiled. "I see."

YOSSI LEANED OVER GAL and showed her a mistake she'd made. They were working on writing down the months; they'd taken down the calendar from the kitchen wall and placed it on the table. She swung her bare feet and twirled her hair, feeling the edges of his body ruffle the edges of hers.

He was coming over twice a week to work with Gal; Matt's lessons with Yossi had become her lessons too as she worked on writing in Hebrew. There was something about Yossi's presence, Matt mused as he watched him focus on the child, one arm on the back of her chair, that made the family a little cuckoo. Although it made him feel like a jerk and he tried very hard not to, sometimes Matt found himself subtly competing with Gal for Yossi's affection and approval. And Daniel too changed imperceptibly around him, his body language more purposeful, less soft, his voice a note lower, Matt could swear, acting with him like a man among Israeli men, speaking in rapid Hebrew that elbowed the others out of the conversation. And Daniel always handled the money. They paid in cash, since Yossi's immigration status forbade him to work, and it somehow always worked out that it was Daniel who peeled off bills from his wallet, the way it was Matt who always brought the coffee or emptied and refilled the ice trays. It felt weird to Matt, as though Daniel were his father paying for his piano lessons, or as though he, Matt, were a housewife on a strict allowance.

Matt's own paper sat in front of him with neatly printed letters. Gal leaned over to look at it and said, "*Yofi*, Matt." Nice.

"Thanks." He and Yossi were working on the names for familial relationships, and starting to get esoteric as they pushed their way into the varieties of queer kinship. Matt had told him a story one of their friends from the shul, Rebecca, had told him about the nurse who'd checked her partner Jen into the hospital the night their son was about to be born. The nurse was visibly peeved about having to do the paperwork five minutes before her shift was supposed to end, and said to Rebecca as she was setting up Jen in bed, "So what will you be called? *Mee*-maw? *Moo*-maw?" honking the names with gleeful scorn.

"How do I say 'I'm your guardian,' although not legally, in kind of a pretend way?" he asked Yossi.

"Pretend is *c'ilu*," Gal said.

Yossi tapped his pen on Gal's paper in a command for her to do her own work. His hand was speckled with tiny flecks of paint.

"When are you going to let me see your studio?" Matt asked.

Gal looked up. Yossi had a trying-to-be-patient expression on his face, the way he looked when Rafi rejected a food before he'd even tasted it. "The law, it's *ha-chok*," he said. "Against the law: *neged ha-chok*. According to the law: *l'fee ha-chok*."

"*Ha-chok*," Matt said, with a juicy guttural *chet*. "Do you, like, incorporate political themes or violence in your work?"

"Why," Yossi said sharply, "because I'm Israeli I must incorporate politics?"

"Sheesh," Matt said. "I was just expressing an interest."

Gal wrote down, in Hebrew, *April May June*. She thought about

Judge Judy, who yelled at people who were too stupid to get a written contract or talked when it wasn't their turn, and she gazed at the calendar with narrowed eyes. Something had been working away at the edges of her memory since they'd sat down, and that, together with the combative tone coming from Yossi and Matt, set her on edge. It was a warm and cloudy afternoon, the kitchen almost dark enough to turn on the lights; a bee batted noisily against the screen door. "You know," Matt was saying, "some people would say that *not* incorporating politics is actually a political act."

Yossi gave him a cool look.

"I'm just saying," Matt said.

"Don't grip the pencil so hard, Gal," she heard Yossi say. "See, your knuckles are white!"

It worked at the edges of her memory and then moved away. She looked down at her hand and let go of the pencil; it rolled off the table and dropped to the floor.

THE STORY ABOUT THEIR family in the local paper was picked up by the AP wires and published by a Springfield paper, and soon after in the *Boston Globe*, as part of a larger story about gay and lesbian foster families; they found out about it from April, who scanned the papers daily. They got a call from a Boston TV station that wanted to feature them on a news program, but they turned it down, agreeing that a local story was one thing, but being a news sensation—and putting the kids in front of television cameras—was another. Gal was about to start school, and they didn't need her to be the object of this kind of attention as she was trying to integrate herself into a class of American first-graders.

At work, Daniel had gotten to a phase where sitting in his office concentrating on editing a story was the only thing that honed and quieted his mind. He reveled in his own expertise as he cut, rearranged, smoothed, corrected emphases, feeling like a carpenter doing fine finish work. They were increasing the magazine's Web presence, and he found that having lived with a graphic designer for four years had rubbed off on him and given him a broad sense of design possibility, so that together with his office's own Web person, he was helping create a fresher and hipper look for the magazine. He felt as though he had answered in the affirmative the unspoken question of whether he would return—really return—to the job they had held for him. Then one day in late August, April called him into her office and handed him a printed email, addressed to her and cc'd to the president. The first paragraph read:

> My deepest condolences to Daniel Rosen on the tragic loss of his brother and sister-in-law. I commend him for taking into his home the youngest victims of a terrorist's bomb, and for raising them in what appears to be a sensitive and caring way. But he appears not to understand that while he has the same right as any citizen to free speech, he holds a high-profile position at the College, and therefore has an obligation to represent it in a way befitting the enlightened values of the liberal arts. To say that he "understands" an act of terror is to defy those values absolutely. His position as College Editor cannot, must not, be used as a platform for what I can only call extremism.

HE LOOKED UP AT April, his heart sinking. "They read the story in the *Globe*," she said, handing it to him with the pages folded back to the article. Terrifyingly prepared, she had highlighted in yellow the paragraph where he talked about the terrorist.

"I wasn't speaking as college editor," he said, scanning it again for signs of extremism, or of having misspoken.

"That's what I told the president."

The president: he absorbed the fact that they had discussed him. "Am I in trouble?" he asked.

"No," she said. "I just wanted to let you know that this is happening. This isn't the only letter; it's the most judicious of the lot." She pulled out another letter. "This one basically says the same thing, but it adds, 'I pity Mr. Rosen, who will realize soon enough that when one has children, one cannot always afford the politically correct position.'" She looked up at him and he wondered why she'd felt compelled to read that to him. "And then there's the one that says, 'What's next? Inviting terrorists to speak on campus?'" The corners of her mouth rose in a wan attempt at wryness.

"What do you want me to do, April?" he asked.

"What's done is done," she said. "I just wanted to alert you to it."

"I didn't go to the *Boston Globe*," he said, provoked by the long-suffering quality he heard in her voice. "It was a local human interest story, for God's sake. I never imagined it would get picked up by the wires." He felt his throat catching with righteous intensity. "I turned down a request to be on a Boston TV news program, did you know that?"

"I didn't know that," April said.

"Are these people who wrote in important donors?" he asked.

She paused, then answered, "Not important ones."

How, he wondered, had he become this person—a needy liability at work, blamed for the bad things that happened to him? He was good at what he did, great at it even, he knew that. But now he felt like one of those single moms who's chronically late for her shitty, low-paying job because she has to take two buses to get there, and one is always late or packed to the gills with passengers and sailing past her as she frantically tries to wave it down.

"They weren't even big donors!" he raged to Matt when he got home. "So why did she feel it necessary to call me out? Did it hurt the college in any way? No. Did it affect my ability to do my job in any way? No. Did it have anything whatsoever to do with the fucking alumni magazine? No."

He was getting into the tight, hyperlogical argumentative mode he got in when he was truly furious. Matt, sitting at his desk, trying to get a little more work done before Michelle brought the kids home, knew that at any moment he might need to duck for cover. "She's an asshole," he said.

"I didn't do anything wrong," Daniel said. "I didn't have any control over it getting picked up by the AP wires—it didn't occur to me for one second that that would happen."

"No, you didn't."

Daniel glared at him. "Don't just say that because you think it's what you're supposed to say. Listen to what I'm saying," he said.

"I am listening! You didn't do anything wrong, Dan. I truly believe that, and I truly believe that April was just taking out some shit on you. She probably got called in by the president or something."

Daniel looked at him, scrutinized him down to his soul, to see if there was any part of him that worried about his competence, because that, truly, would be the last straw. But Matt mostly looked eager to return to his work. Daniel sighed with the petulance of a man who's tried to project his shame out into the world, but failed.

"Baby, I got to finish this," Matt said.

AND THEN IT WAS the end of the summer; Val sang Dar Williams: "It's the end of the summer, when you send your children to the moon." On the recommendation of a friend of Adam and Val's, they'd found a home day care for Noam, run by a woman with a three-year-old, who was only going to take in Noam and one other kid. Her name was Colleen, and Matt and Daniel were immediately taken by her sweet, watchful daughter and by Colleen's gentle energy, and by how, as they sat cross-legged on her living room floor talking to her about Noam's special circumstances, she listened quietly and thoughtfully, without any big reactions, and stroked his hair softly when he came and climbed in her lap.

But after all this time of being a trouper above and beyond what anyone could have expected with his new parents, Noam found day

care to be the last straw. In the first week, when they left him for just
an hour or two at a time, he cried inconsolably, almost the entire time.
Once or twice, gone rigid in the grip of a meltdown, he actually foamed
at the mouth, which, when they talked about it, made them laugh
uncomfortably. It was the first time he'd been even remotely difficult.
Daniel tried to project a sense of calm when he dropped him off in the
mornings, and he couldn't have asked more from Colleen, who crooned
to Noam as he writhed in her arms and never lost her cool or her compassion, but he had to pry Noam's hands off of his legs; and when he
picked him up during his lunch break to bring him home where Matt
would take over, Noam fell asleep almost the moment he was in Daniel's arms, which made Daniel want to die thinking of the effort he must
have put out to hang in there alone. He lugged the baby's deadweight
out to the car seat, where his head lolled as Daniel worked the buckles,
and as he drove him home his mind buzzed unpleasantly with possible
alternatives; he calculated what the family income would be if he quit
his job and stayed home with Noam, and had to keep telling himself
that Noam would have been in full-time day care in Israel, too.

They had enrolled Gal in Jackson Street School, where almost a
quarter of the kids who attended were being raised by queer couples, and
which was adored by everyone they talked to for its sense of community.
Daniel had brought Gal in to meet her new teacher, Ms. Wheeler, and
to see the classroom Gal would be spending the day in. There were five
tables around the room, each with a plastic container full of markers and
scissors set in the middle, surrounded by chairs with tennis balls stuck
onto the bottom of their legs. At one end of the room there was an alcove
with a colorful rug on the floor, for morning meeting. Paper chains and
cardboard birds and butterflies hung from the ceiling, and the walls
were covered with signs, pictures, charts, and a list of playground rules:
You can't say, you can't play, Go down *the slide, Kissing is for your family.* Ms.
Wheeler bent down to Gal when she spoke to her, and had her say her
name several times so she could get the pronunciation just right.

The next day, Matt took her to buy school supplies at Target, where she stared irritably at the ugly Hello Kitty and Dora the Explorer and Pretty Pony lunch boxes. "These ones must be for babies," she said.

"I don't think they are. Babies don't really use lunch boxes," Matt said tactfully. "But I get your point."

"Everything is ugly!" she said, kicking at the display and storming away from Matt, who clearly didn't know where the nice things were, who was going to make her go to her first day of school carrying a Hello Kitty lunch box. He watched her run around the corner, and sighed, bent to pick up the lunch boxes that had clattered onto the floor. The truth was, he didn't know the first thing about what kind of lunch box first-grade girls brought to school, and neither did she, which he knew must feel awful. He went after her and caught up to her, laid his hand on her shoulder to turn her around and talk it through, but she whirled, her face twisted, and dug her fingernails into his arm.

"Ow!" he yelped as she ran off again.

He followed her; each time he approached her she screamed "No!" and struck out at him. He walked out past the cashiers and sat in a chair at the Pizza Hut near the front doors, breathing hard, figuring that she'd be safe as long as she didn't leave the store. A few minutes passed, and then ten, and then he felt that he should look for her. But he was afraid to let the front doors out of his sight.

The pizza and popcorn smell was so intense he felt it must have been concocted in a laboratory somewhere. People were emerging from the cashiers, dazed and stately behind baskets full of bags, diaper boxes, lamps, tall boxes set on the diagonal. He ventured into the long aisle on the store side of the cashiers and began to walk it, his eyes raking over each aisle. He walked all the way to the electronics section, whipping around from time to time to make sure Gal wasn't behind him, then turned and walked back.

He found her standing near the front, gazing into a cooler of sodas and drawing a swirl on the door with her finger. He laid his palm gently on her head. "We'll find you something nice," he said. "I won't make you bring something ugly or babyish to school."

A tremor went through her. She was dreading starting school, where you couldn't kiss people or go up the slide. It seemed to her that once she started, it would mean she was never going back to Israel. And yet the sense of waiting was intolerable, too.

She let Matt lead her into the shimmering parking lot and take her home. They hadn't bought anything, and she hoped, fervently and futilely, that without supplies, there was no way she could go to school.

D ANIEL DROVE GAL to school the first few days and walked her into her classroom, but he soon realized that she was becoming anxious waiting for him to go, and he put her on the bus on the third day. The evening after her fourth day, during dinner, Matt and Daniel got a call from Ms. Wheeler. "Do you have a moment?" she asked Daniel.

"Sure," he said, and took the phone into the other room.

During yesterday's morning meeting, Ms. Wheeler told him, Gal had told the child she was partnered with that her parents were killed when a terrorist put a bomb in a café, and it blew off their heads. So when they were buried in the ground, she said, they didn't have heads. Then, apparently, the boy reported that to the class when it was his turn to show how well he'd listened. "It's not so much that the other children were disconcerted," Ms. Wheeler said, "although I did get a call from a few parents. I'm calling for Gal, to make sure that *she's* all right. And, actually, to find out if she was fabricating. Just so we can know what we're dealing with."

"Whew," Daniel said, his mind blank. "I don't know what to tell you. I am so in over my head here," he said, wincing at the inadvertent pun. "Can I talk to Gal and get back to you?"

He hung up, numb, and went back into the kitchen.

"What?" Matt asked.

Later, he mouthed.

Honestly, he didn't even have it in him to say; he felt dragged down by a lead weight. When, after Gal left the table, Matt finally got him to speak, what came out was sludgy.

"Wow," Matt said. "Why would Gal say that?"

Daniel shrugged. "To get attention? To aggress the other kids?"

They went up to her bedroom and knocked. "Don't be mad at her," Matt said.

"I'm not!" Daniel said, insulted.

She was sitting on her bed with a book, surrounded by all her horses and stuffed animals, which formed a neat ring around her. "Hey, Boo," Matt said.

"Hey," she said.

"Gal," Daniel said, easing himself down onto the corner of the bed. "Your teacher called. She said you told the other kids that your parents were buried without heads?"

Gal blushed furiously.

"Why would you say that?" Daniel asked, sitting on the bed.

"We're not angry, just curious," Matt said.

She looked at him, drawn into his curiosity. She could see Daniel's face in her peripheral vision, and even that glance made her grow hot, made her feel as if there were something wrong with her. She didn't know how to say why. Kids were sharing, and she had had this sudden powerful impulse to take her place among them. It had come from a glistening place in her, the cold water in a lake's deepest spot. Now, though, it seemed so wrong she could hardly look at them. "I wanted to share, too," she said, her voice wavering.

They exchanged glances.

"Gal," Daniel said gently, "your parents did have heads when they were buried."

She looked at him, and her expression was so full of shock and yearning and doubt that tears sprang to his eyes. "I'm not just saying that to make you feel better. You just misremembered. They were buried with heads."

She threw herself facedown onto her pillow. Daniel stroked her back; Matt, who'd been crouching by the bed, sat down heavily on the floor, remembering with a sickening feeling his own avid, terrified scans of their bodies under the sheets they were buried in. She cried something unintelligible into the pillow.

"What?" Daniel asked, lifting her by the shoulders. "I can't hear you, *buba*."

"I told everybody that they didn't!" she cried, her face scarlet and wet with tears.

"But isn't it good that they had heads?" Matt offered. "It must have been terrible to think they didn't."

"Yeah," Gal said, gulping and hiccupping.

She cried some more, and begged them not to make her go back to school, where she'd have to tell the class that what she had said was wrong, and then they would think she didn't even know how her parents were buried. "Please," she said over and over, her teeth chattering, while Daniel and Matt exchanged fierce and meaningful and appalled glances. The memory of her parents was slipping away from her; at night in bed she called to them, but the only images she could conjure were paltry and insubstantial. You couldn't try really hard to imagine them, you couldn't strain; they either came or they didn't.

"Okay," Daniel finally said. "You can stay home tomorrow. For one day only. And you have to let Matt work and not disturb him."

Later, as she and her brother slept in their bed and Daniel and Matt were brushing their teeth, Daniel said, "She's been carrying that image with her this whole time, and we didn't know. What other horrible ideas and images does she carry with her that we don't know about?"

"I know," Matt said through a mouthful of toothpaste. He spat. "I was thinking the same thing. She has this whole secret life in her head, so we can't even comfort her about it because we don't even know how to ask her about it."

"Do you think it's okay to let her stay home from school tomorrow? I don't want to set a precedent where every time she's upset she gets to stay home."

"I think it's okay this once," Matt said.

"Don't make it a huge treat, okay?"

"Okay," Matt said. "I'll make her sit in a corner, and only feed her cabbage."

Daniel realized that he had a pounding headache. Poor Gal, he thought, called on the carpet, for being—what? Inappropriate. Socially inept. A blurter. He knew exactly how she felt, confronted with words that had come from her heart, but which didn't mesh with her environment. The words came back at her blazing and crazy, revealing something deep and frightening about her that couldn't be unsaid. He knew exactly how she felt.

He rubbed the big muscle on the side of his neck. Matt came up behind him and massaged it gently, his other arm clasping Daniel's torso vertically, over his shoulder. He clasped Matt's massaging hand and squeezed it, then eased himself away and into the bedroom.

Early the next morning, Daniel called Gal's teacher and explained that she hadn't been trying to shock or scare the other kids in the class—that she actually believed that her parents were buried without heads, and felt that she was honestly sharing. As Ms. Wheeler murmured, "Oh boy" and "Man oh man," he told her that they'd be keeping her home for the day because she didn't know how to face the other students, now that she realized she'd told them something that wasn't true. "I think it's important to collaborate on a strategy for her, a way to tell the truth without her losing face, or feeling mortified," he said.

She told him she'd talk to the school psychologist for advice on how to help Gal do that.

He hung up and sat down at the table. "Maybe when I get home I can talk with Gal about how to make it comfortable for her to return to school."

"I can do that this afternoon, too," Matt said.

"You don't have to," Daniel said.

Matt closed his eyes, trying not to snap at him. The baby was slumped back on his lap, sucking loudly on a bottle of milk, stopping every once in a while to catch his breath with a big gulping sigh.

"What would you say?"

"I don't know what I'd say, Daniel. From your standpoint, I'd no doubt recommend she do something highly inappropriate." He didn't want to say it because it would sound mean and competitive, but he kind of felt that if Daniel would just leave the house already, he and Gal could work it out. Because he *got* her.

Half an hour later, having sent Daniel off with Noam, he made pancakes, against the small voice in his mind that was reminding him not to make the day a fun one. Gal came into the kitchen as he was spooning a ladle of batter into the pan, a small stack of finished pancakes sitting beside him on a plate on the counter, draped with paper towels.

"Pancakes!" she sighed dreamily, sitting on a kitchen chair in her monkey pajamas and plopping her elbows on the table.

He brought her the finished stack, and set butter and syrup on the table. "Do you want me to pour the syrup for you?" he asked.

"No, I can," she said, with mild indignation. As he returned to the pancakes in the pan, she wrestled the top off the syrup bottle and tipped it carefully, her hand trembling with concentration.

When Matt's pancakes were cooked, he brought them to the table and sat. He pushed the side of his fork into the stack and glanced up at Gal. "So. No heads, huh."

She shook her head through a thick mouthful.

"That must have been a crazy thing to imagine."

She nodded, and crammed another forkful into her mouth.

"Why didn't you say anything to us?"

Her eyes met his as she chewed, cheeks bulging. Yo-yo groaned from his station at Gal's feet and lay back; a lawn mower several doors down sputtered and roared. Gal swallowed. "I thought you already knew about it, and you didn't want to talk about it anymore. Especially Dani."

Matt nodded gently.

"Because if you knew your twin brother didn't have a head . . ." She trailed off and gave him a solemn look.

Sometimes, Matt couldn't believe the conversations he was having, couldn't believe the sequence of words and thoughts uttered in his presence. Had anybody on earth ever uttered that sequence of words, and what were the odds that anybody on earth ever would in the future?

"But *you* had to think that your mother and father didn't have heads! That's even worse!"

Gal considered this, shrugged. "But I knew that in heaven they have their heads."

"Okay." *In heaven,* Matt thought, *everybody will be reunited with his or her head.* "So when you said this in your class, how did the other kids react?"

"They just looked at me."

"Do you think they were freaked out?"

She laughed. "Maybe." She'd finished eating and was dragging the side of her fork into the pool of syrup that remained on her plate, then lifting it toward her outstretched tongue and licking it clean.

He watched her, a faint smile on his lips.

"I don't want to go back there," she said.

"Why?"

She gave him a miserable shrug. "Lots of those kids already know each other. I'm the only one who doesn't know anybody." There were other reasons too, reasons that didn't find their way into her conscious mind. Her accent, which made her the weird kid. The fact that many of them read better than she did in English, when she was used to being the smartest kid in the room.

"You'll make friends, Gal. It's only the first week of school!"

"I don't think I will make friends," she told him.

"Why not? You're a cute and fun kid. You know how to make friends—you had a lot of them in Israel."

She craned her head toward him and lowered her voice. "I don't think I'm so fun anymore." She was thinking about the small groups of kids who milled together talking about things, and how she sat by herself at a table, her stomach churning unpleasantly, trying to look busy with paper or markers or scissors, because she didn't know what to say, and couldn't bring herself to just stand among them silently.

His eyes stung when she said that. "Gal-Gal," he said, then cleared his throat and looked hard at her. "You've had a life unlike any other kid in your school. The hardest thing most of them have had to face is losing their favorite teddy bear, or falling down on the playground and getting a boo-boo."

She cracked a reluctant smile.

"Honestly," he insisted. "Not one of them has had to be as brave as you have to be every day. So if you're not the funnest kid in the class, so be it. You don't have to be like everybody else. Not everybody has to like you. Lots of people didn't like me when I was a kid. Hell—heck—a lot of people don't like me now."

"I know," she said, deadpan.

"Oh, that's hilarious," he said.

That evening he and Daniel snared Cam for an hour of babysitting, tossing at her a bag of Goldfish and vanishing out the door, grabbing the rare chance to take Yo-yo for a walk in the woods behind the abandoned state mental hospital, just the two of them. Yo-yo plunged into the river, wading and slurping, and Daniel threw sticks for him to wear him out in the current. "Drop it," he'd command as Yo-yo emerged from the river, circling with the stick and shaking furiously, until setting it down. Then Daniel would snatch it up and throw it high over the river.

It was a late-summer evening, thick, with a warm wind that seemed to coat their faces and arms. Dogs and their humans walked the paths that ran between the river and the harvested cornfields that looked as if they'd been trampled by a wanton giant. Matt told Daniel about his conversation with Gal, which he was pretty proud of: he felt he'd brought the topic into the light of day and maintained a light touch that encouraged her to confide in him.

Yo-yo emerged from the river, shook himself, then flung himself on his back on a patch of grass, where he writhed ecstatically while they uttered a mild, sad "Oh, Yo-yo," anticipating the dirt he'd be bringing into the house.

"Did you talk to her at all about how to make friends," Daniel asked, "or did you just tell her it was okay for people not to like her?"

Matt paused, said humorously, "I'm not sure I like your tone."

"Well, come on, Matt," Daniel said. "If she doesn't know how to conduct herself, she'll be hurt by people."

"Really?" Matt said, recoiling. "*Conduct* herself? How about being encouraged to *be* herself?" He was physically repulsed; how priggish could you get? He looked at Daniel and saw a thin, bearded man in sneakers and socks, and wondered if he'd look at him twice if he didn't already know him. A small well of panic bubbled in his chest. He was used to wanting sex wanting sex wanting sex. Could it be, he wondered, that he was no longer attracted to Daniel, rather than the other way around? He stopped to fish a pebble out of his sandal, and his eyes blurred as his mind shrank from that possibility.

"I'm calling her therapist," Daniel said. "This is ridiculous."

When they got home, he went up to Matt's study, closed the door, and called Gal's grief counselor, Peggy Sheridan, at home. "Do you have a moment?" he asked, knowing she'd say yes, because having a child whose parents had been killed by terrorists made therapists cut you a lot of slack.

"Sure," she said.

"I just wanted to check in," he said, "because Gal's been pretty volatile at home. And yesterday, she told the kids at school something kind of inappropriate. That her parents were buried without heads."

"Oh dear," Peggy said.

He sat down on the love seat and put his feet up on Matt's Lucite coffee table. "I guess I wanted to ask how you think she's doing."

Peggy was quiet for a moment, and he could hear the clink of dishes in the background, a dishwasher being loaded, or maybe emptied. He conjured her red hair with strands of silver, her freckled skin and clear gray eyes, the Eileen Fisher clothes in earth tones, and wondered if she was in sweats and a T-shirt now, barefoot maybe. Derrick had referred them to her, and Daniel had chosen her without interviewing anyone else based solely on the way she'd first greeted Gal, with a warm seriousness that made Gal visibly relax and open.

"She's struggling," she said. "There's a lot of anger there. She was dreading starting school."

"Do you think there's been any progress?" he asked, careful to keep his tone neutral.

Peggy paused again, and then asked him if he minded holding on for a second while she went someplace quieter. When she returned, she asked, "Are you concerned that the therapy isn't working?"

"No," he lied. "I just thought it might be good to check in."

"I'm glad you did," she said. "You must be having a helluva time yourself. I mean, your twin brother!"

Why was it always the simplest statements that filled your eyes with tears? During that first session, he'd told her what had happened to Gal and she'd said softly, "That's so sad." Just that, and Gal had started to cry. He was quiet for a moment now, knowing his voice would catch if he tried to answer.

"Who's helping you get through this?" she asked gently.

"Well, my partner," Daniel said. "My friends." He paused. "You probably mean I should be in therapy."

"Well," she said, "if it were my twin sister, I'd be running to therapy as fast as my legs could carry me."

Daniel closed his eyes to absorb this. It felt as if she were crossing a line. Was she suggesting that *he* was the problem? His left leg had fallen asleep, crossed under his right up on the coffee table. He uncrossed them and stood and stomped. "We're trying to do right by Gal," he said.

"Of course you are."

"We're trying to be stable and loving, and to help her remember, and put her feelings into language. We've read the books about helping a grieving child. Not to mention consulting with you."

"And you're doing a terrific job," Peggy said. "I guess what I want to say is that she's very attuned to you, Daniel; she's watching, and she takes her cues from you."

That surprised him. Gal was so difficult these days, flinging herself from him, stomping around the house and putting them all on edge—it didn't feel as if she were attached to him at all. He wanted to ask Peggy what she was trying to tell him, but didn't want to come off as confrontational. He told her that he heard Noam crying, and pulled his way off the phone despite some concerned follow-up questions; she knew she'd pissed him off. Then he sat back down, angry that they hadn't had the conversation he'd hoped for. He kicked off his shoes and lay down on the couch with his elbow crooked over his face. Let Matt handle baths and bedtime, thinking he was still on the phone. He knew Matt cheated sometimes in just this way, retreating to the bathroom and sitting there longer than necessary, reading a magazine on the toilet while Daniel was getting the kids into pajamas or reading them stories.

It was starting to get dark in the study now, the sky outside drained of color. He squinted at his watch; it was only six o'clock. The long days of summer would soon come to an end, and his heart was heavy with the thought of coming home from work in the dark. He thought of Gal again and a little starburst of anxiety went off in his chest.

He thought about Peggy saying that Gal was taking her cues from him. What was she trying to tell him? He heard a message there, one that implied that he was sending bad cues. He tried to push aside his defensiveness and to examine himself honestly. He was a mess, he knew that. He was heavy-limbed these days, a little zombielike. But this is what he couldn't get past: How could he not be? Was he supposed to set an example for Gal by being as normal as possible?

He loved her and his heart ached for her, but above all, he wanted to do right by her. He wanted to be a parent she felt safe with, with whom she felt at home. If she didn't, it wasn't fair to get angry at her, he knew that. He closed his eyes and prepared himself to get up and help with bedtime, to enter the fray.

Later that night the principal of Gal's school called. Daniel had never talked to her before, but he'd heard she played trombone in the school band and was known to join in a soccer game when patrolling at recess. At the sound of her voice, Daniel relaxed; she had that ability. When he told her that Gal had actually believed her parents were buried headless, there was silence followed by the sound of nose-blowing. "Poor kid," she said. She said that she wanted the record to be set straight, not just so that the other kids didn't have to imagine something that horrific, but to spare Gal any teasing that might occur. "Because otherwise she's going to be the girl with the headless parents." She said that she'd do it herself the next morning.

"What will you say to them?" Daniel asked.

She paused. "Who the hell knows? Okay. That Gal went through a terrible experience, losing both of her parents when a bomb exploded in a café in Israel. That the experience upset her so much, it's hard for her to remember those days when they were buried. That they actually did have heads, although Gal thought they didn't. And that I'm sure they all want to help Gal, and support her. And I'll ask them if they have any ideas about what might be the most supportive."

"Great," Daniel said.

"May I speak to Gal?" she asked.

Matt went to get her and brought her back, shrinking and shy. "Hello?" she said. "Hi." She listened for a little while, fingering the *chai* necklace her *savta* had given her. "Okay," she said. "Okay. Yes. Okay. Bye."

She hung up and sighed with relief. "Okay, I can go back to school now," she said.

SHE WENT TO SCHOOL the next day, and Daniel called from work to say that Colleen had taken to wearing Noam around in a carrier on her back, which he seemed to like. Matt worked hard all morning, steeling himself against the impulse to clean the house instead. After lunch, he put on the kettle, took out the dog, and got the mail. There were two letters in regular envelopes, addressed to Daniel in handwriting. When he talked to Daniel at lunchtime, he mentioned them, and Daniel told him to go ahead and open them. Matt opened the first.

Dear Daniel,
2 Jews are being marched before the Nazi firing squad, and the executioner asks them, "Do you want to wear a hood?" The first Jew defiantly says, "No, I want them to see my disgust and anger," to which the second Jew whispers, "Shoosh, you might upset them."
You are the second Jew.

The other was typed on a manual typewriter, and the keys had unevenly pressed the letter imprints on the paper.

Dear Daniel Rosen,
I read the newspaper article in which you expressed your understanding of the terrorist who killed your brother and sister-in-law. Please do not talk about things you don't understand. Compassion is a noble impulse but it must always be balanced with WISDOM. If it is not, the result is always foolish stupidity.

MATT LAID THEM CAREFULLY on the kitchen counter, smoothed them with his hand. "Christ," Daniel was saying, and Matt said, "What are the odds that after not receiving any mail at all, you'd get two letters in one morning? And who even sends hate mail via snail mail these days?" Then he thought: *These people know where we live, and they want us to know that.* The thought came gulping up and swallowed him. His eyes scanned the windows. Would he and Daniel be like those abortion doctors, shot in their living rooms by deranged snipers? If one of the kids got hurt . . . At the very thought of that happening, his chest swelled and his blood seemed to roar through his heart.

The whistle of the kettle broke into his consciousness, and he went and turned off the burner. "I gotta go," Daniel was saying. "Let's talk about this when I get home."

Matt opened the letters once more and reread them, and calmed himself with the observation that they didn't seem threatening, just officious, condescending, obnoxious as hell.

CHAPTER 13

H E TRIED TO cultivate a sense of superiority—they didn't deserve to be even considered—but the letters got to Daniel; a reflexive feeling that he'd done something terribly wrong nagged at him, and made it hard to fall asleep.

"That's just what they want you to feel," Matt said hotly. "They want you to think that *you're* the crazy person."

Daniel knew that. Still, sometimes, just sometimes, he had the heart-stopping thought that he'd missed something, or breached an important code of conduct, or failed at some response crucial to the common human enterprise. Wasn't there, just possibly, something strange—even disturbed—about the fact that he couldn't muster any anger at the man who had killed his brother?

Now he looked at Matt, who was sitting cross-legged on the play-room floor and taking apart the foam puzzle alphabet floor. He thought about how irritated Matt was that people who hadn't given him the time of day before suddenly fell all over him in camaraderie once he had kids. Yes, he got why Matt was irritated, but it wasn't entirely sinister, was it? Wasn't having and raising children simply part of the common human enterprise?

"Sometimes," he said, "I wonder, are we so perverse, so used to thinking against the grain that we can't even recognize a normal human sentiment when we stumble upon it? Like, for example, that it's bad to kill people?"

Matt tsked. "We know it's bad to kill people, Daniel. We know that."

"But understandable," Daniel said, feeling the ugliness press at his eyes and face.

Matt looked at him and sighed, stood and put the stack of alphabet floor pieces in the corner. "Is that it?" he asked, looking around the playroom. "Kitchen clean?"

"Yes," Daniel said.

In the living room Daniel threw himself on the couch, covering his face with his crooked arm, while Matt found the newspaper and sank into the armchair. Legs crossed at the knee, swinging a bare foot, he read. The news was all horrendous, the depredations of the Bush administration terrifying; but Matt felt it was his duty to witness it all. So he read and groaned, and his heart sank and swelled.

"What if," Daniel said, sitting up. "What if you said—in print!— that you understood Matthew Shepard's killers? And then the whole gay community turned on you? Would you call *them* lunatics?"

Don't bite, don't bite, Matt told himself, and then he said, "It's *so* not the same thing! When did gay people ever do anything to straight people to warrant being killed?"

"So you think Israelis deserve to be killed!"

"Oh God," Matt groaned.

THEY GOT MORE MAIL, some snail mail, most via email. Much of it— laced with the straining, acid language of political extremism, words like *brutal, mockery, hypocrisy, bloodthirsty, fanatics, agenda*—gave them a headache. *Nothing worse than a Semite who is anti-Semitic. Do your homework before speaking. You're the same type of so-called intelligentsia that propagated Hitler's Holocaust.* A few letters came in the form of long treatises so strenuously argued—one of them was even footnoted—they sounded like the ironclad cases the insane make about their persecution. Then Adam called to tell Daniel that his name was up on a website by a group called TheCancerWithin.com. Matt and Daniel logged on and scrolled down the luridly fonted home page. "Islam, a religion of peace? Or is it preparing to sodomize the world?"

"Lovely," Matt muttered. He pointed to a link titled "His Ugliness Yasser AraFART: decades of stinking lies." "AraFART. Clever!"

"Here," Daniel said, clicking on a link called "Israel-hating Judenrats."

"Oh," Matt said, scanning. "It's everybody who ever signed a petition."

Daniel clicked on the Rs, and scrolled down to his name. There was a tiny picture of him, a cutout of his face from the *Daily Hampshire Gazette* article. "'This Judenrat believes that the terrorist was *right* to kill his brother and sister-in-law. He's a rabid homo—why are we not surprised that he likes to bend over for terrorist cock?'"

"Close it," Matt said.

"Jesus," Daniel said.

"Close it!"

But there were other kinds of letters, too. One was from someone who'd lost a son in 9/11, and wanted to direct Daniel to the group of bereaved family members who'd gone to Afghanistan on a peace mission before the war broke out. One was from a man who ran a workshop called Men Healing From Violence at the Kripalu yoga center; he sent his flyer, on the bottom of which he had written, *I wish your spirit peace, friend.* Daniel read it, feeling, as he always did in the face of the New Age, touched through layers of irony.

There was a letter from a gay man who'd lost his partner in Tower Two and had not received a penny of his estate, or a word of acknowledgment at his funeral, because they hadn't made any legal arrangements, and his partner's bio-family had elbowed him out. *I'm trying not to hate them*, he wrote, *because I want to remember Robert without hatred attached to it. Can you tell me what your secret is for avoiding hatred?*

I don't really have a secret, Daniel wrote back. *I think I'd hate your partner's family, too.*

THE READING ROOM OF the Smith College library was dim, lit by lamps with ornate shades; there was an antique fireplace, and the worn dark leather furniture was pushed against the walls to make room for two sections of folding chairs with an aisle in between them. A long table with water pitchers and cups was set at the head of the room, a small huddle of people talking at one end. In the audience were Smith students, some in tattered jeans and tight shirts and others in head scarves, white girls with dreadlocks, young women pierced in tendentious places, women with blunt features and buzz cuts who were transitioning to manhood. That was what they did these days, instead of living as butches, Daniel thought, regretting the loss of the gender deviance in both men and women that always stirred him. There were older people too, from the community—women in corduroys and wool sweaters with thick gray-streaked hair pulled back in ponytails, men with Abraham Lincoln beards.

Daniel sat next to Derrick in a chair near the door, leaving his coat on, picking out the speakers from the hosts. He'd known about this event for a few weeks, since Derrick had forwarded him the announcement posted on one of his social justice Listservs. It was a discussion by two members of The Families Project, a group of Israelis and Palestinians who had lost a family member to the conflict, who met together seeking peace and reconciliation. A Palestinian and an Israeli man, they were touring the States talking about their group and their friendship, and promoting a peace agenda. Daniel picked them out of the huddle of chatting organizers and faculty members, or was pretty sure he had. The Israeli was in his late thirties or early forties, with glasses and sandy-brown hair brushed evenly over his forehead, the kind of man who perhaps in high school, the army, or university was rejected by women because he wasn't good-looking enough, but who goes on to happily marry in his thirties. The Palestinian was a young man in a worn gray leather bomber jacket, thick dark hair cut short. Chubby, heavy in the chin, with beautiful eyes and lips.

Next to him, Derrick sat with his hands folded, his shaved head stately and gleaming, emanating the scent of his aftershave. He had called Daniel a few hours after emailing him about the event, to ask if he planned on going. Daniel had said he'd try to go, that it depended on what was going on at work. "Don't you think you should make this a priority?" Derrick had asked, and then added, after a chilly silence, "No pressure."

"No pressure," Daniel said.

"It's just that these are *your guys*," Derrick said in a burst. "And I'd like to see you get some support for your . . . your way of being. That's all."

"Support for my way of being, huh?" Daniel said. "You say it a lot nicer than Matt. He says I either come to this event or I stop complaining to him about the hate mail." He continued to compulsively open the messages, instead of—as Matt wanted him to do—deleting them from his email without reading them. The loonies were bad; they called him a faggot, a traitor, a guilty liberal asshole. But it was the ones who debated Middle East policy with him who got to him the most, and his mind scuttled about in constant, heated rebuttal; his lips moved in argument as he went about his day.

Daniel was seized by a fit of yawning, tired from work and depressed as always by the early-winter dark, wanting and not wanting the presentation to be perfect. It was unpleasant sitting there, feeling a kind of scathing irony toward the audience, for he knew that if this peace-loving, gender-queering, intellectually high-flying audience wasn't his ideal community, or very close to it, there was nowhere he belonged. A faculty member with a spray of steel-wool hair came to the front of the room to begin his introduction. He projected the aura of someone popular enough with his audience to extemporize, but he wasn't actually good at it; he had to consult a piece of paper for the key facts, and labored over pronouncing the Israeli and Arab names. At the end, though, he grew grave. "They are the people who are supposed to most desire revenge," he said, "and yet they turned in a different direction, a direction more difficult, more exacting, than retribution. They are here to tell us their stories."

The applause was emphatic and encouraging, and the speakers nodded and said "Thank you" till it died down. The Palestinian man spoke first. His name was Ibrahim and he lived in Ramallah. He had lost his brother in the First Intifada, and spent seven years in an Israeli prison. Strangely, he said in very good English, his Arabic accent like water rolling over rocks, it was there that he developed compassion for Israelis, when he learned a little about Jewish history and about the Holocaust. "For six years I attended the Project's meetings, and met Israelis who were grieving their own losses. I learned that our blood was the same color, that their tears were as bitter as mine, and had the same salty taste."

Then his seven-year-old daughter was killed by a settler on her way home from school, and the IDF spokesman told the newspapers that she wouldn't have been killed if she had been looked after properly. There was a collective intake of breath when he said that, and he paused for a minute. "My faith in peaceful coexistence faltered then," he said, "and I left the Project. I thought that the Israelis I had met must be an aberration. I told myself that they were, after all, only a few. Most Israelis were the savages many Arabs thought they were. But I am not a violent man. I did not seek vengeance—instead, I grew weary, and spent most of my time in bed. I lost my job; I had been a photojournalist. I lost twenty kilos. You can see that I've put them all back." He patted his stomach ruefully, to gentle, relieved laughter. "My wife grew desperate; she had lost her beloved daughter, and now her husband was disappearing, too."

Then someone told him about the Israeli man, Eitan Goldberg, who had just joined the Project after his own young daughter died in his arms after a bus explosion. A Palestinian on the board of directors called him and asked him to reach out to this man. He knew, Ibrahim said, that this was a ruse to bring him back to the Project, and his first impulse was to refuse. But the board member was persuasive. He said,

"So what if it's a ruse? A bereaved man needs support, and Ibrahim, so do you."

"We arranged to meet at Eitan's house in Tel Aviv," Ibrahim said. "It took me many weeks to get there. I was afraid, you see. Afraid that I might look in his eyes and see my own broken image. Afraid I would come to be friends with another Israeli, when I now knew for certain that Jews were evil. There is comfort in knowing that, in living without ambiguity. Much easier to live that way." He paused, gazing at the audience with mild eyes, then picked up briskly. "And then, once I grew brave enough, I had to get a permit, which of course took a long time." He paused and took a sip of water. "When the cab left me off at his address, I walked up and down his street. I was nauseated, I was so nervous."

Eitan cut in. "Meanwhile, I was inside, also nauseated."

The audience laughed.

"Remember," Eitan said, "I was a new member of the Project. My sister had convinced me to try it. She is very important to me, and despite everything that occurred, does not have the least trace of hatred or spite in her heart. And I had not yet met any Palestinian members. My whole life, I had met exactly one Palestinian outside of the army, outside of people trying to pass through the checkpoint I was stationed at. What if I hated him, if he confirmed all the bad ideas I had about Palestinians? And there was part of me, a shameful part, that wondered, can a Palestinian love and grieve as I do?" He paused for effect, and Daniel felt Derrick nodding beside him.

"When he opened the door," Ibrahim said, "we looked at each other, and we embraced without words. I went inside, his wife brought us tea, and we talked for over two hours. We found that we disagreed about many things," Ibrahim said. "But to this we agreed: We must stop this vicious circle of violence. It is a never-ending cycle of murder and retaliation, revenge and punishment, with no winners. It is not a decree of fate. This is not our destiny!"

There was uncertain applause, and then it picked up and became full-fledged. Derrick reached over and took Daniel's hand and squeezed it.

"So! Here are a few of the projects we have done." There was a hotline on which bereaved Israelis could find a Palestinian to talk to, and vice versa. Since the two men became friends they'd gone together to Palestinian high schools and talked with classes of Israeli kids who were about to become soldiers. With two other Palestinian members of the Project, Ibrahim had gone to Magen David Adom, the Israeli Red Cross, to donate blood, while Eitan and several other Israelis made their way across the Green Line to a Palestinian hospital to do the same. "At first they had no idea what to do with us!" Eitan said. "We were trying to make blood flow for peace and healing, instead of from warfare. We were affirming that we all have the *same* blood."

Tears prickled in Daniel's eyes, and he bit his lip.

The moderator opened the floor to questions. There was a longish silence, then a man raised his hand and stood. "I'm sitting in my seat listening to your stunning stories, wondering how to respond, wondering what words could possibly be adequate to follow upon them. And I finally found a single word that does justice to you. 'Bravo.'" He stood for a moment, flushed, until someone started to clap and a string of applause smattered around the room.

"Oh sweet Jesus," Derrick muttered. "Give me a break."

Daniel laughed, which felt like such a great release after his clenched and pent-up listening, he struggled to swallow down the giggles.

A young woman with short hair and a bull ring in her nose, wearing a T-shirt whose writing Daniel tried to make out in her half turn toward him—he was pretty sure it said *Bite me*—stood agitatedly and said, "We learn in college about occupation, nationalism, globalization, migration, oppression . . ." She broke into a grin as a few people laughed. "All those intellectualized concepts! What you have said is simpler and truer than anything I've learned in the classroom."

A bespectacled man in his sixties with disheveled hair stood and spoke. "I commend you for your commitment to peace. I too am agonized by the violence on both sides." Daniel recognized him as one of those Jewish men who speak like a rabbi—heavy-consonanted, sorrow-ful, stooped from the weight of all his great thoughts. "I wish I could believe that yours was the right way. Let's hope that it's you who turn out to be right, and not me." He shook his head woefully and sat back down.

A student with a round, light brown face and a head scarf stood. "My cousin was killed in Jenin last April," she said. "How can my aunt and uncle get in touch with you?"

Eitan began to answer, but Daniel didn't hear him. He stared at the back of the woman's head, his mind buzzing, his heart making an unpleasant whir in his chest. Her cousin was probably killed in the name of his brother and sister-in-law. He wanted to stand and say: *I didn't want it that way. I was not comforted by it.*

He wanted to say these things with a blaze of righteous fury. But he couldn't; something seized his tongue. Derrick was directing a steady, gentle gaze at him—a gaze Daniel knew well and normally loved, but which felt unbearable to him now.

When the event ended, they sat with their hands pressed on their thighs, getting ready to stand. Derrick said, "You should go talk to them."

Daniel looked at the men, who had already been approached by several audience members.

"I can't. I can't hang around here."

"You'll hate yourself if you miss this opportunity."

Daniel shot him an aggrieved look, then sighed and stood, approached the men. Eitan was talking intently to the young woman whose cousin was killed in Jenin. An opening presented itself in front of Ibrahim, so Daniel stepped into it and extended his hand.

Ibrahim had the soft handshake of the Middle Easterner.

"Thank you for your work," Daniel said.

Ibrahim nodded and said, "You're very welcome." Daniel looked at him for a sign that this handshake meant anything at all to him, that he was open to being touched by something Daniel might say. But what he saw was the somewhat distracted politeness of a man who has done this presentation a hundred times and shaken many hands, and is perhaps thinking ahead to dinner, or to being able to take his pants off in his hotel room. He held Ibrahim's gaze for a moment, then turned around, somehow humiliated and tearful. When he joined up with Derrick, he was furious at him.

"Okay," he said, shrugging into his coat and heading for the door. "Let's go."

Derrick grabbed his coat and rushed after him. "That didn't take very long."

Daniel was silent as Derrick fell into step beside him and they headed out into the cold darkness toward the parking lot.

"Are you okay?" Derrick asked.

Daniel stopped abruptly. "What do you want from me, Derrick?" he demanded.

"What do you mean?"

"We didn't have a deep, meaningful conversation, if that's what you're wondering."

"Okay," Derrick said. "That's cool."

He held Daniel's gaze as Daniel stared him down.

They walked quickly to Derrick's car, and Derrick let it idle for a few minutes to warm up. Their breath puffed around them. "I just—I just didn't want to be another sanctimonious Jewish jerk talking about his own pain," Daniel said.

"Man, are you crazy? You're nothing like that."

"*Jesus*, I hate those guys!" Daniel burst out. "They're so *sorry* they don't believe in peace, they're *agonized*"—he made scare quotes with a scathing gesture, his mouth twisted—"about the necessary civilian Palestinian losses in any given conflict. Bullshit! It's all a performance of Jewish moral superiority, and I'm sorry, it's *bullshit*."

"Okay," Derrick said with comic care, as though trying to humor a lunatic. "But you realize that . . . that there's no connection between talking to someone about your own losses and what you're talking about. Right?"

"Whatever," Daniel said.

Derrick shifted into reverse and stretched his arm across Daniel's seat as he backed up. They were quiet during the short ride home, and when they got there, Daniel thanked him for the ride. "You're welcome," Derrick said, adding, as Daniel got out of the car, "And honey, give yourself a break."

Matt was in the bright kitchen, which was warm and steamy from boiling pasta water, sitting at the table with Gal, who had a bowl of pasta and a little container of organic applesauce in front of her. His elbow was on the table and his head rested in his hand as he watched her eat, his own plate cleaned. Noam was in his ExerSaucer, spinning wheels, making beads clatter and little bells ring. He had outgrown it several months ago, but it was enjoying a resurgence of his favor, after he had played in one belonging to the six-month-old twins of a lesbian couple from the shul.

"Hey," Matt said.

"Hey. Did he eat?" Daniel asked, coming into the kitchen in his socks but with his coat still on.

"Yes," Matt said. "How was it?"

"Fine," Daniel said. He went into the hall to hang up his coat, and when he came back, Matt said, "I made pasta with chicken and broccoli and lemons."

Daniel went over to the warm bowl sitting on the counter and helped himself to some pasta, put it in the microwave for a minute, and leaned against the counter.

"Remember all those sitcoms," Matt said, "where the wife is furious because the husband came home late from work and his dinner's cold?"

"Not just sitcoms," Daniel said, loosening his tie and his collar. "*Ordinary People.*"

"No, that was pancakes for the son's breakfast. I think you're confusing *that* Mary Tyler Moore character with Laura Petrie."

"Oh yeah."

"Well, anyhoo, I think the microwave has made that situation obsolete."

"So it has," Daniel said.

"Lucky for us, huh?"

"Are you saying you're mad at me?" Daniel asked, bringing his plate to the table.

Gal looked up with interest.

"Nope. Just making conversation," Matt said. He watched Daniel hunch over his plate and eat. There was a click and then "Pop Goes the Weasel" played, manically cheerful. "I haven't managed to accidentally break the music on that thing yet," Matt said.

Daniel smiled dutifully. Matt looked at him, at the sharp dusty planes of his face, and wondered, again, if he was still in love with him, and if he wasn't, whether he ever had been—because surely a good, real love could get them through tragedy together. The thought didn't pain him, because he put it in a place in his mind marked *On Hold*—things, like his own death, that he would someday have to make it his business to think about, but that he didn't have to think about right now.

"Are you fighting?" Gal asked.

"No," Daniel said, while Matt brushed her hair out of her eyes and said, "Why do you ask that?"

She shrugged. "It looked like you were fighting. Even though you weren't saying anything like 'I'm mad at you' or 'You hurt my feelings.'"

"How can you tell, then?" Matt asked.

She shrugged again, smiling faintly this time. "I just can," she said complacently.

"You can, can you?" He reached over and gave her a squeeze in the ribs, and she slapped his hand away with an aggravated "Stop it!"

"Oh, are *we* fighting now?" he asked.

"Yes!" she shouted.

"Everybody stop fighting," Daniel said.

A song—"London Bridge Is Falling Down"—began to tinkle, loudly and spontaneously, from a toy in the corner of the kitchen. The three of them looked at one another and laughed. "I swear I switched that thing off!" Matt leapt up and grabbed it. "Ha!" he cried, and thrust the toy under each of their noses so they could see the switch on "off." The thing played again in his hands, and he tossed it in the air as if it had burst into flames, which startled Noam. "Oh, sorry, honey," Matt said, running to the small useful-things drawer and pawing through it in search of the tiny Phillips head screwdriver. He unscrewed furiously— the screwdriver tiny and spinning in his hands—one, two, three, four screws; they each hit the table with a tiny click. Then he dug out the D batteries, set the toy on the table. "I'm taking bets that it's like a smoke detector, and will still play," Matt said. "Anyone care to make it interesting?" They waited in suspense. The toy was silent.

"Dang," Matt said.

THAT NIGHT MATT AND Noam read the color book in Matt and Daniel's bed, and then Matt carried him—marveling that they really did get heavier when they started falling asleep—into his own room, and laid him down on his bed. He turned on the humidifier and Noam's Norah Jones CD, his lullaby music. "Good night, monkey," he whispered, running his hand over Noam's hair and putting his little fleece with the puppet head near his hand, so if he awoke in the night he'd know he was in his own bed.

He was drowsy when he went into the bedroom, where Daniel had spilled the basket of clean laundry onto Matt's side of the bed for folding. The water was running in the bathroom down the hall—Gal running herself a bubble bath, about which she'd become a fanatic; every trip to the drugstore now involved the purchase of a fancy potion for her.

Daniel was pulling out all of the kid pajamas from the pile. "Did you turn on the humidifier?" he asked.

"I did," Matt said. He pulled out all the sheets and towels, the things he liked to fold first, to make the laundry pile quickly smaller. He folded the towels, then turned to put them in the linen closet and to go check on Gal.

"Could you check on her?" Daniel asked.

Matt sighed and flashed him a look. "I'm just going to check on her."

"What? Why do you have to be a prick about it?"

"Because ten times a day I'm *in the very process of* picking up a blanket when you tell me to cover the baby with a blanket," Matt said, "or opening a dresser drawer to get a sweater for Gal as you tell me that it's cold and I should put a sweater on her. It's maddening! I know you're the Boss Man, but I'm an adult, too! Jesus."

Daniel stared at him. "Can't you cut me some slack?" he asked. "Think of it as a great-minds-think-alike moment? It's not about you."

Matt took in the semi-hostile apology, unplacated. He sighed. "You didn't used to treat me this way. Now . . ." He shook his head.

" 'Now' what? Do you really want to start a fight right now?"

"Remember yesterday when I came back from the supermarket and was stacking apples in the bowl, and the top one rolled off and hit the floor? What's your response? You laughed! You said, 'I knew it! I could see that one coming.' "

"So what?"

"That's so mean! And you do it all the time."

"You're mad at me because I could see that one coming?"

"I'm mad at you because you treat me like a fuckup." Matt pulled out a pair of jeans and gave them a shake and a snap before laying them on the bed to fold. He knew he was the clown in their family dynamic, the tackler, the tickler, the one who pretended he couldn't find his hat when it was sitting on his head. Most of the time he relished that, and thought it was important to be that way, especially since Daniel was so—what? Deadened. But maybe, he was thinking, it was a mistake, too. One day, he'd reached up to pull the light cord on the kitchen ceiling fan and it had come clear out in his hand. Daniel had gone out and bought a new fan and installed it himself, and for days, Gal had walked around informing people, "Matt broke the ceiling fan, but Dani fixed it."

"Matt made a big steaming pile of doody," he'd said irritably to Brent, "but Daniel cleaned it up. That's what she's saying."

"But just look what a perfect couple that makes you!" Brent offered optimistically. "What if you were both ceiling fan breakers, and neither of you could fix it? Or if you both could fix ceiling fans, but there was no one to break one?"

"Oh please," Daniel said now. "Admit it. This is about sex."

"It is not!" Matt cried. "And what if it is? Is it so terrible for me to want to have sex with you?"

"I knew it," Daniel said with bitter satisfaction.

"Jesus," Matt said, feeling as though he'd just lost a major point. "You make it seem as if I'm an insensitive, shallow jerk for wanting it, so I have to pretend I don't. But I'm tired of pretending, and I'm not shallow and I'm not insensitive. Okay," he said, with an impulse to joke self-deprecatingly to increase his own credibility, "I'm a little shallow and insensitive. But not because I want to have sex with my boyfriend."

Daniel whirled on him. "Don't you think I would if I could? Don't you?"

Matt looked at him with interest, a pair of sweatpants dangling from his hands. "Why can't you?"

"I . . . I just can't. I feel very strongly that I can't."

"Why not?"

"Maybe because my twin brother was blown to smithereens?" Daniel's tone was ugly with suppressed tears.

He was dropping a bomb on the conversation, Matt thought, to make it stop. But Matt pursued it: "So if that happened to his body, then your body can't get any pleasure?"

Daniel shot him a withering look. "Oh, aren't you clever."

The phone rang, and he reached for it, Matt saying with a warning tone, "Don't!" He knew he'd scored, and he didn't want to give up his advantage.

"Hi," Daniel said into the phone.

"That's not cool," Matt said.

Daniel was casting his eyes up, defeated. "It was fine, Val. Thanks for asking. No, I'm not mad, it's just that a lot of people seem to be very interested in how it went, and I feel— No, of course, there's nothing wrong with that."

Matt watched for a minute as Daniel listened impatiently. "Listen," Daniel said, "I'm in the middle of something, can we talk about it tomorrow? Thanks. Thanks." A pause; he was lowering his head toward the telephone base with the receiver against his ear. "Thanks, Val. Okay."

"See?" he said, turning to Matt. "This is what I mean. You, Derrick, Val—everybody knows about the Families Project event, and everyone's on my case about it. 'How was it, Daniel? Did you talk to them, Daniel? Did they show you the right way to grieve?' She keeps trying to give me the name of this therapist she knows."

"Whoa!" Matt said. "You think people think you're grieving wrong?"

"Peggy Sheridan sure does! Don't you?"

Matt sat on the bed, making the pile of little washcloths Daniel had folded cave onto his thigh. "I don't know what that means." He said that even though he sort of knew what it meant. He'd been thinking about it. It was amazing that Daniel didn't feel rage at the terrorist, at the Palestinians. Mostly he thought that was because Daniel was simply an amazing and compassionate person, wise enough to see the big picture. Because he was. But sometimes Matt wondered—he couldn't help it—if that response was entirely real, entirely human. If Daniel could let himself be angry, would things be different?

"It hasn't even been a year!" Daniel said. "But clearly I haven't learned to do it right yet."

"No," Matt said.

"You're messing up my pile! So why is everyone pressuring me?"

"Then fold the laundry on your own freaking side of the bed!" Matt stood and picked up the empty basket to take into the bathroom. "They're not pressuring you."

"Oh, come off it! Sitting next to Derrick at that event was excruciating. He kept turning and gazing into my eyes with this, this soulful expectancy."

Matt laughed. "He always does that, Dan. He does it when he asks if you like his new recipe for tofu stir-fry with shiitake mushrooms, or whatever the fuck."

"He was just dying for me to have a huge catharsis, right there at Smith College."

Matt put the basket into the linen closet in their bathroom. When he came out, he asked carefully, "Do you think therapy's a terrible idea?"

Daniel was hanging a clean shirt in his closet, shaking and smoothing it, buttoning the second button around the hanger. He threw his head back, his eyes closed, his Adam's apple a shard against his throat. "I'm not going into therapy."

"Why not? It's not like you haven't done it before." Matt felt carefully for the words. "I think . . . It's not that you're grieving. It's that you're . . . frozen. You're different."

"What do you think grieving is?" Daniel cried. "Do you think you can really grieve—and I mean grieve *so hard it takes your breath away, day after day after day*—and not be changed?"

Matt was quiet. Was that true?

"Christ!" Daniel said, his face red and his nostrils flared. "It's not—it's not pretty, or ennobling. And if you think therapy can touch it, well—"

Matt stood gazing at him, leaning against his dresser with his arms crossed. Daniel was acting as though Matt had never grieved himself, but as Matt thought resentfully about that he also felt embarrassed, because he had felt his grief for Jay to be a little bit ennobling.

"So excuse me if I'm not exactly lusting after you," Daniel said, sensing an advantage from Matt's pensiveness.

"Stop it," Matt snapped. "You're like straight people, acting like sex is trivial. I can't stand that! And I'll tell you something, we're setting a crappy example of a healthy couple for these kids. They're going to think we hate each other!"

"I don't hate you," Daniel said, his eyes glistening. "I really don't. You've been a total saint, and I don't know what I'd be doing without you."

"Well, thanks," Matt said, thinking, *A total saint: just kill me.*

They sat down on the bed and slumped against each other. "What now?" Matt asked.

"Let me go make sure Gal hasn't flooded the house," Daniel said.

That night, curled against a sleeping Matt, Daniel's mind continued to churn. Therapy! What were they thinking? Sure, he believed in it—back in college, it had been a lifeline as he struggled to become comfortable with his sexuality. But to make him all better from terrorism, from one of the biggest and most violent losses a person could sustain? It felt so galling, so puny and trivial, in the face of what he was going through, so massively deluded as an enterprise. He couldn't get past that. You might as well tell that guy Ibrahim, or the woman whose cousin was killed in Jenin, to go to therapy.

Thinking of them let in a fresh wave of confusion and self-reproach. He'd felt so victimized, as a gay man, in the face of the Israeli legal system. What a joke that was! It mortified him now to even think about it. What an obscene luxury to have all his friends worrying and whispering about his mental health, while the children the Israeli courts had handed to him slept in a safe house that would never get bulldozed, when he would never be stuffed into a tiny strip of land he couldn't get out of and then bombed, or have one of his kids shot and then, on top of that, have the very people who had committed the murder blame him for being a negligent parent.

He didn't know what to do with all that, except to scorn his friends for their naïveté and privilege. His mind stalled there for a while, clotted and pulsing. Who was this man whom his friends said they missed? It was so hard to remember him! He knew, somewhere in the shadows of his mind, that he was a good and loving person, even a charismatic one—or that he *had* been anyway. In their early days together, Matt had prodded him: "You know that that whole shy and sweet thing you've got going on is irresistible, right? Remember fifth grade—'He's cute but he doesn't know it'? That's you." It had been hard to fully believe that Matt was in love with him. Sometimes he still had trouble believing that he could command the attention of such a smart and beautiful man.

His mind cast about for the sweetest moments in his life, the ones where he felt most himself, and most connected to others. Playing guitar, for sure: girls curled up in beanbag chairs in his dorm room, or on his bunk at camp, to listen to him play and to sing with him. He suspected now, although it hadn't occurred to him back then, that more than one of them had been crushed out on him. He remembered sitting barefoot on his bed in the darkened cabin, practicing a new melody line or picking pattern till the fingers of his left hand became red and tender, then calloused, as the shrill voices of campers rose from the moist New Hampshire heat that blanketed the woods and fields outside.

He grew drowsy, and his mind drifted and played in camp memories. He and Joel had loved Camp Ramah, lived for the chance to be away from their parents for four weeks and be steeped in Jewish *ruach*. Camp confirmed for them their sense of the soullessness of their manicured, suburban upbringing, where their accomplishments were paraded by their parents and even their bar mitzvahs seemed like just another opportunity to perform. He remembered the bliss of being without parents, the bracing feeling of competence that came over him when he was freed to take care of himself. To this very day he could conjure it. He remembered the beautiful grove where Shabbat services were held—a lovely peaceful shrine as dusk fell and the smells of dinner drifted in from the dining hall—and the Israeli counselors, who worked there in the summer before or after their army service. They were fair and curly-haired or dark-skinned with thick hair cut short, small and soft-spoken, their masculinity different from the masculinity he'd been, till then, making it his business to emulate. They were unspeakably glamorous, with their Ray-Bans, their flat leather sandals, and their throaty accents. Well into his young adulthood, they played a big role in his erotic fantasy life. His counselor, Ilan, a quiet and gentle soul who went everywhere barefoot and who had been a member of an elite infantry unit, loved hearing him play, and Daniel had basked in his attention—because for whom did he endlessly practice if not for Ilan, hoping for his attention and praise?

Where was Joel all day as he was practicing? Probably in the lake, or on the softball field. He thought of the long, thrilling games of Capture the Flag, and remembered one fine day when Joel actually captured the flag. Daniel himself was the kind of player who didn't imagine he could actually capture the flag. He'd thought of it as a crude, obvious goal, while the less glamorous roles—busting teammates out of jail, drawing a contingent of the other team toward you so another could advance— held risks that were more subtle and complex. Was that true, he wondered now, or was it just the defense of someone who hadn't wanted to take such a big risk? Or someone stepping back so his brother could shine, because his brother wanted to so very badly?

And then his memory shifted and he opened his eyes. Joel had wanted to be elected something or other—he couldn't dredge the desired thing from his memory now—and campaigned by going from bunk to bunk and introducing himself and bringing cookies that he'd had their mother make. Then one night, some of the older camp- ers did a skit in which one of them played Joel, whose Hebrew name was Yisrael, bursting into bunks, singing—instead of *"Hevenu Shalom Aleichem,"* We've brought peace upon you—*"Hevenu Ugiot Eleichem,"* We've brought cookies upon you. It was silly and harmless enough, but the guy who played Yisrael mimicked Joel's ingratiating eager- ness, and the slight childhood speech impediment that made Joel's *n*'s extra heavy, to a tee. Joel was sitting a few rows ahead of Daniel and to the side, and Daniel could see him laugh and then a cloud of uncer- tainty pass over his face, and that killed Daniel right then and there, stabbed him right in the heart. That pain returned to him over the rest of the camp session whenever he saw Joel going about his enthusiastic business—but he was also furious at him, because vulnerability that accrued to Joel accrued to Daniel as well.

He pressed his cheek to Matt's back. Joel had put himself out there, and Daniel, with a mixture of relief and contempt, had let him be the twin who did that. He stayed on the margins, and told himself it was somehow more noble, more interesting, to stay there. Honestly, when it came down to it, he'd just wanted to be distinguishable from Joel. He wanted people to know which one he was.

So who on earth was this man all his friends seemed to miss? Who did they want him to be? Who was the man whom *Matt* missed? Would Mr. Personality have even looked at Daniel twice if Jay hadn't died, if he hadn't had to flee the New York scene to save his own skin?

He blinked into the dark night, his mind throbbing, his heart choked.

THERE WAS A skeleton hanging from Cam's front porch. Gal caught a glimpse of it swaying, antic and ghoulish, through the backseat window one windy gray Saturday afternoon as they pulled into the driveway. *"Ma zeh?"* she asked, whipping around to follow it from the back window.

But by then Noam was crying and the uncles were arguing, as Daniel wrestled him out of the car seat, about Matt driving too fast. She shouted, "I'm going over to Cam's house!" and crossed their lawns and marched up Cam's porch steps, keeping her distance from the skeleton, suddenly determined not to look at it, but not trusting herself to keep her eyes averted, as if in spite of her best effort, they might swivel in their sockets and look.

By the time she rang the doorbell she was terrified of it, could feel it behind her and hear the clicks of its bones as it moved. She heard Xena's wild bark get louder as the dog rocketed toward the front hall, and she took a step back, although she knew that by the time Cam opened the door, Xena would be at a polite, attentive sit-stay by her side.

The door opened and Cam said, "Hey, buddy, how's it going?" She was barefoot, wearing sweatpants and a T-shirt, and her thick dark hair was smashed in one direction, as though it had been fiercely blown and then frozen. "Okay," she instructed the dog, and Xena came forward with a gently wagging tail, thrust her muzzle into Gal's hand. Gal pulled off the new mittens the uncles had bought her for the coldest weather she'd ever known, so Xena could smell her, and she could feel the dog's fur and wet nose.

"Why do you have bones hanging up on your porch?" she demanded, her mind fumbling for the word even in Hebrew but not finding it.

"What? The skeleton? That's James."

"Who's James?"

"The skeleton, that's his name."

Gal stared at her. Was Cam making fun of her? Sometimes Cam played jokes on her, like knock-knock jokes that made her say, "I eat mop who?"

Behind Cam a woman was coming to the door; she had short frosted-blond hair and held a cup of coffee in two hands. She poked out a friendly freckled face. "Hi, cutie!" she said. "Crikey, it's cold out here."

"Don't treat her like a baby," Cam said gruffly. "This is Gal. She's mature."

"Hi," Gal said.

"You can play with him if you want," Cam said. "It's fun to make him dance." She stepped out onto the porch in her bare feet, and as she approached the skeleton Gal let her eyes drift that way too, let them take in the legs and the long, intricate hand bones and move up to the frozen gape of a face. Cam started moving the skeleton's arms and legs around in a grotesque jig. "I'm freezing, give me some skin!" she piped in a high squeaky voice. "Poor James," she sighed in her normal voice. "His eating disorder got out of hand."

Gal reached out and touched a bone of the hand, but she was too embarrassed and too repulsed to play with it, or even to examine it, in front of Cam. Had it really once been a real person named James? She was dying to ask, but feared risking one of Cam's jokes.

Cam smacked him fondly on the shoulder blade. "I got him on Craigslist, from a former yoga teacher who used him to show her students their pelvic floor."

"Okay," Gal said.

Over the next few days Gal began to see skeletons and witches and bloody faces everywhere—in shop windows, on TV commercials, in the front of people's houses. The people in one house on her block hung a spiderweb made of string between two oak trees, a hairy plastic spider the size of a dishwasher suspended inside it. On the front lawn of a house on her school bus route, a headless scarecrow in faded overalls and a checked flannel shirt held his head—a pumpkin with a very surprised expression—under his arm. She didn't know what to make of the gruesomeness that had burst out all over; she could tell that it was supposed to be fun and make her laugh, but it didn't feel fun to her; instead it cast a shadow over her mind and made her move through her days with a sense of foreboding, as if anything she looked at might be gross and terrible. She studiously avoided looking at those houses as the bus passed by, busying herself with her backpack or her shoelaces, but she couldn't shake the feeling that her eyes might look inadvertently, or—and this fear grew and festered over the span of a single afternoon—that her mind would see them even if she managed to keep her eyes averted. At recess, one of the boys told a story about going into a haunted house and putting his hand in a bowl of squishy eyeballs, and several other kids yelled, "It's just peeled grapes!" The image of a bowl of eyeballs tormented Gal.

The next day, Ms. Wheeler told them to come to school next Friday in a costume for Halloween. Gal mouthed the word, her hands tingling. It was a holiday, like Purim. "I'm going to be a ghost!" someone hollered. "Whoo," he said, waving his fingers in the air to express how spooky he was.

She didn't know what a ghost was, although she reasoned that it must be part of Halloween. She thought of waiting till she got home and asking the uncles, but now that she knew a little bit about what she was dealing with, her curiosity became urgent, and she risked sidling up to Hannah as they were waiting for the bus. Hannah was the smartest girl in the class, and asked the best questions during show-and-tell. While most kids asked, "Where did you get it?" Hannah asked things like, "If you lose it do you think your parents will get you another one?" or, if someone brought in a book, "Do you like it better or worse than *Charlotte's Web*?" She was nice to work next to on a project, although she never went out of her way to make friends with Gal. She was friends with Sophia and Lexi and sometimes Ava.

"Hi," Gal said. Hannah greeted her and they stood for a few minutes before Gal mustered her courage and asked, "What's a ghost?"

Hannah turned to her with interest. She had pulled up her hood, and her nose was pink from the cold. "You don't know what a ghost is?"

Gal shook her head, her face growing hot.

"It's someone who died, and then came back. They can move through doors and walls."

Gal's eyes were moving in quick darts as she furiously thought. "What do they look like?"

Hannah pondered that one, her eyes cast up to the sky and blinking hard. "Well, when people dress up as a ghost for Halloween, they sometimes wear a white sheet, with the eyeholes cut out so they can see."

There was a pause. "But I think that's stupid," Hannah said.

"Me too," Gal said.

"Because that's not scary, and a ghost *haunts* people. A ghost looks like—" She screwed her face in thought, and Gal waited, tense with anticipation. "Well, I don't actually know what a ghost looks like, except that you can see through their body."

Gal had never heard of such a thing.

She tried to tell Matt and Daniel about the bowl of eyeballs during dinner, and they frowned and tried to understand as Daniel picked out for her the red peppers, her favorite part, from the salad. "What on earth is the child talking about?" Matt asked Daniel. He turned to Gal. "What is this 'bowl of eyeballs' of which you speak?"

"He was in a special kind of house," Gal persisted, her temper rising.

Daniel's face lit up. "A haunted house?" he asked.

"Yes!" she cried.

"Oh!" they exclaimed. Then Matt leaned forward urgently over his plate and said to Daniel, "Good God, has no one told her about Halloween?"

They looked at each other. "We are pathetic excuses for parents," Daniel said. "Not to mention for gay men."

"Why?" Gal asked.

"Why are we pathetic excuses for gay men?" Daniel asked. "Because many gay men have a special place in their hearts for Halloween."

"Why?"

Matt scratched his face. Since Jay's death he had stopped celebrating Halloween, cold turkey. It was just too painful. He'd buried Halloween deep in his mind, back in some spot near his spine that thoroughly numbed him. It surprised him every time how even that time of year could make him so very heavy and blank; how the sharper cold and the shrill caw of geese moving south, the early dusk, could strip away all the sustaining illusions that made it possible to do things like, say, move his legs to cross the street.

"Because . . . ," he said, and faltered.

"Gay men like dressing up," Daniel said. "We have a really good sense of humor, and we like to make funny costumes."

"People in Israel make funny costumes, too," Gal said in the argumentative tone that could drive Daniel off the deep end, "and they not gay."

"Okay, first of all, some of them *are* gay," Matt said.

Noam took a piece of the cheese slice he'd been eating and rubbed it in his hair. "Honey, just put it down on the tray when you're finished," Matt said, lifting him out of his chair and carrying him to the sink to wash up. Then he set him down on the kitchen floor, and Yo-yo came to clean up inside and under his high chair. The arrival of the kids had been a windfall for him, and Daniel had already put him on a diet.

"I want to have a costume of a ghost," Gal said. "I'm supposed to wear one for school."

"That's not hard," Daniel said. "We'll just get you a white sheet and cut out holes for your eyes."

"No," Gal said decisively. "That's stupid." She paused. "How you say *ghost* in Hebrew?"

"*Ruach refa'im,*" he said. "And you don't have to call me stupid. But I don't think it's the same thing. I don't think you have ghosts in Israel the way we do here. Do Israelis have ghosts?"

"How could you not have ghosts?" Matt asked.

"I wasn't calling *you* stupid," Gal said.

"Well, how do you want to do it, then?" Daniel asked.

"I supposed to be invisible," she said.

"That's the big problem," Matt said, scratching his head in mock perplexity. "How do we make a visible child invisible?"

"Maybe I won't go to school!" Gal shouted.

"Great idea!" Daniel laughed. "'Dear Ms. Wheeler, Gal couldn't be seen in school today, because she came dressed as a ghost. But I want to assure you that she was present, because Gal is a serious student who takes her attendance very seriously.'"

"I have to look like I died and then came back," Gal said.

Matt and Daniel studiously kept their eyes away from each other. Daniel thought: *What the hell is she supposed to do with that information?* He said carefully, "You know that there's no such thing as a real ghost, right?"

"Okay," Gal said.

Later, Daniel said to Matt, "I don't love this new compliant *okay* of hers. What does it even mean? It sounds as if she's saying that she'll play along with whatever horrible or confusing thing you throw at her."

"God, that's so true!" Matt said. "It's like *you* say, 'There's no hope left, there is no God in heaven or goodness in the world,' and then *she* says"—he made his eyes go blank and slackened his face in a spot-on imitation of her—"*Okay.*"

"So what do you think a ghost would look like?" Daniel asked her now.

She thought of Cam's skeleton and then her mind stalled out and she looked at him, finding angry tears gathering between her eyes. "I don't know!" she cried. "You tell me!" She stood, knocked her chair over, and ran out of the room. Noam looked up, startled, and began to wail.

"Here we go," Daniel said, sitting down heavily and patting his knees for Noam to come over.

Matt rose to clear dishes to hide the tears stinging his eyes. "I don't know if I can do this, Dan," he said.

"Let's think it through," Daniel said, lifting Noam onto his lap and grabbing the long transparent plastic tube with the tiny plastic beads that clattered down through a maze, and turning it vertically so Noam could watch them drop. "She needs a costume for school. That's the very minimum. And we should probably count on trick-or-treating, which means a costume for Noam, too."

"I don't think I can handle this," Matt said.

"I heard you," Daniel said.

"So can you take this one?" Matt asked.

"Sure," Daniel said.

"Thanks, honey," Matt said, his voice thickening as he loaded dishes into the dishwasher.

"Are you crying?" Daniel said. "Don't cry." He turned the toy upside down and inhaled sharply in mock surprise as the beads cascaded down again, making Noam laugh. "It's just such a huge bummer," he burst out. "She's totally weird and unpredictable, and now she's being totally morbid. What are we paying the damned therapist for?"

"It's Halloween," Matt said gently. "She's supposed to be morbid."

They were quiet, aside from the sounds of clattering beads, as Matt filled the dishwasher with soap and turned it on, lifted the tray off the high chair and brought it to the sink to wash off the tomato slime and seeds, and the warm, gunky cheese plastered to it. He wanted to thank Daniel more profusely, Daniel who wasn't good at crafts and preferred to leave that stuff to him, but he didn't want to press the volatile Jay issue. He ran the tray under the water, rubbing off the cheese with his fingernails, then shook it off and wiped it with a towel. He looked at

Daniel and Noam, who were watching the tube toy with lazy eyes and the same faint smile, Daniel barefoot in jeans and his Oberlin sweatshirt, the baby slouched against him. Noam's wispy brown hair was darkening, coming in the color of Daniel's, and his eyes, too; they'd become the chocolaty color that Matt had fallen in love with in Daniel.

"I'm going to encourage her to be something more innocuous," Daniel said, "like a Teenage Mutant Ninja Turtle or something."

"Dude, don't," Matt groaned. "That's so twentieth century."

"Or Pocahontas."

"Please."

"Then what? What's an appropriate and benign cultural figure?"

"SpongeBob," Matt said. "Any Harry Potter character. Batman. He's a classic—he never goes out of style."

"Okay," Daniel said, standing and lifting Noam into Matt's arms. "I'm going up. Wish me luck."

He tapped gently on the bedroom door and waited, but didn't hear anything. He opened it slowly and peered in to see Gal sitting cross-legged on her bed with her horses arranged around her.

"Hi," he said. "I have an idea." He came in and stood against the door frame, his arms crossed. "How about dressing up as one of the Harry Potter characters? You could be Hermione."

She'd been waiting for him to come, hoping he would, and now she was torn by the impulses to draw him in and push him out. If she closed her eyes, she could hear her father's voice, and it pained her to have this strange and difficult shadow-father instead of her real one. "I don't want to be a Harry Potter character," she said, pronouncing it scornfully with chewy American *r*'s, instead of the Israeli way with guttural *r*'s—"Herrie *Poe*-tair"—as if it were the English way that was bastardized. "I want to be a ghost."

She eyed him as he lowered his backside to the floor and sat up against the wall. "Why is that so important?" he asked. "You can be anything you'd like."

"I don't know why, it just is," she said. It was the one costume she knew for sure was appropriate, that was one thing. She feared that if she listened to one of his or Matt's suggestions, she'd be dressed as something that would make grown-ups laugh but kids wouldn't even know what she was supposed to be. And she'd looked forward to it! She had a vague but urgent sense that she'd be scary as a ghost, only scary in a way that was acceptable, even fun. Not scary as the girl with the accent, with no-heads parents. She imagined drifting through her school, Hannah looking at her with admiration for wearing something so much better than a white sheet.

"Can you explain why?" he asked. "If you could explain, I'd understand it better."

A hitch of ire, of defeat. *Takshivi la'milim sheli*—Listen to my words—it was something Sari, her teacher in *gan*, used to say, stooping and turning her face toward hers. Why did she have to explain it to him? Hadn't she already explained? She felt winded; talking to him was like trying to blow into a recorder, where you couldn't get your breath to gather into a note and all you could hear was panting and spit. "You never listen!" she said. "Forget it, I don't want your help!" She threw herself facedown on her pillow.

Daniel rubbed his mouth with two fingers, picked up a barrette from under his thigh, closed his hand over it, and looked at the cluster of totemic objects sitting on her desk among the messy piles of workbooks and the spray of pens and pencils: a tiny framed picture of herself with her parents, various rocks, beads, and small plastic animals, a flashlight powered by a hand crank, a coral bracelet Val had brought her back from a trip to Florida, a Lego helicopter. He wanted to help her, but everything he could think of he knew she'd reject. He proposed to himself that her difficulty was bigger than just one of arts and crafts, that it had to do with the concept of returning from the dead. Maybe it was his job to help release her from her painful fixation on that idea. That thought warmed in him and became pressing.

"You know that people don't come back from the dead, right?" he said gently.

"*Oof!*" Gal shouted. She rose abruptly and kicked over the little stool she used as a side table; her clock and cup shot across the room and the clock burst open as it hit the wall, its batteries clattering to the floor. "Why you keep saying that?" she screamed. "You say you're helping me but you're *not* helping me, you never help me!"

"Fine," Daniel said coldly. He got up and left the room, fuming, closing the door behind him, hearing her angry sobs as he went downstairs.

Matt had risen from the couch at the noise, and come to the bottom of the stairs. "What happened?"

Daniel moved past him and sank into an armchair, his face rigidly set. "Nothing. I'm a terrible person who refuses to help. A ghost? It's not even original."

"Did you say that?"

"No," Daniel said, indignant. "Why does everybody keep treating me like a monster?"

Matt regarded him thoughtfully. "I'll tell you what," he said. "I've been thinking, and I've made a decision." He paused for dramatic effect. "I'm going to pull myself up by my bootstraps about this Halloween thing."

"What?" Daniel said, mouth agape. He pounded himself on the ear. "I hear someone saying something, but it's very faint, very foreign, I don't know what language it's in. *Sprechen sie deutsch?*"

"Are you finished?" Matt asked. "Are you pleased with yourself?"

"Kinda," Daniel said.

"Okay, forget it then."

"No, tell me. Tell me your decision."

"Don't condescend to me," Matt said.

"I'm not. I really want to hear."

Matt's hands were on his hips. "Okay. I've decided to use the kids' presence as an opportunity to get over my Halloween issues."

"Really! Good for you, Matt," Daniel said.

Matt shot him a look, a spot check for condescension, and when he saw none, his voice picked up with eagerness. "Don't you think this is a good moment for it? I can honor Jay by channeling his spirit into the holiday. And what do you think about this? I'm thinking of calling Kendrick."

Daniel's eyes widened; this part took him entirely by surprise. "What for?"

"Just to get some closure on it. I ended things with him on such a bad note, and that bitterness isn't a healthy thing for me to carry around. It taints Jay's memory."

Daniel was quiet. He was remembering Matt's stories about Kendrick's self-important bustle around Jay, the way he instructed visitors on how they should behave at Jay's sickbed. Kendrick once gave Matt a list of topics he was not to raise—pets, parties, and the movie *Terms of Endearment*, to name just a few—and Matt had snorted, thinking he was joking, until Kendrick shot him a withering look. After hearing that, Daniel thought that the lengths Matt went to in order to stay close to Jay were nothing short of heroic.

"I know," Matt said. "Risky, right?"

"I don't know if it's risky," Daniel said. "It's just that I don't know if Kendrick's the kind of guy you can get closure with. He'll always say just a little something that'll piss you off, put a little bit of poison out there."

Matt nodded thoughtfully. "Maybe," he said. "It's just that I don't think Jay would want his partner and his best friend to be estranged."

"You're a generous soul, sweetie pie. I just hope it doesn't bite you in the ass."

The next day Matt and Gal went to the craft store, after Matt made her promise that she would not scream at him even if she thought he was doing something wrong; instead, she would explain her objection in a regular tone of voice. They bought gauze, and washable white and black paints for the as-yet-undetermined way they would paint her face. They decided that she would wear white, but not a sheet, white tights and a white T-shirt, and that whiteness and sheerness together would make her seem invisible. They practiced draping after dinner till they had Gal wrapped in a way that she could make the fabric ripple a little, yet still move and not trip. Then Matt said, "Okay, let me paint your face."

"What are you going to do?" she asked warily.

"Just let me do it." He raised his eyebrows when she hesitated. "I'm a trained professional. Just let me."

She came to him and lifted her beautiful face to him, its normal stormy twists smoothing into an obedient expanse of creamy cheek, her mouth closed over the adult front teeth that had recently come in and that her face had yet to grow into, her eyes hooded by her dark lashes. He rubbed a delicate wash of white paint over it, letting some skin show through, used just a touch of black paint to hollow out her eyes. Then he said, "Okay, go," and pushed her toward the mirror.

She opened her eyes and looked at him. "I scared to look!" she said.

He took her by the shoulders and marched her to the mirror and she opened her eyes and took in a breath. She lifted her gauze-covered arms, turned her whitened face this way and that. Her dark hair fell to her shoulders; she raked her fingers gently through the hair on one side and tucked it behind her ear, the first preening gesture Matt had ever seen her make. She turned and looked at him, nodded approvingly.

"Good, right?" he asked. "You look amazing. So much more sophisticated than your normal sheet-on-the-head ghost. Go show Daniel."

They could barely stop her relieved chattering to get her to bed; she made use of every adjective she knew in both English and Hebrew in an attempt to describe the effect of the costume. "It's spooky but not *scary*," she said, and then repeated that, enjoying the fine distinction. "It's sophisticated, don't you think? How do you say *sophisticated* in Hebrew? Where's Dani? How do you say *sophisticated* in Hebrew?"

MATT DECIDED TO DRESS Noam as Mr. Potato Head. "Did you know," he'd said to Daniel as he boned up on Mr. Potato Head on the Web, using the laptop they kept in the kitchen, "that on Mr. Potato Head's fortieth birthday, they announced that he would no longer be a 'couch potato'"—he made ostentatious air quotes with his fingers—"and he received a special award from the President's Council on Physical Fitness? That's awesome. I wonder if he had to do little pull-ups."

Matt spent the day on Noam's costume, sewing elastic into an old brown sheet to close at Noam's neck and thighs, gluing paper plates on for ears, and colored felt and cotton for the facial features. He went to three different stores looking for blue socks to put over Noam's sneakers. He bought a kid-sized hard hat and spray-painted it black. He worked in a swirl of quiet satisfaction, diligent problem solving, and blistering self-irony. He was spending the day making a little kid's Halloween costume. He was a stay-at-home mom—in the lingo of the blogs and message boards, a SAHM! It blew his mind that his life had led him to this point. Not that he was the most ambitious guy in the world. What was his ambition? For a while, at the New York firm among the design hotshots, he'd entertained the fantasy of becoming the next Carson or Sagmeister. But over time, working among incredibly single-minded and talented people, he was forced to admit to himself that while he was good, *very* good, he wasn't a design genius, and didn't quite have the drive and focus to convincingly fake it. The realization pained him, but it didn't devastate him. He liked his work, a lot, liked the quiet focus of it, the visual pleasure of something falling into place and the pride of submitting work that was clean and stylish and impeccable.

And let's face it, he thought, moving away from New York to live with Daniel, who had the talent to be a great musician and writer but who viewed ambition as frivolous and crass, pretty much put the nail in that coffin.

Still, what would he tell Kendrick about what he was doing these days? He gingerly peeled back one of the paper-plate ears, testing the dryness of the glue, wondering if he should put in a few staples for good measure. When identifying himself, should he say, "It's Matt," or "It's Matt Greene"? Should he just catch up with him, or should he actually say that he'd called to bury the hatchet? He reminded himself to stick to "I" statements, as he had been instructed to do in a brief and irritating couples therapy with a short-lived boyfriend. And if Kendrick was an officious fuck, what would he say? His mind ran over various options, honing their wit and cuttingness. Then he grabbed the phone before he could think anymore and dialed.

Kendrick answered on the second ring with a quick and intimate "Hi."

"Hi," Matt said uncertainly, thinking that Kendrick couldn't have recognized him from the caller ID, because their phone was listed under Daniel's name. "It's Matt. Greene."

There was a long pause.

"Jay's friend."

"I know who you are. I thought you were someone else." The voice was slightly peevish, slightly congested.

"How's it going?"

"It's going well," Kendrick said.

"That's great," Matt said. "I'm glad to hear that."

Kendrick didn't reciprocate, but then again, Matt remembered, he'd never acquired the skill of saying "And how are *you?*" If you wanted to say anything about yourself, you had to put a stick of dynamite in the conversation and blast right through it.

"Are you waiting for another call?" Matt asked.

"Yeah, I'm fighting with my credit card company about a finance charge," Kendrick said, "and we got disconnected."

Matt smiled, remembering how Kendrick made a point of keeping excellent medical and financial records, and making sure he didn't get overcharged or double-charged; he checked his credit rating obsessively for errors, and reported everything. "Because otherwise how will they learn?" Matt and Jay loved to use his mantra in their conversations.

"I wanted to call," Matt said, picking up a pen and starting to doodle on the little pad of paper sitting on the kitchen table, "because it's Halloween, which always makes me think of Jay."

"Oh, right," Kendrick said. "So where are you living again? Elmira?"

Matt smiled at the snobbery of the New Yorker. "Northampton. Massachusetts."

"Oh yeah, where all the lesbians are," Kendrick said.

"Right," Matt said. "I'm basically a lesbian now."

Kendrick laughed.

"Listen," Matt said, warmed by that, always a sucker for anybody who laughed at his jokes, "I just wanted to touch base, maybe bury the hatchet. I think Jay would want that."

Kendrick was quiet for a few moments. "Well, I appreciate that, I do," he finally said. "He wished we could get along better; it was painful to him that we couldn't."

"I know," Matt said, and continued to the line he'd practiced before calling: "It's just that—I think that we both loved him so much, and were in so much pain, that we weren't at our best with each other."

There was another pause, and then Kendrick said, "True."

"So I'm sorry for my part," Matt said, thinking that this was easier than he'd thought it would be.

"Thanks, Matt," Kendrick said. "Me too. It's just that— I don't know if I should even say this. No, never mind."

Matt's head rolled back on his neck and he closed his eyes. *Here we go*, he thought.

"It's just that—this may be a fault of mine, but I just can't pretend to be nice to people who hurt the people I love."

"What are you talking about?" Matt said while Kendrick continued, "And it really bothered me how bitchy you were to him for making money and being successful. It was like the minute he stopped being your sidekick, you couldn't handle it anymore. That really hurt his feelings, Matt."

"What are you talking about?" Matt repeated.

"Calling him a corporate tool . . ."

Matt cast his mind back, stunned. "That was a joke!" Matt said. "Jay called *himself* a corporate tool!" He worked in the finance department of Goldman Sachs, a job he had landed straight from college and been incredibly successful at.

"He didn't think it was funny."

"You're so full of shit," Matt said heatedly, propelled to his feet, pacing. "He never said anything to me about it, and believe me, he was no shrinking violet when it came to telling me my flaws."

"Forget it. I thought you wanted to have a genuine conversation, but apparently I was wrong."

"I sincerely wanted to make amends," Matt said. "I didn't call to get attacked by you. Jay and I handled our relationship just fine."

"He was *dying*, Matt! He wasn't about to start some huge drama with you."

Matt's mind was spinning. "Look, I don't have time for this. I'm living with a family that's been devastated by a terrorist attack, raising two orphaned children." He winced as he uttered the word *orphaned*.

"Whoa," Kendrick said.

In Kendrick style, as though devoid of the slightest bit of curiosity, he failed to follow up, leaving Matt to wonder if he was undignified enough to throw more unsolicited details out there himself. *You probably read about the Peace Train bombing in Jerusalem earlier this year. It was all over the papers.*

He hung up, sickened. The thought of trick-or-treating had been drained of all its energy and color. Once, he'd loved the huddle of citizens at dusk scurrying from house to house. So what if the occasional house got pelted with eggs, its trees draped with toilet paper? It was a day when Americans answered the door for other American strangers, which seemed marvelous to him. But now: he'd wanted to honor Jay this Halloween, but now he didn't feel like honoring him at all; he was furious at him for hanging on to that hurt and not telling him about it. It was so stupid—it felt petty and vindictive for him to play the game of calling himself a corporate tool and then turn around and complain to Kendrick about it. They'd both seen the absurdity of Jay's huge success at Goldman. Both of them had! This was the guy who had to ask

his professors for extensions for almost every paper he wrote, who
got behind in his bills, whose house was always a total mess. Then he
turned around and got this high-paying job, and lived in the West Village in a building with a doorman, while Matt, in his first design job,
lived in a studio sublet all the way over on Ninth Avenue, surrounded
by someone else's crappy, tasteless things.

He did have to admit that he'd been jealous; he had never cared
about money until he found he wasn't making very much, at least
by New York standards. But he felt that he and Jay had managed that
well, through the high-level aggressive irony in which they told each
other truths they couldn't say more straightforwardly. Apparently he
was wrong. And Jay had complained to Kendrick, not him. Of everything, that was the thing that sickened him most. He'd always thought
of himself as closer in than Kendrick was, even though Kendrick was
Jay's partner. They'd seen lovers come and go, and dished about them
all, even to Jay's dying day, when they'd rolled their eyes together over
some antic or other of Kendrick's. It was unbearable to think that Jay
and Kendrick rolled their eyes about *him*. Unbearable. And he couldn't
even conjure Jay to be furious at him, because most of his memories
were of Jay after he was already sick, emaciated, with Kaposi's lesions
on his neck and face.

THE NEXT MORNING WAS gray and cold; Matt, wearing only a sweatshirt over his pajamas, shivered as he yelled at Yo-yo to poop, knowing
that if someone was yelling at *him* to poop, he'd never give them the satisfaction. Inside there was a squall of panic, yelling, and frenzied phone
calls, because it turned out that Gal didn't know if they were supposed
to wear their costumes on the bus to school, or bring them and put
them on there. "What if I'm the only one on the school bus wearing a
costume?" she'd asked, eyes wide in panic.

He hoped it was solved before he went back inside, and it was—at
least the kids whose parents they'd reached would be wearing their cos-

tumes on the bus. Matt got busy working on her face. He waited with her in front of the house, said "Look, see?" when the bus pulled up, populated by kids in masks, capes, armored suits. "Just be careful not to step on the gauze," he reminded her for the tenth time. He watched her stomp up the big stairs and felt a pang, knowing he was sending her off to a world with so many land mines, knowing how hard she thought about every step she took, every word she spoke.

Daniel was waiting for him inside. "PHEW!" he bellowed, and they laughed. Matt followed him up the stairs as Daniel went to shave and dress for work.

Gal sat on the bus, adjusting the gauze around her, carefully checking out the other kids' costumes. Emma was dressed as Hermione! And James as Spider-Man. Ava, who brought tofu for lunch, was a kitty cat in a wool striped bodysuit, whiskers painted on her face. What a baby, Gal thought.

Did they know what she was supposed to be? She dreaded someone coming up to her and loudly asking, "What are you supposed to be?" A bigger boy, a third-grader dressed as a knight, stomped up to her row, examined her through his visor, and sat down without a word.

Ms. Wheeler was waiting for the bus, and when Gal stepped off, she said, "Oh, Gal, what a great, scary ghost you are!" and Gal watched carefully to see if she gave similar compliments to the other kids, which would mean she just said that to everybody. She turned at the doors and looked for Hannah but couldn't find her. She noticed that she was the only ghost, which first pleased her, because it might mean she was original, and then scared her, because it might mean that everybody else thought it was stupid. She went in and sat down at her desk, pulling at the gauze where it caught in the chair's joints, listening to the chatter of kids, holding herself in readiness to be addressed.

Ms. Wheeler was clapping her hands to get them to quiet down, and soon her tablemates jostled around. She peered around them, looking for Hannah, but couldn't find her. Hannah was absent today! She knew because Miles and Jake were both on Hannah's bus, and they were there. Maybe, she thought, Hannah had missed the bus, and her mom would come rushing in with her soon, a harried expression on her face.

Jake was a lion with whiskers drawn on his cheeks. "Gali pacholly," he said to her with a look of complacency. "You're the most ghost."

She looked at him with an uncertain smile, trying to figure out if he was teasing her in a nice way or a mean way. A minute later she thought that she should have made up some singsong nonsense, too. She mouthed to herself, *Jakie pachakie.* But by then they were lining up for a parade through the school, and Hannah wasn't there, and Alexis, who was dressed as a princess, was crowding in front of her. Gal felt herself jostled backward, felt a jolt of irritation. Alexis's princess gown trailed on the floor; Gal surreptitiously stepped on the hem. And when they began to walk, there was a rip, and then a howl.

"It was an accident!" Gal said.

Ms. Wheeler came hustling over to examine the ripped and dirty hem. "I'm sure Gal didn't mean to," she said, crouching in front of Alexis like she did when a kid was upset so she could look her in the face.

She hadn't meant to. She told herself that she'd meant just to pull it a little. But seeing Alexis glower tearfully in her direction, Gal decided that it didn't matter, because she was dead anyway, she was invisible, floating through the classroom and through the wall to the hallway, where she drifted, trailing a finger along the bulletin boards and the banks of lockers, looking down on them because they belonged to little kids, while she was so big and so old she was dead.

CHAPTER 15

IN THE DAYS leading up to her grandparents' arrival, Gal grew increasingly excited. Everywhere they went, she wondered aloud whether they'd like it there. A visit to a sushi restaurant gave loose to a torrent of speculation. "Do you think Sabba and Savta have ever eaten sushi?" she asked. She spoke in Hebrew now that Matt could understand most of what she said, although sometimes, when he missed a word but clung to the narrative for dear life, hoping the context would explain it, and then realized he couldn't do without the word after all and was forced to stop her, she heaved a mighty sigh and let out a long-suffering *Oof!* Matt relished the Hebrew he was learning, because it gave him an excuse to be rude. His favorite expression was *"Ma pitom!"*—which meant a combination of "No way!" and "What are you talking about!"—which he loved to exaggerate by uttering it with the loudest, most obnoxious heap of scorn. Or *"Nu?"*—uttered like an elbow to the ribs. He loved that, and he loved the difference in pronunciation between *chet* and *chaf*, the Sephardic *chet* being throatier, gaggier, as *ayin* was to *aleph*.

"I think Savta will love edamame, don't you?" Gal said now. "Because she loves little tasty things like that. Sabba, though, not so much. He likes chicken, and he likes cake. I really can't think of anything else he likes to eat. Oh! Watermelon seeds. I personally"—Matt's and

Daniel's eyebrows rose: *I personally?*—"don't like those as much as sunflower seeds or pumpkin seeds, and when I eat them I just eat the whole thing, because they're so tiny it's not really worth it to get off the skin."

She paused, stabbed a piece of maki with a chopstick, stirred it in the cloudy soy sauce, and nibbled a tiny piece off the edge. "But to get back to Savta and Sabba," she said. "I thought I wouldn't remember them because I didn't see them for such a long time, but as you can see, I remember a lot! Hoo! Spicy!" She reached for her glass of water, gulped it down. "I like spicy foods even though I'm Ashkenazi, and Ashkenazim don't usually like spicy food. Sabba and Savta *definitely* don't like spicy food." She cast Matt a warning look.

"Then we shan't cook spicy food," he said, responding as he normally did, in English. "Any other instructions?"

Gal furrowed her brow and pondered. "You have to be nice to them," she said, her voice lowered. "They had a very hard life."

They looked at her and nodded. Daniel said, "We'll be very nice to them and make them feel very welcome, Gal, okay?"

"I really will make them feel as welcome as I can," Matt later said to Daniel. They were sweeping through the house as they did every night after the kids were asleep, tossing toys into the wooden blanket chest that had become a toy chest, picking up stray socks and jackets, putting the plastic keyboard with the mirror and rattle karaoke microphone, and the toy vacuum cleaner with the popping balls, and the musical phone on wheels with the popping eyes—rotary style, bells ringing as the rotary jiggered and the handset clunked along, a weird anachronistic appendage—into the corners.

Daniel had dug up his old copy of *Survival in Auschwitz*, and over the past week had been reading, flinching now and then at the marginal comments he'd written as a college freshman. "Here's the thing," he told Matt now, his hands and elbows crammed with toy pieces that had to be distributed to their proper toy. "People who survived didn't survive by putting down their heads and being invisible. They schemed, they bartered, they used—or often faked—certain skills, like metalworking or sewing, in order to get in with the SS. They walked away from the edges of a camp or a death march. They jumped into the latrine and hid in the shit.

"But there are also a ton of split-second decisions, sudden pre-monitions—get into this line, not that line! Or arbitrary events like being marched with a group up to the very door of the gas chamber, and a commander comes in yelling that it's the wrong group. Can you imagine the fucked-up messages you'd take from this? You have control over your own survival, and your survival is totally arbitrary. How are you supposed to go on after that, put one foot in front of the other? No wonder Malka loses her mind." He paused. "So you can imagine," he said, "what Israel meant to them."

"Totally," Matt said. "Israel was awesome because it nurtured the delusion that they had control over their own survival."

Daniel laughed. "I wouldn't have put it that way," he said, "but— yeah."

Matt stood and leaned back groaning, hands at his lower back, as Daniel put the plastic cake pieces onto the plastic cake dish, and two crayons into the big plastic bag of crayons, most of whose wrappers Gal had peeled off, in the art supply basket. "I'll be super nice and welcoming. But Jesus Christ, *more* parents? I'm dying here, Daniel."

"It's written into the custody agreement," Daniel said. He'd danced a tortuous and delicate dance with them over the course of several phone conversations, in which he invited them to stay with him and Matt and the kids, certain they couldn't afford two weeks in a hotel, but trying not to mention that fact, knowing that staying with him and Matt was a deeply unpleasant prospect for them. Because he felt that visiting their grandkids shouldn't be a huge financial drain. But he hadn't told Matt that; he'd told him that staying with them was written into the custody agreement. It was easier that way; he just didn't want to have to negotiate *everything*.

"I know! Stop saying that," Matt said from the playroom doorway. "It doesn't mean I have to be happy about it."

"I'm very aware of your feelings, Matt. I'm not exactly thrilled either, and it doesn't help for you to keep bitching about it."

"I'm not *bitching*, Daniel. I'm trying to say something serious." He stared at Daniel till Daniel turned and looked at him. "You know, I never expected to have kids, and that's turned out to be *fine*. It's having three sets of very present parents that's destroying my soul."

Daniel raised his eyebrows. "Destroying your *soul*?"

"Doesn't it bother *you*?"

Daniel shrugged. "I think the more people around, the less I dwell on things."

His honesty softened and disarmed Matt, who said, "Honey."

"But, hey!" Daniel said with a sudden bright idea. "Your Hebrew has gotten really good, so you can talk to them now."

"What am I supposed to talk to them about?"

They were quiet for a second, then Matt said, his spirits lifted because they seemed not to be fighting anymore, "How 'bout that Holocaust! That sure sucked, didn't it."

Daniel cut his eyes at him.

"Oh, is that one of those things I'm not allowed to joke about because I'm not Jewish?"

"Yeah, this might be one of those things," Daniel said drily. "Ask them about fighting for independence, that makes more sense."

"Hmm. So, how 'bout that *Nakba*!" he said, using the Arabic word for "disaster." "It sure sucked for those Palestinians to be driven from their homes, didn't it!"

Daniel shot him an irritated look. "Do you have to do that?"

"What?"

"You always take it a step too far."

"Please! It's not like you believe they were such cowards they just fled."

Daniel sighed. He had just one thing left in his hands, a plastic spotted dog that went with the Legos, and he tossed it into the plastic bin that held them. "It's one thing not to believe that, and another thing to drive the point home, over and over, all the time."

"You mean like the way gay people have to rub it in the faces of straight people over and over, all the time?"

Daniel groaned. "Oh God. That too! That drives me crazy!"

Matt stared at him. "Remind me why we're together again?"

"I don't know!" Daniel said. "Because you keep a lovely home."

"That's true," Matt said complacently.

"And because you deal with the other parents."

Matt thought about those conversations he had with some of the moms during drop-off or pickup from school, where they shrieked with laughter as though everything that came out of his mouth was a camp classic, and called him *darling* in affected theatrical voices. "Well, I'm their gay pet," he said.

He was finding that the why-are-we-together jokes were helpful, that if it was spoken aloud, the idea didn't frighten him so much. When they went upstairs to look at their closets and figure out how to make space for Malka's and Yaakov's clothes, and Daniel emptied his own closet because it was less full than Matt's, and because he knew how much it pained Matt to have his clothes mashed together in the downstairs hall closet, Matt thought: *Ha! Another reason.* Then he was depressed that he was thinking of reasons at all.

His new strategy was to stop acting as though he wanted sex, to hold himself proudly aloof. Brent had laughed when he told him that. "Aloof?! That's not really your thing."

A SNOWSTORM WAS FORECASTED for that night, but it looked as though Malka and Yaakov's flight would just squeak in before it arrived. Daniel took Gal down to pick them up in Hartford, while Matt stayed home and put Noam to bed. Gal was pensive in the car, and Daniel peeked back at her periodically in the rearview mirror to see her gazing out the window, where she'd wiped a clear circle into the fog. It was late, past her bedtime, and her eyes were puffy. A cold sleet was falling; the dusk traffic was heavy; the wipers left a streak across the center of Daniel's vision. The billboards imparted messages from grocery stores, from jewelers and ophthalmologists, of holiday faith and goodwill, the kind of messages that always made him grateful he was Jewish, and therefore not implicated. Gal was relieved to be on vacation; she continued to find school a strain, which pained him. He suspected that as a bilingual kid whose English was still developing, she wasn't considered one of the smartest kids in the class, which was probably excruciating for a superquick and competitive kid like her. What was happening socially, he didn't know; he just knew that she didn't bring friends home, or ask to go over to kids' houses.

He made the perilous merge into Springfield traffic. An enormous Santa and reindeer in lights lit up the office buildings and parking garage to his left. He glanced back again in the rearview mirror and saw Gal drawing imaginary letters on her pants, spelling something out.

The flight from Newark was half an hour late, and they had to wait in a stretch of airport with two rows of four chairs set against the wall, and no shops or restaurants except for the ancient cafeteria, which was already barred shut. Daniel cursed the fact that he hadn't brought anything for them to read or do. He took a stray section of the *Valley Advocate* from the sole empty seat and sat on the floor, facing a monitor, his back against a wall. Gal scuffed her boots along the airport's carpet and watched the people emerging from the gates. "They're not on this flight," he told her. "They haven't landed yet."

"*Oof!*" She wheeled around and scuffed away, and he watched her take a very long drink from the water fountain. She came and asked if she could ride the escalators, and he said he'd rather she didn't because he wouldn't be able to see her when she was downstairs. "You will if you stand at the top," she said. He sighed and stood, and she rode down and back up, down and back up again, solemnly. The thought of seeing Sabba and Savta made her shiver, as if she were under a billowing silk cloak, dark and dangerous and beautiful, waiting for it to drape over her. She tried to conjure their faces. She remembered the constellation of pocks on Sabba's cheeks, and the way she could see his thick tongue resting behind his bottom teeth when he laughed. She remembered the soft feel of Savta's shoulder under a cardigan and her baby powder smell, and then a very clear memory popped out, Savta looking at her with a strange expression, saying, "You are a miracle, you and your brother both. You were not supposed to be born." That had made Gal uneasy even though she didn't know what it meant exactly, and she'd somehow known that it wasn't something she should ask Ema about, because Ema would be mad. She pondered this for a moment, and then her mind moved deftly away from it, concentrating on stepping on and off the escalator at the right moment.

When the flight from Newark finally landed, it seemed to take ages for the passengers to deboard, and by the time people began trickling through the exits, first one or two and then bigger groups, Gal was grinding her fists into her eyes with peevish exhaustion, and Daniel was suddenly finding things wrong with the way she looked—her face white with exhaustion, her hair ratty, a shoelace untied. He actually had a comb in his coat pocket, but he didn't dare bring it to her hair. He detested himself for his worry about her appearance, but he never forgot that his guardianship of her and Noam was provisional.

Then she squirted out from under his arm and ran toward the elderly couple in enormous coats that was coming through the door. They bent over and caught her in a hug that made the people around them smile, exclaiming, "You came!" and "You're still awake? You must be so tired!" The duty-free shopping bag looped over Malka's arm slipped to the floor, along with her purse, and Yaakov stooped to pick them up, then took his beaming granddaughter into an awkward hug, the bags banging on Gal's back.

Malka was wiping tears from her eyes. Daniel hung back, smiling, pained as he felt the reunion from their perspective. They were wearing new matching parkas, shiny navy blue, bought for a harsher winter than they were accustomed to, and carrying shopping bags and plastic bags that looked as if they contained a hundred tin foil–covered paper plates of mandelbrot and rugelach.

They came up to Daniel and he had a moment of uncertainty: kisses or handshakes or neither? Yaakov extended his hand with a bluff, mirthless "Shalom, shalom," and Daniel shook it, saying, "Welcome." Malka lifted her face, with its delicate web of lines, to kiss his cheek. "I look at you and I see your brother, even though you've grown so skinny," she murmured.

"Oh, not that skinny," he said.

She gave him a keen appraising look, very Israeli, and said, "You're really very skinny."

Their suitcases, which Daniel hauled off the carousel, were ancient paisley canvas, pre-wheels vintage. By the time they got to the car, he was panting and sweating, cursing himself for being too cheap to rent a luggage cart. It had begun to snow.

MALKA AND YAAKOV REFUSED to take the master bedroom, insisting that he and Matt sleep in their own bed. Matt and Daniel brought every argument to bear they could. The only TV in the house was in their room. It was so much more private! It was warmer up there! They wouldn't have to share a bathroom! But they were adamant that they didn't want Daniel and Matt to go to any trouble. So Daniel and Matt carried all the clothes back into their closets and re-set up their toiletries in the master bathroom. "This is making more trouble," Matt said. "They'll be in the middle of the house all day, every day."

"Don't," Daniel said. "I'm trying to keep up my morale."

Malka and Yaakov carefully hung up their clothes in the front hall closet. Then Daniel came down and helped them blow up and put sheets on the air mattress, while Gal sat on the couch, gazing at her grandparents beatifically. "I'm so glad it's snowing outside," she said. "Because that's something you don't see in Israel very much."

It snowed all night, the huge, silent flakes that cluster in a moment on hair and eyelashes, and when Matt and Daniel awoke it was still snowing. "Great," Daniel sighed, his heart sinking at the thought of a day at home with grandparents and children. He called the college weather line, which informed him that nonessential personnel did not need to report to work, and as the children slept, he and Matt turned on a local news station without the sound and watched the school closure tickers. They could hear movement downstairs, the toilet flushing, the ding of the toaster. "There," Matt said. "Closed." There was no sound from the kids' room, so they sank back under the covers, Daniel draping his cold legs over Matt's warm ones, and sank back into a rare morning sleep.

Gal awoke buoyant, taking in the snowstorm and the warm, full house, and ran downstairs, where Malka and Yaakov sat at the kitchen table with toast and coffee. She buried her head in their laps and chests and let them stroke her, and showed them how she knew how to make her own breakfast of cereal and milk, with a banana cut on top. She ate with relish, milk slopping over the spoon, talking with her mouth full about snow days and the kinds of things American kids did in the snow.

AT FIRST MATT AND Daniel enjoyed the new and improved Gal, cheerful and cooperative—the "Sure!" that met her grandparents' suggestions or requests. "I'll get them!" she'd yell when Yaakov patted his shirt pocket for his reading glasses, and off she'd go. She talked to Noam in front of them in a fulsome loving voice, and volunteered to set the table every night.

"What!" Daniel and Matt would jocularly exclaim. "Who are you and what have you done with our Gal!" After a while, though, Matt confessed to Daniel that he was finding it a little creepy. "It's just not her!" he said. "There's something about it that makes me sad."

"Really?" Daniel said with surprise. "I think she's just happy to have them here."

Matt shook his head. There was something about them that made you lurch to take care of them. To the naked eye, they were just old folks who drank tea, had a passion for Sudoku, and watched the American nightly news, translated by Daniel, with clucks of the tongue and shaking heads, invariably asking if this or that public figure was Jewish. Their pills and vitamins lined the windowsill above the kitchen sink, doled out carefully by Yaakov every morning. They had set up a five-hundred-piece jigsaw puzzle of a Swiss chalet surrounded by wildflowers on the dining room table, and Malka and Gal worked on it for half an hour before bed, Malka sitting with her glasses on her nose, patiently trying this piece and that, Gal pacing around the table mumbling to herself: "There!" and "*Yofi*, Savta!"

Maybe, Matt thought, it was the way they never asked a follow-up question—so when Gal told them about getting one hundred on a spelling test, they didn't ask what the hardest word was. The bottom just dropped right out of the conversation. Or maybe it was the way there was never the right amount of food in the refrigerator. When Daniel went grocery shopping with Malka, he came home with twice the amount of food he normally did, and then, when the refrigerator was full to bursting, Malka anxiously exhorted everyone to eat the food before it went to waste. "What did we buy this yogurt for, if nobody's going to eat it?" she'd demand. She peered into the pots as Daniel or Matt cooked, and asked whether they were sure there would be enough, whether they should take a bread out of the freezer to supplement the meal. And then, at the end of every meal, Yaakov groaned, "Why did you let me eat so much?" and spent the next few hours with his belt unbuckled, complaining of gas.

It was hard, when Matt and Daniel fell into bed at the end of the day, not to attribute their behaviors to their childhoods in the Holocaust, even though that felt weirdly hushed, ghoulish, fetishistic. They knew only what they'd heard from Ilana, or heard from Ilana via Joel, who said that the information Ilana had was itself spotty and contradictory. She knew, he told them, that her parents didn't want her to know about their lives in the Holocaust, and she wasn't even sure how she did know; she felt as though she'd learned by osmosis. Then she pretended that she didn't know.

They knew that Yaakov had been a child in the Lodz ghetto; that he'd survived by looking bigger and older than his ten years and being sent to work in a Nazi metalworking factory, and by running with a pack of teenagers who stole and shared food. His parents and his two younger brothers had not survived. The aura he projected around them and around Malka was that he was surrounded by a pack of incompetents—lots of condescending laughter and put-upon sighs at the way they blundered. "Do you think he acts that way because everyone around him died?" Matt asked. "Because they just weren't competent enough to stay alive?"

"Beats me," Daniel said. "But the food thing is definitely about having been a hungry kid."

He and Matt peered up at the ceiling and blinked, their minds working at what profound hunger would be like for a child, imagining against their wills being unable to feed Noam and Gal.

One night after the kids were asleep, Daniel invited Malka and Yaakov into the living room to have a conversation about Noam's developmental delays. He sat with a glass of wine in the wood rocker, while Malka warmed her hands around a mug of tea and Yaakov shifted beside her on the couch in a posture of uncomfortable readiness. He'd never had a serious conversation with them by himself, or a conversation where everyone was on the same side, and he found himself turning toward Malka; it was just impossible to maintain eye contact with Yaakov. "He's twenty-one months old now," he said, "and he isn't walking yet or saying very much."

"He's such a good boy," Malka said. "He seems calm and contented."

Daniel suddenly remembered something Ilana had once told him— that Malka hadn't grown up around other children and had never had a normal childhood herself, so when she had Ilana she was at a loss. Ilana said she remembered quite clearly that when she became a toddler demanding independence and throwing tantrums, it was very frightening to her mother.

"I know. We love him very much," Daniel said, conscious of using the word *we*. "There doesn't seem to be anything wrong with him phys-ically. Our pediatrician wanted him tested for neurological disorders and autism." As he said that, he saw Malka's eyes fill with tears. "But till now, we've refused. We think he has suffered very badly, and because he doesn't have the words for what he lost, this is how we're seeing it. But now, more months have passed, and we might have to reconsider."

"*Misken*," Yaakov said. "Poor little boy. So once again, the Arabs fin-ish what the Nazis started."

"Yaakov," Malka murmured.

"You're very right in what you're doing," Yaakov said. "You must stand strong. The doctors have no idea what they're doing."

"Do you need a new doctor?" Malka asked.

"We don't think so, but honestly, we're not sure."

"Maybe you should take him to a specialist," Malka said. "To a . . . what's it called?" She turned to Yaakov, snapping her fingers to bring on the word. "A neurologist."

"They don't know what they're talking about," Yaakov said bitterly. "They think that if they have a fancy degree, they can take the measure of a child who has suffered—who has suffered beyond what they can imagine."

"But maybe the child—"

"The child is fine!" he snapped.

Malka sat back on the couch with a look of resignation and folded her hands. "Okay," she said, her mouth pursed. "I just thought—"

"You thought, you thought!" Yaakov mockingly smacked his hand against his forehead. "That's the trouble, you thinking!"

Daniel felt the blood rise and burn in his face. "I thought it would help me to have this conversation," he said coldly, standing, "but I see I was wrong."

Yaakov's face worked; he put his fingers to the bridge of his nose.

"He's sorry," Malka said. "This is sad, about the child. And with the birthday coming up." Ilana's birthday was in a few days, and they were all dreading it.

"He's not the only one who's sad, Malka," Daniel said.

"Shh, shh, I know," she murmured.

CHRISTMAS CAME WITHOUT NOTICE by anyone but Matt. He drove to Derrick and Brent's house on Christmas Day, listening to holiday songs on the radio, thinking that he didn't really mind missing Christmas in this household of Jews but that he did kind of mind their not noticing that he was missing it. The day was gray and the streets were empty; clusters of cars were parked askew in people's driveways. Derrick and Brent had gone to Derrick's sister's in North Carolina to visit the nieces and nephews, and he was supposed to stop in and feed their two beautiful and haughty tortoiseshell cats, Miles and Ella, twice a day. He parked on the street and let himself in. Their condo was in downtown Northampton, a small but pristine two-story apartment back by the fire department with a galley kitchen whose space they maximized by hanging their pots and pans from a rod they hung from the ceiling, and a living room with a bay window with a bench along it, which was padded with bright cushions and pillows. They'd left the radio on low, and it was playing classical music. Two champagne flutes stood upside down in the dish dryer; the news of Brent's tenure had come right before they left. At the sound of the can opener, the cats sauntered into the kitchen, chirping, and wound themselves around Matt's legs.

He watched them eat for a few minutes. Then he opened the cabinets and contemplated. Derrick was a vegetarian, and glass jars of pasta and grains, some of which Matt didn't recognize—bulgur? quinoa? farro?—lined the shelves in austere harmony. On the top shelf there was a box of schoolboy biscuits covered with dark chocolate, and although Matt preferred milk chocolate, he took out two and ate them, then opened the fridge and swallowed some milk out of the carton. He looked at the calendar hanging on the wall and saw all the dates Derrick and Brent had made in December with other friends. Steve and Bruce—he'd met them once at a concert—were marked down three times, the third time as *S&B*. They were getting ahead of him and Daniel, he thought with anxious rancor. Were they still Derrick and Brent's best friends? Well, it wasn't Steve and Bruce they'd asked to feed the cats, he thought. Surely that meant something.

THE EVENING BEFORE ILANA'S birthday, Matt and Daniel went through the photo albums with Gal and Noam, Noam making the rhythmic *scritch-scritch* sound of hard pacifier sucking, Gal all interruptions and whipping hair and knees on the page and knocking the wind out of them with hard plops onto their laps.

The birthday fell on a Saturday, and after breakfast Daniel gathered them in the living room, where they sat in their separate spaces with their feet on the ground and hands in their laps, made self-conscious by the aura of solemnity. On the coffee table he'd set the most recent photo album, the one taken after Noam was born. He had set a yarhzeit candle beside it, which Yaakov objected to, since it wasn't the anniversary of Ilana's death. "I know, Yaakov," he said, "but I wanted a memorial candle." Gal was cross-legged on the floor, and next to her, Matt sat with his legs spread, Noam between them, playing with a stacking toy.

Daniel scraped a match against the box and it flamed, and nearly went out as he brought it to the candle's wick; then they both blossomed into a glow. They watched the candle wobble in its small glass. "Can I speak about a memory?" Daniel began in Hebrew, leaning against the wall, his arms crossed. "Well, my brother was always a pretty happy guy—successful, tons of friends. But when he got together with Ilana, it was different. His eyes glowed as if he had a special secret. He looked satisfied, completely comfortable in his skin."

They sat in awkward silence for a few minutes, until he said, "That's all." Then Malka reached over and pulled Gal onto her lap on the couch. "I remember, like it was yesterday, the day you were born. Of course, your *ema* read all these books about childbirth, and had ideas of how she wanted it to go. Very strong ideas, as she always had, you know her.

She had a CD she made of songs celebrating life, and children, and the waves, and new beginnings, and when she got to her room at Shaare Zedek they told her the CD player was broken! I thought she'd be furious! She worked very hard on that CD, and wanted you to come into the world with those songs in your ears. But she gave a big laugh and said, 'My first lesson in having children! It just doesn't always go the way you think it will!'"

"Really? She said that?" Gal said, craning around to look into her grandmother's face.

"Yes, she said that. I was so proud of her. She was such a wonderful mother. She loved you two more than anything in the world."

"Yes, she did," Yaakov said. "But for some reason I remember her most as a little girl herself. I remember teaching her to ride a bike, how she howled and howled till she could do it by herself. She was like that with everything—crawling, tying her shoes, every new thing she had to learn, until she learned it, she made our lives miserable. And then suddenly: sunshine! 'And I love you, Abbaleh, and I love you, Shmabbaleh.'" He said that last in a high-pitched, grateful, obsequious way that made Gal laugh and Daniel narrow his eyes, hearing the derision in it, milder and more comic than the derision he'd aimed at his wife, but there just the same.

Then it was Gal's turn; she saw them look at her. She looked at the picture of her mother, looked at herself in the picture, her hair plastered by drying seawater across her forehead. These days she was having more and more trouble remembering her mother, which she kept secret from everybody, even her grief counselor. What remained were tormenting snatches of sense memory: being lifted under the armpits and rising into the air, the pain of a comb being pulled through her hair, her mother's arms bobbing on the water as she encouraged her to swim to her, ballooning huge in the water's reflection, then contracting, the feeling of dark and thunder when her mother was displeased. But no funny stories. Nothing she could tell.

Matt and Daniel were looking at her with unbearable sweetness;

her grandmother's chin rested on the top of her head. Finally, Matt's eyes narrowed. He turned to them with a bright expression on his face. "I have a story," he said.

They looked at him with surprise.

"I know I came late into Ilana's life," he said, blundering forward in Hebrew, "and didn't know her very well, but wow, she made a big impression on me! I remember the first time Joel and Ilana came to visit us here. I was waking up, and I heard yelling downstairs. So I stayed, cowering, in the bedroom. I thought they were having a big fight. I didn't want to interrupt. *Lo na'im!*" He spoke with élan and many hand gestures, stumbling over this word and that, gripping his upper arms with his fists and shivering to convey his fear, suddenly worrying even as he was telling it that his story might be a little inappropriate. It was the familiar feeling of the blurter: he was into it now, and he'd gone too far to turn back. "Finally, I came downstairs and approached the noise, and when I went into the kitchen I saw that they were just having a conversation!"

It didn't go over very well. Malka and Yaakov were looking at him with amazed puzzlement. He was telling Ilana's parents that their daughter was loud. He was a gentile telling Jews that they were loud.

For her part, Gal was still lost in thought, staring at the framed photograph of her mother till her vision blurred, trying to think of something to say. And then it came to her, descended upon her like an angel's touch, and she looked up brightly. "I want to go back to Israel and live with Savta and Sabba," she said.

In the few seconds before the din of dismay and confusion set in, Matt felt relief: This certainly overshadowed his inappropriateness! Then Yaakov slammed his hand on the table, making them all jump, stood abruptly and walked out of the room. Malka squeezed Gal and rocked her, her chin still on her head, her eyes shut. Daniel slumped in his chair with a stunned expression.

Matt stood and went into the kitchen, which held a big messy pile of syrup-covered plates, coffee mugs, a griddle glistening with the residue of melted butter. There were a few cold pancakes left on a plate, and he picked one up with his fingers and tore it in quarters, dragged a piece through the syrup streaks on the top plate, wadded the sweet mess into his mouth. Then he ate the other three quarters as well. From the other room he could hear Gal talking excitedly, saying "No offense," her favorite new expression. "I love you and Matt and Yo-yo. I just think Noam and I should be in Ema's family. Don't you think Ema would be happy if I was?"

Matt found the screw top to the syrup bottle, set it on top, and twisted it closed over a ring of sludge. Then he sighed and headed back into the living room.

"Actually, I don't, sweetie," Daniel said. "Ema and Abba wanted you to live with us, and we have to honor their wishes. And we went to court, and the judge agreed that you and your brother should live with us."

Matt turned around. Gal said, "But back then, I was still pretty little, and didn't know how to talk to him myself. Maybe we should go back to the judge and this time I'll talk to him." She was still sitting on her grandmother's lap, and Malka was pressing her lips against the side of her head, whispering, "Shh, shh." He saw that Gal didn't look so much defiant as exalted, although uncertainty was beginning to cloud her face. The front door slammed: Yaakov taking Yo-yo out for a walk.

"There aren't any do-overs," Daniel said evenly. "The judge thought very carefully about what's best for you, and once he made his decision, we had to obey him. Otherwise we're breaking the law."

Matt opened his mouth with the urge to say something like, "But we understand how much you love Sabba and Savta and how nice it is to be with them," then closed it. It wasn't really his place. Instead, he asked, in Hebrew, "Malka, would you like another cup of coffee?"

But she was standing. "There's no reason to be cruel," she said to Daniel. "'Breaking the law'?"

"That's true, Dani!" Gal said. "There's no reason to be cruel!"

Daniel turned to Matt with a shrug of puzzled and angry dismay.

"It's a hard day for everybody," Matt said.

Gal was sitting by herself on the couch now, crying. She'd tried to make a grand gesture, Matt thought, now sitting heavily beside her, and it had given all the grown-ups a heart attack.

"Oh, sweetie," he said.

THE NEXT MORNING THEY couldn't get Malka out of bed. She lay on the air mattress with her hand splayed over her face, emitting an occasional animal whimper. Yaakov was up and dressed in stocking feet, his steely gray hair standing up, hovering over her with a cold washcloth and a mug of warm tea that shook in his hand. "She has a migraine," he told Daniel.

Daniel nodded, studying them for a moment. They were ashen, both of them. From outside, he heard the loud rumble of the garbage can being wheeled to the curb by Matt. "Let's move her into our bedroom," he said. "Don't say no." And he ran upstairs to change the sheets and straighten up, thinking with strange excitement as he pulled down the fitted corners of the clean sheets, which smelled of a long stay in the linen closet, that this was it, one of Malka's famous breakdowns. Not that he wished it upon her—God, no—and not that he wished it upon Gal, either. And yet, if Gal witnessed her grandmother's incapacity, surely his and Matt's guardianship of her would be settled in her mind, once and for all. And then he berated himself for even having that thought, for who wanted her to accept being in their family because all other options were closed off to her? At six years old?

He grabbed their shaving kits and toothbrushes and toothpaste, the hairbrush and hair gel, brought them downstairs and piled them on the bathroom sink. Matt was stomping his boots on the kitchen entry mat to rid them of snow, then bending to take them off, when Daniel hurried into the kitchen. "You went outside without socks?" Daniel said, as a bare foot emerged from the first boot. "You're nuts."

"Tell me about it," Matt said, giving it a rueful rub.

"Hey, listen, it's happening. One of Malka's breakdowns." Matt looked at him sharply. "Yaakov is calling it a migraine. But I'm pretty sure."

"What should we do?" Matt asked.

"I'm clearing out our bedroom and bathroom so we can move her up there."

"Okay. Do you need help?"

They spoke with quiet urgency. Daniel was imagining Matt stepping into the room where one person was disintegrating and the other was trying to hide it, and apparently so was Matt. "I'm going to leave the house," Matt said. "Not because I don't want to help."

"Okay."

"Because I don't want to add stress to them."

"I know."

Matt looked at his watch. "Yo-yo!" He reached for the leash as the dog came into the kitchen with a quizzical wag.

"Get socks!" Daniel said.

"Believe me," Matt said. They looked at their watches again and agreed that Matt would be home in half an hour.

Back in the living room, Yaakov had gotten Malka into a sitting position, and the kids were sitting on the floor on their heels, watching gravely. "Savta has a migraine," Gal announced. "That's a horrible, horrible headache."

"I know," Daniel said. "So we're going to give her mine and Matt's room, because it's darker and quieter."

Malka was in her nightgown, her feet bare; Yaakov had placed her bathrobe over her shoulders. Her eyes were closed, the lids translucent, and the skin on her face sagged, drawing down the corners of her mouth as if gravity had fought energy and brutally pummeled it. Daniel's impulse was to act quickly, to move this frightening, spectral version of her grandmother away from Gal, and yet, even a few feet away from her, he felt the energy draining from his limbs. He sat down beside Malka, and although a feeling of entropy made him wonder how he'd ever get up again, he draped her arm around his shoulders and helped

Yaakov hoist her off the bed. "Stay down here with your brother," he
told Gal sternly.

They brought her upstairs and laid her on the bed, and hastened
to cover her with the comforter. Daniel pulled down the blinds, and
turned to Yaakov. "Tell me what you need," he said.

"Take away your razors and medications, your scissors and clip-
pers," Yaakov said. "And then go. This happens. I'll stay with her."

Daniel looked at him doubtfully. *"Lech!"* Yaakov barked, flapping
his hand toward the bathroom door. Daniel saw that he was ashamed,
and angry at Daniel for witnessing his shame.

"Okay," Daniel said gently.

He got a plastic grocery bag from under the sink and gathered all
the sharp things and all the medications into it. Then he went downstairs and peeked into the kitchen. Noam had climbed into the Tupperware drawer, and Gal was feeding him Goldfish crackers, placing them
onto his orange, gummy tongue, saying, "Don't worry, Noam."

Over the next few days the house was so silent they became aware
of the refrigerator hum, the water in the pipes, the infuriating tinny
whine of the cable box. They spoke in quiet voices that barely rose from
their throats, and leaned toward each other to hear. Everything had
to be murmured twice or three times, as though it required a running
start before the noise it made could heave itself into something intel-
ligible. They awoke from restless sleep with headaches, blaming the
barometric pressure that had brought in unseasonable warmth. Yaakov
shuffled in his slippers back and forth from the kitchen to the bedroom,
bearing tea and toast Malka didn't touch. Matt and Daniel privately
wondered whether she needed to be hospitalized and put on a drip for
nutrition. They heard Yaakov moving around at night. In the daytime
he fell asleep in the living room rocker, snores blubbering out of his lips.
He was both less himself and more himself, Daniel thought. Quieter
and more shadowy. But also, the sole, stern sentry, the last competent
man on earth.

Gal squatted on the rug and watched him. His chin was squashed double against his neck; his big hands had lost their clasp at his lap, and now the lifeless fingers barely touched. She could see his chest rising and falling above the gut that pushed out his shirt. She had seen Savta sick once, when she'd gone over to their house with Ema. While Ema argued with Sabba in the kitchen, Gal crept into the bedroom. Savta was under the covers, her face as bleached and immobile as stone in sun, and Gal focused fiercely on her chest to see if it was moving. For a second, terror plunged through her. But there—there was the faintest of movements. She imagined Savta in a pile of corpses. She wasn't supposed to know about the pile of corpses, she was pretty sure. Was it cold in there, or warm? She imagined it having this same sick smell. That night, in bed, and for many nights after that, Gal practiced breathing so shallow nobody could see her chest move. She could do it about five or six times before she needed to gulp in air, and felt its clean, beautiful swell inside her. *C'mo gal*, she thought. Like a wave.

DERRICK AND BRENT RETURNED home, and Matt and Daniel planned to spend New Year's with them. But that evening Daniel felt he couldn't leave the kids alone with their grandparents, given Malka's condition, and he didn't want to bring a babysitter into this situation either. He sent Matt over alone, saying, "You have to go, we haven't seen them since Brent got tenure," and promising a thousand times that he didn't really care about New Year's anyway.

When Matt arrived, he could tell Brent was already slightly drunk: his cheeks were flushed and his eyes narrowed and a little watery. Soon he would become cuttingly observant and funny. He also had a tendency, when drunk, to climb onto Matt's lap and kiss him wetly, wondering with sentimental fervor why they'd never gotten together.

They toasted his tenure with tequila shots and beer. "Really, honey," Matt said. "Knowing you can stay here—whew! Because what would I do without you?"

"No kidding," Derrick said. "I was all, 'I can move, my job is portable'—but really, I didn't mean it, I was just trying to be supportive."

Brent laughed. "You talk a good game, Mr. Man, but I saw through that one."

They sat on stools at the kitchen ell, and Matt filled them in on Yaakov and Malka's visit while they winced and sighed. They ordered in pizza, and after they'd eaten, they went into the living room and sprawled out. There was a party Brent had heard about, some rich guy on Pomeroy Terrace, and they'd go in a little while. They watched a *Project Runway* rerun, a challenge in which the designers had to create looks out of salad vegetables, and then another reality show in which contestants apparently made famous from other reality shows were given a series of team challenges on an obstacle course. Matt was deeply relaxed, for the first time in weeks, sunk into an easy chair with a cat on his lap, Derrick and Brent on the couch with their legs draped over each other. They pondered the reality show convention of being challenged to eat disgusting things like insects and maggots, and decided that it was some kind of commentary on Americans consuming such a huge share of the world's resources, although what kind of commentary, they weren't sure. Around eleven thirty, they looked at their watches and at one another. Derrick stretched and groaned, settled more deeply into the couch. "I can't do it," he said. "Too tired. Too old. You guys go. Do you despise me?"

"Yes, we despise you," Brent and Matt said in unison. But Brent wasn't up for going either.

Matt stared at him in exasperation. "Well, as intrigued as I am by the idea of a rich guy on Pomeroy Terrace," Matt said, "if you're not going, I'm not going. I should go kiss Daniel at midnight anyway." He stood and got his jacket. "Thanks for letting me celebrate with you."

He hugged and kissed them both, and stepped out into the Northampton night. Christmas lights from the fire station dotted his peripheral vision and glinted from the puddles; mist rose from the huge piles of melting snow that had been plowed into the meridian, giving the night a billowy movie set feel. He walked through the wet streets of downtown with an unzipped jacket and ungloved hands, stepping around groups of teenagers and families celebrating First Night.

He wasn't in a hurry. He was drunk, and the night was comfortable, and the air cooled his face. Music—bluegrass, swing, zydeco—emerged from various events in the buildings around him. His boots made a pleasing noise as his heels ground the wet, gritty pavement. The house would be quiet by now, Malka and Yaakov huddled under the spare comforter in the dark bedroom, Daniel asleep on the air mattress unless one of the kids was up with nightmares. He thought of the house, the people in it, and it tilted in his mind till he saw it from the perspective of an alien observer. It was a box full of strangers. Strangers: Somehow, out of its billions and billions of people, the universe had hurtled these six from the plots of earth they were born and lived on, across the seas, over the prairie, and into the very same set of rooms. The randomness of it blew his mind. He thought: There wasn't one of them he'd have chosen under normal circumstances. Even Daniel. He was glad he'd chosen him, but he had to be honest about it.

A notion on the very surface of his mind, separate from thought, made him turn toward Pomeroy Terrace instead of toward home. He picked up his pace, his mind nowhere, his will glimmering in twitches of his muscles like the faintest of radio signals, until the sound of dance music and the sight of cars crammed next to each other at the curb indicated which house it was. It was a huge purple Victorian he drove past almost daily, and the party was in a turret.

Inside, a techno baseline thundering in his ears, he nosed his way toward the bar, sidling past clusters of men talking loudly over the music and laughing. The house was broken into several condos, but even still, this one was huge, with lustrous oak floors. He nodded at a colleague of Brent's whose name he'd forgotten; some guys from the gay runner's group he'd run with a few years ago; Jeff Schafer, another designer he knew, who occasionally referred work his way. There were women here and there, spiky-haired, short-skirted, lipsticked—straight, he assessed—but it was mostly men, as though a gay scene had popped up out of nowhere, like those barns and castles and old-woman-who-lived-in-a-shoe shoes that rose, looming and latticed, out of the pages of Noam's storybooks. On the windows, heavy flowered curtains hung from iron rods curiously hammered and curlicued at the ends. Built-in bookcases soared to the ceiling. An enormous flat-screen TV broadcast a New Year's countdown show with the volume off; it was six minutes to midnight.

Who on earth owned this place? Matt found the long table serving as a bar and poured himself a vodka tonic, found a strip of lime next to a wet paring knife and squeezed it in, feeling it bite at a tiny cut on his thumb. He drank it quickly in order to re-kick-start the buzz that had faded. How had he ended up here? He was still wearing his jacket; he would stay for just a few minutes, absorb it as a strange tale he would tell Daniel tomorrow, the story of a gay wonderland that had sprung up in the middle of honest, lesbionic Northampton. The sight of full-speed flirting—bursts of fake laughter, voices brimming with irony, eyes careless and languid and calculating, or darting to gauge the impression a joke had made—made him feel superior, repelled; at the same time, taking in the rich tones of male voices and male scent made him giddy. He quickly finished his drink and poured himself another as people started gathering in front of the TV screen, counting down. At midnight, they gave out a shout and started hugging and kissing.

Happy New Year, Daniel, he thought. *Let's hope it's an improvement on the last one!* He was dying for a cigarette; his eyes sought out and found a pair of elegant French doors leading out to a deck. He went outside with his drink, trying to pick up the smell of cigarette smoke, the glow of an ember. The house was on a fairly busy street, but back here it was quiet except for the occasional celebratory burst of honks from passing cars. On a separate level of the deck a few steps down, a canvas cover wet with melted snow and plastered with dead oak leaves stretched over a hot tub. The bare branches of trees waved gently in the misty sky. There was a couple making out, hands clutching. A man stood smoking at the corner of the wood railing, and as soon as he saw Matt zeroing in on him, he laughed and held out a cigarette pack.

"That obvious, huh?" Matt said. He set his drink on the railing and pulled a cigarette out of the pack, leaned forward as the guy reached toward him with his hand cupped around the flame of his lighter. He was drunk by now, and as he lightly touched the man's hand and drew on the cigarette, he was fully cognizant that he was an utter cliché of a gay man on the prowl, only somehow that very awareness made it unreal, the way a stick figure gestures toward a portrait, or a portrait gestures toward the living, breathing human face.

"Happy New Year," the guy said. "I'm Andrew."

"Matt. Happy New Year." He drew on his cigarette and exhaled with pleasure. Through the dim reflected light coming through the French doors, Matt was taking in this guy's particular brand of beauty. He was bigger and younger than Matt, full in the face; in middle age he'd be cursing what would become a double chin, but now that fullness made him look younger rather than older, at once angelic and sensual. His eyes were clear and wide and he had the expression of someone on the verge of laughter, or amazement.

"Can you believe this place?" Andrew said. "Apparently there are seven bedrooms upstairs."

"You're kidding," Matt said, his heartbeat quickening gleefully.

They drifted back in, languorously, "to explore the house," Matt thought merrily, fingers making big cartoon scare quotes in his mind, and found that people were clustered around the bar, heads thrown back, lips sucking, throats working. Jell-O shots! He slid his way in. They had been set out in trays, artisanal, glistening in layers of fluorescent colors, as gorgeous as tiny pastries, or jewels. He lifted one and Andrew lifted one, and they brought them to their noses first, then their tongues, and then they slurped them down. They looked at each other with narrowed eyes, evaluating: Matt tasted a complicated mix of tequila and lime, and was that something spicy? His tongue and palate tingled on the perfect edge of the pleasant-unpleasant continuum. He ate a pellucid champagne shot with a raspberry suspended in it, and reached for another, this one in the shape of a tiny house. It dawned on him: It was *this* house!—with gables and turrets—the owner must have had them specially made. *Good for you, bucko!* he thought, biting into the house, sucking it in and feeling it slide down his throat. By now he could no longer parse the flavors; they were too layered, too subtle, and his mind was rapidly losing its capacity to make fine distinctions.

He felt fingers touching his own, and a gentle tug; Andrew was leading him away, and upstairs.

The bedrooms were up in the turret, and looking up into the domed ceiling above them, which was whitewashed and crisscrossed by silver braces, Matt grew dizzy. There weren't seven bedrooms, but there were five. Five bedrooms: Matt's mind held on to that as though he might be tested on it later. He stood at the doorways while Andrew went in and handled things: bed ruffles, picture frames, jewelry boxes. Was he going to steal something? Matt wondered vaguely, but it seemed that he was mostly just a toucher. At the doorway of one of the smaller bedrooms he heard a murmur: "Check this out." The clunk of a latch being lifted, then a curve of a tight, patterned shirt as Andrew ducked into a small trapdoor opening in the far wall. Matt looked quickly around the hall, feeling like a cartoon spy, or a cat burglar, then slipped into the room and bent to enter the small space. He expected to be entering a roughed-out storage space, full of suitcases and mouse droppings and milk crates filled with old record albums, but when he heard a tiny click and light warmed the space, he saw that it was somebody's hideaway, with a love seat, a tiny table, and a tiny lamp with birds and butterflies painted on the shade. Even where the roughed-out ceiling peaked highest, it was too cramped to stand. It smelled of wood chips.

"Whoa," they breathed.

They fell onto the couch and kissed the jarring, tooth-clashing kissing of urgent strangers, hands clutching each other's hair. Andrew's lips were full and dry, his breath raucous from cigarettes and alcohol, his tongue a little rude. They pulled down their pants, awkward in the tiny space, seams and belts scraping their thighs, then collapsed back onto the couch, looked at each other nose to nose, eyes crossing, and laughed.

Matt's body absorbed the weight of the man on top of him, the cool scented air, the silence that swathed them after the noise of the party. They kissed and kissed, to the sounds of their own breathing and grunting. Matt's hard-on was warm and rosy. It was exciting to be with someone larger than he was, to watch his face become blind and bloated with need.

Andrew slipped onto the floor and turned Matt away from him, and Matt felt Andrew's fingers slide down his back to his ass. His fingers, and then his tongue. This was a new development; he stiffened with shock and pleasure, feeling himself fondled, tasted, handled like an intriguing object on a dresser. He heard a rip of foil and the snap of a condom. He heard Andrew whisper again, felt the press of his hard-on against him.

"Wait," Matt murmured, his mind arrested, a swamp animal popping its head out of the ooze. Andrew was nuzzling his neck with his lips, stroking him, sliding in by small degrees. He was using lube, thank God; Matt wondered where he had stashed it in those tight pants. He couldn't do this, he knew. One part of him was pulling away; the other was experimenting with just one more moment, one more moment before it really counted. His life outside that tiny room had dimmed and fallen away. Matt breathed and tried to open up, leaned into the pain, leaned into it till it became a glowing ember instead.

He let it happen. He let himself be carried on waves of pleasure, like a sloop, by gentle thrusting. And then it stopped. "Don't stop," he croaked, and then he heard Andrew say, "Shit." And then, fumbling, "Shit. The condom broke."

Matt groaned and rested his head on his forearms, his body tense and hungry. He waited for Andrew to pull out, but he didn't; instead Andrew's arms came around and slid under Matt's shirt, stroked his nipples, his belly. He kissed, and then bit, Matt's shoulder blade. When Matt tried to break away, Andrew's arms tightened around him. He was whispering something, holding Matt down, his breath hot on Matt's neck. Matt made out the word "please," which brought another piercing surge of pleasure. Held by a determined man in this sighing, enfolding space, he felt as if he might fly apart at the seams. He closed his eyes and let his mind swirl, felt a grand, gorgeous submission swell over him. He felt Andrew move inside him again, harder this time, then faster; felt his fingers gripping his hips, and then there was a cry as he came. They rested there for a moment, Andrew's body heaving on top of his. Matt heard the high faint whistle of his own orgasm, approaching and then blasting through him like a blaring bass beat from a teenager's passing car.

He lay wasted and pulsing. When Andrew pulled out of him he was overcome by relief and then a sadness so pungent it made him want to cry. *Daniel, see?* Those were the words that glinted in the dim light of his mind. *This* was a real conversation, *this* was being intimate with someone. He was shattered. It was all he'd ever wanted.

His cheek was pressed into the rough weave of the love seat, his heartbeat swishing in his ear. He was nowhere. *Maybe I'll stay here forever*, he thought.

MALKA AND YAAKOV left two days after New Year's, in a cloud of shame and regret, Gal clinging to them and weeping as they entered the security line, Noam taking his cue from her and letting loose with a fake melodramatic wail. Daniel held Malka's hand in both of his own. "Thank you for coming," he said, his voice raised over the noise of the crying children. "You are welcome anytime." *No matter how you feel.* He wanted to convey that, but she'd recovered only enough to rise from bed and totter tentatively through the house, as though moving through a new element with precarious footing, and he thought he'd mortify her if he actually said so. Instead, he held her hands for an extra moment, then pulled her toward him into an embrace. He squeezed her before letting her go, and she patted his cheek.

"*Yalla,* let's go," Yaakov said. He shook Daniel's hand with the same hearty evasiveness he'd greeted him with, and let his grandchildren hug him before kissing each on the head, rising, and taking Malka's elbow. "Until Purim," he said, and Gal said, "Until Purim." That was when they planned to go back to Israel for the children's mandated yearly visit, and for a memorial for Joel and Ilana.

They watched them stop in front of the first security guard, and Yaakov handed Malka their passports and tickets. They watched him help her off with her coat, and lay it on the conveyor belt with his own, and then, one at a time, they went through the metal detector and disappeared in the crowd of people on the other side.

"Oh, I'm so sad," Gal said as Daniel shepherded her toward the exit, Noam in the stroller in front of them. "I already miss them so much!"

As they stopped at the elevator and Gal pressed the down button, and he made sure the children's coats were zipped, Daniel imagined Malka boarding the plane, sitting down, closing her eyes, and waiting for takeoff. He could see her prepare—which she did perhaps better than anyone else—to sit quietly, hands in her lap, as they tore loose and roared into the sky.

IT SNOWED AND WARMED, then snowed and warmed again, so that it became treacherous to walk outside, and everybody tracked sand inside the front door, an irritant when they walked barefoot or in socks. Gal went back to school after the Christmas holiday, and without her grandparents to come home to, the household felt smaller and more tenuous. Her birthday was approaching, another event to dread and to get through. Her grandparents were going to come, but she didn't want a party with kids. Dani kept asking her if she was sure, and each time he asked, anxiety and embarrassment crept over her because she didn't have any friends. Except Rafi, who didn't really count because none of the girls in her class had a boy for a best friend, and because he was deaf. Dani said she used to have lots of friends when she was little, but it was hard to conjure that person; when he showed her the album of her kindergarten class, the faces gazed out at her, impassive, patterns of light and shadow, each called something that felt like a label on a picture. Peggy said that she did still know how to make friends, she was just dealing with a lot, and that the first year of all the big events and holidays without her parents was the hardest. Dani said that they could just invite her whole class, but she didn't trust him to throw the right kind of party, whatever that was.

She was pretty sure Grandma and Grampa were going to get her horseback riding lessons, and that was the one thing she looked forward to.

WHAT GOT TO MATT was having done something he couldn't tell a soul about, used as he was to enjoying events in retrospect, in storytelling, almost more than he did at the time itself. If he could tell someone about it, he thought, he could work through its strangeness, the sense of radiant connection it had given him. He could work through what had made him cave the very first moment having sex without a condom had presented itself to him as an option, after so many years of disapproval for those who did it. At times, as he worked, his mind drifted back to the party, and he could hardly believe it had even happened. Then he remembered the sensation of being looked at with such intense desire, of being grasped in a man's arms, and he thought he understood what Jay and all the reckless men he'd known and disavowed were searching for.

When he had come to, Andrew was gone. Matt had risen and pulled on his pants, ducked through the little door and into the dark, silent bedroom and hallway. The party was over, and he felt his way down the stairs on the toes of his boots, his heart hammering when the steps creaked, into the living room, then rushed for the door, certain that he would be confronted by a haughty guy in a dressing gown demanding an explanation. He slipped out and closed it as silently as he could, fled down the front porch steps into the neighborhood. He still felt noodly and stoned, a little nauseated, and the night air coated his hot face. He expected to be stopped by the police at any moment. It wasn't till he was six or seven blocks away that his heart slowed.

At the dark doorway of his house, he'd fumbled with the keys, turning and holding them toward the streetlight a few houses down, till he found the right one. He shushed the dog and went into the living room as quietly as he could; he waited till Daniel stopped shifting at the noise, then slipped quickly into the bathroom. In the shower he soaped copiously between his legs, winced at the sting around his ass- hole, worried that he was torn. The adrenaline was wearing off, and he could feel the soreness at his chin where Andrew's beard stubble had rubbed him, bruises at his knees where they'd pressed into the floor. He had been keeping his mind intentionally blank, but as he rubbed himself briskly with a towel, his body felt something coming on, and by the time he was beside Daniel in bed, the sheets clinging to his still-damp body, a great cloud of fear swarmed over and deafened him. What had he done?

Now Malka and Yaakov had gone, at least, and the house was begin- ning to feel like theirs again. Every single day Matt enjoyed being in his own bedroom, enjoyed going downstairs to make breakfast for the kids and not having to make conversation with anybody but the dog. When everybody had gone—to work, day care, school—he took his second cup of coffee up to his study and played computer games for half an hour before getting down to work. He'd bought a new pair of small, high-end speakers for the computer, and he played music turned up loud, the way he'd worked as a young man, singing, embraced and stirred by the clear, powerful sound. Lydia and Sam were coming in a few weeks for Gal's birthday, but they were staying only for a few days this time, and in a hotel, and he thought he could manage that.

The bruises had faded, his chin healed. Most of the time now, the encounter seemed very far away, and his body chaste and contained. Did it have to have happened? Did the reality held in memory have to translate into a raw, physical event at a party somewhere? Wouldn't it exist only if they insisted it had?

A FEW WEEKS LATER, Gal stood with Lydia and Sam inside a drafty pan- eled room, breathing in the smells of hay, horse sweat, manure. There was an old oak reception desk in the front with an appointment ledger flopped open upon it, its pages a mess of scribbles in pencil and pen. Farther in, a few adults and kids sat at the edges of cracked leather couches, in a sitting area with tack hung on the walls, horse magazines splayed on trunks and tables, a fire going in the fireplace. Gal stuffed her coat in Lydia's arms and looked the kids over. She was in a beginner class with three other girls and one boy. Two were wearing jeans and sneakers, and her confidence wobbled for a second: Were they dressed wrong, or was she? But the others were wearing jodhpurs and boots like she was. She'd gotten them, and a helmet, as presents from Matt and Daniel this morning, her birthday.

Their teachers were Briana and Shannon, Briana a ponytailed teenager with a quick smile, Shannon older, weathered, a little stern. It was Shannon who took her into the stall to meet her horse. It was cold, and their breath mingled in the air. "This is Caesar," Shannon said. She explained how Gal should never stand behind a horse, always by its side or shoulders, and cross to the other side in front of it instead of behind. "Don't even do it once," she said. "Don't think, 'Oh, no one's looking, I can just slip around him this one time.' Horses can be unpredictable, and they can kick you to kingdom come." Caesar bent his face down toward her and snorted, and Gal touched the impossibly soft skin around his nostrils. "We call a brown horse with a black mane and tail a bay," Shannon said. "Now, Caesar here is a bit of a clown, and if you let him get away with it, he'll do all kinds of shenanigans. So I'm assigning him to you, because you look like a girl who doesn't take nonsense from other people. Am I right?"

Gal didn't know what shenanigans were, but she did understand nonsense, and the way Shannon described her set off a little rush of delight and pride.

Shannon set a footstool near Caesar's neck and gestured for Gal to step up on it. She left the stall for a second and returned holding a bridle by the crown. "I'm going to show you how to bridle him. You're a little short, so I'll do the top part. Here's your job: putting the bit in his mouth. It's the hardest and most important part of the process."

She showed Gal how to hold the bit in front of Caesar's mouth, and slip her thumb into the back of his mouth. Gal felt the warm slime of his spit, the spongy tongue. He shifted with a groan. "Slip it in!" Shannon said, and she did, feeling it clonk against his teeth, then settle.

"Nice work." Shannon put the crown over his ears, showed her the correct tightness of the throat latch. Gal wiped her hand on her pants, then surreptitiously gave it a smell. If she had to go home right that moment, she thought, she'd have had a fantastic time.

They saddled Caesar, Shannon inviting Gal to run her hand between the cinch and his gut, to see how tight it should be. Then she led him from the stall and tied him in the barn's big hallway, and boosted Gal up onto him. Dizzied by the unexpected height, Gal gripped his mane, but Shannon showed her how to gather and hold the reins, how to pull back to stop him. There were three already mounted as well, but Gal tuned them out, sat back, and reveled in stable music: the saddle's creak as she shifted on it, horses heaving and snuffling, the *slap slap* of the straps as Shannon adjusted the stirrups, Caesar's munch on the bit.

Five helmeted kids rode in circles in a chilly ring, Shannon and Briana calling out instructions from the middle, stopping them sometimes to demonstrate on one kid the way the foot should sit in the stirrup, the height at which the reins should be held. Shannon said, "Horses are flight animals, not fight animals. Do you know what that means?" Parents lined the sides of the ring behind the barrier; Gal glanced at Sam when she passed him, got a thumbs-up. She nudged along Caesar's immense body with her heels and thighs, swaying with his rhythms, feeling the pull in her calves as she strained to keep her heels down, the jolt of the trot that yanked her forward and made her teeth clatter till she could get into a posting rhythm for a second or two before her tailbone smacked back onto the saddle. She watched the swishing tail of the horse in front of her, which lifted for a moment as its anus turned inside out and released steaming grassy turds. The cold encased her cheeks and fingers; she felt the bones in her butt and the warm rub on her crotch, saw her breath materializing in front of her. And when she'd dismounted and Shannon took Caesar's bridle and saddle off and handed her a curry brush, she brushed his coat where it was dark and wet from the saddle, stroking hard with the grain and grooving fine lines into the hair, then moving to his rear and brushing, dust and dirt motes swirling in the air, till she was sweaty and her arms ached. Briana brought her a carrot and showed her how to offer it to Caesar, and Gal laughed as his big lips scrabbled on her open palm, and he chewed it with a deep meditative grind. When she rejoined her grandparents in the reception area, she was beaming. "Did you like it?" they asked, and she flung her arms around them. "Bye, Shannon!" she yelled as her teacher came up to the desk to look at the schedule, and when Shannon looked up and her scowling face broke into a smile, she thought: *She smiled at me!*

After dinner the grandparents and uncles and Rafi and Yossi sang her the Hebrew happy birthday song, and they had a chocolate birthday cake Daniel had made. Yossi handed Rafi the present they'd brought and nudged him toward Gal; he thrust it toward her with a grin. It was two costumes, a police officer and a pirate. Gal and Rafi dressed Noam in the pirate costume, then took turns arresting him in severe authoritarian voices. It was native Hebrew Gal heard from Rafi, but slightly distorted. When you told him something, your words spooled out there and maybe they clicked into the machinery of his ear and maybe they didn't. He always had a slightly distant look, as if he were trying to remember where he'd put his shoes; she thought he might be a little slow, but Matt told her he wasn't. Sometimes she took his chin in her fingers and turned his face toward her before she spoke.

A package from her Israeli grandparents had arrived a few days ago, and Daniel had hidden it till now: it contained bags of Bamba and Bisli and Israeli chocolate and biscuits. There was quick, intense negotiation: Did she have to share with Rafi and Noam, even though it was her birthday? She got a lecture about how, even though she technically didn't have to, it would be nice of her to share, and she and Daniel reached a compromise: She would split one bag of Bisli with the other kids. She ripped open the bag and counted out four for Noam, and while she kept a sharp eye on how many Rafi took, they gorged on the primordial flavors of home.

AFTER THE KIDS HAD gone to bed and his parents to their hotel, Daniel came into the bedroom, where Matt was sprawled on the bed, watching TV. He lay down next to him, moved into the crook of his arm. "Hi," Matt said.

"Hi." Daniel took a deep breath and let it out, closed his eyes and curled against Matt, his knee sliding over his legs. Matt patted his arm absently.

It was the laziest feeling, Daniel's head light and tingly, his prick pressing against his jeans, his legs weightless. He moved his hand onto Matt's thigh and ran it lightly up to his crotch, touching his jeans very very lightly. "Phew, what a relief," he murmured.

Matt raised an eyebrow. "What, getting through the birthday?"

Daniel rose and leaned over him, touched his lips with his, then pressed harder. Matt felt the familiar gentle query of his tongue, breathed in the familiar smell of his breath, which still—after all this!—triggered all kinds of pheromonal happiness, and thought about a silly conversation they'd had when they'd started sleeping together, a conversation that had led through the giddy, winding road of older man/younger man teasing, to his giving Daniel an A-minus grade as a kisser. Daniel had reared back in laughing indignation, and asked, his lashes still lazy from the kiss, "Why, pray tell, the minus?"

"*Pray tell?*" Matt said. "Okay, that just brought you down to a B-plus."

They'd been kneeling on the bed, undressing each other, and Daniel sat back on his haunches with a haughty look. His shirt was unbuttoned, half-revealing the delicate brush of dark hair around his nipples, the cleft between his breasts, and his surprising, disarming, little-boy belly button. "You need to modulate better between wet and dry," Matt said, with the air of the connoisseur. He himself was a world-class kisser, thank you very much.

Now Daniel's hands were in Matt's hair, and he felt himself enormously touched and disquieted. The house was quiet, other than the slurp of the dog washing himself on the floor and static from the baby monitor. Matt's mind began to race through all the things he knew about what was safe and what wasn't, wondering if he could limit this to oral sex, thinking about all the nicks and cuts on their dry winter hands. He could do that, and not tell Daniel.

But when Daniel said, making light of it, "Do you still remember how to do it?" he imagined doing it without telling him, with a condom; he imagined—well, all of it, the whole sweaty, teary, exultant thing, up to the point of Daniel curling up and passing out. He swiftly tried on the idea that in not volunteering the information, he wouldn't be exactly lying to Daniel, the kind of lame sophistry that had served him pretty well when he was younger, and a jerk. But he knew he wouldn't be able to live with himself if he didn't tell him. Even though Daniel had pushed him to the last extremity by denying him all this time and making him feel like shit for wanting him in the first place, and even though he, Matt, deserved to be cut a ton of slack for performing sensationally well under the pressure of this new life. He defied anyone to have done a better job as a partner and a parent! But after all they'd been through, it just seemed tawdry to lie.

Crap, after all these months, who knew that Daniel would suddenly be horny?

"Dan," he murmured. "Honey." He closed his eyes, steeling himself, and turned on the light to Daniel's blinking, rosy, hungry face.

Matt struggled to a sitting position. "Daniel," he said.

Daniel murmured, ran his hand up Matt's chest under his T-shirt.

Matt clasped his hand, over his shirt. "Honey." The word came out hoarse, so he cleared his throat and said it again; this time, as he pressed it out of his throat, it came out loud and harsh. It made Daniel sit up and look at him, his face questioning and a little irritated.

"I don't know how to say this," Matt said.

Daniel was quiet, waiting.

Matt swallowed, feeling blood beat against his face. "It's a really hard thing to say," he said.

Daniel's face grew alarmed. "Are you breaking up with me?"

"No!"

"Phew," Daniel said.

"But this might make you want to break up with me."

Daniel sighed. "Then will you just tell me? What, did you bareback or something?"

"Yes," Matt said.

Daniel snorted, then, seeing Matt's face, grew serious. "Seriously?"

Matt nodded, then rushed to add, "Well, it wasn't really barebacking—the condom broke."

Daniel was bewildered. "Where?"

"At a party."

The words were so strange, it took Daniel some minutes to understand what Matt was saying. *At a party*—what on earth?—it still felt theoretical, as if his mind was testing what it would feel like to hear those words and to attach them to an event. Then his face grew hot, as he felt the rejection, the sheer *No, I won't* response to his advance that he heard, primitively, as *No, go away, disgusting, it's not you I want, it's someone else.* Mortified, he pushed himself away and went into the bathroom and closed the door. Matt pulled the covers over his knees, tense and watchful, only half-resigned to the anger he knew he deserved and was trying to get ready to absorb. His bare feet were cold.

Noam gave out a cry, magnified to a yowl by the monitor. Matt got out of bed, grabbed two pacifiers from the dresser, and went down to his bedroom, where he put one in Noam's mouth and one in his hand. These days Noam slept with three pacifiers, two stuffed dogs, and his special blanket, and Matt wondered if he was waking more often because he had trouble hanging on to all of them at once. On the way out, Matt stepped on two of the pacifiers that had made their way out of the crib, and took them back into the bedroom, where he determined to sit and wait for Daniel to emerge and respond.

Daniel was sitting on the toilet with his head in his hands, his mind blank. It seemed as if it would take a tremendous effort to make it produce a thought, and that it just wasn't worth the effort. He'd think about it after his parents left. He knew that it was bad, very bad; he could also sense, if not quite make contact with, the minor-key pleasure of being aggrieved and in the right. Other than that, all he could feel was his left leg getting numb. And his swollen, itchy eyes.

Matt turned on the TV, but without the sound, so Daniel wouldn't accuse him of checking out during a fight. He held the remote with his thumb on the power switch, ready to turn it off the moment he saw the bathroom doorknob turn. Twenty minutes passed, and a new sit-com cycle began, and still Daniel hadn't emerged. "Daniel?" he called, then, when there was no answer, he went to the door and slowly turned the knob.

Daniel was still sitting on the toilet, sleeping.

Matt roused him and led him to the bed, turned back the covers for him. "Don't touch me," Daniel mumbled, getting into bed and curling himself into a ball facing away from Matt's side.

Matt awoke the next morning with the knowledge that he'd have to face Daniel's wrath, not to mention the last morning of Sam and Lydia's visit; he groaned and rose to get the baby's bottle. Daniel got up and got into the shower, and all through breakfast—which was taken up by Lydia's exclamations of "I'm going to miss you so much!" and Gal's "I'm going to miss you even more!"—he gave him the cold shoulder. Matt wanted to talk about it—they needed to—but they couldn't yet, certainly not till Lydia and Sam had left.

After they'd all left the house in a flurry of kisses and "I love you's," Matt went upstairs to work. He sat down and booted up his computer, and instead of opening his design software, opened the word processor and began composing an email message to Daniel. He caught a whiff of Lydia's scent on him from their good-bye hug. Maybe he'd send the message, maybe he wouldn't, he thought; but he had to write it.

"Daniel," he began:

I can't tell you how sorry I am about what I did. I knew
the minute I got back home that I'd done one of the worst
things I've ever done. I feel like a huge hypocrite, and a terrible
partner. I want to explain how it happened, but I don't think
you'd particularly want to hear about it. If I'm wrong about
that, let me know.

    It's just, I love and miss you so much, and the less
contact I had with you, the more intense contact it seemed I
needed. Okay, I just explained how it happened, when I said I
wouldn't.

He wiped his eyes with his sleeve.

    Anyway, I hope we can talk. I miss that too, it seems like
all we talk about these days is the kids. And I hope you can
find it in your heart to forgive me. Not right away, of course, I
don't expect that.
    I love you, honey.

He sent it before he could second-guess himself, and then, exhausted,
took a nap on the couch, his coffee cooling on his desk.

When he awoke he immediately checked his email; there was no
response yet. He went downstairs and got himself a fresh cup of coffee, came back up and checked his email one more time before getting
down to work. Over the course of the day he logged back onto his email
account incessantly. He knew Daniel hadn't responded in the morning
because he had a meeting, but as the hours went by, he realized that
Daniel was going to let him flap in the breeze.

MATT PICKED UP NOAM from day care, arriving home as Gal was getting off the bus. "Take off your shoes," he said as she pushed inside,
backpack sagging on her back.

"I'm starving," she said in Hebrew.

He sat her down at the kitchen table and gave her a granola bar and a glass of milk; hair in her eyes, feet swinging, humming something tuneless, she dunked it and ate the wet parts in tiny rodent gnaws. Matt lifted Noam into his high chair and cut up a banana onto his tray, watched him mouth a piece off his palm. "Use your fingers, honey," Matt said, picking up a piece. Noam had the small-motor coordination to do that, but still ate baby-style a lot of the time, one of the many small things that continued to make them anxious about his development. *You'd better not leave me alone with these kids*, he silently warned Daniel. It was something he said whenever Daniel set out for work, alongside *Drive safely*. But now he caught himself: Daniel was more likely to *take* the kids than to leave them with him. Waiting for a conversation with him was like waiting for a verdict, head spinning, mouth dry. Daniel hadn't called, hadn't let him know when he'd be home, and Matt had decided the only thing to do was to keep moving; if his life wasn't going to be normal, he was going to put his head down and pretend it was.

He was cubing tofu for a stir-fry and working himself into a state when he heard the key at the door, then the clatter of keys on the counter. He was too afraid to look up. But then he heard footsteps recede: Daniel was going upstairs.

Gal drifted into the room. "I hate tofu," she said.

"Actually, you don't," Matt said, his knife gliding through it. He would fry it till it was golden, add garlic and ginger and soy sauce.

At dinner, Daniel was a model of smooth parental dedication and guidance, but his eyes glided over Matt without seeing him, like skis in glassy waters. Did the kids detect the rage under that warm surface? They didn't seem to: Gal was letting Daniel draw her out about her day at school, where one boy had gotten in trouble for calling another boy fat, and a loser.

"He *should* get in trouble," Daniel said, and although Matt agreed, the words sounded ominous.

. . . .

AFTER DINNER DANIEL WENT upstairs while Matt cleared up and put the dishes in the dishwasher, his mind bubbling with bad feeling. Noam had crawled out of the kitchen and into the living room, and by the time Matt had emerged from the kitchen, he found him halfway up the stairs. "Holy moly, Noam!" he cried, poking his face in between two balusters. "Look at you!"

Noam, on hands and knees, looked down at him, then raised a knee to take another step. He placed it on the very edge and it slipped off, and, flattened on his stomach, he slid down a few stairs and bumped his chin on one of the stairs. Matt ran up the steps to pick him up just as he started crying.

Daniel came running down at the sound of thumping and crying. "Jesus Christ," he said. "Can't I leave him with you for a second?"

When Noam started to fall, Matt had been just about to follow him up. "Will you just stop it?" he snapped. "I can take care of him."

"Obviously, you can't! Did you just stand here watching him go higher and higher?"

"I was trying to help him feel competent." He was patting Noam's back and searching for a pacifier.

"Well, he's not competent!"

"And why do you think that is?" Matt said. "Why do you think he's not walking? It's all the fear locked up in his body."

"What kind of New Age crap is that?" Daniel said, taking Noam from him and cradling his head with his hand, examining his face.

"He's fine," Matt said.

"He's bleeding," Daniel said, turning him toward Matt so Matt could see the smudge of blood where Noam had bitten his lip.

Damn it. Matt followed them into the kitchen, where Daniel sat down with Noam on his lap. Matt went to the freezer and got him a frozen teething ring. "Here, honey," he said, touching Noam's hair. "Suck this."

Daniel grabbed it from him before Noam could take it, tossed it in the sink, and got a different one from the freezer. Noam, squeezed on his hip, grunted and squalled.

"C'mon," Matt said, coloring.

"Stop," Daniel said. "I'm not fighting in front of them."

"Who started the fight?" Matt whispered furiously.

"I'm not fighting in front of him," he said again. "Wait till they go to sleep."

Gal came down the stairs. "Are you fighting?" she asked with great interest.

"No," they said.

"Okay, whatever."

Efficiently and with careful cheerfulness, they got the kids bathed and Noam put to bed. As Daniel went into Gal's room to tell her it was time to stop reading and turn off the light, Matt sat on the bed, waiting.

Daniel came into the room, avoiding his eyes.

"Hey," Matt said.

Daniel sat down beside him. "Matt," he said, looking at the hands in his lap. "This isn't working out."

"And by 'this' you mean . . . ?"

"Any of it. You living here. Our being together."

"What? Are you kidding me?"

"I'm not kidding. I can't do this anymore."

Matt sat back on the pillows, stunned. "Why?! Because I let Noam go up the stairs?"

Daniel gave him a look. "You know why."

Matt's face grew hot. "Because I had unprotected sex?"

"That's just part of it," Daniel said. "That's just a symptom of the whole thing. I feel that it's not safe to have you around."

"Oh please," Matt said.

"Oh please?" Daniel said. "You bareback!"

"*Barebacked* once! The condom broke!"

Daniel rolled his eyes. "Do you realize how pathetic you sound? *The condom broke?*" His voice was withering. "You drive like a maniac. When you take them to the playground by yourself, I spend the whole time worrying that they're going to kill themselves because you let them do whatever they want. I can't handle it! If I'm the only one keeping this family safe, I'm better off doing it on my own."

"I didn't just let Noam go up those stairs. I was watching the whole time." When Daniel threw another derisive look his way, he burst out, "You have to make a calculation! You have to balance between safety and his sense of competence, autonomy."

"Don't condescend to me," Daniel said. "I know that. I make those calculations all the time."

"No, you don't," Matt said. "You just grab the kids and pull them back. Gal complains about it all the time! You don't hear it, but I do."

Daniel flushed. "I need you to get out of here."

"We're not even going to talk this through?"

"No," Daniel said.

Matt stared at him. "You want to do a whole get-out-of-my-house scene instead? Can't we do any better than that?"

"This isn't a joke! Do I look like I'm kidding?"

He very much did not look like he was kidding, Matt thought, looking at Daniel's haggard face and cold eyes. But he was not going to let himself panic, and damned if he was going to let Daniel see him break down. "Do you even *get* to kick me out of the house?" he asked.

"Yes, I do!" Daniel cried. "It's my name, not yours, on the mortgage. My name as the kids' guardian. Where's your name, Matt? Where's *your* fucking name?"

He spat the words while Matt looked at him, shocked, thinking that he sounded as if he'd consulted a lawyer, which made this way more serious than he'd imagined. "Dan," Matt said. "I hear that you're furious and very hurt, and also scared."

"I said don't condescend to me," Daniel said. "Look," he said quietly. "I can handle the sexual betrayal. It hurts, a lot, but I know I've turned my back on you for a long time, and I get it, fair is fair. I can get over that." He was looking steadily at Matt. "But I can't get over the sense of danger I feel when you're around. I've been trying, but I can't. I have no choice but to ask you to leave."

"I'm not leaving the house!" Matt shouted, making Daniel shush him furiously and close the door. "Okay? I live here! I'm not going outside and shiver on the front lawn while you throw my clothes out the window like a betrayed wife with mascara running down her face!" He grabbed a pillow and hugged it.

"I don't want you here," Daniel said, his face red and twisted. "I don't want you here anymore. Do you know what these kids have been through? I can't believe you! What if you got sick? Do you think they could take another loss like that? Or if you got *me* sick, or *them*?"

Daniel brushed his forearm against his eyes, and Matt sat quietly. *I won't get sick!* is what he wanted to say, but he knew he couldn't, he knew that once you're thunderstruck, you no longer live in a country where the natives can decipher that kind of utterance. How he wished it was six months from now!—and the apologies and drama and penance and feeling like a horrible person were over, and he'd been tested and found negative. "I'm so so sorry, Daniel," he said, his voice hoarse.

"I'm sure you are," Daniel said. "And I accept your apology. I do. But that's the best I can do; it doesn't change how I feel."

Despite his best efforts, Matt felt his eyes begin to prickle. "I *told* you, didn't I? I didn't have to do that!"

"Oh my God!" Daniel said. "You want to be congratulated for that? You want me to throw you a big party because you didn't knowingly give me HIV?!"

Matt flushed angrily. "Of course not!" he said, embarrassed, because he did think he'd behaved decently. "But isn't it proof that I can be trusted to observe precautions?"

"Proof that you can be trusted would be not spreading your ass for strangers!"

Matt flung himself facedown onto the bed, acting as if this was a regular fight, hoping that if he acted that way, it would be.

"Please go, Matt," Daniel said. "I can't have you here. It makes me feel . . ." He put his hand on his chest and tried to continue, but he couldn't find the air. "Panicky," he whispered. For a second, until the breath came, he thought he might be having a heart attack. He was focused like a laser on Matt leaving the house, it was his sole need, it was all he could do not to scream *Go!* a thousand times. He sucked in air with the sound of a screeching engine. "I can't," he panted. "I can't have you here, I can't take the vigilance, I can't be reassuring you night and day that you're still a good person, I can't go back to feeling the way I did when Joel died. . . ."

Dismay flared in Matt's chest, and he thought, *Just for now, just for now.* He forced himself to his feet, got his gym bag from the closet, and threw it at Daniel, who fended it off with his forearm. He'd go to Derrick and Brent's. He got dressed and began packing, just a change of clothes, and then, in the bathroom, his toiletries. He took, without hesitation, the things they shared: toothpaste and shaving cream, the hairbrush. He scanned the bathroom, then took the Ativan and all the vitamins from the cabinet. He left the bedroom without looking at Daniel, the bag slung over his shoulder, and went downstairs. From the kitchen, he took a bag of oranges, the mint Milanos, all the beer in the fridge, and the vodka and scotch from the cabinet. He set the bag down at the back door and went back upstairs.

Daniel was lying facedown on the bed, his face buried in the crook of his arm. "I'm going to say good-bye to the kids," Matt said.

Daniel looked up quickly, his face red. "Don't you dare wake them up! I'll tell them in the morning."

"What will you tell them? That I up and left? Don't you dare blame me."

"I won't," Daniel said. "I promise."

"What are you going to tell them?" Matt demanded. "I want to hear the exact words."

"Please," Daniel said, sitting now cross-legged and slumped. "I'm really tired. Let me sleep on it."

Matt's lips tightened and he got a surge of adrenaline at getting the upper hand for the first time. "I'm not leaving till I hear what you're going to tell them."

Daniel sighed tremulously and rubbed his eye hard with his forefinger. "My mind is drawing a blank," he said.

"Tell them you kicked me out of the family."

"I'm not saying that."

"So you're going to lie? I don't want it sounding even mutual, Daniel. You're so big on taking responsibility—*you* fucking take responsibility."

Daniel rubbed his face hard, exhausted from the energy it had taken to get Matt to agree to leave. "I'll tell them that you didn't want to leave, because you love them—"

"Love *us*. Say 'because he loves us.' And why did I leave, then?"

"Because I decided it wasn't safe for you to live with us."

"No—I don't accept that."

They wrangled for another twenty minutes, for each proposition, Matt posing the difficult follow-up questions he knew Gal would ask. Finally, they decided on "I'm very angry at Matt for something he did, and I told him I don't want to live with him anymore. What he did is between him and me. And he didn't want to go, because he loves us."

Matt nodded tiredly. His mouth was dry, and tasted terrible. He thought he should also demand visitation rights with the kids, but didn't have the energy for it right now.

The dog followed him back down to the kitchen, and he stooped and kissed him on the snout. He called Derrick and Brent from the freezing car as he waited for it to warm, his breath billowing and his fingers aching from the cold. He woke Derrick up, so he told him to go back to sleep, that he was coming over but he'd let himself in. When he got there, Brent emerged sleepily in a bathrobe and said, "Big fight?"

"Big fight," Matt said, taking off his jeans and putting on sweats, which, cold from the car, encased his legs in cold.

"What'd you do?"

"Funny," Matt said. "Can I have a blanket?"

"Sure," Brent said, and went back into the bedroom, from which

Matt heard a quick conference in low voices between him and Derrick.

He took two sleeping pills and went to sleep on their couch, a cat curled behind his knees, thinking of all the smart retorts he'd failed to make—*Haven't you learned by now that nobody can keep anybody safe? Safety isn't the only value in the world!*—and vowing to remember them for later, when he and Daniel spoke again. Noam, he thought, would be up a few times during the night coughing, but that was Daniel's problem. If he, Matt, had no rights—what a shit Daniel was to say that!—at least he would now have the right to a good night's sleep. His mind spun and spun, and finally sleep came over him.

DANIEL OPENED THE CABINET and cursed Matt when he discovered the Ativan was missing. He went back into the bedroom, lay down on the bed, and pulled the covers up to his chin. His heart was hammering in his ears and fingers, and when he thought of Matt, panic tickled inside his chest with intolerably pestering fingers till he shuddered. Just as he'd felt when he'd heard about Joel, as if there were something tormenting inside him that he couldn't get out. To go out and court unnecessary danger—as if they hadn't been blown, like fish hunted with guns, into the bloody welter of those who lived every single grim, aching, horrible day with its consequences!

Crying would have helped ease him out of that free fall, but he couldn't muster more than a humid and itchy tingle around the eyes. He'd cried enough over this past year, he thought bitterly, and he was not going to spill more tears over Matt. He had an urge to call someone, call Derrick, but everyone would think he was crazy for kicking Matt out; they'd think he wasn't considering the kids. But now, honestly, he felt that he should have broken up with him as soon as he brought the kids home. Matt had tried to be there for them, because he needed so badly for people to think he was a good person. And sure, fine, he was good with them, especially with Gal, who didn't have the intense entanglement with him she had with Daniel. But what good did it do to make an ace Halloween costume when he never pulled the harness in the baby's car seat tight enough?

He got up and took a hot bath, lay in the tub reading Matt's *Entertainment Weekly* to still his thoughts, feeling the hot water encase his limbs but not penetrate. When he got out, his skin was red. Yo-yo came in and licked his wet feet. Daniel dried off, put on pajamas, and sat on top of the bed, flipping channels. The heat of his bath hit him belatedly and he broke out into an unpleasant prickle and then a sweat. He closed his eyes. He felt like a mangled crustacean on a hot beach littered with soda cans and cigarette butts. He knew he had no right to complain, since he was the one who'd done the breaking up, but he felt awful, and angry for being forced into it, too.

The TV flashed its disturbing late-night images, the ads for weight loss and call girls, the waxen or battered faces of murdered people being studied by medical examiners. He drifted to sleep and then woke up again, and sometime later he pushed off the bed and left the room, walked softly up the stairs to Matt's study.

It was warmer up on the top floor. He turned on the nearest lamp, habituated from long cohabitation with Matt not to use the overheads. The red walls gave off a muted glow against off-white wainscoting. Matt had moved into the smaller, less comfortable space when Gal and Noam arrived, and cast his magic over it, so that it now looked like an ideal design space—comfortable, modern, lovely. On his desk stood a chunk of engraved Lucite, a Best Young Designer award he'd won long ago, along with framed pictures of Matt with Daniel, with the kids. On the bulletin board was pinned the *Ma'ariv* front page with Matt in the photograph. Daniel gazed at it. His expression in the photograph was inscrutable behind the sunglasses, but you had to hand it to the man, he was gorgeous. Being loved by him had been an awesome treat. There was a hitch at Daniel's heart, and for a second, he felt faint. He sat down on Matt's swivel chair and closed his eyes. In the beginning, Matt was so beautiful to him that Daniel had had to learn to re-see him through a human lens rather than a purely aesthetic one. He had broken down that beauty in his mind and constructed a new one, so that the Matt he saw and loved was fresher and more real than the Matt their culture held up as the beauty standard for men. It was a beauty he believed only he could see.

And now—now Matt had let some other man in, some man who could see only the obvious beauty, and let him in closer than he'd ever invited even Daniel.

Daniel sank into the chair, becoming heavy and inert. After a few minutes he became aware that something was hurting. His jaw; he unclenched his teeth, opened his mouth wide, waggled his jaw from side to side.

Against the back wall stood a file cabinet, where they kept all the information about the mortgage, property taxes, and home repair, as well as their passports, the legal information about Daniel's guardianship of the kids, the kids' medical records. Daniel rose and opened the drawer, pulling out those files and stacking them neatly on the floor. He didn't know what he was going to do with them, he was going on instinct, and hadn't meant to look into the file cabinets in the first place. He felt ridiculous, like a character in a heist movie. If Matt forgot something and walked in, he didn't know what he'd say.

He bent and took up his stack of legal documents, removing Matt's passport and tossing it on the floor, and brought them over to the small pearl-colored sofa, sat down with them on his lap, and put his feet up on the coffee table, on which sat some brochures Matt had designed and a coffee cup filled with crayons and markers for Gal's visits up there. These were the things he had: the kids, the house. These were the things he would tend, safeguard, cherish. He fell asleep with the files cradled to his chest.

MATT WAS DAZED. He kept thinking it wasn't possible, that for Daniel to break up with him while he was already destroyed by loss, for him to prefer parenting the kids alone to having him in the house—it seemed insane. For the first few weeks, Matt crashed on Derrick and Brent's couch, protected from utter devastation by his belief that, soon, Daniel would come to his senses. Because what could he possibly tell the kids? Could he really look them in the eye and tell them that yet another parent had vanished from their lives? Could he really be that cruel? Or so furious and implacable that he'd rather take on the burden of dealing with Gal than have Matt in his house? He felt sorry, and guilty, and contrite about what he'd done, but Daniel's reaction was so huge—so outsized and disproportionate, so utterly punitive to the kids, so fucking *crazy*—that he felt that it outweighed even his own crime, and that he and the kids were the ones who had been wronged.

Derrick and Brent were bewildered and appalled by this turn of events. When Matt told him what he'd done, Brent said, "Are you kidding me? You of all people!"

Derrick turned his face away and went into the bedroom. A few minutes later he emerged again into the living room, where Brent and Matt were sitting silently, hands in their laps. "Well, you showed him, didn't you," he said, sarcasm twisting his normally placid face. "You don't have to be responsible if you don't want to. You don't have to put your family first—you're too hot for that."

"Derrick," Brent said.

"For God's sake, Matt," Derrick said, sitting down heavily. "You know better than anyone else how terrible things happen to people in the world. Why would you go out and look for danger?"

They stayed up late, worrying and analyzing, drinking the booze Matt had taken from home. They speculated about his behavior, which he found kind of interesting and pleasurable—who didn't love being the riddle to which his friends' searching analytical attention was tuned?—until it quickly became irritating. "Like Derrick said—only nicer—I can totally imagine rebelling against your new domestic status," Brent said, "that's totally understandable. Or rebelling against Daniel, who, let's face it, can be an arrogant prick at times. But in a way that harms yourself?! That's what I'm struggling with. I mean, I never pegged you as self-destructive or suicidal. . . ."

That word made them all look at one another. "First of all, I told you the condom broke. Second, Christ, it was the *opposite* of that," Matt protested. "It was— It made me feel more alive than I had in months."

"It's not just about you, though," Derrick said. "When you have kids, it's not just about you anymore."

"Oh, for Christ's sake, Derrick, could there be a more self-righteous cliché?" Matt snapped. "Even I wouldn't say that, and I *have* kids!"

"You *had* kids," Derrick said.

Matt's face grew hot. He'd never been talked to that way by Derrick, who was one of the least judgmental people he knew. And he was conscious of deserving it, which made him feel even worse.

"Maybe it was a cry for help," Brent interposed. "A cry for help, to get Daniel to notice you and your own pain."

Matt sighed and sat up, placed his beer bottle on the coffee table. "Okay, let's stop talking about this," he said.

"Well," Derrick said, interlacing his fingers and reaching his palms up in a big stretch, "you wouldn't be the first gay man to fuck without a condom because it made him feel more alive."

"Was it at least good?" Brent asked.

Matt considered what to tell them, and settled upon a simple "Yes."

"Well, at least that," Brent said, while Derrick leveled at him a disapproving stare.

"At least that," Matt said. He was sitting at the edge of their big armchair; it was late at night and they had already said "Okay, time to go to bed" three or four times.

Derrick and Brent were standing now, and collecting bottles and glasses from the living room tables; Matt went into the kitchen to get a damp sponge. Derrick disappeared and came back with a pillow and blanket as he was wiping off the coffee table. "Are you scared?" he asked.

It was one of those moments where Derrick reached out simply and touched your very soul. "Yes," Matt whispered.

"MATT WENT BYE-BYE" WAS the way Daniel told Noam. To Gal he said, "Honey, I have to tell you something. Matt's not going to live here anymore."

"Did you have a fight?" she asked.

"Yes," he said, setting a bowl of cereal in front of her.

"I knew it," she said.

It was a cold January morning, and the radiators were clanging as the heat came on. He sat down opposite her, moving her orange juice away from the edge of the table, and told her the things he'd promised Matt he'd say: that Matt loved them and didn't want to leave, that it was his, Daniel's, decision, because Matt did something that made him very angry. His eyes were dry and grainy and each time he blinked he felt as though his corneas were being scratched. He needed to get some coffee into his body. Still, he was conscious as he spoke of doing a good job using age-appropriate language, and of being conscientious to Matt's demands.

Gal watched him, taking it in. Her lips were smeared past their edges with lip balm—the effort to heal their chronic winter cracks had obviously been an impatient one—and she pressed them together in a blotting motion. "Maybe you could marry a girl now," she said.

"Gal," he sighed. "Is that all you have to say?"

What was she supposed to say, she wondered, gazing at her uncle. His face was worn and dotted with bumps and bristles. Without his glasses she could see the purple under his eyes. Her bare feet were cold; her cereal was puffing up in the milk. Noam's eyes were flitting back and forth from her to Daniel, staticky filaments of his hair stirring gently in the air. "Bye-bye," he whispered.

"I'll take you to school today," Daniel said. "So we don't have to rush for the bus."

Gal put down her spoon, went up to her room, closed the door without slamming it so that Daniel wouldn't follow, and lay down on the unmade bed. With an irritated grunt, she twisted and pulled out the pajamas that were balled under her hip, flung them on the floor. She knew without question that she was never going to see Matt again. Something awful seeped over her, a sludge of panic and helplessness. Hatred of Daniel, for making Matt leave. She told herself that actually it was okay, Matt wasn't really a parent anyway. It wasn't like her parents dying. But who, she wondered, would take her to her riding lessons? If Daniel made her give them up, she would never talk to him again; she would live silently in this house till all the heavy silent air made it burst like a balloon, or a bomb.

About ten minutes later Daniel came up and sat next to her on the bed. Her face was turned away; she was curled up in a ball; his weight plunging down the mattress and the intolerable sound of his breathing made her feel like she was about to scream. *Go away go away go away*, she mouthed to herself. *Go away*.

"Ready to head out?" he said.

She staggered to her feet, avoiding his gaze. Downstairs, she put on her coat and hugged her backpack to her, and climbed into the car without a word. He dropped off Noam, and she waited in the cold silence of the car as he spoke with Colleen. Then he got back in and started the engine and she felt the heat blast back on. At school, she got out of the car and walked by herself to class before he could follow.

Daniel watched her march away from him, wanting to rush and tighten her backpack straps, but turned toward the principal's office instead, to let her know about Gal's changed circumstances.

"Oh, poor Gal," she said, shoulders sagging. "Not again."

"Nobody died," he said.

"Of course not," she hastened to say.

His friends came over to see if they were okay, flooding in again as they had when they'd first come back to the States after Joel's death. It was hard not to feel the parallel, to feel that their solicitude made things a little worse. Hard too to explain that he was feeling kind of good, even a little exhilarated by the clean anger hurtling through him. His days were utterly grueling, a chaos of work, child care, endless cooking and chores; the kids were brittle and God only knew how he was going to keep their financial ship afloat without Matt's income. But when he fell into bed at night, he occupied his light, living body restfully, feeling the tiredness tingle in his arms, his thighs and genitals. His thoughts would drift to Matt, and as rage mounted in him he breathed through it and calmed his own heartbeat.

"Tell me you didn't bring a casserole," he said when he opened the door to Adam and Val; Val swept him into her arms and rocked him back and forth, smashing his cheek against her earring. "Geez, Val," he said, and she released him, took him by the arms and held him at arm's length to look deeply into his sheepish face.

Gal came downstairs and accosted them in the front hall. "Dani decided he didn't want to be partners with Matt anymore," she announced to Adam. "Are you on Dani's side or Matt's side?"

"Nobody's side," Adam said, taking Lev's and Val's coats and reaching into the closet for a hanger. "I'm just sad."

They went into the kitchen while Lev scuttled into the playroom, where the toys were always more scintillating than his own. Gal barged into the kitchen just as they'd huddled around the table to talk, complaining that Lev was touching one of her bead necklaces. "Lev!" Val called, while Daniel said, "Try to be patient, Gal, he's littler than you are." Gal tried to palm off on him a plastic duck instead, but its lameness deeply offended him; his whole idiom and belief system were about bigger/smaller, older/younger, and he cried "That's for babies!" as his mother took him by the shoulders and gave him a little push out of the kitchen. There was a flurry of complaint from the playroom, then the sound of escalating objections. Daniel groaned, and he and Adam rose.

"Guys!" he said. In the playroom, a vaudeville "Yankee Doodle" was tootling merrily from Noam's plastic scooting car; he was sitting on it, gripping the handles hard, as Lev tried to pull him off, while Gal was blithely swinging a collapsible rod from her toy tent, pretending to be a ninja. Daniel caught her wrist and said, "Careful!"

She swung it around again, once, experimentally, her eyes on his face. "Seriously?" he said. "I will take that away from you and put you in your room so fast you won't even know what's happening." Adam was prying Lev's fingers off the car's handles. "Lev, you gotta take it easy, honey," he said. "You want to draw?" He went to the bookcase where the art supplies were stacked, Lev flailing on his hip, found crayons and construction paper.

"Look," Daniel said, "come sit at our new table"—pointing to the bright blue kid-sized plastic table with four chairs—and settled him on one of the chairs.

"I want the green chair," Lev said stoutly, hopping to his feet.

"No problem," said Adam.

"I'ma make a card for Mommy."

"Good thinking," Daniel said.

"Why am I always stuck playing with babies?" Gal was saying as they returned to the kitchen.

Val was eating a banana and leafing through a *New Yorker*, and the coffeepot was gurgling. Daniel sat down and she laid her hand on his wrist. He looked down at the silver rings on her fingers. She had been leaving I-just-wanted-to-see-how-you're-doing messages on his machine for days, and her desire to be there for him and the kids exhausted him. Now she and Adam clearly wanted to feel him out on the juicy details. He'd been avoiding them because he didn't feel he could tell anyone why he and Matt had broken up. Especially straight people, for whom the information would just confirm their stereotypes of gay men, even if they tried not to let it. He looked into their intense empathic eyes and said, "I really can't go into it."

"Whatever it was," Val ventured, "it must have been something pretty terrible. Because—well, because you've been through so much together, and you've done it so beautifully, and seemed so rock-solid as a couple."

Adam was mouthing the patch of beard below his lip and watching Daniel carefully, as if he might at any moment have to apologize for Val.

"Really, Val, I can't," Daniel said. Keeping Matt's secret, being put in that position, was compounding his outrage, he found, and his sense of clarity about having done the right thing. "You know what, though? I'm doing okay. Surprisingly okay."

"I don't think I've ever known someone as strong as you," Val said, and he didn't tell her that it wasn't really a question of strength.

There was a cry from the playroom, a shocked, breath-snatching cry—Noam. They leapt to their feet. He was sitting on the rug, his eyes wide and shocked and his mouth agape in the silence before a scream, his hand clapped to his face. Gal had poked him in the face with the tent pole, and put a gash under his eye. The scream came. Daniel lifted him and sat him on his knees on the couch while Adam ran for the first-aid kit in the upstairs linen closet. "Jesus, Gal," Daniel fumed. "I told you again and again. Do you know how close you came to poking him in the eye?"

Adam returned with sterile pads, and Daniel ripped one open and pressed it gently to Noam's cheek. The gash was about an inch long, and beading with blood; the skin underneath was starting to turn bruise colors. Gal stood on the stand of the floor lamp with her legs and arms twisted around the pole, frozen, watching.

Lev had run into the kitchen and come back with an ice pack, which he was trying to administer to Noam's face. "Lev, honey, step back a little; you're crowding them," Adam said, reaching out and taking him by the elbows.

"But he needs ice!" Lev cried. "And Band-Aids!"

"It's really nice and helpful for you to bring it, honey," Adam said as his son struggled in his grasp. Lev started to cry too, big half-fake sobs. "I know, buddy," Adam said. "It's hard to see your friend hurt."

The extra drama was not helping, Daniel thought. He peeled back the gauze to see if it was still bleeding, and when Noam saw his blood on it, he broke into fresh tears. "You could have blinded him, Gal!" Daniel said. "And you would have felt bad about that your whole life!"

"No I wouldn't," she shouted. "I wouldn't care at all!"

"Gal, sweetie, come here," Val said from the futon couch, patting her lap.

"Why don't you just mind your own business?" Gal said. "You're not in our family, we didn't ask you to come over."

"Gal!" Daniel barked while Val looked at her, hurt, and said, "I'm sorry you feel that way. Because I think of you as family."

"It's a stupid *defective* family," Gal said.

"Gal," Daniel said, his voice deadly. "Get into your room *now*. Damn," he said, "this thing is still bleeding. I'm going to take him to the emergency room."

Gal was on her way up the stairs; she turned and looked down. "We'll stay here with her," Val said, while Adam stroked her arm and said, "You know she's crazy about you."

Up in her room, the knowledge that she'd done something very bad was clawing at Gal, making her quiver between abjection and defiance. She threw herself on the bed, electric with anticipation for Daniel to come storming in, trying to summon him with the force of her hatred. *Oh, he was mad!* The thought brought a painful, agitated laugh. She imagined his grip on her arm, the glare of fully awakened eyes into hers.

She heard stomping downstairs, but nothing approaching her bedroom door. She stood and took down one of her two favorite horses, Cochav, whom she sometimes called by his English name, Star. She sat on the edge of her bed and pressed his plastic hoof into her arm, where it made a small, precise indented square. She carefully fit the hoof inside the square and pressed again, till the plastic mashed her skin up against the bone. Then she made another, till there was a satisfying pattern of squares on her throbbing forearm. She'd known even as she said those words to Val that she was being stupid, a baby nobody would listen to.

She put her arm to her nose and smelled but it didn't smell like anything. She stood and crept into her bed, pulling everything around her: Star, her stuffed dog, her comforter. Her arm still ached from the press of plastic.

Lying there with the covers pulled over her head, her face warmed and moistened by her own breath, she felt something work away at the edges of her memory. She twitched with irritation, as if she were being poked by an obnoxious kid. When the memory broke through, her breath stilled. She was shoulder to shoulder with Abba, kneeling on a chair at the kitchen table, the big calendar before them. Ema was in France, staying for a week with her friend whose mother had died. Gal was drawing a big *X* with a red marker into the square of the day that had passed, as she did each evening Ema was gone. The memory stunned her. The triumph of drawing that last *X*, and then Ema picking her up from school the next day, how her shirt smelled and the feel of her hair falling around Gal's face. Waking up the next morning and the sweet jolt of remembering that Ema was there. *Don't go away again!* she'd said, and Ema said, *I won't.* But it was just one morning. When she woke up the next day, Ema was gone, and Abba too, and everyone was crying. *Did Ema go back to France?* she'd asked.

The memory slopped against her; she had to make a conscious

effort to draw air into her lungs. The one night when they were all together after Ema returned, she'd melted down and ruined their Shabbat dinner. She didn't know why—she remembered the sensation of even then not knowing why, just tearing loose in the wind and there being nothing to catch onto as she shuddered and howled, knowing she was ruining everything.

Now, a metallic taste leached into her mouth; she put her finger inside her lip and when she removed it, it had blood on it. When Sabba told her, he'd tried to pull her into his arms, but she'd stiffened, bringing up her elbows to steel herself against the ugly wailing sounds he was making, the explosion of wetness and slime on her face and neck. She'd sensed that she needed to remain very still and dignified in the face of this degrading display of agony. Something of that old sense unfurled over her now. She imagined herself on horseback, sitting tall and stern next to her teacher Shannon, who wanted to go riding with her. She imagined Daniel watching her as she did something amazing. She heard the front door open and then shut hard, then the sound of the car's reluctant winter sputter before it broke into a roar.

AT THE EMERGENCY ROOM, sitting in an orange plastic chair with Noam on his lap, the irony wasn't lost on Daniel. He'd kicked Matt out for being impervious to the family's need for safety, and here he was in the ER for the first time since they'd brought the kids home. He felt stupid and careless for not having taken the pole away from Gal, because she was fragile, and he was feeling bad for her. He just hoped Matt never found out about it. And what would the social worker say? Maybe, he thought, he should have kicked out Gal instead of Matt. If she just mourned like other people—crying, maybe, or moping—it'd be easier to help her. But she was so mean and provocative and obnoxious. A headache pressed at his temples. Telling Val to mind her own business: He knew that if Matt were here, they'd be admiring the perfection of that insult even as they were deploring it.

The nurse called in the only other people in the waiting room, a mom with frazzled hair and a large teenager with patches of acne on his face and neck, who was pressing his elbow and upper arm against his chest and whimpering. It took forty-five minutes for Daniel's name to be called, and after a nurse finally examined Noam's cheek and eye, she said, "That'll need a stitch or two. We'll need to call down a plastic surgeon, because it's right there on the face." She put a Band-Aid on it and escorted them into an interior waiting room, and Daniel sat down with a sigh. He took out his cell phone and called Adam on speed dial, and Adam said they'd made quesadillas with the leftover chicken and cheese in the fridge, and were just sitting down to eat lunch. Gal was fine, he reported; she'd settled down and come out of her room. "I think she feels really bad about what she did," Adam said.

"Good," said Daniel.

They waited for another hour before the plastic surgeon showed up. By then Daniel had bought them a lunch of Pop-Tarts, pretzels, and lemonade from the vending machine, and relented and set Noam down on the floor, where he shredded a magazine and the arts section of the free local paper. He had to accost another nurse when the blood started seeping through Noam's Band-Aid. When they were called back in, the plastic surgeon said it was almost too late to put in stitches, and Daniel refrained from complaining that they'd been waiting forever for *him*, because there was no reason to anger someone working on his baby's face. The surgeon put some numbing gel on Noam's face. After a few minutes, he had Daniel hold Noam on his lap with his arms wrapped around his body, pinning down his arms, and washed it, then gave him a little shot in the cheek that made Noam cry out and Daniel blanch. As he leaned to put in the stitches, Daniel could smell his breath and the latex gloves on his hands, and he turned away, leaning his cheek on Noam's head.

When he was done, and Daniel, wild with his own relief, was nuzzling Noam and praising him for being a brave boy, the surgeon said, "There. Nobody will ever notice." He snapped off his gloves and tossed

them into the garbage, ruffled Noam's hair. "You're good as new, Noah,"
he said. "Stay away from your sister."

"Noam," Daniel said.

"It will leave a small scar, but it should become imperceptible over
time."

They waited again, this time for the nurse to return with a prescription for antibiotics. Another nurse came and leaned against the doorway, chirped, "Hi, honey! I heard you were super brave!"

Noam was crawling toward the wheels on a stretcher; he turned
and sat down, cast her a friendly look. "Not walking yet, huh," she said
in a loud, falsely reassuring voice, like a colonial administrator. "How
old is he?"

"Twenty-two months," Daniel said.

She looked surprised. "Well, you wait till you're good and ready,"
she said to Noam, which sounded in Daniel's ears like saying that Noam
was a spoiled brat just killing time.

"He's been through a lot," Daniel said, staunch in the face of this
irritant but newly anxious about the baby. "He lost both his parents in
a terrorist attack."

"Goodness!" she said, flinching in a way that was highly gratifying
to him. "I'm so sorry to hear that!"

ON SUNDAY, YOSSI CAME over for Gal's and Matt's lesson, unaware that
Matt wasn't there anymore. "Oh shoot!" Daniel said, staring at him as
he stood on the stoop.

"Dani and Matt broke apart!" Gal announced. "And Dani won't let
Matt live here anymore!" Yossi looked at Daniel in surprise, and then,
as Daniel opened his mouth to explain, he cut him off with pieties about
his own impartiality, as if fearing to be drawn into a catfight. "It's none
of my business," he said, waving his hand to stop Daniel's imaginary
insistence on spilling all the juicy and inappropriate details. "The main
thing is taking good care of the kids, helping them feel safe."

Daniel sighed, half wishing at that moment that Matt was there to walk into the idiotic slight and throw open the blinds by saying something like "Geez, Yossi, it's not like I'm about to start talking about the mechanics of sodomy." He was worried about paying for these lessons now, feeling strapped without Matt's salary, but he knew he couldn't cut Yossi's regular lessons out of Gal's routine. One day he mentioned to Yossi that he was thinking that he might have to cancel the cleaning lady, and the next time Yossi came, he proposed a barter arrangement: He'd give Gal an hour lesson around noon on Sundays, and then he'd go out for a few hours to paint, leaving Rafi there to play with Gal.

For her part, Gal relished getting Yossi to herself. She sat next to this man whose language felt like home—sure, Daniel could speak Hebrew and even Matt could speak a little, but they didn't sound *Israeli*—feeling her sleeves brush against his, smelling his special Yossi-smell, soapy with an undercurrent of body smell. At his house, where they met once in a while, they had little glasses for coffee, an electric *kumkum*, clementines in a bowl and chocolate spread in the refrigerator, and Yossi's wife, Anat, and the two older boys came in and out in a burst of Hebrew and a flurry of signing hands. Yossi pressed Gal's small hand in his large, warm one to encourage the curve or veer of a Hebrew letter, or encouraged her to watch his own hand as he drew, and sometimes she'd reach out with her finger and touch the little sprigs of hair coming from his knuckles and chuckle, "Hairy!" He asked her what happened this week, and she was supposed to tell him in Hebrew. So she told him about a classmate whose mother had died—"of *cancer*," she whispered. "Everyone feels terrible for her," she said. Where she faltered, he wrote down a word, until each week he had five new Hebrew words for her to learn. He called her a *yalda chachama*, a smart girl, held out his palm so she could give him five, beseeching her for a gentle one, and then howled with mock betrayal when she gave it a hard smack instead.

Rafi had become like another brother; she took his presence for granted without seeking it. He was the only kid around who lived in a more complicated linguistic ecosystem than she did, and her official position on him was pity. Once, she had asked Yossi if he was sad Rafi was deaf, and he'd said, "I've only ever known Rafi deaf. If he wasn't deaf, he wouldn't be Rafi." That was an intriguing philosophical revelation to her, and she mulled and mulled it. Rafi could be wild—he could plow through a house with maniacal energy, leaping off of furniture and landing with an explosion of noise you didn't think his small body could create, grabbing cherished or fragile objects and making the grown-ups have to chase him to snatch them out of his hands. Gal sometimes suspected he was just pretending he couldn't hear so that he wouldn't have to listen to anybody. But his blithe oblivion, which had been off-putting at first, had come to feel relaxing to her. When they were bored, he taught her signs in Israeli Sign Language, and in those few moments where they sat, moving only their fingers, palms, wrists, there was a strange pleasure in the silence, in pretending she was deaf.

MATT STOPPED CALLING, RESPECTED Daniel's wishes not to be in touch. Derrick, who went over to pick up his computer and printer, told Matt that he'd tried to talk to Daniel, only to be told that he welcomed Derrick's support and friendship as long as they didn't involve his agitating on Matt's behalf. Matt knew there were things Derrick wasn't telling him, too: When he asked about seeing Gal and Noam, Derrick was evasive, and said, "Just give it a little time."

After a few weeks, Matt found a house in Derrick and Brent's neighborhood to sublet. It was owned by an anthropologist couple from Smith who were going into the field for a semester, and they were charging him next to nothing in exchange for his taking care of their deaf elderly springer spaniel, Molly. They worked in Japan, so the house was filled with Japanese prints and paintings and sacred objects that made him feel loud and hairy and big-footed, and at times, under the tranquil eye of the Buddha, pleasantly reverent. In the big sunny study the owners shared, the dog slumbering at his feet, Matt threw himself into his work, finishing a few projects that he had procrastinated over.

Cam came over at night to visit, as did Brent, and they shook their heads woefully and recalled their own traumatic breakups. He made movie dates with a few people he liked but whose friendship he'd never had time, or was too complacent in his couple-hood, to pursue. He had dinner at Val and Adam's, and endured a wearying meal of watery vegetarian lasagna, during which the older kids answered questions about school in monosyllables, hair flopped over their faces, and Lev, tired and irritable, baited his parents by throwing food on the floor. After Lev finally went to bed, Matt discovered that Daniel hadn't told Adam and Val what he had done to make Daniel kick him out, and had to tell them himself, knowing even as he spoke that they wouldn't have invited him over to dinner if they'd known. They tried to be cosmopolitan about the mysteries of queer desire and behavior, but they were clearly shocked. For the rest of the evening, Val couldn't keep exasperation out of her voice. He suspected that she had planned to get them back together, but was sensing now that this breakup confounded even her abilities. He couldn't wait to get out of there, and excused himself wearily as soon as he could without being rude.

He called Yossi, whose company he missed, and left a message, but Yossi didn't call him back. He wondered if he'd gotten the message; it was a chaotic household and someone could have deleted it. He wondered if Yossi knew what he'd done, in which case, okay, he deserved to be dumped. But if Val and Adam didn't know, he didn't think Yossi would either. After a week had passed, he figured that Yossi just didn't want to be friends. He tried to be a grown-up about it; if he didn't want to be friends, Matt couldn't force him. But he'd thought they had a genuine connection, and as the days went on, the thought that he was so easily dispensable made him increasingly bitter.

He put one foot in front of the other, functioning on the very edge of believing the breakup was final. He just didn't believe that it could be, although he also vowed not to be one of those boyfriends who sent obsessive emails and left phone messages dark with meaning—beginning with a low, terse "It's me"—one of those guys who refused to see the evidence staring him in the face, the evidence all of his creeped-out friends could see. One day, he fell over the edge, and then the agony of his loss shocked him. He'd lost his family because he'd failed them. He'd tried and tried to rise to the occasion of their loss, and he'd done a great job until the effort had become just too great. And then what? The most ignominious of failures, he simply couldn't keep it in his pants. Was that the true Matt? The thought that there might be something fundamentally selfish and childish about him distressed him. And it made him rethink his whole relation to Jay's illness, too. Had Kendrick been right, and he'd just been a big handful the whole time? He spent that day stunned and immobilized in bed, while the stiff old spaniel snored and twitched on the floor beside him.

Other days, though, there was a glimmer of chilly optimism, a little piece of him that felt freed. In a few years, he thought, surely this whole awful, demented interlude would seem like a dream. In the quiet, scholarly rental house, it was sometimes hard to believe it had happened. Terrorism! The Occupation! The Holocaust! The grieving grandparents and stricken children! His house teeming with toys, diapers, strewn bedding, strange people washing dishes or cooking food. *Jesus Christ,* he thought at those moments, *what a freaking melodrama!* And what a stupid, deluded, paltry role he'd played in it. He *so* didn't belong with those people: Hadn't they made that abundantly clear?

He thought about being in Israel, about every door that had slammed in his face, and every time, back home, that Daniel acted surprised when Matt did something that hinted of being an actual parent. Anger would worm into his throat then: they'd exploited him, and he'd let them. Had Daniel been waiting the whole time to pull out that legal crap that he alone was the legal guardian and the sole owner of the house? Throughout this whole nightmare, Matt had reassured himself that Daniel still loved him, but that his love was like a tiny sacred object buried under layers of grief and confusion, so he couldn't find it. Now he thought that Daniel hadn't loved him after all, and just kept him around because it was too hard to parent on his own. Maybe he even did it consciously; he could just imagine the cold calculus of need, affection, dissimulation, self-justification.

And he—he'd reveled in the poignancy of being there to soothe the brokenhearted, the glamour of being a handsome man riding to their rescue. It made his face burn now to recall all that welling up of deep, tender feeling, as if he'd just come across and read his adolescent journal.

Released, he could do as he pleased. He could break through this whole carapace of grief and horror and emerge, gleaming and tender, into a new life. Would he go back to New York, where any respectable gay man would choose to live? He knew he could be picked up by a design firm and make a fair living there, even though rents in Manhattan had gone through the roof in the years he'd been gone. There would be more than three excellent restaurants in walking distance, and things to do after dark; the thought of hanging out and drinking with more than two gay men made his lips twitch with a smile. And art! He missed art so much.

He went through a few weeks of purification, cutting out smoking and eating meat, running in a pattern of two days on, one day off. He joined the gym so he could do weights. He circled the date of his sexual encounter on his calendar, counted six months and circled the date in June he'd get himself tested. He slept late in the mornings, enjoying not having a toddler who awoke at six, and kept the house super tidy, washing strange dishes and using up the laundry detergent in their laundry room, which made him experience a new, not unpleasant smell in his life that it took a few days to identify with his newly washed clothing.

WHEN IT HAD BECOME clear that they would become a couple, Daniel and Matt had made a half-joking pact never to tell Daniel's parents if they broke up, because they knew how gratified they'd be. Even these years later, with all the water under the bridge, Daniel couldn't bring himself to tell his parents right away. He did, though, call the social worker, Christine, thinking it wisest to be up-front about his change in status. She came for a visit late one afternoon, files jutting out of the big purse beside her on the couch, her feet puffing against the strictures of her pumps. "I won't lie to you, Daniel," she said. "I was happier when you and Matt were together."

He shrugged.

"I don't like these kids experiencing another loss so soon, and I don't like seeing them so dark and quiet."

"Do you think *I* do?" he asked, stung that she thought that. He'd actually been feeling pretty good with them, feeling that, as a parent, he was on his game. Last night at supper they'd both been on edge, Noam whining in his booster—he had a stuffed nose, and had been up a lot during the night because he couldn't suck his passy and breathe at the same time—while Gal complained bitterly that she hated every single bit of food in front of her; and Daniel had sat down with them, his mind chugging about how to salvage dinner. "Remember the time we went to the fair and that llama spat on Cam?" he finally asked. "Wow, was she ever covered in llama spit!" Their scowling faces turned toward him. He imitated Cam touching her hair and bringing her hand away, looking at it with revulsion. Simultaneously, they laughed, disarmed, and dinner was saved.

"Of course not." Christine's composed professional face relaxed for a moment, and the expression was kind and weary. "Look, it's none of my business why you fellas broke up. Or to encourage an unhappy relationship. But if you can find your way back to each other, that would be the optimal situation for these kids."

Daniel was silent. Wasn't it a commonplace that staying together for the sake of the kids was a bad idea, because it modeled a bad marriage for them?

"And if you can't, I sure hope you're figuring out some arrangement where the kids can see him. He was an involved parent. They're close to him."

"I will," he said. "Just not yet."

"When?" she asked, waiting him out as he groaned and rolled his head on his neck.

"Do I even have to, from a legal standpoint?" he challenged. "I'm the one who has full custody."

"Legally? No," she said. "But I think you know this isn't only about the letter of the law."

"Gal hasn't even asked to see Matt."

Christine was quiet for a moment. Then she said, "That's for a reason you don't have access to, Daniel. For all you know, she's just used to the world taking parents away, and can't imagine that she has any control over it."

That surprised him, and wounded him too, her thinking of him as some pitiless force crushing his child; and it was still rankling when he opened the door to let her out. He was the one betrayed—how had he become the bad guy? He jammed his leg in front of Yo-yo, who was trying to barrel out into the cold, and watched as, with a jangle of a massive key chain, Christine got into her dinky Prizm.

That night Derrick called, and they were barely into the conversation when he asked Daniel when Matt would be able to see the kids.

"Did he ask you to ask me?" Daniel said, his voice sharp. He muted the bedroom TV, where he'd been watching a police procedural while drinking a glass of scotch.

"So what if he did? There's nothing underhanded about that," Derrick said with some exasperation. "You won't talk to him . . ."

Daniel was quiet. "If I felt it was the wrong thing to do," he finally told Derrick, "I'd really be struggling. But I know that it isn't. I feel good, Derrick. So angry sometimes I can hardly see, but weirdly good. I know the kids are suffering, but I think I'm doing right by them."

"'Doing right by them'? Are you sure? What must they think? I don't mean to pull my professional training on you, but—"

"Then don't," Daniel said. "Just don't."

There was a long pause. Then: "He feels used. And you can sort of see why."

The subtitles on the TV indicated that the detectives suspected the husband of the murdered socialite. "Maybe I did use him a little," Daniel conceded. "Sometimes I think I stayed with him because I couldn't imagine coming home with the kids alone."

Derrick paused, then said, "Really? I don't really buy that."

"What don't you buy?" Daniel asked, irritated; apparently he couldn't get anything right.

"You're saying that you didn't love him anymore at that point. But I think you did."

"You always think people are better than they really are," Daniel said. "I haven't felt anything for him for a while."

Derrick shot back, "You haven't felt much of anything, *period*, for a while. Including anger at the person who killed your brother. But Matt you can get angry with, Matt you can call a danger to your family."

Daniel groaned. "Did you call to harass me, Derrick?"

"No," Derrick said. "But I think you should let him see the kids."

"I'll think about it," Daniel said, willing to say anything at that point to get Derrick off the phone. He still needed to make the kids' lunches for tomorrow and take out the dog. He hung up and lay there for a minute, regretting having settled down with a drink in the first place before finishing his evening chores. He was tired of everybody being on his case. Derrick knew what Matt had done, and he was *still* giving him a hard time. He wished he had asked him what he would have done if *Brent* had barebacked—Derrick would have gone on a tirade about responsibility and consequences so furious it would have set Brent's hair afire. And *of course* he'd let the kids see Matt at some point soon; he wasn't a monster, he knew it was wrong to make him just vanish, as their parents had. But he couldn't bring himself to do it just yet.

THE LONGEST JANUARY HE had ever lived through passed into February, and Matt was learning to live alone again, without a partner and without kids. He handled his anger at Daniel for cutting Noam and Gal out of his life by spitefully luxuriating, when he awoke in the morning, in visions of Daniel having to wake them, dress them, feed them, and hustle them out of the house by himself, along with feeding and taking out the dog. He'd relearned the austere pleasures of making coffee for one, fishing clean laundry out of the basket when he was ready to wear it instead of folding it and putting it in drawers, sprawling on the queen-sized bed and watching HGTV at night and groaning over the idiots who rejected a home simply because they didn't like the color of the paint on the walls, downloading new music on his iPod for the first time in months. He revived a few friendships he'd been pursuing just when Joel and Ilana had been killed, which he hadn't had the time or energy to pursue after that; he drank martinis at dinner parties and slept a full eight hours a night. He ran and worked out at the gym, and got something of his old lean muscle back, although there remained a little too much paunch for comfort, a sign of getting older that he deplored. He aggressively pursued a few big jobs, and got a piece of one of them, with the promise of more. Derrick had been working for a while on setting up an LGBT version of Big Brothers Big Sisters, pairing queer and questioning high schoolers with queer adults in the Pioneer Valley, and Matt volunteered to be a big brother if it got off the ground.

It was exciting to revive his old self—fun, a good conversationalist, a sexual player. But he wasn't, of course, his old self; he had so much baggage now, he told people, he practically had to hire a porter to come with him everywhere. One night, he had a drink with Alex Connor, Northampton's one gay cop; he had a shaved blond head and an earring in one ear that he wore only when off duty, and his T-shirt stretched over his shoulders. Matt wasn't into the whole Aryan thing, the pale lashes, but he found the tension between Alex's sense of duty and his sense of irony appealing, and enjoyed Alex's stories about Northampton's seamy side. As he told Alex the story of his relationship with Daniel and the last year, Alex reacted with a series of "Whoa's," and he felt uncomfortable about how glamorously tragic it made him seem; he found himself underplaying things and omitting others, like the custody fight with the Holocaust-survivor grandparents. At the end of the story, he said, "So he just couldn't deal with a partner; he had to scapegoat somebody in the end, and it was me." He didn't like the way he sounded when he said that, either; if he'd been Alex, listening to him, he'd wonder what bad behavior of Matt's own he was leaving untold.

"Did you like being a parent?" Alex asked.

Matt thought. "I did. I didn't think I would, but I did."

"Do you feel like"—Alex's voice lowered dramatically, a little sardonically—"you never knew what it meant to love, till then?"

Matt looked at him sharply. "Of course not," he said. "That's bullshit. What did those people spend their lives doing before kids, jerking off?" As he spoke, he knew that he was overstating his objection to that cliché, out of worry that he was being mocked. Certainly he'd been willing to give up a whole lot for Gal and Noam, and sometimes he'd be walking down the street with them and know—just calmly know—that if a car swerved toward them, he'd fling his body between it and them. But somehow, that didn't feel like noble parental self-sacrifice, it just felt like the right thing to do. And would he have done any of this if he hadn't loved Daniel with his whole heart—if he hadn't longed to soothe that deep, deep grief?

"What's next for you?" Alex asked, his eyes traveling in a friendly manner over Matt's face and body.

"Not sure," Matt said. "I'm thinking about returning to New York."

Through a friend of Val's, he put down a deposit for a three-month-long sublet in the West Village, thinking he would go back and give living there a trial run before actually moving there. But the closer the time got to the beginning of the sublet, the less New York seemed to shimmer with promise, and he began to wonder whether, at this point, its wonder and excitement were just the mechanical fantasy of a queer living in the boondocks. He found himself getting lethargic each time he was supposed to be packing, and even if it was a total long shot, he felt he had to stick around in case he got to see Gal and Noam. Then his Jetta broke down and needed a new transmission, and for three days he obsessed over whether to continue investing in it—it had ninety-four thousand miles on it—or buy a new car. Either way, it was going to cost a fortune—and if he gave up his sublet, he'd lose his $1,700 security deposit as well.

What was wrong with him? He felt lazy and boring; it felt like an unconscious unwillingness to truly part from Daniel, and he dreaded being the pathetic ex-without-a-clue. He worried that the kids were just an excuse. He'd left New York four years ago because he couldn't take the scene anymore, because he was afraid of the drugs and the self-destruction, because he knew the answer to the game of Who's the Hottest Man in the Room?, and it didn't gratify him anymore. Did he fear that, at thirty-two, with just that infinitesimal thickening, he might not be in the game anymore? And even if he was, he didn't know yet whether he had HIV, and would have to conduct a sex life full of honest confessions and intense precautions with men he didn't even yet know, which wearied him just thinking about it. He had clumsily extricated himself from Alex Connor's muscular arms after their drink for that very reason.

He decided, finally, to stay in Northampton through the summer and consider going back to New York in the fall. It was money down the drain, but you couldn't push this kind of thing. And the truth was, he kind of loved Northampton. Unwillingly, and with a tremendous sense of self-irony, but he did: He'd turned into a nature-loving, dog-loving, hiking New Englander who knows the best local ponds and lakes to swim in, who gorges on farm-stand corn and berries in the summer, and gets his woodpile ready for winter so he can sit in the woodstove's warmth and watch the flames flicker behind the door. Not to mention his love of the cafés crowded with academics writing on their laptops or grading papers, the fantastic bookstores, the organic this and fair-trade that, the fiery debates in local newspapers about the Fourth of July or the Pride parade, or the whole development versus conservation problem. And the lesbians! Could he live without the lesbians now? His tenderness for them was no less deep for its comical condescension. How could you not love the jocks who returned from summer vacations at P-town and the Hamptons and Ogunquit with deep tans and new girl-friends; the buzz-cut butches with their husky laughs; the lesbian moms who were gamely supportive of their daughters who insisted on wear-ing nothing but tutus and tiaras and pink pink pink?

He didn't see Gal and Noam anywhere around town; it figured that in a small town where you saw everybody all the time, he wouldn't see the people he was actually dying to see. He kept himself from driving past Gal's school and Noam's day care, and past Daniel's house, and he didn't ask their mutual friends about them either because asking would have made him feel too pathetic. But he heard this and that from Val and Adam, Brent and Derrick, and Cam. That the kids missed him. That Daniel was still making plans to take them to Israel for the year anniversary. That he wouldn't keep Matt from seeing them forever. He couldn't, Matt thought. Surely he couldn't.

CHAPTER 18

"WHERE AM I going to sleep?" Gal asked.

It was early March, and they were in the car on the way to the Newark airport, a four-hour drive to begin their trip to Israel. Noam, strapped into his car seat next to Gal, was sucking his pacifier and clutching his doggie and two wool hats. Over the past few weeks he'd begun saying a few words other than *yeah* and *no*. His newest word was *doggie*. "What's your doggie's name?" people would ask, and he would reply, "Doggie." His second word was *more*, which he uttered with a huge astonished veer upward, in imitation of the few times they'd teased him about wanting even more of something.

"In your old bed, I guess," Daniel said to Gal. "And I could put Noam's crib into the little guest room if you want, so you can have your own room."

"Uh-huh," Gal murmured, thinking about that. "I think maybe he should sleep in the same room as me, because it's a new place for him."

"Okay," Daniel said. Lately, since Noam's cheek injury, she'd been solicitous to him, running to get his passy when he cried and wedging it into his mouth till he sucked; the other day Daniel had come into their bedroom to read a story and found them sitting on Gal's bed, holding hands.

"Where are *you* going to sleep?" Gal asked.

Daniel paused. "I thought I'd sleep in your parents' old room."

"No," she said. "I don't think that's a good idea."

She said it in her most carefully reasoning tone.

"Really?" he asked.

"Because what if I have a bad dream and I get up and go into their room? I'll think I'm going to Ema and Abba but then they won't be there, and then I'll feel even worse."

Daniel was quiet. Over the past few weeks she'd been full of anxious questions about their visit. Were they staying with her grandparents? Would she sleep over at Leora's house all by herself? Would they lock the doors when they were in the house? Suddenly she couldn't remember the Hebrew word for *Popsicle*, or for *sidewalk*, and her face flooded with relief when he reminded her.

"Why don't we play it by ear," he said.

His mind had been going over the vital things he'd packed or zipped into his inside winter coat pocket: wallet, passports, tickets, the kids' legal papers, the keys to the apartment in Jerusalem. His stomach and throat were tight, and for a few days, it had been hard to get food down. When he thought about opening the door to Joel and Ilana's apartment, he wondered what on earth he'd been thinking when he'd agreed with his father to keep it for a while. He imagined how stale and dusty the apartment would be, how half-vacated, how they'd keep coming across pieces of baby gear or freezer-burned food, every object haunted. He couldn't, for the life of him, remember whether they'd gotten rid of Joel and Ilana's clothes.

Gal gazed out the window at bare trees and dirty snow. Her brother's eyes were falling shut and then opening again. She'd wanted to go back so badly, to see Leora and her classmates and her grandparents, to be home. But as the time had approached, she'd had trouble falling asleep at night, as her mind spun with anxious conjecture. What if she got killed by terrorists? Or didn't remember how to say things? Or missed her parents even more? And Noam, too. The scar under his eye, which no longer needed a bandage, was healing slowly—you couldn't see the stitch marks anymore, but it hadn't yet turned white, either. It made him look fragile and damaged, and Gal dreaded everybody asking what had happened to his cheek, and finding out that she had been the one who hurt him.

She'd wanted to tell Daniel she wasn't going to go, but the thought of being separated from him frightened her. And what about her grandparents? She knew that their looking forward to her visits was what kept them alive, her grandfather had told her that. Daniel had tried to talk to her about the trip, asking her how she felt about going back, and she'd looked at him with door stoppers in her throat, words bumping against hard rubber. He sat next to her, wearing a T-shirt fraying around the collar, his hand warm on her leg. He told her that it was going to be hard, and sad, but also fun to see Leora and Shai and Ruti and her other friends.

"You know what the important thing is?" he asked Gal.

She looked in his face, which was serious and sweet. She knew the right answer was something like "That we all love each other."

"The important thing is that we'll all be together," he said.

"Is Matt coming, too?" she asked.

He sighed. "No, Gal. You know he's not."

She stirred and tried, with a deep breath, to disperse the bad feeling sifting through her like dust motes turning in a shaft of sun; she hadn't asked the question to be fresh or mean.

"But Yossi and Rafi are," Daniel reminded her. Yossi had been talking for a while about taking the family to Israel to visit his aging parents in Petach Tikva, and a few weeks ago, he had decided to go alone with Rafi. He planned it so they and Daniel and the kids could fly back and forth together, and so he and Rafi could come to the memorial. The news had flooded Gal with relief; she had the vague and scary sense of the family dwindling, failing, like the feeble trickle from a faucet after the water runs out.

"Is Rafi going to sleep over?" she asked now, her voice rising over the din of the car. "Where will he sleep?"

"I don't know yet, Gal-Gal. If he does, it'll just be for one night, and we'll figure it out."

"Why isn't Anat coming?"

"She's staying home with Ezra and Udi, remember? Because they have school and practices they didn't want to miss."

"Does she have to go to the lab?" Rafi's mother, Anat, who was doing a postdoc in physics, was famous for spending ungodly hours in the lab; Gal knew the Israeli Sign Language sign for *lab*.

"Yes," Daniel said.

When they arrived at the gate three hours later, flushed and hassled from parking and the shuttle bus and the long security line, Yossi and Rafi were already there. The lounge area wasn't even open yet; it was barricaded off till the security officers could arrive. They wandered around looking for a place nearby to settle and dump their stuff, Noam slumped in his stroller with his passy listless in his mouth; he'd been up three times in the night, and both he and Daniel were haggard. Gal and Rafi examined electronics and iPod accessories and sunglasses and inflatable neck pillows, prodded repeatedly by Yossi and Daniel to move along and keep within eyeshot. In the newspaper store, as the men bought magazines and chewing gum, they fingered the travel-sized items—toothpaste and collapsible toothbrushes, tiny bottles of shampoo and ibuprofen and moisturizer and hand sanitizer, miniature sets of Scrabble and chess. Each time Rafi went with his parents to the supermarket, he begged them for one trial-sized item, and in his room he had a bin of products in deliciously tiny containers that he and Gal loved to plunge their hands into, removing individual items to examine and caress.

On the flight, Gal and Yossi switched seats so she could sit next to Rafi, and she watched movies with a headset while Rafi worked tiny travel puzzles and a Game Boy with his thumbs. He sat slumped with his heels on the seat, tucked under his butt, and sometimes he'd gaze at the screen on the seat back in front of her, blinking with sleepy absorption, and she wondered, as she often did when they watched TV together—the sound turned up and the English subtitles making her eyes scramble all over the screen—how much he could understand. She took off her own headset and just watched the pictures, to see if she could follow the story, and he looked sideways at her, his lips curling up in a smile, then fished out his own headset from the seat pocket. He mimed putting them on and turning up the volume, and arranged his face into an expression of sage contemplation, and she laughed; he was showing her that he could hear if he put those on. He'd gotten a haircut for Israel, which made him look older, less elfin.

It was thrilling to choose and examine and eat their own dinner without the help of a parent. Yossi came by and poked his head in, but they yelled at him to go away till he slunk off, hands raised in surrender. They found the little packets of salt and pepper, the tiny tubs of margarine for their rolls—and they agreed with great pleasure that the meal was disgusting except for the carrot cake.

THEY PARTED FROM YOSSI and Rafi at the Pelephone booth outside of customs, where Daniel needed to stop and rent a cell phone. When Yossi lifted Gal and hugged her, she wrapped her legs around his back and laid her head on his shoulder. She felt his back vibrate as he murmured in her ear, and then he looked in her face and rubbed his beard stubble on her cheek, making her swat at him. "We'll see you next week at the memorial," he said. He put her down and bent to kiss Noam's head. Rafi waggled his fingers good-bye and slipped something into her coat pocket; when she took it out, she found it was a trial-sized tube of Jergens Ultra Healing moisturizer. She watched them walk off with a throb of unease.

The sound of native Hebrew jingled in her ears, and her brain rearranged itself with a smart click, like a metal washer onto a magnet. After he'd signed for the phone, Daniel put his wallet back in his pocket and ushered them away from the line, gesturing for Gal to wheel Noam in the little folding stroller while he wheeled the cart with the suitcases. He stopped, peered at the phone in his palm, and dialed Yaakov's cell phone. "Yaakov?" he said loudly. "It's Daniel!" He listened for a while, and Gal heard a torrent of noisy, distorted male speech come from the phone on his ear. Sabba, she realized with alarm, wasn't at the airport. Daniel kept trying to cut in and tell him it was no problem, they'd take a *sherut*. "Don't worry," he said. "Yaakov. Yaakov. Don't worry. Okay, *le'hitraot*. See you soon."

"Okay, guys," he told the kids. "Sabba isn't going to make it—he got a flat tire. So we're taking a *sherut*. C'mon. Gal, you push your brother, okay?"

"Did he get into an accident?" Gal asked as he herded her out the doors and into the crowd. Would Daniel know how to get them to Jerusalem, and remember that he had to pay with shekels, not dollars?

"No, no," he said. "He got a flat tire when the car was parked in front of the house."

"Are we still going to see him?" She was hurrying with the stroller to keep up with him.

"What?"

"Are we still going to see him? Wait for me!"

"Of course!"

The air smelled of exhaust and cigarette smoke, the high whine of idling planes punctuated by quick blasts of car horns and brake squeals. People were holding up signs, exclaiming, hugging. Taxi drivers approached and solicited his business in English, and Daniel waved them off till he saw a Shemesh van. *"Yerushalayim?"* he asked the driver, and when he nodded, Daniel wheeled the bags to the back, supervised their getting lifted into the trunk, and lifted Gal's backpack off her back so she could get in. He tossed it in after her, lifted Noam out of his stroller and struggled to collapse it with one hand, sweating in his winter coat, remembering the woman in the security line who'd said, "I'd help you with that, but I don't have a degree in advanced engineering."

He handed the folded stroller to the driver to stow away, lifted Noam into the van, and sat him next to Gal in the middle row, then climbed in beside him. The van vibrated loudly. In the back sat a religious couple with two little girls wearing sweatshirts over dresses. Daniel unzipped his coat and squirmed it off, feeling his shirt stick to his back and a trickle of sweat on his temple. "Whoosh," he sighed. "One more little drive and we're there."

They were the last ones in the van; the driver got in and pulled away. Now that Daniel was settled and had caught his breath, he remembered sitting in a van with his parents and Matt a year ago, the one that had taken them to the morgue, and for a moment something of the old shock came over him. When he could breathe again, he was glad to be alone, without his parents to manage and ward off, without reporters in his face. He put his arm around Noam and scooted him in closer.

He dozed, and was awoken when the van lurched into low gear as they began to ascend. It was warm in the van, and one of the little girls behind him was kicking at his seat; just when he was about to turn around, she'd stop, and then when he settled down, she'd kick again. He looked down at Gal, who was nodding and dozing with her head resting on the window. A scent memory of the morgue floated past him, and he concentrated on it for a second, trying to make it comprehensible, before letting it go in revulsion. The swing of the van through curves and the slash of sunlight in and out of his field of vision began to nauseate him. He closed his eyes, and when he opened them again, it was dark, the sun blocked by the massive wall of the cemetery where his brother was buried. Tears sprang to his eyes. His brother—*brother*—never had a word pierced his heart so sharply. A silent cry rushed through his chest and head.

Matt!

The slip was startling—although, he quickly reminded himself, it certainly wasn't the first time he'd called Joel "Matt," or vice versa. After all, hadn't Joel been his first beloved, the model for all future beloveds? He rubbed his eyes before the tears could fall, and shrugged off the soreness and longing in his heart.

THE APARTMENT WAS CHILLY and dark, the blinds on the porch making a hollow shuddering sound in the wind. They entered, sniffing and twitching. There was a faint smell of cleaning chemicals; Malka had had her housekeeper clean it.

Daniel dumped his bags in the hall and helped Gal off with her backpack. He turned on all the lights within reach, and flipped on the boiler switch next to the bathroom. He wheeled Noam into the kitchen and opened the refrigerator, peering in as if it would offer him the key to an important mystery. It was empty except for some condiments in the door—mustard, mayonnaise, capers—and had been wiped out by someone who'd done a half-assed job; tiny crumbs lined the edges of the vegetable drawers, and there was an intractable juice syrup spot with tiny shreds of paper towel fuzzed around its edges.

Gal went automatically to her after-school destination, the snack drawer, sliding it open and finding a few loose Bamba and pretzel pieces and crumbs in the corners. She put a piece of Bamba in her mouth but when she bit down on it, it felt like biting into a sponge and she spat it into her hand. She looked around for the garbage, or a paper towel, then held her hand with the tooth-marked yellow paste out to Daniel, and he wrinkled his nose and brought her by the wrist to the sink. The faucet coughed loudly twice before water came out and washed it off.

She wandered into the living room; there were the blue couch and the leather lounge chair around the pocked octagonal wood coffee table that she had jumped off of thousands of times—first, as a little kid, onto the couch, landing on her knees, and then, later, with a big thud onto the floor, making her parents scold her about disturbing the downstairs neighbors. There, on a shelf under the TV, were the DVDs: *The Sound of Music*, Uzi Chitman, *The Little Mermaid*. The TV had a light film of dust over its face. She put her finger to it to draw her name, and was nipped by an electric shock. Her heartbeat sped up, then slowed down. An unnatural quiet saturated the house; she wanted to speak into the silence but couldn't coax the sound out of her throat.

She walked down the hall to her room, studiously avoiding looking into her parents' room ahead of her. Her room was dim and stripped: just her bed and Noam's crib, no sheets or pillowcases, comforters uncovered and folded; no toys. With only its thin mattress, the crib looked like a tiny jail cell. The pictures were up, though, and in the middle of the floor, the rug with the frog. Sunlight bled through the blinds' closed slats. She sat down on her bed, then curled up around the cold, bare pillow and put her thumb in her mouth. She was chilled. She thought she could fall asleep.

She heard Daniel's footsteps and felt his shadow come over her. "Your grandparents are on their way," he said. "When they get here I'll go to the *makolet* and get some food into this house." He stood there for a few more moments; she could hear him breathing and then scratching his cheek stubble. "Okay," he said.

A minute later there was a knock on the door, light and peppy. Gal sat up, and from Daniel's delighted greeting she registered that it wasn't her grandparents. She came out of her bedroom to see who was there, slowed shyly. There stood Leora, wearing glasses!, and holding a plastic-wrapped plate with cookies and candy. And her mother, Gabrielle, in flowing bell-bottoms, a flowered blouse, and silver trinkets at her neck and wrists. "Welcome back!" Gabrielle cried as she and Daniel embraced. She caught sight of Gal over his shoulder. "Kookie, are you shy?" she said, her voice suffused with amused tenderness.

Gal blushed and trotted over, let herself be lifted and squeezed, her face tickled by Gabrielle's hair, her nostrils by her scent, which was like cucumbers. Gabrielle set her down and beamed at her. "You've gotten so big! How many teeth have you lost?" She peered into Gal's mouth, which was opened for inspection, and said "Psssh!" with an impressed expression. She caught sight of Noam sitting on the living room rug and crouched beside him. "Do you remember me? *Oy vey*, what happened to your poor cheek?" He reached out his hand and touched her face. "Num-num," she growled, pretending to gnaw on his hand. "Where's Matt? What, he didn't come?"

"Hi," Gal was saying to Leora, a little shy because Leora looked older and more serious with glasses on.

"Here's a Purim *mana*," Leora said, and thrust it at her with a smile.

IT WAS PURIM, AND the little-girl Queen Esthers in their pretty dresses were out in force. As were the teenagers with their faces minimally, wittily painted, and the men in drag, one of whom waited on Daniel in the coffee shop the next morning when the kids were at their grandparents'—a miniskirt encasing his slender hips, his breasts askew, his Adam's apple a-bobbing. That evening, Malka and Yaakov took the kids to shul for the reading of the book of Esther, and Daniel spent that time at home unpacking and cleaning up, then pouring himself a scotch and looking all over the house, fruitlessly, for a Bible, so he could reread Esther himself. He finally gave up and turned on his computer to check for wireless coverage, not very hopeful, although as the chord and the white apple greeted him, he marveled at how the sight of his own computer booting up could help him feel just a little more at home. And the wireless was working! Either his father had continued paying for Internet, or Netvision had forgotten to turn it off.

He read, sipping scotch. Vashti, the first queen, a feminist hero, who refused to dance for the king and his court. Then Esther, and her shadowy, ambiguous uncle/counselor/friend Mordechai. And at the end of the story, massacre. That surprised him, even though he'd read it before. Skimming along a chain of Google pages, he found a commentary from Elie Wiesel:

> I confess I never did understand this part of the Book of Esther. After
> all, the catastrophe was averted; the massacre did not take
> place. Why then this call for bloodshed? Five hundred men were
> slain in Shushan in one day and three hundred the next. Seventy-five
> thousand persons lost their lives elsewhere. . . . Is this why we are

told to get drunk and forget? To erase the boundaries between reality
and fantasy—and think that it all happened only in a dream?

Daniel wondered how much of the story Gal was understanding, and he wished Matt was there to appreciate and deplore with him the way things hadn't changed in this latest version of Jewish nationhood, where disproportionate revenge remained such a central tactic. The scotch was beginning to warm him and soften the edges of his vigilant consciousness, and for a minute or two he allowed himself to miss Matt, to feel how much he picked up the slack, both parentally and emotionally. Who else would understand by a mere glance how Daniel felt reading the book of Esther? Without Matt to carry the indignation over the Occupation for the two of them, he now had to carry it himself. Along with ironic, queeny commentary about all aesthetic affronts. It was exhausting. Sure, Matt might snort a little too vociferously, jump to judgment a little too quickly and without sufficient nuance, but if he was being fair about it, shouldn't Daniel acknowledge that you really couldn't ask anybody always to have the most exact and perfect moral touch?

That thought came and then receded, too complex to hold on to in the vague glow of his buzz, but it left him feeling lonely. His eyes skirted the kitchen where he sat, the essential foods—coffee, crackers, cereal, two cans of cracked Syrian olives, two ripening avocados, the crunchy oily treat called "eastern cookies" that Gal loved, a few bars of Elite chocolate—that he'd lined neatly on the counter instead of actually putting into a cabinet, and the apartment's cold provisional half-emptiness made him feel provisional and half-empty, too. He thought he might write Derrick an email, and got up to pour himself another scotch beforehand. He sat and logged on, and found emails from work, from the producer of Joel's old show asking when the memorial would be and inviting him to the studio to look at the new editing room they'd dedicated to Joel's memory, and from an old friend of Daniel's from Oberlin who had married an Israeli man and moved to Jerusalem.

Debra Frankel had been a smart, spiky presence around the edges of his social circle at college, and he had seen her at his ten-year reunion, where they'd ended up in line together at a sandwich shop, joking about her impression of him back then as an aloof aesthete and his impression of her as someone who might eat him alive. It turned out that since the Peace Train bombing she'd been keeping track of him, which kind of touched him but also made him think, *You couldn't send a card?* He wrote to Joel's producer to set up a time, and left Debra's email for another day when he was less tired and vulnerable, more sober.

He heard the moan of the elevator door and a bustle and a knock. When he opened the door Gal burst in, excitedly spinning her noisemaker, which made a hideous noise indeed. "I saw a person throwing up on the sidewalk, and Savta said he was drunk!" she said. "And every time they said the word *Haman*, everybody made all this noise!"

"Awesome," Daniel said mildly, smiling at Malka, who'd come in with her as Yaakov wrestled the stroller, with a sleeping Noam, out of the elevator.

Gal pirouetted on the point of her sneaker, and Malka shushed her as Daniel stooped to unbuckle Noam's straps, picked him up and put him on his shoulder, and took him to his crib, where he dumped him as gracefully as he could, then leaned over to take off his shoes with stealthy fingers. Malka came in and looked over his shoulder. "Did you change him?" Daniel whispered.

"Yes, right before we put him in the car." She kissed her fingers and touched them softly to the baby's cheek.

They went back into the hallway, where Yaakov was standing with his hands in his pocket, watching Gal twirl. "Because that's what happens when you drink too much," she was saying. "Does beer make you throw up? Does wine make you throw up? Does . . . whiskey make you throw up?"

"Everything can make you throw up if you drink too much of it," Yaakov said.

"Even Coke?"

"No, no, just alcohol."

"Oh." She stopped moving and staggered over to her grandfather, collapsed against his legs. "Dizzy!" She laughed.

The three adults stood with indulgent smiles in the austere hallway, patches and holes here and there in the white walls where they'd taken down pictures to bring to Daniel's house or to the grandparents'. They were more relaxed on their home turf, Daniel thought, and Matt's absence probably helped as well.

Gal was still chirping when he helped her get into pajamas and brush her teeth. The women had had to sit separately from the men, she told him, but when you thought about it, on Purim, how would you even know? "Maybe a woman would dress up as a man so she could sit in the front of the *bet knesset!*" she said with a spray of toothpaste. "Maybe there was a man sitting back there with us, and we just couldn't tell! Wouldn't that be funny, Dani?"

"Funny," he said. He hadn't seen her so cheerful and relaxed in ages.

She spat into the sink and studied the string of saliva and toothpaste with interest, then swiped her mouth hard with her pajama sleeve. What a little savage, Daniel thought. He could just see her whirling that noisemaker in shul, eyes bright and teeth bared.

DURING THE DAYS WHEN the children were at their grandparents', Daniel spent the mornings working from home, corresponding with his staff via email. In the afternoons he took long walks, out from their neighborhood, past the playgrounds and the newer, smoother-hewn buildings of Yefe Nof. The almond trees were just starting to blossom, and from hillside lots he caught the scents of sage and rosemary just as they vanished. Above him, from apartment balconies, came the sounds of swishing mops and the thuds of women beating carpets. In the Jerusalem Forest, the paths were knobby and spongy from pine needles, and the treetops shifted against the swift-moving clouds.

He took Gal and Noam to dinner at Gabrielle and Moti's house,

staying past the kids' bedtimes as they played Hearts, the adults sipping a sweet aperitif, Leora and Gal solemn with importance to be playing with the grown-ups, growling and slapping Moti away as he tried
to coach them. He went to the *Israel Today* studio, where editors and
soundpeople racing from one room to another with headphones on
and clipboards in their hands lurched to a stop, clutched their hearts,
and grasped his hand, asked him about the children before looking at
their watches with alarm and rushing off. Rotem, Joel's old producer, ushered him into the new editing room with its state-of-the-art console, its
plush, ergonomic chairs, and a small gleaming plaque on the door,
dedicating it to Joel's memory. He was introduced to Joel's replacement,
Mark Weitzman, a broad-faced, telegenic fellow who'd been a reporter
for the *Hartford Courant* before making *aliyah*, who gripped Daniel's
shoulder and said rather theatrically that he could only hope to live up
to Joel's example as a journalist and as a human being.

He contacted Debra Frankel and she invited him over to her Gilo
apartment for coffee. Her study was lined with titles in English, Hebrew,
and Arabic; policy papers were heaped and scattered chaotically across
her desk. She gave him thick Turkish coffee with cardamom whose
grounds he tongued off his palate, and they were interrupted several
times by excitable, brown-skinned sons wearing soccer clothes. Debra
worked for a nonprofit that worked on fair labor rights for the large
migrant population that had come to Israel in recent years. When Daniel told her he worked as the editor of a college alumni magazine, she
said, "Huh!" And then: "You know, I always imagined you'd do something bigger than that. You were such a good writer. Remember *Rags
and Bones*?" That had been the name of a campus literary magazine, not
the official one, but the more edgy one he and some of his friends had
launched. "I always went straight to your stories first. Remember the
one where the grandfather is buying a boy his first expensive violin?"
Debra was smiling and musing, coffee glass suspended in her hand.
"They're all on display in cases in this shop where you have to have an
appointment to get in, and the boy is trying them out. Your description

of the differences in tone quality was so amazing. I've never looked at violins the same way since. And I remember thinking I'd kill to be able to write like that."

"Thanks," Daniel said, remembering that story, remembering how in the fiction-writing workshop he was taking, the professor had loved that part too, but pressed him to create a stronger conflict. She'd told the class that being conflict-averse might be a workable life strategy for some of them, but that it would not help them in fiction; and he'd sat there for the rest of the class wondering if he was conflict-averse. He was shocked and flattered that Debra remembered the story all these years later. And at the same time, a little irritated: Who was she to comment on his life?

As he was leaving, Debra said, "If you wanted to come work for us, I could probably make that happen." The editor of their newsletter and promotional materials had just left for another job. He thought about that on the bus ride home as he wedged past women with babushkas and men with briefcases and soldiers with traces of acne, whose weapons were propped against their thighs, and dropped hard into a seat in the back. When a pregnant woman approached, the handles of her straining shopping bag digging into white, puffy fingers, he stood to offer her his seat and leaned against a pole. He didn't know whether the job offer was serious, or just impulsive: he thought their Oberlin connection might have made Debra assume she knew more about him than she really did, and want to help him more than she was actually able. Surely there were people who worked in the nonprofit world who were more qualified than he was.

One chilly afternoon, when the sun started to glint through after a rainy morning, he walked into town to see the Peace Train Café. He'd been putting it off for days, but had decided by this point that he'd regret not going more than he dreaded going. It was rebuilt now, a slender Ethiopian guard with a rifle and a yellow vest at the door, the memorial plaque screwed into the stone facing. He stepped around a man in a white oxford, *tzitziot* dangling from his pants and a cell phone plastered to his ear, and suddenly remembered a moment with Joel from his last visit before Joel died: They'd gone to the hospital to visit a friend of Joel's who'd just had a baby, and because it was after hours—Joel had had to work late—they exited through the emergency room. There they saw a man, bloodied, clothes shredded, being rushed into the ER on a stretcher by the EMTs, one trotting alongside him holding his wrapped arm and an IV bag, another leaning over him pumping his chest, the doors sliding open with pneumatic alacrity, the ambulance light whirling in the dark. And the patient was talking on his cell phone. They'd marched out into the parking lot, turned toward each other, and died laughing.

He approached the plaque, found Joel's and Ilana's names on the white, dappled marble, ran his fingers over the elegant etched Hebrew letters. He didn't go inside; he didn't want to see the reconstructed, bustling space, the shiny state-of-the-art espresso machines. Instead he walked over to the café he'd gone to with Matt the time they visited the bombed-out site a year ago. He ordered a cappuccino and took it outside onto the flagstone terrace, wiped the wetness off an iron chair with a fistful of napkins, and sat in that viny, cultivated space, chilly and a little weepy and thinking the whole time that he ought to go sit inside. The coffee's warm foam brushed his lips, and he thought about how they'd sat at that table over there, Matt gazing moistly into his face. He remembered the clench in his stomach and shoulders, the cramp in his very soul. For some reason, it was so much easier to *feel* now. This whole crappy, horrific year, his insides had felt like a carnival, all garish lights and noise, whirling, grotesquery, nausea. Now the carnival had left town, the sawdust had been wetted and raked, and the wind blew clean and sharp through the abandoned stables and arenas.

It made him wonder whether he should just take the kids and move to Israel. He was surprised at how much he felt okay about being here, around Joel's friends and even Ilana's parents. The sheer beauty of the city was a source of constant pleasure. Matt had been the major impediment before now. A flood of memory came rushing at him—the two of them sitting on the floor, Matt convincing him to go back to the States to honor Ilana's wishes. The rawness of his eyes and nostrils from crying, the chasm that had broken open in him at the prospect of leaving Joel behind, Matt's panicky face and his fingers brushing Daniel's cheek, their hands clutching. It had seemed at that moment that he was being forced to choose between Joel and Matt.

He noticed that the sweat had dried on his back, and that he was shivering. He drained his coffee and brought the cup inside, and when he went back onto the street, he felt too tired to walk home and hailed a cab instead.

That night, the kids sleeping and the house quiet, he lay in bed, warm under the covers, his nose cold from the night air coming through the cracked-open window. He heard a car door shut and an engine sputter to life. The idea of moving the kids back to Israel was taking root in him. He thought of Noam, drowsy on Gabrielle's shoulder as she absently brushed her cheek against his hair. He was picking up some Hebrew—*sheli*, mine; *od pa'am*, again. Was it Daniel's imagination that he was learning it more quickly than English? And he thought about Gal hopping up and down with plans and ideas like a regular kid. Why couldn't he just stay here, where they clearly thrived, and where he could magically make an elderly couple happy? If four people—four devastated people—could be made happier by his moving to Israel, wasn't it his obligation to do so?

He wasn't forgetting Ilana's wish that they be taken away from Israel. But maybe, he thought, his thoughts moving gently and clearly, Ilana hadn't made the best decision; maybe her background had made her more punitive toward her parents than wise about her kids' futures. And he didn't have control over the whole geopolitical nightmare here. He didn't. What he had control over was one small piece of the world, four people, and he could make their lives better. That seemed incontrovertible.

He should stay: the thought jolted him awake, and he remained awake for much of the night, thinking. They would return to the U.S. so he could quit his job and discharge his obligations there, and put his house on the market. His mind spun around a thousand details: the furniture, much of which was Matt's, what his boss and colleagues would say, Gal's school. His parents: he was scared to tell them. He wished he had someone besides Debra to talk to about it all. He didn't want to raise hopes when the prospect of moving was so daunting, or to be persuaded out of it, which he thought he might be if he talked to Derrick. He would miss Derrick! The thought came with a stab.

He rose the next morning exhausted, and over the next few days he went about his business imagining that he lived in this city, in this apartment. He went to the offices of Debra Frankel's nonprofit and applied for a job, and over coffee they talked about the politics of migrant labor in a country with many thousands of unemployed and immobilized Palestinians. He asked her if she didn't think the migrants were like scab labor. Her position was: perhaps, but they're here, and if they're here, I can help protect their basic rights. And that felt right to him, or right enough.

THE AIR COOLED GAL'S clammy hand as Daniel released it to open his backpack for the soldier at the entrance to the Machane Yehuda market. It was an early Friday afternoon, three hours or so before the start of Shabbat, and a fog of bad mood, of sadness churning into anger, hung over her. Daniel had just picked her up at Leora's house. The soldier returned Daniel's backpack and Daniel zipped it up and slung it over his shoulder.

As they stepped into the market, the sun was abruptly cut off and they were engulfed by a wave of color and noise. She used to come there with Abba on Friday afternoons, and before coming back, she hadn't been able to remember those trips anymore. She just knew they'd taken them, because the story was told so often, and because she'd been quizzed on it. *What did he buy you there, Gal-Gal, do you remember? Half a falafel. And we'd split a can of Coke.* But now, taking in the market smell of cigarette smoke and citrus and roasted nuts and spices, she remembered again. Ahead of her, legs shuffled impatiently behind other legs and swinging plastic shopping baskets; to the sides were stalls with colorful and bountiful displays of fruits and vegetables, nuts, candy, presided over by brusque brown-skinned men who threw bags of produce onto scales and held out their fingers, cupped and upside down, waiting to drop change into customers' hands. She remembered holding her father's hand as he steered them through the crowd, as she held Daniel's now; she felt the combative jostle of shoppers and the small dirty boys on errands running against the tide; the taste of grapes came to her lips, and she remembered taking them out of the bag in Abba's shopping basket—one, two, three off the stems without him noticing—and feeling the dry, dusty unwashed outsides with her tongue and then the sweet spurt of juice. For a moment she was back in her old life, with her father. She always looked forward to going, but the feeling of being overwhelmed and a little scared when she was actually there was familiar to her, too. There were times when they didn't go to the *shuk* at all, because the Arabs put bombs there that killed people.

That wash of complicated sense memory came over her now as irritation, and she began to lag behind, causing Daniel to pull her a little harder. "Ow!" she yelled. "Stop pulling so hard!"

He stopped and turned, causing a woman wearing a head scarf to bump into him and give him an exasperated stare. "Sorry," he said. "Sorry, Gal-Gal."

Her face was so stricken and so vulnerable he asked her if she wanted him to pick her up.

"I'm not a baby," she said stoutly.

"Oh, honey, I know that," Daniel said. When he left her at Leora's, she was being yanked by Leora down the hall to her bedroom. When he returned, they were eating a snack of crackers and avocado at the kitchen table with Gabrielle. Gal was sitting barefoot and cross-legged on her chair, talking loudly with a mouthful of crumbs and green mush. Leora was trying to talk over her, one admonishing finger held aloft, and Gabrielle, her elbow on the table, her chin resting in her hand, was listening to them gabble with a lazy, amused expression on her face.

"Can't you just stay here forever?" she said teasingly to Daniel. "I'm just crazy about this little girl."

Gal looked expectantly at him, then her expression corrected itself self-consciously as she realized it was just idle love-talk on Gabrielle's part. She'd been struck hard by Gabrielle's affection, Daniel saw, and he'd stepped toward her and laid his hand gently on her hair, wanting to tell her that they *could* stay there forever, they could, but knowing it wasn't the time. She moved it away, and turned slightly to block him from her sight. He felt a surge of empathy for her.

"I'll tell you what," he'd said. "Why don't you stay here for another hour, and I'll come back and get you on my way to the *shuk*."

"Okay," she'd said blithely.

He'd found a kiosk that sold newspapers, and sat in a nearby park reading for an hour before returning to pick her up, with a promise she could come back the next day. She was shut down and unresponsive in the car. He was conscious that he'd been sensitive toward her, and that she hadn't thanked him or even acknowledged that he'd been nice. *That, my friend*, he told himself, *is parenthood*.

"C'mon," he said now. "Let's buy some vegetables for dinner and then we'll go have falafel."

She allowed herself to be led again, looking straight ahead and down at blue jeans, women's calves encased in nylons, thick ankles emerging from pumps and sneakers, sprigs of greens fanning from plastic bags, squashed fruit smears and discarded peels on the cobblestones. She thought about Leora, who was taking a martial arts course, and who had shown her some moves, inexpertly trying in slow motion to wrestle her mother to the ground as Gabrielle laughed and mock gagged and complained facetiously, and finally collapsed gently onto the floor. Gal twitched at the sound of a man speaking Arabic nearby, looked up into his face; he was intently explaining something to someone, his thumb and forefingers pinched and jabbing the air for emphasis. She tripped on something, righted herself.

They passed a candy store that was one of the prettiest sights she'd ever seen, more candy than you could even imagine in brightly colored wrappers, stacked, fanned, bunched, and binned. She stopped and gazed into the little stall, pulling her fingers out of Daniel's hand gradually, experimentally. She waited for him to grab her hand again, but when she looked for him he was at the next stall, picking out change from his palm as a man tossed a plastic bag of carrots on a scale. She took a few steps in the other direction, self-conscious under the gaze of the candy stall proprietor. Would it scare Daniel if he couldn't find her for a minute? The moment she thought that, the impulse to scare him—not entirely conscious, just fizzing at the edges of her mind—intensified.

And then, so quickly it bewildered her, she'd drawn away, and couldn't see or hear him anywhere. She thought she heard him call her name, but when she turned in that direction a different man was calling something else. She tried to retrace her steps back to the vegetable stand where she'd seen him buying carrots, but found herself at a different vegetable stand with a woman in charge. She opened her mouth to call his name, but felt too self-conscious to call attention to herself, and closed it again.

Just then she noticed a cardboard box, unattended at the side of a stall, its top flaps loosely folded in on one another. Her attention worked it over for a long minute. She was supposed to report an unattended package or bag; it had been drilled into her so often, she had to retrain herself at the Jackson Street School not to go to the teacher about every backpack she saw lying in some random place. But it occurred to her now that she didn't know who she was supposed to report it to. She looked for a soldier, but none passed by. She looked at the faces of the people around her—stern and engrossed as they examined fruit, held out money, felt fabric in their fingers—and panic seeped through her body. She turned and began to walk away, then broke into a run, her sneakers pounding the stones. It wasn't hard to dodge people; to anticipate the curbs and gaps in the sidewalk. She picked up speed, and as she ran she felt an echo, a shadow, a hot presence at her heels: her parents, running hard, being led by her to safety. She headed for brighter light, where the covered market ended and the street began, and when she reached it, she stopped, making people cry out "Little girl!" and lurch around her to avoid knocking her over. She looked behind her. She waited, panting. She went over to a wall and sat down on the ground, catching her breath, and waited some more. Her heartbeat roared in her ears.

There was no explosion. No panic, no screaming, no glass or limbs flying through the air, no spray of blood. No burning smell, no smoke, no sirens, no Ema and Abba lying dead. She cautiously let relief trickle though her, but with it barged in a loneliness so powerful she started to cry. *"Ema!"* she whimpered.

She sat there for a minute or two, exhausted, until a shadow passed over her. A big man in a dirty white apron was kneeling down in front of her. "I saw you running!" he said. "Are you lost?"

"Yes," she whispered.

"Did you lose your *ema*?"

"Yes," she said.

"Come with me," he said, holding out his hand, "and we'll find her."

She hesitated, too embarrassed to set him straight.

"Your *ema* probably told you not to go off with strangers," the man said. "But I'm no stranger. I'm Chezzi, and everybody knows me." He took her hand and walked her back into the market to a fish stall, where he gestured to a small battered chair beside the counter. "I'm just going to sit you right there," he said, "where everybody can see you."

He spoke with strong gutturals like Abba's friend Avram, the Hebrew of a Sephardic Israeli, and the words bounced in Gal's ears like a jeep on a rutted road. She saw the chair and thought it would be okay to sit in it, especially since nobody around her seemed frightened or upset. The smell of fish was overpowering. People were jostling in front of the counter, their eyes on the moist silver heaps of fish on display, shouting, "Give me a kilo of this!" and "Give me a kilo of that!" Behind her, a teenage boy wearing bunny ears and pink lipstick was hacking at a salmon on a slippery counter. Heaping a pile of fish on a scale, the fish man turned his head and yelled at him, "Stop stop stop! Smoothly! You're not cutting down a tree!" He muttered a few words to himself. "Come here and work the counter for a second. I have to take care of this little girl. C'mon, can't you see there's a line?"

The teenager tossed down the knife and moved to the counter, muttering, "Okay, okay!"

"What's your name, *motek*?" the fish man asked, taking a cell phone from his apron pocket and dialing.

"Gal."

"Gal! Isn't that a boy's name? Gal what?"

Gal shrugged anxiously. "Gal Rosen."

"What?"

"Rosen."

"I thought Gal was a boy's name," he said again, his ear pressed to the phone. *"Allo!"* he said. He talked with great volume and excitement for a minute or so, then cried, "Yes! He called! Tell him to come to Chezzi's fish counter—just ask anyone—okay. And to keep a closer eye on his niece!" He looked at Gal, nodding, still listening. "Okay. Okay."

He ended the call and said, "Your uncle is looking for you. He's terrified! He's coming to get you." He studied her, hands on his hips. "Do you want to learn how to fillet a fish?"

He put an apron loop over her head and wrapped the cloth several times around her body, tied it tight. "Come," he said, and positioned her in front of him before the counter; her nose was level with the salmon's belly, so he told her to wait a second and went to get the chair so she could stand on it. She stepped up. The fish was huge and shiny, and Gal looked down into its dead, rimmed eye.

"He's already taken out the guts and scaled it," the fish man said, and then muttered, "And that's all he'll be doing in the future." He gestured toward a pail with glop quivering in it and opened the fish at the slit with his thumbs to show clean, pink meat.

"Now, the first thing, your knife must be very sharp. Do you hear me? Very sharp. And you must wet it with water"—he shook some water over it from a liter Coke bottle with its label half peeled off—"so that it doesn't catch on the meat. You never saw at it, like that *ahabal* over there, because that rips the flesh. Look at this!" He tsked, gesturing toward a small jagged part at the beginning of the cut. "What you do is, you make a nice, long movement."

She watched him finish the cut behind the fin, down to the backbone. "See?" he said. "Now you cut along the backbone. You should be able to feel the knife sliding along it."

His knife hand slid gracefully halfway down the length of the fish's body. Gal stood between his arms, looking at the bones on the underside of the fish's head, which was now only half attached. She felt a great, debilitating wave of fatigue wash over her. "You try," the fish man said. He took her hand and closed it around the knife handle, then put his own large and damp one over hers, and together they moved the knife the rest of the way down the fish, to the tail. It made Gal queasy, the gleaming pink flesh and the white-white bones.

"Wait, you didn't tell me you've done this before!"

"I never did!"

"What! Did you hear that?" he bellowed jovially to the people in line at the counter. "This little girl is lying to my face!" He removed the fillet and turned the fish over, and just when Gal was ready for the teasing and the fish filleting to be over, she heard Daniel call her name.

His face was pale as he lifted her off the chair and held her so tightly her ribs hurt. He was saying "Thank you, thank you, thank you" in Hebrew to the fish man. He was babbling about how Gal didn't know his cell phone number, and asking her whether she knew her Jerusalem address. "I thought I'd lost you!" he was saying. "I was so scared!"

She could feel his hands clutching her, the warm dampness of his shirt, his pounding heart. A sense of cold triumph filled her. But when he finally put her down, holding her away from him by the shoulders to examine whether she was okay, it was pity she felt, and embarrassment. She suddenly wanted to drag him away, so the onlookers, who were crowding around with jovial commentary, wouldn't see his naked, haunted face.

IT TOOK DANIEL A few days to recover, for the sensation of racing through the market, hot with panic, to dissipate into ordinary memory. *I can't spare her*: that was the thought that had pounded at his mind as he called for Gal, first tentatively and then with a scream that made people's heads whip around. And then, starting to run: *Ilana's going to kill me*—which now, in retrospect, he was able to laugh about. When he finally had Gal in his grasp, it felt as though he couldn't get her close enough to him, even as he was crushing her to his chest.

In the meantime, he had to put up with Gal compulsively telling everyone she knew the story of how he'd lost her in the *shuk*, which included flourishes like "If the fish man hadn't found me, I might still be lost today, or kidnapped!" and "I was so scared I thought I was going to die!" In her telling, Chezzi was the crafty, streetwise hero and Daniel the incompetent idiot, and that irritated Daniel to no end, although he went secretly to the *shuk* a few days later to bring Chezzi an expensive bottle of wine, which the fishmonger accepted with a blush and an "It's not necessary" before setting it carefully on the ground beside his lunch bag. He also had to put up with Yaakov taking him aside and reminding him that Gal was just a little girl, and he had to be careful when he took her into crowds. Clearly he and Malka had had a talk about the best way to handle this. "Malka and I were very surprised and disappointed to hear this," Yaakov admonished, shaking his head gravely. "You of all people should know that Jerusalem can be a very dangerous place."

At bedtime, Daniel arranged Gal's blanket and stuffed monkey around her chin, the way she liked them, sat at the edge of the bed and brushed the hair off her face with his palm. "You know I would have found you no matter what," he said. "With Chezzi, without Chezzi, I would have flown like Superman throughout that *shuk* till I found you."

"You didn't look very much like Superman when you found me," she told him.

He gave her a look. What a tough little stinker she was. Being on the other end of the sharp, speculative gaze she was leveling at him was daunting, and she was only seven. On the rare occasion he'd imagined the kids he might have one day, he'd never imagined one like this. Then again, he thought, leaning down to brush her temple with his lips, was *anyone* able to imagine their kid, the one that actually came to exist in the world?

Shabbat passed and the new week began, along with the playing-hooky feeling they got when the bus stops crowded once again with people heading to work. He'd borrowed Malka and Yaakov's car, and ferried the children to their house, to Leora's, to Gal's friend Ruti's. One evening he took Gal's hand and led her into her parents' bedroom, which she'd been phobic about even looking into for the week they'd been there. "What are you afraid of?" he'd asked, and she'd said, "Everything."

"It's mostly my stuff now," he told her.

"But does it smell like them?" she asked, yanking her hand away when he reached for her.

"I don't think it does anymore," he said. "Do you want me to go in and give it one more sniff?"

"I'm gonna hold my nose," she said, and she held it the entire time they were in there—held it sitting at the edge of the bed, peeking into the bathroom, and turning the TV on and off.

"This is where you used to come late at night and early in the morning, right?" he said gently, standing at the door. He didn't want to press it, but he did want to acknowledge it. "And when you were sick or scared."

"Yeah," she said in a small, nasal voice.

"Gal, you're making me laugh sitting there holding your nose."

"Don't!" she said reproachfully.

MALKA HAD TOLD HIM that she wanted to take him somewhere; she wouldn't say where, but they'd arranged to go on Tuesday morning. It was all very hush-hush; when they left, leaving the kids with Yaakov, she didn't even tell Yaakov where they were going. Daniel drove her car on the honking, bleating, chaotic Jerusalem streets, buses barreling by them in the bus lane and snorting huge blasts of exhaust, obeying her directions and stealing the occasional glance at her face. "Right here," she finally said.

"Har Herzl?" He slowed the car, looked at the gate, and pulled into visitor parking. They got out into the cool dry air and slammed the car doors shut.

"Come," she said.

She led him out of the parking lot and into the cool, spacious rock tunnel that served as the entrance to the national military cemetery, and he felt the chill of flagstones untouched by sun. He remembered visiting this place during his junior year abroad, when the Jerusalem memorial sites had affected him deeply, conjuring images of young Jewish warriors, men like himself, only called by history to be more selfless and valiant, and forming, astonishingly, the best army in the world. He'd wonder how he would have fared as a soldier during the early days of the state, and feel privileged and soft, and decide that he really couldn't know, because as an Israeli soldier he just wouldn't have been the same person he was back then. Then he'd wonder if that was just the easy way out.

He didn't feel that way anymore. Now the old romance seemed just that, romance. For one, he'd been a gay man for years now, and he understood how that vague shame over being soft came uncomfortably close to shame about being gay. For another, well, there'd been a lot of water under the bridge in his relationship to the State of Israel, and its idealized self-image. He prepared himself for some kind of lesson from Malka in national sacrifice, or national pride. It was a nice day, and he didn't have anywhere else to be; he could indulge her, he thought, especially since she'd been easy and kind since they'd arrived.

They emerged into a large sunny plaza and stepped up to the cemetery map. The areas were coded by number, and by places or wars in which the soldiers were killed: "Road to Jerusalem," "Yom Kippur," "Mount Castel." Then Malka led him into the cemetery. They walked among beautifully tended stone graves that resembled coffin-shaped raised gardens, with plaques on the headstones and small rocks placed by mourners here and there on the headstones or the edges of the grave. It was quiet here; through breaks in the pines along the edges of the hill, Jerusalem glinted, bright and dusty. Malka pointed toward a crane in the distance of the cemetery. "I wanted to show you this," she said.

Daniel followed her, his gaze lingering on the details of this grave and that, skipping over the Hebrew dates to find the dates he could recognize, reading the names of men who were born in South Africa, Poland, Germany, and died in battles he'd never heard of. Walking quietly with Malka, who wore slacks and a sweater and sneakers he'd brought her from the U.S., and large sunglasses that gave her the look of an aging incognito movie star, he felt more comfortable with her than he ever had before. After a few minutes he heard the ping of chisel on stone, multiple pings, then hollow hammering, and soon they came to a large space surrounded by a crane, a flatbed truck, several vans, and men at work. On a white stone wall was written, in iron Hebrew letters, *Monument to the Memory of the Victims of Terrorism*. There was a large rectangular stone sculpture standing on its end, with a hole with wavy sides carved into it; a flight of stairs led down to a plaza surrounded by stone walls on which bronze plaques with engraved names had begun to be mounted.

"Wow," he said. He studied the rectangle, and said, "So that's supposed to be a wall with a hole blown into it?"

"Ah," she said. "I hadn't thought of that."

"You know, stylized."

"Maybe."

"Do you think we can go down inside?"

Malka looked around at the workers. "I don't think so," she said. "It's not supposed to open for a few weeks, on Memorial Day."

He was quiet, then it occurred to him to ask, "Are Joel's and Ilana's names on one of those plaques?"

She nodded, and told him that she'd gone onto a website through which the National Insurance Institute was tracking names, and corroborated their information.

Men were calling out to one another, and two of them were consulting a map laid out on the bed of a truck. Daniel went up to a few of the plaques that were already hung and peered at them, but they were all dated much earlier. He looked around for a place to sit, and finally just stepped up alongside Malka and put his arm gently around her shoulders. They stood there for a few moments, and then she stepped out of his arm and gave his hand a squeeze before letting it go. "There's been a lot of controversy about this memorial," she said.

"Really?" Daniel said. "Why?"

"This is a military cemetery," she said. "The victims of terrorist attacks are civilians, not heroes. So the families of young men killed in war believe that it's unfair. The victims of terror are also going to be honored on Memorial Day from now on, and they don't like that either."

Daniel thought about that. "I guess I can see that," he said. "Their sons and brothers died fighting, while ours were—"

"Sitting in cafeterias and coffee shops," Malka said.

They turned to walk back. "How do *you* feel about it?" Daniel asked.

She shrugged. "I'm used to it. It reminds me of survivors of the Holocaust."

He tried to make the link in his mind.

"We are everything they don't want to be," she said, her face weary and bitter. "Victims. Weaklings. Everything this country does is supposed to be in our name, but really, they despise us."

He'd always wondered about that, but he was shocked that Malka thought it. "Do you think they despise victims of terrorism?" he asked.

She was quiet, then she gestured toward the military graves they were passing. "The message of this cemetery is: This is what we did to protect you. The message of the new memorial is: We can't protect you. How is anybody supposed to tolerate that?"

Whoa, he thought.

She sighed. *"Ain ma la'asot,"* she said, "there's nothing to do about it."

He glanced at her. Her mouth had tightened; she'd reverted back into banality, drawn back that tantalizingly sharp and trenchant part of herself. They turned back to the parking lot; she was no longer looking at him, and he thrust his hands in his pockets. He wondered if he'd ever see that part of her again.

JOEL'S PRODUCER, ROTEM, HAD wanted to have lunch with him, but her schedule didn't open up till the day before the memorial. She was a middle-aged woman with fancy glasses and sleek black hair that fell to her shoulders; she came from a famous military family, and projected an aura of cool authority. Joel—who called her *ha-mefakedet,* Commander—had told Daniel more than once that he would have looked like a total clown on camera without her supervision. Now, at a small, crowded café nestled among boutiques in a square near the TV station, Daniel watched her drench her salad with the dressing she'd asked for on the side, and this little war between discipline and appetite made him remember her husband, whom he'd met once at a dinner party at Joel's. What was his name again? He remembered that he was voluble and balding with ginger tufts of hair that sprang out from above his ears, and had a ready laugh that gobbled into a snort.

When Rotem had put down the small dressing cup, she leaned on her elbows and looked warmly into his face. "So," she said.

"So," he smiled, looking her over, assessing her as a possible friend.

"I was wondering if you'd like to be on our show."

He'd been about to take a bite out of a fancy little sandwich with prosciutto and goat cheese and esoteric greens, but now he lowered it to his plate. "For the year anniversary," Rotem explained. "We're planning a short retrospective, showing clips from some of the more famous shows Joel did. And we thought it might be interesting, and touching, to follow that up with an interview with you in the studio."

Daniel rubbed his chin with his hand. "I don't think so, Rotem," he said. "I just—I honestly don't know how I'd talk about my life." His relation to the terrorist attack, he said, was clearly unbelievable or repugnant to most people. And after some hesitation, knowing that Joel had probably already told her, he told her that he was gay, with that old familiar feeling of making a big deal out of nothing.

Rotem looked at him shrewdly, the journalist in her sizing him up. "So you think nobody's ever reacted to the death of a family member from terror the way you have? That your life is beyond the pale of what Israelis can hear, because you're gay and left-wing?"

"No," he said, feeling heat rise into his face, hearing in her questions the implication that he was emotionally fragile, self-congratulatory in his politics. Or else—the thought moved swiftly through him—she was just Israeli, and would be totally shocked to hear that her straightforward questions had given offense. "But look, I was already burned once for an interview I did in the U.S., and that was for a teeny local paper in Northampton." He told her about what he'd said in the interview, and the hate mail that ensued. "The *nicest* comment I got was that I was a self-hating Jew," he said. "But it was more like I was a faggot who wanted to be fucked by terrorists." He spat the word *faggot* in English, because Hebrew didn't have, as far as he was aware, a slur quite as juicy and potent.

"Idiots," Rotem said with a grimace. "Idiots. I'm sorry."

He sat back, mostly mollified, and picked up his sandwich, bit into the crunchy end of the baguette. He realized that with Rotem he was speaking in his straight register, his hands still, his voice compressed into a shorter range of notes; and as soon as he realized that, he realized that he'd been speaking like that since arriving in Israel, and that a strange fatigue was coming over him. Rotem was stabbing lettuce, peppers, chickpeas onto her fork with quick precision.

"Did you know," Daniel said, "that Ilana wanted the kids taken out

of the country if anything happened to her and Joel? She was a daughter
of Holocaust survivors." Rotem nodded. "She told me, if anything happens to us, get them out of here. I can't imagine an interview where I
wasn't asked why I was raising them in the U.S. How could I explain
that on Israeli TV?"

"That's a thought-provoking feature story," Rotem said.

"But I don't want to provide a thought-provoking feature story," he
said heatedly. "If I did the interview, it would be to honor them, not to
make people scrutinize their choices."

He saw that that displeased and disappointed her, and they were
quiet for a few minutes, eating. The waiter came by to ask if everything
was satisfactory. Daniel wondered how much he needed, or wanted, to
tell Rotem, whom he was experiencing as something of a shark—"a
thought-provoking feature story!"—and strangely, as something of a
confessor. She'd been close to his brother, and that meant something to
him. Finally, he ventured, "And I've broken up with my partner. So now
the kids are being raised by a single parent on top of everything else."

She looked up from her food with interest, clearly lifted out of her
brooding about the show. "So what, you're worried about looking like
a failure on Israeli TV?"

"Yes," he said. "When gay people break up, it just goes to show that
their relationships aren't lasting and legitimate."

"But marriages break up after a family member dies in a terrorist
incident all the time," she said. "It's very common."

He sat back in his chair with a rush of feeling. It made total sense,
but it stunned him, too, stunned and moved him to think that after the
attack, he and Matt had been fighting against the odds. Why, he wondered, hadn't anybody told him that before? It might have helped!

"What's his name?" she asked.

"Matt," Daniel said. "Matthew Greene. He's younger than I am.
He's handsome—I don't know why I said that, it doesn't really matter—
and funny, and he took on the kids with enthusiasm, against every
expectation I had."

"So what was the problem?"

His eyes fluttered closed and he shook his head. What *was* the problem? "He did something that broke my trust," he told Rotem, and the words sounded grandiose and unconvincing.

Rotem studied his face for a few minutes, and then wiped her mouth and set her crumpled napkin on top of the salad remnants on her plate. "Well, tell me you'll at least think about doing the show," she said. "Mark is a wonderful interviewer. And it would mean a lot to people to see Joel's face again."

A laugh sprung out of him. "You do realize that I'm not Joel, right?" he said drolly.

"I do," she said.

He'd hurt her feelings, he saw. He felt bad about that, although there was the slightest flicker of satisfaction that he had that power.

An awkward silence followed, then they both spoke at once. "Which shows were the famous ones?" Daniel asked, just as Rotem was bursting out with "It's just so amazing, how much you look, and sound, alike!"

"Oh, quite a few," she said, sitting back. "The profile of Amos Oz, where Joel got him to sing with him. The one about the security barrier. He interviewed the construction workers who were building it. There are parodies of it all over the place all the time." She laughed. "A columnist in *Ha'aretz* compared it to the gravedigger scene in *Hamlet*."

She put her finger up for the waiter, and when he came over she ordered an espresso, and Daniel said he'd have one, too. Another silence opened up the air. Then Daniel spoke. "You miss him," he said.

"I do," Rotem said, her eyes glistening.

"I do, too," he said, but he was thinking something else. *It would mean a lot to people to see Joel's face again.* What would Joel have said about that comment? Daniel imagined viewers from all over the country seeing him on their televisions, gasping, recovering, gabbling to their spouses about how fooled they'd been. Twinsism, of course, that's what Joel would have called it. Because how was it different from one of them sitting in on the other's exam? And then a thought followed that sank and spread into his chest. He was staying in Israel, sleeping in his brother's bed, raising his children in his house, taking on Joel's friends as his own. How was *that* different?

They parted outside in the windy square, Rotem's hair whipping across her face. *"Ad machar,"* they said. Until tomorrow. Daniel watched her walk back toward the station, hitching her purse higher on her shoulder. He walked to the bus stop and stood under the Plexiglas shelter with the cleaning women going home for the day. The wind battering its sides made his thoughts whirl like debris caught up in it. People stood and crowded toward the curb as the bus approached. He shouldered his way forward, snaking his arm around several bodies and clasping the cool bar to hoist himself in.

He could stay here and be Joel, fulfill the life Joel had been robbed of. But as he handed the driver his *cartisia*, saw the strong blunt fingers curled around the hole punch, he remembered that time so many years ago when he'd been staying in Joel's house, when stealing out of bed at night and hurrying out into the Jerusalem darkness to find men like himself had been his heart's desire.

THE UNVEILING HAD BEEN held at the *shloshim*, thirty days after the burial, but they'd decided to hold a service at the twelve-month anniversary as well, now that they could all come together without a custody battle to divide them. They stood on the outcropping of rock looking over the city, whose colors were muted under cloudy skies, the stone chalky and pale, the conifers dark gray-green, listening to the rabbi praying. Daniel held Noam on his hip, *kipot* on both their heads; lately, Noam had taken to putting his arm around Daniel's neck when he held him that way, which Daniel found totally heartbreaking. He counted around seventy people clustered about the headstones, which stated the dates of Joel's and Ilana's births and deaths in Hebrew and English, their love of their children, the love of their children for them. Their colleagues were there, standing with hands behind their backs and heads bowed, including the teachers and school administrators Daniel had come to know and Joel's coworkers too, Mark, Rotem and her husband, and the others.

The warm wind whipped at their hair and the women's skirts. Daniel's eye kept being drawn to movement in the distance, and he realized that part of him thought Matt might magically appear, surprise them as he had a year ago, the day before they loaded up their ark and sailed to Northampton. But when he looked up, it would just be a tree branch, or once, a solitary mourner approaching someone else's grave. Across from him, Gal stood next to Leora and Rafi, who had a *kipa* pinned to his hair and the spaced-out look he got when undirected speech was going on around him. Looking at them, Daniel saw that Gal did have friends, that among these children she didn't count as awkward or inappropriate at all, and that gladdened him. *I'm doing my best with them*, he silently told his brother and sister-in-law. *I really am*. He also vowed to do better.

Noam shifted on his hip and pointed to the headstones, let out an interested, tuneful cluck that made the people around them smile. "Ema and Abba," Daniel whispered into his ear. He'd been thinking about Rotem's assertion that it was common for couples to break up after they lost a child to a terrorist attack. Thinking that terrorism had broken him and Matt up, not a sex act at a party. Standing there half-listening to the rabbi's singsong, he thought about the blast of rage with which he'd cast Matt out, and felt shaken for a moment by the residue of that commotion. He handed Noam to Yaakov and stood for a second with his hands on his knees, like a winded runner. Who was he kidding? Matt wasn't dangerous. A fool maybe, for wantonly flirting with danger in a world that held plenty of horrors even if you just sat home in your chair all day and read a book. But he wasn't the cause of danger in the world, or at least not more than most people were. Daniel himself had almost lost Gal.

People looked at him with kind, inquiring looks that made his face grow hot. He closed his eyes and felt the pulses beating in his eyelids.

He straightened and let out a shaky sigh. The rabbi had finished praying and they recited the mourner's kaddish, Daniel and a few others reading it off a sheet of paper they'd been handed. Malka and Yaakov, he noticed without surprise, knew it by heart. He took Noam back from his grandfather and settled him into his stroller. As mourners started to wind through the rows of headstones to the cemetery exit, Daniel waited for Gal and put his hand on her head. "Come here for one second," he said in Hebrew. He steered her toward the headstones, and kneeled.

"What now?" she asked, kneeling.

He kissed his fingers and touched the cool granite of first Ilana's headstone, then Joel's. Gal solemnly kissed her own fingers, and touched each of her parents' graves.

THE RECEPTION AT THEIR apartment brought back many of the same people who'd come to the *shiva*, but to Daniel it felt sweeter and quieter, as if the explosion itself had finally stopped echoing and been folded into the air. His parents weren't there, for one; they'd intended to come but had been detained in the U.S. by the death and funeral of their old friend Lou Fried. Lydia didn't even give Daniel a hard time about it, or make him reassure her that she was making the right choice; she just said, wearily, with rare understatement, "It's been a hard year." And Matt wasn't there, of course. For a moment Daniel imagined him coming through the door, remembered how when Matt breezed into a room he seemed to change the very climate—to crisp and freshen the air there.

He let Gal take the other kids into her room, and when he looked in on them, the girls were practicing cartwheels in their jumpers and tights while Noam sat on Rafi's lap. He was slapping Rafi's *kipa* on his own head and tilting it so that it would slide off, then craning his neck to look at Rafi with an antic, expectant expression, and Rafi was saying dutifully, "That's funny." When he got back to the living room, someone was telling a long story about how Joel had gained the trust of his

Israeli crew when his predecessor, whom they'd loved, had been fired, and another did an imitation of an exasperated Ilana going off first on negligent parents and then on overinvolved ones, with a mixture of rudeness and comedy that was so spot-on, tears ran down their faces from laughter. As he wiped his eyes, Daniel felt a soft hand on his forearm; it was Malka's.

After everybody had left, stopping and turning at the door to take Daniel's hands in theirs and make him promise to keep in touch, Daniel sat with Gal and Noam in the living room, too tired to clean up all the empty glasses, the plates with blocks of half-eaten cheese surrounded by cracker crumbs, the bowls with dip crusting at the edges, the *bourekas* plate just flakes and oil. He'd turned on the TV to a cartoon. He closed his eyes and smiled again thinking of Ilana's friend's imitation of her, felt laughter pushing at his throat. His thoughts began to drift, curling pleasantly around Matt. He didn't resist them; it was as if all the Joel-love in the room had opened the spring of love in his heart, which then splashed noisily, refreshingly, over Matt as well.

"Noam!" Gal said in a high, bright voice.

Daniel looked over and caught his breath: Noam was on his feet, walking shakily over to him with a look Daniel could only describe as merry. He stumbled and fell against Daniel's legs, and Daniel picked him up and kissed him noisily on his plump, flushed cheek, saying, "Good job, buddy!" He looked at Gal and held up his hand for a high five; she gave it a resounding smack.

He shook out his stinging hand, smiling. "When we get back," he said, "I think we should see Matt."

She looked quickly at him, her face wavering with incredulity.

"Okay?" he asked.

She broke into a faint smile. "Okay," she said.

ON A WARM evening in early April, Matt hauled out the gas grill his landlords kept in their tiny shed and opened the lid to see what kind of shape it was in, nodded approvingly when he saw that they'd cleaned it before storing it. He didn't know how much gas was left in the tank, but hoped there was enough to cook a piece of fish, which was marinating in the kitchen. He lit the grill and stepped through the screen door from the patio into the kitchen, just in time to hear the doorbell ring. He went to answer the door, prepared to be irritated at anyone standing there with a clipboard in his hands.

It was Daniel, standing there alone with his hands in his pockets and his shoulders hunched. He was wearing a jacket and tie, evidently on his way home late from work; Matt wondered who was home with the kids. He had a grave expression that softened when he greeted Matt. "Hi," he said.

"Hi." Matt stood in front of the door, regarding him coolly as his heart buzzed. He wondered whether he should turn off the grill.

"Can I come in?"

Matt stood aside so he could enter.

Daniel came into the living room and looked around approvingly at the simple couches, the prints, the muted grays, beiges, and blacks of the room. "This is nice," he said.

Matt took this in with an acerbic little cocktail of feelings. Wasn't this ironic—Daniel's praise of the house he'd had to rent because he'd been kicked out of his own?

"Can I sit down?" Daniel asked, gesturing toward the couch. Matt nodded but remained standing himself. He worried that he was looking like a prick. He didn't mean to be one. It was just that he was pretty sure Daniel had come over to invite him to see the kids, but still, he felt he needed to guard against surprises. His whole perception of Daniel felt different; to his eyes, Daniel's seriousness now had a ruthless tinge to it, and his gentle kindness seemed like an attempt to mask that.

Daniel sat, leaning forward with his elbows on his knees, looking earnestly at him. "Matt," he said. It took some time, as he stammered out an apology and told him he loved him, for it to register to Matt that he wanted him back. It felt so unreal hearing the words he'd despaired of ever hearing, that Matt couldn't even revel in his own vindication. He sank into a chair, shocked, as Daniel talked.

He'd done a lot of thinking, Daniel said, about how badly he'd treated him. "I just didn't let you in at all," Daniel said. "I was grieving, Matt, and I didn't know how to let you help me."

Never had Matt wished more to be the kind of cool customer that could wait him out and make him squirm than when he began blurting, "I wanted to be part of it! I wanted to share responsibility. I wanted some freaking *credit* for being a partner in parenting. It was like you refused to let us go through it together! Was that the kind of love you wanted?"

"No, I didn't want *any* love!" Daniel said.

"Why not?"

"I . . ." Daniel paused, and put his hand to his forehead as if checking for a fever. "I just felt unworthy of it, and it felt like a huge pressure."

Matt sat, stumped. "That's just so . . . wrong," he said.

Daniel laughed, a sight so unexpectedly ravishing that Matt had to look away. "But I'm trying to say that now, I—I recognize you. Recognize what you were going through during this whole year."

"And what was I going through?"

Daniel paused, thinking. "You were someone thrust into this impossible situation, surrounded by grieving people, trying to help us," he said. "You threw out there all your generosity and intelligence and love and ingenuity, and you kept doing it even though we often threw it all back in your face."

Matt felt his face twitch, once, twice, and then tears stung his eyes.

"If we can manage to find our way back to each other," Daniel said, "I promise I'll try to make things different. Better."

That was all Matt could handle for a first conversation. "I just need some time alone," he said. He stood stiffly in Daniel's good-bye hug, like a straight man worried that the gay man hugging him might get the wrong idea. He closed the door behind him and watched from the window as Daniel, whistling, got into his car. *Wasn't he a merry fellow,* he thought. He went back into the kitchen, remembered that the grill was still on, went and turned it off. Then he called Brent and announced, "He wants me back."

"Shut up!" Brent shouted.

At his urging, Matt went over to brood. Daniel had said the exact words he'd always wanted him to say, he told Brent, who sat there with such a pink and rosy expression Matt expected him at any moment to break into song. But it wasn't that easy! It was one thing to be apologized to and acknowledged, and another to get back those feelings.

"You don't feel it anymore?" Brent asked, crestfallen. "If you don't feel it—"

"And now, if I don't go back, it's going to be *my* fault that the kids have to shuttle back and forth between us," Matt fumed.

Brent laughed before realizing he was serious. They were standing in the kitchen, leaning on the small island, Matt popping pretzels into his mouth and chewing furiously. On cutting boards arrayed around him were neatly chopped vegetables ready to be cooked. He looked at his watch. "Am I keeping you from dinner? Do you have a beer?"

"Nah, Derrick called and said he's going to be late." Brent went to the refrigerator to get him a beer. Matt opened it and took a long swig, set it down on the counter. "What should I do?" he asked. "I don't want to go back to him just because I'd feel guilty *not* going back."

"No," Brent agreed. "That can't be the only reason. Do you love him?"

Matt was quiet for a few minutes. "I've just spent the past two and a half months learning how to *stop* loving him."

"I have an idea," Brent said. "Let's make a list of things you love about him, and things you don't love about him."

They pulled up the bar stools and sat down with a pad of paper, and spent the next half hour drinking and brainstorming. Brent told him that when he and Derrick had hit ten years together, they'd stopped playing the Three Things I Love About You game, and started playing Three Things I Hate About You instead, which caused a small explosion of beer from Matt's mouth. When Matt was done with his list, he pushed the paper so it was between him and Brent and placed his palms on the table. "Okay," he said, "that should cover it."

LOVE ABOUT DANIEL:

Yummy Jewish looks
Smells delicious at almost every time of day
Can be sweet sweet sweet
Beautiful singing voice, can imitate k.d. lang imitating Elvis
Has been through hell ("That's not technically a thing you love
    about him," Brent pointed out.)
Thinks I'm hilarious
A good kind of quietness, until recent events
Smart enough for me
Conscientious about his kids
Good politics

DON'T LOVE ABOUT DANIEL:

Treated me like shit
Threw me out like trash
Judgmental, condescending prick
Craves the approval of straight people
Stiff and humorless at times
His parents!

They sat quietly and read, till Brent sat back and crossed his ankle over his knee. One of the cats had jumped onto the counter and was rubbing against Matt's pencil. "Dude," Brent said, "you should totally get back together."

"Really?" Matt said, looking at his lists again. "Where do you get that? 'Threw me out like trash' didn't impress you?"

"It did," Brent said, "but 'smells delicious'—you can't buy that kind of pheromonal compatibility, especially after so many years."

"Hmph," Matt said.

"You know, you don't have to decide right now. You could just go on a date with him."

"I don't know," Matt said. Something else was pushing at him, making him uneasy, and he cautiously let it enter his conscious mind. The thought of being back in that house with the kids full-time: it was daunting. In the months that had passed, his memory of the house, and everything that had happened in it, had gradually darkened, till it seemed like a dream that has the power to frighten even when its details have been forgotten. He was glad he would see Gal and Noam again—he missed them—but there lingered in him a strange hesitancy, even reluctance.

"Honestly, I don't know if I want kids," he told Brent with a challenging, defensive look. "Do you think I'm a terrible person?"

Irony and impatience flickered over Brent's face; Matt saw it and realized, his face growing hot, that whenever he asked that, he was being a needy pain in the ass. He made a silent vow never to ask it again.

Brent was sliding the salt and pepper shakers back and forth along the counter. Something dawned on him, and his hands stilled. "You know what I think?" he said. "I think that when they first came to live with you, it happened so fast and was such a crisis that you just took them in and didn't question it. Because let's face it, you really didn't have a choice. But now you do have a choice. Now it's not the heat of the moment anymore. And maybe you're absorbing only now the kinds of losses that come with kids. Honestly, I was surprised you didn't complain more at the time. You just—presto!—became Mr. Dad."

Matt listened, registering his own hunger to be praised, his relief to be back in Brent's good graces.

"Frankly, it creeped me out a little," Brent said.

"Shut up."

Brent laughed. "No, it was beautiful. Don't roll your eyes, I'm serious." He stood and rubbed his hands together. "Look," he said. "It's just one date." For him, it was settled.

"When's Derrick getting home?" Matt asked.

"Why? So you can deliberate all over again, and hope he'll guide you to a different conclusion? You know he won't."

Matt closed his eyes and groaned.

THEY MET AT THE bar at Spoleto. Daniel's parents were visiting, so a babysitter was not a problem. Daniel had dressed up a little, Matt noticed, which was sweet; and he was wearing a leather and silver bracelet Matt had bought him as a birthday present some years ago. His voice, which had become unpleasantly flat since Joel died, had regained—what was it?—musicality; something Matt had perceived without it quite reaching his conscious mind when Daniel had come over a few days ago. And his gaze had recovered some of its old searching, teasing quality. Warmth. *I remember this man*, Matt mused. He ordered a vodka tonic and Daniel ordered a glass of wine.

"You seem better," Matt said.

"Do I?" Daniel asked eagerly. "I feel better. I feel like I'm finally . . ." He paused as his voice broke. "Mourning." He laughed self-consciously as he coughed back the tears. "See? Better," he joked. "But seriously, it's so much better than that horror show I went through all year. Now I just miss my brother and Ilana, and I feel that, and cry for them, and feel my heart breaking."

Matt looked at him, thinking: Upside: more alive, and therefore handsomer; downside: still crying all the time. He wondered if he could just sit still and listen, or whether his mind would rush to assess everything Daniel said in pros and cons.

"It's a little disconcerting for Gal and Noam," Daniel said, "but I think it's better than an atmosphere of dread and guilt. Oh—I don't think I told you: I've enrolled Gal in karate. She starts next week. She's just— I think she's trying to figure out how much power she does and doesn't have in the world. Horseback riding has been great, but I thought that an activity that had controlled violence in it might help her."

"I don't know why we didn't think of that earlier," Matt said.

"I know."

They were quiet for a few minutes, sipping their drinks and looking down at the bar, Matt swirling his forefinger on the ring his drink had formed on a cocktail napkin. "Your parents must be thrilled I'm not there," he said.

Daniel hesitated. "I'm not gonna lie," he said, and they laughed. "I know we promised not to, but I had to tell them we'd broken up, because I really needed some help."

"What did your mom say?" Matt asked.

"I told her I didn't want her to comment, ever," Daniel said, and his eyes glinted in a way that told Matt she had commented anyway. "She said she was sorry I had to go through this alone."

Matt narrowed his eyes. "What did you tell her about why we broke up?" he asked.

Daniel took a sip of wine, and set his glass down carefully.

"I might get sick, you know," Matt blurted. And then, challenging him: "I might get sick. We don't know—it's still three months before a test result will be at all reliable."

"Don't you think I've been doing the math?" Daniel asked.

"And have you thought about what your response will be if I end up positive?"

"I've tried," Daniel said, his face coloring. "But I can't be sure."

"So there's a possibility you'll think it's my own damn fault, and with all you've gone through, you can't take on one more hard thing," Matt said, surprised at his own hard tone. "Or that you can't put the kids through another possible loss, and if it's between me and them . . ."

"Please don't set this up as a you versus them thing, Matt. That's really unfair, and really . . . unhelpful."

They were quiet, stunned that things had blown up so quickly, regretting being in such a public space, where people brushed against the backs of their chairs on the way to their tables and murmured, "Hey, how's it going." Matt didn't even know what he wanted Daniel to say; he'd just hurtled forward, needing to slam against this wall to see if it would hold. Finally, Daniel leaned forward and burst out quietly, "What do you want me to say? That I'll never think that we could have avoided this? Not even let it broach my thoughts for one millisecond? That I'll feel fine about having to put safety precautions into place, and about the prospect of you slowly dying in our house?"

"No!" Matt lied. "How about that you'll be really sad—and take care of me!"

Daniel sat back with an irritated sigh. "For Christ's sake, doesn't that go without saying?"

"No! It could use a little saying," Matt said. "I'm the guy who got kicked out."

Daniel shook his head wearily. He was willing to take his licks, he was; but Matt's need for him to say it aloud was insulting. As if he was such a monster he'd let him die alone! He took his wallet out of his pocket, consulted the check, and tossed his credit card on the table.

How had it happened that Daniel was dismissing *him*? Matt reached into his pocket and withdrew a crumpled ten, which he lay on the bar and smoothed out with his hands.

"You don't have to," Daniel said.

Matt shrugged, sardonic.

They walked silently through the downtown, hands in their jacket pockets, past a lot of couples out on a warm night and a line at the movie theater. They passed a few places where each of them could have turned off to his own house, both of them wondering what would happen when they parted, and when they reached the last possible point, they stopped. *Tell him you'd take care of him and cherish him to the end,* Daniel thought, *that's what he wants to hear.* But somehow, the words stuck in his craw. Instead, he said, "What's next?"

"I don't know," Matt said.

"I love you," Daniel said. "I didn't want this to end with a fight."

"Neither did I," Matt said. He was tired, his mind gummed-up.

They said their good-byes quietly, and when Matt got home, he knew it was over. Luckily, he hadn't let his hopes get too high. He dropped down on the couch with the dog and buried his face in her neck, and she snuffled and sighed, and he fell asleep there.

The doorbell sounded first in his dreams, and when he surfaced, chilled, his eyes searching out the light of the one lit lamp, he felt a spasm of primitive fear at the unexpected late-night phone call or knock at the door. He rose and went to the door, turned on the porch light, and peered out. Daniel stood there in his leather jacket.

When he opened the door for him, Daniel grabbed him by the belt and pulled him to him, slipped his hand between his legs, and cupped him hard. Matt let himself be led up to the bedroom and pushed onto the bed, let Daniel open his belt and fly, pull down his pants, kneel over him with his knee between Matt's legs, and kiss him roughly. "Turn over," he said, reaching for his own belt, and Matt obeyed, kicking his pants off his ankles. He heard Daniel pull his own pants down, then the rip of a condom wrapper and the small snap of his putting it on.

"In the drawer," Matt said, and he heard it open and Daniel's hand scurrying inside in search of the lube.

Daniel entered him awkwardly, rested there. He was still wearing his shirt and jacket and shoes. "Is this what you wanted?" he grunted.

Matt's eyes were closed, his ass burning like hell. As Daniel fucked him, his mind groped for the oblivion he craved, but he couldn't let go of the awareness that Daniel was playing a role. After all these years, he thought, it would take a prodigious act of imagination he probably wasn't capable of to get into this rough-trade fantasy. That ship had so sailed! Where to get the pleasure from, then? From the sheer brutality of the thrust? From gratitude that Daniel was still trying? From the danger Daniel was half-facing? From the idea that Daniel was angry, and punishing him?

It felt okay, it just didn't blow his mind. It wasn't really what he wanted. He rested, his cheek pressed into the mattress, and waited for Daniel to finish. After he did, Daniel eased out of him, both of them wincing, and flopped down next to him, on his back. His face was flushed. It was a large bed on a low wood platform, with a wood headboard; its sheets, blanket, and bedspread were various lovely shades of white. They lay there breathing and sweating. "This is an awesome bed," Daniel said.

"Other people's beds are always more comfortable than your own," Matt said. "I don't know why." He lifted the covers and they got undressed and crawled under. Daniel turned away and scooted gently backward so that Matt was spooning him. They fell asleep that way, and Matt awoke a few hours later with his face mashed into Daniel's hair. The windows were open and it was chilly on his bare shoulders, and he could hear the wind rustling in the tender new leaves of the trees. The only light came in from down the hall at the top of the stairs, and the room was dusky and soft. He lay there for a few minutes, taking in the smells of Daniel's shampoo, his breath, lubricant, and semen, Daniel's sweat or maybe his own. He was thirsty. He pulled away gently and wiped the tickle from his nose. Daniel stirred, then slipped around and was in his arms so quickly it shocked him. Daniel kissed his neck and face and mouth, Matt's hair in his fists; he was moaning, making a sound so private and full of need it was almost hard to hear. Matt felt his tears on his face, heard him say his name, over and over.

"Okay, okay," he said. "Okay." Until Daniel became still in his arms. Then Matt gently pushed him onto his back and kneeled over him, licking and sucking his nipples, his ribs, his stomach, his thighs, and his balls, and he had barely taken him into his mouth when Daniel came with a cry of surprise and pleasure. Matt straightened and wiped his mouth. "It's like making love to a teenager!" he said, which made Daniel laugh—and it was, and *that* was hot, giving pleasure to someone who had forgotten that such pleasure was to be had, who came quickly and hard even when Matt tried to calm him down and draw it out.

He made love to him on and off, and they slept in between. Once, he reached for him and Daniel said, "Ow, enough. I can't anymore," but then he could and did, and they fell back on the bed, hot and sticky, and laughed.

As morning broke, Daniel dreamed about a hike he'd taken in the hills outside Jerusalem with some religious friends, one Shabbat his junior year abroad. They'd taken along the two small, indispensable books for religious hikers, an Old Testament and a botany pocket guide, picked figs from trees and wild grapes from the vine, and when they stopped to drink and rest, one of them had read verses from one of the Samuels, and showed how the events had probably happened right in that very place. A sense of peaceful joy had filled Daniel at the beauty of the rugged stony hills, the comfortable power of his body in vigorous exercise, the ease of giving himself over to his companions' knowledge of where they were going, the feeling that there was no truer Israeli experience he could possibly have. The feeling of this being so much truer and purer than his stifling upbringing.

Later that afternoon they'd entered an Arab village, and an elderly man in a *keffiye* had greeted them as they passed his house, inviting them to stop and rest. They'd sat cross-legged with him on the stone patio in front of his house as his wife brought out a tray with warm pita, tomatoes, and tiny cups of harsh coffee, and while they hadn't been able to understand each other very well, Daniel's companions vigorously affirmed what the old man said as they stood to leave, in Arabic words that were close to the Hebrew: that Isaac and Ishmael were brothers.

It had been a beautiful, beautiful day, and he hadn't thought about it for ages.

He awoke into the faint light to see Matt lying on his back, his head resting on his hands, elbows akimbo, his eyes open, thinking. "I had a dream," Daniel told him. "More a memory, I can't tell if I was awake or not."

"What about?"

Daniel told him about it, tears pressing painfully at his face but not breaking. "Why does it make me want to cry? I have no idea. When I think about it now, I have no idea where we were, on whose land, or what town we entered. It must have been right before the First Intifada. That encounter with the Arab man could never happen now."

"Was Joel there?"

"No," said Daniel, "and I was probably really happy that I was having a more authentic experience than he was right then."

Matt smiled.

"I was such a different person," Daniel said. "So naïve." He paused, blinking up at the ceiling, then turned and looked at Matt. "Do I have to be all ironic about that experience now?"

Matt gazed at him and touched his face. "I'm afraid so, honey," he said.

Daniel was quiet for a while, then asked, "Where does the beauty go?"

Matt thought for a few moments, then slid his arms around Daniel's chest. "Right here," he said, kissing his shoulder. "Right here," he said, laying his palm on Daniel's back. "Where I can feel your heart beating."

Daniel buried his head in Matt's chest, moved and shy. "And then we weren't in Israel anymore, we were in Japan," he said, his voice muffled. "And my mother was there."

Matt laughed.

DANIEL SPENT THE NEXT four nights at Matt's, taking advantage of his parents' presence. The first night, he'd just slipped out and slipped back home at five A.M., and was in the shower before anybody woke up. But after that, he thought he ought to put someone in charge.

His father was asleep, but his mother was in the living room watching TV in her pajamas. She was nodding off, but her head snapped up when he sat down beside her. "Hi, honey," she said. "I've taken a sleeping pill." She took his cold hand in her two warm ones, and chafed it between them.

He perched beside her on the arm of the couch and watched the documentary for a few minutes. They were crazy little critters, meerkats; a laugh bubbled out of him when they rose on their hind legs to do sentry duty, the camera capturing their little heads popping up from behind sand dunes, their quick and alert little faces. They were led by a fierce and ruthless alpha female.

At the commercial, he stood. "Listen, Mom, I'm going over to Matt's for the night. So if the kids wake up—tell them I'm visiting him. I guess."

"Are you sure you won't be getting their hopes up?" Lydia asked. "If you don't end up getting back together, I mean?"

"Mom," Daniel said.

"I know you think I'm saying that because I hope you don't get back together," she interrupted. "But I'm not."

"Really?" he asked, with a penetrating look.

"I'm not an idiot, Daniel," she said. "I can tell when you're happy and when you're not."

"Oh," he said. "In that case—" He gave her a smooch on the cheek. "I'll have my cell phone on me."

He straightened, and then she spoke again, quiet but steady, her head resting against the back of the sofa. "Your brother is looking down on you, Daniel. He's so proud of you, and so grateful that you're here to care for his children."

He turned to look at her, surprised tears springing into his eyes.

THE NIGHTS HAD THE otherworldly feel of first-in-love. The moment Matt let him in the door, they were kissing. They had long, leisurely sex punctuated by surprises that made them laugh; they raided the kitchen, watched TV in bed with their bare legs entwined, eating a bowl of ice cream or drinking a scotch, had sex again. The old dog lay on the rug at the foot of the bed, snorting and farting, and the night deepened until day broke in soft shades of gray.

After Daniel left in the morning, unshaven and wearing the clothes he'd come in, Matt would get coffee brewing and get in the shower. He moved through his day languidly, his body airy and sated, finding himself jerking awake at the computer screen. He had no interest in food. At odd moments he'd find something unpleasant come over him, a flicker of rancor which, the moment he recognized it, was followed by despair, and he'd wonder for a second where it came from. Then he'd remember what Daniel had done, how he'd used Matt's very queerness, and the tenuous status it gave him in the family and the house, against him. Maybe, he'd think, the Daniel who was coming nightly to his bed—open, avid, loving—was the real Daniel, and that other, closed-off, brutal one an aberration. But it was one thing to have broken up with Matt, and quite another to take advantage of his legal vulnerability as a queer partner, to be the type of person who would do that. He just didn't know how to forgive that. He didn't know whether Daniel even registered that he'd done it.

He quizzed Brent and Derrick about it, and they insisted that Daniel *did* realize what he'd done. But it wasn't until the last night of Daniel's parents' visit, the last night they could carry on their affair in this strange, inviting house, that Daniel said something. They were in the kitchen, Matt making a sandwich because he'd hardly eaten that day, Daniel poking around in the fascinating cupboards of strangers and disapproving of the fact that the kitchen hadn't been updated since the '70s. It had pale green linoleum counters and a grubby wooden spice rack above the stove, crammed with spices bought at Asian specialty stores. "It's the only part of the house that isn't lovely," he said.

"I know," Matt said.

"How do you feel about moving back in and rejoining our family?" Daniel asked.

Matt's head whipped around. "Talk about your non sequiturs!" he said.

"I couldn't figure out how to work my way toward it more gradually."

Matt put his knife down and turned toward him, studied his face. They'd been so intertwined for the past week, pulling back and looking at each other felt solemn and intimate. Daniel was tense, his blinking deliberate, his teeth gnawing at the inside of his lip.

"I—" Matt said, and cleared his throat. "The thing is, it's hard for me to let go of what you did to me. The whole thing about my having no legal rights."

Daniel nodded. "I know," he said. "I wish I hadn't done it. I could have done it so differently."

He studied Daniel, wondering if that admission was enough for him. Finally, he said, "How can I be sure you won't do it again?"

Daniel scratched his cheek in mock ponder. "If only there were an institution designed to support couples who have vowed to stay together, and to legally protect them," he said.

Matt laughed, taken aback. "Seriously?"

Daniel shrugged, his eyes growing playful and warm. "It's going to be legal in Massachusetts in"—he looked at his watch—"three weeks."

"Okay, I really don't know how to think about that," Matt said with a small laugh. He turned back around and stared at the turkey and cheese sandwich he'd made, picked it up and took an enormous bite out of it. Then he hiked himself up on the counter and chewed.

"Well, give it some thought," Daniel said. "I know we haven't been very keen on the idea of marriage, but it's a way—it's my way—of helping you feel protected."

Matt took another bite, contemplated Daniel as he chewed. "What a lame proposal," he said.

"I know," Daniel said with a laugh that was more air than noise. "But I mean it. I want you to come back, and I want you to feel safe in our family."

"Okay," Matt said.

"Is that one of those robotic, compliant Gal *okays*?"

Matt scratched his chin. "I sort of understand now what she means by it!" he said. "It's like, 'Okay, I hear you and I get what you mean, but I have to go sit in my room by myself for a while now.'"

"I want you to be happy," Daniel said, coming up to the counter and standing between Matt's knees, resting his hands on Matt's thighs. "I want you to be psyched." His face crinkled into a mischievousness so rare and enchanting, Matt almost died of love right on the spot. "When Daddy comes home, it's a happy sound," Daniel sang, his voice husky. "Daddy!"

Matt laughed and touched Daniel's cheek. "I *am* psyched," he said. "I am. Let me just think about it."

MATT SAT IN THE car outside the Jackson Street School, waiting for the kids to start coming out. In the front of the low, long brick building stood a line of idling school buses, but Gal had been told to look for his car instead. It was a mild day, and he had the driver's-side window open and his sunglasses on. The trees still sent their bare spindles into the sky, but in front and side yards the forsythia was in bloom, the bushes that only days ago had looked like messy, snarled balls of wire now bursting with yellow flowers.

It had taken a week for Matt to even take seriously the idea of marriage. It felt like such a cliché!—as though Daniel was a cheating husband who'd gone out and bought him a fur coat or a Lamborghini so he'd forgive him. He'd just never aspired to marriage; the very idea seemed like a turnoff, like joining a church or moving to the Midwest. And he'd always worried, since the push for gay marriage in Massachusetts began, that the right to marry would become the expectation to marry, which would create two classes of gay people: the good ones who were normal and committed and monogamous, and the queers and deviants.

One day, he ran into his lawyer on the street, who told him that as far as he was concerned, the best thing about gay marriage was going to be gay divorce. "Meaning?" Matt said.

"Meaning that before, gays and lesbians in Massachusetts could screw each other financially, or in terms of custody, when we broke up. And believe me, we did! But now we're going to be subject to the same divorce laws as straight people."

"Right," Matt said, and that made an impression, especially the vision of legions of Massachusetts queers being screwed just as he had been. He had no illusions that gay people were more ethical in love than straight people, but thinking of his attorney routinely going to court on behalf of stay-at-home partners bilked out of alimony, or non-bio-moms having their kids taken away, gave him a slightly different vision of queer Northampton than he'd had, and bolstered the ironic stance he took toward the married state.

"But didn't he mean it as an argument *for* getting married?" Brent asked him, as Matt enlarged upon his critique with cutting pleasure.

"Oh," Matt said with comic deflation. "Right."

The school door opened and the first kids stepped outside, then a few clusters, some lining up for the buses, some taking off and racing for their parents' cars. And there was Gal, coming out by herself. She was wearing her parka, unzipped, and it looked as if Daniel hadn't taken her for a haircut since they'd broken up. He watched as she scanned for his car and then found it; he opened his eyes and mouth wide in a happy surprised expression, and she grinned and ran over. She opened the back door and swung her backpack off her shoulders, heaving it into the seat in front of her. "Mordechai, you're back!" she said. She climbed in and threw her arms around his neck from behind. "Did Uncle Dani let you come back?"

Matt tried to retain his dignity in the midst of the choke hold and the slightly demeaning question. "Uncle Dani and I agreed that you guys should come over for a sleepover," he said. They'd planned at first to have him reunite with the kids at dinner at Daniel's, but after a few days' thought, he'd realized he just wasn't ready yet to go over there, to resume his role in the family, with all the expectations that would raise in everybody. So they'd settled on telling Gal that they were a couple again, but that Matt was staying in his own house because he'd committed to taking care of the dog.

"Phew," she said, plopping herself back onto the seat. "TGIF. So you have a dog over there, right?"

He glanced, smiling at the American slang, into the rearview mirror. "I do. I mean, I'm taking care of her for these people."

He swung by and picked up Noam at Colleen's, where he was shocked to see him just get up, thank you very much, and run over to him, a faint, rakish scar on his right cheek. He picked him up—he was heavier!—and squeezed him, said "Kiss?" and was rewarded with Noam's patented air-kiss, a flat-lipped *pop*. "Do you know you're coming over to my house?" Matt asked him.

"We've been talking about it all day," Colleen said. "Daniel said he'll come by with their stuff after work."

"What happened here?" he asked, smoothing the scar with his thumb.

"There was an incident with a toy tent pole," she said.

He brought them back to his house and let them explore as he went into the kitchen to find them a snack. Gal ran upstairs and then came back down. "Are we sleeping here?" she asked, leaning against the doorway.

"Yep," he said, handing her a granola bar. "It's a sleepover, remember? Just us." He and Daniel had realized just yesterday that he was assuming that Daniel would sleep over, and Daniel was assuming he wouldn't; it was only when Daniel said, with slow, comic, burning intensity, "It would be my first night without kids for, like, a year," that Matt had laughed and agreed to take them by himself.

"What's that?" Gal said, pointing to a Buddha on a little altar on the fireplace mantel across the living room.

"That's the Buddha. He's a religious figure. He's supposed to be very wise."

She looked doubtfully at its secret, serene expression. "I think he's weird," she said. "There's one upstairs, too."

He couldn't really settle in with them till Daniel had come and gone; for reasons he couldn't pinpoint, he'd been nervous about it all day. When the doorbell rang, something went off in his chest, like a wind burst sending dust and candy wrappers flying. Daniel was wearing work clothes, a jacket and a loosened tie, and had in his hands and at his feet what seemed like an inordinate number of suitcases and stuffed paper bags. Molly caught sight of him and barked, and hustled to the door looking very in charge to make up for not having heard him ring the bell. She sniffed him with a wheezy harrumph, her stumpy tail quivering in greeting. Gal called from the kitchen door, "Who's that? You're not supposed to be here!" Daniel took just a few steps into the house, and stayed just long enough to show Matt the dose of Noam's antibiotics for his ear infection.

Matt brought the suitcases and paper bags into the house as Daniel kissed the kids good-bye and said have fun and reminded them that he would pick them up tomorrow morning. Matt set bibs and bottles and medicine on the shelf above the kitchen sink, and hauled the Pack 'n Play up to the TV room down the hall from his bedroom. The room was furnished with a futon couch facing a small television, a woven oval rug, and bookcases with novels and biographies and rows of Lonely Planet guides. He popped up the frame's locking sides and pressed the center down, put the mattress in and pushed in the corners.

He'd planned to have Gal sleep on the futon next to her brother;
he'd found some double-bed sheets for it in the linen closet and washed
them to get out the dust smell. But she wanted to sleep in the tiny third
bedroom with the whitewashed paneled walls and the curtains with a
leaf pattern in fall colors. There was a very old bed in it, a relic, sized for
a child but so tall Gal had to run across the carpet and leap onto it. Matt
scratched his head. "If you fall out of that thing, you *know* who's going
to get in trouble."

"You!" she shouted.

"Right you are," he said.

He'd ordered pizza, and he ran downstairs when the doorbell rang,
telling Gal to keep an eye on her brother. Noam was walking, and he
wasn't a baby anymore. It was as though, Matt discovered over the
course of the evening, becoming ambulatory had released a whole new
personality; the placid chubby baby had become a worker bee, a mover
of furniture, a carrier of things back and forth. After feeding the dog,
Matt watched Noam squat, diapered butt brushing the floor, and carefully pour the remaining kibbles into a Tupperware container. "Not for
eating, Noam," Matt said, but he realized as Noam poured them carefully back into the dog bowl, that far from eating them, Noam was more
likely to perform a Montessori activity with them. He could say *my* and
mine, and had developed a very impressive screech to enforce those categories. He said *ee-eye-ee-eye-oh* and knew what a cow says and what a bird
says, and when Matt sang "The babies on the bus go—" he made obnoxious whining noises. "That's how he says *wah wah wah*," Gal explained.

After dinner, he bathed Noam in the claw-foot tub and brought him
into the bedroom, dug his fingers under the flap of the box of diapers
he'd bought, and pried it open. Then he opened the suitcase Daniel had
brought, and found it entirely filled with diapers. He diapered Noam
and set him on the floor as he looked for pajamas, finding them in a different suitcase. "Here ya go, buddy," he said. Holding the pants at the
waist, close to the floor, with his thumbs and forefingers, he waited for
Noam to step into them. From down there, a curl of pain winding along

his lower back, his view was chubby little legs scuttling back and forth. Finally, he grabbed him. He was sweating when Gal came in the room, asking, "Can we get a dog for this house?"

Matt said, "Honey, we have a dog."

"I mean a real dog," she said.

He sat on the futon couch with a child on each side, reading *Night-Night, Little Pookie*, shouting, in unison with Gal, when little Pookie is asked whether he wants to wear the pajamas with the cars or the ones with the stars: "Stars *and* cars!" Daniel had also sent over an alphabet book illustrated with animals. Noam pointed to the bird under *B* and said, "Pitty teet-teet."

Matt laughed, and looked at Gal, amazed. "What did he say? A pretty tweet-tweet?"

It took Noam a long time to fall asleep; first he sang to himself for a while—if it could be called singing, Matt thought; it was actually more of a drone—and then he cried a vexed, overstimulated cry. Matt kept the hall light on, and after racing upstairs three times, plopped himself down on the hall floor. After a few minutes, he heard the quick, quiet thumping of Gal coming up the stairs in bare feet, saw her peek around the corner at the top. She'd taken off her sweater and socks. He put a finger to his lips and motioned his head toward Noam's room.

She tiptoed up to him and sat down on the floor beside him, cross-legged, and he laid a hand on her knee. "How's it going?" he whispered.

"Good," she said.

"Hey, how was Israel?" he murmured.

"That was a long time ago," she said, twisting and untwisting the fringe of the runner that ran the length of the hall.

"Was it good to see everybody?"

She nodded, and Matt tried to think of a better question, one that would draw her out. When she started school, he'd found that asking "Did anybody cry today?" could sometimes elicit a juicy story.

"What was the best part and what was the worst part?" he asked.

There was a cry from Noam, and they were quiet, ears straining, till they heard him start sucking his passy again. Gal gazed up at the ceiling and frowned. "A real head-scratcher, huh," Matt said.

"What?"

"A head-scratcher. That's a hard question you have to think about a lot."

"The best part," she said slowly, her voice going thoughtfully high on *best*, "was definitely playing with Leora. And seeing Sabba and Savta." She added this last in a rush, nodding and gesturing as if to say that it went without saying, which is why she hadn't mentioned it first.

"And the worst thing?"

She shrugged. She didn't have words for the soreness and longing, the feeling of being home-but-not-home, the wild fear of being lost, the fleeting sense of triumph and the loneliness that had overwhelmed her when she crumpled to the sidewalk, her throat opening and closing like the gills of a salmon yanked into the air. Matt peeked down at her without moving his head, saw her hands lying limp in her lap. "Noam's asleep," he said quietly. "Should we get into pajamas and read a story?"

After he'd read to her, she lay on the high, narrow, strange bed trying to sleep. She'd asked to sleep in this room, but now she felt that had been a mistake; she felt like a dead child laid out in a coffin. And she couldn't stop casting her eyes anxiously at the shadows cast by a streetlight into the room, imagining Buddhas emerging from the window, hordes of them marching in with their secret smiles, with beards and jumpsuits; they'd become, in her hectic mind, a mash-up of Buddhas and the Keebler Elves on her cookie packages.

At around four in the morning, she awoke with a cry. Matt awoke, adrenaline coursing through him, and ran into her room, saying, "What? What? What?" He lifted her by the armpits till she was sitting.

"I want to go home," she said. "This house is weird. I don't like it."

"I thought you liked this bedroom," Matt said.

"I thought we were going to Dani's," she said, staring at him vacantly; he wondered if she was fully awake. "Dani said that you were going to bring us to our own house."

"No, he told you you were coming to *my* house," Matt said.

"No," she insisted. "He didn't."

He was totally perplexed. "So why do you think he was dropping off all that stuff?"

She shrugged with confused misery.

"Why didn't you say anything? Like when I made you dinner and unpacked your pajamas and put you to bed?"

"I don't know."

He thought, *This is a bad idea; she doesn't know if we're really together or not, and we'd better give her a clearer message soon.* They sat there looking at each other in the dim room, a cone of light cast across the floor by the hall light through the half-open door. The old Gal, he knew, would have screamed at him the moment they'd pulled up at his house, refused to get out of the car. She wasn't a little beast anymore, he realized; she was growing up, and the sharp edges were wearing down as age and grief rubbed at them with patient, chastening hands. Even her crying had a different, less outraged tenor: it seemed to express surprise that the world had even more pain in store for her, when she'd thought she couldn't be surprised anymore. It saddened him. Maybe it was just developmental, he thought, and this is how she would have turned out anyway. Maybe it was a good thing, a better way of being for the long haul. Maybe she'd turn back into a beast when she hit twelve.

He ran his hands over his arms, chilled in his undershirt and boxer shorts. "Do you think you can go back to sleep?" he asked.

"Can I sleep with you?"

He thought of the knees and elbows that would pound him as she slept her strenuous sleep. "Okay," he sighed. He helped her down and gathered her pillow and stuffed monkey, ushered her down the hall with his hand on her back. As they got into bed, Gal paused on her knees and peered at the big Japanese painting. "I wonder what that's a painting of," she said, fully awake and intrigued.

"Oh no you don't," he said sternly, switching off the bedside table lamp. "No chitchat."

They lay still for a while, till she flounced onto her side with a groan. "Sleep, Gal," Matt said.

"I can't," she said. "I'm scared."

"What could you possibly be scared of? I'm right here, next to you."

"I'm still scared," she said in Hebrew.

"What are you scared of? Should we make a list?"

There was a pause. Then she said, "That Dani will be mad at me. That I'll try to be good but be bad by accident. That robbers or bears will come into the house. That Noam's scar will never go away. How many is that?"

"Four." He understood her perfectly, but replied in English, thinking that for this conversation, they might each need their full linguistic capacity.

"That I'll never see you again," she said.

He took her arm and gave it a little shake. "I'm right here! And I'm not going anywhere."

"You know what else I'm scared of?" she asked. She didn't sound spooked anymore; she was warming to her theme, getting late-night philosophical. This could be a long night, Matt told himself. "That I'll be at a scary movie and I won't be able to run out of there before the scary parts happen, and even after I'm in the lobby, I'll still hear the sounds, and even if I go into the bathroom, I'll still hear the sounds."

"Yikes," said Matt, remembering his similar fears around the time *The Shining* came out. "What about falling off a horse?"

"*Pshh*. I'm not scared of that." He smiled in the darkness at the dismissive pride in her voice. "But I'm scared my body will get ripped up, and it will hurt so bad."

"That *is* scary."

"Don't tell Dani."

"Why not?"

"Just don't."

His mind swirled around this, fighting the fatigue that was thickening it, like cornstarch. Which part was important to keep from Daniel? He wondered whether he should ask, and then he did. "Is he mad at you a lot?"

She thought about it for a while. Actually, he wasn't anymore; he was different since Israel. He touched her sometimes—her hair, her cheek—and his face would come alive again, like something kissed in a fairy tale. "Not really," she said.

She was on her side, facing him, fists at her chin, her eyes slowly blinking. "Gal," Matt said sleepily, "you're scared that something bad will happen, but what's really scary is that something bad *already* happened."

"But bad things can still happen."

"They can," he conceded, as the thought of HIV pushed darkly into his mind. "But I'm pretty sure it'll never be as bad as that. That's like a once-in-a-lifetime bad thing."

"How do you know?"

"I just do."

"Sabba and Savta had *two* bad things happen to them."

He couldn't argue with that.

Gal said, mournfully, "I think they must be the unluckiest people in the whole world."

He was on the verge of sleep, but through the dim gleam of his consciousness he felt he couldn't let the conversation end that way. He'd be letting Ilana down if he let her daughter carry the weight of her grandparents' unfathomable suffering, or, God forbid, compare their suffering to her own, and find herself wanting. But he couldn't think of anything reassuring to say. So he turned her gently away from him and pulled her by the hips, wrapped his arms around her as she squirmed backward and settled into his chest. Thinking about his own health, trying to reassure himself with the thought that even if he got HIV, people lived for a long time with it these days, kept him awake long after Gal had fallen asleep.

IN THE END, IT was Gal who helped Matt warm to the idea of getting married. "Wow!" she said, her eyes alight, her mouth stretched into a comic rictus of glee, when he and Daniel told her. "Wow! That's all I have to say: Wow!" She told everybody she knew, "Wow! That's all I could think of when they told me!" She was so thrilled by the prospect, he decided that if he had the capacity to make her feel safe and happy, he owed it to her. And seeing a wedding through her eyes—the dignity, solemnity, and joy of it, the knitting together of their family— the tendrils of Matt's imagination began to wind around the idea. He imagined a justice of the peace or a clergyperson saying, "By the authority invested in me by the Commonwealth of Massachusetts . . ." and got a little goose-bumpy. He hadn't moved back home yet; he was sleeping at Daniel's but was still responsible for Molly for another few months, so he'd left most of his clothes and his computer at his own place, and spent the days there, the windows open to the May breeze, after the kids went to day care and school. It suited him. He knew he'd have to move all the way back soon, take up his place as a full-time partner and dad. But sometimes, sitting at a desk in the pretty book-lined study, he wished that this was how he'd gotten involved with the Rosens in the first place: enjoying outings with the kids, gaining their confidence and affection over time, urgently making out with Daniel outside the front door before they tore themselves apart and he went home to his own, quiet refuge.

THEY MET FOR LUNCH on a summery Tuesday, at a café halfway between Northampton and Amherst; they sat outside on the same side of the table, crowding into the shade of the umbrella. Daniel was trying to tell Matt about this upsetting thing he'd read in the materials he got from B'Tselem, the Israeli human rights organization, while Matt was examining the inside of his sandwich to make sure they'd put Dijon mustard on it, as he'd requested, instead of honey mustard, which he hated. "Are you listening to me?" Daniel said. He clunked his shoulder against Matt's.

"Stop, I am," Matt said.

"There's this new Israeli law," he said. "Actually, I think it might be an extension of an old law."

A shadow fell across the table, and they looked up to see Yossi, his face bright and benign, standing over them. His hair, which had grown out since Matt had last seen him, was disheveled, his T-shirt dark with sweat. He had a gym bag slung over his shoulder and a cup of coffee with a lid on it in his hand. Matt's heart popped with surprise and revived anger, the inevitable ribbon of attraction tied around the whole messy package.

"I was just getting my coffee," Yossi said. "I understand that mazal tovs are in order!"

Daniel stood and they hugged, while Matt remained seated, watching their hands clap each other's backs in the way of straight men while Yossi held out his coffee cup so it wouldn't spill. He didn't know how he was supposed to greet Yossi, who had clearly decided he wasn't worth remaining friends with after the breakup; he refused to stand and hug him. But he was conscious of sitting there, slumped and sullen, like a big baby.

"I'm very happy for you," Yossi said in Hebrew, beaming at them. "I, for one, support gay marriage a hundred percent."

"Great!" Matt said, and felt Daniel give him a sharp look. A sparrow landed a few feet away, and he broke off a tiny piece of bread and tossed it in its direction, onto the stone terrace ground, then watched as the bird bustled over, seized it in its beak, and flew off. Yossi and Daniel were making a plan for a Rafi drop-off later that afternoon after school, looking at their watches. *"Metzuyan,"* Daniel said. Excellent.

When Yossi had left, Daniel sat back down and took a bite out of his sandwich. Matt sensed his gaze on him, and turned. "What?"

Daniel raised an eyebrow.

"How about a little loyalty?" Matt asked heatedly. "You know he dumped me as a friend, right? And still, you're nice to him."

Daniel flushed and blinked as he took in Matt's anger. He swallowed his food. "I'm sorry. It's just—he's really been there for me and the kids. Coming to Israel for the memorial—"

"Well, he wasn't there for me," Matt said flatly. "Do you care at all about that?"

"I do, Matt." Daniel leaned over and slipped his arm around Matt's waist, nuzzled his cheek. "I do. But maybe you're madder at me than you are at him? Maybe *I'm* the one who wasn't there for you?"

Matt sat stiffly, accepting his embrace and kiss, half mollified. "He's always been a condescending prick with me. He's not like that with you."

"No," Daniel said.

"Like I'd lost sleep over his support of gay marriage! Give me a break."

Daniel laughed, and they ate in silence for a while, Matt fretting over the various slights he'd experienced from Yossi. They weren't exactly slights, he thought—they didn't even rise to that level; it was as if Yossi didn't take him seriously enough to slight him. As soon as he thought that, he wondered if it was true—or whether it was just his own insecurity that made him feel like a less substantial person than Yossi.

"This Israeli law I was telling you about?" Daniel was saying. "Get this: The law states that if a Palestinian living in Jerusalem marries someone from the West Bank, they can't live legally together in either place. In either place! Can you believe it?" He was looking at Matt, waiting to see the information register on his face. "And did you know that if a Palestinian kid lives with one of its parents in Jerusalem, that kid has to leave Jerusalem when it turns eighteen and go live on the West Bank?"

"What? Why?" Matt turned his head in Daniel's direction, bewildered; it sounded nonsensical, and he thought that maybe he'd missed the initial sentences while he was brooding about Yossi, the ones that explained what the hell Daniel was talking about.

"Why? They always say it's for security reasons. But this is about demographics. About keeping the Jew-to-Arab ratio in Jerusalem stable." Daniel had read about the law quickly, when the materials from B'Tselem had first had arrived, and then more slowly and carefully; but it was so convoluted and had so many poisonous ramifications, it had taken him a while to even understand it. He'd read the testimonials from Palestinians about standing outside in line all night at the Interior

Ministry with their infants and documents, only to be told they were missing a document, or to return in three months, or that their claims were denied, or that the ministry was closing early so clerks could get home for an approaching Jewish holiday. It had made him think how pathetic and subhuman a long weary line of humans always looked, like refugees or convicts with their wooden bowls, waiting for their portion of rice. It made him think that a big strategy of the Occupation was to flood the brain space of Palestinians with the countless cryptic details of petty bureaucracy. And it made him think, irately: *Sorry, Joel, but how is that not like apartheid?*

"I just don't know what to do with this information," he told Matt now, irate all over again. "Seriously. What am I supposed to do with it? Just be glad that I get to get married, and to hell with everybody else?"

"I don't have the slightest idea what you're supposed to do with that information." Matt couldn't say it, but he was secretly glad that Daniel also had complicated feelings about getting married. It made him feel less alone with it.

Daniel took the straw out of his iced tea, sucked on it, and laid it on the table. "I called the Bereaved Families Forum," he said.

Matt turned sharply and looked at him. "Seriously? When? What did they say?"

"The guy's going to call me back on Tuesday."

"Good for you, honey! I'm glad."

Daniel shrugged. "Yeah, they probably don't let American Jews join—it's a group for Israelis and Palestinians—but maybe, if not, they can suggest another group."

"I'm glad," Matt said.

He'd disarmed him, Daniel knew; Matt had been wanting him to join an activist group for a while now. Even if they did let him join, which he doubted, he didn't know what kind of role he'd have, and what kind of travel that might entail. He didn't know if it was the right way to enter the fray. But a yearning had overtaken him, to connect in a human way with Palestinian people. Maybe the impulse was silly or naïve. It was hard to explain, even to Matt. But his fate was tied so intimately to people he'd never met in the flesh—unless you counted that hot, shocking moment when flesh was blown off of bodies. Unless you counted his brief handshake with that Palestinian man, Ibrahim, at the Smith College panel, who'd been too busy or distracted to focus on him. Or maybe he hadn't been. Maybe, it occurred to Daniel as he diffusely took in the heat of the afternoon, the murmur of people's conversations around him, he'd needed so much from Ibrahim at that moment—so much that he couldn't even name—that no response could have lived up to his hopes.

Matt ran his hand gently over Daniel's, and Daniel turned over his palm and entwined his fingers with his. He appreciated how lucky he was to have Matt in the flesh, not to be kept apart from him by a sinkhole of military and legal space. He squeezed Matt's hand hard, to feel him, because it was hard sometimes to feel Matt's presence even when he was right there. Hard to be there for him, when sometimes the dead and the dispossessed felt more real than the man breathing right beside him.

And yet, Matt—Matt had been there for him. He'd been an ark to him and to the kids, carrying them out of dark, catastrophic waters. Solid, durable, sensual, he'd carried them through.

THE UNCLES WERE GETTING married. They said that men could marry each other now, and they weren't teasing her, it was really true. Gal sat aboard Caesar, swaying easily with his walk, while Matt watched, forearms resting on the ring's railing and chin propped on his folded hands. She was waiting for permission to canter and feeling the cool air encase her bare arms; right before she went in, she'd stripped down to her T-shirt and tossed her sweatshirt to Matt. It was hard to wait, because cantering was the most thrilling thing she'd ever done in her entire life. Her heels were down and straight, her thighs pressed easily into the saddle, the reins looped around her soft, able hands. She remembered being at weddings in Israel, running around with other kids in huge, brilliant banquet halls, round tables with white tablecloths as far as her eye could see, flower arrangements and dishes of hummus and olives and wine bottles and glasses of water placed on them, the grown-ups talking in loud voices over the deafening music. Dancing with her father, straddling his hip, while he held her hand straight out in front of them and put on a pompous dancing-master face. The memory moved through her with a languorous ache, like a pearl falling through honey. She gathered in her reins to raise Caesar's head and grazed him with her heels, gathering him, keeping her eye on Briana, who was the teacher today, and who was reminding them to pull the rein near the railing and nudge the horse with that heel. She didn't need to hear that instruction again. She was ready. Her body was light and airy, a knitted baby blanket, a round crystal glass with water shimmering inside.

"Okay," Briana said, and Gal broke into a canter.

Behind a dozen other couples and a crowd of kids, Daniel, Matt, Gal, and Noam stood in line at the Northampton courthouse, waiting for a marriage license on the first day they would be issued to gay couples in the United States. Some courthouses in Cambridge and Provincetown, Matt knew, had opened at midnight to let their gay citizens be the very first in the U.S. to receive marriage certificates. Despite that gall to his competitive spirit, he took in with pleasure the sun warming his shoulders, the feel of Gal's hand resting in his, the sheer gorgeousness of the blue spring sky, doubly precious because they'd earned it by slogging through the grueling, grueling winter. Lesbian couples stood in front and in back of them, wearing their pretty dresses, their suits, whatever counted for them as finery. He himself was sporting bright blue shoes and a fedora. A butch passed by them, scanning for someone in line and muttering to herself; she was wearing a cowboy dress shirt with pearl buttons tucked into black jeans. Matt whispered, "Check out Farmer Brown over there."

Daniel slapped his arm. *"It's her wedding day,"* he admonished.

Around them, people milled and called out to each other. "Tying the knot?" "Taking the plunge?" "Making an honest homo out of him?" They laughed at the idea that those everyday expressions could have anything to do with them. A small Asian-American girl passed by on her father's shoulders, playing the "Wedding March" on a child-sized violin. Several people circulated in caterers' clothes—black pants, white dress shirt—proffering trays of canapés, business cards stacked prettily around the trays' edges. Matt watched them, a smile pulling at his lips at their entrepreneurial spirit.

History had come down and tapped them on the shoulder, and it was hard to know what to feel in the moment. Marriage wouldn't have been Matt's fight, but now it had happened, and that was pretty remarkable. He was proud to live in Massachusetts, USA; other than that, he drew something of a blank. Maybe, he thought, you could only feel these moments in retrospect. He remembered the day that *Lawrence v. Texas*, the Supreme Court case that had overturned Texas's sodomy law, had come down, the Court's majority writing that *Bowers v. Hardwick*—to gay people, an infamously repulsive decision—had been misguided and wrong. He and Daniel had happened to be at Derrick and Brent's for dinner, and they'd all lifted their wineglasses and looked at one another with bemusement, at a loss for the right words, the right emotions, until Brent piped up, "To sodomy!" and they'd all laughed and touched glasses.

The line inched forward. Noam, who was wearing a T-shirt with a bow tie and tuxedo front silk-screened on it, and whose stroller's handlebars had been bedecked with a small rainbow flag, said, "Out! Out!" and Matt unbuckled him, lifted him out, and set him down. "This is taking forever," he said to Daniel. "I'm going to take a walk with him. C'mon, Shorty." Matt let Noam lead him around, a tiny hand clasping his pointer finger. People smiled at the sight of the tall, graceful gay man with the toddler chugging along at his side. They walked to the edges of the crowd and Matt stood watching while Noam stooped to pick up and examine some gravel pebbles at the edges of the parking lot.

"Hey," he heard behind him. It was Brent, smiling, wearing jeans and a blue T-shirt with the big yellow equals sign on the front, a baseball cap to protect his head where his hair was thinning. "We found Daniel in line, and he said you guys had gone for a walk."

"Change your mind?" Matt grinned.

"No," he said. "We just came to join the celebration." He and Derrick had decided not to get married. "It's not for us," Derrick had said in tactful nonjudgment. "At least not right now." They'd been together for fifteen years, since freshman year in college, with only an experimental break when Brent had gone abroad to Paris his junior year.

Now Brent looked into his friend's face with an expression both sweet and keen, and slid his arm around his shoulder.

"I've been thinking about Ilana and Joel today," Matt said.

Brent nodded.

"I think they'd be happy. They trusted us. They trusted us together." He stepped forward abruptly. "No, honey, that's yucky," he said to Noam, before Noam's fingers could close over a cigarette butt on the ground.

"Dass yucky," Noam repeated. He turned to Brent. "Dass yucky," he said solemnly.

"Yes it is," Brent said. "And let me commend you on your good talking!"

"It turns out I wasn't so trustworthy," Matt said. "I don't know why. Well, I do know why. I didn't want to have to spend the rest of my life worrying about being safe. Or something."

Brent was quiet, his thoughts playing across his face.

"It feels good to say fuck you to the universe!" Matt said. He scanned the courthouse, the peaceable crowd, the cars passing by with supportive beeps, the serene blue sky, and he and Brent laughed, struck at the same time by how very benign the universe was looking at that moment. "Seriously, though," he said. "That's what this marriage is, too. A leap of faith. Like: We're not going to wait to climb this mountain till they've put up guardrails and signage along all the cliff faces. We're not! Because we want to climb."

Noam came over to Matt and gave him a handful of stones and street sand left over from the winter plows. "What am I supposed to do with this?" Matt asked, looking at the dirty pile in his hand.

"Take home," Noam replied.

Matt looked at him, sighed, and emptied it into the pocket of his clean, pressed pants. "Nothing," he said to Brent, "and I mean *nothing*, makes me feel like a parent more than holding out my hand so they can spill or gag or spit disgusting shit into it." He rubbed his hands together to clean them off and picked Noam up, raked his bangs back from his forehead with his fingers. "You're a good friend," he said to Brent. "I'm sorry I haven't been a very present one lately."

Brent waved his hand and shook his head, his face pinking with little blots of emotion. "It's okay—"

"It's not okay," Matt said, and Brent clasped his shoulder hard.

When they got back to the line, Daniel and Gal had gotten almost to the courthouse door, and Daniel was anxiously looking around for him. Gal was watching as a little boy on the verge of a tantrum was alternately diverted and scolded by his moms, who were worried their impending moment would be ruined by a screaming toddler. A middle-aged lesbian couple in a suit and a dress were emerging from the courthouse's other door, and raising their clasped hands in the air as reporters took photos of them; there was a wave of applause, then it became rhythmic, and people began to chant, "Thank you! Thank you!" Matt cocked his ear toward a woman next to him. "Goodridge," she told him. "One of the couples who filed the lawsuit."

Then Daniel was holding the door open for him, peering into the paneled, crowded hallways in front of them, and then they'd stepped inside. Standing around tables and sitting on benches against the walls, couples were bent over forms, writing. Four clerks behind the long counter were handing out forms, gesturing and talking, collecting money. Daniel and Matt took theirs from a middle-aged woman with curly hair, big glasses, and a face pink from the humid warmth of bodies, who said in a voice whose hassled quality was just barely covered by mirth, "Good luck finding a place to sit down!"

Daniel, who attributed his ability to slice through lines and crowds to the years he'd spent getting on buses in Israel, disappeared for a second, and when Matt found him, he'd slipped onto the corner of a bench and was patting it in an invitation to sit next to him. Matt sat, excused himself to the woman he was making shift over, and smoothed the form over his thigh; they sat and wrote, knees touching. Addresses, parents' names, city of birth. There was a burst of joyful noise, and they looked up—it was two of the Jewish lesbians; their rabbi had arrived, and was singing a *shehechianu*. Gal and Noam had disappeared down the hall, and just as Matt turned to ask Daniel where they were, they returned, Gal holding a hunk of cake on a paper plate, both of their mouths covered with frosting; in a room down the hall, the city of Northampton was celebrating the right of its gay and lesbian citizens to marry with a wedding cake. "Give me a bite," Daniel said, leaning forward chin-first. He leveled a stern look at Gal when the plastic forkful she offered had just cake on it, no frosting, and she rolled her eyes and stabbed the fork into a gooey heap of white frosting, held it out to him. He grunted with approval, eyes glinting, and took it in his mouth. Matt turned back to his form with a smile.

Their own wedding would be a tiny one at home, a few weeks, or maybe a month from now. They were still debating whether to have a justice of the peace or a rabbi preside. For Daniel, the main appeal of a Jewish wedding was the chance to break the glass at the end, to symbolize the shattering of their lives when Joel and Ilana died, and the continued shattering of Palestinian lives. But he was still trying to figure out whether he'd be satisfied with the one Jewish custom at the end of a secular service. They were also still thinking about whether to invite Malka and Yaakov, along with their parents and their best friends. Or whether to invite anybody but the kids and Yo-yo. They were trying to have a wedding and dodge the idea of a wedding.

"Here we go," Daniel murmured, his lips grazing Matt's ear. He laid his forefinger on the signature line, and signed.

ACKNOWLEDGMENTS

FOR VARIOUS FORMS of vital and enlivening support, I am grateful to the National Endowment for the Arts, the Corporation of Yaddo, the MacDowell Colony, and the Dean of Faculty's office at Amherst College. Warm thanks to Ellen Geiger and David Highfill for their faith in the book, and for shepherding it through multiple revisions, each better than the last.

In Jerusalem, the David family—Paula, Uri, Maya, and Tamar—took loving care of me during my research trips, accompanying me to the sites of café bombings, watching sad documentaries with me, introducing me to various professionals, cooking delicious food. Gila Parizian and Ruth Matot talked with me about the various aspects of the work social workers do when there is a terrorist attack in Jerusalem; I thank them for their generosity with their time, and for their emotional energy.

Anston Bosman, Edmund Campos, Stephanie Grant, and the Sánchez-Eppler family made crucial interventions in the novel at various points, and I thank them and my colleagues in the English Department at Amherst College for their enthusiastic and challenging engagement with it. Alexander Chee, Amity Gaige, Daniel Hall, Amelie Hastie, Catherine Newman, Andrew Parker, Paul Statt, Susan Stinson, and Elizabeth Young provided encouragement, advice, and support; I cherish their collegiality and friendship. Amy Kaplan's friendship is one of my greatest pleasures, and her thoughtfulness and erudition about Israel/Palestine made her an essential interlocutor.

Elizabeth Garland is my first and last reader. I thank her for the rigor and conviction with which she approaches my work and for buoying me, always, with her outsized faith in my abilities. Abigail and Claire were born when I was midway through writing; they slowed the process down, but they also provided loads of new material, which is, of course, what having children is all about. I love them all dearly.

This book is dedicated to my mother, brother, and sister. We moved to Israel in 1976, and the consequences of that move continue to reverberate in our lives even though three of us have been back in the U.S. for decades. Thank you, Tony and Paula, for being my companions through our Israeli experiment and its aftermath, for the openness and humanity of your political views, for your equanimity about my plundering aspects of our lives for fiction, and for your love.

My mother died while this book was in proofs. She had already read it several times; it was on a topic dear to her heart, as her relation to Israel/Palestine had undergone a sea change late in her life. She read my work with wonder and appreciation. I love you, Mom, and I'll miss you.

About the book

Read on

Insights,
Interviews
& More . . .

My Mother's Israel
An Essay by Judith Frank about Writing *All I Love and Know*

FIVE YEARS AFTER our father's death, when my sister Paula and I were seventeen and my brother Tony fourteen, my mother moved us to Israel. It was an unlikely move for a family like ours: we were secular Jews living in the Chicago suburbs—my siblings and I third-generation Americans—we had no relatives in Israel, and other than a trip my parents took there shortly after the Six-Day War, Israel had never played a big part in our lives. None of us but our mother wanted to move. My brother had no choice but to go; he was only fourteen. Nearly eighteen, my sister and I could have gone on to college in the United States, as had been our plan. But our father had committed suicide, after years of depression, when we were only twelve, and his death had frightened us, taught us the bitter lesson that loving us was not enough to tether anyone to this earth. We weren't ready to be so drastically separated from our remaining parent. We left the States with a sense of dread.

I'm writing this seven months after my mother's death. She struggled with health problems for much of her life, but had such a powerful life force that for months after her death, my siblings and I would hang out on the phone mumbling stupidly, "I can't believe she actually died." She died shortly before *All I Love and Know* was published, having read two drafts of it, having bragged about it to every Jew in the greater Chicago area. She would have loved the physical book, which is uncommonly gorgeous, and the reviews and responses. My own deep gratification about the publication of the novel I worked on for so many years has been laced with grief that she is not here to see it.

My siblings and I have our theories about what made the idea of *aliyah*—the Hebrew word for moving to Israel, literally, "rising"— so compelling and urgent for our mother. After five years of mourning the death of her husband, not to mention the years trying to keep a profoundly depressed man alive, she understandably needed to get away—from her grief, her parents, the community she and our father had lived in together. But I think there were other elements to her thinking, conscious or not. I think there might have been something there of the fantasy about Israel as a cure for the enervating effects of the Diaspora—the hope that, like the emaciated and victimized postwar European Jews who in Israel became robust tillers of the earth, my siblings and I, damaged by our father's death, would somehow be transformed. I also wonder, now that I'm at the age where many of my peers have young adult children who flit uneasily and sometimes obnoxiously in that space between dependence on their parents and leaving the nest, whether my mother had decided that having been left widowed with three grieving children at thirty-five, it was *her* turn to fledge. I was furious even then that at this moment when most American children move into the first stages of independence from home, my mother had decided to preempt us by leaving home instead, leaving more audaciously than we could even imagine, as if our dreams of a residential college were puny and uninspired. It felt like a huge ethical violation.

Israel was a time of depression for me, especially in the first years. I was a verbal kid with a highly developed sense of humor, coming from a place where I was deeply rooted and had many friends, now living in a culture where I didn't know a soul and didn't speak the language. I spent a year feeling literally struck dumb. I felt it to be a metaphysical dumbness, I felt I simply had nothing to say. Maybe I was dead like my father, I thought. Much later, I would explore that strange, deadened mourning state in my first novel, *Crybaby Butch*; indeed, mourning continued to preoccupy me in *All I Love and Know*. Only later would I think, Well geez, I didn't know the language! I was mourning my father, but I was also going through culture shock, a shock I could only fully register once it had abated.

I spent the first year with a group of young Americans in a Jewish Agency program in which we studied Hebrew and then became volunteers at a kibbutz in the Galilee. I hated the people in my group, I can now say definitively; but back then I was simply baffled and cowed by them. These decades later I can't get a handle on who they were, exactly. I think I must have been the youngest, and I think that at least some of them must have been sent to Israel by parents who hoped that a military society would shape them up. There was a worldly jadedness about the group, a kind of grossness that passed as humor, that depressed me. We volunteers lived on the edges of the kibbutz in primitive little shacks. Even forty years later, I can conjure the feeling of being a stranger on the margins of a community, and my intense loneliness and shame that it wasn't easier to make friends.

But I also have vivid, pleasurable sense memories from that time. We gathered in kibbutz-issued work clothes at chilly daybreak, where we were warmed by hot, sweet, milky coffee from canisters as the apple-picking trucks idled. Lined on benches on the beds of the trucks, we clattered on dirt roads and dipped below the fog line into the glistening, dewy apple orchards. Each apple picker drove a "michelson," a cherry picker, using the controls to swing ▶

My Mother's Israel *(continued)*

herself or himself into the branches of an apple tree. We were supposed to pick quickly and carefully. I remember lowering my load of apples with a crank, as slowly and gently as possible, into the large crates at the end of rows, and eating apples so gloriously crisp and flavorful they made me an apple snob for the rest of my life, the family member who leaves the soft or bland apples in the bowl for others to soldier their way through. I remember break time, when the American boys tossed bruised apples into the air like baseballs, and smashed them with sticks used as bats.

All the while I was learning Hebrew as though it would be my salvation. After apple season was over I got a job assisting in a children's house for seven-year-olds. Back then kibbutz children were still raised communally, eating, sleeping, and going to school under the care of a *metapelet*, a caretaker, in a house for their age group, visiting their parents during certain hours of the afternoon. It was there, conversing on a daily basis with children, that my Hebrew really got going. I remember their comical frustration at the limitations of my understanding; it was rejuvenating to be treated like a person worthy of frustration and teasing and instruction. Their parents started taking an interest in me, bringing me just a little closer into the life of the kibbutz. The other thing I remember from the children's house is changing thirteen comforter covers every Thursday, which makes me, to this day, as opinionated about how to put on a comforter cover as I am about apples.

When the program ended I went to university. There I was on slightly surer footing; I had always thrived in school. I studied English literature and made some friends, including an Israeli roommate, Rivka, who was to become my closest friend. Rivka was religious, a bright, pragmatic soul. I'd ask, "Can I scratch my back with a milk fork?" and she'd say "As long as you don't break the skin." I'd say, "I don't think I could ever be religious, because I don't believe in God," and she'd say, "Oh Judy, in Judaism the last thing you need to become religious is to believe in God." She loved language, and under her warm, engaged tutelage my Hebrew refined. We would sit talking in the bare, slummy dorm room we shared—in those days, at least, Israeli dorms were extremely rudimentary, as the country is small enough for most students to go home over weekends—eating bread and butter, olives, clementines, soft-boiled eggs out of the shell. I remember those foods, and Israeli folk dancing, which I loved, and working very hard at learning the lyrics to Israeli songs. That last effort made it into *All I Love and Know*, where I made Daniel the guitarist I've always wished I was, and had him learning chords on his guitar and poring over his Hebrew-English dictionary to learn the words.

As you can tell, visceral, sensory Israel stays with me still, almost forty years later: the feel of the language on my tongue, palate, and throat; the light and smells and food. And anyone who's lived in Jerusalem remembers in their very bones the slap of sandals on stone, pale pink light off the Jerusalem buildings, cool mountain air at night, the bark and cough and blasts of

4

exhaust from Egged buses, the sight of people scurrying home carrying challot and cakes for Shabbat. When my brother fought in the Lebanon war, my family endured that quintessential Israeli experience—the one David Grossman's protagonist Ora famously flees to avoid in his devastating *To the End of the Land*—of dreading the unexpected ring of the doorbell. ("It's me, it's me!" people quickly called out at the door, over intercoms, so we wouldn't think they were the army notifiers.)

After six years in Israel, I came back to the United States for graduate school, going into the PhD program in English at Cornell. It was there that I made the intense friendships many Americans make in college, and I caught up on other things American kids learn in college, too, like feminism. I encountered gay people for the first time, which was a revelation. These days you can meet young gay people who lived in isolation in small towns all over the United States, and who nonetheless came out at fourteen and fifteen. They have the Internet, sure, but even so, their powerful senses of self are pretty remarkable. For me, it took seeing a vision of thriving gay life to be able to let myself know that I was gay, and to venture out of the closet.

In graduate school, I also started realizing there was a critique of Israel I hadn't had much access to. I can't quite specify how I slowly came to distrust the received narratives about Israel and the Palestinians, except to say that reading feminist and queer theory created in me the disposition to distrust *many* kinds of received narratives. I tried to express the connection between these things in *All I Love and Know*, in the flashback to Joel's Israeli wedding, where Daniel remembers feeling marginal and unseen because he is gay: "And his increasingly keen awareness of the way oppression operated by making certain things invisible to the eye—things like his own emotional life— began to bleed into distaste and anger about the things he himself couldn't see because Israel made them invisible."

My reading taught me that these things Daniel can't see, by which he means Palestinian life, are invisible by design; Israeli roads and architecture are designed to make big swaths of Jerusalem invisible to a Jewish person in a car or on a bus. I found it stunning that while I knew Israel so intimately in some ways, my geopolitical education couldn't begin until I'd left; for like many Diaspora Jews, I'd grown up with the idea that unless I lived in Israel, I couldn't understand it well enough to judge its policies. Writing *All I Love and Know* was partly a way to explore the question of what you can see from close up, and what you can see from far away. Matt, for example, has had a lifelong critique of the Israeli occupation, but talking to his beloved Shoshi, the social worker in charge of guiding the family through identifying Joel's body, challenges his perceptions: "But her struggle to help grieving and traumatized people . . . pressed upon his worldview and scrambled it a little." And Daniel has a painful argument with his parents about his brother Joel's failure as a television reporter to probe deeply enough into the injustices of the occupation and the treatment of Israeli Arabs, in which they call him arrogant for thinking he can know more about the situation than his brother did. ▶

Roughly a decade later, my mother, who had had a thriving career in Jerusalem as a social worker and a university lecturer, started going through the same process. My sister Paula, who met and married an Israeli man, ended up the only one of us who stayed. My mother and brother returned, one by one, to the Chicago area in the nineties, and in the last decade or so of her life, my mother belonged to Jewish Reconstructionist Congregation in Evanston, Illinois. An expert in early childhood development, she worked as a consultant for the synagogue's nursery school; for several years, baffled and alienated the entire time by the mysterious language of management and bureaucracy, she served on the JRC board. JRC was the center of her social and professional life. She also befriended JRC's rabbi, Brant Rosen. While my siblings and I initially joked that Brant was "the good son," her relationship with him came to take on the intense and combative character of many of her close relationships. And it was with Brant, who is an activist for justice for Palestinians, that my mother's own geopolitical education about Israel took root.

A turning point came for her in 2010, when Rabbi Brant took a delegation of JRC members to the West Bank and East Jerusalem, where they met Palestinian activists and did homestays at Palestinian refugee camps. My mother's health was poor at the time, and she made the trip in a wheelchair, but the experience was transformative for her. Upon their return, she, Brant, and another member of the delegation were interviewed on *Worldview*, on WBEZ, Chicago Public Radio. The podcast of that interview is the place where I can go to hear my mother's voice again. She says of the years she lived in Israel, "The whole time I lived there I paid no attention to the fact that there was an issue here. . . . If I ever had a conversation with a Palestinian it was to buy something. And when I came back I . . . slowly became more aware. I'm very upset with myself. I felt that I had to go back to see what's going on." The families she met were warm and loving, she said. "These people were so like Jews! . . . They could have been my family." She also said something that the radio host described as "eye-popping": "When one country is oppressed and occupied by another, there's only one side to the story, and that's the story of the oppressed. I'm not wiping out any history, I just think that in order to be able to talk about this history, you have to have people who are free to talk about it with you."

My mother died on a bitterly cold day in February 2014. That winter was a particularly hard one in Chicago; as I flew back and forth during her last months, Lake Michigan, I could see from the air, was almost frozen over, lunar and sublime. The roof of my mother's house had such enormous ice dams, we had to have roofers come out so we could wrench open the front door for the shiva, and as we watched chunks of ice and snow sail down I kept thinking that ice had covered her house because her soul had left it. Brant officiated at her funeral—as I write I can conjure him standing before me, gently tearing the black mourning ribbon on my jacket—and his friendship to me and my siblings is something we'll never forget; we felt so lucky to have a rabbi who knew and got our mother, who both loved her and was as irreverent about her as we were.

Three months later, we sold our mother's house, and experienced that new wave of loss, the loss of the family gathering place. Six months later, during the Israeli attack on Gaza, Brant Rosen resigned as rabbi of JRC, feeling that his activism was putting untenable pressures on both him and the congregation. He had never been my rabbi, but his departure felt like yet another loss of home.

For months after she died, my siblings and I were grateful and relieved that our mother had died the death she'd wished for. She wasn't in pain; she didn't linger in dementia or disability; the bodily indignities she suffered were grueling, but manageable. In her last months she was even able to achieve a measure of the tranquility that had eluded her until then. Because she was a chronically ill person, we'd been anxious for a long time about how our mother would die. And now we knew. And now that the ending has occurred, I can look back and see the entire shape of her life. I do so with a novelist's eye, searching out event, causality, proportion, irony. It's an amazing story. My mother was galling and formidable and difficult. She was also astonishingly perceptive and open-minded and capable of change. I will never write her story as it occurred, because I'm a novelist, not a biographer or a memoirist. But of course she's in all of my stories, including this one. ∾

The podcast of the interview with Marjorie Frank, Brant Rosen, and Michael Deheeger: http://www.wbez.org/episode-segments/evanston-rabbi-takes -congregation-west-bank-and-east-jerusalem

Questions for Discussion

1. The first forty-five pages of *All I Love and Know* are narrated from Matt's point of view. Why might Frank have chosen him as the initial point-of-view character in this novel? How does Matt's outsider status—as a young gay man, as a non-Jew, as "the goyfriend"—put him in an awkward or advantageous position as Daniel's partner in this crisis? What about as a parent to Noam and Gal?

2. In what ways is *All I Love and Know* about the experience of being a twin? What does being a twin mean to Daniel, and how does it affect his thinking about rebuilding his life after Joel's death? We're told that he and Joel "invented the semifacetious idea of *twinsism*: the act of stereotyping or fetishizing twins." What does that running joke tell us about their feelings about twinship?

3. *All I Love and Know* can be read as a novel about parenting and being parented: as these gay men become sudden parents, they are thrust into contact with their own parents and confront their feelings about being their parents' children. What are the aspects of parenting that the novel asks you to think about? What do you think Daniel and Matt's relative strengths are as parents to Gal and Noam?

4. Matt moved to Northampton after his best friend Jay died of AIDS. How does Jay's death change the way he handles this new crisis? How does this AIDS story relate to the central narrative of terrorism and trauma? What is at stake in the fight Matt and Daniel have over the relative "innocence" of Jay's and Joel's deaths?

5. Why do you think Frank decided to make Malka and Yaakov Holocaust survivors?

What does their experience add to the novel's story of survival? At the military cemetery, Malka surprises Daniel by comparing victims of terror to Holocaust survivors and claims that Israelis despise them both. What is the connection, in her mind? Does her bitterness make you think differently about her?

6. Israel is very important to many American Jews, and it appeals to the Rosen sons in different ways. What does Israeli culture have to offer Daniel and Joel as young men from an affluent Jewish-American family?

7. In a central event of the novel, talking to a reporter, Daniel says of the terrorist who killed his brother, ". . . I can understand trying to violently place yourself within the Israelis' field of vision, in a way they can't ignore. I don't condone it, but I do understand it." He receives hate mail in response, and wonders whether he has "breached an important code of conduct, or failed at some response crucial to the common human enterprise." What do you make of Daniel's response to the terrorist attack? Is he doing something wrong? Does the novel make you think any differently about terrorism?

8. Daniel has a left-of-center position about the Israeli occupation. From what kinds of sources does he get his information? What factors from his personal life contribute to the way he feels about Israel's policies? And conversely, how does his political position impact or impede his mourning process? What do you think the novel is trying to say about the tension between the personal and the political?

9. Daniel grieves throughout the novel, sometimes in alienating ways. He believes Matt and his friends are pressuring him for "grieving wrong," and feels they're trying to push him into therapy. Matt believes that Daniel has become "frozen" and "different." What are the factors that have made Daniel's process especially grueling? How did you respond to the ways in which he becomes "frozen"?

10. Does Gal get lost accidentally or on purpose in the Jerusalem *shuk*? What kind of internal drama is being enacted as she races away from the suspicious box, feeling her parents at her heels? What kind of figure is Chezzi the fishmonger? What does this frightening event express about Gal's relationship with Daniel?

11. The idea of gay marriage comes up in this story, and it takes one character some time to warm to the idea. In this era of victory for marriage equality in many U.S. states, why do you think some gay and lesbian people might be ambivalent about getting married? ᴄ◡

What I Was Reading While I Was Writing *All I Love and Know*

Children of the Holocaust:
Conversations with Sons and Daughters
of Survivors
by Helen Epstein

Hearing the stories of children of Holocaust survivors helped me imagine the silences that structured the lives of Ilana and her parents.

Independence Park:
The Lives of Gay Men in Israel
by Amir Fink and Jacob Press

Ethnography is one of the most useful ways I learn to imagine how people experience their lives.

To the End of the Land
by David Grossman

This is a searing novel about loss, war, and parenting, by one of Israel's best writers and its moral conscience.

My Happiness Bears No Relation to Happiness:
A Poet's life in the Palestinian Century
by Adina Hoffman

I learned a lot about Palestinian village life from this biography, which also has an unforgettable description of the arrival of Israeli forces in 1948, and the expulsion of a community from its village.

Losing a Parent to Death in the Early Years:
Guidelines for the Treatment of Traumatic
Bereavement in Infancy and Early Childhood
by Alicia F. Lieberman

This book, by a leading expert in early childhood trauma, helped me grasp the experience of Gal and Noam.

Palestine Inside Out:
An Everyday Occupation
by Saree Makdisi

This book taught me about the banal, everyday hurdles that Palestinian people experience as they try to navigate the bureaucracy of the occupation.

A Tale of Love and Darkness
by Amos Oz

Anyone attempting to write well about Jerusalem should read Oz's enchanting description of his childhood there during the 1940s and 1950s.

The Question of Zion
by Jacqueline Rose

I learned from this book that there was a dissenting strand of Zionism that warned from the start about the ethics and possible consequences of displacing the Arab population in Palestine.

Wrestling in the Daylight:
A Rabbi's Path to Palestinian Solidarity
by Brant Rosen

This is a collection of blog posts by a peace activist and former rabbi at a Jewish Reconstructionist Congregation in Evanston, Illinois; I went often to the blog for incisive writing on everything from checkpoints to biblical *parashot*.

The Counterlife
by Philip Roth

Roth's novel is a noisy, engaging, and provocative meditation on Israel and American Jewish masculinity.

The Lemon Tree:
An Arab, a Jew, and the Heart of the Middle East
by Sandy Tolan

A story about what happens when a young Palestinian man returns to the house his family had lived in before their expulsion in 1948, and the fraught, unlikely friendship he strikes up ▶

What I Was Reading While I Was Writing
All I Love and Know (continued)

with the nineteen-year-old Israeli college
student whose family has lived there since.

Hollow Land:
Israel's Architecture of Occupation
by Eyal Weizman

It's from this book, by an Israeli professor of
architecture, that I took the material about
Jerusalem stone that appears in a conversation at
the shiva for Joel and Ilana. ✍

Discover great authors,
exclusive offers, and more
at hc.com.

PENGUIN BOOKS

CAT SENSE

'Bradshaw does a great job of explaining to the clueless cat owner what science has discovered about their pet ... [A] fascinating bookshelf essential for anyone who's ever looked at their cat and wondered what's going on behind those big eyes' *Express*

'A fascinating book every cat owner should read' *Irish Times*

'Witty, surprising writing ... There is his delight in detail, a talent for dismantling myths, but most importantly an ability to build a coherent and entertaining theory from an apparent contradiction that all cat-lovers will recognise: we seek to understand cats even though it is our lack of understanding that makes us love them' *The Herald*

'For any who may wonder what their feline companions are really thinking, *Cat Sense*, by John Bradshaw, provides the best answers that science can give for the time being ... *Cat Sense* will teach you much about the biology of cats that you never suspected' *The New York Times*

'Bradshaw, who has been studying the behaviour of domesticated animals for over 30 years, reveals some fascinating explanations for why cats act the way they do around humans' *Time*

'Engaging from the start, this book tracks feline development and domestication from ancient times, exploring their complex relationship with man in detail. Current assumptions are re-examined with surprising results. This is a must-read for cat owners and anyone interested in how we live within the world around us' *The Lady*

'Following in the paw prints of his bestselling *In Defence of Dogs*, John Bradshaw, a biologist, traces the evolution of felines from wildcats into the world's most popular pet ... the combination of folklore and scientific research offers some illuminating insights' Lowenna Waters, *Financial Times*

'[A] definitive guide to the origins, evolution and modern-day needs of our furry friends ... A must-read for any cat lover, the book offers humane insights about the domestic cat that challenge the most basic assumptions and promise to dramatically improve our pets' lives' *Cat Fancy*

'Bradshaw is ... a dedicated scientist, with much to teach us about our furry darlings' *Daily Telegraph*

'This fascinating book will be a bible for cat owners'
Booklist, Starred Review

'Insightful . . . Using cutting-edge research, Bradshaw takes us into the mysterious mind of the domestic cat, explaining the cat's nature and needs, and, in doing, so deepens our understanding of our wild housemates and improves our relationships with them' *Modern Cat*

'This fascinating book is one of the finest ever written about cats. There was hardly a page where I did not learn something new' Jeffrey Moussaieff Masson, author of *When Elephants Weep* and *The Nine Emotional Lives of Cats*

'In order to understand the species fully, Bradshaw advocates realising that however superficially domesticated cats are they are still subject to primeval instincts, natural hunters and scavengers facing a barrage of contemporary challenges. His erudite and entertaining guide to feline behaviour will prove enlightening and should foster much deeper appreciation of the world cats inhabit' *Good Book Guide*

ABOUT THE AUTHOR

John Bradshaw is a biologist who founded and directs the world-renowned Anthrozoology Institute, based at the University of Bristol. He has been studying the behaviour of domestic cats and their owners for over twenty-five years, and is the author of many scientific articles, research papers and reviews.

JOHN BRADSHAW

Cat Sense

The Feline Enigma Revealed

PENGUIN BOOKS

PENGUIN BOOKS

Published by the Penguin Group
Penguin Books Ltd, 80 Strand, London WC2R ORL, England
Penguin Group (USA) Inc., 375 Hudson Street, New York, New York 10014, USA
Penguin Group (Canada), 90 Eglinton Avenue East, Suite 700, Toronto, Ontario, Canada M4P 2Y3
(a division of Pearson Penguin Canada Inc.)
Penguin Ireland, 25 St Stephen's Green, Dublin 2, Ireland (a division of Penguin Books Ltd)
Penguin Group (Australia), 707 Collins Street, Melbourne, Victoria 3008, Australia
(a division of Pearson Australia Group Pty Ltd)
Penguin Books India Pvt Ltd, 11 Community Centre, Panchsheel Park, New Delhi – 110 017, India
Penguin Group (NZ), 67 Apollo Drive, Rosedale, Auckland 0632, New Zealand
(a division of Pearson New Zealand Ltd)
Penguin Books (South Africa) (Pty) Ltd, Block D, Rosebank Office Park,
181 Jan Smuts Avenue, Parktown North, Gauteng 2193, South Africa

Penguin Books Ltd, Registered Offices: 80 Strand, London WC2R ORL, England

www.penguin.com

First published by Allen Lane 2013
Published in Penguin Books 2014
001

Copyright © John Bradshaw, 2013

The moral right of the author has been asserted

Typeset by Jouve (UK), Milton Keynes
Printed in Great Britain by Clays Ltd, St Ives plc

A CIP catalogue record for this book is available from the British Library

ISBN: 978-0-241-96045-5

www.greenpenguin.co.uk

MIX
Paper from
responsible sources
FSC
www.fsc.org   FSC® C018179

Penguin Books is committed to a sustainable
future for our business, our readers and our planet.
This book is made from Forest Stewardship
Council™ certified paper.

To Splodge (1988–2004) – A Real Cat

Contents

Dogs look up to us: cats look down on us.
                                        – *Winston Churchill*

When a man loves cats, I am his friend and comrade, without
further introduction.
                                              – *Mark Twain*

Preface

What is a cat? Cats have intrigued people ever since they first came to live among us. Irish legend has it that 'a cat's eyes are windows enabling us to see into another world' – but what a mysterious world that is! Most pet owners would agree that dogs tend to be open and honest, revealing their intentions to anyone who will pay them attention. Cats, on the other hand, are elusive: we accept them on their terms, but they in turn never quite reveal what those terms might be. Winston Churchill, who referred to his cat Jock as his 'special assistant', famously once observed of Russian politics, 'It is a riddle, wrapped in a mystery, inside an enigma; but perhaps there is a key'; he might as well have been talking about cats.

Is there a key? I'm convinced that there is, and moreover that it can be found in science. I've shared my home with quite a few cats – and have become aware that 'ownership' is not the appropriate term for this relationship. I've witnessed the birth of several litters of kittens, and nursed my elderly cats through their heartbreaking final declines into senility and ill health. I've helped with the rescue and relocation of feral cats, animals that literally wanted to bite the hand that fed them. Still, I don't feel that, on its own, my personal involvement with cats has taught me very much about what they are really like. Instead, the work of scientists – field biologists, archaeologists, developmental biologists, animal psychologists, DNA chemists and anthrozoologists such as myself – has provided me with the pieces that, assembled, begin to reveal the cat's true nature. We are still missing some pieces, but the definitive picture is emerging. This is an opportune moment to take stock of what we know, what is still to be discovered, and, most important, how we can use our knowledge to improve cats' daily lives.

Getting an idea of what cats are thinking should not detract from the pleasures of 'owning' them. One theory holds that we can enjoy our pets' company only through pretending that they are 'little people' – that we keep animals merely to project our own thoughts and needs on to them, secure in the knowledge that they can't tell us how far off the mark we are. Taking this viewpoint to its logical conclusion, forcing us to concede that they neither understand nor care what we say to them, we might suddenly find that we no longer love them. I do not subscribe to this idea. The human mind is perfectly capable of simultaneously holding two apparently incompatible views about animals, without one negating the others. The idea that animals are in some ways like and in others quite unlike humans is behind the humour of countless cartoons and greetings cards; these simply would not be funny if the two concepts cancelled each other out. In fact, quite the opposite: the more I learn about cats, both through my own studies and through other research, the more I appreciate being able to share my life with them.

Cats have fascinated me since I was a child. We had no cats at home when I was growing up, nor did any of our neighbours. The only cats I knew lived on the farm down the lane, and they weren't pets, they were mousers. My brother and I would occasionally catch intriguing glimpses of one of them running from barn to outhouse, but they were busy animals and not over-friendly to people, especially small boys. Once the farmer showed us a nest of kittens among the hay bales, but he made no special effort to tame them: they were simply his insurance against vermin. At that age, I thought that cats were just another farm animal, like the chickens that pecked around the yard or the cows that were driven back to the byre every evening for milking.

The first pet cat I ever got to know was the polar opposite of these farm cats, a neurotic Burmese by the name of Kelly. Kelly belonged to a friend of my mother's who had bouts of illness, and no neighbour to feed her cat while she was hospitalized. Kelly boarded with us; he could not be let out in case he tried to run back home, he yowled incessantly, he would eat only boiled cod, and he was evidently used to receiving the undivided attention of his besotted owner. While he was with us, he spent most of his time hiding behind the couch, but within a few seconds of the telephone ringing, he would emerge, make sure that my mother's attention was occupied by the person on the other end of the line, and then sink his long Burmese canines deep into her calf. Regular callers became accustomed to the idea that twenty seconds in, the conversation would be interrupted by a scream and then a muttered curse. Understandably, none of us became particularly fond of Kelly, and we were always relieved when it was time for him to head back home.

Not until I had pets of my own did I begin to appreciate the pleasures of living with a normal cat – that is to say, a cat that purrs when it is stroked and greets people by rubbing around their legs. These qualities were probably also appreciated by the first people to give houseroom to cats, thousands of years ago; such displays of affection are also the hallmark of tamed individuals of the African wildcat, the domestic cat's indirect ancestor. The emphasis placed on these qualities has gradually increased over the centuries. While most of today's cat owners value them for their affection above all else, for most of their history, domestic cats have had to earn their keep as controllers of mice and rats.

As my experience with domestic cats grew, so did my appreciation of their utilitarian origins. Splodge, the fluffy black-and-white kitten we bought for our daughter as compensation for having to relocate, quickly grew into a large, shaggy and rather bad-tempered hunter. Unlike many cats, he was fearless in the face of a rat, even an adult. He soon learned that depositing a rat carcass on our kitchen floor for us to find when we came downstairs for breakfast was not appreciated, and after that he kept his predatory activities private – without, I suspect, giving the rats themselves any respite.

However brave he was against a rat, Splodge usually kept away from other cats. Every now and then, we would hear the cat-flap clatter as he arrived home in a tearing hurry, and a quick glance out the window would usually reveal one of the older cats in the neighbourhood, glaring in the general direction of our back door. He had a favourite hunting area in the park nearby, but kept himself inconspicuous when travelling there and back. His diffidence towards other cats, especially males, was not just typical of many cats; it also exemplified a weakness in social skills that is perhaps the greatest difference between cats and dogs. Most dogs find it easy to get along with other

Splodge

dogs; cats generally find other cats a challenge. Yet many of today's owners expect their cats to accept other cats without question – either when they themselves wish to get a second cat, or when they decide to move, depositing their unsuspecting cat into what another cat thinks is its territory.

For cats, a stable social environment is not enough; they rely on their owners to provide a stable physical environment as well. Cats are fundamentally territorial animals that put down powerful roots in their surroundings. For some, their owner's home is all the territory they need. Lucy, another of my cats, showed no interest in hunting, despite being Splodge's great-niece; she barely strayed more than a dozen yards from the house – except when she came into season and disappeared over the garden wall for hours on end. Libby, Lucy's daughter and born in my home, was as brave a hunter as Splodge had been, but preferred to call the tomcats to her rather than go to them. Even though they were all related and all lived in the same house most of their lives, Splodge, Lucy and Libby all had distinctive personalities, and if I learned one thing from observing them it was that no cat is completely typical: cats have personalities, just as humans do. This observation inspired me to study how such differences come about.

The transformation of the cat from resident exterminator to companion cohabitee is both recent and rapid, and – especially from the cat's perspective – evidently incomplete. Today's owners demand a different set of qualities from their cats than would have been the norm even a century ago. In some ways, cats are struggling with their newfound popularity. Most owners would prefer that their cats did not kill defenceless little birds and mice, and those people who are more interested in wildlife than in pets are becoming increasingly vocal in their opposition to the cat's predatory urges. Indeed, cats now probably face more hostility than at any time in the past two centuries. Can cats possibly shake off their legacy as humankind's vermin exterminator of choice, and in just a few generations at that?

Cats themselves are oblivious to the controversy caused by their predatory natures, but they are all too aware of the difficulties they encounter in their dealings with other cats. Their independence, the quality that makes cats the ideal low-maintenance pet, probably stems from their solitary origins, but it has left them poorly equipped to cope with many owners' assumptions that they should be as adaptable as dogs. Can cats become more flexible in their social needs, so that they are unfazed by the proximity of other cats, without compromising their unique appeal?

One of my reasons for writing this book is to project what the typical cat might be like fifty years from now. I want people to continue to enjoy the company of an undoubtedly delightful animal, but I'm not sure that the cat, as a species, is heading in the right direction for this to be sustained. The more I've studied cats, from the wildest feral to the most cosseted Siamese, the more I've become convinced that we can no longer afford to take cats for granted: a more considered approach to cat keeping and cat breeding is necessary if we are to ensure their future.

Acknowledgements

I began studying cat behaviour more than thirty years ago, first at the Waltham Centre for Pet Nutrition, later at the University of Southampton, and now at the University of Bristol's Anthrozoology Institute. Much of what I've learned has come from painstaking observation of cats themselves: my own, my neighbours', cats in re-homing centres, the family of cats that used to share the Anthrozoology Institute's offices, and many ferals and farm cats.

Compared to the large number of canine scientists, rather few academics specialize in feline science, and even fewer make the domestic cat the focus of their attention. Those I've had the privilege of working with and who've helped me to form my ideas about how cats see the world include Christopher Thorne, David Macdonald, Ian Robinson, Sarah Brown, Sarah Benge (*née* Lowe), Deborah Smith, Stuart Church, John Allen, Ruud van den Bos, Charlotte Cameron-Beaumont, Peter Neville, Sarah Hall, Diane Sawyer, Suzanne Hall, Giles Horsfield, Fiona Smart, Rhiann Lovett, Rachel Casey, Kim Hawkins, Christine Bolster, Elizabeth Paul, Carri Westgarth, Jenna Kiddie, Anne Seawright, Jane Murray and others too numerous to list.

I've also learned a great deal from discussions with colleagues both at home and abroad, including the late Professor Paul Leyhausen, Dennis Turner, Gillian Kerby, Eugenia Natoli, Juliet Clutton-Brock, Sandra McCune, James Serpell, Lee Zasloff, Margaret Roberts and her colleagues at Cats Protection, Diane Addie, Irene Rochlitz, Deborah Goodwin, Celia Haddon, Sarah Heath, Graham Law, Claire Bessant, Patrick Pageat, Danielle Gunn-Moore, Paul Morris, Kurt Kotrschal, Elly Hiby, Sarah Ellis, Britta Osthaus, Carlos Driscoll, Alan Wilson, and the late and much missed Penny Bernstein. My thanks also to the University of Bristol's School of Veterinary Medicine, especially Professors Christine Nicol and Mike Mendl, and Doctors David Main and Becky Whay, for nurturing the Anthrozoology Institute and its research.

My studies of cats have relied on the cooperation of many hundreds of volunteer cat owners (and their cats!), to whom I will always be grateful. Much of our research would have been impossible without the unstinting assistance of the UK's re-homing charities, including the RSPCA, the Blue Cross and St Francis Animal Welfare, and I am especially grateful to Cats Protection for two decades of practical and financial assistance.

Summarizing nearly thirty years of research on cat behaviour into a form intended to be appreciated by the average cat owner has not been an easy task. I have had expert guidance from Lara Heimert and Tom Penn, my editors at Basic and Penguin respectively, and my indefatigable agent Patrick Walsh. Thank you all.

As in my previous books, I've turned to my dear friend Alan Peters to bring some of the animals to life in the illustrations, and just as before, he's done me more than proud.

Finally, I must thank my family for their forbearance for my enforced absences in what my granddaughter Beatrice calls 'Pops' office'.

Introduction

The domestic cat is the most popular pet in the world today. Across the globe, domestic cats outnumber 'man's best friend', the dog, by as many as three to one.[1] As more of us have come to live in cities – environments for which dogs are not ideally suited – cats have, for many, become the lifestyle pet of choice. More than a quarter of UK families have one or more cats, and they are found in about one third of US households. Even in Australia, where the domestic cat is routinely demonized as a heartless killer of innocent endangered marsupials, about a fifth of households own cats. All over the world, images of cats are used to advertise all kinds of consumer goods, from perfume to furniture to confectionery. The cartoon cat 'Hello Kitty' has appeared on more than 50,000 different branded products in more than sixty countries, netting her creators billions of dollars in royalties. Even though a significant minority of people – perhaps as many as one person in five – don't like cats, the majority who do show no sign of relinquishing even a fraction of their affection for their favourite animal.

Cats somehow manage to be simultaneously affectionate and self-reliant. Compared to dogs, cats are low-maintenance pets. They do not need training. They groom themselves. They can be left alone all day without pining for their owners as many dogs do, but they will nonetheless greet us affectionately when we get home (well – *some* will). Their mealtimes have been transformed by today's pet-food industry from a chore into a picnic. They remain unobtrusive most of the time, yet seem delighted to receive our affection. In a word, they are *convenient*.

Despite their apparently effortless transformation into urban sophisticates, however, cats still have three out of four feet firmly planted in their wild origins. The dog's mind has been radically altered from that of its ancestor, the grey wolf; cats, on the other hand, still think like wild hunters. Within a couple of generations, cats can revert back to the independent way of life that was the exclusive preserve of their predecessors some 10,000 years ago. Even today, many millions of cats worldwide are not pets but feral scavengers and hunters, living alongside people but inherently distrustful of them. Due to the astonishing flexibility with which kittens learn the difference between friend and foe, cats can move between these dramatically different lifestyles within a generation, and the offspring of a feral mother and feral father can become indistinguishable from any pet cat. A pet that is abandoned by its owner and cannot find another may turn to scavenging; a generation or two on, and its descendants will be indistinguishable from the thousands of feral cats that live shadowy existences in our cities.

As cats become more popular and ever more numerous, those who revile them are beginning to raise their voices, but with more venom now than for several centuries before. Cats have never shared the 'unclean' tag foisted on the dog and the pig,[2] but despite cats' superficially universal acceptance, a minority of people across all cultures finds cats disagreeable, and as many as one in twenty say that they find them repulsive. When asked, few Westerners will admit that they don't like dogs: those who do usually turn out either not to like animals in general[3] or can trace their aversion to a specific experience, perhaps being bitten in childhood. Cat-phobia[4] is more deeply seated and less widespread than common phobias of snakes and spiders – phobias that have a logical basis in helping the sufferer to avoid poisonous varieties – but is just as powerful an experience for those who suffer from it. Cat-phobics were very probably at the forefront of the religious persecution that led to the killing of millions of cats in medieval Europe, and cat-phobia was in all probability just as common then as it is today. Thus, there can be no guarantee that the cat's popularity will last. Indeed, without our intervention, the twentieth century may turn out to have been the cat's golden age.

Today, the cat is especially coming under attack on the specific grounds that it is a wanton and unnecessary killer of 'innocent' wildlife. These voices are most loudly raised in the Antipodes, but are becoming increasingly strident in the UK and the United States. The anti-cat lobby, at its most extreme, demands that cats no longer be allowed to hunt, that pet cats be kept indoors, and that feral cats should be exterminated. Owners of outdoor cats are vilified for supporting an animal that is portrayed as laying waste to the wildlife around their homes. Veterinary surgeons who seek to manage the welfare of feral cats by neutering and vaccinating them, and then returning them to their original territory, have come under attack from within their own profession, with some experts taking the position that this constitutes (illegal) abandonment that benefits neither the cat nor the adjacent wildlife.[5]

Both sides in this debate admit that cats are 'natural' hunters, but cannot agree on how this behaviour might be managed. In parts of Australia and New Zealand, cats are defined as 'alien' predators introduced from the northern hemisphere, and are banned from some areas and subject to curfews or compulsory microchipping in others. Even in places where cats have lived alongside native wildlife for hundreds of years, such as in the UK and the United States, their increasing popularity as pets has prompted a vocal minority to press for similar restrictions. Cat owners point to a lack of scientific evidence that pet cats contribute significantly to a population decline of any wild bird or mammal, which is caused instead mainly by the recent proliferation of other pressures on wildlife, such as loss of habitat. Consequently, any restrictions imposed on pet cats are unlikely to result in a resurgence of the species that they supposedly threaten.

Cats themselves are of course unaware that we no longer value their hunting prowess. Insofar as they themselves are concerned, the greatest threat to their subjective well-being comes not from people, but instead from other cats. In the same way that cats are not born to love people – this is something they have to learn when they are kittens – they do not automatically love other cats; indeed, their default position is to be suspicious, even fearful, of every cat they meet. Unlike the highly sociable wolves that were forebears to modern dogs, the ancestors of cats were both solitary and territorial. As cats began their association with humankind some 10,000 years ago, their tolerance for one another must have been forced to improve so that they could live at the higher densities that man's provision of food for them – at first accidental, then deliberate – allowed.

Cats have yet to evolve the optimistic enthusiasm for contact with their own kind that characterizes dogs. As a result, many cats spend their lives trying to avoid contact with one another. All the while, their owners inadvertently compel them to live with cats they have no reason to trust – whether the neighbours' cats, or the second cat obtained by the owner to 'keep him company'. As their popularity increases, so inevitably does the number of cats that each cat is forced into contact with, thereby increasing the tensions that each experiences. Finding it ever harder to avoid social conflict, many cats find it nearly impossible to relax; the stress they experience affects their behaviour and even their health.

The well-being of many pet cats falls short of what it should be – perhaps because their welfare does not grab headlines in the way that dogs' does, or perhaps because they tend to suffer in silence. In 2011, a UK veterinary charity estimated that the average pet cat's physical and social environment scored only 64 per cent, with households that owned more than one cat scoring even lower. Owners' understanding of cat behaviour scored little better, at 66 per cent.[6] Without a doubt, if cat owners understood more about what makes their cats 'tick', many cats could live much happier lives.

Faced with such pressures, cats do not need our immediate emotional reactions – irrespective of whether we find them endearing or not – but instead a better understanding of what they want from us. Dogs are expressive; their wagging tails and bouncy greetings tell us in no uncertain terms when they are happy, and they do not hesitate to let us know when they are distressed. Cats, on the other hand, are undemonstrative; they keep their feelings to themselves and rarely tell us what they need, beyond asking for food when they're hungry. Even purring, long assumed to be an unequivocal sign of contentment, is now known to have a more complex significance. Dogs certainly benefit from the knowledge of their true natures that can come only from science, but for cats this comprehension is essential, for they rarely communicate their problems to us until these have become too much to bear. Most of all, cats require our assistance when, as happens far too often, their social lives run awry.

Cats desperately need the kind of research from which dogs have benefited, but unfortunately feline science has not seen the explosion of activity that has recently occurred in canine science. Cats have simply not grabbed the attention of scientists as dogs have. However, the past two decades have provided significant advances, profoundly affecting scientists' interpretations of how cats view the world, and what makes them tick. These exciting discoveries form the core of this book, giving us the first indications on how to help cats adjust to the many demands we now put on them.

Cats have adapted themselves to live alongside people while at the same time retaining much of their wild behaviour. Apart from the minority that belong to a breed, cats are not humankind's creation in the sense that dogs are; rather, they have co-evolved with us, moulding themselves into two niches that we have unintentionally provided for them. The first role for cats in human society was that of pest controller: some 10,000 years ago, wild cats moved in to exploit the concentrations of rodents provided by our first granaries, and adapted themselves to hunting there in preference to the surrounding countryside. Realizing how beneficial this was – cats, after all, had no interest in eating grain and plant foods themselves – people must have begun to encourage cats to stay by making available their occasional surpluses of animal products, such as milk and offal. The cats' second role, which undoubtedly followed hard on the heels of the first but whose origins are lost in antiquity, is that of companion. The first good evidence that we have for pet cats comes from Egypt some 4,000 years ago, but women and children in particular may well have adopted kittens as pets long before this.

Over the past few decades these dual roles of pest controller and companion have abruptly ceased to go hand-in-hand. Although until recently we treasured cats for their prowess as hunters, few owners today express delight when their cat deposits a dead mouse on their kitchen floor.

Cats carry the legacy of their primal pasts, and much of their behaviour still reflects their wild instincts. To understand why a cat behaves as it does, we must understand where it came from and the influences that have moulded it into what it is today. Therefore, the first three chapters of this book chart the cat's evolution from wild, solitary hunter to high-rise apartment-dweller. Unlike dogs, only a small minority of cats has ever been intentionally bred by people – and furthermore, when there has been deliberate breeding, it has been exclusively for appearance. No one has bred cats to guard houses, to herd livestock, or to accompany or assist hunters. Instead, cats have evolved to fill a niche brought about by the development of agriculture, from its beginnings in the harvest and storage of wild grains, to today's mechanized agribusiness.

Of course, when the cat first infiltrated our settlements many thousands of years ago, its other qualities did not go unnoticed. Its appealing features, its childlike face and eyes, the softness of its fur, and, crucially, its ability to learn how to become affectionate towards us led to its adoption as a pet. Subsequently, humankind's passion for symbolism and mysticism elevated the cat to iconic status. Popular attitudes towards cats have been profoundly influenced by such connotations: extreme religious views towards cats have affected not only how they were treated, but their very biology – both how they behave and how they look.

Cats have changed to live alongside humans, but cats and people have very different ways of gathering information about and then interpreting the physical world that we superficially share. Chapters 4 to 6 examine those differences: humans and cats are both mammals, but our senses and brains work in different ways. Cat owners often underappreciate these differences: our natural tendency is to interpret the world around us as if it were the only objective reality. Even in today's world of rationality and science, we still treat the world as if it were sentient, attributing intention to the weather, the sea and the stars in the sky. How easy it is, therefore, to fall into the trap of thinking that because cats are communicative and affectionate, they must be, more or less, little furry humans.

Science, however, reveals that cats are anything but. Beginning with the way that every kitten constructs its own version of the world, with consequences that will last its entire lifetime, this part of the book describes how the cat gathers information about its surroundings, especially the way it uses its hypersensitive sense of smell; how its brain interprets and uses that information; and how its emotions guide its responses to opportunities and challenges alike. In scientific circles, it has only recently become acceptable to talk about animal emotions, and one school of thought still maintains that emotions are a byproduct of consciousness, meaning that no animals except humans and possibly a few primates can possibly possess them. However, common sense dictates that if an animal that shares our basic brain structure and hormone systems looks frightened, it must be experiencing something very like fear – probably not in quite the same way that we experience it, but fear nonetheless.

Most (but not everything) of what biology has revealed about the cat's world fits the idea that cats have evolved as predators first and foremost. Cats are social animals too; otherwise, they could never have become pets as well as hunters. The demands of domestication – first of all, the need to cohabitate with other cats in human settlements, and then the benefits of forming affectionate bonds with people – have extended cats' social repertoires out of all recognition compared to those of their wild ancestors. Chapters 7 to 9 explore these social connections in detail: how cats conceive of and interact with other cats and with people, and why two cats may react very differently in the same situation. In other words, we will examine the science of cat 'personality'.

The book concludes with an examination of the cat's current place in the world, and how this might evolve in the coming decades. Cats are under pressure from many different interests, some well-meaning and others antagonistic. Pedigree cats are still in a minority, and those who breed them are in a position to avoid the practices that have so adversely affected the welfare of pedigree dogs over the past few decades.[7] However, the growing fashion for hybrids between domestic cats and other, wild, species of cat, resulting in 'breeds' such as the Bengal, can have unintended consequences. We must also ask whether the cat is being inadvertently and subtly altered by those who hold cat welfare closest to their hearts. Paradoxically, the drive to neuter as many cats as possible, with its laudable aim of reducing the suffering of unwanted kittens, may be gradually eliminating the characteristics of the very cats best suited to living in harmony with humankind: many of the cats that avoid neutering are those that are most suspicious of people and the best at hunting. The friendliest, most docile cats are nowadays neutered before leaving any descendants, while the wildest, meanest ferals are likely to escape the attention of cat rescuers and breed at will, thus pushing the cat's evolution away from, rather than towards, better integration with human society.

We are in danger of demanding more from our cats than they can deliver. We expect that an animal that has been our pest controller of choice for thousands of years should now give up that lifestyle because we have begun to find its consequences distasteful or unacceptable. We also expect that we should be free to choose our cat's companions and neighbours without regard for their origins as solitary, territorial animals. Somehow, we seem to presume that because dogs can be flexible in their choice of canine companions, cats will be equally tolerant of whatever relationships we expect them to develop, purely for our convenience.

Until about twenty or thirty years ago, cats kept pace with human demands, but they are now struggling to adapt to our expectations, especially that they should no longer hunt, and no longer desire to roam away from home. In contrast to almost every other domestic animal, whose breeding has been strictly controlled for many generations past, the cat's transition from wild to domestic has – with the exception of pedigree cats – been driven by natural selection. Cats have essentially evolved to fit opportunities that we provided. We allowed them to find their own mates, and those kittens that were best suited to living alongside humans, in whatever capacity was required of them at the time, were the most likely to thrive and produce the next generation.

Evolution is not going to produce a cat that has no urge to hunt and that is as socially tolerant as a dog – at least not within a timescale that will be acceptable to the cat's detractors. Ten thousand years of natural selection have provided the cat with enough flexibility to fend for itself when, from time to time, its compact with man breaks down, but not enough to cope with a demand that has grown from nowhere in just a few years. Even for such a prolific breeder as the cat, natural selection would take many generations to move even a token step in this direction. Only deliberate, carefully considered breeding can produce cats that are well suited to the demands of tomorrow's owners, and that will be more acceptable to cat haters.

As well as changing their genetics, we can also do much to improve the lot of cats today. Better socialization of kittens, better understanding of what environments cats really need, more deliberate intervention in teaching cats to cope with situations that they find distressing – all these can help cats to adjust to the demands we now make of them, and can also deepen the bond between cat and owner.

Cats are in many ways the ideal pet for the twenty-first century, but will they be able to adapt to the twenty-second? If they are to continue to remain in our affections – and the persecution they have received in the past indicates that this can hardly be a given – then some consensus must emerge among cat welfare charities, conservationists, and cat-fanciers on how to produce a type of cat that ticks all the boxes. These changes must be guided by science. Initially, the way forward will be for cat owners and the general public alike to understand better where cats came from and why they behave as they do. At the same time, owners can rehabilitate the cat's fraying reputation by learning how to channel their cat's behaviour, not only to discourage them from hunting, but also to make them happier in themselves. In the longer term, the emerging science of behavioural genetics – the mechanics of how behaviour and 'personality' are inherited – will allow us to breed cats that can better adapt to an ever more crowded world.

As history shows, cats can fend for themselves in many ways. However, they cannot face what society now demands of them without human assistance. Our understanding of cats must start with a healthy respect for their essential natures.

I

The Cat at the Threshold

Pet cats are now a global phenomenon, but how they transformed themselves from wild to domestic is still a mystery. Most of the animals around us were domesticated for prosaic, practical reasons. Cows, sheep and goats provide meat, milk and hides. Pigs provide meat; chickens, meat and eggs. Dogs, our second favourite pet, continue to provide humans with many benefits beside companionship: help with hunting, herding, guarding, tracking and trailing, to name but a few. Cats are not nearly as useful as any of these; even their traditional reputation as rodent controllers may be somewhat exaggerated, even though, historically, this was their obvious function as far as humankind was concerned. Therefore, in contrast to the dog, we have no easy answers as to how the cat has insinuated itself so effectively into human culture. Our search for explanations must start some ten millennia ago, when cats probably first arrived at our doorsteps.

Conventional accounts of the domestication of the cat, based on archaeological and historical records, propose that they first lived in human homes in Egypt about 3,500 years ago. This theory, however, has recently been challenged by new evidence coming from the field of molecular biology. Examination of differences between the DNA of today's domestic and wild cats has dated their origins much earlier, anywhere between 10,000 and 15,000 years ago (8000 and 13,000 years BCE). We can safely discount the earliest date in this range – anything earlier than about 15,000 years ago makes little sense in terms of the evolution of our own species, since it is unlikely that stone-age hunter-gatherers would have had the need or resources to keep cats. The minimum estimate, 10,000 years, presumes that domestic cats are derived from several wild ancestors that came from several different locations in the Middle East. In other words, the domestication of the cat happened in several widely separated places, either roughly contemporaneously or over a longer period of time. Even if we assume that cats started to become domesticated around 8000 years BCE, this leaves us with a 6,500-year interval before the first historical records of domestic cats appear in Egypt. So far, few scientists of any kind have studied this first – and longest – phase in the partnership between human and cat.

The archaeological record for this period, such as it is, is not very illuminating. Cats' teeth and fragments of bones dating between 7000 and 6000 BCE have been excavated around the Palestinian city of Jericho and elsewhere in the Fertile Crescent, the 'cradle of civilization' that extended from Iraq through Jordan and Syria to the eastern shores of the Mediterranean and Egypt. However, these fragments are uncommon; moreover, they could well have come from wild cats, perhaps killed for their pelts. Rock paintings and statuettes of catlike animals from the following millennia, discovered in what are now Israel and Jordan, could conceivably depict domesticated cats; however, these cats are not depicted in domestic settings, so they may well be representations of wild cats, possibly even big cats. Yet even if we assume that these pieces of evidence all refer to early forms of the domestic cat, their very rarity still must be explained. By 8000 BCE, humankind's relationship with the domestic dog had already progressed to the extent that dogs were routinely buried alongside their masters in several parts of Asia, Europe and North America, whereas burials of cats first became common in Egypt around 1000 BCE.[1] If cats were indeed domesticated pets during this time, we should have far more tangible evidence of that relationship than has been uncovered.

Our best clues on how the partnership between man and cat began come not from the Fertile Crescent, but instead from Cyprus. Cyprus is one of the few Mediterranean islands that have never been joined to the mainland, even when that sea was at its lowest level. Consequently, its animal population has had to migrate there by flying or swimming – that is, until humans started to travel there in primitive boats some 12,000 years ago. At that point, the Eastern Mediterranean had no domesticated animals, with the likely exception of some early dogs, so the animals that made the crossing with those first human settlers must have been either individually tamed wild animals or inadvertent hitchhikers. Therefore, while we cannot possibly tell whether ancient remains of cats on the mainland are from wild, tame or domesticated animals, cats could clearly have reached Cyprus only by being deliberately transported there by humans – assuming, as we safely may, that cats of that era were as averse to swimming in the ocean as today's cats are. Any remains of cats found there must be those of semi-domesticated or at least captive animals, or their descendants.

On Cyprus, the earliest remains of cats coincide with and are found within the first permanent human settlements, about 7500 years BCE, making it highly likely that they were deliberately transported there. Cats are too large and conspicuous to have been accidentally transported across the Mediterranean in the small boats of the time: we know very little about seagoing boats from that period, but they were probably too small to conceal a stowaway cat. Moreover, we have no evidence for cats living away from human habitations on Cyprus for another 3,000 years. The most likely scenario, then, is that the earliest settlers of Cyprus brought with them wildcats that they had captured and tamed on the mainland. It is implausible that they were the only people to have thought of taming wildcats, so it is feasible that capturing cats and taming them was already an established practice in the Eastern Mediterranean. Confirming this, we also have evidence for prehistoric importations of tamed cats to other large Mediterranean islands, such as Crete, Sardinia and Majorca.

The most likely reason for taming wildcats is also evident from the first settlements on Cyprus. Right from the outset, these habitations, like their counterparts of the time on the mainland, became infested by house mice. Presumably these unwanted mice *were* stowaways, accidentally transported across the Mediterranean in sacks of food or seed corn. The most convincing scenario, therefore, is that as soon as mice became established on Cyprus, the colonizers imported tame or semi-domesticated cats to keep them under control. This might have been ten years or a hundred years after the first settlements were established – the archaeological record cannot reveal such small differences. If this is correct, it suggests that the practice of taming cats to control mice was already entrenched on the mainland as long as 10,000 years ago. No firm evidence for this is ever likely to be found, because the ubiquitous presence of wildcats there makes it impossible to tell whether the remains of a cat, even if found within a settlement, are those of a truly wild cat that had died or been killed when hunting there, or of a cat that had lived there for most or all of its life.

Whatever its exact origins, the tradition of taming wildcats to control vermin continued into modern times, in parts of Africa where domestic cats are scarce and wildcats easy to obtain. While travelling the White Nile in 1869, the German botanist-explorer Georg Schweinfurth found that his boxes of botanical specimens were being invaded by rodents during the night. He recalled:

> One of the commonest animals hereabouts was the wild cat of the steppes. Although the natives do not breed them as domestic animals, yet they catch them separately when they are quite young and find no difficulty in reconciling them to a life about their huts and enclosures, where they grow up and wage their natural warfare against the rats. I procured several of these cats, which, after they had been kept tied up for several days, seemed to lose a considerable measure of their ferocity and to adapt themselves to an indoor existence so as to approach in many ways to the habits of the common cat. By night I attached them to my parcels, which were otherwise in jeopardy, and by this means I could go to bed without further fear of any depredations from the rats.[2]

Like Schweinfurth, those much earlier explorers who first brought wildcats to Cyprus would almost certainly have found that they had to keep their cats tethered. If allowed to run free, the cats would have quickly escaped and wreaked havoc on the native fauna, which up to that point would have had no experience with a predator as formidable as a cat. We know that this is what eventually happened. Several centuries after human settlement, cats indistinguishable from wildcats spread throughout Cyprus and remained there for several thousand years.[3] Most likely, only the cats that were confined to the grain stores would have stayed there to help the early settlers to rid those stores of pests: the others would have left to exploit the local wildlife. The descendants of these escapees may have been captured and even eaten from time to time, since broken cat bones have been found at several other Neolithic sites on Cyprus, as well as those of other predators such as foxes and even domestic dogs.

The practice of taming wildcats to control vermin was probably prompted by the emergence of a new pest in the early granaries, the house mouse (*Mus musculus*); indeed, the histories of these two animals are inextricably interwoven. The house mouse is one of more than thirty species of mouse found worldwide, but the only one that has adapted to living alongside humans and exploiting our food.

House mice have their origins in a wild species from somewhere in northern India that was in existence possibly as long as a million years ago, certainly well before the evolution of humankind. From there they spread both east and west, feeding on wild grains, until some reached the Fertile Crescent, where they eventually encountered the earliest stores of harvested grain: mouse teeth have been found among stored grain dating back 11,000 years in Israel, and a 9,500-year-old stone pendant carved in the shape of a mouse's head was found in Syria. Thus began an association with humankind that continues to the present day. Humans not only provided an abundance of food that mice could exploit, but our buildings also provided both warm, dry places to build nests and protection from predators such as wildcats. Mice that could adapt to these living conditions thrived, while those that could not died out: today's house mice rarely breed successfully away from human habitation, especially where there are wild competitors, such as wood mice.

Humans also provided house mice with a way to colonize new areas. Mice from the south-eastern part of the Fertile Crescent, what is now Syria and northern Iraq, were accidentally transported, presumably in grain being traded between communities, throughout the Near East, up to the eastern shores of the Mediterranean, and then to nearby islands such as Cyprus.

The first culture to be bedevilled by house mice was that of the Natufians, who by extension are the people most likely to have initiated the cat's long journey into our homes. The Natufians inhabited the area that now comprises Israel–Palestine, Jordan, south-western Syria and southern Lebanon from about 11,000 to 8000 BCE. Widely regarded as the inventors of agriculture, they were initially hunter-gatherers like other inhabitants of the region; soon, however, they began to specialize in harvesting the wild cereals that grew abundantly all around them, in a region that was significantly more productive then than it is today. To do this, the Natufians invented the sickle. Sickle blades found at Natufian settlements still show the glossy surfaces that could have been produced only from scything through the abrasive stems of wild grains – wheat, barley and rye.

The early Natufians lived in small villages; their houses were partly below ground, partly above, with walls and floors of stone and brushwood roofs. Until about 10,800 BCE, they rarely planted cereals deliberately, but over the next 1,300 years a rapid change in climate, known as the Younger Dryas, brought about a significant intensification in field-clearing, planting and cultivation. As the amounts of harvested grain increased, so did the need for storage. The Natufians and their successors probably used storage pits built out of mudbrick and constructed like miniature versions of their houses. It was probably this invention that triggered the self-domestication of the house mouse, which, moving into this rich and novel environment, thereby became humankind's first mammalian pest species.

As the numbers of mice grew, they must have attracted the attentions of their natural predators, including foxes, jackals, birds of prey, the Natufians' domestic dogs and, of course, wildcats. Wildcats had two advantages that set them apart from other predators of mice: they were both agile and nocturnal, well adapted to hunting in the near-darkness when the mice became active. However, if these wildcats had been as frightened of man as their modern counterparts are, it is difficult to imagine how they would have exploited this new rich source of food. Almost certainly, therefore, the wildcats in the region inhabited by the Natufians were less wary than those of today.

We have no evidence that the Natufians deliberately domesticated the cat. Like the mouse before it, the cat simply arrived to exploit a new resource that had been created by the beginnings of agriculture. As Natufian agriculture became more complex, involving both an increasing array of crops and the domestication of animals such as sheep and goats, and as agriculture extended to other regions and cultures, so the opportunities available for cats multiplied. These were

THE EVOLUTION OF THE CATS

Every member of the cat family, from the noble lion to the tiny black-footed cat, can trace its ancestry back to a medium-sized catlike animal, Pseudaelurus, *that roamed the steppes of central Asia some 11 million years ago.* Pseudaelurus *eventually went extinct, but not before unusually low sea levels had allowed it to migrate across what is now the Red Sea into Africa, where it evolved into several medium-sized cats, including those we know today as the caracal and the serval. Other* Pseudaelurus *travelled east across the Bering land bridge into North America, where they eventually evolved into the bobcat, lynx and puma. Some 2–3 million years ago, following the formation of the Panama isthmus, the first cats crossed into South America; here they evolved in isolation, forming several species not found anywhere else, including the ocelot and Geoffroy's cat. The big cats – lions, tigers, jaguars and leopards – evolved in Asia and then spread into both Europe and North America, their present-day distributions but a tiny relict of where they used to roam a few million years ago. Remarkably, the distant ancestors of today's domestic cats seem to have evolved in North America about 8 million years ago, and then migrated back into Asia some 2 million years later. About 3 million years ago, these began to evolve into the species we know today, including the wildcat, the sand cat and the jungle cat; a separate Asian lineage, including Pallas's cat and the fishing cat, also began to diverge at about this time.*[4]

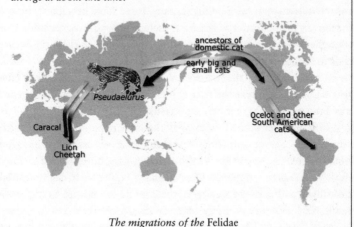

The migrations of the Felidae

not pet cats as we know them today; rather, the cats that exploited these concentrations of mice would have been more like today's urban foxes – capable of adapting to a human environment, but still retaining their essential wildness. Domestication was to come much later.

We know surprisingly little about the wildcats of the Fertile Crescent and surrounding areas (see box, p. 17, 'The Evolution of the Cats'). The archaeological record indicates that 10,000 years ago several species lived in the region, all of which would have been attracted by concentrations of mice. We know that later on, the ancient Egyptians kept tame jungle cats, *Felis chaus*, in considerable numbers; jungle cats, though, are substantially heavier than wildcats, weighing between ten and twenty pounds, and large enough to kill young gazelle and chital. Although their normal diet includes rodents, they may have been too obtrusive to get regular access to granaries. Alternatively, they may simply have been temperamentally unsuited to living alongside man. We do have evidence that the Egyptians tried to tame and even train them as rodent controllers, but apparently without any lasting success.

Coeval with them were sand cats, *Felis margarita*, large-eared nocturnal animals that hunt by night, using their acute hearing. They are, moreover, comparatively unafraid of humans, and hence might be thought good candidates for taming and domestication. However, they are made for life in deserts – the pads on their feet are covered in thick fur to protect them from the hot sand – so few would have found themselves near the first stores of grains: the Natufians generally built their villages in wooded areas.

As civilization spread eastwards through Asia, so it would have come into contact with other cat species. At Chanhudaro, a town built by the Harappan civilization close to the Indus River in what is now Pakistan, archaeologists found a 5,000-year-old mudbrick imprinted with a cat's foot, overlapped by that of a dog. As the newly made brick was drying in the sun, the cat appears to have run across it, closely followed by a dog, possibly in hot pursuit. The footprint is larger than that of a domestic cat, and its webbed feet and extended claws identify it as a fishing cat, *Felis viverrina*, found today from the Indus basin eastwards and south to Sumatra in Indonesia (though not

Jungle cat

Sand cat

in the Fertile Crescent). As its name implies, the fishing cat is a strong swimmer and specializes in catching fish and aquatic birds. Although it will also take small rodents, it is difficult to see how it would switch to a diet consisting predominantly of mice, so it too is an unlikely candidate for domestication.

Farther afield, we know of at least two other species of cat that came in out of the wild to prey on the vermin that plagued humankind's food stores. In Central Asia and ancient China, the local wildcat, the manul (or Pallas's cat, named after the German naturalist who first categorized it) was occasionally even tamed and deliberately kept as a rodent controller. The manul has the shaggiest coat of any member of the cat family, so long that its hair almost completely obscures its ears. In pre-Columbian Central America, meanwhile, an otter-like cat, the jaguarundi, was probably also kept as a semi-tame pest controller. None of these species have ever become fully domesticated; nor are any of them included in the direct ancestry of today's house cats.

Out of all these various wild cats, only one was successfully domesticated. This honour goes to the Arabian wildcat *Felis silvestris lybica*,[5] as confirmed by its DNA. In the past, both scientists and cat-fanciers have suggested that certain breeds within the domestic cat family are hybrids with other species – for example, the Persian's fluffy feet are superficially similar to the sand cat's, and its fine coat is somewhat like that of a manul. However, the DNA of all domestic cats – random-bred, Siamese or Persian – shows no trace of these other species, or indeed any other admixture. Somehow, the Arabian wildcat alone was able to inveigle itself into human society, outcompeting all its rivals, and eventually spreading throughout the world. Although the qualities that gave it this edge are not easy to pin down, they probably occurred in combination only in the wildcats of the Middle East.

The wildcat *Felis silvestris* is currently found throughout Europe, Africa and central Asia, as well as western Asia, the area where it probably first evolved. Like many predators, such as the wolf, it is now found only in isolated and generally remote areas where it can avoid persecution from man. This has not always been the case. Five

Manul

Jaguarundi

thousand years ago, wildcats were evidently regarded as delicacies in some areas; the rubbish pits left by the 'lake dwellers' of Germany and Switzerland contain many wildcat bones.[6] The cats must have been abundant at the time; otherwise, they could hardly have been trapped in such large numbers. Over the centuries they became less common, displaced by the felling of their forest habitat for agriculture, and forced farther into the woods by development and loss of habitat. The invention of firearms led to wildcats being hunted to extinction in many areas. During the nineteenth century, various European countries, including the UK, Germany and Switzerland,[7] classified them as vermin, due to the harm they supposedly caused both wildlife and livestock. Only recently, due to the establishment of wildlife reserves and a more informed attitude to the important role that predators play in stabilizing ecosystems, are wildcats returning to areas such as Bavaria, where they have not been seen for hundreds of years.

The wildcat is now divided into four subspecies or races. These are the European forest cat *Felis silvestris silvestris*, the Arabian wildcat *Felis silvestris lybica*, the Southern African wildcat *Felis silvestris cafra*, and the Indian desert cat *Felis silvestris ornata*.[8] All these cats are rather similar in appearance, and all are capable of interbreeding where their ranges overlap. A possible fifth subspecies is the very rare Chinese desert cat *Felis bieti*, which according to its DNA split off from the main wildcat lineage about a quarter of a million years ago. It's possible that these cats actually form a separate species, as no hybrids are known to exist, but they live in such a small and inaccessible region – part of the Chinese province of Sichuan – that this may be due to lack of opportunity rather than physical impossibility.

Wildcats from different parts of the world differ markedly in how easily they can be tamed. Domestication, moreover, can start only with animals that are already tame enough to raise their young in the proximity of people. Those offspring that are best suited to the company of humans and human environments are, perhaps unsurprisingly, more likely to stay and breed there than those that are not; the latter will most likely revert to the wild. Over several generations, this repeated 'natural' selection will, even on its own, gradually change the genetic makeup of these animals so that they become better adapted to life alongside people. It is also likely that, at the same time, humans will intensify that selection by feeding the more docile animals and driving away those prone to bite and scratch. This process cannot start without some genetic basis for tameness existing beforehand, and in the case of wildcats, this is far from evenly distributed. Today, some parts of the world have little raw material for domestication, while others seem more promising.

We know, for example, that the four subspecies of wildcat differ in how easy they are to tame. The European forest cat is larger and thicker-set than a typical domestic cat, and has a characteristic short tail with a blunt, black tip. This aside, it looks from a distance much like a domestic striped tabby – a distant glimpse is all that most people

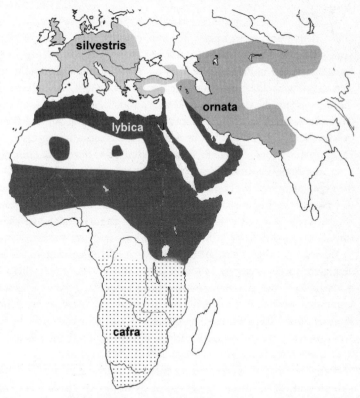

The historical distribution of the subspecies of wildcat

can hope ever to get, however, for it is among the wildest of animals. This is largely due to its genetics, and not the way it is raised: those few people who have tried to produce tame forest cats have met with precious little but rejection. In 1936, natural and wildlife photographer Frances Pitt wrote:

> It has long been stated that the European wildcat is untameable. There was a time when I did not believe this ... My optimism was daunted when I made acquaintance with Beelzebina, Princess of Devils. She came from the Highlands of Scotland, a half-grown kitten that spat and scratched in fiercest resentment. Her pale green eyes glared savage hatred at human-beings, and all attempts to establish friendly relations with her failed. She grew less afraid, but as her timidity departed, her savagery increased.[9]

Pitt then went on to obtain an even younger male kitten, in the hope that Beelzebina had been too old to be socialized when first found. That she named this new kitten Satan perhaps suggests how difficult he was to handle from the outset. As he grew stronger and more confident, he became impossible to touch; he would take food from the hand, but would spit and growl while doing so, and then quickly back away. However, he was not pathologically aggressive – he just hated people. While he was still young, Pitt introduced him to a female domestic kitten, Beauty, towards whom he was 'all gentleness and devotion'. When she was let out of the cage in which he had to be kept, 'this distressed him sorely. He rent the air with harsh cries, for his voice, though loud, was not lovely.' Beauty and Satan produced several litters of kittens, all of which had the characteristic appearance of forest cats. Some, despite being handled from an early age, grew to be as savage as their father; others were more sociable towards Pitt and her parents, though all remained very wary of unfamiliar people. Pitt's experiences of Scottish wildcats seem to be typical: Mike Tomkies, the 'Wilderness Man', was also unable to socialize his two hand-raised wildcat sisters, Cleo and Patra, which he kept at his remote cottage on the shores of a Scottish loch.[10]

We know little about the Indian desert cat, but it is reputedly difficult to tame. This subspecies is found to the south and east of the

Caspian Sea, southwards through Pakistan and into the north-western Indian states of Gujarat, Rajasthan and the Punjab, and eastwards through Kazakhstan into Mongolia. Its coat is usually paler than that of the other wildcats, and is blotchy rather than tabby in pattern. Like other wildcats, it will occasionally base itself near farms, attracted by the concentration of rodents, but it has never taken the next step to domestication – acceptance of humans. We have records from Harappa of tamed caracals, a medium-sized, long-limbed cat with characteristic tufted ears, and jungle cats, to add to the fishing cat that left its footprint there; but we find no indications of any Indian desert cats. For a long time biologists and cat-fanciers alike thought that Siamese cats could be a mixture of domestic and Indian desert cat, the progeny of interbreeding between early domestic cats and local wildcats somewhere around the Indus valley. However, scientists have not found the characteristic DNA signature of the Indian desert cat in any examples of the Siamese and related breeds, which instead are ultimately derived from the wildcats of the Middle East or Egypt – there are no *silvestris* wildcats in South-East Asia, so the original cats of Siam must have been imported from the west as fully domesticated animals.

The wildcats of South Africa and Namibia – 'caffre cats' – are likewise genetically distinctive. They migrated south from the original wildcat population in northern Africa about 175,000 years ago, around the same time as the ancestors of the Indian desert cat migrated east. It is unclear where the boundary between the Southern African and Arabian wildcats lies – no wildcat's DNA has yet been characterized from any part of Africa except Namibia and the Republic of South Africa. The wildcats of Nigeria are shy, aggressive and difficult to tame; those of Uganda are sometimes more tolerant of people, but many do not look like typical wildcats – which in that area have distinctive red-brown backs to their ears – and are probably hybrids, their domesticated genes accounting for their friendly behaviour. Most of the street cats in the same region show signs of some wildcat in their ancestry, so the distinction between wildcat, street cat and random-bred pet is blurred in many parts of Africa.

The wildcats of Zimbabwe – presumably belonging to the Southern

African subspecies – are a case in point. In the 1960s, naturalist and museum director Reay Smithers kept two hand-reared female wildcats, Goro and Komani, at his home in what was then Southern Rhodesia.[11] Both were tame enough to be let out of their pens, though only one at a time, since they would fight whenever they met. Once, Komani disappeared for four months, finally reappearing one evening in the beam of Smithers's flashlight: 'I called my wife, to whom she is particularly attached, and we sat down while she softly called the cat's name. It must have taken a quarter of an hour before Komani suddenly responded and came to her. The reunion was most moving, Komani going into transports of purring and rubbing herself against my wife's legs.'

Such behaviour is identical to that of a pet cat being reunited with its owner, and the similarities with pet cats did not end there. Both Goro and Komani were affectionate towards Smithers's dogs, rubbing themselves on their legs and curling up in front of the fire with them. Every day they demonstrated their affection for Smithers himself by an effusive display of typical pet cat behaviour.

> These cats never do anything by halves; for instance when returning from their day out they are inclined to become super-affectionate. When this happens, one might as well give up what one is doing, for they will walk all over the paper you are writing on, rubbing themselves against your face or hands; or they will jump on your shoulder and insinuate themselves between your face and the book you are reading, roll on it, purring and stretching themselves, sometimes falling off in their enthusiasm and, in general, demanding your undivided attention.

This may be the behaviour of a typical hand-reared 'caffre cat', but it is more likely that Goro and Komani, while undoubtedly wildcats in terms of their markings and their hunting ability, nevertheless contained some DNA from interbreeding with pet cats somewhere in their ancestry. The extent of hybridization between wildcats and domestic cats in South Africa and Namibia was recently revealed by DNA sequences from twenty-four supposed wildcats, eight of which bore the telltale signs of partial descent from domestic cats. In a survey of zoos in the United States, the UK and the Republic of South Africa, I found that ten out of twelve South African wildcats displayed affectionate behaviour towards their keepers, and of these, two would regularly rub and lick them.[12] This kind of behaviour strongly suggests that the latter were hybrids, while those that could not be handled at all were probably genuine wildcats. The eight that were moderately affectionate might have been either.

Hybridization between wildcats and domestic cats is not confined to Africa. In one study, five out of seven wildcats collected in Mongolia carried traces of domestic cat DNA; only two were 'pure' Indian desert cat. In my survey of cats in zoos, I found that out of a dozen cats of this subspecies kept in captivity, only three had ever spontaneously approached their keepers, and only one had ever rubbed on its keeper's leg. From the proportions found in the DNA results, it seems highly likely that all of these were hybrids, even though they all looked like typical Indian desert cats. In the same study of wildcat DNA, almost a third of apparent 'wildcats' sampled in France had some ancestry from domestic pets.[13] With the advent of DNA technology, it is easy to detect hybridization when the local wildcats are genetically distinct from domestic cats – as they are in Southern Africa, central Asia and western Europe alike. Defining what is wild and what is a hybrid is much more problematic in places where domestic cats and wild cats are genetically almost identical, as they are around the Fertile Crescent, home of the Arabian wildcat.

The Arabian wildcat *lybica* is not only the most similar to domestic cats, it is also probably the nearest living representative of the first *Felis silvestris*, all the other subspecies having evolved hundreds of thousands of years ago – a consequence of small numbers of animals migrating east, south or west from the species' origin in the Middle East. The wildcats in Africa north of the Sahara are also probably *lybica*, but their DNA has not yet been tested to confirm this. Like all wildcats, the Arabian/North African wildcat has a 'mackerel'-striped tabby coat, varying in colour from grey to brown – darkest in forest-dwelling animals, palest in those that live on the edges of deserts. It is generally larger and leaner than a typical domestic cat, and both its tail and legs are especially long; indeed, the front legs are so long that when it sits, its posture is characteristically upright, as depicted by the ancient Egyptians in statues of the cat goddess Bastet. While generally nocturnal and therefore rarely seen, it is not particularly rare. Although it is widely claimed that the Arabian wildcat's kittens, if hand-raised, become affectionate towards people, most eyewitness accounts come from central or Southern Africa, and therefore probably refer to *cafra* rather than *lybica*. The explorer Georg Schweinfurth procured his tame wildcats in what is now Southern Sudan, roughly where the ranges of *lybica* and *cafra* merge together, and the most northerly location in Africa to yield reliable accounts of tameable wildcats.

Very little is known of the behaviour of genuine *lybica* wildcats, either in the Middle East or north-east Africa. In the 1990s, conservationist David Macdonald radio-collared six wildcats on the Thumamah reserve in central Saudi Arabia. All except one kept their distance from human activity: the sixth, however, 'often wandered into the vicinity of the pigeon house [in Thumamah town] and would often be found sleeping with the domestic cats in the yard of one of the houses. On one occasion he was seen mating with a [domestic] cat.'[14] Apart from showing just how easily hybridization between wild and domestic cats can occur, these and other observations shed little light on whether the wildcats in this part of the world might have been easy to tame, thousands of years ago.

Tracing the precise geographic origin of the domestic cat is therefore far from easy, for if the archaeological evidence is inconclusive, so is the most recent DNA evidence. The domestic cat's genetic footprint has spread throughout the world and, because it interbreeds so readily, it is now found almost universally in what are, to all outward appearances, 'wildcats'. This is true wherever wildcats have been investigated, from Scotland in the north, to Mongolia in the east, to the southern tip of Africa. Many of these apparent 'wildcats' have DNA characteristic of domestic cats and must therefore be mainly or entirely descended from domestic cats that have gone feral. Others have a mixture – part wildcat DNA, part domestic. Of thirty-six wildcats sampled in France, twenty-three had 'pure' wildcat DNA, eight were indistinguishable from domestic cats, and five were evidently a

The Arabian wildcat – Felis lybica

mixture of the two. The techniques used are sensitive enough only to detect the major contributions to each cat's ancestry: a cat with one domestic and fifteen wild great-great-grandparents, for example, would probably show up as 'pure' wildcat.

Bearing all this in mind, there must be very few entirely 'pure' *Felis silvestris* wildcats left anywhere in the world. At least a millennium of contact between wildcat and domestic cat – and four to ten times as long in the Middle East – means that there must be at least one hybrid in virtually every free-living cat's ancestry. At one extreme, some are domestic pets that have taken to the wild and happen to have the right 'mackerel' coat, such that if they are hit by a vehicle or trapped in some remote area, they are labelled as wildcats – only a sample of their DNA gives away their true identity. At the other end of the spectrum, some wildcats' ancestry might extend back several hundred generations before a domestic type crops up in their otherwise 'unblemished' family tree.

For conservationists anxious to preserve the wildcat in its pristine state, this is an inconvenient truth. In many places in Europe, wildcats are protected animals, and it is an offence to kill one deliberately: feral cats are not offered this status, and may even be treated as vermin. To be clear, a feral cat is a cat that is living wild but is descended from domestic cats: most are distinguishable from wildcats by their markings, which can be any colour found in domestic cats. How is the law to operate if there is no hard-and-fast genetic distinction between ferals and wildcats? The best answer is probably the pragmatic one: if a cat looks like a wildcat and behaves like a wildcat – that is, it lives by hunting rather than scavenging – then it probably is a wildcat, or near enough to a wildcat to make little difference. Domestic cats, even those that grow up in the wild and have to fend for themselves, are rarely as skilled at hunting as genuine wildcats. Furthermore, we can now identify the purest wildcats from their DNA, sampled from just a few hairs: individual cats might therefore be given special protected status in the confidence that they are not just domestic 'lookalikes'.

This near-universal hybridity makes it difficult to pinpoint the origin of the domestic cat – difficult, but not necessarily impossible. Wherever they originated, all the wildcats in that one location should have domestic-type DNA. Following some 4,000 years of coexistence, and presumably interbreeding, each will carry different proportions of wild and domestic genes, but these will be indistinguishable (except for the fifteen to twenty genes, so far unidentified, that make cats easier or harder to socialize to people; these must by definition be different between domestic cats and wildcats).[15] Unfortunately, largely due to the current turmoil in the Middle East and North Africa, it is difficult to obtain sufficient samples of DNA from wildcats in the Fertile Crescent and north-east Africa to probe this hypothesis fully. The most comprehensive study done so far was able to include samples from only two colonies of cats in southern Israel, three individuals collected in Saudi Arabia, and one in the United Arab Emirates. There were no samples from Lebanon, Jordan, Syria or Egypt;[16] nor were any included from North Africa – so even the cats from Libya that give *lybica* its name are still not definitively classified. Until there is more information about the DNA of cats from all these regions, it is impossible to use genetic information to say precisely where domestication began.

What the diversity of DNA among today's cats does suggest is that not just one but several populations of scavenging cats were domesticated. These several domestications may have been more or less contemporary, but it is more likely that they occurred hundreds or even thousands of years apart. We can be reasonably sure that none of those domestications took place in Europe, India or Southern Africa; otherwise, we would find traces of the DNA of wildcats from those regions in modern domestic cats. But precisely where in western Asia and/or north-east Africa those transformations took place awaits further research.

Using the available data, we can posit a convincing scenario, which is that cats were first tamed in one location, probably in the Middle East, for rodent control. The most likely area is therefore that inhabited by the Natufians, but they were not the only early grain-grinding culture in that part of the world. Even earlier, approximately 15,000 years ago in what is now Sudan and southern Egypt, the Qadan culture lived in fixed settlements and harvested wild grains in large quantities. However, some 4,000 years later, following a series of devastating floods in the Nile valley, they were displaced by hunter-gatherers, meaning that if they had tamed their local wildcats to protect their grain stores, this practice may have died out as their culture was destroyed. During roughly the same period, but further north, in the Nile valley, the Mushabians are thought to have independently developed some of the technologies that eventually led to agriculture, including food storage and the cultivation of figs. Again, they might feasibly have tamed wildcats to protect their food stores. About 14,000 years ago some Mushabians left Egypt and moved north-east into the Sinai desert, where, mixing with the local Kebaran people, they became the Natufians.[17] These migratory Mushabians apparently lived as nomadic hunter-gatherers, but it is possible that, even if they had no need or capacity to bring tame cats with them, they nevertheless brought an oral tradition of the usefulness of cats that was absorbed into the Natufian culture.

Even if we give the Natufians sole credit for the first domestication of the cat, the genetic diversity of today's cats must have resulted from domestication in more than one location. Wildcats from any one area tend to be genetically similar because they are territorial animals and rarely migrate. Flow of genes between regions is a very slow process – slow, that is, until more recently, due to humankind's intervention. We know that domestic cats are perfectly able, indeed eager, to mate with members of other subspecies of *Felis silvestris*, even those which, like the Scottish wildcat, have become genetically distinct following tens of thousands of years of separation from the domestic cat's wild ancestors in the Middle East. For some reason, the offspring of such liaisons, while themselves perfectly capable of reproducing, are rarely incorporated into the pet population nowadays; rather, those that survive adopt the wildcat lifestyle. Presumably there is some kind of genetic incompatibility in these hybrids that suppresses the full expression of the genes that would enable them to become socialized to people. Evidently no such incompatibility existed between the earliest domestic cats and the wildcats around them.

As humans began to take cats on their travels, so those cats would have encountered local wildcats belonging to the *lybica* subspecies, and assimilated some of their genes. With no biological barrier to mating, tame females must have been successfully courted by wildcat males. Sometimes, as has been seen recently among cats in Scotland, the resulting kittens would have taken after their father and been unhandleable. Occasionally, however, the kittens would have been easy to tame and stayed with their mother, fusing with the domestic population. This cannot account for all the genetic diversity in today's cats, however, because this process accounts only for new genetic material being introduced from male wildcats. Domestic cats bear the hallmarks of descent from many wildcat males, certainly, but also from about five different individual wildcat females, each of which can be located with some certainty in either the Middle East or North Africa.[18] It is possible that each of these five individuals was domesticated separately, each by a different culture in a different location, and that their descendants were subsequently – perhaps hundreds or even thousands of years later – traded among cultures, until all the genomes became mixed together. However, such an explanation may give too much agency in this process to humans and not enough to the cats themselves.

The ability of those early cats to interbreed with their wild neighbours is what gave them that extra genetic diversity. Every now and then, a tame, semi-domesticated male, lured by the scent and mating calls of a wild female, would have escaped and mated. A few of the resulting offspring could have carried the right genes to be easily tamable; some of these might have been found and adopted as pets by local women or children, and then raised to mate with other domestic cat males. This need not have happened very often: only four or five of these, in addition to the original founding female, have their descendants in today's pets.

The prehistory of the cat is thus the result of many fortuitous interactions between human intent, human affection for cute animals and cat biology. It was a far more haphazard process than the domestications of other animals – sheep, goats, cattle and pigs – that took place at the same time. Domestic dogs of different types were already emerging, showing that people of the time could channel their domestic animals into forms that were more useful and easier to handle than their predecessors. Yet, for thousands of years, the cat remained an essentially wild animal, interbreeding with the local wild populations – such that, in many places, the tame and the wild must have formed a continuum rather than the polar opposites they are today. Moreover, wild and domestic cats would have been almost identical in appearance, and distinguishable only by their behaviour towards people. To earn the tolerance of their human hosts, cats had to be effective hunters: any cat that allowed mice to flourish in its owner's barn, or perhaps let a snake into the house to bite and poison one of the family, would not have lasted long. Docility, low reactivity and a dependence on humans to take the lead – prized characteristics in other domesticated animals – would not have done the cat any favours.

Nevertheless, the first artistic and written records that we have of cats depict them firmly as part of the family, so they evidently inspired feelings of affection in humans at least towards the end of this predomestication phase. Only now is feline science allowing us to understand how and why this has come to be.

2

The Cat Steps out of the Wild

We will never pin down the precise time or place where cats gave up the wild for good. There was no single, dramatic domestication event, the brainwave of some early miller who realized that cats were the ideal solution to his rodent problems. Instead, the cat gradually insinuated itself into our homes and hearts, changing from wild to domestic in fits and starts, over the course of several thousand years.

This progression probably saw many failed beginnings, as one person after another hand-reared some especially tractable kittens in different locations in the Middle East and north-east Africa. These people probably bred two or three litters of cats, and then either lost the habit or lost the cats themselves, which reverted to the wild. These false starts would have occurred from time to time over a period of perhaps 5,000 years, beginning when humankind first started storing food for long enough to attract mice and other vermin, some 11,000 years ago. Some might have lasted for just a few generations of cats, while others may have persisted for decades, perhaps even a century or two. However, temporary liaisons such as these leave little trace in the archaeological record, especially where wild and tame cats lived side by side and differed only in their behaviour.

We have only one well-documented example from this period of a close relationship between humans and cats. In 2001, archaeologists from the Natural History Museum in Paris had been excavating a Neolithic village at Shillourokambos in Cyprus for more than a decade when they discovered a complete cat skeleton, dating to around 7500 BCE, buried in a grave.[1] That the skeleton was still intact and that the grave had been dug deliberately both suggested that the burial had been far from accidental; moreover, the cat lay within fifteen

Cat burial in Cyprus

inches of a human skeleton, whose grave also contained polished stone tools, flint axes and ochre, indicating that this was a human of high status. The cat was not fully grown, probably less than a year old when it died, and although nothing else indicated that it had been killed deliberately, the cat's age suggests that this is indeed what happened.

We can only guess at the relationship between this cat and this person, even though it resulted in their being buried near to each other. Unlike some dog burials of the time, the human and cat were not placed in physical contact, suggesting that the cat was not a treasured pet; instead, there was an arm's-length relationship between the two. Yet the very fact that this cat was buried with such deliberation suggests that someone, perhaps the person in the grave or a surviving relative, valued it highly.

This single cat skeleton gives us a glimpse into an early relationship between cats and humans, but also poses more questions than it answers. No burials of cats have been recorded from the mainland

Middle East until thousands of years later. If cats were fully domesticated pets during this period, some of them should have been buried with the same formality as dogs routinely were at the time. The initial domestication of the cat may just possibly have taken place on Cyprus, and some might have been subsequently exported back to the Middle East to form one of the nuclei that eventually led to today's pets, but we have no evidence to support this idea. More likely, the Cyprus burial represents an anomaly: a very special human and his prized tame wildcat.

For the cat to make the leap into domestication, it almost certainly had to become an object of affection as well as utility: some of the ancestors of today's cats must have been pets in addition to pest controllers. We have little direct evidence for pet-keeping of any kind, apart from dogs, in the Neolithic cultures of the Eastern Mediterranean, but a number of present-day hunter-gatherer societies practise something like it, which may provide clues as to the process by which wildcats originally became first tame and then domestic. In both Borneo and Amazonia, women and children in such societies adopt newly weaned animals taken from the wild, and keep them as pets.[2] Since the habit of creating pets from young wild animals is found in societies that have never had contact with one another, we might consider this a universal human trait. If so, this could account for the possible adoption of wildcat kittens by people on the shores of the Mediterranean, one of which may have been taken by its owner across the sea to Cyprus. The human skeleton buried alongside the cat is that of a man, so pet-keeping was possibly, and somewhat unusually, practised by both men and women at that location and time.

If the first cats to live in human settlements were indeed tamed wildcats, they are unlikely to be the direct ancestors of today's domestic cats. In modern hunter-gatherer societies, young animals taken from the wild, whatever the species, are rarely kept for very long and rarely breed in captivity. Rather, as they grow and their cuteness fades, they may be abandoned, driven away or even eaten, if they are known to be tasty enough and local taboos allow it. For example, such a relationship exists today between the dingo and some Aboriginal tribes of Australia. The dingo is a not a true wild dog, but is descended from domestic dogs that escaped into northern Australia several thousand years ago and became successful predators, rather like the wildcats of Cyprus. Some Aborigines find dingo puppies irresistible and take them from the wild to keep as pets. However, as they grow into adolescence, these puppies become a considerable nuisance, stealing food and harassing children, so they are driven back into the wild. We can easily imagine the affectionate relationship between humans and wildcats beginning in a similar way.

The first clear indications that cats had transformed themselves into pets come from Egypt, just over 4,000 years ago. At that time, cats started to appear in paintings and carvings. It is not always clear what species these cats are – some, especially those without tabby markings, could easily be jungle cats. Indeed, we have evidence that the Egyptians had already been keeping tame jungle cats for hundreds of years – a skeleton of a young jungle cat recovered from a 5,700-year-old grave had healed fractures in its legs, indicating that it must have been nursed for many weeks before it died.[3] There is no indication that these jungle cats were any different from their wild counterparts, so they had not been domesticated in the sense that their genetic makeup had been altered by their association with humankind. Other cats, while clearly striped and therefore presumably *Felis silvestris*, appear in outdoor scenes, often reedbeds, alongside other local wild predators such as genets and mongooses, making it more likely that they are wildcats than domestic cats. Even the cats that appear in indoor scenes are sometimes depicted wearing collars, and so could be tamed wildcats rather than domestic cats. However, early in the Middle Kingdom, about 4,000 years ago, a set of hieroglyphs – 'miw', in translation – was created specifically for the domestic cat. Not long after this, Miw was adopted as a name for girls, a further indication that by that time the domestic cat had become an integral part of Egyptian society.[4]

We see hints of pet cats in Egypt going back a full 2,000 years earlier than this, into the Predynastic era. The tomb of a craftsman, constructed some 6,500 years ago in a town in Middle Egypt, contained the bones of a gazelle and a cat. The gazelle was probably placed there to provide the craftsman with food for the afterlife, but

Tethered cat – Egypt 1450 BCE

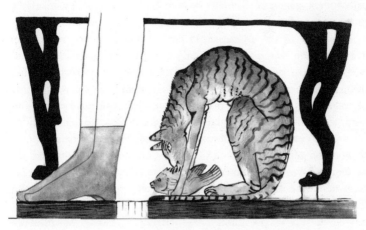

Pet cat – Egypt 1250 BCE

the burial of the cat, perhaps his pet, is reminiscent of the similar burial on Cyprus some 3,000 years earlier. In a cemetery at Abydos in Upper Egypt, 500 miles south of the Mediterranean, a 4,000-year-old tomb contained the skeletons of no fewer than seventeen cats. Alongside them were a number of small pots that had probably contained milk. Although the reason for the burial of so many cats in one place is obscure, that they were buried with their food bowls indicates that these cats must have been pets.

These early pets may have come from stock domesticated locally, or they may have been imported from elsewhere. If cats were indeed domesticated farther north in the Fertile Crescent, or even possibly in Cyprus, long before the rise of Egypt as a centre of civilization, they were likely traded around the region, possibly as exotic novelties. This theory accounts for the scarcity of evidence for domestic cats in Pre-dynastic Egypt. The cats that found their way there would have been valued possessions because their owners had paid well for them, but they might have been too few in number to sustain themselves as domestic animals. Most would have been unable to locate a domesticated member of the opposite sex, and would have mated with, or been mated by, a local wildcat or possibly a tamed wildcat. In this way, the genetic differences between domestic and wild cats at that time would have been swiftly diluted by the wild versions, and each subsequent generation would have become less and less likely to accept a domestic lifestyle.

The domestic role of the cat in Egypt becomes much clearer over the next 500 years, probably reflecting the emergence of a local, self-sustaining, domestic population. Cats sitting in baskets – surely a sign of domesticity – appear in Egyptian temple art between about 4,000 and 3,500 years ago. In paintings dating from about 3,300 years ago, the cats are often depicted sitting – unrestrained – beneath the chair of an important member of the household, often the wife. (The animal beneath the husband's chair is commonly, and perhaps not unexpectedly, a dog.) In one painting from about 3,250 years ago, not only do we see an adult cat sitting under the wife's chair, but also her husband has a kitten on his lap. Members of the Egyptian nobility were evidently deeply attached to their cats, including the eldest son of Pharaoh Amenhotep III, who died at the age of thirty-eight during the same period. He was so fond of his cat Osiris, Ta-Miaut (which translates as Osiris, the she-cat), that when she died he not only had her embalmed, but also had a sarcophagus (stone coffin) carved for her.[5]

Almost all of these cats are depicted in aristocratic surroundings, supporting the idea that cats were still exotic pets, reserved for the privileged few. We find little direct evidence of cats in the homes of working people at this time: this, however, is largely because the tombs and temples, many sited on the edge of the desert, are so much better preserved than ordinary people's dwellings, which were nearer to the Nile. Luckily, the artists who worked on creating the tombs and temples between 3,500 and 3,000 years ago left behind drawings, presumably done for their own pleasure; many are humorous and cartoonlike, in contrast to the formal drawings required for temple decoration. Many of these drawings depict cats – some in ordinary domestic situations, and others in more imaginary contexts, such as an image of a cat carrying a pack on a stick over its shoulder, strangely reminiscent of the later English folktale of Dick Whittington's Cat. These drawings help to confirm that, by this time, pet cats were widespread and commonplace in Egypt.

We have good evidence that the Egyptians, as well as treasuring their cats as companions, also regarded them as useful. Some depictions of cats from about 3,300 years ago show them apparently accompanying Egyptians on hunting trips, but these depictions are almost certainly fanciful; we have no evidence of any other culture using cats for this purpose – and just imagine trying to do anything like this with one of today's domestic cats! It is far more likely that cats were becoming domesticated for their ability to keep pests, such as imported house mice and indigenous wild rodents, out of the granaries and other food stores on which the Egyptian economy depended. One such pest was the Nile rat, smaller and chubbier than the more familiar brown rat, but no less devastating. Agriculture in the Nile valley depended on the annual flooding of the arable land either side of the river, refreshing the soil with much-needed nutrients washed downstream. This

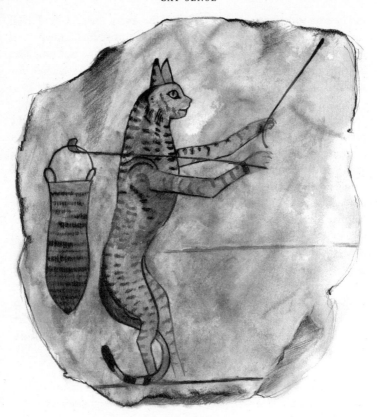

Cartoon cat on a limestone tablet – Egypt 1100 BCE

flooding would also have driven Nile rats, searching for food and shelter, from their communal burrows up to higher ground, where granaries were sited.[6] Cats would have been useful deterrents against such invasions.

The Egyptians seem to have valued cats not only for their ability to keep rodent pests away, but also for their expertise in killing snakes. Venomous snakes were a source of considerable anxiety in ancient Egypt: the Brooklyn Papyrus, dating from about 3,700 years ago, is concerned largely with remedies for snakebites and the venoms of scorpions and tarantulas. The Egyptians used both the mongoose and the genet as snake-exterminators, but these were individually tamed from the wild;[7] the cat was the only domesticated animal capable of killing snakes. The historian Diodorus Siculus, recording life in Egypt more than a millennium later, wrote, 'The cat is very serviceable against the venomous stings of serpents, and the deadly bite of the asp.'[8]

Clearly the Egyptians regarded domestic cats as useful protection against poisonous snakes, although we do not know the extent to which this was based on their actual effectiveness in preventing snakebites. Today's cat owner might be surprised to learn that Egyptian cats would have attacked snakes rather than run away from them. Pet cats rarely kill snakes in Europe – the only reptiles recorded to be eaten there are lizards – and in the United States, cats are known to kill and eat lizards and non-venomous snakes. Only Australia has records of cats killing venomous snakes; many feral cats in Australia kill and eat more reptiles than they do mammals. We have few studies of cats' diets from Africa, and none from Egypt, but English scholars working in Egypt in the 1930s reported seeing cats killing horned vipers, and menacing, if not actually killing, cobras.[9] It is highly unlikely that cats were ever specially bred to prey on snakes – mongooses are much more skilled at this[10] – but incidents like these may have made a lasting impression on the ancient Egyptians who witnessed them. The Egyptians must have used cats mainly to kill mice and other rodents, both in the home and in granaries – a function presumably too mundane to feature in Egyptian art or mythology.

In the next stage of the domestic cat's evolution as a controller of vermin, it encountered a new enemy: the black rat, *Rattus rattus*. Originating from India and South-East Asia, this pest had spread west along trade routes to the civilizations of Pakistan, the Middle East and Egypt by about 2,300 years ago. From there, it hitched a ride on Roman trading vessels, reaching Western Europe by the first century CE. Black rats are more generalist feeders than house mice, eating all kinds of stored foods as well as feeds prepared for domestic livestock. Additionally, they are carriers of disease, and were recognized as such by both the Greeks and the Romans. Had cats been unable to control this new threat, humans might well have given them the cold shoulder. However, the cats of 2,000 years ago, larger than today's cats, appear to have risen to the challenge. A peculiar cat burial on the Red Sea coast 1,800 years ago shows that at least some cats of that era were effective predators of rats. The cat in question was a large young male, typical of the cats of the time but something of a giant by today's standards. Before burial, it had been wrapped in pieces of a woollen cloth decorated in green and purple, beneath a linen shroud similar to that of an Egyptian mummy. However, the cat was not mummified in the conventional way, for its intestines were not removed. Examiners found in its stomach contents the bones of at least five black rats, and at least one more farther down the gut.[11] It is unclear why this cat died and why it was afforded such an elaborate burial, but it may have been special to its owner because of its champion ratting skills.

Egypt esteemed cats for their roles as pets and pest controllers, and also endowed them with spiritual significance: starting about 3,500 years ago, cats became increasingly prominent in Egyptian cults and religion. Depictions of cats begin to feature on tomb walls; depictions of the sun god occasionally have the head of a cat instead of a human, and are referred to as 'Miuty'. The lioness deities Pakhet and Sekhmet (the latter also associated with the caracal) and the leopard goddess Mafdet, although clearly based on big cats known to the Egyptians, nevertheless gradually became associated with domestic cats, presumably because they would have been to most people the most familiar and accessible members of the cat family.

Bastet was the goddess with which the ancient Egyptians came to associate the domestic cat most closely. Worship of Bastet originated in the city of Bubastis, in the Nile delta, some 4,800 years ago. She originally took the form of a woman with a lion's head, carrying a serpent on her forehead. Some 2,000 years later, the Egyptians began to associate her with smaller cats; presumably this followed the arrival of domestic cats in the city, or even a new local domestication. During this period, Bastet still had the head of a lioness, but was sometimes depicted with several smaller, presumably domestic cats as her attendants. Within the next 300 years, some 2,600 years ago, her lion-goddess identity apparently mutated to resemble the domestic cat more closely.

Originally a simple goddess who protected humankind against misfortune, she later became associated with playfulness, fertility, motherhood and female sexuality – all characteristics of domestic cats. Her popularity spread to other parts of Egypt, especially during the Late Period and the Ptolemaic Era (2,600 to 2,050 years ago), as the Egyptian empire gradually crumbled. Her annual feast day was for a time the most important in the calendar, as witnessed by the Greek historian Herodotus:

> Now, when they are coming to the city of Bubastis they do as follows: they sail men and women together, and a great multitude of each sex in every boat; and some of the women have rattles and rattle with them, while some of the men play the flute during the whole time of the voyage, and the rest, both women and men, sing and clap their hands; and when as they sail they come opposite to any city on the way they bring the boat to land, and some of the women continue to do as I have said, others cry aloud and jeer at the women in that city, some dance, and some stand up and pull up their garments. This they do by every city along the riverbank; and when they come to Bubastis they hold festival celebrating great sacrifices, and more wine of grapes is consumed upon that festival than during the whole of the rest of the year.[12]

Presumably because of their association with this cult, the Egyptians seem to have been extremely protective of cats, in ways that may seem absurd to us today. Herodotus reported that when a pet cat died from natural causes, all members of the household shaved their eyebrows as a mark of respect. He even reported seeing Egyptians struggling to prevent cats from entering a burning building in preference to putting out the fire itself.[13] This veneration of cats clearly persisted over time. Some 500 years later, when Egypt was part of the Roman Empire, Diodorus Siculus wrote:

> If any kill a cat, whether wilfully or otherwise, he is certainly dragged away to death by the multitude. For fear of this, if any by chance find any of these creatures dead, they stand aloof, and with lamentable cries and protestations, tell everybody that they found it dead ... It so happened that upon a cat being killed by a Roman, the people in tumult ran to his lodging, and neither the princes sent by the king to dissuade

them, nor the fear of the Romans, could deliver the person from the rage of the people, though he did it [presumably, the killing of the cat] against his will.[14]

In contrast to this behaviour, the Egyptians routinely practised infanticide towards their cats. Herodotus wrote, 'They either take away by force or remove secretly the young from the females and kill them (but after killing they do not eat them).'[15] This account of a convenient method of population control suggests that by his time, and probably much earlier, domestic cats were breeding freely as a self-contained population, more or less isolated from their wild counterparts, and that far more kittens were being born than were needed to become either pest controllers or pets. To modern sensibilities, this brutally pragmatic culling of kittens may seem callous, but before the advent of modern veterinary medicine, it was the simplest way to keep cats' numbers within reasonable bounds. It is presumably least distressing for the perpetrator to dispose of kittens before their eyes open and their faces take on their characteristic appeal. In societies where cats are useful pest controllers first and pets second, this has remained standard practice into the modern era. Describing attitudes to cats in 1940s rural New Hampshire, Elizabeth Marshall Thomas noted that:

> Farm cats, after all, are neither pets nor livestock ... When the cat population got too high for a farmer's liking, the cats were simply put into bags and gassed or drowned. To care for a group of animals for a time, and then to suddenly round them up and dispatch them without warning, is after all what farming is all about.[16]

Even in the twenty-first century, acceptable behaviour towards cats varies widely. Some people view cats as individuals with rights, but others continue to see them as tools that can be discarded when they are no longer useful.

The ancient Egyptians, with their deep reverence for cats, added an additional dimension to cat culture that is abhorrent to us today: the cat as sacrificial object. Cats not only formed an important part of the Egyptian pantheon, but were also ritually buried in large numbers – almost certainly millions. The Egyptians, who placed great emphasis on the afterlife, developed the process of mummification some 4,000 years ago as a way to preserve corpses, both human and animal.

Initially, mummification of cats seems to have been reserved for treasured pets. A mummified cat is depicted on the sarcophagus of Ta-Miaut, so presumably this cat had been mummified and the sarcophagus constructed specifically to house the mummy. This practice probably continued for many hundreds of years, but the numbers of cats involved were tiny compared with the millions that were later mummified as offerings to various cat deities.

The production of 'sacred animals' became a major industry in Egypt between 2,400 and 2,000 years ago. Small cats were by no means the only animal involved: mummies also included lions and jungle cats, cattle, crocodiles, rams, dogs, baboons, mongooses, birds and snakes. Sometimes staggering numbers of animals were treated this way: for example, more than 4 million mummified ibis, a medium-sized wading bird that the Egyptians bred in captivity, were recovered from catacombs at Tuna el-Gebel, and an additional 1.5 million from Saqqara.

Modern analyses show that cat mummification was often performed to a high standard, including many of the techniques used for the mummification of human corpses. To preserve the body, the intestines were removed and replaced with dry sand.[17] Once the corpse was prepared, the cat was wrapped in layers of linen bandages. These were often treated with a preservative, such as natron, a natural desiccant and preservative that forms on the beds of dried-out tropical lakes. Other times, the embalmers used mixtures consisting of animal fats, balsam, beeswax, resins from trees such as cedar and pistacia, and occasionally bitumen brought from the Red Sea coast, more than a hundred miles from where the cats were kept.[18]

Cat 'mummies' varied considerably in external appearance, presumably reflecting the tastes and finances of the prospective purchaser. Some were a simple bundle, with perhaps a plain string of glazed pottery beads for decoration, but others had an outer layer of linen applied with decorative patterns. A 'head' might have been moulded around and above the actual skull, using clay and plaster-soaked linen, or a bronze head might have been added; some were crude, but others depicted every whisker. Many were placed in simple rectangular wooden coffins, but, for others, cat-shaped wooden caskets were constructed, decorated with plaster, and then painted, and sometimes even gilded. Inlaid beads were used to represent the cat's eyes; overall, they must have been astonishingly lifelike when first constructed.

What is more, the sacrificial cats were bred specifically for this purpose. Remains of catteries have been found adjacent to the temples of all the deities associated with cats or other felids. There is little doubt that these cats were deliberately killed for mummification, since X-rays of the mummies show that their necks had been dislocated, and others were probably strangled.[19] Some were killed when they were still kittens, at two to four months old, while others were fully grown, at nine to twelve months: presumably the purveyors of such a commercial operation saw no benefit in feeding a cat for any longer than this unless it had been earmarked for breeding. The mummies would be sold to visitors to the temple, who would then leave them there as offerings to the appropriate deity. As sufficient numbers accumulated, the priests would remove them in batches to dedicated catacombs, where many remained, well preserved, until the pillaging of the cemeteries in the nineteenth and twentieth centuries.

We will never know how many cats were sacrificed this way. The archaeologists who discovered these sites wrote of vast heaps of white

Mummified cats and a casket

cat bones, and dust from disintegrating plaster and linen blowing across the desert. Several other cemeteries were excavated wholesale, and their contents ground up and used as fertilizer – some was used locally, some was exported. One shipment of cat mummies alone, sent to London, weighed nineteen tons, out of which just one cat was removed and presented to the British Museum before the remainder were ground into powder. Out of the millions that were mummified, only a few hundred now survive in museums, and these come from a mere handful of the many cemeteries constructed over a period of several hundred years. As such, these mummies may not be entirely representative of the cats of ancient Egypt.

Examination of some of the few remaining mummies using forensic techniques has revealed much about the animals preserved inside, providing insight into the relationships that the Egyptians had with their cats. All the cats were 'mackerel'-striped tabbies, the same as the wild *lybica*; none were black, or tabby and white, and none had the blotched tabby pattern more common than the striped version in many parts of the world today.

Unequivocal evidence for such colour and pattern variations did not appear in domestic cats until later, and not in Egypt. Each of these changes in appearance is caused by a single mutation that is also common in wild felids. For example, the so-called king cheetah, once thought to be a distinct species, simply has a blotched tabby coat rather than the normal spotted variety. Black ('melanistic') forms of felids abound: they have been recorded from lions, tigers, jaguars, caracals, pumas, bobcats, ocelots, margays and servals. In the wild, their black colour is a handicap because it destroys the camouflaging effect of their normal coat, so they leave few offspring and the gene responsible disappears from the population.[20]

Given this, it seems odd that despite a possible 2,000-year history of domestication, none of these colour varieties are apparent in the Egyptian mummified cats; they all seem to have become established within the next two millennia. Perhaps the Egyptians actively discouraged these 'unnatural' cats on the rare occasions when the mutations occurred, possibly for reasons connected with religion.

Some of the cats in ancient Egypt may have been ginger or

ginger-tabby ('torbie') mixes (see box, 'Why Ginger Cats are Usually Boys'). Some of the wall paintings are a more orange shade of brown than the normal greyish-brown of *lybica*, although this may be the consequence of some artistic licence, or due to yellowing of the pigments over the centuries. Ginger cats are more common in the Egyptian port of Alexandria and the Egyptian-founded city of Khartoum than anywhere else in north-east Africa or the Middle East, suggesting that perhaps ancient Egypt was indeed where the orange mutation originally became incorporated into the domestic cat population, before spreading from there to the rest of the world.[21] Although orange cats look more conspicuous than tabby cats, and may seem less effectively camouflaged, today's orange cats can be very successful hunters, especially in rural areas. Once the mutation had occurred, there seems no reason for it not to have spread through the cat population.[22]

We also know that the mummified cats were about 15 per cent larger than modern pet cats.[23] In almost every other domestic species – cattle, pigs, horses and even dogs – the early domesticated forms are significantly *smaller* than their wild counterparts, mainly because smaller individuals are easier to handle. However, this principle may not apply to the cat, which was small relative to man to begin with. More surprising, the mummified cats were also 10 per cent larger than African wildcats are today. It may be that the Egyptians deliberately favoured large wildcats because they were more effective rodent controllers, and that domestic cats have subsequently become smaller as they gradually transformed from full-time pest controllers into pets.

The attitudes of the ancient Egyptians towards their cats seem paradoxical, almost unthinkable, to modern sensibilities. To the Egyptians, some cats were revered pets, many more were simply pest controllers, used by rich and poor alike, but, uniquely, many were bred specifically to be killed as sacrifices. Apart from the last, all this is not very different from the way that cats were regarded in Europe and the United States in the first half of the twentieth century. Indeed, the Egyptian habit of having elaborate coffins made for favourite pet cats mirrors today's cat cemeteries.

Undoubtedly, the Egyptian association between cats and religion

WHY GINGER CATS ARE USUALLY BOYS

The mutation that causes a cat's coat to be ginger rather than the usual shades of brown and black is inherited differently from other coat colours. In mammals, most genes obey the 'dominance' rule: to affect the appearance of the animal, the 'recessive' version has to be present on both chromosomes, one inherited from the mother and one from the father; otherwise, the other 'dominates'. Usually, animals with one dominant and one recessive gene are indistinguishable on the outside from animals with two dominant versions. However, there is one major exception: if a cat carries one orange and one brown version of the gene, then both appear in the coat, in random patches: in one part of the skin, the chromosome with the orange version has been switched on, and in another it is the brown-black pattern that 'wins', producing a tortoiseshell-tabby (or 'torbie') cat. The precise colour of the patches depends on other coat-colour genes. If the cat also carries (two copies of) the black mutation, then the brown patches are black, so their tabby pattern is obscured (like a regular black cat), while the orange patches, on which the black mutation has no effect, are orange and yellow with the tabby pattern still visible, producing a tortoiseshell or calico.

Second, the gene is carried on the X chromosome. Female cats have two X chromosomes, and males only one, paired with the much smaller Y chromosome that makes them male but carries no information about coat colour. Thus, for a female cat to be orange, it must carry the orange mutation on both chromosomes. If it has only one, it will have a tortoiseshell coat. Although tortoiseshells are much more common, ginger cats can be female. Almost without exception, males are either orange or they're not; in fact, tortoiseshell males do crop up from time to time – they have two X chromosomes and a Y chromosome, the result of an abnormal cell division. A common misperception holds that ginger, or 'marmalade', cats are always male – hence the phrase 'ginger tom'.

seems the most foreign to us. The worshippers who bought ready-prepared mummies as offerings at the temple can hardly have been unaware of what the contents of those mummies were, for the breeding premises and production line for mummies were both nearby, and would have been evident from their smell alone. Presumably these sacrificial cats were regarded in some way as 'different' from household cats, even though they would have been genetically indistinguishable. Perhaps this was reinforced by their being bred in purpose-built catteries. Cats would have been just as prolific breeders in those days as they are now, and mummy manufacturers would have found trapping young feral cats easy. Since both law and custom forbade this, separate breeding of cats must have been the only solution. It is possible that access to the premises used was prohibited to all but the priests who looked after the 'sacred' cats, which were never seen by the worshippers until the cats had been mummified, thus maintaining a distinction between household and sacred cats, even though they were otherwise identical.

The mummies themselves show a paradoxical concern for welfare during life, but no trace of concern for life itself; the procurers of these mummies evidently took great care of their cats, but then killed them in huge numbers. Judging from the sizes of the cats, they were evidently well nourished. Finding sufficient high-quality meat and fish for such large numbers of animals could not have been easy. Although it is not entirely clear how all the cats were killed, it seems most likely that they were strangled in some kind of prescribed, ritual manner. Moreover, although the production of mummies must have been a lucrative business, there seem to have been few attempts to cheat the worshippers; almost all the mummies that were produced to look like cats actually do contain a complete cat skeleton, even though it would presumably have been more profitable to wrap a bundle of reeds in linen and pass it off as a cat mummy. The entire process seems to have been carried out according to strict rules. These rules protected not only the worshippers from the purchase of fake mummies, but also the cats, which were well-fed and cared for, at least by the standards of the time, up to the point when they were sacrificed.

The cats of ancient Egypt were likely the main ancestors of modern-day cats, as several of their qualities attest. We have no credible evidence for large-scale domestication of the cat anywhere else in the world before the birth of Christ. These domestic cats had the wildcat's striped tabby coat, so would have been distinguishable from genuine wildcats only by their affection for, rather than fear of, people. Some were pets, certainly in well-to-do households and most probably in many others. Most would have been useful in keeping food stores and granaries reasonably free of rodent pests. Household cats were venerated, at least during the last few hundred years of Egyptian civilization, as indicated by the illegality of killing them, and the rituals performed when one died.

*

From about 2,500 years ago, keeping cats gradually became more widespread around the eastern and northern shores of the Mediterranean, as Egypt came first under Greek and then Roman influence. Historians have traditionally ascribed the slow northwards spread of the cat to laws that prohibited the export of cats from Egypt. Some accounts even tell of the Egyptians sending out soldiers to retrieve and repatriate cats that had been taken abroad.[24] However, these laws were almost certainly symbolic, connected to cat worship. The cat's independence, hunting ability and rapid rate of reproduction would have made it impossible for Egyptian authorities to prevent domesticated cats from spreading along their trade routes.

As cats spread out of Egypt, they must have come across, and interbred with, wild and semi-domesticated cats in other areas of the Eastern Mediterranean. As the Cyprus cats attest, there must have been tamed cats in other parts of the Middle East for thousands of years before the Egyptians began to transform them into domesticated animals. Egyptian paintings from about 3,500 years ago show cats on board ships, and these cats could plausibly have been either immigrants or emigrants. Between 3,200 and 2,800 years ago, trade in the Eastern Mediterranean was dominated by the seafaring Phoenicians (who may even have domesticated their own wildcats as pest controllers), operating from several city-states in what is now Lebanon and Syria. The Phoenicians probably introduced *lybica* cats, either tamed or partly domesticated, to many of the Mediterranean islands and to mainland Italy and Spain. The spread of the cat was probably delayed not by Egyptian laws, but more by the presence in Greece and Rome of rival rodent controllers, tamed weasels and polecats (the latter becoming domesticated as the ferret).

The domestic cat's migration north from Egypt towards Greece is not well documented. In the Akkadian language, spoken in the eastern part of the Fertile Crescent, separate words for domestic cat and wildcat appear about 2,900 years ago, so domestic cats had probably spread into what is now Iraq by this period.

Domestic cats were most likely common in Greece, at least among the aristocracy, some time before this. We know this from coins minted for use in two Greek colonies. They were made about 2,400 years ago, one for Reggio di Calabria, on the 'toe' of Italy opposite

Sicily, and the other for Taranto, on the 'heel', and both depict their founders, some 300 years previously. Although these were different people, the coins are remarkably similar and may refer to the same legend. Both show a man sitting on a chair, dangling a toy in front of a cat, which is reaching up with its forepaws. That this man is shown with a cat rather than the more usual horse or dog suggests that pet cats were initially unusual in Greece, possibly exotic imports from Egypt, and their possession an indicator of status. A bas-relief carved in Athens at about the same time shows a cat and a dog about to fight, but the cat is leashed, implying a tamed rather than domestic animal.

Domestic cats probably became common in Greece and Italy about 2,400 years ago. Some of the earliest clear evidence comes from Greek paintings, in which cats are shown unleashed and relaxed in the presence of people. Cats also began to be depicted on gravestones, presumably as the pets of the people buried there. Furthermore, by this time, the Greeks had a word specifically for the domestic cat – 'aielouros', or 'waving tail'. In Rome, paintings began to appear showing cats in domestic situations – under benches at a banquet, on a boy's shoulder, playing with a ball of string dangled from a woman's hand. As in Egypt, cats in Rome were women's pets, men generally preferring dogs. And as 'Miw' had been adopted as a name for girls in Egypt, so 'Felicula' – little kitten – became a common name for girls in Rome by about 2,000 years ago. In other parts of the Roman empire, 'Catta' or 'Cattula' were used, the former originating in Roman-occupied North Africa.

As in Egypt, once the cat had been domesticated, it began to be associated with goddesses – particularly Artemis in Greece and Diana in Rome. The Roman poet Ovid wrote of a mythical war between gods and giants in which Diana escaped to Egypt and transformed herself into a cat to avoid detection. Thus, cats became widely associated with paganism, a link that would eventually lead to their persecution in the Middle Ages.

As sea routes opened up between the Middle East, the Indian subcontinent, and the Malay peninsula and Indonesia, so cats – for the first time – were transported out of the native areas of their wild ancestors.

Greek coin – Italy 400 BCE

Roman traders were probably responsible for carrying cats to India, by sea, and later to China through Mongolia, along the Silk Road. Cats were established in China by the fifth century CE, and in Japan about a hundred years later.[25] In both countries, cats became especially valued for their ability to protect the valuable silk moth cocoons from attack by rodents.

The characteristic South-East Asian type of domestic cat – lean-bodied, agile and vocal – is not, as was once thought, a separate domestication of the Indian desert cat, *Felis ornata*. Although archaeological evidence is sparse, the DNA of today's street cats across the Far East – whether from Singapore, Vietnam, China or Korea – shows that they have the same ultimate ancestor as European cats: *Felis lybica* from north-east Africa or the Middle East. So do all the 'foreign' (Far Eastern) purebreds, such as the Siamese, Korat and Burmese.[26] No barrier prevents domestic cats from breeding with Indian desert cats, but evidently their offspring rarely make suitable pets: although wildcats in central Asia carry domestic DNA, their domestic counterparts show no trace of wild DNA.

Precisely dating the appearance of domestic cats in South-East Asia is impossible, and each population seems to have developed in isolation from the others. The DNA of street cats in Korea is fairly similar to that of their counterparts in China and, to a lesser extent, those in Singapore, but the cats of Vietnam are considerably different, implying that there has been little transfer of cats between these countries since they first arrived. The street cats of Sri Lanka are different again, more closely resembling those of Kenya than anywhere in Asia, perhaps due to the transfer of ships' cats across the Indian Ocean.

History paints a conventional picture of the origins and spread of the domestic cat up to the time of the birth of Christ, but this picture is at odds with what we can deduce from biology. Conventional accounts have emphasized human intervention, and presume that the domestication of the cat was a deliberate process. From the cat's perspective, a different picture emerges: one of a gradual shift from wild hunter to opportunist predator, and then, via domestication, to parallel roles as pest controller, companion and symbolic animal.

A biologist would observe that at each stage cats were simply evolving to take advantage of new opportunities provided by human activities. Unlike the dog, which was domesticated much earlier, there would have been no niche for the cat in a hunter-gatherer society. It was not until the first grain stores appeared, resulting in localized concentrations of wild rodents, that it would have been worth any cat's while to visit human habitations – and even then, those that did must have run the risk of being killed for their pelts. It was probably not until after the house mouse had evolved to exploit the new resource provided by human food stores that cats began to appear regularly in settlements, tolerated because they were obviously killing rodents and thereby protecting granaries.

As the practice of agriculture spread, so did the cat, encountering new challenges as it met new pests – for example, the Nile rat in Egypt and, later, the black rat in Europe and Asia. The cat had rivals for the role of vermin exterminator: other carnivores of similar size were tamed, including various members of the weasel family, and the genet and its cousin the Egyptian mongoose. Of these, the ferret was eventually domesticated from the weasels, and the mongoose, most effective as a controller of snakes, was introduced to the Iberian peninsula for that purpose by the occupying Caliphates as late as 750 CE.[27] These various rivals existed in different combinations in different places for many centuries, and it is not clear why the domestic cat was the eventual winner, with the ferret as the only runner-up. Very probably, cats did not have the edge as vermin controllers. The answer, therefore, must lie elsewhere, possibly in the cat's biology. The connection between cats and religion is unlikely to have been crucial, since Egyptians sometimes venerated both mongoose and genet as well.

More likely, the cat managed to become more profoundly domesticated than any of its rivals. However, which was the cause and which the effect? Are cats more 'trustworthy' and predictable than ferrets because they have evolved ways of communicating with humans, or is it the other way around? Since we do not know precisely how the domestic cat's direct ancestors behaved, such questions are impossible to answer. Nevertheless, the cat's capacity to evolve not only into a pest controller but also into a pet animal – its present-day roles – must have been central to its success in the first 2,000 years of its domestication. So what set the cat apart on its millennia-long journey into our homes?

Here, the cat's involvement in Egyptian religion may well have been crucial. It is possible that the Egyptians' veneration of cats gave the cat the time required to evolve fully from wild hunter to domestic pet; otherwise, it might have remained a satellite of human society and not an intrinsic part. It is even possible that the factories which produced the cat mummies forced the evolution of cats that could tolerate being kept in confined spaces and in close proximity with other cats, both qualities that are signally absent from today's strongly territorial wildcats but are essential to life as an urban pet. Although of course most of the cats which carried the relevant genes died young – that was how they were being bred, after all – some must have escaped into the general population, where their descendants would have inherited an improved ability to deal with the close confines of urban society. Such changes take only a few decades in captive carnivores, as exemplified by the Russian fur-fox experiment that turned wild animals docile in just a few generations.[28] Is it possible that today's apartment-dwelling cat owes its very adaptability to the inhabitants of those gruesome Egyptian catteries?

3

One Step Back, Two Steps Forward

The cats of Egypt 2,000 years ago probably differed little in their behaviour from modern cats. These cats were not yet so varied in appearance, and still consisted of a single, rather homogeneous population, with no pedigrees or distinctive types. Few obstacles would then have been apparent to stand in the path of the cat's inexorable rise to universal companion animal. However, this was not to be achieved for another 2,000 years, partly because the cat had only a single practical role. The dog, the cat's primary rival for human affection and attention, has adapted to serve many more functions – guarding, hunting, herding, to name but three – than the less malleable cat. Two other major factors also delayed the cat's rise to prominence, especially in Europe. First, the cat derived from a specialist carnivore, leaving it ill suited to scavenge for a living when prey was scarce. Second, the cat continued a long association with Egyptian religion – at first a blessing, granting the cat time to evolve into a domestic animal, but later a curse.

Surprisingly, Europeans' view of cats continued to be heavily influenced by Egyptian cat worship until as recently as about 400 years ago. Worship of Bastet (Bubastis) and other 'pagan' deities associated with cats, such as Diana and Isis, was popular, in Southern Europe especially, from the second to the sixth centuries CE. In some places, this worship lasted much longer: for example, Ypres, a Belgian city that celebrates its connections with cats to this day, outlawed cat worship only in 962 CE, while a cult based around the goddess Diana lingered in parts of Italy until the sixteenth century. Women managed most of these cults, focusing on motherhood, the family and marriage. When Christianity began to establish itself as the pre-eminent religion of Europe, cats began to suffer from their affiliation with pagan practices.

The spread of cats from the Eastern Mediterranean into Western Europe – and into all strata of society – was hastened by the custom of keeping cats on ships of all sizes. This habit most likely arose for the practical purpose of keeping mice away from cargo, and soon became superstition, with many sailors refusing to sail in ships that had lost their cats. Ships often displayed carved images of cats on the prow to bring good luck.

Their obvious utility aside, cats must have continued to benefit from increasingly warm relationships with their human owners. In many ways, the vicissitudes of the cat's popularity over the past two millennia can be attributed to changes in the balance between two key influences: superstition and affection.

The Romans are often credited with introducing the domestic cat to Britain, but some evidence suggests that it had already arrived several centuries earlier. Cat and house mouse bones were found at two Iron Age hill forts dating to 2,300 years ago, a few dozen miles apart in southern England. The cats were mostly young animals, with the youngest five newborn kittens. These hill forts, inhabited by as many as 300 people led by a local chieftain, were the focal point for several surrounding farmsteads, each of which supplied grain to large stores kept in the fort, perhaps holding twenty times as much as each individual farm. These stores inevitably became infested with mice, so cats would have been a useful addition to the domestic fauna.

These cats must have been brought from the Mediterranean, since it is highly unlikely that the local wildcats, though of the same species (*Felis silvestris silvestris*) could have been tamed, or have even tolerated being in close proximity to people for long enough to produce kittens. Wildcats of European origin are notoriously wary of humans nowadays, and have probably always been so, judging from early Greek accounts of attempts to tame them. The most feasible way in which domestic cats would have reached Britain is on Phoenician ships. The Phoenicians did not colonize Britain, but they did visit, chiefly to buy tin for the manufacture of bronze; and since they often carried cats on their vessels, the presence of domestic cats near the south coast of Britain is unsurprising. Indeed, the grain the Phoenicians brought to Britain on earlier voyages had quite possibly brought the house mice that the cats were called on to eliminate; indeed, the Phoenicians may subsequently also have supplied the cats as a way of clearing up the problem they had themselves created!

Cats probably became widespread in Britain during the Roman occupation. Archaeologists at the Roman town of Silchester, in what is now Hampshire, found a clay floor tile dating from the first century CE bearing the impression of a cat's foot. Presumably, the cat strayed into the drying yard before the tile had set. Other tiles unearthed at the same site bore the footmarks of a dog, a deer, a calf, a lamb, an infant and a man with a hobnailed sandal – indicating that the Romans' reputation for quality control was not infallible.

The wane of Roman influence in Northern Europe seems to have had little effect on the popularity of the cat: for the 500 years of the European Dark Ages, cats were highly valued for their rat- and mouse-catching skills.[1] Several statutes mention cats specifically, showing just how valuable they were. One such statute, from Wales in the tenth century, stated, 'The price of a cat is fourpence. Her qualities are to see, to hear, to kill mice, to have her claws whole, and to nurse and not devour her kittens. If she be deficient in any one of these qualities, one third of her price must be returned.' Note that this refers specifically to a female cat; toms were perhaps not regarded as equally precious. Fourpence was also the value of a full-grown sheep, goat or untrained house-dog. A newborn kitten was valued at one penny, the same as a piglet or a lamb, and a young cat at two. In a divorce, the husband had the right to take one cat from the household, but all the rest belonged to the wife. In Saxony, Germany, the penalty for killing a cat at this time was sixty bushels of grain (almost 500 gallons, or more than 1,500 kilograms), emphasizing the cat's value at keeping granaries free of mice.

Cats must also have helped to slow the spread of the rat-borne bubonic plague that swept through Europe in the sixth century, following the wanton destruction of the drinking water and sewage systems built by the Romans. Cats are themselves susceptible to bubonic plague, so they must also have died in large numbers, but evidently many survived.

Despite their self-evident usefulness and the considerable monetary value placed upon them, cats' welfare was not given the same respect it is today. In Greece, sacrifice and mummification of cats continued much as it had in Egypt, except that drowning rather than strangulation seems to have become the preferred method of killing. An ancient Celtic tradition of burying or killing cats to bring good luck spread across Europe, and given the value evidently placed on female cats, the usual victims were most likely males. A cat would be killed and buried in a newly sown field to ensure the growth of the crop. A new house could be protected from mice and rats by putting a cat – whether dead or alive at the time of interment is unclear – and a rat into a specially constructed hole in an outside wall, or by placing them together under new floorboards.[2] Many European cities had a feast-day custom of putting several cats in a basket together – which would have been stressful enough in itself – and then suspending it over a fire; the screams of the cats were supposed to ward off evil spirits. An alternative was to throw cats from the top of a tower, an event the citizens of Ypres still commemorate every May as the Kattenstoet (Festival of the Cats), using stuffed toys as substitutes for actual cats.

Remarkably, some of these rituals persisted into modern times in their original form. In 1648, Louis XIV presided over one of the last cat-burnings in Paris, lighting the bonfire himself and then dancing in front of it before leaving for a private banquet. The last time live cats were thrown from the bell tower in Ypres was as recently as 1817. However repugnant such rituals may seem today, they cannot have accounted for more than a tiny fraction of the cat population; overall, cats probably thrived during the Dark Ages. Indeed, whenever mice were plentiful, cats would have bred prolifically, producing a surplus of kittens that would need to be culled, often by drowning, to prevent overpopulation. Cats in general were regarded as disposable, like any other farm animal: catskins were commonly used in clothing, and butchery marks on cat bones recovered from medieval sites show that many were killed specifically for their fur as soon as they were fully grown. Such practices would presumably have contributed to a prevailing notion that cats' lives were disposable, making their ritual sacrifice much less abhorrent then than it would be today.

Initially benevolent, the attitude of the Church towards cats gradually became more hostile as the Dark Ages gave way to the Middle Ages. The Roman Catholic Church first set itself on a road that ended in the wholesale persecution of cats, when in 391 CE the emperor Theodosius I banned all pagan (and 'heretical' Christian) worship, including all the cults devoted to Bastet and Diana. Initially the worshippers themselves, not their cats, were targeted. Indeed, cats seem to have been favoured animals in the early Irish Church. The Book of Kells, an eighth-century Irish illuminated book of the Gospels, features several illustrations of cats, some demonic and others depicted in domestic settings. Irish clerics may have encouraged an appreciation of cats as companions. The poem 'Pangur Bán', by a ninth-century monk, compared the writer's life to that of his cat:

> Myself and Pangur, cat and sage
> Go each about our business;
> I harass my beloved page,
> He his mouse . . .
> And his delight when his claws
> Close on his prey
> Equals mine when sudden clues
> Light my way.[3]

In the Middle Ages, monasteries must have been particularly valuable to cats because of their fishponds, used to raise the fish eaten during Lent, the liturgical season of the late winter and early spring when meat-eating was forbidden. Fish were plentiful and great sources of protein, and livestock were slaughtered months before because little fodder was available to feed them in the winter months. Cats, often pregnant during these months, would have been happy to turn from hunting mice to scavenging fish scraps, thereby gaining nutrition essential to the well-being of their unborn kittens, and an advantage over their heathen counterparts on nearby farms.

The relationship between Church and cat became seriously antagonistic from the thirteenth to seventeenth centuries, threatening the very survival of the domestic species in some parts of continental Europe. In 1233, the Catholic Church began a concerted attempt to exterminate cats from the continent. On 13 June of that year, Pope Gregory IX's notorious *Vox in Rama* was published. In this papal Bull, cats – especially black cats – were identified specifically with Satan. Over the next 300 years, millions of cats were tortured and killed, along with hundreds of thousands of their mainly female owners, who were suspected of witchcraft. Urban populations of cats were decimated. The justification for this barbarism was essentially the same as it had been in the fourth century – the extermination of cults that still included cats in their worship, and the demonization of rival religions such as Islam – but now it was the cats themselves that bore the brunt of the Church's wrath.

Outside Western Europe, cats were generally better tolerated at this time. The Eastern (Greek) Orthodox Church appears to have had little quarrel with cat-keeping. Islam has a tradition of kindness to cats, so cats continued to thrive in the Middle East. In Cairo, the Sultan Baibars, ruler of Egypt and Syria, founded what was probably the first sanctuary for homeless cats in 1280 CE.

Even within the reach of the Church of Rome, cats were not universally reviled. In Britain, cats feature in fourteenth-century poetry, including Geoffrey Chaucer's *Canterbury Tales*. If the 'Steward's Tale' is accurate, then cats were well tended at that time, as well as appreciated for their mouse-catching skills:

> Let's take a cat and raise him well with milk
> And tender meat, and make his couch of silk,
> Then let him see a mouse go by the wall –
> At once he'll leave the milk and meat and all,
> And every dainty that is in the house,
> Such appetite he has to eat a mouse.[4]

Moreover, it appears that cats were secretly popular even in ecclesiastical circles. Carvings of cats adorn the choir stalls of medieval churches right across Europe, including Britain, France, Switzerland, Belgium, Germany and Spain. These cats are depicted not as demons, but in natural or domestic situations – washing themselves, caring for kittens, and sitting by the fireside. It may be that such carvings were deliberately placed out of view of the general congregation, since presumably sermons sometimes referred to cats as demonic. Although cats and the women who doted on them were sporadically persecuted, cats were generally tolerated for their usefulness – not least in rural areas, where the reach of the Church was weakest and the services cats provided were most appreciated.

Did this reversal in its fortunes have any lasting impact on the cat as a domesticated animal? No physical trace of the persecution of black cats in Western Europe remains: today, the black mutation is as common in Germany and France as it is in Greece, Israel or North Africa, all of which were outside the influence of the medieval Catholic Church. Sometime during the Middle Ages, cats, which were significantly larger and more wildcat-like up until Roman times, became smaller – in some locations, even smaller than the average cat of today. Although persecution might have influenced this, it is difficult to pinpoint the time or place that the changes in size occurred. In part this is because it is rare for sufficiently large numbers of cat bones to be found in one place to give an accurate picture of what the 'average cat' might have looked like: for example, researchers would presume that the remains of a single large cat found anywhere in Europe are those of a wildcat, and an extra-small cat the product of malnutrition.

In Western Europe, the cat seems to have changed in size over the centuries, but not consistently. For example, in York in the tenth and eleventh centuries, domestic cats were the same size they are today, but at the same period in Lincoln, a scant eighty miles away, cats were mostly small by today's standards. However, by the twelfth and thirteenth centuries, York cats had become smaller than their counterparts of 200 years earlier. In Hedeby, Germany, cats of the ninth to eleventh centuries were roughly the same size as they are today, but in Schleswig, also in Germany, some of the cats recovered from eleventh- to fourteenth-century remains were tiny. A staggering and unexplained 70 per cent reduction in bone lengths seems to have occurred between the eleventh and fourteenth centuries: many of the cats found in Schleswig, which seem to have left no descendants, would look tiny compared to a typical twenty-first-century cat.[5] We might be tempted to ascribe this miniaturization to the persecution that began in the fourteenth century, but we have no direct evidence that this was the case; indeed, the reduction in size in England predates the papal proclamation. As such, the cause of these shifts towards smaller cats remains a mystery, and we do not know when cats grew larger again.

Likewise, we might be tempted to link the persecution of cats to the Black Death, a pandemic of rat-borne bubonic plague that swept from China to Britain from 1340 to 1350. More than a third of Europe's human population died, along with many of its cats. However, the plague was just as devastating in India, the Middle East and North Africa, where cats remained unpersecuted, as it was in Western Europe. Evidently the bacillus was simply too virulent to be contained, and indeed plague continued to break out in Europe occasionally over the next 500 years. The last major epidemic in Britain was the Great Plague of London of 1665–6, and this time cats, not rats, were blamed; 200,000 cats were slaughtered on the Lord Mayor of London's orders.[6]

Seventeenth-century Britain was not a good time and place to be a cat; nor were the new colonies in North America. As a result of their link to the remnants of paganism in rural communities, cats – again, especially black cats – had become associated with witchcraft. We see remnants of this association today in horror films and Halloween decorations. When communities tried witches for their 'crimes', they often claimed that the witches could transform themselves into cats; they also mentioned other animals, including dogs, moles, and frogs, but cats were the most common. Thus, the Church of Rome gave its official sanction to cruelty towards cats. Anyone coming upon a cat after dark was justified in killing or maiming it, on the grounds that it might be a witch in disguise. On the Scottish island of Mull, one black cat after another was roasted alive for four days and four nights in an exorcism referred to as the Taigherm.[7] Colonial leaders brought these same prejudices to Massachusetts, culminating in the Salem Witch Trials of 1692–3.

The reputation of the cat began to improve in mid-eighteenth-century Europe. Louis XV, the great-grandson of the same Louis XIV who had lit a Paris bonfire under a basket of cats, was at least tolerant of them, allowing his wife Maria and her courtiers to indulge their pet cats' every whim. It became fashionable for such pets to be incorporated into paintings of French ladies of title, and special tombs were built for favoured animals when they died. However, such attitudes were far from universal: around the same time, the naturalist Georges

Witches with their 'familiars' – a cat, a rat and an owl

Buffon wrote, in his definitive thirty-six-volume *Histoire Naturelle, Générale et Particulière*: 'The cat is an unfaithful domestic, and kept only through necessity to oppose to another domestic which incommodes us still more, and which we cannot drive away.'[8]

Meanwhile, in England, cats were growing in popularity. The eighteenth-century writers Christopher Smart and Samuel Johnson not only valued the company of cats, but also wrote about them. Smart's poem 'For I Will Consider My Cat Jeoffry' begins:

> For I will consider my Cat Jeoffry.
> For he is the servant of the Living God duly and daily serving him.
> For at the first glance of the glory of God in the East he worships in
> his way.
> For this is done by wreathing his body seven times round with elegant
> quickness.

– implying that Smart saw no link between cats and devil worship: indeed, quite the opposite. Smart was also an acute observer of cat behaviour. The poem continues:

> For first he looks upon his forepaws to see if they are clean.
> For secondly he kicks up behind to clear away there.
> For thirdly he works it upon stretch with the forepaws extended.
> For fourthly he sharpens his paws by wood.
> For fifthly he washes himself.
> For sixthly he rolls upon wash.
> For seventhly he fleas himself, that he may not be interrupted upon the beat.
> For eighthly he rubs himself against a post.
> For ninthly he looks up for his instructions.
> For tenthly he goes in quest of food.

Likewise, Samuel Johnson adored his cats Hodge and Lily. His biographer, James Boswell, wrote, 'I never shall forget the indulgence with which he treated Hodge, his cat', possibly referring to Johnson's habit of feeding Hodge oysters – which, it must be said, were not the luxury food then that they are now.

Towards the end of the nineteenth century, the cat completed its transformation to domestic status. In Britain, Queen Victoria kept a succession of pet cats: her Angora, 'White Heather', was one of the consolations of her old age, surviving her to become the pet of her son, Edward VII. In the United States, Mark Twain was not only a cat enthusiast but also, like Smart, an acute observer of their nature:

> By what right has the dog come to be regarded as a 'noble' animal? The more brutal and cruel and unjust you are to him the more your fawning and adoring slave he becomes; whereas, if you shamefully misuse a cat once she will always maintain a dignified reserve towards you afterwards – you will never get her full confidence again.

By the nineteenth century, cats became far more varied in appearance than their ancestors in Egypt. At different times and in various places in Europe and the Middle East, new coat types appeared due to spontaneous genetic mutations. Sometimes these must have disappeared after a few generations, particularly if cat owners regarded the mutations as freakish. However, sometimes unusual-looking cats must have found sympathetic owners who treasured these unique differences. If this preference came to be shared by local owners, and then spread to other places, the underlying mutation might gradually move through the general population, and thereby became part of the range of variation that we see in today's cats – different colours, different patterns, both long and short hair. Remarkably, we can still trace the origins and spread of some of these changes, even in today's multifarious cat populations.

Geneticists credit the comparative homogeneity of household cats across Europe and the Middle East to the local habit of keeping cats on ships. For example, we can easily imagine a litter of kittens conceived in Lebanon being born two months later in Marseilles after their mother had jumped ship. Seagoing Phoenicians, Greeks and Romans spread cats around the Mediterranean, and the genetics of cats in France still shows traces of the trade route up the river Rhône from the Mediterranean and then down the Seine to the English Channel. The distribution of the orange tabby mutation in Northern Europe still shows the effects of its popularity with Viking invaders, almost a thousand years ago.[9]

The first evidence for domestic cats that did not have striped coats comes not long after the beginning of the Christian era. The Greeks first described black cats and white cats in the sixth century CE, but the black mutation, which occurs quite regularly, may have been spreading through the domestic population for several centuries before. Many of the cats that carry this mutation are not actually black. The black colour is caused by an inherited inability to produce the normal pale hair tips that give wildcats their brownish appearance, which is known technically as 'agouti'. The hairs then revert to their basic colour, black, but only if the cat carries two copies of this mutation – one inherited from its mother and one from its father. If it carries one normal copy and one mutant, then the normal copy is dominant and its coat will be the usual tabby. Thus, a male and female pair of such cats, outwardly tabby, could produce a black kitten alongside their other, tabby, kittens. The black mutation is widespread among today's cats, wherever in the world they are found, suggesting that it may have originated before the Phoenicians and Greeks began spreading domestic cats around Europe.

Black cats and white cats are not only opposites in terms of colour; they are also opposites in terms of their relationship with humankind. Cats can be all white either because they are albino, in which case their eyes will be pink, or because they carry a mutation, 'dominant white'. Both tend to be less healthy than normal cats; not only are they prone to skin cancer, but blue-eyed 'dominant white' cats are often deaf. Perhaps more importantly, unlike their striped counterparts, all-white cats stand out against almost any background, so are unlikely to find it easy to catch enough food to sustain themselves. Outside the pedigree population, in which dominant white coats have been deliberately bred into some breeds, all-white cats are uncommon, rarely forming more than 3 per cent of the free-ranging cat population.

By contrast, the black mutation is so common and widespread that it must not bring any major biological disadvantage to the cats that carry it. In some places, more than 80 per cent of cats carry this mutation – not that all or even most of these cats will actually have black coats, since many will have only one copy of the mutation and will therefore appear striped. Today, black is commonest in Britain and Ireland, in Utrecht in the Netherlands, in the city of Chiang Mai in northern Thailand, in a few US cities such as Denton, Texas (holding the current record at almost 90 per cent incorporation), in Vancouver, and also in Morocco.

Since black has not always been everyone's favourite colour for a cat, this ubiquity is difficult to fathom. Since cultural explanations appear not to fit, scientists have proposed a biological basis for the pervasiveness of the black mutation: that possession of this mutation, even one invisible copy (the 'heterozygote'), somehow makes the cat more friendly to people and/or other cats, thereby giving the cats that carry it an advantage in high-density living situations or in prolonged, unavoidable contact with people, such as onboard a ship.[10]

This hypothesis runs counter to a recent study of cats in Latin America.[11] Here, roughly 72 per cent of cats carry the black mutation, similar to the proportion in Spain, from where most South American cats must have come. We can estimate the number of long journeys that cats must have taken between Spain and each of the various Hispanic colonies by tracing their paths along the trade routes. The ancestors of the cats of La Paz, 13,000 feet above sea level in the Andes, completed many such journeys, but black cats are no more common here than in Spain; any cat that travelled this far must have been remarkably tolerant of people. Thus, we cannot yet convincingly explain either the overall numbers of black cats or their local variations.

The 'classic' or blotched tabby pattern exhibits the most remarkable distribution, although the reasons for its prevalence in some areas and not in others are not entirely clear. The cat's wild ancestor had a striped, or 'mackerel', tabby coat, and all domestic cats probably carried the genes for this pattern until at least 2,000 years ago, and possibly even more recently.[12] The mutation for the blotched tabby pattern probably first took hold sometime in the late Middle Ages, and almost certainly in Britain, where it is the commonest pattern today.

Like the black mutation, blotched tabby is recessive: for a cat to have a blotched tabby coat, it must have two copies of the blotched version of the gene, one inherited from its mother and one from its father. One striped, one blotched, and the cat will have a striped coat. Despite this apparent handicap, in Britain and in many parts of the United States blotched tabbies outnumber striped tabbies about two to one, meaning that more than 80 per cent of cats carry the blotched version of the gene. In many parts of Asia, blotched tabbies are rare or even absent. The main exceptions are a few former British colonies such as Hong Kong, which were presumably simultaneously colonized by British cats, either ships' cats or the pets of the settlers.

For a new version of a gene, especially a recessive gene, to spread through a population, it must provide some advantage. Since (striped) cats had been in Britain since Roman times and probably earlier, blotched tabbies must have been rare to begin with. They probably reached 10 per cent of the population by about 1500 CE, and then increased year after year until they reached their current near-ubiquity. In Britain, blotched tabby is sometimes referred to as 'classic' tabby, as if the striped version were the mutation, not the other way around.

The reason for the ascendancy of the blotched pattern is still unknown. British cat owners do not prefer the blotched to the striped

Blotched and striped tabbies

coat, at least not to the extent that this could account for their proportions among British pets; in fact, when asked, they express a small preference for striped tabby, perhaps simply because it is (now) relatively unusual. Blotched tabby does not seem to provide any better or worse camouflage than striped, at least in the countryside. There has been a suggestion that the pollution caused by the Industrial Revolution, coating British cities in soot, favoured darker cats – both blotched tabby and black – because they were less conspicuous, but this has never been confirmed.[13] Still, we know that almost all genes have multiple effects, even though most are named for the most obvious change they bring about. Therefore, the blotched version of the gene possibly produces some other advantage, nothing to do with the coat, that somehow suited cats to life in Britain.

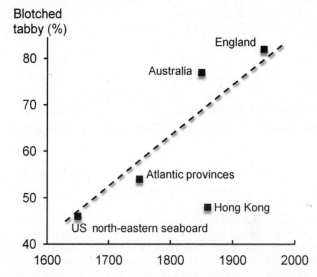

How the percentage of the blotched tabby allele varied between locations colonized from England between 1650 and 1900, compared to England in 1950

We see the rise of the blotched tabby gene in Britain reflected in the proportion of blotched tabbies in former British colonies all around the world. In the north-eastern United States – New York, Philadelphia, and Boston – settled by Europeans in the 1650s, only about 45 per cent of cats carry the blotched tabby gene, but this is considerably more than in originally Spanish-settled areas, such as Texas, at around 30 per cent – where cats look much like those in Spain today. As shown in the chart above, the Atlantic provinces of Canada, settled some 100 years later, have more blotched tabbies. European colonies settled in the nineteenth century are more variable: Hong Kong in particular has fewer than it should, probably because there was already a striped-tabby population of Chinese origin there, thus diluting the effect of British immigration. Australia on the other hand has more than it should, possibly the result of later waves of British immigrants in the twentieth century bringing their cats with them. The proportion in Britain was over 80 per cent in the 1970s, and may have continued to rise since then.

We can explain this trend by making two assumptions. The first is that the proportion of blotched tabbies in Britain has been rising steadily since about 1500, for some reason unique to that country – otherwise the same change should have taken place in, for example, New York, Nova Scotia, Brisbane and Hong Kong, resulting in blotched tabbies reaching 80 per cent of the population today in those places as well. The second is that once a population of cats becomes established in a particular place, the proportion of blotched to striped doesn't change. The latter assumption holds for other places and

RECONSTRUCTING THE ORIGINS OF THE CATS OF HUMBOLDT COUNTY, CALIFORNIA

Domestic cats arrived on the West Coast of the USA by a variety of routes – by sea from the south and the north, and overland from the east. From the sixteenth to eighteenth centuries, Humboldt County, on northern California's Redwood Coast, received a succession of visitors and settlers, including Russians, British and Spanish vessels exploring the Pacific Coast, and farmers from both Missouri to the east and Oregon to the north. Feral cats, probably escapees from trading ships, were first recorded in Humboldt County in the 1820s, before the arrival of the first farmers, so today's cats could be the descendants of either – or both.

In the 1970s, biologist Bennett Blumenberg recorded the coat colours and patterns of 250 local cats, and from these determined the proportions of the different versions of each gene. For example, 56 per cent of the cats were black or black and white, from which he was able to estimate that the black ('non-agouti') version of the gene was present in 75 per cent of the population – the difference being made up of cats that were carrying one black version and one tabby, and were therefore outwardly tabby. He also recorded the numbers of orange and tortoiseshell cats, blotched vs striped tabbies, pale coats, long and short hair, all-white cats, and cats with white feet and bib: each one of these variations is controlled by a different and well-understood gene. He then compared these with cats from other parts of North America.[14]

The most similar were the cats of San Francisco, Calgary and Boston, indicating that the ancestors of today's Humboldt County cats had mainly arrived overland with farmers and prospectors, or in the fur-traders' vessels sailing from Boston. However, he also found traces of cats of Spanish origin, left behind after the demise of New Spain and its occupation of much of what is now California. Some otherwise unaccounted for similarities were detectable with the cats of Vladivostok, home port of the Russian–American Trading Company. Their ships also sailed from ports that are now in China, and could feasibly have carried cats of Chinese origin, but Blumenberg found no trace of Chinese cat genes in the Californian cats.

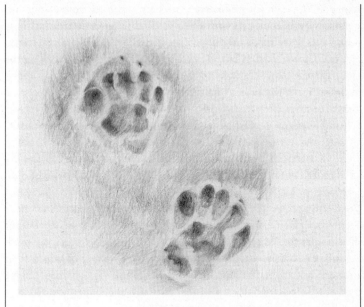

Polydactyl footprints

Another rare mutation, known as polydactyly, gives cats an extra toe on each foot. Early in the establishment of Boston, one newly arrived cat must have produced a kitten with extra toes, and that kitten became the ancestor of many more, such that by 1848 extra-toed cats were common there; today, they form about 15 per cent of the population. Cats with extra toes are also common in Yarmouth, Nova Scotia, a seaport founded by immigrants from Boston, whereas in nearby Digby, settled by New York Loyalists at the end of the Civil War, polydactyly is as rare as it is everywhere else.[15]

variations in coat colour, too, so it may be a universal (see box, 'Reconstructing the Origins of the Cats of Humboldt County, California'): however, given that it seems not to have occurred anywhere else, the rise of the blotched tabby in Britain becomes even more curious.

Relatively few of the domestic cats that colonized South America from Spain and Portugal were blotched tabbies, so scientists have had to turn to other variations in appearance to trace their history. Here also, it seems that once a population of cats becomes established, its genetics don't change much, even over several centuries. It seems plausible that the cat population is set up when the initial (human) colonists bring their cats with them, and subsequent immigrants only adopt cats from the local population. For example, in the nineteenth century, Catalans from Barcelona established several towns along the river Amazon, and the cats of at least two of those towns, Leticia-Tabatinga and Manaus, remain similar to the cats of Barcelona more than a century later.[16]

As in Hispanic-settled parts of the United States, and in Spain itself, orange and tortoiseshell cats are more common in South America than in most other places. The exceptions, where these colours are even more common, are Egypt – possibly one origin of this mutation (see box, p. 51, 'Why Ginger Cats are Usually Boys'); the islands off the north and west coasts of Scotland; and Iceland. Researchers have attributed these exceptions to a hypothetical preference for orange cats among the Vikings, who colonized those places around the ninth century CE, but it is unclear whether the Vikings first obtained their orange cats from the Eastern Mediterranean, or whether orange appeared spontaneously and independently somewhere in Norway and was then transported around the Norwegian Sea in Viking ships.

Today, cats come in many colours and coat types, and many of these variations are undoubtedly the result of human preferences – even leaving aside pedigree cats, whose breeding is strictly under human control. The basic colours of cats – black, tabby (striped or blotched), ginger – are well established in populations all around the world, albeit in slightly different proportions. These colours persist in cats that have gone feral, so they do not seem to produce any major advantage – or disadvantage – to their wearers. However, many other variations in appearance seem to persist mainly because people like them. Cats with white feet and variable amounts of white on the body (the gene that controls this is rather imprecise in its effects) are less well-camouflaged than their plainer counterparts, putting the cat at a disadvantage when hunting. However, many people prefer their cats to carry white patches, especially the black-and-white 'tuxedo' cat. Some people also favour cats that carry a gene that dilutes their coat colour, such that black cats become a fetching shade of grey (often referred to as 'blue'), and other colours are a few shades lighter than usual.

Some people like long-haired cats. Although it seems self-evident that these cats, which, like all cats, cannot sweat through their coats, should be at a natural disadvantage in warm climates, a recent study of Latin American cats indicates that human preference is a much more potent factor than the weather,[17] although a thick coat, such as that of the Maine Coon and the Norwegian Forest Cat, is undoubtedly beneficial for outdoor cats in cold climates. In temperate climates, the main disadvantage of long hair is not that the cat overheats, but that its coat easily becomes matted, which, if left unattended, leads to infection or infestation of the skin. Long-haired cats are rarely seen in feral colonies, testifying to their unsuitability for a life without attention from humans.

The striped tabby pattern evidently suits wildcats the best, possibly because it provides the most effective camouflage for hunting. Presumably, mutations that affect appearance have occurred from time to time, but the wildcats that happened to carry them fared worse than their 'normal' counterparts, so the mutation quickly died out. For a domestic cat, camouflage is probably less critical, allowing other coat colours to spread through the population.

A similar variety of colours and coat types has, of course, also become a feature of many other types of domesticated animal – dogs, horses and cattle, for example. In the case of the cat, external appearance reflects two distinct factors, both of which affect how many offspring a cat is likely to have, and therefore how common its coat colour and type are likely to be in the next generation. The first is whether these factors impede the cat's hunting ability; this may not be so important today, but it certainly was in the past. The second is how appealing the cat is to its owner. Because human tastes vary from person to person and culture to culture, this second factor has produced many variations.

What seems to be missing here is any trace of each cat's own preferences. Although never studied directly, we have no evidence for 'colour prejudice' among cats. Tabby females do not seem to spurn black toms in favour of other tabbies: white bib and socks seem to be neither an advantage nor a disadvantage when it comes to finding a mate, except perhaps indirectly, if the cat's conspicuousness has resulted in it catching less prey and thus looking less healthy than its better-camouflaged rival. Whatever criteria cats use to choose a mate, coat colour seems to be well down the list.

Even today, most domestic cats exert a remarkable amount of control over their own lives, significantly more than other domestic animals, such as dogs. If we leave the pedigree breeds to one side for a moment (and these are still in a minority), most cats go where they please and choose their own mates (unless they are neutered – a relatively recent phenomenon). For this reason alone, cats cannot be considered completely domesticated.[18] Full domestication means that humankind has complete control over what an animal eats, where it goes, and most crucially, which individuals are allowed to breed and which are not.

We certainly provide domestic cats with most or all of their food, but in this respect, too, cats are an anomaly. Science classifies them as obligate carnivores, animals that have to obtain a mostly meat-based diet if they are to thrive (see box, 'Cats are the True Carnivores'). For a female cat to breed successfully, she must have a high proportion of flesh in her diet, especially in late winter, when she is preparing to come into season, and subsequently while she is pregnant. The domestication of such an animal takes some explaining; until recently, meat and even fish formed only a minor part of most people's diets, and were often only seasonally available. Most domesticated animals will thrive on foods that we ourselves cannot eat, unlocking sources of nourishment that would otherwise be unavailable to us: cows turn grass, which we can't digest, into milk and meat, which we can. (Though classified as carnivores, even dogs are actually omnivores; they may prefer meat, but cereal-based foods can, if necessary, give them all the nutrition they need.)

For most of their coexistence with humankind, cats were valued primarily for their skill as hunters. Since mice contain all the nourishment a cat needs, a successful hunter automatically ate a balanced diet; starvation was always possible for the less adept or the unlucky, but diseases due to specific nutritional deficiencies were unlikely. However, even historically, few domestic cats would have lived by hunting alone, most being provided with at least some food by their owners, supplementing their diet by scavenging. So long as some of their diet came from fresh meat, usually in the form of prey they had

CATS ARE THE TRUE CARNIVORES

Cats are carnivores not by choice, but by necessity. Many of their relatives in the animal kingdom, though referred to as Carnivora, are actually omnivores – including domestic dogs, foxes and bears – and some, like pandas, have reverted to being vegetarian. The whole cat family, from the lion down to the tiny black-footed cat from Southern Africa, has the same nutritional needs. At some point many millions of years ago, the ancestral cat became such a specialized meat-eater that it lost the ability to live on plants: it became a 'hypercarnivore'. Once lost, such capabilities rarely re-evolve. Domestic cats might have been more successful if they could have got by, as dogs can, living on scraps, but they are stuck firmly in the nutritional dead end their ancestors bequeathed to them.

Cats require far more protein in their diet than dogs or humans do, because they get most of their energy not from carbohydrates but from protein. Other animals, faced with a shortage of protein in the diet, can channel all the protein they do get into maintaining and repairing their bodies, but cats cannot. Cats also need particular types of protein, especially those that contain the amino acid taurine, a component that occurs naturally in humans, but not in cats.

Cats can digest and metabolize fats, some of which must come from animal sources so that the cat can use them to make prostaglandins, a type of hormone essential for successful reproduction. Most other mammals can make prostaglandins from plant oils, but cats cannot. Female cats must get enough animal fat during the winter to be ready for their normal reproductive cycle, mating in late winter and giving birth in the spring.

Cats' vitamin requirements are also more stringent than ours. They need vitamin A in their diet (if needs be, we can make ours from plant sources), sunshine doesn't stimulate their skin to make vitamin D as ours does, and they need lots of the B vitamins niacin and thiamine.[19]

None of this is a problem if the cat can get plenty of meat – although raw fish, which contains an enzyme that destroys thiamine, can cause a deficiency if eaten in excess. It is just possible to construct a vegetarian diet for cats, but only if every single one of the cat's nutritional peculiarities is carefully compensated for. Their taste buds also differ substantially from our own, having evolved to focus better on an all-meat diet. They cannot taste sugars; instead, they are much more sensitive than we are to how 'sweet' some kinds of flesh are, compared to others, which they find bitter.

Cats do have two notable nutritional advantages over humans. First, their kidneys are very efficient, as expected for an animal whose ancestors lived on the edge of deserts, and many cats drink little water, getting all the moisture they need from the meat they eat. Second, cats do not require vitamin C. Taken together, these make cats well suited to shipboard life: they don't compete with sailors for precious drinking water, getting all they need from the mice they catch, and they are not afflicted by scurvy, a common disease among mariners to the middle of the eighteenth century, when it was found it could be prevented by eating citrus fruits.

killed themselves, scavenging would not have tipped them into nutritional imbalance; still, giving up hunting entirely would have been risky.

Cats do not scavenge at random; they have some ability to make informed choices. They subsequently avoid foods that make them feel seriously and instantly ill. When eating food that they have not killed for themselves, they also deliberately seek out a varied diet, thereby avoiding a buildup of anything that might make them sick long-term, but might slip beneath the radar of immediate malaise.

To demonstrate this behaviour, I laid out individual pieces of dry cat food on a grid on the ground, some of one brand, some of another, and then allowed rescued strays to forage over them, one at a time. In this way, I could record in precisely what order each cat picked up and ate the pieces of the two foods. When there were equal numbers of each type of food, the cats roamed across the grid, eating both foods but more of whichever food they liked better. However, when one of the two foods made up 90 per cent of the total, every cat, whatever its preference, stopped grazing indiscriminately within a couple of minutes and started actively seeking out the rarer food. Thus, these cats demonstrated a primitive 'nutritional wisdom', as if they assumed that eating a variety of food was more likely to produce a balanced diet than simply eating the food that was easiest to find (even though both the foods offered were nutritionally complete).[20] When I gave similar choices to pet cats that had always had a balanced diet, few responded this way, most continuing to eat whichever of the two foods they liked better from the outset, or were just easy to find. Thus, although all cats probably have the capacity to deliberately vary their diets, it seems that this ability must be 'awakened' by some experience of having to scavenge for a living, as most of the stray cats in our original experiment must have done before they were rescued.[21]

Most other animals have more varied diets than cats do. Rats, the best-studied example, are omnivores with extremely wide tastes that suit them perfectly for a scavenging lifestyle. They employ several strategies that enable them to pick the right foods from the wide but unpredictable choices available to them. New foods are only nibbled at until the rat is sure that they're not poisonous. As soon as each food starts to be digested, the rat's gut sends information to its brain about

Cats foraging on a grid

its energy, protein and fat content, enabling the rat to switch to another food with a different nutritional content if necessary. Cats are much less sophisticated in this regard, having travelled a different evolutionary path based on mainly eating fresh prey, which is by definition nutritionally balanced.

Given their limited ability to subsist by scavenging alone, cats were locked into the hunting lifestyle until as recently as the 1980s. Until science revealed all of their nutritional peculiarities, it would have been a matter of luck whether a cat that wasn't able to hunt obtained a nutritionally balanced diet, unless its owner was both willing and able to give it fresh meat and fish every day. Although commercial cat foods have been available for over a century, there was initially little understanding that cats had very different requirements to dogs, and much of this food must have been nutritionally unbalanced. Commercial cat food that is guaranteed to be nutritionally complete has been widely available for only thirty-five years or so – only 1 per cent of the total time since domestication began.

In evolutionary terms, this is just a blink of an eye, and we have yet to see the full effects of this improvement in nutrition on cats' lifestyles. Just a few dozen generations ago, the cat that was a skilful and successful hunter was also the cat that stood the best chance of breeding successfully. Those cats that depended entirely on man for their food would usually obtain enough calories to keep them going day-to-day, but many would not have bred successfully, because a large number of the cat's unusual nutrient requirements are essential for reproduction. Nowadays, any cat owner can go to the supermarket and buy food that keeps their cat in optimum condition for breeding. That is, of course, if the cat has not been neutered – another development that has yet to show its full effect on the cat's nature.

Today's cat is thereby a product of historical turmoil and misconception. What would today's cats be like if they had not gone through centuries of persecution? It is possible that the effects may not have been particularly long-lasting. After all, since serious attempts were made to exterminate black cats in continental Europe because of their supposed association with witchcraft, they should still be uncommon there today – and they're not. Although undoubtedly many individual cats did suffer horribly, little lasting damage seems to have been done to the species as a whole. This is probably because, for most of the time and in most places, particularly in the countryside, cat-keeping was both enjoyable and practically beneficial, even if occasionally interrupted by an outburst of religious persecution. Changes have taken place – cats today are significantly smaller and more varied in colour than when they left Egypt – but they appear to have been mainly local rather than global.

Thus, following the origin of their partnership in ancient Egypt, cats and humans continued to live alongside one another, for a further 2,000 years, without the cat ever becoming fully domesticated. Then, due to the nutritional discoveries of the 1970s, all cats, and not just the pets of the well-off, were relieved of the necessity to hunt for a living. However, their predatory past, so essential to their survival until recently, cannot be obliterated overnight. One of the most significant challenges facing today's cat enthusiasts is how to allow their cats to express their hunting instincts without causing wildlife the damage which evokes so much criticism from the anti-cat lobby.

4

Every Cat Has to Learn
to be Domestic

Cats are not born attached to people; they're born ready to learn how to attach themselves to people. Any kitten denied experience with people will revert towards its ancestral wild state and become feral. Something in their evolution has given domestic cats the inclination – and it's no more than that – to trust people during a brief period when they're tiny kittens. This minute advantage enabled a few wildcats to leave their origins behind and find their place in environments created by the planet's dominant species. Only one other animal has done this more successfully than the domestic cat, and that, of course, is the domestic dog.[1] Like puppies, kittens arrive into the world helpless, and then have just a few weeks in which to learn about the animals around them – an even shorter time for cats than for dogs – before they must make their own way in the world. By comparison with our own infants, which are dependent on us for years, this is a very brief period. Even in their wild ancestors, the wolf and the wildcat, this window must have been open just a crack, waiting for evolution to allow the young animals of these two species to learn to trust us, and thereby become domesticated.

Kittens and puppies alike become more closely integrated into human society than any other animal can, but the way the two species achieve this differs. Early scientific studies of dogs from the 1950s established the notion of a primary socialization period, a few weeks in the puppy's life when it is especially sensitive to learning how to interact with people. A puppy handled every day from seven to fourteen weeks of age will be friendly towards people and virtually indistinguishable from a puppy whose handling started four weeks earlier. For the next quarter-century, scientists generally assumed that kittens must be the same, and that it was not essential to handle kittens until they were seven weeks old. In the 1980s, when researchers finally performed corresponding tests on cats, those recommendations had to change.

These experiments confirmed that the concept of a socialization period could indeed be applied to cats, but that this period was comparatively curtailed in kittens. The researchers handled some kittens from three weeks old, some from seven weeks old, and the rest not until the testing started at fourteen weeks. The kittens started learning about people much earlier than puppies do. As expected, the kittens handled from their third week were happy to sit on a lap when they reached fourteen weeks old, but those whose contact with people had been delayed to seven weeks jumped off within half a minute – though not as quickly as those that had never been handled during their first fourteen weeks, which typically stayed put for less than fifteen seconds.

Could this be explained by the seven-week-handled kittens being more active than the three-week ones – in other words, no less happy to be on a person's lap, just more eager to explore their surroundings? It quickly became obvious that this could not be the cause. When each kitten was subsequently given the opportunity to cross a room towards one of its handlers, only the three-week kittens did so reliably – and were quick to do it, too, giving every impression that they were attracted to the person, who was by then very familiar to them. The seven-week and unhandled kittens did not seem unduly frightened of the person, and would occasionally get close to her. Some even apparently asked to be picked up, but these two groups were more or less indistinguishable in their behaviour.

The handling that those seven-week kittens received up to the point of testing had not produced the powerful attraction to people that was obvious from the behaviour of the three-week kittens. For the scientists taking part, the tests simply formalized what was already obvious from the kittens' behaviour. As the leader of the research team noted, 'In observing and interacting with these cats during testing and in their home rooms, it was obvious to everyone working in the lab that the late-handled [i.e. seven-week] cats behaved more like the unhandled cats.'[2]

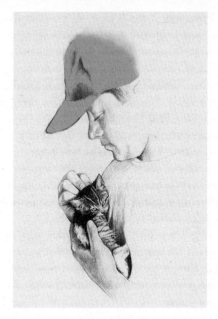

Handling a feral kitten

The scientists concluded that cats need to start learning about people much earlier than dogs must. Dog breeders ought to handle puppies before they are eight weeks old, but if puppies are not handled until that age, then with the right remedial treatment they can still become perfectly happy pets. A kitten that encounters its first human in its ninth week is likely to be anxious when near people for the rest of its life. The paths that lead to an affectionate pet on one hand and a wild scavenger on the other diverge early in the cat's life; indeed, if it were any earlier, few cats would be able to forge relationships with us.

Even though the most crucial changes start in the third week, the first two weeks of the kitten's life are far from uneventful. For the first fourteen days of a kitten's life, the most important feature in its world is its mother. Kittens are born blind, deaf and incapable of moving more than a few inches unaided. They cannot regulate their own body temperatures. Especially if the litter is larger than average, and the kittens are correspondingly small, they carry little in the way of energy reserves, and even the loss of a fraction of an ounce in weight can lead to weakness and, if outside intervention is not forthcoming, death. Their survival, then, depends on their mother's capabilities. Tomcats play no part in rearing offspring, and many mothers that give birth outside the home raise their kittens without help. The mother's choice of nest site is crucial, especially when the luxury of giving birth indoors is not available. Kittens must be well protected from the weather and from potential predators. After the first twenty-four hours, which all mother cats spend suckling and grooming their kittens, she may have to leave them to find food; and if that involves hunting, as it would in the wild, that may take some time.

Once kittens are a few days old, the mother may move them to a different nest site if her instincts make her feel uncomfortable about the original den. Kittens have a special 'scruffing' reflex that enables her to do this quickly and quietly, without drawing attention to their vulnerability: she grasps them in her mouth by the loose skin on the back of their necks, and they instantly go limp and apparently oblivious to their surroundings, until she drops them in the new nest, when they appear confused but otherwise unaffected (see box, 'Clipnosis').

Many mother cats try to move their litters at least once before they wean them, but science has yet to find out why. In the wild, a mother cat will inevitably carry a few fleas, and because she has to spend so much time in the nest, flea eggs accumulate there; when they become adult fleas three or four weeks later, a single hop will take them on to a kitten. Removing the kittens from such an obvious source of infestation seems a good strategy and may be one explanation for nest-moving, but so far no evidence has been found that this reduces the number of fleas that kittens carry. Nest-moving may simply be a response to a disturbance that made the mother anxious, or may sometimes be strategic, bringing the kittens closer to the source of food on to which their mother intends to wean them. The kittens may suffer if the mother cat moves them too early or chooses the wrong new nest site. Kittens are vulnerable to becoming chilled, especially in damp weather that also favours the transmission of respiratory

'CLIPNOSIS'

Unlike much infantile behaviour, in some cats the 'scruff' reflex mother cats use when carrying their kittens persists into adulthood. For those individuals, scruffing can be used as a gentle and humane method of quieting a fearful cat. The cat is simply grasped firmly by the skin on the back of its neck and, if the reflex is triggered, may go into what appears to be a trance, enabling it to be picked up and carried; its weight must be supported by the other hand. Veterinary nurses sometimes use a hands-free version, applying a line of several clothespegs to the area of skin between the top of the head and the shoulders. By doing so, the nurses can complete an examination of the cat without causing it too much stress.[3]

viruses; many feral kittens, particularly those born in the autumn, succumb to cat flu.

As my own experience shows, not all cats are innately skilled at parenthood. My cat Libby, having a nervous disposition, was not the best mother. As the time for her to have her litter approached, we tried to keep her in the same room where she had herself been born, presuming she would find the surroundings reassuring. But she was restless, patrolling the house and looking into every open cupboard and drawer, as if undecided as to the safest location. At least she showed no inclination to give birth outdoors. Eventually, she decided to produce her kittens within a few feet of where she herself had come into the world.

We should not have relaxed: a few days later, we discovered the kittens scattered all around the house. For a few hours after the birth, Libby lay with her three kittens and allowed them to suckle, but after that she appeared to lose interest, spending too much time away from them. Her mother Lucy was intrigued by the kittens, but at this stage played no part in looking after them. When we checked the kittens' weights, they seemed to be growing, so we were not unduly worried until Libby began to try to pick them up in her mouth and carry them away from the den we had built for her. Her inexperience as a first-time mother showed immediately, as she grasped the kittens rather roughly by the head, only occasionally and apparently accidentally gripping them correctly by their scruffs. Once she had got the hang of carrying them, she began to look for places to hide them.

Without our intervention, Libby's kittens would surely have perished. She would find a secluded place to hide the first kitten, and then return to the other two, pick up another, and take that one somewhere else, ignoring the cries of the first. After taking the third to yet another location, Libby would wander off as if unsure what to do next. Each time this happened, we searched out all the kittens and put them back in the original den. Once or twice, we tried constructing a new den – in the same room, but with completely new bedding so that it smelled nothing like the first, hoping this might fool Libby into believing she had successfully moved the whole litter herself. Still, the removals persisted. Finally, grandmother Lucy, her maternal instincts aroused, began to retrieve the kittens herself. Libby, perhaps sensing that she should follow her mother's lead, gradually gave up trying to move the litter. She continued to feed them, and they grew stronger, but from then on it was Lucy who groomed them and kept them together until they were ready to be weaned.

Lucy seemed to know the kittens by their appearance and by their smell, but first-time mothers can behave as if they do not immediately 'know' what a kitten is. Rather, they respond to a single powerful stimulus that ensures that they take care of their newborns. This is the kitten's high-pitched distress call, uttered if it is cold, hungry or out of contact with its littermates. When the mother cat hears this sound coming from outside the nest, indicating that a kitten has strayed away, she should instantly begin a search and, when she finds the kitten, retrieve it by its scruff. If the kittens are all in the nest and calling together, her instinct is to lie down and encircle them with her paws, drawing them on to her abdomen and allowing them to suckle. Gradually, over the course of their first couple of weeks of life, she seems to recognize the kittens as independent animals, though whether she ever comes to know them as individuals is unclear.

Kittens are so vulnerable in the first few weeks of their lives that their survival depends almost entirely on their mother's skill. Libby seemed to lack several components of maternal instinct, but even if just one is defective, the kittens' chances become slim. Yet if cats are as little removed from the wild as many researchers consider they are, they should – and most do – retain the ability to get everything right the first time, without practice. Research on free-ranging cats has pro-

Libby's kittens preferred to curl up with Lucy

duced little evidence to support the idea that first-time mothers are less successful than second-time,[4] although Libby's inability to locate her kittens' scruffs is reportedly quite common in inexperienced mother cats (known as queens). Of course, domestication has provided an obvious safety net: the intervention of human owners.

For about the first two weeks of their lives, kittens define their world through smell and touch. At birth, their eyes and ears are still sealed, providing them with little useful information. Kittens recognize their mother immediately, initially just by her warmth and feel, and rapidly also learn her characteristic smell. They probably have little idea of what she is 'supposed' to smell like; orphaned kittens fed on an artificial 'mother' that smells nothing like a cat quickly learn its scent instead – a kind of 'imprinting'. In one classic series of experiments, researchers constructed a surrogate mother from artificial fur fabric, through which latex teats protruded, only some of which provided milk. Each teat was scented differently, for example with cologne or oil of wintergreen. The kittens quickly learned which scent indicated a milk-delivering teat.[5]

Each kitten gradually develops a nipple preference, based also on the nipple's odour rather than its position, since each kitten knows precisely where it wants to suckle whichever way its mother is lying. They find their preferred nipple by following the odour trail made up of their own saliva, and probably secretions from scent glands under their chins, that are left behind on their mother's fur as they approach the nipple.[6]

Kittens are unusually flexible when bonding with their mothers, a quality that works in their favour when their mothers are part of a social group. Often these groups are composed of close relatives, say a female and her adult daughters, which have grown up together and know one another well enough to overcome their natural mistrust of other cats. Such cats will spontaneously share nests and pool their kittens.

The local authority once asked me how to handle such a cat colony living underneath some temporary buildings. Having pointed them towards humane alternatives to putting out poison, I located an animal charity to trap the cats and relocate them.[7] It was springtime, and three of the females were heavily pregnant; they gave birth within a few days of one another. Even though they were given three separate boxes, the mothers soon put all the kittens together, and each fed them indiscriminately. Ten kittens feeding from three queens, all within a few inches of one another, produced the loudest chorus of purring I have ever heard.

As this implies, mother cats can be equally indiscriminate when identifying their own kittens from those of other cats – or at least, those of their relatives, which may smell similar. For cats, the general rule appears to be that if a kitten is in your nest, it must be yours. Some cat rescue organizations exploit this quality to raise orphaned kittens: some mother cats will readily accept an extra kitten that is gently slipped in with their own, even if their ages don't match up. Some will even suckle entire litters introduced to them as their own kittens are removed after weaning. This doesn't seem to do the mother any harm, provided, of course, she gets enough to eat throughout.

Both mother cat and kittens are unusually trusting during the first few weeks after birth. For the mother, this is due to a wave of the hormone oxytocin, which drives her to make her kittens her top priority. For her kittens, the factor may not be a hormone such as oxytocin, but instead their early inability to produce stress hormones such as adrenalin. A kitten that suckles for a few seconds too long, and is accidentally dragged out of the nest as its mother leaves, should be terrified; after all, this is potentially the most traumatic experience it has had in its short life. We can see the latent danger in this situation: the last thing such a kitten should do is make an association between the mother's smell and the shock of falling to the ground outside the nest. If it does, when the mother returns it might shy away from her, rather than immediately attaching to her to feed as it should. However, thankfully, kittens' inability to produce stress hormones means that such incidents leave no lasting impression.

Once a kitten reaches two weeks of age, its eyes and ears open and it begins to take its first faltering steps around the nest (see figure, p. 92). Its stress mechanisms then begin to function, enabling it to learn both what's bad and what's good about the world. From this point, what the kittens learn depends on whether their mother is present. If she's there, the kittens take their lead from her, but do not become stressed, so may not remember much about anything untoward that happens to them. Only if she is absent, and they must make their own decisions on how to react, do their stress levels rise abruptly, cementing their memory of the trauma and whether they dealt with it effectively or not.

This 'social buffering' is probably adaptive for cats in the wild. A mother that is absent for long periods is probably having difficulty finding enough food for her litter or to replenish her milk, so the kittens must start to learn about the world soon if they are to stand any chance of survival. Kittens whose mother is usually with them in the

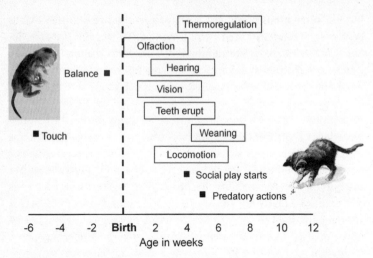

The development of the senses and other critical events in the life of a kitten

nest can delay learning about any perils that may await them, because they can rely on their mother to protect them.

The personalities of cats are powerfully affected by what they learn when they're tiny kittens. Most kittens born in houses will be looked after both by their mothers and by their mothers' owners, but those unfortunate enough to undergo prolonged stress in their first few weeks of life may grow up to have enduring emotional and cognitive problems. For example, kittens that are abandoned by their mothers and are then hand-raised can become excessively attention-seeking towards their first owners, though some subsequently seem to 'grow out of' this. Based on what we know about other mammals in similar situations, we can assume that after the mother's departure, the kittens' brains endure high levels of stress hormones. These consistently high levels cause permanent changes in their developing brains and stress hormone systems, such that they may overreact to unsettling events later in life.

Such cats may not make particularly satisfying pets, but this is by no means to say that they are mentally defective. Rather, their apparently abnormal behaviour is an evolved adaptation. A mother that has struggled to raise her kittens was most likely affected by some difficulty that has made food hard to find. A kitten whose mother has struggled to raise it therefore expects to emerge into an uncertain world, in which it may have to live on its wits and thereby outcompete its littermates and any other kittens born in the vicinity. The kittens of a relaxed, well-fed mother are likely to be able to depend on a more stable world, one in which they will have the time to hone their social skills and reproduce several times over a period of years. Such kittens, of course, are likely to make better pets than kittens that have been stressed in early life.

As a kitten begins its third week, it embarks on the most crucial six weeks of its life, as far as its development is concerned (see box overleaf, 'Stages of Development'). From this point onwards, its eyes, ears and legs begin to function reliably, and, guided by its hormones, it begins to make decisions about whom and what it should interact with, and whom and what it should keep away from. At the same time, its brain is growing rapidly, every day adding thousands of new nerve cells and millions of new connections among them, establishing the framework for storing all the new knowledge it accumulates. Its mother is still a crucial influence during this period, but from now on a kitten gradually becomes able to distinguish its littermates from one another, and to learn about the other animals around it, including people. Kittens born in the wild also begin to learn how to hunt, for within a few short weeks they will need to feed themselves.

Most of the kittens' interactions with one another are playful, and for the first half of the socialization period most of their play is directed at other kittens. However, we do not know if early on each kitten recognizes that what it is playing with is another kitten; most of the actions performed are similar to those used later towards objects. Bouts of play are short and disorganized, and it may be that the movements of the other kitten trigger each attempt at play. By the time they are six weeks old, though, kittens will play on their own with the objects around them, poking, pouncing, chasing, batting them with their paws and tossing them in the air. These are all actions adult cats use when they capture prey, so biologists have looked for an elusive link between the amount of play that kittens perform and their hunting ability when they grow up. While play with objects hones the kittens' general coordination, it's probably not the most

STAGES OF DEVELOPMENT

The way a cat reacts to the world around it develops for at least the first year of its life, but most of the crucial changes take place in the first three or four months. Biologists divide this into four periods, each of which has a different significance for the growing kitten.

During the prenatal period, *the second month of the queen's pregnancy, the kitten is largely – but not entirely – isolated from the outside world. The composition of the amniotic fluid and the blood in the placenta both reflect the mother's environment. For example, if the mother eats a strongly flavoured food during this period, the kittens may prefer to be weaned on to a food with the same flavour, showing that they gain the ability to learn well before they emerge into the world. Female kittens that are adjacent to male kittens in the womb absorb some of their testosterone and are briefly more aggressive in their social play than kittens in all-female litters. Such inclinations are likely to be short-lived, but more far-reaching changes are also possible. Based on what we know of other mammals, if the mother is highly stressed during her pregnancy, her stress hormones may cross the placenta and impair the development of her kittens' brains and endocrine systems.*

During most of the neonatal period, *from birth to about two and a half weeks of age, the kitten is deaf and blind, relying on its senses of smell and touch to bond to its mother.*

The socialization period *begins as the eyes and ears open and begin to function in the third week of life, enabling the kitten to start learning about the world around it, including the people that are caring for it and its mother. At the same time, it learns to walk and then to run. When they are not sleeping, kittens spend much of this period engaged in play, initially with one another and then increasingly with objects.*

The beginning of the juvenile period, *at eight weeks of age, coincides with the customary time to rehome a kitten (except pedigree kittens, traditionally homed at thirteen weeks). By this point, the sensitive period for socialization is virtually over. The juvenile period ends at sexual maturity, sometime between seven months and one year of age; many pet cats will of course be neutered before the end of the first year.*

important factor in determining whether a cat grows up to be capable of catching enough prey to keep itself fed.

For feral kittens, their mother enables them to learn how to fend for themselves. As soon as they are old enough, she brings recently killed prey back to the nest; as they become better coordinated, she brings back prey that is still alive. This gives the kittens the opportunity both to handle prey and to find out what it tastes like. The mother doesn't seem actively to teach them how to deal with prey; rather, she simply places it in front of them and allows their predatory instincts to take over. If they show no interest, she may draw attention to the prey by starting to feed on it herself, stopping when the kittens begin to join in. Of course, this process rarely happens with owned cats, unless the mother happens to be an accomplished and habitual hunter herself, in which case small, gory 'presents' may find their way into the nest.

Whether a cat is destined to be a hunter or (more likely) not, among the most important events in a kitten's life is when its mother decides to start weaning it. This typically occurs in the fourth or fifth week of the kitten's life, but may be earlier if the litter is large – six or more kittens – or if the mother is unwell or stressed. Whatever the circumstances, the mother cat drives this process; kittens rarely if ever decide to wean themselves. At the decisive moment, the mother starts to spend time away from the kittens or simply blocks access to her milk by lying or crouching with her abdomen pressed firmly to the ground. Not surprisingly, the kittens begin to get hungry, and for a few days their weight gain, steady since birth, slows down or even stops. Hunger drives them to become much more inquisitive about other possible sources of food.

In the home, with human owners supplying the grub, the new source of food should be special kitten food. In the wild, mother cats bring prey back to the nest and dissect it, making it easier for small mouths to chew. The kittens continue to pester her for milk, but for the next couple of weeks or so she will ration them, to force them to develop their ability to eat – and digest – meat. As their eating habits change, so do their insides. Meat takes longer to digest than milk, so kittens' intestines become lined with villi, small finger-shaped projections that increase the amount of nutrients that can be absorbed. Lactase, the enzyme that breaks down milk sugar, is permanently replaced by sucrase to break down the sugars in muscle, such that many adult cats find milk indigestible. The mother cat is simply being cruel to be kind: when the kittens become fully weaned at about eight weeks of age, she may spontaneously allow them to suckle occasionally, possibly as a way of reinforcing family ties – although in a domestic situation, they may no longer be with her.

Scientists have sometimes portrayed the weaning process as a conflict between mother and offspring. One theory holds that an animal such as a cat that can have several litters in a lifetime should behave in a way that balances out the survival of each of her litters. For example, the demands of an extra-large litter might become excessive, jeopardizing her own health and therefore her chance of having any more litters. In some mammals, including mice and prairie dogs, mothers with large litters may kill one or two of the weakest members, presumably to ensure the survival of the rest. However, this tactic has never been recorded with cats, although a sickly kitten may simply be ignored by its mother, presumably because it does not produce the right signals to induce her to care for it.

Each kitten must do its best to survive, regardless of whether it is its mother's favourite; if it does not survive to maturity, it will never leave any offspring of its own. Given that female cats tend towards promiscuity,[8] no kitten can be sure that it is closely related even to its littermates, let alone to any of the members of its mother's next litter. It therefore has to put its own interests first, even more so than if it could be sure that it shared both parents with its littermates. So it has no incentive to give up suckling, even to the point of weakening its mother.

A mother cat cannot afford to be too hardhearted towards her offspring; after all, she cannot be at all certain that she will have the chance to breed again. She therefore carefully assesses their needs, keeping them hungry enough to want to try meat while not significantly compromising their health. For example, if her milk temporarily dries up before she's finished weaning them, she will start nursing them again before weaning is over, as soon as her milk comes in again; this ensures that they don't miss out on any essential nutrients. Likewise, the kittens themselves cannot be too aggressive in demanding milk from their mother, for (in the wild) they need to keep her on their side for several weeks longer, as she teaches them essential hunting skills. Furthermore, if her milk supply starts to fail early, kittens *increase* the amount of time they spend playing, presumably to prepare themselves for learning how to hunt. While most young animals – mice, for example – play *less* when they're hungry, presumably to conserve energy, for kittens play is preparation for hunting behaviour. Responding to their mother's predicament, such kittens are thereby preparing themselves for premature independence.

Play prepares kittens not just for hunting, but also for getting along with other cats. If domestic cats were as solitary as their ancestors, they would have little need for social graces. For animals whose individual contact is restricted to brief courtship and mating, and then the raising of each litter by its mother, social play is unsophisticated and brief. For domestic kittens, play with littermates becomes increasingly sophisticated as they get older, and no longer revolves around the elements of hunting behaviour.

By about six to eight weeks of age, kittens begin to use specific signals aimed at persuading their littermates to play with them, such as rolling on to their backs (see 'Belly-Up' in the drawing, p. 98), placing their mouth over another kitten's neck ('Stand-Up'), or rearing on to their hind legs ('Vertical Stance'). By ten weeks – assuming the litter is still together, since many kittens are homed at eight weeks old – each kitten will have come to learn the 'correct' response to each of these – Belly-Up for Stand-Up (and vice versa), and Belly-Up for Vertical Stance. As the kittens get older, play tends to get rougher, and occasionally one of the kittens gets hurt. To avoid any confusion between play and a real fight, kittens will use a 'Play Face' to indicate their friendly intentions, particularly when in the vulnerable Belly-Up position. They may also use special movements of their tails to signal playfulness, but so far no scientist has been able to decode these. Older kittens also have a special signal showing when they want to stop playing: they arch their back, curl their tail upwards, and then leap off the ground.

If a litter is left together after the normal age for homing, social play occupies more and more of the kittens' time, peaking somewhere between nine and fourteen weeks of age. All this sophistication confirms that domestic kittens are designed to become social adults, a process that begins when they are just a few weeks old and, unless interrupted, continues for several months.

Surprisingly, we know little about the optimum time for cats to learn how to interact with other cats. Experiments pinpointing the sensitive period for socialization to people have yet to be repeated to uncover the same for cat interaction, but we can assume that there is more than one sensitive period, each tailored to the social environment in which the kitten finds itself. The first period spans the kitten's first two weeks, when kittens form their attachment to their mother, based on olfaction.

During the first four weeks or so of life, each kitten learns how to interact with its siblings; it may have little need to recognize its littermates as individuals, but that probably follows soon after. Kittens are probably born with a template as to what another kitten looks like, but this is easily overwritten if there are no other kittens available. Thus, a kitten raised in a litter of puppies accepts the puppies as its littermates, and does not appear to 'know' that it itself is a kitten. However, if a puppy is introduced into a litter of kittens, even though they are perfectly friendly towards the puppy, the kittens still prefer one another's company. Cats' brains must be constructed in such a way that they form stronger attachments to cats than to other four-legged animals.

From the fifth week onwards, kittens certainly learn a great deal from their littermates, in particular the most effective way to play. If

Kittens performing Belly-Up with a Play-Face (left) and Stand-Up (right)

Kitten inviting play using Vertical Stance

a kitten from a litter of one is introduced to a kitten that has grown up with other kittens, it will play much more roughly than normal. Hand-raised kittens are even more inept: some turn out to be so aggressive that other kittens actively avoid them. Others become excessively bonded to their human owners and seem barely to realize that they are cats at all.[9] We do not yet know why some go one way and some the other, but possibly some important interactions between socialization to cats and socialization to people help to produce a cat that doesn't overreact to new situations – a balanced individual, if you like. Hand-reared kittens may develop extreme personalities because they miss out on these interactions, due to their lack of contact with other cats.

Littermates that are homed together usually form a stronger bond with one another than two unrelated cats. In August and September of 1998, a student and I studied this by recording the behaviour of pairs of cats in boarding catteries (people who have a pair of cats that get along together at home will usually ask for them to be housed together when they board them). We compared fourteen pairs of littermates that had lived together since birth with eleven pairs of unrelated individuals that had not met each other until at least one of the pair was more than one year old. Despite the hot weather, all the littermate pairs slept in contact with each other, but we observed only five of the unrelated pairs ever lying in contact with each other, and even those only occasionally. Many of the littermate pairs groomed each other; the unrelated pairs never did. Almost all the littermates were happy to feed side by side; we had to feed most of the unrelated pairs from separate bowls or in turns.[10]

This study does not clarify whether just being littermates makes cats friendly to one another, but this seems the most likely explanation. It's unlikely that it was simply the age difference between the unrelated pairs that made them unfriendly, since if a kitten is kept with its mother rather than being homed, the mother and kitten generally remain friends for life. However, scientists have yet to investigate whether littermates can recognize one another as relations, say if they are separated and reintroduced months later (as dogs can), or whether cats use a simple rule of paw, and try to remain friends with any cat that they've lived with continuously since the second month of their life – that is, during the socialization period.

Unlike most kittens born in homes, feral kittens can continue to interact with their littermates, and any other nearby litters, until they are at least six months old. Most kittens born outdoors are born in the spring. By autumn, their mother severs all ties with her male offspring and may actively drive them away – a sensible precaution against risk of inbreeding. Up to that point, the kittens will have had many opportunities to learn more about what it means to be a cat, opportunities generally denied to pet cats of the same age. Female kittens, on the other hand, often do not leave their natal group until they are several years old, so they have even more scope for learning feline social graces.

We often see a corresponding difference between the sexes in kittens' choice of company. As they grow, feral male kittens spend most of their time with brothers from the same litter. They rarely interact with kittens from other litters, even those they are related to; in any one year, most litters born within a feral colony will be first or second cousins. Male cats, assuming they avoid being neutered, are destined to lead solitary lives and, when they reach maturity, must compete with one another for female attention. Female feral kittens initially spend most time with their littermate sisters, but at a few months old will probably also regularly interact with both their aunts and their aunts' or other female relatives' kittens.

The third and fourth months of a kitten's life are full of play, regardless of whether they are male or female. We do not know whether denying kittens the opportunity to play with other kittens during this period has significant consequences. Perhaps because cats are often conceived of as solitary creatures for which a social life is a luxury, not a necessity, no one has investigated this topic scientifically. However, it seems possible that continued interaction with their peer group during adolescence could make a major contribution to cats' development as social animals.

The most important social skill a cat must learn to become a pet is, of course, not how to interact with cats (though that is useful), but how to interact with people. In this respect, cats rank second only to dogs. Like dogs, cats can learn how to behave towards their own kind and towards people, not only virtually simultaneously, but also without confusing the two. Nearly all other domestic animals are not as adaptable. For example, a lamb that has to be hand-raised will attach itself very powerfully to the person that feeds it, as if that person were its mother. Unless introduced to other, mother-reared lambs as quickly as possible, its behaviour may be abnormal for the rest of its life. Moreover, whether sheep are tame or not, their social behaviour is always primarily directed at other sheep.

Cats, like dogs, are capable of multiple socialization, the ability to become attached to animals of several different species – and not just people and other cats. Kittens raised in a household with a cat-friendly dog will continue to be friendly towards that dog, and potentially other similar dogs, for their entire lives. We do not know precisely how cats (or dogs) achieve this, but we can speculate that cats keep the 'rules' for interacting with each separate species in discrete parts of their brains, as the human brain stores different languages in physically distinct areas of the frontal lobes.

Between the ages of four and eight weeks, kittens form their view of people, or at least the people they meet. Kittens that meet only women during that period, as can happen in some breeding catteries, may turn out fearful of men or children once they are homed. A kitten that is handled by only one person may become very strongly attached to that person, purring whenever it is picked up and insistently pestering that person for attention[11] – an intensity that suggests that the person has, in the kitten's mind, taken the place of its mother.

Kittens with a dog

Introducing a kitten to a wide variety of people before the age of eight weeks seems to produce an approachable cat. Doing so seems to block the development of a strong attachment to one person, and instead builds a general picture of the human race in the cat's mind. Whether (say) three categories – men, women, children – develop simultaneously, or whether kittens learn to place all humans in a single category is unknown, but the end result is self-evident: a cat that is not fearful of humans.

Kittens need a lot of daily exposure to people to become optimally socialized to them. In one study, fifteen minutes handling each day produced a kitten that would approach people, but not as enthusiastically as a kitten that had been handled for forty minutes per day. Likewise, the fifteen-minute kitten would not stay on a lap for as long as the forty-minute one.[12] Fortunately for them, most kittens born in homes get this much attention without any special effort being taken, thanks to their irresistible cuteness.

Kittens born in animal shelters may not have the same luxury. Concerns over transmission of disease between litters may stand in the way of optimal socialization. The standard way of looking after mother cats with kittens, in which most contact with people occurs during routine feeding and cleaning, produces reasonably friendly kittens, but these will almost inevitably not have as much human contact as kittens born in a home. However, veterinary behaviour specialist Rachel Casey and I found that additional handling and play, involving several people rather than just one – even as little as a few minutes extra each day – from their third week to their ninth week, produced a dramatic improvement in how friendly these kittens were. This increased interaction they affected their relationships with the people who adopted them, who were kept unaware as to whether or not their kitten had received extra handling. As they reached their first birthdays, the kittens given extra handling were noticeably more relaxed than those raised in the standard way; likewise, their owners reported that they felt closer to them. The extra handling had produced a long-term effect on the strength of the bond between cat and owner.[13]

In the UK, eight weeks old – the end of weaning – is the traditional time to home a 'moggie' (non-pedigree cat), but neither our studies nor any other published research have yet addressed whether eight weeks of age is the right time for a kitten to move to its new home – especially from the viewpoint of how well it will bond with its new owners. From the new owner's perspective, this age seems entirely understandable: after all, kittens are at their cutest at around eight weeks of age. However, pedigree cats are generally not homed until they are thirteen weeks of age; the Governing Council of the Cat Fancy, one of the bodies that regulates cat breeding in the UK, strongly recommends that no kitten should be permitted to go to a new home any earlier than this, because until then it has not received its initial course of vaccinations and is therefore susceptible to disease. Unfortunately, this difference in traditions cannot tell us whether age of homing affects the relationship with the new owner. The personalities of the main types of pedigree breeds – Persians/longhairs and Orientals/Siamese – differ so much from one another and from most house cats that it would swamp any impact of even a four-week difference in the age of homing.

Kittens of any age must surely be affected by being moved to a new home. Everything they have come to know disappears at a stroke, and everything about their new home is novel. They leave the security of their mother, who has probably recently finished weaning them and has just relaxed the arm's-length attitude she had used to persuade them to accept solid food. They are plucked from the company of their littermates, whom they have got to know as individuals over the past month, and who have been their willing play partners. They leave the security of surroundings that they know well and smell reassuringly of their mother, brothers and sisters. The attention of unfamiliar humans, however well-meaning, is unlikely to comfort them during this period of change.[14]

Whether such dislocation happens at eight or thirteen weeks, or sometime in between, it takes place when the kitten is much younger than the age at which it would spontaneously leave its family group. It's a tribute to the cat's behavioural flexibility that this process works at all; indeed, provided that they receive a reasonable amount of handling from their mothers' owners, most kittens evidently adapt to their new surroundings and become attached to their new owners. They may also – although this is by no means certain – adapt to living alongside their owners' other cats.

*

Handling between four and eight weeks of age seems essential to a kitten becoming a contented pet. But what happens when handling is delayed until six, seven or eight weeks, or even later? Many kittens are born to mothers who, because they are feral or stray, are wary of people, and are not discovered until they begin to make their own first faltering steps into the world. In the 1990s, I worked with the UK charity Cats Protection to study this topic. Rehoming charities are frequently called in when such kittens are found, and naturally these organizations wish to help. What is the best course of action?

Our study found that the older the kitten when it was first handled, the less friendly it seemed to be – at least to begin with. Kittens that had received no human contact until they were six weeks old behaved distinctly from normal kittens, even after they had settled into their new surroundings at the rehoming centres. If rescued at six weeks, they were not easy to handle, and very few purred when stroked.[15] Kittens not rescued until eight weeks of age were difficult to handle, and those not found until ten weeks were, at least to begin with, virtually wild. The exceptions were a few litters of kittens that, although they had not been picked up for the first time until they were eleven weeks old, had allowed themselves to be stroked occasionally while in their nests a few weeks earlier. These kittens behaved more like those rescued at seven weeks – initially wary of people and difficult to handle. This confirms that socialization to people has to *start* within the first six or seven weeks if it is to become effective, but that once started the process continues for several weeks more, especially if the initial exposure has been brief.

The way the kittens were handled once rescued also affected how quickly they became friendly. If they had been handled by two or more people, they were more relaxed and playful when introduced to unfamiliar people than if they had been looked after by only one person. Again, it appears that attachment to an individual and socialization to people in general progress in parallel at this age. Kittens who know only one person become attached to that particular person, but may remain wary of other humans; kittens who meet several different people at roughly the same time may not become so attached, but are later much more accepting of people in general.

Most of these rescued feral kittens became perfectly satisfactory pets, the same as kittens who were born in the same rescue centres and were therefore handled from a very early age. In fact, the feral kittens had received *extra* attention to compensate for the socialization they hadn't been able to receive before they were rescued, so many turned out to be more friendly at one year old than their shelter-born counterparts. However, the few kittens that were difficult to socialize at all were still unapproachable at the same age.[16]

Kittens that don't meet a human until the age of ten weeks or older are unlikely to become pets, except in extreme circumstances. Instead, they live as 'stray' or 'feral' cats, living on the fringes of human activity but never becoming part of it. Most hunt to some extent, but virtually all depend on food and shelter provided by people, both accidentally and deliberately. Their only window of opportunity for accepting and then becoming attached to people has passed. The cat's social brain changes suddenly at about eight weeks of age, and altering its basic social inclinations after that is usually impossible.

The general rule is, once a feral, always a feral – unless it experiences severe physical and mental trauma, such as being hit by a motor vehicle. Occasionally, some kindhearted soul will take a feral cat that has been the victim of an accident to a veterinary hospital. Many such cats are beyond saving, but those that cheat death and are nursed slowly back to health can go through an unexpected change in personality; they become attached to whoever has looked after them the most, in a manner reminiscent of a hand-raised kitten. Researchers have recorded similar changes in cats that have suffered severe and protracted fevers. Apparently, the deluge of stress hormones released in a cat that is close to death can scramble the brain enough to go through the socialization process all over again.

The importance of the socialization period to a kitten's future welfare cannot be underestimated. In just six short weeks, beginning as it turns two weeks of age, this period constructs the foundations for all its subsequent social life. If the kitten is unlucky enough to have no brothers and sisters, and has no other kittens nearby, its view of what it is to be a cat is incomplete; although cat mothers will play with single kittens, they are much less inclined to do so than other kittens. If a kitten's mother keeps it away from people, usually because she is herself not socialized to humans, the kitten is unlikely to become a pet. If it is handled by only one person, it will become attached to that person but may form too narrow a view of what humans are like, and thus become wary of strangers. If the kitten has to be hand-reared, it misses out on learning how to be a cat and its entire social and cognitive development may be impaired.

Cats don't suddenly stop learning about people or other animals when they pass the eight-week watershed. At this point, the general course of their attachments is set, but the details of their journey through life are far from predetermined. We know that they learn a great deal more about how to interact with people throughout the first year of their life, and there's every reason to suppose that the same applies to how they adapt when they come into contact with other cats, although little research has been done on this. The way a kitten's personality develops over that first year depends not only on its experiences, but also on genetics: like other animals, individual cats adopt different strategies for dealing with the same events, and these differences are often the product of their genes.

5

The World According to Cat

We may easily overlook the simple fact that cats live in a world that is – subjectively speaking – quite distinct from ours. We share just enough overlap between our different perceptions of the world to be able to relate to one another, each species having evolved its senses to fit its lifestyle. It is unreasonable to consider cats' abilities as inferior – or superior – to our own. Biologists abandoned the idea of one species being 'superior' to another decades ago, though cat owners may suspect that their cats feel otherwise. We now consider each species as having evolved to fit a particular way of life; cats are good at being cats, because their ancestors evolved sense organs and brains to suit that role.

Because the domestication of the cat is still incomplete, that role is still in a state of flux – for example, cats are still adapting to urban living – while their sense organs have remained more or less unchanged. One major difference between cats and people is that cats have evolved genetically, from wild to domestic, while over the same timescale we ourselves have evolved culturally, from hunter-gatherer to city dweller. Genetic evolution is a much slower process than cultural evolution, and the 4,000 years over which cats have adapted to living alongside humankind is not long enough for any major change in sensory or mental abilities. Thus, cats today have essentially the same senses, the same brains and the same emotional repertoire as their wildcat forebears: not enough time has passed for them to break free of their origins as hunters. As far as we know, all that has changed in their brains is a new ability to form social attachments to people, while their senses remain completely unaltered.

Cat behaviour that seems baffling to us may stem from cats' ability to sense things around them to which we are oblivious – and vice versa. A complete understanding of cats requires that we try to visualize the world they live in, which is a world quite different from what our own instincts tell us it should be. Indeed, I use the word 'visualize' because that's how our imaginations work: we conjure pictures in our heads of past events, or of what might happen in the future. Scientists doubt that cats' brains work that way; not only is it unlikely that their brains are capable of such 'time travel', but also their world, unlike ours, is not based on appearance. Smell is at least as important to cats as vision is, so even if they could imagine, they might well conjure up what something smells like rather than what it looks like. A few humans can do this – professional perfumers and sommeliers, for example – but usually only after extensive training.

This fundamental emphasis on other senses is not the only difference in the way cats and humans perceive the world. Each of our individual senses also works differently too, so that, for example, a cat and a person looking out of the same window will see two dissimilar pictures.

Human eyes and cat eyes share some similarities – we're both mammals, after all – but cat eyes have evolved as superefficient aids to hunting prey. The wild ancestors of the modern cat needed to maximize the time they could spend hunting, so their eyes enabled them to see in the merest glimmer of light. This has affected the structure of cats' eyes in several ways. First, they are huge in comparison with the size of their heads; indeed, their eyes are almost the same actual size as our own. In darkness, their pupils expand to three times the area ours do. The efficiency with which their eyes capture light is further enhanced by a reflective layer behind the retina, known as the tapetum. Any incoming light that misses the receptor cells in the retina bounces off the tapetum and back through the retina again, where some will happen to strike a receptor cell from behind, enhancing the sensitivity of the eye by up to 40 per cent. Any light that misses the second time around will pass back out through the pupil, giving the cat its characteristic green eye shine whenever a light is shone into its eyes in the dark.

The receptor cells on the retina are also arranged differently from ours. They fall into the same two basic types – rods for black-and-white vision in dim light, and cones for colour vision when it's bright – but cats' eyes have mainly rods, whereas ours have mainly cones. Instead of each rod connecting to a single nerve, cats' rods are first connected together in bundles; as a result, cats' eyes have ten times fewer nerves travelling between their eyes and their brains than ours. The advantage of this arrangement is that the cat can see in the near-dark, when our eyes are nearly useless. The disadvantage is that in brighter light, cats miss out on finer details; their brains are not being told precisely which rod is firing, only a general area on the retina on to which the light is falling.

The result of this disadvantage is that in full daylight, cats cannot see as well as we can. The rods become overloaded, as ours do under the same conditions, and have to be switched off. The small number of cones that cats do have are spread all over their retinas, rather than concentrated in the centre of the retina, in the fovea, as ours are, so they get a general and not very detailed picture of their surroundings during the day. Because their pupils are so large when wide open, they cannot be shrunk to a pinprick in bright sunlight, as ours can. Instead, cats have evolved the ability to contract their pupils to narrow vertical slits, less than a millimetre wide, which protects their sensitive retinas from being overwhelmed with light. They can further reduce the amount of light entering by half-shutting their eyes, thereby covering the top and bottom of the slit and leaving only the centre exposed.

Cats also show little interest in colour; among mammals, colour seems a uniquely primate, especially human, obsession.[1] Like dogs, cats have only two types of cones and see only two colours, blue and yellow; in humans, we call this red-green colour blindness. To cats, both red and green probably look greyish.[2] Moreover, even colours they can distinguish seem to be of little relevance to them. Their brains contain only a few nerves dedicated to colour comparisons, and it is difficult to train cats to distinguish between blue and yellow objects. Any other difference between objects – brightness, pattern, shape or size – seems to matter more to cats than does colour.

Another drawback of having such large eyes is that they are not easy to focus. We have muscles in our eyes that distort the shape of the lens to allow close vision; cats seem to have to move their whole lens back and forth, as happens in a camera, a much more cumbersome process. Perhaps because it is just too much effort, they often don't bother to focus at all, unless something exciting, such as a bird flying past, catches their attention. Close focus, anything nearer than about a foot away, is also out of the question with such large eyes. Furthermore, the muscles that focus the lens seem to set themselves according to the environment the cat grows up in: outdoor cats are slightly long-sighted, whereas all-indoor cats tend to be shortsighted. Despite the largeness of their eyes, cats can swivel them quickly to keep track of rapidly moving prey. To avoid image blurring, the eyes do not move smoothly but in a series of jerks, known as saccades, about a quarter of a second apart, so that the cat's brain can process each separate image clearly.

Like humans, cats have binocular vision. The signals from each of their forward-facing eyes are matched up in their brains, and are converted there into three-dimensional pictures. Most mammalian carnivores have eyes that point forward to provide them with binocular vision, so that they can gauge precisely how far away potential prey is, and judge their pounce accordingly. Presumably because their eyes don't focus any closer than about a foot away from their noses, cats don't bother to converge their eyes on objects any closer than this.[3] To compensate, cats can swing their whiskers forward to provide a 3-D tactile 'picture' of objects that are right in front of their noses.

Binocular vision is the best way of judging how far away something is, but it's not the only method available. Cats that lose an eye because of disease or injury can compensate by making exaggerated bobbing movements of their heads, monitoring how the images of the various objects they can see move relative to one another. Prey animals such as rabbits commonly do this: because their eyes are on the sides of their heads to maximize surveillance, they have little or no binocular vision, and have to rely on other, slightly cruder ways of judging distance.

The cat's ability to detect tiny movements is another legacy of its predatory past. The visual cortex, the part of the brain that receives signals from the eyes, does not simply construct pictures as if the eyes were two still cameras; it also analyses what has changed between one picture and the next. The cat's visual cortex compares these 'pictures' sixty times each second – slightly more frequently than our visual cortex does, meaning that cats see fluorescent lights and older TV screens as flickery. Dedicated brain cells analyse movements in various directions – up and down, left to right, and along both diagonals – and even local brightening or dimming of specific parts of the image. Thus, the most important features of the image – the parts that are changing rapidly – are instantly singled out for attention.

Cats learn how to integrate all this information when they are kittens – unlike amphibians, for example, which already have specialized prey-detector circuits formed in their brains when they metamorphose from tadpole to adult. Cats use their movement detectors to behave flexibly when they're hunting, paying equal attention to a mouse it spots attempting to make an escape, or to a movement of the grass that betrays the mouse's position. Both help the hunting cat to find a meal.

We can plainly see the cat's origins as a predator of small rodents in its remarkable hearing abilities – remarkable both in the range of sounds it can hear and in pinpointing the source of the sound. The cat's hearing range extends two octaves higher than ours, into the region that – because we can't hear it – we refer to as ultrasound. This extended range enables cats to hear the ultrasonic pulses bats use to orient themselves while flying in the dark, and the high-pitched squeaks of mice and other small rodents. Cats can also tell different types of rodents apart by their squeaks.

In addition to this sensitivity to ultrasound, cats can hear the same full range of frequencies we can, from the lowest bass notes to the highest treble. Almost no other mammal exhibits such a wide range, about eleven octaves in total. Because cats' heads are smaller than ours, their hearing range should be shifted to higher frequencies, so their ability to hear ultrasound is perhaps not all that remarkable; rather, it's their ability to hear low notes that is unexpected. The cat's ability to hear sounds lower than it should, based on the size of its head, is possible because they have an exceptionally large resonating chamber behind the eardrum. The capacity to hear ultrasound despite this arises from a feature of this chamber not seen in other mammals: it divides into two interconnecting compartments, thereby increasing the range of frequencies over which the eardrum will vibrate.

Mobile, erect ears are the cat's direction finders, essential when tracking a mouse rustling through the undergrowth. Cats' brains analyse the differences between the sounds reaching the right and left ear, enabling the cat to pinpoint the source. For lower-pitched sounds that fall into our hearing range – for example, when we talk to our cats – the sound arrives at one ear slightly out of sync with the other. Also, higher frequencies are muffled by the time they reach the ear farthest from the source, providing a further clue to where the source is. This is essentially the way that we too determine where a sound is coming from, but cats have an extra trick: the external parts of the ears are independently mobile, and can be pointed at or away from the sound to confirm its direction. When it comes to ultrasounds, which are above our hearing range, such as a mouse's squeak, the phase differences become too small to be useful, but the muffling effect gets larger and therefore becomes more informative. Therefore, a cat has little difficulty determining whether a sound is coming from the right or the left.

In addition, the structure of their external ears – the visible part of the ears, technically referred to as pinnae – also enables cats to tell with some accuracy how high up the source of a sound is. First and foremost, the corrugations inside the pinnae add stiffness and keep the ears upright, but they also cause complex changes to any sound as it passes into the ear canal; these changes vary depending on how far above or below the cat the sound is coming from. Somehow, the cat's brain decodes these changes, which must be difficult, given that the pinnae may be moving. The pinnae are also directional amplifiers, but rather than being tuned to pick up mouse squeaks, they are especially sensitive to the frequencies found in other cats' vocalizations, enabling male cats to pick up the calls made by females as they come into season, and vice versa. This is perhaps the only feature of the cat's ears not refined specifically for detecting prey.

Cats' hearing is therefore superior to ours in many ways, but inferior in one respect: the ability to distinguish minor differences between sounds, both in pitch and intensity. If it was possible to train a cat to sing, it couldn't sing in tune (bad news for Andrew Lloyd Webber). Human ears are outstanding at telling similar sounds apart, probably an adaptation to our use of speech to communicate, and associated with that is our ability to recognize subtle intricacies of intonation that indicate the emotional content of what we are hearing – even when the speaker is trying to disguise his or her voice. Such subtleties are probably lost on cats, although they do seem to prefer us to talk to them in a high-pitched voice. Perhaps gruff male voices remind them of the rumbling growl of an angry tomcat.

As with hearing, the cat's sense of touch features refinements that help with hunting. Cats' paws are exceptionally sensitive, which explains why many cats don't like having their feet handled. Not only are a cat's pads packed with receptors that tell it what is beneath or between its paws, but the claws are also packed with nerve endings that enable the cat to know both how far each claw has been extended and how much resistance it is experiencing. Since wild cats generally first catch their prey with their forepaws before biting, their pads and claws must provide essential clues on the efforts the prey is making to escape. Cats' long canine teeth are also especially sensitive to touch, enabling the hunting cat to direct its killing bite accurately, sliding one of these teeth between the vertebrae on its victim's neck and killing it instantly and almost painlessly. The bite itself is triggered by special receptors on the snout and the lips, which tell the cat precisely when to open and then close its mouth.

The cat's whiskers are basically modified hairs, but where the whiskers attach to the skin around the muzzle they are equipped with receptors that tell the cat how far each whisker is being bent back, and how quickly. Cat's whiskers are not as mobile as a rat's, but a cat can sweep its whiskers both forward, compensating for longsighted-ness when pouncing, and backwards, to prevent the whiskers from being damaged in a fight. Cats also have tufts of stiffened hairs just above the eyes, triggering the blink reflex if the eyes are threatened, and on the sides of the head and near the ankles. All of these, in tan-dem with the whiskers, enable cats to judge the width of openings they can squeeze through.

Information gathered from these hairs helps keep the cat upright, but the vestibular system, in the inner ear, contributes most to the cat's exquisite sense of balance. Unlike our other senses, balance operates almost entirely at the subconscious level, and we barely notice it until something causes it to malfunction – for example, motion sickness. Although the information that it produces is used more effectively, the cat's vestibular system is actually similar to ours.

This system consists of five fluid-filled tubes. In each, sensory hairs on the inside detect any movement of the fluid, which occurs only when the cat's head twists suddenly; because of inertia, the fluid doesn't move as quickly as the sides of the tube do, dragging the hairs to one side (if you're reading this with a cup of coffee in front of you, try gently rotating the cup: the liquid in the middle of the cup remains where it is). Three of the tubes are curved into half-circles, aligned at right angles to one another to detect movement in all three dimensions. In the other two, the hairs are attached to tiny crystals, which make the hairs hang downwards under gravity, enabling the cat to know which way is up, and also how fast it is moving forward.

One reason cats are agile is simply that they walk on four legs rather than two. Four legs need coordinating if they are to work effectively as a team, and the cat has two separate groups of nerves that do this. One group relays information about each leg's position to the other three, without involving the brain; the other sends information to the brain for comparison with what the inner-ear balance organ relates about the cat's position. More reflexes in the neck enable the cat to hold its head steady even when it is moving quickly over uneven ground – a necessity for keeping its eyes on its prey.

When walking from place to place, cats pay close attention to where they are going. Because of their poor close vision, they have little reason to look down at their front feet, so instead they look three or four paces ahead and briefly memorize the terrain in front, allowing them to step over any obstacles in their path. Scientists have recently determined that if a cat is distracted with a dish of tasty food while walking, it forgets what the ground in its path looks like and has to have another look before setting off again. In the experiment, researchers switched off overhead lights while the cat was distracted into looking to one side; it then had to feel its way gingerly forward, indicating that its view of the path had vanished from its short-term memory. However, if the cat was distracted after it had stepped over an obstacle with its front paws, and while the obstacle was right under its belly, it remembered that it should lift its hind paws when it

How a cat rights itself after a sudden fall

started walking again, even after a ten-minute delay – and even if the obstacle, unbeknown to the cat, had been moved out of the way. Somehow the visual memory of the obstacle is converted from ephemeral to long-lasting by the simple act of stepping over it with the front feet.[4]

A cat's gravity-detecting system is most impressive when it either jumps voluntarily or accidentally slips and falls. Less than a tenth of a second after all four feet lose contact with a surface, the balance organs sense which way up the head is, and reflexes cause the neck to rotate so that the cat can then look downwards towards where it will land. Other reflexes cause first the forelegs and then hind legs to rotate to point downwards. All this happens in thin air, with nothing for the cat to push on. While the front legs are being rotated, they tuck up to reduce their inertia, while the back legs remain extended; then the front legs are extended while the back legs are briefly tucked up (see figure opposite). Ice skaters use the same principle to speed up spins, simply by retracting their arms and the spare leg. The cat also briefly curves its flexible back away from its feet as it rotates, which helps to prevent the twist at the back end cancelling out the twist at the front.[5] Many cats also counter-rotate their tails to stabilize their fall. Finally, all four legs extend in preparation for landing, while the back is arched to cushion the impact.

While this intricate midair ballet is happening, the cat could have already fallen as far as ten feet. As such, it's possible for a short fall to injure the cat as much as, and possibly more than, a longer fall, if there is insufficient time for the cat to prepare itself for landing. If a cat falls out of a high-rise building or a tall tree, it has another trick available: forming a 'parachute' by spreading all four legs out sideways, before adopting the landing position at the last minute. Laboratory simulations suggest that this limits the falling speed to a maximum of fifty-three miles per hour. This tactic apparently allows some cats to survive falls from high buildings with only minor injuries.

Like dogs, cats rely greatly on their sense of smell. Cats' balance, hearing and night vision are all superior to our own, but it's in their sense of smell that they really outperform humans. Everybody knows that dogs have excellent noses, something humankind has made use of for millennia, and this prowess is located, in part, in their large olfactory bulbs, the part of the brain where smells are first analysed. Relative to their size, cats have smaller olfactory bulbs than dogs, but theirs are still considerably larger than ours. Although scientists have not studied the cat's olfactory ability in as much detail as the dog's, we have no reason to suppose that a cat's sense of smell is much less acute. Without a doubt, it is certainly much better than our own.

Like those of dogs, the insides of cats' noses have far more surface area devoted to trapping smells than ours do – about five times as much. Indeed, it's *Homo sapiens* who appears particularly deficient in this respect. During the evolution of our primate ancestors, we seem to have traded most of our olfactory ability for the benefits of three-colour vision, which biologists theorize enabled us to discriminate red ripe fruits and tender pink leaves from their generally less nutritious green counterparts. Cats' sense of smell is more or less typical of mammals, and that of dogs is more acute than the average. As in most mammals, air passing into the nose is first cleaned, moistened and warmed if necessary as it passes over skin supported on a delicate honeycomb of bones, the maxilloturbinals. The air then reaches the surface that extracts and decodes the odour, the olfactory membrane, which is supported on another bony maze, the ethmoturbinals. Because, unlike dogs, cats do not pursue their prey over long distances, their maxilloturbinals are not especially large; dogs must sniff and run at the same time, and while they're doing this their olfactory membranes are constantly at risk from damage by dust, or by dry or cold air. Cats' habit of sitting and waiting for their prey places much less strain on the air-conditioning system in their noses.

Nerve endings in the olfactory membrane trap the molecules that make up the smell. The tips of the nerves are far too delicate to come into contact with air themselves, so they are covered in a protective film of mucus, through which the molecules pass. This film has to be very thin; otherwise, the molecules would take several seconds to move from the airflow to the nerve endings. If this were the case, then the information conveyed by the odour would be out of date before the cat knew it was there. To facilitate a speedy response, the mucus has to be spread so thinly that the nerve endings become damaged from time to time – for example, they may dry out when they become temporarily exposed to the air – and they therefore regenerate about once a month.

The other ends of the olfactory nerves are connected together in bundles of between ten and a hundred before transmitting their information to the brain. Cats have several hundred kinds of olfactory receptors, and the information arises from whichever of these has been triggered by the odour passing through the nose. Each bundle contains only nerves with the same kind of receptor, to amplify the signal without muddling up the data it contains. In the brain, the input from the different receptors is compared to build up a picture of the odour in question.

This system is unlike that of the eye, where images are built up by each section of the retina transmitting its information directly to the brain. The nose does not build up a 'two-dimensional' image, as each eye does; as the cat breathes in, the air is swirled around so much in the nostrils that whatever receptor each odour molecule strikes is a matter of pure chance. It's even unclear whether, unlike their vision and hearing, cats can make any sense of the slightly different amounts of odour entering their left and right nostrils.

Cats are probably capable of distinguishing among many thousands of different smells, so they cannot have one receptor dedicated to each one. Rather, cats deduce the character of each odour they encounter from which type of receptor is being stimulated, and by how much, in comparison with other types. Although scientists do not yet know precisely how the resulting information is combined together in any species of mammal, the potential resolution of such a system is staggering. Consider that our brains can generate a million or so distinct colours from just three types of cones. Several hundred olfactory receptors must therefore have the capacity to discriminate among billions of different odours. Whether cats achieve this is difficult to say; we do not even know precisely how many different odours can be discriminated by our own noses, and we have only about one third to a half the number of receptor types cats have. Based on these extrapolations, the mammalian olfactory receptor system seems rather overengineered, and science has not yet resolved why this might be. Suffice it to say that a cat should theoretically be able to distinguish between more smells than it is likely to encounter in a lifetime.

CATNIP AND OTHER STIMULANTS

Rolling on catnip

Scientists do not yet understand why cats respond to catnip, a traditional constituent of cat toys. Not all cats respond to it. A single gene governs whether or not the cat responds, and in many cats, perhaps as many as one in three, both copies of this gene are defective, with no apparent effect on behaviour or general health.

The behaviour released by catnip is a bizarre mixture of play, feeding and female sexual behaviour, whether the cat itself is male or female. Cats may first play with a catnip toy as if they think it is a small item of prey, but they quickly switch into bouts of a seemingly ecstatic combination of face-rubbing and body-rolling, reminiscent of a female cat in season. Most cats also drool and attempt to lick the catnip. This behaviour may continue for several minutes at a time, until the cat eventually recovers and walks away – but if the toy is left where it is, the cat may repeat the whole sequence, albeit with less intensity, twenty or thirty minutes later.

A few other plants elicit the same response, notably the Japanese cat shrub or silver vine, and the roots of the kiwifruit vine, which despite its name originated in southern China. In the 1970s, the first growers of kiwi vines in France learned this when they found to their distress that cats had excavated and chewed their seedlings. All three plants contain similar fragrant chemicals, thought to be responsible for the cats' responses.

By some accident of evolution, these chemicals most likely stimulate the cat's nose to trigger circuits in the brain that would never normally be activated at the same time, somehow bypassing the normal mechanisms that ensure that cats don't perform two incompatible actions at once. A cat in the throes of catnip-induced oblivion would seem vulnerable to attack, and since cats presumably don't get any lasting benefit from their experience, evolution should have weeded out the gene responsible. Most species in the cat family, from lions to domestic cats, respond to these plants the same way, so the gene must have evolved several million years ago. Why it did so remains a mystery.

Scientists know little about how cats make use of their sensitive noses. Cats' most dramatic response is to the odour of catnip, but this seems to be an aberration (see box, 'Catnip and Other Stimulants'). We know a great deal about the olfactory capabilities of dogs because we have harnessed dogs' noses for various purposes: finding game, tracking fugitives and detecting contraband, to name but three. If cats were as easy to train as dogs are, we'd probably discover that their olfactory performance is close to that of dogs. A few minutes' cursory observation of any cat will reveal that it sniffs its surroundings all the time, confirming that it places a premium on what things smell like. Remarkably, however, it was only in 2010 that the first scientific account of cats using olfaction in hunting was published.[6]

This study showed that cats do indeed locate prey using their scent marks. Many of the rodents that cats hunt, especially mice, communicate with one another using scent signals carried in their urine. As cats and mice are mammals, their noses work in much the same way, so it is highly unlikely that mice can disguise their scent marks so that cats cannot detect them. Australian biologists proved this by collecting samples of sand from mouse cages and placing them on the ground on roadside verges. Almost all these patches of sand were visited by predators – mostly foxes, but tracks of feral cats were also apparent – while clean sand was not. The collected data did not show how far away the cats had travelled from, but it is possible that significant distances were involved – that is, the cats probably navigated upwind towards the odour sources, rather than only investigating the patches of sand because they looked unusual. We know that many dogs prefer to hunt using their noses, and can detect and then locate sources of odour from hundreds of feet away. While cats prefer to use vision when hunting in daylight, they probably switch to using their sense of smell when hunting at night, when sight, even their sensitive night vision, becomes less reliable.

Finding prey from the odours it produces can be difficult. Scent marks rarely indicate the current position of the animal that left them, only where it was when it made the mark, perhaps hours earlier. In the sand experiment, the urine samples continued to attract cats for at least a couple of days. It's possible that cats, as sit-and-wait hunters, use the scent marks to see whether they will attract other members of the same species that made them. Mice use urine marks to signal to other mice, and the marks contain a great deal of useful information about the mouse that produced them. Thus, the scent-marker doesn't put itself at risk, so much as other members of the same species that show up to examine the mark.

In addition, odours spread out from their sources in ways that are not predictable. We know intuitively that light travels in straight lines but not around obstacles, and that sound travels in all directions, including around obstacles. However, because we rely so little on odour to give us directional information, it's not immediately obvious what problems animals face when determining where an odour is emanating from. Of course, odours outdoors are carried by the air – downwind, not upwind – but air movements close to the ground, where cats operate, are usually highly complex. While the wind may be blowing in a consistent direction a few yards above the ground, friction caused by its contact with the ground and especially with vegetation causes it to break up into eddies of various sizes. These carry 'pockets' of odour away from the source, so that a cat somewhere downwind of a mouse's nest will get intermittent bursts of mouse smell.

Tracing these bursts to their source, especially in thick cover, is likely to require diligent searching and possibly some backtracking. Once a cat has located a source of mouse odour, it is potentially able to use the fact that odours don't travel upwind to position itself downwind of the odour source so its own smell can't be detected by the mouse, and then wait for mice to turn up. While sit-and-wait is a well-documented feline hunting method, we do not know whether cats routinely prefer patrolling the downwind sides of, for example, hedgerows, to avoid their own scent betraying their presence. However, it seems likely that a predator as smart as a cat could quickly learn this tactic, even if it is not instinctive.

Cats possess a second olfactory apparatus, which humans lack: the vomeronasal organ (VNO; also called the Jacobson's organ).[7] A pair of tubes, the nasopalatine canals, run from the roof of the cat's mouth, just behind the upper incisors, up to the nostrils; connected roughly halfway up each one of these tubes is a sac, the VNO itself, filled with chemical receptors. Unlike the nose, the entire VNO is full of fluid, so odours must be dissolved in saliva before they can be detected. Moreover, the ducts connecting the VNOs to the canals are only about one hundredth of an inch wide, so thin that the odours must be pumped in and out of the sacs by a dedicated set of tiny muscles.[8] This gives the cat precise control over when it uses the VNO – unlike the nose, which automatically receives odour every time the cat breathes. Thus, the VNO's function lies somewhere between our senses of smell and taste. Appreciating how cats make use of this faculty requires a great leap of imagination.

Cats, unlike dogs, perform an obvious facial contortion when bringing the VNO into play. They pull their top lip upwards slightly, uncovering the top teeth, while the mouth is held partially open. This pose is usually held for several seconds: it's sometimes known as the 'gape' response, although it's usually referred to by its German name, 'Flehmen'. Researchers theorize that during this pose, the tongue is squeezing saliva up into the canals, from where the pumping mechanism delivers it to the VNO.

Cats perform Flehmen exclusively in social situations, so by implication they must use their VNO to detect the smells of other cats.[9] Male cats perform it after sniffing urine marks left by females, including during courtship, and female cats will do the same towards urine marks left by tomcats, although usually only if the tom is not present.

The cat's VNO can probably detect and analyse a wide range of 'smells', since it contains at least thirty different kinds of receptors; more than the dog's, which has only nine. These receptors are distinct from those found in the nose, and are connected to their own dedicated area of the brain, known as the accessory olfactory bulb.

Cat displaying 'Flehmen' – using its vomeronasal organ to detect the odour of a cat that has cheek-rubbed the twig

Why do cats – and, indeed, most mammals, apart from primates – need two olfactory systems? The answer seems to change from species to species. Mice have highly sophisticated VNOs, with several hundred receptor types and two distinct connections to the accessory olfactory bulb, rather than the cat's one; the odorants mice pick up regulate reproduction, as well as allowing recognition of every other mouse in the neighbourhood from its unique odour 'fingerprint'. In many species, some odour communication takes place through the VNO and some through the nose. For example, in rabbits, chemical communication between adults involves the VNO, but the scent emanating from the mother that stimulates her kittens to suckle is picked up by their noses. Sometimes the balance between the two changes as the animal matures: the VNO and the nose are used in tandem during a guinea pig's first breeding season, but the following year its nose alone will suffice. Although cats have not been studied in this amount of detail, it's feasible that they also interpret olfactory information in such a flexible way.

If we accept that the VNO is primarily designed to analyse odours coming from other members of the same species, then the fact that dogs are generally *more* sociable than cats doesn't really fit the fact that their VNOs are *less* discriminating. Dogs, descended from social ancestors, conduct much of their relationships with other dogs face to face, and thus use visual cues to confirm who another dog is and what it is likely to do next, so their VNOs may not be required very often.

The domestic cat's solitary ancestors only rarely had the opportunity to meet one another; the exceptions are males when they are courting females, and females interacting with their litters for a few months. In the wild, much of the social life of cats must be conducted through scent marks, which can be deposited for another cat to sniff days, sometimes weeks later. Since wild cats rarely get to meet other members of their own species, any information they can pick up from scent marks is crucial for making decisions on how to act when they do encounter each other. Most critically for the survival of her offspring, a female cat must assess her various male suitors, who themselves have been attracted by the change in her own scent as she comes into season. She may already have gained useful information about each of them by sniffing the scent marks they have left as they roamed through her territory, information she can use to supplement what she can see of their condition and behaviour when she finally meets them. She may also be able to distinguish those that are unrelated to her from those that are – perhaps a son who has roamed away and then happened to return to the area a few years later – thereby avoiding inbreeding. Scientists have not yet studied any of these possibilities in cats, but we know that they occur in other species.

Cats' sense of smell has evolved not purely for hunting, but also for social purposes. Successful hunting was, until domestication, crucial to the survival of every individual cat. However, it cannot in itself ensure the survival of an individual cat's genes; that also requires an effective mating strategy. Each female cat tries to select the best male for her purposes every time she mates to ensure that her genes pass down to successive generations. Ideally, she should take a long-term view, trying to gauge not only her own offspring's chances of survival, but also how successful they are likely to be when they in turn become old enough to breed. If she picks the strongest and healthiest male(s) to mate with, then her male kittens will in all likelihood be strong and healthy too when they are old enough to mate. She will of course be able to make a judgement based on her suitors' appearance, but she may be able to obtain a better idea of how healthy they are based on their odour. Her sense of smell may thus provide her with extra information to make these crucial mating decisions.

Cats probably perceive most of the scents that have social meaning using the nose and the VNO in tandem. While both may be needed the first time a particular smell is encountered – for example, the first time a young male detects a female in oestrus – on subsequent occasions either one will do the job, the brain presumably using memories of previous encounters to 'fill in' the missing input.

Like dogs, cats pay a great deal of attention to scent marks left by other cats, both those carried in urine and those that they rub on to prominent objects, using the glands around the mouth. To distinguish it from the rubbing that cats perform on people and on one another, which is mainly a tactile display, this is sometimes referred to as 'bunting', a term whose origins are obscure. Cats' faces have numerous scent-producing glands, one under the chin, one at each corner of the mouth, and one beneath the areas of sparse fur between eye and ear, while the pinna itself produces a characteristic odour. We know little about how cats use these scent marks, but they certainly display an interest in the scents other cats produce. For example, male cats can distinguish between females at different stages in their estrus cycle based on their facial gland secretions alone. Each gland produces a unique blend of chemicals, some of which have even been used in commercial products that can have a positive effect on reducing stress in anxious cats.[10]

Apart from the social role of the VNO, and to a lesser extent the nose, all the cat's other senses are exquisitely tuned to the hunting lifestyle of their ancestors. They have quite an arsenal at their disposal: they can locate prey visually, their eyes effective in the half-light of early dawn and late dusk; aurally, detecting high-pitched squeaks and rustles; or olfactorily, through detecting the odours that rodents leave in scent marks. As they approach their prey, cats' exquisite sense of balance and the sensory hairs on their cheeks and elbows allow them to do so silently and stealthily. As they pounce, the whiskers on their faces sweep forward to act as a short-range radar, guiding the mouth and teeth to precisely the right place to deliver the killing bite. Cats evolved as hunters, something domestication has done little to change.

What the cat senses is only half the story. Its brain has to make sense of the vast amounts of information that its eyes, ears, balance organs, nose and whiskers produce, and then turn that information into action, whether correcting the cat's balance as it tiptoes along the top of a fence, deciding on the precise moment to pounce on a mouse, or checking the garden for the scent of cats that have visited during the night. The sheer volume of data that each sense organ generates has to be filtered every waking second. An analogy might be the vast banks of TV screens and monitors at NASA headquarters during the launch of a spacecraft: at any one moment, only a minute fraction of what they display is important, and it takes a highly trained observer to know which ones to watch and which can safely be ignored. Unfortunately at present we know much less about how sensory information is processed than how it is generated.

The size and organization of cats' brains can give us some clues as to their priorities in life. The basic form of the felid brain, as shown by the shape of the skull, evolved at least 5 million years ago. Some parts of the brain, especially the cerebellum, are disproportionally geared to processing information relating to balance and movement, reflecting cats' prowess as athletes. While this is apparently contradicted by the occasions that cats get stuck up trees, the problem here is not their intelligence or their sense of balance, but rather that their claws all face forward, so they cannot be used as brakes when descending. The part of the cortex that deals with hearing is well-developed; so too, as we have seen, are the olfactory bulbs.

In cats, the parts of the brain that seem to be important in regulating social interactions are also less well-developed than they are in the most social members of the Carnivora, such as the wolf and the African hunting dog. This is unsurprising, given the solitary lifestyle of the domestic cat's immediate ancestors. Nevertheless, domestic cats are remarkably adaptable in their social arrangements; some form deep attachments with people, and others remain in a colony with other cats for their entire lives, their only interactions with humans consisting of running away and hiding. Once made, these choices cannot be reversed, since they are set during socialization: the cat as a species can adapt to a number of social environments, but individual cats generally cannot. This lack of flexibility must ultimately lie in the way that their brains are constructed, and in particular, the parts of their brains that process social information. Science has yet to unravel the factors that lie behind these constraints, so that today's cats have limited options when faced with changes in their social milieu.

6

Thoughts and Feelings

Historically, scientists have avoided words such as 'thinking' and 'feeling' when talking about animals. 'Thinking' runs the risk of being too imprecise: it can mean anything from simply paying attention to something ('I'm thinking about cats'), to complex comparisons between memories and projections into the future ('I'm thinking about the best way to get my cat to come in at night'), to expressions of opinion ('I think that cats are such fussy eaters because of their unusual nutritional needs'). To avoid the implication that animals such as cats possess human-type consciousness, biologists tend to use the term 'cognition' to refer to their mental processing of information.

With 'feelings', our intuitive grasp of our own emotions is bound up in our consciousness: we are aware of our emotions to an extent that cats almost certainly are not.[1] However, new scientific techniques such as brain imaging have revealed that all mammals, and therefore cats, have the mental machinery necessary to produce many of the same emotions we feel, even though they probably experience them in a much more in-the-moment way than we do. We do not have to presume that cats are conscious animals to allow that they are capable of making decisions – decisions based not just on information they are receiving and their memories of similar events, but also their emotional reactions to that information. In other words, it's now scientifically acceptable to explain their behaviour in terms of what they 'think' and 'feel' as long as we bear in mind that cats' thought processes and their emotional lives are both significantly different from our own.

Bearing this in mind is a challenge: we are accustomed to thinking about cat behaviour on our own terms. Part of the pleasure of owning a pet comes from projecting our thoughts and feelings on to the animal, treating it as if it were almost human. We talk to our cats as if they could understand our every word, while knowing full well that they certainly can't. We use adjectives like 'aloof' and 'mischievous' and 'sly' to describe cats – well, other people's cats, anyway – without really knowing whether these are just how we imagine the cat to be, or whether the cat knows it possesses these qualities (and is secretly proud of them).

Nearly a century ago, pioneering psychologist Leonard Trelawny Hobhouse wrote, 'I once had a cat which learned to "knock at the door" by lifting the mat outside and letting it fall. The common account of this proceeding would be that the cat did it to get in. It assumes the cat's action to be determined by its end. Is the common account wrong?'[2] As this illustrates, scientists have long struggled to find a coherent way to interpret cats' behaviour rationally and objectively. Scientists still argue about the extent to which cats and other mammals can solve problems by thinking them through in advance, as we do. We can easily interpret cat behaviour as if it had purpose behind it, but is this mere anthropomorphism? Are we assuming that because we would solve a problem in a particular way, cats must be using similar mental processes? Often, we find that cats can solve what appear to be difficult problems by applying much simpler learning processes.

Cognitive processes – 'thoughts' – begin in the sense organs and end in memory. At every stage, information is filtered out: there is simply not enough room in the cat's brain (or for that matter the human brain) to store a representation of every scrap of data picked up by its sense organs. Some of the filtering takes place as the sense organs relay their information to the brain; for example, the motion detectors in the cat's visual cortex draw attention to what is changing in the cat's field of vision, enabling it for an instant to ignore everything else. Within the brain, representations of what is happening are generated and held for a few seconds in *working memory* before most are discarded. A small fraction of these representations, particularly those that have triggered changes in emotion, transfer into *long-term memory*, enabling them to be recalled later on. Short-term memory, long-term memory and emotion are all used when a cat needs to make a decision as to what action to take.

*

Much of the everyday behaviour we observe in our pet cats can be explained by simple mental processes. First, the information gathered by the sense organs has to be categorized: is the animal over there a rat or could it be a mouse? Then it must be compared with the situation as it was a few moments before: has the rat moved or is it still in the same place? More or less at the same time, the cat's long-term memory is being trawled for similar situations: what happened the last time it saw a rat?

As far as we can tell, recollection of such memories affects the cat's decisions through two mechanisms. The first is an emotional reaction: a cat that has been bitten by rats in the past will immediately feel fear and/or anxiety, and a cat skilled at killing and eating rats will feel something like excitement. The second mechanism guides the cat in selecting the most appropriate action for the situation – depending on the emotional reaction, either the best way of getting out of the rat's way or the hunting tactic that has worked best on previous rats.

Our minds continually categorize objects without being aware of what we are doing, a process that requires sophisticated mental processes. Scientists are now studying whether cats' minds use the same processes, and if their brains can fill in gaps, as ours can. Let's say a cat sees a mouse's nose and tail, but the mouse's body is obscured behind a plant. Can the cat imagine the mouse's body in between, or does it perceive the nose and tail as somehow belonging to two separate animals? Cats can be trained to distinguish drawings that – to our eyes – create visual illusions, such as the one shown on p. 132, from those that do not, so it is likely they can indeed 'join the dots' and visualize the body of the mouse between its head and tail. Cats can also use changes in texture to piece together shapes of particular interest to them – to a cat, a negative image of a bird, with the contrasts shifted the wrong way around, is still recognizably a bird.[3] However, they do not seem to have an inbuilt rat/mouse detector as such – unlike toads, for example, which reflexively pounce on anything wormlike.

Cats presumably do not know in advance what type of prey is likely to be available when they first leave their mothers and start hunting for themselves, so they rely on what they've learned as kittens, rather than robotically pouncing on mice or other prey.

Cats can also make sophisticated judgements on how large or small

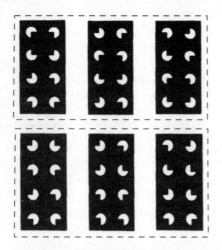 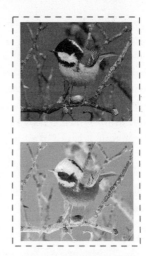

Cats can recognize outlines even when they are broken up or unusual.
They know the difference between pictures that produce an illusion, like the
'falling square' in the three pictures at top left, and those that don't, like the
three at bottom left. They also recognize the negative image as a bird.

something is. If they are trained to pick out the smallest or largest of three objects, they continue to pick out the smallest when all three objects are made smaller, so that what was originally the small object is no longer the smallest of the three. Prey will appear larger or smaller depending on how far away it is, so making a judgement about relative size is important in deciding whether to run away (from a large rat, still some distance away) or attack (a small rat, close by). Mysteriously, cats also seem to classify shapes according to whether they are closed – for example, a filled circle or square – or open – for example, an uppercase I or U. We do not know why this skill evolved as it did, since its contribution to cats' survival is obscure.

That all these examples relate to vision is a consequence of our own biases: because we are a visual species, scientists tend to focus on an animal's visual abilities to get an idea of how their brains work. Cats must also be able to classify what they hear, and although we don't know how they categorize sounds, we can guess from their hunting behaviour that they probably have categories for each of the sounds made by the various species they prey upon. Presumably they also have categories for the odours that they pick up with their noses and their vomeronasal organs, but with our comparatively poor sense of smell we have trouble imagining how such a system might work.

Humans also categorize events by when they happened, but cats probably do not. We know little about cats' conception of time, but they are definitely much better at judging short durations than long ones. Cats have been successfully trained to discriminate sounds that last four seconds from those that last five, and also to delay their response to a cue for a few seconds (because they only get the reward if they wait for the correct time).[4] However, cats are poor at discriminating longer periods of time, and their perception is most likely limited to the few seconds provided by their working memory. We have no evidence to suggest that cats can spontaneously recall memories and place those events as having happened a few days ago, as opposed to a few hours or weeks previous – something we find easy to do.

Cats have a general sense of the rhythm of the day. They have a free-running daily rhythm that is reset every day by the onset of daylight, and they also take other cues from their environment about what time of day it is. Some are natural, such as the sun rising and setting, and some are learned, such as their owner feeding them at roughly the same time every day. Still, they don't seem to think *about* time passing, in the way that we do.

Once a cat has worked out what it is observing through sight, smell or hearing, it must work out what to do next. If its survival might be threatened, the cat may need to act first and think later. When a cat is startled, say by a sudden loud noise, it instantly prepares itself for action through a set of preprogrammed and coordinated reflexes. It crouches, ready to run if necessary. Its pupils dilate while its eyes quickly focus as closely as possible, regardless of whether there is anything there to focus on; this presumably maximizes the chances of pinpointing the threat if it is close by. If the threat is still far away, then the cat has less urgency to identify what it is.

Almost every other reaction a cat makes changes with experience: over time, its reactions change. Even the startle reflex gradually wanes and may eventually disappear, say if the same loud noise is repeated over and over again. In this process, habituation, something initially excites the cat, but then becomes progressively less interesting until it eventually evokes no reaction at all.

For example, cats are renowned for quickly getting 'bored' with toys. Intrigued as to why this should be, in 1992 I set up a research project at the University of Southampton to look into cats' motivation for playing with objects. Do they literally 'play' for the sheer fun of it, as a child might, or are their intentions more 'serious'? The manner in which cats play with toys is highly reminiscent of the way that they attack prey, so we designed our experiments with the presumption that whatever was going on in their heads, it was probably related to their hunting instincts. My graduate student Sarah Hall and I found that habituation is the main underlying reason for this apparent boredom. We presented cats with toys – mouse-sized, fake-fur-covered 'pillows' tied to a piece of cord – and at first they usually played intensely, appearing to treat the toy as if it was indeed a mouse. However, many cats stopped playing within a matter of a couple of minutes. When we took the toys away for a while and then presented them again, most of the cats started playing again, but neither as intensely nor for as long as the first time. By the third presentation, many of the cats would scarcely even begin to play. They clearly became 'bored' with the toy.

If we switched the toy for a slightly different one – a different colour (say, black to white, since cats' perception of colours is different from ours), texture or odour – almost all of the cats would start playing again. Thus, they were 'bored' not by the game, but by the toy. In fact, the frustration of being offered the same toy repeatedly actually *increased* their desire to play. If the interval between the last game with the original toy and the first game with the new toy was about five minutes, they attacked the second toy with even more vigour than they did the first one.[5]

To understand why playing with a toy would make a cat frustrated, we considered what might motivate cats to play in the first place. Kittens sometimes play with toys as if they were fellow kittens, but adult cats invariably treat toys as if they were prey: they chase, bite, claw and pounce on toys just as if the toys were mice or rats. To test the idea that cats think of toys in the same way they think of prey, we tried different kinds of toys to see which ones cats prefer. Our findings showed that, unsurprisingly, they like mouse-sized toys that are furry, feathered or multi-legged – toy spiders, for example. Even indoor cats that had never hunted showed these preferences, so they must be hardwired in the cat's brain. The cats played with rat-sized toys covered in fake fur in a subtly different way from the mouse-sized toys. Instead of holding them in their front paws and biting them, most cats would hold the rat-sized toys at arm's length and rake them with their hind claws – just as hunting cats do with real rats. The cats were apparently thinking of their toys as if they were real animals, and as if their size, texture, and any simulated movement (such as our pulling on the toy's string) had triggered hunting instincts.

We then examined whether a cat's appetite has similar effects on the way it hunts and the way it plays with toys. If cats play with toys just for their own amusement, as many people assume they do, then they should be less inclined to play when they are hungry, since their minds should be focused instead on how to get something to eat. Conversely, as a hunting cat gets hungrier, it will hunt more intensely and become more inclined to take on larger prey than usual. We found exactly the latter when we offered toys to our cats. If their first meal of the day had been delayed, they played more intensely than usual with a mouse-sized toy – for example, biting it more frequently. Moreover, many of the cats that normally refused to play with a rat-sized toy at all were now prepared to attack it.[6] This convinced us that adult cats do think that they are hunting when they're playing with toys.

Cats don't easily get 'bored' with hunting, so we were still puzzled as to why our cats stopped playing with most toys so quickly. Indeed, they appeared to get 'bored' with most commercially available toys and with the kinds of toys we made for our first experiments. The few toys that sustained our cats' interest all shared one quality: they fell apart as the cat was playing with them.[7] Although we had to abandon experiments that involved these toys, which came apart at the seams as our cats batted them about, we noticed that several of the cats were extremely reluctant to give them up. We then realized that our original swapping experiments mimicked one aspect of what happens when a cat rips a toy apart: when we exchanged the toy for a slightly different one, the cat's senses told it that the toy had changed. It didn't seem to matter to the cat that it had not caused the change itself; what was important was that a change seemed to have occurred.

We deduced that not only do cats think they are hunting when they're playing with toys, but their behaviour is being controlled by the same four mechanisms whether they're hunting or playing. One of these mechanisms is affected by hunger, and the same one that makes a cat more likely to play with a toy makes it likely to make a kill when it's hungry.[8] The second is triggered by the appearance – and presumably the smell and sound – of prey, and certain specific features, such as fur, feathers and legs, that the cat recognizes instinctively are likely to belong to prey animals. The third mechanism is affected by the size of the toy or prey. Attacking a mouse puts the cat in much less danger than attacking a rat, so the cat attacks the rat much more carefully; likewise, cats treat large toys much more circumspectly than small toys, as if they were capable of fighting back. Even though cats should quickly learn that the toys are unlikely to retaliate, most cats don't seem to do so. The fourth mechanism is the source of the cat's apparent frustration: if all that biting and clawing doesn't seem to have any effect on its target, then either the target wasn't a meal, or if it *is* prey, then it's proving difficult to subdue. A toy that starts to disintegrate, or is taken away but looks different when it comes back (as in our original experiment), mimics the early stages of a kill, thus encouraging the cat to persist.

Overall, many of the cat's hunting tactics can be explained in terms of simple reflexes, modified by emotion – specifically, the fear of getting hurt by large prey animals – and habituation, which ensures that the cat continues to grapple with its prey only if it is likely to end up with a meal. However, these are only the basic building blocks of hunting behaviour; cats undoubtedly perfect their hunting skills through practice, by learning how to assemble the various elements in the most productive ways.

Habituation can explain many short-term changes in a cat's behaviour, but its effects wear off after a few minutes; longer-term, more permanent changes in the way a cat reacts require a different explanation. These must be based on learning and memory.

Fundamentally, cats learn the same way as dogs, even though dogs are self-evidently much easier to train. Two factors lie behind this difference between cats and dogs. First, most cats do not find human attention rewarding in its own right, whereas dogs do; we therefore train cats using food as a reward, rather than affection. Second, dogs instinctively behave in ways we can easily shape into something useful: for example, the herding behaviour of a sheepdog is composed of elements from the hunting behaviour of the wolf, the dog's ancestor. Cat behaviour features little that we can usefully refine by training, except for our own amusement. Obviously, we have benefited from the cat's hunting abilities for ages. However, we usually leave cats to their own devices: they will seek out the mice that invade our grain stores regardless of whether we want them to do so. Dogs, on the other hand, are specialized for cooperative hunting of much larger prey. They are a nuisance when unsupervised and useful only when trained. We take on the responsibility of gearing their attention towards particular prey, when that is what we need from them.

Much of what cats learn is based on two fundamental psychological processes: classical and operant conditioning. Both of these involve new associations forming in the cat's mind. The first involves two events that regularly occur closely together in time; the second involves something the cat does or does not do and a predictable consequence of that action, which may be good for the cat (a reward) or bad (a punishment). Because cats seem to have little or no instinctive appreciation either of how humans behave or the best ways to interact with them, virtually all their dealings with us are built up through this sort of learning.

Classical conditioning is also known as Pavlovian conditioning, after Ivan Pavlov, the first scientist to map out how such learning works in a series of experiments with dogs in the 1890s. In fact, his principles apply equally well to cats.[9] A hungry cat that smells food will instinctively seek it out and then eat it. For a wild cat, food is the result of a successful hunting expedition; for a pet cat, the owner makes this trip unnecessary by buying food at the supermarket and presenting it to the cat. Cats don't need to learn that food can appear without being preceded by hunting, because this is precisely what happens when, in the wild, their mother brings food back to the nest.

What they do learn, via classical conditioning, are the cues that indicate that food is on its way – for example, the sound of a can opener. In psychologist's jargon, this action by the owner is the conditioned stimulus, which becomes associated in the cat's mind with the unconditioned ('instinctive') stimulus, the smell of the food. Nothing in the cat's evolution has prepared it to respond automatically to the sound of a can opener: the association is something that every cat would have to learn for itself. Of course, this is hardly a difficult lesson; nor is the underlying process complex: scientists have found such behaviour even in bees and caterpillars. Nevertheless, classical conditioning is the main way that cats find out how the world around them is constructed: which parts occur in predictable sequences, and which do not.

The result – the unconditioned response – doesn't have to be a 'reward', such as food. In fact, learning occurs more quickly when it helps the animal to avoid something unpleasant or painful. A cat that is attacked by another, larger cat will certainly experience fear and possibly pain, and will instinctively try to run away. It will also probably remember what the attacking cat looked like, associating its appearance with the unpleasant feelings it experienced at the time.[10] The next time it sees that cat, it will feel the fear before any attack takes place – and may immediately run away, as it ultimately did the first time they met. However, relatively sophisticated animals such as cats can respond flexibly: they do not automatically have to perform the original response simply because stimuli are similar. In this way, the cat may not run away immediately, but instead 'freeze', hoping to avoid detection, having previously learned that running away can invite a chase.

This simple learning has one major constraint: the events that a cat associates together must occur either at precisely the same moment or no more than a second or two apart. Say a cat has done something that its owner doesn't like – for example, depositing a dead mouse on the floor. The cat's owner finds the mouse several minutes after the cat has left it there and shouts at the cat. In this case, classical conditioning does not link the two events together: rather, it links the unpleasantness of being shouted at with whatever happened immediately before the shout – probably the owner's arrival in the room.

This rule has one exception: if a cat eats something that makes it feel ill, it will thereafter avoid foods with the same flavour. Moreover, forging this association requires only one such experience. This food-aversion learning differs from classical conditioning both in the speed with which the lesson is learned and in the delay between the sensation – the odour of the food – and the consequence – the upset stomach. It is obviously in the cat's best interest to avoid repeating any action that could kill it, which accounts for the irreversibility of this learning. Likewise, there would be little point in the cat associating its first feelings of sickness with something else that occurred at the same time – the problem food would have been eaten many minutes, even hours, before. Nevertheless, this is still classical conditioning, except that the 'rule' for the time frame has been both extended and made much more specific, to the flavour of the last food that the cat ate before feeling ill; other cues, such as the characteristics of the room where it ate the meal, are ignored as irrelevant. Of course, feeling nauseous can also be a symptom of an infection unconnected with something the cat ate, so this mechanism occasionally has unexpected consequences: a cat that succumbs to a virus may then go off its regular food even after it has recovered, because it has incorrectly associated the illness with the meal that happened to precede it.

Cats can also learn spontaneously, when there is no obvious reward or penalty involved. This becomes especially useful when they are building up a mental map of their surroundings. A cat will learn that a particular shrub it passes every day has a particular smell. If the cat sees a similar shrub elsewhere, it will expect that shrub to have the same odour as the first one. If it turns out not to – perhaps because an unfamiliar animal has scent-marked it – the cat will give it an especially thorough inspection. Such 'behaviourally silent' learning can be explained by classical Pavlovian learning – that is, if the cat spontaneously feels rewarded by the information it has gained. In other words, cats are programmed to enjoy their explorations; otherwise, they wouldn't learn anything from them.

This kind of learning allows cats to relax in what must be, for them, the highly artificial indoor environments we provide for them. Domesticated cats are happy once they have been able to set up a complete set of associations between what each feature of that environment looks, sounds and smells like. This explains why cats immediately pay attention to anything that changes – move a piece of furniture from one side of the room to the other, and your cat, finding that its predictable set of associations have been broken, will feel compelled to inspect it carefully before it can settle down again. To cope with such changes, cats can gradually unlearn associations that no longer work, a process known technically as extinction.

All animals make some associations more easily than others; evolution has built in certain responses that are difficult to overwrite. For cats, one of these is the likelihood that high-pitched sounds will come from prey. In one experiment, two Hungarian scientists taught some rats that whenever a high-pitched clicking sound came from a loudspeaker at one end of a corridor, a piece of food would appear at the other end, about seven feet away. The rats had to run quickly from the speaker to the food dispenser, otherwise the food would disappear. They learned this quickly and reliably, such that they would sit and wait for the clicking noise, and then on hearing it, run in the correct direction. To the experimenters' surprise, cats took a great deal longer to learn the same exercise: many of the cats required hundreds of repetitions before they would perform reliably. They quickly learned that food was available in the corridor when the clicking sound occurred, but almost invariably started running towards the sound rather than away from it in the direction of the food. While they were still learning the task, some of the cats appeared to become so confused that they refused to eat the food even if they reached it in time. Even when they had completely learned the task, they often glanced briefly at where the sound was coming from before proceeding towards the food, something the rats had given up doing at an early stage.[11]

The difference between the cats' and the rats' performance in this task does not mean that rats are smarter than cats. Rather, for a hungry cat, high-pitched noises are too important to ignore. For the rats, the clicking noise was an arbitrary cue, just as the sound of a can opener is for a cat; such a sound only comes to have meaning because of its association with the arrival of food. For the cats, the clicking noise instinctively meant 'Food is likely to be over here', something they had great difficulty in learning to ignore.

*

Like other animals, cats can learn to perform a particular action every time a particular situation occurs. This forms the basis for much of animal training, and is technically known as operant conditioning. Contrary to popular myth, cats can be trained, but few people bother, apart from the professionals who produce performing cats for movies and TV. Cats are much more difficult to train than dogs are for at least three reasons. First, their behaviour shows less intrinsic variety than that of dogs, so there is less raw material with which to work. Training any animal to do something that it would never do naturally is a difficult process; most training consists of changing the cues that lead to a piece of normal behaviour, rather than inventing a piece of behaviour the animal has never performed in its life. Second, and perhaps most important, cats are less naturally attentive towards people than dogs are. Domestic dogs have evolved to be exceptionally observant of what people want from them, because virtually every use that human-kind has ever had for them has favoured dogs that could interpret human behaviour over those that could not. Cats are surprisingly good at following simple pointing gestures, but when they encounter a problem they cannot solve, they tend not to look to their owners for help – something that dogs automatically do.[12] Third, although dogs are powerfully rewarded by simple physical contact from their owner, few cats are: professional cat trainers generally have to rely on food rewards. These trainers also use secondary reinforcers extensively, rewards that are initially arbitrary but that become rewarding through association with the arrival of food. Nowadays, cat owners can emulate this using training aids such as clickers (see box overleaf, 'Clicker Training').

Cats can be trained to perform normal behaviour out of its usual context. In the process known as shaping, the cat is initially rewarded for any behaviour approximating the desired result that it performs immediately after the cue given by its trainer. Only behaviour that is close to the result is rewarded, until finally only exactly the right response gets the reward. To take a simple example, most cats will (sensibly!) not jump over an obstacle if they can walk around it. To train a cat to jump on command, the trainer rewards it for walking over a stick that is lying on the ground, and then for stepping over it when it is raised slightly. Then if the trainer raises the stick further, she rewards the cat only for actual jumps. Once the habit is established,

CLICKER TRAINING

Like most animals (with the notable exception of dogs), many cats can be trained only with food rewards. However, delivering the reward to the cat at exactly the right moment to reinforce the desired piece of behaviour can be tricky; also, the cat may be distracted from what it is supposed to be learning by the smell of the food 'concealed' in the trainer's hand. Cats can be trained much more easily if a secondary reinforcer is used – a distinctive cue that signals to the cat that a piece of food is on its way, instantly making it feel good, thereby reinforcing the performance of whatever it was doing when the cue appeared.

Although in principle almost anything could be used as a secondary reinforcer, in practice distinctive sounds are the most convenient and practical, partly because they can be timed very precisely, and partly because the cat cannot avoid perceiving them even if it is some distance away and looking in the opposite direction. Animal trainers used to use whistles, but nowadays the cue of choice is often the clicker, a tensioned piece of metal in a plastic case that makes a distinctive click-clack sound when pressed and released.

Clicker-training a cat

Cats must be taught to like the sound of the clicker, which has little or no instinctive significance for them, by classical conditioning. This is simply done by attracting the cat's attention with a handful of its favourite treats when it's hungry, and then offering the treats one at a time, each preceded with one click-clack from the clicker. (Some cats are hypersensitive to metallic sounds – either hold the clicker away from the cat or use a quieter sound, for example the plunger on a retractable ballpoint pen.) After a few sessions, the sound of the clicker will have become firmly associated in the cat's mind with something pleasant, and this sound will gradually become pleasant in its own right.

Once this has become established, the clicker can be used to reward other pieces of behaviour. For example, many cats can be trained to come consistently when called, initially by clicking when they turn and start to approach, but then gradually delaying the click until the cat arrives at the trainer's feet. Once the click has been established as a reward, it doesn't have to be followed by food every single time, although if the cat hears the sound over and over again without food appearing, the association may start to be lost. It is therefore usually most effective to intersperse sessions of training to come when called (when it is impossible to deliver the reward immediately after the click, because the cat is too far away) with repeat sessions of the original click-treat pairings that re-establish the link.

Instructions on how to clicker-train cats can be found at www.humaneso ciety.org/news/magazines/2011/05-06/it_all_clicks_together_join.html.

trainers can ingrain it further by rewarding only some successful performances and not others. This may seem counterintuitive, but animals usually concentrate harder when they know that the outcome is slightly uncertain than when it is guaranteed. Humans show this same quality under some circumstances – behaviour that is perfectly exploited in the payout schedule of fruit machines.

More complex tricks and 'performances' are usually taught piece by piece, each step becoming linked together in the cat's mind through chaining. The easiest way to put a sequence together is to start at the end with the final action and its reward, and progressively add the preceding steps – backwards chaining. For example, to train a cat to turn around once and then offer its paw to be shaken, the paw-shake is shaped first, and once that is perfected, the turn is shaped to precede it. Although it would seem more logical to train the first action first – forward chaining – most animals, including cats, find this much more difficult, indicating that their abilities to think ahead are limited.

Operant conditioning is not confined to deliberate training; it is one way that cats learn how to deal with whatever surroundings they find themselves in. Cats have not (yet) evolved to live in apartments; their instinctive behaviour is still tuned to hunting in the open air. The fact that they can adapt to indoor living is testament to their learning abilities. Not only can they make sense of their surroundings by means of associations built up by classical conditioning, they are also able to learn how to manipulate objects around them to get what they want.

For example, many cats learn how to open a door fitted with a lever-type handle by jumping up and grabbing it with their forepaws. A superficially 'clever' trick such as this one can be explained by operant conditioning. Of course, doors that unlatch with a handle and swing open on hinges do not form part of the world in which cats have done most of their evolving, so the final, successful, version of this behaviour cannot be natural. However, it most probably starts with something that cats will do instinctively when they are unable to get somewhere they want to go, which is to jump up on to a vantage point to see whether there is an alternative route. If the cat tries to jump up on to the lever, which from the ground will look like a fixed platform, it will find that when the lever moves, not only does it lose its footing, but also that the door may swing open. The cat then gets the reward of being able to explore the room on the other side of the door – and cats, as territorial animals, find exploration of novel areas rewarding in itself. The cat will remember the association between its action and the reward. After trying various alternative actions on the handle, it will progressively arrive at the most efficient solution, which is to raise a single paw and gently pull the lever downwards.

Pet cats learn how to use the same techniques on their owners. Even the most ardent cat-lovers sometimes describe them as manipulative, but much of a cat's so-called manipulative behaviour is built up by operant conditioning. Feral cats are remarkably silent compared to domestic cats (except during fighting and courtship, notoriously noisy activities); in particular, such cats rarely meow at one another, whereas the meow is the pet cat's best-known call. The meow is usually directed at people, so rather than being an evolved signal it's more likely to have been shaped by some kind of reward.

Cats need to meow because we humans are generally so unobservant. Cats constantly monitor their surroundings (except when they're asleep, of course) but we often fix our gaze on newspapers and books, TVs and computer screens. We do, however, reliably look up when we hear something unusual, and cats quickly learn that a meow will grab our attention. For a few cats this may be rewarding in itself, but the meow will often also produce the reaction that the cat is hoping for, such as a bowl of food or an opened door. Some cats then shape their own behaviour to increase the precision of their request. Some will deliver the meow at specific locations – by the door means 'Let me out', and in the middle of the kitchen means 'Feed me.' Others find that different intonations lead to different results, and so 'train' themselves to produce a whole range of different meows. These are generally different for every cat, and can be reliably interpreted only by the cat's owner, showing that each meow is an arbitrary, learned, attention-seeking sound rather than some universal cat–human 'language'.[13] Thus, a secret code of meows and other vocalizations develops between each cat and its owner, unique to that cat alone and meaning little to outsiders.

Classical and operant conditioning are not the only feasible explanations for why cats behave as they do, but they are often the simplest. Still, cats are undoubtedly much more than mere stimulus–response machines. Disentangling cat intelligence is a challenge, partially because we tend to believe willingly that much pet behaviour is driven by rational thought. Even the earliest animal psychologists recognized this tendency. In his 1898 book *Animal Intelligence*, Edward L. Thorndike wrote, with his tongue firmly in his cheek:

> Thousands of cats on thousands of occasions sit helplessly yowling, and no one takes thought of it or writes to his friend, the professor; but let one cat claw at the knob of a door supposedly as a signal to be let out, and straightway this cat becomes the representative of the cat-mind in all the books.[14]

We also lack scientific research on cat intelligence: the past decade has seen an explosion in studies of the mental abilities of dogs, but cats, popular subjects for such studies in the 1960s and 1970s, have subsequently been eclipsed by 'man's best friend' – simply because dogs are easier to train.

Some recent studies have focused on cats' understanding of the way the world around them works – their grasp of physics and engineering, if you will. Cats may seem entirely *au fait* with their surroundings, but their capacity to translate the phenomena they encounter into mental pictures evolved when they were wild animals; it has not caught up with humankind's manipulations. I realized this first hand when I noticed that my cat Splodge always inspected the bumpers of cars parked outside my house. Sometimes after sniffing he looked around nervously, and I guessed that he must have picked up a scent mark from another cat, probably deposited a few hours previously when the car had been parked elsewhere, miles away. This happened day after day, month after month, but Splodge, who was otherwise a perfectly intelligent cat, never seemed to understand the possibility that the scent marks might have arrived already on the car: he always seemed to presume that they belonged to an unfamiliar cat that must have just invaded our neighbourhood. In nature, scent marks stay where they've been left, so there would be no need to evolve an understanding that scent marks might move with objects on which they've been deposited.

We have little research on cats' comprehension of physics, but one recent experiment has confirmed that it may be extremely rudimentary. Scientists trained pet cats to retrieve a food treat from beneath a mesh cover by pulling on a handle connected to the treat by a string (see nearby illustration). Many of them learned to do this quite easily, giving the impression that they 'understood', as you or I would without thinking twice, that the handle was connected to the food by the string. However, we can also explain this behaviour by simple operant conditioning – pull the handle and a food reward arrives – in which the handle-pulling is, so far as the cat is concerned, just an arbitrary action. The researchers exposed the cats' lack of understanding of the connection by adding another string and handle alongside the first one; the crucial difference, which the cats could easily have seen, was that only the first handle was connected to the food. Although the cats could easily have seen that this was the case, they continued to pull on the handles, but were unable to predict which handle would produce the reward, showing that, for them, the handle was an arbitrary object, not physically linked to the piece of food. Unsurprisingly, the

*Cats appear not to understand that one string has food
on the end and the other doesn't*

cats performed equally badly when the strings were crossed over.[15] Extrapolating from this experiment, it seems likely that cats, unlike crows or apes, are mentally incapable of learning to use tools.

Their inability to understand that a piece of string can physically link two other things together highlights just how different cats' minds are to our own. We not only find such an idea obvious, we routinely extrapolate it to other situations in which the physical connection is much less obvious, such as the electronic connection between the cursor on the screen in front of me and the (computer) mouse in my hand. Cats fail at the first hurdle, the comprehension of a physical connection between three objects, and their inability to perform such manipulations is not, as some would jokingly have it, simply due to their lack of opposable thumbs.

Yet cats do have a sophisticated understanding of three-dimensional space, as we would expect of an opportunistic hunter. They probably have little need for this when indoors, instead relying on what are known as egocentric cues – 'This is where I turn left', 'This is where I turn right', 'This is where I jump up.' However, when outdoors and in familiar territory, cats can take shortcuts, showing that during their earlier explorations they have constructed a mental map – 'The last time I caught a rat, I first went to the oak tree and then turned left down the hedge, so this time I will go diagonally across the field and through the hedge; I already know that the rats' hole is just beyond the hedge.' They are capable of using this information efficiently;

given a choice of routes to a destination that cannot be seen from where they are, cats will pick the shortest one. Likewise, as many people also do, they prefer a route that starts out in roughly the right direction; a slightly shorter route that involves initially walking in the wrong direction is usually shunned.

As hunters, cats should be able to work out where objects that have gone out of sight are likely to be. No wild cat would give up hunting a mouse immediately after it disappeared from sight under the mistaken impression that it had ceased to exist. As expected, cats do seem to remember where prey has disappeared, although they store this information for only a few seconds, in 'working' memory; not until the cat actually makes contact with the prey does the memory become longer-lasting. Presumably, it is not worthwhile for a cat to continue to search a particular location for highly mobile prey for much longer than this; by that point, the prey has either made its escape or gone to ground.

Scientists recently demonstrated that cats do indeed remember the last place they saw a mouse, rather than merely keeping their eyes fixed on it or even just heading in that general direction. In the apparatus illustrated, scientists allowed the cat to watch a food treat being pulled behind a small barrier on a piece of cord, through the transparent section of the screen. The cat was then allowed to walk into the apparatus, but – as the remainder of the screen was opaque – this action temporarily blocked the cat's view of the location of the food. Nevertheless, the cat usually picked the right place to look for the food. Interestingly, many of the cats tested sometimes went the long way around – they set off and entered the apparatus from the 'wrong' side, but then immediately crossed to the correct side to retrieve the food. This is similar to a common hunting tactic: if cats are in hot pursuit of a mouse or rat, they will often briefly take a more roundabout route, possibly to make their prey think that they have mistaken where it has hidden.[16]

The cat's mental abilities are specifically tuned to their hunting lifestyle, rather than being part of a more general spatial intelligence. Cats perform remarkably badly in tests designed to track the development of such abilities in human infants. Many children of eighteen months can understand that if an object is hidden in a container, and

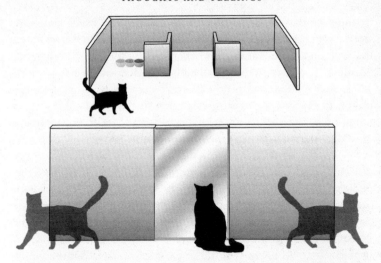

Cats sometimes take the most direct route to the place where food has disappeared (left), but on other occasions they seem to deliberately take a more indirect route (right), as if they were hunting and wanted to confuse their prey

then the container itself is hidden, the object ought to be in the container when it reappears. If they then find that it isn't, they look next in the place where the container disappeared. They not only understand that an object they have seen must still be somewhere even when they can't see it, but can also use their imagination to guess where it might be. Cats cannot do this at all, probably because it is not a situation that their ancestors encountered while hunting. Mice hide, certainly, but they do not hide inside objects that are themselves capable of moving around.

The cat's ability to reason seems limited, especially when determining cause and effect. They rely on simple associations built up through conditioning, and can easily be 'fooled' by our manipulations of their surroundings, which must seem arbitrary in their view of the world (as if they were thinking 'How did that bag arrive in the middle of the kitchen floor?' or 'Why does my owner talk into that thing in her hand?'). Nevertheless, it is entirely possible that scientists have yet to design experiments that allow cats to demonstrate their true abilities.

It could be that the small number of situations in which cats have been tested happen to be those in which their evolution has favoured reliance on simple learning and short-term, rather than long-term, memory. Scientists studying canine intelligence, which has received considerable attention over the past two decades, have only recently begun to find ways of testing dogs that fit their particular way of interpreting the world. Cats, with their enigmatic reputation, may still be hiding the true extent of their brainpower.

Cats are masters at concealing their thoughts, and are even better at hiding their emotions. Several cartoons show an array of cats with identical expressions, each labelled with a different emotion, ranging from 'Frisky' to 'Content' to 'Sad', and in one instance, with irony, 'Alive.' One version that I treasure, by British cartoonist Steven Appleby, has no fewer than thirty cat faces, of which twenty-nine have identical expressions (the captions range from 'About to do nothing at all' to 'Slightly irritated but concealing it well'); the thirtieth, 'Asleep', differs from the others only by its closed eyes.[17]

Biology provides good reasons why most animals keep their emotions to themselves. Dog owners may find this idea absurd, since both dogs and humans express their emotions spontaneously. Indeed, we must often suppress our feelings when social mores dictate. Nevertheless, we humans have evolved a very sophisticated ability to detect tiny flickers of emotion in others, telltale signs that help us predict what that person is likely to do next. Dogs, in their way, are similar to us in this respect; not only have they evolved the ability to guess our intentions from our body language, but they also express their emotions openly, partly because we generally respond in ways that are beneficial to them – backing away when they growl, or giving them a pat if they're wagging their tails. Dogs and humans are both social species that usually live in stable groups, and such stability means that emotional honesty is unlikely to be penalized.

Cats are descended from a species with a solitary lifestyle, and therefore much of their behaviour is guided by the need to compete, not to collaborate. In the wild, a male cat will live alone. The only way he can be sure of leaving any descendants is first to convince a female to accept him as a mate, and second to convince any rival males to back off. Macho behaviour, laced with a generous portion of bluff, is therefore essential to their success. Although female domestic cats do cooperate when raising kittens, this habit, which may have evolved during domestication, seems to have had little effect on their capacity to express their emotions.

Historically, scientists have changed their mind several times over whether animals' emotions should be used when discussing their behaviour. In the nineteenth century, researchers often ascribed human emotions to cats. For example, in his 1886 book *Animal Intelligence*, physiologist George S. Romanes wrote:

> The only other feature in the emotional life of cats which calls for special notice is that which leads to their universal and proverbial treatment of helpless prey. The feelings that prompt a cat to torture a captured mouse can only, I think, be assigned to the category to which by common consent they are ascribed – delight in torturing for torture's sake.[18]

By the beginning of the twentieth century, such anthropomorphism had been abandoned, and the guiding principle in animal psychology was Morgan's canon: 'In no case may we interpret an action as the outcome of the exercise of a higher psychical faculty, if it can be interpreted as the outcome of the exercise of one which stands lower [that is, simpler] in the psychological scale.'[19] For a while, indeed, scientists conceived of animals as if they were robotic stimulus–response machines, leaving no room for any consideration of emotion. Recently, however, we have come to realize that it is difficult to explain much animal behaviour without invoking the idea of emotion. In addition, MRI scanning has enabled us to see where in the human brain emotions are generated, and the simpler, 'gut-feeling' emotions occur in parts of our brains that we share with other mammals, including cats.

The current view holds that emotions are a necessary component of the mechanisms that drive animal behaviour – and indeed our behaviour as well. They can be prompts to shortcuts, enabling our brains to choose the best response to a situation when fast action is called for. In this, cats are no different from ourselves. A cat that sees another, larger, unfamiliar cat approaching will immediately become alert, crouch down and prepare to flee. The anxiety it feels at seeing a potential adversary enables it to take these actions immediately, without having to think the situation through and evaluate all possible strategies and outcomes.

Emotions also explain spontaneous and apparently functionless behaviour. Kittens engage in play during most of their waking moments, and explaining why they do so is not straightforward. In the wild, play is a mildly risky activity, exposing the kittens to danger and possibly attracting the attention of a predator – surely it seems safer for kittens to stay quietly in their nest and wait for their mother to return with food. Furthermore, kittens do sometimes nip each other when playing, but this doesn't seem to put them off playing with that same kitten again, which it should do if they are simple stimulus–response machines.

The simplest explanation for why kittens feel they ought to play, and why they continue to play even following a slight mishap, is that play is *fun*. Neuroscientists have found in young rats that when they play, the neurohormone profile of the brain changes. Moreover, these changes are not the consequences of play, they appear to be its cause: they occur as soon as the rats are given the signal that it's time to play. As such, the mere sight of a sibling ready to play is likely enough to make a kitten want to join in, because the brain signals 'fun' before the playing has even begun.

Of course, hormones are not the same as emotions, but changes in certain hormones are often a sign that emotions are being experienced. We are all aware of the racing heartbeat, hyperventilation, hyperalertness, and sweaty palms induced by adrenalin, the 'fight-or-flight' hormone associated with feelings of fear and panic. Some of us are familiar with the elation we sometimes feel after strenuous exercise, caused by the release of endorphins and other hormones into the brain. Although not all hormones are so closely connected to emotions, many are, and can provide an indicator of immediate emotion or underlying mood.

We can therefore conceive of animal emotions as manifestations of the brain and the nervous system and their associated hormones, sometimes enabling decisions to be made quickly, other times directing learning. Sometimes, information coming into the brain from the cat's senses has to trigger an immediate reaction. A cat that slips while walking along the top of a fence must correct its balance immediately:

the emotional panic that almost certainly follows will help train the cat to be more careful next time. On other occasions, the emotion triggers the behaviour. Indeed, the sight of its owner coming home will cause a cat to feel affectionate, and as a consequence it will raise its tail upright and begin to walk towards her.

Some people who don't like cats – and even some who do – would claim that love, especially towards its human owner, is not part of the cat's behavioural repertoire: as the popular adage goes, 'Dogs have masters, cats have staff.' True, the average cat does not outwardly demonstrate love for its owner in the same way as, say, a Labrador retriever would. Still, that tells us little about what is going on inside the cat's head.

In the animal world, lavish outward displays of emotion are usually manipulative. Consider, for example, the incessant chirping of baby birds in a nest, each essentially calling out, 'Feed me first, feed me first!' Evolution has ensured that where such displays occur, they work: the baby bird that makes the least fuss is ignored by its parents, which often produce more offspring than they can comfortably feed, and it may perish as a result. Wildcats are solitary and self-sufficient except for a few weeks at the beginning of their lives, and so have little need for sophisticated signals. Although domestic cats now depend on us for food, shelter and protection, they have not done so consistently for long enough to have evolved the average dog's effusive greeting. That doesn't mean that cats are incapable of love, merely that their ways of showing love are somewhat limited.

Cats become extravagantly demonstrative only when they are angry or afraid. A fearful cat either will make itself look as small as possible by crouching, and then slink away, or, if it judges that running away may provoke a chase, will make itself look as large as possible, arching and raising the fur on its back. The raw emotion does *not* therefore provoke an automatic and invariable reaction; instead, the brain selects the more appropriate response based on other information available to it.

The angry cat will not only try to look as large as possible, but will also stand head-on towards the threat (usually another cat) with its ears forward, either yowling or growling loudly and lashing its tail side to side. We may be inclined to read these postures as expressions of emotion, but they are fundamentally expressions of intention, as well as attempts to manipulate the animal the cat is confronting.

Even when a cat is demonstrably trying to manipulate its opponent's behaviour, such manipulation need not be conscious. We can explain the cat's behaviour by its adhering to a set of rules that have served its ancestors well; which have, in the past, achieved the best possible outcome from an aggressive encounter. We must not forget, however, that the bluff is being directed at an animal with similar brainpower, and therefore evolution will also have favoured animals capable of 'mindreading' the other's intentions. One cat confronting another will expect one of two possible reactions: either a sign that the other cat is fearful and will probably back down, or that it is not fearful and so a fight is imminent. In this way, the behaviour, whether indicating fear or anger, becomes ritualized: any cat that adopts neither posture, or does something different, is likely to be attacked.

To explain their behaviour, we must thus allow that cats feel joy, love, anger and fear. What other emotions do they possess? Can they feel the full gamut of emotions that we can? To answer these questions, we must consider which are most likely the product of human consciousness, and therefore unknown to animals.

People do not agree on the range of emotions their cats can feel. A 2008 survey of British cat owners[20] revealed that almost all think their cat could feel affection, joy and fear. Nearly one fifth of these owners – perhaps those who own very timid cats – were unsure whether anger is within the cat's repertoire.

We all know the old saw 'Curiosity killed the cat', and, indeed, most owners acknowledge the cat's characteristic nosiness. The original version of this proverb, from its first appearance in the sixteenth century until the end of the nineteenth, was 'Care killed the cat' – 'care' in the sense of worry, anxiety or sorrow. Apparently, the idea that cats could become so anxious that they could even die from it was once common (and is now being revisited by veterinary surgeons). Despite this, about a quarter of the owners surveyed in 2008 thought their cat incapable of feeling anxiety or sadness.

If asked, scientists would now agree that the old version of the proverb contained a germ of truth: anxiety does constitute a serious

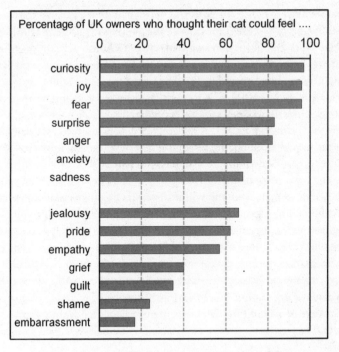

Percentage of UK owners who thought their cat could feel ....

curiosity
joy
fear
surprise
anger
anxiety
sadness

jealousy
pride
empathy
grief
guilt
shame
embarrassment

Owners' opinions about their cats' emotional capabilities

and real affliction for many cats. Anxiety, if simply defined as a fear of something that is not currently happening, has a reliable basis in physiology. Some anti-anxiety drugs developed for humans have also been found to reduce symptoms of anxiety in cats, so although we cannot be sure that cats experience anxiety in precisely the same way we do, we know that they feel something similar.

The most common cause of anxiety in cats is probably the worry that their territory is likely to be invaded by other cats in the neighbourhood, or even by another cat in the same household. When I surveyed ninety cat owners in suburban Hampshire and rural Devon in 2000, they reported that almost half of their cats regularly fought with other cats, and two out of five were fearful of cats in general. My colleague Rachel Casey, a veterinary surgeon specializing in cat behavioural disorders, regularly diagnoses anxiety and fear as the main factors driving cats to urinate and defecate indoors, outside the litter tray. Some cats spray the walls or furniture with urine, possibly to deter other cats from entering their owner's house believing it to be cat-free; others find the point in the house farthest from the cat-flap and urinate there, seemingly terrified of attracting the attention of any other cat. Some will defecate on the bedsheets, desperately trying to mingle their own odour with their owner's to establish 'ownership' of the core of the house. When the conflict is between two cats that live in the same house, one may spend much of its time hiding, or obsessively groom itself until its coat becomes patchy.[21]

The stress of being forced to live with cats it does not trust can often be severe enough to affect the cat's health. One illness now known to be closely linked to psychological stress is cystitis, referred to by veterinary surgeons as idiopathic cystitis because no disease or other medical cause is apparent. As many as two thirds of cats taken to vets for urination problems – blood in the urine, difficult or painful urination, urinating in inappropriate places – have no obvious medical problems, other than inflammation of the bladder and intermittent blockage of the urethra by mucus thereby displaced from the bladder wall. The factors triggering such episodes of cystitis are therefore psychological, and research has identified conflict with other cats living in the same household as being perhaps the most important of these. Less easy to quantify, but possibly just as important, are conflicts with neighbours' cats: certainly cats prone to cystitis usually run away from cats they meet in their own gardens, rather than standing up to them, which suggests that they find contact with other cats particularly stressful. Idiopathic cystitis is less common in female cats than in males: the conventional medical explanation is that the tube leading out of the bladder, the urethra, is generally narrower in males and therefore more prone to blockage. However, tom cats are generally more territorial and less sociable than females, so the latter may find it easier to resolve or avoid conflicts with other cats before stress affects their health.

Colleagues of mine at Bristol University Veterinary School documented one case involving a five-year-old male cat that was having great difficulty urinating, and when he did, his urine was bloody. He also groomed his abdomen excessively, but otherwise was entirely healthy. The cat was one of six within the household, but was friendly with none of the other cats. Moreover, cats from neighbouring households had recently attacked him. His symptoms gradually disappeared once his owners had implemented the changes recommended by the clinic: his own exclusive area within the house, his own food bowl, and his own litter tray that the other cats could not access. At the same time, his owners blocked his view of the garden by covering over the glass at the bottom of the windows in his part of the house, so he could not see any cats that were coming into the garden. Six months later his symptoms returned, but on investigation, it turned out he had been accidentally shut in with the other cats a couple of days previously. His owners vowed never to allow this to happen again, and the cat soon recovered.[22] Anxiety, a useful emotion if experienced for a few minutes, can become the bane of a cat's existence if prolonged for weeks or months, leading to chronically elevated levels of stress hormones, (presumably) a nagging and ever-present sense of dread, and eventually to deterioration in health.

In the same survey, cat owners were also asked about their cats' more complex emotions – jealousy, pride, shame, guilt and grief. Almost two thirds believed that their cat could feel jealous or proud. Only shame, guilt and grief were ruled out by a majority of the owners.

Basic emotions such as anger, affection, joy, fear and anxiety are 'gut feelings' that appear spontaneously. The most primitive part of the cat's brain produces these emotions – the same part that evolved hundreds of millions of years ago before there were any mammals, let alone cats. More complex emotions, such as jealousy, empathy and grief, require the cat to have some understanding of the mental processes of animals other than themselves, and hence psychologists sometimes refer to them as *relational* emotions.

Take jealousy, for example. When we experience jealousy, we are not only aware that whoever we are feeling jealous of is another human being, we can also guess what that other person is feeling; we have what psychologists call theory of mind, the idea that other humans have their own thoughts that may be different from ours. We are also capable of becoming obsessively jealous, thinking about the incident that triggered the original feeling long afterwards, even when the person we were jealous of is no longer present. We have little evidence that cats have the brainpower or the imagination to do either of these.

Cats undoubtedly recognize other cats as cats, and can evidently react to what they see them *doing*. However, even dogs, which are much more highly evolved socially than cats, show no evidence of understanding what other dogs are *thinking*, so it's unlikely that cats can either. Moreover, cats seem to live in the present, neither reflecting on the past nor planning for the future. Still, at its heart, jealousy is an emotion first experienced in the here and now; it does not require the cat to understand what its rival is thinking, or even that it is capable of thinking at all. All that jealousy requires is that the cat merely perceive that another cat is getting more of something than it should. Thus, cats are almost certainly capable of feeling jealous, even if not quite as demonstratively, or as commonly, as dogs. Although not something that my cats have ever indulged in, countless owners have regaled me with stories of how one of their cats would always intervene when they tried to stroke the other.

Many people think that cats are capable of grief, because they behave oddly when another cat that they have known disappears. What they actually feel is probably a temporary anxiety, which disappears once all traces of the missing cat have disappeared. A mother cat may search for her kitten for a day or two after it has been homed. She probably has a memory of that kitten, and may even count the remaining kittens to check that one is missing. This behaviour would be the same if that kitten had temporarily got lost; in the wild, it would be in the mother cat's interest to seek it out and continue to look after it until it was old enough to become independent of her. She cannot 'know' that it has gone to a good home where it will be well cared for, as nothing in her evolution will have prepared her to embrace that concept. For a few days, the mother is reminded of that particular kitten by the lingering traces of its individual odour, the kind of cue that is often meaningless to us. We know that the kitten has gone because we can no longer see or hear it. Once the kitten's odour has faded below her threshold, the mother cat probably forgets all about the departed kitten. While she can still smell it, she may well feel an anxiety that drives her to continue to look for it. This, however, is not the same as grief.

Emotions such as guilt and pride would require cats to possess a further level of cognitive sophistication, the ability to compare their actions with a set of rules or standards that they have worked out for themselves. When we feel guilty, we compare the memory of something we've just done with our sense of what is wrong. Such feelings are sometimes referred to as self-conscious emotions, because they require a degree of self-awareness to be experienced. So far, science has yet to reveal any evidence for self-awareness in cats, or even in dogs. Dogs are widely believed to display a 'guilty look' when their owners discover that they've done something that's forbidden, but a clever experiment has shown that this is all in the owners' imagination.[23] The researcher asked the owners to command their dogs not to touch a tempting food treat, and then leave the room. Then, unbeknown to the owners, she encouraged some of the dogs, but not others, to eat the treat. When the owners came back into the room, they were all told that their dog had stolen the treat – whereon all of the dogs immediately began to look guilty, whether or not they actually had something to feel guilty about. The 'guilty look' was nothing more than each dog's reaction to its owner's body language, which had changed subtly as soon as he or she had been told of the dog's misdeed, whether real or invented. If dogs' 'guilty looks' are a figment of their owners' imaginations, it follows that they – and, by extension, cats – are incapable of feeling guilt. The same is probably true for pride, but no scientist seems to have studied it in any relevant animal.

Cats' emotional lives are more elaborate than their detractors would have us think, but not quite as sophisticated as the most ardent cat-lover would probably like to believe. Unlike dogs, cats hide their emotions – not primarily from us but from one another, a legacy of their evolutionary history as solitary, competitive animals. We have every reason to believe that they possess the basic range of emotions, the gut feelings, shared by all mammals, because having these empowers them to make quick decisions, whether that is to run away (fear), play with a ball of string (joy) or curl up on their owner's lap (love). However, cats are not as socially sophisticated as dogs are: they are undoubtedly intelligent, but much of that intelligence relates to obtaining food and defending territory. Emotions that relate to relationships, such as jealousy, grief and guilt, are probably beyond their reach, as is the ability to comprehend social relationships with any great sophistication. This leaves them ill-equipped for the demands of living closely with other cats, as domestication has progressively required them to do.

7

Cats Together

Cats can be very affectionate, but they are choosy about the objects of their affection. This apparent fastidiousness stems from the cat's evolutionary past: wildcats, especially males, live much of their lives with no adult company, and regard most other members of their species as rivals rather than as potential colleagues. Domestication has not only inhibited the wildcat's intrinsic distrust of people, but has also tempered some of their wariness of other cats.

The bond between cat and owner must have its origins in the bond between cat and cat; such behaviour has no other plausible evolutionary source. Although the cat's immediate ancestor, the wildcat, is not a social animal, adult felids of other species, such as lions, do cooperate. As such, cats of any species could potentially become more sociable in the right conditions. We may therefore find clues to the source of the domestic cat's affection for its owners through a brief survey of the social life of the entire cat family.

Both male and female tigers are solitary, exemplifying the pattern that almost all members of the cat family, big and small alike, live alone. The females hold non-overlapping territories, which they defend from one another; each territory is large enough to provide food not just for that female, but also for the litters of cubs she rears. Young males are usually nomadic, and when they become mature, they try to set up their own large territories. These will contain far more prey than the male will ever need to satisfy his hunger, but that is not their purpose. The male is trying to achieve exclusive access to as many females as possible: especially successful males may hold territories that overlap those of up to seven females.

Cheetah males, especially brothers, are a bit more sociable than tiger males. Female cheetahs are as solitary as female tigers, but male cheetahs sometimes band together in twos or threes to seduce females, many of which are migratory, as they pass nearby. Even though only one of the brothers will be the father of the resulting litter, biologists have shown that over his lifetime each brother will father more cubs than if he had tried to attract females on his own. Male cheetahs do occasionally try to hunt together as well, but are rarely successful, apparently lacking the skills to coordinate their efforts.

The best-known exception to the standard felid pattern is the lion, the only member of the cat family to have several males and several females living together. In Africa, the lion pride is usually constructed from one family of female lions, with the males originating from a different family (thereby preventing inbreeding). While still young, related males band together, sometimes adding unrelated males to swell their ranks, until their numbers are sufficient to challenge and eject the resident males from a pride. Once they have taken over the pride, they may kill all the cubs, and by doing so bring all the females into season within a few months. The males must then keep control of the pride until the females have given birth to their progeny and raised them to independence. For their part, the females not only have to raise the cubs, but they also do most of the hunting, while the males do little but protect the females from other bands of males. Thus, the superficial image of lion society as generally harmonious is something of a myth; rather, it is the result of tension between the benefits of cooperation and competition, with each individual lion employing tactics that maximize its own breeding success.

Biologists still debate why lions live in such groups. In India, lions are often solitary animals, males and females meeting only for mating, so members of this species can evidently choose whether or not to live together. Although the females in a pride generally hunt together, they do not cooperate as selflessly as their 'brave' image suggests: if the prey is large and potentially dangerous, the more experienced females usually hold back and let the younger, more impetuous lionesses take the risks. The main benefit of numbers, and especially the presence of the fierce males, may come after the kill, when the valuable meat must be defended from other animals, particularly hyenas.

Scientists once considered lions and cheetahs the only social cats, and added the domestic cat to that exclusive list only recently. It had long been clear that wherever there was a regular source of suitable food, a group of feral cats would spring up, but these groups were originally considered mere aggregations of individuals that had some-how agreed to tolerate one another, as happens when animals of many species come together to drink at a waterhole. Cat breeders also knew that their queens would sometimes suckle one another's litters, but scientists dismissed this behaviour as the result of the artificial condi-tions under which humans usually keep pedigree cats. In the late 1970s, however, David Macdonald's documentary about cats on a farm in Devon showed that this was in fact natural behaviour – that free-living females, especially related females, will spontaneously cooperate to raise their kittens together.[1]

At the start of the study, the colony consisted of just four cats: a female, Smudge; her daughters, Pickle and Domino; and their father, Tom. When not in the farmyard, they kept to themselves – domestic cats, unlike lions, do not hunt together – but when their visits coin-cided, they usually curled up together in apparent contentment. They evidently regarded the farmyard and the food and shelter it provided as 'theirs', since the three females would join together to drive away three other cats that lived nearby – a female, Whitetip, her son Shadow, and her daughter Tab. Tom, though, was aggressive only towards Shadow, presumably regarding him as a potential rival, whereas he might need to court the two females should he lose his own 'pride' at some point in the future.

Pickle and Domino were the first to reveal how female cats come together to help one another. Early in May, Pickle produced three kit-tens in a nest in a straw stack. For the first couple of weeks, she looked after her kittens on her own, just as any other mother cat would. Then, suddenly, her sister Domino appeared in the nest and gave birth to five more kittens – ably assisted by Pickle, who helped with their delivery and with cleaning them up. Then, despite their difference in ages, all eight kittens settled down together and were nursed and cared for indiscriminately by both their mothers. Sadly, all eight kit-tens subsequently succumbed to cat flu, a common scourge of litters born outdoors in the UK. However, when their grandmother Smudge

Domino and Lucky playing

produced a single male kitten a few weeks later, the aptly named Lucky, both Domino and Pickle helped with caring for him, including playing with him and bringing back mice they had caught, to save Smudge leaving him alone while she went out hunting for herself.

Subsequent studies have revealed that such cooperation between related female cats is the rule, not the exception. I observed this in my own home when my cat Libby gave birth to her first litter: Libby's own mother, Lucy, shared their care, grooming them and curling around them to keep them warm. Indeed, when they grew old enough to move around the house, Libby's kittens generally preferred their grandmother's company to their mother's.

Cat society is based on females from the same family. In feral or farm cats, it rarely involves more than two (sisters and their kittens) or three (mother, daughter[s], and kittens) generations. However, we see little indication that the participants are consciously helping one another. Rather, many female cats, especially those with kittens, simply seem not to distinguish between their own offspring and those of other cats with whom they are already friendly; in the wild, these are most likely their own daughters or sisters, cats they have known and trusted all their lives. Some mother cats that have recently given birth will accept almost any kitten they are presented with, and some humane organizations make use of such cats as wet nurses for mother-less litters.

Larger colonies of feral cats usually consist of more than one family, and while these families continue to cooperate among themselves, they also compete with one another. The size of a cat colony is determined by the amount of food available on a regular basis, and where this is plentiful – for example, in a traditional fishing village where the catch is processed *in situ* – colonies can build up until several hundred cats are all living in close proximity to one another. Cats are prolific breeders, and numbers can grow quickly until food becomes scarce, at which point the cats on the edge of the colony will either leave or succumb to disease brought about by malnutrition.

Each family group strives to monopolize the best sites for dens in which kittens can be born, and to stay as close as possible to the best places to find food. However, as the most successful families grow, tensions increase among its members, even when there is enough food. Cats appear to be incapable of sustaining a large number of friendly relationships, even when all their neighbours are close relatives. Squabbles break out, and eventually some members of the family are forced out – and because all the prime space in the colony will already be occupied by other cats, they may have to find a place alongside the new arrivals on the very fringes of the colony, where pickings are slim.

Cat colonies are therefore far from being well-regulated societies: rather, they are spontaneous gatherings of cats that occur around a localized concentration of food. If the food supply is limited, a single family may monopolize it. When food is especially plentiful, several families compete for the best and biggest share, although warfare between the various clans is generally conducted through threats and careful skirting around one another, punctuated only occasionally by overt violence. In such situations, being able to call on family to assist is essential to holding on to prime territory: a female cat on her own, especially if she has kittens to feed, is unlikely to thrive.

The cooperation within families that undoubtedly occurs in larger colonies is based on the same bonds of kinship that form in much smaller colonies consisting of a single family. Cats seem incapable of forming alliances between family groups, unlike, for example, some primates; negotiation skills of this sophistication lie beyond their capabilities.

Biologists are uncertain about the precise origins of these family ties. They could be accidental, caused by female cats' inability to distinguish their own kittens from others. Looking back to their wildcat ancestors, every female holds her own territory, which she defends against all other females, so the chance that two litters could ever be born in the same place is virtually zero. A female cat, wild or domestic, probably follows a simple rule of looking after all the kittens that she finds in the nest she has made: she sees no need to sniff each kitten carefully to check that it is not an interloper before settling down to nurse it. However, this is unlikely to form the sole basis for cooperation among adult cats. The thousands of generations over which domestic cats have evolved away from their wild ancestors provide enough time for more sophisticated social mechanisms to have evolved.

Cats' social behaviour probably started to evolve as soon as humankind's invention of food storage first made concentrated sources of food available. Any cats that maintained their natural antagonism towards all members of their own species could not have exploited this new resource as efficiently as those able to recognize their relations, and both give and receive help from them.

Biologists distinguish two different ways in which cooperative behaviour can be beneficial to both parties. One is reciprocal altruism, continuing to do favours only for those who have done favours for you. This could theoretically take place between any two animals that live near each other, irrespective of whether they were related. However, if they are related, a second reason why it would be a good idea to cooperate is kin selection. Cats that are sisters share half their genes, a much greater proportion than two unrelated female cats would. Their kittens, even if fathered by different tomcats, each share a quarter of their genes with their aunt. Thus, whichever of those kittens goes on to have kittens of its own (it's a sad fact of life that not all of them will), each kitten shares genes with both their mother and their aunt.[2] Since neither sister knows which of their offspring is most likely to survive to maturity, they should, all other things being equal, try to raise both litters. Thus, the genes that favour cooperation between cats that are related can flourish, at the expense of rival genes that promote antagonism, even between sisters.[3]

Reciprocal altruism and kin selection are useful mechanisms preventing selfish behaviour, but cooperative behaviour itself will evolve only if its benefits outweigh its costs. For the first domestic cats, the initial advantage of living in family groups would have been that the abundant food – whether prey infesting food stores, scraps provided by people, or a mix of the two – could be shared without constant strife. However, putting several litters into one nest means that if one kitten gets sick, they all do; this can be fatal, as Domino and Pickle's experience illustrates. When in 1978 South African scientists introduced a virus to exterminate cats that were causing havoc among the ground-nesting seabirds on Marion Island in the Indian Ocean, cats that had retained their wild ancestors' habit of nesting on their own mostly survived, but family groups perished. Elsewhere, this disadvantage may be outweighed by the benefit of having several mothers on hand to protect kittens from predators: a solitary mother must leave her litter from time to time to find food, or her milk will dry up.

Two or more mother cats that pool their kittens can guard them much more effectively than can a lone mother, who has to leave her kittens alone in order to hunt. This benefit must outweigh the increased risk of disease wiping out the whole litter, or the ability to cooperate like this would never have evolved. Domestic cats living among humans have probably always had two main enemies: stray dogs and other cats. Twenty years ago, while on holiday in a Turkish village with my wife and our youngest son, our apartment was visited by a heavily pregnant calico stray we christened Arikan. After disappearing for a couple of days, she returned, much thinner and starving hungry, so we knew that she must have given birth nearby. We found a supermarket that sold cat food (receiving puzzled looks from the cashier, who seemed not to expect tourists to make such a purchase). When we followed Arikan after she ate, she disappeared into some derelict farm buildings farther up the road. After that, we fed her morning and evening, until one night we were awoken by pitiful wailing: Arikan was outside our door, carrying a dead kitten that showed signs of having been mauled. Arikan immediately ran off, and moments later returned with another dead kitten, which she deposited alongside the first on our doorstep.

A dog may conceivably have been the culprit. Small packs of 'latch-key' dogs did roam the village in the evenings, badgering diners at outdoor restaurants for table scraps and chasing cats. If a pack of dogs found a cat's nest, they would probably dismantle it, but possibly not eat the kittens – although on one occasion, I did witness a dog 'playing' with a dead kitten. Under other circumstances, dogs can be effective predators of cats: in Australia, dingoes – originally domestic dogs, gone wild – keep feral cats in check, enabling local small marsupials to thrive.[4] Still, despite a long history and reputation for being the cat's prime nemesis, dogs were probably not to blame for these kittens' deaths.

Because Arikan's loss occurred at night, the culprit was more likely to have been another cat, the dogs having returned to their owners' homes at dusk. Infanticide is a regular occurrence in lions, but only a few instances have been documented in domestic cats.[5] Male lions kill cubs that are not their own because doing so brings the mother lion back into season almost immediately; otherwise, the males must endure a nineteen-month interval between births, and by that time those males might have lost control of the females.

Female cats are often ready to mate as soon as their kittens are weaned, or earlier if they do not survive infancy, so the intruding male cats that have carried out all recorded instances of infanticide probably gained little from their cruel act, at least in terms of increasing their opportunities for mating. Infanticide appears to be most common in small, single-family cat colonies on farms, rather than – perhaps surprisingly – in the large multi-group colonies where aggression is much more generally evident. In those larger colonies, females often mate with more than one male, thereby making it much more difficult for those males to work out which kittens are theirs and which are not. In this way, males should kill only the kittens of females they can be sure they have never met before.

If the mother is present, she defends her kittens with all her might, so males are wise to target unguarded litters. A pooled litter with two or more females in attendance will be better protected against marauding males than litters kept in separate nests, even though they are less well isolated from infections. Perhaps the unfortunate Arikan had no surviving sisters with whom she could have joined forces.

Family life provides opportunities for cats to learn from one another, rather than working everything out for themselves. As we have seen, mother cats instruct their kittens on how to handle prey by bringing it back to them. We have no evidence that she actively *teaches* them: she simply provides them with opportunities to learn what prey is like, but in the safe environment of the nest. Also, although kittens naturally pay great attention to everything their mothers do, it is unlikely that they deliberately imitate her. True imitation involves complex mental processes; the animal must first know what the relevant actions are, and then translate what it has seen into movements of its own muscles. Because we ourselves find it easy to imitate, we tend to assume that other animals can do the same, but research indicates that true imitation – deliberate copying of another animal's actions – may be restricted to primates.

We know of simpler ways that kittens learn from their mothers, without directly imitating her actions. Instead, the mother draws the kittens' attention to an appropriate target, and they then direct their own instinctive behaviour towards it. In a 1967 experiment, scientists demonstrated that mothers teach their kittens best when challenging them to perform an arbitrary task to get food. The experiment consisted of allowing a kitten to explore a box that had a lever sticking out of one wall.[6] The kitten would usually ignore the lever, apart from giving it a sniff, unless it had watched its mother pawing the lever and being rewarded with food, in which case it paid great attention to the lever and quickly learned that pawing it produced a reward. Usually, kittens will spontaneously pat an object that moves, but only rarely pat something that appears inanimate and fixed. As other experiments have shown, that both mother and kitten ended up pawing the lever was probably not due to direct imitation – the lever was designed to work best when pawed – but instead to the kitten's realization that the lever it had seen its mother manipulating looked the same as the one in its own box, and was therefore something it should investigate closely. Kittens invariably use their paws to investigate something novel, so they didn't need to imitate their mother's actions; they simply did what came naturally. In a similar experiment, other kittens were allowed to watch unfamiliar female cats performing the task. These kittens either took a long time to learn to paw the lever or didn't learn it at all, showing that it is specifically the mother that kittens feel comfortable watching. They are probably just too inhibited by the presence of an unfamiliar adult cat to learn anything.

Mother cats can pass some of their hard-won expertise on to their kittens by providing them with novel experiences, but this is equally easy for solitary mothers and those that live socially, in families. Can adult cats benefit from living socially by learning from one another? We know little about this intriguing possibility, but one obscure experiment done more than seventy years ago suggests that they can.[7] Several six-month-old cats were given the opportunity to obtain a bowl of food placed on a turntable out of their reach, as shown in the illustration. A ratchet under the turntable ensured that a single swipe of a paw was not sufficient to bring the food within reach, and it took many sessions before the cats had learned that careful manipulation with one paw was needed to pull the food within reach. However, two cats that had never used the apparatus themselves, but had watched their sisters successfully rotate the turntable and eat the food, both solved the problem in less than a minute. It was probably no coincidence that it was sisters, not unrelated cats, that found it easy to learn from one another. Transmission of skills between family members may be mutually beneficial and give family groups an advantage over solitary cats, which can learn only by trial and error.

Whether young cats ever learn much from cats that are not members of their family is doubtful. Underlying distrust probably focuses their minds exclusively on staying out of trouble, overriding any curi-

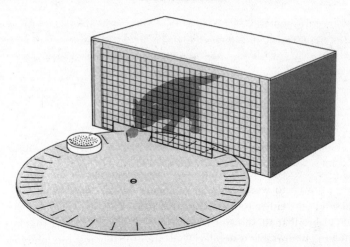

The turntable used to test cats' ability to learn from other cats. The cat can get the food by gradually rotating the table until the bowl passes through the gap.

osity about what another cat is doing. However, within a close-knit family group, younger members may benefit from watching how older, more experienced members of the group solve everyday problems. Because cats hunt alone, this is most likely to occur when the cats are in their shared core territory, perhaps when scavenging for food or interacting with people.

Although we may logically assume that cats began to live in family groups only since they started to associate with humans, wildcats also may have (or may have had) this ability. The formation of a group of cats seems to have only one essential requirement: a reliable source of food that can feed more than one cat and her litter of kittens. The only felid that has consistently achieved this leap is the lion, which has adopted group hunting as a way to prey on large animals. However, other felids might once have lived in small groups even without developing this additional skill.

Before man's domination of the environment in the twentieth century led to the depletion of the small cats and their favourite prey, wildcats might occasionally have lived in colonies. Several accounts left by early twentieth-century European explorers of Africa give tantalizing glimpses of this possibility. Willoughby Prescott Lowe, one of the last noted collectors of animals for the British Museum of Natural History, describes a specimen he took from near Darfur in the Sudan in 1921:

> I trapped an interesting cat near Fasher. Something like a domestic cat – but v. different in coloration. The curious thing is that they live in colonies in holes in the open plain – all the holes are close together – just like a rabbit warren. I'm told they are v. local – Anyhow a cat with these habits was quite new to me! They feed on gerbils which swarm everywhere and the ground is always a mass of holes.[8]

Ten years later, on an expedition in the Ahaggar Mountains in the centre of the Sahara desert, Lowe again recorded colonies of wildcats, living in burrows previously dug by fennec foxes.

Both these cats looked like typical African wildcats, but their sociability need not have come from their wildcat ancestry. The DNA of apparent wildcats from farther south in Africa, and also from the Middle East, reveals extensive interbreeding between domestic cats and wildcats. What Lowe saw may have been colonies of hybrids, which had retained the domestic cat's ability to live in family groups while outwardly appearing to be wildcats. That social groups of these *Felis lybica* have been recorded so infrequently suggests that when they do occur, their social skills may have originated in previous interbreeding with domestic cats.

The switch from solitary animal to social living requires a huge leap in communication skills. For an animal as well-armoured and suspicious as a cat, a simple tiff between sisters might well escalate into a family bust-up – unless, that is, a system of signalling evolved that allowed each cat to assess the others' moods and intentions. And this, it seems, is precisely what happened.

For domestic cats, my own research has shown that the key signal is the familiar straight-up tail. In cat colonies, when two cats are working out whether to approach each other, one usually raises its tail vertically; if the other is happy to reciprocate, it usually raises its tail also, and the two will walk up to each other.[9] If the second cat does not raise its tail and the first is feeling especially bold, it may approach nevertheless, but obliquely. If the second cat then turns away, the first cat occasionally meows to attract its attention – among the very few occasions when feral cats meow. Otherwise, the first cat lowers its tail and heads off in another direction, presumably judging that the other is not in the mood to be friendly. Hesitation can be risky. My research team documented instances when a cat moving in the wrong direction, even with its tail upright, was chased off by another, usually larger, cat determined to be left alone.

Observations such as these do not prove conclusively that the upright tail is a signal; it could conceivably be something that happens when two friendly cats meet, with no meaning for either. To isolate the raised tail from everything else that a real cat might do to indicate its intentions, we cut life-size silhouettes of cats from black paper and stuck them to the skirting boards of cat owners' houses. When the resident cat saw an upright-tail silhouette, it usually approached and sniffed it; when the silhouette had a horizontal tail, the cat backed away.[10]

The tail-up signal has almost certainly evolved since domestication, arising from a posture kittens use when greeting their mothers. Adults of other cat species raise their tails only when they are about to spray urine, simply for hygiene. A few individuals of *Felis lybica* in zoos do raise their tails when about to rub on their keepers' legs, but these, of course, could have some domestic cat in their ancestry. Adults of the other races of *Felis silvestris* do not raise their tails in greeting, but their kittens do hold their tails upright when approaching their mother; no one has tested whether this holds any significance for the mother, so we do not know whether kittens do this as a signal or whether it's purely incidental. Therefore, it seems most plausible that the upright tail evolved from a posture into a signal during the early stages of domestication. This would have required two changes in how cats organize their behaviour: one, for adult cats to perform the kitten's raised-tail posture when approaching other cats,[11] and two, for other cats to recognize instinctively that a cat with its tail raised is not a threat. Once both these changes had occurred, the posture would have evolved into a signal, one that enabled adult cats to live in close proximity to each other with less risk of quarrelling.[12]

Once an exchange of tail-ups has established that both cats are happy to approach each other, one of two things occurs; which of the two seems to be influenced by both the cats' moods and the relationship they have with each other. If the cats are in the middle of doing something else, and/or one cat is significantly older or larger than the other, they usually walk up to or alongside each other. Then, keeping their tails upright, they come into physical contact and rub their heads, flanks or tails – or a combination of all of them – on each other, before separating and walking on. Any two cats from the same group will perform this occasionally, but it is typically performed by female cats greeting males, and young cats of either sex greeting females.

The precise significance of this rubbing ritual is still unclear. The physical contact in itself may reinforce the friendship between the two participants, and thereby keep the group together – a ritual that counteracts the natural tendency of cats to regard others as rivals, not allies. The act of rubbing together also inevitably transfers scent from one cat to the other, so repeated rubbing could cause a 'family odour' to build up. We know that some of the cat's carnivore relatives exchange scent via rubbing rituals: for example, badgers from the same sett create a 'clan odour' by rubbing their back ends together, exchanging scent between their subcaudal glands, wax-filled pockets of skin that lie just beneath their tails.[13] Cats may not deliberately exchange odour when they rub on one another; if they were doing so, they would probably concentrate their rubs on scent-producing areas of their bodies, such as the glands at the corners of their mouths, which they use to scent-mark prominent objects in their territories – but they generally don't. As such, the rubbing ritual may be mainly tactile, a reaffirmation of trust between two animals, which by accumulation reduces the likelihood of the group splintering apart.

The other social exchange that can follow the tail-up signal is mutual licking, or allogrooming. Cats spend much time licking their coats, so it is hardly surprising that when two cats lie down side by side, they often lick each other. Moreover, they tend to groom the top of the other cat's head and between the shoulders. These are areas that the supplest of cats finds hardest to groom for itself – not impossible, of course, since cats with no grooming buddy use their wrists to wipe those areas, and then in turn lick their wrists – and all cats use this method to clean their mouths after eating.

One interpretation of allogrooming holds that it is entirely acciden-tal: two cats sitting together groom those areas that smell the least clean, oblivious that those areas belong to another cat. However, we know that allogrooming has a profound social significance in many other animals, especially in primates, in which it has been linked with pair-bonding, the building of coalitions, and in reconciliations between family members who have recently quarrelled. In cats, allogrooming most probably performs the same function as mutual rubbing: cement-ing an amicable relationship. Consistent with this is the observation that in large groups of cats consisting of more than one family, most allogrooming takes place between relatives.[14]

Some evidence shows that allogrooming does reduce conflict. In arti-ficial colonies, such as those established by cat rescue organizations,

Libby grooming Lucy

aggression is often much less prevalent than might be expected from tensions caused by forcing unrelated animals to live together; significantly, however, allogrooming is common. Moreover, the most aggressive cats often do most of the allogrooming, implying that licking another cat may be an 'apology' for a recent loss of temper. Alternatively, a cat that allows itself to be groomed does so because it remembers that it was recently attacked by the same cat, and being groomed is much more pleasant than being bitten. This latter interpretation conceives allogrooming as an alternative to aggression, so placing it in a 'dominance' framework, whereby one animal controls another's activities.

Some scientists have proposed that cat societies are indeed structured according to dominance hierarchies, with larger, stronger, more experienced and more aggressive cats imposing themselves on those that are smaller, younger, or more timid. The dominance concept has long been applied to domestic dogs and their ancestor the grey wolf, but has recently been the source of much controversy. Most biologists now agree that while groups of dogs (and wolves) may sometimes appear to establish and maintain hierarchies using aggression and threat, they do so only under extreme circumstances, when their natural tendencies to form amicable relationships have been thwarted.[15]

As with dogs, the apparent formation of a dominance hierarchy in cats may be a result of external pressures. Social tensions arise when unrelated cats live together, either in one of the large outdoor colonies that form around large concentrations of food, such as fishing villages, or in a household with many unrelated cats obtained at different times from multiple sources. No hierarchies are apparent in small, one-family colonies, or indeed within family groups that form part of a larger colony.

Cat society is not as highly evolved as canid society. Domestic cat society is matriarchal: each unit begins with one female and her offspring, and if enough food is available on a regular basis, her daughters will stay with her; and when they produce litters of their own, care of the kittens will be shared between them. This situation is more equitable – and less highly evolved – than in wolf society, where juveniles assist their parents in raising the next generation of cubs but refrain from breeding themselves that year.[16] Moreover – and in contrast to the situation in the wolf pack, which typically consists of roughly equal numbers of males and females, male cats do not help with raising kittens. In some colonies, female cats have been observed as super-affectionate towards the resident male – presumably the father of their most recent litters – possibly regarding him as a first line of defence against infanticide by other males. A typical small cat colony might thus consist of a mother, her grown-up daughters, their most recent litters of kittens, and one or two tomcats.

Family groups cannot expand ad infinitum, of course, because they would inevitably outstrip their food supply. Young males start to leave their colonies at about six months of age, sometimes maintaining a shadowy existence around the fringes for a year or two, but eventually forging out on their own to look for females elsewhere – thereby incidentally preventing inbreeding. Among females, relationships become increasingly strained as they must compete for space and food. Any major event, perhaps the death of the matriarch, can trigger a breakdown in the relationships between some of the cats; aggression increases and the once-peaceful colony may irrevocably split into two or more groups. The members of the minority group may be forced to leave the area entirely, something that will have serious consequences for them; thereafter, deprived of the resources around which the original colony formed, they are unlikely to raise many offspring to maturity. In this way, over the years the central family group will usually persist, but the more successful it becomes, the more likely that some of its female members will become outcasts. The composition of the central group is also likely to be disrupted, both by other cats trying to get access to the food and shelter the original group are monopolizing, and also by humans, who often attempt to cull the cats as their numbers rise. As a result, cat society rarely remains stable for more than a few years at a stretch.

The benefits of cooperation, while not powerful enough to produce sophisticated social behaviour, have evidently been sufficient for a limited range of social communication to have evolved: the tail-up posture, mutual rubbing and allogrooming. In the absence of evidence to the contrary, we can reasonably assume that this change did not start until cats began their association with humankind, some 10,000 years ago. If so, it has happened remarkably quickly, but not impossibly so. Although we usually conceive of evolution by natural selection operating over time scales of hundreds of thousands or even millions of years, examples of exceptionally rapid change or 'explosive speciation' have recently been documented in wild animals that have stumbled on new and hitherto unexploited environments, such that completely new species can emerge in just a few hundred generations.[17] Furthermore, if the tail-up signal has evolved from a posture performed by kittens into a sign whose meaning is recognized by every adult cat, then it is the only documented example of a new signal having evolved as a consequence of domestication; every other documented domestic species communicates using a subset of signals performed by its wild ancestor.

Male domestic cats, in contrast to females, appear largely untouched by domestication, apart from their capacity to become socialized to people when they are kittens. Each one precisely resembles Rudyard Kipling's 'cat that walked by himself'.[18] Unlike lions and cheetahs, male domestic cats do not form alliances with one another, remaining resolutely competitive for the whole of their lives – which, as a result, are often both eventful and rather short. Female cats (and neutered males) try to avoid one another when they can, but when two males meet, and neither wishes to back down, their fighting can be brutal (see box, 'Bluff and Bluster').

Because most owners have their cats neutered, mature tomcats are something of a rarity in Western society. Few people keep them as pets, and many of those who try are subsequently discouraged by the pungency of the urine tomcats spray around the garden (or, worse, the house); by the wounds they receive from stronger, more experienced tomcats in the neighbourhood; and by their weeklong absences as they journey off in search of receptive females. Most owners of male cats never get to this point, taking the advice of their veterinary surgeon to have their kitten neutered before testosterone starts to kick in at about six months of age. Male cats that have been neutered during their first year behave much more like females than males, and are usually as sociable towards other cats as a female would be under the same circumstances; that is, most will remain friendly towards other cats that they have known since birth (usually, but not necessarily, their blood relations), and a few will be even more outgoing.

Tomcat spraying

BLUFF AND BLUSTER

When two rival cats meet, each will try to persuade the other to back down without either having to resort to physical contact. Cats are too well armed to risk fighting unless this is unavoidable; they therefore resort to adopting postures that attempt to persuade their opponent that they are bigger than they really are.

Each cat will draw itself up to its full height, turn partially sideways, and make its hair stand on end, all designed to make its profile seem as big as possible. Of course, since both cats do this, neither gains any advantage, but that also means that neither can risk not performing this display to its maximum extent. The only clue that such a cat may be less than confident about winning is when it pulls its ears towards the back of its head: the ears are very vulnerable to being damaged in a fight, as testified by how ragged they can become even when they belong to the most successful of toms.

At the same time, each cat tries to add to the general effect by uttering a variety of calls, each designed to enhance the general impression that it is not to be trifled with. These include guttural yowls and snarls, violent spitting, and especially low-pitched growls – the lower the sound, the larger the voice box must be, and therefore, by implication, the larger the cat. These vocalizations usually continue even if the visual posturing fails and actual fighting begins.

Cats, lacking the dog's rich repertoire of visual signals, find it difficult to signal an intention to back down. Fights usually end with one cat fleeing, with the victor in hot pursuit. If neither cat wishes to fight, one will gradually adopt a much less threatening posture, with its body crouched and its ears flattened, and then attempt to creep slowly away, frequently looking over its shoulder to check that the other cat is not about to launch an attack.

Tomcat behaviour gives us insight on how the cat may be evolving today. A tomcat's main goal is to compete for the attention of as many females as possible. As a consequence, wildcat toms evolved to be 15 to 40 per cent heavier than females. This is also true of domestic cats today; tomcats' physicality appears to have been affected little by domestication.

By definition, half the genes in each new generation of kittens come from their fathers. Because successful tomcats can mate with many females over the course of a lifetime, those tomcats that leave the most offspring have a disproportionate effect on the next generation. Most owners of unneutered female cats allow them to mate with any tomcat in the neighbourhood, so the decision over which tomcats leave the most offspring is usually determined by the cats themselves, and not by people.

The tactics tomcats employ to maximize their chances of successfully mating are affected by how many females live nearby. Where females are widely dispersed, as with wildcats and rural domestic cats, males try to defend large territories that overlap with those of as many females as possible, typically three or four. Even allowing that tomcats are larger than females, the amount of available food in such large territories is far more than they need, but their primary goal is access to females, not nourishment. Inevitably, there are not enough females for all males to monopolize more than one female – male and female cats are born in roughly equal numbers – so some tomcats, usually the younger ones, must adopt a different strategy, that of roaming around, trying to find unclaimed females while avoiding bumping into those that are established territory-holders.

This overtly competitive system inevitably breaks down when large colonies of cats form around an abundant source of food. Although tomcats' tactics seem to have evolved prior to domestication, when all females were solitary and lived in separate territories, there appears to have been no great need for males to change their behaviour when females began to live in small family groups, attracted by the fairly modest concentrations of food stemming from human activity. This arrangement continues to this day, for example on farms that can support just a handful of cats.

In places where scores of females are concentrated into one area – fishing ports, towns with many outdoor restaurants, or where several feral cat-feeders operate together – no single male, however strong and fierce, could succeed in monopolizing several females, or even one. In these situations, there is a buildup of large colonies that include both males and females, some of which act on their own, and others cooperating in family groups. Each male is essentially in competition with all the others for the attention of the females, but, as we have seen, they somehow manage mostly to avoid the overt fighting that occurs around smaller colonies. Moreover, males in these large groups are often even less aggressive when some of the females become receptive to mating, almost as if they knew they needed to be on their best behaviour for a female to accept them as a mate.

Most of the time, female cats avoid contact with males, particularly those they don't know well, presumably for fear of being attacked. There are some exceptions. In the small, single-family colony that David Macdonald studied, all the females behaved affectionately towards the resident tomcat, possibly hoping that he would defend their kittens against any marauding males attempting to take over the group. Of course, this antipathy changes as the female begins to come into season. When she is in the pro-estrus phase, the few days prior to actual mating, she becomes both more attractive to males and more tolerant of them, although at this stage she will not allow more than fleeting contact. She becomes more restless than usual, and repeatedly deposits scent by rubbing against prominent objects in her territory. If there are no males in the vicinity, she begins to roam away from her usual haunts, scent-marking and uttering a characteristic guttural cry as she goes. She probably also advertises her imminent willingness to mate by changes in her scent, which may be detected by males as far away as several miles downwind. Then, as estrus approaches, she begins to roll over and over on the ground, purring all the while, interspersed with bouts of stretching, kneading the ground with her claws, and more restless scent-marking. By this time, several males are usually in attendance. While she now lets them approach, she does not allow them to mount her, fighting off any that try with her claws and teeth.

As each male attempts to maximize the numbers of kittens they sire, each female tries to maximize the genetic quality of the limited number of kittens she can produce in a lifetime; she uses her courtship period to select between the males that she has attracted. She may already know something about them from the scent marks they have deposited in her territory (see box, 'That Catty Smell'), but she can make a more balanced assessment from observing their behaviour towards one another and towards other females. She may then decide – or be forced – to accept more than one for mating.

THAT CATTY SMELL

Female cats can be very choosy when it comes to selecting a father for their kittens, so tomcats need to advertise just how successful they are, preferably before they ever actually meet the female. They probably do this through the pungent smell of their urine – repellent to our noses, but presenting vital information to a cat's. To make sure that this smell is picked up by as many other cats as possible, the tom doesn't squat down before urinating, as other cats do, but instead backs towards a prominent object such as a gatepost, raises his tail, stands on the tips of his hind toes, and sprays his urine on to the object as high up as he can.

The powerful odour of a tomcat's urine, much stronger than that of a female's or a neutered male's, is caused by a mixture of sulphur-containing molecules called thiols, similar to those that give garlic its characteristic smell.[19] These do not appear in the urine until it has actually been voided and come into contact with the air – otherwise the tomcat himself would smell as if he ate garlic every day. In the bladder, they are stored in an odourless form, as an amino acid that was first discovered in cats and hence was given the name felinine. Felinine in turn is generated in the bladder by a protein called cauxin.

Felinine

In tomcat urine, the signal is probably not the protein (cauxin) but the felinine, which is made from one of two amino acids, cysteine and methionine, both of which contain the sulphur atom necessary for the eventual generation of the pungent odour. Cats cannot make either of these amino acids for themselves, meaning that the amount of felinine they can make is determined by the amount of high-quality protein in their diets. In a wild cat, this is in turn determined by how successful a hunter that cat is. Thus, the smellier the urine mark is, the more felinine it contains, indicating that the cat which made the mark must be good at obtaining food.

The urine mark must also contain information about the identity of the cat that produced it; otherwise, a female could not know which of the several males in front of her was the best hunter. So far, scientists have not investigated this part of the message, but it is presumably something other than the pungent sulphur compounds. Other species use the vomeronasal organ to detect individual odour 'signatures'.

However repellent to us, the cat-urine odour is a genuine badge of quality. A sickly or incompetent male is simply unable to get enough food to make its urine pungent. The evolution of this signal was therefore probably driven by the females, which selected males based on how smelly their urine was: males unable to make felinine, however good their diet, would not have been favoured by females. Using these criteria, tomcats whose owners feed them high-quality commercial food are technically cheats, but this has happened too recently to have had any effect on female behaviour – and, anyway, I guess nobody has told them yet.

As her hormones take her into full estrus, the female's behaviour changes abruptly. In between bouts of rolling, she crouches with her head close to the ground, treading with hind legs partially extended, and holding her tail to one side, inviting the males to copulate. The boldest of those in attendance then mounts her, grasping the scruff of her neck in his teeth. A few seconds later, in apparent contradiction to her invitation, she screams in pain, turns on him, and drives him away, spitting and scratching. This abrupt change of mood is brought about by the pain she undoubtedly experiences during copulation: the male cat's penis is equipped with 120 to 150 sharp spines, designed to trigger her ovulation (cats, unlike humans, do not ovulate spontaneously, but require this stimulus). Happily, she appears to forget this discomfort quickly; within a few minutes, she displays herself to the males all over again – a cycle that continues at a gradually decreasing rate for a day or two. Her receptive period over, she removes herself from the area and the males disperse. If she has not become pregnant, she comes into season again every couple of weeks, until she successfully conceives.

Much of this complex ritual evolved long before domestication, when every female cat lived in her own territory, perhaps several miles away from the nearest male. Scientists think that the female's delayed ovulation evolved to give her plenty of time to locate a mate, since wildcats, unlike many carnivores, do not usually form pair bonds. This drawn-out courtship would be unnecessary if only one male was attracted at a time. Instead, it seems designed for the female first to attract several males, presuming that there are a good few ones in the area, and then to observe them for many hours or even days, so she can gauge which is likely to provide the best genes for her kittens – which is all she can hope to get from their father, since paternal care is unknown in cats.

The optimum strategy for males probably changed once man began to provide cats with food, at the beginning of the journey to domestication. Female territories became smaller and reliably focused on prime hunting locations around granaries, rich areas for scavenging, and any places where people deliberately provided food. It then became efficient for males to compete all year for territories that encompassed those of several females, and to monopolize those females when they came into season. Males that adopted the 'old-fashioned' tactic of roaming widely, expecting to pick up the scent of receptive females by chance, were likely to be less successful. The few studies that have investigated male mating patterns show that the most successful males are often those that combine these tactics, staying 'at home' when their own females were most likely coming into season, but also making brief forays to other groups and solitary females nearby in the hope of achieving successful mating there also.[20] Such a no-holds-barred lifestyle takes its toll, however: males are rarely strong or experienced enough to compete effectively until they are three years old, and many do not survive beyond six or seven, the victims of road traffic accidents or infections spreading from wounds incurred in fights.

When many cats of both sexes all live in one small area, tomcats are forced to change their tactics. Monopolizing even one female risks becoming unprofitable, since while his back is turned to deal with one challenger, another may have sneaked in and successfully mated with 'his' female. Under these circumstances, the toms appear to accept that each female will inevitably copulate with several males; instead of attempting to attach themselves to any one or two individuals, they try to mate with as many females as possible.

This strategy probably did not evolve specifically to allow cats to live at such very high densities. Indeed, such high-density cat colonies probably occur rarely in nature, although they attract a disproportionate amount of attention from scientists where they do, given how convenient they are to study. Instead, males that grow up in such large groups probably learn which tactics work best – or, perhaps more likely, which tactics should be avoided because they risk injury – from a combination of personal experience and observation of how older males in the colony conduct themselves. They may also use this knowledge as the older males become too infirm to compete: in the few large colonies that have been studied, young males rarely emigrate, the opposite of the situation in smaller colonies. This situation may result in some inbreeding, given the enhanced risk that a male who remains in his family group will mate with a close female relative. Still, immigration by males and females from outside, attracted by abundant resources – usually a 'cluster' of dedicated cat-feeders – prevents such potential inbreeding from becoming debilitating.

For some time, scientists have known that the coat colours of the kittens in some litters can be accounted for only if some had one father, and some another. If a female attracts several males, she will sometimes refuse all but one; often, however, she will choose to mate with two or even more. Multiple paternity within a single litter is therefore always a possibility, but we cannot reliably detect it by coat colour alone, especially in large colonies where the males may all look similar. DNA testing has enabled much more reliable examination of how females' opportunities for choices at mating translate into actual choices of fathers for their kittens.

In small colonies with one resident male, females do not appear to have exerted much choice at the time of mating: only about one litter in five exhibits DNA from any other male. The females may, however, have settled on their choice of male long beforehand, when they allowed him to live alongside them. Alternatively, he may simply have imposed himself on them, giving them little option but to wait for another, larger male to turn up if they had doubts about the quality of his genes. At present, we have little scientific evidence either way.

In larger colonies, females not only mate with several males in sequence, but the large majority of their litters also contain the DNA of more than one of these. The females may be exerting some choice – they sometimes show a preference for males from outside their group, thus preventing inbreeding, and also those males from their own group which are able to defend the largest territories.

The female's practice of offering herself to several males one after the other may have another purpose: protecting her future offspring from infanticide. Each male has observed her being mated by others, but cannot know which of her kittens are his and which not. Likewise, since each of the larger males has mated with several females, none has any incentive to kill any litters.

Most urban males today are faced with a new and different problem: how to locate females that are capable of breeding. Nowadays, an increasing proportion of pet cats are neutered before they are old enough to reproduce. Animal welfare charities not only promote the spaying of all females before they have even one litter, they also attempt to seek out and neuter the feral colonies that remain.[21] The urban tomcat is unlikely to locate, let alone defend, a harem of reproductive females. In built-up environments, most tomcats probably adopt the same roaming lifestyle as their wild forebears, hoping to stumble on a young female whose owners have delayed spaying either because they want her to have a litter or simply because they are unaware that today's reliable nutrition enables females to mature more quickly than ever before and that they can come into season when they are as young as six months old.

Judging by my admittedly casual observations, tomcats seem unable to distinguish between neutered females that form the large majority in many towns and cities, and the few, mostly young, females that are still reproductively intact. Roaming toms still visited annually in late winter to check out my two females, even ten years after they had been neutered (having produced one and three litters respectively). Spayed females may be difficult to distinguish from intact females between seasons, certainly not by the way they behave and possibly not even by their odour, to which tomcats are presumably very sensitive.

Urban toms thus face a needle-in-a-haystack problem: they are surrounded by hundreds of females, only an otherwise indistinguishable few of which will ever present them with the opportunity to sire any kittens. The tomcats must therefore roam as widely as possible, endlessly straining their senses for the yowl and odour of the rare female that is coming into season. Such toms are shadowy animals; some are theoretically 'owned' – though their owners rarely see them – and many feral. Because they make themselves inconspicuous except when they have located a prize female, there are probably far more of them than most people realize. When it first became possible to obtain a cat's DNA fingerprint from just a few hairs, my research team attempted to locate every litter born in homes in a couple of districts of Southampton. From what we'd read, we expected to find that just a few 'dominant' tomcats had sired most of the litters in each district; instead, we found that out of more than seventy kittens, virtually all litters had different fathers, only one of which we were able to locate. We found no evidence for littermates having different fathers, which implied that most estrous females had attracted only one male. Apparently, by inadvertently 'hiding' the few reproductive queens that remain in a sea of spayed females, the widespread adoption of neutering is making it difficult for even the fiercest, strongest tomcat to do much more than search at random, thereby giving all the males in the area an even chance of reproducing.

Cats of both sexes have shown remarkable flexibility in adapting their sexual behaviour to the various scenarios that we humans have, over the course of time, imposed on them. One reason that they have coped so well is simply that female domestic cats are very fecund, capable of producing as many as a dozen kittens per year. Even when conditions for reproduction are difficult, most free-living female cats will leave at least two or three descendants, enough to maintain the population even if many of her litters do not survive to adulthood.

Cat society has even adapted to life at high densities, despite origins in territorial rivalry. Logically, that heritage should result in mayhem, totally unsuitable for raising defenceless infants. Females seem to have resolved this problem by accepting the advances of several males each time they come into season, thereby making each male uncertain which kittens are his, and so banishing all thoughts of infanticide. When cat colonies are smaller, females choose to live in small family groups, and may bond with only one male, whom they accept as being both the most suitable father for their kittens and the most effective at driving away marauding rivals. When they are deprived of the company of their female relatives, either because food is insufficient for more than one cat, or due to human intervention, females are equally capable of bringing up litters without any assistance whatsoever. This remarkable flexibility must have contributed to the cat adapting to such a wide range of niches.

Male cats have also adapted remarkably well, though in a different way to females. Since in theory one male cat can sire many hundreds of kittens, the number of males in any one area is never likely to be the factor that limits the size of the cat population. Nevertheless, each individual male has no interest in the survival of his species, only in producing as many offspring of his own as he can. When breeding females are few and far between, a male must search as widely as possible for mating opportunities, pausing only to grab enough food to keep him on the move. If he can be the first and ideally only male to reach a female at the crucial moment, she is unlikely to be choosy about his quality. If he happens to be in an area where there are several females, and some of these live in groups, it may benefit him to form a pair bond or harem – although this seems not to inhibit him from searching for additional females elsewhere, when he judges that he can get away with it. He will also keep an eye out for other groups of females that he might try to take over in the future, and it is most likely males that are in this frame of mind which commit the occasional act of infanticide. However, if he finds himself living in a vast colony with many potential rivals as well as many potential mates, he will learn to curb his natural aggression, this being the only sensible strategy that will allow him to father some kittens without sustaining mortal injury.

These tales of sex and violence seem far removed from the cosy world of cat and devoted owner, but these are of course the ways in which the next generation of cats is created. Only about 15 per cent of cats in the Western world come from planned matings, the great majority arising from liaisons initiated by the cats themselves. Since most pets are now neutered before they become sexually mature, most cat owners are only dimly aware of the shenanigans that undoctored cats get up to; spayed females behave as if permanently stuck between cycles of reproductive activity, and males that are neutered young never develop characteristic tomcat behaviour, instead behaving more like neutered females. Tolerance of other cats is improved by neutering, but only up to a point, and family bonds established between brothers and sisters, or mothers and their offspring, are still apparent if the cats continue to live in the same house. Unrelated cats that are brought together by their owners to live in the same household, or that meet on the boundaries between adjacent gardens, often still display the natural antipathy that they have inherited from their wild ancestors. However, unlike those ancestors, today's domestic cats can also establish close bonds with humans, bringing a new dimension to their social networks.

8

Cats and Their People

The relationship between cat and owner is fundamentally affectionate, surpassed in its richness and complexity only by the bond between
dog and master. Cynics often suggest that cats trick people into providing food and shelter through false displays of affection, and that
cat owners merely project their own emotions on to their cats, imagining that the love they feel for their pet is reciprocated.

We cannot dismiss these claims lightly, but surely we feel such affection
for cats with good reason. Ferrets, which can be just as effective at pest
control as cats, have never found a place in the hearts of the majority –
although they do, of course, have their fans. Our emotional bond with
cats does not stem from gratitude for mere utility; in fact, many of
today's cat owners find themselves disgusted by their cat's hunting
prowess, while continuing to love them as pets. So it is indeed possible
that we humans are somewhat credulous, drawn in by some quality
cats possess that encourages us to anthropomorphize their behaviour.

The most obvious reason we might think of cats as little people is the
humanlike qualities of their facial features. Their eyes face forward, like
ours and unlike those of most animals – including ferrets – which point
more or less sideways. Their heads are round and their foreheads are
large, reminding us of a human baby's face. Infants' faces are powerful
releasers of caring behaviour in humans, especially in women of childbearing age. The effects of cats on humans can be remarkable: for
example, scientists have found that simply viewing pictures of 'cute'
puppies and kittens temporarily enhances people's fine-motor dexterity,
as if preparing them to care for a fragile infant.[1]

Our preference for baby-faced animals is exemplified by the 'evolution' of the teddy bear. Originally naturalistic depictions of brown

bears, teddy bears changed over the course of the twentieth century, gradually becoming more and more infantile: their bodies shrank, their heads – especially their foreheads – grew, and their pointed snouts were transmogrified into the button nose of a baby.[2] The 'selection pressure' that caused these changes did not come from the children that played with the bears – children of four and under are equally happy with a naturalistic bear – but instead the adults, mostly women, who bought them. Cats' faces did not have to evolve to appeal to us; they have always had the right combination of features to appeal to people. That's not to say they have achieved their maximum 'cuteness': freed from the constraints of biological practicality, cat images have continued to evolve, reaching their apotheosis in the Japanese cartoon figure 'Hello Kitty', whose head is bigger than her body, and whose forehead is larger than the rest of her head.

Cats have a built-in visual appeal that we find attractive, but while this may persuade us that it might be pleasurable to interact with them, it cannot possibly be sufficient to sustain an affectionate relationship. Indeed, pandas look very appealing – for much the same reasons – and their image has helped raise millions of pounds for the World Wildlife Fund, which adopted the panda as its logo more than fifty years ago. The WWF acknowledges the key role that the panda's apparent cuteness has played in its success, with fund-raising campaigns such as 'The Panda Made Me Do It'.[3] Yet no one who has encountered a panda would assert that it would make a great pet. They simply don't like people – or each other, much. Thus superficial cuteness, while important, cannot be the only quality that endears cats to us.

Cats' success as pets is not just because of their looks, but because they are open to building relationships with humankind. As they became domesticated, they evolved an ability to interact with us in a way that we find appealing, and it is this that has enabled them to make the transition from vermin killer to treasured companion. Our need for cats as pest controllers has waned, but despite this they have increased in numbers, with the majority now pets first and foremost.

We feel affection for our cats, but what do they feel for us? Wildcats generally regard people as enemies, so the answer must lie in the way cats have changed during domestication. Cats have not travelled as far down this road as dogs. Dogs have largely worked *with* man, herding, hunting and guarding, and have therefore evolved a unique ability to pay close attention to human gestures and facial expressions. Cats have worked *independently* of man, going about their pest-controlling tasks alone and acting on their own initiative; their primary focus had to be on their surroundings, not on their owners. Historically, they have never needed to form as close an attachment to humans as dogs have. Nevertheless, even at the earliest stages of domestication, cats needed humans to protect and feed them during the times when the vermin they were supposed to eradicate were in short supply. The cats that thrived were those that were able to combine their natural hunting ability with a newfound capacity to reward people with their company.

Cats' attachment to people cannot be merely utilitarian; it must have an emotional basis. Since we now know that cats have the capacity to feel affection for other cats, why should they not feel the same emotion towards their owners? Domestication has enabled cats to extend their amicable social bonds to include not only members of their own (feline) family, but also the members of the human family that takes care of them. Because cat society is nowhere near as sophisticated as canine society, we cannot expect the same degree of devotion from every cat as dogs typically display towards their masters. The lasting loyalty feral cats can show towards members of their own family is the raw material on which evolution has worked, resulting in a new capacity to form affectionate bonds towards humans as well.

Every time I'm tempted to think that the sceptics might be right, and that cats only pretend to love us, I think back to one of my own cats, Splodge. He was a neutered, long-haired moggy-cat, as standoffish as his mother and sisters were outgoing and affectionate. He liked to sit on his own in a corner of the room, never on anyone's lap. If visitors came to the house, he would get up with an air of supreme reluctance, stretch himself, and slowly leave the room. He wasn't afraid of people; he just didn't like being disturbed. Yet Splodge did like a couple of select people. One was a research student of mine who came to the house to play games with him as part of her doctoral studies. After the first few times, he came running as soon as he heard her voice at the door, presumably recalling the fun he'd had on her previous visit.

The other target of Splodge's affections was, thankfully, me. Whenever he noticed I had taken the car to work, he would sit in the front garden all day, even if it was raining, and wait for me to come home. On seeing my car return home, he would come running across the driveway and sit by the car. As soon as I opened the car door, he would push his way in, purring loudly. After a brief but excited tour of the car's interior, he would stand with his hind legs on the passenger seat and his front paws on my leg, and rub his face on mine. It is hard to argue that such a display was not driven by a deeply felt emotion, and by all appearances that emotion must have been affection. This affection was unlikely to have been motivated by a desire for food or reward – my wife usually fed Splodge, yet he never behaved in this way towards her.

The most convincing indicator that cats feel genuinely happy when they're with people was found by accident more than twenty years ago. Scientists were investigating why some wild felids were proving especially difficult to breed in captivity, guessing that many of the females were so stressed by being kept in small enclosures that they were unable to conceive.[4] To develop a method for assessing stress, the scientists relocated two pumas, four Asian leopard cats and one Geoffroy's cat from their familiar enclosure into an unfamiliar one. These are all territorial species, so the loss of their familiar surroundings should have caused them considerable anxiety. The scientists measured how much stress hormone (cortisol) appeared in each cat's urine, and, as they expected, it increased dramatically on the first day after the move, settling gradually over the next ten days or so as the cats adjusted to their new surroundings.

By way of comparison, they also analysed the urine of eight domestic cats that were kept in zoo-type enclosures. Four of these were known to be very affectionate towards people, whereas the other four were somewhat unfriendly. All eight were given a daily veterinary examination, something many cats find mildly stressful, and, as expected, this caused an increase in the amount of cortisol excreted by the four less sociable cats, showing that they had indeed felt stressed. When they were in their usual enclosures, the level of stress hormone in the four affectionate cats' urine was slightly higher than in the other four, suggesting that they specifically did not like being caged; when the additional daily handling by the veterinary staff began, their stress levels went down. Thus, these cats appeared to be mildly upset when left alone, but contact with people – even contact that the average pet cat might object to – had a calming effect. Although it is probably going too far to suggest that these cats were suffering from 'separation anxiety', they seem to have been happiest when they were receiving attention from people.

With no access to a hormone testing lab, owners can judge their cats' emotions only by their actions, and cats do not wear their hearts on their sleeves as dogs do. For most animals besides dogs, we can more logically examine the way they communicate as attempts to manipulate the behaviour of other animals. Apart from animals that spend their entire lives in permanent social groups, evolution selects against total transparency. If every other member of its species is potentially a rival, it is not in an animal's best interest to shout with joy every time it finds something tasty to eat, a safe place to sleep or an ideal mate. Conversely, if an animal is in pain or unwell, it attempts to hide all outward signs of discomfort for fear that this weakness will encourage a rival to drive it away. In solitary animals such as cats, exaggerated displays of emotion are therefore unlikely because evolution would have selected out these behaviours. Individuals that give little away leave more offspring than those whose behaviour betrays their fortune, both good and bad.

Honest indicators of an animal's strength and health, such as a peacock's tail or (in my opinion) a tomcat's pungent urine, usually evolve only when the interests of one set of animals – in both these instances, the females – are distinct from those of another set – the males. For their part, females evolve a way they can discriminate between males that are successful hunters from those that are not, one that the males cannot fake. The male peacock's huge tail is the classic example, requiring its bearer to be supremely healthy; a less-than-perfect tail clearly indicates to peahens that they should look elsewhere for a mate. Likewise, any tomcat that produces urine that stinks of the breakdown products of animal protein must be a good hunter, with no room for faking.

On the other hand, using a signal is a low-cost way of getting something – a means of obtaining something from another animal without a fight. For example, when kittens are tiny, their mother has no choice but to feed them: it is the only way they can survive, and she has already invested two months of her life in them. As they get older, it is in her best interest to persuade them to take solid food, but they often try to continue to take milk from her – and one way they do this is by purring.

Here we have the first indicator that purring, the classic sign of a contented cat, might also mean something else. Purring is a rather quiet vocalization (see box, 'The Rumble: How Cats Purr'), audible only over short distances, which almost certainly evolved as a signal produced by kittens, not between adult cats. In the cat's wild relatives, the only close-quarters interactions that occur, apart from mating, are those between mother and kittens. The kittens begin purring when they start to suckle, and the mother sometimes joins in. And as they start to suckle, the kittens knead their mother's belly to stimulate the flow of milk.

Cats don't purr only when they are in physical contact: some will also purr when they're walking around, trying to get their owner to feed them. This purr takes on a more urgent quality, particularly effective at getting the owner's attention. Some cats continue to purr even when their body language, for example a fluffed-up tail, says they are getting angry with their owner.[5] Not so obvious to the average owner, adult cats purr also when there are no people in the vicinity. Studies performed with remote radio microphones show that cats may purr when they're greeting another cat that they're friendly with, when they're grooming or being groomed by another cat, or simply resting in contact with another cat. Occasionally, cats have also been heard purring when they were in deep distress, perhaps following an injury or even during the moments before death.

Purring therefore seems to convey a general request: 'Please settle down next to me.' In the gentlest possible way, the purring cat is asking someone else, whether cat or human, to do something for it. When they purr, kittens are asking their mother to lie still for long enough to allow them to feed – something they cannot take for granted. As in the wild, where purring evolved, there may come a time when she will

THE RUMBLE: HOW CATS PURR

Purring is an unusual sound for an animal to make; although it appears to come from the region of the voice box, it is (almost) continuous. For this reason, scientists once thought it to have been produced by the cat somehow making its blood rumble through its chest. A close examination of the sound reveals that it changes subtly between the in-breath and the out-breath, and almost stops for a moment in between. To see this in action, read the chart, known as a sonogram, from left to right: the higher the spikes, the louder the noise. The in-breaths are shorter and louder, and the out-breaths are longer.

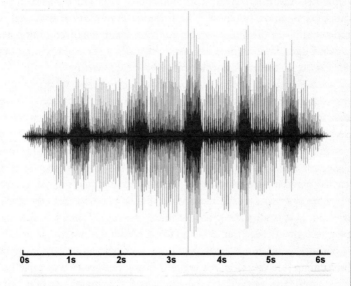

Sonagram of purring: reading from left to right, the in-breaths are shown by the dense 'spikes', with quieter out-breaths in between.

The rumbling sound is produced as the vocal cords are vibrated by a special set of muscles, like a low-pitched hum. The difference between purring and a hum is that the basic sound is not produced by air passing across the vocal cords and making them vibrate, but rather by the vocal cords themselves banging together, like an old-fashioned football rattle. Often the cat will also hum at the same time, but this is possible only on the out-breaths, reinforcing the sound of the purr and giving it a more rhythmic quality.

Some cats can add a further meow-like sound to their purr, making it seem more urgent to the human listener.[26] These cats often use their 'urgent *purr' when soliciting food from their owners, reverting to the normal purr when they are more content. This version of the purr has not yet been recorded from kittens or from ownerless cats, so it may be that, like the meow, this is something individual cats learn as an effective way to get something they want.*

feel too hungry and exhausted to stay with them, and she may have to choose between feeding them and going hunting to feed herself. Although scientists have not studied this systematically, when adult cats purr to one another, they are presumably asking the other cat to remain still. I have heard my cat Libby purring while grooming her mother, Lucy, in an almost aggressive manner, sometimes placing one paw across her mother's neck as if to hold her down.

Purring conveys information to those with an ear for it, but not necessarily the emotional state of the cat. Of course, it may occur when the cat is happy; indeed, this may be the norm. But often a cat – whether a kitten suckling from its mother or a pet enjoying being stroked by its owner – purrs not to show that it is contented, but instead to prolong the circumstances that are making it so. On other occasions, the purring cat may be hungry or mildly anxious because it is unsure how its owner or another cat is going to react; it may even be experiencing fear or pain. Under all these circumstances, the cat instinctively uses the purr to try to change the situation to its advantage.

Mark Twain lightheartedly acknowledged that a purring cat might be conning him when he observed, 'I simply can't resist a cat, particularly a purring one. They are the cleanest, cunningest, and most intelligent things I know . . .'[7] To say that cats are cunning probably overstates their mental abilities: they do not deliberately and consciously deceive their owners and each other through purring. Rather, each cat simply learns that purring under certain circumstances makes its life run more smoothly.

With the purr in mind, we can see that the way our cats behave towards us can be widely misinterpreted. Science has demonstrated that a signal many owners interpret as a sign of love may sometimes mean something else. Insofar as we know, purring is not central to affectionate relationships in cat society, apart from its original role in the bond between a mother cat and her kittens. However, other signals that we tend to overlook may in fact be more genuine displays of affection. Relationships between adult cats seem to be sustained mainly through mutual licking and rubbing, so we should examine whether these also indicate affection when our cats direct such behaviour towards us.

Many cats lick their owners on a regular basis, but scientists have not yet investigated why this should be. Cats that do *not* lick their owners may have been put off because their owners resisted being licked in the past; the cat's tongue is covered with backwards-facing spines that work well at disentangling fur, but can feel harsh on human skin. Conceivably, some cats may lick their owners because they like the taste: some researchers speculate that they lick us for the salt on our skins, but cats don't seem to have a strong preference for salty flavours.[8] The most likely explanation is a social one, that the cat is trying to convey something to its owner about their relationship. The question is what that something is. It may vary from one cat to another, as also seems to be the case when one cat grooms another (allogrooming).

The reason must be basically affectionate, because two cats that don't like each other never groom each other, although grooming can apparently reunite two cats which have recently quarrelled. Cats licking their owners may sometimes be attempting to 'apologize' for something the cat thinks it has done wrong – possibly something the owner has not even noticed, but that has some significance for the cat. However, a cat that licks its owner's hand with one paw placed over her wrist may be attempting to exert some sort of control over her. Until we know more about why cats groom one another, we can only speculate on why they groom us.

Cat owners also engage in a tactile ritual with their cats, of course, when they stroke them. Most owners stroke their cats simply because it gives them pleasure, and because the cat also seems to enjoy it, but stroking may also have symbolic meaning for the cat, possibly substituting for allogrooming in some and possibly for rubbing in others. Most cats prefer to be stroked on their heads rather than any other part of the body, precisely the area towards which cats direct their grooming; studies show that fewer than one in ten cats likes to be stroked on the belly or around the tail.

Many cats do not simply accept their owner's stroking passively; rather, they regularly invite their owners to stroke them, perhaps by jumping on their laps or rolling over in front of them. These rituals may not have any underlying significance, simply being mutually agreed exchanges that particular cats and their owners have learned will lead to pleasurable interactions. But while the owner has to initiate the actual stroking, most cats then indicate precisely where they wish to be stroked by offering that part of the body, or by shifting their position to place it under the owner's stroking hand.[9] By accepting our petting, cats are doing more than enjoying themselves: in their minds, they are almost certainly engaging in a social ritual that is reinforcing the bond with their owner.

Some scientists have speculated further that the cat is also deliberately inviting its owner to take up its scent. Cats may prefer to be stroked around the cheeks and ears because those areas are equipped with skin glands that emit perfumes that appeal to other cats, and the cat wishes the owner to take on the smell of these specific glands.[10] Cats have similar glands on areas of skin that they don't generally like their owners to touch, such as at the base of the tail, so this theory implies that the cat does not want its owner to smell of these other areas. The subtle smell of the cat, virtually undetectable to our noses, will inevitably be transferred on to the owner's hand by the act of stroking, but this exchange may not have much social significance for the cat. If it did, cats would presumably be constantly sniffing our hands; while this does sometimes happen, cats do not do so obsessively. More likely, the primary function of the stroking ritual lies in its tactile component.

While touch is very important to cats, it's a common visual signal, the upright tail, that is probably the clearest way cats show their affection for us. In the same way that an upright tail is a sign of friendly intentions between two cats, so it must be when directed at a person. When cats raise their tails to another cat, they usually wait to see whether the other will reciprocate before approaching, but this is obviously impossible when the recipient is human. Presumably each cat learns enough about their owner's body language to be able to work out, first, whether they've been noticed – they tend not to raise their tails until they have been – and, second, whether the owner is ready to interact. Or at least, most cats do: my long-haired cat Splodge sometimes startled me by approaching while my back was turned, and jumping up to rub his head against the side of my knee.

Since this tail-up signal seems unique to the domestic cat, we do not know whether it evolved first as a signal to be directed at people, and then became useful to maintain amicable relationships with other cats, or vice versa. The latter seems more likely, however: because the raised tail has its origins in kitten–mother interactions, all cats are presumably born with an innate sense of its significance, and adults are therefore able to extend its use for interactions with other cats. The alternative explanation seems more far-fetched, since we would have to assume that the first people to domesticate the cat found this gesture so appealing that they deliberately favoured cats that did it every time they met them.

As when two cats meet, a cat approaching its owner with tail raised will often rub on its owner's legs. The form that the rub takes seems to vary from cat to cat, and despite years of research I am still uncertain whether there is any significance in which part of the body the cat uses to rub. Some rub just with the side of their head, others continue the rub down their flank, and some routinely make contact with head, flank, and tail. Many simply walk past without making any contact at all. A few, like Splodge, jump as they initiate the rub, so that the side of the head makes contact with the owner's knee, and the flank caresses the owner's calf.

Some more nervous cats often prefer to perform their rubs on a physical object nearby, such as a chair leg or the edge of a door. Splodge's great-great niece Libby was a classic example. Even confident cats will sometimes do this when they don't know the person well, even though they are perfectly happy to rub on their owner's leg. Indeed, most times this happens, the cat is probably just redirecting its rub on to an object because it is confident that the object, unlike a familiar person, will not push it away. However, sometimes when this happens it looks as though the cat is also scent-marking the object with the glands on the side of its head. Scent is certainly deposited: when I've invited such cats to rub on posts covered in paper, those pieces of paper excite a great deal of interest when presented to cats in other households. However, the redirected rubbing behaviour is not performed in precisely the same way as when a cat is deliberately scent-marking an object. The difference can easily be seen if the same cat is presented at head height with the blunt end of a pencil, mimicking the protruding twigs that are many cats' favourite targets for 'bunting' with their heads.

Rubbing can only be a sign of affection. Because many cats rub most intensely when they are about to be fed, they have been accused of showing nothing more than what we British call cupboard love. However, few cats confine their rubbing to occasions when they are expecting to receive a tangible reward. When two cats rub on each other, they exchange no food or any other currency; after the rub, each usually continues with what it was doing before. Such an exchange of rubs is a declaration of affection between the two animals – nothing more, nothing less.

Cats also rub on animals other than cats and humans, even animals that do not understand the significance of the ritual and are unlikely to give anything in return. Splodge used to perform the tail-up/rubbing ritual on our Labrador retriever, Bruno. Bruno was already a couple of years old when Splodge arrived in our house as an eight-week-old kitten; although he had not been brought up with cats, he was too laid back to think about chasing them, so Splodge regarded him as a friend from the very start. Of course, Bruno never fed Splodge – quite the opposite: as a typical Lab he was all too eager to finish up any uneaten cat food – so the cupboard love explanation cannot possibly apply. Again, the only plausible significance must be social.

Scent must become transferred from cat to owner during rubbing, but this does not seem to hold any particular significance for the cat. Most owners certainly seem oblivious to this possibility – although apparently not Mark Twain, who once observed, 'That cat will write her autograph all over your leg if you let her.'[11] If the primary motivation for rubbing was to leave scent behind, cats should constantly try to sniff people's legs to discover if any other cat has left its scent there. Of course, our habit of changing our clothes regularly cannot help, but the resulting confusion might lead to more sniffing rather than less. All the evidence points to rubbing, like stroking, as a primarily tactile display.

When two cats rub each other, they don't do so in equal measures, and a similar asymmetry seems to apply when cats rub on humans and other animals. When two cats of a different size approach each other, the smaller cat usually rubs on the larger, which usually doesn't reciprocate. When Splodge rubbed on Bruno, who was substantially larger, Splodge's instincts probably told him not to count on any particular response. Likewise, when our cats rub on us, our greater height, along with their knowledge that we are in control of most of the resources in the house, probably lead them to expect the rub to be one-sided. They are showing their affection for us in a way that doesn't demand a response – which is just as well, because unless we bend down and stroke them, we generally don't reply, at least not at the time.

Cats presumably find rubbing on us rewarding in its own right – if they didn't, they'd probably give up doing it – and like most of their attempts to communicate with us, they learn how to do it gradually. Kittens spontaneously rub on older cats with which they are friendly, and continue to do this as they get older. However, after they arrive in their new homes at around eight weeks of age, young cats (especially females) may take several weeks or even months to start rubbing on their new owners, as if they need time to work out how best to use this behaviour to cement the relationship. Once the habit is formed, however, it seems to become fixed.[12]

Cats are more than intelligent enough to learn how to get our attention when they need to. Many use purring to persuade us to do something they want us to, and a few invent their own personal rituals, such as jumping on to laps, or walking along the mantelpiece dangerously close to valued ornaments. However, the meow comes nearest to being their universal method of attracting our attention.

Purring is too quiet and low-pitched to be of much use for this sort of summons. Cats do also have a greeting call that they use towards one another, a brief, soft 'chirrup' sound; for example, mothers use this when returning to their kittens.[13] Some cats will also use this chirrup to greet their owners: my cat Splodge used to greet me with this sound when he came back from a roam around the garden. Knowing a bit about cat behaviour, I would try to chirrup back at him – something he evidently appreciated, as this exchange became something of a ritual between us.

The meow is part of the cat's natural repertoire, but they rarely use it to communicate with other cats, and its meaning in cat society is somewhat obscure. Feral cats occasionally meow when one is following another, perhaps to get the cat in front to stop and participate in a friendly exchange of rubs. However, feral cats are generally rather silent animals, nowhere near as vocal as their domestic counterparts. While all cats are apparently born knowing how to meow, each has to learn how to use it to communicate most effectively.

The meow is much the same wherever the cat happens to live, confirming that it is instinctive. Every human language has a linguistic representation of this type of call:

> The English cat 'mews', the Indian cat 'myaus', the Chinese cat says 'mio', the Arabian cat 'naoua' and the Egyptian cat 'mau'. To illustrate how difficult it is to interpret the cat's language, her 'mew' is spelled in thirty-one different ways [in English alone], five examples being maeow, me-ow, mieaou, mouw, and murr-raow.[14]

Domestication appears to have subtly modified the sound of the cat's meow. All *Felis silvestris* wildcats can make a meow sound, wherever they live, whether the north of Scotland or South Africa. Meows performed by Southern African wildcats, *Felis silvestris cafra*, are lower-pitched and more drawn-out than typical domestic cat meows. When researchers played recordings of these wildcat meows to cat owners, the owners rated them significantly less pleasant than domestic cat meows.[15] During the course of domestication, humans may have selected for a cat with a meow that is easier on our ears. However, it's equally possible that the meow of the direct ancestor of the domestic cat, *Felis (silvestris) lybica*, was different from that of its Southern African cousin.

Feral cat meows are not as guttural as wildcat meows, but not as sweet-sounding as those of pet cats. Keep in mind that feral cats are genetically almost identical to pet cats, which suggests that their calls – as also applies to much else in cat behaviour – are profoundly affected by each individual's early experiences of people. Pet kittens don't start meowing until after they're weaned, so as they become old enough to meow, they most likely try out a range of meows on their owners, quickly finding that higher-pitched versions produce a more positive reaction. As with so much of cat behaviour, differences between the wild meow and the domestic meow seem to be partly genetic and partly learned; domestication has enhanced cats' ability to learn how to use their meow, but may have also altered its basic sound.

Cats can also modify their meows to suit different situations: some are coaxing, and others more urgent and demanding. They do this by altering their pitch and duration, or by combining the meow with another of their calls, perhaps a chirrup or a growl. Owners often say that they know what their cats want from the tone of their meow. However, when scientists recorded meows from twelve cats and then asked owners to guess the circumstances under which the meow had been uttered, few guessed correctly. Angry meows had a characteristic tone, as did affectionate meows, but meows requesting food, asking for a door to be opened, and appealing for help were not identifiable as such, even though they made sense to each cat's owner in the context in which they were uttered.[16] Therefore, once cats have learned that their owners respond to meows, many probably develop a repertoire of different meows that, by trial and error, they learn are effective in specific circumstances. How this unfolds will depend on which meows get rewarded by the owner, through achieving what the cat wants – a bowl of food, a rub on the head, opening a door. Each cat and its owner gradually develop an individual 'language' that they both understand, but that is not shared by other cats or other owners. This is, of course, a form of training; but unlike the formalities of dog training, the cat and the owner are unwittingly training each other.

If we can decode them, the meows that we inadvertently teach each of our cats to use may provide us with a window into their emotional lives. Our universal recognition of the 'angry meow' and the 'affectionate meow' suggests that each has an underlying and invariant emotional component, as the names I've used for them imply. The cat uses the others, the 'request meows', simply to attract its owner's attention. The context within which they occur provides clues to what

Meowing to be let indoors

the cat wants – whether it is sitting beside a closed door or walking around the kitchen gazing at the cupboard where the food is kept. The meows themselves are probably emotionally neutral.

Cats thus demonstrate great flexibility in how they communicate with us, which rather contradicts their reputation for aloofness. Cats come to realize that human beings do not always pay attention to them, so often need to be alerted with a meow. They learn that purring has a calming effect on most of us, as it did on their mothers when they were kittens. They learn that we like to communicate our affection for them through stroking, which fortuitously mimics the grooming and rubbing rituals in which friendly cats indulge with one another. They may even learn, through our lack of reaction, that we are oblivious to the delicate odour marks that they leave behind on our furniture and even our legs.

We could consider some of this behaviour manipulative, but only to the extent that two friends negotiate the details of their relationship.

The underlying emotion on both sides is undoubtedly affection: cats show this in the way they communicate with their owners, using the same patterns of behaviour that they employ to form and maintain close relationships with members of their own feline family.

Owners who expect long, intense interactions with their cat are frequently disappointed. Unlike most dogs, cats are not always ready to chat, often preferring to choose a moment that suits them. Cats are also nervous of any indication of a threat, however imaginary that might be; as such, many do not like being stared at, staring often being an indicator of impending aggression if it comes from another cat. The most satisfying exchanges between cat and owner are often those that the cat chooses to initiate, rather than those in which the owner approaches the cat, which may regard such uninvited advances with suspicion.[17]

Do cats think of us as surrogate mothers, equals or even as kittens? Biologist Desmond Morris considered that at least two of these might apply, depending on the circumstances. When cats bring freshly caught prey home to 'present' it to their owners, Morris asserts that 'although usually they look upon humans as pseudoparents, on these occasions they view them as their family – in other words, their kittens'.[18] Mother cats do bring prey back to the nest, but presumably their behaviour must be activated by some combination of hormones and the presence of kittens. Male cats and females without kittens don't do this, nor do female cats attempt to treat their owners as their kittens in any other way.[19] A much more likely explanation for the unwelcome 'gift' deposited on the kitchen floor is that the cat has simply brought its prey home, intending to consume it at its leisure. The place where it caught the prey will almost certainly contain scent marks indicating that other cats may be nearby, so what better way of avoiding an ambush than to return to the protection of its owner's home? However, when the cat gets there, it seems to remember that while mice are good to catch, they are not nearly as tasty as commercial cat food – hence the prey is abandoned, to its owner's revulsion.

It seems implausible that cats think of human beings as their kittens, given the size difference between us. On the other hand, it is logical to assume that they regard their owners as mother substitutes.

'Presenting' a dead vole

Much of the cat's social repertoire appears to have evolved from mother–kitten communication. Our cats' behaviour indicates that they take our greater size and upright stance into account when they interact with us. For example, many cats routinely jump up on to furniture to 'talk' to their owners, and many others would probably like to do so, but recall that their owners haven't approved in the past. That they rub on us without necessarily expecting a rub in return, and the apparent exchange of grooming when they lick us and we stroke them, suggests that while they do not regard us as their mothers, they do acknowledge us as being in some way superior to them. Perhaps this is simply because we are physically larger than they are, so we trigger behaviour in them that they would under different circumstances direct towards a bigger or more senior member of their feline family. Perhaps it is because we control their food supply, or at least (for a cat that hunts outdoors) the tastiest options available, mimicking the situation in which a few individuals can limit access to food for other cats in a large feral colony. Both of these analogies refer to situations that wildcats never encounter, and which have existed only since cats began to become domesticated, so the underlying behaviour has presumably only evolved during the past 10,000 years. Hence, we must assume that their relationship with us is still in flux. A definitive answer on how cats perceive us thus remains elusive; for the time being, the most likely explanation for their behaviour towards us is that they think of us as part mother substitute, part superior cat.

An affectionate relationship with people is not most cats' main reason for living. Our cats' behaviour shows us that they are still trying to balance their evolutionary legacy as hunters with their acquired role as companions. They form strong attachments not just to the people they live with, but also to the place where they live – the 'patch' that encompasses their supply of food. Most domestic dogs, in stark contrast, bond to their owners first, other dogs second, and their physical surroundings third. This is why it is easier to take a dog on a vacation than a cat: most cats must feel uneasy when they're uprooted from their familiar surroundings, and certainly behave as if they do. They generally prefer to be left at home when their owner goes away.

Considered logically, well-fed neutered cats should not feel the need for a territory of their own, neither for sexual purposes nor for nutrition. Most cats that have got into a daily routine of being fed high-quality food by their owners do not hunt. Those that do hunt are not particularly enthusiastic – after all, they don't need the nourishment – nor do they usually consume the prey they catch, which is generally less tasty than commercial food. Nevertheless, most do still patrol an area around their homes, if their owners allow them to do so. In urban areas, many do not stray far – in one study, some only ventured about twenty-five feet from the cat-flap, and none more than fifty-five yards. In rural areas, this increased to between roughly twenty and one hundred yards, depending on the cat.[20] But what motivates these cats to pursue what appears to be an unnecessary remnant of their ancestral territorial behaviour?

Regular food certainly seems to reduce the area cats patrol. Socialized cats without a permanent owner, who cannot rely on a regular food supply, travel significantly farther from their 'home' base, perhaps a couple of hundred yards. This is still nowhere near as far as unsocialized feral cats travel, even those that have been neutered and are therefore no longer roaming in search of mates; these cats may range for a mile or more. Neutering of males once they become adults does not substantially reduce the distance they travel, as they are still in the habit of locating as many receptive females as possible, even though they no longer have the ability to do anything if they were to find one. It is clear that any cat which realizes it cannot rely on a regular source of food instinctively increases the size of its range to compensate.

That the ranges of well-fed owned cats are so small suggests that many are not deliberately hunting at all. If the opportunity presents itself, they may grasp it; but without hunger goading them on, they may not do so with single-mindedness. Nevertheless, the cat's brain does not link hunting and hunger together tightly, and for good evolutionary reasons. A single mouse provides few calories, so a wildcat must kill and eat several each day. If cats waited to start each hunting trip until they felt hungry, they'd be unlikely to get enough to eat. So even a well-fed cat, seeing a mouse within catching distance, is likely to grasp the moment – or, rather, the mouse.

Since most pet cats do not hunt seriously, it seems curious that they spend so much time outdoors, apparently sitting and doing nothing or meandering between the same locations they visited the previous day. When my cat Splodge was about eighteen months old, I borrowed a lightweight radio-tracking transmitter and fixed it to an elasticated 'safety' collar so I could locate him wherever he went.[21] I already knew that he spent about a third of his time in our garden or on the roof of a nearby garage. Once the collar was on, I learned that he crossed the garden behind the apartment block next door into a strip of woodland beyond, about an acre in area. An older male cat lived in the apartments, accounting for Splodge's disinclination to remain there for more time than absolutely necessary: I'd already seen the two engaged in stand-offs on several occasions, so they were undoubtedly aware of each other. Splodge rarely ventured beyond the trees – to my great relief, since there was a busy road not far beyond. He would sometimes remain in the same location for hours at a time, usually one of a few favoured vantage points such as a branch of a fallen tree, before moving on to another site or returning home. He rarely seemed to be hunting: occasionally, he caught a mouse or a young rat, but would let birds fly past him without batting an eyelid. I often wondered, and still do, what was going through his mind as he maintained his surveillance of the same small area, day after day, year after year.

Even the best-fed cats seem inclined to pursue this outdated territorial agenda. They clearly feel the need to maintain space of their own, and many are prepared to fight other cats to hang on to it, even though they no longer need to hunt to survive. Their instinct to hunt is dampened, though not entirely eliminated, by their never going hungry. Both sides of this behaviour are understandable from an evolutionary perspective. Hunting puts cats at risk, so they possess a mechanism that dampens the need to hunt actively when they have not gone hungry for a long time. However, few of today's pet cats are more than a small number of generations away from feral cats that have had to live on their own resources, and for whom a productive territory was a necessity. Going back a few generations further, when commercial cat food was neither universally available nor nutritionally complete, virtually every cat would have had to hunt for some of its food, and would therefore have to defend an area in which it had exclusive access to prey. Too few generations have elapsed for this instinctive need to have disappeared – however archaic it may seem to a pet cat's owner.

Each cat's desire to establish and then defend a territory inevitably brings it into conflict with other cats. In the countryside, pet cats live mostly in clusters, dictated by our habit of living in villages rather than evenly spread across the landscape – which would presumably be their preference, since that would match their own ancestral pattern. In this situation, they reduce conflict with other cats by each foraging out in different directions, the pattern of territories resembling the petals of a flower with the village or hamlet at its centre. The somewhat relaxed notions of 'ownership' of cats in rural areas, with farm cats becoming pets and vice versa, also mean that if two cats find themselves living too close together for comfort, one can usually find a vacant niche nearby.

Most cat owners nowadays expect their cat to live wherever the owners choose. Perhaps not fully understanding the cat's need to form an attachment to its physical environment, owners assume that it is enough to provide food, shelter and human company, and that, if they do, the cat will have no reason not to stay put. In reality, many cats adopt a second 'owner', and sometimes migrate permanently.[22]

Surveys I have performed in the UK confirm this picture: many cats stray and get 'lost' even from apparently high-quality homes. We see some clues as to what happens to many of these cats from the significant proportion of owners – as many as one quarter in some areas – who, when asked where they obtained their cat, reply, 'He just turned up one day.' These were not feral cats: that they were so keen to adopt a new home shows that they had recently been someone else's pet and were desperate to find a new owner. A few of these cats may have been genuinely lost, still searching unsuccessfully for their original home, but most were probably voluntary migrants, looking for a better place to live than their original owner could provide. For the few instances of this that I could trace back to the original home, the cat had evidently left not because it wasn't being fed properly or was unloved; something else must have gone seriously wrong for the cat to abandon the certainties of a regular food supply and, in most cases, feelings of attachment towards its original owner. The most likely explanation is that these cats could not establish an area where they could feel relaxed, safe from challenges from other cats.

The threat could have come from the next-door cat, or even from another cat living in the same household. Within the home, opportunities for conflict are rife. Just because two cats have the same owner does not mean they are going to get along. Many pay heed to the cardinal rule of cat society: proceed with caution when meeting any cat that has not been a part of your (cat) family for as long as you can remember. Many cat owners seem oblivious to this principle, blithely assuming that when they obtain a second cat, the two will quickly become friends. Although this is generally true of dogs, cats are more likely to merely tolerate one another (see box, 'Signs That Cats in a Household Do or Don't Get Along with One Another'). To reduce conflict, they often set up separate, if overlapping, territories within the house, but may continue to scrap with each other sporadically. In surveys of owners with two cats, roughly one third report that their cats always avoid each other if they can, and about a quarter say that they fight occasionally. The two cats will probably each come to respect the other's favourite places to rest – the larger or original cat will generally take the prime spots – but tension may remain if both cats are fed in the same room or if there is only one litter tray. They may also compete for the cat-flap, if one cat claims it as being within its core territory. Feeding each cat in a different room and providing several litter trays in different locations (not the rooms used for feeding) can often make the situation more tolerable for both cats.

SIGNS THAT CATS IN A HOUSEHOLD DO OR DON'T GET ALONG WITH ONE ANOTHER[23]

Cats that see themselves as part of the same social group generally:

- *hold their tails upright when they see one another*
- *rub on one another, either when walking past or alongside one another*
- *regularly sleep in contact with one another*
- *play gentle, 'mock-fighting' games with one another*
- *share their toys*

Cats that have set up separate territories within the house will tend to:

- *chase or run away from one another*
- *hiss or spit when they meet*
- *avoid contact with one another: one cat may always leave the room when another enters*
- *sleep in widely separated places: often, one will sleep high up, perhaps on a shelf, to avoid another*
- *sleep defensively: the cat has its eyes closed and looks as if it is asleep, but its posture is tense and its ears may twitch*
- *apparently restrict one another's movements on purpose – for example, one cat sitting for hours by the cat-flap, or at the top of the stairs*
- *watch one another intently*
- *look unusually tense when they're in the same room*
- *interact separately with their owner – for example, they may sit either side of the owner to avoid physical contact with one another*

For any cat that is allowed outdoors, other cats in the neighbourhood will also be a source of conflict and stress. When a cat comes into a new household, whether or not it was previously cat-free, it will most likely find that it has been parachuted into the middle of a mosaic of existing cat territories. If there are already cats on two, three, or even all four sides, the owner's garden will almost certainly 'belong' to one or more other cats; for cats, garden walls are highways, not boundaries to be respected. The new cat will have to establish its right to roam in 'its own' garden, and it will be able to do this only by standing up to the other cats that previously had undisputed use of the space. Challenges over territorial boundaries may continue for years: in one survey, two thirds of owners reported that their cat actively avoided contact with other cats in the neighbourhood – and, frankly, the other third probably hadn't looked out of their windows often enough. One third reported that they had witnessed actual fights between their own cat and their neighbour's.

Surprisingly few owners seem particularly bothered about such conflicts until they begin to affect their cat's health: a bite can turn into an abscess requiring veterinary treatment. More ominously, the cat may become so stressed, or its movements so restricted, that it begins to urinate or defecate in the house (see box, 'Signs That a Cat is Failing to Establish a Territory outside Its Owner's House'). Even if the various cats in an area eventually arrive at a truce, owners may inadvertently reignite the conflict by temporarily removing their cat, perhaps boarding it elsewhere for a couple of weeks while they go on holiday. Encouraged by the signs that the cat may have left for good, such as fading scent marks or absence of sightings, one or more of the neighbours' cats may start to encroach into what was previously that cat's territory. When that cat returns, it may have to re-establish its rights all over again.

Increasingly, cat owners are avoiding such problems by keeping their cats indoors, although their motivation may be more to protect their pet from traffic, disease or potential thieves (especially if it is a valuable pedigree animal) than from social stress. Restricting the cat to one relatively small area for its entire life can induce stresses of its own. Although the practice of keeping cats indoors has been common among apartment-dwellers for more than thirty years, we have little

SIGNS THAT A CAT IS FAILING TO ESTABLISH A TERRITORY OUTSIDE ITS OWNER'S HOUSE[24]

- *Not leaving the house even when encouraged to do so*
- *Waiting to be let out by the owner rather than using its cat-flap (because there might be a rival cat ready to ambush it on the other side)*
- *Neighbour's cats entering the house through the cat-flap*
- *Leaving the house only if the owner is in the garden*
- *Excessive time spent watching out of windows*
- *Running away from windows and hiding when another cat is spotted in the garden*
- *Running into the house and immediately to a place of safety, far from the access point*
- *Tense interaction with the owner, including rough play*
- *Urinating and defecating in the house, by a cat that usually goes outside to do this but feels too insecure to do so*
- *Spraying urine (scent-marking) in the house, especially if near to access points such as doors and cat-flaps (more likely in male cats than females)*
- *Other signs of psychological stress, such as excessive grooming*

systematic research into whether domestic cats find this confinement stressful. To see how we should expect indoor cats to behave if they were stressed by confinement, we must therefore look further afield, to their wild ancestors.

Wild felids often react badly to being confined. Both 'big cats', such as lions, and 'small cats', such as jungle and leopard cats, are prone to the habit, once commonplace in zoos all over the world, of pacing to and fro in their cages.[25] Of other types of animal, only bears are as badly affected, and like most of the cat family they are also solitary territorial carnivores. We do not fully understand why these animals pace, but the reasons probably arise from a mixture of frustration at not having access to a large enough hunting territory, even though their nutritional needs are being more than satisfied, and 'boredom': well-fed carnivores do instinctively sleep for much of the time, but many seem to crave mental stimulation when they are awake. Changing the way the wild cat is fed can provide the latter: rather than simply providing one daily meal that can be wolfed down in seconds, zookeepers now provide food several times each day, and the cats must make an effort to get at least some of it – for example, by feeding bones that have to be cracked open, or placing the food in puzzle feeders which the cat has to work at for an extended period of time.

When considering whether domestic cats kept indoors are likely to suffer, we might first examine whether they show signs of objecting to being spatially restricted, and whether they show signs of 'boredom'. Repetitive pacing is surprisingly rare in domestic cats, considering that this is the most common abnormal behaviour observed in cats kept in zoos. This difference may have already evolved prior to domestication; when in captivity, the domestic cat's wild ancestor (*Felis silvestris*) is more prone to 'apathetic resting' (taking no notice of its surroundings) than to pacing. The difference could also be a consequence of domestication. Whichever the culprit, domestic cats seem to have lost much of their ancestors' spontaneous 'drive' to roam. We do not know why this loss would have benefited cats: for most of their 10,000-year history, they have had to hunt for their living.

Domestication may have given the cat a much greater flexibility in its territorial behaviour. Wild felids generally feed on prey dispersed over the landscape around them, and therefore have always needed a large territory: they may need to venture farther afield if food is scarce, but in all their evolutionary history they would never have encountered a situation where food was so locally plentiful that they could afford not to go out foraging day after day. Domestic cats, by contrast, have adapted to hunting in and around what are, by comparison, very small areas – human settlements – while retaining the ability to expand their hunting ranges quickly if food becomes scarce, provided that other cats don't prevent them from doing so.

Feral domestic cats can thus have territories 10,000 times larger than those of some owned cats that are allowed twenty-four-hour outdoor access. However, just because the species as a whole shows this flexibility does not mean to say that individual cats are so adaptable. Much depends on their previous lifestyle and what expectations they have acquired. A feral cat accustomed to hunting across fifty acres and then suddenly confined to a pen will be almost as distressed as its wildcat counterpart. A pet cat that has never had to hunt to survive would most likely perish if abandoned somewhere remote.

Domestic cats have probably become so flexible in their demands for space that they can, under the right circumstances, adapt adequately to indoor living. Very few cats that are allowed outdoors voluntarily restrict themselves to an area as small as even the most spacious apartment, and those that do would probably venture farther away if they were not anxious about meeting other cats. However, the additional restriction does not appear to cause undue stress. Cats that have grown up wandering wherever they choose will almost certainly be stressed by being suddenly confined indoors, even when this becomes necessary to protect the cat's health. Thus cats that are destined for a life indoors should probably never be allowed outdoors, so that they can't miss what they've never had.

Space that is restricted needs to be quality space. It's unlikely that wild cats value open space for the simple joy of the view into the distance; rather, they presumably gain satisfaction from how many places they can see that might be concealing their next meal. Zoo-keepers have tried giving big cats access to wide open spaces, but this usually had no effect on their habitual pacing, and in fact they rarely visit the additional territory. However, making the same amount of space more interesting was a much more successful strategy; zoos adapted the enclosures so that the cat could not see the entire area from any one place, requiring the cat to move around.

An indoor cat must also be kept busy, since it cannot experience the variety automatically provided by the outdoors – nor, admittedly, the anxiety of being ambushed by another cat. For the owner, this requires extra effort (see box overleaf, 'Keeping an Indoor Cat Happy'), which must be balanced against the relative ease of allowing a cat to seek much of its mental stimulation outdoors. In particular, owners should allow the cat to perform as much of its 'natural' behaviour as possible. Although there is no specific scientific evidence to support such a recommendation for the domestic cat, it is one of the guiding principles of animal welfare that have been established for vertebrate animals in general.

The owner can provide the cat with social behaviour either by spending time with it or by keeping two compatible cats together. The easiest way to achieve the latter is probably to obtain two kittens from the same litter, although even this is not guaranteed to be

KEEPING AN INDOOR CAT HAPPY[26]

- *Allow the cat as much space to roam around as possible.*
- *Site the litter tray in a secluded place, away from windows from which it can see other cats.*
- *If possible, provide an enclosed outdoor area for the cat, perhaps on a balcony. While we have no evidence that cats need 'fresh air' as such, the sights, sounds and smells of the outdoors keep it interested.*
- *Indoors, provide two beds of different types. One should be on the floor, with a roof and three walls; cats are often happy with a cardboard carton placed on its side. The other should be placed up high, near the ceiling but easily accessible, with a good view of the entrance to the house or out of a window. Not all cats will use both, but most will feel safe in one or the other.*
- *Provide at least one scratching post.*
- *Play with the cat several times a day. Games with prey-like toys may satisfy the cat's urge to hunt, especially if it has been viewing birds through the window. Change the toys often to sustain the cat's interest.*
- *Try using a puzzle feeder containing a small amount of dry cat food. A plastic drink bottle with a few holes of appropriate size cut in the sides will keep some cats busy for hours. More complex devices are available commercially.[27]*

An activity-feeder made from a plastic bottle

- *Provide a pot of live 'cat grass'. Many cats like to chew on these oat seedlings,* Avena sativa, *although why they do it is somewhat obscure.*
- *Don't overfeed: indoor cats are at greater risk of obesity than outdoor cats.*
- *If you don't yet have a cat, consider getting two littermates: they will be good company for each other.*
- *If you already have one indoor cat, plan ahead before getting another cat for 'company'. Cats that have never met before are unlikely to adapt spontaneously to sharing a confined space.*

successful – sibling rivalry is not unheard of among cats. Hunting behaviour can be simulated by giving the cat a view of some 'natural' space, through 'play' with prey-sized toys (since cats react to these as if they really are prey), and feeding dry cat food in a device that requires the cat to perform predatory behaviour to release each piece (simulation of hunting behaviour has been successfully used to restore normal behaviour in captive wildcats,[28] so it should also benefit indoor domestic cats). None of these may be entirely satisfactory substitutes, but any stress that the cat feels at being restricted or not allowed to carry out all its natural behaviour may be counterbalanced by its being removed from the stress of being 'bullied' by other cats in the neighbourhood.

Considering how little time has elapsed since they were first domesticated, cats demonstrate remarkable flexibility when it comes to the amount of space they need. However, we must be careful not to provide them with too little space, or space that contains incipient threats. Pet cats have no practical need to maintain a hunting territory any more, but it is too soon for evolution to have removed the desire to do so. Unfortunately for the cats, this perceived need to roam can bring them into daily conflict with other cats, each with the same agenda. Cats, having a relatively unsophisticated repertoire for communicating with other cats, take time to 'negotiate' their territory boundaries, time that increasingly we no longer provide them with.

Cats face great pressure to change their ways – and not only to adapt to modern urban lifestyles. The conservation lobby, from Australasia to the United States to Great Britain, increasingly objects to their maintaining any kind of hunting territory. To change, cats must evolve new ways to organize their behaviour, at an unprecedented speed. Evolution requires variation: cats must differ from one another in the way they perceive and react to their environment, both social and physical. We still see great variation among cats in their personalities, and somewhere among these we might find the combination of characteristics for the ideal twenty-first-century cat.

9

Cats as Individuals

Cats have much in common with one another; as a species, they are highly distinctive, so what is true of one cat is also likely to be true of another. But cats are also unquestionably individuals, both in appearance and – more significantly for their relationship with their owners and for their future – in the way they behave. Even scientists now talk freely of cats having their own personalities. The existence of many different personality types among today's cats gives us hope that they, as a species, have the potential to adapt to the demands of the twenty-first century and beyond. Somewhere hidden among the cats that live around us today are the genes that will enable their offspring to evolve into a slightly different kind of cat; for example, one that is better adapted to living indoors.

Of course, genes alone cannot drive such changes; the environment in which a cat finds itself plays a powerful role in guiding the development of its personality. Furthermore, cats do not have to make these changes on their own; we as owners have a wealth of strategies we can employ to help them to lead happier lives. If cats' genes were as unvarying as those of some pedigree dog breeds – many of which contain little more variation in total than does the average human extended family – then no amount of breeding for temperament would achieve much: the only way forward would be for cat owners to change the way they relate to their cats. But knowing that cats are so genetically variable, even today, provides us with two, complementary ways to help them adapt to our world.

The crucial question is: how much influence do genes have? Much of the cat's personality depends on other factors. For example, whether a cat will tolerate people depends on whether it has had contact – and the right kind of contact – with people during the first eight weeks of its life. Cats that do receive such contact nevertheless vary greatly in how friendly they are to people in general, and even towards their owner. How much of this variation, not fully explained by the basic process of socialization, is inherited? Is each cat's ability to tolerate other cats due simply to whether it grows up with other cats, or are some born to be more adaptable than others?

Decoding the inheritance of personality is nowhere near as simple as the inheritance of the colour or length of a cat's coat. We can track most of those visible differences between cats to twenty or so well-defined genes that operate in a highly predictable manner. If a cat's parents both have black coats, then the cat will also be black; this is not affected by whether it is born in a hedge or in a kitchen.

Genes and environment can interact in complex ways, however. Even coat colours can be affected by the environment: for example, the darker 'points' on a Siamese cat's face, paws and ears come from a temperature-sensitive mutation that prevents the hairs from taking up their usual colour at normal body temperature. As newborns, these cats are whitish all over because their mother's womb is uniformly warm. As they grow and the extremities of the body become cooler, the hair there grows darker, producing the characteristic 'pointed' coat. Finally, as the cat enters old age and the circulation of blood in its skin deteriorates slightly, it gradually turns brown all over.

The relationship between genetics and environment is evident in personality as well. Cat personality is influenced by hundreds of genes and a lifetime of experience, interacting together to produce the cats we see today.

To search for evidence that personality can be inherited, we might start with pedigree cats. Unlike dogs, which have been bred for different functions for many centuries, pedigree cats have been bred mainly for their looks. Deliberate selection is probably not to blame for any consistent differences in behaviour between different cat breeds; we cannot expect to find differences as great as those between, say, a border collie and a Labrador retriever. However, because all pedigree cats are raised by breeders, and, at least within each country, in much the same way, any consistent behavioural differences between them are likely to be due to genetics.

The breeding of pedigree or 'show' cats is regulated by standards laid down by the individual 'breed clubs', and the best cats from each breed compete in cat shows run by organizations such as the Cat Fanciers' Association and the International Cat Association, in the United States, and the Governing Council of the Cat Fancy, in the UK. Well-known breeds or groups of breeds include the Persian or 'Exotic' breeds, stocky cats with long hair and flat faces; the 'Foreign' breeds, fine-boned, long-limbed cats such as the Siamese, Burmese, and Abyssinian; and the Domestic breeds, which as their name implies were originally derived from ordinary domestic cats local to the British Isles. Some individual breeds can be characterized by a single mutation, such as the short, wavy coat of the Cornish Rex, the downy hair of the Sphynx and the short tail of the Manx.

Many of the newer breeds of cat are simply colour variations on existing breeds. For example, the Havana Brown is genetically indistinguishable from the Siamese, except that it lacks the mutation that causes most of the Siamese's coat to stay cream-coloured. Though some of the longer-established breeds claim ancient ancestry – for example, the Siamese breed is apparently described in the 'Cat-Book Poems' written in the ancient Siamese city of Ayutthaya sometime between 1350 and 1750 – but their DNA shows that the breeds have become separate entities only during the past 150 years or so.[1]

This recent evidence separates the breeds into roughly six groups, each seemingly derived from – or possibly allowed to interbreed with – local street cats. The DNA of the Siamese, Havana Brown, Singapura, Burmese, Korat and Birman shows not only that they are closely related, but that they are also genetically similar to the street cats of South-East Asia from which they were undoubtedly derived. The Bobtail, a traditional Japanese breed, is genetically close to the moggies of Korea, China and Singapore (and presumably those of Japan, which were not included in the study). The Turkish Van cat, as its name implies, is related to non-pedigree cats from Turkey, as well as Italy, Israel and Egypt. The Siberian and Norwegian Forest cats are derived from long-haired Northern European moggies, while the superficially similar Maine Coon finds its closest non-pedigree relatives in New York State. Most of the stockier breeds – the American and British Shorthairs, the Chartreux, the Russian Blue – and, surprisingly, the Persian and Exotic breeds, are all closely related and are presumably derived from Western European stock. The modern Persian, even if some of its distant ancestors did come from the Middle East, seems to have lost most traces of those origins, possibly due to recent breeding to produce the flat (brachycephalic) face preferred by its devotees.

The various breed clubs usually describe typical personalities for their cats. For example, the Governing Council of the Cat Fancy (GCCF) describes the Ocicat, an American breed derived from Abyssinian, Siamese and American Shorthair lines, as follows:

> Many owners remark on the almost doglike tendencies of the Breed, in that they are devoted to people, are easily trained and respond well to the voice, but retain their independence as a proper cat should, and are very intelligent. Because of their adaptability they are a joy to be with, they are not demanding in any way and seem to take life in their stride. Ocicats are reasonably vocal and do not like being left alone for long periods, but do make ideal companions for households with other pets, and are confident with children.[2]

Although such formal recognition permeates the world of cat enthusiasts, scientists have devoted little attention to investigating whether cat breeds have distinctive personalities. The line-breeding necessary to develop cats that breed 'true' – that is, where the offspring look the same as their parents – has led to some behavioural abnormalities that have a genetic basis (see box overleaf, 'Fabric Eating in Pedigree Oriental Cats'). Because these are essentially pathologies, and isolated within a single breed or group of breeds, scientists do not classify these abnormalities as aspects of 'personality'. Turning to more universal cat behaviour, Siamese and other Oriental cats are remarkably vocal; many develop so many variations on the meow that they seem to 'talk' to their owners. Longhaired cats, especially Persians, have a reputation for being lethargic and not terribly fond of close contact with people, perhaps because these cats overheat easily. Beyond such self-evident differences, we have little hard information on precisely how breeds differ in personality and how those differences arise. Most of the information we have is based on surveys of experts – veterinary surgeons or cat show judges, for example – who tend to see most cats when they are away from their normal territories, and therefore may not always get a complete picture of their behaviour.

FABRIC EATING IN PEDIGREE ORIENTAL CATS

Siamese, Burmese and other Oriental cat breeds are susceptible to developing an unusual form of pica, the eating of non-nutritive substances. For reasons we do not yet understand, some house cats develop the habit of chewing unusual items, such as elastic bands and rubber gloves, but a significant proportion of pedigree Oriental cats not only chew but also eat fabrics. Their fabric of choice is usually wool, closely followed by cotton; synthetic fabrics such as nylon and polyester are less popular. Most of these cats start by chewing woollen items: many then progress to swallowing the chewed-off fabric chunks, or move on to other materials. In these cases, the cats appear to confuse fabrics with food. I have seen a Siamese cat dragging an old sock up to its food bowl, and then alternately taking one mouthful of one, and one mouthful of the other.

A Siamese cat eating a piece of cloth

We also have yet to understand their predilection for wool over other fabrics. One theory held that these cats might have a craving for the natural lanolin in wool, but when I tested this directly, the idea did not stand up.

Because wool eating is largely restricted to a small number of closely related breeds, it must have a genetic basis. However, it does not seem to be inherited directly. When I surveyed the owners of seventy-five kittens produced by seven mothers, three of which were fabric eaters and four of which were not, one third of the kittens had become fabric eaters themselves – but many of these had 'normal' mothers (their fathers' habits were unknown). Neither simple genetic factors, nor imitation of the mother's behaviour, could explain why some had developed this problem while others had not.

Many of the fabric-eating cats did also show other types of abnormal behaviour, such as biting their owners and excessive scratching. These also occur in non-pedigree cats and are often a sign of anxiety and stress. Among Oriental cats, fabric eating often starts within a few weeks of the cat being rehomed, when the cat may be feeling stressed by the change in its environment. Onset can also occur at around one year of age even without a move, when the cat is becoming sexually mature and starting to come into conflict with other cats either within the household or outside (even though they were valuable pedigree animals, few of the cats in my study were totally confined indoors).

Fabric eating may therefore start as a soothing oral behaviour that these cats adopt when they feel especially stressed, rather like thumb sucking in human infants. Why they choose fabrics, and why chewing often turns into ingestion, is still unclear.

One small-scale study conducted in Norway confirmed that Siamese and Persian cats do indeed behave in characteristic ways in their owners' homes.[3] Although the cats' personalities were recorded by the owners themselves (which in itself could have introduced some biases) rather than through direct observation, the Siamese were reported to be more contact-seeking, more vocal, and more playful and active than standard moggies. One in ten Siamese were regularly aggressive towards people, compared to one in twenty moggies and one in sixty Persians. Persians were generally less active than other cats, and apparently more tolerant of unfamiliar people and cats – although their apparent laziness might have simply made them disinclined to run away.

It's highly implausible that every single variation in cat personality will be traced to a different gene. Rather, breed characteristics seem to emerge during kittenhood as general tendencies, such as when making the choice whether to explore or to move away from novel objects or situations. In turn, these tendencies profoundly affect what each kitten learns, and thus how its behaviour develops: tactics it learns are useful in one particular circumstance may become general strategies, used in many situations. The underlying processes have scarcely been investigated in pedigree cats, but in one study researchers found that the ability of Norwegian Forest kittens to remember novel situations develops more slowly than those of other pedigree cats (Oriental breeds and Abyssinians), whose brains may develop somewhat more quickly than those of ordinary moggies.[4] Such slowing down and speeding up of the rates at which different parts of the brain grow might have long-term effects on cat personality. Many of the self-evident differences in behaviour between dog breeds result from changes in the speed at which different areas of the brain develop: for example, Siberian Huskies display a full range of wolf-type behaviour, while breeds with 'baby faces', such as bulldogs, signal to one another in a similar way to wolf cubs of just a few weeks old.[5] However, scientists have not yet documented any such link for cats.

Differences among breeds provide useful insights into whether cat behaviour might be influenced by genetics, and pedigree breeds are useful in this regard because each cat's parentage is documented. Popular males can sire many kittens, yet rarely even see any of them, so their influence on their offspring must be genetic. In the Norwegian study, playfulness, fearfulness and confidence in encounters with unfamiliar people were all distinctively different between the offspring of different fathers, although some other traits, such as aggression towards cats or people, were not. Because this study was small-scale, and carried out in only one country, its details may not apply everywhere; still, the principle that some aspects of a cat's behaviour are influenced by its father's genes seems likely to stand.[6]

Non-pedigree cats also vary greatly in their 'personalities', spurring on the myth that a cat's temperament and its coat colour are inextricably linked.[7] The British refer to tortoiseshell cats as 'naughty torties'; likewise, blotched tabbies are 'real homebodies', mackerel tabbies are 'independent', and white patches on a cat's coat have a 'calming effect' on the animal. It seems part of human nature to link outward appearance and inner character, and to continue to see those links even when evidence is to the contrary. Some scientists have speculated that the specific biochemistry that generates different coat colours also somehow affects the way an animal's brain works, showing a genetic effect referred to as pleiotropy, but little evidence has been found to support this idea in cats.[8]

Links between coat colour and personality do occasionally occur among pedigree cats, and these provide an opportunity for proper investigation because the family trees are available. The relatively restricted gene pool for each colour within each breed does result in certain temperaments accidentally becoming associated with particular coat colours. At any one time, only a limited number of high-quality tomcats within each breed are available to produce the desired colour; as a result, the temperament of the most popular of those tomcats – or at least those aspects affected by genetics – tends to become predominant within that section of the breed. For example, twenty years ago, Scotland's British Shorthair cats with tortoiseshell, cream and especially red (a rare, un-patterned version of orange) coats were relatively difficult to handle; scientists traced this characteristic back to one male with a particularly difficult temperament.[9] Likewise, cats with dark 'points' on their paws and ears, even if not pedigree Siamese, are likely to be unusually vocal, because the gene that causes the points to appear is very rare in any cat without at least one Siamese in its recent ancestry.

Coat colour and some aspect of personality can also become linked if the gene that controls the colour and a gene affecting the way the brain develops happen to occur very close together on the same chromosome. Because genes are grouped together on chromosomes – cats have thirty-eight: eighteen pairs, plus two sex chromosomes – not all combinations are passed on randomly from one generation to the next. If two genes occur on different chromosomes, then the chances that a kitten will receive any particular combination of the two are essentially random. However, two genes that occur on the same chromosome tend to be inherited together. This is not inevitable, because matching pairs of chromosomes do occasionally swap sections between each other, by a mechanism known as crossing over; if the swap happens in between the two genes in question, they are then inherited separately. Such exchanges rarely occur between genes that are sited close together on the same chromosome. For example, the gene that causes a white coat ('dominant white', that is; different from albino) is situated on the same chromosome and close to another gene that causes both eyes to be blue and the cat to be deaf, a rare example of one gene affecting both appearance and (indirectly) behaviour. Blue-eyed, white cats are thus almost invariably deaf.[10] In the case of the ginger cats in rural France, the gene that suits those cats to the feral lifestyle might simply be very close to the O(range)-gene (on the X-chromosome), rather than being a direct effect of the cat being orange.

Making assumptions about a cat's personality based solely on its appearance is often misleading, but cats undoubtedly do behave in individual ways, irrespective of their colour. Until about twenty years ago, most scientists considered that only humans could have 'personalities', yet now this concept is widely applied to animals – and not just to domestic animals. Even wild animals behave in consistently different ways that reflect differences in how they react to the world around them: over the past few years, the concept of 'personality' has been applied to animals as diverse as lizards, crickets, bees, chimpanzees and geese. Some individuals may be particularly bold, and therefore the first to exploit a new food source, whereas others are particularly shy and therefore less likely to run headlong into dangerous situations. The success of each strategy is likely to vary depending on what the environment is like, and if that changes, so sometimes bold individuals will do best, at other times they will be the ones who perish first. In this way, the genes that influence both types persist in the species.

Some of the most complex effects of personality occur in social situations. Sticklebacks, fish that sometimes swim in shoals, can be classed as either bold or shy. When a fish has a choice of shoals consisting entirely of bold or shy individuals, it will choose to join the bold shoal, irrespective of whether it is bold or shy itself. Bold shoals usually find more food, and a shy fish will find the middle of a shoal of bold fish a good place to hide. However, to keep up with the bold shoal, it must swim faster than usual, so it temporarily starts behaving more like a bold fish. Although we don't yet know much about social effects on cat personality, such observations raise the fascinating possibility that each cat may be able to adjust its personality to fit in with those of the other animals – human, feline and canine – in the household in which it finds itself.

We have two broad approaches to studying cat personality: watching the cats or asking their owners. Because owners are likely to be biased, observing the cat's behaviour is the only way an impression of its personality can be gained. For this reason, most of my own studies have involved recording cats' behaviour. To ensure that outdoor cats would be home, I chose to observe them just before and just after their usual feeding time.[11] Since many cats interact most intensely with their owners when expecting food, and since hunger usually affects the way they interact, this arrangement had the additional advantage that all the cats would have been hungry when the observation started and sated at the end.

While their food was being prepared, the thirty-six cats in the study acted as cats usually do when expecting to be fed: walking around the kitchen with their tails upright, meowing, and rubbing on their owners' legs. After the meal, some went straight outdoors, while others sat and groomed themselves; some interacted with their owners again, while others investigated the unfamiliar human in the room – that is, the person making the observations. So far, so obvious; but the first objective of our study was to find out whether each cat behaved in a characteristic way every time. We repeated these visits once a week for eight weeks, and found that they were indeed fairly consistent – so what we had measured was probably a reflection of the cat's personality, or at least its 'personal style'.

From their behaviour before they were fed, we separated the cats into various types. Some always rubbed around their owner's legs, purring all the while; others never did. Some walked around the kitchen much more than others, and some continually tried to attract their owner's attention by meowing; their owners didn't seem to find this particularly endearing – they stroked the quiet ones more often. Only about half of the cats took any of these tendencies to extremes; the others split their time between rubbing and meowing, and were moderately active – unsurprising given that all these traits are typical of cats.

After they were fed, some of the younger cats went straight outdoors – possibly more of a habit than a personality trait. Most, however, stayed in the kitchen for a few minutes. Several of the cats

A bold cat studies a scientist

that had been more active than the others before the meal continued to interact vigorously with their owners, walking around with their tails up and meowing. Those that had paid most attention to the unfamiliar person before the meal continued to do so.

We rounded out our observations by talking to the cats' owners. Some of the differences between cats we observed seemed to reflect their personalities, but we did watch them only in one (convenient) situation. Would we have seen other sides to each cat's character if we'd also watched it when it was out exploring, socializing with (or avoiding) other cats, or curled up while its owner watched television? Several studies have examined differences in cats' reactions to people by asking owners or other caregivers to report on their cats' behaviour. Inevitably, these surveys provide little information on how the cat behaves when it's alone, and owners with only one cat won't necessarily know how well it gets along with other cats.

Three aspects or dimensions of cat personality have emerged from such studies, despite their limitations.[12] The first is whether or not the cat gets along well with other cats in the same household or another social group; some cats seem to be more outgoing towards other cats and some less so – at least, ones that they know well. Second is how sociable the cat is towards people in the household; some cats seem to value close contact with their owners more than others. Third, and possibly most fundamental, is how bold and active or steady and cautious the cat is in general. An individual cat may possess any one of the eight possible combinations of these three basic traits: for example, one cat could be shy and retiring, but affectionate towards its owner and the other cats in the house; another might be highly active and equally affectionate towards its owner, but might keep its distance from another cat in the household. While these traits are defined by their extremes, in real life most cats are intermediate on one, two or even all three. Insofar as their owners are concerned, there may be no such thing as an 'average cat' – but many do in fact approximate to that description.

The bold/shy dimension is perhaps the most important of all, because it affects not only how the cat behaves on a minute-by-minute basis, but also how much and what each cat learns. In some situations, a bold cat learns more from a new experience than a cat that holds back. However, if the bold cat behaves over-confidently and is hurt as a consequence – for example, if it struts up to a belligerent tomcat – then not only may it get injured, but it may also learn less from its experience than a more circumspect cat that simply stands by and watches the encounter.

Whether a cat gets on with other cats, or is especially affectionate towards people, seems strongly influenced by its experiences as a kitten and during its adolescence. At least, we have yet to detect a strong and lasting genetic influence among ordinary house cats. Scientists once thought that some cats carried 'friendly' genes and others 'unfriendly' ones, but when they investigated this in more depth, they found that the differences were in fact due to genes which affected how bold the cats were. Bold and shy cats learn differently how to interact with cats and people. This is not to say that bold cats are necessarily friendlier than shy cats, or vice versa, although they are likely to express their affection in slightly different ways.

The notion that bold and shy cats learn in subtly different ways emerged from a classic experiment in which the offspring of two tom-cats, one with a reputation for producing 'friendly' kittens and the other 'unfriendly', were raised in groups that were socialized a little differently, some given minimal handling, while others were handled daily.[13] At one year old, the offspring were compared by placing them in an arena with an unfamiliar object: a cardboard box they'd never seen before. The offspring of the 'friendly' father explored the box most rapidly and most thoroughly, and the offspring of the 'unfriendly' father tended to hold back. The genetic difference between the two fathers thus influenced something more fundamental than just how friendly they had become; it affected how their kittens reacted to any-thing they hadn't encountered before.

Similarly, how the kittens interacted with people during their social-ization period was affected by their boldness. The kittens with the bold father approached people spontaneously, and as a result learned quickly how to interact with them. The shy kittens took longer to achieve the same level of confidence with people. However, given enough handling, these shy kittens could turn out just as friendly as the kittens with the bold father – though, as expected, they tended to show their friendliness in a less 'pushy' way than the kittens with the bold father. The shy father's kittens became fearful of people only if they were not handled every day: even at a year old these kittens, like their father, moved away from people, hissing and flattening their bodies to the ground. The amount of exposure to people they had received was, for the most timid, significantly less than the average kitten born in a typical home experiences, so the study did not pre-cisely replicate normal conditions. However, it does provide a valuable insight into how vulnerable the offspring of shy tomcats may be to interruptions in their socialization.

Kittens born in someone's home will in all likelihood receive enough handling to end up at least reasonably friendly to people, regardless of whether they are genetically bold, shy or somewhere in between. The ways they show their affection may differ, however, and this seems to interact in a complex way with their early experience. In 2002, my team researched this interaction in a study on twenty-nine cats from nine litters born in ordinary homes.[14] The amount of handling the litters received in their second month varied from twenty minutes to more than two hours per day. When these kittens were eight weeks old, just before they were homed, we tried picking them up, one at a time. Those that had received the least handling were definitely the most inclined to jump down; we could hold those that had received the most handling for several minutes at a time. The amount of handling they had received seemed to have had more of an effect on their behaviour than any genetic effects; all the litters had different mothers, and although we had no idea who their fathers were, the homes they'd been born in were far enough apart to make it unlikely that any two had the same father.

When we repeated our test two months later, after the great majority of the kittens had been moved to new homes, we found exactly the opposite: the kittens that had received the most handling during their second month of life were now the *most* restless, and those that had received the least were now the quietest.

This apparent contradiction probably demonstrates that not only does socialization to people in general start during the second month, so too does attachment to specific people. Very few of the cats appeared distressed when they were picked up at eight weeks old, so all must have received more than enough socialization to create a generally friendly kitten. Nevertheless, those handled the least were still not entirely confident when picked up by a stranger. Two months later, these kittens had gone through the process of learning about a new set of people – their new owners – and showed through their behaviour that they were perfectly content to be picked up by anyone. The kittens that had received a great deal of handling in their original home may consequently have become extremely attached to their original owners, and therefore found the transfer to their new home particularly unsettling. Despite the two months of acclimatization that had passed, when we returned to test them again they may still have been anxious in these new homes.

The handling they'd received seemed to set these kittens' personalities off in different directions, but all effects of the differences in handling during kittenhood gradually disappeared as these cats matured. At one year of age, they varied in how much they liked being picked up by a person they hadn't seen for eight months, but this bore no relation to how much handling they'd received as kittens, or indeed to their genetics; cats that had originally been littermates were no longer similar to one another. When we tested them again at two and three years old, we found that they had changed little from the way they were at twelve months; so, by the end of their first year, each cat had already developed its own distinctive way of reacting to people.

Somehow, the way cats react to being picked up by unfamiliar people changes as they grow through their first year. This change is probably influenced by their new owners' lifestyles and how they interact with the cats' developing personality. However, once they are about one year old, their reactions vary much less. For example, some cats presumably become accustomed to being in a busy house and are unfazed by strangers; others prefer the company of their owners and hide when visitors stop by. The way cats arrive at these states of equanimity is affected by the amount of handling they receive before they leave their mothers, and almost certainly also by their genetics, but the end result appears to be roughly the same whatever the route they have travelled.

Most cats are extraordinarily sensitive to human body language, much more so than they usually receive credit for. This sensitivity enables them to adapt their behaviour to the people they meet. People who dislike cats often complain that they are the first person in the room a cat makes a beeline for, so I decided to test this theory by staging encounters between cats and people who either liked cats or found them repulsive.[15] The people – all men, since we could not find any women who admitted to hating cats – were instructed to sit on a couch and not to move when a cat came into the room, even if it tried to sit on their laps. However, we could not prevent the cat-haters from looking away from the cat, which they usually did within ten seconds of first seeing it. The cats, for their part, seemed to sense the disposition of the people they were meeting within a few seconds of entering the room. They rarely approached the cat-phobics, preferring to sit near the door and look away from them. It was unclear how the cats were detecting the difference between the two types of men: perhaps they could sense that the cat-phobics were tenser, or smelled different, or glanced nervously at the cats. Nevertheless, the cats' reactions show that they can be keenly perceptive when encountering someone for the first time. However, one of our eight cats, while apparently equally perceptive, behaved contrariwise to the other seven, singling out the cat-phobics for the most attention, jumping on their laps and purring loudly, to their evident disgust. Cats such as this one presumably make a lasting impression on cat-phobics, rather than the majority of cats that sensibly avoid them.

Young cats especially seem to be much more adaptable animals than their detractors – and even some of their supporters – might have us believe. During the first year of their lives, they effectively tailor their personalities as much as they can to suit the particular household, or indeed other environment, in which they find themselves. Investigations on how they do this are still in their infancy, and the process is likely to be both drawn-out and contain features that are intrinsically private; still, intriguing links are emerging between cat behaviour and their owners' personality. For example, owners who have intensely emotional relationships with their cats tend to have cats that are very happy to be picked up and cuddled.[16] This could be due to the cat simply adapting to the owner's demands, although studies have suggested that cats tend to resist being picked up when they're not ready for it. It's possible, therefore, that people who obtain an adult cat and want one that loves to be picked up deliberately select one with that kind of personality, rather than the cat changing its ways to suit its owner's demands. However, young cats and kittens are almost certainly more adaptable than older cats are.

A typical cat's relationship with its owner is apparently not rigidly determined by whether the cat is genetically bold or shy, even though both these personality types persist in the general cat population. More important than its personality is the amount of handling the cat receives when it is a kitten, which alters the way it behaves for the first few months of its life; after this time, most cats successfully adapt their behaviour to the demands of their new owners. Some kittens do not receive much handling, perhaps because they have been born in a cat shelter where the staff are overstretched, or because their mother, being shy herself, has hidden them away. If such kittens also have an inherited genetic tendency towards shyness, inherited from their mother or indeed their father, they may be at risk of never developing a fully affectionate relationship with their new owners. In all the studies that trace the development of kittens' personalities, some cats have disappeared from their owner's homes. While we have never been able to explain this fully, we have suspected that some were somewhat unsuited to being pets and had chosen to become feral.

Continued gentle interaction with people can buffer the effects of genetic shyness, so that the young cat learns to come out of its shell. If a cat that is genetically disposed towards shyness does not receive this handling, then the innate shyness may persist into adulthood. These cats, if allowed to breed, will still carry the 'shy' genes they inherited from their parents; so if they mate with another 'shy' individual, these genes will persist throughout the cat population.

We know little about how a cat's genetics affects its sociability towards other cats. What research there is has focused instead on how a kitten's early experience of other cats alters its behaviour as an adult. Kittens hand-raised on their own behave abnormally towards other cats, and kittens hand-raised alongside a littermate less so – nevertheless, all display a bizarre combination of fascination and fear on encountering another cat.[17] The presence of the mother, or in her absence another friendly adult cat, is apparently necessary for kittens to develop normal social behaviour.

Cats raised in the normal way by their mothers also differ from one another in how friendly they are to other cats, albeit not exhibiting the extremes found in hand-raised cats. Much of this variation may also stem from different experiences during kittenhood: kittens born into extended families normally find it easier to learn social skills than those born to solitary mothers. For example, in parts of New Zealand, some feral cats live around farmyards, subsisting on a diet of rodents and scraps provided by the farmer, much like farm cats in the UK or the United States. However, because of less competition from native predators than elsewhere, other cats live in the bush nearby, feeding exclusively on prey they have hunted for themselves and adopting a way of life that must be much like that of undomesticated *Felis lybica*.[18] Males roam between the two populations, keeping them genetically mixed, but females seem to adopt their mother's lifestyle: those born on the farms stay there and share their mothers' territories, while those in the bush strike out on their own. Cats thus appear to inherit a form of social 'culture' from their mothers that may have little to do with their genetics.

Even cats that have lived their whole lives in groups can differ markedly in how they react to other cats, hinting at genetic as well as cultural influences. In one study of two small indoor colonies (seven females each), researchers found that the individual cats varied consistently in their calmness while interacting with the others, and varied also in the extent to which they chose to be close to or keep away from them. These aspects of their personalities were distinct from how sociable these cats were towards people, or how generally active and inquisitive they were.[19] Each cat appeared to have worked out its own way of interacting with the cats around it, which was not simply a reflection of how 'bold' it was.

Each cat's boldness would have affected the way it had initially approached other cats when it was first introduced to them, since 'boldness' is a trait that underlies all first encounters with novel situations. However, in repeated encounters with the same individuals, each had developed a new and eventually stable personality trait, sociability to cats, which was unrelated to how bold they were. We can only guess at the reasons behind these emergent differences, since we know little of how such traits are formed. For example, if the outcome of just the first few encounters fixes each cat's strategy for dealing with cats permanently, then its personality might be profoundly affected by whether it happened to be smaller and weaker, or bigger and stronger, than the cats it met early on in its life. However, if this aspect of personality develops over many encounters, then the subsequent differences between each cat could conceivably be driven by genetic factors, distinct from those that affect whether a cat is bold or shy.

Indeed, the domestic cat's capacity to live amicably with other cats should be genetically variable. Its wildcat ancestors seem incapable of extending their affiliations beyond temporary bonds between mother and offspring, but many domestic cats seem capable of forming affectionate bonds with adult cats. It seems highly unlikely that this change has already evolved as far as it can. Some cats, at least anecdotally, are unusually outgoing towards other cats, while others prefer to be virtually solitary. Dissimilarities in early life experience certainly caused some of these differences, but surely genetics also plays a part. We should still see variation between today's cats in how easy they find it to forge bonds with others. How shy or bold they are may affect this variation, although, as with affection for people, boldness or shyness may have more influence on how the cat approaches another cat than on whether or not they become friends or enemies.

On the face of it, we would not expect much genetic variation underlying the domestic cat's ability to hunt. Not only is the cat descended from a specialist predator, but the primary function of the cat in human society has been, until recently, to kill rodent pests. Moreover, until the appearance of nutritionally balanced cat food some forty years ago, cats that were incompetent predators would not have bred as successfully as those that were. Scientific studies have confirmed that, given enough exposure to real prey, all cats have the potential to become competent predators by the time they are six months old. The way each cat hunts – whether it moves around constantly or sits and waits for hours where it knows that prey will appear – varies a great deal from individual to individual. So too does the type of prey in which each cat specializes: some cats seem incapable of catching a bird, and others catch more birds than rodents. We could regard these differences as aspects of 'personality'. However, these differences probably stem from each cat's experiences as it refines its hunting skills, since it will most likely repeat tactics that have led to a meal. We have no evidence that some cats are born bird-hunters and others innate mouse-catchers.

Surprisingly, research *has* revealed considerable differences among kittens in their prey-catching competence, particularly during their third month of life. By this stage in their development, all kittens are capable of performing their basic repertoire of predatory behaviour –

stalking, pouncing, biting, and raking with the claws – which they have practised for the past several weeks through play with inanimate objects around the nest, as well as in mock predation on their litter-mates. Despite all this practice, kittens between two and three months old vary greatly in effectively putting these actions together, in assessing what they can probably catch and what they should avoid, and in selecting the appropriate tactics for the prey in question – for example, not chasing after birds that are already flying away.[20] Three months later, however, they are all equally competent; somehow, the laggards catch up. Scientists have found no developmental reasons for the differences between kittens during their third month, so it is possible that these variations at least are genetically influenced. Genetics undoubtedly affects the rate at which kittens develop in general – for example, the age at which their eyes open – so this hypothesis is reasonable.

As every cat owner knows, cats differ not just on the outside. Inner and outer qualities are both affected by genes and the environment in which the cat grows up, but to different extents and in different ways. Cats' personalities develop according to a highly complex interplay between genetics and what the cat experiences during the first year or so of its life. These experiences can have extremely powerful effects that can all but obliterate any trace of genetics. Yet among cats that receive what is, for their species, a 'normal' upbringing within a human household, signs of genetic effects on personality are apparent.

Cats also vary in terms of how quickly they learn to hunt. Although experience again plays a large part in determining this aspect of a cat's personality, it also seems likely that genetic factors are at work. Cats are not only able to adapt as individuals to the circumstances in which they find themselves; they are also members of a species that contains a significant amount of genetic variation which affects their behaviour, giving them the potential to evolve further as our demands upon them change. Today, the most significant challenge facing cats is a growing reputation as destroyers of wildlife, but even their most vociferous critics have to admit that not all cats are to blame. If hunting ability is linked to personality, and personality has a genetic basis, then it may become possible to predict which cats are likely to cause least offence.

IO

Cats and Wildlife

Few topics get wildlife enthusiasts as hot under the collar as predation by domestic cats. In the wrong environment, cats can undoubtedly cause substantial damage to other species, especially where there is little competition in the shape of wild predators. Although many pet cats do undeniably go out hunting, it has proved remarkably difficult to pin down the impact of that hunting – in other words, whether it does have a significant effect on wildlife numbers. Indeed, when the balance of wildlife changes in a particular place, cats become convenient scapegoats. Well-fed pet cats should not need to hunt to supplement their diet, and in that sense any damage they do is unnecessary. Moreover, their habit of bringing their kill home rather than eating it on the spot does make it easy for their detractors to point the finger at them – it can seem as though they are killing for 'sport' – while deaths due to wilder predators tend to be ignored.

More insidiously, general anti-cat sentiments can creep into scientific literature addressing wildlife conservation. A group of scientists in Australia has recently called for 'restrictions on the maximum number of cats allowed per household, mandatory sterilization and registration of pet cats, curfews, requiring pet cats roaming outdoors to wear collar-mounted predation-deterrents or compulsory confinement of cats to their owners' premises',[1] even though it is far from clear that any of these restrictions would lead to a recovery in the local wildlife.

In 1997, the UK's Mammal Society produced an estimate of 275 million animals killed in Britain each year by pet cats. These figures derived from forms completed by their youth wing, 'Mammalaction': data from the 696 cats surveyed were extrapolated up to the 9 million cats then in the UK. However, when the full analysis was finally published in 2003,[2] it became clear that very few cats – less than 9 per cent – had been included that did not hunt at all, even though most other studies had concluded that only about half of pet cats ever bring any prey home; fewer in urban areas, slightly more in the countryside.[3] The reason for this bias appeared to be in the design of the questionnaire, which encouraged Mammalaction members to submit their results only if their cat had brought in some prey during the five months of the survey.

Despite these shortcomings, the figure of 275 million is still widely quoted by many influential organizations, including the Royal Society for the Protection of Birds, the British Trust for Ornithology and the Bat Conservation Trust. When the figures were first announced in 2001, British wildlife TV presenter Chris Packham, a self-confessed 'cat-hater', appeared on BBC radio describing cats as 'sly, greedy, insidious murderers', and calling for them to be 'shot'; more recently, he asserted that all cats should be given 'ASBOs' (Anti-Social Behaviour Orders).[4] Similarly, when the University of Georgia's Kitty Cams revealed that a small minority of cats in Athens, Georgia, were killing a couple of lizards each week, the *Los Angeles Times*' Paul Whitfield wrote, 'So they're slaughtering wildlife, and you can't trust them. Seems like grounds for government action . . . Present owners can keep their cats. But as the tabbies die off, so does cat ownership.'[5] A January 2013 *New York Times* report of an estimate of predation by cats across the United States made by scientists from the Smithsonian Institute generated more email responses than any other story that day. The headline of another report on the same study read, 'Domestic Cats are Destroying the Planet'.[6]

Looking at this situation more objectively, the impact cats actually have on wildlife varies enormously from one type of environment to another. The most dramatic effects undoubtedly occur on small, oceanic islands on to which cats have been introduced. Many of these islands contain unique fauna that have evolved due to their isolation from the mainland. Others are refuges for seabirds that raise their young in safety there, undisturbed by predators. When cats appear, they can cause havoc. Occasionally, these cats have been pets, perhaps the most notorious being the lighthouse-keeper's cat that killed the last specimen of the Stephens Island wren in 1894.[7] Usually, however, the cats have either escaped from visiting ships, or have been deliberately introduced to suppress pests such as rabbits, rats and mice – usually accidental introductions in themselves. Lacking competition from other mammalian predators, cats can thrive in such environments, making easy prey of the local wildlife that has previously been unexposed to such hunters. With such an abundance of food available, cats breed prolifically, producing large populations of ferals. Perhaps counterintuitively, these feral cats sometimes do most harm on islands where they are not the only introduced animal: some researchers have suggested that an abundance of house mice, for example, provides the cats with a stable diet, thereby enabling them to increase in numbers to the point where they can exterminate the more vulnerable local wildlife.

We must keep the effects of feral cats in perspective, even when considering the island cat situation. Island species account for 83 per cent of all documented extinctions of mammals: isolated from many of the diseases, parasites and predators that plague their relatives on the mainland, these species are intrinsically vulnerable. Yet scientists have been able to implicate feral cats in only about 15 per cent of such extinctions and, even in these, other introduced predators have to take their share of the responsibility. Foxes, cane toads, mongooses and especially rats can be equally, if not more, devastating. Black ('ship') rats probably do more damage than any other introduced predator, and because cats are effective hunters of this species, their presence can sometimes even be beneficial.

For example, on Stewart Island off the coast of New Zealand, feral cats have existed for more than 200 years side by side with an endangered flightless parrot, the kakapo. These cats feed mainly on introduced species of rats (black and brown), which have been held responsible for the extinction of several other species of birds in the same region. Removal of the cats in such places might lead to an increase in the rat population, and could therefore potentially lead to the extinction of the kakapo.[8] However, we cannot deny that eradicating cats from islands has in some cases led to dramatic recoveries in the populations of threatened vertebrate species: examples include iguanas on Long Cay in the West Indies, deer mice on Coronados

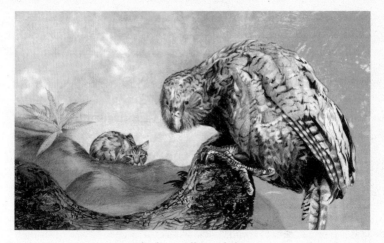

A feral cat stalking a kakapo

Island in the Gulf of California, and a rare bird, the saddleback, on Little Barrier Island in New Zealand.

On the mainland, feral cats can undoubtedly be effective predators in some locations, but their impact is much more difficult to quantify. Nevertheless, the sheer numbers of stray and feral cats in the world, somewhere between 25 and 80 million in the United States[9] and around 12 million in Australia, suggests that they might have a major impact. Feral domestic cats are 'alien' predators throughout much of their range: indeed, they have been in the United States for less than 500 years. In most places where they have been introduced, cats seem able to compete quite effectively with local, 'native' predators, even though the latter should be better adapted to local conditions.

Feral cats do have three advantages over other predators. First, their numbers are constantly added to by cats straying from the pet population, or emigrating from farms where cats are still kept for pest control. Second, because they are generally less fearful of humans than many wild carnivores, they can better take advantage of food accidentally provided by people, such as at rubbish tips, to sustain themselves when prey is hard to find. Third, because they resemble pet cats in everything but behaviour, they attract the sympathy of many people, some of whom devote their lives to providing them with food and even veterinary care.

The most scientific attention to this problem, and perhaps the most public outcry, has occurred in Australia and New Zealand, where cats seem to be relatively recent introductions.[10] In both countries, many small marsupials and flightless birds have undoubtedly gone extinct, but the main culprit may be loss of habitat, not predation. Even where predators have been a major factor, the responsibility is often shared among cats, rats, introduced red foxes and (in Australia) dingoes. According to Christopher R. Dickman, of the Institute of Wildlife Research in Sydney, 'the effects of cats on prey communities remain speculative'.[11]

In some situations, cats can be a major cause of decline; in others, they may be protective. Predation from cats appears to have made a major contribution to the decline of some threatened native Australian species, such as the eastern barred bandicoot in Victoria and the rufous hare-wallaby in the Northern Territory. On the other hand, in a study of remnant patches of forest in suburban Sydney, the presence of cats *protected* tree-nesting birds, apparently because the cats were hunting rats and other animals that would normally have raided the nests.[12] Cats can also suppress the numbers of introduced mammals, such as mice and rabbits, that compete for food with the native wildlife.

Despite the equivocal evidence, several Australian municipalities have pressed ahead with measures to reduce the impact of cats on wildlife. These include confinement of cats to owners' premises at all times, prohibiting cat ownership in new suburbs, night-time curfews, and impounding free-roaming cats in declared conservation areas – even though only the last of these would control the activities of the feral cats that are probably causing the most damage.

Researchers have yet to evaluate the effectiveness of such control measures comprehensively. However, a recent survey of four areas of the City of Armadale, Western Australia, suggests that cats may not be the primary culprits after all. One area in this study was a no-cat zone, where cat ownership was strictly prohibited; the second was a curfew zone, in which pet cats had to be belled during the day and kept indoors at night; and in the other two areas cats went unrestricted. The main prey species in the area were brushtail possums, southern brown bandicoots and the mardo, a small predatory marsupial a little bigger than a mouse, which was predicted to be the most vulnerable of the three to cat predation. In fact, researchers found more mardos in the unregulated areas than in the curfew or no-cat areas, and saw little difference in the numbers of the other two prey species across any of the sites. What variation there was could be best accounted for by the amount of vegetation available: in other words, habitat degradation, and not cats, may have been the major factor limiting the numbers of small marsupials. The draconian control measures against pet cats had, at least in this one location, produced no benefit to wildlife.[13]

How much long-term damage to wildlife do pet cats cause? Estimates of what proportion of pet cats ever kill anything vary considerably, but figures of between 30 per cent and 60 per cent seem reasonable, even when those cats kept indoors without access to prey are excluded. We have little reliable information on how many animals those cats that do hunt actually catch, because such events are rarely observed. What is usually recorded is not how many animals are caught, but how many are brought back dead to their owners – and then a 'correction factor' is used to calculate the number killed, to account for those prey items that are eaten where they were killed, or simply discarded. The number brought home per cat is often quite low: for example, 4.4 animals per cat, per year in a recent UK study.[14]

The proportion of prey brought home has been calculated only twice, coming out at around 30 per cent (although one of the two studies examined only eleven cats). Recently, a new study in the United States has provided a much more detailed picture, both metaphorically and literally, as the cats were fitted with Kitty Cams, lightweight video camcorders that provided a view of everywhere they went for a week or more. These cats took home around a quarter of their prey, they ate another quarter, and left the remaining half uneaten at the capture site. What may make this study somewhat atypical is that the main prey taken was a lizard, the Carolina anole, which many cats find unappetizing. In places where the main prey consists of mammals – such as the more palatable woodmouse commonly taken in the UK – both the proportion brought home and the proportion eaten might well be higher.

Once we take these 'correction factors' into account, and the figures are scaled up to the whole of an area's cat population, the total number of prey taken can at first sight seem alarming. The Mammal Society's figures of 275 million per year might be overstating the case, but between 100 and 150 million may be a reasonable estimate for the entire UK. The recent Smithsonian study produced an estimate of between 430 million and 1.1 billion birds killed annually by pet cats in the mainland United States.[15] Furthermore, individual anecdotes, taken in isolation, do at first glance suggest that cats might be capable of bringing about local exterminations. For example, biologist Rebecca Hughes from Reading University reported that, in the cold winter of 2009–10, 'One cat that lived beside a woodland brought in a blue tit every single day for a fortnight.'[16]

Whether such levels of predation make any significant difference to wildlife populations in the long term is far less easy to assess. To take the blue tit as an example, the UK has an estimated 3.5 million breeding pairs, each producing seven or eight young per year – about 25 million more young birds than would be required to keep the population constant. So, some 25 million blue tits must die during the course of most years. Some do not make it out of the nest and some are victims of predation, but many starve during cold winters because their metabolism runs so quickly that they are barely able to store enough food to keep themselves alive overnight. Some of the birds brought home by the cat referred to above may well have died of natural causes during the night, and were then retrieved by the cat in the morning. In fact, the numbers of blue tits in UK gardens have increased by a quarter over the past fifty years, so pet cats are unlikely to be having any major effect on their numbers year on year. Most of the cat's favourite prey species are equally profligate breeders – in built-up environments in the UK, these include woodmice (fifteen to twenty young per pair per year), brown rats (fifteen to twenty-five), and robins (ten to fifteen).

Rather than contributing to the decline in wildlife populations, cats may simply be killing (or collecting) animals that are in any case not destined to survive for much longer – those that are ill or malnourished. Such animals are by their very nature the easiest to catch. One study that examined the condition of birds brought home by cats tended to confirm this idea: these birds were generally underweight and in poor condition.[17]

Recent evidence shows that garden birds may be evolving strategies to cope with cats. In rural areas, the main predators of European songbirds are usually the sparrowhawk and the kestrel; in urban gardens, the main predator is often the cat. By comparison with their country cousins, common birds living in urban gardens such as sparrows, robins, blue tits and finches were found to wriggle less, were more likely to 'play dead', were less aggressive, and made fewer shrieks and alarm calls, all by comparison with their country cousins. The longer an area had been urbanized, the greater the difference, which suggests that the urban birds had not simply learned about avoiding cats, but had actually evolved a new set of defence mechanisms over the hundred or so generations since large-scale urbanization began in the mid nineteenth century.[18]

What seems to irritate wildlife enthusiasts the most is not that pet cats hunt at all, but that they should not have to hunt, since the majority are well fed by their owners. Cats are therefore often portrayed as committing 'murder', as opposed to other predators, which kill 'legitimately', to survive. Because they are fed, pet cats can exist at a much higher density than they ever could if they had to catch every meal for themselves. Thus, even occasional hunting could have a substantial impact, simply because there are so many cats.

Cats have not yet lost their desire to hunt; too few generations separate them from the rodent controllers of the nineteenth and early twentieth centuries. They will go out hunting even if well fed – in the past, when they were mousers, a single catch did not provide enough calories to allow them to relax between meals – but hunger does affect how intensely they hunt. Feral cats, even those that obtain most of their food from scraps, spend on average twice as much time hunting as pet cats do. Mother cats with kittens to feed will hunt almost continuously if they are not themselves being fed by someone.

By contrast, pet cats rarely hunt 'seriously', often watching potential prey without bothering to stalk it. A hungry cat will pounce several times until the prey either escapes or is caught; a well-fed pet will pounce halfheartedly and then give up, probably explaining why

Feral cats foraging in rubbish bins

pet cats, when they do kill birds, usually succeed only when they target individuals already weakened by hunger or disease. Furthermore, pet cats rarely consume their prey, often bringing it home as if to consume it there, but then abandoning it.

The quality of a cat's diet also affects its desire to hunt. In one recent study conducted in Chile, cats fed on household scraps were four times more likely to kill and eat a mouse than cats fed on modern pet food. In another, cats eating low-quality cat food would break off to chase and kill a rat, but cats eating fresh salmon ignored the same opportunity to hunt.[19] These and other similar observations suggest that cats fed on scraps or nutritionally unbalanced cat food are strongly motivated to hunt, in particular by an impulse that they must supplement their diet to maintain their health. The domestic cat, in common with all its wild felid cousins, has highly specialized nutritional requirements that can be met from only one of two sources: either modern, nutritionally balanced commercial cat food, or prey (see box, p.79, 'Cats are the True Carnivores'). Scraps and low-quality cat food tend to be high in carbohydrates. If eaten day after day, carbohydrates seem to give cats a craving for protein-rich food, which in their world means flesh. Commercial pet foods are of much better quality than they were half a century ago, so most modern pet cats are likely to have received a nutritionally balanced diet every day since they were weaned, and so are unlikely to become prolific hunters. Cats that have been neglected or have strayed at some time in their lives may have been driven to hunt through nutritional necessity: once they have acquired the habit, it may be difficult to lose, so such cats may require extra precautions to prevent them from hunting unnecessarily (see box, 'How Can We Prevent Cats from Hunting?')

HOW CAN WE PREVENT CATS FROM HUNTING?

Surveys show that the large majority of pet cats catch very few birds or mammals. If your cat is part of this majority, then you need not take any countermeasures, unless you happen to live next door to a nature reserve.

If your cat is a prolific hunter, one of the following may reduce its impact:

- *Equip your cat with a belled collar. Although some studies have found little effect, several have shown significant reductions in the number of prey caught, both mammals and birds.*
- *Add a neoprene bib[20] to your cat's collar. This interferes with its ability to pounce and may reduce the number of birds that it catches.*
- *Add an ultrasonic device to your cat's collar to warn potential prey of its approach.*
- *Keep your cat indoors at night. This may reduce the number of mammals it catches, and slightly reduces its own risk of being hit by a car.*
- *Play with your cat, and allow it to 'hunt' prey-like toys. This may reduce its motivation to hunt, although this has never been scientifically evaluated.*

Any collar you put on your cat should be of the snap-open type, as other types could strangle the cat; see www.fabcats.org/owners/safety/collars/info.html for additional information.

Additionally, cat owners can mitigate any damage their cat might cause to the local wildlife by taking positive steps to provide food and refuges. Feeding birds at a cat-proof bird table[21] and building a log pile in the corner of the garden as shelter for small mammals are just two measures that could counteract the effect of the cat's hunting.

*

Of course, we all want to minimize the damage cats do to wildlife. The best approach to this problem will vary depending on what kind of cat we are dealing with, and particularly how closely the cat in question is associated with people. Pets and ferals require different solutions. On oceanic islands, cats are invariably introduced 'aliens', largely or completely unsocialized to people, and occupying a niche that would otherwise have remained vacant, since medium-sized land mammals cannot reach such places without man's help. Whether the cats were introduced deliberately, or are the descendants of escaped ships' cats or settlers' pets does not matter; either way, they are now essentially wild animals. Eradication of these cats, by humane means, is usually the only means whereby each island's unique ecosystem can be restored, although this should not be carried out in isolation: other 'alien' species, such as rats, may themselves decimate the local fauna once they are liberated from the pressure of being preyed on by cats. Perhaps surprisingly, given the publicity that the damage that cats can do receives, only about a hundred such eradications have taken place so far, with thousands more islands still affected by the presence of feral cats.[22] Ultimately, however, widespread humane eradication may be the only way to fully restore fragile island ecosystems.

Minimizing the impact of feral cats on wildlife is much more difficult when they live near pet cats – which, on the mainland, is almost everywhere. We have few reliable estimates on how much damage such feral cats do, mainly because they are rarely the only predator present, competing with both their native equivalents and also introduced species such as the red fox and the rat. Feral cats, even those that obtain some of their food from handouts or scavenging, are of necessity much more 'serious' hunters than the vast majority of pet cats, and so per capita must be responsible for more damage to wildlife.

In many locations, human activity has reduced areas of conservation interest ('biodiversity value') into small 'islands', albeit islands surrounded by concrete rather than water. For example, urbanization has broken the once-contiguous heathland habitat of the sand lizard on the south coast of England into fragments, making each isolated population highly vulnerable to extinction by brush fires. In other, similarly fragmented habitats feral cats could potentially cause considerable damage, although well-documented examples remain scarce.

Eradication of feral cats from areas where they coexist with pet cats is both problematic and ultimately unproductive. Unless all pet cats are curfewed, or kept permanently indoors, or compulsorily registered and microchipped, it is virtually impossible to be certain that a cat that has been trapped is feral, particularly if it is somewhat socialized to people. Even if local eradication were achieved, the niche formerly occupied by the feral cats would still exist, and would soon be filled by stray cats or by ferals migrating from other areas.

Although they rarely say so outright, it is difficult to avoid the impression that conservationists and wildlife enthusiasts would like to exterminate all feral cats. This would account for their vehement objection to Trap-Neuter-Return (TNR) schemes, in which feral cats are, for welfare reasons, neutered and then returned to the site where they were originally trapped. Although such schemes might, in theory, eventually lead to the disappearance of the feral cat population in the locality in question, due to reduced breeding, this has rarely actually been achieved. Un-neutered cats migrate into the area to which the neutered cats have been returned, and soon restore the original breeding capacity. Indeed, such schemes can inadvertently generate 'hotspots' for the abandonment of unwanted cats, their owners believing, possibly mistakenly, that the cat will join the feral colony and be allowed to share its food. Even where the site is fairly well isolated and trapping and neutering are maintained for years, the feral cats rarely disappear completely.

I studied one such colony that had formed around a partly derelict hospital in the south of England, originally built in the nineteenth century as an insane asylum, and – as such places usually were – located several miles from the nearest village. Prior to the introduction of TNR, the colony had consisted of several hundred cats and kittens; several years later, numbers had reduced to about eighty cats. Many of these were members of the original colony, now neutered and gradually becoming elderly, but at least one tomcat and several females had evaded capture and were continuing to breed. In addition, pregnant females would appear periodically, presumably having been 'dumped' there – although, being well socialized, these were easy enough to trap and re-home via a humane charity. Overall, the colony stayed the same size, residual breeding and immigration replacing those of the original

Neutered feral cats at the hospital

group that were dying of old age, sustained by the food provided by the dwindling band of remaining long-stay patients.

Supporters of TNR maintain that once a colony has been neutered and its food supply stabilized, its impact on wildlife should reduce. However, little reliable evidence has been found to support this position. The cats presumably continue to hunt: better nutrition may result in less consumption of prey items, but, having caught the habit of hunting every day, they nevertheless continue to kill and harass wildlife. However, the neutered cats do at least occupy space that, had they been euthanized rather than neutered and returned, would have soon become occupied by other cats. From the perspective of assigning finite resources to wildlife conservation, it may be better for conservationists to allow cat enthusiasts to assist in managing a cat population, if it is not causing catastrophic damage to wildlife. The much-touted alternative, the extermination of feral cats on a regular basis, is likely to alienate those of their supporters who care equally for cats and wildlife.

Since feral cats present such a slippery target where they coexist with free-roaming pets, conservationists tend to concentrate their efforts on restricting owned cats – this, despite an almost complete lack of hard evidence that pet cats are causing significant and lasting damage to wildlife. In an apparent attempt to fill the loophole caused by this lack of evidence, scientists at the University of Sheffield have proposed a 'fear effect' hypothesis: that pet cats suppress breeding in bird populations, their very presence triggering fear responses in the birds that inhibit foraging and depress fertility.[23] However, this theory discounts the idea that urban birds seem to have evolved strategies to overcome the impact of cats. Furthermore, the mere presence of one lazy and ineffective predator must surely have less impact than the fear engendered by rats, magpies, crows and other 'serious' predators of small birds and their young.

When targeting pet cats for criticism, bird enthusiasts often fail to mention that other predators may make much more of an impact on bird numbers than cats do. Magpies, major predators of songbird nests, have tripled in number in the UK since 1970 to between 1 and 2 million individuals – with most of the increase occurring in towns where, coincidentally, cats have also increased. The Royal Society for the Protection of Birds – pledged to protect magpies, as well as their prey – investigated this increase in case it was tied to reductions in songbird populations over the same period. They concluded:

> The study ... found no evidence that increased numbers of magpies have caused declines in songbirds and confirms that populations of prey species are not determined by the numbers of their predators. [Presumably, these include domestic cats, although they don't say so specifically.] Availability of food and suitable nesting sites are probably the main factors limiting songbird populations ... We discovered that the loss of food and habitats caused by intensive farming have played a major role in songbird declines.[24]

Cats rarely catch magpies, but they may inadvertently assist smaller birds by suppressing the populations of some of their other enemies.

A magpie killing a blackbird chick

The UK has at least ten brown rats for every cat, and while rats are omnivores, their impact on bird and small mammal populations around the world has been well documented. Moreover, since young brown rats are among cats' favourite prey items,[25] if cats suppress rat populations in towns, they may indirectly be helping birds. Cat owners may therefore be able to do more for wildlife by improving habitats for small birds (and mammals other than rats) in their gardens than by confining their cats indoors (see box, p. 249, 'How Can We Prevent Cats from Hunting?').

Such precautions may not be enough to silence the cat's most vocal critics. Furthermore, most of today's owners revile or endure, rather than admire, their cat's hunting prowess. Unlike their ancestors, pet cats no longer need to hunt to stay healthy, so a reduction in their desire to hunt will do them no harm. Ideally, the cat of the future will have less inclination to hunt than the cat of today.

11

Cats of the Future

We have more pet cats today than at any time in history. Over the past half-century, the growth of organizations devoted to re-homing unwanted cats, together with advances in veterinary medicine and in nutritional science, have ensured that today's cats are far healthier than cats as a whole have ever been. Despite these auspicious trends, we now also see signs that their very popularity is adversely affecting their well-being. These effects will increase in the coming decades, so we cannot take the future of the cat for granted.

Humans are tending to cats' physical needs to an extent never experienced before. However, cats' emotional needs are still the cause of widespread misapprehensions. Cats are widely perceived as being far more socially adaptable than they actually are. Owners polled for a recent survey said that half of pet cats avoid (human) visitors to the house; almost all pet cats either get into fights with cats from neighbouring houses, or avoid any contact with them; and half of the cats that share households with other cats either fight or avoid one another.[1] Research confirms that cats find such conflicts highly stressful: they experience fear during the event itself, and anxiety in anticipation of the next encounter. They are constantly hypervigilant for cues we are unaware of, such as the odour of a rival cat. Chronic anxiety can lead to deteriorating health and may reduce life expectancy. Unfortunately, we do not know enough about how to mitigate this situation, made worse by the ever-increasing number of cats kept as pets.

Owners also face increasing pressure to keep cats indoors, either permanently or just at night. Charities concerned with cats' welfare point out that urban environments present many hazards, including injury from traffic, wounds from fighting with other cats, exposure to diseases and parasites, and accidental poisoning. Most prominent are conservationists and wildlife enthusiasts, who call stridently for cats to be kept indoors to prevent them from killing wildlife. Perhaps surprisingly, we have very little research on whether cats are adversely affected by being kept in one small area for all or part of the day, although it seems that some cats adapt much more readily to confinement than others.

Looking ahead, there has been virtually no discussion anywhere on what the cat of the future might be like. We seem to share an unvoiced assumption that because cats have always been around, they always will be; but, as discussed in previous chapters, their circumstances are changing rapidly, and we cannot take their continued popularity for granted.

A century ago, the world was often, by today's standards, excessively cruel to cats, even those lucky enough to be chosen as pets; tying a lighted firecracker to a kitten's tail was considered amusing, and 'kicking the cat' was so unremarkable as to pass into the vernacular as a metaphor for releasing frustration. Sentiments have changed radically since then: for example, in 2012 two Las Vegas teenagers accused of drowning two kittens in a cup of water were charged with animal cruelty, now considered a felony in Nevada.[2] We now have the resources to minimize cruelty – even if this is not uniformly exercised – and at the same time to curb cat populations by humane means.

Cats are prolific breeders. Left to their own devices, females produce many more kittens than are needed to keep the population stable, and in the past most of these kittens would have died before reaching adulthood, their lives not only short but also fairly miserable. Indeed, many unwanted kittens were drowned by their owners, and many of those that survived succumbed to debilitating respiratory diseases for which no vaccine yet existed. Over the past few decades, humane charities have promoted the use of neutering as the method of choice for restricting the numbers of house cats, setting themselves the goal of ensuring that every cat and kitten should find a loving home. To date, only a few more affluent locations have achieved this goal. This can be compensated for by the transfer of cats from areas where neutering rates are low, so that they can be re-homed in areas where cats – or at least young, appealing cats – are in short supply. Some owners, now increasingly branded as irresponsible, still allow their young female cats to have one litter before they get them spayed. Others are caught unaware because on modern diets females can conceive at six months old, whereas many owners do not get around to thinking about neutering until towards the end of their cat's first year. Other kittens may enter the pet population when stray females are rescued when they are pregnant or are found with new-born litters. Conversely, undoctored tomcats are rarely kept as pets nowadays, at least in urban areas (raising the question as to where the six-month-old females find fathers for their litters). For the time being, we have more cats available for adoption than owners wanting them, but as neutering becomes ever more widely practised, kittens, especially, can become difficult to find.

If at some time in the future random-bred cats do become difficult to find, then prospective owners will presumably turn to pedigree cat breeders, who currently supply no more than 15 per cent of pet cats, and less than 10 per cent in many countries. Luckily for cats, few of the mutations that have produced such extremes of appearance in the domestic dog seem to have been incorporated into cat breeds. The few that have, such as the dwarfing gene responsible for the munchkin cat's short legs, have been carefully scrutinized by geneticists anxious that cats should not go down the same road as dogs. However, some of the most popular pedigree cat breeds have begun to succumb to the afflictions of breeding for appearance, as well as the side effects of too much inbreeding (see box overleaf, 'Pedigree Cats: The Dangers of Breeding for Extremes'). Moreover, the behaviour of pedigree cats, while it differs somewhat from that of random-bred house cats, provides little variation that is not already found in random-bred cats, a situation quite different from that in dogs, where many breeds were originally derived for their behaviour, not their appearance. Simply replacing random-bred cats with cats from today's pedigree breeds will not only perpetuate those genetic problems that already exist, but also it cannot solve the problems that the cat is facing as a species.

PEDIGREE CATS: THE DANGERS OF BREEDING FOR EXTREMES

In the past few years, the media have paid much attention to problems created for pedigree dogs by indiscriminate breeding for looks.[13] *The same plight for cats has been less newsworthy, but similar issues might appear in the future – indeed, some are already evident.*

Breeding for appearance can create two problems. First, breeding for exaggerated features may cause the animal distress or result in chronic ill health. Among cat breeds, the classic example is the snub-nosed or peke-faced (technically, 'brachycephalic') Persian. Traditionally, Persian cats have faces that are somewhat rounder ('doll-faces') than those of ordinary cats, and were derived from a variety of longhaired breeds, including the Turkish Angora. The mutation that causes the flat face appeared in the 1940s in the United States and was quickly adopted as the ideal for the breed. Further selection led to the nose becoming even shorter and higher in the skull, to the point where the nose became squashed between the eyes; this extreme form is now discouraged by the breed clubs. All brachycephalic cats are prone to breathing difficulties, eye problems and malformed tear ducts, and difficulties when giving birth, with a high proportion of stillborn kittens. Pet owners today seem to prefer the traditional style of Persian, as reflected in a fourfold drop in registrations of peke-faced Persians in the UK between 1988 and 2008.

A peke-faced Persian

Other breeds face health concerns as a result of breeding: surprisingly, one, the Manx, has been exhibited in cat shows for more than a century. The gene that gives the Manx cat its stumpy tail is essentially a defect, often lethal: a kitten that has inherited two copies of this gene, one from its father and one from its mother, is likely to die before birth. Cats with one copy of the gene grow tails of varying lengths, and some with partial tails are prone to arthritis that may produce severe pain. The gene can also affect the growth of not just the tail but also the back, damaging the spinal cord and causing a form of spina bifida. Manx cats are also prone to bowel disease.

A different skeletal malformation characterizes the 'squitten' or 'twisty cat' (not a recognized breed), which has incomplete development of the long bone in the front legs, resulting in the paw being twisted and attached at the shoulder, a deformity that has been likened to the effects of Thalidomide on human infants. Such cats cannot walk, run or dig properly, and cannot defend themselves; they do, however, sit upright in a 'cute' manner, which presumably accounts for their 'twisted' appeal.

In other breeds, problems caused by breeding for appearance are less obvious. For example, the gene that gives the Scottish Fold its characteristic lop-eared appearance also causes malformations of the cartilage elsewhere in the body, and as a result many of these cats develop severely painful joints at a relatively early age.

The second type of problem arises as a side effect of so-called line breeding, which is effectively inbreeding. The quest for the perfect specimen can result in the perpetuation of genes that disadvantage the cats that carry them – genes that would be quickly selected out if they appeared in alley cats, because they must impede hunting. For example, many Siamese cats have poor stereoscopic vision due to a lack of nerves in their brains to compare signals from the left and right eyes. As a result, they may see double, or one eye may shut down completely, sometimes causing a squint to develop. Another separate malformation in the retina leads to their vision blurring every time they move their heads. In wishing to sustain the Siamese cat's distinctive appearance, breeders inadvertently allowed this defect to continue from generation to generation.

A reduced motivation to hunt and kill prey is just one of several factors that will enable cats to adapt better to twenty-first-century living. Allowing a little anthropomorphism: if cats could write themselves a wish list for self-improvement, a set of goals to allow them to adapt to the demands we place on them, it might look something like this:

• *To get along better with other cats, so that social encounters are no longer a source of anxiety.*

- *To understand human behaviour better, so that encounters with unfamiliar people no longer feel like a threat.*
- *To overcome the compulsion to hunt even on a full stomach.*

The corresponding requests from owners:

- *I'd like to have more than one cat at a time, and for my cats to be company – not just for me, but also for one another.*
- *I wish my cat didn't disappear into the bedroom to urinate on the carpet every time I have visitors.*
- *I wish my cat didn't bring gory 'presents' through the cat-flap.*

We currently know of two ways to achieve these goals. First, we can train individual cats to change how they interpret and react to their surroundings. The advantage of this approach is that its effects would be immediate; the disadvantage is that it must be repeated for each successive generation of cats. Second, because the cat's genome is not yet fully domesticated, there is still scope to genetically adapt their behaviour and personalities to twenty-first-century lifestyles. The benefits of selective breeding towards our goals will become apparent only after several decades, but these changes would be permanent.

Cats are intelligent, and (up to a point) adaptable animals, so we can achieve some of these goals through directing cats' learning – providing them with the right experiences to enable them to conform to the demands placed upon them. This will almost certainly involve a certain amount of formal 'training'. Although most dog owners know that they must train their dogs to make them socially acceptable, such a thought scarcely crosses cat owners' minds, or if it does, they reject it as only appropriate for 'performing cats'. Providing the right sort of experiences during the first few months of a kitten's life most likely produces long-lasting effects, considering that this is the time when cats' personalities are forged, but more research is needed into precisely what those experiences should be.

The genetic basis for the cat's behaviour must have changed as it adapted to living alongside man, even though the details are now lost in prehistory and are ultimately impossible to trace. It is feasible that the average cat's personality is still changing, as some personality types fit modern conditions better than others. However, such haphazard change will not come about quickly enough to keep up with the pace of change that we now demand of our pets, as our own life-styles change, so more direct intervention will be needed if the cat is to adapt at an acceptable pace.

We value our cats for their affectionate behaviour, yet this trait has rarely been deliberately bred for – and then, only as an afterthought. This trait must have been accidentally selected for in the past, as loving cats get the best food![4] Nevertheless, 'unfriendly' tendencies have persisted even among pet cats: in the 1980s experiments that defined the cat's socialization period, the experimenters noted 'a small but constant percentage of the cats (about 15 per cent) seem to have a temperament that is resistant to socialization.'[5] Even today, cats seem to possess a large range of variation in the genes that underpin temperament, learning and behaviour, providing the raw material for work on selective breeding for behaviour and 'personality', rather than just appearance.

As cat owners, we have various resources available to help individual cats adapt to today's crowded conditions, but many people seem unaware of many of these. Our challenge is to use these tools early in the cat's life, when it is still learning about its surroundings. The second and third months of life are the crucial period, during which the growing kitten learns how to interact socially – with other cats, with people and with other household animals. As we have seen, it is during this period of its life that the cat learns both how to identify its social partners, and how to behave towards them in a way that will produce the desired outcome – a friendly tail-up, a lick behind the ear, a bowl of food or a cuddle. More generally, this is also the time when cats learn how to cope with the unexpected – whether to be curious, accepting the risk of approaching and inspecting new things, or whether to play it safe and run away. Research shows that a cat's capacity to take risks can be subject to a strong genetic influence, but learning must also play a part.

A cat that has had only limited exposure to different kinds of people during its second and third months of life may become timid, retreating to its safe place whenever people it regards as unfamiliar come to the house. Without exposure to people before eight weeks of age a cat will become fearful of humans in general. However this is not the end of the process of socialization, just the necessary beginning: kittens must have the opportunity to make their own connections with different types of humans.

Many kittens homed at eight weeks may miss out on useful socialization experience with other kittens. The third month of life is when play with other kittens peaks, and feral kittens maintain strong social links with their peer group until they are about six months old. Veterinary surgeons often (sensibly) advise that kittens should be kept indoors for the first few weeks after homing, to prevent them from straying: however, if there are no other cats in the house, they may miss out on a crucial phase in the development of their social skills.

Individual cats adopt different strategies when encountering the unfamiliar. Many withdraw, hide or climb to a safe vantage point. A minority may become aggressive, perhaps those that have not been given the opportunity to retreat on previous occasions. Their owner may have run after them and scooped them up rather than allow them to withdraw. These cats quickly learn that the stress of an undesired encounter can be prevented by scratching, hissing and biting. Some of these cats develop this tactic even further, preemptively striking out at people they don't know or who have previously been forced on them.

Cats also develop their own preferred tactics for dealing with other cats they do not know. When making their first social encounters as kittens, some simply flee; others attempt to stand their ground, and often get a swipe or worse for their efforts. Few attempt to engage in a friendly greeting, and even fewer find such a greeting reciprocated. Flight or fight thus often becomes the young cat's default response when meeting unfamiliar cats.

Owners who wish to add another cat to their household have an opportunity to manage the introduction to have a positive outcome for all concerned. We cannot take for granted that cats will immediately like one another. The new cat is likely to feel stressed at being suddenly uprooted from its familiar surroundings and dropped into what it perceives as another cat's territory, and the resident cat will probably resent the intrusion. Therefore, it is usually best to start by keeping the new cat in a part of the house that the resident cat rarely uses, allowing it to establish a small 'territory' of its own and getting to know its new owners before facing the challenge of meeting the resident cat face to face. The two cats will undoubtedly be aware of each other's presence, if only by smell, but this will be less stressful at this early stage than being able to see each other. Owners can build up some degree of familiarity between the two cats before a meeting takes place by periodically taking toys and bedding from each of the two cats and introducing them to the other while rewarding that cat with food treats or a game. This builds up a positive emotional link with the other cat's odour. The actual introduction should wait until after both cats no longer show any adverse reaction to the other's smell, and should be carried out in stages, starting with allowing the cats to be together for just a few minutes.[6]

Because cats carry a reputation for being untrainable, most owners are unaware that training can reduce the stress that cats can feel in situations where they would much rather run away. For example, owners can use clicker training (see chapter 6) to entice a cat to walk into its cat carrier, rather than forcing it in.[7] Similar training could help cats overcome their initial fear of other potentially stressful situations – for example, encounters with new people. In general, cats need persuasion, not force, if they are to adopt a calm approach to new situations. If more owners understood the value of training, a great deal of stress could be avoided – for the cats, certainly, but also for the owner, if the cat's stress results in deposits of urine or faeces around the house.

Training can also help cats to adapt to indoor living. Training a cat is a one-on-one activity that is mentally stimulating for the cat, and also enhances the bond between cat and owner. It may also be useful in reducing some of the negatives of keeping a cat indoors. Cats need to express their natural behaviour, and many owners understandably object to the damage to household furnishings that their cats unwittingly cause, for instance when sharpening their claws. In some countries, veterinary surgeons remove the cat's claws surgically, but this may not be in the cat's best interest, and in some countries this intervention is illegal (see box overleaf, 'Declawing'). A cat without claws may not only experience phantom pains from its missing toes, but is also unable to defend itself if attacked by other cats. Training the cat to claw only in specific places is a far more humane and straightforward alternative, especially if the cat has not yet developed a preference for soft furnishings.[8]

DECLAWING

Cats instinctively scratch objects with their front claws. Perhaps they do this to leave behind an odour or a visible sign of their presence, to alert other cats. They may also scratch because their claws are itchy: periodically, the whole of the outside of the claw detaches, revealing a new, sharp claw within. If this is not shed, maybe because the cat is arthritic and finds scratching painful, the whole claw may overgrow and cause the pad to become infected.

Some owners who object to scratch marks on their furniture seek to have its front claws (and occasionally, too, its back claws) removed. Few veterinary procedures excite as much controversy as declawing (known technically as onychectomy). This is regarded as routine in the United States and the Far East, but is illegal in many places, including the European Union, Brazil and Australia.

Declawing is a surgical procedure that involves amputation of the first joint of the cat's toes. The initial pain resulting from the procedure may be controlled with analgesics, but we do not know whether cats subsequently feel phantom pain due to the nerves that have been severed. However, cats and humans have nearly identical mechanisms for feeling pain, and four *out of five people who have fingers amputated have phantom pain, so cats most likely do as well. (I myself experienced phantom pain for more than ten years after most of the nerves in one fingertip were severed in an accident. I learned to ignore the pain because I knew it was meaningless – something cats are unlikely to be able to do.) Declawed cats are more likely to urinate outside their litter trays than other indoor cats, possibly because of the stress of this phantom pain.*

Claws are an essential defence mechanism for cats. While owners of indoor cats will argue that their cat never meets other cats, and so should never need their claws, a declawed cat that is picked up roughly by a person may resort to biting, unable to scratch to indicate its discomfort, and thereby cause a much more significant wound.[9]

Although untested so far, training might also be useful in reducing cats' desire to hunt – or at least curtail their effectiveness as predators of wildlife. We know that when cats appear to be playing with toys, they think they're hunting, but we have no information on whether playing in this way reduces – or, just conceivably, enhances – their desire to hunt for real. If play does have an effect on this desire, how long does the effect last? Would a daily 'hunting' game between owner and cat save the lives of garden birds and mammals? Is it possible to train a cat to inhibit its pounce?

We also know little about how experience affects the hunting habit in general. Cats vary enormously in how keen they are to go out hunting. That the basis for this is mainly genetic is unlikely, since only a few generations have elapsed since all cats had to hunt to obtain the right kind of food. Anecdotally, one of the arguments for allowing a female house cat to have one litter is that this is usually born in the spring, distracting the cat (provided its owners feed it well) from going out hunting and thereby learning its trade. Is there a 'sensitive period' for perfecting predatory skills, after which the desire to hunt is unlikely to develop fully? Further study of this might not only save animals' lives, but also a great deal of aggravation between cat and wildlife enthusiasts.

Today's cats find themselves in a delicate situation. On the one hand, they must adapt to meet our changing needs; on the other, they have a reputation for being a pet that is easy to maintain. Persuading many cat owners to train their cats, to spend that extra time and effort to change their pets' behaviour, may be difficult. As such, we must focus on a genetic shift as well, taking the cat further down the road towards full domestication.

Ideally, cats that are predisposed to adapt to modern living conditions – to achieve the three goals outlined above – should be identified and then prioritized for breeding. This will not be entirely straightforward, since cats' personalities continue to develop after the normal age of neutering, so before any such breeding programme can begin, research will be needed to separate the effects of the desired genes from those of the cat's social environment. Moreover, there is probably no single 'perfect' set of genes that will enable cats to fit all the lifestyles that humankind will demand of them. The ideal indoor cat will almost certainly be genetically distinct from the ideal outdoor cat, since, among other differences, the owner can have far more influence on relationships with other cats if the cat is confined indoors.

We have three potential sources for such genes: moggies, pedigree cats and hybrids. Conventional pedigree cats have been produced almost exclusively for their looks, not their behaviour, so they are unlikely to be a rich source of new behaviour traits.[10] Pedigree cats are derived entirely from cats that have only ever had two functions: to hunt vermin and to be good companions. In most breeds, there seems to have been little direct selection for behaviour, only looks. There are, however, a few interesting exceptions.

The Ragdoll is a semi-longhaired breed that was originally named for its extremely placid temperament. The first examples to be exhibited, bred in the early 1990s, went limp when picked up, almost as if the scruffing reflex was triggered by touch anywhere on the body, not just the back of the neck. It was once rumoured that these cats were insensitive to pain, and animal welfare organizations raised concerns that people might be tempted to toss these cats around like cushions. The breed no longer shows such extreme behaviour, but is still renowned for its easy-going temperament. A similar breed derived from the same original stock, the RagaMuffin, is described thus: 'The only extreme allowed in this breed is its friendly, sociable and intelligent nature. These cats love people and are extremely affectionate.'[11] The genetic basis for these cats' relaxed sociality, at least towards people, is unknown, but could potentially be transferred to other cats by crossbreeding. Unfortunately for their welfare, ragdoll-type cats are reputedly vulnerable to attack from neighbourhood cats, perhaps because they are simply too trusting, and for this reason many breeders advise prospective owners to keep them indoors.

Hybrids, crosses between *Felis catus* and other species, while initially produced mainly for their 'exotic' appearance, have brought new genetic material into the domain of the domestic cat. Their behaviour is often quite distinctive, so hybrids might, at first sight, provide a source of genes influencing behaviour that are not currently found in ordinary domestic cats.

The most widespread of these hybrids, the Bengal cat, may not offer any solution to adapting the domestic cat to the twenty-first century, since its personality appears to have headed back towards that of its wild ancestors. The Bengal is a hybrid between domestic cats and the Asian leopard cat *Prionailurus bengalensis*. The latter species is separated by more than 6 million years of evolution from the domestic cat, and has never been domesticated in its own right; therefore, it would seem an unlikely starting point for a new breed of cat, were it not for its attractive spotted coat (referred to as 'rosettes'). Domestic cats and Asian leopard cats will mate with one another if given no other option, but the resulting offspring are essentially untamable. During the 1970s, repeated breeding between these hybrids and domestic cats produced some offspring that retained the leopard cat's spots on the back and flanks, creating the current Bengal 'breed'.

Unfortunately, many Bengals possess not only wild-type coats, but also wild-type behaviour, as this information from the Bengal Cat Rescue Website confirms:

> This breed has a strong and sometimes dominant personality and although affectionate, lots are not simple lap cats. They can respond aggressively to discipline and to being handled ... Their commonest problems are aggression and spraying ... Also hardly a week goes by when someone doesn't contact me about having bought or adopted a pair that are trying to kill each other ... Bengals enjoy climbing and this includes your clothes and curtains. They like exploring and are no

respecter of ornaments or photographs. Often cat-aggressive, many will terrorise not just their own household but can actively seek out neighbours' cats and enter their homes to hurt them. They are not playing, they mean it.[12]

From the perspective of producing a docile pet, the Asian leopard cat was never going to be a good candidate for hybridization. This species is one of the few small wildcats that is not threatened with extinction; nevertheless, many zoos keep one or two specimens. These animals are, however, virtually untamable: zookeepers report that they are impossible to approach, let alone touch.[13]

From the perspective of seeking genes that could be useful for changing the domestic cat, some of the smaller South American cats could be better candidates for hybridization. In particular, Geoffroy's cat, similar in size to the domestic cat, and the slightly larger margay are often friendly to their keepers when kept in zoos, and might therefore provide genetic material useful to the continued evolution of the domestic cat. The South American cats lost one pair of chromosomes soon after they diverged from the rest of the cat family some 8 million years ago; this *should* make the offspring of a domestic cat and a South American cat sterile, but, surprisingly, hybrids with Geoffroy's cat can be fertile. The resulting 'breed', usually known as the 'Safari', was first created in the 1970s, but is still rare: it is usually still produced by mating the two original species, and the kittens, which grow into extra-large cats, fetch thousands of pounds. Breeding between these first crosses and ordinary domestic cats, the method used to produce the Bengal, seems to produce fertile offspring, but breeders apparently chose not to pursue this option. Hybrids with the margay, once referred to as the 'Bristol', suffer from fertility problems and are apparently no longer bred. The margay is a tree-dwelling cat with double-jointed ankles, enabling it to climb down tree trunks as easily as other cats climb upwards, to hang one-footed from branches like a monkey, and to leap twelve feet from one perch to another: such agility, if passed on to its hybrids, might be appealing, but also excessive for most domestic purposes.

Several other types of cat have been produced through hybridization with other felids, but all have been bred for their 'wild' looks, and none

Bengal cat (above) and Safari cat (beneath)

seem to offer more than curiosity value to the domestic cat's genome. These include the Chausie, a domestic cat crossed with the jungle cat *Felis chaus*, and the Savannah (serval *Leptailurus serval*), as well as many other oddities of doubtful provenance. Some are classified as wild animals rather than as pets, much as wolf–dog hybrids are.[14]

These various hybrid breeds appear more of a side issue than a

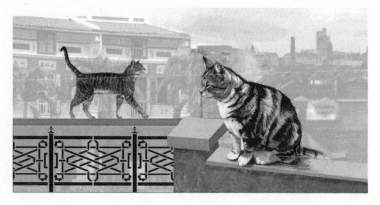

Moggies from the Far East (left) and Western Europe (right)

potential source of new genetic material to enrich the genome of *Felis catus*. The most promising of the species in behavioural terms, the more docile of the South American cats, are genetically incompatible with the domestic cat. The Old World cats that are better matched genetically produce hybrids that are wilder, not calmer, than today's moggies, so have little to offer.

Existing variation within *Felis catus* seems to be the best starting point for the completion of the cat's domestication. Plenty of modern cats combine an easy-going nature with a disinclination to hunt. Research has not yet indicated precisely how much of this variation is underpinned by genetics, but a significant proportion must be. Our goals should be to identify those individual cats with the best temperaments and to ensure that their progeny are available to become tomorrow's pets.

One potential source of genetic variation has only recently emerged. Although house cats the world over are superficially similar, their DNA reveals that they are genetically distinct – as different under the skin as, say, a Siamese and a Persian are on the surface. Interbreeding between, for example, ordinary pet cats from China with their counterparts from the UK or the United States might produce some novel temperaments, some of which might be better suited to indoor life, or be more sociable, than any of today's cats.

*

Selection for the right temperament among house cats requires delib-erate intervention; natural evolutionary processes, which have served the cat well so far, will not be enough. One obstacle is the increasingly widespread practice of neutering cats before they breed. With so many unwanted cats euthanized every year, arguing against the widespread use of this procedure is difficult. Still, if taken too far, widespread neutering is likely to favour unfriendly cats over friendly. Encourag-ing owners not to allow their cats to produce any offspring whatsoever prevents all the genes that these cats carry from being passed on to the next generation. Some of those genes have contributed to making those cats into valued pets.

When almost every pet house cat has been neutered – a situation that already applies in some parts of the UK – then we must have concern for the next generations of cats. These will then mainly be the offspring of those that live on the fringes of human society – feral males, stray females, as well as the female cats owned by people who either do not care whether their cat is neutered or not, or have an ethical objection to neutering. The qualities that allow most ferals and strays to thrive and produce offspring are, unfortunately, those same behaviours we want to eliminate: wariness of people and effectiveness at self-sustaining hunting.

These cats will undoubtedly adapt their behaviour to cope with whatever situations they find themselves in, but they are also likely to be genetically slightly 'wilder' than the average pet cat – therefore dis-tinctly different from the 'ideal' pet cat. Initially, the difference will probably be small, since some of the breeding cats will be strays that are genetically similar to pet cats. But as the decades pass, as fewer and fewer reproductively intact cats are available to stray, most of the kittens born each year will come from a long line of semi-wild cats – since these are the only cats that are able to breed freely. Thus the widespread adoption of early neutering by the most responsible cat owners risks pushing the domestic cat's genetics back gradually towards the wild, away from their current domesticated state.

A study that I conducted in 1999 suggests that such extrapolation cannot be dismissed as science fiction.[15] In one area of Southampton, we found that more than 98 per cent of the pet cat population had been neutered. So few kittens were being born that potential cat owners had to travel outside the city to obtain their cats. This situation had clearly existed for some time: from talking to the owners of the older cats, we calculated that the cat population in that area had last been self-sustaining some ten years previously, in the late 1980s. We located ten female pets in the area that were still being allowed to breed and tested the temperament of their kittens after homing, when the kittens were six months old. Our hypothesis was that feral males must have fathered many of these kittens, since so few intact males were being kept as pets in the area, and all of these were young and unlikely to compete effectively with the more wily ferals. We found that, on average, the kittens in those ten litters were much less willing to settle on their owners' laps than kittens born in another area of the city that still had a significant number of undoctored pet tomcats. There was no systematic difference in the way these two groups of kittens had been socialized, and the mother cats in the two areas were indistinguishable in temperament. We therefore deduced that even if only one of the two parents comes from a long line of ferals, the kittens will be less easy to socialize than if both parents are pets. The study was too small to draw any firm conclusions, but in the years since it was carried out, blanket neutering has become more widespread, and so the cumulative effects of this on the temperament of kittens should be becoming more obvious.

Neutering is an extremely powerful selection pressure, the effects of which have been given little consideration. At present, it is the only humane way of ensuring that there are as few unwanted cats as possible, and it is unlikely ever to become so widely adopted that the house cat population begins to shrink. However, over time it is likely to have unintended consequences. Consider a hypothetical situation. A century or more ago, when feline surgery was still crude, society generally accepted that most cats would reproduce. Imagine that a highly contagious parasite had appeared which sterilized cats of both sexes while they were still kittens, but otherwise left them unaffected, so that they lived as long as an unaffected cat. Any cats that happened to be resistant to that parasite would be the only cats able to breed – so within a few years the parasite, deprived of susceptible hosts, would die out.

The only significant difference between such a hypothetical parasite and neutering is that the latter does not require a host (a cat) to continue: it lives as an idea and so is detached from its effects.[16] Because neutering inevitably targets those cats that are being best cared for, it must logically hand the reproductive advantage to those cats that are least attached to people, many of which are genetically predisposed to remain unsocialized. We must consider the long-term effects of neutering carefully: for example, it might be better for the cats of the future as a whole if neutering programmes were targeted more at ferals, which are both the unfriendliest cats and also those most likely to damage wildlife populations.

We need a fresh approach to cat breeding. Pedigree cats are bred largely for looks, not with the primary goal of ensuring an optimal temperament – although an adequate temperament is, of course, taken into account in the majority of breeds. Moggies are under siege from neutering; even if this widespread practice is not making each successive generation a little wilder than the previous, it is highly unlikely to be having the opposite effect. So while cats' looks and welfare both have their champions, the cat's future has none.

Then again, why should it? Cats have always outnumbered potential owners. Why should that situation change? Cats have become more popular, not less, so there should be more homes available for them, not fewer, than there were a few decades ago. Apart from the (significant) minority of cat-haters, the general public is more tolerant of cats than of dogs. We cannot guarantee, however, that these apparent givens will continue.

Recent decades have witnessed immense changes to the way dogs are kept, especially in urban areas, with a proliferation of 'clean up after your dog' regulations, no-dog parks and legislation aimed at protecting the public from dog bites. We expect dogs to behave in a much more controlled and civilized way than they did half a century ago. Are similar restrictions on cat-keeping just around the corner? Will gardeners and wildlife enthusiasts unite to produce legislation that restricts cats to their owners' property? If such pressures do appear, they will be easier to head off if cat-lovers are already taking steps towards producing a more socially acceptable cat. At the same time, the cats themselves will benefit if they find it easier to cope with the vagaries of their owners' social lives.

Ultimately, the future of cats lies in the hands of those who breed them – not those whose eye is primarily on success in the show ring, but those who can be persuaded that an improved temperament, not good looks, should be the goal. The genetic material is available, although more science is needed to devise the temperament tests that will locate which individual cats carry it; many cats that appear well-adapted to life with people will have received an optimal upbringing, rather than being anything special genetically. The relevant genes are probably scattered all over the globe, so ideally we need collaboration between cat enthusiasts in different parts of the world.

Such human-friendly cats, however cute, are unlikely ever to command much of a price. Expectations that non-pedigree kittens should be free, or nearly so, will take a long time to die out. Commercial breeding of non-pedigree cats may never be viable. Well-adjusted kittens need a wealth of early experience that even some pedigree breeders struggle to provide. Providing this level of care is cost-effective only if kittens are bred in people's homes, the very type of environment into which they will move when they become pets.

Meanwhile, the way that cats are socialized has much room for improvement. Both breeders and owners can play a part in this, since kittens adapt to their surroundings throughout their second and third months of life. In this context, the continuing policy of some cat breeders' associations to prohibit homing until a kitten is twelve weeks of age demands careful scrutiny: it may provide extra socialization with littermates, but often at the cost of learning about different kinds of people, and the development of a robust strategy for dealing with the unfamiliar. For adult cats, training, both in the general sense of providing the right learning experiences as well as teaching them how to behave calmly in specific situations, could improve each cat's lot considerably, if only its value were more widely appreciated.

Finally, we must continue to research why some cats are strongly motivated to hunt, while the majority are content to doze in their beds. Science has not yet revealed to what extent such differences are due to early experience, and how much to genetics, but ultimately it should be possible to breed cats that are unlikely to feel the need to become predators, now that we can easily provide them with all the nutrition they need.

Cats need our understanding – both as individual animals that need our help to adjust to our ever-increasing demands, and also as a species that is still in transition between the wild and the truly domestic. If we can agree to support them in both these ways, cats will be assured a future in which they are not only popular and populous, but also more relaxed, and affectionate, than they are today.

Further Reading

Most of my source material for this book has consisted of papers in academic journals, which are often difficult to access for those without a university affiliation. I've included references to the most important of these in the notes, with web links if they appear to be in the public domain. For those readers who wish to take their study of cats further without first requiring a degree in biology, I can recommend the following books, most of them written by knowledgeable academics but with a more general audience in mind.

The Domestic Cat: The Biology of Its Behaviour, edited by Professors Dennis Turner and Patrick Bateson, is now available in three editions; all are published by Cambridge University Press, the most recent in 2013. These books consist of chapters written by experts in different aspects of cat behaviour.

My own *The Behaviour of the Domestic Cat*, 2nd edition (Wallingford: CAB International, 2012), co-authored by Drs Sarah L. Brown and Rachel Casey, provides an integrated introduction to the science of cat behaviour, aimed at an advanced undergraduate audience. *Feline Behavior: A Guide for Veterinarians* by Bonnie V. Beaver (Philadelphia and Kidlington: Saunders, 2003) is, as its title indicates, aimed at veterinary surgeons and veterinary students.

For the various stages in the history of the cat's life with humankind, Jaromir Malek's *The Cat in Ancient Egypt* (London: British Museum Press, 2006), Donald Engels's *Classical Cats* (London and New York: Routledge, 1999), and Carl Van Vechten's *The Tiger in the House* (London: Cape, 1938) provide specialist accounts.

Carrots and Sticks: Principles of Animal Training (Cambridge: Cambridge University Press, 2008) by Professors Paul McGreevy and

Bob Boakes from the University of Sydney, is a fascinating book of two halves: the first explains learning theory in accessible language, and the second contains fifty case histories of animals (including cats) trained for specific purposes, ranging from film work to bomb detection, each illustrated with colour photographs of the animals and how they were trained.

For cat owners seeking guidance on a problem cat, there is often no substitute for a one-to-one consultation with a genuine expert, but these can be hard to find. The advice given in books by Sarah Heath, Vicky Halls or Pam Johnson-Bennett may be helpful. Celia Haddon's books should also provide some light relief.

Notes

All Web addresses mentioned in the Notes are active as of April 2013.

INTRODUCTION

1. This ratio takes many millions of unowned animals into account, and also incorporates a guess as to the numbers in Muslim countries, where dogs are rare.

2. The Prophet Muhammad is said to have loved his cat Muezza so much that 'he would do without his cloak rather than disturb one that was sleeping on it'. Minou Reeves, *Muhammad in Europe* (New York: NYU Press, 2000), 52.

3. Rose M. Perrine and Hannah L. Osbourne, 'Personality Characteristics of Dog and Cat Persons', *Anthrozoös: A Multidisciplinary Journal of the Interactions of People & Animals* 11 (1998): 33–40.

4. A recognized medical condition, referred to as 'ailurophobia'.

5. David A. Jessup, 'The Welfare of Feral Cats and Wildlife', *Journal of the American Veterinary Medical Association* 225 (2004): 1377–83; available online at www.avma.org/News/Journals/Collections/Documents/javma_225_9_1377.pdf.

6. The People's Dispensary for Sick Animals, 'The State of Our Pet Nation . . .: The PDSA Animal Wellbeing (PAW) Report 2011', Shropshire, 2011; available online at tinyurl.com/b4jgzjk. Dogs scored a little better for social and physical environments (71 per cent) but worse for behaviour (55 per cent).

7. The situation for pedigree dogs in the UK has been summarized in several expert reports, including those commissioned by the Royal Society for the Prevention of Cruelty to Animals (www.rspca.org.uk/allaboutanimals/pets/dogs/health/pedigreedogs/report), the Associate Parliamentary Group for Animal Welfare (www.apgaw.org/images/stories/PDFs/Dog-Breeding-Report-2012.pdf) and the UK Kennel Club in partnership with the re-homing charity DogsTrust (breedinginquiry.files.wordpress.com/2010/01/final-dog-inquiry-120110.pdf).

1. THE CAT AT THE THRESHOLD

1. Darcy F. Morey, *Dogs: Domestication and the Development of a Social Bond* (Cambridge: Cambridge University Press, 2010).

2. Quoted in C. A. W. Guggisberg, *Wild Cats of the World* (New York: Taplinger, 1975), 33–4.

3. These cats are now extinct on Cyprus, displaced by the red fox, another introduction, which is now the only land-based carnivorous mammal on the island.

4. For a more detailed account of these migrations, see Stephen O'Brien and Warren Johnson's 'The Evolution of Cats', *Scientific American* 297 (2007): 68–75.

5. The spelling *lybica* should more correctly be *libyca*, 'from Libya', but most modern accounts use the original (incorrect) version.

6. These 'lake dwellers' built villages on sites that now lie beneath the margins of lakes, but were probably fertile dry land at the time.

7. Frances Pitt (see note 9 below) claimed that the Scottish wildcat would have joined its English and Welsh counterparts in extinction, had it not been for the call-up of the younger gamekeepers to fight in the Great War

8. Carlos A. Driscoll, Juliet Clutton-Brock, Andrew C. Kitchener and Stephen J. O'Brien, 'The Taming of the Cat', *Scientific American* 300 (2009): 68–75; available online at tinyurl.com/akxyn9c.

9. From Frances Pitt, ed., *The Romance of Nature: Wild Life of the British Isles in Picture and Story*, vol. 2 (London: Country Life Press, 1936). Pitt (1888–1964) was a pioneering wildlife photographer who lived near Bridgnorth in Shropshire.

10. Mike Tomkies, *My Wilderness Wildcats* (London: Macdonald and Jane's, 1977).

11. This and the following two quotations are from Reay H. N. Smithers's 'Cat of the Pharaohs: The African Wild Cat from Past to Present', *Animal Kingdom* 61 (1968): 16–23.

12. Charlotte Cameron-Beaumont, Sarah E. Lowe and John W. S. Bradshaw, 'Evidence Suggesting Preadaptation to Domestication throughout the Small Felidae', *Biological Journal of the Linnean Society* 75 (2002): 361–6; available online at www.neiu.edu/~jkasmer/Biol498R/Readings/essay1-06.pdf. In this paper, which came before Carlos Driscoll's DNA study making *cafra* a separate subspecies, the Southern African cats are listed as *Felis silvestris libyca*.

13. Carlos Driscoll et al., 'The Near Eastern Origin of Cat Domestication', *Science (Washington)* 317 (2007): 519–23; available online at www.mobot.

org/plantscience/resbot/Repr/Add/DomesticCat_Driscoll2007.pdf. The data discussed can be found in the online Supplemental Information, Figure S1.

14. David Macdonald, Orin Courtenay, Scott Forbes and Paul Honess, 'African Wildcats in Saudi Arabia', in David Macdonald and Françoise Tattersall, eds., *The WildCRU Review: the Tenth Anniversary Report of the wildlife Conservation Research Unit at Oxford University* (Oxford: University of Oxford Department of Zoology, 1996), 42.

15. The estimate of fifteen to twenty comes from Carlos Driscoll of the Laboratory of Genomic Diversity at the National Cancer Institute in Frederick, Maryland, who is currently working to pinpoint where these genes lie on the cat's chromosomes, and how they may work.

16. See note 13 above.

17. O. Bar-Yosef, 'Pleistocene Connexions between Africa and Southwest Asia: An Archaeological Perspective', *The African Archaeological Review* 5 (1987), 29–38.

18. Carlos Driscoll and his colleagues have discovered five distinct types of mitochondrial DNA in today's domestic cats; mitochondrial DNA is inherited only through the maternal line. The common maternal ancestor of these five cats lived about 130,000 years ago; over the next 120,000 years, her descendants gradually moved around the Middle East and North Africa, their mitochondrial DNA mutating slightly over time, before a few of them happened to become the ancestors of today's pet cats.

2. THE CAT STEPS OUT OF THE WILD

1. J.-D. Vigne, J. Guilane, K. Debue, L. Haye and P. Gérard, 'Early Taming of the Cat in Cyprus', *Science* 304 (2004): 259.

2. James Serpell, *In the Company of Animals: A Study of Human–Animal Relationships*, Canto edn (Cambridge and New York: Cambridge University Press, 1996); Stefan Seitz, 'Game, Pets and Animal Husbandry among Penan and Punan Groups', in Peter G. Sercombe and Bernard Sellato, eds., *Beyond the Green Myth: Borneo's Hunter-Gatherers in the Twenty-First Century* (Copenhagen: NIAS Press, 2007).

3. Veerle Linseele, Wim Van Neer and Stan Hendrickx, 'Evidence for Early Cat Taming in Egypt', *Journal of Archaeological Science* 34 (2007): 2081–90 and 35 (2008): 2672–3; available online at tinyurl.com/aotk2e8.

4. Jaromír Málek, *The Cat in Ancient Egypt* (London: British Museum Press, 2006).

5. This stone coffin is now in the Museum of Egyptian Antiquities in Cairo. On its side, alongside pictures of Ta-Miaut herself and the deities Nephthys and Isis,

are several inscriptions. Words spoken by Osiris: 'Ta-Miaut is not tired, nor weary is the body of Ta-Miaut, justified before the Great God.' Words spoken by Isis: 'I embrace you in my arms, Osiris.' Words spoken by Nephthys: 'I envelop my brother, Osiris Ta-Miaut, the Triumphant.' See www.mafdet. org/tA-miaut.html.

6. At the same time, cats may have been implicated in the first outbreaks of bubonic plague. Although this disease was later spread into Europe by black rats, its natural host is apparently the Nile rat. The disease is usually transmitted from the Nile rat to humans via the rat flea but cat fleas are also sometimes responsible. See Eva Panagiotakopulu, 'Pharaonic Egypt and the Origins of Plague', *Journal of Biogeography* 31 (2004): 269–75; available online at tinyurl.com/ba52zuv.

7. Both genets and mongooses are occasionally kept as domestic pets, but these are genetically unaltered from their wild ancestors, not domesticated animals, and consequently difficult to keep.

8. From *The Historical Library of Diodorus the Sicilian*, Vol. 1, Chap. VI, trans. G. Booth (London: Military Chronicle Office, 1814), 87.

9. Frank J. Yurko, 'The Cat and Ancient Egypt', *Field Museum of Natural History Bulletin* 61 (March–April 1990): 15–23.

10. Mongooses have been introduced to many parts of the world in an attempt to control snakes, especially on islands such as Hawaii and Fiji, which lack other predators of snakes.

11. Angela von den Driesch and Joachim Boessneck, 'A Roman Cat Skeleton from Quseir on the Red Sea Coast', *Journal of Archaeological Science* 10 (1983): 205–11.

12. Herodotus, *The Histories (Euterpe)* 2:60, trans. G. C. Macaulay (London and New York: Macmillan & Co, 1890).

13. Herodotus, *Histories*, 2:66.

14. From *The Historical Library of Diodorus the Sicilian*, trans. Booth, 84.

15. Herodotus, *Histories*, 2:66.

16. Elizabeth Marshall Thomas, *The Tribe of Tiger: Cats and Their Culture* (New York: Simon & Schuster, 1994), 100–101.

17. Paul Armitage and Juliet Clutton-Brock, 'A Radiological and Histological Investigation into the Mummification of Cats from Ancient Egypt', *Journal of Archaeological Science* 8 (1981): 185–96.

18. Stephen Buckley, Katherine Clark and Richard Evershed, 'Complex Organic Chemical Balms of Pharaonic Animal Mummies', *Nature* 431 (2004): 294–9.

19. Armitage and Clutton-Brock, 'A Radiological and Histological Investigation'.

20. The 'black panther', a melanistic form of the leopard, is common in the rainforests of Southern Asia. Presumably so little light penetrates to the forest floor that camouflage is not as much of an issue as for a normally spotted leopard hunting in the African bush.

21. Neil B. Todd, who collected this data, instead suggests that the orange mutation first arose in Asia Minor (roughly, modern Turkey), even though it is less common there than in Alexandria. 'Cats and Commerce', *Scientific American* 237 (1977): 100–107.

22. Dominique Pontier, Nathalie Rioux and Annie Heizmann, 'Evidence of Selection on the Orange Allele in the Domestic Cat *Felis catus*: The Role of Social Structure', *Oikos* 73 (1995): 299–308.

23. Terence Morrison-Scott, 'The Mummified Cats of Ancient Egypt', *Proceedings of the Zoological Society of London* 121 (1952): 861–7.

24. See chapter 16 of Frederick Everard Zeuner's *A History of Domesticated Animals* (New York: Harper & Row, 1963).

25. This rapid acceptance of cats contrasts with the Japanese refusal to admit dogs for thousands of years after they had become widely adopted in China.

26. Monika Lipinski et al., 'The Ascent of Cat Breeds: Genetic Evaluations of Breeds and Worldwide Random-Bred Populations', *Genomics* 91 (2008): 12–21; available online at tinyurl.com/cdop2op.

27. Cleia Detry, Nuno Bicho, Hermenegildo Fernandes and Carlos Fernandes, 'The Emirate of Córdoba (756–929 AD) and the Introduction of the Egyptian Mongoose (*Herpestes ichneumon*) in Iberia: The Remains from Muge, Portugal', *Journal of Archaeological Science* 38 (2011): 3518–23. The related Indian mongoose has been introduced into many parts of the world in an attempt to control snakes, especially islands such as Hawaii and Fiji, which lack other snake predators.

28. Lyudmila N. Trut, 'Early Canid Domestication: The Farm-Fox Experiment', *American Scientist* 87 (1999): 160–69; available online at www.terrierman.com/russianfoxfarmstudy.pdf.

3. ONE STEP BACK, TWO STEPS FORWARD

1. Perhaps fortunately for the domestic cat's popularity, the brown rat, *Rattus norvegicus*, much larger and more formidable than the black rat, did not spread across Europe until the late Middle Ages. As it advanced, it gradually displaced the plague-carrying black rat from the towns and cities; now, black rats are generally found only in warmer places. Most cats are not powerful or skilful enough to take on a full-grown brown rat, although they can be an effective deterrent to brown rat colonization or recolonization. See Charles

Elton, 'The Use of Cats in Farm Rat Control', *British Journal of Animal Behaviour* 1 (1953), 151–5.

2. Researchers have found numerous examples of this in Britain, France and Spain, so this superstition must have been such a discovery in an organ pipe in Dublin's Christ Church Cathedral, although the official story holds that they were trapped there by accident.

3. Translation by Eavan Boland; see homepages.wmich.edu/~cooneys/poems/pangur.ban.html. *Bán* means 'white' in Old Irish, so presumably that was the colour of the writer's cat.

4. Ronald L. Ecker and Eugene J. Crook, *Geoffrey Chaucer: The Canterbury Tales – A Complete Translation into Modern English* (online edn; Palatka, Fl.: Hodge & Braddock, 1993); english.fsu.edu/canterbury.

5. Tom P. O'Connor, 'Wild or Domestic? Biometric Variation in the Cat *Felis silvestris* Schreber', *International Journal of Osteoarchaeology* 17 (2007): 581–95; available online at eprints.whiterose.ac.uk/3700/1/OConnor_Cats-IJOA-submitted.pdf.

6. At this time, cats were also considered generally detrimental to good health. The French physician Ambroise Paré described the cat as 'a venomous animal which infects through its hair, its breath and its brains', and in 1607 the English cleric Edward Topsell wrote, 'It is most certain that the breath and savour of cats . . . destroy the lungs.'

7. Carl Van Vechten, *The Tiger in the House*, 3rd edn (London: Cape, 1938), 100.

8. J. S. Barr, *Buffon's Natural History*, Vol. VI, translated from the French (1797), 1.

9. Neil Todd, 'Cats and Commerce', *Scientific American* 237 (May 1977): 100–107.

10. Ibid.

11. Manuel Ruiz-García and Diana Alvarez, 'A Biogeographical Population Genetics Perspective of the Colonization of Cats in Latin America and Temporal Genetic Changes in Brazilian Cat Populations', *Genetics and Molecular Biology* 31 (2008): 772–82.

12. Even black cats carry the genes for one or other of the 'tabby' patterns, but because the hairs that should be brown at the tips are black, the pattern doesn't show – at least, not until the cat gets old, when the hairs that would be brown if they weren't black fade to a dark, rusty colour. A tabby pattern can also be just discernible in black kittens for a few weeks. Another variation of the tabby gene, 'Abyssinian', restricts the black stripes to the head, tail and legs, while the body is covered in brown-tipped hairs; this is quite rare except in the pedigree cats of the same name.

13. See Todd, 'Cats and Commerce', footnote 9.

14. Bennett Blumenberg, 'Historical Population Genetics of *Felis catus* in Humboldt County, California', *Genetica* 68 (1986): 81–6.

15. Andrew T. Lloyd, 'Pussy Cat, Pussy Cat, Where Have You Been?', *Natural History* 95 (1986): 46–53.

16. Ruiz-García and Alvarez, 'A Biogeographical Population Genetics Perspective'.

17. Manuel Ruiz-García, 'Is There Really Natural Selection Affecting the L Frequencies (Long Hair) in the Brazilian Cat Populations?', *Journal of Heredity* 91 (2000): 49–57.

18. Juliet Clutton-Brock, formerly of the British Museum of Natural History in London, pointed this out in her 1987 book *A Natural History of Domesticated Mammals* (Cambridge and New York: Cambridge University Press, 1987). Indian elephants, camels and reindeer are among other domestic animals that exist, like the domestic cat, somewhere between wildness and full domestication.

19. For more detail on cat nutrition and how it interacts with their lifestyles, see Debra L. Zoran and C. A. T. Buffington, 'Effects of Nutrition Choices and Lifestyle Changes on the Well-Being of Cats, a Carnivore That Has Moved Indoors', *Journal of the American Veterinary Medical Association* 239 (2011): 596–606.

20. The idea of 'nutritional wisdom' comes from Chicago-based paediatrician Clara Marie Davis's classic 1933 experiment, which showed that human infants, allowed to choose from thirty-three 'natural' foodstuffs, would choose a balanced diet, even though each infant preferred a different combination of foods.

21. Stuart C. Church, John A. Allen and John W. S. Bradshaw, 'Frequency-Dependent Food Selection by Domestic Cats: A Comparative Study', *Ethology* 102 (1996): 495–509.

4. EVERY CAT HAS TO LEARN TO BE DOMESTIC

1. I suspect – and this is only conjecture – that it is no coincidence that both cats and dogs are members of the Carnivora.

2. Dennis C. Turner and Patrick Bateson, eds., *The Domestic Cat: The Biology of Its Behaviour* (Cambridge and New York: Cambridge University Press, 1988), 164. Professor Eileen Karsh and her team carried out their study at Temple University in Philadelphia. Remarkably, this revolutionary work has never been published in peer-reviewed journals; however, no one since has fundamentally disagreed with its conclusions.

3. M. E. Pozza, J. L. Stella, A.-C. Chappuis-Gagnon, S. O. Wagner and C. A. T. Buffington, 'Pinch-Induced Behavioural Inhibition ("Clipnosis") in Domestic Cats', *Journal of Feline Medicine and Surgery* 10 (2008): 82–7.

4. John M. Deag, Aubrey Manning and Candace E. Lawrence, 'Factors Influencing the Mother–Kitten Relationship', in Dennis C. Turner and Patrick Bateson, eds., *The Domestic Cat: The Biology of Its Behaviour*, 2nd edn (Cambridge and New York: Cambridge University Press, 2000), 23–39.

5. Jay S. Rosenblatt, 'Suckling and Home Orientation in the Kitten: A Comparative Developmental Study', in Ethel Tobach, Lester R. Aronson and Evelyn Shaw, eds., *The Biopsychology of Development* (New York and London: Academic Press, 1971), 345–410.

6. R. Hudson, G. Raihani, D. González, A. Bautista and H. Distel, 'Nipple Preference and Contests in Suckling Kittens of the Domestic Cat are Unrelated to Presumed Nipple Quality', *Developmental Psychobiology* 51 (2009): 322–32.

7. St Francis Animal Welfare in Fair Oak, Hampshire.

8. Female cats sometimes mate with several males in succession, such that the members of a litter may be half-siblings. See the chapter by Olof Liberg, Mikael Sandell, Dominique Pontier and Eugenia Natoli in Turner and Bateson, eds., *The Domestic Cat*, 2nd edn, 119–47.

9. Hand-reared kittens often end up spending their entire lives with the person that hand-reared them. Whether this is because the kittens are difficult to home or whether their human foster parents cannot bear to give them away seems to be unknown.

10. John Bradshaw and Suzanne L. Hall, 'Affiliative Behaviour of Related and Unrelated Pairs of Cats in Catteries: A Preliminary Report', *Applied Animal Behaviour Science* 63 (1999): 251–5.

11. Roberta R. Collard, 'Fear of Strangers and Play Behaviour in Kittens with Varied Social Experience', *Child Development* 38 (1967): 877–91.

12. See note 2 above.

13. We measured the closeness of the relationship by asking the owners how likely they would be to turn to their cat for emotional support in each of nine situations – for example, after a bad day at work or when they were feeling lonely. See Rachel A. Casey and John Bradshaw, 'The Effects of Additional Socialisation for Kittens in a Rescue Centre on Their Behaviour and Suitability as a Pet', *Applied Animal Behaviour Science* 114 (2008): 196–205.

14. Practical steps for minimizing the stress of being moved to a new house – for both kittens and cats – can be found on the Cats Protection website: www.cats.org.uk/uploads/documents/cat_care_leaflets/EG02-Welcomehome. pdf.

15. Although purring is not always a reliable indicator of how friendly a kitten is, it probably was in this instance.

16. Perhaps surprisingly, the 'owners' of these half-wild cats didn't seem to mind – some people seem to value cats for their wildness, and may even deliberately choose a cat with a personality to match.

5. THE WORLD ACCORDING TO CAT

1. Birds, much more visual creatures than cats, see four colours, including ultraviolet, invisible to mammals of all kinds.

2. At least, we know that people who are red–green colour-blind see colours this way. A very small number of people also have one normal eye and one red–green colour-blind eye, and can develop a normal vocabulary for colour using their 'good' eye, and then use that vocabulary to report what they see with only their colour-blind eye open.

3. You can try this by placing a finger on the page of this book, and then moving the finger a little way towards your nose while continuing to focus on the print. We can choose to fix our gaze on either the print or the finger, but if we had a cat's eyes, at this distance, we would be unable to fix on the finger.

4. David McVea and Keir Pearson, 'Stepping of the Forelegs over Obstacles Establishes Long-Lasting Memories in Cats', *Current Biology* 17 (2007): R621–3.

5. See also the animation at en.wikipedia.org/wiki/Cat_righting_reflex.

6. Nelika K. Hughes, Catherine J. Price and Peter B. Banks, 'Predators are Attracted to the Olfactory Signals of Prey', *PLoS One* 5 (2010): e13114, doi: 10.1371.

7. A vestigial Jacobson's organ can be detected in the human foetus, but it never develops functional nerve connections.

8. Ignacio Salazar, Pablo Sanchez Quinteiro, Jose Manuel Cifuentes and Tomas Garcia Caballero, 'The Vomeronasal Organ of the Cat', *Journal of Anatomy* 188 (1996): 445–54.

9. Whereas mammals seem to use their VNOs exclusively for social and especially sexual functions, reptiles use them more diversely. Snakes use their forked tongues, which do not have taste buds, to deliver different samples of odorants to their left and right VNOs, useful when they are tracking prey or a snake of the opposite sex.

10. See Patrick Pageat and Emmanuel Gaultier, 'Current Research in Canine and Feline Pheromones', *The Veterinary Clinics: North American Small Animal Practice* 33 (2003): 187–211.

6. THOUGHTS AND FEELINGS

1. However, science has recently revealed that some of our emotions never surface into consciousness but nevertheless affect the way we behave; for example, images and emotions that we never become aware of affect the way we drive our cars. See Ben Lewis-Evans, Dick de Waard, Jacob Jolij and Karel A. Brookhuis, 'What You May Not See Might Slow You Down Anyway: Masked Images and Driving', *PLoS One* 7 (2012): e29857, doi: 10.1371/journal.pone.0029857.

2. Leonard Trelawny Hobhouse, *Mind in Evolution*, 2nd edn (London: Macmillan and Co., 1915).

3. For details of the experiments, see M. Bravo, R. Blake and S. Morrison, 'Cats See Subjective Contours', *Vision Research* 18 (1988): 861–5; F. Wilkinson, 'Visual Texture Segmentation in Cats', *Behavioural Brain Research* 19 (1986): 71–82.

4. Further details of the discriminatory abilities of cats can be found in John W. S. Bradshaw, Rachel A. Casey and Sarah L. Brown, *The Behaviour of the Domestic Cat*, 2nd edn (Wallingford: CAB International, 2012), chap. 3.

5. Sarah L. Hall, John W. S. Bradshaw and Ian Robinson, 'Object Play in Adult Domestic Cats: The Roles of Habituation and Disinhibition', *Applied Animal Behaviour Science* 79 (2002): 263–71. Compared to 'classic' habituation as studied in laboratory rats, the timescale over which cats remain habituated to toys is very long – minutes rather than seconds. We subsequently found that the same applies to dogs.

6. Sarah L. Hall and John W. S. Bradshaw, 'The Influence of Hunger on Object Play by Adult Domestic Cats', *Applied Animal Behaviour Science* 58 (1998): 143–50.

7. Commercially available toys don't come apart for a good reason: occasionally a cat can choke on a piece of toy, or get fragments lodged in its gut.

8. Although cats will go out hunting whether they're hungry or not, they're more likely to make a kill if they're hungry; see chap. 10.

9. For a (very) alternative view, look online for comedian Eddie Izzard's 'Pavlov's Cat', currently at tinyurl.com/dce6lb.

10. Psychologists generally classify pain as a feeling rather than an emotion, but there is no doubt that both feelings and emotions are equally involved in how animals learn about the world.

11. Endre Grastyán and Lajos Vereczkei, 'Effects of Spatial Separation of the Conditioned Signal from the Reinforcement: A Demonstration of the Conditioned Character of the Orienting Response or the Orientational Character of Conditioning', *Behavioural Biology* 10 (1974): 121–46.

12. Ádam Miklósi, Péter Pongrácz, Gabriella Lakatos, József Topál and Vilmos Csányi, 'A Comparative Study of the Use of Visual Communicative Signals in Interactions between Dogs (*Canis familiaris*) and Humans and Cats (*Felis catus*) and Humans', *Journal of Comparative Psychology* 119 (2005): 179–86; available online at www.mtapi.hu/userdirs/26/Publika ciok_Topal/Miklosietal2005JCP.pdf.

13. Nicholas Nicastro and Michael J. Owren, 'Classification of Domestic Cat (*Felis catus*) Vocalizations by Naive and Experienced Human Listeners', *Journal of Comparative Psychology* 117 (2003): 44–52.

14. Edward L. Thorndike, *Animal Intelligence: An Experimental Study of the Associative Processes in Animals*, chap. 2 (New York: Columbia University Press, 1898); available online at tinyurl.com/c4bl6do.

15. Emma Whitt, Marie Douglas, Britta Osthaus and Ian Hocking, 'Domestic Cats (*Felis catus*) Do Not Show Causal Understanding in a String-Pulling Task', *Animal Cognition* 12 (2009): 739–43. The same scientists had earlier shown that the crossed-strings arrangement defeats most dogs, even those which, unlike the cats, had earlier successfully solved the parallel-strings problem – thus, dogs' understanding of physics seems to be better than that of cats.

16. Claude Dumas, 'Object Permanence in Cats (*Felis catus*): An Ecological Approach to the Study of Invisible Displacements', *Journal of Comparative Psychology* 106 (1992): 404–10; Claude Dumas, 'Flexible Search Behaviour in Domestic Cats (*Felis catus*): A Case Study of Predator–Prey Interaction', *Journal of Comparative Psychology* 114 (2000): 232–8.

17. For other works by this cartoonist, visit www.stevenappleby.com.

18. George S. Romanes, *Animal Intelligence* (New York: D. Appleton & Co., 1886); available online at www.gutenberg.org/files/40459/40459-h/40459-h. htm.

19. C. Lloyd Morgan, *An Introduction to Comparative Psychology* (New York: Scribner, 1896); available online at tinyurl.com/crehpj9.

20. Paul H. Morris, Christine Doe and Emma Godsell, 'Secondary Emotions in Non-Primate Species? Behavioural Reports and Subjective Claims by Animal Owners', *Cognition and Emotion* 22 (2008): 3–20.

21. More detail of the causes of such problematic behaviour can be found in chaps. 11 and 12 of my book *The Behaviour of the Domestic Cat*, 2nd edn, coauthored with Rachel Casey and Sarah Brown (Wallingford: CAB International, 2012).

22. Anne Seawright et al., 'A Case of Recurrent Feline Idiopathic Cystitis: The Control of Clinical Signs with Behaviour Therapy', *Journal of Veterinary Behaviour: Clinical Applications and Research* 3 (2008): 32–8. For background

information on feline cystitis, see the Feline Advisory Bureau's website, www.
fabcats.org/owners/flutd/info.html.

23. Alexandra Horowitz, a professor of cognitive psychology at New York's
Barnard College, performed this study. See her paper 'Disambiguating the
"Guilty Look": Salient Prompts to a Familiar Dog Behaviour', *Behavioural
Processes* 81 (2009): 447–52, and her book *Inside of a Dog: What Dogs See,
Smell, and Know* (New York: Scribner, 2009).

7. CATS TOGETHER

1. *The Curious Cat*, filmed for the BBC's *The World about Us* series (1979).
A delightful account of the making of this film is included in its companion
volume of the same title, written by Michael Allaby and Peter Crawford
(London: Michael Joseph, 1982). Similar studies were being conducted at
roughly the same time by Jane Dards in Portsmouth dockyard, Olof Liberg
in Sweden, and Masako Izawa in Japan.

2. Strictly speaking, the term 'gene' refers to a single location on a particular
chromosome, and the competing versions of the same gene are alleles; one
example already discussed is the blotched and striped alleles of the 'tabby'
gene.

3. This is likely to be true even though we know little about how such genes
might work, since almost all cooperation between animals occurs between
members of the same family. Genes code for proteins, and it is difficult to
imagine a protein that could promote family loyalty as such. Rather, many
genes must be involved, each contributing a small piece to the whole: for
example, one might increase the threshold for aggression towards other cats
in general, while another enables the recognition of odours characteristic of
family members, through changes in the accessory olfactory bulb, the part of
the brain that processes information coming from the vomeronasal organ.

4. Christopher N. Johnson, Joanne L. Isaac and Diana O. Fisher, 'Rarity of a
Top Predator Triggers Continent-Wide Collapse of Mammal Prey: Dingoes
and Marsupials in Australia', *Proceedings of the Royal Society B* 274 (2007):
341–6.

5. Dominique Pontier and Eugenia Natoli, 'Infanticide in Rural Male Cats
(*Felis catus* L.) as a Reproductive Mating Tactic', *Aggressive Behaviour*
25 (1999): 445–9.

6. Phyllis Chesler, 'Maternal Influence in Learning by Observation in Kittens',
Science 166 (1969): 901–3.

7. Marvin J. Herbert and Charles M. Harsh, 'Observational Learning by
Cats', *Journal of Comparative Psychology* 31 (1944): 81–95.

8. Transcribed from the original letter in the British Museum (Natural History) collections.

9. These studies were mainly conducted by my colleagues Sarah Brown and Charlotte Cameron-Beaumont. For more detail, see chap. 8 of my book, *The Behaviour of the Domestic Cat*, 2nd edn, coauthored by Rachel Casey and Sarah Brown (Wallingford: CAB International, 2012).

10. This silhouette trick fooled most cats only once; the second one they came across elicited almost no reaction at all.

11. Researchers think that the retention of juvenile characteristics into adulthood, referred to as neoteny, was a major factor in the domestication of many animals, especially the dog. For example, at first sight the skull of a Pekinese is nothing like that of its ancestor, the wolf, but in fact it is roughly the same shape as the skull of a wolf foetus. Although the domestic cat's body has not been neotenized, some of its behaviour may have been, including the upright tail and some other social signals.

12. A fuller account of the evolution of signalling in the cat family can be found in John W. S. Bradshaw and Charlotte Cameron-Beaumont, 'The Signalling Repertoire of the Domestic Cat and Its Undomesticated Relatives', in Dennis Turner and Patrick Bateson, eds., *The Domestic Cat: The Biology of Its Behaviour*, 2nd edn (Cambridge: Cambridge University Press, 2000), 67–93.

13. Christina D. Buesching, Pavel Stopka and David W. Macdonald, 'The Social Function of Allo-marking in the European Badger (*Meles meles*)', *Behaviour* 140 (2003): 965–80.

14. Terry Marie Curtis, Rebecca Knowles and Sharon Crowell-Davis, 'Influence of Familiarity and Relatedness on Proximity and Allogrooming in Domestic Cats (*Felis catus*)', *American Journal of Veterinary Research* 64 (2003): 1151–4. See also Ruud van den Bos, 'The Function of Allogrooming in Domestic Cats (*Felis silvestris catus*): A Study in a Group of Cats Living in Confinement', *Journal of Ethology* 16 (1998): 1–13.

15. See my book *In Defence of Dogs* (London: Penguin Books, 2012).

16. Feral dogs, the direct descendants of wolves, show little of their ancestors' social sophistication. Although groups of males and females band together to form packs that share common territory, all the adult females attempt to breed, and most of the puppies are cared for only by their mother – although occasionally two litters may be pooled, and some records show fathers bringing food to their litters.

17. One well-researched instance of explosive speciation is the cichlid fish of Lake Victoria, which despite now being the world's largest tropical lake was dry land only 15,000 years ago. Today it contains many hundreds of cichlid

species, none of which are found in any of the other African great lakes, and most of which have evolved in the 14,000 years since the lake last filled with water. See, for example, Walter Salzburger, Tanja Mack, Erik Verheyen and Axel Meyer, 'Out of Tanganyika: Genesis, Explosive Speciation, Key Innovations and Phylogeography of the Haplochromine Cichlid Fishes', *BMC Evolutionary Biology* 5 (2005): 17.

18. Rudyard Kipling, *Just So Stories for Little Children* (New York: Doubleday, Page & Company, 1902); available online at www.boop.org/jan/justso/cat.htm.

19. Our noses are particularly sensitive to thiols: minute traces are added to natural gas, which in itself is completely odourless, to make it easier to detect leaks.

20. Ludovic Say and Dominique Pontier, 'Spacing Pattern in a Social Group of Stray Cats: Effects on Male Reproductive Success', *Animal Behaviour* 68 (2004): 175–80.

21. See, for example, the policies of Cats Protection, which is as of 2011 'the largest single cat neutering group in the world': www.cats.org.uk/what-we-do/neutering/.

8. CATS AND THEIR PEOPLE

1. Gary D. Sherman, Jonathan Haidt and James A. Coan, 'Viewing Cute Images Increases Behavioural Carefulness', *Emotion* 9 (2009): 282–6; available online at tinyurl.com/bxqg2u6.

2. Robert A. Hinde and Les A. Barden, 'The Evolution of the Teddy Bear', *Animal Behaviour* 33 (1985): 1371–3.

3. See www.wwf.org.uk/how_you_can_help/the_panda_made_me_do_it/.

4. Kathy Carlstead, Janine L. Brown, Steven L. Monfort, Richard Killens and David E. Wildt, 'Urinary Monitoring of Adrenal Responses to Psychological Stressors in Domestic and Nondomestic Felids', *Zoo Biology* 11 (1992): 165–76.

5. Susan Soennichsen and Arnold S. Chamove, 'Responses of Cats to Petting by Humans', *Anthrozoös: A Multidisciplinary Journal of the Interactions of People & Animals* 15 (2002): 258–65.

6. Karen McComb, Anna M. Taylor, Christian Wilson and Benjamin D. Charlton, 'The Cry Embedded within the Purr', *Current Biology* 19 (2009): R507–8.

7. Henry W. Fisher, *Abroad with Mark Twain and Eugene Field: Tales They Told to a Fellow Correspondent* (New York: Nicholas L. Brown, 1922), 102. It's worth noting the end of the quotation as well: '. . . outside of the girl you love, of course'.

8. Some manufacturers add salt to dry cat food, but not for its taste: it's mainly there to stimulate cats to drink, thereby minimizing their risk of developing bladder stones.

9. The late Penny Bernstein conducted a detailed study of stroking, details of which sadly remained unpublished when she died in 2012. For a summary, see Tracy Vogel's 'Petting Your Cat – Something to Purr About' at www.pets.ca/cats/articles/petting-a-cat/, and Bernstein's own review, 'The Human–Cat Relationship', in Irene Rochlitz, ed., *The Welfare of Cats* (Dordrecht: Springer), 47–89.

10. Soennichsen and Chamove, 'Responses of Cats'.

11. Mary Louise Howden, 'Mark Twain as His Secretary at Stormfield Remembers Him: Anecdotes of the Author Untold until Now', *New York Herald*, 13 December 1925, 1–4; available online at www.twainquotes.com/howden.html.

12. Sarah Lowe and John W. S. Bradshaw, 'Ontogeny of Individuality in the Domestic Cat in the Home Environment', *Animal Behaviour* 61 (2001): 231–7.

13. To hear two Bengal cats yowling and chirruping to each other, go to tiny-url.com/crb5ycj. The noise that many cats make when they see birds through a window is sometimes referred to as 'chirping', but is more correctly 'chattering'; see tinyurl.com/cny83rd.

14. Mildred Moelk, 'Vocalizing in the House-Cat: A Phonetic and Functional Study', *American Journal of Psychology* 57 (1944): 184–205.

15. Nicholas Nicastro, 'Perceptual and Acoustic Evidence for Species-Level Differences in Meow Vocalizations by Domestic Cats (*Felis catus*) and African Wild Cats (*Felis silvestris lybica*)', *Journal of Comparative Psychology* 118 (2004): 287–96. When this paper was published, it was common practice to refer to all African wildcats as *lybica*; however, these Southern African wildcats, now known as *cafra*, are not particularly closely related to domestic cats, having diverged from the Middle Eastern/North African *lybica* more than 150,000 years ago.

16. Nicholas Nicastro and Michael J. Owren, 'Classification of Domestic Cat (*Felis catus*) Vocalizations by Naive and Experienced Human Listeners', *Journal of Comparative Psychology* 117 (2003): 44–52.

17. Dennis C. Turner, 'The Ethology of the Human–Cat Relationship', *Swiss Archive for Veterinary Medicine* 133 (1991): 63–70.

18. Desmond Morris, *Catwatching: The Essential Guide to Cat Training* (London: Jonathan Cape, 1986).

19. Of course, many cats do groom their owners, but cats also groom other adult cats.

20. Maggie Lilith, Michael Calver and Mark Garkaklis, 'Roaming Habits of Pet Cats on the Suburban Fringe in Perth, Western Australia: What Size Buffer Zone is Needed to Protect Wildlife in Reserves?', in Daniel Lunney, Adam Munn and Will Meikle, eds., *Too Close for Comfort: Contentious Issues in Human–Wildlife Encounters* (Mosman, NSW: Royal Zoological Society of New South Wales, 2008), 65–72. See also Roland W. Kays and Amielle A. DeWan, 'Ecological Impact of Inside/Outside House Cats around a Suburban Nature Preserve', *Animal Conservation* 7 (2004): 273–83; available online at www.nysm.nysed.gov/staffpubs/docs/15128.pdf.

21. The transmitter and its battery could be carried by a bird the size of a thrush, so it was extremely light. These radio collars emit 'beeps' every few seconds that are picked up on a portable aerial and receiver; the aerial is directional, producing the strongest signal when pointed directly at the animal. When used for tracking wildlife, the operator keeps at a distance once a reasonably strong signal has been picked up, to avoid disturbing the animal, taking several recordings from different angles to map the animal's exact location. With a pet cat, it's easier to simply walk towards the radio source until the cat is sighted.

22. This feline unfaithfulness was exposed by the University of Georgia's Kitty Cam project: fifty-five cats in Athens, Georgia, wore lightweight video recorders, revealing that four often visited second households, where they received food and/or affection. See the website for 'The National Geographic & University of Georgia Kitty Cams (Crittercam) Project: A Window into the World of Free-Roaming Cats' (2011), www.kittycams.uga.edu/research.html.

23. Adapted from material provided by Rachel Casey. See John W. S. Bradshaw, Rachel Casey and Sarah Brown, *The Behaviour of the Domestic Cat*, 2nd edn (Wallingford: CAB International, 2012), chap. 11.

24. Ibid.

25. Ronald R. Swaisgood and David J. Shepherdson, 'Scientific Approaches to Enrichment and Stereotypes in Zoo Animals: What's Been Done and Where Should We Go Next?', *Zoo Biology* 24 (2005): 499–518.

26. Adapted from the RSPCA webpage 'Keeping Cats Indoors' (2013), www.rspca.org.uk/allaboutanimals/pets/cats/environment/indoors.

27. See Cat Behaviour Associates, 'The Benefits of Using Puzzle Feeders for Cats' (2013), www.catbehaviourassociates.com/the-benefits-of-using-puzzle-feeders-for-cats/.

28. Marianne Hartmann-Furter, 'A Species-Specific Feeding Technique Designed for European Wildcats (*Felis s. silvestris*) in Captivity', *Säugetierkundliche Informationen* 4 (2000): 567–75.

9. CATS AS INDIVIDUALS

1. Monika Lipinski et al., 'The Ascent of Cat Breeds: Genetic Evaluations of Breeds and Worldwide Random-Bred Populations', *Genomics* 91 (2008): 12–21.

2. See www.gccfcats.org/breeds/oci.html.

3. Bjarne O. Braastad, I. Westbye and Morten Bakken, 'Frequencies of Behaviour Problems and Heritability of Behaviour Traits in Breeds of Domestic Cat', in Knut Bøe, Morten Bakken and Bjarne Braastad, eds., *Proceedings of the 33rd International Congress of the International Society for Applied Ethology, Lillehammer, Norway* (Ås: Agricultural University of Norway, 1999), 85.

4. Paola Marchei et al., 'Breed Differences in Behavioural Response to Challenging Situations in Kittens', *Physiology & Behaviour* 102 (2011): 276–84.

5. See chap. 11 of my book *In Defence of Dogs* (London: Penguin Books, 2012).

6. Obviously, the mother cat makes genetic contributions to the kittens as well, but she can also influence the development of her kittens' personalities through the way she raises them. Thus, the effects of maternal genetics, while undoubtedly as strong as those of the father, are harder to pin down.

7. For a more detailed discussion, see Sarah Hartwell, 'Is Coat Colour Linked to Temperament?' (2001), www.messybeast.com/colour-tempment.htm.

8. Michael Mendl and Robert Harcourt, 'Individuality in the Domestic Cat: Origins, Development and Stability', in Dennis C. Turner and Patrick Bateson, eds., *The Domestic Cat: The Biology of Its Behaviour*, 2nd edn (Cambridge: Cambridge University Press, 2000), 47–64.

9. Rebecca Ledger and Valerie O'Farrell, 'Factors Influencing the Reactions of Cats to Humans and Novel Objects', in Ian Duncan, Tina Widowski and Derek Haley, eds., *Proceedings of the 30th International Congress of the International Society for Applied Ethology* (Guelph: Col. K. L. Campbell Centre for the Study of Animal Welfare, 1996), 112.

10. Caroline Geigy, Silvia Heid, Frank Steffen, Kristen Danielson, André Jaggy and Claude Gaillard, 'Does a Pleiotropic Gene Explain Deafness and Blue Irises in White Cats?', *The Veterinary Journal* 173 (2007): 548–53.

11. John W. S. Bradshaw and Sarah Cook, 'Patterns of Pet Cat Behaviour at Feeding Occasions', *Applied Animal Behaviour Science* 47 (1996): 61–74.

12. For a review, see Michael Mendl and Robert Harcourt, as above.

13. Sandra McCune, 'The Impact of Paternity and Early Socialisation on the Development of Cats' Behaviour to People and Novel Objects', *Applied Animal Behaviour Science* 45 (1995): 109–24.

14. Sarah E. Lowe and John W. S. Bradshaw, 'Responses of Pet Cats to being Held by an Unfamiliar Person, from Weaning to Three Years of Age', *Anthrozoös: A Multidisciplinary Journal of the Interactions of People & Animals* 15 (2002): 69–79.

15. The technical term for an inveterate cat-hater is an ailurophobe. I carried out my research here with the assistance of a former colleague, Dr Deborah Goodwin.

16. Kurt Kotrschal, Jon Day and Manuela Wedl, 'Human and Cat Personalities: Putting Them Together', in Dennis C. Turner and Patrick Bateson, eds., *The Domestic Cat: The Biology of Its Behaviour*, 3rd edn (Cambridge: Cambridge University Press, 2013).

17. Jill Mellen, 'Effects of Early Rearing Experience on Subsequent Adult Sexual Behaviour Using Domestic Cats (*Felis catus*) as a Model for Exotic Small Felids', *Zoo Biology* 11 (1992): 17–32.

18. Nigel Langham, 'Feral Cats (*Felis catus* L.) on New Zealand Farmland. II. Seasonal Activity', *Wildlife Research* 19 (1992): 707–20.

19. Julie Feaver, Michael Mendl and Patrick Bateson, 'A Method for Rating the Individual Distinctiveness of Domestic Cats', *Animal Behaviour* 34 (1986): 1016–25.

20. See Patrick Bateson, 'Behavioural Development in the Cat', in Turner and Bateson, eds., *The Domestic Cat*, 2nd edn, 9–22.

10. CATS AND WILDLIFE

1. Michael C. Calver, Jacky Grayson, Maggie Lilith and Christopher R. Dickman, 'Applying the Precautionary Principle to the Issue of Impacts by Pet Cats on Urban Wildlife', *Biological Conservation* 144 (2011): 1895–1901.

2. Michael Woods, Robbie Mcdonald and Stephen Harris, 'Predation of Wildlife by Domestic Cats *Felis catus* in Great Britain', *Mammal Review* 33 (2003): 174–88; available online at tinyurl.com/ah6552e. This paper does not note that the survey was largely completed by children, nor does it provide any information about the format of the questionnaire used.

3. See, for example, Britta Tschanz, Daniel Hegglin, Sandra Gloor and Fabio Bontadina, 'Hunters and Non-Hunters: Skewed Predation Rate by Domestic Cats in a Rural Village', *European Journal of Wildlife Research* 57 (2011): 597–602. The University of Georgia Kitty Cam project recorded 30 per cent of outdoor cats capturing and killing prey; see www.wildlifeextra.com/go/news/domestic-cat-camera.html. This was reduced to 15 per cent if indoor-only cats were included.

4. See tinyurl.com/ak8c4ne.

5. Keen gardeners also seem to detest cats; a 2003 survey commissioned by the UK's Mammal Society as further grist for its campaign against cat ownership found that cats were rated alongside rats and moles as the mammals gardeners least like to see in their gardens.

6. Natalie Anglier, 'That Cuddly Kitty is Deadlier Than You Think', *The New York Times*, 29 January 2013, tinyurl.com/bb4nmpb; and Annalee Newitz, 'Domestic Cats are Destroying the Planet', io9, 29 January 2013, tinyurl.com/adhczar.

7. Ross Galbreath and Derek Brown, 'The Tale of the Lighthouse-Keeper's Cat: Discovery and Extinction of the Stephens Island Wren (*Traversia lyalli*)', *Notornis* 51 (2004): 193–200; available online at notornis.osnz.org.nz/system/files/Notornis_51_4_193.pdf.

8. B. J. Karl and H. A. Best, 'Feral Cats on Stewart Island: Their Foods and Their Effects on Kakapo', *New Zealand Journal of Zoology* 9 (1982): 287–93. Despite this study, the cats on Stewart Island were subsequently exterminated, but (as predicted from the study) the kakapo continued to decline, and eventually scientists moved all the survivors to another, predator-free island.

9. Scott R. Loss, Tom Will and Peter P. Marra, 'The Impact of Free-Ranging Domestic Cats on Wildlife of the United States', *Nature Communications* (2013): DOI: 10.1038/ncomms2380.

10. Cats may not be a recent introduction to Australia: it has been suggested that feral cats actually spread there several thousand years ago from South-East Asia, following the same route as the dingo, the Australian feral dog. See Jonica Newby, *The Pact for Survival: Humans and Their Companion Animals* (Sydney: ABC Books, 1997), 193.

11. Christopher R. Dickman, 'House Cats as Predators in the Australian Environment: Impacts and Management', *Human–Wildlife Conflicts* 3 (2009): 41–8.

12. Ibid.

13. Maggie Lilith, Michael Calver and Mark Garkaklis, 'Do Cat Restrictions Lead to Increased Species Diversity or Abundance of Small and Medium-Sized Mammals in Remnant Urban Bushland?', *Pacific Conservation Biology* 16 (2010): 162–72.

14. James Fair, 'The Hunter of Suburbia', *BBC Wildlife*, November 2010, 68–72; available online at www.discoverwildlife.com/british-wildlife/cats-and-wildlife-hunter-suburbia. The study Fair reports on was conducted by Rebecca Thomas at the University of Reading.

15. Loss, Will and Marra, 'The Impact of Free-Ranging Domestic Cats', note 9.

16. Ibid.

17. Philip J. Baker, Susie E. Molony, Emma Stone, Innes C. Cuthill and Stephen Harris, 'Cats About Town: Is Predation by Free-Ranging Pet Cats *Felis catus* Likely to Affect Urban Bird Populations?', *Ibis* 150, Suppl. 1 (2008): 86–99.

18. Andreas A. P. Møller and Juan D. Ibáñez-Álamo, 'Escape Behaviour of Birds Provides Evidence of Predation being Involved in Urbanization', *Animal Behaviour* 84 (2012): 341–8.

19. Eduardo A. Silva-Rodríguez and Kathryn E. Sieving, 'Influence of Care of Domestic Carnivores on Their Predation on Vertebrates', *Conservation Biology* 25 (2011): 808–15. The cat and rat experiment was conducted in the early 1970s, when the ethics of animal experimentation were different from how they are today: Robert E. Adamec, 'The Interaction of Hunger and Preying in the Domestic Cat (*Felis catus*): An Adaptive Hierarchy?', *Behavioural Biology* 18 (1976): 263–72.

20. See the video at 'Cat's Bibs Stop Them Killing Wildlife', Reuters, 29 May 2007; tinyurl.com/c9jfn36.

21. For more detailed advice, see www.rspb.org.uk/advice/gardening/unwantedvisitors/cats/birdfriendly.aspx.

22. David Cameron Duffy and Paula Capece, 'Biology and Impacts of Pacific Island Invasive Species. 7. The Domestic Cat (*Felis catus*)', *Pacific Science* 66 (2012): 173–212.

23. Andrew P. Beckerman, Michael Boots and Kevin J. Gaston, 'Urban Bird Declines and the Fear of Cats', *Animal Conservation* 10 (2007): 320–25.

24. See www.rspb.org.uk/wildlife/birdguide/name/m/magpie/effect_on_songbirds.aspx.

25. James Childs, 'Size-Dependent Predation on Rats (*Rattus norvegicus*) by House Cats (*Felis catus*) in an Urban Setting', *Journal of Mammalogy* 67 (1986): 196–9.

11. CATS OF THE FUTURE

1. John W. S. Bradshaw, Rachel Casey and Sarah Brown, *The Behaviour of the Domestic Cat*, 2nd edn (Wallingford: CAB International, 2012), chap. 11.

2. Darcy Spears, 'Contact 13 Investigates: Teens Accused of Drowning Kitten Appear in Court', 28 June 2012, www.ktnv.com/news/local/160764205.html.

3. Summaries are available in several expert reports, including those commissioned by the Royal Society for the Prevention of Cruelty to Animals, the Associate Parliamentary Group for Animal Welfare, and the UK Kennel Club in partnership with the rehoming charity Dogs Trust. See www.rspca.org.uk/allaboutanimals/pets/dogs/health/pedigreedogs.

4. Domestic dogs have, of course, been selected for this trait throughout their association with man, since it is primarily their affection for us that makes them trainable.

5. Eileen Karsh, 'Factors Influencing the Socialization of Cats to People', in Robert K. Anderson, Benjamin L. Hart and Lynette A. Hart, eds., *The Pet Connection: Its Influence on Our Health and Quality of Life* (Minneapolis: University of Minnesota Press, 1984), 207–15.

6. You can find additional details of the introduction procedure on the Cats Protection website, www.cats.org.uk/cat-care/cat-care-faqs.

7. See the box in chap. 6 on clicker training. You can view a video of Dr Sarah Ellis using clicker training to persuade a cat to walk into its cat carrier at www.fabcats.org/behaviour/training/videos.html.

8. See Vicky Halls's article, for example, on the Feline Advisory Bureau website, www.fabcats.org/behaviour/scratching/article.html.

9. For more information on declawing, written by a veterinarian, see 'A Rational Look at Declawing from Jean Hofve, DVM' (2002), declaw.lisaviolet.com/declawdrjean2.html.

10. This constraint does not apply so much to dogs. Most pedigree dog breeds were originally derived from working types – terriers, herding dogs, guard dogs, pack hounds, and so on – and although the show-ring has diluted out much of their characteristic behaviour, some still remains. Moreover, some working-breed clubs have deliberately kept their lines separate to perpetuate the genes that enable their dogs to perform their traditional functions.

11. The Governing Council of the Cat Fancy, 'The Story of the RagaMuffin Cat' (2012), www.gccfcats.org/breeds/ragamuffin.html.

12. Debbie Connolly, 'Bengals as Pets' (2003), www.bengalcathelpline.co.uk/bengalsaspets.htm.

13. Charlotte Cameron-Beaumont, Sarah Lowe and John Bradshaw, 'Evidence Suggesting Preadaptation to Domestication throughout the Small *Felidae*', *Biological Journal of the Linnean Society* 75 (2002): 361–6. This study included sixteen leopard cats and six Geoffroy's cats.

14. Susan Saulny, 'What's Up, Pussycat? Whoa!', *The New York Times*, 12 May 2005, www.nytimes.com/2005/05/12/fashion/thursdaystyles/12cats.html.

15. John W. S. Bradshaw, Giles F. Horsfield, John A. Allen and Ian H. Robinson, 'Feral Cats: Their Role in the Population Dynamics of *Felis catus*', *Applied Animal Behaviour Science* 65 (1999): 273–83.

16. In this context, neutering can be conceived of as a 'meme', a concept that spreads, rather like a virus, from one human brain to another, producing biological consequences. See Susan J. Blackmore, *The Meme Machine* (Oxford and New York: Oxford University Press, 1999).

Index

Diagrams and pictures are given in italics, notes etc. are marked 'n'.

ALLEN LANE
an imprint of
PENGUIN BOOKS

Recently Published

Alexander Watson, *Ring of Steel: Germany and Austria-Hungary at War, 1914-1918*

Richard Vinen, *National Service: Conscription in Britain, 1945-1963*

Paul Dolan, *Happiness by Design: Finding Pleasure and Purpose in Everyday Life*

Mark Greengrass, *Christendom Destroyed: Europe 1517-1650*

Hugh Thomas, *World Without End: The Global Empire of Philip II*

Richard Layard and David M. Clark, *Thrive: The Power of Evidence-Based Psychological Therapies*

Uwe Tellkamp, *The Tower: A Novel*

Zelda la Grange, *Good Morning, Mr Mandela*

Ahron Bregman, *Cursed Victory: A History of Israel and the Occupied Territories*

Tristram Hunt, *Ten Cities that Made an Empire*

Jordan Ellenberg, *How Not to Be Wrong: The Power of Mathematical Thinking*

David Marquand, *Mammon's Kingdom: An Essay on Britain, Now*

Justin Marozzi, *Baghdad: City of Peace, City of Blood*

Adam Tooze, *The Deluge: The Great War and the Remaking of Global Order 1916-1931*

John Micklethwait and Adrian Wooldridge, *The Fourth Revolution: The Global Race to Reinvent the State*

Steven D. Levitt and Stephen J. Dubner, *Think Like a Freak: How to Solve Problems, Win Fights and Be a Slightly Better Person*

Alexander Monro, *The Paper Trail: An Unexpected History of the World's Greatest Invention*

Jacob Soll, *The Reckoning: Financial Accountability and the Making and Breaking of Nations*

Gerd Gigerenzer, *Risk Savvy: How to Make Good Decisions*

James Lovelock, *A Rough Ride to the Future*

Michael Lewis, *Flash Boys*

Hans Ulrich Obrist, *Ways of Curating*

Mai Jia, *Decoded: A Novel*

Richard Mabey, *Dreams of the Good Life: The Life of Flora Thompson and the Creation of* Lark Rise to Candleford

Danny Dorling, *All That Is Solid: The Great Housing Disaster*

Leonard Susskind and Art Friedman, *Quantum Mechanics: The Theoretical Minimum*

Michio Kaku, *The Future of the Mind: The Scientific Quest to Understand, Enhance and Empower the Mind*

Nicholas Epley, *Mindwise: How we Understand what others Think, Believe, Feel and Want*

Geoff Dyer, *Contest of the Century: The New Era of Competition with China*

Yaron Matras, *I Met Lucky People: The Story of the Romani Gypsies*

Larry Siedentop, *Inventing the Individual: The Origins of Western Liberalism*

Dick Swaab, *We Are Our Brains: A Neurobiography of the Brain, from the Womb to Alzheimer's*

Max Tegmark, *Our Mathematical Universe: My Quest for the Ultimate Nature of Reality*

David Pilling, *Bending Adversity: Japan and the Art of Survival*

Hooman Majd, *The Ministry of Guidance Invites You to Not Stay: An American Family in Iran*

Roger Knight, *Britain Against Napoleon: The Organisation of Victory, 1793-1815*

Alan Greenspan, *The Map and the Territory: Risk, Human Nature and the Future of Forecasting*

Daniel Lieberman, *Story of the Human Body: Evolution, Health and Disease*

Malcolm Gladwell, *David and Goliath: Underdogs, Misfits and the Art of Battling Giants*

Paul Collier, *Exodus: Immigration and Multiculturalism in the 21st Century*

John Eliot Gardiner, *Music in the Castle of Heaven: Immigration and Multiculturalism in the 21st Century*

Catherine Merridale, *Red Fortress: The Secret Heart of Russia's History*

Ramachandra Guha, *Gandhi Before India*

Vic Gatrell, *The First Bohemians: Life and Art in London's Golden Age*

Richard Overy, *The Bombing War: Europe 1939-1945*

Charles Townshend, *The Republic: The Fight for Irish Independence, 1918-1923*

Eric Schlosser, *Command and Control*

Sudhir Venkatesh, *Floating City: Hustlers, Strivers, Dealers, Call Girls and Other Lives in Illicit New York*

Sendhil Mullainathan and Eldar Shafir, *Scarcity: Why Having Too Little Means So Much*

John Drury, *Music at Midnight: The Life and Poetry of George Herbert*

Philip Coggan, *The Last Vote: The Threats to Western Democracy*

Richard Barber, *Edward III and the Triumph of England*

Daniel M Davis, *The Compatibility Gene*

John Bradshaw, *Cat Sense: The Feline Enigma Revealed*

Roger Knight, *Britain Against Napoleon: The Organisation of Victory, 1793-1815*

Thurston Clarke, *JFK's Last Hundred Days: An Intimate Portrait of a Great President*

Jean Drèze and Amartya Sen, *An Uncertain Glory: India and its Contradictions*

Rana Mitter, *China's War with Japan, 1937-1945: The Struggle for Survival*

Tom Burns, *Our Necessary Shadow: The Nature and Meaning of Psychiatry*

Sylvain Tesson, *Consolations of the Forest: Alone in a Cabin in the Middle Taiga*

George Monbiot, *Feral: Searching for Enchantment on the Frontiers of Rewilding*

Ken Robinson and Lou Aronica, *Finding Your Element: How to Discover Your Talents and Passions and Transform Your Life*

David Stuckler and Sanjay Basu, *The Body Economic: Why Austerity Kills*

Suzanne Corkin, *Permanent Present Tense: The Man with No Memory, and What He Taught the World*

Daniel C. Dennett, *Intuition Pumps and Other Tools for Thinking*

Adrian Raine, *The Anatomy of Violence: The Biological Roots of Crime*

Eduardo Galeano, *Children of the Days: A Calendar of Human History*

Lee Smolin, *Time Reborn: From the Crisis of Physics to the Future of the Universe*

Michael Pollan, *Cooked: A Natural History of Transformation*

David Graeber, *The Democracy Project: A History, a Crisis, a Movement*

Brendan Simms, *Europe: The Struggle for Supremacy, 1453 to the Present*

Oliver Bullough, *The Last Man in Russia and the Struggle to Save a Dying Nation*

Diarmaid MacCulloch, *Silence: A Christian History*

Evgeny Morozov, *To Save Everything, Click Here: Technology, Solutionism, and the Urge to Fix Problems that Don't Exist*

David Cannadine, *The Undivided Past: History Beyond Our Differences*

Michael Axworthy, *Revolutionary Iran: A History of the Islamic Republic*

Jaron Lanier, *Who Owns the Future?*

John Gray, *The Silence of Animals: On Progress and Other Modern Myths*

Paul Kildea, *Benjamin Britten: A Life in the Twentieth Century*

Jared Diamond, *The World Until Yesterday: What Can We Learn from Traditional Societies?*

Nassim Nicholas Taleb, *Antifragile: How to Live in a World We Don't Understand*

Alan Ryan, *On Politics: A History of Political Thought from Herodotus to the Present*

Roberto Calasso, *La Folie Baudelaire*

Carolyn Abbate and Roger Parker, *A History of Opera: The Last Four Hundred Years*

Yang Jisheng, *Tombstone: The Untold Story of Mao's Great Famine*

Caleb Scharf, *Gravity's Engines: The Other Side of Black Holes*

Jancis Robinson, Julia Harding and José Vouillamoz, *Wine Grapes: A Complete Guide to 1,368 Vine Varieties, including their Origins and Flavours*

David Bownes, Oliver Green and Sam Mullins, *Underground: How the Tube Shaped London*

Niall Ferguson, *The Great Degeneration: How Institutions Decay and Economies Die*

Chrystia Freeland, *Plutocrats: The Rise of the New Global Super-Rich*

David Thomson, *The Big Screen: The Story of the Movies and What They Did to Us*

Halik Kochanski, *The Eagle Unbowed: Poland and the Poles in the Second World War*

Kofi Annan with Nader Mousavizadeh, *Interventions: A Life in War and Peace*

Mark Mazower, *Governing the World: The History of an Idea*

Anne Applebaum, *Iron Curtain: The Crushing of Eastern Europe 1944-56*

Steven Johnson, *Future Perfect: The Case for Progress in a Networked Age*

Christopher Clark, *The Sleepwalkers: How Europe Went to War in 1914*

Neil MacGregor, *Shakespeare's Restless World*

Nate Silver, *The Signal and the Noise: The Art and Science of Prediction*

Chinua Achebe, *There Was a Country: A Personal History of Biafra*

John Darwin, *Unfinished Empire: The Global Expansion of Britain*

Jerry Brotton, *A History of the World in Twelve Maps*

Patrick Hennessey, *KANDAK: Fighting with Afghans*

Katherine Angel, *Unmastered: A Book on Desire, Most Difficult to Tell*

David Priestland, *Merchant, Soldier, Sage: A New History of Power*

Stephen Alford, *The Watchers: A Secret History of the Reign of Elizabeth I*

Tom Feiling, *Short Walks from Bogotá: Journeys in the New Colombia*

Pankaj Mishra, *From the Ruins of Empire: The Revolt Against the West and the Remaking of Asia*

Geza Vermes, *Christian Beginnings: From Nazareth to Nicaea, AD 30-325*

Steve Coll, *Private Empire: ExxonMobil and American Power*

Joseph Stiglitz, *The Price of Inequality*

Dambisa Moyo, *Winner Take All: China's Race for Resources and What it Means for Us*

Robert Skidelsky and Edward Skidelsky, *How Much is Enough? The Love of Money, and the Case for the Good Life*

Frances Ashcroft, *The Spark of Life: Electricity in the Human Body*

Sebastian Seung, *Connectome: How the Brain's Wiring Makes Us Who We Are*

Callum Roberts, *Ocean of Life*

Orlando Figes, *Just Send Me Word: A True Story of Love and Survival in the Gulag*

Leonard Mlodinow, *Subliminal: The Revolution of the New Unconscious and What it Teaches Us about Ourselves*

John Romer, *A History of Ancient Egypt: From the First Farmers to the Great Pyramid*

Ruchir Sharma, *Breakout Nations: In Pursuit of the Next Economic Miracle*

Michael J. Sandel, *What Money Can't Buy: The Moral Limits of Markets*

Dominic Sandbrook, *Seasons in the Sun: The Battle for Britain, 1974-1979*

Tariq Ramadan, *The Arab Awakening: Islam and the New Middle East*

Jonathan Haidt, *The Righteous Mind: Why Good People are Divided by Politics and Religion*

Ahmed Rashid, *Pakistan on the Brink: The Future of Pakistan, Afghanistan and the West*

Tim Weiner, *Enemies: A History of the FBI*

Mark Pagel, *Wired for Culture: The Natural History of Human Cooperation*

George Dyson, *Turing's Cathedral: The Origins of the Digital Universe*

Cullen Murphy, *God's Jury: The Inquisition and the Making of the Modern World*

Richard Sennett, *Together: The Rituals, Pleasures and Politics of Co-operation*

Faramerz Dabhoiwala, *The Origins of Sex: A History of the First Sexual Revolution*

Roy F. Baumeister and John Tierney, *Willpower: Rediscovering Our Greatest Strength*

Jesse J. Prinz, *Beyond Human Nature: How Culture and Experience Shape Our Lives*

Robert Holland, *Blue-Water Empire: The British in the Mediterranean since 1800*

Jodi Kantor, *The Obamas: A Mission, A Marriage*

Philip Coggan, *Paper Promises: Money, Debt and the New World Order*

Charles Nicholl, *Traces Remain: Essays and Explorations*

Daniel Kahneman, *Thinking, Fast and Slow*

Hunter S. Thompson, *Fear and Loathing at* Rolling Stone*: The Essential Writing of Hunter S. Thompson*

Duncan Campbell-Smith, *Masters of the Post: The Authorized History of the Royal Mail*

Colin McEvedy, *Cities of the Classical World: An Atlas and Gazetteer of 120 Centres of Ancient Civilization*

Heike B. Görtemaker, *Eva Braun: Life with Hitler*

Brian Cox and Jeff Forshaw, *The Quantum Universe: Everything that Can Happen Does Happen*

Nathan D. Wolfe, *The Viral Storm: The Dawn of a New Pandemic Age*

Norman Davies, *Vanished Kingdoms: The History of Half-Forgotten Europe*

Michael Lewis, *Boomerang: The Meltdown Tour*

Steven Pinker, *The Better Angels of Our Nature: The Decline of Violence in History and Its Causes*

Robert Trivers, *Deceit and Self-Deception: Fooling Yourself the Better to Fool Others*

Thomas Penn, *Winter King: The Dawn of Tudor England*

Daniel Yergin, *The Quest: Energy, Security and the Remaking of the Modern World*

Michael Moore, *Here Comes Trouble: Stories from My Life*

Ali Soufan, *The Black Banners: Inside the Hunt for Al Qaeda*

Jason Burke, *The 9/11 Wars*

Timothy D. Wilson, *Redirect: The Surprising New Science of Psychological Change*

Ian Kershaw, *The End: Hitler's Germany, 1944-45*

T M Devine, *To the Ends of the Earth: Scotland's Global Diaspora, 1750-2010*

Catherine Hakim, *Honey Money: The Power of Erotic Capital*

Douglas Edwards, *I'm Feeling Lucky: The Confessions of Google Employee Number 59*

John Bradshaw, *In Defence of Dogs*

Chris Stringer, *The Origin of Our Species*

Lila Azam Zanganeh, *The Enchanter: Nabokov and Happiness*

David Stevenson, *With Our Backs to the Wall: Victory and Defeat in 1918*

Evelyn Juers, *House of Exile: War, Love and Literature, from Berlin to Los Angeles*

Henry Kissinger, *On China*

Michio Kaku, *Physics of the Future: How Science Will Shape Human Destiny and Our Daily Lives by the Year 2100*

David Abulafia, *The Great Sea: A Human History of the Mediterranean*

John Gribbin, *The Reason Why: The Miracle of Life on Earth*

Anatol Lieven, *Pakistan: A Hard Country*

William Cohen, *Money and Power: How Goldman Sachs Came to Rule the World*

Joshua Foer, *Moonwalking with Einstein: The Art and Science of Remembering Everything*

Simon Baron-Cohen, *Zero Degrees of Empathy: A New Theory of Human Cruelty*

Manning Marable, *Malcolm X: A Life of Reinvention*

David Deutsch, *The Beginning of Infinity: Explanations that Transform the World*

David Edgerton, *Britain's War Machine: Weapons, Resources and Experts in the Second World War*

John Kasarda and Greg Lindsay, *Aerotropolis: The Way We'll Live Next*

David Gilmour, *The Pursuit of Italy: A History of a Land, Its Regions and Their Peoples*

Niall Ferguson, *Civilization: The West and the Rest*

Tim Flannery, *Here on Earth: A New Beginning*

Robert Bickers, *The Scramble for China: Foreign Devils in the Qing Empire, 1832-1914*

Mark Malloch-Brown, *The Unfinished Global Revolution: The Limits of Nations and the Pursuit of a New Politics*

King Abdullah of Jordan, *Our Last Best Chance: The Pursuit of Peace in a Time of Peril*

Eliza Griswold, *The Tenth Parallel: Dispatches from the Faultline between Christianity and Islam*